Business Statistics

3rd Edition

Business Statistics

3rd Edition

Norean R. Sharpe
Georgetown University

Richard D. De Veaux
Williams College

Paul F. Velleman
Cornell University

With Contributions by David Bock

PEARSON

Boston   Columbus   Indianapolis   New York   San Francisco   Upper Saddle River
Amsterdam   Cape Town   Dubai   London   Madrid   Milan   Munich   Paris   Montrèal   Toronto
Delhi   Mexico City   São Paulo   Sydney   Hong Kong   Seoul   Singapore   Taipei   Tokyo

Editor in Chief: Deirdre Lynch
Senior Content Editor: Chere Bemelmans
Assistant Editor: Sonia Ashraf
Senior Marketing Manager: Erin Lane
Marketing Assistant: Kathleen DeChavez
Senior Managing Editor: Karen Wernholm
Associate Managing Editor: Tamela Ambush
Senior Production Project Manager: Peggy McMahon
Digital Assets Manager: Marianne Groth
Senior Author Support/Technology Specialist: Joe Vetere
Associate Director of Design, USHE EMSS/HSC/EDU: Andrea Nix
Program Design Lead: Barbara T. Atkinson

Cover Photo: Silhouette of business women in a skyscraper, ©Yvan Dubé/Getty Images
Cover and Text Design: Studio Montage
Image Manager: Rachel Youdelman
Permissions Liaison Manager: Joseph Croscup
Media Producer: Aimee Thorne
Project Supervisor, MyStatLab: Robert Carroll
QA Manager, Assessment Content: Marty Wright
Procurement Specialist: Debbie Rossi
Full-Service Project Management, Composition, and Illustrations:
 PreMediaGlobal
Printer/Binder: Webcrafters
Cover Printer: Lehigh-Phoenix Color/Hagerstown

Credits and acknowledgments borrowed from other sources and reproduced, with permission, in this textbook appear on the appropriate page within text or in Appendix C, which is hereby made part of this copyright page.

The student edition of this book has been cataloged by the Library of Congress as follows:

Library of Congress Cataloging-in-Publication Data
Sharpe, Norean Radke.
 Business statistics / Norean R. Sharpe, Richard D. De Veaux, Paul F. Velleman; with contributions by David Bock.—3rd ed.
  p. cm.
 ISBN 978-0-321-92583-1
 1. Commercial statistics. I. De Veaux, Richard D. II. Velleman, Paul F., 1949- III. Title.
 HF1017.S468 2014
 519.5—dc23

                                                                    2012012980

10 9 8 7 6 5 4 3—WC—16 15 14

PEARSON

ISBN 10: 0-321-92583-1
ISBN 13: 978-0-321-92583-1

To my husband, Peter, for his patience and support

—*Norean*

To my family

—*Dick*

To my father, who taught me about ethical business practice by his constant example as a small businessman and parent

—*Paul*

Meet the Authors

Norean Radke Sharpe (Ph.D. University of Virginia) has developed an international reputation as an educator, administrator, and consultant on assessment and accreditation. She is currently a professor at the McDonough School of Business at Georgetown University, where she is also Senior Associate Dean and Director of Undergraduate Programs. Prior to joining Georgetown, Norean taught business statistics and operations research courses to both undergraduate and MBA students for fourteen years at Babson College. Before moving into business education, she taught statistics for several years at Bowdoin College and conducted research at Yale University. Norean is coauthor of the recent text, *A Casebook for Business Statistics: Laboratories for Decision Making*, and she has authored more than 30 articles—primarily in the areas of statistics education and women in science. Norean currently serves as Associate Editor for the journal *Cases in Business, Industry, and Government Statistics*. Her scholarship focuses on business forecasting, statistics education, and student learning. She is co-founder of the DOME Foundation, a nonprofit foundation that works to increase Diversity and Outreach in Mathematics and Engineering, and she currently serves on two other nonprofit boards in the Washington, D.C. area. Norean has been active in increasing the participation of women and underrepresented students in science and mathematics for several years and has two children of her own.

Richard D. De Veaux (Ph.D. Stanford University) is an internationally known educator, consultant, and lecturer. Dick has taught statistics at a business school (Wharton), an engineering school (Princeton), and a liberal arts college (Williams). While at Princeton, he won a Lifetime Award for Dedication and Excellence in Teaching. Since 1994, he has taught at Williams College, although he returned to Princeton for the academic year 2006–2007 as the William R. Kenan Jr. Visiting Professor of Distinguished Teaching. He is currently the C. Carlisle and Margaret Tippit Professor of Statistics at Williams College. Dick holds degrees from Princeton University in Civil Engineering and Mathematics and from Stanford University in Dance Education and Statistics, where he studied with Persi Diaconis. His research focuses on the analysis of large data sets and data mining in science and industry. Dick has won both the Wilcoxon and Shewell awards from the American Society for Quality. He is an elected member of the International Statistics Institute (ISI) and a Fellow of the American Statistical Association (ASA). He currently serves on the Board of Directors of the ASA. Dick is also well known in industry, having consulted for such *Fortune* 500 companies as American Express, Hewlett-Packard, Alcoa, DuPont, Pillsbury, General Electric, and Chemical Bank. He was named the "Statistician of the Year" for 2008 by the Boston Chapter of the American Statistical Association for his contributions to teaching, research, and consulting. In his spare time he is an avid cyclist and swimmer. He also is the founder and bass for the doo-wop group the Diminished Faculty and is a frequent singer and soloist with various local choirs, including the Choeur Vittoria of Paris, France. Dick is the father of four children.

Paul F. Velleman (Ph.D. Princeton University) has an international reputation for innovative statistics education. He designed the Data Desk® software package and is also the author and designer of the award-winning ActivStats® multimedia software, for which he received the EDUCOM Medal for innovative uses of computers in teaching statistics and the ICTCM Award for Innovation in Using Technology in College Mathematics. He is the founder and CEO of Data Description, Inc. (www.datadesk.com), which supports both of these programs. He also developed the Internet site *Data and Story Library* (DASL; lib.stat.cmu.edu/DASL/), which provides data sets for teaching Statistics. Paul coauthored (with David Hoaglin) the book *ABCs of Exploratory Data Analysis*. Paul teaches Statistics at Cornell University in the Department of Statistical Sciences and in the School of Industrial and Labor Relations, for which he has been awarded the MacIntyre Prize for Exemplary Teaching. His research often focuses on statistical graphics and data analysis methods. Paul is a Fellow of the American Statistical Association and of the American Association for the Advancement of Science. Paul's experience as a professor, entrepreneur, and business leader brings a unique perspective to the book.

Richard De Veaux and Paul Velleman have authored successful books in the introductory college and AP High School market with David Bock, including *Intro Stats*, Fourth Edition (Pearson, 2014); *Stats: Modeling the World*, Fourth Edition (Pearson, 2015); and *Stats: Data and Models*, Third Edition (Pearson, 2012).

Contents

Preface

The question that should motivate a business student's study of Statistics should be "How can I make better decisions?"[1] As entrepreneurs and consultants, we know that in today's data-rich environment, knowledge of Statistics is essential to survive and thrive in the business world. But, as educators, we've seen a disconnect between the way business statistics is traditionally taught and the way it should be used in making business decisions. In *Business Statistics*, we try to narrow the gap between theory and practice by presenting relevant statistical methods that will empower business students to make effective, data-informed decisions.

Of course, students should come away from their statistics course knowing how to think statistically and how to apply statistics methods with modern technology. But they must also be able to communicate their analyses effectively to others. When asked about statistics education, a group of CEOs from *Fortune* 500 companies recently said that although they were satisfied with the technical competence of students who had studied statistics, they found the students' ability to communicate their findings to be woefully inadequate.

Our Plan, Do, Report rubric provides a structure for solving business problems that mimics the correct application of statistics to solving real business problems. Unlike many other books, we emphasize the often neglected thinking (Plan) and communication (Report) steps in problem solving in addition to the methodology (Do). This approach requires up-to-date, real-world examples and data. So we constantly strive to illustrate our lessons with current business issues and examples.

What's New in This Edition?

We've been delighted with the reaction to previous editions of *Business Statistics*. We've streamlined the third edition further to help students focus on the central material. And, of course, we continue to update examples and exercises so that the story we tell is always tied to the ways Statistics informs modern business practice.

- **Recent data.** We teach with real data whenever possible, so we've updated data throughout the book. New examples reflect current stories in the news and recent economic and business events. The brief cases have been updated with new data and new contexts.

- **Improved organization.** We have retained our "data first" presentation of topics because we find that it provides students with both motivation and a foundation in real business decisions on which to build an understanding.
  - Chapters 1–4 have been streamlined to cover collecting, displaying, summarizing, and understanding data in four chapters. We find that this provides students with a solid foundation to launch their study of probability and statistics.
  - Chapters 5–9 introduce students to randomness and probability models. They then apply these new concepts to sampling. This provides a gateway to the core material on statistical inference. We've moved the discussion of probability trees and Bayes' rule into these chapters.
  - Chapters 10–14 cover inference for both proportions and means. We introduce inference by discussing proportions because most students are better acquainted with proportions reported in surveys and news stories. However, this edition ties in the discussion of means immediately so students can appreciate that the reasoning of inference is the same in a variety of contexts.
  - Chapters 15–19 cover regression-based models for decision making.
  - Chapters 20–24 discuss special topics that can be selected according to the needs of the course and the preferences of the instructor.

---

[1]Unfortunately, not the question most students are asking themselves on the first day of the course.

- **Streamlined design.** Our goal has always been an accessible text. This edition sports a new design that clarifies the purpose of each text element. The major theme of each chapter is more linear and easier to follow without distraction. Supporting material is clearly boxed and shaded, so students know where to focus their study efforts.
- **Enhanced Technology Help with expanded Excel 2013 coverage.** We've updated Technology Help and added detailed instructions for Excel 2013 to almost every chapter.
- **Updated Ethics in Action features.** We've updated more than half of our Ethics in Action features. Ethically and statistically sound alternative approaches to the questions raised in these features and a link to the American Statistical Association's Ethical Guidelines are now presented in the Instructor's Solutions Manual, making the Ethics features suitable for assignment or class discussion.
- **Updated examples to reflect the changing world.** The time since our last revision has seen marked changes in the U.S. and world economies. This has required us to update many of our examples. Our chapter on time series was particularly affected. We've reworked those examples and discussed the real-world challenges of modeling economic and business data in a changing world. The result is a chapter that is more realistic and useful.
- **Increased focus on core material.** Statistics in practice means making smart decisions based on data. Students need to know the methods, how to apply them, and the assumptions and conditions that make them work. We've tightened our discussions to get students there as quickly as possible, focusing increasingly on the central ideas and core material.

Our Approach

Statistical Thinking

For all of our improvements, examples, and updates in this edition of *Business Statistics* we haven't lost sight of our original mission—writing a modern business statistics text that addresses the importance of *statistical thinking* in making business decisions and that acknowledges how Statistics is actually used in business.

Statistics is practiced with technology, and this insight informs everything from our choice of forms for equations (favoring intuitive forms over calculation forms) to our extensive use of real data. But most important, understanding the value of technology allows us to focus on teaching statistical thinking rather than calculation. The questions that motivate each of our hundreds of examples are not "How do you find the answer?" but "How do you think about the answer?", "How does it help you make a better decision?", and "How can you best communicate your decision?"

Our focus on statistical thinking ties the chapters of the book together. An introductory Business Statistics course covers an overwhelming number of new terms, concepts, and methods, and it is vital that students see their central core: how we can understand more about the world and make better decisions by understanding what the data tell us. From this perspective, it is easy to see that the patterns we look for in graphs are the same as those we think about when we prepare to make inferences. And it is easy to see that the many ways to draw inferences from data are several applications of the same core concepts. And it follows naturally that when we extend these basic ideas into more complex (and even more realistic) situations, the same basic reasoning is still at the core of our analyses.

Our Goal: Read This Book!

The best textbook in the world is of little value if it isn't read. Here are some of the ways we made *Business Statistics* more approachable:

- **Readability.** We strive for a conversational, approachable style, and we introduce anecdotes to maintain interest. Instructors report (to their amazement) that their students read ahead of their assignments voluntarily. Students tell us (to *their* amazement) that they actually enjoy the book. In this edition, we've tightened our discussions to be more focused on the central ideas we want to convey.

- **Focus on assumptions and conditions.** More than any other textbook, *Business Statistics* emphasizes the need to verify assumptions when using statistical procedures. We reiterate this focus throughout the examples and exercises. We make every effort to provide templates that reinforce the practice of checking these assumptions and conditions, rather than rushing through the computations. Business decisions have consequences. Blind calculations open the door to errors that could easily be avoided by taking the time to graph the data, check assumptions and conditions, and then check again that the results and residuals make sense.

- **Emphasis on graphing and exploring data.** Our consistent emphasis on the importance of displaying data is evident from the first chapters on understanding data to the sophisticated model-building chapters at the end. Examples often illustrate the value of examining data graphically, and the Exercises reinforce this. Good graphics reveal structures, patterns, and occasional anomalies that could otherwise go unnoticed. These patterns often raise new questions and inform both the path of a resulting statistical analysis and the business decisions. Hundreds of new graphics found throughout the book demonstrate that the simple structures that underlie even the most sophisticated statistical inferences are the same ones we look for in the simplest examples. This helps tie the concepts of the book together to tell a coherent story.

- **Consistency.** We work hard to avoid the "do what we say, not what we do" trap. Having taught the importance of plotting data and checking assumptions and conditions, we are careful to model that behavior throughout the book. (Check the Exercises in the chapters on multiple regression or time series and you'll find us still requiring and demonstrating the plots and checks that were introduced in the early chapters.) This consistency helps reinforce these fundamental principles and provides a familiar foundation for the more sophisticated topics.

- **The need to read.** In this book, important concepts, definitions, and sample solutions are not always set aside in boxes. The book needs to be read, so we've tried to make the reading experience enjoyable. The common approach of skimming for definitions or starting with the exercises and looking up examples just won't work here. (It never did work as a way to learn about and understand Statistics.)

Coverage

The topics covered in a Business Statistics course are generally mandated by our students' needs in their studies and in their future professions. But the *order* of these topics and the relative emphasis given to each is not well established. *Business Statistics* presents some topics sooner or later than other texts. Although many chapters can be taught in a different order, we urge you to consider the order we have chosen.

We've been guided in the order of topics by the fundamental goal of designing a coherent course in which concepts and methods fit together to provide a new understanding of how reasoning with data can uncover new and important truths. Each new topic should fit into the growing structure of understanding that students develop throughout the course. For example, we teach inference concepts with proportions first and then with means. Most people have a wider experience with proportions, seeing them in polls and advertising. And by starting with proportions, we can teach inference with the Normal model and then introduce inference for means with the Student's t distribution.

We introduce the concepts of association, correlation, and regression early in *Business Statistics*. Our experience in the classroom shows that introducing these fundamental ideas early makes Statistics useful and relevant even at the beginning of the course. By Chapter 4, students can discuss relationships among variables in a meaningful way. Later in the semester, when we discuss inference, it is natural and relatively easy to build on the fundamental concepts learned earlier and enhance them with inferential methods.

GAISE Report

We've been guided in our choice of what to emphasize by the GAISE (Guidelines for Assessment and Instruction in Statistics Education) Report, which emerged from extensive studies of how students best learn Statistics (**www.amstat.org/education/gaise/**). Those recommendations, now officially adopted and recommended by the American Statistical Association, urge (among other detailed suggestions) that Statistics education should:

1. Emphasize statistical literacy and develop statistical thinking.
2. Use real data.
3. Stress conceptual understanding rather than mere knowledge of procedures.
4. Foster active learning.
5. Use technology for developing conceptual understanding and analyzing data.
6. Make assessment a part of the learning process.

In this sense, this book is thoroughly modern.

Syllabus Flexibility

But to be effective, a course must fit comfortably with the instructor's preferences. The early chapters—Chapters 1–14—present core material that will be part of any introductory course. Chapters 15–20—multiple regression, time series, model building, and Analysis of Variance—may be included in an introductory course, but our organization provides flexibility in the order and choice of specific topics. Chapters 21–24 may be viewed as "special topics" and selected and sequenced to suit the instructor or the course requirements. Here are some specific notes:

- Chapter 4, Correlation and Linear Regression, may be postponed until just before covering regression inference in Chapters 15 and 16. (But we urge you to teach it where it appears.)
- Chapter 18, Building Multiple Regression Models, must follow the introductory material on multiple regression in Chapter 17.
- Chapter 19, Time Series Analysis, requires material on multiple regression from Chapter 17.
- Chapter 20, Design and Analysis of Experiments and Observational Studies, may be taught before the material on regression—at any point after Chapter 13.

The following topics can be introduced in any order (or omitted) after basic inference has been covered:

- Chapter 14, Inference for Counts: Chi-Square Tests
- Chapter 21, Quality Control
- Chapter 22, Nonparametric Methods
- Chapter 23, Decision Making and Risk
- Chapter 24, Introduction to Data Mining

Continuing Features

A textbook isn't just words on a page. A textbook is many elements that come together to form a big picture. The features in *Business Statistics* provide a real-world context for concepts, help students apply these concepts, promote problem solving, and integrate technology—all of which help students understand and see the big picture of Business Statistics.

Providing Real-World Context

Motivating Vignettes. Each chapter opens with a motivating vignette, often taken from the authors' consulting experiences. Companies featured include Amazon.com, Zillow.com, Keen Inc., and Whole Foods Market. We analyze data from or about the companies in the motivating vignettes throughout the chapter.

Brief Cases. Each chapter includes one or more Brief Cases that use real data and ask students to investigate a question or make a decision. Students define the objective, plan the process, complete the analysis, and report a conclusion. Data for the Brief Cases are available on the CD and website, formatted for various technologies.

Case Studies. Each of the five parts of the book ends with a Case Study. Students are given realistically large data sets (on the CD) and challenged to respond to open-ended business questions using the data. Students can bring together methods they have learned throughout the book to address the issues raised. Students will have to use a computer to work with the large data sets that accompany these Case Studies.

What Can Go Wrong? In each chapter, What Can Go Wrong? highlights the most common statistical errors and the misconceptions about Statistics. The most common mistakes for the new user of Statistics often involve misusing a method—not miscalculating a statistic. One of our goals is to arm students with the tools to detect statistical errors and to offer practice in debunking misuses of Statistics, whether intentional or not.

Applying Concepts

For Examples. Almost every section of every chapter includes a focused example that illustrates and applies the concepts or methods of that section to a real-world business context.

Step-by-Step Guided Examples. The answer to a statistical question is almost never just a number. Statistics is about understanding the world and making better decisions with data. Guided Examples model a thorough solution in the right column with commentary in the left column. The overall analysis follows our innovative **Plan, Do, Report** template. Each analysis begins with a clear question about a business decision and an examination of the data (**Plan**), moves to calculating the selected statistics (**Do**), and finally concludes with a **Report** that specifically addresses the question. To emphasize that our goal is to address the motivating question, we present the **Report** step as a business memo that summarizes the results in the context of the example and states a recommendation if the data are able to support one. To preserve the realism of the example, whenever it is appropriate, we include limitations of the analysis or models in the concluding memo, as one should in making such a report.

By Hand. Even though we encourage the use of technology to calculate statistical quantities, we recognize the pedagogical benefits of occasionally doing a calculation by hand. The By Hand boxes break apart the calculation of some of the simpler formulas and help the student through the calculation of a worked example.

Reality Check. We regularly offer reminders that Statistics is about understanding the world and making decisions with data. Results that make no sense are probably wrong, no matter how carefully we think we did the calculations. Mistakes are often easy to spot with a little thought, so we ask students to stop for a reality check before interpreting results.

Notation Alert. Throughout this book, we emphasize the importance of clear communication. Proper notation is part of the vocabulary of Statistics, but it can be daunting. We've found that it helps students when we are clear about the letters and symbols statisticians use to mean very specific things, so we've included Notation Alerts whenever we introduce a special notation that students will see again.

Math Boxes. In many chapters, we present the mathematical underpinnings of the statistical methods and concepts. We set proofs, derivations, and justifications apart from the narrative, so the underlying mathematics is there for those who want greater depth, but the text itself presents the logical development of the topic at hand without distractions.

What Have We Learned? Each chapter ends with a What Have We Learned? summary that includes learning objectives and definitions of terms introduced in the chapter. Students can think of these as study guides.

Promoting Problem Solving

Just Checking. Throughout each chapter we pose short questions to help students check their understanding. The answers are at the end of the exercise sets in each chapter to make them easy to check. The questions can also be used to motivate class discussion.

Ethics in Action. Statistics is not just plugging numbers into formulas; most statistical analyses require a fair amount of judgment. Ethics in Action vignettes—updated for this edition—in each chapter provide a context for some of the judgments needed in statistical analyses. Possible errors, a link to the American Statistical Association's Ethical Guidelines, and ethically and statistically sound alternative approaches are presented in the Instructor's Solutions Manual.

Section Exercises. The exercises for each chapter begin with straightforward exercises targeted at the topics in each section. These are designed to check understanding of specific topics. Because they are labeled by section, it is easy to turn back to the chapter to clarify a concept or review a method.

Chapter Exercises. These exercises are designed to be more realistic than Section Exercises and to lead to conclusions about the real world. They may combine concepts and methods from different sections, and they contain relevant, modern, and real-world questions. Many come from news stories; some come from recent research articles. The exercises marked with a **T** indicate that the data are provided on the CD (and at the book's companion website, **www.pearsonhighered.com/sharpe**) in a variety of formats. We pair the exercises so that each odd-numbered exercise (with answer in the back of the book) is followed by an even-numbered exercise on the same Statistics topic. Exercises are roughly ordered within each chapter by both topic and by level of difficulty.

Integrating Technology

Data and Sources. Most of the data used in examples and exercises are from real-world sources and whenever we can, we include URLs for Internet data sources. The data we use are usually on the CD and on the companion website, **www.pearsonhighered.com/sharpe**.

Videos with Optional Captioning. Videos, featuring the *Business Statistics* authors, review the high points of each chapter. The presentations feature the same student-friendly style and emphasis on critical thinking as the textbook. In addition, 10 *Business Insight Videos* feature Deckers, Southwest Airlines, Starwood, and other companies and focus on statistical concepts as they pertain to the real world. Videos are available with captioning. They can also be viewed from within the online MyStatLab course.

Technology Help. In business, Statistics is practiced with computers using a variety of statistics packages. In Business-school Statistics classes, however, Excel is the software most often used. In Technology Help at the end of each chapter, we summarize what students can find in the most common software, often with annotated output. Updated for this edition, we offer extended guidance for Excel 2013, and start-up pointers for Minitab, SPSS, and JMP, formatted in easy-to-read bulleted lists. This advice is not intended to replace the documentation for any of the software, but rather to point the way and provide start-up assistance.

Student Supplements

Business Statistics, for-sale student edition. (ISBN-13: 978-0-321-92583-1; ISBN-10: 0-321-92583-1)

Student's Solutions Manual, by Linda Dawson, University of Washington, and Rose Sebastianelli, University of Scranton, provides detailed, worked-out solutions to odd-numbered exercises. (ISBN-13: 978-0-321-93940-1; ISBN-10: 0-321-93940-9)

Study Cards for Business Statistics Software: This series of study cards, available for Excel 2013 with XLSTAT (0-321-92579-3), Excel 2013 with Data Analysis Toolpak (0-321-92581-5), Minitab (0-321-64421-2), JMP (0-321-64423-9), SPSS (0-321-64422-0), and StatCrunch (0-321-74472-1) provide students with easy step-by-step guides to the most common business statistics software.

Instructor Supplements

Instructor's Edition contains answers to all exercises. (ISBN-13: 978-0-321-93939-5; ISBN-10: 0-321-93939-5)

Instructor's Resource Guide (download only), written by the authors, contains chapter-by-chapter comments on the major concepts, tips on presenting topics (and what to avoid), teaching examples, suggested assignments, basic exercises, and web links and lists of other resources. Available within MyStatLab or at www.pearsonhighered.com/irc.

Online Test Bank (download only), by Linda Dawson, University of Washington, and Rose Sebastianelli, University of Scranton, includes chapter quizzes and part level tests. The Test Bank is available at www.pearsonhighered.com/irc.

Instructor's Solutions Manual (download only), by Linda Dawson, University of Washington and Rose Sebastianelli, University of Scranton, contains detailed solutions to all of the exercises. The Instructor's Solutions Manual is available at www.pearsonhighered.com/irc.

Technology Resources

MyStatLab™ Online Course (access code required)

MyStatLab from Pearson is the world's leading online resource in statistics, integrating interactive homework, assessment, and media in a flexible, easy-to-use format. MyStatLab is a course management system that delivers proven results in helping individual students succeed.

MyStatLab can be implemented successfully in any environment—lab-based, hybrid, fully online, traditional—and demonstrates the quantifiable difference that integrated usage has on student retention, subsequent success, and overall achievement.

MyStatLab's comprehensive online gradebook automatically tracks students' results on tests, quizzes, homework, and in the study plan. Instructors can use the gradebook to provide positive feedback or intervene if students have trouble. Gradebook data can be easily exported to a variety of spreadsheet programs, such as Microsoft Excel. You can determine which points of data you want to export, and then analyze the results to determine success.

MyStatLab provides engaging experiences that personalize, stimulate, and measure learning for each student. In addition to the resources below, each course includes a full interactive online version of the accompanying textbook.

- **Tutorial Exercises with Multimedia Learning Aids:** The homework and practice exercises in MyStatLab align with the exercises in the textbook, and most regenerate algorithmically to give students unlimited opportunity for practice and mastery. Exercises offer immediate helpful feedback, including guided solutions, sample problems, animations, and videos.
- **Adaptive Study Plan:** Pearson now offers an optional focus on adaptive learning in the study plan to allow students to work on just what they need to learn when it makes the most sense to learn it. The adaptive study plan maximizes students' potential for understanding and success.
- **Additional Question Libraries:** In addition to algorithmically regenerated questions that are aligned with your textbook, MyStatLab courses come with two additional question libraries. **450 Getting Ready for Statistics** questions cover the developmental math topics students need for the course. These can be assigned as a prerequisite to other assignments, if desired. The **1000 Conceptual Question Library** requires students to apply their statistical understanding.
- **StatCrunch®:** MyStatLab includes web-based statistical software, StatCrunch, within the online assessment platform so that students can analyze data sets from exercises and the text. In addition, MyStatLab includes access to www.StatCrunch.com, a web site where users can access tens of thousands of shared data sets, conduct online surveys, perform complex analyses using the powerful statistical software, and generate compelling reports.
- **Integration of Statistical Software:** We make it easy to copy our data sets, both from the ebook and the MyStatLab questions, into software such as StatCrunch, Minitab, Excel, and more. Students have access to a variety of support tools—Technology Instruction Videos, Technology Study Cards, and Manuals for select titles—to learn how to use statistical software.
- **Business Insight Videos:** Ten engaging videos show managers at top companies using statistics in their everyday work. Assignable questions encourage debate and discussion.
- **StatTalk Videos:** Fun-loving statistician Andrew Vickers takes to the streets of Brooklyn, New York, to demonstrate important statistical concepts through interesting stories and real-life events. This series of 24 videos includes available assessment questions and an instructor's guide.
- **Expert Tutoring:** Although many students describe the whole of MyStatLab as "like having your own personal tutor," students also have access to live tutoring from qualified statistics instructors via MyStatLab.

MyStatLab™ Ready to Go Course (access code required)

These new Ready to Go courses provide students with all the same great MyStatLab features that you're used to, but make it easier for instructors to get started. Each course includes pre-assigned homework and quizzes to make creating your course even simpler. Ask your Pearson representative about the details for this particular course or to see a copy of this course.

MathXL® for Statistics Online Course (access code required)

MathXL® is the homework and assessment engine that runs MyStatLab. (MyStatLab is MathXL plus a learning management system.) With MathXL for Statistics, instructors can:

- Create, edit, and assign online homework and tests using algorithmically generated exercises correlated at the objective level to the textbook.
- Create and assign their own online exercises and import TestGen tests for added flexibility.
- Maintain records of all student work, tracked in MathXL's online gradebook.

With MathXL for Statistics, students can:

- Take chapter tests in MathXL and receive personalized study plans and/or personalized homework assignments based on their test results.
- Use the study plan and/or the homework to link directly to tutorial exercises for the objectives they need to study.
- Students can also access supplemental animations and video clips directly from selected exercises.
- Knowing that students often use external statistical software, we make it easy to copy our data sets, both from the ebook and the MyStatLab questions, into software like StatCrunch™, Minitab, Excel, and more.

MathXL for Statistics is available to qualified adopters. For more information, visit our website at www.mathxl.com, or contact your Pearson representative.

StatCrunch®

StatCrunch is powerful web-based statistical software that allows users to perform complex analyses, share data sets, and generate compelling reports of their data. The vibrant online community offers tens of thousands data sets for students to analyze.

- **Collect.** Users can upload their own data to StatCrunch or search a large library of publicly shared data sets, spanning almost any topic of interest. An online survey tool allows users to collect data via web-based surveys.
- **Crunch.** A full range of numerical and graphical methods allows users to analyze and gain insights from any data set. Interactive graphics help users understand statistical concepts, and are available for export to enrich reports with visual representations of data.
- **Communicate.** Reporting options help users create a wide variety of visually appealing representations of their data.

Full access to StatCrunch is available with a MyStatLab kit, and StatCrunch is available by itself to qualified adopters. For more information, visit our website at www.StatCrunch.com, or contact your Pearson representative.

TestGen®

TestGen® (www.pearsoned.com/testgen) enables instructors to build, edit, print, and administer tests using a computerized bank of questions developed to cover all the objectives of the text. TestGen is algorithmically based, so instructors can create multiple but equivalent versions of the same question or test with the click of a button. Instructors can also modify test bank questions or add new questions. The software and testbank are available for download from Pearson Education's online catalog.

PowerPoint® Lecture Slides

PowerPoint® Lecture Slides provide an outline to use in a lecture setting, presenting definitions, key concepts, and figures from the text. These slides are available within MyStatLab and in the Instructor Resource Center at www.pearsonhighered.com/irc.

Active Learning Questions

Prepared in PowerPoint®, these questions are intended for use with classroom response systems. Several multiple-choice questions are available for each chapter of the book, allowing instructors to quickly assess mastery of material in class. The Active Learning Questions are available to download from within MyStatLab® and in the Instructor Resource Center at www.pearsonhighered.com/irc.

XLStat for Pearson

XLStat for Pearson is an Excel® add-in that offers a wide variety of functions to enhance the analytical capabilities of Microsoft Excel, making it the ideal tool for your everyday data analysis and statistics requirements. Developed in 1993, XLStat is used by leading businesses and universities around the world. XLStat is compatible with all Excel versions from version 97 to version 2013 (except Mac 2008) including PowerPC and Intel-based Mac systems.

Student Edition of Minitab

The Student Edition of Minitab is a condensed edition of the Professional release of Minitab statistical software. It offers the full range of statistical methods and graphical capabilities, along with worksheets that can include up to 10,000 data points. Individual copies of the software can be bundled with the text. (ISBN-13: 978-0-13-143661-9; ISBN-10: 0-13-143661-9)

JMP Student Edition

JMP Student Edition is an easy-to-use, streamlined version of JMP desktop statistical discovery software from SAS Institute, Inc., and is available for bundling with the text. (ISBN-13: 978-0-321-89164-8; ISBN-10: 0-321-89164-3)

Acknowledgments

This book would not have been possible without many contributions from David Bock, our coauthor on several other texts. Many of the explanations and exercises in this book benefit from Dave's pedagogical flair and expertise. We are honored to have him as a colleague and friend.

Many people have contributed to this book from the first day of its conception to its publication. *Business Statistics* would have never seen the light of day without the assistance of the incredible team at Pearson. Our Editor in Chief, Deirdre Lynch, was central to the support, development, and realization of the book from day one. Chere Bemelmans, Senior Content Editor, kept us on task as much as humanly possible. Peggy McMahon, Senior Production Project Manager, and Nancy Kincade, Project Manager at PreMediaGlobal, worked miracles to get the book out the door. We are indebted to them. Sonia Ashraf, Assistant Editor; Erin Lane, Senior Marketing Manager; Kathleen DeChavez, Marketing Associate; and Dona Kenly, Senior Market Development Manager, were essential in managing all of the behind-the-scenes work that needed to be done. Aimee Thorne, Media Producer, put together a top-notch media package for this book. Barbara Atkinson, Senior Designer, and Studio Montage are responsible for the wonderful way the book looks. Procurement Specialist Debbie Rossi worked miracles to get this book and CD in your hands, and Greg Tobin, President, was supportive and good-humored throughout all aspects of the project.

We'd also like to thank our accuracy checkers whose monumental task was to make sure we said what we thought we were saying: James Lapp; Joan Saniuk, Wentworth Institute of Technology; Sarah Streett; and Dirk Tempelaar, Maastricht University.

We also thank those who provided feedback through focus groups, class tests, and reviews:

Hope M. Baker, Kennesaw State University

John F. Beyers, University of Maryland—University College

Scott Callan, Bentley College

Laurel Chiappetta, University of Pittsburgh

Anne Davey, Northeastern State University

Joan Donohue, The University of South Carolina

Robert Emrich, Pepperdine University

Michael Ernst, St. Cloud State

Mark Gebert, University of Kentucky

Kim Gilbert, University of Georgia

Nicholas Gorgievski, Nichols College

Clifford Hawley, West Virginia University

Kathleen Iacocca, University of Scranton

Chun Jin, Central Connecticut State University

Austin Lampros, Colorado State University

Roger Lee, Salt Lake Community College

Monnie McGee, Southern Methodist University

Richard McGowan, Boston College

Mihail Motzev, Walla Walla University

Robert Potter, University of Central Florida

Eugene Round, Embry-Riddle Aeronautical University

Sunil Sapra, California State University—Los Angeles

Dmitry Shishkin, Georgia Gwinnett College

Courtenay Stone, Ball State University

Gordon Stringer, University of Colorado—Colorado Springs

Arnold J. Stromberg, University of Kentucky

Joe H. Sullivan, Mississippi State University

Timothy Sullivan, Towson University

Minghe Sun, University of Texas—San Antonio

Patrick Thompson, University of Florida

Jackie Wroughton, Northern Kentucky University

Ye Zhang, Indiana University—Purdue Indianapolis

Schiro Withanachchi, Queens College

Finally, we want to thank our families. This has been a long project, and it has required many nights and weekends. Our families have sacrificed so that we could write the book we envisioned.

Norean Sharpe

Index of Applications

1

Data and Decisions

E-Commerce

E-Commerce and mobile commerce have dramatically changed the way the world shops. Online shoppers can buy clothes, food, even cars with the click of a mouse and a digital swipe of their credit card—24 hours a day, 7 days a week. Companies now reach their customers in ways no one could even imagine just a generation ago. Online sales in some sectors, such as clothing and electronics, already account for over 15% of total sales, which is about double what it was five years ago. U.S. adults, on average, currently spend about $1200 a year online, but some projections put that number at nearly $2000 a year by 2016.

The trend in online shopping is worldwide. The amount Australians spend online is expected to grow by $10B in the next five years. The research firm Forrester estimates that global digital retailing is headed toward 15 to 20% of total sales worldwide in the near future.

A few generations ago, many store owners knew their customers well. With that knowledge, they could personalize their suggestions, guessing which items that particular customer might like. Online marketers rely on similar information about customers and potential customers to make decisions. But in today's digital age retailers never meet their customers, so, that information has to be obtained in other ways. How do today's companies know which ads to place on your browser or what order to list the websites from your search? How do marketers know what to advertise and to whom?
The answer is …
Data.

What Are Data?

"Data is king at Amazon. Clickstream and purchase data are the crown jewels at Amazon. They help us build features to personalize the website experience."

—Ronny Kohavi,
Former Director of Data
Mining and
Personalization,
Amazon.com

"It is the mark of a truly intelligent person to be moved by statistics."

—George Bernard Shaw

> **Q:** What is Statistics?
>
> **A:** Statistics is a way of reasoning, along with a collection of tools and methods, designed to help us understand the world.
>
> **Q:** What are statistics?
>
> **A:** Statistics (plural) are quantities calculated from data.
>
> **Q:** So what is data?
>
> **A:** You mean, "what *are* data?" Data is the plural form. The singular is datum.
>
> **Q:** So, what are data?
>
> **A:** Data are values along with their context.

Businesses have always relied on data for planning and to improve efficiency and quality. Now, more than ever before, businesses rely on the information in data to compete in the global marketplace. Every time you make an online purchase, much more information is actually captured than just the details of the purchase itself. What pages did you search in order to get to your purchase? How much time did you spend looking at each? Companies use this information to make decisions about virtually all phases of their business, from inventory to advertising to website design. These data are recorded and stored electronically, in vast digital repositories called **data warehouses.**

In the past few decades these data warehouses have grown enormously in size, but with the use of powerful computers, the information contained in them is accessible and used to help make decisions. The huge capacity of these warehouses has given rise to the term **Big Data** to describe data sets so large that traditional methods of storage and analysis are inadequate. Even though the data amounts are huge, some decisions can be made quickly. When you pay with your credit card, for example, the information about the transaction is transmitted to a central computer where it is processed and analyzed. A decision whether to approve or deny your purchase is made and transmitted back to the point of sale, all within a few seconds. But data alone can't help you make better business decisions. You must be able to summarize, model, and understand what the data can tell you. That collection of tools and its associated reasoning is what we call "Statistics."

Statistics plays a role in making sense of our complex world in an astonishing number of ways. Statisticians assess the risk of genetically engineered foods or of a new drug being considered by the Food and Drug Administration (FDA). Statisticians predict the number of new cases of AIDS by regions of the country or the number of customers likely to respond to a sale at the supermarket. And statisticians help scientists, social scientists, and business leaders understand how unemployment is related to environmental controls, whether enriched early education affects the later performance of school children, and whether vitamin C really prevents illness. Whenever you have data and a need to understand the world or make an informed decision, you need Statistics.

If we want to analyze student perceptions of business ethics (a question we'll come back to in a later chapter), should we administer a survey to every single university student in the United States—or, for that matter, in the world? Well, that wouldn't be very practical or cost-effective. Instead, we can try to obtain survey responses from a smaller, representative group of students. Statistics can help us make the leap from a smaller sample of data we have at hand to an understanding of the world at large. We talk about the specifics of sampling in Chapter 8, and the theme of generalizing from the specific to the general is one that we revisit throughout this book. We hope this text will empower *you* to draw conclusions from data and make valid business decisions in response to such questions as:

- Will the new design of our website increase click-through rates and result in more sales?
- What is the effect of advertising on sales?
- Do aggressive, "high-growth" mutual funds really have higher returns than more conservative funds?
- Is there a seasonal cycle in your firm's revenues and profits?
- What is the relationship between shelf location and cereal sales?
- Do students around the world perceive issues in business ethics differently?
- Are there common characteristics about your customers and why they choose your products?—and, more importantly, are those characteristics the same among those who aren't your customers?

Our ability to answer questions such as these and make sound business decisions with data depends largely on our ability to understand *variation.* That may not be the term you expected to find at the end of that sentence, but it is the essence of Statistics. The key to learning from data is understanding the variation that is all around us.

Data vary. People are different. So are economic conditions from month to month. We can't see everything, let alone measure it all. And even what we do measure, we measure imperfectly. So the data we wind up looking at and basing our decisions on provide, at best, an imperfect picture of the world. Variation lies at the heart of what Statistics is all about. How to make sense of it is the central challenge of Statistics.

Companies use data to make decisions about nearly every aspect of their business. By studying the past behavior of customers and predicting their responses, they hope to better serve their customers and to compete more effectively. This process of using data, especially of **transactional data** (data collected for recording the companies' transactions), to make decisions and predictions is sometimes called **data mining** or *predictive analytics*. The more general term **business analytics** (or sometimes simply analytics) describes *any* use of data and statistical analysis to drive business decisions from data whether the purpose is predictive or simply descriptive.

Leading companies are embracing business analytics. Reed Hastings, a former computer science major, is the founder and CEO of Netflix. Netflix uses analytics on customer information both to recommend new movies and to adapt the website that customers see to individual tastes. Netflix offered a $1 million prize to anyone who could improve on the accuracy of their recommendations by more than 10%. That prize was won in 2009 by a team of statisticians and computer scientists using data-mining techniques. The Oakland Athletics use analytics to judge players instead of the traditional methods used by scouts and baseball experts for over a hundred years. The book and movie *Moneyball* document how business analytics enabled them to put together a team that could compete against the richer teams in spite of the severely limited resources available to the front office. eBay used analytics to examine its own use of computer resources. Although not obvious to their own technical people, once they crunched the data they found huge inefficiencies. According to Forbes, they were able to "save millions in capital expenditures within the first year."

To begin to make sense of **data**, we first need to understand its context. Whether the data are numerical (consisting only of numbers), alphabetic (consisting only of letters), or alphanumerical (mixed numbers and letters), they are useless unless we know what they represent. Newspaper journalists know that the lead paragraph of a good story should establish the "Five W's": *who, what, when, where,* and (if possible) *why*. Often, we add *how* to the list as well. Answering these questions can provide a **context** for data values and make them meaningful. The answers to the first two questions are essential. If you can't answer *who* and *what*, you don't have data, and you don't have any useful information.

We can make the meaning clear if we add the context of *who* the data are about and *what* was measured and organize the values into a **data table** such as this one.

Table 1.1 shows purchase records from an online music retailer. Each row represents a purchase of a music album. In general, rows of a data table correspond to individual **cases** about which we've recorded some characteristics called **variables**.

THE W'S:
WHO
WHAT
WHEN
WHERE
WHY

Order Number	Name	State/Country	Price	Area Code	Album Download	Gift?	Stock ID	Artist
105-2686834-3759466	Katherine H.	Ohio	5.99	440	Identity	N	B0000015Y6	James Fortune & Flya
105-9318443-4200264	Samuel P.	Illinois	9.99	312	Port of Morrow	Y	B000002BK9	The Shins
105-1872500-0198646	Chris G.	Massachusetts	9.99	413	Up All Night	N	B000068ZVQ	Syco Music UK
103-2628345-9238664	Monique D.	Canada	10.99	902	Fallen Empires	N	B0000010AA	Snow Patrol
002-1663369-6638649	Katherine H.	Ohio	11.99	440	Sees the Light	N	B002MXA7Q0	La Sera

Table 1.1 Example of a data table. The variable names are in the top row. Typically, the *Who* of the table are found in the leftmost column.

Cases go by different names, depending on the situation. Individuals who answer a survey are referred to as **respondents**. People on whom we experiment are **subjects** or (in an attempt to acknowledge the importance of their role in the experiment) **participants**, but animals, plants, websites, and other inanimate subjects are often called **experimental units**. Often we call cases just what they are: for example, *customers*, *economic quarters*, or *companies*. In a database, rows are called **records**—in this example, purchase records. Perhaps the most generic term is cases. In Table 1.1, the cases are the individual orders.

The column titles (variable names) tell *what* has been recorded. What does a row of Table 1.1 represent? Be careful. Even if people are involved, the cases may not correspond to people. For example, in Table 1.1, each row represents a different order and not the customer who made the purchases (notice that the same person made two different orders). A common place to find the *who* of the table is the leftmost column. It's often an identifying variable for the cases, in this example, the order number.

If you collect the data yourself, you'll know what the cases are and how the variables are defined. But, often, you'll be looking at data that someone else collected. The information about the data, called the metadata, might have to come from the company's database administrator or from the *information technology* department of a company. **Metadata** typically contains information about *how*, *when*, and *where* (and possibly *why*) the data were collected; *who* each case represents; and the definitions of all the variables.

A general term for a data table like the one shown in Table 1.1 is a **spreadsheet**, a name that comes from bookkeeping ledgers of financial information. The data were typically spread across facing pages of a bound ledger, the book used by an accountant for keeping records of expenditures and sources of income. For the accountant, the columns were the types of expenses and income, and the cases were transactions, typically invoices or receipts. These days, it is common to keep modest-size datasets in a spreadsheet even if no accounting is involved. It is usually easy to move a data table from a spreadsheet program to a program designed for statistical graphics and analysis, either directly or by copying the data table and pasting it into the statistics program.

Although data tables and spreadsheets are great for relatively small data sets, they are cumbersome for the complex data sets that companies must maintain on a day-to-day basis. Try to imagine a spreadsheet from a company the size of Amazon with customers in the rows and products in the columns. Amazon has tens of millions of customers and millions of products. But very few customers have purchased more than a few dozen items, so almost all the entries would be blank—not a very efficient way to store information. For that reason, various other database architectures are used to store data. The most common is a relational database.

In a **relational database**, two or more separate data tables are linked together so that information can be merged across them. Each data table is a *relation* because it is about a specific set of cases with information about each of these cases for all (or at least most) of the variables ("fields" in database terminology). For example, a table of customers, along with demographic information on each, is such a relation. A data table of all the items sold by the company, including information on price, inventory, and past history, is another relation. Transactions may be held in a third "relation" that references each of the other two relations. Table 1.2 shows a small example.

In statistics, analyses are typically performed on a single relation because all variables must refer to the same cases. But often the data must be retrieved from a relational database. Retrieving data from these databases may require specific expertise with that software. In the rest of the book, we'll assume that the data have been retrieved and placed in a data table or spreadsheet with variables listed as columns and cases as the rows.

Customers

Customer Number	Name	City	State	Zip Code	Customer since	Gold Member?
473859	R. De Veaux	Williamstown	MA	01267	2007	No
127389	N. Sharpe	Washington	DC	20052	2000	Yes
335682	P. Velleman	Ithaca	NY	14580	2003	No
...						

Items

Product ID	Name	Price	Currently in Stock?
SC5662	Silver Cane	43.50	Yes
TH2839	Top Hat	29.99	No
RS3883	Red Sequined Shoes	35.00	Yes
...			

Transactions

Transaction Number	Date	Customer Number	Product ID	Quantity	Shipping Method	Free Ship?
T23478923	9/15/13	473859	SC5662	1	UPS 2nd Day	N
T23478924	9/15/13	473859	TH2839	1	UPS 2nd Day	N
T63928934	10/20/13	335682	TH2839	3	UPS Ground	N
T72348299	12/22/13	127389	RS3883	1	Fed Ex Ovnt	Y

Table 1.2   A relational database shows all the relevant information for three separate relations linked together by customer and product numbers.

FOR EXAMPLE   Identifying variables and the W's

Carly, a marketing manager at a credit card bank, wants to know if an offer mailed 3 months ago has affected customers' use of their cards. To answer that, she asks the information technology department to assemble the following information for each customer: total spending on the card during the 3 months before the offer (*Pre Spending*); total spending for 3 months after the offer (*Post Spending*); the customer's *Age* (by category); what kind of expenditure they made (*Segment*); if customers are enrolled in the website (*Enroll?*); what offer they were sent (*Offer*); and the amount each customer spent on the card in their segment (*Segment Spend*). She gets a spreadsheet whose first six rows look like this:

Account ID	Pre Spending	Spending	Age	Segment	Enroll?	Offer	Segment Spend
393371	$2,698.12	$6,261.40	25–34	Travel/Ent	NO	None	$887.36
462715	$2,707.92	$3,397.22	45–54	Retail	NO	Gift Card	$5,062.55
433469	$800.51	$4,196.77	65+	Retail	NO	None	$673.80
462716	$3,459.52	$3,335.00	25–34	Services	YES	Double Miles	$800.75
420605	$2,106.48	$5,576.83	35–44	Leisure	YES	Double Miles	$3,064.81
473703	$2,603.92	$7,397.50	<25	Travel/Ent	YES	Double Miles	$491.29

(*continued*)

QUESTION   Identify the cases and the variables. Describe as many of the W's as you can for this data set.

ANSWER   The cases are individual customers of the credit card bank. The data are from the internal records of the credit card bank for the past 6 months (3 months before and 3 months after an offer was sent to the customers). The variables include the account ID of the customer (*Account ID*) and the amount charged on the card before (*Pre Spending*) and after (*Post Spending*) the offer was sent out. Also included are the customer's *Age*, marketing *Segment*, whether they enrolled on the website (*Enroll?*), what offer they were sent (*Offer*), and how much they charged on the card in their marketing segment (*Segment Spend*).

1.2   Variable Types

When the values of a variable are simply the names of categories we call it a **categorical, or qualitative, variable**. When the values of a variable are measured numerical quantities with **units,** we call it a **quantitative variable**.

Descriptive responses to questions are often categories. For example, the responses to the questions "What type of mutual fund do you invest in?" or "What kind of advertising does your firm use?" yield categorical values. An important special case of categorical variables is one that has only two possible responses (usually "yes" or "no"), which arise naturally from questions like "Do you invest in the stock market?" or "Do you make online purchases from this website?"

Categorical, or Quantitative?

When area codes were first introduced all phones had dials. To reduce wear and tear on the dials and to speed calls, the lowest-digit codes (the fastest to dial—those for which the dial spun the least) were assigned to the largest cities. So, New York City was given 212, Chicago 312, LA 213, and Philadelphia 215, but rural upstate New York was 607, Joliet was 815, and San Diego 619. Back then, the numerical value of an area code could be used to guess something about the population of its region. But after dials gave way to push buttons, new area codes were assigned without regard to population and area codes are now just categories.

Question	Categories or Responses
Do you invest in the stock market?	___ Yes ___ No
What kind of advertising do you use?	___ Newspapers ___ Internet ___ Direct mailings
What is your class at school?	___ Freshman ___ Sophomore ___ Junior ___ Senior
I would recommend this course to another student.	___ Strongly Disagree ___ Slightly Disagree ___ Slightly Agree ___ Strongly Agree
How satisfied are you with this product?	___ Very Unsatisfied ___ Unsatisfied ___ Satisfied ___ Very Satisfied

Table 1.3   Some examples of categorical variables.

Many measurements are quantitative. In a purchase record, price, quantity, and time spent on the website are all quantitative values with units (dollars, count, and seconds). For quantitative variables, the units tell how each value has been measured. Even more important, units such as yen, cubits, carats, angstroms, nanoseconds, miles per hour, or degrees Celsius tell us the *scale* of measurement, so we know how far apart two values are. Without units, the values of a measured variable have no meaning. It does little good to be promised a raise of 5000 a year if you don't know whether it will be paid in euros, dollars, yen, or Estonian krooni. An essential part of a quantitative variable is its units.

The distinction between categorical and quantitative variables seems clear, but there are reasons to be careful. First, some variables can be considered as either categorical or quantitative, depending on the kind of questions we ask about them. For example, the variable *Age* would be considered quantitative if the responses were numerical and they had units. A doctor would certainly consider *Age* to be quantitative. The units could be years, or for infants, the doctor would want even more precise units, like months, or even days. On the other hand, a retailer might lump together the values into categories like "Child (12 years or less)," "Teen (13 to 19)," "Adult (20 to 64)," or "Senior (65 or over)." For many purposes, like knowing which song download coupon to send you, that might be all the information needed. Then *Age* would be a categorical variable.

How to classify some variables as categorical or quantitative may seem obvious. But be careful. Area codes may look quantitative, but are really categories. What about ZIP codes? They are categories too, but the numbers do contain information. If you look at a map of the United States with ZIP codes, you'll see that as you move West, the first digit of ZIP codes increases, so treating them as quantitative might make sense for some questions.

Another reason to be careful about classifying variables comes from the analysis of Big Data. When analysts want to decide what advertisement to send to the web page you're looking at, or what the probability is that you'll renew your phone contract, they use automatic methods involving dozens or even hundreds of variables. Usually the software used to do the analysis has to guess the type of variable from its values. When the variable contains symbols other than numbers, the software will correctly type the variable as categorical, but just because a variable has numbers doesn't mean it is quantitative. We've seen examples (area code, order number) where that's just not the case. Data miners spend much of their time going back through data sets to correctly retype variables as categorical or quantitative to avoid silly mistakes of misuse. Chapter 2 discusses summaries and displays of categorical variables more fully. Chapter 3 discusses quantitative variables, which require different summaries and displays.

Identifiers

A special kind of categorical variable is worth mentioning. **Identifier variables** are categorical variables whose only purpose is to assign a unique identifier code to each individual in the data set. Your student ID number, social security number, and phone number are all identifiers.

Identifier variables are crucial in this era of Big Data because by uniquely identifying the cases, they make it possible to combine data from different sources, protect confidentiality, and provide unique labels. Your school's grade transcripts are likely in a different relation than your bursar bill records. Your student ID is what links them. Most companies keep such relational databases. The identifier is crucial to linking one data table to another in a relational database. The identifiers in Table 1.2 are the *Customer Number, Product ID*, and *Transaction Number*. Variables like *UPS Tracking Number* and *Social Security Number*, are other examples of identifiers.

Other Data Types

Many companies follow up with customers after a service call or sale with an online questionnaire. They might ask:

"How satisfied were you with the service you received?"

1) Not satisfied; 2) Somewhat satisfied; 3) Moderately satisfied; or 4) Extremely satisfied.

Is this variable categorical or quantitative? There is certainly an *order* of perceived worth; higher numbers indicate higher perceived worth. An employee whose customer responses average around 4 seems to be doing a better job than one whose average is around 2, but are they *twice* as good? These values are not strictly number, so we can't really answer that question. When the values of a categorical variable have an intrinsic order, we can say that the variable is **ordinal**. By contrast, a categorical variable with unordered categories

Year	Total Revenue (in $M)
2002	3288.9
2003	4075.5
2004	5294.2
2005	6369.3
2006	7786.9
2007	9441.5
2008	10,383.0
2009	9774.6
2010	10,707
2011	11,700
2012	13,300

Table 1.4   Starbucks's total revenue (in $M) for the years 2002 to 2012.

is sometimes called **nominal.** Values can be individually ordered (e.g., the ranks of employees based on the number of days they've worked for the company) or ordered in classes (e.g., Freshman, Sophomore, Junior, Senior). Ordering is not absolute; how the values are ordered depends on the purpose of the ordering. For example, are the categories Infant, Youth, Teen, Adult, and Senior ordinal? Well, if we are ordering on age, they surely are and how to order the categories is clear. But if we are ordering on purchase volume, it is likely that either Teen or Adult will be the top group.[1]

Cross-Sectional and Time Series Data

The quantitative variable *Total Revenue* in Table 1.4 is an example of a time series. A **time series** is an ordered sequence of values of a single quantitative variable measured at regular intervals over time. Time series are common in business. Typical measuring points are months, quarters, or years, but virtually any consistently-spaced time interval is possible. Variables collected over time hold special challenges for statistical analysis, and Chapter 19 discusses these in more detail.

By contrast, most of the methods in this book are better suited for **cross-sectional data,** where several variables are measured at the same time point. If we collect data on sales revenue, number of customers, and expenses for last month at *each* Starbucks (more than 20,000 locations as of 2012) at one point in time, this would be cross-sectional data. Cross-sectional data may contain some time information (such as dates), but it isn't a time series because it isn't measured at regular intervals. Because different methods are used to analyze these different types of data, it is important to be able to identify both time series and cross-sectional data sets.

FOR EXAMPLE   Identifying the types of variables

QUESTION   Before she can continue with her analysis, Carly (from the example on page 5) must classify each variable as being quantitative or categorical (or possibly both), and whether the data are a time series or cross-sectional. For quantitative variables, what are the units? For categorical variables, are they nominal or ordinal?

ANSWER

Account ID – categorical (nominal, identifier)

Pre Spending – quantitative (units $)

Post Spending – quantitative (units $)

Age – categorical (ordinal). Could be quantitative if we had more precise information

Segment – categorical (nominal)

Enroll? – categorical (nominal)

Offer – categorical (nominal)

Segment Spend – quantitative (units $)

The data are cross-sectional. We do not have successive values over time.

---

[1]Some people differentiate quantitative variables according to whether their measured values have a defined value for zero. This is a technical distinction and usually not one we'll need to make. (For example, it isn't correct to say that a temperature of 80°F is twice as hot as 40°F because 0° is an arbitrary value. On the Celsius scale those temperatures are 26.67°C and 4.44°C—a ratio of 6.) The term *interval scale* is sometimes applied to quantitative variables that lack a defined zero, and the term *ratio scale* is applied to measurements for which such ratios are appropriate.

1.3   Data Sources: Where, How, and When

We must know *who*, *what*, and *why* to analyze data. Without knowing these three, we don't have enough to start. Of course, we'd always like to know more because the more we know, the more we'll understand and the better our decisions will be. If possible, we'd like to know the *where*, *how*, and *when* of data as well. Values recorded in 1947 may mean something different than similar values recorded last year. Values measured in Abu Dhabi may differ in meaning from similar measurements made in Mexico.

How the data are collected can make the difference between insight and nonsense. As we'll see later, data that come from a voluntary survey on the Internet are almost always worthless. In a recent Internet poll, 84% of respondents said "no" to the question of whether subprime borrowers should be bailed out. While it may be true that 84% of those 23,418 respondents did say that, it's dangerous to assume that that group is representative of any larger group. To make inferences from the data you have at hand to the world at large, you need to ensure that the data you have are representative of the larger group. Chapter 8 discusses sound methods for *designing* a *survey* or poll to help ensure that the inferences you make are valid.

Another way to collect valid data is by performing an experiment in which you actively manipulate variables (called factors) to see what happens. Most of the "junk mail" credit card offers that you receive are actually experiments done by marketing groups in those companies. They may make different versions of an offer to selected groups of customers to see which one works best before rolling out the winning idea to the entire customer base. Chapter 20 discusses both the design and the analysis of experiments like these.

Sometimes, the answer to a question you may have can be found in data that someone or some organization has already collected. Internally, companies may analyze data from their own databases or data warehouse. They may also supplement or rely entirely on data collected by others. Many companies, nonprofit organizations, and government agencies collect vast amounts of data via the Internet. Some organizations may charge you a fee for accessing or downloading their data. The U.S. government collects information on nearly every aspect of life in the United States, both social and economic (see for example www.census.gov, or more generally, www.usa.gov), as the European Union does for Europe (see ec.europa.eu/eurostat). International organizations such as the World Health Organization (www.who.org) and polling agencies such as Pew Research (www.pewresearch.org) offer information on a variety of current social and demographic trends. Data like these are usually collected for different purposes than to answer your particular business question. So you should be cautious when generalizing from data like these. Unless the data were collected in a way that ensures that they are representative of the population in which you are interested, you may be misled. Chapter 24 discusses data mining, which attempts to use Big Data to make hypotheses and draw insights.

There's a World of Data on the Internet

These days, one of the richest sources of data is the Internet. With a bit of practice, you can learn to find data on almost any subject. We found many of the data sets used in this book by searching on the Internet. The Internet has both advantages and disadvantages as a source of data. Among the advantages are the fact that often you'll be able to find even more current data than we present. One disadvantage is that references to Internet addresses can "break" as sites evolve, move, and die. Another disadvantage is that important metadata—information about the collection, quality, and intent of the data—may be missing.

Our solution to these challenges is to offer the best advice we can to help you search for the data, wherever they may be residing. We usually point you to a website. We'll sometimes suggest search terms and offer other guidance.

(continued)

Some words of caution, though: Data found on Internet sites may not be formatted in the best way for use in statistics software. Although you may see a data table in standard form, an attempt to copy the data may leave you with a single column of values. You may have to work in your favorite statistics or spreadsheet program to reformat the data into variables. You will also probably want to remove commas from large numbers and such extra symbols as money indicators ($, ¥, £, €); few statistics packages can handle these.

Throughout this book, we often provide a margin note for a new dataset listing some of the W's of the data. When we can, we also offer a reference for the source of the data. It's a habit we recommend. The first step of any data analysis is to know why you are examining the data (what you want to know), whom each row of your data table refers to, and what the variables (the columns of the table) record. These are the *Why*, the *Who*, and the *What*. Identifying them is a key part of the *Plan* step of any analysis. Make sure you know all three before you spend time analyzing the data.

FOR EXAMPLE   Identifying data sources

On the basis of her initial analysis, Carly asks her colleague Ying Mei to e-mail a sample of customers from the Travel and Entertainment segment and ask about their card use and household demographics. Carly asks another colleague, Gregg, to design a study about their double miles offer. In this study, a random sample of customers receives one of three offers: the standard double miles offer; a double miles offer good on any airline; or no offer.

QUESTION   For each of the three data sets—Carly's original data set and Ying Mei's and Gregg's sets—state whether they come from a designed survey or a designed experiment or are collected in another way.

ANSWER   Carly's data set was derived from transactional data, not part of a survey or experiment. Ying Mei's data come from a designed survey, and Gregg's data come from a designed experiment.

JUST CHECKING

An insurance company that specializes in commercial property insurance has a separate database for their policies that involve churches and schools. Here is a small portion of that database.

Policy Number	Years Claim Free	Net Property Premium ($)	Net Liability Premium ($)	Total Property Value ($000)	Median Age in ZIP Code	School?	Territory	Coverage
4000174699	1	3107	503	1036	40	FALSE	AL580	BLANKET
8000571997	2	1036	261	748	42	FALSE	PA192	SPECIFIC
8000623296	1	438	353	344	30	FALSE	ID60	BLANKET
3000495296	1	582	339	270	35	TRUE	NC340	BLANKET
5000291199	4	993	357	218	43	FALSE	OK590	BLANKET
8000470297	2	433	622	108	31	FALSE	NV140	BLANKET
1000042399	4	2461	1016	1544	41	TRUE	NJ20	BLANKET
4000554596	0	7340	1782	5121	44	FALSE	FL530	BLANKET
3000260397	0	1458	261	1037	42	FALSE	NC560	BLANKET
8000333297	2	392	351	177	40	FALSE	OR190	BLANKET
4000174699	1	3107	503	1036	40	FALSE	AL580	BLANKET

1 List as many of the W's as you can for this data set.

2 Classify each variable as to whether you think it should be treated as categorical or quantitative (or both); if quantitative, identify the units.

WHAT CAN GO WRONG?

- **Don't label a variable as categorical or quantitative without thinking about the data and what they represent.** The same variable can sometimes take on different roles.

- **Don't assume that a variable is quantitative just because its values are numbers.** Categories are often given numerical labels. Don't let that fool you into thinking they have quantitative meaning. Look at the context.

- **Always be skeptical.** One reason to analyze data is to discover the truth. Even when you are told a context for the data, it may turn out that the truth is a bit (or even a lot) different. The context colors our interpretation of the data, so those who want to influence what you think may slant the context. A survey that seems to be about all students may in fact report just the opinions of those who visited a fan website. The question that respondents answered may be posed in a way that influences responses.

ETHICS IN ACTION

Sarah Potterman, a doctoral student in educational psychology, is researching the effectiveness of various interventions recommended to help children with learning disabilities improve their reading skills. One particularly intriguing approach is an interactive software system that uses analogy-based phonics.

Sarah contacted the company that developed this software, RSPT Inc., to obtain the system free of charge for use in her research. RSPT Inc. expressed interest in having her compare its product with other intervention strategies and was quite confident that its approach would be the most effective. Not only did the company provide Sarah with free software, but RSPT Inc. also generously offered to fund her research with a grant to cover her data collection and analysis costs.

- Identify the ethical dilemma in this scenario.

- What are the undesirable consequences?

- Propose an ethical solution that considers the welfare of all stakeholders.

Jim Hopler is operations manager for a local office of a top-ranked full-service brokerage firm. With increasing competition from both discount and online brokers, Jim's firm has redirected attention to attaining exceptional customer service through its client-facing staff, namely brokers. In particular, management wished to emphasize the excellent advisory services provided by its brokers.

Results from surveying clients about the advice received from brokers at the local office revealed that 20% rated it poor, 5% rated it *below average*, 15% rated it *average*, 10% rated it *above average*, and 50% rated it *outstanding*. With corporate approval, Jim and his management team instituted several changes in an effort to provide the best possible advisory services at the local office. Their goal was to increase the percentage of clients who viewed their advisory services as *outstanding*.

Surveys conducted after the changes were implemented showed the following results: 5% *poor*, 5% *below average*, 20% *average*, 40% *above average*, and 30% *outstanding*. In discussing these results, the management team expressed concern that the percentage of clients who considered their advisory services *outstanding* fell from 50% to 30%.

One member of the team suggested an alternative way of summarizing the data. By coding the categories on a scale from 1 = poor to 5 = outstanding and computing the average, they found that the average rating increased from 3.65 to 3.85 as a result of the changes implemented. Jim was delighted to see that their changes were successful in improving the level of advisory services offered at the local office. In his report to corporate, he only included average ratings for the client surveys.

- Identify the ethical dilemma in this scenario.

- What are the undesirable consequences?

- Propose an ethical solution that considers the welfare of all stakeholders.

WHAT HAVE WE LEARNED?

Learning Objectives	**Understand that data are values, whether numerical or labels, together with their context.**
	• *Who, what, why, where, when* (and *how*)—the W's—help nail down the context of the data.
	• We must know *who*, *what*, and *why* to be able to say anything useful based on the data. The *who* are the cases. The *what* are the variables. A variable gives information about each of the cases. The *why* helps us decide which way to treat the variables.
	• Stop and identify the W's whenever you have data, and be sure you can identify the cases and the variables.
	Identify whether a variable is being used as categorical or quantitative.
	• Categorical variables identify a category for each case. Usually we think about the counts of cases that fall in each category. (An exception is an identifier variable that just names each case.)
	• Quantitative variables record measurements or amounts of something; they must have units.
	• Sometimes we may treat the same variable as categorical or quantitative depending on what we want to learn from it, which means some variables can't be pigeonholed as one type or the other.
	Consider the source of your data and the reasons the data were collected. That can help you understand what you might be able to learn from the data.

Terms	
Big Data	The collection and analysis of data sets so large and complex that traditional methods typically brought to bear on the problem would be overwhelmed.
Business analytics	The process of using statistical analysis and modeling to drive business decisions.
Case	A case is an individual about whom or which we have data.
Categorical (or qualitative) variable	A variable that names categories (whether with words or numerals) is called categorical or qualitative.
Context	The context ideally tells *who* was measured, *what* was measured, *how* the data were collected, *where* the data were collected, and *when* and *why* the study was performed.
Cross-sectional data	Data taken from situations that vary over time but measured at a single time instant is said to be a cross-section of the time series.
Data	Recorded values whether numbers or labels, together with their context.
Data mining	The process of using a variety of statistical tools to analyze large data bases or data warehouses.
Data table	An arrangement of data in which each row represents a case and each column represents a variable.
Data warehouse	A large data base of information collected by a company or other organization usually to record transactions that the organization makes, but also used for analysis via data mining.
Experimental unit	An individual in a study for which or for whom data values are recorded. Human experimental units are usually called subjects or participants.
Identifier variable	A categorical variable that records a unique value for each case, used to name or identify it.
Metadata	Auxiliary information about variables in a database, typically including *how*, *when*, and *where* (and possibly *why*) the data were collected; *who* each case represents; and the definitions of all the variables.
Nominal variable	The term "nominal" can be applied to a variable whose values are used only to name categories.
Ordinal variable	The term "ordinal" can be applied to a variable whose categorical values possess some kind of order.
Participant	A human experimental unit. Also called a subject.
Quantitative variable	A variable in which the numbers are values of measured quantities with units.
Record	Information about an individual in a database.

Relational database	A relational database stores and retrieves information. Within the database, information is kept in data tables that can be "related" to each other.
Respondent	Someone who answers, or responds to, a survey.
Spreadsheet	A spreadsheet is layout designed for accounting that is often used to store and manage data tables. Excel is a common example of a spreadsheet program.
Subject	A human experimental unit. Also called a participant.
Time series	Data measured over time. Usually the time intervals are equally spaced or regularly spaced (e.g., every week, every quarter, or every year).
Transactional data	Data collected to record the individual transactions of a company or organization.
Units	A quantity or amount adopted as a standard of measurement, such as dollars, hours, or grams.
Variable	A variable holds information about the same characteristic for many cases.

TECHNOLOGY HELP: Data

Most often we find statistics on a computer using a program, or *package*, designed for that purpose. There are many different statistics packages, but they all do essentially the same things.

If you understand what the computer needs to know to do what you want and what it needs to show you in return, you can figure out the specific details of most packages pretty easily.

For example, to get your data into a computer statistics package, you need to tell the computer:

- Where to find the data. This usually means directing the computer to a file stored on your computer's disk or to data on a database. Or it might just mean that you have copied the data from a spreadsheet program or Internet site and it is currently on your computer's clipboard. Usually, the data should be in the form of a data table. Most computer statistics packages prefer the *delimiter* that marks the division between elements of a data table to be a tab character and the delimiter that marks the end of a case to be a *return* character.

- Where to put the data. (Usually this is handled automatically.)

- What to call the variables. Some data tables have variable names as the first row of the data, and often statistics packages can take the variable names from the first row automatically.

EXCEL

To open a file containing data in Excel:

- Choose **File > Open**.

- Browse to find the file to open. Data files provided with this text are tab-delimited text files (.txt) or comma-delimited text files (.csv). Excel supports many other file formats.

- You can also copy tables of data from other sources, such as Internet sites, and paste them into an Excel spreadsheet. Excel can recognize the format of many tables copied this way, but this method may not work for some tables.

- When opening a data file, Excel may not recognize the format of the data. If data include dates or other special formats ($, €, ¥, etc.), identify the desired format. Select the cells or columns to reformat and choose **Format > Cell**. Often, the General format is the best option.

Brief **Case**

Credit Card Bank

Like all credit and charge card companies, this company makes money on each of its cardholders' transactions. Thus, its profitability is directly linked to card usage. To increase customer spending on its cards, the company sends many different offers to its cardholders, and market researchers analyze the results to see which offers yield the largest increases in the average amount charged.

On your disk (in the file **Credit Card Bank**) is part of a database like the one used by the researchers. For each customer, it contains several variables in a spreadsheet.

Examine the data in the data file. List as many of the W's as you can for these data and classify each variable as categorical or quantitative. If quantitative, identify the units.

EXERCISES

SECTION 1.1

1. A real estate major collected information on some recent local home sales. The first 6 lines of the database appear below. The columns correspond to the house identification number, the community name, the ZIP code, the number of acres of the property, the year the house was built, the market value, and the size of the living area (in square feet).

a) What does a row correspond to in this data table? How would you best describe its role: as a participant, subject, case, respondent, or experimental unit?
b) How many variables are measured on each row?

House_ID	Neighborhood	Mail_ZIP	Acres	Yr_Built	Full_Market_Value	Size
413400536	Greenfield Manor	12859	1.00	1967	$1,00,400	960
4128001474	Fort Amherst	12801	0.09	1961	$1,32,500	906
412800344	Dublin	12309	1.65	1993	$1,40,000	1620
4128001552	Granite Springs	10598	0.33	1969	$67,100	900
412800352	Arcady	10562	2.29	1955	$1,90,000	1224
413400322	Ormsbee	12859	9.13	1997	$1,26,900	1056

2. A local bookstore is keeping a database of its customers to find out more about their spending habits so that the store can start to make personal recommendations based on past purchases. Here are the first five rows of their database:

a) What does a row correspond to in this data table? How would you best describe its role: as a participant, subject, case, respondent, or experimental unit?
b) How many variables are measured on each row?

Transaction ID	Customer ID	Date	ISBN Number of Purchase	Price	Coupon?	Gift?	Quantity
29784320912	4J438	11/12/2009	345-23-2355	$29.95	N	N	1
26483589001	3K729	9/30/2009	983-83-2739	$16.99	N	N	1
26483589002	3K729	9/30/2009	102-65-2332	$9.95	Y	N	1
36429489305	3U034	12/5/2009	295-39-5884	$35.00	N	Y	1
36429489306	3U034	12/5/2009	183-38-2957	$79.95	N	Y	1

SECTION 1.2

3. Referring to the real estate data table of Exercise 1,

a) For each variable, would you describe it as primarily categorical, or quantitative? If quantitative, what are the units? If categorical, is it ordinal or simply nominal?
b) Are these data a time series, or are these cross-sectional? Explain briefly.

4. Referring to the bookstore data table of Exercise 2,

a) For each variable, would you describe it as primarily categorical, or quantitative? If quantitative, what are the units? If categorical, is it ordinal or simply nominal?
b) Are these data a time series, or are these cross-sectional? Explain briefly.

SECTION 1.3

5. For the real estate data of Exercise 1, do the data appear to have come from a designed survey or experiment? What concerns might you have about drawing conclusions from this data set?

6. A student finds data on an Internet site that contains financial information about selected companies. He plans to analyze the data and use the results to develop a stock investment strategy. What kind of data source is he using? What concerns might you have about drawing conclusions from this data set?

CHAPTER EXERCISES

For each description of data in Exercises 7 to 26, identify the W's, name the variables, specify for each variable whether its use indicates it should be treated as categorical or quantitative, and for any quantitative variable identify the units in which it was measured (if they are not provided, give some possible units in which they might be measured). Specify whether the data come from a designed survey or experiment. Are the variables time series or cross-sectional? Report any concerns you have as well.

7. The news. Find a newspaper or magazine article in which some data are reported (e.g., see *The Wall Street Journal*, *Financial Times*, *Business Week*, or *Fortune*). For the data discussed in the article, answer the questions above. Include a copy of the article with your report.

8. The Internet. Find an Internet site on which some data are reported. For the data found on the site, answer as many of the questions above as you can. Include a copy of the URL with your report.

9. Survey. An automobile manufacturer wants to know what college students think about electric vehicles. They ask you to conduct a survey that asks students, "Do you think there will be more electric or gasoline powered vehicles on the road in 2025?" and "How likely are you to buy an electric vehicle in the next 10 years?" (scale of 1 = not at all likely to 5 = very likely).

10. Your survey. Think of a question that you'd like to know the answer to that might be answered with a survey. What are the questions? Identify the variables and answer the questions above.

11. World databank. The World Bank provides economic data on most of the world's countries at their website (databank.worldbank.org/data/home.aspx). Select 5 indicators that they provide and answer the questions above for these variables.

12. Arby's menu. A listing posted by the Arby's restaurant chain gives, for each of the sandwiches it sells, the type of meat in the sandwich, number of calories, and serving size in ounces. The data might be used to assess the nutritional value of the different sandwiches.

13. MBA admissions. A school in the northeastern United States is concerned with the recent drop in female students in its MBA program. It decides to collect data from the admissions office on each applicant, including: sex of each applicant, age of each applicant, whether or not they were accepted, whether or not they attended, and the reason for not attending (if they did not attend). The school hopes to find commonalities among the female accepted students who have decided not to attend the business program.

14. MBA admissions II. An internationally recognized MBA program outside of Paris intends to also track the GPA of the MBA students and compares MBA performance to standardized test scores over a six-year period (2009–2014).

15. Pharmaceutical firm. Scientists at a major pharmaceutical firm conducted an experiment to study the effectiveness of an herbal compound to treat the common cold. They exposed volunteers to a cold virus, then gave them either the herbal compound or a sugar solution known to have no effect on colds. Several days later they assessed each patient's condition using a cold severity scale ranging from 0–5. They found no evidence of the benefits of the compound.

16. Start-up company. A start-up company is building a database of customers and sales information. For each customer, it records name, ID number, region of the country (1 = East, 2 = South, 3 = Midwest, 4 = West), date of last purchase, amount of purchase, and item purchased.

17. Vineyards. Business analysts hoping to provide information helpful to grape growers sent out a questionnaire to a sample of growers requesting these data about vineyards: size, number of years in existence, state, varieties of grapes grown, average case price, gross sales, and percent profit.

18. Spectrem Group polls. The Spectrem provides services for the affluent and retirement markets. In a recent survey, they found that millionaires tend to prefer dogs to cats from a question asking them to list the pets they own. They also found that senior executives are more likely to buy treats and toys for their pet than regular investors by asking, "What services and products do you buy for your pet?" (www.spectrem.com/news/life-ruff-ruff-529).

19. EPA. The Environmental Protection Agency (EPA) tracks fuel economy of automobiles. Among the data EPA analysts collect from the manufacturer are the manufacturer (Ford, Toyota, etc.), vehicle type (car, SUV, etc.), weight, horsepower, and gas mileage (mpg) for city and highway driving.

20. Consumer Reports. In 2013, Consumer Reports published an article comparing smart phones. It listed 46 phones, giving brand, price, display size, operating system (Android, iOS, or Windows Phone), camera image size (megapixels), and whether it had a memory card slot.

21. Zagat. Zagat.com provides ratings from customer experiences on restaurants. For each restaurant, the percentage of customers that liked it, the average cost and ratings of the food, decor, and service (all on a 30-point scale) are reported.

22. L.L. Bean. L.L. Bean is a large U.S. retailer that depends heavily on its catalog sales. It collects data internally and tracks the number of catalogs mailed out, the number of square inches in each catalog, and the sales ($ thousands) in the four weeks following each mailing. The company is interested in learning more about the relationship (if any) among the timing and space of their catalogs and their sales.

23. Stock market. An online survey of students in a large MBA Statistics class at a business school in the northeastern United States asked them to report their total personal investment in the stock market ($), total number of different stocks currently held, total invested in mutual funds ($), and the name of each mutual fund in which they have invested. The data were used in the aggregate for classroom illustrations.

24. Theme park sites. A study on the potential for developing theme parks in various locations throughout Europe in 2013 collects the following information: the country where the proposed site is located, estimated cost to acquire site, size of population within a one-hour drive of the site, size of the site, and availability of mass transportation within

five minutes of the site. The data will be used to present to prospective developers.

25. Indy 2009. The 2.5-mile Indianapolis Motor Speedway has been the home to a race on Memorial Day nearly every year since 1911. Even during the first race there were controversies. Ralph Mulford was given the checkered flag first but took three extra laps just to make sure he'd completed 500 miles. When he finished, another driver, Ray Harroun, was being presented with the winner's trophy, and Mulford's protests were ignored. Harroun averaged 74.6 mph for the 500 miles. Here are the data for the first few and six recent Indianapolis 500 races.

Year	Winner	Car	Time (hrs)	Speed (mph)	Car #
1911	Ray Harroun	Marmon Model 32	6.7022	74.602	32
1912	Joe Dawson	National	6.3517	78.719	8
1913	Jules Goux	Peugeot	6.5848	75.933	16
...					
...					
2007	Dario Franchitti	Dallara/Honda	3.2943	151.774	27
2008	Scott Dixon	Dallara	3.4826	143.567	9
2009	Hélio Castroneves	Dallara	3.3262	150.318	3
2010	Dario Franchitti	Dallara/Honda	3.0936	161.623	10
2011	Dan Wheldon	Dallara/Honda	2.9366	170.265	98
2012	Dario Franchitti	Dallara/Honda	2.9809	167.734	50

26. Kentucky Derby. The Kentucky Derby is a horse race that has been run every year since 1875 at Churchill Downs, Louisville, Kentucky. The race started as a 1.5-mile race, but in 1896 it was shortened to 1.25 miles because experts felt that three-year-old horses shouldn't run such a long race that early in the season. (It has been run in May every year but one—1901—when it took place on April 29.) The table at the bottom of the page shows the data for the first few and a few recent races. http://www.kentuckyderby.ag/kentuckyderby-results.php and http://horseracing.about.com/od/history/l/blderbywin.htm

Date	Winner	Margin (lengths)	Jockey	Winner's Payoff ($)	Duration (min:sec)	Track Condition
May 17, 1875	Aristides	2	O. Lewis	2850	2:37.75	Fast
May 15, 1876	Vagrant	2	B. Swim	2950	2:38.25	Fast
May 22, 1877	Baden-Baden	2	W. Walker	3300	2:38.00	Fast
May 21, 1878	Day Star	1	J. Carter	4050	2:37.25	Dusty
May 20, 1879	Lord Murphy	1	C. Shauer	3550	2:37.00	Fast
...						
May 2, 2008	Big Brown	4 3/4	Kent Desormeaux	2,000,000.00	2:01.82	Fast
May 2, 2009	Mine That Bird	6 3/4	Calvin Borel	2,000,000.00	2:02.66	Fast
May 1, 2010	Super Saver	2 3/4	Calvin Borel	2,000,000.00	2:04.45	Fast
May 7, 2011	Animal Kingdom	2 1/2	John R. Velazquez	2,000,000.00	2:02.04	Fast
May 5, 2012	I'll Have Another	1 1/2	Mario Gutierrez	2,000,000.00	2:01.83	Fast

When you organize data in a spreadsheet, it is important to lay it out as a data table. For each of these examples in Exercises 27 to 30, show how you would lay out these data. Indicate the headings of columns and what would be found in each row.

27. Mortgages. For a study of mortgage loan performance: amount of the loan, the name of the borrower.

28. Employee performance. Data collected to determine performance-based bonuses: employee ID, average contract closed (in $), supervisor's rating (1–10), years with the company.

29. Company performance. Data collected for financial planning: weekly sales, week (week number of the year), sales predicted by last year's plan, difference between predicted sales and realized sales.

30. Command performance. Data collected on investments in Broadway shows: number of investors, total invested, name of the show, profit/loss after one year.

For the following examples in Exercises 31 to 34, indicate whether the data are time-series or cross-sectional.

31. Car sales. Number of cars sold by each salesperson in a dealership in September.

32. Motorcycle sales. Number of motorcycles sold by a dealership in each month of 2014.

33. Cross sections. Average diameter of trees brought to a sawmill in each week of a year.

34. Series. Attendance at the third World Series game recording the age of each fan.

JUST CHECKING ANSWERS

1 Who—policies on churches and schools

 What—policy number, years claim free, net property premium ($), net liability premium ($), total property value ($000), median age in ZIP code, school?, territory, coverage

 How—company records

 When—not given

2 Policy number: identifier (categorical)

 Years claim free: quantitative

 Net property premium: quantitative ($)

 Net liability premium: quantitative ($)

 Total property value: quantitative ($)

 Median age in ZIP code: quantitative

 School?: categorical (true/false)

 Territory: categorical

 Coverage: categorical

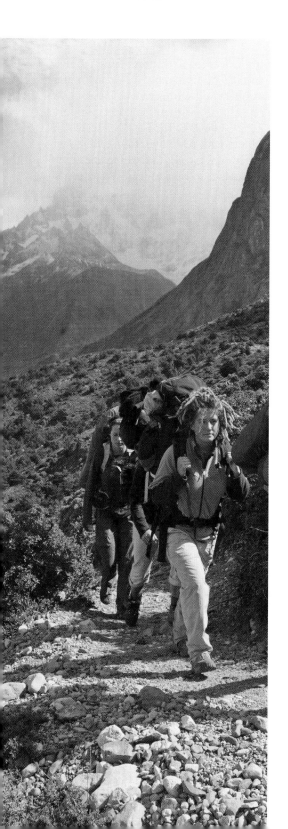

2

Displaying and Describing Categorical Data

KEEN, Inc.

KEEN, Inc. was started to create a sandal designed for a variety of water activities. The sandals quickly became popular due to their unique patented toe protection—a black bumper to protect the toes when adventuring out on rivers and trails. Today, the KEEN brand offers over 300 different outdoor performance and outdoor inspired casual footwear styles as well as bags and socks.

Few companies experience the kind of growth that KEEN has in its first nine years. Amazingly, they've done this with relatively little advertising and by selling primarily to specialty footwear and outdoor stores, in addition to online outlets.

After the 2004 Tsunami disaster, KEEN cut its advertising budget almost completely and donated over $1 million to help the victims and establish the KEEN Foundation to support environmental and social causes. Philanthropy and community projects continue to play an integral part of the KEEN brand values. In fact, KEEN has established a giving program with a philanthropic effort devoted to helping the environment, conservation, and social movements involving the outdoors.

WHO	Visits to the KEEN, Inc. website
WHAT	Source (search engine or other) that led to KEEN's website
WHEN	February 2013
WHERE	Worldwide
HOW	Data compiled by KEEN
WHY	To understand customer use of the website and how they got there

KEEN, Inc., like most companies, collects data on visits to its website. Each visit to the site and each subsequent action the visitor takes (changing the page, entering data, etc.) is recorded in a file called a usage, or access weblog. These logs contain a lot of potentially worthwhile information, but they are not easy to use. Here's one line from a log:

```
245.240.221.71 -- [1/Apr/2013:13:15:08-0800]" GET http://
www.keenfootwear.com/us/en/product/shoes/men/cnx/clear
water%20cnx/forest%20night!rust "http://www.google.com/"
"Mozilla/5.0WebTV/1.2 (compatible; MSIE 2.0)"
```

Unless the company has the analytic resources to deal with these files, it must rely on a third party to summarize the data. KEEN, like many other small and mid-sized companies, uses *Google Analytics* to collect and summarize its log data.

Imagine a whole table of data like the one above—with a line corresponding to every visit. In February 2013, there were 226,925 visits to the KEEN site, which would be a table with as many rows. The problem with a file like this—and in fact even with data tables—is that we can't see what's going on. And seeing is exactly what we want to do. We need ways to show the data so that we can see patterns, relationships, trends, and exceptions.

2.1 Summarizing a Categorical Variable

KEEN might be interested to know how people find their website. They might use the information to allocate their advertising revenue to various search engines, putting ads where they'll be seen by the most potential customers. The variable *Source* records, for each visit to KEEN's website, where the visit came from. The categories are all the search engines used, plus the label "Direct", which indicates that the customer typed in KEEN's web address (or URL) directly into the browser. To make sense of the 226,925 visits for which they have data, they'd like to summarize the variable and display the information in a way that can easily communicate the results to others.

Frequency Tables

A **frequency table** records the counts for each of the categories of the variable. Some tables report percentages, and many report both. For example, Table 2.1 shows the ways that customers found their way to the KEEN website.

Source	Visits	Visits by %
Google	130,158	57.36
Direct	52,969	23.34
E-mail	16,084	7.09
Bing	9,581	4.22
Yahoo	7,439	3.28
Facebook	2,253	0.99
Mobile	1,701	0.75
Other	6,740	2.97
Total	**226,925**	**100.00**

Table 2.1 A frequency table of the *Source* used by visitors to the KEEN, Inc. website. Notice the label "Other". When the number of categories gets too large, we often lump together values of the variable into "Other". When to do that is a judgment call, but it's a good idea to have fewer than about a dozen categories. (Source: KEEN, Inc., personal communication.)

> **FOR EXAMPLE** Making frequency and relative frequency tables
>
> The Super Bowl, the championship game of the National Football League of the United States, is an important annual social event for Americans, with tens of millions of viewers. The ads that air during the game are expensive: a 30-second ad during the 2013 Super Bowl cost about $4M. The high price of these commercials makes them high-profile and much anticipated, and so the advertisers feel pressure to be innovative, entertaining, and often humorous. Some people, in fact, watch the Super Bowl mainly for the commercials. Polls often ask whether respondents are more interested

Figure 2.10 A mosaic plot for *Class by Survival*. The plot is just like the segmented bar chart in Figure 2.9 except that the space has been taken out between the categories on the *x*-axis and the rectangles are proportional to the number of cases of the *x* variable as well. We can easily see that the number of survivors was far less than the nonsurvivors, something that we can't in the bar charts.

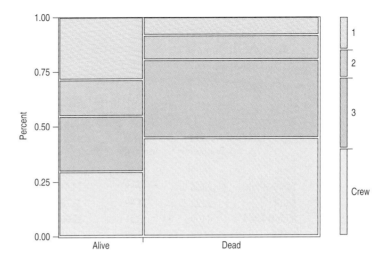

GUIDED EXAMPLE   Food Safety

Food storage and food safety are major issues for multinational food companies. A client wants to know if people of all age groups have the same degree of concern so GfK Roper Consulting asked 1500 people in five countries whether they agree with the following statement: "I worry about how safe the food I buy is." We would want to report to the client how concerns about food safety are related to age.

 PLAN   **Setup**
- State the objectives and goals of the study.
- Identify and define the variables.
- Provide the time frame of the data collection process.

Determine the appropriate analysis for data type.

The client wants to examine the distribution of responses to the food safety question and see whether they are related to the age of the respondent. GfK Roper Consulting collected data on this question in the fall of 2005 for their 2006 Worldwide report. We will use the data from that study.

The variable is *Food Safety*. The responses are in nonoverlapping categories of agreement, from Agree Completely to Disagree Completely (and Don't Know). There were originally 12 age groups, which we can combine into five:

Teen	13–19
Young Adult	20–29
Adult	30–39
Middle Aged	40–49
Mature	50 and older

Both variables, *Food Safety* and *Age*, are ordered categorical variables. To examine any differences in responses across age groups, it is appropriate to create a contingency table and a side-by-side bar chart. Here is a contingency table of "Food Safety" by "Age".

(continued)

DO **Mechanics** For a large data set like this, we rely on technology to make tables and displays.

		Food Safety						
		Agree Completely	**Agree Somewhat**	**Neither Disagree Nor Agree**	**Disagree Somewhat**	**Disagree Completely**	**Don't Know**	**Total**
Age	**Teen**	16.19	27.50	24.32	19.30	10.58	2.12	**100%**
	Young Adult	20.55	32.68	23.81	14.94	6.98	1.04	**100%**
	Adult	22.23	34.89	23.28	12.26	6.75	0.59	**100%**
	Middle Aged	24.79	35.31	22.02	12.43	5.06	0.39	**100%**
	Mature	26.60	33.85	21.21	11.89	5.82	0.63	**100%**

A side-by-side bar chart is particularly helpful when comparing multiple groups.

A side-by-side bar chart shows the percent of each response to the question by age group.

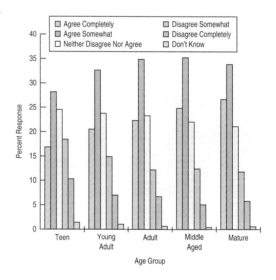

REPORT **Summary and Conclusions** Summarize the charts and analysis in context. Make recommendations if possible and discuss further analysis that is needed.

MEMO

Re: Food safety concerns by age

Our analysis of the GfK Roper Reports™ Worldwide survey data shows a weak pattern of concern about food safety that generally increases from youngest to oldest.

Our analysis thus far has not considered whether this trend is consistent across countries. If it were of interest to your group, we could perform a similar analysis for each of the countries.

The enclosed tables and plots provide support for these conclusions.

2.5   Simpson's Paradox

Here's an example showing that combining percentages across very different values or groups can give confusing results. Suppose there are two sales representatives, Peter and Katrina. Peter argues that he's the better salesperson, since he managed to close 83% of his last 120 prospects compared with Katrina's 78%. But let's look at the data a little more closely. Here (Table 2.7) are the results for each of their last 120 sales calls, broken down by the product they were selling.

Springfield Industries

Founded	1983
Employees	8536
Stock price	12.625
Average	3510.54

		Product		
		Printer Paper	**USB Flash Drive**	**Overall**
Sales Rep	**Peter**	90 out of 100 90%	10 out of 20 50%	100 out of 120 83%
	Katrina	19 out of 20 95%	75 out of 100 75%	94 out of 120 78%

Table 2.7   Look at the percentages within each Product category. Who has a better success rate closing sales of paper? Who has the better success rate closing sales of Flash Drives? Who has the better performance overall?

Look at the sales of the two products separately. For printer paper sales, Katrina had a 95% success rate, and Peter only had a 90% rate. When selling flash drives, Katrina closed her sales 75% of the time, but Peter only 50%. So Peter has better "overall" performance, but Katrina is better selling each product. How can this be?

This problem is known as **Simpson's Paradox**, named for the statistician who described it in the 1960s. Although it is rare, there have been a few well-publicized cases of it. As we can see from the example, the problem results from inappropriately combining percentages of different groups. Katrina concentrates on selling flash drives, which is more difficult, so her *overall* percentage is heavily influenced by her flash drive average. Peter sells more printer paper, which appears to be easier to sell. With their different patterns of selling, taking an overall percentage is misleading. Their manager should be careful not to conclude rashly that Peter is the better salesperson.

The lesson of Simpson's Paradox is to be sure to combine only comparable measurements for comparable individuals. Be especially careful when combining across different levels of a second variable. It's usually better to compare percentages *within* each level, rather than across levels.

Discrimination?

One famous example of Simpson's Paradox arose during an investigation of admission rates for men and women at the University of California at Berkeley's graduate schools. As reported in an article in *Science*, about 45% of male applicants were admitted, but only about 30% of female applicants got in. It looked like a clear case of discrimination. However, when the data were broken down by school (Engineering, Law, Medicine, etc.), it turned out that within each school, the women were admitted at nearly the same or, in some cases, much *higher* rates than the men. How could this be? Women applied in large numbers to schools with very low admission rates. (Law and Medicine, for example, admitted fewer than 10%.) Men tended to apply to Engineering and Science. Those schools have admission rates above 50%. When the total applicant pool was combined and the percentages were computed, the women had a much lower *overall* rate, but the combined percentage didn't really make sense.

WHAT CAN GO WRONG?

- **Don't violate the area principle.** This is probably the most common mistake in a graphical display. Violations of the area principle are often made for the sake of artistic presentation. Consider this pie chart of ways that respondents said they commute to work.

Would it surprise you to learn that the fraction who "Shared" rides to work is 33%, while the fraction who "Drive Alone" is 41%? This pie chart was made in Excel, but overuse of features that make it look interesting has hurt its ability to convey accurate information.

- **Keep it honest.** Here's a pie chart that displays data on the percentage of high school students who engage in specified dangerous behaviors as reported by the Centers for Disease Control. What's wrong with this plot?

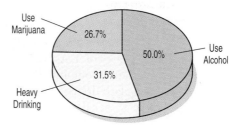

Try adding up the percentages. Or look at the 50% slice. Does it look right? Then think: What are these percentages of? Is there a "whole" that has been sliced up? In a pie chart, the proportions shown by each slice of the pie must add up to 100%, and each individual must fall into only one category. Of course, showing the pie on a slant makes it even harder to detect the error.

Here's another one. This chart shows the average number of texts in various time periods by American cell phone customers in the period 1999 to 2013.

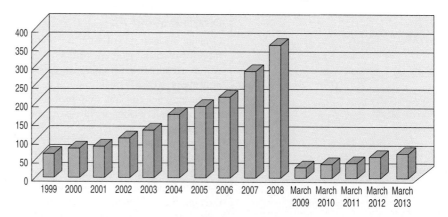

It may look as though text messaging decreased suddenly some time around 2009, which probably doesn't seem right to you. In fact, this chart has several problems. First, it's not a bar chart. Bar charts display counts of categories. This bar chart is a plot of a quantitative variable (average number of texts) against time—although to make it worse, some of the time periods are missing. Of course, the real problem is that starting in 2009, they reported the data for only one month instead of for the entire year.

- **Don't confuse percentages.** Many percentages based on conditional and joint distributions sound similar, but are different (see Table 2.4):

  - The percentage of Russians who answered "Yes": This is 500/1010 or 49.5%.
  - The percentage of those who answered "Yes" who were Russian: This is 500/2175 or 23%.
  - The percentage of those who were Russian *and* answered "Yes": This is 500/5039 or 9.92%.

  In each instance, pay attention to the wording that makes a restriction to a smaller group (those who are French, those who answered "Don't Know," and all respondents, respectively) before a percentage is found. This restricts the who of the problem and the associated denominator for the percentage. Your discussion of results must make these differences clear.

- **Don't forget to look at the variables separately, too.** When you make a contingency table or display a conditional distribution, be sure to also examine the marginal distributions. It's important to know how many cases are in each category.

- **Be sure to use enough individuals.** When you consider percentages, take care that they are based on a large enough number of individuals (or cases). Take care not to make a report such as this one:

  We found that 66.67% of the companies surveyed improved their performance by hiring outside consultants. The other company went bankrupt.

- **Don't overstate your case.** Independence is an important concept, but it is rare for two variables to be *entirely* independent. We can't conclude that one variable has no effect whatsoever on another. Usually, all we know is that little effect was observed in our study. Other studies of other groups under other circumstances could find different results.

ETHICS IN ACTION

Mount Ashland Promotions Inc. is organizing one of its most popular events, the ZenNaturals Annual Trade Fest. At this trade show, producers, manufacturers, and distributors in the natural foods market display the latest trends in organic foods, herbal supplements, and natural body care products. The Trade Fest attracts a wide variety of participants, from large distributors who display a wide range of products to small, independent companies.

As in previous years, Nina Li and her team at Mount Ashland are in charge of managing the event, which includes all advertising and publicity as well as arranging spots for exhibitors. The success of this event depends on Nina's ability to attract large numbers of small independent retailers in the natural foods market who are looking to expand their product lines. She knows that these small retailers tend to be zealously committed to the principles of healthful lifestyle. Moreover, many are members of the Organic Trade Federation (OTF), an organization that advocates ethical consumerism.

The OTF has been known to boycott trade shows that include too many products with controversial ingredients such as ginkgo biloba, hemp, or kava kava. Nina is aware that some herbal diet teas have been receiving lots of negative attention lately in trade publications and the popular press. These teas claim to be "thermogenic" or fat burning, and typically contain ma huang (or ephedra). Ephedra is particularly controversial, not only because it

can be unsafe for people with certain existing health conditions, but because this fast-acting stimulant commonly found in diet and energy products is contrary to the OTF's principles and values.

Worried that too many products at the ZenNaturals Trade Fest may be thermogenic teas, Nina decides to take a closer look at vendors already committed to participate in the event. Based on the data that her team pulled together, she finds that more than 33% of them do indeed include teas in their product lines. She was quite surprised to find that this percentage is so high. She decides to categorize the vendors into four groups: (1) those selling herbal supplements only; (2) those selling organic foods and herbal supplements; (3) those selling organic foods, herbal supplements, and natural body care products; and (4) all others. She finds that only 2% of groups 1, 2, and 4 include tea in their product lines, while 34% of the third group do. Even though group 3 contains most of the vendors, Nina instructs her team to use the average percentage 10% in its communications, especially with the OTF, about the upcoming ZenNaturals Annual Trade Fest.

- Identify the ethical dilemma in this scenario.

- What are the undesirable consequences?

- Propose an ethical solution that considers the welfare of all stakeholders.

WHAT HAVE WE LEARNED?

Learning Objectives

Make and interpret a frequency table for a categorical variable.

- We can summarize categorical data by counting the number of cases in each category, sometimes expressing the resulting distribution as percentages.

Make and interpret a bar chart or pie chart.

- We display categorical data using the area principle in either a **bar chart** or a **pie chart**.

Make and interpret a contingency table.

- When we want to see how two categorical variables are related, we put the counts (and/or percentages) in a two-way table called a **contingency table**.

Make and interpret bar charts and pie charts of marginal distributions.

- We look at the **marginal distribution** of each variable (found in the margins of the table). We also look at the **conditional distribution** of a variable within each category of the other variable.
- Comparing conditional distributions of one variable across categories of another tells us about the association between variables. If the conditional distributions of one variable are (roughly) the same for every category of the other, the variables are **independent**.

Terms

Area principle   In a statistical display, each data value is represented by the same amount of area.

Bar chart (relative frequency bar chart)   A chart that represents the count (or percentage) of each category in a categorical variable as a bar, allowing easy visual comparisons across categories.

Cell	Each location in a contingency table, representing the values of two categorical variables, is called a cell.
Column percent	The proportion of each column contained in the cell of a frequency table.
Conditional distribution	The distribution of a variable restricting the *who* to consider only a smaller group of individuals.
Contingency table	A table displaying the frequencies (sometimes percentages) for each combination of two or more variables.
Distribution	The distribution of a variable is a list of: • all the possible values of the variable • the relative frequency of each value
Frequency table (relative frequency table)	A table that lists the categories in a categorical variable and gives the number (the percentage) of observations for each category.
Independent variables	Variables for which the conditional distribution of one variable is the same for each category of the other.
Marginal distribution	In a contingency table, the distribution of either variable alone. The counts or percentages are the totals found in the margins (usually the right-most column or bottom row) of the table.
Mosaic plot	A mosaic plot is a graphical representation of a (usually two-way) contingency table. The plot is divided into rectangles so that the area of each rectangle is proportional to the number of cases in the corresponding cell.
Pie chart	Pie charts show how a "whole" divides into categories by showing a wedge of a circle whose area corresponds to the proportion in each category.
Row percent	The proportion of each row contained in the cell of a frequency table.
Segmented bar chart	A segmented bar chart displays the conditional distribution of a categorical variable within each category of another variable.
Simpson's paradox	A phenomenon that arises when averages, or percentages, are taken across different groups, and these group averages appear to contradict the overall averages.
Total percent	The proportion of the total contained in the cell of a frequency table.

TECHNOLOGY HELP: Displaying Categorical Data

Although every package makes a slightly different bar chart, they all have similar features:

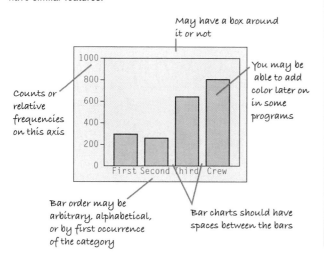

May have a box around it or not

Counts or relative frequencies on this axis

You may be able to add color later on in some programs

Bar order may be arbitrary, alphabetical, or by first occurrence of the category

Bar charts should have spaces between the bars

Sometimes the count or a percentage is printed above or on top of each bar to give some additional information. You may find that your statistics package sorts category names in annoying orders by default. For example, many packages sort categories alphabetically or by the order the categories are seen in the data set. Often, neither of these is the best choice.

EXCEL

Excel offers a versatile and powerful tool it calls a *PivotTable*. A pivot table can summarize, organize, and present data from an Excel spreadsheet. Pivot tables can be used to create frequency distributions and contingency tables. They provide a starting point for several kinds of displays. Pivot tables are linked to data in your Excel spreadsheet so they will update when you make changes to your data. They can also be linked directly to a *PivotChart* to display the data graphically.

In a pivot table, all types of data are summarized into a row-by-column table format. Pivot table cells can hold counts, percentages, and descriptive statistics.

To create a pivot table:

- Open a data file in Excel. At least one of the variables in the dataset should be categorical.

- Choose **Insert > PivotTable** or **Data > PivotTable** (Mac). If you are using a PC, choose to put the pivot table in a new worksheet. Macintosh users should choose the option to create a custom pivot table.

- The *PivotTable* builder has five boxes:
  - *Field List* (top): variables from the data set linked to the *PivotTable*. (The *PivotTable* tool calls the variables "fields.") Fields can be selected using the checkbox or dragged and dropped into one of the areas below in the *PivotTable* builder.
  - *Report Filter* (middle left): Variables placed here filter the data in the pivot table. When selected, the filter variable name appears above the pivot table. Use the drop-down list to the right of the variable name to choose values to display.
  - *Row Labels* (bottom left): Values of variables placed here become row labels in the pivot table.
  - *Column Labels* (middle right): Values of variables placed here become column labels in the pivot table.
  - *Values* (bottom right): Variables placed here are summarized in the cells of the table. Change settings to display count, sum, minimum, maximum, average, and more or to display percentages and ranks.

To create a frequency distribution pivot table:

- Drag a categorical variable from the Field List into **Row Labels**.

- Choose another variable from the data set and drag it into **Values**. Use a unique identifier variable (e.g., subject number) if possible.

- To change what fact or statistics about the **Values** variable is displayed, click the arrow next to the variable in the **Values** box and open the **Value Field Settings**. For a frequency distribution, select **count of [VARIABLE].** When changing **Value Field Settings**, note the tab **Show Values As,** which provides other display options (e.g., % of row, % of column).

The result will be a frequency table with a column for count.

To create a contingency table using *PivotTable*:

Row Labels	Count of Cut
Excellent	1276
Good	165
Ideal	185
Very Good	1064
Grand Total	**2690**

- Drag a categorical variable from the Field List into **Row Labels**.

- Drag a second categorical variable from the Field List into **Column Labels**.

- Choose another variable from the dataset and drag it into **Values**. The resulting pivot table is a row-by-column contingency table.

Count of Cut	Column Labels							
Row Labels	IF	SI1	SI2	VS1	VS2	VVS1	VVS2	Grand Total
Excellent	92	278	196	184	220	160	146	1276
Good	4	39	47	33	26	4	12	165
Ideal	22	24	24	20	24	41	30	185
Very Good	26	283	263	155	190	64	83	1064
Grand Total	**144**	**624**	**530**	**392**	**460**	**269**	**271**	**2690**

NOTE: As with the frequency distribution, you can use the **Value Field Settings** to change the type of summary.

To create a chart from a pivot table frequency distribution or contingency table:

- Place the cursor anywhere on the pivot table.

- Click **PivotTable Tools > PivotChart**.

- Choose the type of chart: options include pie chart, bar chart, and segmented bar graph.

- Move the chart to a new worksheet by right-clicking the chart and selecting **Move chart.**

- In a bar chart created from a contingency table, by default, rows display on the *x*-axis and the columns are separate bars. To change this, place cursor in chart and choose **PivotChart Tools > Design > Switch Row/Column**.

- On Macs, choose the **Charts** tab and select your chart from the ribbon or choose a chart type from the **Chart** menu.

XLSTAT

To create a contingency table from unsummarized data:

- On the XLStat tab, choose **Preparing data**.

- From the menu, choose **Create a contingency table**.

- In the dialog box, enter your data range on the General tab. Your data should be in two columns, one of which is the row variable and the other is the column variable.

- On the Outputs tab, check the box next to **Contingency table** and optionally choose **Percentages/Row or Column** to see the conditional distributions.

JMP

JMP makes a bar chart and frequency table together.

- From the **Analyze** menu, choose **Distribution**.

- In the Distribution dialog, drag the name of the variable into the empty variable window beside the label **Y, Columns**; click **OK**.

To make a pie chart,

- Choose **Chart > Graph** menu.

- In the Chart dialog, select the variable name from the Columns list, click on the button labeled **Statistics**, and select **N** from the drop-down menu.

- Click the "**Categories, X, Levels**" button to assign the same variable name to the *x*-axis.

- Under Options, click on the second button—labeled "**Bar Chart**"— and select **Pie Chart** from the drop-down menu.

MINITAB

To make a bar chart,

- Choose **Bar Chart** from the **Graph** menu.
- Then select a Simple, Cluster, or Stack chart from the options and click **OK**.
- To make a **Simple** bar chart, enter the name of the variable to graph in the dialog box.
- To make a relative frequency chart, click **Chart Options**, and choose **Show Y as Percent.**
- In the Chart dialog, enter the name of the variable that you wish to display in the box labeled "Categorical variables."
- Click **OK.**

SPSS

To make a bar chart,

- Open the **Chart Builder** from the **Graphs** menu.
- Click the **Gallery** tab.
- Choose **Bar Chart** from the list of chart types.
- Drag the appropriate bar chart onto the canvas.
- Drag a categorical variable onto the x-axis drop zone.
- Click **OK.**

Comments

A similar path makes a pie chart by choosing **Pie chart** from the list of chart types.

Brief **Case**

Credit Card Bank

In Chapter 1, you identified the W's for the data in the file **Credit Card Bank**. For the categorical variables in the data set, create frequency tables, bar charts, and pie charts using your software. What might the bank want to know about these variables? Which of the tables and charts do you find most useful for communicating information about the bank's customers? Write a brief case report summarizing your analysis and results.

EXERCISES

SECTION 2.1

1. As part of the human resource group of your company you are asked to summarize the educational levels of the 512 employees in your division. From company records, you find that 164 have no college degree (None), 42 have an associate's degree (AA), 225 have a bachelor's degree (BA), 52 have a master's degree (MA), and 29 have PhDs. For the educational level of your division:

a) Make a frequency table.
b) Make a relative frequency table.

2. As part of the marketing group at Pixar, you are asked to find out the age distribution of the audience of Pixar's latest film. With the help of 10 of your colleagues, you conduct exit interviews by randomly selecting people to question at 20 different movie theaters. You ask them to tell you if they are younger than 6 years old, 6 to 9 years old, 10 to 14 years old, 15 to 21 years old, or older than 21. From 470 responses, you find out that 45 are younger than 6, 83 are 6 to 9 years old, 154 are 10 to 14, 18 are 15 to 21, and 170 are older than 21. For the age distribution:

a) Make a frequency table.
b) Make a relative frequency table.

SECTION 2.2

3. From the educational level data described in Exercise 1:

a) Make a bar chart using counts on the *y*-axis.
b) Make a relative frequency bar chart using percentages on the *y*-axis.
c) Make a pie chart.

4. From the age distribution data described in Exercise 2:

a) Make a bar chart using counts on the *y*-axis.
b) Make a relative frequency bar chart using percentages on the *y*-axis.
c) Make a pie chart.

5. For the educational levels described in Exercise 1:

a) Write two to four sentences summarizing the distribution.
b) What conclusions, if any, could you make about the educational level at other companies?

6. For the ages described in Exercise 2:

a) Write two to four sentences summarizing the distribution.
b) What possible problems do you see in concluding that the age distribution from these surveys accurately represents the ages of the national audience for this film?

SECTION 2.3

7. From Exercise 1, we also have data on how long each person has been with the company (tenure) categorized into three levels: less than 1 year, between 1 and 5 years, and more than 5 years. A table of the two variables together looks like:

	None	AA	BA	MA	PhD
<1 Year	10	3	50	20	12
1–5 Years	42	9	112	27	15
More Than 5 Years	112	30	63	5	2

a) Find the marginal distribution of the tenure. (*Hint*: Find the row totals.)
b) Verify that the marginal distribution of the education level is the same as that given in Exercise 1.

8. In addition to their age levels, the movie audiences in Exercise 2 were also asked if they had seen the movie before (Never, Once, More than Once). Here is a table showing the responses by age group:

	Under 6	6–9	10–14	15–21	Over 21
Never	39	60	84	16	151
Once	3	20	38	2	15
More Than Once	3	3	32	0	4

a) Find the marginal distribution of their previous viewing of the movie. (*Hint:* Find the row totals.)
b) Verify that the marginal distribution of the ages is the same as that given in Exercise 2.

SECTION 2.4

9. For the table in Exercise 7:

a) Find the column percentages.
b) Looking at the column percentages in part a, does the *tenure* distribution (how long the employee has been with the company) for each educational level look the same? Comment briefly.
c) Make a sebmented or stacked bar chart showing the *tenure* distribution for each educational level.
d) Is it easier to see the differences in the distributions using the column percentages or the segmented bar chart?
e) How would a mosaic plot help to accurately display these data?

10. For the table in Exercise 8:

a) Find the column percentages.
b) Looking at the column percentages in part a, does the distribution of how many times someone has seen the movie look the same for each age group? Comment briefly.
c) Make a segmented bar chart, showing the distribution of viewings for each age level.
d) Is it easier to see the differences in the distributions using the column percentages or the segmented bar chart?
e) How would a mosaic plot represent these data more appropriately?

CHAPTER EXERCISES

11. Graphs in the news. Find a bar graph of categorical data from a business publication (e.g., *Bloomberg Businessweek, Fortune, The Wall Street Journal*, etc.).

a) Is the graph clearly labeled?
b) Does it violate the area principle?
c) Does the accompanying article tell the W's of the variable?
d) Do you think the article correctly interprets the data? Explain.

12. Graphs in the news, part 2. Find a pie chart of categorical data from a business publication (e.g., *Bloomberg Businessweek, Fortune, The Wall Street Journal*, etc.).

a) Is the graph clearly labeled?
b) Does it violate the area principle?
c) Does the accompanying article tell the W's of the variable?
d) Do you think the article correctly interprets the data? Explain.

13. Tables in the news. Find a frequency table of categorical data from a business publication (e.g., *Bloomberg Businessweek, Fortune, The Wall Street Journal*, etc.).

a) Is it clearly labeled?
b) Does it display percentages or counts?
c) Does the accompanying article tell the W's of the variable?
d) Do you think the article correctly interprets the data? Explain.

14. Tables in the news, part 2. Find a contingency table of categorical data from a business publication (e.g., *Bloomberg Businessweek*, *Fortune*, *The Wall Street Journal*, etc.).

a) Is it clearly labeled?
b) Does it display percentages or counts?
c) Does the accompanying article tell the W's of the variable?
d) Do you think the article correctly interprets the data? Explain.

15. U.S. market share. An article in the *The Wall Street Journal* (March 18, 2011) reported the 2010 U.S. market share of leading sellers of carbonated soft drinks, summarized in the following pie chart:

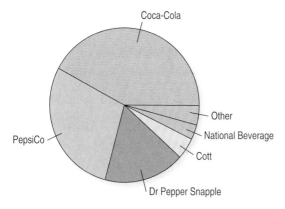

a) Is this an appropriate display for these data? Explain.
b) Which company had the largest share of the market?

16. World market share. *The Wall Street Journal* article described in Exercise 15 also indicated the market share of the leading *brands* of carbonated beverages. The following bar chart displays the values:

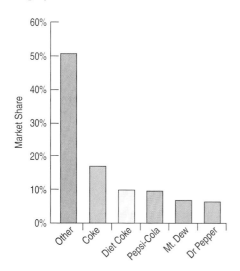

a) Is this an appropriate display for these data? Explain.
b) Which brand had the largest share of the beverage market?
c) Which brand had the larger market share—Mountain Dew or Dr Pepper?

17. Market share again. Here's a bar chart of the data in Exercise 15.

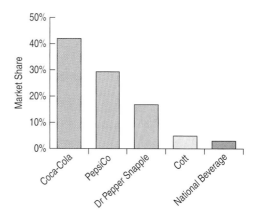

a) Compared to the pie chart in Exercise 15, which is better for displaying the relative portions of market share? Explain.
b) What is missing from this display that might make it somewhat misleading?

18. World market share again. Here's a pie chart of the data in Exercise 16.

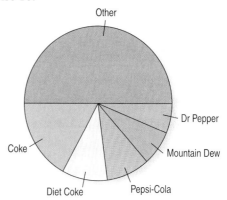

a) Which display of these data is best for comparing the market shares of these brands? Explain.
b) Does Mountain Dew or Dr Pepper have a bigger market share? Is that comparison easier to make with the pie chart or the bar chart of Exercise 16?

19. Insurance company. An insurance company is updating its payouts and cost structure for their insurance policies. Of particular interest to them is the risk analysis for customers currently on heart or blood pressure medication. The Centers for Disease Control and Prevention (www.cdc.gov) lists causes of death in the United States during one year as follows.

Cause of Death	Percent
Heart disease	30.3
Cancer	23.0
Circulatory diseases and stroke	8.4
Respiratory diseases	7.9
Accidents	4.1

a) Is it reasonable to conclude that heart or respiratory diseases were the cause of approximately 38% of U.S. deaths during this year?

b) What percent of deaths were from causes not listed here?

c) Create an appropriate display for these data.

20. College value? In March and April of 2011, the Pew Research Center asked 2142 U.S. adults and 1055 college presidents whether they would "rate the job the higher education system is doing in providing value for the money spent by students and their families" as Excellent, Good, Only Fair, or Poor.

	Poor	Only Fair	Good	Excellent	No Answer/ Don't Know
U.S. Adults	321	900	750	107	64
College Presidents	32	222	622	179	0

a) Compare the distribution of opinions between U.S. adults and college presidents on the value of higher education.

b) Is it reasonable to conclude that 5.00% of *all* U.S. adults think that the higher education system provides an excellent value?

21. SaaS. According to a 2013 report by Synergy Research Group (www.informationweek.com/telecom /unified-communications/cisco-rules-saas-uc-conferencing -market/231601562) the market for desktop conferencing apps has been growing rapidly, spurred by a 33% jump in software-as-a-service-delivered conferencing apps revenue. Cisco Systems has a 58% share of this market, followed by Citrix with a 13% share and Microsoft with 11%. Create an appropriate graphical display of this information and write a sentence or two that might appear in a newspaper article about the market share.

22. Mattel. In their 2013 annual report, Mattel Inc. reported that their domestic market sales were broken down as follows: 49.6% Mattel Girls and Boys brand, 36.1% Fisher-Price brand, and the rest of their over $3.5 billion revenues were due to their American Girl brand. Create an appropriate graphical display of this information and write a sentence or two that might appear in a newspaper article about their revenue breakdown.

23. Small business productivity. The Wells Fargo/Gallup Small Business Index asked 604 small business owners in October 2011 "how difficult or easy do you think it will be for your company to obtain credit when you need it?" 22% said "Very difficult," 21% "Somewhat difficult," 28% "About Average," 11% "Somewhat easy," and 11% "Very Easy."

a) What do you notice about the percentages listed? How could this be?

b) Make a bar chart to display the results and label it clearly.

c) Would a pie chart be an effective way of communicating this information? Why or why not?

d) Write a couple of sentences on how small businesses felt about the difficulty of obtaining credit in late 2011.

24. Small business hiring. The Wells Fargo/Gallup Small Business Index survey from Exercise 23 also asked 604 small businesses about their cash flow over the next 12 months. 13% responded "Very Good," 37% "Somewhat good," 21% "Neither good nor poor," 20% "Somewhat poor," and 7% "Very poor."

a) What do you notice about the percentages listed?

b) Make a bar chart to display the results and label it clearly.

c) Would a pie chart be an effective way of communicating this information? Why or why not?

d) Write a couple of sentences on the responses of small business owners about their cash flow in the next 12 months.

25. Environmental hazard 2012. Data from the International Tanker Owners Pollution Federation Limited (www.itopf .com) give the cause of spillage for 455 large oil tanker accidents from 1970 to 2012. Here are the displays. Write a brief report interpreting what the displays show. Is a pie chart an appropriate display for these data? Why or why not?

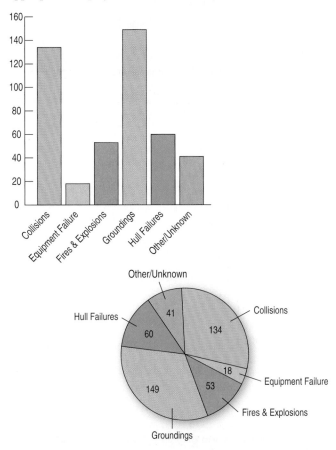

26. Olympic medals. In the history of the modern Olympics, the United States has won more medals than any other country. But the United States has a large population. Perhaps a better measure of success is the number of medals won *per capita*—that is the number of medals divided by the population. By that measure, the leading countries are Liechtenstein (255.42 medals/cap), Norway (95.271), Finland (86.514), and Sweden (66.455). The following table summarizes the medals/capita counts for the 100 countries with the most medals.

a) Try to make a display of these data. What problems do you encounter?

b) Can you find a way to organize the data so that the graph is more successful?

Medals/capita	# Countries	Medals/capita	# Countries
0	72	130	0
10	13	140	0
20	3	150	0
30	3	160	0
40	2	170	0
50	0	180	0
60	1	190	0
70	0	200	0
80	1	210	0
90	1	220	0
100	0	230	0
110	0	240	0
120	0	250	1

27. Importance of wealth. GfK Roper Reports Worldwide surveyed people, asking them "How important is acquiring wealth to you?" The percent who responded that it was of more than average importance were: 71.9% China, 59.6% France, 76.1% India, 45.5% U.K., and 45.3% U.S. There were about 1500 respondents per country. A report showed the following bar chart of these percentages.

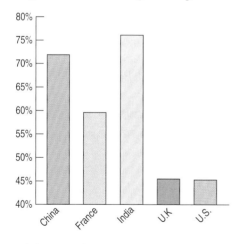

a) How much larger is the proportion of those who said acquiring wealth was important in India than in the United States?

b) Is that the impression given by the display? Explain.

c) How would you improve this display?

d) Make an appropriate display for the percentages.

e) Write a few sentences describing what you have learned about attitudes toward acquiring wealth.

28. Importance of power. In the same survey as that discussed in Exercise 27, GfK Roper Consulting also asked "How important is having control over people and resources to you?" The percent who responded that it was of more than average importance are given in the following table:

China	49.1%
France	44.1%
India	74.2%
U.K.	27.8%
U.S.	36.0%

Here's a pie chart of the data:

a) List the errors you see in this display.

b) Make an appropriate display for the percentages.

c) Write a few sentences describing what you have learned about attitudes toward acquiring power.

29. Google financials. Google Inc. derives revenue from three major sources: advertising revenue from their websites, advertising revenue from the thousands of third-party websites that comprise the Google Network, and licensing and miscellaneous revenue. The following table shows the percentage of all revenue derived from these sources for the period from 2008 to 2012.

	2008	2009	2010	2011	2012
Google Websites	66%	67%	66%	69%	68%
Google Network Members' Websites	31%	30%	30%	28%	27%
Other Revenues	3%	3%	4%	3%	5%

a) Are these row or column percentages?

b) Make an appropriate display of these data.

c) Write a brief summary of this information.

30. Real estate pricing. A study of a sample of 1057 houses in upstate New York reports the following percentages of houses falling into different Price and Size categories.

		Price			
		Low	Med Low	Med High	High
Size	**Small**	61.5%	35.2%	5.2%	2.4%
	Med Small	30.4%	45.3%	26.4%	4.7%
	Med Large	5.4%	17.6%	47.6%	21.7%
	Large	2.7%	1.9%	20.8%	71.2%

a) Are these column, row, or total percentages? How do you know?
b) What percent of the highest priced houses were small?
c) From this table, can you determine what percent of all houses were in the low price category?
d) Among the lowest priced? houses, what percent were small or medium small?
e) Write a few sentences describing the association between *Price* and *Size*.

31. Stock performance. The following table displays information for 470 of the S&P 500 stocks, on how their one-day change on October 24, 2011 (a day on which the S&P 500 index gained 1.23%) compared with their year to date change.

		Year to Date	
		Positive Change	Negative Change
October 24, 2011	Positive Change	164	233
	Negative Change	48	25

a) What percent of the companies reported a positive change in their stock price over the year to date?
b) What percent of the companies reported a positive change in their stock price over both time periods?
c) What percent of the companies reported a negative change in their stock price over both time periods?
d) What percent of the companies reported a positive change in their stock price over one period and a negative change in the other period?
e) Among those companies reporting a positive change in their stock price on October 24 over the prior day what percentage also reported a positive change over the year to date?
f) Among those companies reporting a negative change in their stock price on October 24 over the prior day what percentage reported a positive change over the year to date?
g) What relationship, if any, do you see between the performance of a stock on a single day and its year-to-date performance?

32. New product. A company started and managed by business students is selling campus calendars. The students have conducted a market survey with the various campus constituents to determine sales potential and identify which market segments should be targeted. (Should they advertise in the Alumni Magazine and/or the local newspaper?) The following table shows the results of the market survey.

		Buying Likelihood			
		Unlikely	Moderately Likely	Very Likely	Total
Campus Group	Students	197	388	320	905
	Faculty/Staff	103	137	98	338
	Alumni	20	18	18	56
	Town Residents	13	58	45	116
	Total	333	601	481	1415

a) What percent of all these respondents are alumni?
b) What percent of these respondents are very likely to buy the calendar?
c) What percent of the respondents who are very likely to buy the calendar are alumni?
d) Of the alumni, what percent are very likely to buy the calendar?
e) What is the marginal distribution of the campus constituents?
f) What is the conditional distribution of the campus constituents among those very likely to buy the calendar?
g) Does this study present any evidence that this company should focus on selling to certain campus constituents?

33. Real estate. The *Greenville, South Carolina Real Estate Hub* keeps track of home sales in their area. They reported that sales were down in 2010 by about 3.7% from the previous year. Here are the number of homes sold in Greenville for the last 5 months of 2009 and 2010:

	August	September	October	November	December
2010	475	466	502	423	495
2009	607	597	596	581	447

a) What percent of all homes in these ten months were sold in October of 2009?
b) What percent of all homes in these 10 months were sold in 2010?
c) What percent of all homes in these 10 months were sold in December?
d) How did the percent of homes sold in November change from 2009 to 2010?

34. Google financials, part 2. Google Inc. divides their total costs and expenses into five categories: Costs of Revenues, Research and Development, Sales and Marketing, General and Administrative, and Dept of Justice charges (amounts in $Millions).

	2008	2009	2010	2011	2012
Cost of Revenues	$8612	$8844	$10,417	$13,188	$20,634
Research and Development	$2793	$2843	$3762	$5162	$6793
Sales and Marketing	$1946	$1984	$2799	$4589	$6143
General and Administrative	$1803	$1667	$1962	$2724	$3845
Dept of Justice	$0	$0	$0	$500	$0
Total Costs and Expenses	$15,154	$15,338	$18,940	$26,163	$37,415

a) What percent of total costs and expenses were sales and marketing in 2008? In 2012?
b) What percent of total costs and expenses were due to research and development in 2008? In 2012?
c) Have general and administrative costs grown as a percentage of total costs and expenses over this time period?

35. Movie ratings. The movie ratings system is a voluntary system operated jointly by the Motion Picture Association of America (MPAA) and the National Association of Theatre Owners (NATO). The ratings themselves are given by a board of parents who are members of the Classification and Ratings Administration (CARA). The board was created in response to outcries from parents in the 1960s for some kind of regulation of film content, and the first ratings were introduced in 1968. Here is information on the ratings of 279 movies that came out in 2011, also classified by their genre.

		Rating			
	G	**PG**	**PG-13**	**R or NC-17**	**Total**
Action/Adventure	3	19	23	18	63
Comedy	1	8	13	34	56
Drama	2	13	36	65	116
Thriller/Suspense	0	1	20	23	44
Total	6	41	92	140	279

(Genre labels the rows)

a) Find the conditional distribution (in percentages) of movie ratings for action/adventure films.
b) Find the conditional distribution (in percentages) of movie ratings for thriller/suspense films.
c) Create a graph comparing the ratings for the four genres.
d) Are *Genre* and *Rating* independent? Write a brief summary of what these data show about movie ratings and the relationship to the genre of the film.

36. CyberShopping. It has become more common for shoppers to "comparison shop" using the Internet. Respondents to a Pew survey in 2013 who owned cell phones were asked whether they had, in the past 30 days, looked up the price of a product while they were in a store to see if they could get a better price somewhere else. Here is a table of their responses by income level.

	<$30K	$30K–$49.9K	$50K–$74.9K	>$75K
Yes	207	115	134	204
No	625	406	260	417

(Source: www.pewinternet.org/Reports/2012/In-store-mobile-commerce.aspx)

a) Find the conditional distribution (in percentages) of income distribution for those who do not compare prices on the Internet.
b) Find the conditional distribution (in percentages) of income distribution for shoppers who do compare prices.
c) Create a graph comparing the income distributions of those who compare prices with those who don't.
d) Do you see any differences between the conditional distributions? Write a brief summary of what these data show about Internet use and its relationship to income.

37. MBAs. A survey of the entering MBA students at a university in the United States classified the country of origin of the students, as seen in the table.

		MBA Program		
		Two-Year MBA	**Evening MBA**	**Total**
Origin	**Asia/Pacific Rim**	31	33	64
	Europe	5	0	5
	Latin America	20	1	21
	Middle East/Africa	5	5	10
	North America	103	65	168
	Total	164	104	268

a) What percent of all MBA students were from North America?
b) What percent of the Two-Year MBAs were from North America?
c) What percent of the Evening MBAs were from North America?
d) What is the marginal distribution of origin?
e) Obtain the column percentages and show the conditional distributions of origin by MBA Program.
f) Do you think that origin of the MBA student is independent of the MBA program? Explain.

38. MBAs, part 2. The same university as in Exercise 37 reported the following data on the gender of their students in their two MBA programs.

		Type		
		Two-Year	**Evening**	**Total**
Sex	**Men**	116	66	182
	Women	48	38	86
	Total	164	104	268

a) What percent of all MBA students are women?
b) What percent of Two-Year MBAs are women?
c) What percent of Evening MBAs are women?
d) Do you see evidence of an association between the *Type* of MBA program and the percentage of women students? If so, why do you believe this might be true?

T 39. Top-producing movies. The following table shows the Motion Picture Association of America (MPA; www.mpaa.org) ratings for the top 20 grossing films in the United States for each of the 10 years from 2003 to 2012. (Data are number of films.)

		Rating			
	G	**PG**	**PG-13**	**R/NC-17**	**Total**
2012	0	6	12	2	20
2011	1	4	11	4	20
2010	1	9	9	1	20
2009	0	7	12	1	20
2008	2	4	10	4	20
2007	1	5	11	3	20
2006	1	4	13	2	20
2005	1	4	13	2	20
2004	1	6	10	3	20
2003	1	3	11	5	20
Total	9	52	112	27	200

(Year labels the rows)

a) What percent of all these top 20 films are G rated?

b) What percent of all top 20 films in 2005 were G rated?

c) What percent of all top 20 films were PG-13 and came out in 2010?

d) What percent of all top 20 films produced in 2008 or later were PG-13?

e) What percent of all top 20 films produced from 2003 to 2007 were rated PG-13 or R/NC-17?

f) Compare the conditional distributions of the ratings for films produced in 2008 or later to those produced from 2003 to 2008. Write a couple of sentences summarizing what you see.

T **40.** Movie admissions 2011. The following table shows attendance data collected by the Motion Picture Association of America during the period 2009 to 2011. Figures are the number (in millions) of frequent moviegoers in each age group.

Frequent Moviegoers (M)		Age						
		2–11	12–17	18–24	25–39	40–49	50–59	60+
	2011	2.5	5.7	6.6	9.7	3.3	3.1	4.1
	2010	3.1	6.1	7.4	7.7	3.5	3.0	4.3
	2009	2.8	5.7	6.3	6.3	4.5	2.9	3.4

a) What percent of all frequent moviegoers during this period were people between the ages of 12 and 24?

b) What percent of the frequent moviegoers in 2011 were people between the ages of 12 and 39?

c) What percent of *all* frequent moviegoers during this period were people between the ages of 18 and 24 who went to the movies in 2009?

d) What percent of frequent moviegoers in 2010 were people 60 years old and older?

e) What percent of *all* frequent moviegoers in this period were people 60 years old and older who went to the movies in 2010?

f) Compare the conditional distributions of the age groups across years. Write a couple of sentences summarizing what you see.

41. Tattoos. A study by the University of Texas Southwestern Medical Center examined 626 people to see if there was an increased risk of contracting hepatitis C associated with having a tattoo. If the subject had a tattoo, researchers asked whether it had been done in a commercial tattoo parlor or elsewhere. Write a brief description of the association between tattooing and hepatitis C, including an appropriate graphical display.

	Tattoo Done in Commercial Parlor	Tattoo Done Elsewhere	No Tattoo
Has Hepatitis C	17	8	18
No Hepatitis C	35	53	495

42. Poverty and region 2012. In 2012, the following data were reported by the U.S. Census Bureau. The data show the number of people (in thousands) living above and below the poverty line in each of the four regions of the United States. Based on these data do you think there is an association between region and poverty? Explain.

	Below Poverty Level	Above Poverty Level
Northeast	12,728	86,932
Midwest	13,055	82,459
South	17,287	85,913
West	17,031	93,753

43. Being successful. In a random sample of U.S. adults surveyed in December 2011, Pew research asked how important it is "to you personally" to be successful in a high-paying career or profession. Here is a table reporting the responses. (Percentages may not add to 100% due to rounding.) (Data from www.pewsocialtrends.org/files/2012/04/Women-in-the-Workplace.pdf)

	Women		Men	
Age	18–34	35–64	18–34	35–64
One of the most important things	18%	7%	11%	9%
Very important, but not the most	48%	35%	47%	34%
Somewhat important	26%	34%	31%	37%
Not important	8%	24%	10%	20%
	100%	100%	100%	100%

a) What percent of young women consider it very important or one of the most important things for them personally to be successful?

b) How does that compare with young men?

c) From this table, can you determine what percent of all women responding felt this way? Explain.

d) Write a few sentences describing the association between the sex of young respondents and their attitudes toward the importance of financial or professional success.

T **44.** Minimum wage workers. The U.S. Department of Labor (www.bls.gov) collects data on the number of U.S. workers who are employed at or below the minimum wage. Here is a table showing the number of hourly workers by *Age* and *Sex* and the number who were paid at or below the prevailing minimum wage:

		Hourly Workers (in thousands)		At or Below Minimum Wage (in thousands)	
		Men	Women	Men	Women
Age	16–24	7978	7701	384	738
	25–34	9029	7864	150	332
	35–44	7696	7783	71	170
	45–54	7365	8260	68	134
	55–64	4092	4895	35	72
	65+	1174	1469	22	50

a) What percent of the women were ages 16–24?

b) Using side-by-side bar graphs, compare the proportions of the men and women who worked at or below minimum wage at each *Age* group. Write a couple of sentences summarizing what you see.

45. Moviegoers and ethnicity. The Motion Picture Association of America studies the ethnicity of moviegoers to understand changes in the demographics of moviegoers over time. Here are the numbers of moviegoers (in millions) classified as to whether they were Hispanic, African-American, Caucasian, and Other for the year 2010. Also included are the numbers for the general U.S. population and the number of tickets sold.

	Caucasian	Hispanic	African-American	Other	Total
Population	204.6	49.6	37.2	18.6	**310**
Moviegoers	88.8	26.8	16.9	8.5	**141**
Tickets	728	338	143	91	**1300**
Total	**1021.4**	**414.4**	**197.1**	**118.1**	**1751**

a) Compare the conditional distribution of *Ethnicity* for all three groups: the entire population, moviegoers, and ticket holders.

b) Write a brief description of the association between population groups and *Ethnicity*.

46. Department store. A department store is planning its next advertising campaign. Since different publications are read by different market segments, they would like to know if they should be targeting specific age segments. The results of a marketing survey are summarized in the following table by *Age* and *Shopping Frequency* at their store.

			Age		
	Shopping	**Under 30**	**30–49**	**50 and Over**	**Total**
Frequency	Low	27	37	31	95
	Moderate	48	91	93	232
	High	23	51	73	147
	Total	98	179	197	474

a) Find the marginal distribution of *Shopping Frequency*.

b) Find the conditional distribution of *Shopping Frequency* within each age group.

c) Compare these distributions with a segmented bar graph.

d) Write a brief description of the association between *Age* and *Shopping Frequency* among these respondents.

e) Does this prove that customers ages 50 and over are more likely to shop at this department store? Explain.

47. Success II. Look back at the table in exercise 43 concerning desires for success and a high-paying career. That table presented only the percentages, but Pew Research reported the numbers of respondents in the major categories:

	Women		Men	
Age	18–34	35–64	18–34	35–64
Count	610	571	703	605

With this additional information you should be able to answer these questions. (Note: Percentages were rounded to whole numbers, so estimated cell counts will have fractions. You need not round estimated cell counts to whole numbers for the purpose of answering these questions.)

a) What percentage of 18–34 year olds (both male and female) reported that being successful in a high-paying career or profession was "one of the most important things" to them personally?

b) What percentage of 18–34 year olds who said that such success was "one of the most important things" were women?

c) Write a few sentences describing how the opinions of young women differ from those of older female respondents.

48. Advertising. A company that distributes a variety of pet foods is planning their next advertising campaign. Since different publications are read by different market segments, they would like to know how pet ownership is distributed across different income segments. The U.S. Census Bureau (www.allcountries.org/uscensus/424_household_pet_ownership_and_by_selected.html) reports the number of households owning various types of pets. Specifically, they keep track of dogs, cats, birds, and horses.

a) Do you think the income distributions of the households who own these different animals would be roughly the same? Why or why not?

Percent Distribution of Households Owning Pets

		Pets			
		Dog	**Cat**	**Bird**	**Horse**
Income Range	**Under $12,500**	12.7	13.9	17.3	9.5
	$12,500 to $24,999	19.1	19.7	20.9	20.3
	$25,000 to $39,999	21.6	21.5	22.0	21.8
	$40,000 to $59,999	21.5	21.2	17.5	23.1
	$60,000 and over	25.2	23.7	22.3	25.4

b) The table shows the percentages of income levels for each type of animal owned. Are these row percentages, column percentages, or total percentages?

c) Do the data support that the pet food company should not target specific market segments based on household income? Explain.

49. Insurance company, part 2. An insurance company that provides medical insurance is concerned with recent data. They suspect that patients who undergo surgery at large hospitals have their discharges delayed for various reasons—which results in increased medical costs to the insurance company. The recent data for area hospitals and two types of surgery (major and minor) are shown in the following table.

		Discharge Delayed	
		Large Hospital	Small Hospital
Procedure	Major Surgery	120 of 800	10 of 50
	Minor Surgery	10 of 200	20 of 250

a) Overall, for what percent of patients was discharge delayed?
b) Were the percentages different for major and minor surgery?
c) Overall, what were the discharge delay rates at each hospital?
d) What were the delay rates at each hospital for each kind of surgery?
e) The insurance company is considering advising their clients to use large hospitals for surgery to avoid postsurgical complications. Do you think they should do this?
f) Explain, in your own words, why this confusion occurs.

50. Delivery service. A company must decide which of two delivery services they will contract with. During a recent trial period, they shipped numerous packages with each service and have kept track of how often deliveries did not arrive on time. Here are the data.

Delivery Service	Type of Service	Number of Deliveries	Number of Late Packages
Pack Rats	Regular	400	12
	Overnight	100	16
Boxes R Us	Regular	100	2
	Overnight	400	28

a) Compare the two services' overall percentage of late deliveries.
b) Based on the results in part a, the company has decided to hire Pack Rats. Do you agree they deliver on time more often? Why or why not? Be specific.
c) The results here are an instance of what phenomenon?

51. Graduate admissions. A 1975 article in the magazine *Science* examined the graduate admissions process at Berkeley for evidence of gender bias. The following table shows the number of applicants accepted to each of four graduate programs.

Program	Males Accepted (of Applicants)	Females Accepted (of Applicants)
1	511 of 825	89 of 108
2	352 of 560	17 of 25
3	137 of 407	132 of 375
4	22 of 373	24 of 341
Total	1022 of 2165	262 of 849

a) What percent of total applicants were admitted?
b) Overall, were a higher percentage of males or females admitted?
c) Compare the percentage of males and females admitted in each program.
d) Which of the comparisons you made do you consider to be the most valid? Why?

52. Simpson's Paradox. Develop your own table of data that is a business example of Simpson's Paradox. Explain the conflict between the conclusions made from the conditional and marginal distributions.

JUST CHECKING ANSWERS

1 50.0%

2 40.0%

3 25.0%

4 15.6% Nearsighted, 56.3% Farsighted, 18.8% Need Bifocals

5 18.8% Nearsighted, 62.5% Farsighted, 18.8% Need Bifocals

6 40% of the nearsighted customers are female, while 50% of customers are female.

7 Since nearsighted customers appear less likely to be female, it seems that they may not be independent. (But the numbers are small.)

3

Displaying and Describing Quantitative Data

AIG

The American International Group (AIG) was once the 18th largest corporation in the world. AIG was founded nearly 100 years ago by Cornelius Vander Starr who opened an insurance agency in Shanghai, China. As the first Westerner to sell insurance to the Chinese, Starr grew his business rapidly until 1949 when Mao Zedong and the People's Liberation Army took over Shanghai. Starr moved the company to New York City, where it continued to grow, expanding its markets worldwide. In 2004, AIG stock hit an all-time high of $76.77, putting its market value at nearly $300 billion.

According to its own website, "By early 2007 AIG had assets of $1 trillion, $110 billion in revenues, 74 million customers and 116,000 employees in 130 countries and jurisdictions. Yet just 18 months later, AIG found itself on the brink of failure and in need of emergency government assistance." AIG was one of the largest beneficiaries of the U.S. government's Troubled Asset Relief Program (TARP), established in 2008 during the financial crisis to purchase assets and equity from financial institutions. TARP was an attempt to strengthen the financial sector and avoid a repeat of a depression as severe as the 1930s. Many banks quickly repaid the government part or all of the money given to them under the TARP program, but AIG, which received $170 billion, took until the end of 2012 to repay the government completely.

Even though AIG stock today is on solid financial footing, its stock price is only a fraction (adjusted for splits) of what it was before the 2008 crisis. Between 2007 and 2009 AIG stock lost more than 99% of its value, hitting $0.35 in early March. That same month AIG became embroiled in controversy when it disclosed that it had paid $218 million in bonuses to employees of its financial services division. AIG's drop in stock price represented a loss of nearly $300 billion for investors. Portfolio managers typically examine stock prices and volumes to determine stock volatility and to help them decide which stocks to buy and sell. Were there early warning signs in AIG's data?

Table 3.1 gives the monthly average stock price (in dollars) for the six years leading up to the company's crisis. Were there clues to warn of problems?

	Jan.	Feb.	Mar.	Apr.	May	June	July	Aug.	Sept.	Oct.	Nov.	Dec.
2002	77.26	72.95	73.72	71.57	68.42	65.99	61.22	64.10	58.04	60.26	65.03	59.96
2003	59.74	49.57	49.41	54.38	56.52	57.88	59.80	61.51	59.39	60.93	58.73	62.37
2004	69.02	73.25	72.06	74.21	70.93	72.61	69.85	69.58	70.67	62.31	62.17	65.33
2005	66.74	68.96	61.55	51.77	53.81	55.66	60.27	60.86	60.54	62.64	67.06	66.72
2006	68.33	67.02	67.15	64.29	63.14	59.74	59.40	62.00	65.25	67.02	69.86	71.35
2007	70.45	68.99	68.14	68.25	71.78	71.75	68.64	65.21	66.02	66.12	56.86	58.13

Table 3.1   Monthly stock price in dollars of AIG stock for the period 2002 through 2007.

It's hard to tell very much from tables of values like this. You might get a rough idea of how much the stock cost—usually somewhere around $60 or so, but that's about it.

3.1   Displaying Quantitative Variables

The first rule of data analysis is to make a picture. AIG's stock price is a *quantitative* variable, whose units are dollars, so a bar chart or pie chart won't work. For quantitative variables, there are no categories. Instead, we usually slice up all the possible values into **bins** and then count the number of cases that fall into each bin. The bins, together with these counts, give the **distribution** of the quantitative variable and provide the building blocks for the display of the distribution, called a **histogram**.

Histograms

Here are the monthly prices of AIG stock displayed in a histogram.

WHO	Months
WHAT	Monthly average price for AIG's stock (in dollars)
WHEN	2002 through 2007
WHERE	New York Stock Exchange
WHY	To examine AIG stock volatility

Figure 3.1   Monthly average prices of AIG stock. The histogram displays the distribution of prices by showing for each "bin" of prices, the number of months having prices in that bin.

A histogram plots the bin counts as the heights of bars. It counts the number of cases that fall into each bin, and displays that count as the height of the corresponding bar. In this histogram of monthly average prices, each bin has a width of $5, so, for example, the height of the tallest bar says that there were 24 months whose average price of AIG stock was between $65 and $70. In this way, the histogram displays the entire distribution of prices. Unlike a bar chart, which puts gaps between bars to separate the categories, there are no gaps between the bars of a histogram unless there are actual gaps in the data. **Gaps** indicate a region where there are no values. Gaps can be important features of the distribution so watch out for them and point them out.

For categorical variables, each category got its own bar. The only choice was whether to combine categories for ease of display. For quantitative variables, we have to choose the width of the bins. It isn't hard to make a histogram by hand, but we almost always use technology. Many statistics programs allow you to adjust the bin width yourself.

From the histogram, we can see that in these months the AIG stock price was typically near $65 and usually between $55 and $75. Keep in mind that this histogram is a static picture. We have treated these prices simply as a collection of months, not as a time series, and shown their distribution. Later in the chapter we will discuss when this is appropriate and add time to the story.

Does the distribution look as you expected? It's often a good idea to imagine what the distribution might look like before making a display. That way you're less likely to be fooled by errors either in your display or in the data themselves.

The vertical axis of a histogram shows the number of cases falling in each bin. An alternative is to report the percentage of cases in each bin, creating a **relative frequency histogram**. The shape of the two histograms is the same; only the vertical axis and labels are different. A relative frequency histogram is faithful to the area principle by displaying the *percentage* of cases in each bin instead of the count.

Figure 3.2   A relative frequency histogram looks just like a frequency histogram except that the *y*-axis now shows the percentage of months in each bin.

FOR EXAMPLE   Creating a histogram

As the chief financial officer of a music download site, you've just secured the rights to offer downloads of a new album. You'd like to see how well it's selling, so you collect the number of downloads per hour for the past 24 hours:

(continued)

Hour	Downloads	Hour	Downloads
12:00 a.m.	36	12:00 p.m.	25
1:00 a.m.	28	1:00 p.m.	22
2:00 a.m.	19	2:00 p.m.	17
3:00 a.m.	10	3:00 p.m.	18
4:00 a.m.	5	4:00 p.m.	20
5:00 a.m.	3	5:00 p.m.	23
6:00 a.m.	2	6:00 p.m.	21
7:00 a.m.	6	7:00 p.m.	18
8:00 a.m.	12	8:00 p.m.	24
9:00 a.m.	14	9:00 p.m.	30
10:00 a.m.	20	10:00 p.m.	27
11:00 a.m.	18	11:00 p.m.	30

QUESTION   Make a histogram for this variable.

ANSWER   Create a frequency table of bins of width five from 0 to 40 and put values at the ends of bins into the right bin:

Downloads	Number of Hours
0–5	2
5–10	2
10–15	3
15–20	5
20–25	6
25–30	3
30–35	2
35–40	1
Total	**24**

The histogram looks like this:

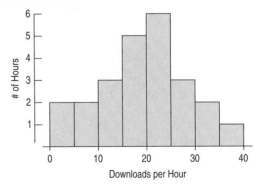

*Stem-and-Leaf Displays

Stem-and-leaf displays are like histograms, but they also show the individual values. They are easy to make by hand for data sets that aren't too large, so they're a great way to look at a small batch of values quickly.[1] Here's a stem-and-leaf display for the AIG stock data, alongside a histogram of the same data.

---

*Sections marked with an asterisk may be optional. Check with your Instructor.
[1]The authors like to make stem-and-leaf displays whenever data are presented (without a suitable display) at committee meetings or working groups. The insights from just that quick look at the distribution are often quite valuable.

Figure 3.3 The AIG monthly average stock prices displayed both by a histogram (left) and stem-and-leaf display (right). Stem-and-leaf displays are typically made by hand, so we are most likely to use them for small data sets. For much larger data sets, we use a histogram.

```
4 | 99
5 | 134
5 | 5667888999999
6 | 0000011122222344
6 | 555556666777788888889999
7 | 0001111222334
7 | 7
```

How Stem-And-Leaf Displays Work

A stem-and-leaf display breaks each number into two parts: the stem shown to the left of the solid line and the leaf, to the right. For the AIG data, each price, for example $67.02, is first truncated to two digits, $67. Then it is split into two components: 6|7. The line 5|134 displays the values $51, $53, and $54 and corresponds to the histogram bin from $50 to $55. The stem-and-leaf in Figure 3.3 uses a bin width of 5. Another choice would be to increase the bin size and put all the prices from $50 to $60 on one line:

$$5 | 1345667888999999$$

That would decrease the number of bins to 4, but makes the bin from $60 to $70 too crowded:

```
4 | 99
5 | 1345667888999999
6 | 00000111222223445555566667777788888889999
7 | 00011112223347
```

Before making a stem-and-leaf display, or a histogram, you should check the **Quantitative Data Condition**: The data must be values of a quantitative variable whose units are known.

Although a bar chart and a histogram may look similar, they're not the same display. You can't display categorical data in a histogram or quantitative data in a bar chart. Always check the condition that confirms what type of data you have before making your display.

3.2 Shape

Once you've displayed the distribution in a histogram or stem-and-leaf display, what can you say about it? When you describe a distribution, you should pay attention to three things: its **shape**, its **center**, and its **spread**.

We describe the shape of a distribution in terms of its modes, its symmetry, and whether it has any gaps or outlying values.

Mode

Does the histogram have a single, central hump (or peak) or several, separated humps? These humps are called **modes**. Formally, the mode is the single, most frequent value, but we rarely use the term that way.[2] The AIG stock prices have a single mode around $65. We

---
[2]Technically, the mode is the value on the *x*-axis of the histogram below the highest peak, but when asked to identify the mode, most people would point to the peak itself.

Where's the Mode?

The mode is typically defined as the single value that appears most often. That definition is fine for categorical variables because we only need to count the number of cases for each category. For quantitative variables, the meaning of *mode* is more ambiguous. For example, what's the mode of the AIG data? No two prices were exactly the same, but 7 months had prices between $68 and $69. Should that be the mode? Probably not—that seems a little arbitrary. For quantitative data, it makes more sense to use the word *mode* in the more general sense of "peak in a histogram," rather than as a single summary value.

Pie à la Mode

Is there a connection between pie and the mode of a distribution? Actually, there is! The mode of a distribution is a *popular* value near which a lot of data values gather. And à la mode means "in style"— *not* "with ice cream." That just happened to be a *popular* way to have pie in Paris around 1900.

often use modes to describe the shape of the distribution. A distribution whose histogram has one main hump, such as the one for the AIG stock prices, is called **unimodal**; distributions whose histograms have two humps are **bimodal**, and those with three or more are called **multimodal**. For example, here's a bimodal distribution.

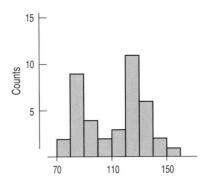

Figure 3.4   A bimodal distribution has two apparent modes.

A bimodal histogram is often an indication that there are two groups in the data. It's a good idea to investigate when you see bimodality. But don't get overly excited by minor fluctuations in the histogram, which may just be artifacts of where the bin boundaries fall. To be a true mode, the hump should still be there when you display the histogram with slightly different bin widths.

A distribution whose histogram doesn't appear to have any mode and in which all the bars are approximately the same height is called **uniform**. (Chapter 5 gives a more formal definition.)

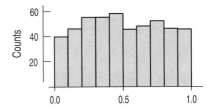

Figure 3.5   In a uniform distribution, bars are all about the same height. The histogram doesn't appear to have a mode.

Symmetry

Could you fold the histogram along a vertical line through the middle and have the edges match pretty closely, as in Figure 3.6, or are more of the values on one side, as in the histograms in Figure 3.7? A distribution is **symmetric** if the halves on either side of the center look, at least approximately, like mirror images.

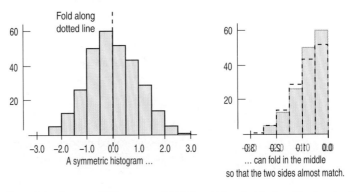

Figure 3.6   A symmetric histogram can fold in the middle so that the two sides almost match.

The (usually) thinner ends of a distribution are called the **tails**. If one tail stretches out farther than the other, the distribution is said to be **skewed** to the side of the longer tail.

Figure 3.7 Two skewed histograms showing the age (left) and hospital charges (right) for all female heart attack patients in New York State in one year. The histogram of Age (in blue) is skewed to the left, while the histogram of Charges (in purple) is skewed to the right.

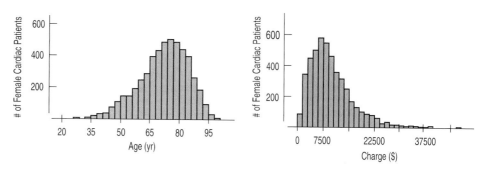

Skewed Right or Left?

Amounts of things (dollars, employees, waiting times) can't be negative so they run up against zero. But they have no natural upper limit. So, they often have distributions that are skewed to the right. Grades on a test where most students do well are often skewed to the left with many scoring near the top, but a few straggling off to the low end.

Outliers

Do any values appear to stick out? Often such values tell us something interesting or exciting about the data. You should always point out any stragglers or **outliers** that stand off away from the body of the distribution. For example, if you're studying the personal wealth of Americans and Bill Gates is in your sample, he would certainly be an outlier. Because his wealth would be so obviously atypical, you'd want to point it out as a special feature.

Outliers can affect almost every method we discuss in this book, so we'll always be on the lookout for them. An outlier can be the most informative part of your data, or it might just be an error. Either way, you shouldn't throw it away without comment. Treat it specially and discuss it when you report your conclusions about your data. (Or find the error and fix it if you can.)

Using Your Judgment

How you characterize a distribution is often a judgment call. Do the two humps in the histogram really reveal two subgroups, or will the shape look different if you change the bin width slightly? Are those observations at the high end of the histogram truly unusual, or are they just the largest ones at the end of a long tail? These are matters of judgment on which different people can legitimately disagree. There's no automatic calculation or rule of thumb that can make the decision for you. Understanding your data and how they arose can help. What should guide your decisions is an honest desire to understand what is happening in the data. That's what you'll need to make sound business decisions.

Viewing a histogram at several different bin widths can help you to see how persistent some of the features are. Some technologies offer ways to change the bin width interactively to get multiple views of the histogram. If the number of observations in each bin is small enough so that moving a couple of values to the next bin changes your assessment of how many modes there are, be careful. Be sure to think about the data, where they came from, and what kinds of questions you hope to answer from them.

FOR EXAMPLE   Describing the shape of a distribution

QUESTION   Describe the shape of the distribution of downloads from the example on page 51.

ANSWER   It is symmetric and unimodal with no outliers.

3.3   Center

Look again at the AIG prices in Figure 3.1. If you had to pick one number to describe a *typical* price, what would you pick? When a histogram is unimodal and fairly symmetric, most people would point to the center of the distribution, where the histogram peaks. The typical price is around $65.00.

If we want to be more precise and *calculate* a number, we can *average* the data. In the AIG example, the average monthly price is $64.48, about what we might expect from the histogram. You probably know how to average values, but this is a good place to introduce notation that we'll use throughout the book. We'll call the generic variable x, and use the Greek capital letter sigma, Σ, to mean "sum" (sigma is "S" in Greek), and write[3]:

NOTATION ALERT

A bar over any symbol indicates the mean of that quantity.

$$\bar{x} = \frac{Total}{n} = \frac{\Sigma x}{n}.$$

According to this formula, we add up all the values of the variable, x, and divide that sum (*Total*, or Σx) by the number of data values, n. We call the resulting value the **mean** of x.[4]

Although the mean is a natural summary for unimodal, symmetric distributions, it can be misleading for skewed data or for distributions with gaps or outliers. The histogram of AIG monthly prices in Figure 3.1 is unimodal, and nearly symmetric, with a slight left skew. A look at the total volume of AIG stock sold each month for the same 6 years tells a very different story. Figure 3.8 shows a unimodal but strongly right-skewed distribution with two gaps. The mean monthly volume was 170.1 million shares. Locate that value on the histogram. Does it seem a little high as a summary of a typical month's volume? In fact, more than two out of three months have volumes that are less than that value. It might be better to use the **median**—the value that splits the histogram into two equal *areas*. The median is commonly used for variables such as cost or income, which are likely to be skewed.

Figure 3.8   The median splits the area of the histogram in half at 135.9 million shares. The mean is the point on which the histogram would balance. Because the distribution is skewed to the right, the mean 170.1 million shares is *higher* than the median. The points at the right have pulled the mean toward them, away from the median.

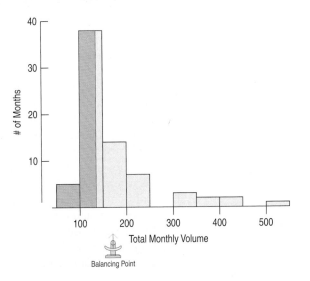

[3]You may also see the variable called y and the equation written $\bar{y} = \frac{Total}{n} = \frac{\Sigma y}{n}$. We actually prefer to call a single variable y instead of x, because in the next chapter we'll need x to name a variable that predicts another (which we'll call y), but when you have only one variable either name is common. Most calculators call a single variable x.

[4]Once you've averaged the data, you might logically expect the result to be called the *average*. But average is used too colloquially as in the "average" home buyer, where we don't sum up anything. Even though average *is* sometimes used in the way we intend, as in the Dow Jones Industrial Average (which is actually a weighted average) or a batting average, we'll usually use the term *mean* throughout the book.

That's because the median is *resistant* to unusual observations and to the shape of the distribution. For the AIG monthly trading volumes, the median is 135.9 million shares, which seems like a more appropriate summary.

Does it really make a difference whether we choose a mean or a median? The mean monthly price for the AIG stock is $64.48. Because the distribution of the prices is roughly symmetric, we'd expect the mean and median to be close. In fact, we compute the median to be $65.23. But for variables with skewed distributions, the story is quite different. For a right-skewed distribution like the monthly volumes in Figure 3.8, the mean is larger than the median: 170.1 compared to 135.9. The two give quite different summaries. The difference is due to the overall shape of the distributions.

BY HAND   Finding the Median

Finding the median of a batch of n numbers is easy as long as you remember to order the values first. If n is odd, the median is the middle value. Counting in from the ends, we find this value in the $\dfrac{n + 1}{2}$ position.

When n is even, there are two middle values. So, in this case, the median is the average of the two values in positions $\dfrac{n}{2}$ and $\dfrac{n}{2} + 1$.

Here are two examples:

Suppose the batch has the values 14.1, 3.2, 25.3, 2.8, −17.5, 13.9, and 45.8. First we order the values: −17.5, 2.8, 3.2, 13.9, 14.1, 25.3, and 45.8. There are 7 values, so the median is the $(7 + 1)/2 = $ 4th value counting from the top or bottom: 13.9.

Suppose we had the same batch with another value at 35.7. Then the ordered values are −17.5, 2.8, 3.2, 13.9, 14.1, 25.3, 35.7, and 45.8. The median is the average of the 8/2, or 4th, and the $(8/2) + 1$, or 5th, values. So the median is $(13.9 + 14.1)/2 = 14.0$.

The mean is the point at which the histogram would balance. A value far from the center has more leverage, pulling the mean in its direction. It's hard to argue that a summary that's been pulled aside by only a few outlying values or by a long tail is what we mean by the center of the distribution. That's why the median is usually a better choice for skewed data.

However, when the distribution is unimodal and symmetric, the mean offers better opportunities to calculate useful quantities and draw interesting conclusions. It will be the summary value we work with throughout the rest of the book.

FOR EXAMPLE   Finding the mean and median

QUESTION   From the data on page 52, what is a typical number of downloads per hour?

ANSWER   The mean number is 18.7 downloads per hour. The median is 19.5 downloads per hour. Because the distribution is unimodal and roughly symmetric, we shouldn't be surprised that the two are close. There are a few more hours (in the middle of the night) with small numbers of downloads that pull the mean lower than the median, but either one seems like a reasonable summary to report.

3.4   Spread of the Distribution

We know that the typical price of the AIG stock is around $65, but knowing the mean or median alone doesn't tell us about the entire distribution. A stock whose price doesn't move away from its center isn't very interesting.[5] The more the data vary, the less a measure of center can tell us. We need to know how spread out the data are as well.

One simple measure of spread is the **range**, defined as the difference between the extremes:

$$\text{Range} = max - min.$$

For the AIG price data, the range is $77.26 - $49.41 = $27.85. Notice that the range is *a single number* that describes the spread of the data, not an interval of values—as you might think from its use in common speech. If there are any unusual observations in the data, the range is not resistant and will be influenced by them. Concentrating on the middle of the data avoids this problem.

The **lower quartile, Q1**, is defined as the value for which one quarter of the data lie below it and the **upper quartile, Q3**, is the value for which one quarter of the data lie above it. In this way, the quartiles frame the middle 50% of the data. The **interquartile range (IQR)** summarizes the spread by focusing on the middle half of the data. It's defined as the difference between the two quartiles:

$$\text{IQR} = Q3 - Q1.$$

BY HAND   Finding Quartiles

Quartiles are easy to find in theory, but more difficult in practice. The three quartiles, Q1 (lower quartile), Q2 (the median), and Q3 (the upper quartile) split the sorted data values into quarters. So, for example, 25% of the data values will lie at or below Q1. The problem lies in the fact that unless your sample size divides nicely by 4, there isn't just one way to split the data into quarters. The statistical software package SAS offers at least five different ways to compute quartiles. The differences are usually small, but can be annoying. Here are two of the most common methods for finding quartiles by hand or with a calculator:

1. The Tukey Method

    Split the sorted data at the median. (If n is odd, include the median with each half). Then find the median of each of these halves—use these as the quartiles.

    Example: The data set $\{14.1, 3.2, 25.3, 2.8, -17.5, 13.9, 45.8\}$

    First we order the values: $\{-17.5, 2.8, 3.2, 13.9, 14.1, 25.3, 45.8\}$. We found the median to be 13.9, so form two data sets: $\{-17.5, 2.8, 3.2, 13.9\}$ and $\{13.9, 14.1, 25.3, 45.8\}$. The medians of these are $3.0 = (2.8 + 3.2)/2$ and $19.7 = (14.1 + 25.3)/2$. So we let $Q1 = 3.0$ and $Q3 = 19.7$.

2. The TI calculator method

    The same as the Tukey method, except we *don't* include the median with each half. So for $\{14.1, 3.2, 25.3, 2.8, -17.5, 13.9,$ and $45.8\}$ we find the two data sets:

    $\{-17.5, 2.8, 3.2\}$ and $\{14.1, 25.3, 45.8\}$ by not including the median in either.

---

[5]And not much of an investment, either.

Now the medians of these are Q1 = 2.8 and Q3 = 25.3.

Notice the effect on the IQR. For Tukey:

IQR = Q3−Q1 = 19.7−3.0 = 16.7, but for TI,
IQR = 25.3−2.8 = 22.5.

For both of these methods, notice that the quartiles are either data values, or the average of two adjacent values. In Excel and other software, the quartiles are *interpolated*, so they may not be simple averages of two values. Be aware that there may be differences, but the idea is the same: the quartiles Q1, Q2, and Q3 split the data roughly into quarters.

> **Waiting in Line**
>
> Why do banks favor a single line that feeds several teller windows rather than separate lines for each teller? It does make the average waiting time slightly shorter, but that improvement is very small. The real difference people notice is that the time you can expect to wait is less variable when there is a single line, and people prefer consistency.

For the AIG data, Q1 = \$60.11, Q3 = \$69.01.[6] So the IQR = Q3 − Q1 = \$69.01 − \$60.11 = \$8.90.

The IQR is a reasonable summary of spread, but because it uses only the two quartiles of the data, it ignores much of the information about how individual values vary. By contrast, the standard deviation, takes into account how far each value is from the mean. Like the mean, the standard deviation is appropriate only for symmetric data and can be influenced by outlying observations.

As the name implies, the standard deviation uses the *deviations* of each data value from the mean. The average[7] of the *squared* deviations is called the **variance** and is denoted by s^2:

$$s^2 = \frac{\sum (x - \bar{x})^2}{n - 1}.$$

The variance plays an important role in statistics, but as a measure of spread, it has a problem. Whatever the units of the original data, the variance is in *squared* units. We want measures of spread to have the same units as the data, so we usually take the square root of the variance. That gives the **standard deviation**.

$$s = \sqrt{\frac{\sum (x - \bar{x})^2}{n - 1}}.$$

For the AIG stock prices, $s = \$6.12$.

FOR EXAMPLE Describing the spread

QUESTION   For the data on page 52, describe the spread of the number of downloads per hour.

ANSWER   The range of downloads is 36 − 2 = 34 downloads per hour.
The quartiles are 13 and 24.5, so the IQR is 24.5 − 13 = 11.5 downloads per hour.
The standard deviation is 8.94 downloads per hour.

---

[6]In general, we use the Tukey method in this book unless stated otherwise.
[7]For technical reasons, we divide by $n - 1$ instead of n to take this average. We'll discuss this more in Chapter 11.

JUST CHECKING

Thinking about Variation

1 The U.S. Census Bureau reports the median family income in its summary of census data. Why do you suppose they use the median instead of the mean? What might be the disadvantages of reporting the mean?

2 You've just bought a new car that claims to get a highway fuel efficiency of 31 miles per gallon (mpg). Of course, your mileage will "vary." If you had to guess, would you expect the IQR of gas mileage attained by all cars like yours to be 30 mpg, 3 mpg, or 0.3 mpg? Why?

3 A company selling a new MP3 player advertises that the player has a mean lifetime of 5 years. If you were in charge of quality control at the factory, would you prefer that the standard deviation of life spans of the players you produce be 2 years or 2 months? Why?

3.5   Shape, Center, and Spread—A Summary

What should you report about a quantitative variable? Report the shape of its distribution, and include a center and a spread. But which measure of center and which measure of spread? The guidelines are pretty easy.

- If the shape is skewed, point that out and report the median and IQR. You may want to include the mean and standard deviation as well, explaining why the mean and median differ. The fact that the mean and median do not agree is a sign that the distribution may be skewed. A histogram will help you make the point.
- If the shape is unimodal and symmetric, report the mean and standard deviation and possibly the median and IQR as well. For unimodal symmetric data, the IQR is usually a bit larger than the standard deviation. If that's not true for your data set, look again to make sure the distribution isn't skewed or multimodal and that there are no outliers.
- If there are multiple modes, try to understand why. If you can identify a reason for separate modes, it may be a good idea to split the data into separate groups.
- If there are any clearly unusual observations, point them out. If you are reporting the mean and standard deviation, report them computed with and without the unusual observations. The differences may be revealing.
- Always pair the median with the IQR and the mean with the standard deviation. It's not useful to report a measure of center without a corresponding measure of spread. Reporting a center without a spread can lead you to think you know more about the distribution than you do. Reporting only the spread omits important information.

> **FOR EXAMPLE** Summarizing data
>
> **QUESTION**   Report on the shape, center, and spread of the downloads data; see page 52.
>
> **ANSWER**   The distribution of downloads per hour over the past 24 hours is unimodal and roughly symmetric. The mean number of downloads per hour is 18.7 and the standard deviation is 8.94. There are several hours in the middle of the night with very few downloads, but none seem to be so unusual as to be considered outliers.

3.6   Standardizing Variables

A real estate agent in California covers two markets. One is near Stanford University, filled with old homes and tree lined streets in an area called Old Palo Alto. The other is a newer neighborhood, in Foster City, created when part of the San Francisco Bay was filled in to create space for more housing.

Here are summaries of the prices of a sample of houses in these two neighborhoods as found on Zillow.com:

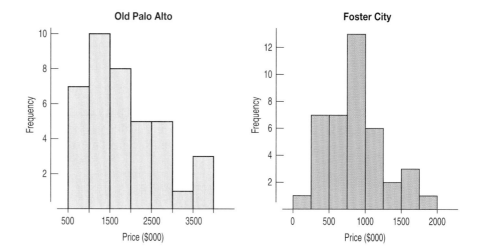

Figure 3.9 Prices of houses from samples from Old Palo Alto (left) and Foster City (right). Note that the horizontal scale is quite different for the two neighborhoods. Prices are in $1000's.

The average house in Old Palo Alto was worth $1,930,436 with a standard deviation of $914,523, while the average Foster City house cost $711,400 with a standard deviation of $318,177. So, a $1,000,000 home in Foster City is on the expensive side, but for Old Palo Alto, that's just over half the average cost.

Which would be more unusual, a $2M home in Foster City, or a $3.5M home in Old Palo Alto?

Using the standard deviation as a way to measure distance helps us answer this question. In Foster City, a $2M home is $1,288,600 over the average. In Old Palo Alto, a $3.5M home is $1,569,564 over its average. It might seem to be more unusual. But look at the standard deviations. That excess of $1,288,600 is over 4 standard deviations above the mean for Foster City. But in Old Palo Alto, the standard deviation is nearly $1M, so the $3.5M home is "only" 1.72 standard deviations above the mean. If you look at the histogram, you can see that $2M (2000) is off the right side for Foster City, but for Old Palo Alto, $3.5M (3500) is still in the histogram.

Using the mean and standard deviation this way gives us a way to standardize values in different distributions to compare them.

How Does Standardizing Work?

We first need to find the mean and standard deviation of each variable for the prices in each town.

	Mean ($000)	SD ($000)
Old Palo Alto	1930.4	914.5
Foster City	711.40	318.2

Next we measure how *far* each of our values is from the mean of its variable. We subtract the mean and then divide by the standard deviation:

$$z = (x - \bar{x})/s$$

We call the resulting value a **standardized value** and denote it with the letter z. Usually, we just call it a **z-score**. The z-score tells us how many standard deviations a value is from its mean.

Let's look at Old Palo Alto first.

To compute the z-score for the $3.5M house, take its value (3500 in $000 units), subtract the mean (1930.4) and divide by the standard deviation, 914.5:

$$z = (3500 - 1930.4)/914.5 = 1.72$$

So this house's price is 1.72 standard deviations *above* the mean price of all the houses we sampled in Old Palo Alto. How about that $2M home in Foster City? Standardizing it for the mean and standard deviation of Foster City prices, we find

$$z = (2000 - 711.4)/318.2 = 4.05$$

So this house's price is over 4 standard deviations above the mean for its location! Standardizing enables us to compare values from different distributions to see which is more unusual in context.

> **Standardizing into z-Scores:**
> - Shifts the mean to 0.
> - Changes the standard deviation to 1.
> - Does not change the shape.
> - Removes the units.

FOR EXAMPLE   Comparing values by standardizing

QUESTION   A real estate analyst finds from data on 350 recent sales, that the average price was $175,000 with a standard deviation of $55,000. The size of the houses (in square feet) averaged 2100 sq. ft. with a standard deviation of 650 sq. ft. Which is more unusual, a house in this town that costs $340,000, or a 5000 sq. ft. house?

ANSWER   Compute the z-scores to compare. For the $340,000 house:

$$z = \frac{x - \bar{x}}{s} = \frac{(340,000 - 175,000)}{55,000} = 3.0$$

The house price is 3 standard deviations above the mean.
For the 5000 sq. ft. house:

$$z = \frac{x - \bar{x}}{s} = \frac{(5000 - 2100)}{650} = 4.46$$

This house is 4.46 standard deviations above the mean in size. That's more unusual than the house that costs $340,000.

3.7   Five-Number Summary and Boxplots

The **five-number summary** of a distribution reports its median, quartiles, and extremes (maximum and minimum). The five-number summary of the monthly trading volumes of AIG stock for the period 2002–2007 looks like this (in millions of shares).

Max	515.62
Q3	182.32
Median	135.87
Q1	121.04
Min	83.91

Table 3.2   The five-number summary of monthly trading volume of AIG shares (in millions of shares) for the period 2002–2007.

Figure 3.10 Boxplot of monthly volumes of AIG stock traded in the period 2002–2007 (in millions of shares).

The five-number summary provides a good overall look at the distribution. We can see that on half of the days the volume was between 121.04 and 182.32 million shares, and that it was never above 515.62 or below 83.91 million shares.

We can display the information from a five-number summary in a **boxplot** (see Figure 3.10).

A boxplot highlights several features of the distribution of a variable. The central box shows the middle half of the data, between the quartiles. Because the top of the box is at the upper quartile (Q3) and the bottom is at Q1, the height of the box is equal to Q3 − Q1 which is the IQR. (For the AIG data, it's 61.28.) The median is displayed as a horizontal line. If the median is roughly centered between the quartiles, then the middle half of the data is roughly symmetric. If it is not centered, the distribution is skewed. In extreme cases, the median can coincide with one of the quartiles.

The whiskers reach out from the box to the most extreme values that are not considered outliers. The boxplot nominates points as outliers if they fall farther than 1.5 IQRs beyond either quartile (for the AIG data, 1.5 IQR = 1.5 × 61.28 = 91.92). Outliers are displayed individually, both to keep them out of the way for judging skewness and to encourage you to give them special attention. They may be mistakes or they may be the most interesting cases in your data. This rule is not a definition of what makes a point an outlier. It just nominates cases for special attention. And it is not a substitute for careful analysis and thought about whether an extreme value deserves to be treated specially.

Boxplots are especially useful for comparing several distributions side by side. From the shape of the box in Figure 3.10, we can see that the central part of the distribution of volume is skewed to the right (upward here) and the dissimilar length of the two whiskers shows that the skewness continues into the tails of the distribution. We also see several high-volume and some extremely high-volume months. Those months may warrant some inquiries into why trading volume was so high.

Why Use 1.5 IQRs for Nominating Outliers?

Nominate a point as a potential outlier if it lies farther than 1.5 IQRs beyond either the lower (Q1) or upper (Q3) quartile. Some boxplots also designate points as "far" outliers if they lie more than 3 IQRs from the quartiles (as in Figure 3.10). The prominent statistician John W. Tukey, the originator of the boxplot, was asked (by one of the authors) why the outlier nomination rule cut at 1.5 IQRs beyond each quartile. He answered that the reason was simple—1 IQR would be too small and 2 IQRs would be too large.

FOR EXAMPLE The boxplot rule for nominating outliers

QUESTION From the histogram on page 52, we saw that no download times seemed to be so far from the center as to be considered outliers. Use the 1.5 IQR rule to see if it nominates any points as outliers.

ANSWER The quartiles are 13 and 24.5 and the IQR is 11.5, and 1.5 × IQR = 17.25. A value would have to be larger than 24.5 + 17.25 = 41.75 downloads per hour or smaller than 13 − 17.25 = −4.25. The largest value was 36 downloads per hour and all values must be nonnegative, so there are no points nominated as outliers.

GUIDED EXAMPLE   Credit Card Bank Customers

To focus on the needs of particular customers, companies often segment their customers into groups with similar needs or spending patterns. A major credit card bank wanted to see how much a particular group of cardholders charged per month on their cards to understand the potential growth in their card use. The data for each customer was the amount he or she spent using the card during a recent three-month period. Boxplots are especially useful for one variable when combined with a histogram and numerical summaries. Let's summarize the spending of this market segment.

PLAN	**Setup** Identify the *variable*, the time frame of the data, and the objective of the analysis.	We want to summarize the average monthly charges (in dollars) made by 500 cardholders from a market segment of interest during a three-month period. The data are quantitative, so we'll use histograms and boxplots, as well as numerical summaries.

DO

Mechanics Select an appropriate display based on the nature of the data and what you want to know about it.

REALITY CHECK ▶ It is always a good idea to anticipate the shape of the distribution so you can check whether the histogram is close to what you expected. Are these data reasonable amounts for customers to charge on their cards in a month? A typical value is a few hundred dollars. That seems like the right ballpark.

Note that outliers are often easier to see with boxplots than with histograms, but the histogram provides more details about the shape of the distribution. The computer program that made this boxplot "jitters" the outliers in the boxplot so they don't lie on top of each other, making them easier to see.

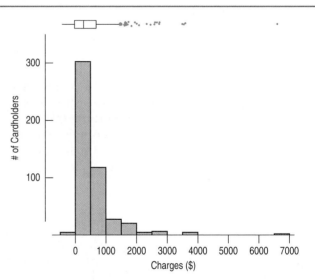

Both graphs show a distribution that is highly skewed to the right with several outliers and an extreme outlier near $7000.

Summary of Monthly Charges	
Count	500
Mean	544.749
Median	370.65
StdDev	661.244
IQR	624.125
Q1	114.54
Q3	738.665

The mean is much larger than the median. The data have a skewed distribution.

REPORT

Interpretation Describe the shape, center, and spread of the distribution. Be sure to report on the symmetry, number of modes, and any gaps or outliers.

Recommendation State a conclusion and any recommended actions or analysis.

MEMO

Re: Report on segment spending

The distribution of charges for this segment during this time period is unimodal and skewed to the right. For that reason, we have summarized the data with the median and interquartile range (IQR).

The median amount charged was $370.65. Half of the cardholders charged between $114.54 and $738.67.

In addition, there are several high outliers, with one extreme value at $6745.

There are also a few negative values. We suspect that these are people who returned more than they charged in a month, but because the values might be data errors, we suggest that they be checked.

Future analyses should look at whether charges during these three months were similar to charges in the rest of the year. We would also like to investigate if there is a seasonal pattern and, if so, whether it can be explained by our advertising campaigns or by other factors.

3.8 Comparing Groups

Stock prices can sometimes reflect turmoil within a company. Could an investor have seen signs of trouble in the AIG stock prices? Figure 3.11 shows the daily closing prices for the first two years of our data, 2002 and 2003:

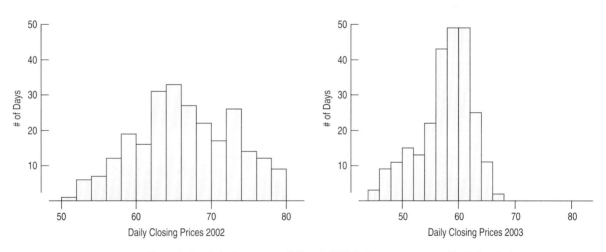

Figure 3.11 Daily closing prices of AIG on the NYSE for the two years 2002 and 2003. How do the two distributions differ?

Prices were generally lower in 2003 than 2002. The price distribution for 2002 appears to be symmetric with a center in the high $60s while the 2003 distribution is left skewed with a center below $60. For comparison, we displayed the two histograms on the same scale. Histograms with very different centers and spreads can appear similar unless you do that.

When we compare several groups, boxplots usually do a better job. Boxplots offer an ideal balance of information and simplicity, hiding the details while displaying the overall summary information. And we can plot them side by side, making it easy to compare multiple groups or categories.

When we place boxplots side by side, we can compare their centers and spreads. We can see past any outliers in making these comparisons because the outliers are displayed individually. We can also begin to look for trends in both the centers and the spreads.

GUIDED EXAMPLE   AIG Stock Price

What really happened to the AIG stock price from the beginning of the period we've been studying through the financial crisis of 2008/2009? We will use the daily closing prices of AIG stock for these nine years.

PLAN

Setup Identify the variables, report the time frame of the data, and state the objective.

We want to compare the daily prices of AIG shares traded on the NYSE from 2002 through 2009.

The daily price is quantitative and measured in dollars. We can partition the values by year and use side-by-side boxplots to compare the daily prices across years.

DO

Mechanics Plot the side-by-side boxplots of the data.

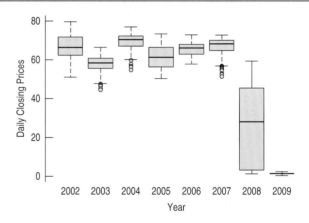

What happened in 2008? We'd better look there with a finer partition. Here are boxplots by month for 2008.

Display any other plots suggested by the analysis so far.

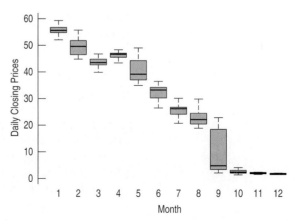

REPORT

Conclusion Report what you've learned about the data and any recommended action or analysis.

MEMO

Re: Research on price of AIG stock

We have examined the daily closing prices of AIG stock on the NYSE for the period 2002 through 2009. Prices were relatively stable for the period 2002 through 2007. Prices were a bit lower in 2003 but recovered and stayed generally above $60 for 2004 through 2007. Then throughout the first 9 months of 2008, prices dropped dramatically, and remained low throughout 2009. A boxplot by month during 2008 shows that the decline in price was sharpest in September. Most analysts point to that month as the beginning of the financial meltdown, but clearly there were signs in the price of AIG that trouble had been brewing for much longer. By October, and for the rest of the year, the price was very low with almost no variation.

FOR EXAMPLE Comparing boxplots

QUESTION For the data on page 52, compare the a.m. downloads to the p.m. downloads by displaying the two distributions side-by-side with boxplots.

ANSWER There are generally more downloads in the afternoon than in the morning. The median number of afternoon downloads is around 22 as compared with 14 for the morning hours. The p.m. downloads are also much more consistent. The entire range of the p.m. hours, 15, is about the size of the IQR for a.m. hours. Both distributions appear to be fairly symmetric, although the a.m. hour distribution has some high points which seem to give some asymmetry.

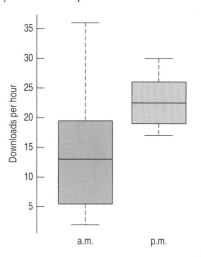

3.9 Identifying Outliers

We've just seen that the price of AIG shares dropped precipitously during the year 2008. Figure 3.12 (next page) shows the daily sales volume by month.

Cases that stand out from the rest of the data deserve our attention. Boxplots have a rule for nominating extreme cases to display as outliers, but that's just a rule of thumb—not a definition. The rule doesn't tell you what to do with them. It's never a substitute for careful thinking about the data and their context.

So, what *should* we do with outliers? The first thing to do is to try to understand them in the context of the data. Once you've identified likely outliers, you should always investigate them. Some outliers are not plausible and may simply be errors. A decimal point may have been misplaced, digits transposed, digits repeated

Figure 3.12   In January, there was a high-volume day of 38 million shares that is nominated as an outlier for that month. In February there were three outliers with a maximum of over 100 million shares. In most months one or more high-volume days are identified as outliers for their month. But none of these high-volume days would have been considered unusual during September, when the median daily volume of AIG stock was 170 million shares. Days that may have seemed ordinary for September if placed in another month would have seemed extraordinary and *vice versa*. That high-volume day in January certainly wouldn't stand out in September or even October or November, but for January it was remarkable.

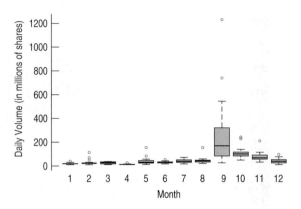

or omitted, or the wrong value transcribed. Or, the units may be wrong. If you saw the number of AIG shares traded on the NYSE listed as 2 shares for a particular day, you'd know something was wrong. It could be that it was meant as 2 million shares, but you'd have to check to be sure. If you can identify the error, then you should certainly correct it.

Other outliers are not wrong; they're just different. These are the cases that often repay your efforts to understand them. You may learn more from the extraordinary cases than from summaries of the overall dataset.

What about those two days in September that stand out as extreme even during that volatile month? Those were September 15 and 16, 2008. On the 15th, 740 million shares of AIG stock were traded. That was followed by an incredible volume of over 1 billion shares of stock from a single company traded the following day. Here's how Barron's described the trading of September 16:

Record Volume for NYSE Stocks, Nasdaq Trades Surge
Beats Its July Record

Yesterday's record-setting volume of 8.14 billion shares traded of all stocks listed on the New York Stock Exchange was pushed aside today by 9.31 billion shares in NYSE Composite volume. The biggest among those trades was the buying and selling of American International Group, with 1.11 billion shares traded as of 4 p.m. today. The AIG trades were 12% of all NYSE Composite volume.

FOR EXAMPLE   Identifying outliers and summarizing data

QUESTION   A real estate report lists the following prices for sales of single family homes in a small town in Virginia (rounded to the nearest thousand). Write a couple of sentences describing house prices in this town.

155,000	329,000	172,000	122,000	260,000
139,000	178,000	339,435,000	136,000	330,000
158,000	194,000	279,000	167,000	159,000
149,000	160,000	231,000	136,000	128,000

ANSWER A box plot shows an extreme outlier:

That extreme point is a home whose sale price is listed at $339.4 M.

A check on the Internet shows that the most expensive homes ever sold are less than $200 M. This is clearly a mistake.

Setting aside this point, we find the following histogram and summary statistics:

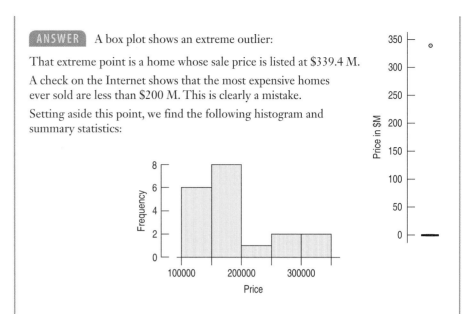

The distribution of prices is strongly skewed to the right. The median price is $160,000. The minimum is $122,000 and the maximum (without the outlier) is $330,000. The middle 50% of house prices lie between $144,000 and $212,500 with an IQR of $68,500. (Calculated using the Tukey method.)

3.10 Time Series Plots

A histogram can provide information about the distribution of a variable, but it can't show any pattern over time. Whenever we have time series data, it is a good idea to look for patterns by plotting the data in time order. The histogram we saw in the beginning of the chapter (Figure 3.1) was an appropriate display for the distribution of prices because during that period from 2002 to 2007 the monthly prices were fairly stable.

When a time series has no strong trend or change in variability we say that it is **stationary**.[8] A histogram can provide a useful summary of a stationary series. When your data are measured over time, you should look for patterns by plotting the data in time order. For example, when we examine the daily prices for the year 2007 (Figure 3.13 on the next page), we see that prices started to change during the last quarter.

A display of values against time is called a **time series plot**. This plot reveals a pattern that we were unable to see in either a histogram or a boxplot. Now we can see that although the price rallied in the spring of 2007, after July there were already signs that the price might not stay above $60. By October, that pattern was clear.

---

[8]Sometimes we separate the properties and say the series is stationary with respect to the mean (if there is no trend) or stationary with respect to the variance (if the spread doesn't change). But unless otherwise noted, we'll assume that all the statistical properties of a stationary series are constant over time.

Figure 3.13 *A time series plot of daily closing Price of AIG stock for the year 2007 shows the overall pattern and changes in variation.*

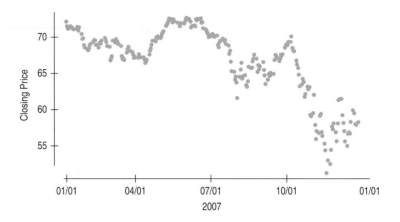

Time series plots often show a great deal of point-to-point variation, as Figure 3.13 does, so you'll often see time series plots drawn with all the points connected (as in Figure 3.14), especially in financial publications.

Figure 3.14 *The Daily Prices of Figure 3.13, drawn with lines connecting all the points. Sometimes this can help us see an underlying pattern.*

Often it is better to try to smooth out the local point-to-point variability. After all, we usually want to see past this variation to understand any underlying trend and think about how the values vary around that trend—the time series version of center and spread. There are many ways for computers to find a smooth trace through a time series plot.

A smooth trace can highlight long-term patterns and help us see them through the more local variation. Figure 3.15 shows the daily prices of Figures 3.13 and 3.14 with a typical smoothing function, available in many statistics programs. With the smooth trace, it's a bit easier to see a pattern. The trace helps our eye follow the main trend and alerts us to points that don't fit the overall pattern.

It is always tempting to try to extend what we see in a timeplot into the future. Sometimes that makes sense. Most likely, the NYSE volume follows some regular patterns throughout the year. It's probably safe to predict more volume on triple witching days (when contracts expire) and less activity in the week between Christmas and New Year's Day.

Figure 3.15   The *2007 Daily Prices* of Figure 3.13, with a smooth trace added to help your eye see the long-term pattern.

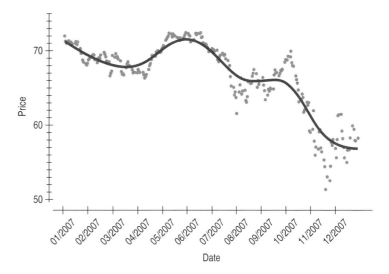

Other patterns are riskier to extend into the future. If a stock's price has been rising, how long will it continue to go up? No stock has ever increased in value indefinitely, and no stock analyst has consistently been able to forecast when a stock's value will turn around. Stock prices, unemployment rates, and other economic, social, or psychological measures are much harder to predict than physical quantities. The path a ball will follow when thrown from a certain height at a given speed and direction is well-understood. The path that interest rates will take is much less clear.

Unless you have strong (nonstatistical) reasons for doing otherwise, you should resist the temptation to think that any trend you see will continue indefinitely. Statistical models often tempt those who use them to think beyond the data. We'll pay close attention later in this book to understanding when, how, and how much we can justify doing that.

Look at the prices in Figures 3.13 through 3.15 and try to guess what happened in the subsequent months. Was that drop from October to December a sign of trouble ahead, or was the increase in December back to around $60 where the stock had comfortably traded for several years a sign that stability had returned to AIG's stock price? Perhaps those who picked up the stock for $51 in early November really got a bargain. Let's look ahead to 2008:

Figure 3.16   A time series plot of daily AIG *Price* in 2008 shows a general decline followed by a sharp collapse in September.

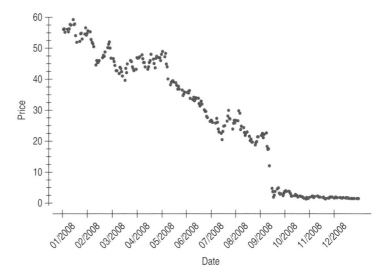

Even through the spring of 2008, although the price was gently falling, nothing prepared traders following only the time series plot for what was to follow. In September the stock lost nearly all of its value. But, by 2012, it was trading in the mid $30's.

FOR EXAMPLE Plotting time series data

QUESTION The download times from the example on page 51 are a time series. Plot the data by hour of the day and describe any patterns you see.

ANSWER For this day, downloads were highest at midnight with about 36 downloads per hour then dropped sharply until about 5–6 a.m. when they reached their minimum at 2–3 per hour. They gradually increased to about 20 per hour by noon, and then stayed in the twenties until midnight, with a slight increase during the evening hours. When we ignored the time order, as we did earlier, we missed this pattern entirely.

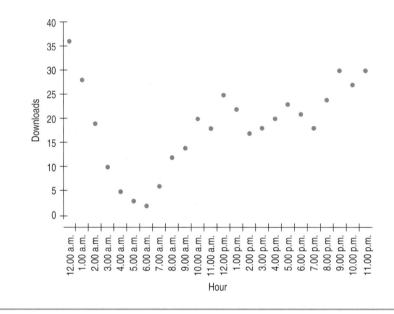

The histogram we saw in the beginning of the chapter (Figure 3.1) summarized the distribution of prices fairly well because during that period the prices were fairly stable; the price series appears to be stationary. However, when the time series is not stationary as was the case for AIG prices after 2007, be careful. A histogram is unlikely to capture what is really of interest. Then, a time series plot is the best graphical display to use to display the behavior of the data.

*3.11 Transforming Skewed Data

When a distribution is skewed, it may not be appropriate to summarize the data simply with a center and spread, and it can be hard to decide whether the most extreme values are outliers or just part of the stretched-out tail. How can we say anything useful about such data? The secret is to apply a simple function to each data value. One function that can change the shape of a distribution is the logarithm function. Let's examine an example in which a set of data is severely skewed.

In 1980, the average CEO made about 42 times the average worker's salary. In the two decades that followed, CEO compensation soared when compared with the average worker's pay; by 2000, the multiple had jumped to 525.[9] What does the distribution of the largest 500 companies' CEOs look like? Figure 3.17 shows a boxplot and a histogram of the CEO compensation from a recent year.

Figure 3.17 The total compensation for CEOs (in $M) of the 500 largest companies is skewed and includes some extraordinarily large values.

These values are reported in *millions* of dollars. The boxplot indicates that some of the 500 CEOs received extraordinarily high compensation. The first bin of the histogram, containing more than half the CEOs, covers the range $0 to $10,000,000. The reason that the histogram seems to leave so much of the area blank is that the largest observations are so far from the bulk of the data, as we can see from the boxplot. Both the histogram and boxplot make it clear that this distribution is very skewed to the right.

Total compensation for CEOs consists of their base salaries, bonuses, and extra compensation, usually in the form of stock or stock options. Data that add together several variables, such as the compensation data, can easily have skewed distributions. It's often a good idea to separate the component variables and examine them individually, but we don't have that information for the CEOs.

Skewed distributions are difficult to summarize. It's hard to know what we mean by the "center" of a skewed distribution, so it's not obvious what value to use to summarize the distribution. What would you say was a typical CEO total compensation? The mean value in 2011 was $9,027,780, while the median is "only" $5,955,000. Each tells something different about how the data are distributed.

One way to make a skewed distribution more symmetric is to **re-express**, or **transform**, the data by applying a simple function to all the data values. It is common to take the logarithm of variables like income, corporate earnings, and prices, which tend to be skewed to the right. Economists do this as a matter of course in many of their models.

> **Dealing with Logarithms**
>
> You may think of logarithms as something technical, but they are just a function that can make some values easier to work with. You have probably already seen logarithmic scales in decibels, Richter scale values, pH values, and others. You may not have realized that logs had been used. Base 10 logs are the easiest to understand, but natural logs are often used as well. (Either one is fine.) You can think of the base 10 log of a number as roughly one less than the number of digits you need to write that number. So 100, which is the smallest number to require 3 digits, has a $\log_{10}$ of 2. And 1000 has a $\log_{10}$ of 3. The $\log_{10}$ of 500 is between 2 and 3, but you'd need a calculator to find that it's approximately 2.7. All salaries of "six figures" have $\log_{10}$ between 5 and 6. Fortunately, with technology, it is easy to re-express data by logs.

[9]Sources: United for a Fair Economy, *Business Week* annual CEO pay surveys, Bureau of Labor Statistics, "Average Weekly Earnings of Production Workers, Total Private Sector." Series ID: EEU00500004.

The histogram of the logs of the total CEO compensations in Figure 3.18 is nearly symmetric, so we can say that a typical log compensation is between 6.0 and 7.0, which means that it lies between $1 million and $10 million. To be more precise, the mean log_{10} value is 6.73, while the median is 6.67 (that's $5,370,318 and $4,677,351, respectively). Note that nearly all the values are between 6.0 and 8.0—in other words, between $1,000,000 and $100,000,000 per year. Logarithmic transformations are common, but other transformations like square root and reciprocal are also used. Because computers and calculators are available to do the calculating, you should consider transformation as a helpful tool whenever you have skewed data.

Figure 3.18   Taking logs makes the histogram of CEO total compensation nearly symmetric.

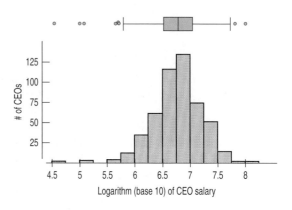

FOR EXAMPLE   Transforming skewed data

QUESTION   *Fortune* magazine publishes a list of the 100 best companies to work for (money.cnn.com/magazines/fortune/bestcompanies/2010/). One statistic often looked at is the average annual pay for the most common job title at the company. Can we characterize those pay values? Here is a histogram of the average annual pay values and a histogram of the logarithm of the pay values. Which would provide the better basis for summarizing pay?

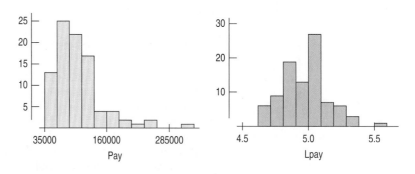

ANSWER   The pay values are skewed to the high end. The logarithmic transformation makes the distribution more nearly symmetric, making it more appropriate to summarize with a mean and standard deviation.

WHAT CAN GO WRONG?

A data display should tell a story about the data. To do that it must speak in a clear language, making plain what variable is displayed, what any axis shows, and what the values of the data are. And it must be consistent in those decisions.

The task of summarizing a quantitative variable requires that we follow a set of rules. We need to watch out for certain features of the data that make summarizing them with a number dangerous. Here's some advice:

- **Don't make a histogram of a categorical variable.** Just because the variable contains numbers doesn't mean it's quantitative. Here's a histogram of the insurance policy numbers of some workers. It's not very informative because the policy numbers are categorical. A histogram or stem-and-leaf display of a categorical variable makes no sense. A bar chart or pie chart may do better.

Figure 3.19 It's not appropriate to display categorical data like policy numbers with a histogram.

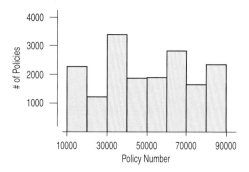

- **Choose a scale appropriate to the data.** Computer programs usually do a pretty good job of choosing histogram bin widths. Often, there's an easy way to adjust the width, sometimes interactively. Figure 3.20 shows the AIG price histogram with two other choices for the bin size. Neither seems to be the best choice.

Figure 3.20 Changing the bin width changes how the histogram looks. The AIG stock prices look very different with these two choices.

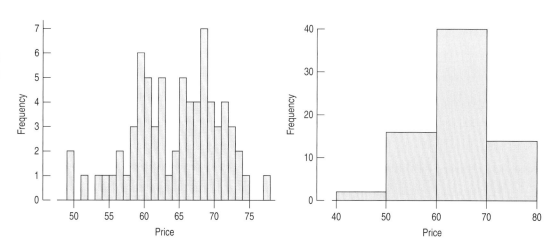

- **Avoid inconsistent scales.** Parts of displays should be mutually consistent—it's not fair to change scales in the middle or to plot two variables on different scales on the same display. When comparing two groups, be sure to draw them on the same scale.

- **Label clearly.** Variables should be identified clearly and axes labeled so a reader knows what the plot displays.

Here's a remarkable example of a plot gone wrong. It illustrated a news story about rising college costs. It uses time series plots, but it gives a misleading impression. First, think about the story you're being told by this display. Then try to figure out what has gone wrong.

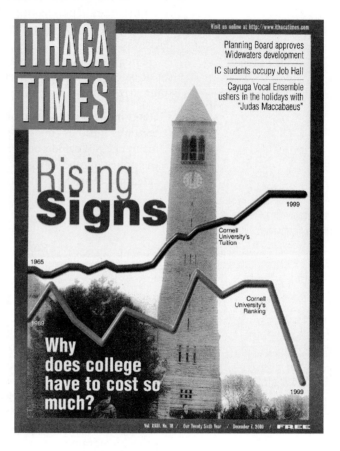

What's wrong? Just about everything.

- **The horizontal scales are inconsistent.** Both lines show trends over time, but for what years? The tuition sequence starts in 1965, but rankings are graphed from 1989. Plotting them on the same (invisible) scale makes it seem that they're for the same years.

- **The vertical axis isn't labeled.** That hides the fact that it's using two different scales. Does it graph dollars (of tuition) or ranking (of Cornell University)?

This display violates every rule we can think of. And it's even worse than that. It violates a rule that we didn't even consider. The two inconsistent scales for the vertical axis don't point in the same direction! The line for Cornell's rank shows that it has "plummeted" from 15th place to 6th place in academic rank. Most of us think that's an *improvement*, but that's not the message of this graph.

- **Do a reality check.** Don't let the computer (or calculator) do your thinking for you. Make sure the calculated summaries make sense. For example, does the mean look like it is in the center of the histogram? Think about the spread. An IQR of 50 mpg would clearly be wrong for a family car. And no measure of spread can be negative. The standard deviation can take the value 0, but only in the very unusual case that all the data values equal the same number. If you see the IQR or standard deviation equal to 0, it's probably a sign that something's wrong with the data.

- **Don't compute numerical summaries of a categorical variable.** The mean ZIP code or the standard deviation of Social Security numbers is not meaningful. If the variable is categorical, you should instead report summaries such as percentages. It is easy to make this mistake when you let technology do the summaries for you. After all, the computer doesn't care what the numbers mean.

- **Watch out for multiple modes.** If the distribution—as seen in a histogram, for example—has multiple modes, consider separating the data into groups. If you cannot separate the data in a meaningful way, you should not summarize the center and spread of the variable.

- **Beware of outliers.** If the data have outliers but are otherwise unimodal, consider holding the outliers out of the further calculations and reporting them individually. If you can find a simple reason for the outlier (for instance, a data transcription error), you should remove or correct it. If you cannot do either of these, then choose the median and IQR to summarize the center and spread.

ETHICS IN ACTION

Beth Tully owns Zenna's Café, an independent coffee shop located in a small Midwestern city. Since opening Zenna's in 2002, she has been steadily growing her business and now distributes her custom coffee blends to a number of regional restaurants and markets. She operates a microroaster that offers specialty grade Arabica coffees recognized by some as the best in the area.

In addition to providing the highest quality coffees, Beth also wants her business to be socially responsible. Toward that end, she pays fair prices to coffee farmers and donates funds to help charitable causes in Panama, Costa Rica, and Guatemala. In addition, she encourages her employees to get involved in the local community.

Recently, one of the well-known multinational coffeehouse chains announced plans to locate shops in her area. This chain is one of the few to offer Certified Free-Trade coffee products and work toward social justice in the global community. Consequently, Beth thought it might be a good idea for her to begin communicating Zenna's socially-responsible efforts to the public, but with an emphasis on their commitment to the local community.

Three months ago she began collecting data on the number of volunteer hours donated by her employees per week. She has a total of 12 employees, of whom 10 are full time. Most employees volunteered less than 2 hours per week, but Beth noticed that one part-time employee volunteered more than 20 hours per week. She discovered that her employees collectively volunteered an average of 15 hours per month (with a median of 8 hours). She planned to report the average number and believed most people would be impressed with Zenna's level of commitment to the local community.

- Identify the ethical dilemma in this scenario.
- What are the undesirable consequences?
- Propose an ethical solution that considers the welfare of all stakeholders.

WHAT HAVE WE LEARNED?

Learning Objectives

Make and interpret histograms to display the distribution of a variable.

- We understand distributions in terms of their shape, center, and spread.

Describe the shape of a distribution.

- A **symmetric** distribution has roughly the same shape reflected around the center.
- A **skewed** distribution extends farther on one side than on the other.
- A **unimodal** distribution has a single major hump or mode; a bimodal distribution has two; multimodal distributions have more.
- **Outliers** are values that lie far from the rest of the data.

Compute the mean and median of a distribution, and know when it is best to use each to summarize the center.

- The **mean** is the sum of the values divided by the count. It is a suitable summary for unimodal, symmetric distributions.
- The **median** is the middle value; half the values are above and half are below the median. It is a better summary when the distribution is skewed or has outliers.

Compute the standard deviation and interquartile range (IQR), and know when it is best to use each to summarize the spread.

- The **standard deviation** is the square root of the average squared difference between each data value and the mean. It is the summary of choice for the spread of unimodal, symmetric variables.
- The **IQR** is the difference between the quartiles. It is often a better summary of spread for skewed distributions or data with outliers.

Standardize values and use them for comparisons of otherwise disparate variables.

- We standardize by finding **z-scores**. To convert a data value to its z-score, subtract the mean and divide by the standard deviation.
- z-scores have no units, so they can be compared to z-scores of other variables.
- The idea of measuring the distance of a value from the mean in terms of standard deviations is a basic concept in Statistics and will return many times later in the course.

Find a five-number summary and, using it, make a boxplot. Use the boxplot's outlier nomination rule to identify cases that may deserve special attention.

- A **five-number summary** consists of the median, the quartiles, and the extremes of the data.
- A **boxplot** shows the quartiles as the upper and lower ends of a central box, the median as a line across the box, and "whiskers" that extend to the most extreme values that are not nominated as outliers.
- Boxplots display separately any case that is more than 1.5 IQRs beyond each quartile. These cases should be considered as possible outliers.

Use boxplots to compare distributions.

- Boxplots facilitate comparisons of several groups. It is easy to compare centers (medians) and spreads (IQRs).
- Because boxplots show possible outliers separately, any outliers don't affect comparisons.

Make and interpret time plots for time series data.

- Look for the trend and any changes in the spread of the data over time.

Terms	
Bin	In a histogram, the range of possible values are split into intervals called bins, over which the frequencies are displayed.
Bimodal	Distributions with two modes.
Boxplot	A boxplot displays the 5-number summary as a central box with whiskers that extend to the nonoutlying values. Boxplots are particularly effective for comparing groups.
Center	The middle of the distribution, usually summarized numerically by the mean or the median.
Distribution	The distribution of a variable gives:

- possible values of the variable
- frequency or relative frequency of each value or range of values

Five-number summary	A five-number summary for a variable consists of: • The minimum and maximum • The quartiles Q1 and Q3 • The median
Gap	A region of a distribution where there are no values
Histogram (relative frequency histogram)	A histogram uses adjacent bars to show the distribution of values in a quantitative variable. Each bar represents the frequency (relative frequency) of values falling in an interval of values.
Interquartile range (IQR)	The difference between the lower and upper quartiles. IQR = Q3 − Q1.
Mean	A measure of center found as $\bar{x} = \sum x/n$.
Median	The middle value with half of the data above it and half below it.
Mode	A peak or local high point in the shape of the distribution of a variable. The apparent location of modes can change as the scale of a histogram is changed.
Multimodal	Distributions with more than two modes.
Outliers	Extreme values that don't appear to belong with the rest of the data. They may be unusual values that deserve further investigation or just mistakes; there's no obvious way to tell.
Quartile	The lower quartile (Q1) is the value with a quarter of the data below it. The upper quartile (Q3) has a quarter of the data above it. The median and quartiles divide the data into four equal parts.
Range	The difference between the lowest and highest values in a data set: Range = *max* − *min*.
*Re-express or transform	To re-express or transform data, take the logarithm, square root, reciprocal, or some other mathematical operation on all values of the data set. Re-expression can make the distribution of a variable more nearly symmetric and the spread of groups more nearly alike.
Shape	The visual appearance of the distribution. To describe the shape, look for: • single vs. multiple modes • symmetry vs. skewness
Skewed	A distribution is skewed if one tail stretches out farther than the other.
Spread	The description of how tightly clustered the distribution is around its center. Measures of spread include the IQR and the standard deviation.
Standard deviation	A measure of spread found as $s = \sqrt{\dfrac{\sum (x - \bar{x})^2}{n - 1}}$.
Standardized value	We standardize a value by subtracting the mean and dividing by the standard deviation for the variable. These values, called z-scores, have no units.
Stationary	A time series is said to be stationary if its statistical properties don't change over time.
*Stem-and-leaf display	A stem-and-leaf display shows quantitative data values in a way that sketches the distribution of the data. It's best described in detail by example like the one on page 53.
Symmetric	A distribution is symmetric if the two halves on either side of the center look approximately like mirror images of each other.
Tail	The tails of a distribution are the parts that typically trail off on either side.
Time series plot	A time series plot displays the values of a time series plotted against time. Often, successive values are connected with lines to show trends more clearly.
Uniform	A distribution that's roughly flat is said to be uniform.
Unimodal	Having one mode. This is a useful term for describing the shape of a histogram when it's generally mound-shaped.
Variance	The standard deviation squared.
z-Score	A standardized value that tells how many standard deviations a value is from the mean; z-scores have a mean of 0 and a standard deviation of 1.

TECHNOLOGY HELP: Displaying and Summarizing Quantitative Variables

Almost any program that displays data can make a histogram, but some will do a better job of determining where the bars should start and how they should partition the span of the data (see the figure below).

Many statistics packages offer a prepackaged collection of summary measures. The result might look like this:

```
Variable: Weight
N = 234
Mean = 143.3      Median = 139
St. Dev = 11.1    IQR = 14
```

Alternatively, a package might make a table for several variables and summary measures:

```
Variable   N     mean    median    stdev    IQR
Weight     234   143.3   139       11.1     14
Height     234   68.3    68.1      4.3      5
Score      234   86      88        9        5
```

It is usually easy to read the results and identify each computed summary statistic. You should be able to read the summary statistics produced by any computer package.

Packages often provide many more summary statistics than you need. Of course, some of these may not be appropriate when the data are skewed or have outliers. It is your responsibility to check a histogram or stem-and-leaf display and decide which summary statistics to use.

It is common for packages to report summary statistics to many decimal places of "accuracy." Of course, it is rare to find data that have such accuracy in the original measurements. The ability to calculate to six or seven digits beyond the decimal point doesn't mean that those digits have any meaning. Generally, it's a good idea to round these values, allowing perhaps one more digit of precision than was given in the original data.

Displays and summaries of quantitative variables are among the simplest things you can do in most statistics packages.

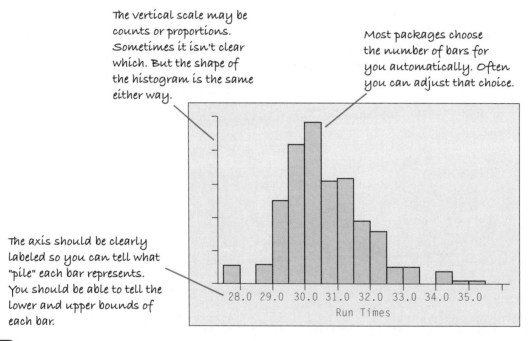

The vertical scale may be counts or proportions. Sometimes it isn't clear which. But the shape of the histogram is the same either way.

Most packages choose the number of bars for you automatically. Often you can adjust that choice.

The axis should be clearly labeled so you can tell what "pile" each bar represents. You should be able to tell the lower and upper bounds of each bar.

Run Times

EXCEL

To make a histogram in Excel 2010 or 2013, use the Data Analysis add-in. If you have not installed that, you must do that first:

- On the File tab, click **Options,** and then click **Add-Ins**.
- Near the bottom of the Excel Options dialog box, select **Excel add-ins** in the Manage box, and then click **Go**.
- In the Add-Ins dialog box, select the check box for Analysis ToolPak, and then click **OK**.
- If Excel displays a message that states it can't run this add-in and prompts you to install it, click **Yes** to install the add-in.

To make a histogram,

- From Data, select the **Data Analysis add-in**.
- From its menu, select **Histograms**.

- Indicate the range of the data whose histogram you wish to draw.
- Indicate the bin ranges that are up to and including the right end points of each bin.
- Check **Labels** if your columns have names in the first cell.
- Check **Chart output** and click **OK**.
- Right-click on any bar of the resulting graph and, from the menu that drops down, select **Format Data Series ...**
- In the dialog box that opens, select **Series Options** from the sidebar.
- Slide the Gap Width slider to **No Gap**, and click **Close**.
- In the pivot table on the left, use your pointing tool to slide the bottom of the table up to get rid of the "more" bin.
- Edit the bin names in Column A to properly identify the contents of each bin.

- You can right click on the legend or axis names to edit or remove them.
- Following these instructions, you can reproduce Figure 3.1 using the data set AIG stock series.

Alternatively, you can set up your own bin boundaries and count the observations falling within each bin using an Excel function such as FREQUENCY (Data array, Bins array). Consult your Excel manual or help files for details of how to do this.

To create a time series plot in Excel:

- Open a time-series data file sorted in ascending order by time.
- Highlight the column(s) holding the values of the quantitative variable(s) measured over a period of time.
- Choose **Insert** > **Charts** > **Line** > **2-D Line.**
- Click the chart and choose **Select Data** from the **Chart Tools** > **Design menu.**
- Choose **Select Data Source** > **Edit** under Horizontal (Category) Axis Labels and select the time data.

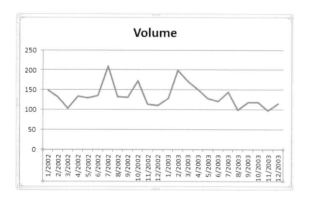

XLStat

To make a box plot:

- Choose **Visualizing data**, and then select **Univariate plots**.
- Enter the cell range of your data in the **Quantitative** or **Qualitative data** field.
- Select the type of chart on the **Charts** tab.

NOTE: XLStat scales side-by-side boxplots individually, so they are not suitable for comparing groups.

JMP

To make a histogram and find summary statistics:

- Choose **Distribution** from the **Analyze** menu.

- In the **Distribution** dialog, drag the name of the variable that you wish to analyze into the empty window beside the label "**Y, Columns.**"
- Click **OK**. JMP computes standard summary statistics along with displays of the variables.

To make boxplots:

- Choose **Fit Y By X**. Assign a continuous response variable to **Y, Response** and a nominal group variable holding the group names to **X, Factor,** and click **OK**. JMP will offer (among other things) dot-plots of the data. Click the red triangle and, under **Display Options**, select **Box Plots**. Note: If the variables are of the wrong type, the display options might not offer boxplots.

Alternatively

- Chose **Graph** > **Graph Builder**. Drag the quantitative variable to **Y** and the categorical variable to **X**. Right click on the points and change Points to **Box Plots**

To make a time series plot in JMP:

- From the **Analyze** menu, choose **Fit Y by X**.
- Move the y variable (measured over time) into the **Y, Response** box.
- Move the x variable (time) into the **X, Factor** box.
- Press **OK**.
  - To connect the points select **Fit Each Value** from the red triangle next to Bivariate Fit.
- To put a smooth through the points, select either **Kernel Smoother** or **Fit Spline** under the red triangle.

Comments

For either the **Kernel Smoother** or **Spline** a slider bar appears to adjust the amount of smoothing.

Alternatively,

- Select **Graph** > **Graph Builder**.
- Drag the *y* variable into the Y window and the x variable (time) into the X window.
- The default shows the points and a smoother.
  - Right click on the graph and select **Smoother** > **Change to** > **Line** to connect the points instead.

MINITAB

To make a histogram:

- Choose **Histogram** from the **Graph** menu.
- Select **Simple** for the type of graph and click **OK**.
- Enter the name of the quantitative variable you wish to display in the box labeled "Graph variables." Click **OK**.

To make a boxplot:

- Choose **Boxplot** from the **Graph** menu and specify your data format.

To calculate summary statistics:

- Choose **Basic Statistics** from the **Stat** menu. From the **Basic Statistics** submenu, choose **Display Descriptive Statistics**.
- Assign variables from the variable list box to the Variables box. MINITAB makes a Descriptive Statistics table.

SPSS

To make a histogram or boxplot in SPSS open the Chart Builder from the Graphs menu.

- Click the **Gallery** tab.
- Choose **Histogram** or **Boxplot** from the list of chart types.
- Drag the icon of the plot you want onto the canvas.
- Drag a scale variable to the *y*-axis drop zone.

- Click **OK**.

To make side-by-side boxplots, drag a categorical variable to the *x*-axis drop zone and click **OK**.

To calculate summary statistics:

- Choose **Explore** from the **Descriptive Statistics** submenu of the **Analyze** menu. In the **Explore** dialog, assign one or more variables from the source list to the Dependent List and click the **OK** button.

Brief **Case**

Detecting the Housing Bubble

The S&P/Case-Shiller Home Price Indices provide measures of the U.S. residential housing market. They track changes in the value of residential real estate nationally and in 20 metropolitan regions. (Some of these indices are actually traded on the Chicago Mercantile Exchange). The dataset **Case-Shiller** gives the monthly index values for each of the 20 cities tracked by the Case-Shiller index and two national composite series. Examine these values and write a report on them.

Some suggestions:
First consider the Composite.20 series, which combines (seasonally adjusted) data for the 20 cities. Describe the distribution of prices overall, then look at a time series plot and discuss the trend over time especially the period from 2007 to 2008.

Then select several cities to compare. For example, you might compare Miami, Boston, and Detroit. Write a report discussing how trends in housing prices changed over time and how these changes differed from city to city.

Socio-Economic Data on States

The dataset **States** contains various educational and economic measures of the 50 U.S. states, including the District of Columbia. Examine the variables, commenting on their shape, center, and spread and any unusual features. If you see any unusual cases, set them aside if appropriate, comment on why you took them out, and redo the analysis without them.

EXERCISES

SECTION 3.1

1. As part of the marketing team at an Internet music site, you want to understand who your customers are. You send out a survey to 25 customers (you use an incentive of $50 worth of downloads to guarantee a high response rate) asking for demographic information. One of the variables is the customer's age. For the 25 customers the ages are:

20	32	34	29	30
30	30	14	29	11
38	22	44	48	26
25	22	32	35	32
35	42	44	44	48

a) Make a histogram of the data using a bar width of 10 years.
b) Make a histogram of the data using a bar width of 5 years.
c) Make a relative frequency histogram of the data using a bar width of 5 years.
d) *Make a stem-and-leaf plot of the data using 10s as the stems and putting the youngest customers on the top of the plot.

2. As the new manager of a small convenience store, you want to understand the shopping patterns of your customers. You randomly sample 20 purchases from yesterday's records (all purchases in U.S. dollars):

39.05	2.73	32.92	47.51
37.91	34.35	64.48	51.96
56.95	81.58	47.80	11.72
21.57	40.83	38.24	32.98
75.16	74.30	47.54	65.62

a) Make a histogram of the data using a bar width of $20.
b) Make a histogram of the data using a bar width of $10.
c) Make a relative frequency histogram of the data using a bar width of $10.
d) *Make a stem-and-leaf plot of the data using $10 as the stems and putting the smallest amounts on top and round the data to the nearest $.

SECTION 3.2

3. For the histogram you made in Exercise 1a:

a) Is the distribution unimodal or multimodal?
b) Where is (are) the mode(s)?
c) Is the distribution symmetric?
d) Are there any outliers?

4. For the histogram you made in Exercise 2a:

a) Is the distribution unimodal or multimodal?
b) Where is (are) the mode(s)?
c) Is the distribution symmetric?
d) Are there any outliers?

SECTION 3.3

5. For the data in Exercise 1:

a) Would you expect the mean age to be smaller than, bigger than, or about the same size as the median? Explain.
b) Find the mean age.
c) Find the median age.

6. For the data in Exercise 2:

a) Would you expect the mean purchase to be smaller than, bigger than, or about the same size as the median? Explain.
b) Find the mean purchase.
c) Find the median purchase.

SECTION 3.4

7. For the data in Exercise 1:

a) Find the quartiles using your calculator.
b) Find the quartiles using Tukey's method (page 58).
c) Find the IQR using the quartiles from part b.
d) Find the standard deviation.

8. For the data in Exercise 2:

a) Find the quartiles using your calculator.
b) Find the quartiles using Tukey's method (page 58).
c) Find the IQR using the quartiles from part b.
d) Find the standard deviation.

SECTION 3.5

9. The histogram shows the December charges (in $) for 5000 customers from one marketing segment from a credit card company. (Negative values indicate customers who received more credits than charges during the month.)

a) Write a short description of this distribution (shape, center, spread, unusual features).
b) Would you expect the mean or the median to be larger? Explain.
c) Which would be a more appropriate summary of the center, the mean or the median? Explain.

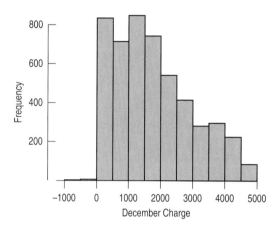

10. Adair Vineyard is a 10-acre vineyard in New Paltz, New York. The winery itself is housed in a 200-year-old historic Dutch barn, with the wine cellar on the first floor and the tasting room and gift shop on the second. Since they are relatively small and considering an expansion, they are curious about how their size compares to that of other vineyards. The histogram shows the sizes (in acres) of 36 wineries in upstate New York.

a) Write a short description of this distribution (shape, center, spread, unusual features).
b) Would you expect the mean or the median to be larger? Explain.
c) Which would be a more appropriate summary of the center, the mean or the median? Explain.

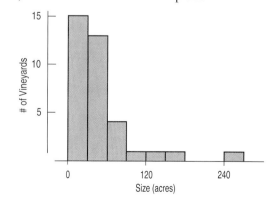

SECTION 3.6

11. Using the ages from Exercise 1:

a) Standardize the minimum and maximum ages using the mean from Exercise 5b and the standard deviation from Exercise 7d.
b) Which has the more extreme z-score, the min or the max?
c) How old would someone with a z-score of 3 be?

12. Using the purchases from Exercise 2:

a) Standardize the minimum and maximum purchase using the mean from Exercise 6b and the standard deviation from Exercise 8d.
b) Which has the more extreme z-score, the min or the max?
c) How large a purchase would a purchase with a z-score of 3.5 be?

SECTION 3.7

13. For the data in Exercise 1:

a) Draw a boxplot using the quartiles from Exercise 7b.
b) Does the boxplot nominate any outliers?
c) What age would be considered a high outlier?

14. For the data in Exercise 2:

a) Draw a boxplot using the quartiles from Exercise 8b.
b) Does the boxplot nominate any outliers?
c) What purchase amount would be considered a high outlier?

15. Here are summary statistics for the sizes (in acres) of upstate New York vineyards from Exercise 10.

Variable	N	Mean	StDev	Minimum	Q1	Median	Q3	Maximum
Acres	36	46.50	47.76	6	18.50	33.50	55	250

a) From the summary statistics, would you describe this distribution as symmetric or skewed? Explain.
b) From the summary statistics, are there any outliers? Explain.
c) Using these summary statistics, sketch a boxplot. What additional information would you need to complete the boxplot?

16. A survey of major universities asked what percentage of incoming freshmen usually graduate "on time" in 4 years. Use the summary statistics given to answer these questions.

	% on time
Count	48
Mean	68.35
Median	69.90
StdDev	10.20
Min	43.20
Max	87.40
Range	44.20
25th %tile	59.15
75th %tile	74.75

a) Would you describe this distribution as symmetric or skewed?
b) Are there any outliers? Explain.
c) Create a boxplot of these data.

SECTION 3.8

17. The survey from Exercise 1 had also asked the customers to say whether they were male or female. Here are the data:

Age	Sex	Age	Sex	Age	Sex	Age	Sex	Age	Sex
20	M	32	F	34	F	29	M	30	M
30	F	30	M	14	M	29	M	11	M
38	F	22	M	44	F	48	F	26	F
25	M	22	M	32	F	35	F	32	F
35	F	42	F	44	F	44	F	48	F

Construct boxplots to compare the ages of men and women and write a sentence summarizing what you find.

18. The store manager from Exercise 2 has collected data on purchases from weekdays and weekends. Here are some summary statistics (rounded to the nearest dollar):

Weekdays:　n = 230

Min = 4, Q1 = 28, Median = 40, Q3 = 68, Max = 95

Weekends:　n = 150

Min = 10, Q1 = 35, Median = 55, Q3 = 70, Max = 100

From these statistics, construct side-by-side boxplots and write a sentence comparing the two distributions.

19. Here are boxplots of the weekly sales (in $ U.S.) over a two-year period for a regional food store for two locations. Location #1 is a metropolitan area that is known to be residential where shoppers walk to the store. Location #2 is a suburban area where shoppers drive to the store. Assume that the two towns have similar populations and that the two stores are similar in square footage. Write a brief report discussing what these data show.

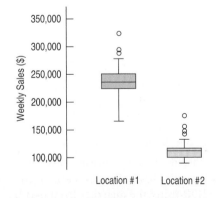

20. Recall the distributions of the weekly sales for the regional stores in Exercise 19. Following are boxplots of weekly sales for this same food store chain for three stores of similar size and location for two different states: Massachusetts (MA) and Connecticut (CT). Compare the distribution of sales for the two states and describe in a report.

SECTION 3.9

21. The five-number summary for the total revenue (in $M) of the top 100 movies of 2012 looks like this:

Min	Q1	Med	Q3	Max
28.8	44.9	64.1	123.0	623.4

Are there any outliers in these data? How can you tell? What might your next steps in the analysis be?

22. The five-number summary for the ages of 100 respondents to a survey on cell phone use looks like this:

Min	Q1	Med	Q3	Max
13	24	38	49	256

Are there any outliers in these data? How can you tell? What might your next steps in the analysis be?

SECTION 3.10

23. Are the following data time series? If not, explain why.
a) Quarterly earnings of Microsoft Corp.
b) Unemployment in August 2010 by education level.
c) Time spent in training by workers in NewCo.
d) Numbers of e-mails sent by employees of SynCo each hour in a single day.

24. Are the following data time series? If not, explain why.
a) Reports from the Bureau of Labor Statistics on the number of U.S. adults who are employed full time in each major sector of the economy.
b) The quarterly Gross Domestic Product (GDP) of France from 1980 to the present.
c) The dates on which a particular employee was absent from work due to illness over the past two years.
d) The number of cases of flu reported by the CDC each week during a flu season.

SECTION 3.11

25. The histogram of the total revenues (in $M) of the movies in exercise 21 looks like this:

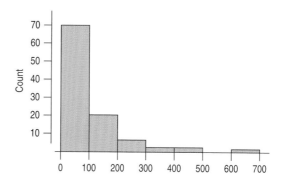

What might you suggest for the next step of the analysis?

26. The histogram of the ages of the respondents in exercise 22 looks like this:

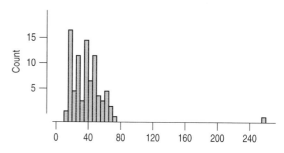

What might you suggest for the next step of the analysis?

CHAPTER EXERCISES

27. Statistics in business. Find a histogram that shows the distribution of a quantitative variable in a business publication (e.g., *The Wall Street Journal, Business Week,* etc.).
a) Does the article identify the W's?
b) Discuss whether the display is appropriate for the data.
c) Discuss what the display reveals about the variable and its distribution.
d) Does the article accurately describe and interpret the data? Explain.

28. Statistics in business, part 2. Find a graph other than a histogram that shows the distribution of a quantitative variable in a business publication (e.g., *The Wall Street Journal, Business Week,* etc.).
a) Does the article identify the W's?
b) Discuss whether the display is appropriate for the data.
c) Discuss what the display reveals about the variable and its distribution.
d) Does the article accurately describe and interpret the data? Explain.

29. Shirt sizes. A clothing manufacturer wants to study men's neck sizes to plan how many shirts of different sizes to produce (shirt sizes are generally one-half inch larger than measured neck sizes and rounded to the nearest half inch). The following histogram shows the distribution of neck sizes of 248 random volunteers for a health study conducted in Utah.

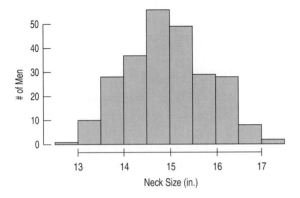

a) Write a short description of this distribution (shape, center, spread, unusual features).
b) What two bins hold the most values for neck size?
c) If we add half an inch to the neck size and round up to the nearest half inch to get the shirt size, what are the two most popular shirt sizes?

30. Gas prices 2013. The website LosAngelesGasPrices.com has current gasoline prices all over the United States. In the week of February 5, 2013, the following histogram shows the gas prices at 55 stations in the San Francisco Bay Area. Describe the shape of this distribution (shape, center, spread, unusual features).

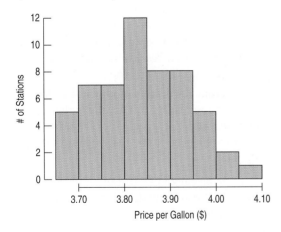

31. Mutual funds 2013. In 2013, the Standard & Poor's (S&P) 500 stock index reached a new all time high in early April. For the first quarter of 2013, the index was up 10.0%. Here is a histogram of the returns for Money Magazine's top 70 mutual funds for the same period (money.cnn.com/magazines/moneymag/bestfunds/index.html).

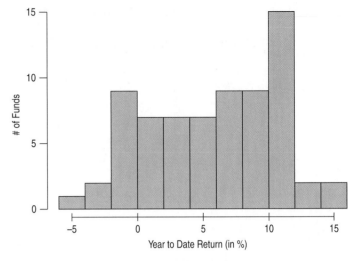

a) From the histogram, give a short summary of the distribution (shape, center, spread, unusual features).
b) In general, how did these funds perform compared to the S&P 500?

32. Car discounts. A researcher, interested in studying gender differences in negotiations, collects data on the prices that men and women pay for new cars. Here is a histogram of the discounts (the amount in $ below the list price) that men and women received at one car dealership for the last 100 transactions (54 men and 46 women). Give a short summary of this distribution (shape, center, spread, unusual features). What do you think might account for this particular shape?

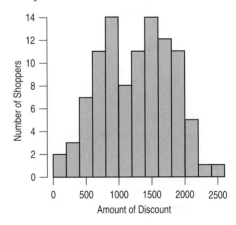

33. Mutual funds 2013, part 2. Use the actual data set of Exercise 31 to answer the following questions.

a) Find the five-number summary for these data.
b) Find appropriate measures of center and spread for these data.
c) Create a boxplot for these data.
d) What can you see, if anything, in the histogram that isn't clear in the boxplot?

T 34. Car discounts, part 2. Use the data set of Exercise 32 to answer the following questions.

a) Find the five-number summary for these data.
b) Create a boxplot for these data.
c) What can you see, if anything, in the histogram of Exercise 32 that isn't clear in the boxplot?

T *35. Vineyards. The data set provided contains the data from Exercises 10 and 15. Create a stem-and-leaf display of the sizes of the vineyards in acres. Point out any unusual features of the data that you can see from the stem-and-leaf.

T *36. Gas prices 2013, again. The data set provided contains the data from Exercise 30 on the price of gas for 55 stations around San Francisco in January 2013. Create a stem-and-leaf display of the data. Point out any unusual features of the data that you can see from the stem-and-leaf.

37. Gretzky. During his 20 seasons in the National Hockey League, Wayne Gretzky scored 50% more points than anyone else who ever played professional hockey. He accomplished this amazing feat while playing in 280 fewer games than Gordie Howe, the previous record holder. Here are the number of games Gretzky played during each season:

79, 80, 80, 80, 74, 80, 80, 79, 64, 78, 73, 78, 74, 45, 81, 48, 80, 82, 82, 70

*a) Create a stem-and-leaf display.
b) Sketch a boxplot.
c) Briefly describe this distribution.
d) What unusual features do you see in this distribution? What might explain this?

38. McGwire. In his 16-year career as a player in major league baseball, Mark McGwire hit 583 home runs, placing him eighth on the all-time home run list (as of 2008). Here are the number of home runs that McGwire hit for each year from 1986 through 2001:

3, 49, 32, 33, 39, 22, 42, 9, 9, 39, 52, 58, 70, 65, 32, 29

* a) Create a stem-and-leaf display.
b) Sketch a boxplot.
c) Briefly describe this distribution.
d) What unusual features do you see in this distribution? What might explain this?

39. Gretzky returns. Look once more at data of hockey games played each season by Wayne Gretzky, seen in Exercise 37.

a) Would you use the mean or the median to summarize the center of this distribution? Why?
b) Without actually finding the mean, would you expect it to be lower or higher than the median? Explain.
c) A student was asked to make a histogram of the data in Exercise 33 and produced the following. Comment.

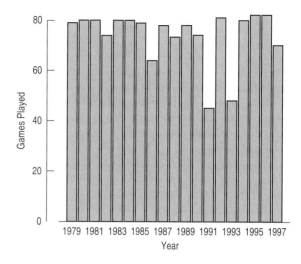

40. McGwire, again. Look once more at data of home runs hit by Mark McGwire during his 16-year career as seen in Exercise 38.

a) Would you use the mean or the median to summarize the center of this distribution? Why?
b) Find the median.
c) Without actually finding the mean, would you expect it to be lower or higher than the median? Explain.
d) A student was asked to make a histogram of the data in Exercise 38 and produced the following. Comment.

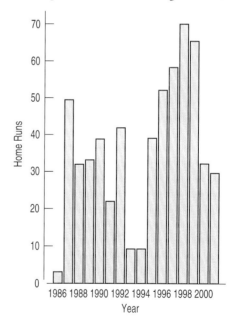

T 41. Pizza prices. The weekly prices of one brand of frozen pizza over a three-year period in Dallas are provided in the data file. Use the price data to answer the following questions.

a) Find the five-number summary for these data.
b) Find the range and IQR for these data.
c) Create a boxplot for these data.
d) Describe this distribution.
e) Describe any unusual observations.

T **42.** Pizza prices, part 2. The weekly prices of one brand of frozen pizza over a three-year period in Chicago are provided in the data file. Use the price data to answer the following questions.

a) Find the five-number summary for these data.
b) Find the range and IQR for these data.
c) Create a boxplot for these data.
d) Describe the shape (center and spread) of this distribution.
e) Describe any unusual observations.

T **43.** Gasoline usage 2011. The U.S. Energy Information Administration (EIA) collects data on the total energy consumption by sector for each state and the District of Columbia. The following data show the per capita consumption in the year 2011 used for transportation (converted to gallons of gasoline per person). Write a report on the gasoline usage by states in the year 2011, being sure to include appropriate graphical displays and summary statistics.

Alabama	522.08	Montana	472.52
Alaska	369.80	Nebraska	428.15
Arizona	392.94	Nevada	385.55
Arkansas	458.55	New Hampshire	513.87
California	375.26	New Jersey	453.92
Colorado	398.60	New Mexico	441.01
Connecticut	394.11	New York	274.01
Delaware	461.95	North Carolina	433.05
District of Columbia	152.63	North Dakota	571.79
Florida	414.99	Ohio	409.87
Georgia	468.55	Oklahoma	460.96
Hawaii	328.77	Oregon	366.62
Idaho	399.26	Pennsylvania	385.86
Illinois	350.41	Rhode Island	341.92
Indiana	438.93	South Carolina	541.17
Iowa	501.71	South Dakota	514.50
Kansas	401.85	Tennessee	478.81
Kentucky	478.58	Texas	462.78
Louisiana	478.86	Utah	370.14
Maine	483.32	Vermont	489.71
Maryland	442.93	Virginia	459.65
Massachusetts	407.75	Washington	379.01
Michigan	436.93	West Virginia	426.35
Minnesota	436.86	Wisconsin	416.28
Mississippi	509.22	Wyoming	528.63
Missouri	495.03		

T **44.** OECD 2011. Established in Paris in 1961, the Organisation for Economic Co-operation and Development (OECD) (www.oecd.org) collects information on many economic and social aspects of countries around the world. Here are the 2011 GDP growth rates (in percentages) of 35 industrialized countries. Write a brief report on the

2011 GDP growth rates of these countries being sure to include appropriate graphical displays and summary statistics.

Country	2011 GDP Growth Rate	Country	2011 GDP Growth Rate
Australia	2.25	Luxembourg	1.66
Austria	2.7	Mexico	3.92
Belgium	1.78	Netherlands	0.99
Canada	2.41	New Zealand	1.08
Chile	5.99	Norway	1.22
Czech Republic	1.89	Poland	4.32
Denmark	1.1	Portugal	−1.55
Estonia	8.28	Slovak Republic	3.23
Finland	2.74	Slovenia	0.6
France	1.7	Spain	0.42
Germany	3.03	Sweden	3.71
Greece	−7.11	Switzerland	1.93
Hungary	1.65	Turkey	8.5
Iceland	2.56	United Kingdom	0.92
Israel	4.6	United States	1.8
Italy	0.44	Russian Federation	4.34
Japan	−0.75	South Africa	3.46
Korea	3.63		

T **45.** Golf courses. A start-up company is planning to build a new golf course. For marketing purposes, the company would like to be able to advertise the new course as one of the more difficult courses in the state of Vermont. One measure of the difficulty of a golf course is its length: the total distance (in yards) from tee to hole for all 18 holes. Here are the histogram and summary statistics for the lengths of all the golf courses in Vermont.

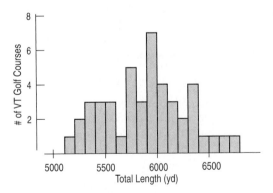

Count	45
Mean	5892.91 yd
StdDev	386.59
Min	5185
Q1	5585.75
Median	5928
Q3	6131
Max	6796

a) What is the range of these lengths?

b) Between what lengths do the central 50% of these courses lie?

c) What summary statistics would you use to describe these data?

d) Write a brief description of these data (shape, center, and spread).

46. Real estate. A real estate agent has surveyed houses in 20 nearby ZIP codes in an attempt to put together a comparison for a new property that she would like to put on the market. She knows that the size of the living area of a house is a strong factor in the price, and she'd like to market this house as being one of the biggest in the area. Here is a histogram and summary statistics for the sizes of all the houses in the area.

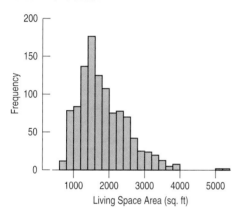

Count	1057
Mean	1819.498 sq. ft
StdDev	662.9414
Min	672
Q1	1342
Median	1675
Q3	2223
Max	5228
Missing	0

a) What is the range of these sizes?

b) Between what sizes do the central 50% of these houses lie?

c) What summary statistics would you use to describe these data?

d) Write a brief description of these data (shape, center, and spread).

47. Food sales. Sales (in $) for one week were collected for 18 stores in a food store chain in the northeastern United States. The stores and the towns they are located in vary in size.

a) Make a suitable display of the sales from the data provided.

b) Summarize the central value for sales for this week with a median and mean. Why do they differ?

c) Given what you know about the distribution, which of these measures does the better job of summarizing the stores' sales? Why?

d) Summarize the spread of the sales distribution with a standard deviation and with an IQR.

e) Given what you know about the distribution, which of these measures does the better job of summarizing the spread of stores' sales? Why?

f) If we were to remove the outliers from the data, how would you expect the mean, median, standard deviation, and IQR to change?

48. Insurance profits. Insurance companies don't know whether a policy they've written is profitable until the policy matures (expires). To see how they've performed recently, an analyst looked at mature policies and investigated the net profit to the company (in $).

a) Make a suitable display of the profits from the data provided.

b) Summarize the central value for the profits with a median and mean. Why do they differ?

c) Given what you know about the distribution, which of these measures might do a better job of summarizing the company's profits? Why?

d) Summarize the spread of the profit distribution with a standard deviation and with an IQR.

e) Given what you know about the distribution, which of these measures might do a better job of summarizing the spread in the company's profits? Why?

f) If we were to remove the outliers from the data, how would you expect the mean, median, standard deviation, and IQR to change?

49. iPod failures. In the early days of the iPod, MacInTouch (www.macintouch.com/reliability/ipodfailures.html) surveyed readers about reliability. Of the 8926 iPods owned at that time, 7510 were problem-free while the other 1416 failed. From the data on the CD, compute the failure rate for each of the 17 iPod models. Produce an appropriate graphical display of the failure rates and briefly describe the distribution. (To calculate the failure rate, divide the number failed by the sum of the number failed and the number OK for each model and then multiply by 100.)

50. Unemployment 2012. The data set provided contains 2012 (2nd quarter) unemployment rates for 34 developed countries (www.oecd.org). Produce an appropriate graphical display and briefly describe the distribution of unemployment rates. Report and comment on any outliers you may see.

51. Gas prices 2012. A driver has recorded and posted on the Internet (www.randomuseless.info/gasprice/gasprice.html) the price he paid for gasoline at every purchase from 1979 to 2012. Since 1984 all purchases were self-serve and all were for premium (92-93 octane) gas. He has also standardized the prices to April 1979 dollars. Here are boxplots for 2003, 2006, 2009, and 2012:

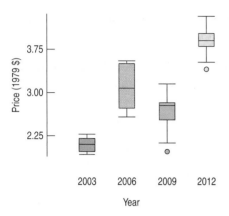

a) Compare the distribution of prices over the four years.
b) In which year were the prices least stable (most volatile)? Explain.

52. Fuel economy. American automobile companies are becoming more motivated to improve the fuel efficiency of the automobiles they produce. It is well known that fuel efficiency is impacted by many characteristics of the car. Describe what these boxplots tell you about the relationship between the number of cylinders a car's engine has and the car's fuel economy (mpg).

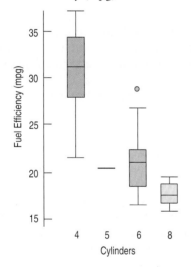

53. Wine prices 2013. The boxplots display bottle prices (in dollars) of dry Riesling wines produced by vineyards along three of the Finger Lakes in upstate New York.

a) Which lake region produced the most expensive wine?
b) Which lake region produced the cheapest wine?
c) In which region were the wines generally more expensive?
d) Write a few sentences describing these prices.

54. Ozone. Historic ozone levels (in parts per billion, ppb) were recorded at sites in New Jersey monthly. Here are boxplots of the data for each month (over 46 years) lined up in order (January = 1).

a) In what month was the highest ozone level ever recorded?
b) Which month has the largest IQR?
c) Which month has the smallest range?
d) Write a brief comparison of the ozone levels in January and June.
e) Write a report on the annual patterns you see in the ozone levels.

55. Derby speeds. How fast do horses run? Kentucky Derby winners top 30 mph, as shown in the graph. This graph shows the percentage of Kentucky Derby winners that have run *slower* than a given speed. Note that few have won running less than 33 mph, but about 95% of the winning horses have run less than 37 mph. (A cumulative frequency graph like this is called an **ogive**.)

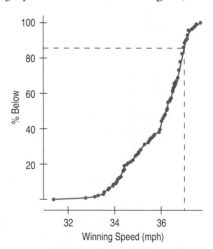

a) Estimate the median winning speed.
b) Estimate the quartiles.
c) Estimate the range and the IQR.
d) Create a boxplot of these speeds.
e) Write a few sentences about the speeds of the Kentucky Derby winners.

56. Mutual funds, historical. Here is an ogive of the distribution of monthly returns for a group of aggressive (or high growth) mutual funds over a period of 25 years. (Recall from Exercise 55 that an ogive, or cumulative relative frequency graph, shows the percent of cases at or below a certain value. Thus this graph always begins at 0% and ends at 100%.)

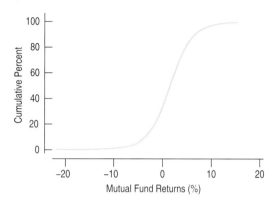

a) Estimate the median.
b) Estimate the quartiles.
c) Estimate the range and the IQR.

57. Test scores. Three Statistics classes all took the same test. Here are histograms of the scores for each class.

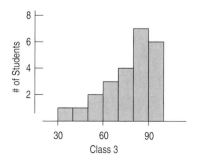

a) Which class had the highest mean score?
b) Which class had the highest median score?
c) For which class are the mean and median most different? Which is higher? Why?
d) Which class had the smallest standard deviation?
e) Which class had the smallest IQR?

58. Test scores, again. Look again at the histograms of test scores for the three Statistics classes in Exercise 57.

a) Overall, which class do you think performed better on the test? Why?
b) How would you describe the shape of each distribution?
c) Match each class with the corresponding boxplot.

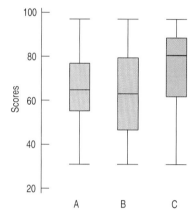

59. Quality control holes. Engineers at a computer production plant tested two methods for accuracy in drilling holes into a PC board. They tested how fast they could set the drilling machine by running 10 boards at each of two different speeds. To assess the results, they measured the distance (in inches) from the center of a target on the board to the center of the hole. The data and summary statistics are shown in the table.

	Fast	Slow
	0.000101	0.000098
	0.000102	0.000096
	0.000100	0.000097
	0.000102	0.000095
	0.000101	0.000094
	0.000103	0.000098
	0.000104	0.000096
	0.000102	0.975600
	0.000102	0.000097
	0.000100	0.000096
Mean	**0.000102**	**0.097647**
StdDev	**0.000001**	**0.308481**

Write a report summarizing the findings of the experiment. Include appropriate visual and verbal displays of the distributions, and make a recommendation to the engineers if they are most interested in the accuracy of the method.

T **60. Fire sale.** A real estate agent notices that houses with fireplaces often fetch a premium in the market and wants to assess the difference in sales price of 60 homes that recently sold. The data and summary are shown in the table.

No Fireplace	Fireplace
142,212	134,865
206,512	118,007
50,709	138,297
108,794	129,470
68,353	309,808
123,266	157,946
80,248	173,723
135,708	140,510
122,221	151,917
128,440	235,105,000
221,925	259,999
65,325	211,517
87,588	102,068
88,207	115,659
148,246	145,583
205,073	116,289
185,323	238,792
71,904	310,696
199,684	139,079
81,762	109,578
45,004	89,893
62,105	132,311
79,893	131,411
88,770	158,863
115,312	130,490
118,952	178,767
	82,556
	122,221
	84,291
	206,512
	105,363
	103,508
	157,513
	103,861
Mean 116,597.54	7,061,657.74
Median 112,053	136,581

Write a report summarizing the findings of the investigation. Include appropriate visual and verbal displays of the distributions, and make a recommendation to the agent about the average premium that a fireplace is worth in this market.

61. Customer database. A philanthropic organization has a database of millions of donors that they contact by mail to raise money for charities. One of the variables in the database, *Title*, contains the title of the person or persons printed on the address label. The most common are Mr., Ms., Miss, and Mrs., but there are also Ambassador and Mrs., Your Imperial Majesty, and Cardinal, to name a few others. In all, there are over 100 different titles, each with a corresponding numeric code.

Code	Title	Code	Title
000	MR.	127	PRINCESS
001	MRS.	128	CHIEF
1002	MR. and MRS.	129	BARON
003	MISS	130	SHEIK
004	DR.	131	PRINCE AND PRINCESS
005	MADAME	132	YOUR IMPERIAL MAJESTY
006	SERGEANT	135	M. ET MME.
009	RABBI	210	PROF.
010	PROFESSOR	⋮	⋮
126	PRINCE		

An intern who was asked to analyze the organization's fundraising efforts presented these summary statistics for the variable *Title*.

Mean	54.41
StdDev	957.62
Median	1
IQR	2
n	94,649

a) What does the mean of 54.41 mean?
b) What are the typical reasons that cause measures of center and spread to be as different as those in this table?
c) Is that why these are so different?

62. CEOs. For each CEO, a code is listed that corresponds to the industry of the CEO's company. Here are a few of the codes and the industries to which they correspond:

Industry	Industry Code	Industry	Industry Code
Financial services	1	Energy	12
Food/drink/tobacco	2	Capital goods	14
Health	3	Computers/ communications	16
Insurance	4	Entertainment/ information	17
Retailing	6	Consumer non-durables	18
Forest products	9	Electric utilities	19
Aerospace/defense	11		

A recently hired investment analyst has been assigned to examine the industries and the compensations of the CEOs. To start the analysis, he produces the following histogram of industry codes.

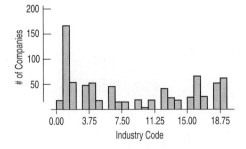

a) What might account for the gaps seen in the histogram?

b) What advice might you give the analyst about the appropriateness of this display?

63. Mutual fund types. The 70 mutual funds of Exercise 31 are classified into four types: U.S. Domestic Equity Funds, Bond Funds, International Funds, and Other Funds. Compare the 12 month returns of the four types of funds using an appropriate display and write a brief summary of the differences.

64. Car discounts, part 3. The discounts negotiated by the car buyers in Exercise 32 are classified by whether the buyer was Male (code = 0) or Female (code = 1). Compare the discounts of men vs. women using an appropriate display and write a brief summary of the differences.

65. Houses for sale. Each house listed on the multiple listing service (MLS) is assigned a sequential ID number. A recently hired real estate agent decided to examine the MLS numbers in a recent random sample of homes for sale by one real estate agency in nearby towns. To begin the analysis, the agent produces the following histogram of ID numbers.

a) What might account for the distribution seen in the histogram?

b) What advice might you give the analyst about the appropriateness of this display?

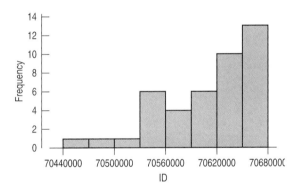

66. ZIP codes. Holes-R-Us, an Internet company that sells piercing jewelry, keeps transaction records on its sales. At a recent sales meeting, one of the staff presented the following histogram and summary statistics of the ZIP codes of the last 500 customers, so that the staff might understand where sales are coming from. Comment on the usefulness and appropriateness of this display.

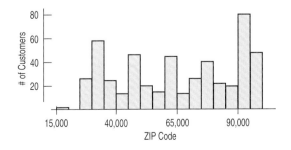

67. Hurricanes. Buying insurance for property loss from hurricanes has become increasingly difficult since Hurricane Katrina caused record property loss damage. Many companies have refused to renew policies or write new ones. The data set provided contains the total number of hurricanes by every full decade from 1851 to 2000 (from the National Hurricane Center). Some scientists claim that there has been an increase in the number of hurricanes in recent years.

a) Create a histogram of these data.

b) Describe the distribution.

c) Create a time series plot of these data.

d) Discuss the time series plot. Does this graph support the claim of these scientists, at least up to the year 2000?

68. Hurricanes, part 2. Using the hurricanes data set, examine the number of major hurricanes (category 3, 4, or 5) by every full decade from 1851 to 2000.

a) Create a histogram of these data.

b) Describe the distribution.

c) Create a timeplot of these data.

d) Discuss the timeplot. Does this graph support the claim of scientists that the number of major hurricanes has been increasing (at least up through the year 2000)?

69. Productivity study. The National Center for Productivity releases information on the efficiency of workers. In a recent report, they included the following graph showing a rapid rise in productivity. What questions do you have about this?

70. Productivity study revisited. A second report by the National Center for Productivity analyzed the relationship between productivity and wages. They used the graph from Exercise 69, with the *x*-axis labeled "wages". Comment on any problems you see with their analysis.

71. Real estate, part 2. The 1057 houses described in Exercise 46 have a mean price of $167,900, with a standard deviation of $77,158. The mean living area is 1819 sq. ft., with a standard deviation of 663 sq. ft. Which is more unusual, a house in that market that sells for $400,000 or a house that has 4000 sq. ft of living area? Explain.

72. Tuition, 2008. The data set provided contains the average tuition of private four-year colleges and universities as well as the average 2007–2008 tuitions for each state. The mean tuition charged by a public two-year college was $2763, with a standard deviation of $988. For private four-year colleges the mean was $21,259, with a standard deviation of $6241. Which would be more unusual: a state whose average public two-year college is $700 or a state whose average private four-year college tuition was $10,000? Explain.

73. Food consumption. FAOSTAT, the Food and Agriculture Organization of the United Nations, collects information on the production and consumption of more than 200 food and agricultural products for 200 countries around the world. Here are two tables, one for meat consumption (per capita in kg per year) and one for alcohol consumption (per capita in gallons per year). The United States leads in meat consumption with 267.30 pounds, while Ireland is the largest alcohol consumer at 55.80 gallons. Using z-scores, find which of these two countries is the larger consumer of both meat and alcohol together.

Country	Alcohol	Meat	Country	Alcohol	Meat
Australia	29.56	242.22	Luxembourg	34.32	197.34
Austria	40.46	242.22	Mexico	13.52	126.50
Belgium	34.32	197.34	Netherlands	23.87	201.08
Canada	26.62	219.56	New Zealand	25.22	228.58
Czech Republic	43.81	166.98	Norway	17.58	129.80
Denmark	40.59	256.96	Poland	20.70	155.10
Finland	25.01	146.08	Portugal	33.02	194.92
France	24.88	225.28	Slovakia	26.49	121.88
Germany	37.44	182.82	South Korea	17.60	93.06
Greece	17.68	201.30	Spain	28.05	259.82
Hungary	29.25	179.52	Sweden	20.07	155.32
Iceland	15.94	178.20	Switzerland	25.32	159.72
Ireland	55.80	194.26	Turkey	3.28	42.68
Italy	21.68	200.64	United Kingdom	30.32	171.16
Japan	14.59	93.28	United States	26.36	267.30

74. World Bank. The World Bank, through their Doing Business project (www.doingbusiness.org), ranks nearly 200 economies on the ease of doing business. One of their rankings measures the ease of starting a business and is made up (in part) of the following variables: number of required start-up procedures, average start-up time (in days), and average start-up cost (in % of per capita income). The following table gives the mean and standard deviations of these variables for 95 economies.

	Procedures (#)	Time (Days)	Cost (%)
Mean	7.9	27.9	14.2
SD	2.9	19.6	12.9

Here are the data for three countries.

	Procedures	Time	Cost
Spain	10	47	15.1
Guatemala	11	26	47.3
Fiji	8	46	25.3

a) Use z-scores to combine the three measures.
b) Which country has the best environment after combining the three measures? Be careful—a lower rank indicates a better environment to start up a business.

75. Regular gas. The data set provided contains U.S. regular retail gasoline prices (cents/gallon) from August 20, 1990 to January 2, 2012, from a national sample of gasoline stations obtained from the U.S. Department of Energy.

a) Create a histogram of the data and describe the distribution.
b) Create a time series plot of the data and describe the trend.
c) Which graphical display seems the more appropriate for these data? Explain.

76. Home price index. Standard and Poor's Case-Shiller® Home Price Index measures the residential housing market in metropolitan regions across the United States. The national index, Composite.10, is a composite of 10 regions, and can be found in the data set provided for the years 1987 to 2007.

a) Create a histogram of the data and describe the distribution.
b) Create a time series plot of the data and describe the trend.
c) Which graphical display seems the more appropriate for these data? Explain.

*77. Unemployment rate, 2013. The histogram shows the monthly U.S. unemployment rate from January 2003 to January 2013 (data.bls.gov/timeseries/LNS14000000).

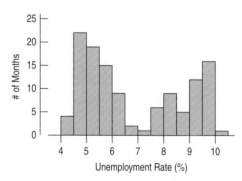

Here is the time series plot for the same data.

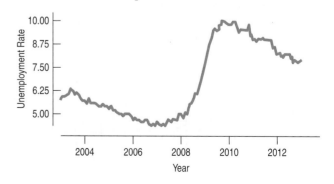

a) What features of the data can you see in the histogram that aren't clear in the time series plot?

b) What features of the data can you see in the time series plot that aren't clear in the histogram?

c) Which graphical display seems the more appropriate for these data? Explain.

d) Write a brief description of unemployment rates over this time period in the United States.

*78. Consumer Price Index (CPI). Here is a histogram of the monthly CPI as reported by the Bureau of Labor Statistics (ftp://ftp.bls.gov/pub/special.requests/cpi/cpiai.txt) from 2008 through 2012:

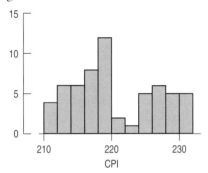

Here is the time series plot for the same data.

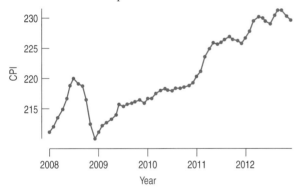

a) What features of the data can you see in the histogram that aren't clear from the time series plot?

b) What features of the data can you see in the time series plot that aren't clear in the histogram?

c) Which graphical display seems the more appropriate for these data? Explain.

d) Write a brief description of monthly CPI over this time period.

79. Assets. Here is a histogram of the assets (in millions of dollars) of 79 companies chosen from the *Forbes* list of the nation's top corporations.

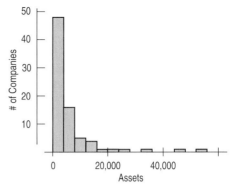

a) What aspect of this distribution makes it difficult to summarize, or to discuss, center and spread?

b) What would you suggest doing with these data if we want to understand them better?

80. Assets, again. Here are the same data you saw in Exercise 79 after re-expressions as the square root of assets and the logarithm of assets.

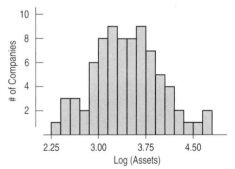

a) Which re-expression do you prefer? Why?

b) In the square root re-expression, what does the value 50 actually indicate about the company's assets?

JUST CHECKING ANSWERS

1 Incomes are probably skewed to the right and not symmetric, making the median the more appropriate measure of center. The mean will be influenced by the high end of family incomes and not reflect the "typical" family income as well as the median would. It will give the impression that the typical income is higher than it is.

2 An IQR of 30 mpg would mean that only 50% of the cars get gas mileages in an interval 30 mpg wide. Fuel economy doesn't vary that much. 3 mpg is reasonable. It seems plausible that 50% of the cars will be within about 3 mpg of each other. An IQR of 0.3 mpg would mean that the gas mileage of half the cars varies little from the estimate. It's unlikely that cars, drivers, and driving conditions are that consistent.

3 We'd prefer a standard deviation of 2 months. Making a consistent product is important for quality. Customers want to be able to count on the MP3 player lasting somewhere close to 5 years, and a standard deviation of 2 years would mean that life spans were highly variable.

4

Correlation and Linear Regression

Amazon.com

Amazon.com opened for business in July 1995, billing itself even then as "Earth's Biggest Bookstore," with an unusual business plan: They didn't plan to turn a profit for four to five years. Although some shareholders complained when the dotcom bubble burst, Amazon continued its slow, steady growth, becoming profitable for the first time in 2002. Since then, Amazon has remained profitable and has continued to grow. By 2011, sales had topped $48 billion, of which 44% were international sales. In 2012 Amazon was ranked the 20th most valuable brand by *Business Week*. Amazon's selection of merchandise has expanded to include almost anything you can imagine, from $400,000 necklaces, to yak cheese from Tibet, to the largest book in the world.

Amazon R&D is constantly monitoring and evolving their website to best serve their customers and maximize their sales performance. To make changes to the site, they experiment by collecting data and analyzing what works best. As Ronny Kohavi, former director of Data Mining and Personalization, said, "Data trumps intuition. Instead of using our intuition, we experiment on the live site and let our customers tell us what works for them."

WHO	Books sold by Amazon
WHAT	List Price and Weight
UNITS	$ and Ounces
WHEN	2012
WHERE	Online
WHY	Originally collected as a class project

ven with the rapid growth of e-books (about 15% growth per year), sales of traditional ink on paper books have held their own. Of course, one difference between e-books and print books is that a print book has weight, and that can help predict its price. The weight can account for the materials in the book's manufacture as well as other related costs. Amazon makes a variety of facts available for most books it sells, including the shipping weight (in ounces), the number of pages, the dimensions, and of course, the price.

Figure 4.1 shows a plot of *List Price* ($) against (shipping) *Weight* (oz) for 307 books selected[1] from Amazon's offerings. Clearly price and weight are related. If you were asked to summarize the relationship, what would you say?

Figure 4.1   *List Price* ($) vs *Weight* (oz) for 307 books sold by Amazon

There is an overall trend; heavier books tend to cost more. But the relationship is far from perfect. This plot is an example of a **scatterplot**. It plots one quantitative variable against another. Just by looking at a scatterplot, you can see patterns, trends, relationships, and the occasional unusual cases standing apart from the general pattern. Scatterplots are the best way to start observing the relationship between two *quantitative* variables.

Relationships between variables are often at the heart of what we'd like to learn from data.

- Is consumer confidence related to oil prices?
- Are customers who consult online help sites as satisfied with a company's customer relations as those who speak with human customer support specialists?
- Is an increase in money spent on advertising related to sales?
- What is the relationship between a stock's sales volume and its price?

Questions such as these relate two quantitative variables and ask whether there is an **association** between them. Scatterplots are the ideal way to picture such associations.

4.1   Looking at Scatterplots

The Texas Transportation Institute, which studies the mobility provided by the nation's transportation system, issues an annual report on traffic congestion and its costs to society and business. Figure 4.2 shows a scatterplot of the annual *Congestion Cost* Per Person of traffic delays (in dollars) in 65 cities in the United States against the Peak Period *Freeway Speed* (mph).

---

[1]The books were selected by "walking" randomly through Amazon's offerings, starting at a variety of haphazardly selected books and then selecting a randomly chosen book from the "Customers who bought this item also bought" list, and continuing the randomly generated thread. Although it is not a random sample, for our purposes it can be regarded as a representative collection of books.

WHO	Cities in the United States
WHAT	*Congestion Cost Per Person* and *Peak Period Freeway Speed*
UNITS	*Congestion Cost Per Person* ($ per person per year); *Peak Period Freeway Speed* (mph)
WHEN	2000
WHERE	United States
WHY	To examine the relationship between congestion on the highways and its impact on society and business

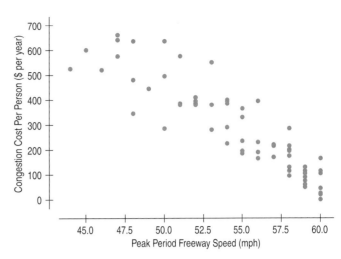

Figure 4.2 *Congestion Cost Per Person* ($ per year) of traffic delays against *Peak Period Freeway Speed* (mph) for 65 U.S. cities.

Everyone looks at scatterplots. But many people would find it hard to say what to look for in a scatterplot. What do *you* see? Try to describe the scatterplot of *Congestion Cost* against *Freeway Speed*.

You might say that the **direction** of the association is important. As the peak freeway speed goes up, the cost of congestion goes down. A pattern that runs from the upper left to the lower right   is said to be **negative**. A pattern running the other way   , as we saw for the price and weight of books, is called **positive**.

> Look for **Direction**: What's the sign—positive, negative, or neither?

The second thing to look for in a scatterplot is its **form**. If there is a straight line relationship, it will appear as a cloud or swarm of points stretched out in a generally consistent, straight form. For example, the scatterplot of traffic congestion has an underlying **linear** form, although some points stray away from it.

Scatterplots can reveal many different kinds of patterns. Often they will not be straight, but straight line patterns are both the most common and the most useful for statistics.

If the relationship isn't straight, but curves gently, while still increasing or decreasing steadily,   we can often find ways to straighten it out. But if it

> Look for **Form**: Straight, curved, something exotic, or no pattern?

curves sharply—up and then down, for example,   —then you'll need more advanced methods.

The third feature to look for in a scatterplot is the **strength** of the relationship.

At one extreme, do the points appear tightly clustered in a single stream (whether straight, curved, or bending all over the place)? Or, at the other extreme, do the points seem to be so variable and spread out that we can barely discern

> Look for **Strength**: How much scatter?

any trend or pattern?   The traffic congestion plot shows moderate scatter around a generally straight form. That indicates that there's a moderately strong linear relationship between cost and speed.

Finally, always look for the unexpected. Often the most interesting discovery in a scatterplot is something you never thought to look for. One example of such a

> Look for **Unusual Features**:
> Are there unusual observations or subgroups?

surprise is an unusual observation, or **outlier**, standing away from the overall pattern of the scatterplot. Such a point is almost always interesting and deserves special attention. You may see entire clusters or subgroups that stand away or show a trend in a different direction than the rest of the plot. That should raise questions about why they are different. They may be a clue that you should split the data into subgroups instead of looking at them all together.

FOR EXAMPLE Creating a scatterplot

The first automobile crash in the United States occurred in New York City in 1896, when a motor vehicle collided with a "pedalcycle" rider. Cycle/car accidents are a serious concern for insurance companies. About 53,000 cyclists have died in traffic crashes in the United States since 1932. Demographic information such as this is often available from government agencies. It can be useful to insurers, who use it to set appropriate rates, and to retailers, who must plan what safety equipment to stock and how to present it to their customers. This becomes a more pressing concern when the demographic profiles change over time.

Here's data on the mean age of cyclists killed each year during the decade from 1998 to 2010. (Source: National Highway Transportation Safety Agency, found at www-nrd.nhtsa.dot.gov/Pubs/811624.pdf)

Year	Mean Age
1998	32
1999	33
2000	35
2001	36
2002	37
2003	36
2004	39
2005	39
2006	41
2007	40
2008	41
2009	41
2010	42

QUESTION Make a scatterplot and summarize what it says.

ANSWER The mean age of cyclist traffic deaths has been increasing almost linearly during this period. The trend is a strong one.

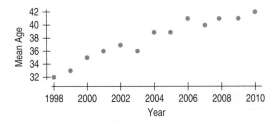

4.2   Assigning Roles to Variables in Scatterplots

Scatterplots were among the first modern mathematical displays. The idea of using two axes at right angles to define a field on which to display values can be traced back to René Descartes (1596–1650), and the playing field he defined in this way is formally called a *Cartesian plane*, in his honor.

The two axes Descartes specified characterize the scatterplot. The axis that runs up and down is, by convention, called the *y*-axis, and the one that runs from side to side is called the *x*-axis. These terms are standard.[2]

To make a scatterplot of two quantitative variables, assign one to the *y*-axis and the other to the *x*-axis. As with any graph, be sure to label the axes clearly, and indicate the scales of the axes with numbers. Scatterplots display *quantitative* variables. Each variable has units, and these should appear with the display—usually near each axis. Each point is placed on a scatterplot at a position that corresponds to values of these two variables. Its horizontal location is specified by its *x*-value, and its vertical location is specified by its *y*-value variable. Together, these are known as *coordinates* and written (*x*, *y*).

Descartes was a philosopher, famous for his statement *cogito, ergo sum*: I think, therefore I am.

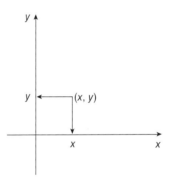

Scatterplots made by computer programs (such as the two we've seen in this chapter) often do not—and usually should not—show the *origin*, the point at $x = 0$, $y = 0$ where the axes meet. If both variables have values near or on both sides of zero, then the origin will be part of the display. If the values are far from zero, though, there's no reason to include the origin. In fact, it's far better to focus on the part of the Cartesian plane that contains the data. In our example about books none of the books were free and all weighed something so the computer drew the scatterplot in Figure 4.1 with axes that don't quite meet.

Which variable should go on the *x*-axis and which on the *y*-axis? What we want to know about the relationship can tell us how to make the plot. Amazon may have questions such as:

- How are prices related to sales volume?
- Are increased sales at Amazon reflected in its stock price?
- What offers will encourage shoppers to browse the Amazon site for a longer time?

In all of these examples, one variable plays the role of the **explanatory** or **predictor variable**, while the other takes on the role of the **response variable**. We place the explanatory variable on the *x*-axis and the response variable on the *y*-axis. When you make a scatterplot, you can assume that those who view it will think this way, so choose which variables to assign to which axes carefully.

---

[2]The axes are also called the "ordinate" and the "abscissa"—but we can never remember which is which because statisticians don't generally use these terms. In Statistics (and in all statistics computer programs) the axes are generally called "*x*" (abscissa) and "*y*" (ordinate) and are usually labeled with the names of the corresponding variables.

The roles that we choose for variables have more to do with how we *think* about them than with the variables themselves. Just placing a variable on the x-axis doesn't necessarily mean that it explains or predicts *anything*, and the variable on the y-axis may not respond to it in any way. The Amazon marketing department may want to predict prices leading to *Price* as the response variable in Figure 4.1. But the shipping department is likely to be more interested in predicting the weights of books, so for them, *Weight* would be a natural response variable.

The x- and y-variables are sometimes referred to as the **independent** and **dependent** variables, respectively. The idea is that the y-variable *depends* on the x-variable and the x-variable acts *independently* to make y respond. These names, however, conflict with other uses of the same terms in Statistics. Instead, we'll sometimes use the terms "explanatory" or "predictor variable" and "response variable" when we're discussing roles, but we'll often just say *x-variable* and *y-variable*.

> ## FOR EXAMPLE   Assigning roles to variables
>
> **QUESTION**   When examining the ages of victims in cycle/car accidents, why does it make the most sense to plot *year* on the x-axis and *mean age* on the y-axis? (See the example on page 100.)
>
> **ANSWER**   We are interested in how the age of accident victims might change over time, so we think of the year as the basis for prediction and the mean age of victims as the variable that is predicted.

4.3   Understanding Correlation

If you had to put a number (say, between 0 and 1) on the strength of the linear association between book prices and weights in Figure 4.1, what would it be? Your measure shouldn't depend on the choice of units for the variables. After all, Amazon sells books in euros as well as in dollars and book weights can be recorded in grams rather than ounces, but regardless of the units, the scatterplot would look the same. When we change units, the direction, form, and strength won't change, so neither should our measure of the association's (linear) strength.

We saw a way to remove the units in the previous chapter. We can standardize each of the variables, finding $z_x = \left(\dfrac{x - \bar{x}}{s_x} \right)$ and $z_y = \left(\dfrac{y - \bar{y}}{s_y} \right)$. With these, we can compute a measure of strength that you've probably heard of—the **correlation coefficient**:

$$r = \frac{\sum z_x z_y}{n - 1}.$$

Keep in mind that the x's and y's are paired. For each book we have a price and a weight. To find the correlation we multiply each standardized value by the standardized value it is paired with and add up those *cross products*. We divide the total by the number of pairs minus one, $n - 1$.[3]

---

[3]The same $n - 1$ we used for calculating the standard deviation.

There are alternative formulas for the correlation in terms of the variables x and y. Here are two of the more common:

$$r = \frac{\sum (x - \bar{x})(y - \bar{y})}{\sqrt{\sum (x - \bar{x})^2 \sum (y - \bar{y})^2}} = \frac{\sum (x - \bar{x})(y - \bar{y})}{(n - 1)s_x s_y}.$$

These formulas can be more convenient for calculating correlation by hand, but the form using z-scores is best for understanding what correlation means. No matter which formula you use, the correlation between *List Price* and *Weight* for the Amazon books is 0.498.

FOR EXAMPLE Finding the correlation coefficient

QUESTION What is the correlation of *mean age* and *year* for the cyclist accident data on page 100?

ANSWER Working by hand:

$$\bar{x} = 2004, s_x = 3.89$$
$$\bar{y} = 37.85, s_y = 3.26$$

The sum of the cross product of the deviations is found as follows:

$$\sum (x - \bar{x})(y - \bar{y}) = 147$$

Putting the sum of the cross products in the numerator and $(n - 1) \times s_x \times s_y$ in the denominator, we get

$$\frac{147}{(13 - 1) \times 3.89 \times 3.26} = 0.96$$

For *mean age* and *year*, the correlation coefficient is 0.96. That indicates a strong linear association. Because this is a time series, we refer to it as a strong "trend."

Correlation Conditions

Correlation measures the strength of the *linear* association between two *quantitative* variables. Before you use correlation, you must check three *conditions:*

- **Quantitative Variables Condition:** Correlation applies only to quantitative variables. Don't apply correlation to categorical data masquerading as quantitative. Check that you know the variables' units and what they measure.
- **Linearity Condition:** Sure, you can *calculate* a correlation coefficient for any pair of variables. But correlation measures the strength only of the *linear* association and will be misleading if the relationship is not straight enough. What is "straight enough"? This question may sound too informal for a statistical condition, but that's really the point. We can't verify whether a relationship is linear or not. Very few relationships between variables are perfectly linear, even in theory, and scatterplots of real data are never perfectly straight. How nonlinear looking would the scatterplot have to be to fail the condition? This is a judgment call that you just have to think about. Do you think that the underlying relationship is curved? If so, then summarizing its strength with a correlation would be misleading.
- **Outlier Condition:** Unusual observations can distort the correlation and can make an otherwise small correlation look big or, on the other hand, hide a large correlation. It can even give an otherwise positive association a negative correlation coefficient (and vice versa). When you see an outlier, it's often a good idea to report the correlation both with and without the point.

Each of these conditions is easy to check with a scatterplot. Many correlations are reported without supporting data or plots. You should still think about the conditions. You should be cautious in interpreting (or accepting others' interpretations of) the correlation when you can't check the conditions for yourself.

Throughout this course, you'll see that doing Statistics right means selecting the proper methods. That means you have to think about the situation at hand. An important first step is to check that the type of analysis you plan is appropriate. These conditions are just the first of many such checks.

JUST CHECKING

For the years 1992 to 2002, the quarterly stock prices of the semiconductor companies Cypress and Intel have a correlation of 0.86.

1 Before drawing any conclusions from the correlation, what would you like to see? Why?

2 If your coworker tracks the same prices in euros, how will this change the correlation? Will you need to know the exchange rate between euros and U.S. dollars to draw conclusions?

3 If you standardize both prices, how will this affect the correlation?

4 In general, if on a given day the price of Intel is relatively low, is the price of Cypress likely to be relatively low as well?

5 If on a given day the price of Intel stock is high, is the price of Cypress stock definitely high as well?

GUIDED EXAMPLE   Customer Spending

A major credit card company sends an incentive to its best customers hoping that the customers will use the card more. Market analysts wonder how often they can offer the incentive. Will repeated offerings of the incentive result in repeated increased credit card use? To examine this question, an analyst took a random sample of 184 customers from their highest use segment and investigated the charges in each of the two months following the date that customers received the incentive.

PLAN	**Setup** State the objective. Identify the quantitative variables to examine. Report the time frame over which the data have been collected and define each variable. (State the W's.)	Our objective is to investigate the association between the amount that a customer charges in each of the two months after they receive an incentive. The customers have been randomly selected from among the highest use segment of customers. The variables measured are the total credit card charges (in $) in the two months of interest.

✓ **Quantitative Variable Condition.** Both variables are quantitative. Both charges are measured in dollars.

Make the scatterplot and clearly label the axes to identify the scale and units.

Because we have two quantitative variables measured on the same cases, we can make a scatterplot.

Check the conditions.		✓ **Linearity Condition.** The scatterplot is straight enough.
		✓ **Outlier Condition.** There are no obvious outliers.

DO	**Mechanics** Once the conditions are satisfied, calculate the correlation with technology.	The correlation is −0.391.
		The negative correlation coefficient confirms the impression from the scatterplot.

REPORT	**Conclusion** Describe the direction, form, and the strength of the plot, along with any unusual points or features. Be sure to state your interpretation in the proper context.	MEMO
		Re: credit card spending
		We have examined some of the data from the incentive program. In particular, we looked at the charges made in each of the first two months of the program. We noted that there was a negative association between charges in the second month and charges in the first month. The correlation was −0.391, which is only moderately strong, and indicates substantial variation.
		We've concluded that although the observed pattern is negative, these data do not allow us to find the causes of this behavior. It is likely that some customers were encouraged by the offer to increase their spending in the first month, but then returned to former spending patterns. It is possible that others didn't change their behavior until the second month of the program, increasing their spending at that time. Without data on the customers' pre-incentive spending patterns it would be hard to say more.
		We suggest further research, and we suggest that the next trial extend for a longer period of time to help determine whether the patterns seen here persist.

Correlation Properties

Because correlation is so widely used as a measure of association it's a good idea to remember some of its basic properties. Here's a useful list of facts about the correlation coefficient:

- **The sign of a correlation coefficient gives the direction of the association.**
- **Correlation is always between −1 and +1.** Correlation *can* be exactly equal to −1.0 or +1.0, but watch out. These values are unusual in real data because they mean that all the data points fall *exactly* on a single straight line.
- **Correlation treats *x* and *y* symmetrically.** The correlation of *x* with *y* is the same as the correlation of *y* with *x*.
- **Correlation has no units.** This fact can be especially important when the data's units are somewhat vague to begin with (customer satisfaction, worker efficiency, productivity, and so on).
- **Correlation is not affected by changes in the center or scale of either variable.** Changing the units or baseline of either variable has no effect on the correlation coefficient because the correlation depends only on the z-scores.
- **Correlation measures the strength of the *linear* association between the two variables.** Variables can be strongly associated but still have a small correlation if the association is not linear.
- **Correlation is sensitive to unusual observations.** A single outlier can make a small correlation large or make a large one small.

How Strong Is Strong?

There's little agreement on what the terms "weak," "moderate," and "strong" mean. The same correlation might be strong in one context and weak in another. A correlation of 0.7 between an economic index and stock market prices would be exciting, but finding "only" a correlation of 0.7 between a drug dose and blood pressure might be seen as a failure by a pharmaceutical company. Use these terms cautiously and be sure to report the correlation and show a scatterplot so others can judge the strength for themselves.

Correlation Tables

Sometimes you'll see the correlations between each pair of variables in a dataset arranged in a table. The rows and columns of the table name the variables, and the cells hold the correlations.

	#Pages	Width	Thick	Pub year
#Pages	1.000			
Width	0.003	1.000		
Thick	0.813	0.074	1.000	
Pub year	0.253	0.012	0.309	1.000

Table 4.1   A correlation table for some variables collected on a sample of Amazon books.

Correlation tables are compact and give a lot of summary information at a glance. The diagonal cells of a correlation table always show correlations of exactly 1.000, and the upper half of the table is symmetrically the same as the lower half (can you see why?), so by convention, only the lower half is shown. A table like this can be an efficient way to start looking at a large dataset, but be sure to check for linearity and unusual observations or the correlations in the table may be misleading or meaningless. Can you be sure, looking at Table 4.1, that the variables are linearly associated? Correlation tables are often produced by statistical software packages. Fortunately, these same packages often offer simple ways to make all the scatterplots you need to look at.[4]

4.4   Lurking Variables and Causation

An educational researcher finds a strong association between height and reading ability among elementary school students in a nationwide survey. Taller children tend to have higher reading scores. Does that mean that students' height *causes* their reading scores to go up? No matter how strong the correlation is between two variables, there's no simple way to show from observational data that one variable causes the other. A high correlation just increases the temptation to think and to say that the *x*-variable *causes* the *y*-variable. Just to make sure, let's repeat the point again.

No matter how strong the association, no matter how large the *r* value, no matter how straight the form, there is no way to conclude from a high correlation *alone* that one variable causes the other. There's always the possibility that some third variable—a **lurking variable**—is affecting both of the variables you have observed. In the reading score example, you may have already guessed that the lurking variable is the age of the child. Older children tend to be taller and have stronger reading skills. But even when the lurking variable isn't as obvious, resist the temptation to think that a high correlation implies causation. Here's another example.

---

[4]A table of scatterplots arranged just like a correlation table is sometimes called a *scatterplot matrix*, or SPLOM, and is easily created using a statistics package.

Figure 4.3 *Life Expectancy* and numbers of *Doctors per Person* in 40 countries shows a fairly strong, positive, somewhat linear relationship with a correlation of 0.705.

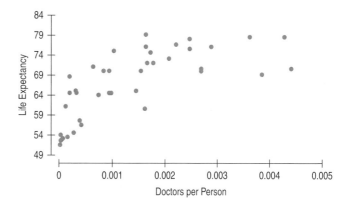

Figure 4.3 shows the *Life Expectancy* (average of men and women, in years) for each of 40 countries of the world, plotted against the number of *Doctors per Person* in each country. The strong positive association ($r = 0.705$) seems to confirm our expectation that more *Doctors per Person* improves health care, leading to longer lifetimes and a higher *Life Expectancy*. Perhaps we should send more doctors to developing countries to increase life expectancy.

If we increase the number of doctors, will the life expectancy increase? That is, would adding more doctors *cause* greater life expectancy? Could there be another explanation of the association? Figure 4.4 shows another scatterplot. *Life Expectancy* is still the response, but this time the predictor variable is not the number of doctors, but the number of *Televisions per Person* in each country. The positive association in this scatterplot looks even *stronger* than the association in the previous plot. If we wanted to calculate a correlation, we should straighten the plot first, but even from this plot, it's clear that higher life expectancies are associated with more televisions per person. Should we conclude that increasing the number of televisions extends lifetimes? If so, we should send televisions instead of doctors to developing countries. Not only is the association with life expectancy stronger, but televisions are cheaper than doctors.

Figure 4.4 *Life Expectancy* and number of *Televisions per Person* shows a strong, positive (although clearly not linear) relationship.

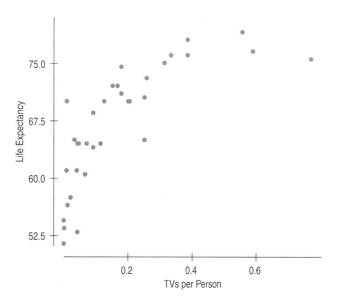

What's wrong with this reasoning? Maybe we were a bit hasty earlier when we concluded that doctors *cause* greater life expectancy. Maybe there's a lurking variable here. Countries with higher standards of living have both longer life expectancies *and* more doctors. Could higher living standards cause changes in the other variables? If so, then improving living standards might be expected to pro-long lives, increase the number of doctors, and increase the number of televisions. From this example, you can see how easy it is to fall into the trap of mistakenly inferring causality from a correlation. For all we know, doctors (or televisions) *do* increase life expectancy. But we can't tell that from data like these no matter how much we'd like to. Resist the temptation to conclude that *x* causes *y* from a correla-tion, no matter how obvious that conclusion seems to you.

FOR EXAMPLE   Understanding causation

QUESTION   An insurance company analyst suggests that the data on ages of cyclist accident deaths are actually due to the entire population of cyclists getting older and not to a change in the safe riding habits of older cyclists (see page 100). What would we call the *mean cyclist age* if we had that variable available?

ANSWER   It would be a lurking variable. If the entire population of cyclists is aging then that would lead to the average age of cyclists in accidents increasing.

4.5   The Linear Model

"Statisticians, like artists, have the bad habit of falling in love with their models."

—GEORGE BOX, FAMOUS
STATISTICIAN

Let's return to the relationship between Amazon book prices and weights. In Figure 4.1 (repeated here) we saw a moderate, positive, linear relationship, so we can summarize its strength with a correlation. For this relationship, the correlation is 0.498.

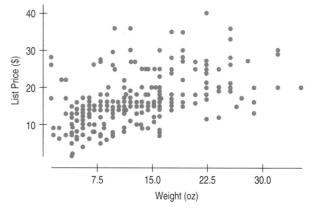

That's moderately strong, but the strength of the relationship is only part of the picture. Amazon's management might want a deeper understanding of prices for trade books to compare with prices in the rapidly growing e-book market. That's a reasonable business need but to meet it we'll need a model for the trend. The correlation says that there seems to be a linear association between the vari-ables, but it doesn't tell us what that association is.

Of course, we can say more. We can model the relationship with a line and give the equation. Specifically, we can find a linear model to describe the relationship we saw in Figure 4.1 between *Price* and *Weight*. A **linear model** is just an equation of a straight line through the data. The points in the scatterplot don't all line up, but a straight line can summarize the general pattern with only a few parameters. This model can help us understand how the variables are associated.

Residuals

We know the model won't be perfect. No matter what line we draw, it won't go through many of the points. The best line might not even hit *any* of the points. Then how can it be the "best" line? We want to find the line that somehow comes *closer* to all the points than any other line. Some of the points will be above the line and some below. Any linear model can be written as $\hat{y} = b_0 + b_1x$, where b_0 and b_1 are numbers estimated from the data and $\hat{y}$ (pronounced *y*-hat) is the **predicted value**. We use the *hat* to distinguish the predicted value from the observed value y. The difference between these two is called the **residual**:

$$e = y - \hat{y}.$$

The residual value tells us how far the model's prediction is from the observed value at that point. To find the residuals, we always subtract the predicted values from the observed ones.

Our question now is how to find the right line.

The Line of "Best Fit"

When we draw a line through a scatterplot, some residuals are positive, and some are negative. We can't assess how well the line fits by adding up all the residuals—the positive and negative ones would just cancel each other out. We need to find the line that's closest to all the points, and to do that, we need to make all the distances positive. We faced the same issue when we calculated a standard deviation to measure spread. And we deal with it the same way here: by squaring the residuals to make them positive. The sum of all the squared residuals tells us how well the line we drew fits the data—the smaller the sum, the better the fit. A different line will produce a different sum, maybe bigger, maybe smaller. The **line of best fit** is the line for which the sum of the squared residuals is smallest—often called the **least squares line**.

This line has the special property that the variation of the data around the model, as seen in the residuals, is the smallest it can be for any straight line model for these data. No other line has this property. Speaking mathematically, we say that this line minimizes the sum of the squared residuals. You might think that finding this "least squares line" would be difficult. Surprisingly, it's not, although it was an exciting mathematical discovery when Legendre published it in 1805.

4.6 Correlation and the Line

Any straight line can be written as:

$$y = b_0 + b_1x.$$

If we were to plot all the (x, y) pairs that satisfy this equation, they'd fall exactly on a straight line. We'll use this form for our linear model. Of course, with real data, the points won't all fall on the line. So, we write our model as $\hat{y} = b_0 + b_1x$, using $\hat{y}$ for the predicted values, because it's the predicted values (not the data values) that fall on the line. If the model is a good one, the data values will scatter closely around it.

For the Amazon book data, the line is:

$$\widehat{Price} = 10.35 + 0.477\ Weight.$$

What does this mean? The **slope**, 0.477, says that we can expect a book that weighs an ounce more to cost about $0.48 more. Slopes are always expressed in *y*-units per *x*-units. They tell you how the response variable changes for a one unit step in the predictor variable. So we'd say that the slope is 0.477 dollars per ounce.

The **intercept**, 10.35, is the value of the line when the x-variable is zero. Of course a weightless physical book isn't possible, so we wouldn't use these data to predict such a price, and we would choose to treat the intercept as just a "starting point" for our model.

JUST CHECKING

A scatterplot of sales per month (in thousands of dollars) vs. number of employees for all the outlets of a large computer chain shows a relationship that is straight, with only moderate scatter and no outliers. The correlation between *Sales* and *Employees* is 0.85, and the equation of the least squares model is:

$$\widehat{Sales} = 9.564 + 122.74 \; Employees$$

6 What does the slope of 122.74 mean?

7 What are the units of the slope?

8 The outlet in Dallas, Texas, has 10 more employees than the outlet in Cincinnati. How much more *Sales* do you expect it to have?

How do we find the slope and intercept of the least squares line? The formulas are simple. The model is built from the summary statistics we've used before. We'll need the correlation (to tell us the strength of the linear association), the standard deviations (to give us the units), and the means (to tell us where to locate the line).

The slope of the line is computed as:

$$b_1 = r\frac{s_y}{s_x}.$$

We've already seen that the correlation tells us the sign and the strength of the relationship, so it should be no surprise to see that the slope inherits this sign as well. If the correlation is positive, the scatterplot runs from lower left to upper right, and the slope of the line is positive.

Correlations don't have units, but slopes do. How x and y are measured—what units they have—doesn't affect their correlation, but does change the slope. The slope gets its units from the ratio of the two standard deviations. Each standard deviation has the units of its respective variable. So, the units of the slope are a ratio, too, and are always expressed in units of y per unit of x.

How do we find the intercept? If you had to predict the y-value for a data point whose x-value was average, what would you say? The best fit line predicts $\bar{y}$ for points whose x-value is $\bar{x}$. Putting that into our equation and using the slope we just found gives:

$$\bar{y} = b_0 + b_1\bar{x}$$

and we can rearrange the terms to find:

$$b_0 = \bar{y} - b_1\bar{x}.$$

It's easy to use the estimated linear model to predict the price of a book from its weight. Consider, for example, Peter Drucker's book *Innovation and Entrepreneurship*. According to Amazon, the book weighs 6.4 ounces. Our model predicts its price as:

$$\widehat{Price} = 10.35 + 0.477 \times 6.4 = \$13.40$$

In fact, the book's list price is $16.99. The difference between the observed value and the value predicted by the regression equation is called the **residual**. For Drucker's book, the residual is $16.99 - 13.40 = \$3.59$.

Least squares lines are commonly called **regression lines**. Although this name is an accident of history (as we'll soon see), "regression" almost always means "the linear model fit by least squares." Clearly, regression and correlation are closely related. We'll need to check the same conditions before computing a regression as we did for correlation:

1. **Quantitative Variables Condition**
2. **Linearity Condition**
3. **Outlier Condition**

A little later in the chapter we'll add two more.

FOR EXAMPLE **Interpreting the equation of a linear model**

QUESTION The data on cyclist accident deaths show a linear pattern. Find and interpret the equation of a linear model for that pattern. Refer to the values given in the answer to the example on page 103.

ANSWER

$$b_1 = 0.96 \times \frac{3.26}{3.89} = 0.80$$

$$b_a = 37.85 - 0.80 \times 2004 = -1565.35$$

$$\widehat{MeanAge} = -1565.35 + 0.80 \, Year$$

The mean age of cyclists killed in vehicular accidents has increased by about 0.80 years of age (about 10 months) per year during the years observed by these data.

Understanding Regression from Correlation

The correlation coefficient has no units. (It is found from z-scores, which have no units.) When we multiply r by the ratio of the standard deviations of the two variables to find the slope, we introduce their units. As a result, $b_1 = r\dfrac{s_y}{s_x}$ is in *y-units* per *x-unit*. For the Amazon books, the slope is in dollars per ounce.

What happens to the regression equation if we standardize both the predictor and response variables and regress z_y on z_x? Both standardized variables have standard deviation = 1 and mean = 0. So, the slope is just r, and the intercept is 0 (because both $\bar{y}$ and $\bar{x}$ are now 0), and we have the simple equation

$$\hat{z}_y = r\, z_x.$$

Although we don't usually standardize variables for regression, thinking in z-scores is a good way to understand what the regression equation is doing. The equation says that cases that deviate by one standard deviation from the mean in x are predicted to have a value of y that is r standard deviations away from the mean in y.

Let's be more specific. For the Amazon books the correlation is 0.498. So, we know immediately that:

$$\hat{z}_{Price} = 0.498\, z_{Weight}.$$

That means that a book that is one standard deviation heavier than the mean book is predicted by our model to cost about half a standard deviation more than the mean book.

4.7   Regression to the Mean

Sir Francis Galton was the first to speak of "regression," although others had fit lines to data by the same method.

Suppose you were told of a book and, without any additional information, you were asked to guess its price. What would be your guess? A good guess would be the mean price of books. Now suppose you are also told that this book has an ISBN (International Standard Book Number) that is 2 standard deviations (SDs) above the mean ISBN. Would that change your guess? Probably not. The correlation between ISBN and *Price* is near 0, so knowing the ISBN doesn't tell you anything and doesn't move your guess. (And the standardized regression equation, $\hat{z}_y = r\, z_x$ tells us that as well, since it says that we should move 0×2 SDs from the mean.)

On the other hand, if you were told that, measured in euros, the book's price was 2 SDs above the mean, you'd know the price in dollars. There's a perfect correlation between *Price* in dollars and *Price* in euros ($r = 1$), so you know it's 2 SDs above mean *Price* in dollars as well.

What if you were told that the book was 2 SDs above the mean in number of pages? Would you still guess that its list price is average? You might guess that it costs more than average, since there's a positive correlation between Price and number of pages. But would you guess 2 SDs above the mean? When there was no correlation, we didn't move away from the mean at all. With a perfect correlation, we moved our guess the full 2 SDs. Any correlation between these extremes should lead us to move somewhere between 0 and 2 SDs above the mean. (To be exact, our best guess would be to move $r \times 2$ standard deviations away from the mean.)

Notice that if x is 2 SDs above its mean, we won't ever move more than 2 SDs away for y, since r can't be bigger than 1.0. So each predicted y tends to be closer to its mean (in standard deviations) than its corresponding x was. This property of the linear model is called **regression to the mean**. This is why the line is called the regression line.

The First Regression

Sir Francis Galton related the heights of sons to the heights of their fathers with a regression line. The slope of his line was less than 1. That is, sons of tall fathers were tall, but not as much above the average height as their fathers had been above their mean. Sons of short fathers were short, but generally not as far from their mean as their fathers. Galton interpreted the slope correctly as indicating a "regression" toward the mean height—and "regression" stuck as a description of the method he had used to find the line.

Harold Hotelling was a prominent statistician and economic theorist. He taught statistics to (among others) Nobel prize winners Milton Friedman and Kenneth Arrow.

Business Tales about Regression to the Mean

During the Great Depression, Northwestern University professor Horace Secrist followed the fortunes of 49 department stores, measuring the ratio of net profit or loss to net sales. He divided the stores into four groups, took the average performance of each group, and followed those averages from 1920 to 1930. He found that stores that had been above average tended to perform worse, while those that were below average tended to improve.

A careful scientist, he then examined other types of business. All 73 of the different industries he examined showed the same pattern! He solicited comments and criticisms from economists and statisticians. He then published a book entitled *Triumph of Mediocrity in Business* (Secrist 1933) announcing his discovery. Initial reviews were favorable, but the prominent statistician Harold Hotelling pointed out in a scathing review that Secrist had simply rediscovered regression to the mean, which is a mathematical certainty and not a new principle of economics or business.

Although Secrist wrote 13 books on economics and statistics and was director of Northwestern University's bureau of business research, his name is still largely associated with the fallacious interpretation of regression to the mean.

More recently, the psychologist Daniel Kahneman, winner of the 2002 Nobel Prize in Economics, explained (see his book *Thinking, Fast and Slow*) that regression to the mean can make managers believe that praising employees who do well doesn't work, but punishing them when they do badly does. Employees who score a success are likely to do a bit less well the next time (just due to random fluctuation), whether they are praised or not. Those who make a big error are likely to do better next time, whether they were chastised or not. But managers like to believe that their management actions have consequences and will therefore conclude that praise causes workers to do worse, but criticism encourages workers to improve.

MATH BOX   Equation of the line of best fit

Where does the equation of the line of best fit come from? To write the equation of any line, we need to know a point on the line and the slope. It's logical to expect that an average x will correspond to an average y, and, in fact, the line does pass through the point $(\bar{x}, \bar{y})$. (This is not hard to show as well.)

To think about the slope, we look once again at the z-scores. We need to remember a few things.

1. The mean of any set of z-scores is 0. This tells us that the line that best fits the z-scores passes through the origin (0, 0).

2. The standard deviation of a set of z-scores is 1, so the variance is also 1. This means that $\dfrac{\sum(z_y - \bar{z}_y)^2}{n-1} = \dfrac{\sum(z_y - 0)^2}{n-1} = \dfrac{\sum z_y^2}{n-1} = 1$, a fact that will be important soon.

3. The correlation is $r = \dfrac{\sum z_x z_y}{n-1}$, also important soon.

Remember that our objective is to find the slope of the best fit line. Because it passes through the origin, the equation of the best fit line will be of the form $\hat{z}_y = m z_x$. We want to find the value for m that will minimize the sum of the squared errors. Actually we'll divide that sum by $n - 1$ and minimize this mean squared error (MSE). Here goes:

$$\text{Minimize:} \qquad MSE = \frac{\sum(z_y - \hat{z}_y)^2}{n-1}$$

$$\text{Since } \hat{z}_y = m z_x: \qquad = \frac{\sum(z_y - m z_x)^2}{n-1}$$

$$\text{Square the binomial:} \qquad = \frac{\sum(z_y^2 - 2m z_x z_y + m^2 z_x^2)}{n-1}$$

$$\text{Rewrite the summation:} \qquad = \frac{\sum z_y^2}{n-1} - 2m\frac{\sum z_x z_y}{n-1} + m^2\frac{\sum z_x^2}{n-1}$$

4. Substitute from (2) and (3): $= 1 - 2mr + m^2$

   This last expression is a quadratic. A parabola in the form $y = ax^2 + bx + c$ reaches its minimum at its turning point, which occurs when $x = \dfrac{-b}{2a}$. We can minimize the mean of squared errors by choosing

$$m = \frac{-(-2r)}{2(1)} = r.$$

The slope of the best fit line for z-scores is the correlation, r. This fact leads us immediately to two important additional results:

A slope with value r for z-scores means that a difference of 1 standard deviation in z_x corresponds to a difference of r standard deviations in $\hat{z}_y$.

Who Was First?

One of history's most famous disputes of authorship was between Gauss and Legendre over the method of "least squares." Legendre was the first to publish the solution to finding the best fit line through data in 1805, at which time Gauss claimed to have known it for years. There is some evidence that, in fact, Gauss may have been right, but he hadn't bothered to publish it, and had been unable to communicate its importance to other scientists.[5] Gauss later referred to the solution as "*our* method" (principium *nostrum*), which certainly didn't help his relationship with Legendre.

---

[5]Stigler, Steven M., "Gauss and the Invention of Least Squares," **Annals of Statistics**, 9, (3), 1981, pp. 465–474.

Why *r* for *Correlation*?

In his original paper on correlation, Galton used *r* for the "index of correlation"—what we now call the correlation coefficient. He calculated it from the regression of *y* on *x* or of *x* on *y* after standardizing the variables, just as we have done. It's fairly clear from the text that he used *r* to stand for (standardized) regression.

Translate that back to the original *x* and *y* values: "Over one standard deviation in *x*, up *r* standard deviations in $\hat{y}$."

The slope of the regression line is $b = \dfrac{rs_y}{s_x}$.

We know choosing $m = r$ minimizes the sum of the squared errors (SSE), but how small does that sum get? Equation (4) told us that the mean of the squared errors is $1 - 2mr + m^2$. When $m = r$, $1 - 2mr + m^2 = 1 - 2r^2 + r^2 = 1 - r^2$. This is the percentage of variability *not* explained by the regression line. Since $1 - r^2$ of the variability is *not* explained, the percentage of variability in *y* that *is* explained by *x* is r^2. This important fact will help us assess the strength of our models.

And there's still another bonus. Because r^2 is the percent of variability explained by our model, r^2 is at most 100%. If $r^2 \le 1$, then $-1 \le r \le 1$, proving that correlations are always between -1 and $+1$.

4.8   Checking the Model

The linear regression model may be the most widely used model in all of Statistics. It has everything we could want in a model: two easily estimated parameters, a meaningful measure of how well the model fits the data, and the ability to predict new values. It even provides a self-check in plots of the residuals to help us avoid all kinds of mistakes. For the linear model, we start by checking the same conditions we checked earlier in this chapter for using correlation.

Linear models only make sense for quantitative data. The **Quantitative Data Condition** is pretty easy to check, but don't be fooled by categorical data recorded as numbers. You probably don't want to predict zip codes from credit card account numbers.

The regression model *assumes* that the relationship between the variables is, in fact, linear—the **Linearity Assumption**. If you try to model a curved relationship with a straight line, you'll usually get what you deserve. We can't ever verify that the underlying relationship between two variables is truly linear, but an examination of the scatterplot will let you check the **Linearity Condition** as we did for correlation. If you don't judge the scatterplot to be straight enough, stop. You can't use a linear model for just *any* two variables, even if they are related. The two variables must have a *linear* association, or the model won't mean a thing and decisions you base on the model may be wrong. Some nonlinear relationships can be saved by re-expressing—or transforming—the data to make the scatterplot more linear. (See Section 4.11.)

Watch out for outliers. The linearity assumption also requires that no points lie far enough away to distort the line of best fit. Check the **Outlier Condition** to make sure no point needs special attention. Outlying values may have large residuals, and squaring makes their influence that much greater. Outlying points can dramatically change a regression model. Unusual observations can even change the sign of the slope, misleading us about the direction of the underlying relationship between the variables.

Another assumption that is usually made when fitting a linear regression is that the residuals are independent of each other. We don't strictly need this assumption to fit the line, but we will need it to draw conclusions beyond the data. We'll come back to it when we discuss inference. We can't be sure that the **Independence**

Assumptions and Conditions

Most models are useful only when specific assumptions are true. Of course, assumptions are hard—often impossible—to check. That's why we *assume* them. But we should check to see whether the assumptions are *reasonable*. Fortunately, there are often *conditions* that we can check. Checking the conditions provides information about whether the assumptions are reasonable, and whether it's safe to proceed with the model.

Check the Scatterplot!

Check the scatterplot. The shape must be linear, or you can't use regression for the variables in their current form. And watch out for outliers.

Assumption is true, but we are more willing to believe that the cases are independent if the cases are a random sample from the population.

We can also check displays of the regression residuals for evidence of patterns, trends, or clumping, any of which would suggest a failure of independence. In the special case when we have a time series, a common violation of the Independence Assumption is for successive errors to be correlated with each other (autocorrelation). The error our model makes today may be similar to the one it made yesterday. We can check this violation by plotting the residuals against time and looking for patterns.

When our goal is just to explore and describe the relationship, independence isn't essential. However, when we want to go beyond the data at hand and make inferences for other situations (in Chapter 15) this will be a crucial assumption, so it's good practice to think about it even now, especially for time series.

We always check conditions with a scatterplot of the data, but we can learn even more after we've fit the regression model. There's extra information in the residuals that we can use to help us decide how reasonable our model is and how well the model fits. So, we plot the residuals and check the conditions again.

The residuals are the part of the data that *hasn't* been modeled. We can write

$$Data = Predicted + Residual$$

or, equivalently,

$$Residual = Data - Predicted.$$

Or, as we showed earlier, in symbols:

$$e = y - \hat{y}.$$

A scatterplot of the residuals versus the x-values should be a plot without patterns. It shouldn't have any interesting features—no direction, no shape. It should stretch horizontally, showing no bends, and it should have no outliers. If you see nonlinearities, outliers, or clusters in the residuals, find out what the regression model missed.

Let's examine the residuals from our regression of Amazon book prices on weight.[6]

> **Why *e* for *Residual*?**
>
> The easy answer is that *r* is already taken for correlation, but the truth is that *e* stands for "error." It's not that the data point is a mistake but that statisticians often refer to variability not explained by a model as error.

Figure 4.5 Residuals of the regression model predicting Amazon book prices from weights.

Not only can the residuals help check the conditions, but they can also tell us how well the model performs. The better the model fits the data, the less the

---

[6]Most computer statistics packages plot the residuals as we did in Figure 4.5, against the predicted values, rather than against *x*. When the slope is positive, the scatterplots are virtually identical except for the axes labels. When the slope is negative, the two versions are mirror images. Since all we care about is the patterns (or, better, lack of patterns) in the plot, either plot is useful.

Equal Spread Condition

This condition requires that the scatter is about equal for all *x*-values. It's often checked using a plot of residuals against predicted values. The underlying assumption of equal variance is also called *homoscedasticity*.

residuals will vary around the line. The standard deviation of the residuals, s_e, gives us a measure of how much the points spread around the regression line. Of course, for this summary to make sense, the residuals should all share the same underlying spread. So we must *assume* that the standard deviation around the line is the same wherever we want the model to apply.

This new assumption about the standard deviation around the line gives us a new condition, called the **Equal Spread Condition**. The associated question to ask is does the plot have a consistent spread or does it fan out? We check to make sure that the spread of the residuals is about the same everywhere. We can check that either in the original scatterplot of *y* against *x* or in the scatterplot of residuals (or, preferably, in both plots). We estimate the **standard deviation of the residuals** in almost the way you'd expect:

$$s_e = \sqrt{\frac{\sum e^2}{n - 2}}$$

We don't need to subtract the mean of the residuals because $\bar{e} = 0$. Why divide by $n - 2$ rather than $n - 1$? We used $n - 1$ for *s* when we estimated the mean. Now we're estimating both a slope and an intercept. Looks like a pattern—and it is. We subtract one more for each parameter we estimate.

When we predicted the price of Peter Drucker's book *Innovation and Entrepreneurship* our model made an error of $3.59. The standard deviation of the errors is $s_e = \$5.49$, so that's a fairly typical size for a residual because it's within one standard deviation.

FOR EXAMPLE   Examining the residuals

Here is a scatterplot of the residuals for the linear model found in the example on page 111 plotted against the predicted values:

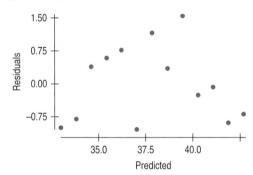

QUESTION   Show how the plotted values were calculated. What does the plot suggest about the model?

ANSWER   The predicted values are the values of $\widehat{MeanAge}$ found for each year by substituting the year value in the linear model. The residuals are the differences between the actual mean ages and the predicted values for each year.

The plot shows some remaining pattern in the form of four possible, nearly parallel, lower left to upper right trends. A further analysis may want to determine the reason for this pattern.

4.9   Variation in the Model and R^2

How is the thickness of a book related to the number of pages? We certainly expect books with more pages to be thicker, but can we find a model to relate these two variables? Here's a scatterplot of the data:

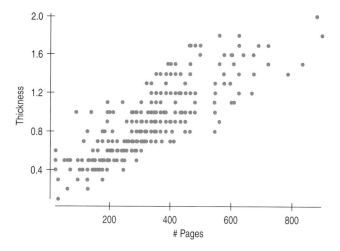

Figure 4.6   Naturally enough, the thickness of a book grows with the number of pages.

The regression model is

$$\widehat{Thickness} = 0.28 + 0.00189\,Pages$$

which says that books start out about 0.28 inches thick (due to covers and binding, perhaps) and then have about 0.00189 inches per page of thickness. We can see that the residuals vary less than the original thickness values did. That shows that we can get a better prediction of the thickness of a book by using a model rather than just using the mean to estimate the thickness of all the books.

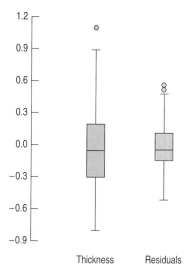

Figure 4.7   Thickness and the regression residuals compared. The thickness values have their mean subtracted for the comparison. The smaller variation of the residuals shows the success of the regression model.

If the linear model were perfect, the residuals would all be zero and would have a standard deviation of 0. If knowing about the number of pages gave us no information about the thickness of a book, then we'd just use the mean thickness and not bother with the regression.

We can construct a measure that tells us where our model falls between being perfect and being useless. One measure we could use is the correlation between the data y and the predicted values $\hat{y}$. In a perfect regression model, the predictions would match the observed values and the correlation would be 1.0. In the worthless regression, we'd expect a correlation of 0.

All regression models fall somewhere between the two extremes of zero correlation and perfect correlation. We'd like to gauge where our model falls. But a regression model with correlation $+0.5$ is doing as well as one with correlation -0.5. They just have different directions. If we *square* the correlation coefficient, we'll get a value between 0 and 1, and the direction won't matter. But that's not the real reason for squaring the correlation. In fact, the squared correlation, r^2, gives the *fraction of the data's variation accounted for by the model*, and $1 - r^2$ is the fraction of the original variation left in the residuals. For the thickness and pages model, $r^2 = 0.822^2 = 0.676$, and $1 - r^2$ is 0.324, so 32.4% of the variability in *Thickness* has been left in the residuals.

All regression analyses include this statistic, although by tradition, it is written with a capital letter, R^2, and pronounced "**R-squared**." Because R^2 is a fraction of a whole, it is often given as a percentage.[7] An R^2 of 0% means that none of the variance in the data is in the model; all of it is still in the residuals. An R^2 of 100% sounds great, but means you've probably made a mistake.[8]

We can see how R^2 relates to the variance. The variance of *Thickness* is 0.128. The variance of the residuals is 0.0415.[9] That's $0.0415/0.128 = 0.324$, or 32.4% of the variance of *Thickness* left behind in the residuals. So $100\% - 32.4\% = 67.6\%$ is the R^2 of the regression. The appropriate way to report this as part of a regression analysis is to say that 67.6% of the variance *is accounted for by the regression*.

r and R^2

Is a correlation of 0.80 twice as strong as a correlation of 0.40? Not if you think in terms of R^2. A correlation of 0.80 means an R^2 of $0.80^2 = 64\%$. A correlation of 0.40 means an R^2 of $0.40^2 = 16\%$—only a quarter as much of the variability accounted for. A correlation of 0.80 gives an R^2 *four* times as strong as a correlation of 0.40 and accounts for four times as much of the variability.

JUST CHECKING

Let's go back to our regression of sales ($000) on number of employees again.

$$\widehat{Sales} = 9.564 + 122.74 \, Employees$$

The R^2 value is reported as 72.25%.

9 What does the R^2 value mean about the relationship of *Sales* and *Employees*?

10 Is the correlation of *Sales* and *Employees* positive or negative? How do you know?

11 If we measured the *Sales* in thousands of euros instead of thousands of dollars, would the R^2 value change? How about the slope?

Some Extreme Tales

One major company developed a method to differentiate between proteins. To do so, they had to distinguish between regressions with R^2 of 99.99% and 99.98%. For this application, 99.98% was not high enough.

The president of a financial services company reports that although his regressions give R^2 below 2%, they are highly successful because those used by his competition are even lower.

How Big Should R^2 Be?

The value of R^2 is always between 0% and 100%. But what is a "good" R^2 value? The answer depends on the kind of data you are analyzing and on what you want to do with it. Just as with correlation, there is no value for R^2 that automatically determines that the regression is "good." Data from scientific experiments often have R^2 in the 80% to 90% range and even higher. Data from observational studies and surveys, though, often show relatively weak associations because it's so difficult to measure reliable responses. An R^2 of 30% to 50% or even lower might be taken as evidence of a useful regression. The standard deviation of the residuals can give us more information about the usefulness of the regression by telling us how much scatter there is around the line.

---

[7]By contrast, we usually give correlation coefficients as decimal values between -1.0 and 1.0.

[8]Well, actually, it means that you have a perfect fit. But perfect models don't happen with real data unless you accidentally try to predict a variable from itself.

[9]This isn't quite the same as squaring s_e which we discussed previously, but it's very close.

FOR EXAMPLE Understanding R^2

QUESTION Find and interpret the R^2 for the regression of cyclist death ages vs. time found in the example on page 100. (Hint: The calculation is a simple one.)

ANSWER We are given the correlation, $r = 0.96$. R^2 is the square of this, or 0.92. It tells us that 92% of the variation in the mean age of cyclist deaths can be accounted for by the trend of increasing age over time.

As we've seen, an R^2 of 100% is a perfect fit, with no scatter around the line. The s_e would be zero. All of the variance would be accounted for by the model with none left in the residuals. This sounds great, but it's too good to be true for real data.[10]

4.10 Reality Check: Is the Regression Reasonable?

Statistics don't come out of nowhere. They are based on data. The results of a statistical analysis should reinforce common sense. If the results are surprising, then either you've learned something new about the world or your analysis is wrong.

Whenever you perform a regression, think about the coefficients and ask whether they make sense. Is the slope reasonable? Does the direction of the slope seem right? The small effort of asking whether the regression equation is plausible will be repaid whenever you catch errors or avoid saying something silly or absurd about the data. It's too easy to take something that comes out of a computer at face value and assume that it makes sense.

Always be skeptical and ask yourself if the answer is reasonable.

GUIDED EXAMPLE Home Size and Price

Real estate agents know the three most important factors in determining the price of a house are *location*, *location*, and *location*. But what other factors help determine the price at which a house should be listed? Number of bathrooms? Size of the yard? A student amassed publicly available data on thousands of homes in upstate New York. We've drawn a random sample of 1000 homes from that larger dataset to examine house pricing. Among the variables she collected were the total living area (in square feet), number of bathrooms, number of bedrooms, size of lot (in acres), and age of house (in years). We will investigate how well the size of the house, as measured by living area, can predict the selling price.

PLAN **Setup** State the objective of the study.

Identify the variables and their context.

We want to find out how well the living area of a house in upstate NY can predict its selling price.

We have two quantitative variables: the living area (in square feet) and the selling price ($). These data come from public records in upstate New York in 2006.

(continued)

---

[10]If you see an R^2 of 100%, it's a good idea to investigate what happened. You may have accidentally regressed two variables that measure the same thing.

Model We need to check the same conditions for regression as we did for correlation. To do that, make a picture. Never fit a regression without looking at the scatterplot first.

✓ **Quantitative Variables Condition**

Check the **Linearity**, **Equal Spread**, and **Outlier Conditions**.

✓ **Linearity Condition** The scatterplot shows two variables that appear to have a fairly strong positive association. The plot appears to be fairly linear.

✓ **Equal Spread Condition** The scatterplot shows a consistent spread across the x-values.

✓ **Outlier Condition** There appear to be a few possible outliers, especially among large, relatively expensive houses. A few smaller houses are expensive for their size. We will check their influence on the model later.

We have two quantitative variables that appear to satisfy the conditions, so we will model this relationship with a regression line.

DO   **Mechanics** Find the equation of the regression line using a statistics package. Remember to write the equation of the model using meaningful variable names.

Our software produces the following output.

```
Dependent variable is: Price
1000 total cases
R squared = 62.43%
s = 57930 with 1000 − 2 = 998 df
Variable          Coefficient
Intercept         6378.08
Living Area       115.13
```

Once you have the model, plot the residuals and check the Equal Spread Condition again.

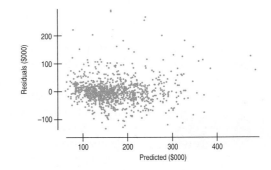

The residual plot appears generally patternless. The few relatively expensive small houses are evident, but setting them aside and refitting the model did not change either the slope or intercept very much so we left them in. There is a slight tendency for cheaper houses to have less variation, but the spread is roughly the same throughout.

REPORT   **Conclusion** Interpret what you have found in the proper context.

MEMO

Re: Report on housing prices

We examined how well the size of a house could predict its selling price. Data were obtained from recent sales of 1000 homes in upstate New York. The model is:

$$\widehat{Price} = \$6378.08 + 115.13 \times Living\ Area$$

In other words, from a base of $6378.08, houses cost about $115.13 per square foot in upstate NY.

This model appears reasonable from both a statistical and real estate perspective. Although we know that size is not the only factor in pricing a house, the model accounts for 62.4% of the variation in selling price.

As a reality check, we checked with several real estate pricing sites (www.realestateabc.com, www.zillow.com) and found that houses in this region were averaging $100 to $150 per square foot, so our model is plausible.

Of course, not all house prices are predicted well by the model. We computed the model without several of these houses, but their impact on the regression model was small. We believe that this is a reasonable place to start to assess whether a house is priced correctly for this market. Future analysis might benefit by considering other factors.

4.11 Nonlinear Relationships

Everything we've discussed in this chapter requires that the underlying relationship between two variables be linear. But what should we do when the relationship is nonlinear and we can't use the correlation coefficient or a linear model? There are three basic approaches, each with its advantages and disadvantages.

Let's consider an example. The Human Development Index (HDI) was developed by the United Nations as a general measure of quality of life in countries around the world. It combines economic information (GDP), life expectancy, and education. The growth of cell phone usage has been phenomenal worldwide. Is cell phone usage related to the developmental state of a country? Figure 4.8 shows a scatterplot of number of *Cell Phones* vs. *HDI* for 152 countries of the world.

We can look at the scatterplot and see that cell phone usage increases with increasing HDI. But the relationship is not straight. In Figure 4.8, we can easily see the bend in the form. But that doesn't help us summarize or model the relationship.

Figure 4.8 The scatterplot of number of *Cell Phones* (000s) vs. *HDI* for countries shows a bent relationship not suitable for correlation or regression.

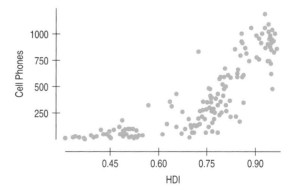

You might think that we should just fit some curved function such as an exponential or quadratic to a shape like this. But using curved functions is complicated, and the resulting model can be difficult to interpret. And many of the convenient associated statistics (which we'll see in Chapters 17 and 18) are not appropriate for such models. So this approach isn't often used.

Another approach allows us to summarize the strength of the association between the variables even when we don't have a linear relationship. The **Spearman rank correlation**[11] works with the *ranks* of the data rather than their values. To find the ranks we simply count from the lowest value to the highest so that rank 1 is assigned to the lowest value, rank 2 to the next lowest, and so on. Using ranks for both variables generally straightens out the relationship, as Figure 4.9 shows.

Figure 4.9 Plotting the ranks results in a plot with a straight relationship.

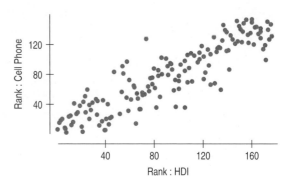

Now we can calculate a correlation on the ranks. The resulting correlation[12] summarizes the degree of relationship between two variables—but not, of course, of the degree of *linear* relationship. The Spearman correlation for these variables is 0.876. That says there's a reasonably strong relationship between *Cell Phones* and *HDI*. We don't usually fit a linear model to the ranks because that would be difficult to interpret and because the supporting statistics (as we said, see Chapters 17 and 18) wouldn't be appropriate.

A third approach to a nonlinear relationship is to transform or re-express one or both of the variables by a function such as the square root, logarithm, or reciprocal. We saw in Chapter 3 that a transformation can improve the symmetry of the distribution of a single variable. In the same way—and often with the same transforming function—transformations can make a relationship more nearly linear. Figure 4.10, for example, shows the relationship between the log of the number of *Cell Phones* and the *HDI* for the same countries.

Figure 4.10 Taking the logarithm of *Cell Phones* results in a more nearly linear relationship.

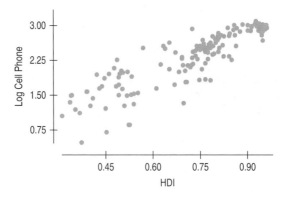

The advantage of re-expressing variables is that we *can* use regression models, along with all the supporting statistics still to come. The disadvantage is that we must interpret our results in terms of the re-expressed data, and it can be difficult to explain what we mean by the logarithm of the number of cell phones in

---

[11]Due to Charles Spearman, a psychologist who did pioneering work in intelligence testing.
[12]Spearman rank correlation is a *nonparametric* statistical method. You'll find other nonparametric methods in Chapter 22.

a country. We can, of course, reverse the transformation to transform a predicted value or residual back to the original units. (In the case of a logarithmic transformation, calculate 10^y to get back to the original units.)

Which approach you choose is likely to depend on the situation and your needs. Statisticians, economists, and scientists generally prefer to transform their data, and many of their laws and theories include transforming functions.[13] But for just understanding the shape of a relationship, a scatterplot does a fine job, and as a summary of the strength of a relationship, a Spearman correlation is a good general-purpose tool.

FOR EXAMPLE   Re-expressing for linearity

Consider the relationship between a company's *Assets* and its *Sales* as reported in annual financial statements. Here's a scatterplot of those variables for 79 of the largest companies:

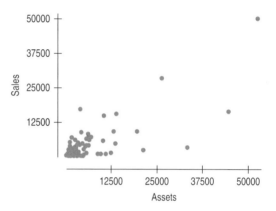

The Pearson correlation is 0.746, and the Spearman rank correlation is 0.50. Taking the logarithm of both variables produces the following scatterplot:

QUESTION   What should we say about the relationship between *Assets* and *Sales*?

ANSWER   The Pearson correlation is not appropriate because the scatterplot of the data is not linear. The Spearman correlation is a more appropriate summary. The scatterplot of the log transformed variables is linear and shows a strong pattern. We could find a linear model for this relationship, but we'd have to interpret it in terms of *log Sales* and *log Assets*.

---

[13]In fact, the HDI itself includes such transformed variables in its construction.

WHAT CAN GO WRONG?

- **Don't say "correlation" when you mean "association."** How often have you heard the word "correlation"? Chances are pretty good that when you've heard the term, it's been misused. It's one of the most widely misused Statistics terms, and given how often Statistics are misused, that's saying a lot. One of the problems is that many people use the specific term *correlation* when they really mean the more general term *association*. Association is a deliberately vague term used to describe the relationship between two variables.

  Correlation is a precise term used to describe the strength and direction of a linear relationship between quantitative variables.

- **Don't correlate categorical variables.** Be sure to check the Quantitative Variables Condition. It makes no sense to compute a correlation of categorical variables.

- **Make sure the association is linear.** Not all associations between quantitative variables are linear. Correlation can miss even a strong nonlinear association. And linear regression models are never appropriate for relationships that are not linear. A company, concerned that customers might use ovens with imperfect temperature controls, performed a series of experiments[14] to assess the effect of baking temperature on the quality of brownies made from their freeze-dried reconstituted brownies. The company wants to understand the sensitivity of brownie quality to variation in oven temperatures around the recommended baking temperature of 325°F. The lab reported a correlation of −0.05 between the scores awarded by a panel of trained taste-testers and baking temperature and a regression slope of −0.02, so they told management that there is no relationship. Before printing directions on the box telling customers not to worry about the temperature, a savvy intern asks to see the scatterplot.

Figure 4.11 The relationship between brownie taste *Score* and *Baking Temperature* is strong, but not linear.

The plot actually shows a strong association—but not a linear one. Don't forget to check the Linearity Condition.

- **Beware of outliers.** You can't interpret a correlation coefficient or a regression model safely without a background check for unusual observations.

---

[14]Experiments designed to assess the impact of environmental variables outside the control of the company on the quality of the company's products were advocated by the Japanese quality expert Dr. Genichi Taguchi starting in the 1980s in the United States.

Here's an example. The relationship between *IQ* and *Shoe Size* among comedians shows a surprisingly strong positive correlation of 0.50. To check assumptions, we look at the scatterplot.

Figure 4.12 *IQ* vs. *Shoe Size*

From this "study," what can we say about the relationship between the two? The correlation is 0.50. But who *does* that point in the upper right-hand corner belong to? The outlier is Bozo the Clown, known for his large shoes and widely acknowledged to be a comic "genius." Without Bozo the correlation is near zero.

Even a single unusual observation can dominate the correlation value. That's why you need to check the Unusual Observations Condition.

- **Don't confuse correlation with causation.** Once we have a strong correlation, it's tempting to try to explain it by imagining that the predictor variable has *caused* the response to change. Putting a regression line on a scatterplot tempts us even further. Humans are like that; we tend to see causes and effects in everything. Just because two variables are related does not mean that one *causes* the other.

Does Cancer Cause Smoking?

Even if the correlation of two variables is due to a causal relationship, the correlation itself cannot tell us what causes what.

Sir Ronald Aylmer Fisher (1890–1962) was one of the greatest statisticians of the 20th century. Fisher testified in court (paid by the tobacco companies) that a causal relationship might underlie the correlation of smoking and cancer:

> Is it possible, then, that lung cancer . . . is one of the causes of smoking cigarettes? I don't think it can be excluded . . . the pre-cancerous condition is one involving a certain amount of slight chronic inflammation . . .
>
> A slight cause of irritation . . . is commonly accompanied by pulling out a cigarette, and getting a little compensation for life's minor ills in that way. And . . . is not unlikely to be associated with smoking more frequently.

Ironically, the proof that smoking indeed is the cause of many cancers came from experiments conducted following the principles of experiment design and analysis that Fisher himself developed.

Scatterplots, correlation coefficients, and regression models never prove causation. This is, for example, partly why it took so long for the U.S. Surgeon General to get warning labels on cigarettes. Although there was plenty of evidence that increased smoking was *associated* with increased levels of lung cancer, it took years to provide evidence that smoking actually *causes* lung cancer. (The tobacco companies used this to great advantage.)

(continued)

- **Watch out for lurking variables.** A scatterplot of the damage (in dollars) caused to a house by fire would show a strong correlation with the number of firefighters at the scene. Surely the damage doesn't cause firefighters. And firefighters actually do cause damage, spraying water all around and chopping holes, but does that mean we shouldn't call the fire department? Of course not. There is an underlying variable that leads to both more damage and more firefighters—the size of the blaze. You can often debunk claims made about data by finding a lurking variable behind the scenes.

- **Don't fit a straight line to a nonlinear relationship.** Linear regression is suited only to relationships that are, in fact, linear.

- **Beware of extraordinary points.** Data values can be extraordinary or unusual in a regression in two ways. They can have y-values that stand off from the linear pattern suggested by the bulk of the data. These are what we have been calling outliers; although with regression, a point can be an outlier by being far from the linear pattern even if it is not the largest or smallest y-value. Points can also be extraordinary in their x-values. Such points can exert a strong influence on the line. Both kinds of extraordinary points require attention.

- **Don't predict far beyond the data. A linear model will often do a reasonable job of summarizing a relationship in the range of observed x-values.** Once we have a working model for the relationship, it's tempting to use it. But beware of predicting y-values for x-values that lie too far outside the range of the original data. The model may no longer hold there, so such extrapolations too far from the data are dangerous.

- **Don't choose a model based on R^2 alone.** Although R^2 measures the *strength* of the linear association, a high R^2 does not demonstrate the *appropriateness* of the regression. A single unusual observation, or data that separate into two groups, can make the R^2 seem quite large when, in fact, the linear regression model is simply inappropriate. Conversely, a low R^2 value may be due to a single outlier. It may be that most of the data fall roughly along a straight line, with the exception of a single point. Always look at the scatterplot.

ETHICS IN ACTION

Rebekkah Greene, owner of Up with Life Café and Marketplace, is a true believer in the health and healing benefits of food. She offers her customers pure, wholesome, and locally sourced products. Recently, she decided to add a line of hearty "made to order" cereals that she prepares according to each customer's expressed preferences. To do this, she keeps a wide variety of ingredients on hand from which her customers can choose to "design" their own unique cereal mix. These not only include organic grains, nuts, and dried fruits typically found in cereals, like oat bran and wheat germ, but also a wide assortment of sprouted grains.

Rebekkah is following the lead of food innovators who understand that sprouting grains activates food enzymes, increases vitamin content, and decreases starch—all of which improve digestion and absorption. She finds that sprouted grains are particularly delicious choices for warm breakfast cereals. Being a purest, Rebekkah decided that she would take care of the sprouting process herself. She therefore invested in the equipment and designed a "sprouting" space with appropriate temperature and humidity controls.

At the onset, her "made to order" cereal mixes were a big hit. But after the novelty wore off, she noticed that sales began to decline. Since most of her regular customers are young to middle-aged women, Rebekkah now considered the possibility that most are weight conscious as well as health conscious. She suspects that many ultimately decided to give up eating cereal for breakfast, even if it can provide superior health benefits, to opt for lower carb alternatives to maintain or lose weight.

Given her sizeable investment in sprouting grains, Rebekkah realizes she needs to do something to get more of her cereals back on the breakfast table! She began to do some research on the topic to better educate her customers. While she found a number of studies suggesting that sprouted grains are particularly healthful, she focused her attention on findings that emphasize the relationship between eating breakfast (specifically cereal) and weight loss. In her weekly flyer on "Up

with Life Food Facts" she cited one study she found in a dietetic association journal that showed regular cereal eaters had fewer weight problems than infrequent cereal eaters. She stressed this positive correlation in her advice to customers. *The more often you eat cereal for breakfast the more weight you can lose… more cereal = more weight lost!* She did fail to mention, however, that this particular study was funded by the big cereal companies.

- Identify the ethical dilemma in this scenario.

- What are the undesirable consequences?

- Propose an ethical solution that considers the welfare of all stakeholders.

WHAT HAVE WE LEARNED?

Learning Objectives

Make a scatterplot to display the relationship between two quantitative variables.

- Look at the direction, form, and strength of the relationship, and any outliers that stand away from the overall pattern.

Provided the form of the relationship is linear, summarize its strength with a correlation, *r*.

- The sign of the correlation gives the direction of the relationship.
- $-1 \le r \le 1$; A correlation of 1 or -1 is a perfect linear relationship. A correlation of 0 is a lack of linear relationship.
- Correlation has no units, so shifting or scaling the data, standardizing, or even swapping the variables has no effect on the numerical value.
- A large correlation is not a sign of a causal relationship

Model a linear relationship with a least squares regression model.

- The regression (best fit) line doesn't pass through all the points, but it is the best compromise in the sense that the sum of squares of the residuals is the smallest possible.
- The slope tells us the change in *y* per unit change in *x*.
- The R^2 gives the fraction of the variation in *y* accounted for by the linear regression model.

Recognize regression to the mean when it occurs in data.

- A deviation of one standard deviation from the mean in one variable is predicted to correspond to a deviation of *r* standard deviations from the mean in the other. Because *r* is never more than 1, we predict a change toward the mean.

Examine the residuals from a linear model to assess the quality of the model.

- When plotted against the predicted values, the residuals should show no pattern and no change in spread.

Terms

Association

- **Direction:** A positive direction or association means that, in general, as one variable increases, so does the other. When increases in one variable generally correspond to decreases in the other, the association is negative.

- **Form:** The form we care about most is straight, but you should certainly describe other patterns you see in scatterplots.
- **Strength:** A scatterplot is said to show a strong association if there is little scatter around the underlying relationship.

Correlation coefficient

A numerical measure of the direction and strength of a linear association.

$$r = \frac{\sum z_x z_y}{n - 1}$$

Explanatory or independent variable (x-variable)

The variable that accounts for, explains, predicts, or is otherwise responsible for the y-variable.

Intercept

The intercept, b_0, gives a starting value in y-units. It's the $\hat{y}$ value when x is 0.

$$b_0 = \bar{y} - b_1 \bar{x}$$

Least squares

A criterion that specifies the unique line that minimizes the variance of the residuals or, equivalently, the sum of the squared residuals.

Linear model (Line of best fit)

The linear model of the form $\hat{y} = b_0 + b_1 x$ fit by least squares. Also called the regression line. To interpret a linear model, we need to know the variables and their units.

Lurking variable

A variable other than x and y that simultaneously affects both variables, accounting for the correlation between the two.

Outlier

A point that does not fit the overall pattern seen in the scatterplot.

Predicted value

The prediction for y found for each x-value in the data. A predicted value, $\hat{y}$, is found by substituting the x-value in the regression equation. The predicted values are the values on the fitted line; the points $(x, \hat{y})$ lie exactly on the fitted line.

Re-expression or transformation

Re-expressing one or both variables using functions such as log, square root, or reciprocal can improve the straightness of the relationship between them.

Residual

The difference between the actual data value and the corresponding value predicted by the regression model—or, more generally, predicted by any model:

$$e = y - \hat{y}.$$

Regression line

The particular linear equation that satisfies the least squares criterion, often called the line of best fit.

Regression to the mean

Because the correlation is always less than 1.0 in magnitude, each predicted y tends to be fewer standard deviations from its mean than its corresponding x is from its mean.

Response or dependent variable (y-variable)

The variable that the model is intended to explain or predict.

R^2

- The square of the correlation between y and x
- The fraction of the variability of y accounted for by the least squares linear regression on x
- An overall measure of how successful the regression is in linearly relating y to x

Scatterplot

A graph that shows the relationship between two quantitative variables measured on the same cases.

Slope

The slope, b_1, is given in y-units per x-unit. Differences of one unit in x are associated with differences of b_1 units in predicted values of y:

$$b_1 = r \frac{s_y}{s_x}.$$

Spearman rank correlation

The correlation between the ranks of two variables may be an appropriate measure of the strength of a relationship when the form isn't straight.

Standard deviation of the residuals

s_e is found by:

$$s_e = \sqrt{\frac{\sum e^2}{n - 2}}.$$

TECHNOLOGY HELP: Correlation and Regression

All statistics packages make a table of results for a regression. These tables may differ slightly from one package to another, but all are essentially the same—and all include much more than we need to know for now. Every computer regression table includes a section that looks something like this:

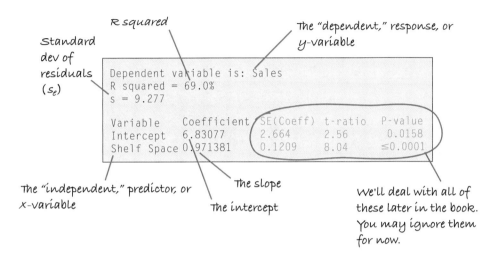

The slope and intercept coefficient are given in a table such as this one. Usually the slope is labeled with the name of the *x*-variable, and the intercept is labeled "Intercept" or "Constant." So the regression equation shown here is

$$\widehat{Sales} = 6.83077 + 0.971381\, Shelf\ Space.$$

EXCEL

To make a scatterplot in Excel:

- Arrange data in worksheet so that *x*-variable and *y*-variable are in columns next to each other in that order.
- Highlight data in *x*-variable and *y*-variable columns.
- Navigate to **Insert > Scatter.** (Mac users choose **Marked Scatter.**)
- Choose **Scatter With Only Markers.**
- The scatterplot appears. Shown here is a scatterplot of the Real Estate data.

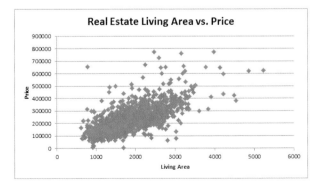

- To move the scatterplot to a new worksheet choose **Chart Tools > Design > Move Chart.**
- To add a linear regression Line to a scatterplot, choose **Chart Tools > Layout > Trendline > Linear Trendline.** (Mac users choose **Analysis > Trendline > Linear Trendline.**)

- Design, Layout, and Format options now show at the top of the screen as Chart Tools. Use these to change chart layouts, labels, and colors.
- By default, Excel includes in the intercept in the plot. If your data values are all far from zero, you may need to re-format your scatterplot. (See the discussion of Format axis below.)

To carry out a Linear Regression in Excel:

- First, make sure that you've installed the Data Analysis add-in, as follows:
  - On the **File** tab, click **Options,** and then click **Add-Ins.**
  - Near the bottom of the **Excel Options** dialog box, select **Excel Add-ins** in the **Manage** box, and then click **Go.**
  - In the **Add-Ins** dialog box, select the check box for **Analysis ToolPak,** and then click **OK.**
  - If Excel displays a message that states it can't run this add-in and prompts you to install it, click **Yes** to install the add-in.
- Navigate to **Data > Data Analysis.**
- Select **Regression.**

- Choose the cells of the spreadsheet holding the *x* and *y* variables.
- Check the **Labels** box if your data columns have variable names in the first row.

- Select where the output will appear.
- Check the **Line Fit Plots** box to display a scatterplot of the data with the Least Squares Regression Line.

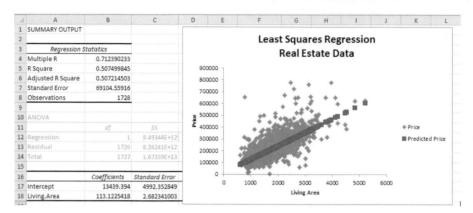

- The series displayed in red is the predicted values for price based on the Linear Regression Model. These points make up the Least Squares Regression Line.
- The R^2 value is in cell **B5.**
- The *y*-intercept and slope are in cells **B17** and **B18** respectively.
- The Design, Layout, and Format options now show at the top of the screen as Chart Tools. Use these to change chart layouts, labels, and colors.

But we aren't quite done yet. Excel always scales the axes of a scatterplot to show the origin (0, 0). But most data are not near the origin, so you may get a plot that, like this one, is bunched up in one corner.

- Right-click on the *x*-axis labels. From the menu that drops down, choose **Format axis**…
- Choose **Scale**.
- Set the *x*-axis minimum value. One useful trick is to use the dialog box itself as a straightedge to read over to the *x*-axis so you can estimate a good minimum value. Here 500 seems appropriate.
- Repeat the process with the *y*-axis if necessary.

JMP

To make a scatterplot and compute correlation:
- Choose **Fit Y by X** from the **Analyze** menu.
- In the **Fit Y by X** dialog, drag the Y variable into the **"Y, Response"** box, and drag the X variable into the **"X, Factor"** box.
- Click the **OK** button.

Once JMP has made the scatterplot, click on the red triangle next to the plot title to reveal a menu of options.

- Select **Density Ellipse** and select **.95**. JMP draws an ellipse around the data and reveals the Correlation tab.
- Click the blue triangle next to Correlation to reveal a table containing the correlation coefficient.

To compute a regression,
- Choose **Fit Y by X** from the **Analyze** menu. Specify the Y variable in the — Select Columns box and click the **Y, Response** button.

- Specify the *x*-variable and click the **X, Factor** button.
- Click **OK** to make a scatterplot.
- In the scatterplot window, click on the red triangle beside the heading labeled **"Bivariate Fit…"** and choose **Fit Line**. JMP draws the least squares regression line on the scatterplot and displays the results of the regression in tables below the plot.

MINITAB

To make a scatterplot,
- Choose **Scatterplot** from the Graph menu.
- Choose **Simple** for the type of graph. Click **OK**.
- Enter variable names for the *Y*-variable and *X*-variable into the table. Click **OK**.

To compute a correlation coefficient,
- Choose **Basic Statistics** from the Stat menu.
- From the Basic Statistics submenu, choose **Correlation**. Specify the names of at least two quantitative variables in the "Variables" box.
- Click **OK** to compute the correlation table.

SPSS

To make a scatterplot in SPSS, open the Chart Builder from the Graphs menu. Then
- Click the **Gallery** tab.
- Choose **Scatterplot** from the list of chart types.
- Drag the scatterplot onto the canvas.
- Drag a scale variable you want as the response variable to the *y*-axis drop zone.
- Drag a scale variable you want as the factor or predictor to the *x*-axis drop zone.
- Click **OK**.

To compute a correlation coefficient,

- Choose **Correlate** from the Analyze menu.
- From the Correlate submenu, choose **Bivariate**.
- In the Bivariate Correlations dialog, use the arrow button to move variables between the source and target lists. Make sure the Pearson option is selected in the Correlation Coefficients field.

To compute a regression, from the Analyze menu, choose

- **Regression** > **Linear** … In the Linear Regression dialog, specify the Dependent (*y*), and Independent (*x*) variables.
- Click the **Plots** button to specify plots and Normal Probability Plots of the residuals. Click **OK**.

Brief **Case**

Fuel Efficiency

Both drivers and auto companies are motivated to raise the fuel efficiency of cars. Recent information posted by the U.S. government proposes some simple ways to increase fuel efficiency (see www.fueleconomy.gov): avoid rapid acceleration, avoid driving over 60 mph, reduce idling, and reduce the vehicle's weight. An extra 100 pounds can reduce fuel efficiency (mpg) by up to 2%. A marketing executive is studying the relationship between the fuel efficiency of cars (as measured in miles per gallon) and their weight to design a new compact car campaign. In the file **Fuel Efficiency** you'll find data on the variables below.[15]

- Model of Car
- Engine Size
- Cylinders
- MSRP (Manufacturer's Suggested Retail Price in $)
- City (mpg)

- Highway (mpg)
- Carbon footprint
- Transmission type (Automatic or Manual)
- Fuel type (Regular or premium)

Describe the relationship of *MSRP* and *Engine Size* with *Fuel Efficiency* (both City and Highway) in a written report. Only in the U.S. is fuel efficiency measured in miles per gallon. The rest of the world uses liters per 100 kilometers. To convert mpg to l/100 km, compute 235.215/mpg. Try that form of the variable and compare the resulting models. Be sure to plot the residuals.

Cost of Living

The Numbeo website (www.numbeo.com) provides access to a variety of data. One table lists prices of certain items in selected cities around the world. They also report an overall cost-of-living index for each city compared to the costs of hundreds of items in New York City. For example, London at 110.69 us 10.69% more expensive than New York. You'll find the data for 322 cities as of March 23, 2013 in the file **Cost of living 2013**. Included are the *Cost of Living Index*, a *Rent Index*, a *Groceries Index*, a *Restaurant price Index*, and a *Local Purchasing Power Index* that measures the ability of the average wage earner in a city to buy goods and services. All indices are measured relative to New York City, which is scored 100.

Examine the relationship between the *Cost of Living Index* and the *Cost Index* for each of these individual items. Verify the necessary conditions and describe the relationship in as much detail as possible. (Remember to look at direction, form, and strength.) Identify any unusual observations.

Based on the correlations and linear regressions, which item would be the best predictor of overall cost in these cities? Which would be the worst? Are there any surprising relationships? Write a short report detailing your conclusions.

(continued)

---

[15]Data are from the 2004 model year and were compiled from www.Edmonds.com.

Mutual Funds

According to the U.S. Securities and Exchange Commission (SEC), a mutual fund is a professionally-managed collection of investments for a group of investors in stocks, bonds, and other securities. The fund manager manages the investment portfolio and tracks the wins and losses. Eventually the dividends are passed along to the individual investors in the mutual fund. The first group fund was founded in 1924, but the spread of these types of funds was slowed by the stock market crash in 1929. Congress passed the Securities Act in 1933 and the Securities Exchange Act in 1934 to require that investors be provided disclosures about the fund, the securities, and the fund manager. The SEC drafted the Investment Company Act, which provided guidelines for registering all funds with the SEC. By the end of the 1960s, funds reported $48 billion in assets and, by October 2007 there were over 8,000 mutual funds with combined assets under management of over $12 trillion.

Investors often choose mutual funds on the basis of past performance, and many brokers, mutual fund companies, and other websites offer such data. In the file **Mutual fund returns 2013**, you'll find the 3-month return, the annualized 1 yr, 5 yr, and 10 yr returns, and the return since inception of 64 funds of various types. Which data from the past provides the best predictions of the recent 3 months? Examine the scatterplots and regression models for predicting 3-month returns and write a short report containing your conclusions.

EXERCISES

The calculations for correlation and regression models can be very sensitive to how intermediate results are rounded. If you find your answers using a calculator and writing down intermediate results, you may obtain slightly different answers than you would have had you used statistics software. Different programs can also yield different results. So your answers may differ in the trailing digits from those in the Appendix. That should not concern you. The meaningful digits are the first few; the trailing digits may be essentially random results of the rounding of intermediate results.

SECTION 4.1

1. Consider the following data from a small bookstore.

Number of Sales People Working	Sales (in $1000)
2	10
3	11
7	13
9	14
10	18
10	20
12	20
15	22
16	22
20	26
$\bar{x} = 10.4$	$\bar{y} = 17.6$
$SD(x) = 5.64$	$SD(y) = 5.34$

a) Prepare a scatterplot of *Sales* against *Number of Sales People Working*.
b) What can you say about the direction of the association?
c) What can you say about the form of the relationship?
d) What can you say about the strength of the relationship?
e) Does the scatterplot show any outliers?

2. Disk drives have been getting larger. Their capacity is now often given in *terabytes* (TB) where 1 TB = 1000 gigabytes, or about a trillion bytes. A survey of prices for external disk drives found the following data:

Capacity (in TB)	Price (in $)
.150	35.00
.200	299.00
.250	39.95
.320	49.95
1.0	75.00
2.0	110.00
3.0	140.00
4.0	325.00

a) Prepare a scatterplot of *Price* against *Capacity*.
b) What can you say about the direction of the association?
c) What can you say about the form of the relationship?
d) What can you say about the strength of the relationship?
e) Does the scatterplot show any outliers?

SECTION 4.2

3. The human resources department at a large multinational corporation wants to be able to predict average salary for a given number of years' experience. Data on salary (in $1000s) and years of experience were collected for a sample of employees.

a) Which variable is the explanatory or predictor variable?
b) Which variable is the response variable?
c) Which variable would you plot on the *y* axis?

4. A company that relies on Internet-based advertising linked to key search terms wants to understand the relationship between the amount it spends on this advertising and revenue (in $).

a) Which variable is the explanatory or predictor variable?
b) Which variable is the response variable?
c) Which variable would you plot on the *x* axis?

SECTION 4.3

5. If we assume that the conditions for correlation are met, which of the following are true? If false, explain briefly.

a) A correlation of -0.98 indicates a strong, negative association.
b) Multiplying every value of *x* by 2 will double the correlation.
c) The units of the correlation are the same as the units of *y*.

6. If we assume that the conditions for correlation are met, which of the following are true? If false, explain briefly.

a) A correlation of 0.02 indicates a strong positive association.
b) Standardizing the variables will make the correlation 0.
c) Adding an outlier can dramatically change the correlation.

SECTION 4.4

7. A larger firm is considering acquiring the bookstore of Exercise 1. An analyst for the firm, noting the relationship seen in Exercise 1, suggests that when they acquire the store they should hire more people because that will drive higher sales. Is his conclusion justified? What alternative explanations can you offer? Use appropriate statistics terminology.

8. A study finds that during blizzards, online sales are highly associated with the number of snow plows on the road; the more plows, the more online purchases. The director of an association of online merchants suggests that the organization should encourage municipalities to send out more plows whenever it snows because, he says, that will increase business. Comment.

SECTION 4.5

9. True or False. If False, explain briefly.

a) We choose the linear model that passes through the most data points on the scatterplot.
b) The residuals are the observed *y*-values minus the *y*-values predicted by the linear model.
c) Least squares means that the square of the largest residual is as small as it could possibly be.

10. True or False. If False, explain briefly.

a) Some of the residuals from a least squares linear model will be positive and some will be negative.
b) Least Squares means that some of the squares of the residuals are minimized.
c) We write $\hat{y}$ to denote the predicted values and *y* to denote the observed values.

SECTION 4.6

11. For the bookstore sales data in Exercise 1, the correlation of number of sales people and sales is 0.965.

a) If the number of people working is 2 standard deviations above the mean, how many standard deviations above or below the mean do you expect sales to be?
b) What value of sales does that correspond to?
c) If the number of people working is 1 standard deviation below the mean, how many standard deviations above or below the mean do you expect sales to be?
d) What value of sales does that correspond to?

12. For the hard drive data in Exercise 2, some research on the prices discovered that the 200 GB hard drive was a special "hardened" drive designed to resist physical shocks and work under water. Because it is completely different from the other drives, it was removed from the data. For the remaining 7 drives, the correlation is now 0.927 and other summary statistics are:

Capacity (in TB)	Price (in $)
$\bar{x} = 1.531$	$\bar{y} = 110.70$
$SD(x) = 1.515$	$SD(y) = 102.05$

a) If a drive has a capacity of 3.046 TB (or 1 SD above the mean of 1.531 TB), how many standard deviations above or below the mean price of $110.70 do you expect the drive to cost?
b) What price does that correspond to?

13. For the bookstore of Exercise 1, the manager wants to predict *Sales* from *Number of Sales People Working*.

a) Find the slope estimate, b_1.
b) What does it mean, in this context?

c) Find the intercept, b_0.
d) What does it mean, in this context? Is it meaningful?
e) Write down the equation that predicts *Sales* from *Number of Sales People Working*.
f) If 18 people are working, what *Sales* do you predict?
g) If sales are actually $25,000 when 18 people are working, what is the value of the residual?
h) Have we overestimated or underestimated the sales?

14. For the disk drives in Exercise 2 (as corrected in Exercise 12), we want to predict *Price* from *Capacity*.

a) Find the slope estimate, b_1.
b) What does it mean, in this context?
c) Find the intercept, b_0.
d) What does it mean, in this context? Is it meaningful?
e) Write down the equation that predicts *Price* from *Capacity*.
f) What would you predict for the price of a 3.0 TB disk?
g) You have found a 3.0 TB drive for $175. Is this a good buy? How *much would you* save compared to what you expected to pay?
h) Did the model overestimate or underestimate the pricing?

SECTION 4.7

15. A CEO complains that the winners of his "rookie junior executive of the year" award often turn out to have less impressive performance the following year. He wonders whether the award actually encourages them to slack off. Can you offer a better explanation?

16. An online investment blogger advises investing in mutual funds that have performed badly the past year because "regression to the mean tells us that they will do well next year." Is he correct?

SECTION 4.8

17. Here are the residuals for a regression of *Sales* on *Number of Sales People Working* for the bookstore of Exercise 1:

Sales People Working	Residual
2	0.07
3	0.16
7	−1.49
9	−2.32
10	0.77
10	2.77
12	0.94
15	0.20
16	−0.72
20	−0.37

a) What are the units of the residuals?
b) Which residual contributes the most to the sum that was minimized according to the Least Squares Criterion to find this regression?
c) Which residual contributes least to that sum?

18. Here are residual plots (residuals plotted against predicted values) for three linear regression models. Indicate which condition appears to be violated (linearity, outlier, or equal spread) in each case.

a)

b)

c)
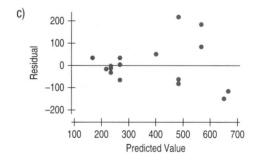

SECTION 4.9

19. For the regression model for the bookstore of Exercise 1, what is the value of R^2 and what does it mean?

20. For the disk drive data of Exercise 2 (as corrected in Exercise 12), find and interpret the value of R^2.

SECTION 4.11

21. When analyzing data on the number of employees in small companies in one town, a researcher took square roots of the counts. Some of the resulting values, which are reasonably symmetric were:

$$4, 4, 6, 7, 7, 8, 10$$

What were the original values, and how are they distributed?

22. You wish to explain to your boss what effect taking the base-10 logarithm of the salary values in the company's database will have on the data. As simple, example values you compare a salary of $10,000 earned by a part-time shipping clerk, a salary of $100,000 earned by a manager, and the CEO's $1,000,000 compensation package. Why might the average of these values be a misleading summary? What would the logarithms of these three values be?

CHAPTER EXERCISES

23. Association. Suppose you were to collect data for each pair of variables. You want to make a scatterplot. Which variable would you use as the explanatory variable and which as the response variable? Why? What would you expect to see in the scatterplot? Discuss the likely direction and form.

a) Cell phone bills: number of text messages, cost.
b) Automobiles: Fuel efficiency (mpg), sales volume (number of autos).
c) For each week: Ice cream cone sales, air conditioner sales.
d) Product: Price ($), demand (number sold per day).

24. Association, part 2. Suppose you were to collect data for each pair of variables. You want to make a scatterplot. Which variable would you use as the explanatory variable and which as the response variable? Why? What would you expect to see in the scatterplot? Discuss the likely direction and form.

a) T- shirts at a store: price each, number sold.
b) Real estate: house price, house size (square footage).
c) Economics: Interest rates, number of mortgage applications.
d) Employees: Salary, years of experience.

25. Scatterplots. Which of the scatterplots show:

a) Little or no association?
b) A negative association?
c) A linear association?
d) A moderately strong association?
e) A very strong association?

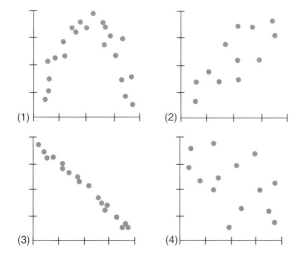

26. Scatterplots, part 2. Which of the scatterplots show:

a) Little or no association?
b) A negative association?
c) A linear association?
d) A moderately strong association?
e) A very strong association?

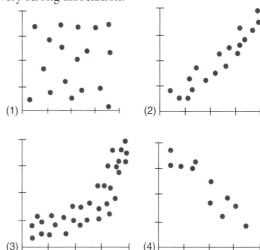

27. Manufacturing. A ceramics factory can fire eight large batches of pottery a day. Sometimes a few of the pieces break in the process. In order to understand the problem better, the factory records the number of broken pieces in each batch for three days and then creates the scatterplot shown.

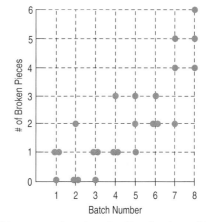

a) Make a histogram showing the distribution of the number of broken pieces in the 24 batches of pottery examined.
b) Describe the distribution as shown in the histogram. What feature of the problem is more apparent in the histogram than in the scatterplot?
c) What aspect of the company's problem is more apparent in the scatterplot?

28. Coffee sales. Owners of a new coffee shop tracked sales for the first 20 days and displayed the data in a scatterplot (by day).

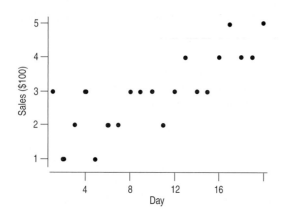

a) Make a histogram of the daily sales since the shop has been in business.

b) State one fact that is obvious from the scatterplot, but not from the histogram.

c) State one fact that is obvious from the histogram, but not from the scatterplot.

29. Matching. Here are several scatterplots. The calculated correlations are −0.923, −0.487, 0.006, and 0.777. Which is which?

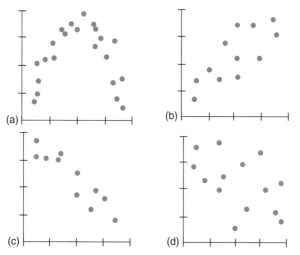

30. Matching, part 2. Here are several scatterplots. The calculated correlations are −0.977, −0.021, 0.736, and 0.951. Which is which?

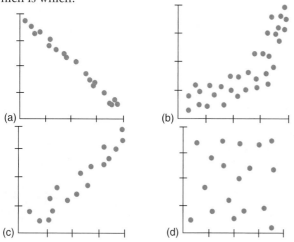

31. Pizza sales and price. A linear model fit to predict weekly *Sales* of frozen pizza (in pounds) from the average *Price* ($/unit) charged by a sample of stores in the city of Dallas in 39 recent weeks is:

$$\widehat{Sales} = 141{,}865.53 - 24{,}369.49\ Price.$$

a) What is the explanatory variable?

b) What is the response variable?

c) What does the slope mean in this context?

d) What does the *y*-intercept mean in this context? Is it meaningful?

e) What do you predict the sales to be if the average price charged was $3.50 for a pizza?

f) If the sales for a price of $3.50 turned out to be 60,000 pounds, what would the residual be?

32. Used Honda prices 2013. A linear model to predict the *Price* of a 2012 Honda Civic EX (in $) from its *Mileage* (in miles) was fit to 18 cars that were available during the week of March 1, 2013 (Kelly's Blue Book, www.kbb.com) within 200 miles of San Francisco, CA. The model was:

$$\widehat{Price} = 21{,}253.58 - 0.11097\ Mileage.$$

a) What is the explanatory variable?

b) What is the response variable?

c) What does the slope mean in this context?

d) What does the *y*-intercept mean in this context? Is it meaningful?

e) What do you predict the price to be for a car with 50,000 miles on it?

f) If the price for a car with 50,000 miles on it was selling for $14,000, what would the residual be?

g) Would that car for $14,000 and 50,000 miles seem like a good deal or a bad deal? Explain.

33. Football salaries 2013. Is there a relationship between to-tal team salary and the performance of teams in the National Football League (NFL)? For the 2012–2013 season, a linear model predicting *Wins* (out of 16 regular season games) from the total team *Salary* ($M) for the 32 teams in the league is:

$$\widehat{Wins} = -16.32 + 0.219\ Salary$$

a) What is the explanatory variable?

b) What is the response variable?

c) What does the slope mean in this context?

d) What does the *y*-intercept mean in this context? Is it meaningful?

e) If one team spends $10 million more than another on sal-ary, how many more games on average would you predict them to win?

f) If a team spent $120 million on salaries and won 8 games, would they have done better or worse than predicted?

g) What would the residual of the team in part f be?

h) The residual standard deviation is 2.78 games. What does that tell you about the likely practical use of this model for predicting wins?

34. Baseball salaries 2012. In 2012, the New York Yankees won 95 games and spent $198 million on salaries for their players (*USA Today*). Is there a relationship between salary and team performance in Major League Baseball? For the 2012 season, a linear model fit to the number of *Wins* (out of 162 regular season games) from the team *Salary* ($M) for the 30 teams in the league is:

$$\widehat{Wins} = 76.45 + 0.046\ Salary.$$

a) What is the explanatory variable?

b) What is the response variable?

c) What does the slope mean in this context?

d) What does the *y*-intercept mean in this context? Is it meaningful?

e) If one team spends $10 million more than another on salaries, how many more games on average would you predict them to win?

f) If a team spent $110 million on salaries and won half (81) of their games, would they have done better or worse than predicted?

g) What would the residual of the team in part f be?

h) The R^2 for this model is 2.05% and the residual standard deviation is 12.0 games. How useful is this model likely to be for predicting the number of wins?

35. Pizza sales and price, part 2. For the data in Exercise 31, the average *Sales* was 52,697 pounds (SD = 10,261 pounds), and the correlation between *Price* and *Sales* was = −0.547. If the *Price* in a particular week was one SD higher than the mean *Price*, how much pizza would you predict was sold that week?

36. Used Honda prices 2013, part 2. The 18 cars in Exercise 32 had an average *Price* of $19,843.50 (SD = $1853.59), and the correlation between *Price* and *Mileage* was = −0.889. If the *Mileage* of a 2012 Honda Civic EX was 1 SD below the average number of miles, what *Price* would you predict for it?

37. Packaging. A CEO announces at the annual shareholders meeting that the new see-through packaging for the company's flagship product has been a success. In fact, he says, "There is a strong correlation between packaging and sales." Criticize this statement on statistical grounds.

38. Insurance. Insurance companies carefully track claims histories so that they can assess risk and set rates appropriately. The National Insurance Crime Bureau reports that Honda Accords, Honda Civics, and Toyota Camrys are the cars most frequently reported stolen, while Ford Tauruses, Pontiac Vibes, and Buick LeSabres are stolen least often. Is it correct to say that there's a correlation between the type of car you own and the risk that it will be stolen?

39. Sales by region. A sales manager for a major pharmaceutical company analyzes last year's sales data for her 96 sales representatives, grouping them by region (1 = East Coast United States; 2 = Mid West United States; 3 = West

United States; 4 = South United States; 5 = Canada; 6 = Rest of World). She plots *Sales* (in $1000) against *Region* (1–6) and sees a strong negative correlation.

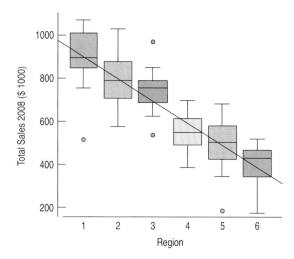

She fits a regression to the data and finds:

$$\widehat{Sales} = 1002.5 − 102.7\ Region$$

The R^2 is 70.5%.

Write a few sentences interpreting this model and describing what she can conclude from this analysis.

40. Salary by job type. At a small company, the head of human resources wants to examine salary to prepare annual reviews. He selects 28 employees at random with job types ranging from 01 = Stocking clerk to 99 = President. He plots *Salary* ($) against *Job Type* and finds a strong linear relationship with a correlation of 0.96.

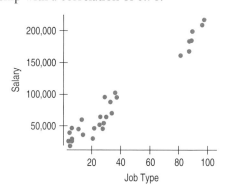

The regression output gives:

$$\widehat{Salary} = 15827.9 + 1939.1\ Job\ Type$$

Write a few sentences interpreting this model and describing what he can conclude from this analysis.

41. Carbon footprint 2013. The scatterplot shows, for 2013 cars, the carbon footprint (tons of CO_2 per mile) vs. the new Environmental Protection Agency (EPA) highway mileage for 76 family sedans as reported by the U.S.

government (www.fueleconomy.gov/feg/byclass.htm). There are seven cars (two points in the scatterplot are pairs of overlapping cars) with high highway mpg and low carbon footprint. They are all hybrids.

a) The correlation is −0.959. Describe the association.
b) Are the assumptions and conditions met for computing correlation?
c) Using technology, find the correlation of the data when the hybrid cards are not included with the others. Can you explain why it changes in that way?

42. EPA mpg 2013. In 2008, the EPA revised their methods for estimating the fuel efficiency (mpg) of cars—a factor that plays an increasingly important role in car sales. How do the new highway and city estimated mpg values relate to each other? Here's a scatterplot for 76 family sedans as reported by the U.S. government. These are the same cars as in Exercise 41.

a) The correlation of these two variables is 0.896. Describe the association.
b) If the hybrids were removed from the data, what would you expect to happen to the slope (increase, decrease, or stay pretty much the same) and to the correlation (increase, decrease, the same)? Try it using technology. Report and discuss what you find.

43. Real estate. Is the number of total rooms in the house associated with the price of a house? Here is the scatterplot of a random sample of homes for sale:

a) Is there an association?
b) Check the assumptions and conditions for correlation.

44. Economic analysis 2012. An economics student is studying the American economy and finds that the correlation between the inflation-adjusted Dow Jones Industrial Average and the Gross Domestic Product (GDP) (also inflation adjusted) is 0.81 for the years 1946 to 2011. (www.measuringworth.com). From that he concludes that there is a strong linear relationship between the two series and predicts that a drop in the GDP will make the stock market go down. Here is a scatterplot of the adjusted DJIA against the GDP (in the years 1946 to 2011). Describe the relationship and comment on the student's conclusions.

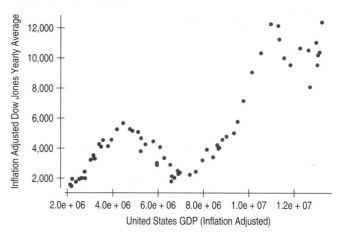

45. GDP growth 2012. Is economic growth in the developing world related to growth in the industrialized countries? Here's a scatterplot of the growth (in % of Gross Domestic Product) of 180 developing countries vs. the growth of 33 developed countries as grouped by the World Bank (www.ers.usda.gov/data/macroeconomics). Each point represents one of the years from 1970 to 2011. The output of a regression analysis follows.

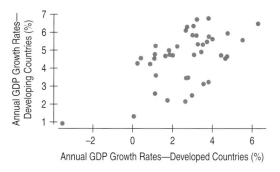

Dependent variable: GDP Growth Developing Countries
R² = 31.64%
s = 1.201

Variable	Coefficient
Intercept	3.38
GDP Growth Developed Countries	0.468

a) Check the assumptions and conditions for the linear model.
b) Explain the meaning of R^2 in this context.
c) What are the cases in this model?

46. European GDP growth 2012. Is economic growth in Europe related to growth in the United States? Here's a scatterplot of the average growth in 25 European countries (in % of Gross Domestic Product) vs. the growth in the United States. Each point represents one of the years from 1970 to 2011.

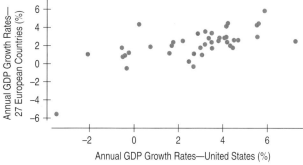

Dependent variable: European Countries GDP Growth
R² = 44.92%
s = 1.352

Variable	Coefficient
Intercept	0.693
U.S. GDP Growth	0.534

a) Check the assumptions and conditions for the linear model.
b) Explain the meaning of R^2 in this context.

47. GDP growth 2012, part 2. From the linear model fit to the data on GDP growth in Exercise 45:
a) Write the equation of the regression line.

b) What is the meaning of the intercept? Does it make sense in this context?
c) Interpret the meaning of the slope.
d) In a year in which the developed countries grow 4%, what do you predict for the developing world?
e) In 2007, the developed countries experienced a 2.65% growth, while the developing countries grew at a rate of 6.09%. Is this more or less than you would have predicted?
f) What is the residual for this year?

48. European GDP growth 2012, part 2. From the linear model fit to the data on GDP growth of Exercise 46:
a) Write the equation of the regression line.
b) What is the meaning of the intercept? Does it make sense in this context?
c) Interpret the meaning of the slope.
d) In a year in which the United States grows at 0%, what do you predict for European growth?
e) In 2010, the United States experienced a 3.00% growth, while Europe grew at a rate of 1.78%. Is this more or less than you would have predicted?
f) What is the residual for this year?

49. Attendance 2012. American League baseball games are played under the designated hitter rule, meaning that weak-hitting pitchers do not come to bat. Baseball owners believe that the designated hitter rule means more runs scored, which in turn means higher attendance. Is there evidence that more fans attend games if the teams score more runs? Data collected from Major League games from both major leagues during the 2012 season have a correlation of 0.477 between *Runs Scored* and the *Home Attendance* (espn.go.com/mlb/attendance).

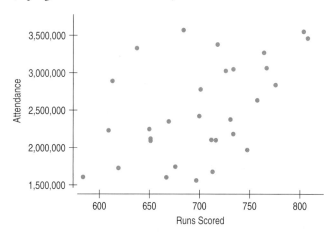

a) Does the scatterplot indicate that it's appropriate to calculate a correlation? Explain.
b) Describe the association between attendance and runs scored.
c) Does this association prove that the owners are right that more fans will come to games if the teams score more runs?

T 50. Attendance 2012, part 2. Perhaps fans are just more interested in teams that win. Here are displays of other variables in the dataset of exercise 49 (espn.go.com). Are the teams that win necessarily those that score the most runs?

	Correlation		
	Wins	**Runs**	**Attend**
Wins	1.000		
Runs	0.437	1.000	
Attend	0.133	0.477	1.000

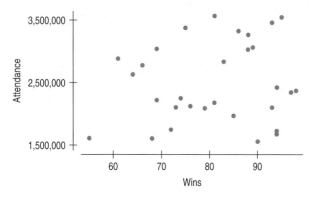

a) Do winning teams generally enjoy greater attendance at their home games? Describe the association.

b) Is attendance more strongly associated with winning or scoring runs? Explain.

c) How strongly is scoring more runs associated with winning more games?

T 51. Mutual fund flows. As the nature of investing shifted in the 1990s (more day traders and faster flow of information using technology), the relationship between mutual fund monthly performance (*Return*) in percent and money flowing (*Flow*) into mutual funds ($ million) shifted. Using only the values for the 1990s (we'll examine later years in later chapters), answer the following questions. (You may assume that the assumptions and conditions for regression are met.)

The least squares linear regression is:

$$\widehat{Flow} = 9747 + 771 \; Return.$$

a) Interpret the intercept in the linear model.

b) Interpret the slope in the linear model.

c) What is the predicted fund *Flow* for a month that had a market *Return* of 0%?

d) If during this month, the recorded fund *Flow* was $5 billion, what is the residual using this linear model? Did the model provide an underestimate or overestimate for this month?

52. Online clothing purchases. An online clothing retailer examined their transactional database to see if total yearly *Purchases* ($) were related to customers' *Incomes* ($). (You may assume that the assumptions and conditions for regression are met.)

The least squares linear regression is:

$$\widehat{Purchases} = -31.6 + 0.012 \; Income.$$

a) Interpret the intercept in the linear model.

b) Interpret the slope in the linear model.

c) If a customer has an *Income* of $20,000, what is his predicted total yearly *Purchases*?

d) This customer's yearly *Purchases* were actually $100. What is the residual using this linear model? Did the model provide an underestimate or overestimate for this customer?

53. Residual plots. Tell what each of the following residual plots indicates about the appropriateness of the linear model that was fit to the data.

54. Residual plots, again. Tell what each of the following residual plots indicates about the appropriateness of the linear model that was fit to the data.

T 55. Consumer spending. An analyst at a large credit card bank is looking at the relationship between customers' charges to the bank's card in two successive months. He selects 150 customers at random, regresses charges in *March* ($) on charges in *February* ($), and finds an R^2 of 79%. The intercept is $730.20, and the slope is 0.79. After verifying all the data with the company's CPA, he concludes that the model is a useful one for predicting one month's charges from the other. Examine the data on the CD and comment on his conclusions.

T 56. Insurance policies. An actuary at a mid-sized insurance company is examining the sales performance of the company's sales force. She has data on the average size of the policy ($) written in two consecutive years by 200 salespeople. She fits a linear model and finds the slope to be 3.00 and the R^2 is 99.92%. She concludes that the predictions for next year's policy size will be very accurate. Examine the data on the CD and comment on her conclusions.

57. What slope? If you create a regression model for predicting the sales ($ million) from money spent on advertising the prior month ($ thousand), is the slope most likely to be closer to 0.03, 300, or 3000? Explain.

58. What slope, part 2? If you create a regression model for estimating a student's business school GPA (on a scale of 1–5) based on his math SAT (on a scale of 200–800), is the slope most likely to be closer to 0.01, 1, or 10? Explain.

59. Misinterpretations. An advertising agent who created a regression model using amount spent on *Advertising* to predict annual *Sales* for a company made these two statements. Assuming the calculations were done correctly, explain what is wrong with each interpretation.

a) My R^2 of 93% shows that this linear model is appropriate.

b) If this company spends $1.5 million on advertising, then annual sales will be $10 million.

60. More misinterpretations. An economist investigated the association between a country's *Literacy Rate* and *Gross Domestic Product (GDP)* and used the association to draw the following conclusions. Explain why each statement is incorrect. (Assume that all the calculations were done properly.)

a) The *Literacy Rate* determines 64% of the *GDP* for a country.

b) The slope of the line shows that an increase of 5% in *Literacy Rate* will produce a $1 billion improvement in *GDP*.

61. Business admissions. An analyst at a business school's admissions office claims to have developed a valid linear model predicting success (measured by starting salary ($) at time of graduation) from a student's undergraduate performance (measured by GPA). Describe how you would check each of the four regression conditions in this context.

62. School rankings. A popular magazine annually publishes rankings of both U.S. business programs and international business programs. The latest issue claims to have developed a linear model predicting the school's ranking (with "1" being the highest ranked school) from its financial resources (as measured by size of the school's endowment). Describe how you would apply each of the four regression conditions in this context.

63. Used BMW prices 2013. A business student needs cash, so he decides to sell his car. The car is a valuable BMW 850CSi that was only made over the course of a few years in the 1990s. He would like to sell it on his own, rather than through a dealer so he'd like to predict the price he'll get for his car's model year.

a) Make a scatterplot for the data on used BMW 850SCi's provided.

b) Describe the association between year and price.

c) Do you think a linear model is appropriate?

d) Computer software says that $R^2 = 57.3\%$. What is the correlation between year and price?

e) Explain the meaning of R^2 in this context.

f) Why doesn't this model explain 100% of the variability in the price of a used BMW 850CSi?

64. Used BMW prices 2013, part 2. Use the advertised prices for BMW 850s given in Exercise 63 to create a linear model for the relationship between a car's *Model Year* and its *Price*.

a) Find the equation of the regression line.

b) Explain the meaning of the slope of the line.

c) Explain the meaning of the intercept of the line.

d) If you wanted to sell a 1997 BMW 850, what price seems appropriate?

e) You have a chance to buy one of two cars. They are about the same age and appear to be in equally good condition. Would you rather buy the one with a positive residual or the one with a negative residual? Explain.

65. Expensive cities. The *Worldwide Cost of Living Survey City Rankings* determine the cost of living in the most expensive cities in the world as an index. This index scales New York City as 100 and expresses the cost of living in other cities as a percentage of the New York cost. For example, in 2007, the cost of living index in Tokyo was 122.1, which means that it was 22% higher than New York. The scatterplot shows the index for 2013 plotted against the 2007 index for the 15 most expensive cities of 2007.

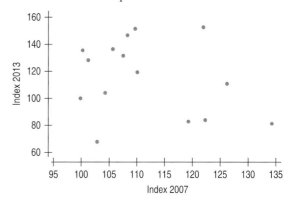

a) Describe the association between cost of living indices in 2007 and 2013.

b) The R^2 for the regression equation is 0.070. Interpret the value of R^2.

c) Find the correlation.

d) Using the data provided, find the least squares fit of the 2013 index to the 2007 index.

e) Predict the 2013 cost of living index of Moscow and find its residual.

66. Lobster prices 2012. The demand for lobster has grown steadily for several decades. The Maine lobster fishery is carefully controlled to protect the lobster population from over-fishing. The number of fishing licenses and the number of traps are both limited. During the years from 1974 to 2006, the price of lobster also grew, as shown in this plot.

a) Describe the increase in the *Price* of lobster during this period.

b) The R^2 for the regression equation is 87.42%. Interpret the value of R^2.

c) Find the correlation.

d) Find the linear model.

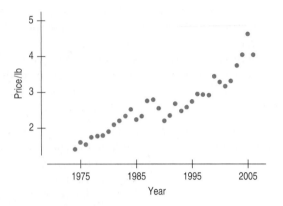

The years from 2007 to 2012 have seen a change in this pattern. Here is the scatterplot.

e) How would you suggest dealing with these new cases to model the change in prices?

67. El Niño. Concern over the weather associated with El Niño has increased interest in the possibility that the climate on Earth is getting warmer. The most common theory relates an increase in atmospheric levels of carbon dioxide (CO_2), a greenhouse gas, to increases in temperature. Here is a scatterplot showing the mean annual CO_2 concentration in the atmosphere, measured in parts per million (ppm) at the top of Mauna Loa in Hawaii, and the mean annual air temperature over both land and sea across the globe, in degrees Celsius (C).

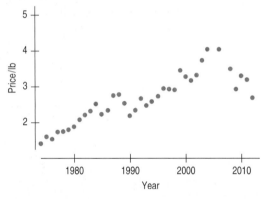

A regression predicting *Mean Temperature* from CO_2 produces the following output table (in part).

```
Dependent variable: Temperature
R-squared = 33.4%

Variable                Coefficient
Intercept                   15.3066
CO2                           0.004
```

a) What is the correlation between CO_2 and *Mean Temperature*?
b) Explain the meaning of R-squared in this context.
c) Give the regression equation.
d) What is the meaning of the slope in this equation?
e) What is the meaning of the intercept of this equation?
f) Here is a scatterplot of the residuals vs. CO_2. Does this plot show evidence of the violations of any of the assumptions of the regression model? If so, which ones?

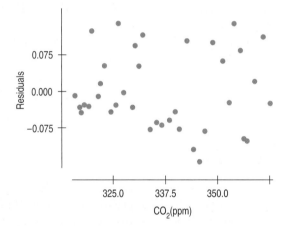

g) CO_2 levels may reach 364 *ppm* in the near future. What *Mean Temperature* does the model predict for that value?

T 68. U.S. birthrates. The table shows the number of live births per 1000 women aged 15–44 years in the United States, starting in 1965. (National Center for Health Statistics, www.cdc.gov/nchs/)

Year	1965	1970	1975	1980	1985
Rate	19.4	18.4	14.8	15.9	15.6

Year	1990	1995	2000	2005	2010
Rate	16.4	14.8	14.4	14.0	13.0

a) Make a scatterplot and describe the general trend in *Birthrates*. (Enter *Year* as years since 1900: 65, 70, 75, etc.)
b) Find the equation of the regression line.
c) Check to see if the line is an appropriate model. Explain.
d) Interpret the slope of the line.
e) The table gives rates only at 5-year intervals. Estimate what the rate was in 1978.
f) In 1978, the birthrate was actually 15.0. What was the residual?
g) Predict what the *Birthrate* will be in 2012. Comment on your faith in this prediction.
h) Predict the *Birthrate* for 2050. Comment on your faith in this prediction.

JUST CHECKING ANSWERS

1 We know the scores are quantitative. We should check to see if the *Linearity Condition* and the *Outlier Condition* are satisfied by looking at a scatterplot of the two scores.

2 It won't change.

3 It won't change.

4 They are more likely to do poorly. The positive correlation means that low closing prices for Intel are associated with low closing prices for Cypress.

5 No, the general association is positive, but daily closing prices may vary.

6 For each additional employee, monthly sales increase, on average, $122,740.

7 Thousands of $ per employee.

8 $1,227,400 per month.

9 Differences in the number of employees account for about 71.4% of the variation in the monthly sales.

10 It's positive. The correlation and the slope have the same sign.

11 R^2, No. Slope, Yes.

Case **Study**

Paralyzed Veterans of America

Philanthropic organizations often rely on contributions from individuals to finance the work that they do, and a national veterans' organization is no exception. The Paralyzed Veterans of America (PVA) was founded as a congressionally chartered veterans' service organization more than 60 years ago. It provides a range of services to veterans who have experienced spinal cord injury or dysfunction. Some of the services offered include medical care, research, education, and accessibility and legal consulting. In 2008, this organization had total revenue of more than $135 million, with more than 99% of this revenue coming from contributions.

An organization that depends so heavily on contributions needs a multifaceted fundraising program, and PVA solicits donations in a number of ways. From its website (www.pva.org), people can make a one-time donation, donate monthly, donate in honor or in memory of someone, and shop in the PVA online store. People can also support one of the charity events, such as its golf tournament, National Veterans Wheelchair Games, and Charity Ride.

Traditionally, one of PVA's main methods of soliciting funds was the use of return address labels and greeting cards (although still used, this method has declined in recent years). Typically, these gifts were sent to potential donors about every six weeks with a request for a contribution. From its established donors, PVA could expect a response rate of about 5%, which, given the relatively small cost to produce and send the gifts, kept the organization well funded.

But fundraising accounts for 28% of expenses, so PVA wanted to know who its donors are, what variables might be useful in predicting whether a donor is likely to give to an upcoming campaign, and what the size of that gift might be. On your CD is a dataset **Case Study 1**, which includes data designed to be very similar to part of the data that this organization works with. Here is a description of some of the variables. Keep in mind, however, that in the real dataset, there would be hundreds more variables given for each donor.

Variable Name	Units (if applicable)	Description	Remarks
Age	Years		
Own Home?	H = Yes; U = No or unknown		
Children	Counts		
Income		1 = Lowest ; 7 = Highest	Based on national medians and percentiles
Sex	M = Male; F = Female		
Total Wealth		1 = Lowest; 9 = Highest	Based on national medians and percentiles
Gifts to Other Orgs	Counts	Number of Gifts (if known) to other philanthropic organizations in the same time period	
Number of Gifts	Counts	Number of Gifts to this organization in this time period	
Time Between Gifts	Months	Time between first and second gifts	
Smallest Gift	$	Smallest Gift (in $) in the time period	See also Sqrt(Smallest Gift)
Largest Gift	$	Largest Gift (in $) in the time period	See also Sqrt(Largest Gift)

Variable Name	Units (if applicable)	Description	Remarks
Previous Gift	$	Gift (in $) for previous campaign	See also Sqrt(Previous Gift)
Average Gift	$	Total amount donated divided by total number of gifts	See also Sqrt(Average Gift)
Current Gift	$	Gift (in $) to organization this campaign	See also Sqrt(Current Gift)
Sqrt(Smallest Gift)	Sqrt($)	Square Root of Smallest Gift in $	
Sqrt(Largest Gift)	Sqrt($)	Square Root of Largest Gift in $	
Sqrt(Previous Gift)	Sqrt($)	Square Root of Previous Gift in $	
Sqrt(Average Gift)	Sqrt($)	Square Root of Average Gift in $	
Sqrt(Current Gift)	Sqrt($)	Square Root of Current Gift in $	

Let's see what the data can tell us. Are there any interesting relationships between the current gift and other variables? Is it possible to use the data to predict who is going to respond to the next direct-mail campaign?

Recall that when variables are highly skewed or the relationship between variables is not linear, reporting a correlation coefficient is not appropriate. You may want to consider a transformed version of those variables (square roots are provided for all the variables concerning gifts) or a correlation based on the ranks of the values rather than the values themselves.

Suggested Study Plan and Questions

Write a report of what you discover about the donors to this organization. Be sure to follow the Plan, Do, Report outline for your report. Include a basic description of each variable (shape, center, and spread), point out any interesting features, and explore the relationships between the variables. In particular you should describe any interesting relationships between the current gift and other variables. Use these questions as a guide:

- Is the age distribution of the clients a typical one found in most businesses?
- Do people who give more often make smaller gifts on average?
- Do people who give to other organizations tend to give to this organization?

Describe the relationship between the Income and Wealth rankings. How do you explain this relationship (or lack of one)? (*Hint*: Look at the age distribution.)

What variables (if any) seem to have an association with the Current Gift? Do you think the organization can use any of these variables to predict the gift for the next campaign?

Optional: This file includes people who did not give to the current campaign. Do your answers to any of the questions above change if you consider only those who gave to this campaign?

5

Randomness and Probability

Credit Reports and the Fair Isaacs Corporation

You've probably never heard of the Fair Isaacs Corporation, but they probably know you. Whenever you apply for a loan, a credit card, or even a job, your credit "score" will be used to determine whether you are a good risk. And because the most widely used credit scores are Fair Isaacs' FICO® scores, the company may well be involved in the decision. The Fair Isaacs Corporation (FICO) was founded in 1956, with the idea that data, used intelligently, could improve business decision making. Today, Fair Isaacs claims that their services provide companies around the world with information for more than 180 billion business decisions a year.

Your credit score is a number between 350 and 850 that summarizes your credit "worthiness." It's a snapshot of credit risk today based on your credit history and past behavior. Lenders of all kinds use credit scores to predict behavior, such as how likely you are to make your loan payments on time or to default on a loan. Lenders use the score to determine not only whether to give credit, but also the cost of the credit that they'll offer. There are no established boundaries, but generally scores over 750 are considered excellent, and applicants with those scores get the best rates. An applicant with a score below 620 is generally considered to be a poor risk. Those with very low scores may be denied credit outright or only offered "subprime" loans at substantially higher rates.

It's important that you be able to verify the information that your score is based on, but until recently, you could only hope that your score was based on correct information. That changed in 2000, when a California law gave mortgage applicants the right to see their credit scores. Today, the credit industry is more open about giving consumers

147

access to their scores and the U.S. government, through the Fair and Accurate Credit Transaction Act (FACTA), now guarantees that you can access your credit report at no cost, at least once a year.[1]

Companies have to manage risk to survive, but by its nature, risk carries uncertainty. A bank can't know for certain that you'll pay your mortgage on time—or at all. What can they do with events they can't predict? They start with the fact that, although individual outcomes cannot be anticipated with certainty, random phenomena do, in the long run, settle into patterns that are consistent and predictable. It's this property of random events that makes Statistics practical.

5.1   Random Phenomena and Probability

When a customer calls the 800 number of a credit card company, he or she is asked for a card number before being connected with an operator. As the connection is made, the purchase records of that card and the demographic information of the customer are retrieved and displayed on the operator's screen. If the customer's FICO score is high enough, the operator may be prompted to "cross-sell" another service—perhaps a new "platinum" card for customers with a credit score of at least 750.

Of course, the company doesn't know which customers are going to call. Call arrivals are an example of a random phenomenon. With **random phenomena,** we can't predict the individual outcomes, but we can hope to understand characteristics of their long-run behavior. We don't know whether the *next* caller will qualify for the platinum card, but as calls come into the call center, the company will find that the percentage of platinum callers who qualify for cross-selling will settle into a pattern, like that shown in the graph in Figure 5.1.

Part of a call center operator's earnings might be based on the number of platinum cards she sells. To figure out what her potential bonus might be, an operator might first want to know what percentage of all callers qualifies. She decides to write down whether the caller from each call she gets today qualifies or not. The first caller today qualified. Then the next five callers' qualifications were no, yes, yes, no, and no. If we plot the percentage who qualify against the number of calls she's made so far the graph would start at 100% because the first caller qualified (1 out of 1, for 100%). The next caller didn't qualify, so the accumulated percentage dropped to 50% (1 out of 2). The third caller qualified (2 out of 3, or 67%), then yes again (3 out of 4, or 75%), then no twice in a row (3 out of 5, for 60%, and then 3 out of 6, for 50%), and so on (Table 5.1). Each new call is a smaller fraction of the total number, so the percentages change less after each call. After a while, the graph starts to settle down and we can see that the fraction of customers who qualify is about 35% (Figure 5.1).

When talking about long-run behavior, it helps to define our terms. For any random phenomenon, each attempt, or **trial**, generates an **outcome.** For the call center, each call is a trial. Something happens on each trial, and we call whatever happens the outcome. Here the outcome is whether the caller qualifies or not. We use the more general term **event** to refer to outcomes or combinations of outcomes. For example, suppose we categorize callers into 6 risk categories and number these outcomes from 1 to 6 (of increasing credit worthiness). The three outcomes 4, 5, or 6 could make up the event "caller is at least a category 4."

We sometimes talk about the collection of *all possible outcomes*, a special event that we'll refer to as the **sample space.** We denote the sample space **S**; you may also

> A **random phenomenon** consists of **trials**. Each trial has an **outcome**. Outcomes combine to make **events**.

---

[1]However, the score you see in your report will be an "educational" score intended to show consumers how scoring works. You still have to pay a "reasonable fee" to see your FICO score.

Figure 5.1 The percentage of credit card customers who qualify for the premium card.

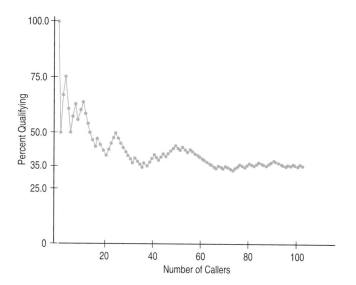

Table 5.1 Data on the first six callers showing their FICO score, whether they qualified for the platinum card offer, and a running percentage of number of callers who qualified.

Call	FICO Score	Qualify?	Running % Qualify
1	750	Yes	100
2	640	No	50
3	765	Yes	66.7
4	780	Yes	75
5	680	No	60
6	630	No	50
⋮	⋮		⋮

> **Probability as Long-Run Frequency**
>
> The **probability** of an event is its long-run relative frequency. A relative frequency is a fraction, so we can write it as $\frac{35}{100}$, as a decimal, 0.35, or as a percentage, 35%.

see the Greek letter Ω used. But whatever symbol we use, the sample space is the set that contains all the possible outcomes. For the calls, if we let Q = qualified and N = not qualified, the sample space is simple: $\mathbf{S} = \{Q, N\}$. If we look at two calls together, the sample space has four outcomes: $\mathbf{S} = \{QQ, QN, NQ, NN\}$. If we were interested in at least one qualified caller from the two calls, we would be interested in the event (call it $\mathbf{A}$) consisting of the three outcomes QQ, QN, and NQ, and we'd write $\mathbf{A} = \{QQ, QN, NQ\}$.

Although we may not be able to predict a *particular* individual outcome, such as which incoming call represents a potential upgrade sale, we can say a lot about the long-run behavior. Look back at Figure 5.1. If you were asked for the probability that a random caller will qualify, you might say that it was 35% because, in the *long run*, the percentage of the callers who qualify is about 35%. That's exactly what we mean by **probability**.

When we think about what happens with a series of trials, it really simplifies things if the individual trials are independent. Roughly speaking, **independence** means that the outcome of one trial doesn't influence or change the outcome of another. Recall, that in Chapter 2, we called two variables *independent* if the value of one categorical variable did not influence the value of another categorical variable.

(We checked for independence by comparing relative frequency distributions across variables.) There's no reason to think that whether the one caller qualifies influences whether another caller qualifies, so these are independent trials. We'll see a more formal definition of independence later in the chapter.

You might think that we just got lucky when the percentage of the qualifying calls settled down to a number. But for independent events, we can depend on a principle called the **Law of Large Numbers (LLN)**, which states that if the events are independent, then as the number of trials increases, the long-run relative frequency of any outcome gets closer and closer to a single value. This gives us the guarantee we need and makes probability a useful concept.

Because the LLN guarantees that relative frequencies settle down in the long run, we can give a name to the value that they approach. We call it the probability of that event. For the call center, we can write $P(\text{qualified}) = 0.35$. Because it is based on repeatedly observing the event's outcome, this definition of probability is often called **empirical probability**.

> **Law of Large Numbers (LLN)**
>
> The *long-run relative frequency* of repeated, independent events eventually produces the *true relative frequency* as the number of trials increases.

5.2   The Nonexistent Law of Averages

The Law of Large Numbers is often misunderstood to be a "law of averages." Many people believe, for example, that an outcome of a random event that hasn't occurred in many trials is "due" to occur. The original "dogs of the Dow" strategy for buying stocks recommended buying the 10 worst performing stocks of the 30 that make up the Dow Jones Industrial Average, figuring that these "dogs" were bound to do better next year. The thinking was that, since the relative frequency will settle down to the probability of that outcome in the long run, we'll have some "catching up" to do. That may seem logical, but random events don't work that way. In fact, Louis Rukeyser (the former host of *Wall Street Week*) said of the "dogs of the Dow" strategy, "that theory didn't work as promised."

Here's why. We actually know very little about the behavior of random events in the short run. The fact that we are seeing independent random events makes each individual result impossible to predict. Relative frequencies even out *only* in the long run. And the long run referred to in the LLN is really long. The "Large" in the law's name means *infinitely* large. Sequences of random events don't compensate in the short run and don't need to do so to get back to the right long-run probability. Any short-run deviations will be overwhelmed in the long run. If the probability of an outcome doesn't change and the events are independent, the probability of any outcome in another trial never changes, no matter what has happened in other trials.

Many people confuse the Law of Large numbers with the so-called Law of Averages, which says that things have to even out in the short run. But even though the Law of Averages doesn't exist at all, you'll hear people talk about it as if it does. Is a good hitter in baseball who has struck out the last six times *due* for a hit his next time up? If the stock market has been down for the last three sessions, is it *due* to increase today? No. This isn't the way random phenomena work. There is no Law of Averages for short runs—no "Law of Small Numbers." A belief in such a "law" can lead to poor business decisions.

"Slump? I ain't in no slump. I just ain't hittin'."

—Yogi Berra

You may think it's obvious that the frequency of repeated events settles down in the long run to a single number. The discoverer of the Law of Large Numbers thought so, too. The way Jacob Bernoulli put it was: *"For even the most stupid of men is convinced that the more observations have been made, the less danger there is of wandering from one's goal."*

> **Keno and the Law of Averages**
>
> Of course, sometimes an apparent drift from what we expect means that the probabilities are, in fact, *not* what we thought. If you get 10 heads in a row, maybe the coin has heads on both sides! Here's a true story that illustrates this.
>
> Keno is a simple casino game in which numbers from 1 to 80 are chosen. The numbers, as in most lottery games, are supposed to be equally likely. Payoffs are made

depending on how many of those numbers you match on your card. A group of graduate students from a Statistics department decided to take a field trip to Reno. They (*very* discreetly) wrote down the outcomes of the games for a couple of days, then drove back to test whether the numbers were, in fact, equally likely. It turned out that some numbers were *more likely* to come up than others. Rather than bet on the Law of Averages and put their money on the numbers that were "due," the students put their faith in the LLN— and all their (and their friends') money on the numbers that had come up before. After they pocketed more than $50,000, they were escorted off the premises and invited never to show their faces in that casino again. Not coincidentally, the ringleader of that group currently makes his living on Wall Street.

"In addition, in time, if the roulette-betting fool keeps playing the game, the bad histories [outcomes] will tend to catch up with him."

—NASSIM NICHOLAS TALEB IN
FOOLED BY RANDOMNESS

The Law of Averages Debunked

You've just flipped a fair coin and seen six heads in a row. Does the coin "owe" you some tails? Suppose you spend that coin and your friend gets it in change. When she starts flipping the coin, should she expect a run of tails? Of course not. Each flip is a new event. The coin can't "remember" what it did in the past, so it can't "owe" any particular outcomes in the future. Just to see how this works in practice, we simulated 100,000 flips of a fair coin on a computer. In our 100,000 "flips," there were 2981 streaks of at least 5 heads. The "Law of Averages" suggests that the next flip after a run of 5 heads should be tails more often to even things out. Actually, in this particular simulation the next flip was heads more often than tails: 1550 times to 1431 times. That's 51.9% heads. You can perform a similar simulation easily.

JUST CHECKING

1 It has been shown that the stock market fluctuates randomly. Nevertheless, some investors believe that they should buy right after a day when the market goes down because it is bound to go up soon. Explain why this is faulty reasoning.

5.3   Different Types of Probability

Model-Based (Theoretical) Probability

Model-based Probability

We can write:

$$P(\mathbf{A}) = \frac{\# \text{ of outcomes in } \mathbf{A}}{\text{total } \# \text{ of outcomes}}$$

and call this the **(theoretical) probability** of the event.

We've discussed *empirical probability*—the relative frequency of an event's occurrence as the probability of an event. There are other ways to define probability as well. Probability was first studied extensively by a group of French mathematicians who were interested in games of chance. Rather than experiment with the games and risk losing their money, they developed mathematical models of probability. To make things simple (as we usually do when we build models), they started by looking at games in which the different outcomes were equally likely. Fortunately, many games of chance are like that. Any of 52 cards is equally likely to be the next one dealt from a well-shuffled deck. Each face of a die is equally likely to land up (or at least it should be).

When we have equally likely outcomes, we write the **(theoretical) probability** of an event $\mathbf{A}$, as $P(\mathbf{A}) = \#$ of outcomes in $\mathbf{A}$/total # of outcomes possible. When outcomes are equally likely, the probability that one of them occurs is easy to compute—it's just 1 divided by the number of possible outcomes. So the probability of rolling a 3 with a fair die is one in six, which we write as 1/6. The probability of picking the ace of spades from a well-shuffled deck is 1/52.

It's almost as simple to find probabilities for events that are made up of several equally likely outcomes. We just count all the outcomes that the event contains. The probability of the event is the number of outcomes in the event divided by the total number of possible outcomes.

For example, Pew Research[2] reports that of 10,190 randomly generated working phone numbers called for a survey, the initial results of the calls were as follows:

Result	Number of Calls
No Answer	311
Busy	61
Answering Machine	1336
Callbacks	189
Other Non-Contacts	893
Contacted Numbers	7400

The phone numbers were generated randomly, so each was equally likely. To find the probability of a contact, we just divide the number of contacts by the number of calls: $7400/10,190 = 0.7262$.

But don't get trapped into thinking that random events are always equally likely. The chance of winning a lottery—especially lotteries with very large payoffs—is small. Regardless, people continue to buy tickets.

Personal Probability

What's the probability that gold will sell for more than $2000 an ounce at the end of next year? You may be able to come up with a number that seems reasonable. Of course, no matter what your guess is, your probability should be between 0 and 1. In our discussion of probability, we've defined probability in two ways: 1) in terms of the relative frequency—or the fraction of times—that an event occurs in the long run or 2) as the number of outcomes in the event divided by the total number of outcomes. Neither situation applies to your assessment of gold's chances of selling for more than $2000.

We use the *language* of probability in everyday speech to express a degree of uncertainty without necessarily basing it on long-run relative frequencies. Your personal assessment of an event expresses your uncertainty about the outcome. We call this kind of probability a subjective, or **personal probability**.

Although personal probabilities may be based on experience, they are typically not based on long-run relative frequencies or on equally likely events. But, like the two other probabilities we defined, they need to satisfy the same rules as both empirical and theoretical probabilities that we'll discuss in the next section.

> **Equally Likely?**
>
> In an attempt to understand why someone would buy a lottery ticket, an interviewer asked someone who had just purchased one "What do you think your chances are of winning the lottery?" The reply was, "Oh, about 50–50." The shocked interviewer asked, "How do you get that?" to which the response was, "Well, the way I figure it, either I win or I don't!" The moral of this story is that events are not always equally likely.

---

[2] www.pewinternet.org/pdfs/PIP_Digital_Footprints.pdf.

Probability Rules

NOTATION ALERT

We often represent events with capital letters (such as **A** and **B**), so *P*(**A**) means "the probability of event **A**."

"Baseball is 90% mental. The other half is physical."

—YOGI BERRA

For some people, the phrase "50/50" means something vague like "I don't know" or "whatever." But when we discuss probabilities, 50/50 has the precise meaning that two outcomes are *equally likely*. Speaking vaguely about probabilities can get you into trouble, so it's wise to develop some formal rules about how probability works. These rules apply to probability whether we're dealing with empirical, theoretical, or personal probability.

Rule 1. If the probability of an event occurring is 0, the event won't occur; likewise if the probability is 1, the event will *always* occur. Even if you think an event is very unlikely, its probability can't be negative, and even if you're sure it will happen, its probability can't be greater than 1. So we require that:

A probability is a number between 0 and 1.

For any event A, $0 \leq P(A) \leq 1$.

Rule 2. If a random phenomenon has only one possible outcome, it's not very interesting (or very random). So we need to distribute the probabilities among all the outcomes a trial can have. How can we do that so that it makes sense? For example, consider the behavior of a certain stock. The possible daily outcomes might be:

A: The stock price goes up.
B: The stock price goes down.
C: The stock price remains the same.

When we assign probabilities to these outcomes, we should be sure to distribute all of the available probability. Something always occurs, so the probability of *something* happening is 1. This is called the **Probability Assignment Rule**:

The probability of the set of all possible outcomes must be 1.

$$P(S) = 1$$

where **S** is the sample space.

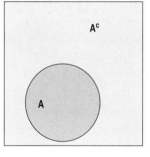

The set **A** and its complement **A**^{C}. Together, they make up the entire sample space **S**.

Rule 3. Suppose the probability that you get to class on time is 0.8. What's the probability that you don't get to class on time? Yes, it's 0.2. The set of outcomes that are *not* in the event **A** is called the "complement" of **A** and is denoted **A**^{C}. This leads to the **Complement Rule**:

The probability of an event occurring is 1 minus the probability that it doesn't occur.

$$P(A) = 1 - P(A^C)$$

FOR EXAMPLE **Applying the Complement Rule**

Lee's Lights sells lighting fixtures. Some customers are there only to browse, so Lee records the behavior of all customers for a week to assess how likely it is that a customer will make a purchase. Lee finds that of 1000 customers entering the store during the week, 300 make purchases. Lee concludes that the probability of a customer making a purchase is 0.30.

QUESTION   If *P*(purchase) = 0.30, what is the probability that a customer *doesn't* make a purchase?

ANSWER   Because "no purchase" is the complement of "purchase,"

$$P(\text{no purchase}) = 1 - P(\text{purchase})$$
$$= 1 - 0.30 = 0.70$$

There is a 70% chance a customer won't make a purchase.

Rule 4. Whether or not a caller qualifies for a platinum card is a random outcome. Suppose the probability of qualifying is 0.35. What's the chance that the next two callers qualify? The **Multiplication Rule** says that to find the probability that two independent events occur, we multiply the probabilities. For two independent events **A** and **B**, the probability that both **A** and **B** occur is the product of the probabilities of the two events:

$$P(A \text{ and } B) = P(A) \times P(B), \text{ provided that A and B are independent.}$$

Thus if **A** = {customer 1 qualifies} and **B** = {customer 2 qualifies}, the chance that both qualify is:

$$0.35 \times 0.35 = 0.1225$$

Of course, to calculate this probability, we have used the assumption that the two events are independent. We'll expand the multiplication rule to be more general later in this chapter.

FOR EXAMPLE   Using the Multiplication Rule

Lee knows that the probability that a customer will make a purchase is 30%.

 QUESTION   If we can assume that customers behave independently, what is the probability that the next two customers entering Lee's Lights both make purchases?

 ANSWER   Because the events are independent, we can use the multiplication rule.

$P(\text{first customer makes a purchase } and \text{ second customer makes a purchase})$

$$= P(\text{purchase}) \times P(\text{purchase})$$

$$= 0.30 \times 0.30 = 0.09$$

There's about a 9% chance that the next two customers will both make purchases.

Rule 5. Suppose the card center operator has more options. She can **A**: offer a special travel deal, **B**: offer a platinum card, or **C**: decide to send information about a new affinity card. If she can do one, but only one, of these, then these outcomes are **disjoint** (or **mutually exclusive**). To see whether two events are disjoint, we separate them into their component outcomes and check whether they have any outcomes in common. For example, if the operator can choose to both offer the travel deal and send the affinity card information, those events would not be disjoint. The **Addition Rule** allows us to add the probabilities of disjoint events to get the probability that *either* event occurs:

$$P(A \text{ or } B) = P(A) + P(B), \text{ provided that A and B are disjoint.}$$

Thus the probability that the caller *either* is offered a platinum card *or* is sent the affinity card information is the sum of the two probabilities, since the events are disjoint.

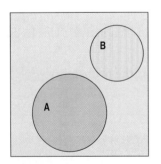

Two disjoint sets, **A** and **B**.

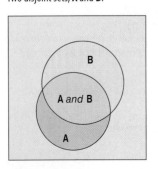

Two sets **A** and **B** that are not disjoint.
The event (**A** and **B**) is their intersection.

FOR EXAMPLE   Using the Addition Rule

Some customers prefer to see the merchandise but then make their purchase later using Lee's Lights' website. Lee offers a promotion to attempt to track customer behavior. Customers leaving the store without making a purchase are offered a "bonus code" to use at the Internet site. Using these codes, Lee determines that there's a 9% chance of a customer making a purchase using the code later. We know that about 30% of customers make purchases when they enter the store.

QUESTION   What is the probability that a customer who enters the store will not make a purchase at all?

ANSWER   We can use the Addition Rule because the alternatives "no purchase at all," "purchase in the store," and "purchase online" are disjoint events.

$$P(\text{purchase in the store } or \text{ online}) = P(\text{purchase in store}) + P(\text{purchase online})$$
$$= 0.30 + 0.09 = 0.39$$

$$P(\text{no purchase at all}) = P(\text{not (purchase in the store } or \text{ purchase online)})$$
$$= 1 - P(\text{in store } or \text{ online})$$
$$= 1 - 0.39 = 0.61$$

NOTATION ALERT

You may see the event (**A** or **B**) written as (**A** $\cup$ **B**). The symbol $\cup$ means "union" and represents the outcomes in event **A** or event **B**. Similarly the symbol $\cap$ means intersection and represents outcomes that are in *both* event **A** and event **B**. You may see the event (**A** and **B**) written as (**A** $\cap$ **B**).

Rule 6. Suppose we would like to know the probability that either of the next two callers qualifies for a platinum card? We know $P(\mathbf{A}) = P(\mathbf{B}) = 0.35$, but $P(\mathbf{A} \text{ or } \mathbf{B})$ is not simply the sum $P(\mathbf{A}) + P(\mathbf{B})$ because the events **A** and **B** are not disjoint in this case. Both customers could qualify. So we need a new probability rule.

We can't simply add the probabilities of **A** and **B** because that would count the outcome of *both* customers qualifying twice. So, if we started by adding the two probabilities, we could compensate by subtracting out the probability that both qualify. In other words,

$P(\text{customer A } or \text{ customer B qualifies}) =$

$P(\text{customer A qualifies}) + P(\text{customer B qualifies}) - P(\text{both customers qualify})$

$= (0.35) + (0.35) - (0.35 \times 0.35) \text{ (since events are independent)}$

$= (0.35) + (0.35) - (0.1225)$

$= 0.5775$

It turns out that this method works in general. We add the probabilities of two events and then subtract out the probability of their intersection. This gives us the **General Addition Rule**, which does not require disjoint events:

$$P(\mathbf{A} \text{ or } \mathbf{B}) = P(\mathbf{A}) + P(\mathbf{B}) - P(\mathbf{A} \text{ and } \mathbf{B}) \text{ for any two events A and B.}$$

FOR EXAMPLE   Using the General Addition Rule

Lee notices that when two customers enter the store together, their purchases are not disjoint. In fact, there's a 20% chance they'll *both* make a purchase.

QUESTION   When two customers enter the store together, what is the probability that *at least one* of them makes a purchase?

ANSWER   Now we know that the events are not disjoint, so we must use the General Addition Rule.

$$P(\text{at least one purchases}) = P(\text{A purchases } or \text{ B purchases})$$
$$= P(\text{A purchases}) + P(\text{B purchases})$$
$$- P(\text{A and B both purchase})$$
$$= 0.30 + 0.30 - 0.20 = 0.40$$

JUST CHECKING

2 Even successful companies sometimes make products with high failure rates. One (in)famous example is the Apple 40GB click wheel iPod, which used a tiny disk drive for storage. According to Macintouch.com, 30% of those devices eventually failed. It is reasonable to assume that the failures were independent. What would a store that sold these devices have seen?

a) What is the probability that a particular 40GB click wheel iPod failed?

b) What is the probability that two 40GB click wheel iPods sold together *both* failed?

c) What is the probability that the store's first failure problem was the third one they sold?

d) What is the probability the store had a failure problem with at least one of the five that they sold on a particular day?

GUIDED EXAMPLE   **M&M's Modern Market Research**

In 1941, when M&M's® milk chocolate candies were introduced to American GIs in World War II, there were six colors: brown, yellow, orange, red, green, and violet. Mars®, the company that manufactures M&M's, has used the introduction of a new color as a marketing and advertising event several times in the years since then. In 1980, the candy went international adding 16 countries to their markets. In 1995, the company conducted a "worldwide survey" to vote on a new color. Over 10 million people voted to add blue. They even got the lights of the Empire State Building in New York City to glow blue to help announce the addition. In 2002, they used the Internet to help pick a new color. Children from over 200 countries were invited to respond via the Internet, telephone, or mail. Millions of voters chose among purple, pink, and teal. The global winner was purple, and for a brief time, purple M&M's could be found in packages worldwide (although in 2013, the colors were brown, yellow, red, blue, orange, and green). In the United States, 42% of those who voted said purple, 37% said teal, and only 19% said pink. But in Japan the percentages were 38% pink, 36% teal, and only 16% purple. Let's use Japan's percentages to ask some questions.

1. What's the probability that a Japanese M&M's survey respondent selected at random preferred either pink or teal?
2. If we pick two respondents at random, what's the probability that they *both* selected purple?
3. If we pick three respondents at random, what's the probability that *at least one* preferred purple?

PLAN   **Setup** The probability of an event is its long-term relative frequency. This can be determined in several ways: by looking at many replications of an event, by deducing it from equally likely events, or by using some other information. Here, we are told the relative frequencies of the three responses.

The M&M's website reports the proportions of Japanese votes by color. These give the probability of selecting a voter who preferred each of the colors:

$$P(pink) = 0.38$$
$$P(teal) = 0.36$$
$$P(purple) = 0.16$$

Make sure the probabilities are legitimate. Here, they're not. Either there was a mistake or the other voters must have chosen a color other than the three given. A check of other countries shows a similar deficit, so probably we're seeing those who had no preference or who wrote in another color.

Each is between 0 and 1, but these don't add up to 1. The remaining 10% of the voters must have not expressed a preference or written in another color. We'll put them together into "other" and add $P(\text{other}) = 0.10$.

With this addition, we have a legitimate assignment of probabilities.

Question 1: What's the probability that a Japanese M&M's survey respondent selected at random preferred either pink or teal?

PLAN | **Setup** Decide which rules to use and check the conditions they require. | The events "pink" and "teal" are individual outcomes (a respondent can't choose both colors), so they are disjoint. We can apply the General Addition Rule anyway.

DO | **Mechanics** Show your work. |

$$P(\text{pink or teal}) = P(\text{pink}) + P(\text{teal})$$
$$- P(\text{pink and teal})$$
$$= 0.38 + 0.36 - 0 = 0.74$$

The probability that both pink and teal were chosen is zero, since respondents were limited to one choice.

REPORT | **Conclusion** Interpret your results in the proper context. | The probability that the respondent said pink or teal is 0.74.

Question 2: If we pick two respondents at random, what's the probability that they both said purple?

PLAN | **Setup** The word "both" suggests we want $P(\mathbf{A} \text{ and } \mathbf{B})$, which calls for the Multiplication Rule. Check the required condition. | **Independence**

It's unlikely that the choice made by one respondent affected the choice of the other, so the events seem to be independent. We can use the Multiplication Rule.

DO | **Mechanics** Show your work.

For both respondents to pick purple, each one has to pick purple. |

$P(\text{both purple})$
$= P(\text{first respondent picks purple and}$
$\quad \text{second respondent picks purple})$
$= P(\text{first respondent picks purple})$
$\quad \times P(\text{second respondent picks purple})$
$= 0.16 \times 0.16 = 0.0256$

REPORT | **Conclusion** Interpret your results in the proper context. | The probability that both respondents pick purple is 0.0256.

(continued)

Question 3: If we pick three respondents at random, what's the probability that at least one preferred purple?

PLAN	**Setup** The phrase "at least one" often flags a question best answered by looking at the complement, and that's the best approach here. The complement of "at least one preferred purple" is "none of them preferred purple."	$P(\text{at least one picked purple})$ $= P(\{\text{none picked purple}\}^c)$ $= 1 - P(\text{none picked purple}).$
	Check the conditions.	**Independence.** These are independent events because they are choices by three random respondents. We can use the Multiplication Rule.
DO	**Mechanics** We calculate $P(\text{none purple})$ by using the Multiplication Rule.	$P(\text{none picked purple}) = P(\text{first not purple})$ $\hspace{3cm} \times P(\text{second not purple})$ $\hspace{3cm} \times P(\text{third not purple})$ $\hspace{3cm} = [P(\text{not purple})]^3.$ $P(\text{not purple}) = 1 - P(\text{purple})$ $\hspace{2cm} = 1 - 0.16 = 0.84.$
	Then we can use the Complement Rule to get the probability we want.	So $P(\text{none picked purple}) = (0.84)^3 = 0.5927.$ $P(\text{at least 1 picked purple})$ $= 1 - P(\text{none picked purple})$ $= 1 - 0.5927 = 0.4073.$
REPORT	**Conclusion** Interpret your results in the proper context.	There's about a 40.7% chance that at least one of the respondents picked purple.

5.5   Joint Probability and Contingency Tables

As part of a Pick Your Prize Promotion, a chain store invited customers to choose which of three prizes they'd like to win (while providing name, address, phone number, and e-mail address). At one store, the responses could be placed in the contingency table in Table 5.2.

		Prize preference			
		MP3	**Camera**	**Bike**	**Total**
Sex	**Man**	117	50	60	**227**
	Woman	130	91	30	**251**
	Total	**247**	**141**	**90**	**478**

Table 5.2   Prize preference for 478 customers.

If the winner is chosen at random from these customers, the probability we select a woman is just the corresponding relative frequency (since we're equally likely to select any of the 478 customers). There are 251 women in the data out of a total of 478, giving a probability of:

$$P(\text{woman}) = 251/478 = 0.525$$

This is called a **marginal probability** because it depends only on totals found in the margins of the table. The same method works for more complicated events. For example, what's the probability of selecting a woman whose preferred prize is the camera? Well, 91 women named the camera as their preference, so the probability is:

$$P(\text{woman } and \text{ camera}) = 91/478 = 0.190$$

Probabilities such as these are called **joint probabilities** because they give the probability of two events occurring together.

The probability of selecting a customer whose preferred prize is a bike is:

$$P(\text{bike}) = 90/478 = 0.188$$

> A **marginal probability** uses a marginal frequency (from either the Total row or Total column) to compute the probability.

FOR EXAMPLE Marginal probabilities

Lee suspects that men and women make different kinds of purchases at Lee's Lights (see the example on page 153). The table shows the purchases made by the last 100 customers.

	Utility Lighting	Fashion Lighting	Total
Men	40	20	**60**
Women	10	30	**40**
Total	**50**	**50**	**100**

QUESTION   What's the probability that one of Lee's customers is a woman? What is the probability that a random customer is a man who purchases fashion lighting?

ANSWER   From the marginal totals we can see that 40% of Lee's customers are women, so the probability that a customer is a woman is 0.40. The cell of the table for Men who purchase Fashion lighting has 20 of the 100 customers, so the probability of that event is 0.20.

5.6 Conditional Probability

Since our sample space is these 478 customers, we can recognize the relative frequencies as probabilities. What if we are given the information that the selected customer is a woman? Would that change the probability that the selected customer's preferred prize is a bike? You bet it would! The pie charts in Figure 5.2 on the next page show that women are much less likely to say their preferred prize is a bike than are men. When we restrict our focus to women, we look only at the women's row of the table, which gives the conditional distribution of preferred prizes given "woman." Of the 251 women, only 30 of them said their preferred prize was a bike. We write the probability that a selected customer wants a bike *given* that we have selected a woman as:

$$P(\text{bike}|\text{woman}) = 30/251 = 0.120$$

Figure 5.2   Conditional distributions of *Prize Preference* for *Women* and for *Men*.

NOTATION ALERT

$P(\mathbf{B}|\mathbf{A})$ is the conditional probability of $\mathbf{B}$ *given* $\mathbf{A}$.

For men, we look at the conditional distribution of preferred prizes given "man" shown in the top row of the table. There, of the 227 men, 60 said their preferred prize was a bike. So, $P(\text{bike}|\text{man}) = 60/227 = 0.264$, more than twice the women's probability (see Figure 5.2).

In general, when we want the probability of an event from a *conditional* distribution, we write $P(\mathbf{B}|\mathbf{A})$ and pronounce it "the probability of $\mathbf{B}$ *given* $\mathbf{A}$." A probability that takes into account a given *condition* such as this is called a **conditional probability**.

Let's look at what we did. We worked with the counts, but we could work with the probabilities just as well. There were 30 women who selected a bike as a prize, and there were 251 women customers. So we found the probability to be 30/251. To find the probability of the event $\mathbf{B}$ *given* the event $\mathbf{A}$, we restrict our attention to the outcomes in $\mathbf{A}$. We then find in what fraction of *those* outcomes $\mathbf{B}$ also occurred. Formally, we write:

$$P(\mathbf{B}|\mathbf{A}) = \frac{P(\mathbf{A} \text{ and } \mathbf{B})}{P(\mathbf{A})}$$

We can use the formula directly with the probabilities derived from the contingency table (Table 5.2) to find:

$$P(\text{bike}|\text{woman}) = \frac{P(\text{bike } and \text{ woman})}{P(\text{woman})} = \frac{30/478}{251/478} = \frac{30}{251} = 0.120 \text{ as before.}$$

The formula for conditional probability requires one restriction. The formula works only when the event that's given has probability greater than 0. The formula doesn't work if $P(\mathbf{A})$ is 0 because that would mean we had been "given" the fact that $\mathbf{A}$ was true even though the probability of $\mathbf{A}$ is 0, which would be a contradiction.

Rule 7. Remember the Multiplication Rule for the probability of $\mathbf{A}$ *and* $\mathbf{B}$? It said

$$P(\mathbf{A} \text{ and } \mathbf{B}) = P(\mathbf{A}) \times P(\mathbf{B})$$

when $\mathbf{A}$ and $\mathbf{B}$ are independent. Now we can write a more general rule that doesn't require independence. In fact, we've already written it. We just need to rearrange the equation a bit.

The equation in the definition for conditional probability contains the probability of $\mathbf{A}$ *and* $\mathbf{B}$. Rearranging the equation gives the **General Multiplication Rule** for compound events that does not require the events to be independent:

$$P(\mathbf{A} \text{ } and \text{ } \mathbf{B}) = P(\mathbf{A}) \times P(\mathbf{B}|\mathbf{A}) \text{ for any two events } \mathbf{A} \text{ and } \mathbf{B}.$$

The probability that two events, $\mathbf{A}$ and $\mathbf{B}$, both occur is the probability that event $\mathbf{A}$ occurs multiplied by the probability that event $\mathbf{B}$ also occurs *given* that event $\mathbf{A}$ occurs.

Of course, there's nothing special about which event we call $\mathbf{A}$ and which one we call $\mathbf{B}$. We should be able to state this the other way around. Indeed we can. It is equally true that:

$$P(\mathbf{A} \text{ } and \text{ } \mathbf{B}) = P(\mathbf{B}) \times P(\mathbf{A}|\mathbf{B}).$$

Let's return to the question of just what it means for events to be independent. We said informally in Chapter 2 that what we mean by independence is that the outcome of one event does not influence the probability of the other. With our new notation for conditional probabilities, we can write a formal definition. Events $\mathbf{A}$ and $\mathbf{B}$ are **independent** whenever:

$$P(\mathbf{B}|\mathbf{A}) = P(\mathbf{B}).$$

Independence

If we had to pick one key idea in this chapter that you should understand and remember, it's the definition and meaning of independence.

Now we can see that the Multiplication Rule for independent events is just a special case of the General Multiplication Rule. The general rule says

$$P(\mathbf{A} \textit{ and } \mathbf{B}) = P(\mathbf{A}) \times P(\mathbf{B}|\mathbf{A})$$

whether the events are independent or not. But when events **A** and **B** are independent, we can write $P(\mathbf{B})$ for $P(\mathbf{B}|\mathbf{A})$ and we get back our simple rule:

$$P(\mathbf{A} \textit{ and } \mathbf{B}) = P(\mathbf{A}) \times P(\mathbf{B}).$$

Sometimes people use this statement as the definition of independent events, but we find the other definition more intuitive. When events are independent, the fact that one has occurred does not affect the probability of the other.

Using our earlier example, is the probability of the event *choosing a bike* independent of the sex of the customer? We need to check whether

$$P(\text{bike}|\text{man}) = \frac{P(\text{bike } \textit{and } \text{man})}{P(\text{man})} = \frac{0.126}{0.475} = 0.264$$

is the same as $P(\text{bike}) = 0.188$.

Because these probabilities aren't equal, we can say that prize preference is *not* independent of the sex of the customer. Whenever at least one of the joint probabilities in the table is *not* equal to the product of the marginal probabilities, we say that the variables are not independent.

Independent *vs.* Disjoint

Are disjoint events independent? Both concepts seem to have similar ideas of separation and distinctness about them, but in fact disjoint events *cannot* be independent.[3] Let's see why. Consider the two disjoint events {you get an A in this course} and {you get a B in this course}. They're disjoint because they have no outcomes in common. Suppose you learn that you *did* get an A in the course. Now what is the probability that you got a B? You can't get both grades, so it must be 0.

Think about what that means. The fact that the first event (getting an A) occurred changed the probability for the second event (down to 0). So these events aren't independent.

Mutually exclusive events can never be independent. They have no outcomes in common, so knowing that one occurred means the other didn't. A common error is to treat disjoint events as if they were independent and apply the Multiplication Rule for independent events. Don't make that mistake.

Are events A and B independent or disjoint?	
Independent	Check whether $P(\mathbf{B}\|\mathbf{A}) = P(\mathbf{B})$ or Check whether $P(\mathbf{A}\|\mathbf{B}) = P(\mathbf{A})$ or Check whether $P(\mathbf{A} \text{ and } \mathbf{B}) = P(\mathbf{A}) \times P(\mathbf{B})$
Disjoint	Check whether $P(\mathbf{A} \text{ and } \mathbf{B}) = 0$ or Check whether events **A** and **B** overlap in a sample space diagram or Check whether the two events can occur together

---

[3]Technically two disjoint events *can* be independent, but only if the probability of one of the events is 0. For practical purposes, we can ignore this case, since we don't anticipate collecting data about things that don't happen.

QUESTION   Using the table from the example on page 159, if a customer purchases a Fashion light, what is the probability that the customer is a woman?

ANSWER $P(\text{Woman} \mid \text{Fashion}) = P(\text{Woman } and \text{ Fashion})/P(\text{Fashion})$
$$= 0.30/0.50 = 0.60$$

5.7   Constructing Contingency Tables

Sometimes we're given probabilities without a contingency table. You can often construct a simple table to correspond to the probabilities.

A survey of real estate in upstate New York classified homes into two price categories (Low—less than $175,000 and High—over $175,000). It also noted whether the houses had at least 2 bathrooms or not (True or False). We are told that 56% of the houses had at least 2 bathrooms, 62% of the houses were Low priced, and 22% of the houses were both. That's enough information to fill out the table. Translating the percentages to probabilities, we have:

		At Least 2 Bathrooms		
		True	**False**	**Total**
Price	**Low**	0.22		**0.62**
	High			
	Total	**0.56**		**1.00**

The 0.56 and 0.62 are marginal probabilities, so they go in the margins. What about the 22% of houses that were both low priced and had at least 2 bathrooms? That's a *joint* probability, so it belongs in the interior of the table.

Because the cells of the table show disjoint events, the probabilities always add to the marginal totals going across rows or down columns.

		At Least 2 Bathrooms		
		True	**False**	**Total**
Price	**Low**	0.22	0.40	**0.62**
	High	0.34	0.04	**0.38**
	Total	**0.56**	**0.44**	**1.00**

Now, finding any other probability is straightforward. For example, what's the probability that a high-priced house has at least 2 bathrooms?

$P(\text{at least 2 bathrooms} \mid \text{high-priced})$

$= P(\text{at least 2 bathrooms } and \text{ high-priced})/P(\text{high-priced})$

$= 0.34/0.38 = 0.895 \text{ or } 89.5\%.$

JUST CHECKING

3 Suppose a supermarket is conducting a survey to find out the busiest time and day for shoppers. Survey respondents are asked 1) whether they shopped at the store on a week-day or on the weekend and 2) whether they shopped at the store before or after 5 p.m. The survey revealed that:

- 48% of shoppers visited the store before 5 p.m.
  27% of shoppers visited the store on a weekday (Mon.–Fri.)

- 7% of shoppers visited the store before 5 p.m. on a weekday.

a) Make a contingency table for the variables *time of day* and *day of week*.

b) What is the probability that a randomly selected shopper who shops on a weekday also shops before 5 p.m.?

c) Are time and day of the week disjoint events?

d) Are time and day of the week independent events?

5.8   Probability Trees

Some business decisions involve more subtle evaluation of probabilities. Given the probabilities of various states of nature, we can use a picture called a probability tree or **tree diagram** to help think through the decision-making process. A tree shows sequences of events as paths that look like branches of a tree. This can enable us to compare several possible scenarios. Here's a manufacturing example.

Personal electronic devices, such as smart phones and tablets, are getting more capable all the time. Manufacturing components for these devices is a challenge, and at the same time, consumers are demanding more and more functionality and increasing sturdiness. Microscopic and even submicroscopic flaws that can cause intermittent performance failures can develop during their fabrication. Defects will always occur, so the quality engineer in charge of the production process must monitor the number of defects and take action if the process seems out of control.

Let's suppose that the engineer is called down to the production line because the number of defects has crossed a threshold and the process has been declared to be out of control. She must decide between two possible actions. She knows that a small adjustment to the robots that assemble the components can fix a variety of problems, but for more complex problems, the entire production line needs to be shut down in order to pinpoint the problem. The adjustment requires that production be stopped for about an hour. But shutting down the line takes at least an entire shift (8 hours). Naturally, her boss would prefer that she make the simple adjustment. But without knowing the source or severity of the problem, she can't be sure whether that will be successful.

If the engineer wants to predict whether the smaller adjustment will work, she can use a probability tree to help make the decision. Based on her experience, the engineer thinks that there are three possible problems: (1) the motherboards could have faulty connections, (2) the memory could be the source of the faulty connections, or (3) some of the cases may simply be seating incorrectly in the assembly line. She knows from past experience how often these types of problem crop up and how likely it is that just making an adjustment will fix each type of problem. *Motherboard* problems are rare (10%), *memory* problems have been showing up about 30% of the time, and *case* alignment issues occur most often (60%). We can put those probabilities on the first set of branches in Figure 5.3 on the next page.

Figure 5.3   Possible problems and their probabilities.

Notice that we've covered all the possibilities, and so the probabilities sum to one. To this diagram we can now add the *conditional* probabilities that a minor adjustment will fix each type of problem. Most likely the engineer will rely on her experience or assemble a team to help determine these probabilities. For example, the engineer knows that motherboard connection problems are not likely to be fixed with a simple adjustment: $P(\text{Fix}|\text{Motherboard}) = 0.10$. After some discussion, she and her team determine that $P(\text{Fix}|\text{Memory}) = 0.50$ and $P(\text{Fix}|\text{Case alignment}) = 0.80$. At the end of each branch representing the problem type, we draw two possibilities (*Fix* or *Not Fixed*) and write the conditional probabilities on the branches.

Figure 5.4   Extending the tree diagram, we can show both the problem class and the outcome probabilities. The outcome (Fixed or Not fixed) probabilities are conditional on the problem type, and they change depending on which branch we follow.

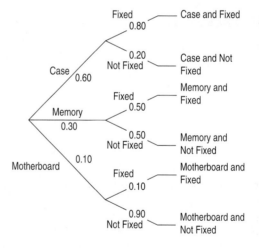

At the end of each second branch, we write the *joint event* corresponding to the combination of the two branches. For example, the top branch is the combination of the problem being Case alignment, and the outcome of the small adjustment is that the problem is now Fixed. For each of the joint events, we can use the general multiplication rule to calculate their joint probability. For example:

$$P(\textit{Case and Fixed}) = P(\textit{Case}) \times P(\textit{Fixed} \,|\, \textit{Case})$$
$$= 0.60 \times 0.80 = 0.48$$

We write this probability next to the corresponding event. Doing this for all branch combinations gives us Figure 5.5.

Figure 5.5 We can find the probabilities of compound events by multiplying the probabilities along the branch of the tree that leads to the event, just the way the General Multiplication Rule specifies.

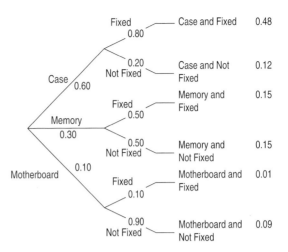

All the outcomes at the far right are disjoint because at every node, all the choices are disjoint alternatives. And those alternatives are *all* the possibilities, so the probabilities on the far right must add up to one.

Because the final outcomes are disjoint, we can add up any combination of probabilities to find probabilities for compound events. In particular, the engineer can answer her question: What's the probability that the problem will be fixed by a simple adjustment? She finds all the outcomes on the far right in which the problem was fixed. There are three (one corresponding to each type of problem), and she adds their probabilities: $0.48 + 0.15 + 0.01 = 0.64$. So 64% of all problems are fixed by the simple adjustment. The other 36% require a major investigation.

*5.9   Reversing the Conditioning: Bayes' Rule

The engineer in our story decided to try the simple adjustment and, fortunately, it worked. Now she needs to report to the quality engineer on the next shift what she thinks the problem was. Was it more likely to be a case alignment problem or a motherboard problem? We know the probabilities of those problems beforehand, but they change now that we have more information. What are the likelihoods that each of the possible problems was, in fact, the one that occurred?

Unfortunately, we can't read those probabilities from the tree in Figure 5.5. For example, the tree gives us $P(Fixed\ and\ Case) = 0.48$, but we want $P(Case\,|\,Fixed)$. We know $P(Fixed\,|\,Case) = 0.80$, but that's not the same thing. It isn't valid to reverse the order of conditioning in a conditional probability statement. To "turn the probability around," we need to go back to the definition of conditional probability.

$$P(Case\,|\,Fixed) = \frac{P(Case\ and\ Fixed)}{P(Fixed)}$$

We can read the probability in the numerator from the tree, and we've already calculated the probability in the denominator by adding all the probabilities on the final branches that correspond to the event *Fixed*. Putting those values in the formula, the engineer finds:

$$P(Case\,|\,Fixed) = \frac{0.48}{0.48 + 0.15 + 0.01} = 0.75$$

She knew that 60% of all problems were due to case alignment, but now that she knows the problem has been fixed, she knows more. Given the additional information that a simple adjustment was able to fix the problem, she now can increase the probability that the problem was case alignment to 0.75.

It's usually easiest to solve problems like this by reading the appropriate probabilities from the tree. However, we can write a general formula for finding the reverse conditional probability. To understand it, let's review our example again. Let $A_1 = \{Case\}, A_2 = \{Memory\}$, and $A_3 = \{Motherboard\}$ represent the three types of problems. Let $B = \{Fixed\}$, meaning that the simple adjustment fixed the problem. We know $P(B \mid A_1) = 0.80, P(B \mid A_2) = 0.50$, and $P(B \mid A_3) = 0.10$. We want to find the reverse probabilities, $P(A_i \mid B)$, for the three possible problem types. From the definition of conditional probability, we know (for any of the three types of problems):

$$P(A_i \mid B) = \frac{P(A_i \; and \; B)}{P(B)}$$

We still don't know either of these quantities, but we use the definition of conditional probability again to find $P(A_i \; and \; B) = P(B \mid A_i)P(A_i)$, both of which we know. Finally, we find $P(B)$ by adding up the probabilities of the three events.

$$P(B) = P(A_1 \; and \; B) + P(A_2 \; and \; B) + P(A_3 \; and \; B) =$$
$$P(B \mid A_1)P(A_1) + P(B \mid A_2)P(A_2) + P(B \mid A_3)P(A_3)$$

In general, we can write this for n events A_i that are mutually exclusive (each pair is disjoint) and exhaustive (their union is the whole space). Then:

$$P(A_i \mid B) = \frac{P(B \mid A_i)P(A_i)}{\sum\limits_{j} P(B \mid A_j)P(A_j)}$$

This formula is known as Bayes' rule, after the Reverend Thomas Bayes (1702–1761), even though historians don't really know if Bayes first came up with the reverse conditioning probability. When you need to find reverse conditional probabilities, we recommend drawing a tree and finding the appropriate probabilities as we did at the beginning of the section, but the formula gives the general rule.

WHAT CAN GO WRONG?

- **Beware of probabilities that don't add up to 1.** To be a legitimate assignment of probability, the sum of the probabilities for all possible outcomes must total 1. If the sum is less than 1, you may need to add another category ("other") and assign the remaining probability to that outcome. If the sum is more than 1, check that the outcomes are disjoint. If they're not, then you can't assign probabilities by counting relative frequencies. (And if they are, you must locate the error.)

- **Don't add probabilities of events if they're not disjoint.** Events must be disjoint to use the Addition Rule. The probability of being under 80 *or* a female is not the probability of being under 80 *plus* the probability of being female. That sum may be more than 1.

- **Don't multiply probabilities of events if they're not independent.** The probability of selecting a customer at random who is over 70 years old *and* retired is not the probability the customer is over 70 years old *times* the probability the customer is retired. Knowing that the customer is over 70 changes the probability of his or her being retired. You can't multiply these probabilities. The multiplication of probabilities of events that are not independent is one of the most common errors people make in dealing with probabilities.

- **Don't confuse disjoint and independent.** Disjoint events *can't* be independent. If $A = \{you \; get \; a \; promotion\}$ and $B = \{you \; don't \; get \; a \; promotion\}$, A and B are disjoint. Are they independent? If you find out that A is true, does that change the probability of B? Yes, if A is true, then B cannot be true, so they are not independent.

ETHICS IN ACTION

Fabrizio Rivetti is an entrepreneur who has recently started a wine importing business. While he currently has an exclusive relationship with only one premier winery in Tuscany, he is hoping to expand his importing business to include other wineries as well as artisan Italian food products, such as cheeses and specialty meats.

With plans to expand, Fabrizio is in need of extra funds. As a first step, he approaches a friend and fellow entrepreneur who has considerable experience dealing with angel investors, Chas Mulligan. Chas has successfully obtained funds from angel investors for his social networking start-up company, so Fabrizio is hopeful that Chas can provide some sound advice. Chas explains to Fabrizio that most angel investors bear considerable risk and consequently favor ventures that are in high-growth areas, such as software, healthcare, and biotech. He also mentions that many angel investors, like venture capitalists, want to exercise some control over the start-up companies in which they invest, either by securing a seat on the company's board of directors or having veto power.

Fabrizio is now a bit unsure about seeking angel investments, so Chas puts him in contact with a consultant, Paula Foxx, who can help him make the right decision. Paula is well connected with a network of angel investors, understands the types of start-ups they prefer to invest in, and, most importantly, knows how to prepare the perfect pitch. At their first meeting, Paula is quick to inform Fabrizio of her consultancy fee schedule. Next, she assures Fabrizio that she is acquainted with a number of angels whom she believes might be interested in his wine importing business. Fabrizio expresses to Paula his reservations about sharing too much control of his start-up with investors, and is particularly wary of granting investors veto power.

He is reluctant to hire Paula on the spot, so Paula suggests they meet again after she has had the opportunity to pull together data on some of her most successful clients. Paula's objective is to direct clients to angels who tend to make large initial investments. In this way, her clients reach their goals more quickly and she can spend less time with each client. She decides to compile some data only for angel investors who have made significant initial investments in her clients' start-ups (in excess of $250,000). She came up with the following contingency table for this group of investors.

		Veto Power?		
		Yes	No	Total
Board Seat?	Yes	.05	.45	.50
	No	.45	.05	.50
	Total	.50	.50	1.00

She was happy to find that 50% did not get veto power and 50% did not sit on the board. By multiplying these two probabilities, she arrived at a figure she thought would help persuade Fabrizio to pursue angels and hire her to do so. She planned to tell him that 25% of angels who make large investments are not interested in either veto power or a seat on the board in the start-ups they fund. She called her administrative assistant to arrange another meeting with Fabrizio as soon as possible.

- Identify the ethical dilemma in this scenario.

- What are the undesirable consequences?

- Propose an ethical solution that considers the welfare of all stakeholders

WHAT HAVE WE LEARNED?

Learning Objectives

Apply the facts about probability to determine whether an assignment of probabilities is legitimate.

- Probability is long-run relative frequency.
- Individual probabilities must be between 0 and 1.
- The sum of probabilities assigned to all outcomes must be 1.

Understand the Law of Large Numbers and that the common understanding of the "Law of Averages" is false.

Know the rules of probability and how to apply them.

- The **Complement Rule** says that $P(\text{not } \mathbf{A}) = P(\mathbf{A}^{\mathbf{C}}) = 1 - P(\mathbf{A})$.
- The **Multiplication Rule** for independent events says that $P(\mathbf{A} \text{ and } \mathbf{B}) = P(\mathbf{A}) \times P(\mathbf{B})$ provided events $\mathbf{A}$ and $\mathbf{B}$ are independent.

- The **General Multiplication Rule** says that $P(\mathbf{A}\ and\ \mathbf{B}) = P(\mathbf{A}) \times P(\mathbf{B}|\mathbf{A})$ for any events **A** and **B**.
- The **Addition Rule** for disjoint events says that $P(\mathbf{A}\ or\ \mathbf{B}) = P(\mathbf{A}) + P(\mathbf{B})$ provided events A and B are disjoint.
- The **General Addition Rule** says that $P(\mathbf{A}\ or\ \mathbf{B}) = P(\mathbf{A}) + P(\mathbf{B}) - P(\mathbf{A}\ and\ \mathbf{B})$ for any events **A** and **B**.

Know how to construct and read a contingency table.

Know how to define and use independence.

- Events A and B are independent if $P(\mathbf{A}|\mathbf{B}) = P(\mathbf{A})$.

Know how to construct tree diagrams and use them to calculate and understand conditional probabilities.

Know how to use Bayes' Rule to compute conditional probabilities.

Terms

Addition Rule

If **A** and **B** are disjoint events, then the probability of **A** or **B** is

$$P(\mathbf{A}\ or\ \mathbf{B}) = P(\mathbf{A}) + P(\mathbf{B}).$$

Complement Rule

The probability of an event occurring is 1 minus the probability that it doesn't occur:

$$P(\mathbf{A}) = 1 - P(\mathbf{A}^\mathbf{C}).$$

Conditional probability

$$P(\mathbf{B}|\mathbf{A}) = \frac{P(\mathbf{A}\ and\ \mathbf{B})}{P(\mathbf{A})}.$$

$P(\mathbf{B}|\mathbf{A})$ is read "the probability of **B** *given* **A**."

Disjoint (or Mutually Exclusive) Events

Two events are disjoint if they have no outcomes in common. If **A** and **B** are disjoint, then the fact that **A** occurs tells us that **B** cannot occur. Disjoint events are also called "mutually exclusive."

Empirical probability

When the probability comes from the long-run relative frequency of the event's occurrence, it is an empirical probability.

Event

A collection of outcomes. Usually, we identify events so that we can attach probabilities to them. We denote events with bold capital letters such as **A**, **B**, or **C**.

General Addition Rule

For any two events, **A** and **B**, the probability of **A** *or* **B** is:

$$P(\mathbf{A}\ or\ \mathbf{B}) = P(\mathbf{A}) + P(\mathbf{B}) - P(\mathbf{A}\ and\ \mathbf{B}).$$

General Multiplication Rule

For any two events, **A** and **B**, the probability of **A** and **B** is:

$$P(\mathbf{A}\ and\ \mathbf{B}) = P(\mathbf{A}) \times P(\mathbf{B}|\mathbf{A}).$$

Independence (informally)

Two events are *independent* if the fact that one event occurs does not change the probability of the other.

Independence (used formally)

Events **A** and **B** are independent when $P(\mathbf{B}|\mathbf{A}) = P(\mathbf{B})$.

Joint probabilities

The probability that two events both occur.

Law of Large Numbers (LLN)

The Law of Large Numbers states that the *long-run relative frequency* of repeated, independent events settles down to the *true relative frequency* as the number of trials increases.

Marginal probability

In a joint probability table a marginal probability is the probability distribution of either variable separately, usually found in the rightmost column or bottom row of the table.

Multiplication Rule

If **A** and **B** are independent events, then the probability of **A** *and* **B** is:

$$P(\mathbf{A}\ and\ \mathbf{B}) = P(\mathbf{A}) \times P(\mathbf{B}).$$

Outcome	The outcome of a trial is the value measured, observed, or reported for an individual instance of that trial.
Personal probability	When the probability is subjective and represents one's personal degree of belief, it is called a personal probability.
Probability	The probability of an event is a number between 0 and 1 that reports the likelihood of the event's occurrence. A probability can be derived from a model (such as equally likely outcomes), from the long-run relative frequency of the event's occurrence, or from subjective degrees of belief. We write $P(\mathbf{A})$ for the probability of the event $\mathbf{A}$.
Probability Assignment Rule	The probability of the entire sample space must be 1: $$P(S) = 1.$$
Random phenomenon	A phenomenon is random if we know what outcomes *could* happen, but not which particular values *will* happen in any given trial.
Sample space	The collection of all possible outcome values. The sample space has a probability of 1.
Theoretical probability	When the probability comes from a mathematical model (such as, but not limited to, equally likely outcomes), it is called a theoretical probability.
Trial	A single attempt or realization of a random phenomenon.
Tree diagram (or probability tree)	A display of conditional events or probabilities that is helpful in thinking through conditioning.

TECHNOLOGY HELP: Generating Random Numbers

Most statistics packages generate single or lists of random numbers. You may find them useful for introducing randomness in a study or drawing a random sample. Excel can generate random numbers with the **RAND( )** function.

EXCEL

To generate a random number in Excel:

- In a cell, type **= RAND( )**. A random number between 0 and 1 (a real number to 9 decimal places) appears in the cell.

- To generate more random numbers, copy and paste this cell or select it and **Fill Down** to obtain more random values.

- To generate a random number within a range, type **= RAND( )*(b − a) + a** into the formula bar where **a** is the number at the low end of the range and **b** is the number at the high end of the range.

- You can also use the function **= RANDBETWEEN (a, b)** to generate an integer between a and b.

Random numbers are re-generated each time a change is made to the spreadsheet. To avoid this:

- Highlight the cell containing the random number.

- Copy the value and paste into same cell using the **Paste Values: Values** command.

Brief Case

Global Markets

A global survey firm reports data from surveys taken in several countries. The data file **Global** holds data for 800 respondents in each of five countries. The variables provide demographic information (sex, age, education, marital status) and responses to questions of interest to marketers on personal finance and purchasing.

Write a report that discusses how decisions about personal finance and shopping vary by country and by sex. You'll want to make contingency tables of some variables and consider the contingent probabilities that they show. You may also want to restrict your attention to one country and then consider relationships between variables within that country.

EXERCISES

SECTION 5.1

1. Indicate which of the following represent independent events. Explain briefly.

a) The gender of customers using an ATM machine.
b) The last digit of the social security numbers of students in a class.
c) The scores you receive on the first midterm, second midterm, and the final exam of a course.

2. Indicate which of the following represent independent events. Explain briefly.

a) Prices of houses on the same block.
b) Successive measurements of your heart rate as you exercise on a treadmill.
c) Measurements of the heart rates of all students in the gym.

SECTION 5.2

3. In many state lotteries, you can choose which numbers to play. Consider a common form in which you choose 5 numbers. Which of the following strategies can improve your chance of winning? If the method works, explain why. If not, explain why using appropriate statistics terms.

a) Always play 1, 2, 3, 4, 5.
b) Choose the numbers that did come up in the most recent lottery drawing because they are "hot."

4. For the same kind of lottery as in Exercise 3, which of the following strategies can improve your chance of winning? If the method works, explain why. If not, explain why using appropriate statistics terms.

a) Choose randomly from among the numbers that have *not* come up in the last 3 lottery drawings because they are "due."
b) Generate random numbers using a computer or calculator and play those.

SECTION 5.4

5. A recent survey found that, despite airline requests, about 40% of passengers don't fully turn off their cell phones during takeoff and landing (although they may put them in "airplane mode"). The two passengers across the aisle (in seats A and B) clearly do not know each other.

a) What is the probability that the passenger in seat A does not turn off his phone?
b) What is the probability that he does turn off his phone?
c) What is the probability that both of them turn off their phones?
d) What is the probability that at least one of them turns off his or her phone?

6. At your school, 10% of the class are marketing majors. If you are randomly assigned to two partners in your statistics class,

a) What is the probability that the first partner will be a marketing major?
b) What is the probability that the first partner won't be a marketing major?
c) What is the probability that both will be marketing majors?
d) What is the probability that at least one will be a marketing major?

SECTION 5.5

7. The following contingency table shows opinion about global warming among U.S. adults, broken down by political party affiliation (based on a poll in October 2012 by Pew Research found at http://www.people-press .org/2012/10/15/more-say-there-is-solid-evidence-of -global-warming/).

| | **Opinion on Global Warming** | | |
	Nonissue	Serious Concern	Total
Democratic	85	415	**500**
Republican	290	210	**500**
Independent	70	130	**200**
Total	**445**	**755**	**1200**

(Political Party labels the rows)

a) What is the probability that a U.S. adult selected at random believes that global warming is a serious issue?
b) What type of probability did you find in part a?
c) What is the probability that a U.S. adult selected at random is a Republican and believes that global warming is a serious issue?
d) What type of probability did you find in part c?

8. Multigenerational families can be categorized as having two adult generations such as parents living with adult children, "skip" generation families, such as grandparents living with grandchildren, and three or more generations living in the household. Pew Research surveyed multigenerational households. This table is based on their reported results.

	2 Adult Gens	2 Skip Gens	3 or More Gens	
White	509	55	222	**786**
Hispanic	139	11	142	**292**
Black	119	32	99	**250**
Asian	61	1	48	**110**
	828	**99**	**511**	**1438**

a) What is the probability that a multigenerational family is Hispanic?
b) What is the probability that a multigenerational family selected at random is a Black, two-adult-generation family?
c) What type of probability did you find in parts a and b?

SECTION 5.6

9. Using the table from Exercise 7,

a) What is the probability that a randomly selected U.S. adult who is a Republican believes that global warming is a serious issue?
b) What is the probability that a randomly selected U.S. adult is a Republican given that he or she believes global warming is a serious issue?
c) What is $P(\text{Serious Concern} \mid \text{Democratic})$?

10. Using the table from Exercise 8,

a) What is the probability that a randomly selected Black multigenerational family is a 2 Adult Generation family?
b) What is the probability that a randomly selected multigenerational family is White, given that it is a "skip" generation family?
c) What is $P(3 \text{ or more Generations} \mid \text{Asian})$?

SECTION 5.7

11. A national survey indicated that 30% of adults conduct their banking online. It also found that 40% are under the age of 50, and that 25% are under the age of 50 and conduct their banking online.

a) What percentage of adults do not conduct their banking online?
b) What type of probability is the 25% mentioned above?
c) Construct a contingency table showing all joint and marginal probabilities.
d) What is the probability that an individual conducts banking online given that the individual is under the age of 50?
e) Are *Banking online* and *Age* independent? Explain.

12. Facebook reports that 70% of their users are from outside the United States and that 50% of their users log on to Facebook every day. Suppose that 20% of their users are United States users who log on every day.

a) What percentage of Facebook's users are from the United States?
b) What type of probability is the 20% mentioned above?
c) Construct a contingency table showing all the joint and marginal probabilities.
d) What is the probability that a user is from the United States given that he or she logs on every day?
e) Are *From United States* and *Log on Every Day* independent? Explain.

SECTION 5.8

13. Summit Projects provides marketing services and website management for many companies that specialize in outdoor products and services (www.summitprojects.com). To understand customer Web behavior, the company experiments with different offers and website design. The results of such experiments can help to maximize the probability that customers purchase products during a visit to a website. Possible actions by the website include offering the customer an instant discount, offering the customer free shipping, or doing nothing. A recent experiment found that customers make purchases 6% of the time when offered the instant discount, 5% when offered free shipping, and 2% when no special offer was given. Suppose 20% of the customers are offered the discount and an additional 30% are offered free shipping.

a) Construct a probability tree for this experiment.
b) What percent of customers who visit the site made a purchase?
c) Given that a customer made a purchase, what is the probability that they were offered free shipping?

14. The company in Exercise 13 performed another experiment in which they tested three website designs to see which one would lead to the highest probability of purchase. The first (design A) used enhanced product information, the second (design B) used extensive iconography, and the third (design C) allowed the customer to submit their own product ratings. After 6 weeks of testing, the designs delivered probabilities of purchase of 4.5%, 5.2%, and 3.8%, respectively. Equal numbers of customers were sent randomly to each website design.

a) Construct a probability tree for this experiment.
b) What percent of customers who visited the site made a purchase?
c) What is the probability that a randomly selected customer was sent to design C?
d) Given that a customer made a purchase, what is the probability that the customer had been sent to design C?

SECTION 5.9

15. According to U.S. Census data, 68% of the civilian U.S. labor force self-identifies as White, 11% as Black, and the remaining 21% as Hispanic/Latino or Other. Among Whites in the labor force, 54% are Male, and 46% Female. Among Blacks, 52% are Male and 48% Female, and among Hispanic/Latino/Other, 58% are Male and 42% are Female.

a) Polling companies need to sample an appropriate number of respondents of each gender from each ethnic group. For a randomly selected U.S. worker, fill in the probabilities in this tree:

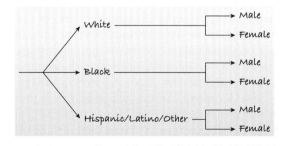

b) What is the probability that a randomly selected worker is a Black Female?
c) For a randomly selected worker, what is $P(Female \mid White)$?
d) For a randomly selected worked what is $P(White \mid Female)$?

16. U.S. Customs and Border Protection has been testing automated kiosks that may be able to detect lies. (www.wired.com/threatlevel/2013/01/ff-lie-detector/all/) One measurement used (among several) is involuntary eye movements. Using this method alone, tests show that it can detect 60% of lies, but incorrectly identifies 15% of true statements as lies. Suppose that 95% of those entering the country tell the truth. The immigration kiosk asks questions such as "Have you ever been arrested for a crime?" Naturally, all the applicants answer "No," but the kiosk identifies some of those answers as lies, and refers the entrant to a human interviewer.

a) Here is the outline of a probability tree for this situation. Fill in the probabilities:

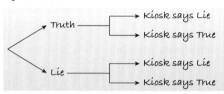

b) What is the probability that a random person will be telling the truth and will be cleared by the Kiosk?
c) What is the probability that a person who is rejected by the kiosk was actually telling the truth?

CHAPTER EXERCISES

17. What does it mean? Part 1. Respond to the following questions:

a) A casino claims that its roulette wheel is truly random. What should that claim mean?
b) A reporter on *Market Place* says that there is a 50% chance that the NASDAQ will hit a new high in the next month. What is the meaning of such a phrase?

18. What does it mean? Part 2. Respond to the following questions:

a) After an unusually dry autumn, a radio announcer is heard to say, "Watch out! We'll pay for these sunny days later on this winter." Explain what he's trying to say, and comment on the validity of his reasoning.
b) A batter who had failed to get a hit in seven consecutive times at bat then hits a game-winning home run. When talking to reporters afterward, he says he was very confident that last time at bat because he knew he was "due for a hit." Comment on his reasoning.

19. Airline safety. Even though commercial airlines have excellent safety records, in the weeks following a crash, airlines often report a drop in the number of passengers, probably because people are afraid to risk flying.

a) A travel agent suggests that since the law of averages makes it highly unlikely to have two plane crashes within a few weeks of each other, flying soon after a crash is the safest time. What do you think?
b) If the airline industry proudly announces that it has set a new record for the longest period of safe flights, would you be reluctant to fly? Are the airlines due to have a crash?

20. Economic predictions. An investment newsletter makes general predictions about the economy to help their clients make sound investment decisions.

a) Recently they said that because the stock market had been up for the past three months in a row that it was "due for a correction" and advised their client to reduce their holdings. What "law" are they applying? Comment.
b) They advised buying a stock that had gone down in the past four sessions because they said that it was clearly "due to bounce back." What "law" are they applying? Comment.

21. Fire insurance. Insurance companies collect annual payments from homeowners in exchange for paying to rebuild houses that burn down.

a) Why should you be reluctant to accept a $300 payment from your neighbor to replace his house should it burn down during the coming year?

b) Why can the insurance company make that offer?

22. Casino gambling. Recently, the International Gaming Technology company issued the following press release:

(LAS VEGAS, Nev.)—Cynthia Jay was smiling ear to ear as she walked into the news conference at the Desert Inn Resort in Las Vegas today, and well she should. Last night, the 37-year-old cocktail waitress won the world's largest slot jackpot—$34,959,458—on a Megabucks machine. She said she had played $27 in the machine when the jackpot hit. Nevada Megabucks has produced 49 major winners in its 14-year history. The top jackpot builds from a base amount of $7 million and can be won with a 3-coin ($3) bet.

a) How can the Desert Inn afford to give away millions of dollars on a $3 bet?

b) Why did the company issue a press release? Wouldn't most businesses want to keep such a huge loss quiet?

23. Toy company. A toy company is preparing to market an electronic game for young children that "randomly" generates a color. They suspect, however, that the way the random color is determined may not be reliable, so they ask the programmers to perform tests and report the frequencies of each outcome. Are each of the following probability assignments possible? Why or why not?

	Probabilities of ...			
	Red	Yellow	Green	Blue
a)	0.25	0.25	0.25	0.25
b)	0.10	0.20	0.30	0.40
c)	0.20	0.30	0.40	0.50
d)	0	0	1.00	0
e)	0.10	0.20	1.20	−1.50

24. Store discounts. Many stores run "secret sales": Shoppers receive cards that determine how large a discount they get, but the percentage is revealed by scratching off that black stuff (what *is* that?) only after the purchase has been totaled at the cash register. The store is required to reveal (in the fine print) the distribution of discounts available. Are each of these probability assignments plausible? Why or why not?

	Probabilities of ...			
	10% Off	20% Off	30% Off	50% Off
a)	0.20	0.20	0.20	0.20
b)	0.50	0.30	0.20	0.10
c)	0.80	0.10	0.05	0.05
d)	0.75	0.25	0.25	−0.25
e)	1.00	0	0	0

25. Quality control. A tire manufacturer recently announced a recall because 2% of its tires are defective. If you just bought a new set of four tires from this manufacturer, what is the probability that at least one of your new tires is defective?

26. Pepsi promotion. For a sales promotion, the manufacturer places winning symbols under the caps of 10% of all Pepsi bottles. If you buy a six-pack of Pepsi, what is the probability that you win something?

27. Auto warranty. In developing their warranty policy, an automobile company estimates that over a 1-year period 17% of their new cars will need to be repaired once, 7% will need repairs twice, and 4% will require three or more repairs. If you buy a new car from them, what is the probability that your car will need:

a) No repairs?

b) No more than one repair?

c) Some repairs?

28. Consulting team. You work for a large global management consulting company. Of the entire work force of analysts, 55% have had no experience in the telecommunications industry, 32% have had limited experience (less than 5 years), and the rest have had extensive experience (5 years or more). On a recent project, you and two other analysts were chosen at random to constitute a team. It turns out that part of the project involves telecommunications. What is the probability that the first teammate you meet has:

a) Extensive telecommunications experience?

b) Some telecommunications experience?

c) No more than limited telecommunications experience?

29. Auto warranty, part 2. Consider again the auto repair rates described in Exercise 27. If you bought two new cars, what is the probability that:

a) Neither will need repair?

b) Both will need repair?

c) At least one car will need repair?

30. Consulting team, part 2. You are assigned to be part of a team of three analysts of a global management consulting company as described in Exercise 28. What is the probability that of your other two teammates:

a) Neither has any telecommunications experience?

b) Both have some telecommunications experience?

c) At least one has had extensive telecommunications experience?

31. Auto warranty, again. You used the Multiplication Rule to calculate repair probabilities for your cars in Exercise 29.

a) What must be true about your cars in order to make that approach valid?

b) Do you think this assumption is reasonable? Explain.

32. Final consulting team project. You used the Multiplication Rule to calculate probabilities about the telecommunications experience of your consulting teammates in Exercise 30.

a) What must be true about the groups in order to make that approach valid?

b) Do you think this assumption is reasonable? Explain.

33. Real estate. In a sample of real estate ads, 64% of homes for sale had garages, 21% have swimming pools, and 17% have both features. What is the probability that a home for sale has:

a) A pool, a garage, or both?

b) Neither a pool nor a garage?

c) A pool but no garage?

34. Human resource data. Employment data at a large company reveal that 72% of the workers are married, 44% are college graduates, and half of the college grads are married. What's the probability that a randomly chosen worker is:

a) Neither married nor a college graduate?

b) Married but not a college graduate?

c) Married or a college graduate?

35. Mars product information. The Mars company says that before the introduction of purple, yellow made up 20% of their plain M&M candies, red made up another 20%, and orange, blue, and green each made up 10%. The rest were brown.

a) If you picked an M&M at random from a pre-purple bag of candies, what is the probability that it was:

   i)   Brown?

   ii) Yellow or orange?

   iii) Not green?

   iv) Striped?

b) Assuming you had an infinite supply of M&M's with the older color distribution, if you picked three M&M's in a row, what is the probability that:

   i)   They are all brown?

   ii) The third one is the first one that's red?

   iii) None are yellow?

   iv) At least one is green?

36. American Red Cross. The American Red Cross must track their supply and demand for various blood types. They estimate that about 45% of the U.S. population has Type O blood, 40% Type A, 11% Type B, and the rest Type AB.

a) If someone volunteers to give blood, what is the probability that this donor:

   i)   Has Type AB blood?

   ii) Has Type A or Type B blood?

   iii) Is not Type O?

b) Among four potential donors, what is the probability that:

   i)   All are Type O?

   ii) None have Type AB blood?

   iii) Not all are Type A?

   iv) At least one person is Type B?

37. More Mars product information. In Exercise 35, you calculated probabilities of getting various colors of M&M's.

a) If you draw one M&M, are the events of getting a red one and getting an orange one disjoint or independent or neither?

b) If you draw two M&M's one after the other, are the events of getting a red on the first and a red on the second disjoint or independent or neither?

c) Can disjoint events ever be independent? Explain.

38. American Red Cross, part 2. In Exercise 36, you calculated probabilities involving various blood types.

a) If you examine one donor, are the events of the donor being Type A and the donor being Type B disjoint or independent or neither? Explain your answer.

b) If you examine two donors, are the events that the first donor is Type A and the second donor is Type B disjoint or independent or neither?

c) Can disjoint events ever be independent? Explain.

39. Tax accountant. A recent study of IRS audits showed that, for estates worth less than $5 million, about 1 out of 7 of all estate tax returns are audited, but that probability increases to 50% for estates worth over $5 million. Suppose a tax accountant has three clients who have recently filed returns for estates worth more than $5 million. What are the probabilities that:

a) All three will be audited?

b) None will be audited?

c) At least one will be audited?

d) What did you assume in calculating these probabilities?

40. Casinos. Because gambling is big business, calculating the odds of a gambler winning or losing in every game is crucial to the financial forecasting for a casino. A standard slot machine has three wheels that spin independently. Each has 10 equally likely symbols: 4 bars, 3 lemons, 2 cherries, and a bell. If you play once, what is the probability that you will get:

a) 3 lemons?

b) No fruit symbols?

c) 3 bells (the jackpot)?

d) No bells?

e) At least one bar (an automatic loser)?

41. Spam filter. A company has recently replaced their e-mail spam filter because investigations had found that the volume of spam e-mail was interrupting productive work on about 15% of workdays. To see how bad the situation was, calculate the probability that during a 5-day work week, e-mail spam would interrupt work:

a) On Monday and again on Tuesday?

b) For the first time on Thursday?

c) Every day?

d) At least once during the week?

42. Tablet tech support. The technical support desk at a college has set up a special service for tablets. A survey shows that 54% of tablets on campus run Apple's iOS, 43% run Google's Android OS, and 3% run Microsoft's Windows. Assuming that users of each of the operating systems are equally likely to call in for technical support what is the probability that of the next three calls:

a) All are iOS?
b) None are Android?
c) At least one is a Windows machine?
d) All are Windows machines?

43. Casinos, part 2. In addition to slot machines, casinos must understand the probabilities involved in card games. Suppose you are playing at the blackjack table, and the dealer shuffles a deck of cards. The first card shown is red. So is the second and the third. In fact, you are surprised to see 5 red cards in a row. You start thinking, "The next one is due to be black!"

a) Are you correct in thinking that there's a higher probability that the next card will be black than red? Explain.
b) Is this an example of the Law of Large Numbers? Explain.

44. Inventory. A shipment of road bikes has just arrived at The Spoke, a small bicycle shop, and all the boxes have been placed in the back room. The owner asks her assistant to start bringing in the boxes. The assistant sees 20 identical-looking boxes and starts bringing them into the shop at random. The owner knows that she ordered 10 women's and 10 men's bicycles, and so she's surprised to find that the first six are all women's bikes. As the seventh box is brought in, she starts thinking, "This one is bound to be a men's bike."

a) Is she correct in thinking that there's a higher probability that the next box will contain a men's bike? Explain.
b) Is this an example of the Law of Large Numbers? Explain.

45. U.S. economic conditions 2013. A Gallup Poll in March 2013 (www.gallup.com/poll/110821/gallup-daily-us-economic-conditions.aspx) asked 1500 U.S. adults to rate economic conditions in the country today as "excellent," "good," "only fair," or "poor." The results are below:

Current Economic Conditions	
Response	Number of Respondents
Excellent/Good	270
Only Fair	645
Poor	585
Total	**1500**

If we select a person at random from this sample of 1500 adults:

a) What is the probability that the person responded "Poor"?
b) What is the probability that the person responded "Fair" or "Poor"?

46. More economic conditions 2013. Exercise 45 shows the results of a Gallup Poll about U.S. economic conditions. Suppose we select three adults at random from this sample.

a) What is the probability that all three responded "Poor"?
b) What is the probability that none responded "Poor"?
c) What assumption did you make in computing these probabilities?
d) Explain why you think that assumption is reasonable.

47. Owning guns. The General Social Survey, run annually, asked respondents "Do you have in your home (or garage) any guns or revolvers?" The responses are given in the table. (sda.berkeley.edu/cgi-bin/hsda?harcsda+gss10)

Gun Ownership	
Response	Number of Respondents
Yes	410
No	815
Don't Know/Refused	45
Total	**1270**

a) If we select a random person from this sample of 1270 adults, what is the probability that their response will be "No"?
b) What is the probability that their response will be "Don't know/refused"?
c) Show another way to calculate the probability in part b. (Hint: use the complement.)

48. Gun ownership, part 2. Exercise 47 shows the results of a poll that asked about gun ownership. Suppose we select three adults at random from this sample.

a) What is the probability that all three respond "Yes"?
b) What is the probability that none responded "Yes"?
c) What assumption did you make in computing these probabilities?
d) Explain why you think that assumption is reasonable.

49. Contract bidding. As manager for a construction firm, you are in charge of bidding on two large contracts. You believe the probability you get contract #1 is 0.8. If you get contract #1, the probability you also get contract #2 will be 0.2, and if you do not get #1, the probability you get #2 will be 0.4.

a) Sketch the probability tree.
b) What is the probability you will get both contracts?
c) Your competitor hears that you got the second contract but hears nothing about the first contract. Given that you got the second contract, what is the probability that you also got the first contract?

50. Extended warranties. A company that manufactures and sells consumer video cameras sells two versions of their popular hard disk camera, a basic camera for $750, and a deluxe version for $1250. About 75% of customers select the basic camera. Of those, 60% purchase the extended warranty for an additional $200. Of the people who buy the deluxe version, 90% purchase the extended warranty.

a) Sketch the probability tree for total purchases.
b) What is the percentage of customers who buy an extended warranty?
c) What is the expected revenue of the company from a camera purchase (including warranty if applicable)?
d) Given that a customer purchases an extended warranty, what is the probability that he or she bought the deluxe version?

51. Tweeting. According to the Pew 2012 News Consumption survey, 50% of adults who post news on Twitter ("tweet") are younger than 30. But according to the U.S. Census, only 23% of adults are less than 30 years old. A separate survey by Pew in 2012 found that 15% of adults tweet.

a) Find the probability that a random adult is both less than 30 years old and a Twitter poster. That is, find $P(\text{Tweet and} <30)$.
b) For a random young (<30) adult, what is the probability he or she is a tweeter? That is, find $P(\text{Tweet} \mid <30)$ (Hint: use Bayes theorem.)

52. Titanic survival. Of the 2201 people on the RMS *Titanic*, only 711 survived. The practice of "women and children first" was first used to describe the chivalrous actions of the sailors during the sinking of the HMS *Birkenhead* in 1852, but became popular after the sinking of the *Titanic*, during which 53% of the children and 73% of the women survived, but only 21% of the men survived. Part of the protocol stated that passengers enter lifeboats by ticket class as well. Here is a table showing survival by ticket class.

	First	Second	Third	Crew	Total
Alive	203	118	178	212	711
	28.6%	16.6%	25.0%	29.8%	100%
Dead	122	167	528	673	1490
	8.2%	11.2%	35.4%	45.2%	100%

a) Find the conditional probability of survival for each type of ticket.
b) Draw a probability tree for this situation.
c) Given that a passenger survived, what is the probability they had a first-class ticket?

53. Coffeehouse survey. A 2011 Mintel report on coffeehouses asked consumers if they were spending more time in coffeehouses. The table below gives the responses classified by age:

a) What is the probability that a randomly selected respondent is spending more time at coffeehouses and donut shops this year than last year?
b) What is the probability that the person is younger than 25 years old?
c) What is the probability that the person is younger than 25 years old and is spending more time at coffeehouses and donut shops compared to last year?
d) What is the probability that the person is younger than 25 years old *or* is spending more time at coffeehouses and donut shops compared to last year?

	Age						
	18–24	25–34	35–44	45–54	55–64	65 +	Total
I am spending less time at coffeehouses and donut shops this year than last year.	78	93	102	104	68	48	493
I am spending about the same time at coffeehouses and donut shops this year as last year.	82	109	106	89	75	67	528
I am spending more time at coffeehouses and donut shops this year than last year.	30	30	18	19	11	6	114
Total	190	232	226	212	154	121	1135

Source: 2011 Mintel Report. Reprinted by permission of Mintel, a leading market research company. www.mintel.com

54. Electronic communications. A Mintel study asked consumers if electronic communications devices influenced whether or not they bought a certain car. The table on the next page gives the results classified by household income:

If we select a person at random from this sample:

a) What is the probability that electronic communication devices somewhat influenced their decisions?

b) What is the probability that the person is earning at least $100K?
c) What is the probability that the person was somewhat influenced by electronic communications *and* earns at least $100K?
d) What is the probability that electronic communications somewhat influenced the purchase *or* that the person earns at least $100K?

Communications influence on car purchase, by household income, July 2011				
Communication (e.g., hands-free calling):	**Income**			
	< $50K	**$50K–99.9K**	**$100K +**	**Total**
Very Much	30	57	41	128
Somewhat	26	39	62	127
Not At All	23	39	35	97
Total	79	135	138	352

Source: Mintel

55. Red Cross Rh. Exercises 36 and 38 discussed the challenges faced by the Red Cross in finding enough blood of various types. But blood typing also depends on the Rh factor, which can be negative or positive. Here is a table of the estimated proportions worldwide for blood types categorized on both type and Rh factor:

		Blood Type			
		O	**A**	**B**	**AB**
Rh	**+**	36.44%	28.27%	20.59%	5.06%
	−	4.33%	3.52%	1.39%	0.45%

For a randomly selected human, what is the probability that he …

a) Is Rh negative given that he is type O
b) Is type O given that he is Rh negative
c) A person with Type A − blood can accept donated blood only of types A− and O−. What is the probability that a randomly selected donor can donate to a recipient given that the recipient's blood type is A−?

56. Automobile inspection. Twenty percent of cars that are inspected have faulty pollution control systems. The cost of repairing a pollution control system exceeds $100 about 40% of the time. When a driver takes her car in for inspection, what's the probability that she will end up paying more than $100 to repair the pollution control system?

57. Pharmaceutical company. A U.S. pharmaceutical company is considering manufacturing and marketing a pill that will help to lower both an individual's blood pressure and cholesterol. The company is interested in understanding the demand for such a product. The joint probabilities that an adult American man has high blood pressure and/or high cholesterol are shown in the table.

		Blood Pressure	
		High	**OK**
Cholesterol	**High**	0.11	0.21
	OK	0.16	0.52

a) What's the probability that an adult American male has both conditions?
b) What's the probability that an adult American male has high blood pressure?

c) What's the probability that an adult American male with high blood pressure also has high cholesterol?
d) What's the probability that an adult American male has high blood pressure if it's known that he has high cholesterol?

58. International relocation. A European department store is developing a new advertising campaign for their new U.S. location, and their marketing managers need to understand their target market better. A survey of adult shoppers found the probabilities that an adult would shop at their new U.S. store classified by age is shown below.

		Shop		
		Yes	**No**	**Total**
Age	**< 20**	0.26	0.04	0.30
	20–40	0.24	0.10	0.34
	> 40	0.12	0.24	0.36
	Total	0.62	0.38	1.00

a) What's the probability that a survey respondent will shop at the U.S. store?
b) What is the probability that a survey respondent will shop at the store given that they are younger than 20 years old?
c) What is the probability that a survey respondent who is older than 40 shops at the store?
d) What is the probability that a survey respondent is younger than 20 or will shop at the store?

59. Pharmaceutical company, again. Given the table of probabilities compiled for marketing managers in Exercise 57, are high blood pressure and high cholesterol independent? Explain.

60. International relocation, again. Given the table of probabilities compiled for a department store chain in Exercise 58, are age and shopping at the department store independent? Explain.

61. Coffeehouse survey, part 2. Look again at the data from the coffeehouse survey in Exercise 53.

a) If we select a person at random, what's the probability we choose a person between 18 and 24 years old who is spending more at coffeehouses?

b) Among the 18- to 24-year olds, what is the probability that the person responded that they are not spending more time at coffeehouses?

c) What's the probability that a person who spends the same amount of time at coffeehouses is between 35 and 44 years old?

d) If the person responded that they spend more time, what's the probability that they are at least 65 years old?

e) What's the probability that a person at least 65 years old spends the same amount of time?

f) Are the responses to the question and age independent?

62. Electronic communications, part 2. Look again at the data in the electronic communications in Exercise 54.

a) If we select a respondent at random, what's the probability that we choose a person earning less than $50 K and responded "somewhat"?

b) Among those earning $50–99.9K, what is the probability that the person responded "not at all"?

c) What's the probability that a person who responded "very much" was earning at least $100K?

d) If the person responded "very much," what is the probability that they earn between $50K and 99.9K?

e) Are the responses to the question and income level independent?

63. Real estate, part 2. In the real estate research described in Exercise 33, 64% of homes for sale have garages, 21% have swimming pools, and 17% have both features.

a) What is the probability that a home for sale has a garage, but not a pool?

b) If a home for sale has a garage, what's the probability that it has a pool, too?

c) Are having a garage and a pool independent events? Explain.

d) Are having a garage and a pool mutually exclusive? Explain.

64. Polling. Professional polling organizations face the challenge of selecting a representative sample of U.S. adults by telephone. This has been complicated by people who only use cell phones and by others whose landline phones are unlisted. A careful survey by Democracy Corps determined the following proportions:

Cell phone only	39%
Both cell and landline	29%
Landline only listed	22%
Landline only unlisted	7%

a) What's the probability that a randomly selected U.S. adult has a landline?

b) What's the probability that a U.S. adult has a landline given that he or she has a cell phone?

c) Are having a cell phone and a landline independent? Explain.

d) Are having a cell phone and a landline disjoint? Explain.

65. Property values. The following table shows a sample of property listings and values from one neighborhood (one ZIP code) in the Washington, DC, area in December 2011:

Property Values in this Neighborhood of Washington, DC

Price	Number of Bedrooms	Number of Stories	Garage	Number of Baths
$1.8MM	3	3	1	3
$1.1MM	2	2	1	3
$430K	1	1	0	1
$339K	1	1	0	1
$255K	0	1	0	1
$200K	0	1	0	1
$169K	0	1	0	1

a) In this sample, what proportion of homes is valued at $500K or less?

b) Are the number of bedrooms and property values independent? Explain.

66. Property values, part 2. A sample of 1800 homes in a different neighborhood of Washington, DC, in 2011 produced the data in the table for the number of bedrooms and house price. Is the price of the house independent of whether it has 3 or more bedrooms?

Property Values in the Washington, DC, Area

		3 or More Bedrooms	
		Yes	No
House Price	Less than $300K	337	491
	$300–450K	202	334
	$450–600K	139	297

67. Used cars. A business student is searching for a used car to purchase, so she posts an ad to a website saying she wants to buy a used Jeep between $18,000 and $20,000. From Kelly's BlueBook.com, she learns that there are 149 cars matching that description within a 30-mile radius of her home. If we assume that those are the people who will call her and that they are equally likely to call her:

		Price		
		$18,000–$18,999	$19,000–$19,999	Total
Car Make	Commander	3	6	9
	Compass	6	1	7
	Grand Cherokee	33	33	66
	Liberty	17	6	23
	Wrangler	33	11	44
	Total	92	57	149

a) What is the probability that the first caller will be a Jeep Liberty owner?

b) What is the probability that the first caller will own a Jeep Liberty that costs between $18,000 and $18,999?

c) If the first call offers her a Jeep Liberty, what is the probability that it costs less than $19,000?

d) Suppose she decides to ignore calls with cars whose cost is ≥$19,000. What is the probability that the first call she takes will offer to sell her a Jeep Liberty?

68. CEO relocation. The CEO of a mid-sized company has to relocate to another part of the country. To make it easier, the company has hired a relocation agency to help purchase a house. The CEO has 5 children and so has specified that the house have at least 5 bedrooms, but hasn't put any other constraints on the search. The relocation agency has narrowed the search down to the houses in the table and has selected one house to showcase to the CEO and family on their trip out to the new site. The agency doesn't know it, but the family has its heart set on a Cape Cod house with a fireplace. If the agency selected the house at random, without regard to this:

		Fireplace?		
		No	**Yes**	**Total**
House Type	**Cape Cod**	7	2	9
	Colonial	8	14	22
	Other	6	5	11
	Total	21	21	42

a) What is the probability that the selected house is a Cape Cod?

b) What is the probability that the house is a Colonial with a fireplace?

c) If the house is a Cape Cod, what is the probability that it has a fireplace?

d) What is the probability that the selected house is what the family wants?

*69. Computer reliability. Laptop computers have been growing in popularity according to a study by Current Analysis Inc. Laptops now represent more than half the computer sales in the United States. A campus bookstore sells both types of computers and in the last semester sold 56% laptops and 44% desktops. Reliability rates for the two types of machines are quite different, however. In the first year, 5% of desktops require service, while 15% of laptops have problems requiring service.

a) Sketch a probability tree for this situation.

b) What percentage of computers sold by the bookstore last semester required service?

c) Given that a computer required service, what is the probability that it was a laptop?

JUST CHECKING ANSWERS

1 The probability of going up on the next day is not affected by the previous day's outcome.

2 a) 0.30

   b) $0.30(0.30) = 0.09$

   c) $(1 - 0.30)^2(0.30) = 0.147$

   d) $1 - (1 - 0.30)^5 = 0.832$

3 a)

		Weekday		
		Yes	**No**	**Total**
Before Five	**Yes**	0.07	0.41	**0.48**
	No	0.20	0.32	**0.52**
	Total	**0.27**	**0.73**	**1.00**

b) $P(\mathbf{BF}|\mathbf{WD}) = P(\mathbf{BF}\ and\ \mathbf{WD})/P(\mathbf{WD}) = 0.07/0.27 = .259$

c) No, shoppers can do both (and 7% do).

d) To be independent, we'd need $P(\mathbf{BF}|\mathbf{WD}) = P(\mathbf{BF})$. $P(\mathbf{BF}|\mathbf{WD}) = 0.259$, but $P(\mathbf{BF}) = \mathbf{0.48}$. They do not appear to be independent.

6

Random Variables and Probability Models

Metropolitan Life Insurance Company

In 1863, at the height of the U.S. Civil War, a group of businessmen in New York City decided to form a new company to insure Civil War soldiers against disabilities and injuries suffered from the war. After the war ended, they changed direction and decided to focus on selling life insurance. The new company was named Metropolitan Life (MetLife) because the bulk of the company's clients were in the "metropolitan" area of New York City.

Although an economic depression in the 1870s put many life insurance companies out of business, MetLife survived, modeling their business on similar successful programs in England. Taking advantage of spreading industrialism and the selling methods of British insurance agents, the company soon was enrolling as many as 700 new policies per day. By 1909, MetLife was the nation's largest life insurer in the United States.

During the Great Depression of the 1930s, MetLife expanded their public service by promoting public health campaigns, focusing on educating the urban poor in major U.S. cities about the risk of tuberculosis. Because the company invested primarily in urban and farm mortgages, as opposed to the stock market, they survived the crash of 1929 and ended up investing heavily in the postwar U.S. housing boom. They were the principal investors in both the Empire State Building (1929) and Rockefeller Center (1931). During World War II, the company was the single largest contributor to the Allied cause, investing more than half of their total assets in war bonds.

Today, in addition to life insurance, MetLife manages pensions and investments. In 2000, the company held an initial public offering and entered the retail banking business in 2001 with the launch of MetLife Bank. The company's public face is well known because of their use of Snoopy, the dog from the cartoon strip "Peanuts."

nsurance companies make bets all the time. For example, they bet that you're going to live a long life. Ironically, you bet that you're going to die sooner. Both you and the insurance company want the company to stay in business, so it's important to find a "fair price" for your bet. Of course, the right price for *you* depends on many factors, and nobody can predict exactly how long you'll live. But when the company averages its bets over enough customers, it can make reasonably accurate estimates of the amount it can expect to collect on a policy before it has to pay out the benefit. To do that effectively, it must model the situation with a probability model. Using the resulting probabilities, the company can find the fair price of almost any situation involving risk and uncertainty.

Here's a simple example. An insurance company offers a "death and disability" policy that pays $100,000 when a client dies or $50,000 if the client is permanently disabled. It charges a premium of $500 per year for this benefit. Is the company likely to make a profit selling such a plan? To answer this question, the company needs to know the *probability* that a client will die or become disabled in any year. From such actuarial information and the appropriate model, the company can calculate the expected value of this policy.

6.1   Expected Value of a Random Variable

To model the insurance company's risk, we need to define a few terms. The amount the company pays out on an individual policy is an example of a **random variable,** called that because its value is based on the outcome of a random event. We use a capital letter, in this case, X, to denote a random variable. We'll denote a particular *value* that it can have by the corresponding lowercase letter, in this case, x. For the insurance company, x can be $100,000 (if you die that year), $50,000 (if you are disabled), or $0 (if neither occurs). Because we can list all the outcomes, we call this random variable a **discrete random variable**. A random variable that can take on any value (possibly bounded on one or both sides) is called a **continuous random variable**. Continuous random variables are common in business applications for modeling physical quantities like heights and weights, and monetary quantities such as profits, revenues, and spending.

Sometimes it is obvious whether to treat a random variable as discrete or continuous, but at other times the choice is more subtle. Age, for example, might be viewed as discrete if it is measured only to the nearest decade with possible values 10, 20, 30, ... In a scientific context, however, it might be measured more precisely and treated as continuous.

For both discrete and continuous variables, the collection of all the possible values and the probabilities associated with them is called the **probability model** for the random variable. For a discrete random variable, we can list the probability of all possible values in a table, or describe it by a formula. For example, to model the possible outcomes of a fair die, we can let X be the number showing on the face. The probability model for X is simply:

$$P(X = x) = \begin{cases} 1/6 & \textit{if } x = 1, 2, 3, 4, 5, \textit{ or } 6 \\ 0 & \textit{otherwise} \end{cases}$$

NOTATION ALERT

The most common letters for random variables are X, Y, and Z, but any capital letter might be used.

Suppose in our insurance risk example that the death rate in any year is 1 out of every 1000 people and that another 2 out of 1000 suffer some kind of disability. The loss, which we'll denote as X, is a discrete random variable because it takes on only 3 possible values. We can display the probability model for X in a table, as in Table 6.1.

Policyholder Outcome	Payout x (cost)	Probability $P(X = x)$
Death	100,000	$\dfrac{1}{1000}$
Disability	50,000	$\dfrac{2}{1000}$
Neither	0	$\dfrac{997}{1000}$

Table 6.1   Probability model for an insurance policy.

Of course, we can't predict exactly what *will* happen during any given year, but we can say what we *expect* to happen—in this case, what we expect the profit of a policy will be. The expected value of a policy is a **parameter** (a numerically valued attribute) of the probability model. In fact, it's the mean. We'll signify this with the notation $E(X)$, for expected value (or sometimes μ to indicate that it is a mean). This isn't an average of data values, so we won't estimate it. Instead, we calculate it directly from the probability model for the random variable. Because it comes from a model and not data, we use the parameter μ to denote it (and *not* $\bar{y}$ or $\bar{x}$).

To see what the insurance company can expect, think about some convenient number of outcomes. For example, imagine that they have exactly 1000 clients and that the outcomes in one year followed the probability model exactly: 1 died, 2 were disabled, and 997 survived unscathed. Then our expected payout would be:

$$\mu = E(X) = \frac{100{,}000(1) + 50{,}000(2) + 0(997)}{1000} = 200$$

So our expected payout comes to $200 per policy.

Instead of writing the expected value as one big fraction, we can rewrite it as separate terms, each divided by 1000.

$$\mu = E(X) = \$100{,}000\left(\frac{1}{1000}\right) + \$50{,}000\left(\frac{2}{1000}\right) + \$0\left(\frac{997}{1000}\right)$$
$$= \$200$$

Writing it this way, we can see that for each policy, there's a 1/1000 chance that we'll have to pay $100,000 for a death and a 2/1000 chance that we'll have to pay $50,000 for a disability. Of course, there's a 997/1000 chance that we won't have to pay anything.

So the **expected value** of a (discrete) random variable is found by multiplying each possible value of the random variable by the probability that it occurs and then summing all those products. This gives the general formula for the expected value of a discrete random variable:[1]

$$E(X) = \Sigma x P(x).$$

---

[1]The concept of expected values for continuous random variables is similar, but the calculation requires calculus and is beyond the scope of this text.

Be sure that *every* possible outcome is included in the sum. Verify that you have a valid probability model to start with—the probabilities should each be between 0 and 1 and should sum to one. (Recall the rules of probability in Chapter 5.)

FOR EXAMPLE   Calculating the expected value of a random variable

QUESTIONS   A fund-raising lottery offers 500 tickets for $3 each. If the grand prize is $250 and 4 second prizes are $50 each, what is the expected value of a single ticket? (Don't count the cost of the ticket in this yet.) Now, including its cost, what is the expected value of the ticket? (Knowing this value, does it make any "sense" to buy a lottery ticket?) The fund-raising group has a target of $1000 to be raised by the lottery. Can they expect to make this much?

ANSWERS   Each ticket has a 1/500 chance of winning the grand prize of $250, a 4/500 chance of winning $50, and a 495/500 chance of winning nothing. So $E(X) = (1/500) \times \$250 + (4/500) \times \$50 + (495/500) \times \$0 = \$0.50 + \$0.40 + \$0.00 = \$0.90$. Including the cost, the expected value is $\$0.90 - \$3 = -\$2.10$. Although no single person will lose $2.10 (they either lose $3 or win $50 or $250), $2.10 is the amount, on average, that the lottery gains per ticket. Therefore, they can expect to make $500 \times \$2.10 = \$1050$.

6.2   Standard Deviation of a Random Variable

Of course, this expected value (or mean) is not what actually happens to any *particular* policyholder. No individual policy actually costs the company $200. We are dealing with random events, so some policyholders receive big payouts and others nothing. Because the insurance company must anticipate this variability, it needs to know the standard deviation of the random variable.

For data, we calculate the standard deviation by first computing the deviation of each data value from the mean and squaring it. We perform a similar calculation when we compute the **standard deviation** of a (discrete) random variable as well. First, we find the deviation of each payout from the mean (expected value). (See Table 6.2.)

Policyholder Outcome	Payout *x* (cost)	Probability $P(X = x)$	Deviation $(x - EV)$
Death	100,000	$\dfrac{1}{1000}$	$(100,000 - 200) = 99,800$
Disability	50,000	$\dfrac{2}{1000}$	$(50,000 - 200) = 49,800$
Neither	0	$\dfrac{997}{1000}$	$(0 - 200) = -200$

Table 6.2   Deviations between the expected value and each payout (cost).

Next, we square each deviation. The **variance** is the expected value of those squared deviations. To find it, we multiply each by the appropriate probability and sum those products:

$$Var(X) = 99,800^2\left(\frac{1}{1000}\right) + 49,800^2\left(\frac{2}{1000}\right) + (-200)^2\left(\frac{997}{1000}\right)$$
$$= 14,960,000.$$

Finally, we take the square root to get the standard deviation:

$$SD(X) = \sqrt{14,960,000} \approx \$3867.82$$

The insurance company can expect an average payout of $200 per policy, with a standard deviation of $3867.82.

Think about that. The company charges $500 for each policy and expects to pay out $200 per policy. Sounds like an easy way to make $300. (In fact, most of the time—probability 997/1000—the company pockets the entire $500.) But would you be willing to take on this risk yourself and sell all your friends policies like this? The problem is that occasionally the company loses big. With a probability of 1/1000, it will pay out $100,000, and with a probability of 2/1000, it will pay out $50,000. That may be more risk than you're willing to take on. The standard deviation of $3867.82 gives an indication of the uncertainty of the profit, and that seems like a fairly large spread (and risk) for an average profit of $300.

Here are the formulas for these arguments. Because these are parameters of our probability model, the variance and standard deviation can also be written as σ^2 and σ, respectively (sometimes with the name of the random variable as a subscript). You should recognize both kinds of notation:

$$\sigma^2 = Var(X) = \sum (x - \mu)^2 P(x) = \sum (x - E(X))^2 P(x), \text{ and}$$

$$\sigma = SD(X) = \sqrt{Var(X)}.$$

FOR EXAMPLE Calculating the standard deviation of a random variable

QUESTION In the lottery example on page 184, we found the expected gain per ticket to be $2.10. What is the standard deviation? What does it say about your chances in the lottery? Comment.

ANSWER

$$\sigma^2 = Var(X) = \sum (x - E(X))^2 P(x) = \sum (x - 2.10)^2 P(x)$$

$$= (250 - 2.10)^2 \frac{1}{500} + (50 - 2.10)^2 \frac{4}{500} + (0 - 2.10)^2 \frac{495}{500}$$

$$= 61,454.41 \times \frac{1}{500} + 2,294.41 \times \frac{4}{500} + 4.41 \times \frac{495}{500}$$

$$= 145.63$$

so $\sigma = \sqrt{145.63} = \$12.07$

That's a lot of variation for a mean of $2.10, which reflects the fact that there is a small chance that you'll win a lot but a large chance you'll win nothing.

GUIDED EXAMPLE   Computer Inventory

As the head of inventory for a computer company, you've had a challenging couple of weeks. One of your warehouses recently had a fire, and you had to flag all the computers stored there to be recycled. On the positive side, you were thrilled that you had managed to ship two computers to your biggest client last week. But then you discovered that your assistant hadn't heard about the fire and had mistakenly transported a whole truckload of computers from the damaged warehouse into the shipping center. It turns out that 30% of all the computers shipped last week were

(continued)

damaged. You don't know whether your biggest client received two damaged computers, two undamaged ones, or one of each. Computers were selected at random from the shipping center for delivery.

If your client received two undamaged computers, everything is fine. If the client gets one damaged computer, it will be returned at your expense—$100—and you can replace it. However, if both computers are damaged, the client will cancel all other orders this month, and you'll lose $10,000.

Question: What is the expected value and the standard deviation of your loss under this scenario?

| **PLAN** | **Setup** State the problem. | We want to analyze the potential consequences of shipping damaged computers to a large client. We'll look at the expected value and standard deviation of the amount we'll lose. |
| | | Let $X =$ amount of loss. We'll denote the receipt of an undamaged computer by **U** and the receipt of a damaged computer by **D**. The three possibilities are: two undamaged computers (**U** and **U**), two damaged computers (**D** and **D**), and one of each (**UD** or **DU**). Because the computers were selected randomly and the number in the warehouse is large, we can assume independence. |

| **DO** | **Model** List the possible values of the random variable, and compute all the values you'll need to determine the probability model. | Because the events are independent, we can use the multiplication rule (Chapter 5) and find: |

$$P(\mathbf{UU}) = P(\mathbf{U}) \times P(\mathbf{U})$$
$$= 0.7 \times 0.7 = 0.49$$
$$P(\mathbf{DD}) = P(\mathbf{D}) \times P(\mathbf{D})$$
$$= 0.3 \times 0.3 = 0.09$$
So, $P(\mathbf{UD}\ or\ \mathbf{DU}) = 1 - (0.49 + 0.09) = 0.42$

We have the following model for all possible values of X.

Outcome	x	$P(X = x)$
Two damaged	10,000	$P(\mathbf{DD}) = 0.09$
One damaged	100	$P(\mathbf{UD}\ or\ \mathbf{DU}) = 0.42$
Neither damaged	0	$P(\mathbf{UU}) = 0.49$

Mechanics Find the expected value.

$$E(X) = 0(0.49) + 100(0.42) + 10,000(0.09)$$
$$= \$942.00$$

Find the variance.

$$Var(X) = (0 - 942)^2 \times (0.49)$$
$$+ (100 - 942)^2 \times (0.42)$$
$$+ (10,000 - 942)^2 \times (0.09)$$
$$= 8,116,836$$

Find the standard deviation.

$$SD(X) = \sqrt{8,116,836} = \$2849.01$$

REPORT	**Conclusion** Interpret your results in context.	MEMO
		Re: Damaged computers
		The recent shipment of two computers to our large client may have some serious problems. Even though there is about a 50% chance that they will receive two perfectly good computers, there is a 9% chance that they will

REALITY CHECK

receive two damaged computers and will cancel the rest of their monthly order. We have analyzed the expected loss to the firm as $942 with a standard deviation of $2849.01. The large standard deviation reflects the fact that there is a real possibility of losing $10,000 from the mistake.

Both numbers seem reasonable. The expected value of $942 is between the extremes of $0 and $10,000, and there's great variability in the outcome values.

6.3 Properties of Expected Values and Variances

Our example insurance company expected to pay out an average of $200 per policy, with a standard deviation of about $3868. The expected profit then was $500 − $200 = $300 per policy. Suppose that the company decides to lower the price of the premium by $50 to $450. It's pretty clear that the expected profit would drop an average of $50 per policy, to $450 − $200 = $250.

What about the standard deviation? We know that adding or subtracting a constant from data shifts the mean but doesn't change the variance or standard deviation. The same is true of random variables:[2]

$$E(X \pm c) = E(X) \pm c,$$
$$Var(X \pm c) = Var(X), \text{and}$$
$$SD(X \pm c) = SD(X).$$

What if the company decides to *double* all the payouts—that is, pay $200,000 for death and $100,000 for disability? This would double the average payout per policy and also increase the variability in payouts. In general, multiplying each value of a random variable by a constant multiplies the mean by that constant and multiplies the variance by the *square* of the constant:

$$E(aX) = aE(X), \text{and}$$
$$Var(aX) = a^2 Var(X).$$

Taking square roots of the last equation shows that the standard deviation is multiplied by the absolute value of the constant:

$$SD(aX) = |a|SD(X).$$

This insurance company sells policies to more than just one person. We've just seen how to compute means and variances for one person at a time. What happens to the mean and variance when we have a collection of customers? The profit on a group of customers is the *sum* of the individual profits, so we'll need to know how to find expected values and variances for sums. To start, consider a simple case with just two customers who we'll call Mr. Ecks and Ms. Wye. With an expected payout of $200 on each policy, we might expect a total of $200 + $200 = $400 to be paid out on the two policies—nothing surprising there. In other words, we have the **Addition Rule for Expected Values of Random Variables**: *The expected value of the sum (or difference) of random variables is the sum (or difference) of their expected values:*

$$E(X \pm Y) = E(X) \pm E(Y).$$

---

[2]The rules in this section are true for both discrete *and* continuous random variables.

The variability is another matter. Is the risk of insuring two people the same as the risk of insuring one person for twice as much? We wouldn't expect both clients to die or become disabled in the same year. In fact, because we've spread the risk, the standard deviation should be smaller. Indeed, this is the fundamental principle behind insurance. By spreading the risk among many policies, a company can keep the standard deviation quite small and predict costs more accurately. It's much less risky to insure thousands of customers than one customer when the total expected payout is the same, assuming that the events are independent. Catastrophic events such as hurricanes or earthquakes that affect large numbers of customers at the same time destroy the independence assumption, and often the insurance company along with it.

But how much smaller is the standard deviation of the sum? It turns out that, if the random variables are independent, we have the **Addition Rule for Variances of (Independent) Random Variables**: *The variance of the sum or difference of two independent random variables is the sum of their individual variances:*

$$Var(X \pm Y) = Var(X) + Var(Y)$$

if X and Y are independent.

MATH BOX   Pythagorean Theorem of Statistics

We often use the standard deviation to measure variability, but when we add independent random variables, we use their variances. Think of the Pythagorean Theorem. In a right triangle (only), the *square* of the length of the hypotenuse is the sum of the *squares* of the lengths of the other two sides:

$$c^2 = a^2 + b^2.$$

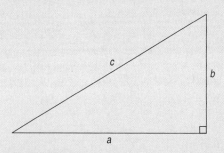

For independent random variables (only), the *square* of the standard deviation of their sum is the sum of the *squares* of their standard deviations:

$$SD^2(X + Y) = SD^2(X) + SD^2(Y).$$

It's simpler to write this with *variances:*

$$Var(X + Y) = Var(X) + Var(Y),$$

but we'll use the standard deviation formula often as well:

$$SD(X + Y) = \sqrt{Var(X) + Var(Y)}.$$

For Mr. Ecks and Ms. Wye, the insurance company can expect their outcomes to be independent, so (using X for Mr. Ecks's payout and Y for Ms. Wye's):

$$
\begin{aligned}
Var(X + Y) &= Var(X) + Var(Y) \\
&= 14{,}960{,}000 + 14{,}960{,}000 \\
&= 29{,}920{,}000.
\end{aligned}
$$

Let's compare the variance of writing two independent policies to the variance of writing only one for twice the size. If the company had insured only Mr. Ecks for twice as much, the variance would have been

$$Var(2X) = 2^2 Var(X) = 4 \times 14{,}960{,}000 = 59{,}840{,}000, \text{ or}$$

twice as big as with two independent policies, even though the expected payout is the same.

Of course, variances are in squared units. The company would prefer to know standard deviations, which are in dollars. The standard deviation of the payout for two independent policies is $SD(X + Y) = \sqrt{Var(X + Y)} = \sqrt{29{,}920{,}000} = \$5469.92$. But the standard deviation of the payout for a single policy of twice the size is twice the standard deviation of a single policy: $SD(2X) = 2SD(X) = 2(\$3867.82) = \$7735.64$, or about 40% more than the standard deviation of the sum of the two independent policies.

If the company has two customers, then it will have an expected annual total payout (cost) of $400 with a standard deviation of about $5470. If they write one policy with an expected annual payout of $400, they increase the standard deviation by about 40%. Spreading risk by insuring many independent customers is one of the fundamental principles in insurance and finance.

Let's review the rules of expected values and variances for sums and differences.

- The expected value of the sum of two random variables is the sum of the expected values.
- The expected value of the difference of two random variables is the difference of the expected values:

$$E(X \pm Y) = E(X) \pm E(Y).$$

- If the random variables are independent, the variance of their sum or difference is always the sum of the variances:

$$Var(X \pm Y) = Var(X) + Var(Y).$$

Do we always *add* variances? Even when we take the *difference* of two random quantities? Yes! Think about the two insurance policies. Suppose we want to know the mean and standard deviation of the *difference* in payouts to the two clients. Since each policy has an expected payout of $200, the expected difference is $200 − $200 = $0. If we computed the variance of the difference by subtracting variances, we would get $0 for the variance. But that doesn't make sense. Their difference won't always be exactly $0. In fact, the difference in payouts could range from $100,000 to −$100,000, a spread of $200,000. The variability in differences *increases* as much as the variability in sums. If the company has two customers, the difference in payouts has a mean of $0 and a standard deviation of about $5470.

For Random Variables, Does $X + X + X = 3X$?

Maybe, but be careful. As we've just seen, insuring one person for $300,000 is not the same risk as insuring three people for $100,000 each. When each instance represents a different outcome for the same random variable, though, it's easy to fall into the trap of writing all of them with the same symbol. Don't make this common mistake. Make sure you write each instance as a *different* random variable. Just because each random variable describes a similar situation doesn't mean that each random outcome will be the same. What you really mean is $X_1 + X_2 + X_3$. Written this way, it's clear that the sum shouldn't necessarily equal 3 times *anything*.

FOR EXAMPLE Sums of random variables

You are considering investing $1000 into one or possibly two different investment funds. Historically, each has delivered 5% a year in profit with a standard deviation of 3%. So, a $1000 investment would produce $50 with a standard deviation of $30.

QUESTION Assuming the two funds are independent, what are the relative advantages and disadvantages of putting $1000 into one, or splitting the $1000 and putting $500 into each? Compare the means and SDs of the profit from the two strategies.

(continued)

ANSWER   Let X = amount gained by putting $1000 into one

$$E(X) = 0.05 \times 1000 = \$50 \text{ and } SD(X) = 0.03 \times 1000 = \$30.$$

Let W = amount gained by putting $500 into each. W_1 and W_2 are the amounts from each fund respectively. $E(W_1) = E(W_2) = 0.05 \times 500 = \$25$. So $E(W) = E(W_1) + E(W_2) = \$25 + \$25 = \$50$. The expected values of the two strategies are the same. You expect on average to earn $50 on $1000.

$$\begin{aligned} SD(W) &= \sqrt{SD^2(W_1) + SD^2(W_2)} \\ &= \sqrt{(0.03 \times 500)^2 + (0.03 \times 500)^2} \\ &= \sqrt{15^2 + 15^2} \\ &= \$21.213 \end{aligned}$$

The standard deviation of the amount earned is $21.213 by splitting the investment amount compared to $30 for investing in one. The expected values are the same. Spreading the investment into more than one vehicle *reduces* the variation. On the other hand, keeping it all in one vehicle increases the chances of both extremely good and extremely bad returns. Which one is better depends on an individual's appetite for risk.[3]

Covariance

In Chapter 4 we saw that the association of two variables could be measured with their correlation. What about random variables? We can talk about the correlation between random variables, too. But it's easier to start with a related concept called covariance.

If X is a random variable with expected value $E(X) = \mu$ and Y is a random variable with expected value $E(X) = \nu$, then the **covariance** of X and Y is defined as

$$Cov(X, Y) = E((X - \mu)(Y - \nu)).$$

The covariance, like the correlation, measures how X and Y vary together ($co = together$).

The covariance gives us the extra information we need to find the variance of the sum or difference of two random variables when they are *not* independent:

$$Var(X \pm Y) = Var(X) + Var(Y) \pm 2Cov(X, Y).$$

When X and Y are independent, their covariance is zero, so we have the Pythagorean theorem of statistics, as we saw earlier. When the variables are positively associated, the variance of their sum (or difference) is increased. This is why it's riskier to invest in two things that are related and less risky to diversify by finding two investments that are nearly independent (and thus have covariance near zero.)

Covariance, unlike correlation, doesn't have to be between -1 and 1, which can make it harder to interpret. To fix this "problem," we divide the covariance by each of the standard deviations to get the **correlation:**

$$Corr(X, Y) = \frac{Cov(X, Y)}{\sigma_X \sigma_Y}.$$

---

[3]The assumption of independence is crucial, but not always (or ever) reasonable. As a March 3, 2010, article on *CNN Money* stated:

> "It's only when economic conditions start to return to normal . . . that investors, and investments, move independently again. That's when diversification reasserts its case. . . ."

money.cnn.com/2010/03/03/pf/funds/diversification.moneymag/index.htm

This is the random variable analogue of the correlation coefficient, r, which we saw in Chapter 4 for data. For random variables, correlation is usually denoted with the greek letter ρ.

JUST CHECKING

1 Suppose that the time it takes a customer to get and pay for seats at the ticket window of a baseball park is a random variable with a mean of 100 seconds and a standard deviation of 50 seconds. When you get there, you find only two people in line in front of you.

a) How long do you expect to wait for your turn to get tickets?

b) What's the standard deviation of your wait time?

c) What assumption did you make about the two customers in finding the standard deviation?

6.4 Bernoulli Trials

Calvin and Hobbes © 1993 Watterson. Distributed by Universal Uclick. Reprinted with permission. All rights reserved.

NOTATION ALERT

Now we have two more reserved letters. Whenever we deal with Bernoulli trials, p represents the probability of success, and q represents the probability of failure. (Of course, $q = 1 - p$.)

When Google Inc. designed their web browser *Chrome*, they worked hard to minimize the probability that their browser would have trouble displaying a website. Before releasing the product, they had to test many websites to discover those that might fail. Although web browsers are relatively new, *quality control inspection* such as this is common throughout manufacturing worldwide and has been in use in industry for nearly 100 years.

The developers of *Chrome* sampled websites, recording whether the browser displayed the website correctly or had a problem. We call the act of inspecting a website a trial. There are two possible outcomes—either the website is displayed correctly or it isn't. The developers thought that whether any particular website displayed correctly was independent from other sites. Situations like this occur often and are called **Bernoulli trials**. To summarize, trials are Bernoulli if:

- There are only two possible outcomes (called *success* and *failure*) for each trial.
- The probability of success, denoted p, is the same on every trial. (The probability of failure, $1 - p$ is often denoted q.)
- The trials are independent. Finding that one website does not display correctly does not change what might happen with the next website.

Common examples of Bernoulli trials include tossing a coin, collecting responses on Yes/No questions from surveys, or even shooting free throws in a basketball game. Bernoulli trials are remarkably versatile and can be used to model a wide variety of real-life situations. The specific question you might ask in different situations will give rise to different random variables that, in turn, have different probability models.

Of course, the *Chrome* developers wanted to find websites that wouldn't display so they could fix any problems in the browser. So for them a "success" was finding a failed website. The labels "success" and "failure" are often applied arbitrarily, so be sure you know what they mean in any particular situation.

One of the important requirements for Bernoulli trials is that the trials be independent. Sometimes that's a reasonable assumption. Is it true for our example? It's easy to imagine that related sites might have similar problems, but if the sites are selected at random, whether one has a problem should be independent of others.

The 10% Condition: Bernoulli trials must be independent. In theory, we need to sample from a population that's infinitely big. However, if the population is finite, it's still okay to proceed as long as the sample is smaller than 10% of the population. In Google's case, they just happened to have a directory of millions of websites, so most samples would easily satisfy the 10% condition.

6.5

Discrete Probability Models

Sam Savage, Professor at Stanford University, says in his book, *The Flaw of Averages*, that plans based only on averages are, on average, wrong. Unfortunately, many business owners make decisions based on averages—the average amount sold last year, the average number of customers seen last month, etc. But averages are just too simple to represent real-world business practice. Fortunately, we can do better by modeling business situations with a probability model. Probability models can play an important role in helping decision makers predict both the outcomes and the consequences of their decision alternatives. In this section we'll see that some fairly simple models let us model a wide variety of business phenomena.

The Uniform Model

We'll start with the simplest probability model of all, the Uniform model. When we first studied probability in Chapter 5, we saw that equally likely events were the simplest case. For example, a single die can turn up 1, 2, . . . , 6 on one toss. A probability model for the toss is Uniform because each of the outcomes has the same probability $(1/6)$ of occurring. Similarly if X is a random variable with possible outcomes 1, 2, . . . , n and $P(X = i) = 1/n$ for each value of i, then we say X has a **discrete Uniform distribution, U[1, . . . , n]**.

Unfortunately, some business decision makers take only one step away from averages and assume that all their unknown outcomes are equally likely. That can put them with the lottery ticket purchaser who thought her chances were 50/50: "either I win or I don't." Let's look at some more realistic (and more useful) probability models.

The Geometric Model

What's the probability that when Google tests *Chrome* on new websites, the first website that fails to display is the second one that they test? They can use Bernoulli trials to build a probability model. Let X denote the number of trials (websites) until the first such "success." For X to be 2, the first website must have displayed correctly (which has probability $1 - p$), and then the second one must have not displayed correctly—a success, with probability p.[4] Since the trials are independent, these probabilities can be multiplied, and so $P(X = 2) = (1 - p)(p)$ or qp. Maybe Google won't find a success until the fifth trial. What are the chances of that? *Chrome* would have to display the first four websites correctly and then choke on the fifth one, so $P(X = 5) = (1 - p)^4(p) = q^4p$.

Whenever the question is how long (how many trials) it will take to achieve the first success, the model that gives this probability is the **geometric probability model**. Geometric models are completely specified by one parameter, p, the probability of success. We denote them Geom(p).

Daniel Bernoulli (1700–1782) was the nephew of Jacob, whom you saw in Chapter 5. He was the first to work out the mathematics for what we now call Bernoulli trials.

> **Geometric Probability Model for Bernoulli Trials: Geom(p)**
>
> p = probability of success (and $q = 1 - p$ = probability of failure)
> X = number of trials until the first success occurs
>
> $$P(X = x) = q^{x-1}p$$
>
> Expected value: $\mu = \dfrac{1}{p}$
>
> Standard deviation: $\sigma = \sqrt{\dfrac{q}{p^2}}$

---

[4] This is an example of applying the term "success" to something we care about—a *failure* of the browser. Don't be confused.

The geometric distribution can tell Google something important about its software. No large complex program is entirely free of bugs. So before releasing a program or upgrade, developers typically ask not whether it is free of bugs, but how long it is likely to be until the next bug is discovered. If the expected number of trials until the next bug discovery is high enough, then it makes business sense to ship the product rather than wait for that next bug report.

The Binomial Model

Suppose Google tests 5 websites. What's the probability that *exactly* 2 of them have problems (2 "successes")? The geometric model tells how long it should take until the first success. Now we want to find the probability of getting exactly 2 successes among the 5 trials. We are still talking about Bernoulli trials, but we're asking a different question.

This time we're interested in the *number of successes* in the 5 trials, which we'll denote by X. We want to find $P(X = 2)$. Whenever the random variable of interest is the number of successes in a series of Bernoulli trials, it's called a **Binomial random variable**. It takes two parameters to define this Binomial probability model: the number of trials, n, and the probability of success, p. We denote this model Binom(n, p).

Suppose that in an early phase of development, 10% of the sites exhibited some sort of problem so that $p = 0.10$. Exactly 2 successes in 5 trials means 2 successes and 3 failures. It seems logical that the probability should be $(p)^2(1 - p)^3$. Unfortunately, it's not *quite* that easy. That calculation would give you the probability of finding two successes and then three failures—*in that order*. But you could find the two successes in a lot of other ways, for example in the 2nd and 4th website you test. The probability of that sequence is $(1 - p)p(1 - p)p(1 - p)$ which is also $p^2(1 - p)^3$. In fact, as long as there are two successes and three failures, the probability will always be the same, regardless of the order of the sequence of successes and failures. The probability will be $(p)^2(1 - p)^3$. To find the probability of getting 2 successes in 5 trials in any order, we just need to know how many ways that outcome can occur.

Fortunately, all the sequences that lead to the same number of successes are *disjoint*. (For example, if your successes came on the first two trials, they couldn't come on the last two.) So once we find all the different sequences, we can add up their probabilities. And since the probabilities are all the same, we just need to find how many sequences there are and multiply $(p)^2(1 - p)^3$ by that number.

Each different order in which we can have k successes in n trials is called a "combination." The total number of ways this can happen is written $\binom{n}{k}$ or $_nC_k$ and pronounced "n choose k:"

$$\binom{n}{k} = \,_nC_k = \frac{n!}{k!(n - k)!} \text{ where } n! = n \times (n - 1) \times \cdots \times 1.$$

For 2 successes in 5 trials,

$$\binom{5}{2} = \frac{5!}{2!(5 - 2)!} = \frac{(5 \times 4 \times 3 \times 2 \times 1)}{(2 \times 1 \times 3 \times 2 \times 1)} = \frac{(5 \times 4)}{(2 \times 1)} = 10.$$

So there are 10 ways to get 2 successes in 5 websites, and the probability of each is $(p)^2(1 - p)^3$. To find the probability of exactly 2 successes in 5 trials, we multiply the probability of any particular order by the number of possible different orders:

$$P(\textit{exactly 2 successes in 5 trials}) = 10p^2(1 - p)^3 = 10(0.10)^2(0.90)^3 = 0.0729$$

In general, we can write the probability of exactly k successes in n trials as

$$P(X = k) = \binom{n}{k}p^k q^{n-k}.$$

If the probability that any single website has a display problem is 0.10, what's the expected number of websites with problems if we test 100 sites? You probably said 10. We suspect you didn't use the formula for expected value that involves multiplying each value times its probability and adding them up. In fact, there is an easier way to find the expected value for a Binomial random variable. You just multiply the probability of success by n. In other words, $E(X) = np$. We prove this in the next Math Box.

The standard deviation is less obvious and you can't just rely on your intuition. Fortunately, the formula for the standard deviation also boils down to something simple: $SD(X) = \sqrt{npq}$. If you're curious to know where that comes from, it's in the Math Box, too.

In our website example, with $n = 100$, $E(X) = np = 100(0.10) = 10$ so we expect to find 10 successes out of the 100 trials. The standard deviation is

$$\sqrt{100 \times 0.10 \times 0.90} = 3 \text{ websites.}$$

Binomial Model for Bernoulli Trials: Binom (n, p)

n = number of trials
p = probability of success (and $q = 1 - p$ = probability of failure)
X = number of successes in n trials

$$P(X = x) = \binom{n}{x} p^x q^{n-x}, \text{ where } \binom{n}{x} = \frac{n!}{x!(n-x)!}$$

Mean: $\mu = np$
Standard deviation: $\sigma = \sqrt{npq}$

MATH BOX   Mean and Standard Deviation
of the Binomial Model

To derive the formulas for the mean and standard deviation of the Binomial model we start with the most basic situation.

Consider a single Bernoulli trial with probability of success p. Let's find the mean and variance of the number of successes.

Here's the probability model for the number of successes:

x	0	1
$P(X = x)$	q	p

Find the expected value:

$$E(X) = 0q + 1p$$
$$E(X) = p$$

Now the variance:

$$Var(X) = (0 - p)^2 q + (1 - p)^2 p$$
$$= p^2 q + q^2 p$$
$$= pq(p + q)$$
$$= pq(1)$$
$$Var(X) = pq$$

What happens when there is more than one trial? A Binomial model simply counts the number of successes in a series of n independent Bernoulli trials. That makes it easy to find the mean and standard deviation of a binomial random variable, Y.

$$\text{Let } Y = X_1 + X_2 + X_3 + \cdots + X_n$$
$$E(Y) = E(X_1 + X_2 + X_3 + \cdots + X_n)$$
$$= E(X_1) + E(X_2) + E(X_3) + \cdots + E(X_n)$$
$$= p + p + p + \cdots + p \text{ (There are } n \text{ terms.)}$$

So, as we thought, the mean is $E(Y) = np$.

And since the trials are independent, the variances add:

$$Var(Y) = Var(X_1 + X_2 + X_3 + \cdots + X_n)$$
$$= Var(X_1) + Var(X_2) + Var(X_3) + \cdots + Var(X_n)$$
$$= pq + pq + pq + \cdots + pq \text{ (Again, } n \text{ terms.)}$$
$$Var(Y) = npq$$

Voila! The standard deviation is $SD(Y) = \sqrt{npq}$.

GUIDED EXAMPLE   The American Red Cross

Every two seconds someone in America needs blood.

The American Red Cross is a nonprofit organization that runs like a large business. It serves over 3000 hospitals around the United States, providing a wide range of high-quality blood products and blood donor and patient testing services. It collects blood from over 4 million donors, provides blood to millions of patients, and is dedicated to meeting customer needs.

Balancing supply and demand is complicated not only by the logistics of finding donors that meet health criteria, but also by the fact that the blood type of donor and patient must be matched. People with O-negative blood are called "universal donors" because O-negative blood can be given to patients with any blood type. Only about 6% of people have O-negative blood, which presents a challenge in managing and planning. This is especially true, since, unlike a manufacturer who can balance supply by planning to produce or to purchase more or less of a key item, the Red Cross gets its supply from volunteer donors who show up more-or-less at random (at least in terms of blood type). Modeling the arrival of samples with various blood types helps the Red Cross managers to plan their blood allocations.

Here's a small example of the kind of planning required. Of the next 20 donors to arrive at a blood donation center, how many universal donors can be expected? Specifically, what are the mean and standard deviation of the number of universal donors? What is the probability that there are 2 or 3 universal donors?

Question 1: What are the mean and standard deviation of the number of universal donors?

Question 2: What is the probability that there are exactly 2 or 3 universal donors out of the 20 donors?

| | **Setup** State the question.

Check to see that these are Bernoulli trials. | We want to know the mean and standard deviation of the number of universal donors among 20 people and the probability that there are 2 or 3 of them.

✓ There are two outcomes:
success = O-negative
failure = other blood types

✓ $p = 0.06$

✓ **10% Condition:** Fewer than 10% of all possible donors have shown up. |
| | **Variable** Define the random variable.

Model Specify the model. | Let X = number of O-negative donors among $n = 20$ people.

We can model X with a Binom(20, 0.06). |

(continued)

DO   **Mechanics** Find the expected value and standard deviation.

Calculate the probability of 2 or 3 successes.

$E(X) = np = 20(0.06) = 1.2$
$SD(X) = \sqrt{npq} = \sqrt{20(0.06)(0.94)} \approx 1.06$
$P(X = 2 \text{ or } 3) = P(X = 2) + P(X = 3)$

$$= \binom{20}{2}(0.06)^2(0.94)^{18}$$
$$+ \binom{20}{3}(0.06)^3(0.94)^{17}$$
$$\approx 0.2246 + 0.0860$$
$$= 0.3106$$

REPORT   **Conclusion** Interpret your results in context.

Memo

Re: Blood Drive

In groups of 20 randomly selected blood donors, we'd expect to find an average of 1.2 universal donors, with a standard deviation of 1.06. About 31% of the time, we'd expect to find exactly 2 or 3 universal donors among the 20 people.

The Poisson Model

Simeon Denis Poisson was a French mathematician interested in rare events. He originally derived his model to approximate the Binomial model when the probability of a success, p, is very small and the number of trials, n, is very large. Poisson's contribution was providing a simple approximation to find that probability. When you see the formula, however, you won't necessarily see the connection to the Binomial.

Not all discrete events can be modeled as Bernoulli trials. Sometimes we're interested simply in the number of events that occur over a given interval of time or space. For example, we might want to model the number of customers arriving in our store in the next ten minutes, the number of visitors to our website in the next minute, or the number of defects that occur in a computer monitor of a certain size. In cases like these, the number of occurrences can be modeled by a **Poisson model**. The Poisson's parameter, the mean of the distribution, is usually denoted by λ.

Poisson Probability Model for Occurrences: Poisson(λ)
λ = mean number of occurrences
X = number of occurrences

$$P(X = x) = \frac{e^{-\lambda}\lambda^x}{x!}$$

Expected value: $E(X) = \lambda$
Standard deviation: $SD(X) = \sqrt{\lambda}$

For example, data show an average of about 4 hits per minute to a small business website during the afternoon hours from 1:00 to 5:00 p.m. We can use the Poisson model to find the probability of any number of hits arriving. For example, if we let X be the number of hits arriving in the next minute, then $P(X = x) = \frac{e^{-\lambda}\lambda^x}{x!} = \frac{e^{-4}4^x}{x!}$, using the given average rate of 4 per minute. So, the probability of no hits during the next minute would be $P(X = 0) = \frac{e^{-4}4^0}{0!} = e^{-4} = 0.0183$ (The constant e is the base of the natural logarithms and is approximately 2.71828).

One interesting and useful feature of the Poisson model is that it scales according to the interval size. For example, suppose we want to know the probability of no hits to our website in the next 30 seconds. Since the mean rate is 4 hits per

W. S. Gosset, the quality control chemist at the Guinness brewery in the early 20th century who developed the methods of Chapters 11 and 12, was one of the first to use the Poisson in industry. He used it to model and predict the number of yeast cells so he'd know how much to add to the stock. The Poisson is a good model to consider whenever your data consist of counts of occurrences. It requires only that the events be independent and that the mean number of occurrences stays constant.

minute, it's 2 hits per 30 seconds, so we can use the model with $\lambda = 2$ instead. If we let Y be the number of hits arriving in the next 30 seconds, then:

$$P(Y = 0) = \frac{e^{-2}2^0}{0!} = e^{-2} = 0.1353.$$

(Recall that $0! = 1$.) The Poisson model has been used to model phenomena such as customer arrivals, hot streaks in sports, and disease clusters.

Whenever or wherever rare events happen closely together, people want to know whether the occurrence happened by chance or whether an underlying change caused the unusual occurrence. The Poisson model can be used to find the probability of the occurrence and can be the basis for making the judgment.

e and Compound Interest

The constant e equals 2.7182818... (to 7 decimal places). One of the places e originally turned up was in calculating how much money you'd earn if you could get interest compounded more often. If you earn 100% per year simple interest, at the end of the year, you'd have twice as much money as when you started. But if the interest were compounded and paid at the end of every month, each month you'd earn $1/12$ of 100% interest. At the year's end you'd have $(1 + 1/12)^{12} = 2.613$ times as much instead of 2. If the interest were paid every day, you'd get $(1 + 1/365)^{365} = 2.715$ times as much. If the interest were paid every second, you'd get $(1 + 1/3153600)^{3153600} = 2.7182812$ times as much. This is where e shows up. If you could get the interest compounded continually, you'd get e times as much. In other words, as n gets large, the limit of $(1 + 1/n)^n = e$. This unexpected result was discovered by Jacob Bernoulli in 1683.

JUST CHECKING

Roper Worldwide reports that they are able to contact 76% of the randomly selected households drawn for a telephone survey.

2 Explain why these phone calls can be considered Bernoulli trials.

3 Which of the models of this chapter (Geometric, Binomial, or Poisson) would you use to model the number of successful contracts from a list of 1000 sampled households?

4 Roper also reports that even after they contacted a household, only 38% of the contacts agreed to be interviewed. So the probability of getting a completed interview from a randomly selected household is only 0.29 (38% of 76%). Which of the models of this chapter would you use to model the number of households Roper has to call before they get the first completed interview?

FOR EXAMPLE Probability models

A venture capital firm has a list of potential investors who have previously invested in new technologies. On average, these investors invest about 5% of the time. A new client of the firm is interested in finding investors for a mobile phone application that enables financial transactions, an application that is finding increasing acceptance in much of the developing world. An analyst at the firm starts calling potential investors.

QUESTIONS

1. What is the probability that the first person she calls will want to invest?
2. What is the probability that none of the first five people she calls will be interested?
3. How many people will she have to call until the probability of finding someone interested is at least 0.50?
4. How many investors will she have to call, on average, to find someone interested?
5. If she calls 10 investors, what is the probability that exactly 2 of them will be interested?
6. What assumptions are you making to answer these questions?

(continued)

ANSWERS

1. Each investor has a 5% or 1/20 chance of wanting to invest, so the chance that the first person she calls is interested is 1/20.

2. P(first one not interested) $= 1 - 1/20 = 19/20$. Assuming the trials are independent, P(none are interested) $= P$ (1st not interested) $\times P$ (2nd not interested) $\times \cdots \times P$ (5th not interested) $= (19/20)^5 = 0.774$.

3. By trial and error, $(19/20)^{13} = 0.513$ and $(19/20)^{14} = 0.488$, so she would need to call 14 people to have the probability of *no one* interested drop below 0.50, therefore making the probability that someone is interested greater than 0.50.

4. This uses a geometric model. Let $X =$ number of people she calls until the first interested person. $E(X) = 1/p = 1/(1/20) = 20$ people.

5. Using the Binomial model, let $Y =$ number of people interested in 10 calls, then

$$P(Y = 2) = \binom{10}{2}p^2(1 - p)^8 = \frac{10 \times 9}{2}(1/20)^2(19/20)^8 = 0.0746.$$

6. We are assuming that the trials are independent and that the probability of being interested in investing is the same for all potential investors.

WHAT CAN GO WRONG?

- **Probability models are still just models.** Models can be useful, but they are not reality. Think about the assumptions behind your models. Question probabilities as you would data.

- **If the model is wrong, so is everything else.** Before you try to find the mean or standard deviation of a random variable, check to make sure the probability model is reasonable. As a start, the probabilities should all be between 0 and 1 and they should add up to 1. If not, you may have calculated a probability incorrectly or left out a value of the random variable.

- **Watch out for variables that aren't independent.** You can add expected values of *any* two random variables, but you can only add variances of independent random variables. Suppose a survey includes questions about the number of hours of sleep people get each night and also the number of hours they are awake each day. From their answers, we find the mean and standard deviation of hours asleep and hours awake. The expected total must be 24 hours; after all, people are either asleep or awake. The means still add just fine. Since all the totals are exactly 24 hours, however, the standard deviation of the total will be 0. We can't add variances here because the number of hours you're awake depends on the number of hours you're asleep. Be sure to check for independence before adding variances.

- **Don't write independent instances of a random variable with notation that looks like they are the same variables.** Make sure you write each instance as a different random variable. Just because each random variable describes a similar situation doesn't mean that each random outcome will be the same. These are *random* variables, not the variables you saw in Algebra. Write $X_1 + X_2 + X_3$ rather than $X + X + X$.

- **Don't forget:** Variances of independent random variables add. Standard deviations don't.

- **Don't forget:** Variances of independent random variables add, even when you're looking at the difference between them.

- **Be sure you have Bernoulli trials.** Be sure to check the requirements first: two possible outcomes per trial ("success" and "failure"), a constant probability of success, and independence. Remember that the 10% Condition provides a reasonable substitute for independence.

4. A day trader buys an option on a stock that will return $100 profit if the stock goes up today and lose $400 if it goes down. If the trader thinks there is a 75% chance that the stock will go up,

a) What is her expected value of the option's profit?
b) What do you think of this option?

SECTION 6.2

5. Find the standard deviation of the book purchases in Exercise 3.

6. Find the standard deviation of the day trader's option value in Exercise 4.

7. An orthodontist has three financing packages, and each has a different service charge. He estimates that 30% of patients use the first plan, which has a $10 finance charge; 50% use the second plan, which has a $20 finance charge; and 20% use the third plan, which has a $30 finance charge.

a) Find the expected value of the service charge.
b) Find the standard deviation of the service charge.

8. A marketing agency has developed three vacation packages to promote a timeshare plan at a new resort. They estimate that 20% of potential customers will choose the Day Plan, which does not include overnight accommodations; 40% will choose the Overnight Plan, which includes one night at the resort; and 40% will choose the Weekend Plan, which includes two nights.

a) Find the expected value of the number of nights potential customers will need.
b) Find the standard deviation of the number of nights potential customers will need.

SECTION 6.3

9. Given independent random variables, X and Y, with means and standard deviations as shown, find the mean and standard deviation of each of the variables in parts a to d.

a) $3X$
b) $Y + 6$
c) $X + Y$
d) $X - Y$

	Mean	SD
X	10	2
Y	20	5

10. Given independent random variables, X and Y, with means and standard deviations as shown, find the mean and standard deviation of each of the variables in parts a to d.

a) $X - 20$
b) $0.5Y$
c) $X + Y$
d) $X - Y$

	Mean	SD
X	80	12
Y	12	3

11. A broker has calculated the expected values of two different financial instruments X and Y. Suppose that $E(X) = \$100, E(Y) = \$90, SD(X) = \$12$, and $SD(Y) = \$8$. Find each of the following.

a) $E(X + 10)$ and $SD(X + 10)$
b) $E(5Y)$ and $SD(5Y)$
c) $E(X + Y)$ and $SD(X + Y)$
d) What assumption must you make in part c?

12. A company selling glass ornaments by mail-order expects, from previous history, that 6% of the ornaments it ships will break in shipping. You purchase two ornaments as gifts and have them shipped separately to two different addresses. What is the probability that both arrive safely? What did you assume?

SECTION 6.4

13. Which of these situations fit the conditions for using Bernoulli trials? Explain.

a) You are rolling 5 dice and need to get at least two 6s to win the game.
b) We record the distribution of home states of customers visiting our website.
c) A committee consisting of 11 men and 8 women selects a delegation of 4 to attend a professional meeting at random. What is the probability they choose all women?
d) A study (softwaresecure.typepad.com/multiple_choice/2007/05/cheat_cheat_nev.html) found that 56% of M.B.A. students admit to cheating. A business school dean surveys all the students in the graduating class and gets responses that admit to cheating from 250 of 481 students.

14. At the airport entry sites, a computer is used to randomly decide whether a traveler's baggage should be opened for inspection. If the chance of being selected is 12%, can you model your chance of having your baggage opened with a Bernoulli model? Check each of the conditions specifically.

SECTION 6.5

15. At many airports, a traveler entering the U.S. is sent randomly to one of several stations where his passport and visa are checked. If each of the 6 stations is equally likely, can the probabilities of which station a traveler will be sent be modeled with a Uniform model?

16. Through the career services office, you have arranged preliminary interviews at four companies for summer jobs. Each company will either ask you to come to their site for a follow-up interview or not. Let X be the random variable equal to the total number of follow-up interviews that you might have.

a) List all the possible values of X.
b) Is the random variable discrete or continuous?
c) Do you think a uniform distribution might be appropriate as a model for this random variable? Explain briefly.

17. The U.S. Census Bureau's 2007 Survey of Business Owners showed that 28.7% of all non-farm businesses are owned by women. You are phoning local businesses and assume that the national percentage is true in your area. You wonder how many calls you will have to make before you find one owned by a woman. What probability model should you use? (Specify the parameters as well.)

18. As in Exercise 17, you are phoning local businesses. You call three firms. What is the probability that all three are owned by women?

19. A manufacturer of clothing knows that the probability of a button flaw (broken, sewed on incorrectly, or missing) is 0.002. An inspector examines 50 shirts in an hour, each with 6 buttons. Using a Poisson probability model:

a) What is the probability that she finds no button flaws?
b) What is the probability that she finds at least one?

20. Replacing the buttons with snaps increases the probability of a flaw to 0.003, but the inspector can check 70 shirts an hour (still with 6 snaps each). Now what is the probability she finds no snap flaws?

CHAPTER EXERCISES

21. New website. You have just launched the website for your company that sells nutritional products online. Suppose X = the number of different pages that a customer hits during a visit to the website.

a) Assuming that there are n different pages in total on your website, what are the possible values that this random variable may take on?
b) Is the random variable discrete or continuous?

22. New website, part 2. For the website described in Exercise 21, let Y = the total time (in minutes) that a customer spends during a visit to the website.

a) What are the possible values of this random variable?
b) Is the random variable discrete or continuous?

23. Repairs. The probability model below describes the number of repair calls that an appliance repair shop may receive during an hour.

Repair Calls	0	1	2	3
Probability	0.1	0.3	0.4	0.2

a) How many calls should the shop expect per hour?
b) What is the standard deviation?

24. Software company. A small software company will bid on a major contract. It anticipates a profit of $50,000 if it gets it, but thinks there is only a 30% chance of that happening.

a) What's the expected profit?
b) Find the standard deviation for the profit.

25. Commuting to work. A commuter must pass through five traffic lights on her way to work and will have to stop at each one that is red. After keeping a record for several months, she developed the following probability model for the number of red lights she hits:

X = # of Red	0	1	2	3	4	5
$p(X = x)$	0.05	0.25	0.35	0.15	0.15	0.05

a) How many red lights should she expect to hit each day?
b) What's the standard deviation?

26. Defects. A consumer organization inspecting new cars found that many had appearance defects (dents, scratches, paint chips, etc.). While none had more than three of these defects, 7% had three, 11% had two, and 21% had one defect.

a) Find the expected number of appearance defects in a new car.
b) What is the standard deviation?

27. Fishing tournament. A sporting goods manufacturer was asked to sponsor a local boy in two fishing tournaments. They claim the probability that he will win the first tournament is 0.4. If he wins the first tournament, they estimate the probability that he will also win the second is 0.2. They guess that if he loses the first tournament, the probability that he will win the second is 0.3.

a) According to their estimates, are the two tournaments independent? Explain your answer.
b) What's the probability that he loses both tournaments?
c) What's the probability he wins both tournaments?
d) Let random variable X be the number of tournaments he wins. Find the probability model for X.
e) What are the expected value and standard deviation of X?

28. Contracts. Your company bids for two contracts. You believe the probability that you get contract #1 is 0.8. If you get contract #1, the probability that you also get contract #2 will be 0.2, and if you do not get contract #1, the probability that you get contract #2 will be 0.3.

a) Are the outcomes of the two contract bids independent? Explain.
b) Find the probability you get both contracts.
c) Find the probability you get neither contract.
d) Let X be the number of contracts you get. Find the probability model for X.
e) Find the expected value and standard deviation of X.

29. Battery recall. A company has discovered that a recent batch of batteries had manufacturing flaws, and has issued a recall. You have 10 batteries covered by the recall, and 3 are dead. You choose 2 batteries at random from your package of 10.

a) Has the assumption of independence been met? Explain.
b) Create a probability model for the number of good batteries chosen.

c) What's the expected number of good batteries?
d) What's the standard deviation?

30. Grocery supplier. A grocery supplier believes that the mean number of broken eggs per dozen is 0.6, with a standard deviation of 0.5. You buy 3 dozen eggs without checking them.

a) How many broken eggs do you expect to get?
b) What's the standard deviation?
c) Is it necessary to assume the cartons of eggs are independent? Why?

31. Commuting, part 2. A commuter finds that she waits an average of 14.8 seconds at each of five stoplights, with a standard deviation of 9.2 seconds. Find the mean and the standard deviation of the total amount of time she waits at all five lights. What, if anything, did you assume?

32. Defective pixels. For warranty purposes, analysts want to model the number of defects on a screen of the new tablet they are manufacturing. Let X = the number of defective pixels per screen. If X can be modeled by:

X = # of Defective Pixels	0	1	2	3	4 or more
P(X = x)	0.95	0.04	0.008	0.002	0

a) What is the expected number of defective pixels per screen?
b) What is the standard deviation of the number of defective pixels per screen?
c) What is the expected number of defective pixels in the next 100 screens?
d) What is the standard deviation of the number of defective pixels in the next 100 screens?

33. Repair calls. Suppose that the appliance shop in Exercise 23 plans an 8-hour day.

a) Find the mean and standard deviation of the number of repair calls they should expect in a day.
b) What assumption did you make about the repair calls?
c) Use the mean and standard deviation to describe what a typical 8-hour day will be like.
d) At the end of a day, a worker comments "Boy, I'm tired. Today was sure unusually busy!" How many repair calls would justify such an observation?

34. Casino. At a casino, people play the slot machines in hopes of hitting the jackpot, but most of the time, they lose their money. A certain machine pays out an average of $0.92 (for every dollar played), with a standard deviation of $120.

a) Why is the standard deviation so large?
b) If a gambler plays 5 times, what are the mean and standard deviation of the casino's profit?
c) If gamblers play this machine 1000 times in a day, what are the mean and standard deviation of the casino's profit?

35. Bike sale. A bicycle shop plans to offer 2 specially priced children's models at a sidewalk sale. The basic model will return a profit of $120 and the deluxe model $150. Past experience indicates that sales of the basic model will have a mean of 5.4 bikes with a standard deviation of 1.2, and sales of the deluxe model will have a mean of 3.2 bikes with a standard deviation of 0.8 bikes. The cost of setting up for the sidewalk sale is $200.

a) Define random variables and use them to express the bicycle shop's net profit.
b) What's the mean of the net profit?
c) What's the standard deviation of the net profit?
d) Do you need to make any assumptions in calculating the mean? How about the standard deviation?

36. Farmers' market. A farmer has 100 lb of apples and 50 lb of potatoes for sale. The market price for apples (per pound) each day is a random variable with a mean of 0.5 dollars and a standard deviation of 0.2 dollars. Similarly, for a pound of potatoes, the mean price is 0.3 dollars and the standard deviation is 0.1 dollars. It also costs him 2 dollars to bring all the apples and potatoes to the market. The market is busy with eager shoppers, so we can assume that he'll be able to sell all of each type of produce at that day's price.

a) Define your random variables, and use them to express the farmer's net income.
b) Find the mean of the net income.
c) Find the standard deviation of the net income.
d) Do you need to make any assumptions in calculating the mean? How about the standard deviation?

37. Cancelled flights. Mary is deciding whether to book the cheaper flight home college after her final exams, but she's unsure when her last exam will be. She thinks there is only a 20% chance that the exam will be scheduled after the last day she can get a seat on the cheaper flight. If it is and she has to cancel the flight, she will lose $150. If she can take the cheaper flight, she will save $100.

a) If she books the cheaper flight, what can she expect to gain, on average?
b) What is the standard deviation?

38. Day trading. An option to buy a stock is priced at $200. If the stock closes above 30 on May 15, the option will be worth $1000. If it closes below 20, the option will be worth nothing, and if it closes between 20 and 30 (inclusively), the option will be worth $200. A trader thinks there is a 50% chance that the stock will close in the 20–30 range, a 20% chance that it will close above 30, and a 30% chance that it will fall below 20 on May 15.

a) How much does she expect to gain?
b) What is the standard deviation of her gain?
c) Should she buy the stock option? Discuss the pros and cons in terms of your answers to (a) and (b).

39. eBay. A collector purchased a quantity of action figures and is going to sell them on eBay. He has 19 Hulk figures. In recent auctions, the mean selling price of similar figures has been $12.11, with a standard deviation of $1.38. He also has 13 Iron Man figures which have had a mean selling price of $10.19, with a standard deviation of $0.77. His insertion fee will be $0.55 on each item, and the closing fee will be 8.75% of the selling price. He assumes all will sell without having to be relisted.

a) Define your random variables, and use them to create a random variable for the collector's net revenue.
b) Find the mean (expected value) of the net revenue.
c) Find the standard deviation of the net revenue.
d) Do you have to assume independence for the sales on eBay? Explain.

40. Real estate. A real-estate broker in Washington, DC, purchased 3 two-bedroom houses in a depressed market for a combined cost of $1,000,000. He expects the cleaning and repair costs on each house to average $100,000 with a standard deviation of $15,000. When he sells them, after subtracting taxes and other closing costs, he expects to realize an average of $475,000 per house, with a standard deviation of $12,500.

a) Define your random variables, and use them to create a random variable for the broker's net profit.
b) Find the mean (expected value) of the net profit.
c) Find the standard deviation of the net profit.
d) Do you have to assume independence for the repairs and sale prices of the houses? Explain.

41. Bernoulli. Can we use probability models based on Bernoulli trials to investigate the following situations? Explain.

a) Each week a doctor rolls a single die to determine which of his six office staff members gets the preferred parking space.
b) A medical research lab has samples of blood collected from 120 different individuals. How likely is it that the majority of them are Type A blood, given that Type A is found in 43% of the population?
c) From a workforce of 13 men and 23 women, all five promotions go to men. How likely is that, if promotions are based on qualifications rather than gender?
d) We poll 500 of the 3000 stockholders to see how likely it is that the proposed budget will pass.
e) A company realizes that about 10% of its packages are not being sealed properly. In a case of 24 packages, how likely is it that more than 3 are unsealed?

42. Bernoulli, part 2. Can we use probability models based on Bernoulli trials to investigate the following situations? Explain.

a) You survey 500 potential customers to determine their color preference.
b) A manufacturer recalls a doll because about 3% have buttons that are not properly attached. Customers return 37 of these dolls to the local toy store. How likely are they to find any buttons not properly attached?
c) A city council of 11 Republicans and 8 Democrats picks a committee of 4 at random. How likely are they to choose all Democrats?
d) An executive reads that 74% of employees in his industry are dissatisfied with their jobs. How many dissatisfied employees can he expect to find among the 481 employees in his company?

43. Closing sales. A salesman normally makes a sale (closes) on 80% of his presentations. Assuming the presentations are independent, find the probability of each of the following.

a) He fails to close for the first time on his fifth attempt.
b) He closes his first presentation on his fourth attempt.
c) The first presentation he closes will be on his second attempt.
d) The first presentation he closes will be on one of his first three attempts.

44. Computer chip manufacturer. Suppose a computer chip manufacturer rejects 2% of the chips produced because they fail presale testing. Assuming the bad chips are independent, find the probability of each of the following.

a) The fifth chip they test is the first bad one they find.
b) They find a bad one within the first 10 they examine.
c) The first bad chip they find will be the fourth one they test.
d) The first bad chip they find will be one of the first three they test.

45. Side effects. Researchers testing a new medication find that 7% of users have side effects. To how many patients would a doctor expect to prescribe the medication before finding the first one who has side effects?

46. Credit cards. College students are a major target for advertisements for credit cards. At a university, 65% of students surveyed said they had opened a new credit card account within the past year. If that percentage is accurate, how many students would you expect to survey before finding one who had not opened a new account in the past year?

47. Missing pixels. A company that manufactures large LCD screens knows that not all pixels on their screen light, even if they spend great care when making them. In a sheet 6 ft by 10 ft (72 in. by 120 in.) that will be cut into smaller screens, they find an average of 4.7 blank pixels. They believe that the occurrences of blank pixels are independent. Their warranty policy states that they will replace any screen sold that shows more than 2 blank pixels.

a) What is the mean number of blank pixels per square foot?
b) What is the standard deviation of blank pixels per square foot?
c) What is the probability that a 2 ft by 3 ft screen will have at least one defect?

d) What is the probability that a 2 ft by 3 ft screen will be replaced because it has too many defects?

48. Bean bags. Cellophane that is going to be formed into bags for items such as dried beans or bird seed is passed over a light sensor to test if the alignment is correct before it passes through the heating units that seal the edges. Small adjustments can be made by the machine automatically. But if the alignment is too bad, the process is stopped and an operator has to manually adjust it. These misalignment stops occur randomly and independently. On one line, the average number of stops is 52 per 8-hour shift.

a) What is the mean number of stops per hour?
b) What is the standard deviation of stops per hour?

49. Hurricane insurance. An insurance company needs to assess the risks associated with providing hurricane insurance. During the 22 years from 1990 through 2011, Florida was hit by 27 major hurricanes (level 3 and above). If hurricanes are independent and the mean has not changed, what is the probability of having a year in Florida with each of the following?

a) No hits?
b) Exactly 1 hit?
c) More than 1 hit?

50. Hurricane insurance, part 2. During the 18 years from 1995 through 2012, there were 144 hurricanes in the Atlantic basin. Assume that hurricanes are independent and the mean has not changed.

a) What is the mean number of major hurricanes per year?
b) What is the standard deviation of the annual frequency of major hurricanes?
c) What is the probability of having a year with no major hurricanes?
d) What is the probability of going three years in a row without a major hurricane?

51. Lefties. A manufacturer of game controllers is concerned that their controller may be difficult for left-handed users. They set out to find lefties to test. About 13% of the population is left-handed. If they select a sample of five customers at random in their stores, what is the probability of each of these outcomes?

a) The first lefty is the fifth person chosen.
b) There are some lefties among the 5 people.
c) The first lefty is the second or third person.
d) There are exactly 3 lefties in the group.
e) There are at least 3 lefties in the group.
f) There are no more than 3 lefties in the group.

52. Arrows. An Olympic archer is able to hit the bull's-eye 80% of the time. Assume each shot is independent of the others. If she shoots 6 arrows, what's the probability of each of the following results?

a) Her first bull's-eye comes on the third arrow.
b) She misses the bull's-eye at least once.

c) Her first bull's-eye comes on the fourth or fifth arrow.
d) She gets exactly 4 bull's-eyes.
e) She gets at least 4 bull's-eyes.
f) She gets at most 4 bull's-eyes.

53. Satisfaction survey. A cable provider wants to contact customers in a particular telephone exchange to see how satisfied they are with the new digital TV service the company has provided. All numbers are in the 452 exchange, so there are 10,000 possible numbers from 452-0000 to 452-9999. If they select the numbers with equal probability:

a) What distribution would they use to model the selection?
b) What is the probability the number selected will be an even number?
c) What is the probability the number selected will end in 000?

54. Manufacturing quality. In an effort to check the quality of their cell phones, a manufacturing manager decides to take a random sample of 10 cell phones from yesterday's production run, which produced cell phones with serial numbers ranging (according to when they were produced) from 43005000 to 43005999. If each of the 1000 phones is equally likely to be selected:

a) What distribution would they use to model the selection?
b) What is the probability that a randomly selected cell phone will be one of the last 100 to be produced?
c) What is the probability that the first cell phone selected is either from the last 200 to be produced or from the first 50 to be produced?
d) What is the probability that the first two cell phones are both from the last 100 to be produced?

55. Web visitors. A website manager has noticed that during the evening hours, about 3 people per minute check out from their shopping cart and make an online purchase. She believes that each purchase is independent of the others and wants to model the number of purchases per minute.

a) What model might you suggest to model the number of purchases per minute?
b) What is the probability that in any 1 minute at least one purchase is made?
c) What is the probability that no one makes a purchase in the next 2 minutes?

56. Quality control. The manufacturer in Exercise 54 has noticed that the number of faulty cell phones in a production run of cell phones is usually small and that the quality of one day's run seems to have no bearing on the next day.

a) What model might you use to model the number of faulty cell phones produced in one day?
b) If the mean number of faulty cell phones is 2 per day, what is the probability that no faulty cell phones will be produced tomorrow?
c) If the mean number of faulty cell phones is 2 per day, what is the probability that 3 or more faulty cell phones were produced in today's run?

57. Lefties, redux. Consider our group of 5 people from Exercise 51.

a) How many lefties do you expect?
b) With what standard deviation?
c) If we keep picking people until we find a lefty, how long do you expect it will take?

58. More arrows. Consider our archer from Exercise 52.

a) How many bull's-eyes do you expect her to get?
b) With what standard deviation?
c) If she keeps shooting arrows until she hits the bull's-eye, how long do you expect it will take?

59. Still more lefties. Suppose we choose 12 people instead of the 5 chosen in Exercise 57

a) Find the mean and standard deviation of the number of right-handers in the group.
b) What's the probability that they're not all right-handed?
c) What's the probability that there are no more than 10 righties?
d) What's the probability that there are exactly 6 of each?
e) What's the probability that the majority is right-handed?

60. Still more arrows. Suppose the archer from Exercise 58 shoots 10 arrows.

a) Find the mean and standard deviation of the number of bull's-eyes she may get.
b) What's the probability that she never misses?
c) What's the probability that there are no more than 8 bull's-eyes?
d) What's the probability that there are exactly 8 bull's-eyes?
e) What's the probability that she hits the bull's-eye more often than she misses?

JUST CHECKING ANSWERS

1 a) $100 + 100 = 200$ seconds
   b) $\sqrt{50^2 + 50^2} = 70.7$ seconds
   c) The times for the two customers are independent.
2 There are two outcomes (contact, no contact), the probability of contact stays constant at 0.76, and random calls should be independent.
3 Binomial
4 Geometric

7

The Normal and Other Continuous Distributions

The NYSE

The New York Stock Exchange (NYSE) was founded in 1792 by 24 stockbrokers who signed an agreement under a buttonwood tree on Wall Street in New York. The first offices were in a rented room at 40 Wall Street. In the 1830s traders who were not part of the Exchange did business in the street. They were called "curbstone brokers." It was the curbstone brokers who first made markets in gold and oil stocks and, after the Civil War, in small industrial companies such as the emerging steel, textile, and chemical industries.

By 1903 the New York Stock Exchange was established at its current home at 18 Broad Street. The curbstone brokers finally moved indoors in 1921 to a building on Greenwich street in lower Manhattan. In 1953 the curb market changed its name to the American Stock Exchange. In 1993 the American Stock Exchange pioneered the market for derivatives by introducing the first exchange-traded fund, Standard & Poor's Depositary Receipts (SPDRs).

The NYSE Euronext holding company was created in 2007 as a combination of the NYSE Group, Inc., and Euronext N.V. And in 2008, NYSE Euronext merged with the American Stock Exchange. The combined exchange is the world's largest and most liquid exchange group.

7.1   The Standard Deviation as a Ruler

WHO	Months
WHAT	CAPE10 values for the NYSE
WHEN	1880 through early 2013
WHY	Investment guidance

Investors have always sought ways to help them decide when to buy and when to sell. Such measures have become increasingly sophisticated. But all rely on identifying when the stock market is in an unusual state—either unusually undervalued (buy!) or unusually overvalued (sell!). One such measure is the Cyclically Adjusted Price/ Earnings Ratio (CAPE10) developed by Yale professor Robert Shiller. The CAPE10 is based on the standard Price/Earnings (P/E) ratio of stocks, but designed to smooth out short-term fluctuations by "cyclically adjusting" them. The CAPE10 has been as low as 4.78, in 1920, and as high as 44.20, in late 1999. The long-term average CAPE10 (since year 1881) is 16.47.

Investors who follow the CAPE10 use the metric to signal times to buy and sell. One mutual fund strategy buys only when the CAPE10 is 33% lower than the long-term average and sells (or "goes into cash") when the CAPE10 is 50% higher than the long-term average. Between January 1, 1971, and October 23, 2009, this strategy would have outperformed such standard measures as the Wiltshire 5000 in both average return and volatility, but it is important to note that the strategy would have been completely in cash from just before the stock market crash of 1987 all the way to March of 2009! 87 Shiller popularized the strategy in his book *Irrational Exuberance.* Figure 7.1 shows a time series plot of the CAPE10 values for the New York Stock Exchange from 1880 until the beginning of 2013. Generally, the CAPE10 hovers around 15. But occasionally, it can take a large excursion. One such time was in 1999 and 2000, when the CAPE10 exceeded 40. But was this just a random peak or were these values really extraordinary?

Figure 7.1   CAPE10 values for the NYSE from 1880 to 2013.

To answer this question, we can look at the overall distribution of CAPE10 values. Figure 7.2 shows a histogram of the same values. Now we don't see patterns over time, but we may be able to make a better judgment of whether values are extraordinary.

Overall, the main body of the distribution looks unimodal and reasonably symmetric. But then there's a tail of values that trails off to the high end. How can we assess how extraordinary they are?

Investors follow a wide variety of measures that record various aspects of stocks, bonds, and other investments. They are usually particularly interested in identifying times when these measures are extraordinary because those often represent times of increased risk or opportunity. But these are quantitative values, not categories.

How can we characterize the behavior of a random variable that can take on any value in a range of values? The distributions of Chapter 6 won't provide the tools we need, but many of the basic concepts still work. The random variables we need are *continuous.*

Figure 7.2   The distribution of the CAPE10 values shown in Figure 7.1.

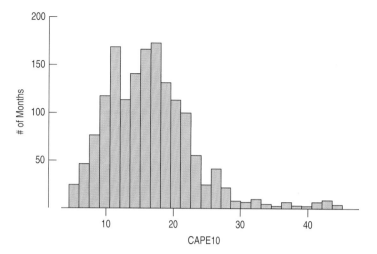

We saw in Chapter 3 that *z*-scores provide a standard way to compare values. In a sense, we use the standard deviation as a ruler, asking how many standard deviations a value is from the mean. That's what a *z*-score reports; the number of standard deviations away from the mean. We can convert the CAPE10 values to *z*-scores by subtracting their mean (16.47) and dividing by their standard deviation (6.55). Figure 7.3 shows the resulting distribution.

Figure 7.3   The CAPE10 values as *z*-scores.

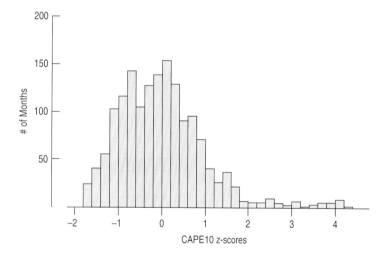

It's easy to see that the *z*-scores have the same distribution as the original values, but now we can also see that the largest of them is above 4. How extraordinary is it for a value to be four standard deviations away from the mean? Fortunately, there's a fact about unimodal, symmetric distributions that can guide us.[1]

The 68–95–99.7 Rule

In a unimodal, symmetric distribution, about 68% of the values fall within 1 standard deviation of the mean, about 95% fall within 2 standard deviations of the mean, and about 99.7%—almost all—fall within 3 standard deviations of the mean. Calling this rule the **68–95–99.7 Rule** provides a mnemonic for these three values.[2]

---

[1] All of the CAPE10 values in the right tail occurred after 1993. Until that time the distribution of CAPE10 values was quite symmetric and clearly unimodal.

[2] This rule is also called the "Empirical Rule" because it originally was observed without any proof. It was first published by Abraham de Moivre in 1733, 75 years before the underlying reason for it—which we're about to see—was known.

Figure 7.4 The 68–95–99.7 Rule tells us how much of most unimodal, symmetric models is found within one, two, or three standard deviations of the mean.

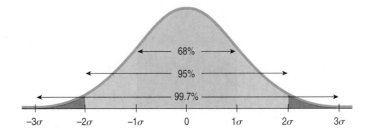

FOR EXAMPLE An extraordinary day for the Dow?

After the financial crisis of 2007/2008, the Dow Jones Industrial Average (DJIA) improved from a low of 7278 on March 20, 2009, to new records over 15,000 just 4 years later. But on August 8, 2011, the Dow dropped 634.8 points. Although that wasn't the most ever lost in a day, it sent shock waves through the financial community. During the year from mid-2011 to mid-2012, the mean daily change in the DJIA was 1.87, with a standard deviation of 155.28 points. A histogram of day-to-day changes in the DJIA looked like this:

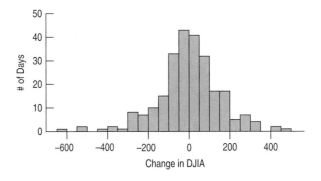

QUESTION Use the 68–95–99.7 Rule to characterize how extraordinary the change on August 8, 2011 was. Is the rule appropriate?

ANSWER The histogram is unimodal and symmetric, so the 68–95–99.7 Rule is an appropriate model. The z-score corresponding to the August 8 change is

$$\frac{-634.8 - 1.87}{155.28} = -4.10$$

A z-score bigger than 3 in magnitude will occur with a probability of less than 0.0015, or about once every 3 years for daily values. A z-score of 4 is even less likely. This was a truly extraordinary event.

7.2   The Normal Distribution

The 68–95–99.7 Rule is useful in describing how unusual a z-score is. But often in business we want a more precise answer than one of these three values. To say more about how big we expect a z-score to be, we need to *model* the data's distribution.

There is no universal standard for z-scores, but there is a model that shows up over and over in Statistics. You've probably heard of "bell-shaped curves." Statisticians call them Normal (or Gaussian) distributions. **Normal distributions** are appropriate models for distributions whose shapes are unimodal and roughly

"All models are wrong—but some are useful."

—GEORGE BOX, FAMOUS
STATISTICIAN

NOTATION ALERT

$N(\mu, \sigma)$ always denotes a Normal. The μ, pronounced "mew," is the Greek letter for "m," and always represents the mean in a model. The σ, sigma, is the lowercase Greek letter for "s," and always represents the standard deviation in a model.

Is Normal Normal?

Don't be misled. The name "Normal" doesn't mean that these are the *usual* shapes for histograms. The name follows a tradition of positive thinking in Mathematics and Statistics in which functions, equations, and relationships that are easy to work with or have other nice properties are called "normal," "common," "regular," "natural," or similar terms. It's as if by calling them ordinary, we could make them actually occur more often and make our lives simpler.

Is the Standard Normal a Standard?

Yes. We call it the "Standard Normal" because it models standardized values. It is also a "standard" because this is the particular Normal model that we almost always use.

symmetric. There is a Normal distribution for every possible combination of mean and standard deviation. We write $N(\mu, \sigma)$ to represent a Normal distribution with a mean of μ and a standard deviation of σ. We use Greek symbols here because this mean and standard deviation are parameters of the model, not summaries based on data. We can compute z-scores based on this model by using the **parameters** μ and σ. We still call these standardized values z-**scores**. We write

$$z = \frac{y - \mu}{\sigma}.$$

Standardized values have mean 0 and standard deviation 1, so by doing this to our values, we'll need only one model—the model $N(0,1)$. The Normal distribution with mean 0 and standard deviation 1 is called the **standard Normal distribution** (or the **standard Normal model**).

But be careful. You shouldn't use a Normal model for just any data set. Remember that standardizing won't change the shape of the distribution. If the distribution is not unimodal and symmetric to begin with, standardizing won't make it Normal.

JUST CHECKING

1 Your Accounting teacher has announced that the lower of your two tests will be dropped. You got a 90 on test 1 and an 80 on test 2. You're all set to drop the 80 until she announces that she grades "on a curve." She standardized the scores in order to decide which is the lower one. If the mean on the first test was 88 with a standard deviation of 4 and the mean on the second was 75 with a standard deviation of 5,
a) Which one will be dropped?
b) Does this seem "fair"?

The Normal distribution differs from the discrete probability distributions we saw in Chapter 6 because now, the random variable can take on any value. So, we need a **continuous random variable**. For any continuous random variable, the distribution of its probability can be shown with a curve called the **probability density function (pdf),** usually denoted as $f(x)$. The curve we use to work with the Normal distribution is called the Normal probability density function.

The probability density function (pdf) doesn't give the probability directly as the probability models for discrete random variables did. Instead the pdf gives the probability from the area below its curve. For the standard Normal, shown in Figure 7.5, we can see that the area below the curve between -1 and 1 is about 68%, which is where the 68–95–99.7 Rule comes from.

Figure 7.5 The standard Normal density function (with mean 0 and standard deviation 1). The probability of finding a z-score in any interval is the area over that interval under the curve. For example, the probability that the z-score falls between -1 and 1 is about 68%, which can be seen approximately from the density function or found more precisely from a table or technology.

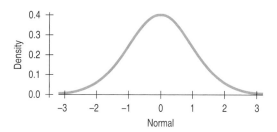

It's important to remember that the probability density function $f(x)$ isn't equal to $P(X = x)$. In fact, for a continuous random variable, X, $P(X = x)$ is 0 for every value of x! That may seem strange at first, but since the probability is the area under the curve over an interval, as the interval gets smaller and smaller, the probability does too. Finally, when the interval is just a point, there is no area—and no probability. (See the box below.)

How Can *Every* Value Have Probability 0?

We can find a probability for any interval of z-scores. But the probability for a single z-score is zero. How can that be? Let's look at the standard Normal random variable, Z. We could find (from a table, website, or computer program) that the probability that Z lies between 0 and 1 is 0.3413.

That's the area under the Normal pdf (in red) between the values 0 and 1.

So, what's the probability that Z is between 0 and 1/10?

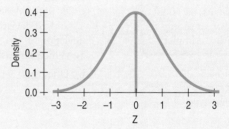

That area is only 0.0398. What is the chance then that Z will fall between 0 and 1/100? There's not much area—the probability is only 0.0040. If we kept going, the probability would keep getting smaller. The probability that Z is between 0 and 1/100,000 is less than 0.0001.

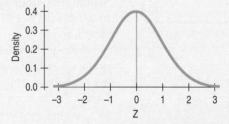

So, what's the probability that Z is *exactly* 0? Well, there's *no* area under the curve right at $x = 0$, so the probability is 0. It's only intervals that have positive probability, but that's OK. In real life we never mean exactly 0.0000000000 or any other value. If you say "exactly 164 pounds," you might really mean between 163.5 and 164.5 pounds or even between 163.99 and 164.01 pounds, but realistically not 164.000000000 . . . pounds.

Finding Normal Percentiles

Finding the probability that a value is at least 1 SD above the mean is easy. We know that 68% of the values lie within 1 SD of the mean, so 32% lie farther away. Since the Normal distribution is symmetric, half of those 32% (or 16%) are more than 1 SD above the mean. But what if we want to know the percentage of observations that fall more than 1.8 SD above the mean? We already know that no more than 16% of observations have z-scores above 1. By similar reasoning, no more than 2.5% of the observations have a z-score above 2. Can we be more precise with our answer than "between 16% and 2.5%"?

Figure 7.6 A table of Normal percentiles (Table Z in Appendix B) lets us find the percentage of individuals in a standard Normal distribution falling below any specified z-score value.

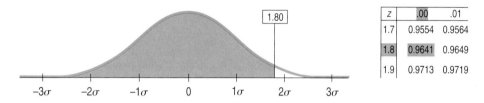

With a z-score we can use the standard Normal distribution to find the probabilities we're interested in. These days, we can find probabilities associated with z-scores using technology such as calculators, statistical software, and websites. We can also look up these values in a table of **Normal percentiles**.[3] Tables use the standard Normal distribution, so we'll have to convert our data to z-scores before using the table. Our value 1.8 SD above the mean is a z-score of 1.80. To use a table, as shown in Figure 7.7, find the z-score by looking down the left column for the first two digits (1.8) and across the top row for the third digit, 0. The table gives the percentile as 0.9641. That means that 96.4% of the z-scores are less than 1.80. Since the total area is always 1, and $1 - 0.9641 = 0.0359$ we know that only 3.6% of all observations from a Normal distribution have z-scores higher than 1.80.

FOR EXAMPLE   GMAT scores and the Normal model

The Graduate Management Admission Test (GMAT) has scores from 200 to 800. Scores are supposed to follow a distribution that is roughly unimodal and symmetric and is designed to have an overall mean of 500 and a standard deviation of 100. In any one year, the mean and standard deviation may differ from these target values by a small amount, but we can use these values as good overall approximations.

QUESTION   Suppose you earned a 600 on your GMAT test. From that information and the 68–95–99.7 Rule, where do you stand among all students who took the GMAT?

ANSWER   Because we're told that the distribution is unimodal and symmetric, we can approximate the distribution with a Normal model. We are also told the scores have a mean of 500 and an SD of 100. So, we'll use a $N(500,100)$. It's good practice at this point to draw the distribution. Find the score whose percentile you want to know and locate it on the picture. When you finish the calculation, you should check to make sure that it's a reasonable percentile from the picture.

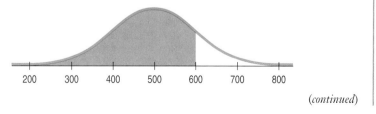

(continued)

---

[3] See Table Z in Appendix B. Many calculators and statistics computer packages do this as well.

A score of 600 is 1 SD above the mean. That corresponds to one of the points in the 68–95–99.7% Rule. About 32% (100% − 68%) of those who took the test were more than one standard deviation from the mean, but only half of those were on the high side. So about 16% (half of 32%) of the test scores were better than 600.

FOR EXAMPLE   More GMAT scores

QUESTION   Assuming the GMAT scores are nearly Normal with $N(500,100)$, what proportion of GMAT scores falls between 450 and 600?

ANSWER   The first step is to find the z-scores associated with each value. Standardizing the scores we are given, we find that for 600, $z = (600 − 500)/100 = 1.0$ and for 450, $z = (450 − 500)/100 = −0.50$. Then, we can label the axis below the picture either in the original values or the z-scores or even use both scales as the following picture shows.

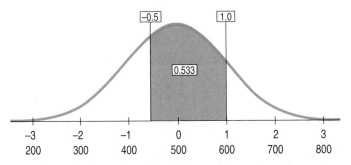

From Table Z, we find the area $z \leq 1.0 = 0.8413$, which means that 84.13% of scores fall below 1.0, and the area $z \leq −0.50 = 0.3085$, which means that 30.85% of the values fall below −0.5, so the proportion of z-scores *between* them is 84.13% − 30.85% = 53.28%. So, the Normal model estimates that about 53.3% of GMAT scores fall between 450 and 600.

Finding areas from z-scores is the simplest way to work with the Normal distribution. Sometimes we start with areas and need to work backward to find the corresponding z-score or even the original data value. For instance, what z-score represents the first quartile, Q1, in a Normal distribution? In our first set of examples, we knew the z-score and used the table or technology to find the percentile. Now we want to find the cut point for the 25th percentile. Make a picture, shading the leftmost 25% of the area. Look in Table Z for an area of 0.2500. The exact area is not there, but 0.2514 is the closest number. That shows up in the table with −0.6 in the left margin and 0.07 in the top margin. The z-score for Q1, then, is approximately $z = −0.67$. Computers and calculators can determine the cut point more precisely (and more easily).[4]

FOR EXAMPLE   An exclusive MBA program

QUESTION   Suppose an MBA program says it admits only people with GMAT scores among the top 10%. How high a GMAT score does it take to be eligible?

---

[4]We'll often use those more precise values in our examples. If you're finding the values from the table you may not get *exactly* the same number to all decimal places as your classmate who's using a computer package.

ANSWER The program takes the top 10%, so their cutoff score is the 90th percentile. Draw an approximate picture like this one.

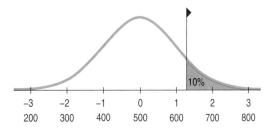

	0.07	0.08	0.09
1.0	0.8577	0.8599	0.8621
1.1	0.8790	0.8810	0.8830
1.2	0.8980	0.8997	0.9015
1.3	0.9147	0.9162	0.9177
1.4	0.9292	0.9306	0.9319

From our picture we can see that the z-value is between 1 and 1.5 (if we've judged 10% of the area correctly), and so the cutoff score is between 600 and 650 or so. Using technology, you may be able to select the 10% area and find the z-value directly. Using a table, such as Table Z, locate 0.90 (or as close to it as you can; here 0.8997 is closer than 0.9015) in the *interior* of the table and find the corresponding z-score (see table above). Here the 1.2 is in the left margin, and the 0.08 is in the margin above the entry. Putting them together gives 1.28. Now, convert the z-score back to the original units. A z-score of 1.28 is 1.28 standard deviations above the mean. Since the standard deviation is 100, that's 128 GMAT points. The cutoff is 128 points above the mean of 500, or 628. Because the program wants GMAT scores in the top 10%, the cutoff is 628. (Actually since GMAT scores are reported only in multiples of 10, you'd have to score at least a 630.)

GUIDED EXAMPLE   Cereal Company

A cereal manufacturer has a machine that fills the boxes. Boxes are labeled "16 oz," so the company wants to have that much cereal in each box. But since no packaging process is perfect, there will be minor variations. If the machine is set at exactly 16 oz and the Normal distribution applies (or at least the distribution is roughly symmetric), then about half of the boxes will be underweight, making consumers unhappy and exposing the company to bad publicity and possible lawsuits. To prevent underweight boxes, the manufacturer has to set the mean a little higher than 16.0 oz. Based on their experience with the packaging machine, the company believes that the amount of cereal in the boxes fits a Normal distribution with a standard deviation of 0.2 oz. The manufacturer decides to set the machine to put an average of 16.3 oz in each box. Let's use that model to answer a series of questions about these cereal boxes.

Question 1: What fraction of the boxes will be underweight?

Setup State the variable and the objective.

Model Check to see if a Normal distribution is appropriate.

Specify which Normal distribution to use.

The variable is weight of cereal in a box. We want to determine what fraction of the boxes risk being underweight.

We have no data, so we cannot make a histogram. But we are told that the company believes the distribution of weights from the machine is Normal.

We use an $N(16.3, 0.2)$ model.

(continued)

DO   **Mechanics** Make a graph of this Normal distribution. Locate the value you're interested in on the picture, label it, and shade the appropriate region.

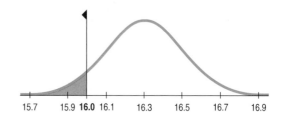

REALITY CHECK Estimate from the picture the percentage of boxes that are underweight. (This will be useful later to check that your answer makes sense.)

(It looks like a low percentage—maybe less than 10%.)

We want to know what fraction of the boxes will weigh less than 16 oz.

$$z = \frac{y - \mu}{\sigma} = \frac{16 - 16.3}{0.2} = -1.50.$$

Convert your cutoff value into a z-score.

Look up the area in the Normal table, or use technology.

$$P(y < 16) = P(z < -1.50) = 0.0668$$

REPORT   **Conclusion** State your conclusion in the context of the problem.

We estimate that approximately 6.7% of the boxes will contain less than 16 oz of cereal.

Question 2: The company's lawyers say that 6.7% is too high. They insist that no more than 4% of the boxes can be underweight. So the company needs to set the machine to put a little more cereal in each box. What mean setting do they need?

PLAN   **Setup** State the variable and the objective.

The variable is weight of cereal in a box. We want to determine a setting for the machine.

Model Check to see if a Normal model is appropriate.

We have no data, so we cannot make a histogram. But we are told that a Normal model applies.

Specify which Normal distribution to use. This time you are not given a value for the mean!

We don't know μ, the mean amount of cereal. The standard deviation for this machine is 0.2 oz. The model, then, is $N(\mu, 0.2)$.

REALITY CHECK We found out earlier that setting the machine to $\mu = 16.3$ oz made 6.7% of the boxes too light. We'll need to raise the mean a bit to reduce this fraction.

We are told that no more than 4% of the boxes can be below 16 oz.

DO   **Mechanics** Make a graph of this Normal distribution. Center it at μ (since you don't know the mean) and shade the region below 16 oz.

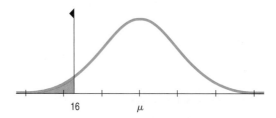

Using the Normal table, a calculator, or software, find the z-score that cuts off the lowest 4%.

The z-score that has 0.04 area to the left of it is $z = -1.75$.

Use this information to find μ. It's located 1.75 standard deviations to the right of 16.	Since 16 must be 1.75 standard deviations below the mean, we need to set the mean at $16 + 1.75 \cdot 0.2 = 16.35$.

REPORT **Conclusion** State your conclusion in the context of the problem.

The company must set the machine to average 16.35 oz of cereal per box.

Question 3: The company president vetoes that plan, saying the company should give away less free cereal, not more. Her goal is to set the machine no higher than 16.2 oz and still have only 4% underweight boxes. The only way to accomplish this is to reduce the standard deviation. What standard deviation must the company achieve, and what does that mean about the machine?

PLAN **Setup** State the variable and the objective.

The variable is weight of cereal in a box. We want to determine the necessary standard deviation to have only 4% of boxes underweight.

Model Check that a Normal model is appropriate.

The company believes that the weights are described by a Normal distribution.

Specify which Normal distribution to use. This time you don't know σ.

Now we know the mean, but we don't know the standard deviation. The model is therefore $N(16.2, \sigma)$.

 REALITY CHECK We know the new standard deviation must be less than 0.2 oz.

DO **Mechanics** Make a graph of this Normal distribution. Center it at 16.2, and shade the area you're interested in. We want 4% of the area to the left of 16 oz.

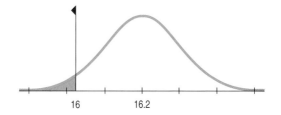

Find the z-score that cuts off the lowest 4%.

We already know that the z-score with 4% below it is $z = -1.75$.

Solve for σ. (Note that we need 16 to be 1.75 σ's below 16.2, so 1.75 σ must be 0.2 oz. You could just start with that equation.)

$$z = \frac{y - \mu}{\sigma}$$

$$-1.75 = \frac{16 - 16.2}{\sigma}$$

$$1.75\sigma = 0.2$$

$$\sigma = 0.114.$$

REPORT **Conclusion** State your conclusion in the context of the problem.

The company must get the machine to box cereal with a standard deviation of only 0.114 oz. This means the machine must be more consistent (by nearly a factor of 2) in filling the boxes.

As we expected, the standard deviation is lower than before—actually, quite a bit lower.

JUST CHECKING

2 As a group, the Dutch are among the tallest people in the world. The average Dutch man is 184 cm tall—just over 6 feet (and the average Dutch woman is 170.8 cm tall—just over 5′7″). If a Normal model is appropriate and the standard deviation for men is about 8 cm, what percentage of all Dutch men will be over 2 meters (6′6″) tall?

3 Suppose it takes you 20 minutes, on average, to drive to work, with a standard deviation of 2 minutes. Suppose a Normal model is appropriate for the distributions of driving times.

a) How often will you arrive at work in less than 22 minutes?
b) How often will it take you more than 24 minutes?
c) Do you think the distribution of your driving times is unimodal and symmetric?
d) What does this say about the accuracy of your prediction? Explain.

7.3   Normal Probability Plots

Before using a Normal model you should check that the data follow a distribution that is at least close to Normal. You can check that the histogram is unimodal and symmetric, but there is also a specialized graphical display that can help you to decide whether the Normal model is appropriate: the **Normal probability plot**. If the distribution of the data is roughly Normal, the plot is roughly a diagonal straight line. Deviations from a straight line indicate that the distribution is not Normal. This plot is usually able to show deviations from Normality more clearly than the corresponding histogram, but it's usually easier to understand *how* a distribution fails to be Normal by looking at its histogram. Normal probability plots are difficult to make by hand, but are provided by most statistics software.

Some data on a car's fuel efficiency provide an example of data that are nearly Normal. The overall pattern of the Normal probability plot is straight. The two trailing low values correspond to the values in the histogram that trail off the low end. They're not quite in line with the rest of the data set. The Normal probability plot shows us that they're a bit lower than we'd expect of the lowest two values in a Normal distribution.

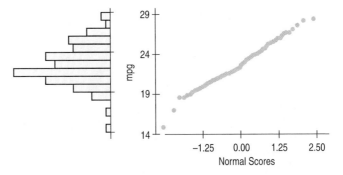

Figure 7.7   Histogram and Normal probability plot for gas mileage (mpg) recorded for a Nissan Maxima. The vertical axes are the same, so each dot on the probability plot would fall into the bar on the histogram immediately to its left.

By contrast, the Normal probability plot of a sample of men's *Weights* in Figure 7.8 from a study of lifestyle and health is far from straight. The weights

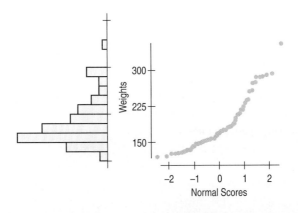

Figure 7.8   Histogram and Normal probability plot for men's weights. Note how a skewed distribution corresponds to a bent probability plot.

are skewed to the high end, and the plot is curved. We'd conclude from these pictures that approximations using the Normal model for these data would not be very accurate.

FOR EXAMPLE   Using a Normal probability plot

A Normal probability plot of the CAPE10 prices from page 211 looks like this:

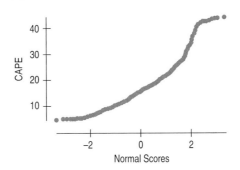

QUESTION   What does this plot say about the distribution of the CAPE10 scores?

ANSWER   The bent shape of the probability plot indicates a deviation from Normality. The upward bend is because the distribution is skewed to the high end. The "kink" in that bend suggest a collection of values that don't continue that skewness consistently. We should probably not use a Normal model for these data.

Figure 7.9   A Normal probability plot lines up the sorted data values against the Normal scores that we'd expect for a sample of that size. The straighter the line, the closer the data are to a Normal model. The mileage data look quite Normal.

How Does a Normal Probability Plot Work?

Figure 7.9 shows a Normal probability plot for 100 fuel efficiency measures for a car. The smallest of these has a z-score of -3.16. The Normal model can tell us what value to expect for the smallest z-score in a batch of 100 if a Normal model were appropriate. That turns out to be -2.58. So our first data value is smaller than we would expect from the Normal.

We can continue this and ask a similar question for each value. For example, the 14th-smallest fuel efficiency has a z-score of almost exactly -1, and that's just what we should expect (-1.1 to be exact). The easiest way to make the comparison, of course, is to graph it.[5] If our observed values look like a sample from a Normal model, then the probability plot stretches out in a straight line from lower left to upper right. But if our values deviate from what we'd expect, the plot will bend or have jumps in it. The values we'd expect from a Normal model are called Normal scores, or sometimes nscores. You can't easily look them up in the table, so probability plots are best made with technology and not by hand.

The best advice on using Normal probability plots is to see whether they are straight. If so, then your data look like data from a Normal model. If not, make a histogram to understand how they differ from the model.

7.4   The Distribution of Sums of Normals

Another reason Normal models show up so often is that they have some special properties. An important one is that the sum or difference of two independent Normal random variables is also Normal.

---

[5]Sometimes the Normal probability plot switches the two axes, putting the data on the x-axis and the z-scores on the y-axis.

A company manufactures small stereo systems. At the end of the production line, the stereos are packaged and prepared for shipping. Stage 1 of this process is called "packing." Workers must collect all the system components (a main unit, two speakers, a power cord, an antenna, and some wires), put each in plastic bags, and then place everything inside a protective form. The packed form then moves on to Stage 2, called "boxing," in which workers place the form and a packet of instructions in a cardboard box and then close, seal, and label the box for shipping.

The company says that times required for the packing stage are unimodal and symmetric and can be described by a Normal distribution with a mean of 9 minutes and standard deviation of 1.5 minutes. (See Figure 7.10.) The times for the boxing stage can also be modeled as Normal, with a mean of 6 minutes and standard deviation of 1 minute.

Figure 7.10   The Normal model for the packing stage with a mean of 9 minutes and standard deviation of 1.5 minutes.

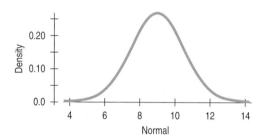

The company is interested in the total time that it takes to get a system through both packing and boxing, so they want to model the sum of the two random variables. Fortunately, the special property that adding independent Normals yields another Normal allows us to apply our knowledge of Normal probabilities to questions about the sum or difference of independent random variables. To use this property of Normals, we'll need to check two assumptions: that the variables are Independent and that they can be modeled by the Normal distribution.

GUIDED EXAMPLE   Packaging Stereos

Consider the company that manufactures and ships small stereo systems that we discussed previously.

If the time required to pack the stereos can be described by a Normal distribution, with a mean of 9 minutes and standard deviation of 1.5 minutes, and the times for the boxing stage can also be modeled as Normal, with a mean of 6 minutes and standard deviation of 1 minute, what is the probability that packing an order of two systems takes over 20 minutes? What percentage of the stereo systems takes longer to pack than to box?

Question 1:   What is the probability that packing an order of two systems takes more than 20 minutes?

	Setup State the problem.	We want to estimate the probability that packing an order of two systems takes more than 20 minutes.
	Variables Define your random variables.	Let P_1 = time for packing the first system P_2 = time for packing the second system T = total time to pack two systems
	Write an appropriate equation for the variables you need.	$T = P_1 + P_2$

Think about the model assumptions.	✓ **Normal Model Assumption.** We are told that packing times are well modeled by a Normal model, and we know that the sum of two Normal random variables is also Normal. ✓ **Independence Assumption.** There is no reason to think that the packing time for one system would affect the packing time for the next, so we can reasonably assume the two are independent.

 Mechanics Find the expected value. (Expected values always add.)

$$E(T) = E(P_1 + P_2)$$
$$= E(P_1) + E(P_2)$$
$$= 9 + 9 = 18 \text{ minutes}$$

Find the variance.

For sums of independent random variables, variances add. (In general, we don't need the variables to be Normal for this to be true—just independent.) Find the standard deviation.

Since the times are independent,

$$Var(T) = Var(P_1 + P_2)$$
$$= Var(P_1) + Var(P_2)$$
$$= 1.5^2 + 1.5^2$$
$$Var(T) = 4.50$$
$$SD(T) = \sqrt{4.50} \approx 2.12 \text{ minutes}$$

Now we use the fact that both random variables follow Normal distributions to say that their sum is also Normal.

We can model the time, T, with a $N(18, 2.12)$ model.

Sketch a picture of the Normal distribution for the total time, shading the region representing over 20 minutes.

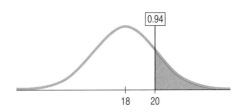

Find the z-score for 20 minutes.

$$z = \frac{20 - 18}{2.12} = 0.94$$

Use technology or a table to find the probability.

$$P(T > 20) = P(z > 0.94) = 0.1736$$

 Conclusion Interpret your result in context.

MEMO

Re: Computer systems packing

Using past history to build a model, we find slightly more than a 17% chance that it will take more than 20 minutes to pack an order of two stereo systems.

Question 2: What percentage of stereo systems take longer to pack than to box?

PLAN **Setup** State the question.

We want to estimate the percentage of the stereo systems that takes longer to pack than to box.

Variables Define your random variables.

Let P = time for packing a system
B = time for boxing a system
D = difference in times to pack and box a system

(continued)

Write an appropriate equation.	$D = P - B$
What are we trying to find? Notice that we can tell which of two quantities is greater by subtracting and asking whether the difference is positive or negative.	A system that takes longer to pack than to box will have $P > B$, and so D will be positive. We want to find $P(D > 0)$.
Remember to think about the assumptions.	✓ **Normal Model Assumption.** We are told that both random variables are well modeled by Normal distributions, and we know that the difference of two Normal random variables is also Normal. ✓ **Independence Assumption.** There is no reason to think that the packing time for a system will affect its boxing time, so we can reasonably assume the two are independent.

 DO

Mechanics Find the expected value.	$$E(D) = E(P - B)$$ $$= E(P) - E(B)$$ $$= 9 - 6 = 3 \text{ minutes}$$
For the difference of independent random variables, the variance is the sum of the individual variances.	Since the times are independent, $$Var(D) = Var(P - B)$$ $$= Var(P) + Var(B)$$ $$= 1.5^2 + 1^2$$ $$Var(D) = 3.25$$
Find the standard deviation.	$SD(D) = \sqrt{3.25} \approx 1.80 \text{ minutes}$
State what model you will use.	We can model D with $N(3, 1.80)$.
Sketch a picture of the Normal distribution for the difference in times and shade the region representing a difference greater than zero.	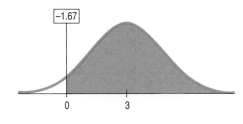
Find the z-score. Then use a table or technology to find the probability.	$$z = \frac{0 - 3}{1.80} = -1.67$$ $$P(D > 0) = P(z > -1.67) = 0.9525$$

REPORT

Conclusion Interpret your result in context.	MEMO **Re: Computer systems packing** In our second analysis, we found that just over 95% of all the stereo systems will require more time for packing than for boxing.

7.5 The Normal Approximation for the Binomial

In the previous chapter we modeled the number of successes of a series of trials with a Binomial. Suppose we send out 1000 flyers advertising a free cup of coffee at our new cafe and we think that the probability that someone will come is about 0.10. We might want to know the chance that at least 120 people will come to claim their coffee. We could use the binomial to calculate that with $n = 1000$ and $p = 0.10$. We know that the probability that exactly 120 people will come is $\binom{1000}{120} \times (0.10)^{120} \times (0.90)^{880}$ (about 0.005). But that's not the answer. We want to know the probability that *at least* 120 will show up, so we have to calculate a probability for 121, 122, 123, ... and all the way up to 1000. There must be a better way. And there is. The Normal distribution can approximate the Binomial.

The Binomial model for our cafe has mean $np = 100$ and standard deviation $\sqrt{npq} \approx 9.5$. We might just try to approximate its distribution with a Normal distribution using the same mean and standard deviation. Remarkably enough, that turns out to be a very good approximation. Using that mean and standard deviation, we can find the *probability*:

$$P(X \geq 120) = P\left(z \geq \frac{120 - 100}{9.5}\right) \approx P(z \geq 2.11) \approx 0.0174$$

There seems to be only about a 1.7% chance that at least 120 people will show up. (Adding up all 881 probabilities using the Binomial agrees with this to 3 decimal places!)

We can't always use a Normal distribution to make estimates of Binomial probabilities. The success of the approximation depends on the sample size. Suppose we are searching for a prize in cereal boxes, where the probability of finding a prize is 20%. If we buy five boxes, the actual Binomial probabilities that we get 0, 1, 2, 3, 4, or 5 prizes are 33%, 41%, 20%, 5%, 1%, and 0.03%, respectively. The histogram just below shows that this probability model is skewed. We shouldn't try to estimate these probabilities by using a Normal model.

But if we open 50 boxes of this cereal and count the number of prizes we find, we'll get the histogram below. It is centered at $np = 50(0.2) = 10$ prizes, as expected, and it appears to be fairly symmetric around that center.

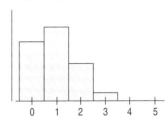

A Normal distribution is a close enough approximation to the Binomial only for a large enough number of trials. And what we mean by "large enough" depends on the probability of success. We'd need a larger sample if the probability of success were very low (or very high). It turns out that a Normal distribution works pretty well if we expect to see at least 10 successes and 10 failures. We can check the Success/Failure Condition.

Success/Failure Condition: A Binomial model is approximately Normal if we expect at least 10 successes and 10 failures:

$$np \geq 10 \text{ and } nq \geq 10.$$

Why 10? Well, actually it's 9, as revealed in the following Math Box.

MATH BOX Why Check $np \geq 10$?

It's easy to see where the magic number 10 comes from. You just need to remember how Normal models work. The problem is that a Normal model extends infinitely in both directions. But a Binomial model must have between 0 and n successes, so if we use a Normal to approximate a Binomial, we have to cut off its tails. That's not very important if the center of the Normal model is so far from 0 and n that the lost tails have only a negligible area. More than three standard deviations should do it because a Normal model has little probability past that.

So the mean needs to be at least 3 standard deviations from 0 and at least 3 standard deviations from n. Let's look at the 0 end.

We require:	$\mu - 3\sigma > 0$
Or, in other words:	$\mu > 3\sigma$
For a Binomial that's:	$np > 3\sqrt{npq}$
Squaring yields:	$n^2p^2 > 9npq$
Now simplify:	$np > 9q$
Since $q \leq 1$, we require:	$np > 9$

For simplicity we usually demand that np (and nq for the other tail) be at least 0 to use the Normal approximation which gives the Success/Failure Condition.[6]

---

*The Continuity Correction

When we use a continuous model to model a set of discrete events, we may need to make an adjustment called the **continuity correction**. We approximated the Binomial distribution $(50, 0.2)$ with a Normal distribution. But what does the Normal distribution say about the probability that $X = 10$? Every specific value in the Normal probability model has probability 0. That's not the answer we want.

---

[6]Looking at the final step, we see that we need $np > 9$ in the worst case, when q (or p) is near 1, making the Binomial model quite skewed. When q and p are near 0.5—for example, between 0.4 and 0.6—the Binomial model is nearly symmetric, and $np > 5$ ought to be safe enough. Although we'll always check for 10 expected successes and failures, keep in mind that for values of p near 0.5, we can be somewhat more forgiving.

Because X is really discrete, it takes on the exact values 0, 1, 2, ... , 50, each with positive probability. The histogram holds the secret to the correction. Look at the bin corresponding to $X = 10$ in the histogram. It goes from 9.5 to 10.5. What we really want is to find the area under the Normal curve *between* 9.5 and 10.5. So when we use the Normal distribution to approximate discrete events, we go halfway to the next value on the left and/or the right. We approximate $P(X = 10)$ by finding $P(9.5 \leq X \leq 10.5)$. For a Binomial $(50, 0.2)$, $\mu = 10$ and $\sigma = 2.83$.

$$\text{So } P(9.5 \leq X \leq 10.5) \approx P\left(\frac{9.5 - 10}{2.83} \leq z \leq \frac{10.5 - 10}{2.83}\right)$$

$$= P(-0.177 \leq z \leq 0.177)$$

$$= 0.1405$$

By comparison, the *exact* Binomial probability is 0.1398.

FOR EXAMPLE Using the Normal distribution

Some LCD panels have stuck or "dead" pixels that have defective transistors and are permanently unlit. If a panel has too many dead pixels, it must be rejected. A manufacturer knows that, when the production line is working correctly, the probability of rejecting a panel is 0.07.

QUESTIONS

1. How many screens do they expect to reject in a day's production run of 500 screens? What is the standard deviation?
2. If they reject 40 screens today, is that a large enough number that they should be concerned that something may have gone wrong with the production line?
3. In the past week of 5 days of production, they've rejected 200 screens—an average of 40 per day. Should that raise concerns?

ANSWERS

1. $\mu = 0.07 \times 500 = 35$ is the expected number of rejects

   $\sigma = \sqrt{npq} = \sqrt{500 \times 0.07 \times 0.93} = 5.7$

2. $P(X \geq 40) = P\left(z \geq \dfrac{40 - 35}{5.7}\right) = P(z \geq 0.877) \approx 0.19$, not an extraordinarily large number of rejects

3. Using the Normal approximation:

   $\mu = 0.07 \times 2500 = 175$

   $\sigma = \sqrt{2500 \times 0.07 \times 0.93} = 12.757$

   $P(X \geq 200) = P\left(z \geq \dfrac{200 - 175}{12.757}\right) = P(z \geq 1.96) \approx 0.025$

   Yes, this seems to be a number of rejects that would occur by chance rarely if nothing were wrong.

7.6   Other Continuous Random Variables

Many phenomena in business can be modeled by continuous random variables. The Normal model is important, but it is only one of many different models. Entire courses are devoted to studying which models work well in different situations, but we'll introduce just two others that are commonly used: the uniform and the exponential.

The Uniform Distribution

We've already seen the discrete version of the uniform probability model. A continuous uniform shares the principle that all events should be equally likely, but with a continuous distribution we can't talk about the probability of a particular value because each value has probability zero. Instead, for a continuous random variable X, we say that the probability that X lies in any interval depends only on the length of that interval. Not surprisingly the density function of a continuous uniform random variable looks flat. It can be defined by the formula

$$f(x) = \begin{cases} \dfrac{1}{b-a} & \text{if } a \leq x \leq b \\ 0 & \text{otherwise} \end{cases}$$

Figure 7.11   The density function of a continuous uniform random variable on the interval from a to b.

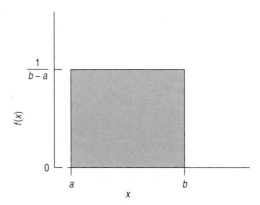

From Figure 7.11, it's easy to see that the probability that X lies in any interval between a and b is the same as any other interval of the same length. In fact, the probability is just the ratio of the length of the interval to the total length: $b - a$. In other words:

For values c and d $(c \leq d)$ both within the interval $[a, b]$:

$$P(c \leq X \leq d) = \frac{(d - c)}{(b - a)}$$

As an example, suppose you arrive at a bus stop and want to model how long you'll wait for the next bus. The sign says that busses arrive about every 20 minutes, but no other information is given. You might assume that the arrival is equally likely to be anywhere in the next 20 minutes, and so the density function would be

$$f(x) = \begin{cases} \dfrac{1}{20} & \text{if } 0 \leq x \leq 20 \\ 0 & \text{otherwise} \end{cases}$$

and would look as shown in Figure 7.12.

Figure 7.12 The density function of a continuous uniform random variable on the interval [0,20]. Notice that the mean (the balancing point) of the distribution is at 10 minutes and that the area of the box is 1.

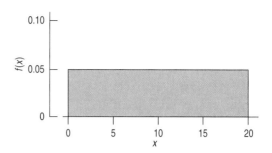

Just as the mean of a data distribution is the balancing point of a histogram, the mean of any continuous random variable is the balancing point of the density function. Looking at Figure 7.12, we can see that the balancing point is halfway between the end points at 10 minutes. In general, the expected value is:

$$E(X) = \frac{a + b}{2}$$

for a uniform distribution on the interval (a, b). With $a = 0$ and $b = 20$, the expected value would be 10 minutes.

The variance and standard deviation are less intuitive:

$$Var(X) = \frac{(b - a)^2}{12}; SD(X) = \sqrt{\frac{(b - a)^2}{12}}.$$

Using these formulas, our bus wait will have an expected value of 10 minutes with a standard deviation of $\sqrt{\frac{(20 - 0)^2}{12}} = 5.77$ minutes.

The Exponential Model

We saw in Chapter 6 that the Poisson distribution is a good model for the arrival, or occurrence, of events. We found, for example, the probability that x visits to our website will occur within the next minute. The exponential distribution with parameter λ can be used to model the time *between* those events. Its density function has the form:

$$f(x) = \lambda e^{-\lambda x} \quad for\, x \geq 0\, and\, \lambda > 0$$

The use of the parameter λ again is not coincidental. It highlights the relationship between the exponential and the Poisson.

Figure 7.13 The exponential density function with $\lambda = 1$.

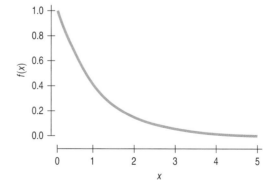

If a discrete random variable can be modeled by a Poisson model with rate λ, then the times between those events can be modeled by an exponential model with the same parameter λ. The mean of the exponential is $1/\lambda$. The inverse relationship between the two means makes intuitive sense. If λ increases and we expect *more*

hits per minute, then the expected time between hits should go down. The standard deviation of an exponential random variable is $1/\lambda$.

Like any continuous random variable, probabilities of an exponential random variable can be found only through the density function. Fortunately, the area under the exponential density between any two values, s and t ($s \leq t$), has a particularly easy form:

$$P(s \leq X \leq t) = e^{-\lambda s} - e^{-\lambda t}.$$

In particular, by setting s to be 0, we can find the probability that the waiting time will be less than t from

$$P(X \leq t) = P(0 \leq X \leq t) = e^{-\lambda 0} - e^{-\lambda t} = 1 - e^{-\lambda t}.$$

The function $P(X \leq t) = F(t)$ is called the **cumulative distribution function (cdf)** of the random variable X. If arrivals of hits to our website can be well modeled by a Poisson with $\lambda = 4/\text{minute}$, then the probability that we'll have to wait less than 20 seconds (1/3 of a minute) for the next hit is $F(1/3) = P(0 \leq X \leq 1/3) = 1 - e^{-4/3} = 0.736$. That seems about right. Arrivals are coming about every 15 seconds on average, so we shouldn't be surprised that nearly 75% of the time we won't have to wait more than 20 seconds for the next hit.

WHAT CAN GO WRONG?

- **Probability models are still just models.** Models can be useful, but they are not reality. Think about the assumptions behind your models. Question probabilities as you would data.

- **Don't assume everything's Normal.** Just because a random variable is continuous or you happen to know a mean and standard deviation doesn't mean that a Normal model will be useful. You must think about whether the **Normality Assumption** is justified. Using a Normal model when it really does not apply will lead to wrong answers and misleading conclusions.

  A sample of CEOs has a mean total compensation of \$10,307,311.87 with a standard deviation of \$17,964,615.16. Using the Normal model rule, we should expect about 68% of the CEOs to have compensations between $-\$7,657,303.29$ and \$28,271,927.03. In fact, more than 90% of the CEOs have annual compensations in this range. What went wrong? The distribution is skewed, not symmetric. Using the 68–95–99.7 Rule for data like these will lead to silly results.

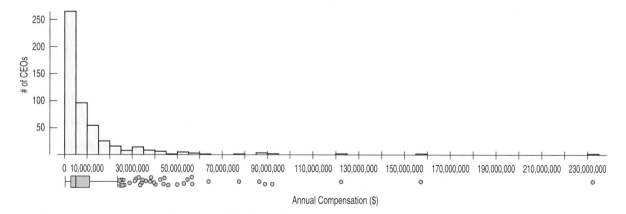

- **Don't use the Normal approximation with small *n*.** To use a Normal approximation in place of a Binomial model, there must be at least 10 expected successes and 10 expected failures.

To calculate Continuous Distribution Probabilities in Excel:

Distribution	Excel Syntax	Example Syntax	Result	Probability Statement
Normal (μ, σ)	NORM.DIST(x, mean, standard dev., cumulative)	=NORM.DIST(16,16.3,0.2,TRUE)	0.0668	P(X<16), N(16.3, 0.2)
	NORM.INV(probability, mean, standard dev.)	=NORM.INV(0.0668,16.3,0.2)	16.0000	P(X<x?) = 0.0668 N(16.3, 0.2)
Standard Normal, N(0,1)	NORM.S.DIST(z, cumulative)	=NORM.S.DIST(-1.75,TRUE)	0.0401	P(Z<-1.75)
	NORM.S.INV(probability)	=NORM.S.INV(0.04)	-1.7507	P(Z<z?)=0.04
Exponential	EXPON.DIST(x, lamda, cumulative)	=EXPON.DIST(1,1.33,TRUE)	0.7355	P(X<1), λ=4/3

Note that the commands here are for Excel 2013. These functions are available in earlier versions of Excel with similar commands (e.g., the pre-2010 Excel command for NORM.DIST was NORMDIST). In general, the functions ending in DIST will calculate a probability given a value from the distribution and the INV functions will calculate a value given a probability. When using the function bar or typing into a cell, Excel will search the functions to find what matches the typed characters, and this can be used to find the proper function.

XLSTAT

XLStat can make Normal probability plots (XLStat calls these Q-Q plots):

- Select **Visualizing data**, and then **Univariate plots**.
- On the General tab, click the **Quantitative** data box and then select the data on your worksheet.
- Click **OK**.
- If prompted, click **Continue**.

JMP

To make a "Normal Quantile Plot" in JMP,

- Make a histogram using **Distributions** from the **Analyze** menu.
- Click on the drop-down menu next to the variable name.
- Choose **Normal Quantile Plot** from the drop-down menu.
- JMP opens the plot next to the histogram.

Comments

JMP places the ordered data on the vertical axis and the Normal scores on the horizontal axis. The vertical axis aligns with the histogram's axis, a useful feature.

MINITAB

To make a "Normal Probability Plot" in MINITAB,

- Choose **Probability Plot** from the **Graph** menu.
- Select "Single" for the type of plot. Click **OK.**
- Enter the name of the variable in the "Graph variables" box. Click **OK.**

Comments

MINITAB places the ordered data on the horizontal axis and the Normal scores on the vertical axis.

SPSS

To make a Normal "P-P plot" in SPSS,

- Choose **Descriptives > P-P Plots** from the **Analyze** menu.
- Select the variable to be displayed and add to "Variable".
- Make sure that "Normal" is selected under "Test Distribution". Leave all other defaults set.

Comments

SPSS places the ordered data on the horizontal axis and the Normal scores on the vertical axis.

Price/Earnings and Stock Value

The CAPE10 index is based on the Price/Earnings (P/E) ratios of stocks. We can examine the P/E ratios without applying the smoothing techniques used to find the CAPE10. The file **CAPE10** holds the data, giving dates, various economic variables, CAPE10 values, and P/E values.

Examine the P/E values. Split the data into two periods: 1870–1989 and 1990 to the present. Would you judge that a Normal model would be appropriate for those values from the 1880s through the 1980s? Explain (and show the plots you made.)

Now consider the more recent P/E values in this context. Do you think they have been extreme? What years, if any, appear to be particularly problematic? Explain.

EXERCISES

Normal model calculations can be performed using a variety of technology or with the tables in Appendix B. Different methods may yield slightly different results.

SECTION 7.1

1. An incoming MBA student took placement exams in economics and mathematics. In economics, she scored 82 and in math 86. The overall results on the economics exam had a mean of 72 and a standard deviation of 8, while the mean math score was 68, with a standard deviation of 12. On which exam did she do better compared with the other students?

2. The first Statistics exam had a mean of 65 and a standard deviation of 10 points; the second had a mean of 80 and a standard deviation of 5 points. Derrick scored an 80 on both tests. Julie scored a 70 on the first test and a 90 on the second. They both totaled 160 points on the two exams, but Julie claims that her total is better. Explain.

3. Your company's Human Resources department administers a test of "Executive Aptitude." They report test grades as z-scores, and you got a score of 2.20. What does this mean?

4. After examining a child at his 2-year checkup, the boy's pediatrician said that the z-score for his height relative to American 2-year-olds was -1.88. Write a sentence to explain to the parents what that means.

5. Your company will admit to the executive training program only people who score in the top 3% on the executive aptitude test discussed in Exercise 3.

a) With your z-score of 2.20, did you make the cut?
b) What do you need to assume about test scores to find your answer in part a?

6. The pediatrician in Exercise 4 explains to the parents that the most extreme 5% of cases often require special treatment or attention.

a) Does this child fall into that group?
b) What do you need to assume about the heights of 2-year-olds to find your answer to part a?

SECTION 7.2

7. The Environmental Protection Agency (EPA) fuel economy estimates for automobiles suggest a mean of 24.8 mpg and a standard deviation of 6.2 mpg for highway driving. Assume that a Normal model can be applied.

a) Draw the model for auto fuel economy. Clearly label it, showing what the 68–95–99.7 Rule predicts about miles per gallon.
b) In what interval would you expect the central 68% of autos to be found?
c) About what percent of autos should get more than 31 mpg?

d) About what percent of cars should get between 31 and 37.2 mpg?
e) Describe the gas mileage of the worst 2.5% of all cars.

8. Some IQ tests are standardized to a Normal model with a mean of 100 and a standard deviation of 16.

a) Draw the model for these IQ scores. Clearly label it, showing what the 68–95–99.7 Rule predicts about the scores.
b) In what interval would you expect the central 95% of IQ scores to be found?
c) About what percent of people should have IQ scores above 116?
d) About what percent of people should have IQ scores between 68 and 84?
e) About what percent of people should have IQ scores above 132?

9. What percent of a standard Normal model is found in each region? Be sure to draw a picture first.

a) $z > 1.5$
b) $z < 2.25$
c) $-1 < z < 1.15$
d) $|z| > 0.5$

10. What percent of a standard Normal model is found in each region? Draw a picture first.

a) $z > -2.05$
b) $z < -0.33$
c) $1.2 < z < 1.8$
d) $|z| < 1.28$

11. In a standard Normal model, what value(s) of z cut(s) off the region described? Don't forget to draw a picture.

a) the highest 20%
b) the highest 75%
c) the lowest 3%
d) the middle 90%

12. In a standard Normal model, what value(s) of z cut(s) off the region described? Remember to draw a picture first.

a) the lowest 12%
b) the highest 30%
c) the highest 7%
d) the middle 50%

SECTION 7.3

13. Speeds of cars were measured as they passed one point on a road to study whether traffic speed controls were needed. Here's a histogram and normal probability plot of the measured speeds. Is a Normal model appropriate for these data? Explain.

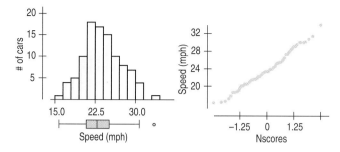

14. Has the Consumer Price Index (CPI) fluctuated around its mean according to a Normal model? Here are some displays. Is a Normal model appropriate for these data? Explain.

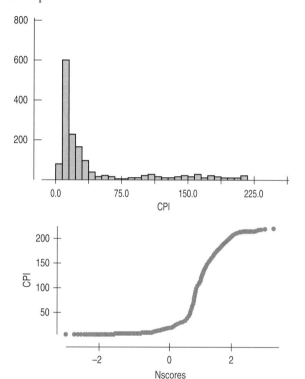

SECTION 7.4

15. For a new type of tire, a NASCAR team found the average distance a set of tires would run during a race is 168 miles, with a standard deviation of 14 miles. Assume that tire mileage is independent and follows a Normal model.

a) If the team plans to change tires twice during a 500-mile race, what is the expected value and standard deviation of miles remaining after two changes?
b) What is the probability they won't have to change tires a third time (and use a fourth set of tires) before the end of a 500-mile race?

16. In the 4 × 100 medley relay event, four swimmers swim 100 yards, each using a different stroke. A college team preparing for the conference championship looks at the times their swimmers have posted and creates a model based on the following assumptions:

- The swimmers' performances are independent.
- Each swimmer's times follow a Normal model.
- The means and standard deviations of the times (in seconds) are as shown here.

Swimmer	Mean	SD
1 (backstroke)	50.72	0.24
2 (breaststroke)	55.51	0.22
3 (butterfly)	49.43	0.25
4 (freestyle)	44.91	0.21

a) What are the mean and standard deviation for the relay team's total time in this event?
b) The team's best time so far this season was 3:19.48. (That's 199.48 seconds.) What is the probability that they will beat that time in the next event?

SECTION 7.5

17. Because many passengers who make reservations do not show up, airlines often overbook flights (sell more tickets than there are seats). A Boeing 767-400ER holds 245 passengers. If the airline believes the rate of passenger no-shows is 5% and sells 255 tickets, is it likely they will not have enough seats and someone will get bumped?

a) Use the Normal model to approximate the Binomial to determine the probability of at least 246 passengers showing up.
b) Should the airline change the number of tickets they sell for this flight? Explain.

18. Shortly after the introduction of the Belgian euro coin, newspapers around the world published articles claiming the coin is biased. The stories were based on reports that someone had spun the coin 250 times and gotten 140 heads—that's 56% heads.

a) Use the Normal model to approximate the Binomial to determine the probability of spinning a fair coin 250 times and getting at least 140 heads.
b) Do you think this is evidence that spinning a Belgian euro is unfair? Would you be willing to use it at the beginning of a sports event? Explain.

SECTION 7.6

19. A cable provider wants to contact customers in a particular telephone exchange to see how satisfied they are with the new digital TV service the company has provided. All numbers are in the 452 exchange, so there are 10,000 possible numbers from 452-0000 to 452-9999. If they select the numbers with equal probability:

a) What distribution would they use to model the selection?

b) The new business "incubator" was assigned the 200 numbers between 452-2500 and 452-2699, but these businesses don't subscribe to digital TV. What is the probability that the randomly selected number will be for an incubator business?

c) Numbers above 9000 were only released for domestic use last year, so they went to newly constructed residences. What is the probability that a randomly selected number will be one of these?

20. In an effort to check the quality of their cell phones, a manufacturing manager decides to take a random sample of 10 cell phones from yesterday's production run, which produced cell phones with serial numbers ranging (according to when they were produced) from 43005000 to 43005999. If each of the 1000 phones is equally likely to be selected:

a) What distribution would they use to model the selection?
b) What is the probability that a randomly selected cell phone will be one of the last 100 to be produced?
c) What is the probability that the first cell phone selected is either from the last 200 to be produced or from the first 50 to be produced?

21. Lifetimes of electronic components can often be modeled by an exponential model. Suppose quality control engineers want to model the lifetime of a hard drive to have a mean lifetime of 3 years.

a) What value of λ should they use?
b) With this model, what would the probability be that a hard drive lasts 5 years or less?

22. Suppose occurrences of sales on a small company's website are well modeled by a Poisson model with $\lambda = 5/\text{hour}$.

a) If a sale just occurred, what it the expected waiting time until the next sale?
b) What is the probability that the next sale will happen in the next 6 minutes?

CHAPTER EXERCISES

For Exercises 23–30, use the 68–95–99.7 Rule to approximate the probabilities rather than using technology to find the values more precisely. Answers given for probabilities or percentages from Exercise 31 on assume that a calculator or software has been used. Answers found from using Z-tables may vary slightly.

23. Mutual fund returns 2013. In the first quarter of 2013, a group of domestic equity mutual funds had a mean return of 6.2% with a standard deviation of 1.8%. If a Normal model can be used to model them, what percent of the funds would you expect to be in each region?

Be sure to draw a picture first.

a) Returns of 8.0% or more
b) Returns of 6.2% or less

c) Returns between 2.6% and 9.8%
d) Returns of more than 11.6%

24. Human resource testing. Although controversial and the subject of some recent law suits (e.g., *Satchell et al. vs. FedEx Express*), some human resource departments administer standard IQ tests to all employees. The Stanford-Binet test scores are well modeled by a Normal model with mean 100 and standard deviation 16. If the applicant pool is well modeled by this distribution, a randomly selected applicant would have what probability of scoring in the following regions?

a) 100 or below
b) Above 148
c) Between 84 and 116
d) Above 132

25. Mutual funds, again. From the mutual funds in Exercise 23 with quarterly returns that are well modeled by a Normal model with a mean of 6.2% and a standard deviation of 1.8%, find the cutoff return value(s) that would separate the

a) highest 50%.
b) highest 16%.
c) lowest 2.5%.
d) middle 68%.

26. Human resource testing, again. For the IQ test administered by human resources and discussed in Exercise 24, what cutoff value would separate the

a) lowest 0.15% of all applicants?
b) lowest 16%?
c) middle 95%?
d) highest 2.5%?

27. Currency exchange rates. The daily exchange rates for the five-year period 2008 to 2013 between the euro (EUR) and the British pound (GBP) can be modeled by a Normal distribution with mean 1.19 euros (to pounds) and standard deviation 0.043 euros. Given this model, what is the probability that on a randomly selected day during this period, the pound was worth

a) less than 1.19 euros?
b) more than 1.233 euros?
c) less than 1.104 euros?
d) Which would be more unusual, a day on which the pound was worth less than 1.126 euros or more than 1.298 euros?

28. Stock prices. For the 300 trading days from January 11, 2012 to March 22, 2013, the daily closing price of IBM stock (in $) is well modeled by a Normal model with mean $197.92 and standard deviation $7.16. According to this model, what is the probability that on a randomly selected day in this period the stock price closed

a) above $205.08?

b) below $212.24?

c) between $183.60 and $205.08?

d) Which would be more unusual, a day on which the stock price closed above $206 or below $180?

29. Currency exchange rates, again. For the model of the EUR/GBP exchange rate discussed in Exercise 27, what would the cutoff rates be that would separate the

a) highest 16% of EUR/GBP rates?

b) lowest 50%?

c) middle 95%?

d) lowest 2.5%?

30. Stock prices, again. According to the model in Exercise 28, what cutoff value of price would separate the

a) lowest 16% of the days?

b) highest 0.15%?

c) middle 68%?

d) highest 50%?

31. Mutual fund probabilities. According to the Normal model $N(0.062, 0.018)$ describing mutual fund returns in the 1st quarter of 2013 in Exercise 23, what percent of this group of funds would you expect to have return

a) over 6.8%?

b) between 0% and 7.6%?

c) more than 1%?

d) less than 0%?

32. Normal IQs. Based on the Normal model $N(100, 16)$ describing IQ scores from Exercise 24, what percent of applicants would you expect to have scores

a) over 80?

b) under 90?

c) between 112 and 132?

d) over 125?

33. Mutual funds, once more. Based on the model $N(0.062, 0.018)$ for quarterly returns from Exercise 23, what are the cut-off values for the

a) highest 10% of these funds?

b) lowest 20%?

c) middle 40%?

d) highest 80%?

34. More IQs. In the Normal model $N(100, 16)$ for IQ scores from Exercise 24, what cutoff value bounds the

a) highest 5% of all IQs?

b) lowest 30% of the IQs?

c) middle 80% of the IQs?

d) lowest 90% of all IQs?

35. Mutual funds, finis. Consider the Normal model $N(0.062, 0.018)$ for returns of mutual funds in Exercise 23 one last time.

a) What value represents the 40th percentile of these returns?

b) What value represents the 99th percentile?

c) What's the IQR of the quarterly returns for this group of funds?

36. IQs, finis. Consider the IQ model $N(100, 16)$ one last time.

a) What IQ represents the 15th percentile?

b) What IQ represents the 98th percentile?

c) What's the IQR of the IQs?

37. Parameters. Every Normal model is defined by its parameters, the mean and the standard deviation. For each model described here, find the missing parameter. As always, start by drawing a picture.

a) $\mu = 20$, 45% above 30; $\sigma = ?$

b) $\mu = 88$, 2% below 50; $\sigma = ?$

c) $\sigma = 5$, 80% below 100; $\mu = ?$

d) $\sigma = 15.6$, 10% above 17.2; $\mu = ?$

38. Parameters, again. Every Normal model is defined by its parameters, the mean and the standard deviation. For each model described here, find the missing parameter. Don't forget to draw a picture.

a) $\mu = 1250$, 35% below 1200; $\sigma = ?$

b) $\mu = 0.64$, 12% above 0.70; $\sigma = ?$

c) $\sigma = 0.5$, 90% above 10.0; $\mu = ?$

d) $\sigma = 220$, 3% below 202; $\mu = ?$

39. SAT or ACT? Each year thousands of high school students take either the SAT or ACT, standardized tests used in the college admissions process. Combined SAT scores can go as high as 1600, while the maximum ACT composite score is 36. Since the two exams use very different scales, comparisons of performance are difficult. (A convenient rule of thumb is $SAT = 40 \times ACT + 150$; that is, multiply an ACT score by 40 and add 150 points to estimate the equivalent SAT score.) Assume that one year the combined SAT can be modeled by $N(1000, 200)$ and the ACT can be modeled by $N(27, 3)$. If an applicant to a university has taken the SAT and scored 1260 and another student has taken the ACT and scored 33, compare these students scores using z-values. Which one has a higher relative score? Explain.

40. Economics. Anna, a business major, took final exams in both Microeconomics and Macroeconomics and scored 83 on both. Her roommate Megan, also taking both courses, scored 77 on the Micro exam and 95 on the Macro exam. Overall, student scores on the Micro exam had a mean of 81 and a standard deviation of 5, and the Macro scores had a mean of 74 and a standard deviation of 15. Which student's overall performance was better? Explain.

41. Low job satisfaction. Suppose that job satisfaction scores can be modeled with $N(100, 12)$. Human resource departments of corporations are generally concerned if the job satisfaction drops below a certain score. What score would you consider to be unusually low? Explain.

42. Low return. Exercise 23 proposes modeling quarterly returns of a group of mutual funds with $N(0.062, 0.018)$. The manager of this group of funds would like to flag any fund whose return is unusually low for a quarter. What level of return would you consider to be unusually low? Explain.

43. Management survey. A survey of 200 middle managers showed a distribution of the number of hours of exercise they participated in per week with a mean of 3.66 hours and a standard deviation of 4.93 hours.

a) According to the Normal model, what percent of managers will exercise fewer than one standard deviation below the mean number of hours?
b) For these data, what does that mean? Explain.
c) Explain the problem in using the Normal model for these data.

44. Customer database. A large philanthropic organization keeps records on the people who have contributed to their cause. In addition to keeping records of past giving, the organization buys demographic data on neighborhoods from the U.S. Census Bureau. Eighteen of these variables concern the ethnicity of the neighborhood of the donor. Here is a histogram and summary statistics for the percentage of whites in the neighborhoods of 500 donors.

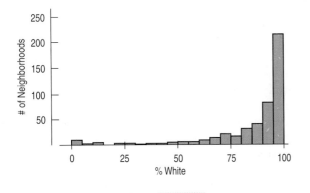

Count	500
Mean	83.59
Median	93
StdDev	22.26
IQR	17
Q1	80
Q3	97

a) Which is a better summary of the percentage of white residents in the neighborhoods, the mean or the median? Explain.

b) Which is a better summary of the spread, the IQR or the standard deviation? Explain.
c) From a Normal model, about what percentage of neighborhoods should have a percent white residents within one standard deviation of the mean?
d) What percentage of neighborhoods actually have a percent white within one standard deviation of the mean?
e) Explain the problem in using the Normal model for these data.

45. Drug company. Manufacturing and selling drugs that claim to reduce an individual's cholesterol level is big business. A company would like to market their drug to women if their cholesterol is in the top 15%. Assume the cholesterol levels of adult American women can be described by a Normal model with a mean of 188 mg/dL and a standard deviation of 24.

a) Draw and label the Normal model.
b) What percent of adult women do you expect to have cholesterol levels over 200 mg/dL?
c) What percent of adult women do you expect to have cholesterol levels between 150 and 170 mg/dL?
d) Estimate the interquartile range of the cholesterol levels.
e) Above what value are the highest 15% of women's cholesterol levels?

46. Tire company. A tire manufacturer believes that the tread life of its snow tires can be described by a Normal model with a mean of 32,000 miles and a standard deviation of 2500 miles.

a) If you buy a set of these tires, would it be reasonable for you to hope that they'll last 40,000 miles? Explain.
b) Approximately what fraction of these tires can be expected to last less than 30,000 miles?
c) Approximately what fraction of these tires can be expected to last between 30,000 and 35,000 miles?
d) Estimate the IQR for these data.
e) In planning a marketing strategy, a local tire dealer wants to offer a refund to any customer whose tires fail to last a certain number of miles. However, the dealer does not want to take too big a risk. If the dealer is willing to give refunds to no more than 1 of every 25 customers, for what mileage can he guarantee these tires to last?

47. Claims. Two companies make batteries for cell phone manufacturers. One company claims a mean life span of 2 years, while the other company claims a mean life span of 2.5 years (assuming average use of minutes/month for the cell phone).

a) Explain why you would also like to know the standard deviations of the battery life spans before deciding which brand to buy.
b) Suppose those standard deviations are 1.5 months for the first company and 9 months for the second company. Does this change your opinion of the batteries? Explain.

T 48. Car speeds. The police department of a major city needs to update its budget. For this purpose, they need to understand the variation in their fines collected from motorists for speeding. As a sample, they recorded the speeds of cars driving past a location with a 20 mph speed limit, a place that in the past has been known for producing fines. The mean of 100 readings was 23.84 mph, with a standard deviation of 3.56 mph. (The police actually recorded every car for a two-month period. These are 100 representative readings.)

a) How many standard deviations from the mean would a car going the speed limit be?
b) Which would be more unusual, a car traveling 34 mph or one going 10 mph?

49. CEOs. A business publication recently released a study on the total number of years of experience in industry among CEOs. The mean is provided in the article, but not the standard deviation. Is the standard deviation most likely to be 6 months, 6 years, or 16 years? Explain which standard deviation is correct and why.

50. Stocks. A newsletter for investors recently reported that the average stock price for a blue chip stock over the past 12 months was $72. No standard deviation was given. Is the standard deviation more likely to be $6, $16, or $60? Explain.

51. Cereal. The amount of cereal that can be poured into a small bowl varies with a mean of 1.5 ounces and a standard deviation of 0.3 ounces. A large bowl holds a mean of 2.5 ounces with a standard deviation of 0.4 ounces. You open a new box of cereal and pour one large and one small bowl.

a) How much more cereal do you expect to be in the large bowl?
b) What's the standard deviation of this difference?
c) If the difference follows a Normal model, what's the probability the small bowl contains more cereal than the large one?
d) What are the mean and standard deviation of the total amount of cereal in the two bowls?
e) If the total follows a Normal model, what's the probability you poured out more than 4.5 ounces of cereal in the two bowls together?
f) The amount of cereal the manufacturer puts in the boxes is a random variable with a mean of 16.3 ounces and a standard deviation of 0.2 ounces. Find the expected amount of cereal left in the box and the standard deviation.

52. Pets. The American Veterinary Association claims that the annual cost of medical care for dogs averages $100, with a standard deviation of $30, and for cats averages $120, with a standard deviation of $35.

a) What's the expected difference in the cost of medical care for dogs and cats?
b) What's the standard deviation of that difference?

c) If the costs can be described by Normal models, what's the probability that medical expenses are higher for someone's dog than for her cat?
d) What concerns do you have?

53. More cereal. In Exercise 51 we poured a large and a small bowl of cereal from a box. Suppose the amount of cereal that the manufacturer puts in the boxes is a random variable with mean 16.2 ounces and standard deviation 0.1 ounces.

a) Find the expected amount of cereal left in the box.
b) What's the standard deviation?
c) If the weight of the remaining cereal can be described by a Normal model, what's the probability that the box still contains more than 13 ounces?

54. More pets. You're thinking about getting two dogs and a cat. Assume that annual veterinary expenses are independent and have a Normal model with the means and standard deviations described in Exercise 52.

a) Define appropriate variables and express the total annual veterinary costs you may have.
b) Describe the model for this total cost. Be sure to specify its name, expected value, and standard deviation.
c) What's the probability that your total expenses will exceed $400?

55. Bikes. Bicycles arrive at a bike shop in boxes. Before they can be sold, they must be unpacked, assembled, and tuned (lubricated, adjusted, etc.). Based on past experience, the shop manager makes the following assumptions about how long this may take:

- The times for each setup phase are independent.
- The times for each phase follow a Normal model.
- The means and standard deviations of the times (in minutes) are as shown:

Phase	Mean	SD
Unpacking	3.5	0.7
Assembly	21.8	2.4
Tuning	12.3	2.7

a) What are the mean and standard deviation for the total bicycle setup time?
b) A customer decides to buy a bike like one of the display models but wants a different color. The shop has one, still in the box. The manager says they can have it ready in half an hour. Do you think the bike will be set up and ready to go as promised? Explain.

56. Bike sale. The bicycle shop in Exercise 55 estimates using current labor costs that unpacking a bike costs $0.82 on average with a standard deviation of $0.16. Assembly costs $8.00 on average with a standard deviation of $0.88 and tuning costs $4.10 with a standard deviation of $0.90. Because the costs are directly related to the times, you can use the same assumptions as in exercise 55.

a) Define your random variables, and use them to express the total cost of the bike set up.
b) Find the mean set up cost.
c) Find the standard deviation of the set up cost.
d) If the next shipment is 40 bikes, what is the probability that the total set up cost will be less than $500?

57. Coffee and doughnuts. At a certain coffee shop, all the customers buy a cup of coffee; some also buy a doughnut. The shop owner believes that the number of cups he sells each day is normally distributed with a mean of 320 cups and a standard deviation of 20 cups. He also believes that the number of doughnuts he sells each day is independent of the coffee sales and is normally distributed with a mean of 150 doughnuts and a standard deviation of 12.

a) The shop is open every day but Sunday. Assuming day-to-day sales are independent, what's the probability he'll sell more than 2000 cups of coffee in a week?
b) If he makes a profit of 50 cents on each cup of coffee and 40 cents on each doughnut, can he reasonably expect to have a day's profit of over $300? Explain.
c) What's the probability that on any given day he'll sell a doughnut to more than half of his coffee customers?

58. Weightlifting. The Atlas BodyBuilding Company (ABC) sells "starter sets" of barbells that consist of one bar, two 20-pound weights, and four 5-pound weights. The bars weigh an average of 10 pounds with a standard deviation of 0.25 pounds. The weights average the specified amounts, but the standard deviations are 0.2 pounds for the 20-pounders and 0.1 pounds for the 5-pounders. We can assume that all the weights are normally distributed.

a) ABC ships these starter sets to customers in two boxes: The bar goes in one box and the six weights go in another. What's the probability that the total weight in that second box exceeds 60.5 pounds? Define your variables clearly and state any assumptions you make.
b) It costs ABC $0.40 per pound to ship the box containing the weights. Because it's an odd-shaped package, though, shipping the bar costs $0.50 a pound plus a $6.00 surcharge. Find the mean and standard deviation of the company's total cost for shipping a starter set.
c) Suppose a customer puts a 20-pound weight at one end of the bar and the four 5-pound weights at the other end. Although he expects the two ends to weigh the same, they might differ slightly. What's the probability the difference is more than a quarter of a pound?

59. Lefties. A lecture hall has 200 seats with folding arm tablets, 30 of which are designed for left-handers. The typical size of classes that meet there is 188, and we can assume that about 13% of students are left-handed. Use a Normal approximation to find the probability that a right-handed student in one of these classes is forced to use a lefty arm tablet.

60. Seatbelts. Police estimate that 80% of drivers wear their seatbelts. They set up a safety roadblock, stopping cars to check for seatbelt use. If they stop 120 cars, what's the probability they find at least 20 drivers not wearing their seatbelt? Use a Normal approximation.

61. Rickets. Vitamin D is essential for strong, healthy bones. Although the bone disease rickets was largely eliminated in England during the 1950s, some people there are concerned that this generation of children is at increased risk because they are more likely to watch TV or play computer games than spend time outdoors. Recent research indicated that about 20% of British children are deficient in vitamin D. A company that sells vitamin D supplements tests 320 elementary school children in one area of the country. Use a Normal approximation to find the probability that no more than 50 of them have vitamin D deficiency.

62. Tennis. A tennis player has taken a special course to improve her serving. She thinks that individual serves are independent of each other. She has been able to make a successful first serve 70% of the time. Use a Normal approximation to find the probability she'll make at least 65 of her first serves out of the 80 she serves in her next match if her success percentage has not changed.

63. Wheel defects. Defects can occur anywhere on the wheel of a car during the manufacturing process. If X is the angle where the defect occurs, measured from a reference line, then X can be modeled as a uniform random variable on the interval from 0 to 360 degrees.

a) What is the probability that the defect is found between 0 and 180 degrees?
b) What is the probability that the defect is found between 0 and 45 degrees or between 315 and 360 degrees?

64. Quitting time. My employee seems to leave work anytime between 5PM and 6PM, uniformly.

a) What is the probability he will still be at work at 5:45 PM?
b) What is the probability he will still be at work at 5:45 PM every day this week (M-F)?
c) What did you assume to calculate b?

65. Web visitors. A website manager has noticed that during the evening hours, about 3 people per minute check out from their shopping cart and make an online purchase. She believes that each purchase is independent of the others.

a) What model might you suggest to model the number of purchases per minute?
b) What model would you use to model the time between events?
c) What is the mean time between purchases?
d) What is the probability that the time to the next purchase will be between 1 and 2 minutes?

66. Monitoring quality. A cell phone manufacturer samples cell phones from the assembly to test. She noticed that the number of faulty cell phones in a production run of cell phones is usually small and that the quality of one day's run seems to have no bearing on the next day.

a) What model might you use to model the number of faulty cell phones produced in one day?

She wants to model the time between the events of producing a faulty phone. The mean number of defective cell phones is 2 per day.

b) What model would you use to model the time between events?

c) What would the probability be that the time to the next failure is 1 day or less?

d) What is the mean time between failures?

8

Surveys and Sampling

Roper Polls

Public opinion polls are a relatively new phenomenon. In 1948, as a result of telephone surveys of likely voters, all of the major organizations—Gallup, Roper, and Crossley—consistently predicted, throughout the summer and into the fall, that Thomas Dewey would defeat Harry Truman in the November presidential election. By October the results seemed so clear that *Fortune* magazine declared, "Due to the overwhelming evidence, *Fortune* and Mr. Roper plan no further detailed reports on change of opinion in the forthcoming presidential campaign . . . ."

Of course, Harry Truman went on to win the 1948 election, and the picture of Truman in the early morning after the election holding up the *Chicago Tribune* (printed the night before), with its headline declaring Dewey the winner, has become legend.

The public's faith in opinion polls plummeted after the election, but Elmo Roper vigorously defended the pollsters. Roper was a principal and founder of one of the first market research firms, Cherington, Wood, and Roper, and director of the *Fortune Survey*, which was the first national poll to use scientific sampling techniques. He argued that rather than abandoning polling, business leaders should learn what had gone wrong in the 1948 polls so that market research could be improved. His frank admission of the mistakes made in those polls helped to restore confidence in polling as a business tool.

For the rest of his career, Roper split his efforts between two projects, commercial polling and public opinion. He established the Roper Center for Public Opinion Research at Williams College as a place to house public opinion archives, convincing fellow polling leaders Gallup and Crossley to participate as well. Now located at the University of Connecticut, the Roper Center is one of the world's leading archives of social science data. Roper's market research efforts started as Roper Research Associates and later became the Roper Organization, which was acquired in 2005 by GfK. Founded in Germany in 1934 as the Gesellschaft für Konsumforschung (literally, "Society for Consumption Research"), GfK now stands for "growth from knowledge." It is the fourth largest international market research organization, with over 130 companies in 70 countries and more than 7700 employees worldwide.

GfK Roper Consulting conducts a yearly, global study to examine cultural, economic, and social information that may be crucial to companies doing business worldwide. These companies use the information provided by GfK Roper to help make marketing and advertising decisions in different markets around the world.

How do the researchers at GfK Roper know that the responses they get reflect the real attitudes of consumers? After all, they don't ask everyone, but they don't want to limit their conclusions to just the people they surveyed. Generalizing from the data at hand to the world at large is something that market researchers, investors, and pollsters do every day. To do it wisely, they need three fundamental ideas.

8.1 Three Ideas of Sampling

Idea 1: Sample—Examine a Part of the Whole

We'd like to know about an entire collection of individuals, called a **population**, but examining all of them is usually impractical, if not impossible. So we settle for examining a smaller group of individuals—a **sample**—selected from the population. For the Roper researchers the population of interest is the entire world, but it's not practical, cost-effective, or feasible to survey everyone. So they examine a sample selected from the population.

We take samples all the time. For example, if a restaurant chef wants to be sure that the vegetable soup she's cooking is up to her standards, she'll taste a spoonful. She doesn't need to consume the whole pot. She can trust that the taste will *represent* the flavor of the population—the entire pot. The idea of tasting is that a small sample, if selected properly, can represent the larger population. Sampling is common in many aspects of business practice. For example, auditors may sample some records rather than reading through all of them. Manufacturers monitor quality by testing a small sample off the line.

The GfK Roper Reports® Worldwide poll is an example of a **sample survey**, designed to ask questions of a small group of people in the hope of learning something about the entire population. Most likely, you've never been selected to be part of a national opinion poll. That's true of most people. So how can the pollsters claim that a sample represents the entire population? As we'll see, a representative sample can often provide a good idea of what the entire population is like. But the sample must be selected with care.

Selecting a sample to represent the population fairly is easy in theory, but in practice, it's more difficult than it sounds. For example, a sample may fail to represent part of the population. If a retail business samples customers as they come in the door, they may be missing an important part of their potential customer population—those who choose to shop elsewhere. Samples that over- or underemphasize

> **The W's and Sampling**
> The population we are interested in is usually determined by the *why* of our study. The participants or cases in the sample we draw will be the *who*. *When* and *how* we draw the sample may depend on what is practical.

some characteristics of the population are said to be biased. When a sample is **biased,** the summary characteristics of a sample differ from the corresponding characteristics of the population it is trying to represent, so they can produce misleading information. Conclusions based on biased samples are inherently flawed. There is usually no way to fix bias after the sample is drawn and no way to salvage useful information from it.

To make the sample as representative as possible, the best strategy is to select individuals for the sample *at random*. This may seem almost careless at first, but, as we will see, it is essential.

Idea 2: Randomize

Think back to our soup example. Suppose the chef adds some salt to the pot (the population). If she samples from the top before stirring, she'll get the misleading idea that the soup is salty. If she samples from the bottom, she'll get the equally misleading idea that it's bland. But by stirring the soup, she'll make each spoonful a more random sample of the soup, distributing the salt throughout the pot, and making each taste more typical of the saltiness of the whole pot. Deliberate randomization is one of the great tools of Statistics.

Randomization can also protect against factors that you aren't aware of. Suppose, while the chef isn't looking, an assistant adds a handful of peas to the soup. The peas sink to the bottom of the pot, mixing with the other vegetables. Stirring in the salt *also* randomizes the peas throughout the pot, making the sample taste more typical of the overall pot *even though the chef didn't know the peas were there*. So randomizing protects us by giving us a representative sample even for effects we were unaware of.

For a survey, we select participants at random, and this helps us represent *all* the features of our population, making sure that *on average* the sample looks like the rest of the population.

The essential feature of randomness is that the selection is "fair." We have discussed many facets of randomness in Chapter 5, and we can use some of those concepts here. What makes the sample fair is that each participant has an equal chance to be selected.

- **Why not match the sample to the population?** Rather than randomizing, we could try to design a sample to include every possible, relevant characteristic: income level, age, political affiliation, marital status, number of children, place of residence, etc. But we can't possibly think of all the things that might be important. Even if we could, we wouldn't be able to match our sample to the population for all these characteristics.

How well can a sample represent the population from which it was selected? Here's an example using the database of the Paralyzed Veterans of America, a philanthropic organization with a donor list of about 3.5 million people. We've taken two samples, each of 8000 individuals at random from the population. Table 8.1 shows how the means and proportions match up on seven variables.

	A	Age (yr)	White (%)	Female (%)	# of children	Income Bracket (1-7)	Wealth Bracket (1-9)	Homeowner? (% Yes)
1								
2	Sample 1	61.4	85.12	56.2	1.54	3.91	5.29	71.36
3	Sample 2	61.2	84.44	56.4	1.51	3.88	5.33	72.3

Table 8.1   Means and proportions for seven variables from two samples of size 8000 from the Paralyzed Veterans of America data. We drew these samples using Microsoft Excel's RAND function (Excel 2013), but you can use almost any statistics software to draw similar random samples. The fact that the summaries of the variables from these two samples are so similar gives us confidence that either one would be representative of the entire population.

The two samples match closely in every category. You can see how well randomizing has stirred the population. We didn't preselect the samples for these variables, but randomizing has matched the results closely. The two samples don't vary much from each other, so we can assume that they don't differ much from the rest of the population either.

Idea 3: The Sample Size Is What Matters

You probably weren't surprised by the idea that a sample can represent the whole. And the idea of sampling randomly to make the sample fair makes sense too. But the third important idea of sampling often surprises people. The third idea is that the *size of the sample* determines what we can conclude from the data *regardless of the size of the population*. Many people think that to provide a good representation of the population, the sample must be a large percentage, or *fraction*, of the population, but in fact all that matters is the size of the sample. The size of the *population* doesn't matter at all.[1] A random sample of 100 students in a college represents the student body just about as well as a random sample of 100 voters represents the entire electorate of the United States. This is perhaps the most surprising idea in designing surveys.

Think about the pot of soup again. The chef is probably making a large pot of soup. But she doesn't need a really big spoon to decide how the soup tastes. She'll get the same information from an ordinary spoonful no matter how large the pot—as long as the pot is sufficiently stirred. That's what randomness does for us. What *fraction* of the population you sample doesn't matter. It's the **sample size** itself that's important. This idea is of key importance to the design of any sample survey, because it determines the balance between how well the survey can measure the population and how much the survey costs.

How big a sample do you need? That depends on what you're estimating, but too small a sample won't be representative of the population. To get an idea of what's really in the soup, you need a large enough taste to be a *representative* sample from the pot, including, say, a selection of the vegetables. For a survey that tries to find the proportion of the population falling into a category, you'll usually need at least several hundred respondents.[2]

- **What do the professionals do?** How do professional polling and market research companies do their work? The most common polling method today is to contact respondents by telephone. Computers generate random telephone numbers for telephone exchanges known to include residential customers; so pollsters can contact people with unlisted phone numbers. The person who answers the phone will be invited to respond to the survey—if that person qualifies. (For example, only adults are usually surveyed, and the respondent usually must live at the residence phoned.) If the person answering doesn't qualify, the caller will ask for an appropriate alternative. When they conduct the interview, the pollsters often list possible responses (such as product names) in randomized orders to avoid biases that might favor the first name on the list.

Do these methods work? The Pew Research Center for the People and the Press reports on survey completion rates about every three years. Pew reports that by 2012 a telephone survey could contact about 62% of households whose

---

[1]Well, that's not exactly true. If the population is smaller than about 10 times the size of the sample it *can* matter. It doesn't matter whenever, as usual, our sample is a very small fraction of the population.
[2]Chapter 9 gives the details behind this statement and shows how to decide on a sample size for a survey.

phone numbers had been randomly generated. However, only 14% of those contacts yielded an interview, amounting to only 9% of the households originally sampled. Nevertheless, Pew concludes that "telephone surveys that include landlines and cell phones and are weighted to match the demographic composition of the population continue to provide accurate data on most political, social and economic measures." (www.people-press.org/2012/05/15/assessing-the-representativeness-of-public-opinion-surveys/)

A Census—Does It Make Sense?

Why bother determining the right sample size? If you plan to open a store in a new community, why draw a sample of residents to understand their interests and needs? Wouldn't it be better to just include everyone and make the "sample" be the entire population? Such a special sample is called a **census**. Although a census would appear to provide the best possible information about the population, there are a number of reasons why it might not.

First, it can be difficult to complete a census. There always seem to be some individuals who are hard to locate or hard to measure. Do you really need to contact the folks away on vacation when you collect your data? How about those with no telephone or mailing address? The cost of locating the last few cases may far exceed the budget. It can also be just plain impractical to take a census. The quality control manager for Hostess® Twinkies® doesn't want to taste *all* the Twinkies on the production line to determine their quality. Aside from the fact that nobody could eat that many Twinkies, it would defeat their purpose: there would be none left to sell.

Second, the population you're studying may change. For example, in any human population, babies are born, people travel, and folks die during the time it takes to complete the census. News events and advertising campaigns can cause sudden shifts in opinions and preferences. A sample, surveyed in a shorter time frame, may actually generate more accurate information.

Finally, taking a census can be cumbersome. A census usually requires a team of pollsters and the cooperation of the population. Even with both, it's almost impossible to avoid errors. Because it tries to count everyone, the U.S. Census records too many college students. Many are included both by their families and in a report filed by their schools. Errors of this sort, of both under- and overcounting can be found throughout the U.S. Census.

FOR EXAMPLE   Identifying sampling terms

A nonprofit organization has taken over the historic State Theater and hopes to preserve it with a combination of attractive shows and fundraising. The organization has asked a team of students to help them design a survey to better understand the customer base likely to purchase tickets. Fortunately, the theater's computerized ticket system records contact and some demographic information for ticket purchasers, and that database of 7345 customers is available.

QUESTIONS What is the population of interest? What would a census be in this case? Would it be practical?

ANSWERS The population is all potential ticket purchasers. A census would have to reach all potential purchasers. We don't know who they are or have any way to contact them.

8.2   Populations and Parameters

> **Statistic**
>
> Any quantity that we calculate from data could be called a "statistic." But in practice, we usually obtain a statistic from a sample and use it to estimate a population parameter.

> **Parameter**
>
> Population model parameters are not just unknown—usually they are unknowable. We take a sample and use the sample statistics to estimate them.

GfK Roper Reports Worldwide reports that 60.5% of people over 50 worry about food safety, but only 43.7% of teens do. What does this claim mean? We can be sure the Roper researchers didn't take a census. So they can't possibly know *exactly* what percentage of teenagers worry about food safety. So what does "43.7%" mean?

To generalize from a sample to the world at large, we need a model of reality. Such a model doesn't need to be complete or perfect. Just as a model of an airplane in a wind tunnel can tell engineers what they need to know about aerodynamics even though it doesn't include every rivet of the actual plane, models of data can give us summaries that we can learn from and use even though they don't fit each data value exactly. It's important to remember that they're only models of reality and not reality itself. But without models, what we can learn about the world at large is limited to only what we can say about the data we have at hand.

Models use mathematics to represent reality. We call the key numbers in those models **parameters**. Sometimes a parameter used in a model for a population is called (redundantly) a **population parameter**.

But let's not forget about the data. We use the data to try to estimate values for the population parameters. Any summary found from the data is a **statistic**. Those statistics that estimate population parameters are particularly interesting. Sometimes—and especially when we match statistics with the parameters they estimate—we use the term **sample statistic**.

We draw samples because we can't work with the entire population. We hope that the statistics we compute from the sample will estimate the corresponding parameters accurately. A sample that does this is said to be **representative**.

JUST CHECKING

1 Various claims are often made for surveys. Why is each of the following claims not correct?

   a) It is always better to take a census than to draw a sample.
   b) Stopping customers as they are leaving a restaurant is a good way to sample opinions about the quality of the food.
   c) We drew a sample of 100 from the 3000 students in a school. To get the same level of precision for a town of 30,000 residents, we'll need a sample of 1000.
   d) A poll taken at a popular website (www.statsisfun.org) garnered 12,357 responses. The majority of respondents said they enjoy doing Statistics. With a sample size that large, we can be sure that most Americans feel this way.
   e) The true percentage of all Americans who enjoy Statistics is called a "population statistic."

8.3   Common Sampling Designs

We've said that every individual in the population should have an equal chance of being selected in a sample. That makes the sample fair, but it's not quite enough to ensure that the sample is representative. Consider, for example, a market analyst who samples customers by drawing at random from product registration forms, half of which arrived by mail and half by online registration. She flips a coin. If it comes up heads, she'll draw 100 mail returns; tails, she'll draw 100 electronic returns. Each customer has an equal chance of being selected, but if tech-savvy customers are different, then the samples are hardly representative.

Simple Random Sample (SRS)

To make the sample representative, we must ensure that our sampling method gives each *combination* of individuals an equal chance as well. A sample drawn in this way is called a **simple random sample**, usually abbreviated **SRS**. An SRS is the sampling method on which the theory of working with sampled data is based and thus the standard against which we measure other sampling methods.

question you ask is important, so state the wording of the question clearly. Be sure that the question is useful in helping you with the overall goal of the survey.

Sampling Practice Specify *when*, *where*, and *how* the sampling will be performed. Specify any other details of your survey, such as how respondents were contacted, any incentives that were offered to encourage them to respond, how nonrespondents were treated, and so on.

The survey will be administered in the middle of the fall semester during October. We have a master list of registered students, which we will randomize by matching it with random numbers from www.random.org and sorting on the random numbers, carrying the names. We will contact selected students by phone or e-mail and arrange to meet with them. If a student is unwilling to participate, the next name from the randomized list will be substituted until a sample of 200 participants is found.

We will meet with students in an office set aside for this purpose so that each will see the puzzle under similar conditions.

REPORT **Summary and Conclusion** This report should include a discussion of all the elements needed to design the study. It's good practice to discuss any special circumstances or other issues that may need attention.

MEMO

Re: Survey plans

Our team's plans for the puzzle market survey call for a simple random sample of students. Because subjects need to be shown the prototype puzzle, we must arrange to meet with selected participants. We have arranged an office for that purpose.

We will also collect demographic information so we can determine whether there is in fact a difference in interest level among classes or between men and women.

The Real Sample

We have been discussing sampling in a somewhat idealized setting. In the real world, things can be a bit messier. Here are some things to consider.

The population may not be as well-defined as it seems. For example, if a company wants the opinions of a typical mall "shopper," who should they sample? Should they only ask shoppers carrying a purchase? Should they include people eating at the food court? How about teenagers just hanging out in the mall? Even when the population is clear, it may not be possible to establish an appropriate sampling frame.

Usually, the practical sampling frame is not the group you *really* want to know about. For example, election polls want to sample from those who will actually vote in the next election—a group that is particularly tricky to identify before election day. The sampling frame limits what your survey can find out.

Then there's your target sample. These are the individuals selected according to your sample design for whom you *intend* to measure responses. You're not likely to get responses from all of them. ("I know it's dinner time, but I'm sure you wouldn't mind answering a few questions. It'll only take 20 minutes or so. Oh, you're busy?") Nonresponse is a problem in many surveys.

Sample designs are usually about the target sample. But in the real world, you won't get responses from everyone your design selects. So in reality, your sample

What's the Sample?

The population we want to study is determined by asking *why*. When we design a survey, we use the term "sample" to refer to the individuals selected, from whom we hope to obtain responses. Unfortunately, the real sample is just those we can reach to obtain responses—the *who* of the study. These are slightly different uses of the same term *sample*. The context usually makes clear which we mean, but it's important to realize that the difference between the two samples could undermine even a well-designed study.

consists of the actual respondents. These are the individuals about whom you *do* get data and can draw conclusions. Unfortunately, they might not be representative of either the sampling frame or the population.

At each step, the group we can study may be constrained further. The *who* of our study keeps changing, and each constraint can introduce biases. A careful study should address the question of how well each group matches the population of interest. The *who* in an SRS is the population of interest from which we've drawn a representative sample. That's not always true for other kinds of samples.

When people (or committees!) decide on a survey, they often fail to think through the important questions about who are the *who* of the study and whether they are the individuals from whom the answers would be interesting or have meaningful business consequences. This is a key step in performing a survey and should not be overlooked.

8.4   The Valid Survey

It isn't sufficient to draw a sample and start asking questions. You want to feel confident your survey can yield the information you need about the population you are interested in. We want a *valid survey*.

To help ensure a valid survey, you need to ask four questions:

- What do I want to know?
- Who are the right respondents?
- What are the right questions?
- What will be done with the results?

These questions may seem obvious, but there are a number of specific pitfalls to avoid:

Know what you want to know. Far too often, decision makers decide to perform a survey without any clear idea of what they hope to learn. Before considering a survey, you must be clear about what you hope to learn and what population you want to learn about. If you don't know that, you can't even judge whether you have a valid survey. The survey *instrument*—the questionnaire itself—can be a source of errors. Perhaps the most common error is to ask unnecessary questions. The longer the survey, the fewer people will complete it, leading to greater nonresponse bias. For each question on your survey, you should ask yourself whether you really want to know this and know what you would do with the responses if you had them. If you don't have a good use for the answer to a question, don't ask it.

Use the right sampling frame. A valid survey obtains responses from appropriate respondents. Be sure you have a suitable sampling frame. Have you identified the population of interest and sampled from it appropriately? A company looking to expand its base might survey customers who returned warrantee registration cards—after all, that's a readily available sampling frame—but if the company wants to know how to make its product more attractive, it needs to survey customers who rejected its product in favor of a competitor's product. This is the population that can tell the company what about its product needs to change to capture a larger market share. The errors in the presidential election polls of 1948 were likely due to the use of telephone samples in an era when telephones were not affordable by the less affluent—who were the folks most likely to vote for Truman.

It is equally important to be sure that your respondents actually know the information you hope to discover. Your customers may not know much about the competing products, so asking them to compare your product with others may not yield useful information.

Ask specific rather than general questions. It is better to be specific. "Do you usually recall TV commercials?" won't be as useful as "How many TV commercials can you recall from last night?" or better, yet, "Please describe for me all the TV commercials you can recall from your viewing last night."

Watch for biases. Even with the right sampling frame, you must beware of bias in your sample. If customers who purchase more expensive items are less likely to respond to your survey, this can lead to **nonresponse bias**. Although you can't expect all mailed surveys to be returned, if those individuals who don't respond have common characteristics, your sample will no longer represent the population you hope to learn about. Surveys in which respondents volunteer to participate, such as online surveys, suffer from **voluntary response bias**. Individuals with the strongest feelings on either side of an issue are more likely to respond; those who don't care may not bother.

Be careful with question phrasing. Questions must be carefully worded. A respondent may not understand the question—or may not understand the question the way the researcher intended it. For example, "Does anyone in your family own a Ford truck?" leaves the term "family" unclear. Does it include only spouses and children or parents and siblings, or do in-laws and second cousins count too? A question like "Was your Twinkie fresh?" might be interpreted quite differently by different people.

Be careful with answer phrasing. Respondents and survey-takers may also provide inaccurate responses, especially when questions are politically or sociologically sensitive. This also applies when the question does not take into account all possible answers, such as a true-false or multiple-choice question to which there may be other answers. Or the respondent may not know the correct answer to the question on the survey. In 1948, there were four major candidates for President,[3] but some survey respondents might not have been able to name them all. A survey question that just asked "Who do you plan to vote for?" might have underrepresented the less prominent candidates. And one that just asked "What do you think of Wallace?" might yield inaccurate results from voters who simply didn't know who he was. We refer to inaccurate responses (intentional or unintentional) as **measurement errors.** One way to cut down on measurement errors is to provide a range of possible responses. But be sure to phrase them in neutral terms.

The best way to protect a survey from measurement errors is to perform a pilot test. In a **pilot test,** a small sample is drawn from the sampling frame, and a draft form of the survey instrument is administered. A pilot test can point out flaws in the instrument. For example, during a staff cutback at one of our schools, a researcher

---

[3] Harry Truman, Thomas Dewey, Strom Thurmond, and Henry Wallace.

surveyed faculty members to ask how they felt about the reduction in staff support. The scale ran from "It's a good idea" to "I'm very unhappy." Fortunately, a pilot study showed that everyone was very unhappy or worse. The scale was re-tuned to run from "unhappy" to "ready to quit."

FOR EXAMPLE   Survey design

A nonprofit organization has enlisted some student consultants to help design a fund-raising survey. The student consultants suggest to the board of directors that they may want to rethink their survey plans. They point out that there are differences among the population, the sampling frame, the target sample contacted by telephone, and the actual sample.

QUESTION   How are the population, sampling frame, target sample, and sample likely to differ?

ANSWER   The population is all potential ticket buyers.

The sampling frame consists of only those who have previously purchased tickets. Anyone who wasn't attracted to previous productions wouldn't be surveyed. That could keep the board from learning of ways to make the theater's offering more attractive to those who hadn't purchased tickets before.

The target sample is those selected from the database who can be contacted by telephone. Those with unlisted numbers or who had declined to give their phone number can't be contacted. It may be more difficult to contact those with caller ID.

The actual sample will be those previous customers selected at random from the database who can be reached by telephone and who agree to complete the survey.

8.5   How to Sample Badly

Bad sample designs yield worthless data. Many of the most convenient forms of sampling can be seriously biased. And there is no way to correct for the bias from a bad sample. So it's wise to pay attention to sample design—and to beware of reports based on poor samples.

Voluntary Response Sample

One of the most common dangerous sampling methods is the voluntary response sample. In a **voluntary response sample,** a large group of individuals is invited to respond, and all who do respond are counted. This method is used by call-in shows, 900 numbers, Internet polls, and letters written to members of Congress. Voluntary response samples are almost always biased, and so conclusions drawn from them are almost always wrong.

It's often hard to define the sampling frame of a voluntary response study. Practically, the frames are groups such as Internet users who frequent a particular website or viewers of a particular TV show. But those sampling frames don't correspond to the population you are likely to be interested in.

Even if the sampling frame is of interest, voluntary response samples are often biased toward those with strong opinions or those who are strongly motivated—and especially from those with strong negative opinions. A request that travelers who have used the local airport visit a survey site to report on their experiences is much more likely to hear from those who had long waits, cancelled flights, and lost luggage than from those whose flights were on time and carefree. The resulting voluntary response bias invalidates the survey.

Convenience Sampling

Another sampling method that doesn't work is convenience sampling. As the name suggests, in **convenience sampling** we simply include the individuals who are convenient. Unfortunately, this group may not be representative of the population. A survey of 437 potential home buyers in Orange County, California, found, among other things, that

> *all but 2 percent of the buyers have at least one computer at home, and 62 percent have two or more. Of those with a computer, 99 percent are connected to the Internet (Jennifer Hieger, "Portrait of Homebuyer Household: 2 Kids and a PC," Orange County Register, July 27, 2001).*

Later in the article, we learn that the survey was conducted via the Internet. That was a convenient way to collect data and surely easier than drawing a simple random sample, but perhaps home builders shouldn't conclude from this study that *every* family has a computer and an Internet connection.

Many surveys conducted at shopping malls suffer from the same problem. People in shopping malls are not necessarily representative of the population of interest. Mall shoppers tend to be more affluent and include a larger percentage of teenagers and retirees than the population at large. To make matters worse, survey interviewers tend to select individuals who look "safe," or easy to interview.

Convenience sampling is not just a problem for beginners. In fact, convenience sampling is a widespread problem in the business world. When a company wants to find out what people think about its products or services, it may turn to the easiest people to sample: its own customers. But the company will never learn how those who *don't* buy its product feel about it.

Do you use the Internet?
Click here ⬤ for yes
Click here ⬤ for no

Internet Surveys

Internet convenience surveys are often worthless. As voluntary response surveys, they have no well-defined sampling frame (all those who use the Internet and visit their site?) and thus report no useful information. Do not use them.

Bad Sampling Frame?

An SRS from an incomplete sampling frame introduces bias because the individuals included may differ from the ones not in the frame. It may be easier to sample workers from a single site, but if a company has many sites and they differ in worker satisfaction, training, or job descriptions, the resulting sample can be biased. There is serious concern among professional pollsters that the increasing numbers of people who can be reached only by cell phone may bias telephone-based market research and polling.

Undercoverage

Many survey designs suffer from **undercoverage,** in which some portion of the population is not sampled at all or has a smaller representation in the sample than it has in the population. Undercoverage can arise for a number of reasons, but it's always a potential source of bias. Are people who use answering machines to screen callers (and are thus less available to blind calls from market researchers) different from other customers in their purchasing preferences?

FOR EXAMPLE   Common mistakes in survey design

A board member proposes that rather than telephoning past customers, they simply post someone at the door to ask theater goers their opinions. Another suggests that it would be even easier to post a questionnaire on the theater website and invite responses there. A third suggests that rather than working with random numbers, they simply phone every 200th person on the list of past customers.

(continued)

QUESTION   Identify the three methods proposed and explain what strengths and weaknesses they have.

ANSWER   Questioning customers at the door would be a convenience sample. It would be cheap and fast but is likely to be biased by the nature and quality of the particular performance where the survey takes place.

Inviting responses on the website would be a voluntary response sample. Only customers who frequented the website and decided to respond would be surveyed. This might, for example, underrepresent older customers or those without home Internet access.

Sampling every 200th name from the customer list would be a systematic sample. It is slightly easier than randomizing. If the order of names on the list is unrelated to any questions asked, then this might be an acceptable method. But if, for example, the list is kept in the order of first purchases (when a customer's name and information were added to the database), then there might be a relationship between opinions and location on the list.

WHAT CAN GO WRONG?

- **Nonrespondents.** No survey succeeds in getting responses from everyone. The problem is that those who don't respond may differ from those who do. And if they differ on just the variables we care about, the lack of response will bias the results. Rather than sending out a large number of surveys for which the response rate will be low, it is often better to design a smaller, randomized survey for which you have the resources to ensure a high response rate.

- **Long, dull surveys.** Surveys that are too long are more likely to be refused, reducing the response rate and biasing all the results. Keep it short.

- **Response bias.** Response bias includes the tendency of respondents to tailor their responses to please the interviewer and the consequences of slanted question wording.

- **Push polls.** Push polls, which masquerade as surveys, present one side of an issue before asking a question. For example, a question like

  Would the fact that the new store that just opened by the mall sells mostly goods made overseas by workers in sweatshop conditions influence your decision to shop there rather than in the downtown store that features American-made products?

  is designed not to gather information, but to spread ill-will toward the new store.

THE WIZARD OF ID   **parker and hart**

The Wizard of Id © 2001 John L. Hart/Distributed by Creators Syndicate. Reprinted with permission. All rights reserved.

HOW TO THINK ABOUT BIASES

- **Look for biases in any survey.** If you design a survey of your own, ask someone else to help look for biases that may not be obvious to you. Do this *before* you collect your data. There's no way to recover from a biased sample or a survey that asks biased questions.

  A bigger sample size for a biased study just gives you a bigger useless study. A really big sample gives you a really big useless study.

- **Spend your time and resources reducing biases.** No other use of resources is as worthwhile as reducing the biases.

- **If you possibly can, pretest or pilot your survey.** Administer the survey in the exact form that you intend to use it to a small sample drawn from the population you intend to sample. Look for misunderstandings, misinterpretation, confusion, or other possible biases. Then redesign your survey instrument.

- **Always report your sampling methods in detail.** Others may be able to detect biases where you did not expect to find them.

ETHICS IN ACTION

The Lackawax River Group is interested in applying for state funds to continue their restoration and conservation of the Lackawax River, a river that has been polluted from years of industry and agricultural discharge. While they have managed to gain significant support for their cause through education and community involvement, the executive committee is now interested in presenting the state with more compelling evidence.

They decided to survey local residents regarding their attitudes toward the proposed expansion of the river restoration and conservation project. With limited time and money (the deadline for the grant application was fast approaching), the executive committee was delighted that one of its members, Harry Greentree, volunteered to undertake the project.

Harry owned a local organic food store and agreed to have a sample of his shoppers interviewed during the next one-week period. One committee member questioned whether a representative sample of residents could be found in this way, but the other members of the committee thought that the customers of Harry's store were likely to be just the kind of well-informed residents whose opinions they wanted to hear. The only instruction the committee decided to give was that the shoppers be selected in a systematic fashion, for instance, by interviewing every fifth person who entered the store. Harry had no problem with this request and was eager to help the Lackawax River Group.

- Identify the ethical dilemma in this scenario.

- What are the undesirable consequences?

- Propose an ethical solution that considers the welfare of all stakeholders.

WHAT HAVE WE LEARNED?

Learning Objectives

Know the three ideas of sampling.
- Examine a part of the whole: A sample can give information about the population.
- Randomize to make the sample representative.
- The sample size is what matters. It's the size of the sample—and not its fraction of the larger population—that determines the precision of the statistics it yields.

Be able to draw a Simple Random Sample (SRS) using a table of random digits or a list of random numbers from technology or an Internet site.
- In a **simple random sample** (SRS), every possible group of n individuals has an equal chance of being our sample.

Know the definitions of other sampling methods:

- **Stratified samples** can reduce sampling variability by identifying homogeneous subgroups and then randomly sampling within each.
- **Cluster samples** randomly select among heterogeneous subgroups that each resemble the population at large, making our sampling tasks more manageable.
- **Systematic samples** can work in some situations and are often the least expensive method of sampling. But we still want to start them randomly.
- **Multistage samples** combine several random sampling methods.

Identify and avoid causes of bias.

- **Nonresponse bias** can arise when sampled individuals will not or cannot respond.
- **Response bias** arises when respondents' answers might be affected by external influences, such as question wording or interviewer behavior.
- **Voluntary response samples** are almost always biased and should be avoided and distrusted.
- **Convenience samples** are likely to be flawed for similar reasons.
- **Undercoverage** occurs when individuals from a subgroup of the population are selected less often than they should be.

Terms

Bias	Any systematic failure of a sampling method to represent its population.
Census	An attempt to collect data on the entire population of interest.
Cluster	A subset of a population aggregated into larger sampling units. These units, chosen for reasons of cost or practicality are often natural groups thought to be representative of the population.
Cluster sampling	A sampling design in which groups, or clusters, representative of the population are chosen at random and a census is then taken of each.
Convenience sampling	A sample that consists of individuals who are conveniently available.
Measurement error	Any inaccuracy in a response, from any source, whether intentional or unintentional.
Multistage sample	A sampling scheme that combines several sampling methods.
Nonresponse bias	Bias introduced to a sample when a large fraction of those sampled fails to respond.
Parameter	A numerically valued attribute of a model for a population. We rarely expect to know the value of a parameter, but we do hope to estimate it from sampled data.
Pilot test	A small trial run of a study to check that the methods of the study are sound.
Population	The entire group of individuals or instances about whom we hope to learn.
Population parameter	A numerically valued attribute of a model for a population.
Randomization	A defense against bias in the sample selection process, in which each individual is given a fair, random chance of selection.
Representative sample	A sample from which the statistics computed accurately reflect the corresponding population parameters.
Response bias	Anything in a survey design that influences responses.
Sample	A subset of a population, examined in hope of learning about the population.
Sample size	The number of individuals in a sample.
Sample survey	A study that asks questions of a sample drawn from some population in the hope of learning something about the entire population.
Sampling frame	A list of individuals from which the sample is drawn. Individuals in the population of interest but who are not in the sampling frame cannot be included in any sample.
Sampling variability (or sampling error)	The natural tendency of randomly drawn samples to differ, one from another.

Simple random sample (SRS)	A sample in which each set of n elements in the population has an equal chance of selection.
Statistic, sample statistic	A value calculated for sampled data, particularly one that corresponds to, and thus estimates, a population parameter. The term "sample statistic" is sometimes used, usually to parallel the corresponding term "population parameter."
Strata	Subsets of a population that are internally homogeneous but may differ one from another.
Stratified random sample	A sampling design in which the population is divided into several homogeneous subpopulations, or strata, and random samples are then drawn from each stratum.
Systematic sample	A sample drawn by selecting individuals systematically from a sampling frame.
Voluntary response bias	Bias introduced to a sample when individuals can choose on their own whether to participate in the sample.
Voluntary response sample	A sample in which a large group of individuals are invited to respond and decide individually whether or not to participate. Voluntary response samples are generally worthless.
Undercoverage	A sampling scheme that biases the sample in a way that gives a part of the population less representation than it has in the population.

TECHNOLOGY HELP: Random Sampling

Computer-generated random numbers are usually quite good enough for drawing random samples. But there is little reason not to use the truly random values available on the Internet. Here's a convenient way to draw an SRS of a specified size using a computer-based sampling frame. The sampling frame can be a list of names or identification numbers arrayed, for example, as a column in a spreadsheet, statistics program, or database:

1. Generate random numbers of enough digits so that each exceeds the size of the sampling frame list by several digits. This makes duplication unlikely. (For example, in Excel, use the RAND function described in detail in Technology Help, Chapter 5 to fill a column with random numbers between 0 and 1. With many digits they will almost surely be unique.)

2. Assign the random numbers arbitrarily to individuals in the sampling frame list. For example, put them in an adjacent column.

3. Sort the list of random numbers, *carrying* along the sampling frame list.

4. Now the first n values in the sorted sampling frame column are an SRS of n values from the entire sampling frame.

Most statistics packages also offer commands to sample from your data, but you should be careful to see that they do what you intend.

EXCEL

To generate random numbers in Excel:

- Choose **Data > Data Analysis > Random Number Generation.** (Note: the Data Analysis add-in must be installed.)

- In the Random Number Generation window, fill in

  - Number of variables = number of columns of random numbers.

  - Number of random numbers = number of rows of random numbers.

- Select a distribution from the drop-down menu. Parameters for your selected distribution will appear below.

- Enter the minimum and maximum bounds for the random numbers. This will be the minimum and maximum of the random numbers generated.

- A list of random numbers will be generated in a new worksheet. The example shown here resulted from parameters of 1 to 100.

- Format cells to obtain values desired.

To sample from a column of data in Excel:

- Choose **Data > Data Analysis > Sampling.**

- Type in or select the cell range containing the data. If this column has a title, place a check in the box marked "Labels".

- Next to Random, indicate the "number of Samples" desired—this is actually the sample size, n.
- Finally, choose a location for the selected sample.

Warning: Excel samples with replacement. This is probably not the sampling method you want for drawing a sample from a population. The method given above using externally generated random numbers may be more appropriate.

MINITAB

To generate a list of random numbers in Minitab:

- Choose **Calc** > **Random Data** > **Uniform.**
- Enter the number of rows.
- Select the column where the random numbers will be stored.
- Click **OK.**

To sample from a variable in Minitab:

- Name a column in the data that will contain the sample; this column will be blank.
- Choose **Calc** > **Random Data** > **Sample From Columns.**
- Enter the number of rows to sample. This is the sample size, n.
- Indicate the column from which to select the data under "From Columns".
- Indicate the column in which the samples data should be placed under "Store Samples In".
- Minitab samples without replacement. To sample with replacement, check the box specifying that alternative.
- Click **OK.**

JMP

To generate a list of random numbers in JMP:

- Create a **New Data Table.**
- Choose **Rows** > **Add Rows** and enter the number of random numbers desired.

- Right-click on the top of Column 1.
- Choose **Formula...**
- Under **Functions (grouped)** choose **Random** > **Random Uniform.**
- Click **OK;** format data as desired.

To sample from a variable in JMP:

- Select the column of data to sample from by clicking the top of the column.
- Select **Tables** > **Subset.**
- Choose **Random – sample size:** and enter the desired sample size, n.
- Choose **Selected columns**.
- Fill in a name for the table where the sample will be stored.

A table will be created containing the random sample.

SPSS

To generate a list of random numbers in SPSS:

- Open a new dataset and assign a new variable with numbers 1 to n where n is the number of random numbers that will be generated.
- In the **Transform** menu, choose **Compute Variable . . .**
- Assign a name to the target variable.
- Under **Numeric Expression**, type **RV.UNIFORM(min,max),** where min = the lowest value of the variable and max = the highest value of the variable. For example, RV.UNIFORM (0, 1) will give you random numbers between 0 and 1.

To select a random sample in SPSS:

- From **Data** menu, choose **Select Cases.**
- Choose **Random sample of cases.**
- Click the **Sample** button to select either a percentage of cases or a number of cases.
- Select the desired output.

Brief Case

Market Survey Research

You are part of a marketing team that needs to research the potential of a new product. Your team decides to e-mail an interactive survey to a random sample of consumers. Write a short questionnaire that will generate the information you need about the new product. Select a sample of 200 using an SRS from your sampling frame. Discuss how you will collect the data and how the responses will help your market research.

The GfK Roper Reports Worldwide Survey

GfK Roper Consulting conducts market research for multinational companies who want to understand attitudes in different countries so they can market and advertise more effectively to different cultures. Every year they conduct a poll worldwide, which asks hundreds of questions of people in approximately 30 different countries. Respondents are asked a variety of questions about food. Some of the questions are simply yes/no (agree/disagree) questions: Please tell me whether you agree or disagree with each of these statements about your appearance: (Agree = 1; Disagree = 2; Don't know = 9).

The way you look affects the way you feel.

I am very interested in new skin care breakthroughs.

People who don't care about their appearance don't care about themselves.

Other questions are asked on a 5-point scale (Please tell me the extent to which you disagree or agree with it using the following scale: Disagree completely = 1; Disagree somewhat = 2; Neither disagree nor agree = 3; Agree somewhat = 4; Agree completely = 5; Don't know = 9).

Examples of such questions include:

I read labels carefully to find out about ingredients, fat content, and/or calories.

I try to avoid eating fast food.

When it comes to food I'm always on the lookout for something new.

Think about designing a survey on such a global scale:

- What is the population of interest?
- Why might it be difficult to select an SRS from this sampling frame?
- What are some potential sources of bias?
- Why might it be difficult to ensure a representative number of men and women and all age groups in some countries?
- What might be a reasonable sampling frame?

EXERCISES

SECTION 8.1

1. Indicate whether each statement below is true or false. If false, explain why.

a) We can eliminate sampling error by selecting an unbiased sample.

b) Randomization helps to ensure that our sample is representative.

c) Sampling error refers to sample-to-sample differences and is also known as sampling variability.

d) It is better to try to match the characteristics of the sample to the population rather than relying on randomization.

2. Indicate whether each statement below is true or false. If false, explain why.

a) To get a representative sample, you must sample a large fraction of the population.

b) Using modern methods, it is best to select a representative subset of a population systematically.

c) A census is the only true representative sample.

d) A random sample of 100 students from a school with 2000 students has the same precision as a random sample of 100 from a school with 20,000 students.

SECTION 8.2

3. An environmental advocacy group is interested in the perceptions of farmers about global climate change. Specifically, they wish to determine the percentage of organic farmers who are concerned that climate change will affect their crop yields. They use an alphabetized list of members of the Northeast Organic Farming Association (www.nofa.org), a nonprofit organization of over 5000 members with chapters in Connecticut, Massachusetts, New Hampshire, New Jersey, New York, Rhode Island, and Vermont. They use Excel to generate a randomly shuffled list of the members. They then select members to contact from this list until they have succeeded in contacting 150 members.

a) What is the population?
b) What is the sampling frame?
c) What is the population parameter of interest?
d) What sampling method is used?

4. An airline company is interested in the opinions of their frequent flyer customers about their proposed new routes. Specifically they want to know what proportion of them plan to use one of their new hubs in the next six months. They take a random sample of 10,000 from the database of all frequent flyers and send them an e-mail message with a request to fill out a survey in exchange for 1500 miles.

a) What is the population?
b) What is the sampling frame?
c) What is the population parameter of interest?
d) What sampling method is used?

SECTION 8.3

5. As discussed in the chapter, GfK Roper Consulting conducts a global consumer survey to help multinational companies understand different consumer attitudes throughout the world. In India, the researchers interviewed 1000 people aged 13–65 (www.gfkamerica.com). Their sample is designed so that they get 500 males and 500 females.

a) Are they using a simple random sample? How do you know?
b) What kind of design do you think they are using?

6. For their class project, a group of Business students decides to survey the student body to assess opinions about a proposed new student coffee shop to judge how successful it might be. Their sample of 200 contained 50 first-year students, 50 sophomores, 50 juniors, and 50 seniors.

a) Do you think the group was using an SRS? Why?
b) What kind of sampling design do you think they used?

7. The environmental advocacy group from Exercise 3 that was interested in gauging perceptions about climate change among organic farmers has decided to use a different method to sample. Instead of randomly selecting members from a shuffled list, they listed the members in alphabetical order and took every tenth member until they succeeded in contacting 150 members. What kind of sampling method have they used?

8. The airline company from Exercise 4, interested in the opinions of their frequent flyer customers about their proposed new routes, has decided that different types of customers might have different opinions. Of their customers, 50% are silver-level, 30% are blue, and 20% are red. They first compile separate lists of silver, blue, and red members and then randomly select 5000 silver members, 3000 blue members, and 2000 red members to e-mail. What kind of sampling method have they used?

For Exercises 9 and 10, identify the following if possible. (If not, say why.)

a) The population
b) The population parameter of interest
c) The sampling frame
d) The sample
e) The sampling method, including whether or not randomization was employed
f) Any potential sources of bias you can detect and any problems you see in generalizing to the population of interest

9. A business magazine mailed a questionnaire to the human resources directors of all *Fortune* 500 companies, and received responses from 23% of them. Those responding reported that they did not find that such surveys intruded significantly on their workday.

10. A question posted on the Lycos website asked visitors to the site to say whether they thought that businesses should be required to pay for their employees' health insurance.

SECTION 8.4

11. An intern for the environmental group in Exercise 3 has decided to make the survey process simpler by calling 150 of the members who attended the recent symposium on coping with climate change that was recently held in Burlington, VT. He has all the phone numbers, so it will be easy to contact them. He will start calling members from the top of the list, which was generated as the members enrolled for the symposium. He has written a script to read to them that follows,

"As we learned in Burlington, climate change is a serious problem for farmers. Given the evidence of impact on crops, do you agree that the government should be doing more to fight global warming?"

a) What is the population of interest?
b) What is the sampling frame?
c) Point out any problems you see either with the sampling procedure and/or the survey itself. What are the potential impacts of these problems?

12. The airline company in Exercise 4 has realized that some of its customers don't have e-mail or don't read it regularly. They decide to restrict the mailing only to customers who have recently registered for a "Win a trip to Miami" contest, figuring that those with Internet access are more likely to read and to respond to their e-mail. They send an e-mail with the following message:

"Did you know that National Airlines has just spent over $3 million refurbishing our brand new hub in Miami? By answering the following question, you may be eligible to win $1000 worth of coupons that can be spent in any of the fabulous restaurants or shops in the Miami airport. Might you possibly think of traveling to Miami in the next six months on your way to one of your destinations?"

a) What is the population?

b) What is the sampling frame?

c) Point out any problems you see either with the sampling procedure and/or the survey itself. What are the potential impacts of these problems?

13. An intern is working for Pacific TV (PTV), a small cable and Internet provider, and has proposed some questions that might be used in the survey to assess whether customers are willing to pay $50 for a new service.

Question 1: If PTV offered state-of-the-art, high-speed Internet service for $50 per month, would you subscribe to that service?

Question 2: Would you find $50 per month—less than the cost of a daily cappuccino—an appropriate price for high-speed Internet service?

a) Do you think these are appropriately worded questions? Why or why not?

b) Which one has more neutral wording? Explain.

14. Here are more proposed survey questions for the survey in Exercise 13:

Question 3: Do you find that the slow speed of DSL Internet access reduces your enjoyment of web services?

Question 4: Given the growing importance of high-speed Internet access for your children's education, would you subscribe to such a service if it were offered?

a) Do you think these are appropriately worded questions? Why or why not?

b) Suggest a question with better wording.

SECTION 8.5

15. Indicate whether each statement below is true or false. If false, explain why.

a) A local television news program that asks viewers to call in and give their opinion on an issue typically results in a biased voluntary response sample.

b) Convenience samples are generally representative of the population.

c) Measurement error is the same as sampling error.

d) A pilot test can be useful for identifying poorly worded questions on a survey.

16. Indicate whether each statement below is true or false. If false, explain why.

a) Asking viewers to call into an 800 number is a good way to produce a representative sample.

b) When writing a survey, it's a good idea to include as many questions as possible to ensure efficiency and to lower costs.

c) A recent poll on a website was valid because the sample size was over 1,000,000 respondents.

d) Malls are not necessarily good places to conduct surveys because people who frequent malls may not be representative of the population at large.

17. For your marketing class, you'd like to take a survey from a sample of all the Catholic Church members in your city to assess the market for a DVD about Pope Francis's first year as pope. A list of churches shows 17 Catholic churches within the city limits. Rather than try to obtain a list of all members of all these churches, you decide to pick 3 churches at random. For those churches, you'll ask to get a list of all current members and contact 100 members at random.

a) What kind of design have you used?

b) What could go wrong with the design that you have proposed?

18. The U.S. Fish and Wildlife Service plans to study the fishing industry around Saginaw Bay. To do that, they decide to randomly select five fishing boats at the end of a randomly chosen fishing day and count the numbers and types of all the fish on those boats.

a) What kind of design have they used?

b) What could go wrong with the design that they have proposed?

CHAPTER EXERCISES

19. Software licenses. The website www.gamefaqs.com asked, as their question of the day to which visitors to the site were invited to respond, "*Do you ever read the end-user license agreements when installing software or games?*" Of the 98,574 respondents, 63.47% said they never read those agreements—a fact that software manufacturers might find important.

a) What kind of sample was this?

b) How much confidence would you place in using 63.47% as an estimate of the fraction of people who don't read software licenses?

20. Drugs in baseball. Major League Baseball, responding to concerns about their "brand," tests players to see whether they are using performance-enhancing drugs. Officials select a team at random, and a drug-testing crew shows up unannounced to test all 40 players on the team. Each testing day can be considered a study of drug use in Major League Baseball.

a) What kind of sample is this?

b) Is that choice appropriate?

21. Pew. Pew Research Center publishes polls on issues important in the news and about American life at its website, www.pewinternet.org. At the end of a report about a survey you can find a paragraph such as this one:

These readings come from a national survey conducted between November 14 and December 9, 2012 of U.S. adults on landline and cell phones and in English and in Spanish. The results reported here come from the 1,802 respondents who are internet users and the margin of error is +/−2.6 percentage points.

a) For this survey, identify the population of interest.
b) Pew performs its surveys by phoning numbers generated at random by a computer program. What is the sampling frame? Does this seem representative of the population?

22. Defining the survey. At its website (www.gallup.com) the Gallup World Poll reports results of surveys conducted in various places around the world. At the end of one of these reports about the reliability of electric power in Africa, they describe their methods, including explanations such as the following:

Results are based on face-to-face interviews with 1,000 adults, aged 15 and older, conducted in 2010 in Botswana, Burkina Faso, Cameroon, Central African Republic, Chad, Ghana, Kenya, Liberia, Mali, Niger, Nigeria, Senegal, Sierra Leone, South Africa, Tanzania, Uganda, and Zimbabwe. For results based on the total sample of national adults, one can say with 95% confidence that the maximum margin of sampling error ranges from ± 3.4 percentage points to ± 4.0 percentage points. The margin of error reflects the influence of data weighting. In addition to sampling error, question wording and practical difficulties in conducting surveys can introduce error or bias into the findings of public opinion polls.[4]

a) Gallup is interested in the opinions of Africans. What kind of survey design are they using?
b) Some of the countries surveyed have large populations. (South Africa is estimated to have over 50 million people.) Some are quite small. (Zimbabwe has fewer than 13,000,000 people.) Nonetheless, Gallup sampled 1000 adults in each country. How does this affect the precision of its estimates for these countries?

23–30. Survey details. *For the following reports about statistical studies, identify the following items (if possible). If you can't tell, then say so—this often happens when we read about a survey.*

a) The population
b) The population parameter of interest
c) The sampling frame
d) The sample
e) The sampling method, including whether or not randomization was employed
f) Any potential sources of bias you can detect and any problems you see in generalizing to the population of interest

---

23. Teens and technology. Pew Internet & American Life Project surveyed 802 pairs of parents and teens (aged 12–17). They report that 93% of teens have access to a computer. 25% of teens access the Internet primarily on their cell phone rather than on a computer.

24. Global warming. The Gallup Poll interviewed 1022 randomly selected U.S. adults aged 18 and older, March 7–10, 2013. Gallup reports that when asked whether respondents thought that global warming was due primarily to human activities, 57% of respondents said it was.

25. At the bar. Researchers waited outside a bar they had randomly selected from a list of such establishments. They stopped every tenth person who came out of the bar and asked whether he or she thought drinking and driving was a serious problem.

26. Election poll. Hoping to learn what issues may resonate with voters in the coming election, the campaign director for a mayoral candidate selects one block at random from each of the city's election districts. Staff members go there and interview all the residents they can find.

27. Toxic waste. The Environmental Protection Agency took soil samples at 16 locations near a former industrial waste dump and checked each for evidence of toxic chemicals. They found no elevated levels of any harmful substances.

28. Housing discrimination. Inspectors send trained "renters" of various races and ethnic backgrounds, and of both sexes to inquire about renting randomly assigned advertised apartments. They look for evidence that landlords deny access illegally based on race, sex, or ethnic background.

29. Quality control. A company packaging snack foods maintains quality control by randomly selecting 10 cases from each day's production and weighing the bags. Then they open one bag from each case and inspect the contents.

30. Contaminated milk. Dairy inspectors visit farms unannounced and take samples of the milk to test for contamination. If the milk is found to contain dirt, antibiotics, or other foreign matter, the milk will be destroyed and the farm is considered to be contaminated pending further testing.

31. Instant poll. A local TV station conducted an "Instant Poll" to predict the winner in the upcoming mayoral election. Evening news viewers were invited to phone in their votes, with the results to be announced on the late-night news. Based on the phone calls, the station predicted that Amabo would win the election with 52% of the vote. They were wrong: Amabo lost, getting only 46% of the vote. Do you think the station's faulty prediction is more likely to be a result of bias or sampling error? Explain.

32. Paper poll. Prior to the mayoral election discussed in Exercise 31, the newspaper also conducted a poll. The paper surveyed a random sample of registered voters stratified by political party, age, sex, and area of residence. This poll predicted that Amabo would win the election with 52% of the vote. The newspaper was wrong: Amabo lost, getting only 46% of the vote. Do you think the newspaper's faulty prediction is more likely to be a result of bias or sampling error? Explain.

33. Cable company market research. A local cable TV company, Pacific TV (PTV), with customers in 15 towns is considering offering high-speed Internet service on its cable lines. Before launching the new service they want to find out whether customers would pay the $75 per month that they plan to charge. An intern has prepared several alternative plans for assessing customer demand. For each, indicate what kind of sampling strategy is involved and what (if any) biases might result.

a) Put a big ad in the newspaper asking people to log their opinions on the PTV website.
b) Randomly select one of the towns and contact every cable subscriber by phone.
c) Send a survey to each customer and ask them to fill it out and return it.
d) Randomly select 20 customers from each town. Send them a survey, and follow up with a phone call if they do not return the survey within a week.

34. Cable company market research, part 2. Four new sampling strategies have been proposed to help PTV determine whether enough cable subscribers are likely to purchase high-speed Internet service. For each, indicate what kind of sampling strategy is involved and what (if any) biases might result.

a) Run a poll on the local TV news, asking people to dial one of two phone numbers to indicate whether they would be interested.
b) Hold a meeting in each of the 15 towns, and tally the opinions expressed by those who attend the meetings.
c) Randomly select one street in each town and contact each of the households on that street.
d) Go through the company's customer records, selecting every 40th subscriber. Send employees to those homes to interview the people chosen.

35. Amusement park riders. An amusement park has opened a new roller coaster. It is so popular that people are waiting for up to three hours for a two-minute ride. Concerned about how patrons (who paid a large amount to enter the park and ride on the rides) feel about this, they survey every tenth person in line for the roller coaster, starting from a randomly selected individual.

a) What kind of sample is this?
b) Is it likely to be representative?
c) What is the sampling frame?

36. Playground. Some people have been complaining that the children's playground at a municipal park is too small and is in need of repair. Managers of the park decide to survey city residents to see if they believe the playground should be rebuilt. They hand out questionnaires to parents who bring children to the park. Describe possible biases in this sample.

37. Another ride. The survey of patrons waiting in line for the roller coaster in Exercise 35 asks whether they think it is worthwhile to wait a long time for the ride and whether they'd like the amusement park to install still more roller coasters. What biases might cause a problem for this survey?

38. Playground bias. The survey described in Exercise 36 asked,

Many people believe this playground is too small and in need of repair. Do you think the playground should be repaired and expanded even if that means imposing an entrance fee to the park?

Describe two ways this question may lead to response bias.

39. (Possibly) Biased questions. Examine each of the following questions for possible bias. If you think the question is biased, indicate how and propose a better question.

a) Should companies that pollute the environment be compelled to pay the costs of cleanup?
b) Should a company enforce a strict dress code?

40. More possibly biased questions. Examine each of the following questions for possible bias. If you think the question is biased, indicate how and propose a better question.

a) Do you think that price or quality is more important in selecting a tablet computer?
b) Given humanity's great tradition of exploration, do you favor continued funding for space flights?

41. Phone surveys. Anytime we conduct a survey, we must take care to avoid undercoverage. Suppose we plan to select 500 names from the city phone book, call their homes between noon and 4 p.m., and interview whoever answers, anticipating contacts with at least 200 people.

a) Why is it difficult to use a simple random sample here?
b) Describe a more convenient, but still random, sampling strategy.
c) What kinds of households are likely to be included in the eventual sample of opinion? Who will be excluded?
d) Suppose, instead, that we continue calling each number, perhaps in the morning or evening, until an adult is contacted and interviewed. How does this improve the sampling design?
e) Random-digit dialing machines can generate the phone calls for us. How would this improve our design? Is anyone still excluded?

42. Cell phone survey. What about drawing a random sample only from cell phone exchanges? Discuss the advantages and disadvantages of such a sampling method compared with surveying randomly generated telephone numbers from non–cell phone exchanges. Do you think these advantages and disadvantages have changed over time? How do you expect they'll change in the future?

43. Change. How much change do you have on you right now? Go ahead, count it.

a) How much change do you have?
b) Suppose you check on your change every day for a week as you head for lunch and average the results. What parameter would this average estimate?
c) Suppose you ask 10 friends to average *their* change every day for a week, and you average those 10 measurements. What is the population now? What parameter would this average estimate?
d) Do you think these 10 average change amounts are likely to be representative of the population of change amounts in your class? In your college? In the country? Why or why not?

44. Fuel economy. Occasionally, when I fill my car with gas, I figure out how many miles per gallon my car got. I wrote down those results after six fill-ups in the past few months. Overall, it appears my car gets 28.8 miles per gallon.

a) What statistic have I calculated?
b) What is the parameter I'm trying to estimate?
c) How might my results be biased?
d) When the Environmental Protection Agency (EPA) checks a car like mine to predict its fuel economy, what parameter is it trying to estimate?

45. Accounting. Between quarterly audits, a company likes to check on its accounting procedures to address any problems before they become serious. The accounting staff processes payments on about 120 orders each day. The next day, the supervisor rechecks 10 of the transactions to be sure they were processed properly.

a) Propose a sampling strategy for the supervisor.
b) How would you modify that strategy if the company makes both wholesale and retail sales, requiring different bookkeeping procedures?

46. Happy workers? A manufacturing company employs 14 project managers, 48 foremen, and 377 laborers. In an effort to keep informed about any possible sources of employee discontent, management wants to conduct job satisfaction interviews with a simple random sample of employees every month.

a) Do you see any danger of bias in the company's plan? Explain.
b) How might you select a simple random sample?
c) Why do you think a simple random sample might not provide the best estimate of the parameters the company wants to estimate?
d) Propose a better sampling strategy.

e) Listed below are the last names of the project managers. Use random numbers to select two people to be interviewed. Be sure to explain your method carefully.

Barrett	Bowman	Chen
DeLara	DeRoos	Grigorov
Maceli	Mulvaney	Pagliarulo
Rosica	Smithson	Tadros
Williams	Yamamoto	

47. Quality control. Sammy's Salsa, a small local company, produces 20 cases of salsa a day. Each case contains 12 jars and is imprinted with a code indicating the date and batch number. To help maintain consistency, at the end of each day, Sammy selects three bottles of salsa, weighs the contents, and tastes the product. Help Sammy select the sample jars. Today's cases are coded 07N61 through 07N80.

a) Carefully explain your sampling strategy.
b) Show how to use random numbers to pick the three jars for testing.
c) Did you use a simple random sample? Explain.

48. Fish quality. Concerned about reports of discolored scales on fish caught downstream from a newly sited chemical plant, scientists set up a field station in a shoreline public park. For one week they asked fishermen there to bring any fish they caught to the field station for a brief inspection. At the end of the week, the scientists said that 18% of the 234 fish that were submitted for inspection displayed the discoloration. From this information, can the researchers estimate what proportion of fish in the river have discolored scales? Explain.

49. Sampling methods. Consider each of these situations. Do you think the proposed sampling method is appropriate? Explain.

a) We want to know what percentage of local doctors accept Medicaid patients. We call the offices of 50 doctors randomly selected from local Yellow Pages listings.
b) We want to know what percentage of local businesses anticipate hiring additional employees in the upcoming month. We randomly select a page in the Yellow Pages and call every business listed there.

50. More sampling methods. Consider each of these situations. Do you think the proposed sampling method is appropriate? Explain.

a) We want to know if business leaders in the community support the development of an "incubator" site at a vacant lot on the edge of town. We spend a day phoning local businesses in the phone book to ask whether they'd sign a petition.
b) We want to know if travelers at the local airport are satisfied with the food available there. We go to the airport on a busy day and interview every tenth person in line in the food court.

JUST CHECKING ANSWERS

1 a) It can be hard to reach all members of a population, and it can take so long that circumstances change, affecting the responses. A well-designed sample is often a better choice.

   b) This sample is probably biased—people who didn't like the food at the restaurant might not choose to eat there.

   c) No, only the sample size matters, not the fraction of the overall population.

   d) Students who frequent this website might be more enthusiastic about Statistics than the overall population of Statistics students. A large sample cannot compensate for bias.

   e) It's the population "parameter." "Statistics" describe samples.

2 a) systematic

   b) stratified

   c) simple

   d) cluster

9

Sampling Distributions and Confidence Intervals for Proportions

Marketing Credit Cards: The MBNA Story

When Delaware substantially raised its interest rate ceiling in 1981, banks and other lending institutions rushed to establish corporate headquarters there. One of these was the Maryland Bank National Association, which established a credit card branch in Delaware using the acronym MBNA. Starting in 1982 with 250 employees in a vacant supermarket in Ogletown, Delaware, MBNA grew explosively in the next two decades.

One of the reasons for this growth was MBNA's use of affinity groups—issuing cards endorsed by alumni associations, sports teams, interest groups, and labor unions, among others. MBNA sold the idea to these groups by letting them share a small percentage of the profit. By 2006, MBNA had become Delaware's largest private employer. At its peak, MBNA had more than 50 million cardholders and had outstanding credit card loans of $82.1 billion, making MBNA the third-largest U.S. credit card bank.

"In American corporate history, I doubt there are many companies that burned as brightly, for such a short period of time, as MBNA," said Rep. Mike Castle, R-Del.[1] MBNA was bought by Bank of America in 2005 for $35 billion. Bank of America kept the brand briefly before issuing all cards under its own name in 2007.

---

[1]Delaware *News Online*, January 1, 2006.

Unlike the early days of the credit card industry when MBNA established itself, the environment today is intensely competitive, with companies constantly looking for ways to attract new customers and to maximize the profitability of the customers they already have. Many of the large companies have millions of customers, so instead of trying out a new idea with all their customers, they almost always conduct a pilot study or trial first, conducting a survey or an experiment on a sample of their customers.

Credit card companies make money on their cards in three ways: they earn a percentage of every transaction, they charge interest on balances that are not paid in full, and they collect fees (yearly fees, late fees, etc.). To generate all three types of revenue, the marketing departments of credit card banks constantly seek ways to encourage customers to increase the use of their cards.

A marketing specialist at one company has an idea of offering double air miles to their customers with an airline-affiliated card if they increase their spending by at least $800 in the month following the offer. Of course, offering double miles is not free. The company has to pay the airline for the added miles they give away. Her finance department tells her that if 20% of all customers increase spending by $800 then, based on past behavior, the double miles offer will be profitable. Unfortunately, she can't know what *all* customers will do until it's too late. So, she decides to send the offer to a random sample of 1000 customers. In that sample, she finds that 211 (21.1%) of the cardholders increase their spending by more than the required $800. Is that good enough? Could another sample of 1000 *different* people show 19.5%? If results vary from sample to sample how can we make good decisions? Variation like this is sometimes called **sampling error** even though no error has been committed. A better name for this variation that you'd expect to see from sample to sample might be **sampling variability**.

Even though we can't control this variability we can *predict* exactly how much different proportions will vary from sample to sample. This will enable us to make sound business decisions based on a single sample.

WHO	Cardholders of a bank's credit card
WHAT	Proportion of cardholders who increase their spending by at least $800 in the subsequent month
WHEN	Now
WHERE	United States
WHY	To predict costs and benefits of a program offer

9.1 The Distribution of Sample Proportions

NOTATION ALERT

We use p for the proportion in the population and $\hat{p}$ for the observed proportion in a sample. We'll also use q for the proportion of failures ($q = 1 - p$), and $\hat{q}$ for its observed value, just to simplify some formulas.

Our marketing manager can't know p, the actual proportion of all cardholders who will increase their spending by more than $800. Her experiment with 1000 cardholders provides only one sample proportion, $\hat{p} = \dfrac{211}{1000} = 0.211$. So how can this single experiment provide useful information?

If we could see how proportions vary across all possible samples that she could have taken, that might help us make decisions about what a *single* experiment can tell us. One way to do that is to *simulate* lots of samples of the same size using the same population proportion. Here's a histogram of 10,000 sample proportions, each for a random sample of size 1000, using $p = 0.2$ as the true proportion:

Figure 9.1 A histogram of 10,000 samples of size 1000 with a true proportion of 0.20. Most of the samples have proportions between 0.175 and 0.225 and nearly all have proportions between 0.16 and 0.24.

Imagine
We see only the sample we actually drew. If we *imagine* the results of all the other possible samples we could have drawn (by modeling or simulating them), we can learn more.

The Sampling Distribution for a Proportion
We have now answered the question raised at the start of the chapter. To discover how variable a sample proportion is, we need to know the proportion and the size of the sample. That's all.

Effect of Sample Size
Because n is in the denominator of $SD(\hat{p})$, the larger the sample, the smaller the standard deviation. We need a small standard deviation to make sound business decisions, but larger samples cost more. That tension is a fundamental issue in Statistics.

What can we see about this distribution? First, not every sample has a sample proportion equal to 0.2. We know that sample proportions vary, and this distribution shows that variation. For example, we can see that sample proportions bigger than 0.24 and smaller than 0.16 are rare, and that most of the sample proportions are between 0.18 and 0.22. From the 10,000 samples, we can also compute the standard deviation of these sample proportions to see how much they vary. In this simulation the standard deviation is 0.0126, or 1.26%. The 68–95–99.7 Rule tells us to expect 95% of the sample proportions to be within 2×0.0126 of the mean (which is 0.20). That is, we expect 95% of the sample proportions to be in the interval (0.175, 0.225) and 99.7% within 3×0.0126 of 0.20 (0.162, 0.238). This matches the histogram pretty well.

The histogram in Figure 9.1 shows a simulation of the **sampling distribution** of $\hat{p}$. The theoretical sampling distribution is the distribution of all the sample proportions that would arise from all possible samples of the same size with a constant probability of a "success."

We actually didn't need to simulate this sampling distribution. We know, from Chapter 7, that the number of successes can be modeled by a Binomial, which, in turn, can be modeled by a Normal distribution as long as np and nq are large enough. The sample proportion is just the number of successes, X, divided by n, so if the distribution of X is Normal, the distribution of $\hat{p}$ should have the same shape. And we know that it should be centered at the true proportion p and have standard deviation $\sqrt{\dfrac{pq}{n}}$. Let's see how well that matches our simulation: $\sqrt{\dfrac{pq}{n}} = \sqrt{\dfrac{(0.2)(0.8)}{1000}} = 0.0126$. Pretty good! With a sample size this large, the Normal approximation really works well.

So, we can say that the sampling distribution of a sample proportion from a sample of size n with true proportion p is Normal with mean p and standard deviation $\sqrt{\dfrac{pq}{n}}$. Here's a picture of that sampling distribution model:

Figure 9.2 A Normal model centered at p with a standard deviation of $\sqrt{\dfrac{pq}{n}}$ is a good model for a collection of proportions found for many random samples of size n from a population with success probability p.

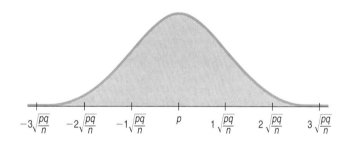

$$-3\sqrt{\dfrac{pq}{n}} \quad -2\sqrt{\dfrac{pq}{n}} \quad -1\sqrt{\dfrac{pq}{n}} \quad p \quad 1\sqrt{\dfrac{pq}{n}} \quad 2\sqrt{\dfrac{pq}{n}} \quad 3\sqrt{\dfrac{pq}{n}}$$

The Sampling Distribution Model for a Proportion
Provided that the sampled values are independent and the sample size is large enough, the sampling distribution of $\hat{p}$ is modeled by a Normal model with mean $\mu(\hat{p}) = p$ and standard deviation $SD(\hat{p}) = \sqrt{\dfrac{pq}{n}}$.

FOR EXAMPLE   **The distribution of a sample proportion**

A supermarket has installed "self-checkout" stations that allow customers to scan and bag their own groceries. These are popular, but because customers occasionally encounter a problem, a staff member must be available to help out. The manager wants

(continued)

to estimate what proportion of customers need help so that he can optimize the number of self-check stations per staff member. He collects data from the stations for 30 days, recording the proportion of customers on each day that need help and makes a histogram of the observed proportions.

QUESTIONS

1. If the proportion needing help is independent from day to day, what shape would you expect his histogram to follow?

2. Is the assumption of independence reasonable?

ANSWERS

1. Normal, centered at the true proportion.

2. Possibly not. For example, shoppers on weekends might be less experienced than regular weekday shoppers and would then need more help.

JUST CHECKING

1 You want to poll a random sample of 100 shopping mall customers about whether they like the proposed location for the new coffee shop on the third floor, with a panoramic view of the food court. Of course, you'll get just one number, your sample proportion, $\hat{p}$. But if you imagined all the possible samples of 100 customers you could draw and imagined the histogram of all the sample proportions from these samples, what shape would it have?

2 Where would the center of that histogram be?

3 If you think that about half the customers are in favor of the plan, what would the standard deviation of the sample proportions be?

How Good Is the Normal Model?

We've seen that the sampling distribution of proportions follows the 68–95–99.7 Rule well. But do all sample proportions really work like this? Stop and think for a minute about what we're claiming. We've said that if we draw repeated random samples of the same size, n, from some population and measure the proportion, $\hat{p}$, we get for each sample, then the collection of these proportions will pile up around the underlying population proportion, p, in such a way that a histogram of the sample proportions can be modeled well by a Normal model.

There must be a catch. Suppose the samples were of size 2, for example. Then the only possible numbers of successes could be 0, 1, or 2, and the proportion values would be 0, 0.5, and 1. There's no way the histogram could ever look like a Normal model with only three possible values for the variable (Figure 9.3).

Well, there *is* a slight catch. The claim is only approximately true. But, the model becomes a better and better representation of the distribution of the sample proportions as the sample size gets bigger.[2] That's one reason we require np and nq to be at least 10. But the distributions of proportions from samples of the size you're likely to see in business do have histograms that are remarkably close to a Normal model.

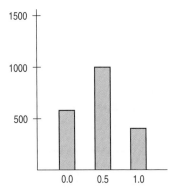

Figure 9.3   Proportions from samples of size 2 can take on only three possible values. A Normal model does not work well here.

FOR EXAMPLE   Sampling distribution for proportions

Time Warner provides cable, phone, and Internet services to customers, some of whom subscribe to "packages" including several services. Nationwide, suppose that 30% of their customers are "package subscribers" and subscribe to all three types of service. A local representative in Phoenix, Arizona, wonders if the proportion in his region is the same as the national proportion.

---

[2]Formally, we say the claim is true in the limit as the sample size (n) grows.

QUESTIONS If the same proportion holds in his region and he takes a survey of 100 customers at random from his subscriber list:

1. What proportion of customers would you expect to be package subscribers?
2. What is the standard deviation of the sample proportion?
3. What shape would you expect the sampling distribution of the proportion to have?
4. Would you be surprised to find out that in a sample of 100, 49 of the customers are package subscribers? Explain. What might account for this high percentage?

ANSWERS

1. Because 30% of customers nationwide are package subscribers, we would expect the same for the sample proportion.
2. The standard deviation is $SD(\hat{p}) = \sqrt{\dfrac{pq}{n}} = \sqrt{\dfrac{(0.3)(0.7)}{100}} = 0.046$.
3. Normal.
4. 49 customers results in a sample proportion of 0.49. The mean is 0.30 with a standard deviation of 0.046. This sample proportion is more than 4 standard deviations higher than the mean: $\dfrac{(0.49 - 0.30)}{0.046} = 4.13$. It would be very unusual to find such a large proportion in a random sample. Either it is a very unusual sample, or the proportion in his region is not the same as the national average.

Assumptions and Conditions

Most models are useful only when specific assumptions are true. In the case of the model for the distribution of sample proportions, there are two assumptions:

> **Independence Assumption:** The sampled values must be *independent* of each other.

> **Sample Size Assumption:** The sample size, *n*, must be *large* enough.

Of course, the best we can do with assumptions is to think about whether they are likely to be true, and we should do so. However, we often can check corresponding *conditions* that provide information about the assumptions as well. Think about the Independence Assumption and check the following corresponding conditions before using the Normal model to model the distribution of sample proportions:

> **Randomization Condition:** If your data come from an experiment, subjects should have been randomly assigned to treatments. If you have a survey, your sample should be a simple random sample of the population. If some other sampling design was used, be sure the sampling method was not biased and that the data are representative of the population.

> **10% Condition:** If sampling has not been made with replacement (that is, returning each sampled individual to the population before drawing the next individual), then the sample size, *n*, should be no larger than 10% of the population. If it is, you must adjust the size of the confidence interval with methods more advanced than those found in this book.

> **Success/Failure Condition:** The Success/Failure condition says that the sample size must be big enough so that both the number of "successes," *np*, and the number of "failures," *nq*, are expected to be at least 10.[3] Expressed without the symbols, this condition just says that we need to expect at least 10 successes and at least 10 failures to have enough data for sound conclusions. For the bank's credit card promotion example, we labeled as a "success" a cardholder

---
[3]We saw where the 10 came from in the Math Box on page 226.

who increases monthly spending by at least $800 during the trial. The bank observed 211 successes and 789 failures. Both are at least 10, so there are certainly enough successes and enough failures for the condition to be satisfied.[4]

These two conditions seem to contradict each other. The Success/Failure condition wants a big sample size. How big depends on p. If p is near 0.5, we need a sample of only 20 or so. If p is only 0.01, however, we'd need 1000. But the 10% condition says that the sample size can't be too large a fraction of the population. Fortunately, the tension between them isn't usually a problem in practice. Often, as in polls that sample from all U.S. adults, or industrial samples from a day's production, the populations are much larger than 10 times the sample size.

FOR EXAMPLE | **Assumptions and conditions for sample proportions**

The analyst conducting the Time Warner survey says that, unfortunately, only 20 of the customers he tried to contact actually responded, but that of those 20, 8 are package subscribers.

QUESTIONS
1. If the proportion of package subscribers in his region is 0.30, how many package subscribers, on average, would you expect in a sample of 20?
2. Would you expect the shape of the sampling distribution of the proportion to be Normal? Explain.

ANSWERS
1. You would expect $0.30 \times 20 = 6$ package subscribers.
2. No. Because 6 is less than 10, we should be cautious in using the Normal as a model for the sampling distribution of proportions. (The number of *observed* successes, 8, is also less than 10.)

GUIDED EXAMPLE | **Foreclosures**

An analyst at a home loan lender was looking at a package of 90 mortgages that the company had recently purchased in central California. The analyst was aware that in that region about 13% of the homeowners with current mortgages will default on their loans in the next year and the houses will go into foreclosure. In deciding to buy the collection of mortgages, the finance department assumed that no more than 15 of the mortgages would go into default. Any amount above that will result in losses for the company. In the package of 90 mortgages, what's the probability that there will be more than 15 foreclosures?

| **PLAN** | **Setup** State the objective of the study. | We want to find the probability that in a group of 90 mortgages, more than 15 will default. Since 15 out of 90 is 16.7%, we need the probability of finding more than 16.7% defaults out of a sample of 90, if the proportion of defaults is 13%. |

---

[4]The Success/Failure condition is about the number of successes and failures we *expect*, but if the number of successes and failures that *occurred* is ≥ 10, then you can use that.

Model Check the conditions.

✓ **Independence Assumption** If the mortgages come from a wide geographical area, one homeowner defaulting should not affect the probability that another does. However, if the mortgages come from the same neighborhood(s), the independence assumption may fail and our estimates of the default probabilities may be wrong.

✓ **Randomization Condition.** For the question asked, these 90 mortgages in the package can be considered as a random sample of mortgages in the region. If there are too many failures, we may doubt that they are a representative sample.

✓ **10% Condition.** The 90 mortgages are less than 10% of the population.

✓ **Success/Failure Condition**

$$np = 90(0.13) = 11.7 \geq 10$$
$$nq = 90(0.87) = 78.3 \geq 10$$

State the parameters and the sampling distribution model.

The population proportion is $p = 0.13$. The conditions are satisfied, so we'll model the sampling distribution of $\hat{p}$ with a Normal model, with mean 0.13 and standard deviation

$$SD(\hat{p}) = \sqrt{\frac{pq}{n}} = \sqrt{\frac{(0.13)(0.87)}{90}} \approx 0.035.$$

Our model for $\hat{p}$ is $N(0.13, 0.035)$. We want to find $P(\hat{p} > 0.167)$.

Plot Make a picture. Sketch the model and shade the area we're interested in, in this case the area to the right of 16.7%.

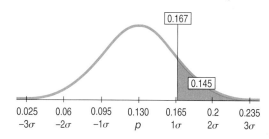

DO

Mechanics Use the standard deviation as a ruler to find the z-score of the cutoff proportion. Find the resulting probability from a table, a computer program, or a calculator.

$$z = \frac{\hat{p} - p}{SD(\hat{p})} = \frac{0.167 - 0.13}{0.035} = 1.06$$
$$P(\hat{p} > 0.167) = P(z > 1.06) = 0.1446$$

REPORT

Conclusion Interpret the probability in the context of the question.

MEMO

Re: Mortgage defaults

Assuming that the 90 mortgages we recently purchased are a random sample of mortgages in this region, there is about a 14.5% chance that we will exceed the 15 foreclosures that Finance has determined as the break-even point.

9.2   A Confidence Interval for a Proportion

To plan their inventory and production needs, businesses use a variety of forecasts about the economy. One important attribute is consumer confidence in the overall economy. Tracking changes in consumer confidence over time can help businesses

NOTATION ALERT

Remember that $\hat{p}$ is our sample estimate of the true proportion p. Recall also that q is just shorthand for $1 - p$, and $\hat{q} = 1 - \hat{p}$.

gauge whether the demand for their products is on an upswing or about to experience a downturn. The Gallup Poll periodically asks a random sample of U.S. adults whether they think economic conditions are getting better, getting worse, or staying about the same. When Gallup polled 3559 respondents in April 2013 (during the week ending April 21), only 1495 thought economic conditions in the United States were getting better—a sample proportion of $\hat{p} = 1495/3559 = 42\%$. We (and Gallup) hope that this observed proportion is close to the population proportion, p, but we know that a second sample of 3559 adults wouldn't have a sample proportion of exactly 42.0%. In fact, Gallup did sample another group of adults just a few days later and found a slightly different sample proportion.

What can we say about consumer confidence in the entire population when the proportion that we measure keeps bouncing around from sample to sample? That's where the sampling distribution model can help. By knowing how much they vary and the shape of their distribution, we'll get a clearer idea of where the true proportion might be and how much we know about it. So, what do we know about our sampling distribution model? We know that it's centered at the true proportion, p, of all U.S. adults who think the economy is improving. But we don't know p. It probably isn't 42.0%. That's the $\hat{p}$ from our sample. What we do know is that the sampling distribution model of $\hat{p}$ is centered at p, and we know that the standard deviation of the sampling distribution is $\sqrt{\dfrac{pq}{n}}$. We also know that the shape of the sampling distribution is approximately Normal, when the sample is large enough.

This is all fine in the model world, but we need to solve problems in the real world. In the real world, we don't know p. (If we did, we wouldn't have bothered to take a sample.) And so, we don't know $\sqrt{pq/n}$ either. But, we'll do the best we can and *estimate* it by using $\sqrt{\hat{p}\hat{q}/n}$. That may not seem like a big deal, but it gets a special name. Whenever we estimate the standard deviation of a sampling distribution, we call it a **standard error (SE)**. Using $\hat{p}$, we find the standard error:

$$SE(\hat{p}) = \sqrt{\dfrac{\hat{p}\hat{q}}{n}} = \sqrt{\dfrac{(0.42)(1 - 0.42)}{3559}} = 0.008$$

Now, we use that to draw our best guess of the sampling distribution for the true proportion who think the economy is getting better as shown in Figure 9.4.

Figure 9.4 The sampling distribution of sample proportions from samples of size 3559 is centered at the true proportion, p, with a standard deviation of 0.008.

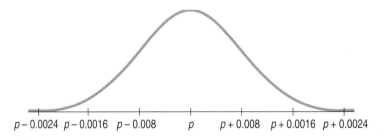

$p - 0.0024 \quad p - 0.0016 \quad p - 0.008 \qquad p \qquad p + 0.008 \quad p + 0.0016 \quad p + 0.0024$

Because the sampling distribution is Normal, we expect that about 68% of all samples of 3559 U.S. adults taken in April 2013 would have sample proportions within 1 standard deviation of p. And about 95% of all these samples will have proportions within $p \pm 2$ SEs. But where is *our* sample proportion in this picture? And what value does p really have? We still don't know!

We do know that for 95% of random samples, $\hat{p}$ will be no more than 2 SEs away from p. So here's the key to using sampling distributions. Let's reverse it and look at it from $\hat{p}$'s point of view. If I'm $\hat{p}$, there's a 95% chance that p is no more than 2 SEs away from me. If I reach out 2 SEs, or 2×0.008, away from me on both sides, I'm 95% sure that p will be within my grasp.

Figure 9.5 Reaching out 2 *SEs* on either side of $\hat{p}$ makes us 95% confident we'll trap the true proportion, *p*.

What Can We Say about a Proportion?

So what can we really say about *p*? Of course, I'm not *sure* that my interval catches *p*. And I don't know its true value, but I can state a probability that I've covered the true value in an interval. Here's a list of things we'd like to be able to say and the reasons we can't say most of them:

1. **"42.0% of *all* U.S. adults thought the economy was improving."** It would be nice to be able to make absolute statements about population values with certainty, but we just don't have enough information to do that. There's no way to be sure that the population proportion is the same as the sample proportion; in fact, it almost certainly isn't. Observations vary. Another sample would yield a different sample proportion.

2. **"It is *probably* true that 42.0% of all U.S. adults thought the economy was improving."** No. In fact, we can be pretty sure that whatever the true proportion is, it's not exactly 42.0%, so the statement is not true.

3. **"We don't know exactly what proportion of U.S. adults thought the economy was improving, but we know that it's within the interval 42.0% $\pm$ 2 $\times$ 0.8%. That is, it's between 40.4% and 43.6%."** This is getting closer, but we still can't be certain. We can't know for sure that the true proportion is in this interval—or in any particular range.

4. **"We don't know exactly what proportion of U.S. adults thought the economy was improving, but the interval from 40.4% to 43.6% *probably* contains the true proportion."** Close! Now, we've fudged twice—first by giving an interval and second by admitting that we only think the interval "probably" contains the true value.

That last statement is true, but it's a bit wishy-washy. We can tighten it up by quantifying what we mean by "probably." We saw that 95% of the time when we reach out 2 SEs from $\hat{p}$, we capture *p*, *so we can be 95% confident that this is one of those times*. After putting a number on the probability that this interval covers the true proportion, we've given our best guess of where the parameter is and how certain we are that it's within some range.

5. **"We are 95% confident that between 40.4% and 43.6% of U.S. adults thought the economy was improving."** Statements like this are called **confidence intervals**. They don't tell us everything we might want to know, but they're the best we can do.

Each confidence interval discussed in this book has a name. You'll see many different kinds of confidence intervals in the following chapters. Some will be about more than *one* sample, some will be about statistics other than *proportions*, and some

"Far better an approximate answer to the right question, … than an exact answer to the wrong question."

—John W. Tukey

will use models other than the Normal. The interval calculated and interpreted here is an example of a **one-proportion z-interval**.[5] We'll lay out the formal definition in the next few pages.

FOR EXAMPLE   Finding a 95% confidence interval for a proportion

The Chamber of Commerce of a mid-sized city has supported a proposal to change the zoning laws for a new part of town. The new regulations would allow for mixed commercial and residential development. The vote on the measure is scheduled for three weeks from today, and the president of the Chamber of Commerce is concerned that they may not have the majority of votes that they will need to pass the measure. She commissions a survey that asks likely voters if they plan to vote for the measure. Of the 516 people selected at random from likely voters, 289 said they would likely vote for the measure.

QUESTIONS
a. Find a 95% confidence interval for the true proportion of voters who will vote for the measure. (Use the 68–95–99.7% Rule.)
b. What would you report to the president of the Chamber of Commerce?

ANSWERS
a. $\hat{p} = \dfrac{289}{516} = 0.56$ So, $SE(\hat{p}) = \sqrt{\dfrac{\hat{p}\hat{q}}{n}} = \sqrt{\dfrac{(0.56)(0.44)}{516}} = 0.022$

A 95% confidence interval for p can be found from $\hat{p} \pm 2\,SE(\hat{p}) = 0.56 \pm 2(0.022) = (0.516, 0.604)$ or 51.6% to 60.4%.

b. We are 95% confident that the true proportion of voters who plan to vote for the measure is between 51.6% and 60.4%. This assumes that the sample we have is representative of all likely voters.

What Does "95% Confidence" Really Mean?

What do we mean when we say we have 95% confidence that our interval contains the true proportion? Formally, what we mean is that "95% of samples of this size will produce confidence intervals that capture the true proportion." This is correct but a little long-winded, so we sometimes say "we are 95% confident that the true proportion lies in our interval." Our uncertainty is about whether the particular sample we have at hand is one of the successful ones or one of the 5% that fail to produce an interval that captures the true value. In this chapter, we have seen how proportions vary from sample to sample. If other pollsters had selected their own samples of adults, they would have found some who thought the economy was getting better, but each sample proportion would almost certainly differ from ours. When they each tried to estimate the true proportion, they'd center their confidence intervals at the proportions they observed in their own samples. Each would have ended up with a different interval.

Figure 9.6 shows the confidence intervals produced by simulating 20 samples. The purple dots are the simulated proportions of adults in each sample who thought the economy was improving, and the orange segments show the confidence intervals found for each simulated sample. The green line represents the true percentage of adults who thought the economy was improving. You can see that most of the simulated confidence intervals include the true value—but one missed. (Note that it is the *intervals* that vary from sample to sample; the green line doesn't move.)

Of course, a huge number of possible samples *could* be drawn, each with its own sample proportion. This simulation approximates just some of them. Each sample can be used to make a confidence interval. That's a large pile of possible confidence intervals, and ours is just one of those in the pile. Did *our* confidence

---

[5]In fact, this confidence interval is so standard for a single proportion that you may see it simply called a "confidence interval for the proportion."

Figure 9.6 The horizontal green line shows the true proportion of people in April 2013 who thought the economy was improving. Most of the 20 simulated samples shown here produced 95% confidence intervals that captured the true value, but one missed.

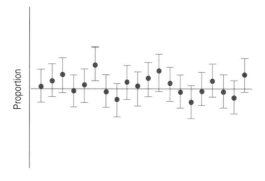

interval "work"? We can never be sure because we'll never know the true proportion of all U.S. adults who thought in April 2013 that the economy was improving. However, the Normal model assures us that 95% of the intervals in the pile are winners, covering the true value, and only 5%, on average, miss the target. That's why we're 95% *confident* that our interval is a winner.

The statements we made about what all U.S. adults thought about the economy were possible because we used a Normal model for the sampling distribution. But is that model appropriate?

As we've seen, all statistical models make assumptions. If those assumptions are not true, the model might be inappropriate, and our conclusions based on it may be wrong. Because the confidence interval is built on the Normal model for the sampling distribution, the assumptions and conditions are the same as those we discussed in section 9.1. But, because they are so important, we'll go over them again.

You can never be certain that an assumption is true, but you can decide intelligently whether it is reasonable. When you have data, you can often decide whether an assumption is plausible by checking a related condition in the data. However, you'll want to make a statement about the world at large, not just about the data. So the assumptions you make are not just about how the data look, but about how representative they are.

Here are the assumptions and the corresponding conditions to check before creating (or believing) a confidence interval about a proportion.

Independence Assumption

You first need to think about whether the independence assumption is plausible. You can look for reasons to suspect that it fails. You might wonder whether there is any reason to believe that the data values somehow affect each other. (For example, might any of the adults in the sample be related?) This condition depends on your knowledge of the situation. It's not one you can check by looking at the data. However, now that you have data, there are two conditions that you can check:

- **Randomization Condition:** Were the data sampled at random or generated from a properly randomized experiment? Proper randomization can help ensure independence.
- **10% Condition:** Samples are almost always drawn without replacement. Usually, you'd like to have as large a sample as you can. But if you sample from a small population, the probability of success may be different for the last few individuals you draw than it was for the first few. For example, if most of the women have already been sampled, the chance of drawing a woman from the remaining population is lower. If the sample exceeds 10% of the population, you will have to adjust the margin of error with methods more advanced than those found in this book. But if less than 10% of the population is sampled, it is safe to proceed without adjustment.

Sample Size Assumption

The model we use for inference is based on the Normal model. So, the sample must be large enough for the Normal sampling model to be appropriate. It turns out that we need more data when the proportion is close to either extreme (0 or 1). This requirement is easy to check with the following condition:

- **Success/Failure Condition:** We must expect our sample to contain at least 10 "successes" and at least 10 "failures." Recall that by tradition we arbitrarily label one alternative (usually the outcome being counted) as a "success" even if it's something bad. The other alternative is then a "failure." So we check that both $n\hat{p} \geq 10$ and $n\hat{q} \geq 10$.

FOR EXAMPLE Assumptions and conditions for a confidence interval for proportions

We previously reported a confidence interval to the president of the Chamber of Commerce.

QUESTION   Were the assumptions and conditions for making this interval satisfied?

ANSWER   Because the sample was randomized, we assume that the responses of the people surveyed were independent so the randomization condition is met. We assume that 516 people represent fewer than 10% of the likely voters in the town so the 10% condition is met. Because 289 people said they were likely to vote for the measure and thus 227 said they were not, both are much larger than 10 so the Success/Failure condition is also met.

All the conditions to make a confidence interval for the proportion appear to have been satisfied.

9.3   Margin of Error: Certainty vs. Precision

We've just claimed that at a certain confidence level we've captured the true proportion of all U.S. adults who thought the economy was improving in April 2013. Our confidence interval stretched out the same distance on either side of the estimated proportion with the form:

$$\hat{p} \pm 2\,SE(\hat{p}).$$

The *extent* of that interval on either side of $\hat{p}$ is called the **margin of error (ME)**. In general, confidence intervals look like this:

$$estimate \pm ME.$$

The margin of error for our 95% confidence interval was 2 SEs. What if we wanted to be more confident? To be more confident, we'd need to capture p more often, and to do that, we'd need to make the interval wider. For example, if we want to be 99.7% confident, the margin of error will have to be 3 SEs.

The more confident we want to be, the larger the margin of error must be. We can be 100% confident that any proportion is between 0% and 100%, but that's not very useful. Or we could give a narrow confidence interval, say, from 41.98% to 42.02%. But we couldn't be very confident about a statement this precise. Every confidence interval is a balance between certainty and precision.

The tension between certainty and precision is always there. There is no simple answer to the conflict. Fortunately, in most cases we can be both sufficiently

> **Confidence Intervals**
> We'll see many confidence intervals in this book. All have the form:
> $$estimate \pm ME.$$
> For proportions at 95% confidence:
> $$ME \approx 2\,SE(\hat{p}).$$

Figure 9.7 Reaching out 3 SEs on either side of $\hat{p}$ makes us 99.7% confident we'll trap the true proportion p. Compare the width of this interval with the interval in Figure 9.5.

certain and sufficiently precise to make useful statements. The choice of confidence level is somewhat arbitrary, but you must choose the level yourself. The data can't do it for you. The most commonly chosen confidence levels are 90%, 95%, and 99%, but any percentage can be used. (In practice, though, using something like 92.9% or 97.2% might be viewed with suspicion.)

Garfield © 1999 Jim Davis/Distributed by Universal Uclick. Reprinted with permission. All rights reserved.

Critical Values

Some common confidence levels and their associated critical values:	
CI	**z^***
90%	1.645
95%	1.960
99%	2.576

In our opening example, our margin of error was 2 SEs, which produced a 95% confidence interval. To change the confidence level, we'll need to change the *number* of SEs to correspond to the new level. A wider confidence interval means more confidence. For any confidence level, the number of SEs we must stretch out on either side of $\hat{p}$ is called the **critical value**. Because it is based on the Normal model, we denote it z^*. For any confidence level, we can find the corresponding critical value from a computer, a calculator, or a Normal probability table, such as Table Z in the back of the book.

For a 95% confidence interval, the precise critical value is $z^* = 1.96$. That is, 95% of a Normal model is found within ± 1.96 standard deviations of the mean. We've been using $z^* = 2$ from the 68–95–99.7 Rule because 2 is very close to 1.96 and is easier to remember. Usually, the difference is negligible, but if you want to be precise, use 1.96.[6]

Suppose we could be satisfied with 90% confidence. What critical value would we need? We can use a smaller margin of error. Our greater precision is offset by our acceptance of being wrong more often (that is, having a confidence interval that misses the true value). Specifically, for a 90% confidence interval, the critical value is only 1.645 because for a Normal model, 90% of the values are within 1.645 standard deviations from the mean (Figure 9.8). By contrast, suppose your

---

[6]It's been suggested that since 1.96 is both an unusual value and so important in Statistics, you can recognize someone who's had a Statistics course by just saying "1.96" and seeing whether they react.

boss demands more confidence. If she wants an interval in which she can have 99% confidence, she'll need to include values within 2.576 standard deviations, creating a wider confidence interval.

Figure 9.8   For a 90% confidence interval, the critical value is 1.645 because for a Normal model, 90% of the values fall within 1.645 standard deviations of the mean.

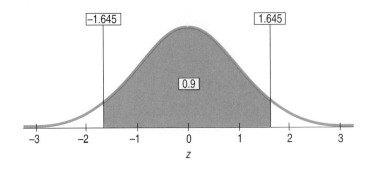

One-Proportion z-Interval

When the conditions are met, we are ready to find the confidence interval for the population proportion, p. The confidence interval is $\hat{p} \pm z^* \times SE(\hat{p})$, where the standard deviation of the proportion is estimated by $SE(\hat{p}) = \sqrt{\dfrac{\hat{p}\hat{q}}{n}}$.

FOR EXAMPLE   Finding confidence intervals for proportions with different levels of confidence

The president of the Chamber of Commerce is worried that 95% confidence is too low and wants a 99% confidence interval.

QUESTION   Find a 99% confidence interval. Would you reassure her that the measure will pass? Explain.

ANSWER   In the example on page 280, we used 2 as the value of z^* for 95% confidence. A more precise value would be 1.96 for 95% confidence. For 99% confidence, the critical z-value is 2.576. So, a 99% confidence interval for the true proportion is

$$\hat{p} \pm 2.576\, SE(\hat{p}) = 0.56 \pm 2.576(0.022) = (0.503, 0.617)$$

The confidence interval is now wider: 50.3% to 61.7%.

The Chamber of Commerce needs at least 50% for the vote to pass. At a 99% confidence level, it looks as if the measure will pass. However, we must assume that the sample is representative of the voters in the actual election and that people vote in the election as they said they will when they took the survey.

GUIDED EXAMPLE   Public Opinion

In March of 2013, workers in the greeting card company Edit66, based in the southern French town of Cabestany, took their bosses hostage. Company chiefs Paul Denis and Merthus Bezemer had informed employees who were to be laid off that they would not receive severance pay that they are legally entitled to. The workers refused to allow their bosses to leave the premises. The town's mayor Jean Vila supported the action. (www.english.rfi.fr/economy/20130329 -greeetings-card-workers-kidnap-bosses-over-unpaid-layoff-pay) There had been a number of similar "bossnappings" in France in 2009. Incidents occurred at SONY, 3M, and Caterpillar plants in France. A poll taken by *Le Parisien* in

WHO	Adults in France
WHAT	Proportion who sympathize with the practice of bossnapping
WHEN	April 2–3, 2009
WHERE	France
HOW	1010 adults were randomly sampled by the French Institute of Public Opinion (l'Ifop) for the magazine *Paris Match*
WHY	To investigate public opinion of bossnapping

April 2009 found 45% of the French "supportive" of such action. A similar poll taken by *Paris Match*, April 2–3, 2009, found 30% "approving" and 63% were "understanding" or "sympathetic" of the action. Only 7% condemned the practice of "bossnapping."

The *Paris Match* poll was based on a random representative sample of 1010 adults. What can we conclude about the proportion of all French adults who sympathize with (without supporting outright) the practice of bossnapping?

To answer this question, we'll build a confidence interval for the proportion of all French adults who sympathize with the practice of bossnapping. As with other procedures, there are three steps to building and summarizing a confidence interval for proportions: Plan, Do, and Report.

PLAN **Setup** State the context of the question.
Identify the *parameter* you wish to estimate. Identify the *population* about which you wish to make statements.

Choose and state a confidence level.

Model Think about the assumptions and check the conditions to decide whether we can use the Normal model.

We want to find an interval that is likely with 95% confidence to contain the true proportion, p, of French adults who sympathize with the practice of bossnapping. We have a random sample of 1010 French adults, with a sample proportion of 63%.

✓ **Independence Assumption:** A French polling agency, l'Ifop, phoned a random sample of French adults. It is unlikely that any respondent influenced another.

✓ **Randomization Condition:** l'Ifop drew a random sample from all French adults. We don't have details of their randomization but assume that we can trust it.

✓ **10% Condition:** Although sampling was necessarily without replacement, there are many more French adults than were sampled. The sample is certainly less than 10% of the population.

✓ **Success/Failure Condition:**
$n\hat{p} = 1010 \times 0.63 = 636 \geq 10$ and
$n\hat{q} = 1010 \times 0.37 = 374 \geq 10$,
so the sample is large enough.

State the sampling distribution model for the statistic. Choose your method.

The conditions are satisfied, so I can use a Normal model to find a one-proportion z-interval.

 DO **Mechanics** Construct the confidence interval. First, find the standard error. (Remember: It's called the "standard error" because we don't know p and have to use $\hat{p}$ instead.)

$n = 1010, \hat{p} = 0.63$, so

$$SE(\hat{p}) = \sqrt{\frac{0.63 \times 0.37}{1010}} = 0.015$$

Next, find the margin of error. We could informally use 2 for our critical value, but 1.96 is more accurate.[7]

Because the sampling model is Normal, for a 95% confidence interval, the critical value $z^* = 1.96$. The margin of error is:

$$ME = z^* \times SE(\hat{p}) = 1.96 \times 0.015 = 0.029$$

(continued)

REALITY CHECK ▶

Write the confidence interval.

Check that the interval is plausible. We may not have a strong expectation for the center, but the width of the interval depends primarily on the sample size—especially when the estimated proportion is near 0.5.

So the 95% confidence interval is:

$$0.63 \pm 0.029 \; or \; (0.601, 0.659).$$

The confidence interval covers a range of about plus or minus 3%. That's about the width we might expect for a sample size of about 1000 (when $\hat{p}$ is reasonably close to 0.5).

REPORT

Conclusion Interpret the confidence interval in the proper context. We're 95% confident that our interval captured the true proportion.

MEMO

Re: Bossnapping survey

The polling agency l'Ifop surveyed 1010 French adults and asked whether they approved, were sympathetic to, or disapproved of recent bossnapping actions. Although we can't know the true proportion of French adults who were sympathetic (without supporting outright), based on this survey we can be 95% confident that between 60.1% and 65.9% of all French adults were. Because this is an ongoing concern, we may want to repeat the survey to obtain more current data. We may also want to keep these results in mind for future corporate public relations.

JUST CHECKING

Think some more about the 95% confidence interval we just created in the guided example for the proportion of French adults who were sympathetic to bossnapping.

4 If we wanted to be 98% confident, would our confidence interval need to be wider or narrower?

5 Our margin of error was about $\pm 3\%$. If we wanted to reduce it to $\pm 2\%$ without increasing the sample size, would our level of confidence be higher or lower?

6 If the organization had polled more people, would the interval's margin of error have likely been larger or smaller?

9.4   Choosing the Sample Size

Every confidence interval must balance precision—the width of the interval—against confidence. Although it is good to be precise and comforting to be confident, there is a trade-off between the two. A confidence interval that says that the percentage is between 10% and 90% wouldn't be of much use, although you could be quite confident that it covered the true proportion. An interval from 43% to 44% is reassuringly precise, but not if it carries a confidence level of 35%. It's a

---

[7]If you are following along on your calculator and not rounding off (as we have done for this example), you'll get $SE = 0.0151944$ and a ME of 0.0297804.

rare study that reports confidence levels lower than 80%. Levels of 95% or 99% are more common.

The time to decide whether the margin of error is small enough to be useful is when you design your study. Don't wait until you compute your confidence interval. To get a narrower interval without giving up confidence, you need to have less variability in your sample proportion. How can you do that? Choose a larger sample.

Consider a company planning to offer a new service to their customers. Product managers want to estimate the proportion of customers who are likely to purchase this new service to within 3% with 95% confidence. How large a sample do they need?

Let's look at the margin of error:

$$ME = z^* \sqrt{\frac{\hat{p}\hat{q}}{n}}$$

$$0.03 = 1.96 \sqrt{\frac{\hat{p}\hat{q}}{n}}.$$

They want to find n, the sample size. To find n, they need a value for $\hat{p}$. They don't know $\hat{p}$ because they don't have a sample yet, but they can probably guess a value. The worst case—the value that makes the SD (and therefore n) largest—is 0.50, so if they use that value for $\hat{p}$, they'll certainly be safe.

The company's equation, then, is:

$$0.03 = 1.96 \sqrt{\frac{(0.5)(0.5)}{n}}.$$

To solve for n, just multiply both sides of the equation by $\sqrt{n}$ and divide by 0.03:

$$0.03\sqrt{n} = 1.96\sqrt{(0.5)(0.5)}$$

$$\sqrt{n} = \frac{1.96\sqrt{(0.5)(0.5)}}{0.03} \approx 32.67$$

Then square the result to find n:

$$n \approx (32.67)^2 \approx 1067.1$$

That method will probably give a value with a fraction. To be safe, always round up. The company will need at least 1068 respondents to keep the margin of error as small as 3% with a confidence level of 95%.

Unfortunately, bigger samples cost more money and require more effort. Because the standard error declines only with the *square root* of the sample size, to cut the standard error (and thus the ME) in half, you must *quadruple* the sample size.

Generally, a margin of error of 5% or less is acceptable, but different circumstances call for different standards. The size of the margin of error may be a marketing decision or one determined by the amount of financial risk you (or the company) are willing to accept. Drawing a large sample to get a smaller ME, however, can run into trouble. It takes time to survey 2400 people, and a survey that extends over a week or more may be trying to hit a target that moves during the time of the survey. A news event or new product announcement can change opinions in the middle of the survey process.

Keep in mind that the sample size for a survey is the number of respondents, not the number of people to whom questionnaires were sent or whose phone numbers were dialed. Also keep in mind that a low response rate turns any study essentially into a voluntary response study, which is of little value for inferring population values. It's almost always better to spend resources on increasing the

What $\hat{p}$ Should We Use?

Often you'll have an estimate of the population proportion based on experience or perhaps on a previous study. If so, use that value as $\hat{p}$ in calculating what size sample you need. If not, the cautious approach is to use $\hat{p} = 0.5$. That will determine the largest sample necessary regardless of the true proportion. It's the *worst case* scenario.

Why 1000?

Public opinion polls often use a sample size of 1000, which gives an ME of about 3% (at 95% confidence) when p is near 0.5. But businesses and nonprofit organizations often use much larger samples to estimate the response to a direct mail campaign. Why? Because the proportion of people who respond to these mailings is very low, often 5% or even less. An ME of 3% may not be precise enough if the response rate is that low. Instead, an ME like 0.1% would be more useful, and that requires a very large sample size.

response rate than on surveying a larger group. A complete or nearly complete response by a modest-size sample can yield useful results.

Surveys are not the only place where proportions pop up. Credit card banks sample huge mailing lists to estimate what proportion of people will accept a credit card offer. Even pilot studies may be mailed to 50,000 customers or more. Most of these customers don't respond. But in this case, that doesn't make the sample smaller. In fact, they did respond in a way—they just said "No thanks." To the bank, the response rate[8] is $\hat{p}$. With a typical success rate below 1%, the bank needs a very small margin of error—often as low as 0.1%—to make a sound business decision. That calls for a large sample, and the bank should take care when estimating the size needed. For our election poll example, we used $p = 0.5$, both because it's safe and because we honestly believed p to be near 0.5. If the bank used 0.5, they'd get an absurd answer. Instead they base their calculation on a value of p that they expect to find from their experience.

How Much of a Difference Can It Make?

A credit card company is about to send out a mailing to test the market for a new credit card. From that sample, they want to estimate the true proportion of people who will sign up for the card nationwide. To be within a tenth of a percentage point, or 0.001 of the true acquisition rate with 95% confidence, how big does the test mailing have to be? Similar mailings in the past lead them to expect that about 0.5% of the people receiving the offer will accept it. Using those values, they find:

$$ME = 0.001 = z^* \sqrt{\frac{pq}{n}} = 1.96 \sqrt{\frac{(0.005)(0.995)}{n}}$$

$$(0.001)^2 = 1.96^2 \frac{(0.005)(0.995)}{n} \Rightarrow n = \frac{1.96^2(0.005)(0.995)}{(0.001)^2}$$

$$= 19,111.96 \ or \ 19,112$$

That's a perfectly reasonable size for a trial mailing. But if they had used 0.50 for their estimate of p they would have found:

$$ME = 0.001 = z^* \sqrt{\frac{pq}{n}} = 1.96 \sqrt{\frac{(0.5)(0.5)}{n}}$$

$$(0.001)^2 = 1.96^2 \frac{(0.5)(0.5)}{n} \Rightarrow n = \frac{1.96^2(0.5)(0.5)}{(0.001)^2} = 960,400.$$

Quite a different result!

FOR EXAMPLE   Sample size calculations for a confidence interval for a proportion

The President of the Chamber of Commerce in the previous examples is worried that the 99% confidence interval is too wide. Recall that it was $(0.503, 0.617)$, which has a width of 0.114.

QUESTIONS   How large a sample would she need to take to have a 99% interval half as wide? One quarter as wide? What if she wanted a 99% confidence interval that was plus or minus 3 percentage points? How large a sample would she need?

---

[8]Be careful. In marketing studies like this *every* mailing yields a response—"yes" or "no"—and response rate means the success rate, the proportion of customers who accept the offer. That's a different use of the term response rate from the one used in survey response.

ANSWERS Because the formula for the confidence interval is dependent on the inverse of the square root of the sample size:

$$\hat{p} \pm z^* \sqrt{\frac{\hat{p}\hat{q}}{n}},$$

a sample size four times as large will produce a confidence interval *half* as wide. The original 99% confidence interval had a sample size of 516. If she wants it half as wide, she will need about $4 \times 516 = 2064$ respondents. To get it a quarter as wide she'd need $4^2 \times 516 = 8256$ respondents!

If she wants a 99% confidence interval that's plus or minus 3 percentage points, she must calculate

$$\hat{p} \pm z^* \sqrt{\frac{\hat{p}\hat{q}}{n}} = \hat{p} \pm 0.03$$

so

$$2.576\sqrt{\frac{(0.5)(0.5)}{n}} = 0.03$$

which means that

$$n \approx \left(\frac{2.576}{0.03}\right)^2 (0.5)(0.5) = 1843.27$$

Rounding up, she'd need 1844 respondents. We used 0.5 because we didn't have any information about the election before taking the survey. Using $p = 0.56$ instead would give $n = 1817$.

WHAT CAN GO WRONG?

- **Don't confuse the sampling distribution with the distribution of the sample.** When you take a sample, you always look at the distribution of the values, usually with a histogram, and you may calculate summary statistics. Examining the distribution of the sample like this is wise. But that's not the sampling distribution. The sampling distribution is an imaginary collection of the values that a statistic might have taken for all the random samples—the one you got and the ones that you didn't get. Use the sampling distribution model to make statements about how the statistic varies.

- **Beware of observations that are not independent.** The CLT depends crucially on the assumption of independence. Unfortunately, this isn't something you can check in your data. You have to think about how the data were gathered. Good sampling practice and well-designed randomized experiments ensure independence.

- **Watch out for small samples.** The CLT tells us that the sampling distribution model is Normal if n is large enough. The Success/Failure condition assures us that if we have at least 10 successes and failures, the Normal model will work well for modeling the sampling distribution of the sample proportion If the population proportion is near 0.50, we could get by with even fewer successes and failures, but the Success/Failure condition is conservative and will protect us no matter how large or small the true underlying proportion happens to be.

Confidence intervals are powerful tools. Not only do they tell us what is known about the parameter value, but—more important—they also tell us what we *don't* know. In order to use confidence intervals effectively, you must be clear about what you say about them.

- **Be sure to use the right language to describe your confidence intervals.** Technically, you should say "I am 95% confident that the interval from 40.4% to 43.6% captures the true proportion of U.S. adults who thought the economy was improving in April 2013." That formal phrasing emphasizes that *your confidence (and your uncertainty) is about the interval, not the true proportion.* But you may choose a more casual phrasing like "I am 95% confident that between 40.4% and 43.6% of U.S. adults thought the economy was improving in April 2013." Because you've made it clear that the uncertainty is yours and you didn't suggest that the randomness is in the true proportion, this is OK. Keep in mind that it's the interval that's random. It's the focus of both our confidence and our doubt.

- **Don't suggest that the parameter varies.** A statement like "there is a 95% chance that the true proportion is between 40.4% and 43.6%" sounds as though you think the population proportion wanders around and sometimes happens to fall between 40.4% and 43.6%. When you interpret a confidence interval, make it clear that *you* know that the population parameter is fixed and that it is the interval that varies from sample to sample.

- **Don't claim that other samples will agree with yours.** Keep in mind that the confidence interval makes a statement about the true population proportion. An interpretation such as "in 95% of samples of U.S. adults the proportion who thought the economy was improving in April 2013 will be between 40.4% and 43.6%" is just wrong. The interval isn't about sample proportions but about the population proportion. There is nothing special about the sample we happen to have; it doesn't establish a standard for other samples.

- **Don't be certain about the parameter.** Saying "between 40.4% and 43.6% of U.S. adults thought the economy was improving in April 2013" asserts that the population proportion cannot be outside that interval. Of course, you can't be absolutely certain of that (just pretty sure).

- **Don't forget: It's about the parameter.** Don't say "I'm 95% confident that $\hat{p}$ is between 40.4% and 43.6%." Of course, you are—in fact, we calculated that our sample proportion was 42.0%. So we already *know* the sample proportion. The confidence interval is about the (unknown) population parameter, p.

- **Don't claim to know too much.** Don't say "I'm 95% confident that between 40.4% and 43.6% of all U.S. adults think the economy is improving." Gallup sampled adults during April 2013, and public opinion shifts over time.

- **Do take responsibility.** Confidence intervals are about *un*certainty. *You* are the one who is uncertain, not the parameter. You have to accept the responsibility and consequences of the fact that not all the intervals you compute will capture the true value. In fact, about 5% of the 95% confidence intervals you find will fail to capture the true value of the parameter. You *can* say "I am 95% confident that between 40.4% and 43.6% of U.S. adults thought the economy was improving in April 2013."

Confidence intervals and margins of error depend crucially on the assumptions and conditions. When they're not true the results may be invalid. For your own surveys, follow the survey designs from Chapter 8. For surveys you read about, be sure to:

- **Watch out for biased sampling.** Just because we have more statistical machinery now doesn't mean we can forget what we've already learned. A questionnaire that finds that 85% of people enjoy filling out surveys still suffers from nonresponse bias even though now we're able to put confidence intervals around this (biased) estimate.

- **Think about independence.** The assumption that the values in a sample are mutually independent is one that you usually cannot check. It always pays to think about it, though.

- **Be careful of sample size.** The validity of the confidence interval for proportions may be affected by sample size. Avoid using the confidence interval on "small" samples.

ETHICS IN ACTION

Gold Key Agency is a regional real estate brokerage firm that features properties in northern Pennsylvania and southern New York. Ann Sheridan has been with the agency for about five years, working out of its Bradford County, PA, office. One of her current clients, Ben Rhodes, has been looking at a fairly large parcel of land with an old farmhouse to renovate. He seems very interested and she has met with him several times, but he has expressed some concern about gas drilling in the region.

Ann is well aware of how natural gas drilling in the area has affected the real estate business. Large reserves located in the Marcellus shale formation, now accessible as a result of advances in horizontal drilling and hydraulic fracturing or "fracking," has created an economic boom: new jobs, an influx of workers, and prosperity to landowners who have leased to gas drilling companies. At the same time, it has had undesirable consequences.

Because drilling companies are not required by law to disclose the chemicals used in fracking, many fear its potential negative effects on the surrounding environment. Indeed, there is evidence that some property values have actually decreased, particularly those depending on well water. Demonstrations in the media of how well water contaminated by fracking chemicals "ignites" has further heightened anxiety. Moreover, some banks and credit unions are reluctant to grant mortgages on properties leased for gas drilling.

Ann is getting ready to meet yet again with Ben. She really wants to close this deal, so she decides to gather some information to help persuade Ben to make the purchase. Ann collects both the selling price and appraised value for each of 20 properties recently sold by agents in her office. She finds that only one of them sold for below its appraised value. Based on these data, Ann constructs a 95% confidence interval and finds the upper limit to be 15%. That value is small enough to please her, so she doesn't bother to look more closely at whether her method is appropriate for her data. Assuming that one of Ben's concerns may be that property values in the region may decline in the future, she plans to use this figure to reassure him. She will tell him that she is 95% sure that no more than 15% of properties in the area run the risk of selling for less than its appraised value. She hopes this will convince Ben to finally make an offer on the property.

- Identify the ethical dilemma in this scenario.

- What are the undesirable consequences?

- Propose an ethical solution that considers the welfare of all stakeholders.

WHAT HAVE WE LEARNED?

Learning Objectives

Model the variation in statistics from sample to sample with a sampling distribution.

- The sampling distribution of the sample proportion is Normal as long as the sample size is large enough.

Understand that, usually, the mean of a sampling distribution is the value of the parameter estimated.

- For the sampling distribution of $\hat{p}$, the mean is p.

Interpret the standard deviation of a sampling distribution.

- The standard deviation of a sampling model is the most important information about it.

- The standard deviation of the sampling distribution of a proportion is $\sqrt{\dfrac{pq}{n}}$ where $q = 1 - p$.

Construct a confidence interval for a proportion, p, as the statistic, $\hat{p}$, plus and minus a margin of error.

- The margin of error consists of a **critical value** based on the sampling model times a **standard error** based on the sample.
- The critical value is found from the Normal model.
- The standard error of a sample proportion is calculated as $\sqrt{\dfrac{\hat{p}\hat{q}}{n}}$.

Interpret a confidence interval correctly.

- You can claim to have the specified level of confidence that the interval you have computed actually covers the true value.

Understand the importance of the sample size, n, in improving both the certainty (confidence level) and precision (margin of error).

- For the same sample size and proportion, more certainty requires less precision and more precision requires less certainty.

Know and check the assumptions and conditions for finding and interpreting confidence intervals.

- Independence Assumption or Randomization Condition
- 10% Condition
- Success/Failure Condition

Be able to invert the calculation of the margin of error to find the sample size required, given a proportion, a confidence level, and a desired margin of error.

Terms

Confidence interval
 An interval of values usually of the form

$$estimate \;\pm\; margin\ of\ error$$

found from data in such a way that a particular percentage of all random samples can be expected to yield intervals that capture the true parameter value.

Critical value
 The number of standard errors to move away from the estimate (mean of the sampling distribution) to correspond to the specified level of confidence. The critical value, denoted z^*, is usually found from a table or with technology.

Margin of error (ME)	In a confidence interval, the extent of the interval on either side of the estimate (the observed statistic value). A margin of error is typically the product of a critical value from the sampling distribution and a standard error from the data. A small margin of error corresponds to a confidence interval that pins down the parameter precisely. A large margin of error corresponds to a confidence interval that gives relatively little information about the estimated parameter.
One-proportion *z*-interval	A confidence interval for the true value of a proportion. The confidence interval is $$\hat{p} \pm z^*SE(\hat{p})$$ where z^* is a critical value from the Standard Normal model corresponding to the specified confidence level and $SE(\hat{p}) = \sqrt{\dfrac{\hat{p}\hat{q}}{n}}$.
Sampling distribution	The distribution of a statistic over many independent samples of the same size from the same population.
Sampling distribution model for a proportion	If the independence assumption and randomization condition are met and we expect at least 10 successes and 10 failures, then the sampling distribution of a proportion is well modeled by a Normal model with a mean equal to the true proportion value, p, and a standard deviation equal to $\sqrt{\dfrac{pq}{n}}$.
Sampling error Sampling variability	The variability we expect to see from sample to sample is often called the sampling error, although sampling variability is a better term.
Standard error (SE)	When the standard deviation of the sampling distribution of a statistic is estimated from the data, the resulting statistic is called a standard error (SE).

TECHNOLOGY HELP: Confidence Intervals for Proportions

Confidence intervals for proportions are so easy and natural that many statistics packages don't offer special commands for them. Most statistics programs want the "raw data" for computations. For proportions, the raw data are the "success" and "failure" status for each case. Usually, these are given as 1 or 0, but they might be category names like "yes" and "no." Often we just know the proportion of successes, $\hat{p}$, and the total count, n. Computer packages don't usually deal with summary data like this easily, but the statistics routines found on many graphing calculators allow you to create confidence intervals from summaries of the data—usually all you need to enter are the number of successes and the sample size.

In some programs you can reconstruct variables of 0's and 1's with the given proportions. But even when you have (or can reconstruct) the raw data values, you may not get *exactly* the same margin of error from a computer package as you would find working by hand. The reason is that some packages make approximations or use other methods. The result is very close but not exactly the same. Fortunately, Statistics means never having to say you're certain, so the approximate result is good enough.

EXCEL

Inference methods for proportions are not part of the standard Excel tool set, but you use Excel's equations to calculate a confidence interval for a proportion in Excel:

	A	B	C	D	E
1	z-Estimate of a Proportion				
2					
3	Sample proportion	0.63	Confidence Interval Estimate		
4	Sample size	1010	0.63	±	0.0298
5	Confidence level	0.95	Lower confidence limit		0.6002
6			Upper confidence limit		0.6598

- Enter the sample proportion in cell B3.
- Enter the sample size in cell B4.
- Enter the confidence level in cell B5.
- In cell C4, type: "=b3".
- In cell E4, type "=NORM.S.INV(0.5+B5/2)*(SQRT(B3*(1-B3)/B4))".

- Type "=C4−E4" in cell E5.
- Type "=C4+E4" in cell E6.

Comments

The method shown here will work for summarized data. When working with raw data, use the COUNTIF function in Excel to quickly count values to compute the sample proportion. You can also use the Pivot Table to quickly summarize the data.

For a categorical variable that holds category labels, the **Distribution** platform includes tests and intervals for proportions.

For raw data:

- Right-click on the column containing data.
- Identify "Modeling Type" as Nominal.
- Choose **Analyze > Distribution**.
- Select data column as **Y, Columns** and click **OK**.
- Expand menu next to variable name in output.
- Select **Confidence Interval** and choose confidence level.

Comments

JMP uses slightly different methods for proportion inferences than those discussed in this text. Your answers are likely to be slightly different, especially for small samples.

Choose **Basic Statistics** from the **Stat** menu.

- Choose **1Proportion** from the Basic Statistics submenu.
- If the data are category names in a variable, assign the variable from the variable list box to the **Samples in columns** box. If you have summarized data, click the **Summarized Data** button and fill in the number of trials and the number of successes.
- Click the **Options** button and specify the remaining details. Leave the Alternative as ≠.
- If you have a large sample, check **Use test and interval based on normal distribution.** Click the **OK** button.

Comments

When working from a variable that names categories, MINITAB treats the last category as the "success" category. You can specify how the categories should be ordered.

SPSS

SPSS does not find confidence intervals for proportions.

Brief **Case**

Has Gold Lost its Luster?

In 2011, when the Gallup organization polled investors, 34% rated gold the best long-term investment. But in April of 2013 Gallup surveyed a random sample of U.S. adults. Respondents were asked to select the best long-term investment from a list of possibilities. Only 241 of the 1005 respondents chose gold as the best long-term investment. By contrast, only 91 choose bonds.

Compute the standard error for each sample proportion. Compute and describe a 95% confidence interval in the context of the question.

Do you think opinions about the value of gold as a long-term investment have really changed from the old 34% favorability rate, or do you think this is just sample variability? Explain.

Forecasting Demand

Utilities must forecast the demand for energy use far into the future because it takes decades to plan and build new power plants. Ron Baker, who worked for New York State Electric and Gas (NYSEG), had the job of predicting the proportion of homes that would choose to use electricity to heat their homes. He was prepared to report a confidence interval for the true proportion, but after seeing his preliminary report, his management demanded a single number as his prediction. Help Ron explain to his management why a confidence interval for the desired proportion would be more useful for planning purposes. Explain how the precision of the interval and the confidence we can have in it are related to each other. Discuss the business consequences of an interval that is too narrow and the consequences of an interval with too low a confidence level.

EXERCISES

SECTION 9.1

1. An investment website can tell what devices are used to access the site. The site managers wonder whether they should enhance the facilities for trading via "smart phones" so they want to estimate the proportion of users who access the site that way (even if they also use their computers sometimes). They draw a random sample of 200 investors from their customers. Suppose that the true proportion of smart phone users is 36%.

a) What would you expect the shape of the sampling distribution for the sample proportion to be?
b) What would be the mean of this sampling distribution?
c) If the sample size were increased to 500, would your answers change? Explain.

2. The proportion of adult women in the United States is approximately 51%. A marketing survey telephones 400 people at random.

a) What proportion of women in the sample of 400 would you expect to see?
b) How many women, on average, would you expect to find in a sample of that size? (*Hint:* Multiply the expected proportion by the sample size.)

3. The investment website of Exercise 1 draws a random sample of 200 investors from their customers. Suppose that the true proportion of smart phone users is 36%.

a) What would the standard deviation of the sampling distribution of the proportion of smart phone users be?
b) What is the probability that the sample proportion of smart phone users is greater than 0.36?
c) What is the probability that the sample proportion is between 0.30 and 0.40?
d) What is the probability that the sample proportion is less than 0.28?
e) What is the probability that the sample proportion is greater than 0.42?

4. The proportion of adult women in the United States is approximately 51%. A marketing survey telephones 400 people at random.

a) What is the sampling distribution of the observed proportion that are women?
b) What is the standard deviation of that proportion?
c) Would you be surprised to find 53% women in a sample of size 400? Explain.
d) Would you be surprised to find 48% women in a sample of size 400? Explain.
e) Would you be surprised to find that there were fewer than 160 women in the sample? Explain.

5. A real estate agent wants to know how many owners of homes worth over $1,000,000 might be considering putting their home on the market in the next 12 months. He surveys 40 of them and finds that 10 of them are considering such a move. Are all the assumptions and conditions for finding the sampling distribution of the proportion satisfied? Explain briefly.

6. A tourist agency wants to know what proportion of visitors to the Eiffel Tower are from the Far East. To find out they survey 100 people in the line to purchase tickets to the top of the tower one Sunday afternoon in May. Are all the assumptions and conditions for finding the sampling distribution of the proportion satisfied? Explain briefly.

7. A marketing researcher for a phone company surveys 100 people and finds that that proportion of clients who are likely to switch providers when their contract expires is 0.15.

a) What is the standard deviation of the sampling distribution of the proportion?
b) If she wants to reduce the standard deviation by half, how large a sample would she need?

8. A market researcher for a provider of iPod accessories wants to know the proportion of customers who own cars to assess the market for a new iPod car charger. A survey of 500 customers indicates that 76% own cars.

a) What is the standard deviation of the sampling distribution of the proportion?
b) How large would the standard deviation have been if he had surveyed only 125 customers (assuming the proportion is about the same)?

SECTION 9.2

9. For each situation below identify the population and the sample and identify p and $\hat{p}$ if appropriate and what the value of $\hat{p}$ is. Would you trust a confidence interval for the true proportion based on these data? Explain briefly why or why not.

a) As concertgoers enter a stadium, a security guard randomly inspects their backpacks for alcoholic beverages. Of the 130 backpacks checked so far, 17 contained alcoholic beverages of some kind. The guards want to estimate the percentage of all backpacks of concertgoers at this concert that contain alcoholic beverages.
b) The website of the English newspaper *The Guardian* asked visitors to the site to say whether they approved of recent "bossnapping" actions by British workers who were outraged over being fired. Of those who responded, 49.2% said "Yes. Desperate times, desperate measures."
c) An airline wants to know the weight of carry-on baggage that customers take on their international routes, so they take a random sample of 50 bags and find that the average weight is 17.3 pounds.

10. For each situation below identify the population and the sample and explain what p and $\hat{p}$ represent and what the value of $\hat{p}$ is. Would you trust a confidence interval for the true proportion based on these data? Explain briefly why or why not.

a) A marketing analyst conducts a large survey of her customers to find out how much money they plan to spend at the company website in the next 6 months. The average amount reported from the 534 respondents is $145.34.

b) A campus survey on a large campus (40,000 students) is trying to find out whether students approve of a new parking policy allowing students to park in previously inaccessible parking lots, but for a small fee. Surveys are sent out by mail and e-mail to all students. Of the 243 surveys returned, 134 are in favor of the change.

c) The human resources department of a large Fortune 100 company wants to find out how many employees would take advantage of an on-site day care facility. They send out an e-mail to 500 employees and receive responses from 450 of them. Of those responding, 75 say that they would take advantage of such a facility.

11. A survey of 200 students is selected randomly on a large university campus. They are asked if they use a laptop in class to take notes. The result of the survey is that 70 of the 200 students responded "yes."

a) What is the value of the sample proportion $\hat{p}$?

b) What is the standard error of the sample proportion?

c) Construct an approximate 95% confidence interval for the true proportion p by taking ± 2 SEs from the sample proportion.

12. From a survey of 250 coworkers you find that 155 would like the company to provide on-site day care.

a) What is the value of the sample proportion $\hat{p}$?

b) What is the standard error of the sample proportion?

c) Construct an approximate 95% confidence interval for the true proportion p by taking ± 2 SEs from the sample proportion.

13. From a survey of coworkers you find that 48% of 200 have already received this year's flu vaccine. An approximate 95% confidence interval is (0.409, 0.551). Which of the following are true? If not, explain briefly.

a) 95% of the coworkers fall in the interval (0.409, 0.551).

b) We are 95% confident that the proportion of coworkers who have received this year's flu vaccine is between 40.9% and 55.1%.

c) There is a 95% chance that a random selected coworker has received the vaccine.

d) There is a 48% chance that a random selected coworker has received the vaccine.

e) We are 95% confident that between 40.9% and 55.1% of the samples will have a proportion near 48%.

14. From the survey in Exercise 11, which of the following are true? If they are not true, explain briefly why not.

a) 95% of the 200 students are in the interval (0.283, 0.417).

b) The true proportion of students who use laptops to take notes is captured in the interval (0.283, 0.417) with probability 0.95.

c) There is a 35% chance that a student uses a laptop to take notes.

d) There is a 95% chance that the student uses a laptop to take notes 35% of the time.

e) We are 95% confident that the true proportion of students who use laptops to take notes is captured in the interval (0.283, 0.417).

SECTION 9.3

15. From the survey in Exercise 11,

a) How would the confidence interval change if the confidence level had been 90% instead of 95%?

b) How would the confidence interval change if the sample size had been 300 instead of 200? (Assume the same sample proportion.)

c) How would the confidence interval change if the confidence level had been 99% instead of 95%?

d) How large would the sample size have to be to make the margin of error half as big in the 95% confidence interval?

16. As in Exercise 13, from a survey of coworkers you find that 48% of 200 have already received this year's flu vaccine. An approximate 95% confidence interval is (0.409, 0.551).

a) How would the confidence interval change if the sample size had been 800 instead of 200?

b) How would the confidence interval change if the confidence level had been 90% instead of 95%?

c) How would the confidence interval change if the confidence level had been 99% instead of 95%?

SECTION 9.4

17. Suppose you want to estimate the proportion of traditional college students on your campus who own their own car. You have no preconceived idea of what that proportion might be.

a) What sample size is needed if you wish to be 95% confident that your estimate is within 0.02 of the true proportion?

b) What sample size is needed if you wish to be 99% confident that your estimate is within 0.02 of the true proportion?

c) What sample size is needed if you wish to be 95% confident that your estimate is within 0.05 of the true proportion?

18. As in Exercise 17, you want to estimate the proportion of traditional college students on your campus who own their own car. However, from some research on other college campuses, you believe the proportion will be near 20%.

a) What sample size is needed if you wish to be 95% confident that your estimate is within 0.02 of the true proportion?
b) What sample size is needed if you wish to be 99% confident that your estimate is within 0.02 of the true proportion?
c) What sample size is needed if you wish to be 95% confident that your estimate is within 0.05 of the true proportion?

19. It's believed that as many as 25% of adults over age 50 never graduated from high school. We wish to see if this percentage is the same among the 25 to 30 age group.

a) How many of this younger age group must we survey in order to estimate the proportion of nongrads to within 6% with 90% confidence?
b) Suppose we want to cut the margin of error to 4%. What's the necessary sample size?
c) What sample size would produce a margin of error of 3%?

20. In preparing a report on the economy, we need to estimate the percentage of businesses that plan to hire additional employees in the next 60 days.

a) How many randomly selected employers must we contact in order to create an estimate in which we are 98% confident with a margin of error of 5%?
b) Suppose we want to reduce the margin of error to 3%. What sample size will suffice?
c) Why might it not be worth the effort to try to get an interval with a margin of error of 1%?

CHAPTER EXERCISES

21. Send money. When they send out their fundraising letter, a philanthropic organization typically gets a return from about 5% of the people on their mailing list. To see what the response rate might be for future appeals, they did a simulation using samples of size 20, 50, 100, and 200. For each sample size, they simulated 1000 mailings with success rate $p = 0.05$ and constructed the histogram of the 1000 sample proportions, shown below. Explain what these histograms say about the sampling distribution model for sample proportions. Be sure to talk about shape, center, and spread.

22. Character recognition. An automatic character recognition device can successfully read about 85% of handwritten credit card applications. To estimate what might happen when this device reads a stack of applications, the company did a simulation using samples of size 20, 50, 75, and 100. For each sample size, they simulated 1000 samples with success rate $p = 0.85$ and constructed the histogram of the 1000 sample proportions, shown here. Explain what these histograms say about the sampling distribution model for sample proportions. Be sure to talk about shape, center, and spread.

23. Send money, again. The philanthropic organization in Exercise 21 expects about a 5% success rate when they send fundraising letters to the people on their mailing list. In Exercise 21 you looked at the histograms showing distributions of sample proportions from 1000 simulated mailings for samples of size 20, 50, 100, and 200. The sample statistics from each simulation were as follows:

n	mean	st. dev.
20	0.0497	0.0479
50	0.0516	0.0309
100	0.0497	0.0215
200	0.0501	0.0152

a) According to the Normal model, what should the theoretical mean and standard deviations be for these sample sizes?

b) How close are those theoretical values to what was observed in these simulations?

c) Looking at the histograms in Exercise 21, at what sample size would you be comfortable using the Normal model as an approximation for the sampling distribution?

d) What does the Success/Failure Condition say about the choice you made in part c?

24. Character recognition, again. The automatic character recognition device discussed in Exercise 22 successfully reads about 85% of handwritten credit card applications. In Exercise 22 you looked at the histograms showing distributions of sample proportions from 1000 simulated samples of size 20, 50, 75, and 100. The sample statistics from each simulation were as follows:

n	mean	st. dev.
20	0.8481	0.0803
50	0.8507	0.0509
75	0.8481	0.0406
100	0.8488	0.0354

a) According to the Normal model, what should the theoretical mean and standard deviations be for these sample sizes?

b) How close are those theoretical values to what was observed in these simulations?

c) Looking at the histograms in Exercise 22, at what sample size would you be comfortable using the Normal model as an approximation for the sampling distribution?

d) What does the Success/Failure Condition say about the choice you made in part c?

25. Stock picking. In a large Business Statistics class, the professor has each person select stocks by throwing 16 darts at pages of the *Wall Street Journal*. They then check to see whether their stock picks rose or fell the next day and report their proportion of "successes." As a lesson, the professor has selected pages of the *Journal* for which exactly half the publicly traded stocks went up and half went down. The professor then makes a histogram of the reported proportions.

a) What shape would you expect this histogram to be? Why?

b) Where do you expect the histogram to be centered?

c) How much variability would you expect among these proportions?

d) Explain why a Normal model should not be used here.

26. Quality management. Manufacturing companies strive to maintain production consistency, but it is often difficult for outsiders to tell whether they have succeeded. Sometimes, however, we can find a simple example. The candy company that makes M&M's candies claims that 10% of the candies it produces are green and that bags are packed randomly. We can check on their production controls by sampling bags of candies. Suppose we open bags containing about 50 M&M's and record the proportion of green candies.

a) If we plot a histogram showing the proportions of green candies in the various bags, what shape would you expect it to have?

b) Can that histogram be approximated by a Normal model? Explain.

c) Where should the center of the histogram be?

d) What should the standard deviation of the proportion be?

27. Bigger portfolio. The class in Exercise 25 expands its stock-picking experiment.

a) The students use computer-generated random numbers to choose 25 stocks each. Use the 68–95–99.7 Rule to describe the sampling distribution model.

b) Confirm that you can use a Normal model here.

c) They increase the number of stocks picked to 64 each. Draw and label the appropriate sampling distribution model. Check the appropriate conditions to justify your model.

d) Explain how the sampling distribution model changes as the number of stocks picked increases.

28. More quality. Would a bigger sample help us to assess manufacturing consistency? Suppose instead of the 50-candy bags of Exercise 26, we work with bags that contain 200 M&M's each. Again we calculate the proportion of green candies found.

a) Explain why it's appropriate to use a Normal model to describe the distribution of the proportion of green M&M's they might expect.

b) Use the 68–95–99.7 Rule to describe how this proportion might vary from bag to bag.

c) How would this model change if the bags contained even more candies?

29. A winning investment strategy? One student in the class of Exercise 25 claims to have found a winning strategy. He watches a cable news show about investing and *during the show* throws his darts at the pages of the *Journal*. He claims that of 200 stocks picked in this manner, 58% were winners.

a) What do you think of his claim? Explain.

b) If there are 100 students in the class, are you surprised that one was this successful? Explain.

30. Even more quality. In a really large bag of M&M's, we found 12% of 500 candies were green. Is this evidence that the manufacturing process is out of control and has made too many greens? Explain.

31. Speeding. State police believe that 70% of the drivers traveling on a major interstate highway exceed the speed limit. They plan to set up a radar trap and check the speeds of 80 cars.

a) Using the 68–95–99.7 Rule, draw and label the distribution of the proportion of these cars the police will observe speeding.

b) Do you think the appropriate conditions necessary for your analysis are met? Explain.

32. Smoking, 2013. The most recent public health statistics available indicate that 19.0% of American adults smoke cigarettes. Using the 68–95–99.7 Rule, describe the sampling distribution model for the proportion of smokers among a randomly selected group of 50 adults. Be sure to discuss your assumptions and conditions.

33. Vision. It is generally believed that nearsightedness affects about 12% of all children. A school district has registered 170 incoming kindergarten children.

a) Can you use the Normal Model to describe the sampling distribution model for the sample proportion of children who are nearsighted? Check the conditions and discuss any assumptions you need to make.

b) Sketch and clearly label the sampling model, based on the 68–95–99.7 Rule.

c) How many of the incoming students might the school expect to be nearsighted? Explain.

34. Mortgages 2013. In early 2013 Realty Trac reported that foreclosures had settled down to 1 in 859 homes per month for a rate of 0.116%, far below the 1.6% seen during the financial crisis of 2007–2008. Suppose a large bank holds 9455 of these mortgages.

a) Can you use the Normal model to describe the sampling distribution model for the sample proportion of foreclosures? Check the conditions and discuss any assumptions you need to make.

b) Sketch and clearly label the sampling model, based on the 68–95–99.7 Rule.

c) How many of these homeowners might the bank expect will default on their mortgages? Explain.

35. Loans. Based on past experience, a bank believes that 7% of the people who receive loans will not make payments on time. The bank has recently approved 200 loans.

a) What are the mean and standard deviation of the proportion of clients in this group who may not make timely payments?

b) What assumptions underlie your model? Are the conditions met? Explain.

c) What's the probability that over 10% of these clients will not make timely payments?

36. Contacts. The campus representative for Lens.com wants to know what percentage of students at a university currently wear contact lens. Suppose the true proportion is 30%.

a) We randomly pick 100 students. Let $\hat{p}$ represent the proportion of students in this sample who wear contacts. What's the appropriate model for the distribution of $\hat{p}$? Specify the name of the distribution, the mean, and the standard deviation. Be sure to verify that the conditions are met.

b) What's the approximate probability that more than one third of this sample wear contacts?

37. Back to school? Best known for its testing program, ACT, Inc., also compiles data on a variety of issues in education. In 2012 the company reported that the national college freshman-to-sophomore retention rate at four-year colleges was about 80.0%. Consider colleges with freshman classes of 400 students. Use the 68–95–99.7 Rule to describe the sampling distribution model for the percentage of those students we expect to return to that school for their sophomore years. Do you think the appropriate conditions are met?

38. Binge drinking. A national study found that 44% of college students engage in binge drinking (5 drinks at a sitting for men, 4 for women). Use the 68–95–99.7 Rule to describe the sampling distribution model for the proportion of students in a randomly selected group of 200 college students who engage in binge drinking. Do you think the appropriate conditions are met?

39. Back to school, again. Based on the 80% national retention rate described in Exercise 37, does a college where 551 of the 603 freshmen returned the next year as sophomores have a right to brag that it has an unusually high retention rate? Explain.

40. Binge sample. After hearing of the national result that 44% of students engage in binge drinking (5 drinks at a sitting for men, 4 for women), a professor surveyed a random sample of 244 students at his college and found that 96 of them admitted to binge drinking in the past week. Should he be surprised at this result? Explain.

41. Polling. Just before a referendum on a school budget, a local newspaper polls 400 voters in an attempt to predict whether the budget will pass. Suppose that the budget actually has the support of 52% of the voters. What's the probability the newspaper's sample will lead them to predict defeat? Be sure to verify that the assumptions and conditions necessary for your analysis are met.

42. Seeds. Information on a packet of seeds claims that the germination rate is 92%. What's the probability that more than 95% of the 160 seeds in the packet will germinate? Be sure to discuss your assumptions and check the conditions that support your model.

43. Apples. When a truckload of apples arrives at a packing plant, a random sample of 150 is selected and examined for bruises, discoloration, and other defects. The whole truckload will be rejected if more than 5% of the sample is unsatisfactory. Suppose that in fact 8% of the apples on the truck do not meet the desired standard. What's the probability that the shipment will be accepted anyway?

44. Genetic defect. It's believed that 4% of children have a gene that may be linked to juvenile diabetes. Researchers hoping to track 20 of these children for several years test 732 newborns for the presence of this gene. What's the probability that they find enough subjects for their study?

45. Catalog sales. A catalog sales company promises to deliver orders placed on the Internet within 3 days. Follow-up calls to a few randomly selected customers show that a 95% confidence interval for the proportion of all orders that arrive on time is 88% ± 6%. What does this mean? Are the conclusions in parts a–e correct? Explain.

a) Between 82% and 94% of all orders arrive on time.
b) 95% of all random samples of customers will show that 88% of orders arrive on time.
c) 95% of all random samples of customers will show that 82% to 94% of orders arrive on time.
d) The company is 95% sure that between 82% and 94% of the orders placed by the customers in this sample arrived on time.
e) On 95% of the days, between 82% and 94% of the orders will arrive on time.

46. Belgian euro. Recently, two students made worldwide headlines by spinning a Belgian euro 250 times and getting 140 heads—that's 56%. That makes the 90% confidence interval (51%, 61%). What does this mean? Are the conclusions in parts a–e correct? Explain your answers.

a) Between 51% and 61% of all euros are unfair.
b) We are 90% sure that in this experiment this euro landed heads between 51% and 61% of the spins.
c) We are 90% sure that spun euros will land heads between 51% and 61% of the time.
d) If you spin a euro many times, you can be 90% sure of getting between 51% and 61% heads.
e) 90% of all spun euros will land heads between 51% and 61% of the time.

47. Confidence intervals. Several factors are involved in the creation of a confidence interval. Among them are the sample size, the level of confidence, and the margin of error. Which statements are true?

a) For a given sample size, higher confidence means a smaller margin of error.
b) For a specified confidence level, larger samples provide smaller margins of error.
c) For a fixed margin of error, larger samples provide greater confidence.
d) For a given confidence level, halving the margin of error requires a sample twice as large.

48. Confidence intervals, again. Several factors are involved in the creation of a confidence interval. Among them are the sample size, the level of confidence, and the margin of error. Which statements are true?

a) For a given sample size, reducing the margin of error will mean lower confidence.
b) For a certain confidence level, you can get a smaller margin of error by selecting a bigger sample.
c) For a fixed margin of error, smaller samples will mean lower confidence.
d) For a given confidence level, a sample 9 times as large will make a margin of error one third as big.

49. Cars. A student is considering publishing a new magazine aimed directly at owners of Japanese automobiles. He wanted to estimate the fraction of cars in the United States that are made in Japan. The computer output summarizes the results of a random sample of 50 autos. Explain carefully what it tells you.

```
z-interval for proportion
With 90.00% confidence
0.29938661 < p(japan) < 0.46984416
```

50. Quality control. For quality control purposes, 900 ceramic tiles were inspected to determine the proportion of defective (e.g., cracked, uneven finish, etc.) tiles. Assuming that these tiles are representative of all tiles manufactured by an Italian tile company, what can you conclude based on the computer output?

```
z-interval for proportion
With 95.00% confidence
0.025 < p(defective) < 0.035
```

51. E-mail. A small company involved in e-commerce is interested in statistics concerning the use of e-mail. A poll found that 38% of a random sample of 1012 adults, who use a computer at their home, work, or school, said that they do not send or receive e-mail.

a) Find the margin of error for this poll if we want 90% confidence in our estimate of the percent of American adults who do not use e-mail.
b) Explain what that margin of error means.
c) If we want to be 99% confident, will the margin of error be larger or smaller? Explain.
d) Find that margin of error.
e) In general, if all other aspects of the situation remain the same, will smaller margins of error involve greater or less confidence in the interval?

52. Biotechnology. A biotechnology firm in Boston is planning its investment strategy for future products and research labs. A poll found that only 8% of a random sample of 1012 U.S. adults approved of attempts to clone a human.

a) Find the margin of error for this poll if we want 95% confidence in our estimate of the percent of American adults who approve of cloning humans.
b) Explain what that margin of error means.
c) If we only need to be 90% confident, will the margin of error be larger or smaller? Explain.
d) Find that margin of error.

e) In general, if all other aspects of the situation remain the same, would smaller samples produce smaller or larger margins of error?

53. Teenage drivers. An insurance company checks police records on 582 accidents selected at random and notes that teenagers were at the wheel in 91 of them.

a) Create a 95% confidence interval for the percentage of all auto accidents that involve teenage drivers.
b) Explain what your interval means.
c) Explain what "95% confidence" means.
d) A politician urging tighter restrictions on drivers' licenses issued to teens says, "In one of every five auto accidents, a teenager is behind the wheel." Does your confidence interval support or contradict this statement? Explain.

54. Advertisers. Direct mail advertisers send solicitations ("junk mail") to thousands of potential customers in the hope that some will buy the company's product. The response rate is usually quite low. Suppose a company wants to test the response to a new flyer and sends it to 1000 people randomly selected from their mailing list of over 200,000 people. They get orders from 123 of the recipients.

a) Create a 90% confidence interval for the percentage of people the company contacts who may buy something.
b) Explain what this interval means.
c) Explain what "90% confidence" means.
d) The company must decide whether to now do a mass mailing. The mailing won't be cost-effective unless it produces at least a 5% return. What does your confidence interval suggest? Explain.

55. Retailers. Some food retailers propose subjecting food to a low level of radiation in order to improve safety, but sale of such "irradiated" food is opposed by many people. Suppose a grocer wants to find out what his customers think. He has cashiers distribute surveys at checkout and ask customers to fill them out and drop them in a box near the front door. He gets responses from 122 customers, of whom 78 oppose the radiation treatments. What can the grocer conclude about the opinions of all his customers?

56. Local news. The mayor of a small city has suggested that the state locate a new prison there, arguing that the construction project and resulting jobs will be good for the local economy. A total of 183 residents show up for a public hearing on the proposal, and a show of hands finds 31 in favor of the prison project. What can the city council conclude about public support for the mayor's initiative?

57. Internet music. In a survey on downloading music, the Gallup Poll asked 703 Internet users if they "ever downloaded music from an Internet site that was not authorized by a record company, or not," and 18% responded "yes." Construct a 95% confidence interval for the true proportion of Internet users who have downloaded music from an Internet site that was not authorized.

58. Economy worries. During the week of April 15, 2013, a Gallup Poll asked 1500 U.S. adults, aged 18 or over, how they rated economic conditions. Only 17% rated the economy as Excellent/Good. Construct a 95% confidence interval for the true proportion of Americans who rated the U.S. economy as Excellent/Good.

59. International business. In Canada, the vast majority (90%) of companies in the chemical industry are ISO 14001 certified. The ISO 14001 is an international standard for environmental management systems. An environmental group wished to estimate the percentage of U.S. chemical companies that are ISO 14001 certified. Of the 550 chemical companies sampled, 385 are certified.

a) What proportion of the sample reported being certified?
b) Create a 95% confidence interval for the proportion of U.S. chemical companies with ISO 14001 certification. (Be sure to check conditions.) Compare to the Canadian proportion.

60. Worldwide survey. GfK Roper surveyed people worldwide asking them "how important is acquiring wealth to you." Of 1535 respondents in India, 1168 said that it was of more than average importance. In the United States of 1317 respondents, 596 said it was of more than average importance.

a) What proportion thought acquiring wealth was of more than average importance in each country's sample?
b) Create a 95% confidence interval for the proportion who thought it was of more than average importance in India. (Be sure to test conditions.) Compare that to a confidence interval for the U.S. population.

61. Business ethics. In a survey on corporate ethics, a poll split a sample at random, asking 538 faculty and corporate recruiters the question: "Generally speaking, do you believe that MBAs are more or less aware of ethical issues in business today than five years ago?" The other half were asked: "Generally speaking, do you believe that MBAs are less or more aware of ethical issues in business today than five years ago?" These may seem like the same questions, but sometimes the order of the choices matters. In response to the first question, 53% thought MBA graduates were more aware of ethical issues, but when the question was phrased differently, this proportion dropped to 44%.

a) What kind of bias may be present here?
b) Each group consisted of 538 respondents. If we combine them, considering the overall group to be one larger random sample, what is a 95% confidence interval for the proportion of the faculty and corporate recruiters that believe MBAs are more aware of ethical issues today?
c) How does the margin of error based on this pooled sample compare with the margins of error from the separate groups? Why?

62. Middle Eastern entrepreneurs. In 2012, Gallup published a report entitled "Qatar's Rising Entrepreneurial Spirit" in which they concluded that the 33% of 1057 Qatari youth they surveyed who responded that they plan to start their own business was the highest in the region. They conducted a variety of face to face and phone interviews with Qatari youth during their survey. They noted that the margin of error was between 6.6 and 7.8 percentage points, and that "in addition to sampling error, question wording and practical difficulties in conducting surveys can introduce error or bias into the findings of public opinion polls."

a) What kinds of bias might they be referring to?
b) Does their margin of error suggest that this was a simple random sample? Explain.

63. Pharmaceutical company. A pharmaceutical company is considering investing in a "new and improved" vitamin D supplement for children. Vitamin D, whether ingested as a dietary supplement or produced naturally when sunlight falls upon the skin, is essential for strong, healthy bones. The bone disease rickets was largely eliminated in England during the 1950s, but now there is concern that a generation of children more likely to watch TV or play computer games than spend time outdoors is at increased risk. A recent study of 2700 children randomly selected from all parts of England found 20% of them deficient in vitamin D.

a) Find a 98% confidence interval for the proportion of children in England who are deficient in vitamin D.
b) Explain carefully what your interval means.
c) Explain what "98% confidence" means.
d) Does the study show that computer games are a likely cause of rickets? Explain.

64. Real estate survey. A real estate agent looks over the 15 listings she has in a particular zip code in California and finds that 80% of them have swimming pools.

a) Check the assumptions and conditions for inference on proportions.
b) If it's appropriate, find a 90% confidence interval for the proportion of houses in this zip code that have swimming pools. If it's not appropriate, explain why.

65. Benefits survey. A paralegal at the Vermont State Attorney General's office wants to know how many companies in Vermont provide health insurance benefits to all employees. She chooses 12 companies at random and finds that all 12 offer benefits.

a) Check the assumptions and conditions for inference on proportions.
b) If conditions are met, find a 95% confidence interval for the true proportion of companies that provide health insurance benefits to all their employees. If conditions are not met, explain why.

66. Awareness survey. A telemarketer at a credit card company is instructed to ask the next 18 customers that call into the 800 number whether they are aware of the new Platinum card that the company is offering. Of the 18, 17 said they were aware of the program.

a) Check the assumptions and conditions for inference on proportions.
b) If conditions are met, find a 95% confidence interval for the true proportion of customers who are aware of the new card. If conditions are not met, explain why.

67. IRS. In a random survey of 226 self-employed individuals, 20 reported having had their tax returns audited by the IRS in the past year. Estimate the proportion of self-employed individuals nationwide who've been audited by the IRS in the past year.

a) Check the assumptions and conditions (to the extent you can) for constructing a confidence interval.
b) Construct a 95% confidence interval.
c) Interpret your interval.
d) Explain what "95% confidence" means in this context.

68. Internet music, again. A Gallup Poll (Exercise 57) asked Americans if the fact that they can make copies of songs on the Internet for free made them more likely—or less likely—to buy a performer's CD. Only 13% responded that it made them "less likely." The poll was based on a random sample of 703 Internet users.

a) Check that the assumptions and conditions are met for inference on proportions.
b) Find the 95% confidence interval for the true proportion of all U.S. Internet users who are "less likely" to buy CDs.

69. Politics. A recent poll of 1005 U.S. adults split the sample into four age groups: ages 18–29, 30–49, 50–64, and 65+. In the youngest age group, 62% said that they thought the U.S. was ready for a woman president, as opposed to 35% who said "no, the country was not ready" (3% were undecided). The sample included 250 18- to 29-year-olds.

a) Do you expect the 95% confidence interval for the true proportion of all 18- to 29-year-olds who think the U.S. is ready for a woman president to be wider or narrower than the 95% confidence interval for the true proportion of all U.S. adults? Explain.
b) Find the 95% confidence interval for the true proportion of all 18- to 29-year-olds who believe the U.S. is ready for a woman president.

70. More Internet music. A random sample of 168 students was asked how many songs were in their digital music library and what fraction of them was legally purchased. Overall, they reported having a total of 117,079 songs, of which 23.1% were legal. The music industry would like a good estimate of the proportion of songs in students' digital music libraries that are legal.

a) Think carefully. What is the parameter being estimated? What is the population? What is the sample size?

that theory. So, to test whether the daily fluctuations in the Dow are equally likely to be up as down, we'll assume that they are and then see if the data are consistent with that hypothesis.

Our starting hypothesis, called the null hypothesis, is that the proportion of days on which the DJIA increases is 50%. The **null hypothesis**, H_0, is a working model that we adopt temporarily or for the sake of argument. It specifies a population model parameter (in this case, the true proportion of "up" days, p) and proposes a value for that parameter. We write $H_0: p = p_0$. This is a concise way to specify the two things we need. It names the parameter we hope to learn about and specifies a value for it. For our hypothesis about the DJIA, our null hypothesis is that $p = 0.5$ so we write $H_0: p = 0.5$.

The **alternative hypothesis**, which we denote H_A, contains all the values of the parameter that we will consider plausible if we reject the null hypothesis. For the stock market, our null hypothesis is $p = 0.5$. What's the alternative? If we are interested in deviations equally likely in either direction, then our alternative is $H_A: p \neq 0.5$.

Now that we have our null hypothesis, what evidence would convince you that the proportion of up days was not 50%? Suppose that the market closed up on 95% of the days you looked at. That would probably convince you that the hypothesis was wrong: it's just too unlikely an event. But if the sample proportion of up days is close to 50%, you might not be sure. After all, observations do vary, so you wouldn't be surprised to see some difference. So, how different from 50% must the sample proportion be before you would be convinced that the true proportion wasn't 50%? That's the crucial question in a hypothesis test. As usual in statistics, when we think about the size of a change, we think of using the standard deviation as the ruler to measure that change.

We learned in Chapter 7 how to estimate the standard deviation of a random proportion using the Binomial model. If we think the probability of an up day is 0.5, then the standard deviation of our random, observed proportion of up days would be

$$SD(\hat{p}) = \sqrt{\frac{pq}{n}} = \sqrt{\frac{(0.5)(1-0.5)}{1112}} = 0.015$$

Why Is This a Standard Deviation and Not a Standard Error?

This is a standard deviation because we are using the model (hypothesized) value for p and *not* the estimated value, $\hat{p}$. Once we assume that the null hypothesis is true, it gives us a value for the model parameter p. With proportions, if we know p then we also automatically know its standard deviation. Because we find the standard deviation from the model parameter, this is a standard deviation and not a standard error. When we found a confidence interval for p, we could not assume that we knew its value, so we estimated the standard deviation from the sample value, $\hat{p}$.

Now, armed with that standard deviation, we want to model the behavior of the sample proportion to judge whether the proportion we've observed is unusually large. For that, we'll need the sampling distribution model. We saw in Chapter 9 how to model the distribution of random proportions with a Normal model. The null hypothesis provides all we need to find the mean and standard deviation. We adopt the null hypothesis temporarily to see whether it does actually describe the data, so we'll use a Normal model with a mean of .50 and a standard deviation of 0.015.

We want to know how likely it would be to see the observed value $\hat{p}$ as far away from 50% as the value of 51.53% that we actually have observed. Looking at Figure 10.2, we can see that 51.53% doesn't look very surprising. With a calculator, computer program, or the Normal table we can find that the probability of a proportion this far from 0.50 is about 0.308. This is the probability of observing

The SD Comes From the Null Hypothesis

To remind us that the parameter value comes from the null hypothesis, it is sometimes written as p_0 and the standard deviation as

$$SD(\hat{p}) = \sqrt{\frac{p_0 q_0}{n}}.$$

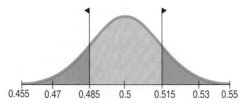

Figure 10.2   How likely is a proportion of more than 51.5% or less than 48.5% when the true mean is 50%? This is what it looks like. Each red area is 0.154 of the total area under the curve.

more than 51.53% up days or more than 51.53% down days if the null model were true. In other words, if the chance of an up day for the Dow is 50%, we'd expect to see stretches of 1112 trading days with 51.53% or more up days about 15.4% of the time and with 51.53% or more down days about 15.4% of the time. That's not terribly unusual, so there's really no convincing evidence that the market did not act randomly.

It may surprise you that even during a bull market, the direction of daily movements is random. In fact, the probability that any given day will end up or down appears to be about 0.5 regardless of the longer-term trends. It may be that when the stock market has a long run up (or possibly down, although we haven't checked that), it does so not by having more days of increasing or decreasing value, but by the actual amounts of the increases or decreases being unequal.

FOR EXAMPLE   Writing hypotheses

Many customers visit your site, and about 60% of all visitors "click-through" to the product page. You're happy with that 60% click-through rate, but one of your colleagues is proposing some major changes to your home page. You worry that the click-through rate might change, so you propose an experiment. To test the new design, you randomly send some visitors to the new site. Of 90 visitors sent to the new site, 57 clicked through.

QUESTION   Does this suggest that the click-through proportion has changed with the new site? What are the right hypotheses for a test?

ANSWER   We'll assume that the click-through proportion is still 60% unless there is enough evidence to suggest that it's different.

$$H_0: p = 0.60$$
$$H_A: p \neq 0.60$$

10.2   A Trial as a Hypothesis Test

We started by assuming that the probability of an up day was 50%. Then we looked at the data and concluded that we couldn't say otherwise because the proportion that we actually observed wasn't far enough from 50%. Does this reasoning seem backwards? That could be because we usually prefer to think about getting things right rather than getting them wrong. But, you've seen this reasoning before in a different context. This is the logic of jury trials.

Let's suppose a defendant has been accused of robbery. In British common law and those systems derived from it (including U.S. law), the null hypothesis is that the defendant is innocent. Instructions to juries are quite explicit about this.

"If the People fail to satisfy their burden of proof, you must find the defendant not guilty."

—NEW YORK STATE JURY
INSTRUCTIONS

The evidence takes the form of facts that seem to contradict the presumption of innocence. For us, this means collecting data. In the trial, the prosecutor presents evidence. ("If the defendant were innocent, wouldn't it be remarkable that the police found him at the scene of the crime with a bag full of money in his hand, a mask on his face, and a getaway car parked outside?") The next step is to judge the evidence. Evaluating the evidence is the responsibility of the jury in a trial, but it falls on your shoulders in hypothesis testing. The jury considers the evidence in light of the *presumption* of innocence and judges whether the evidence against the defendant would be plausible *if the defendant were in fact innocent.*

Like the jury, we ask: "Could these data plausibly have happened by chance if the null hypothesis were true?" If they are very unlikely to have occurred, then the evidence raises a reasonable doubt about the null hypothesis. Ultimately, *you* must make a decision. The standard of "beyond a reasonable doubt" is intentionally ambiguous because it leaves the jury to decide the degree to which the evidence contradicts the hypothesis of innocence. Juries don't explicitly use probability to help them decide whether to reject that hypothesis. But when you ask the same question of your null hypothesis, you have the advantage of being able to quantify exactly how surprising the evidence would be if the null hypothesis were true.

How unlikely is unlikely? Some people set rigid standards. Levels like 1 time out of 20 (0.05) or 1 time out of 100 (0.01) are common. But if *you* have to make the decision, you must judge for yourself in each situation whether the probability of observing your data is small enough to constitute "reasonable doubt."

10.3   P-Values

The fundamental step in our reasoning is the question: "Are the data surprising, given the null hypothesis?" And the key calculation is to determine exactly how likely the data we observed would be if the null hypothesis were the true model of the world. So we need a *probability.* Specifically, we want to find the probability of seeing data like these (or something even less likely) *given* the null hypothesis. This probability is called the **P-value.**

A low enough P-value says that the data we have observed would be very unlikely if our null hypothesis were true. We started with a model, and now that same model tells us that the data we have are unlikely to have happened. That's surprising. In this case, the model and data are at odds with each other, so we have to make a choice. Either the null hypothesis is correct and we've just seen something remarkable, or the null hypothesis is wrong (and, in fact, we were wrong to use it as the basis for computing our P-value). When you see a low P-value, you should reject the null hypothesis. There is no hard and fast rule about how low the P-value has to be. In fact, that decision is the subject of much of the rest of this chapter. Almost everyone would agree, however, that a P-value less than 0.001 indicates very strong evidence *against* the null hypothesis but a P-value greater than 0.05 provides very weak evidence.

When the P-value is *high* (or just not low *enough*), what do we conclude? In that case, we haven't seen anything unlikely or surprising at all. The data are consistent with the model from the null hypothesis, and we have no reason to reject the null hypothesis. Events that have a high probability of happening happen all the time. So, when the P-value is high does that mean we've proved the null hypothesis is true? No! We realize that many other similar hypotheses could also account for the data we've seen. The most we can say is that it doesn't appear to be false. Formally, we say that we "fail to reject" the null hypothesis. That may seem to be a pretty weak conclusion, but it's all we can say when the P-value is not low enough. All that means is that the data are consistent with the model that we started with.

> **Beyond a Reasonable Doubt**
> We ask whether the data were unlikely beyond a reasonable doubt. For the DJIA prices, we calculated how unlikely the data are if the null hypothesis is true. The probability that the observed statistic value (or an even more extreme value) could occur if the null model is true—in this case, 0.308—is the P-value. That probability is certainly not *beyond a reasonable doubt*, so we fail to reject the null hypothesis here.

How low is "low enough"? That's a judgment call that depends on the kind of decision you want to make. People typically select an arbitrary level such as .10, .05, or .01 and resolve to make a decision if the P-value falls below the level they selected. That arbitrary level is called an "alpha level" and (naturally enough) denoted α. We'll say more about alpha levels in Chapter 12.

What to Do with an "Innocent" Defendant

Let's see what that last statement means in a jury trial. If the evidence is not strong enough to reject the defendant's presumption of innocence, what verdict does the jury return? They do not say that the defendant is innocent. They say "not guilty." All they are saying is that they have not seen sufficient evidence to reject innocence and convict the defendant. The defendant may, in fact, be innocent, but the jury has no way to be sure.

Said statistically, the jury's null hypothesis is: innocent defendant. If the evidence is too unlikely (the P-value is low) then, given the assumption of innocence, the jury rejects the null hypothesis and finds the defendant guilty. But—and this is an important distinction—if there is *insufficient evidence* to convict the defendant (if the P-value is *not* low), the jury does not conclude that the null hypothesis is true and declare that the defendant is innocent. Juries can only *fail to reject* the null hypothesis and declare the defendant "not guilty."

In the same way, if the data are not particularly unlikely under the assumption that the null hypothesis is true, then the most we can do is to "fail to reject" our null hypothesis. We never declare the null hypothesis to be true. In fact, we simply do not know whether it's true or not. (After all, more evidence may come along later.)

Imagine a test of whether a company's new website design encourages a higher percentage of visitors to make a purchase (as compared to the site they've used for years). The null hypothesis is that the new site is no more effective at stimulating purchases than the old one. The test sends visitors randomly to one version of the website or the other. Of course, some will make a purchase, and others won't. If we compare the two websites on only 10 customers each, the results are likely *not to be clear*, and we'll be unable to reject the null hypothesis. Does this mean the new design is a complete bust? Not necessarily. It simply means that we don't have enough evidence to reject our null hypothesis. That's why we don't start by assuming that the new design is *more* effective. If we were to do that, then we could test just a few customers, find that the results aren't clear, and claim that since we've been unable to reject our original assumption the redesign must be effective. The Board of Directors is unlikely to be impressed by that argument.

Don't We Want to Reject the Null?

Often, people who collect data or perform an experiment hope to reject the null. They hope the new ad campaign is *better* than the old one, or they hope their candidate is *ahead* of the opponent. But, when we test a hypothesis, we must stay neutral. We can't let our hope bias our decision. As in a jury trial, we must stay with the null hypothesis until we are convinced otherwise. The burden of proof rests with the alternative hypothesis—innocent until proven guilty. When you test a hypothesis, you must act as judge and jury, but not as prosecutor.

Conclusion

If the P-value is "low," reject H_0 and conclude H_A.

If the P-value is not "low enough," then fail to reject H_0 and the test is inconclusive.

JUST CHECKING

1 A pharmaceutical firm wants to know whether aspirin helps to thin blood. The null hypothesis says that it doesn't. The firm's researchers test 12 patients, observe the proportion with thinner blood, and get a P-value of 0.32. They proclaim that aspirin doesn't work. What would you say?

2 An allergy drug has been tested and found to give relief to 75% of the patients in a large clinical trial. Now the scientists want to see whether a new, "improved" version works even better. What would the null hypothesis be?

3 The new allergy drug is tested, and the P-value is 0.0001. What would you conclude about the new drug?

10.4   The Reasoning of Hypothesis Testing

Hypothesis tests follow a carefully structured path. To avoid getting lost, it helps to divide that path into four distinct sections: hypotheses, model, mechanics, and conclusion.

Hypotheses

First, state the null hypothesis. That's usually the skeptical claim that nothing's different. The null hypothesis assumes the default (often the status quo) is true (the defendant is innocent, the new method is no better than the old, customer preferences haven't changed since last year, etc.).

In statistical hypothesis testing, hypotheses are almost always about model parameters. To assess how unlikely our data may be, we need a null model. The null hypothesis specifies a particular parameter value to use in our model. In the usual notation, we write H_0: *parameter = hypothesized value*. The alternative hypothesis, H_A, contains the values of the parameter we consider plausible when we reject the null.

Model

To plan a statistical hypothesis test, specify the *model* for the sampling distribution of the statistic you will use to test the null hypothesis and the parameter of interest. For proportions, we use the Normal model for the sampling distribution. Of course, all models require assumptions, so you will need to state them and check any corresponding conditions. For a test of a proportion, the assumptions and conditions are the same as for a one-proportion z-interval. For the DJIA example, the sample size of 1112 is certainly big enough to satisfy the Success/Failure condition, but doesn't violate the 10% condition either. (We expect $0.50 * 1112 = 556$ daily increases.) And, although the value of the DJIA from day to day is certainly not independent, it may be reasonable to assume that the daily price *changes* are random and independent.

Your model step should end with a statement such as: *Because the conditions are satisfied, we can model the sampling distribution of the proportion with a Normal model.* Watch out, though. Your Model step could end with: *Because the conditions are not satisfied, we can't proceed with the test.* (If that's the case, stop and reconsider.)

Each test we discuss in this book has a name that you should include in your report. We'll see many tests in the following chapters. Some will be about more than one sample, some will involve statistics other than proportions, and some will use models other than the Normal (and so will not use z-scores). The test about proportions is called a **one-proportion z-test**.[1]

> ### One-Proportion *z*-Test
> The conditions for the one-proportion z-test are the same as for the one-proportion z-interval (except that we use the hypothesized values, p_0 and q_0, to check the Success/Failure condition). We test the hypothesis $H_0: p = p_0$ using the statistic
>
> $$z = \frac{(\hat{p} - p_0)}{SD(\hat{p})}.$$
>
> We also use p_0 to find the standard deviation: $SD(\hat{p}) = \sqrt{\dfrac{p_0 q_0}{n}}$. When the conditions are met and the null hypothesis is true, this statistic follows the standard Normal model, so we can use that model to obtain a P-value.

---

[1] It's also called the "one-sample test for a proportion."

"The null hypothesis is never proved or established, but is possibly disproved, in the course of experimentation. Every experiment may be said to exist only in order to give the facts a chance of disproving the null hypothesis."

—Sir Ronald Fisher, *The Design of Experiments*, 1931

When the Conditions Fail …
You might proceed with caution, explicitly stating your concerns. Or you may need to do the analysis with and without an outlier, or on different subgroups, or after re-expressing the response variable. Or you may not be able to proceed at all.

FOR EXAMPLE Checking assumptions and conditions

Consider the test of the new website from page 308.

QUESTION   Are the conditions for inference satisfied?

ANSWER

Independence assumption: This is plausible because the **Randomization Condition** has been met through our decision to send a random selection of visitors to the new site.

The population of potential visitors is large, so we don't have to worry about sampling more than 10% of it.

Success/Failure Condition: We expect $np_0 = 90(.60) = 54$ successes and $nq_0 = 90(.40) = 36$ failures. Both are at least 10.

So the assumptions and conditions appear to be satisfied.

Mechanics

Under "Mechanics" we perform the actual calculation of our test statistic from the data. Different tests we encounter will have different formulas and different test statistics. Usually, the mechanics are handled by a statistics program or calculator. The ultimate goal of the calculation is to obtain a P-value—the probability that the observed statistic value (or an even more extreme value) could occur if the null model were correct. If the P-value is small enough, we'll reject the null hypothesis.

Conclusions and Decisions

The primary conclusion in a formal hypothesis test is only a statement about the null hypothesis. It simply states whether we reject or fail to reject that hypothesis. As always, the conclusion should be stated in context, but your conclusion about the null hypothesis should never be the end of the process. You can't make a decision based solely on a P-value. Business decisions have consequences, with actions to take or policies to change. The conclusions of a hypothesis test can help *inform* your decision, but they shouldn't be the only basis for it.

Business decisions should always take into consideration three things: the statistical significance of the test, the *cost* of the proposed action, and the **effect size** (the difference between the hypothesized and observed value) of the statistic. For example, a cellular telephone provider finds that 30% of their customers switch providers (or *churn*) when their two-year subscription contract expires. They try a small experiment and offer a random sample of customers a free $350 top-of-the-line phone if they renew their contracts for another two years. Not surprisingly, they find that the new switching rate is lower by a statistically significant amount. Should they offer these free phones to all their customers? Obviously, the answer depends on more than the P-value of the hypothesis test. Even if the P-value is statistically significant, the correct business decision also depends on the cost of the free phones and by how much the churn rate is lowered (the effect size). It's rare that a hypothesis test alone is enough to make a sound business decision.

10.5 Alternative Hypotheses

In our example about the DJIA, we were equally interested in proportions that deviate from 50% in *either* direction. So we wrote our alternative hypothesis as $H_A: p \neq 0.5$. Such an alternative hypothesis is known as a **two-sided alternative** because we are equally interested in deviations on either side of the null hypothesis value. For two-sided alternatives, the P-value is the probability of deviating in *either* direction from the null hypothesis value. Figure 10.3 shows the P-value area when the alternative is two-sided.

Figure 10.3 The P-value for a two-sided alternative adds the probabilities in both tails of the sampling distribution model outside the value that corresponds to the test statistic.

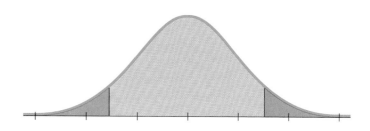

FOR EXAMPLE   Finding a P-value

We have sampled 90 visitors to our new website and 57 of them clicked through to another page (see page 308).

QUESTION   What's the P-value associated with a one-proportion z-test of our null hypothesis?

ANSWER   We have $n = 90$, $x = 57$, and a hypothesized $p = 0.60$

$$\hat{p} = \frac{57}{90} = 0.633$$

$$SD(\hat{p}) = \sqrt{\frac{p_0 q_0}{n}} = \sqrt{\frac{(0.6)(0.4)}{90}} = 0.0516$$

$$\text{So, } z = \frac{\hat{p} - p_0}{SD(\hat{p})} = \frac{0.633 - 0.60}{0.0516} = 0.64$$

P-value $= P(|z| > 0.64) = 0.52$

z (hundredths)

You can find from table z, or other technology that the area in each tail is 0.26, so the P-value is $2 \times 0.26 = 0.52$.

Alternative Hypotheses

Proportions:

Two-sided
$$H_0: p = p_0$$
$$H_A: p \neq p_0$$

One-sided
$$H_0: p = p_0$$
$$H_A: p < p_0 \text{ or } p > p_0$$

The alternative hypothesis gives the values of the parameter that we will consider plausible if we reject the null hypothesis. Sometimes values that deviate from the null in one direction are either not plausible at all or just of no interest to us in making a business decision. For example, suppose we want to test whether the proportion of customers returning merchandise has decreased under our new quality monitoring program. We're only going to continue the program if it has reduced returns, so we would only be interested in a sample proportion *smaller* than the null hypothesis value. We'd write our alternative hypothesis as $H_A: p < p_0$. An alternative hypothesis that focuses on deviations from the null hypothesis value in only one direction is called a **one-sided alternative.**

For a hypothesis test with a one-sided alternative, the P-value is the probability of deviating *only in the direction of the alternative* away from the null hypothesis value. Many business decisions are based on hypothesis tests with one-sided alternatives because the interest is only in increasing sales or profits or in reducing losses or errors rather than in a theoretical understanding of how things might change. Figure 10.4 shows the area of the P-value when the alternative is $H_A: p < p_0$. For $H_A: p > p_0$ the (red) shaded area would be on the right.

Figure 10.4 The P-value for a one-sided alternative considers only the probability of values beyond the test statistic value in the specified direction.

GUIDED EXAMPLE   Credit Card Promotion

A credit card company plans to offer a special incentive program to customers who charge at least $500 next month. The marketing department has pulled a sample of 500 customers from the same month last year and noted that the mean amount charged was $478.19 and the median amount was $216.48. The finance department says that the only relevant quantity is the proportion of customers who spend more than $500. If that proportion is not more than 25%, the program will lose money.

Among the 500 customers, 148 or 29.6% of them charged $500 or more. Has the goal that 25% of all customers charging at least $500 been met?

	Setup State the problem and discuss the variables and the context.	We want to know whether 25% or more of the customers will spend $500 or more in the next month and qualify for the special program. We will use the data from the same month a year ago to estimate the proportion and see whether the proportion was at least 25%.

Hypotheses The null hypothesis is that the proportion qualifying is 25%. The alternative is that it is higher. It's clearly a one-sided test.

The statistic is $\hat{p} = 0.296$, the proportion of customers who charged $500 or more.

$$H_0: p = 0.25$$
$$H_A: p > 0.25$$

Model Check the conditions.

✓ **Independence Assumption.** Customers are not likely to influence one another when it comes to spending on their credit cards.

✓ **Randomization Condition.** This is a random sample from the company's database.

✓ **Success/Failure Condition.** We expect 125 successes and 375 failures, both at least 10. The sample is large enough.

✓ **10% condition.** The sample of 500 customers is less than 10% of all our customers.

| State your method. | Under these conditions, the sampling model is Normal. We'll compute a one-proportion z-test. |

DO **Mechanics** Write down the given information and determine the sample proportion. Find the test statistic and its P-value.

$n = 500$, so

$$\hat{p} = \frac{148}{500} = 0.296 \text{ and}$$

$$SD(\hat{p}) = \sqrt{\frac{(0.25)(0.75)}{500}} = 0.01936$$

so the test statistic is $z = \dfrac{0.296 - 0.250}{0.01936} = 2.38$

From technology or from Table Z at the back of the book, we find that the probability of a z-score ≥ 2.38 is 0.0087, so that is our P-value.

REPORT **Conclusion** Link the test to your decision about the null hypothesis, then state your conclusion in context.

MEMO

Re: Credit card promotion

If the true proportion of customers charging $500 or more were actually 25%, the probability of seeing a success rate at least as large as the 29.6% that we did observe is about 0.0087. This is strong evidence that the true proportion is greater than our target of 25%. However, business judgment is called for to determine whether to go ahead with the new promotion.

Here's a portion of table Z that gives the probability we needed for the hypothesis test. At $z = 2.38$, the table gives the percentile as 0.9913. The upper-tail probability (shaded red) is, therefore, $1 - 0.9913 = 0.0087$; so, for our test, that's the P-value we need.

Figure 10.5 A portion of a Normal table with the look-up for $z = 2.38$ indicated.

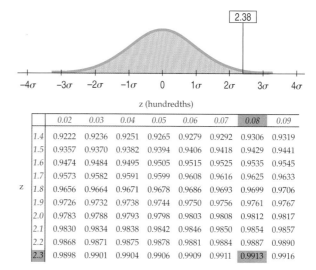

z	0.02	0.03	0.04	0.05	0.06	0.07	0.08	0.09
1.4	0.9222	0.9236	0.9251	0.9265	0.9279	0.9292	0.9306	0.9319
1.5	0.9357	0.9370	0.9382	0.9394	0.9406	0.9418	0.9429	0.9441
1.6	0.9474	0.9484	0.9495	0.9505	0.9515	0.9525	0.9535	0.9545
1.7	0.9573	0.9582	0.9591	0.9599	0.9608	0.9616	0.9625	0.9633
1.8	0.9656	0.9664	0.9671	0.9678	0.9686	0.9693	0.9699	0.9706
1.9	0.9726	0.9732	0.9738	0.9744	0.9750	0.9756	0.9761	0.9767
2.0	0.9783	0.9788	0.9793	0.9798	0.9803	0.9808	0.9812	0.9817
2.1	0.9830	0.9834	0.9838	0.9842	0.9846	0.9850	0.9854	0.9857
2.2	0.9868	0.9871	0.9875	0.9878	0.9881	0.9884	0.9887	0.9890
2.3	0.9898	0.9901	0.9904	0.9906	0.9909	0.9911	0.9913	0.9916

10.6   P-Values and Decisions: What to Tell about a Hypothesis Test

Hypothesis tests are particularly useful when we must make a decision. Is the defendant guilty or not? Should we choose print advertising or television? The absolute nature of the hypothesis test decision, however, makes some people (including the authors) uneasy. Whenever possible, it's a good idea to report a confidence interval for the parameter of interest as well.

How small should the P-value be to reject the null hypothesis? A jury needs enough evidence to show the defendant guilty "beyond a reasonable doubt." How does that translate to P-values? The answer is that there is no good, universal answer. How small the P-value has to be to reject the null hypothesis is highly context-dependent. Sometimes we choose an arbitrary value and reject the null hypothesis if the P-value falls below it. That value is called the **α-level** of the test. When we're screening for a disease and want to be sure we treat all those who are sick, we may be willing to reject the null hypothesis of no disease with a P-value as large as 0.10. That would mean that 10% of the healthy people would be treated as sick and subjected to further testing. We might rather treat (or recommend further testing for) the occasional healthy person than fail to treat someone who was really sick. But a long-standing hypothesis, believed by many to be true, needs stronger evidence (and a correspondingly small P-value) to reject it.

See if you require the same P-value to reject each of the following null hypotheses:

- A start-up engineering firm claims that they have technology that can detect manufacturing flaws using ultrasound technology. You set up a test with 10 samples, some flawed and some not. If the method is just guessing, it will guess right about 50% of the time. So our null hypothesis is that p equals 0.5. If the new technology works, it will get more than 50% correct. Suppose the technology gets 9 of the 10 test samples correct. The P-value associated with that result is 0.011. (In other words, if you tried to guess, you'd get at least 9 out of 10 correct only about 1% of the time.) What do you conclude? Most manufacturers would probably reject the null hypothesis and be convinced that the technology works. Why? Because the P-value is small and we don't have any particular reason to doubt the alternative.
- You are contacted by a new investment advisor. He claims to have psychic powers of precognition that allow him to predict which stocks will rise and which will fall in the next month. To test him you choose 10 stocks and record his projections. Suppose he gets 9 out of 10 right. This also has a P-value of 0.011. Are you willing now to reject this null hypothesis? Are you convinced that he's not just lucky?

  What amount of evidence would convince you? We require more evidence to reject a null hypothesis that would contradict long-standing beliefs or other scientific results. Reliable evidence of precognition would be grounds for a Nobel Prize. But, with sufficient evidence, we should revise our opinions (and scientific theories). That's how science makes progress.

Another factor in choosing the α-level is the importance of the issue being tested. Consider the following two tests:

- A researcher claims that the proportion of college students who hold part-time jobs now is higher than the proportion known to hold such jobs a decade ago. You might be willing to believe the claim (and reject the null hypothesis of no change) with a P-value of 0.05.
- An engineer claims that even though there were several problems with the rivets holding the wing on an airplane in their fleet, they've retested the

"An extraordinary claim requires extraordinary proof."
—MARCELLO TRUZZI

proportion of faulty rivets and now the P-value is small enough to reject the null hypothesis that the proportion is the same. What P-value would be small enough to get you to fly on that plane?

Your conclusion about any null hypothesis should always be accompanied by the P-value of the test. Don't just declare the null hypothesis rejected or not rejected because of some arbitrary α-level. Report the P-value to show the strength of the evidence against the hypothesis and the effect size. This will let each reader decide whether or not to reject the null hypothesis and whether or not to consider the result important if it is statistically significant.

FOR EXAMPLE Stating the conclusion

QUESTION What should we conclude about the new design of the website from page 308?

ANSWER Because the P-value of 0.52 is quite high, we see no evidence to reject the null hypothesis. Even though a proportion slightly higher than 60% was observed, this experiment does not provide enough evidence to conclude that the new website will actually change our click-through rate.

GUIDED EXAMPLE Home Field Advantage

Major league sports are big business. And the fans are more likely to come out to root for the team if the home team has a good chance of winning. Anyone who plays or watches sports has heard of the "home field advantage." Teams tend to win more often when they play at home. Or do they?

If there were no home field advantage, the home teams would win about half of all games played. In the 2012 Major League Baseball season, there were 2430 regular-season games. It turns out that the home team won 1295 of the 2430 games, or 53.29% of the time.

Question: Could this deviation from 50% be explained just from natural sampling variability, or is it evidence to suggest that there really is a home field advantage, at least in professional baseball?

PLAN **Setup** State what we want to know. Define the variables and discuss their context. **Hypotheses** The null hypothesis makes the claim of no home field advantage. We are interested only in a home field *advantage*, so the alternative hypothesis is one-sided. **Model** Think about the assumptions and check the appropriate conditions.	We want to know whether the home team in professional baseball is more likely to win. The data are all 2430 games from the 2012 Major League Baseball season. The variable is whether or not the home team won. The parameter of interest is the proportion of home team wins. If there's no advantage, I'd expect that proportion to be 0.50. $$H_0: p = 0.50$$ $$H_A: p > 0.50$$ ✓ **Independence Assumption:** Generally, the outcome of one game has no effect on the outcome of another game. But this may not be strictly true. For example, if a key player is injured, the probability that the team will win in the next couple of games may decrease slightly, but independence is still roughly true. The data come from one entire season, but I expect other seasons to be similar.

(*continued*)

This is not a random sample. But we can view the 2430 games here as a representative collection of games including those that might be played in the future.

✓ **Success/Failure Condition:** Both

$$np_0 = 2430(0.50) = 1215.0 \text{ and}$$
$$nq_0 = 2430(0.50) = 1215.0 \text{ are at least } 10.$$

Specify the sampling distribution model.

State what test you plan to use.

Because the conditions are satisfied, I'll use a Normal model for the sampling distribution of the proportion and do a **one-proportion z-test**.

DO

Mechanics The null model gives us the mean, and (because we are working with proportions) the mean gives us the standard deviation.

The null model is a Normal distribution with a mean of 0.50 and a standard deviation of

$$SD(\hat{p}) = \sqrt{\frac{p_0 q_0}{n}} = \sqrt{\frac{(0.5)(1 - 0.5)}{2430}}$$
$$= 0.01014$$

The observed proportion, $\hat{p}$, is 0.5329.

Next, we find the z-score for the observed proportion, to find out how many standard deviations it is from the hypothesized proportion.

So the z-value is

$$z = \frac{0.5329 - 0.5}{0.01014} = 3.24$$

From the z-score, we can find the P-value, which tells us the probability of observing a value that extreme (or more).

The sample proportion lies 3.24 standard deviations above the mean.

The probability of observing a sample proportion 3.24 or more standard deviations above the mean of a Normal model can be found by computer, calculator, or table to be < 0.001.

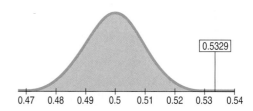

The corresponding P-value is < 0.001.

REPORT

Conclusion State your conclusion about the parameter—in context.

MEMO

Re: Home field advantage

Our analysis of games played during the 2012 season showed a statistically significant home field advantage. The P-value of < 0.001 says that if the true proportion of home team wins were 0.50, then an observed value of 0.5329 (or larger) would occur less than 1 time in 1000.

JUST CHECKING

4 An accountant at an organic food chain is testing whether the customers prefer a new cheese supplier. She surveys 100 customers and finds out that the proportion preferring the new supplier is greater than the previous proportion with a P-value of 0.002. The new supplier costs more, but the P-value is so low. Should she switch to the new supplier?

5 A marketing analyst at a biotechnology firm has just learned that the P-value for testing whether the proportion of people who find pain relief using their new product Z-170 was 0.06. Should he conclude that the product doesn't work?

The Hypothesis Testing Process

Setup	State your problem and identify the variables. Be sure that the identity of the cases and what the variables measure are both clear.
Hypotheses	State your hypotheses: • The null hypothesis, H_0, identifies a parameter and proposes a value for it. • The alternative hypothesis, H_A, specifies what kind of deviations from the null model would be of interest.
Model	Specify the statistic and its sampling distribution model. The sampling distribution model comes from theory and will usually be something you look up. It will likely require you to make assumptions about your data. You can often determine if an assumption is plausible by checking related conditions—usually with graphical displays. If the required assumptions are not plausible, STOP. You can't test your hypothesis with this method or with these data. Otherwise, state clearly what method you will use.
Mechanics	Calculate the test statistic. Usually, you'll use technology to do the work.
Find the P-value	Find the probability of observing the statistic value you found (or values even less likely). The sampling distribution model provides this probability. The hypothesized parameter value will be needed for the sampling distribution model and the alternative hypothesis will indicate what part of the distribution is of interest. Usually, we can use technology to find this probability. The probability is called the P-value. You should report it along with your decision.

Reasoning	Is the P-value small? Then **reject** the null hypothesis.
	    If the null hypothesis were true then we have observed a rare event, and we don't want to base decisions on rare events.
	Is the P-value large? Then **fail to reject** the null hypothesis.
	    We don't know whether the null hypothesis is true, so we can't "accept" it. But we lack strong enough evidence to declare it false.

Judgment	You must decide for yourself what probability would be small enough that you would find an event with that probability rare. Although there are some common values (10%, 5%, and 1% are all used), your decision should be based on the circumstances of the test, including considerations of the costs should your test conclusion prove to be wrong.

WHAT CAN GO WRONG?

- **Don't base your null hypotheses on what you see in the data.** You are not allowed to look at the data first and then adjust your null hypothesis so that it will be rejected. If your sample value turns out to be $\hat{p} = 51.8\%$ with a standard deviation of 1%, don't form a null hypothesis just big enough so you'll be able to reject it like $H_0: \hat{p} = 49.8\%$. The null hypothesis should not be based on the data you collect. It should describe the "nothing interesting" or "nothing has changed" situation.

- **Don't base your alternative hypothesis on the data either.** You should always think about the situation you are investigating and base your alternative hypothesis on that. Are you interested only in knowing whether something has *increased*? Then write a one-tail (upper tail) alternative. Or would you be equally interested in a change in either direction? Then you want a two-tailed alternative. You should decide whether to do a one- or two-tailed test based on what results would be of interest to you, not on what you might see in the data.

- **Don't make your null hypothesis what you want to show to be true.** Remember, the null hypothesis is the status quo, the nothing-is-strange-here position a skeptic would take. You wonder whether the data cast doubt on that. You can reject the null hypothesis, but you can never "accept" or "prove" the null.

- **Don't forget to check the conditions.** The reasoning of inference depends on randomization. No amount of care in calculating a test result can save you from a biased sample. The probabilities you compute depend on the independence assumption. And your sample must be large enough to justify your use of a Normal model.

- **Don't believe too strongly in arbitrary alpha levels.** There's not really much difference between a P-value of 0.051 and a P-value of 0.049, but sometimes it's regarded as the difference between night (having to retain H_0) and day (being able to shout to the world that your results are "statistically significant"). It may just be better to report the P-value and a confidence interval and let the world (perhaps your manager or client) decide along with you.

- **Don't confuse practical and statistical significance.** A large sample size can make it easy to discern even a trivial change from the null hypothesis value. On the other hand, you could miss an important difference if your sample size is too small to detect an effect size that you're interested in seeing.

ETHICS IN ACTION

Shellie Cooper, longtime owner of a small organic food store, specializes in locally produced organic foods and products. Over the years Shellie's customer base has been quite stable, consisting mainly of health-conscious individuals who tend not to be very price sensitive, opting to pay higher prices for better-quality local, organic products. However, faced with increasing competition from grocery chains offering more organic choices, Shellie is now thinking of offering coupons. She needs to decide between the newspaper and the Internet. She recently read that the percentage of consumers who use printable Internet coupons is on the rise but, at 15%, is still much less than the 40% who clip and redeem newspaper coupons. Nonetheless, she is interested in learning more about the Internet and sets up a meeting with Jack Kasor, a Web consultant. She discovers that for an initial investment and continuing monthly fee, Jack would design Shellie's website, host it on his server, and broadcast e-coupons to her customers at regular intervals.

While she was concerned about the difference in redemption rates for e-coupons vs. newspaper coupons, Jack assured her that e-coupon redemptions are continuing to rise and that she should expect between 15% and 40% of her customers to redeem them. Shellie agreed to give it a try. After the first six months, Jack informed Shellie that the proportion of her customers who redeemed e-coupons was significantly greater than 15%. He determined this by selecting several broadcasts at random and found the number redeemed (483) out of the total number sent (3000). Shellie thought that this was positive and made up her mind to continue the use of e-coupons.

- Identify the ethical dilemma in this scenario.

- What are the undesirable consequences?

- Propose an ethical solution that considers the welfare of all stakeholders.

WHAT HAVE WE LEARNED?

Learning Objectives

Know how to formulate a null and alternative hypothesis for a question of interest.

- The null hypothesis specifies a parameter and a (null) value for that parameter.
- The alternative hypothesis specifies a range of plausible values should we fail to reject the null.

Be able to perform a hypothesis test for a proportion.

- The null hypothesis has the form $H_0: p = p_0$.
- We estimate the standard deviation of the sampling distribution of the sample proportion by assuming that the null hypothesis is true:

$$SD(\hat{p}) = \sqrt{\frac{p_0 q_0}{n}}$$

- We compare the statistic $z = \dfrac{\hat{p} - p_0}{SD(\hat{p})}$ to the standard Normal model.

Understand P-values.

- A P-value is the estimated probability of observing a statistic value at least as far from the (null) hypothesized value as the one we have actually observed.
- A small P-value indicates that the statistic we have observed would be unlikely were the null hypothesis true. That leads us to doubt the null.
- A large P-value just tells us that we have insufficient evidence to doubt the null hypothesis. In particular, it does not prove the null to be true.

Know the reasoning of hypothesis testing.

- State the **hypotheses**.
- Determine (and check assumptions for) the sampling distribution **model**.
- Calculate the test statistic—the **mechanics**.
- State your **conclusions and decisions**.

Be able to decide on a two-sided or one-sided alternative hypothesis, and justify your decision.

Know the value of estimating and reporting the effect size.

- A test may be statistically significant, but practically meaningless if the estimated effect is of trivial importance.

Terms

Alpha Level
The threshold P-value that determines when we reject a null hypothesis. Using an alpha level of α, if we observe a statistic whose P-value based on the null hypothesis is less than α, we reject that null hypothesis.

Alternative hypothesis
The hypothesis that proposes what we should conclude if we find the null hypothesis to be unlikely.

Effect size
The difference between the null hypothesis and an observed (or proposed) value.

Null hypothesis
The claim being assessed in a hypothesis test. Usually, the null hypothesis is a statement of "no change from the traditional value," "no effect," "no difference," or "no relationship." For a claim to be a testable null hypothesis, it must specify a value for some population parameter that can form the basis for assuming a sampling distribution for a test statistic.

One-proportion z-test
A test of the null hypothesis that the proportion of a single sample equals a specified value ($H_0: p = p_0$) by comparing the statistic $z = \dfrac{\hat{p} - p_0}{SD(\hat{p})}$ to a standard Normal model.

One-sided alternative
An alternative hypothesis is one-sided (e.g., $H_A: p > p_0$ or $H_A: p < p_0$) when we are interested in deviations in *only one* direction away from the hypothesized parameter value.

P-value	The probability of observing a value for a test statistic at least as far from the hypothesized value as the statistic value actually observed if the null hypothesis is true. A small P-value indicates that the observation obtained is improbable given the null hypothesis and thus provides evidence against the null hypothesis.
Two-sided alternative	An alternative hypothesis is two-sided (e.g., $H_A: p \neq p_0$) when we are interested in deviations in *either* direction away from the hypothesized parameter value.

TECHNOLOGY HELP: Hypothesis Tests

Hypothesis tests for proportions are so easy and natural that many statistics packages don't offer special commands for them. Most statistics programs want to know the "success" and "failure" status for each case. Usually these are given as 1 or 0, but they might be category names like "yes" and "no." Often we just know the proportion of successes, $\hat{p}$, and the total count, n. Computer packages don't usually deal naturally with summary data like this, but see below for a couple of important exceptions (Minitab and JMP).

In some programs you can reconstruct the original values. But even when you have reconstructed (or can reconstruct) the raw data values, often you won't get *exactly* the same test statistic from a computer package as you would find working by hand. The reason is that many packages make approximations. The result is very close, but not exactly the same. If you use a computer package, you may notice slight discrepancies between your answers and the answers in the back of the book, but they're not important.

Reports about hypothesis tests generated by technologies don't follow a standard form. Most will name the test and provide the test statistic value, its standard deviation, and the P-value. But these elements may not be labeled clearly. For example, the expression "Prob > $|z|$" means the probability (the "Prob") of observing a test statistic whose

magnitude (the absolute value tells us this) is larger than that of the one (the "z") found in the data (which, because it is written as "z," we know follows a Normal model). That is a fancy (and not very clear) way of saying two-sided P-value for a test based on the Normal model. In some packages, you can specify that the test be one-sided. Others might report three P-values, covering the ground for both one-sided tests and two-sided tests.

Sometimes a confidence interval and hypothesis test are automatically given together.

Often, the standard deviation of the statistic is called the "standard error," and usually that's appropriate because we've had to estimate its value from the data. That's not the case for proportions, however: We get the standard deviation for a proportion from the null hypothesis value. Nevertheless, you may see the standard deviation called a "standard error" even for tests with proportions.

It's common for statistics packages and calculators to report more digits of "precision" than could possibly have been found from the data. You can safely ignore them. Round values such as the standard deviation to one digit more than the number of digits reported in your data.

Here are the kind of results you might see in typical computer output.

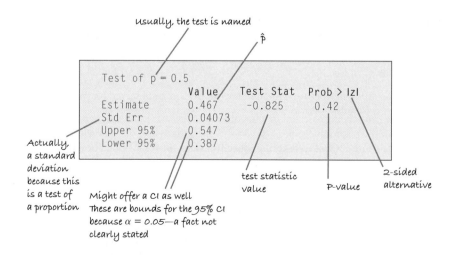

EXCEL

Inference methods for proportions are not part of the standard Excel tool set.

To calculate a *z*-test of a proportion in Excel:

	A	B	C	D	E
1	z-Test of a Proportion				
2					(Expression for Column D)
3	Sample proportion	0.467	z Stat	-0.81	=(B3-B5)/((B5*(1-B5)/B4)^0.5)
4	Sample size	150	P(Z<=z) one-tail	0.2094	=(1-NORM.S.DIST(ABS(D3),TRUE))
5	Hypothesized proportion	0.5	z Critical one-tail	1.6449	=NORM.S.INV(1-B6)
6	Alpha	0.05	P(Z<=z) two-tail	0.4189	=2*D4
7			z Critical two-tail	1.9600	=NORM.S.INV(1-B6/2)

- To calculate the values in cells D3–D7, type the formulas in cells E3 through E7.

- After the formulas are set in column D, enter information for any *z*-test for a proportion in cells B3 through B6, and the results will show in column D. Note that the one- and two-tail critical values given are for the upper end of the distribution. If a lower one-tail test is being conducted, the critical value will be negative, and for a two-tail test the lower tail critical value will be negative.

Note: In pre-2010 versions of Microsoft Excel, the functions used in these calculations are "=NORMSINV" and "=NORMSDIST".

XLSTAT

To find a one-proportion *z* interval:

- Select **Parametric Tests,** and then choose **Tests for one proportion**.

- Under the **General** tab, choose the **Data format** to be either **Frequency** or **Proportion** depending on the form of your data.

- Enter the **frequency** of your variable (or **proportion**) and the **sample size**.

- Enter the **test proportion**.

Under **Data format** choose the appropriate button.

- Under the **Options** tab choose the **Alternative hypothesis** of **Proportion – Test proportion ≠ D**. Enter **0** for the **Hypothesized difference (D)**.

- Enter 5 under **Significance Level.** The output will show the 95% confidence interval.

MINITAB

Choose **Basic Statistics** from the **Stat** menu.

- Choose **1 Proportion** from the Basic Statistics submenu.

- If the data are category names in a variable, assign the variable from the variable list box to the **Samples in columns** box.

- If you have summarized data, click the **Summarized Data** button and fill in the number of trials and the number of successes.

- Mark a check next to **Perform hypothesis test** and enter the hypothesized proportion.

- Click the **Options** button and specify the remaining details.

- If you have a large sample, check **Use test and interval based on Normal distribution.**

- Click the **OK** button.

Comments

When working from a variable that names categories, Minitab treats the last category as the "success" category. You can specify how the categories should be ordered.

SPSS

SPSS does not perform the hypothesis test for one proportion using the Normal approximation.

JMP

For a categorical variable that holds two categories, go to **Analyze > Distribution**. Put the variable containing the categories in the **Y, Columns** box and press **OK**.

- Click the red triangle next to the column name and select **Test Probabilities**.

- Put both p_0 and $1 - p_0$ into the probabilities and click **Done**.

Comments

JMP does not use the Normal distribution to test the proportions and so your answers will differ slightly from the book. For summarized data, you will need to have the frequencies in another column and designate that column as the **Frequencies**.

Brief **Case**

Metal Production

Ingots are huge pieces of metal, often weighing in excess of 20,000 pounds, made in a giant mold. They must be cast in one large piece for use in fabricating large structural parts for cars and planes. If they crack while being made, the crack may propagate into the zone required for the part, compromising its integrity. Airplane manufacturers insist that metal for their planes be defect-free, so the ingot must be made over if any cracking is detected.

Even though the metal from the cracked ingot is recycled, the scrap cost runs into the tens of thousands of dollars. Metal manufacturers would like to avoid cracking if at all possible, but only about 75% of the ingots have been free of cracks. The data from 5000 ingots produced after some changes were made to the process are found in the file **Ingots**. The variable *Crack* indicates whether a crack was found (1) or not (0). The variable *Impurities* shows the amount (in ppm) of impurities found in

(continued)

a sample from each ingot. Select a random sample of 100 ingots and test the claim that the cracking rate has decreased from 25%. Find a confidence interval for the cracking rate as well. Now select a random sample of 500 ingots and test the claim and find the confidence interval again. Prepare a short report about your findings including any differences you see between the conclusions from the two samples.

Loyalty Program

A marketing manager has sent out 10,000 mail pieces to a random sample of customers to test a new web-based loyalty program and see its impact on customer spending. The customers either received nothing (No Offer), a free companion airline ticket (Free Flight), or free flight insurance on their next flight (Free Insurance). The analyst who designed the test used a stratified random sample to ensure that all the market segments are represented, but the manager has several concerns. First, she worries that the *Travel* segment (which comprises 25% of all customers) is underrepresented (variable *Segment*). In addition, she worries that fewer than 1/3 of the customers in that segment were held out as controls and received no offer. Using the data found in the file **Loyalty Program** write a short report to the manager testing the appropriate hypotheses and summarizing your findings. Include in your report 95% confidence intervals for the proportion of customers who responded to the offer by signing up for the loyalty program in the various segments. (The variable *Response* indicates a 1 for responders and 0 for nonresponders.)

EXERCISES -

SECTION 10.1

1. For each of the following situations, write the null and alternative hypotheses in terms of parameter values. Example: We want to know if the proportion of up days in the stock market is 50%. Answer: Let p = the proportion of up days. $H_0: p = 0.5$ vs. $H_A: p \neq 0.5$.

a) A casino wants to know if their slot machine really delivers the 1 in 100 win rate that it claims.

b) A pharmaceutical company wonders if their new drug has a cure rate different from the 30% reported by the placebo.

c) A bank wants to know if the percentage of customers using their website has changed from the 40% that used it before their system crashed last week.

2. As in Exercise 1, for each of the following situations, write the null and alternative hypotheses in terms of parameter values.

a) A recent UMass-Amherst study found that seat-belt compliance in Massachusetts was 73% in 2011. The state wants to know if it has changed.

b) Last year, a survey found that 45% of the employees were willing to pay for on-site day care. The company wants to know if that has changed.

c) Regular card customers have a default rate of 6.7%. A credit card bank wants to know if that rate is different for their Gold card customers.

SECTION 10.3

3. Which of the following are true? If false, explain briefly.

a) A very high P-value is strong evidence that the null hypothesis is false.

b) A very low P-value proves that the null hypothesis is false.

c) A high P-value shows that the null hypothesis is true.

d) A P-value below 0.05 is always considered sufficient evidence to reject a null hypothesis.

4. Which of the following are true? If false, explain briefly.

a) A very low P-value provides evidence against the null hypothesis.

b) A high P-value is strong evidence in favor of the null hypothesis.

c) A P-value above 0.10 shows that the null hypothesis is true.

d) If the null hypothesis is true, you can't get a P-value below 0.01.

SECTION 10.4

5. A consulting firm had predicted that 35% of the employees at a large firm would take advantage of a new company Credit Union, but management is skeptical. They doubt the rate is that high. A survey of 300 employees shows that 138 of them are currently taking advantage of the Credit Union. From the sample proportion

a) Find the standard deviation of the sample proportion based on the null hypothesis.
b) Find the z-statistic.
c) Does the z-statistic seem like a particularly large or small value?

6. A survey of 100 CEOs finds that 60 think the economy will improve next year. Is there evidence that the rate is higher among all CEOs than the 55% reported by the public at large?

a) Find the standard deviation of the sample proportion based on the null hypothesis.
b) Find the z-statistic.
c) Does the z-statistic seem like a particularly large or small value?

SECTION 10.5

7. For each of the following, write out the null and alternative hypotheses, being sure to state whether the alternative is one-sided or two-sided.

a) A company reports that last year 40% of their reports in accounting were on time. From a random sample this year, they want to know if that proportion has changed.
b) Last year, 42% of the employees enrolled in at least one wellness class at the company's site. Using a survey, they want to know if a greater percentage is planning to take a wellness class this year.
c) A political candidate wants to know from recent polls if she's going to garner a majority of votes in next week's election.

8. For each of the following, write out null and the alternative hypotheses, being sure to indicate whether the alternative is one-sided or two-sided.

a) *Consumer Reports* discovered that 20% of a certain computer model had warranty problems over the first three months. From a random sample, the manufacturer wants to know if a new model has improved that rate.
b) The last time a philanthropic agency requested donations, 4.75% of people responded. From a recent pilot mailing, they wonder if that rate has increased.
c) A student wants to know if other students on her campus prefer Coke or Pepsi.

SECTION 10.6

9. Occasionally, a report comes out that a drug that cures some disease turns out to have a nasty side effect. For example, some antidepressant drugs may cause suicidal thoughts in younger patients. A researcher wants to study such a drug and look for evidence that such side effects exist.

a) If the test yields a low P-value and the researcher rejects the null hypothesis, but there is actually no ill side effect of the drug, what are the consequences of such a mistake?

b) If the test yields a high P-value and the researcher fails to reject the null hypothesis, but there is a bad side effect of the drug, what are the consequences of such a mistake?

10. Developing a new drug can be an expensive process, resulting in high costs to patients. A pharmaceutical company has developed a new drug to reduce cholesterol, and it will conduct a clinical trial to compare the effectiveness to the most widely used current treatment. The results will be analyzed using a hypothesis test.

a) If the test yields a low P-value and the researcher rejects the null hypothesis, but it actually is not better, what are the consequences of such a mistake?
b) If the test yields a high P-value and the researcher fails to reject the null hypothesis, but the new drug is more effective, what are the consequences of such a mistake?

CHAPTER EXERCISES

11. Hypotheses. Write the null and alternative hypotheses to test each of the following situations.

a) An online clothing company is concerned about the timeliness of their deliveries. The VP of Operations and Marketing recently stated that she wanted the percentage of products delivered on time to be greater than 90%, and she wants to know if the company has succeeded.
b) A realty company recently announced that the proportion of houses taking more than three months to sell is now greater than 50%.
c) A financial firm's accounting department reports that after improvements in their system, they now have an error rate below 2%.

12. More hypotheses. Write the null and alternative hypotheses to test each of the following situations.

a) A 2010 *Harvard Business Review* article looked at 1109 CEOs from global companies and found that 32% had MBAs. Has the percentage changed?
b) Recently, 20% of cars of a certain model have needed costly transmission work after being driven between 50,000 and 100,000 miles. The car manufacturer hopes that the redesign of a transmission component has solved this problem.
c) A market researcher for a cola company decides to field test a new soft drink flavor, planning to market it only if he is sure that over 60% of the people like the flavor.

13. Deliveries. The clothing company in Exercise 11a looks at a sample of delivery reports. They test the hypothesis that 90% of the deliveries are on time against the alternative that greater than 90% are on time and find a P-value of 0.22. Which of these conclusions is appropriate?

a) There's a 22% chance that 90% of the deliveries are on time.
b) There's a 78% chance that 90% of the deliveries are on time.
c) There's a 22% chance that the sample they drew shows the correct percentage of on-time deliveries

d) There's a 22% chance that natural sampling variation could produce a sample with an observed proportion of on-time deliveries such as the one they obtained if, in fact, 90% of deliveries are on time.

14. House sales. The realty company in Exercise 11b looks at a recent sample of houses that have sold. On testing the null hypothesis that 50% of the houses take more than three months to sell against the hypothesis that more than 50% of the houses take more than three months to sell, they find a P-value of 0.034. Which of these conclusions is appropriate?

a) There's a 3.4% chance that 50% of the houses take more than three months to sell.

b) If 50% of the houses take more than three months to sell, there's a 3.4% chance that a random sample would produce a sample proportion as high as the one they obtained.

c) There's a 3.4% chance that the null hypothesis is correct.

d) There's a 96.6% chance that 50% of the houses take more than three months to sell.

15. P-value. Have harsher penalties and ad campaigns increased seat-belt use among drivers and passengers? Observations of commuter traffic have failed to find evidence of a significant change compared with three years ago. Explain what the study's P-value of 0.17 means in this context.

16. Another P-value. A company developing scanners to search for hidden weapons at airports has concluded that a new device is significantly better than the current scanner. The company made this decision based on a P-value of 0.03. Explain the meaning of the P-value in this context.

17. Ad campaign. An information technology analyst believes that they are losing customers on their website who find the checkout and purchase system too complicated. She adds a one-click feature to the website, to make it easier but finds that only about 10% of the customers are using it. She decides to launch an ad awareness campaign to tell customers about the new feature in the hope of increasing the percentage. She doesn't see much of a difference, so she hires a consultant to help her. The consultant selects a random sample of recent purchases, tests the hypothesis that the ads produced no change against the alternative that the percent who use the one-click feature is now greater than 10%, and finds a P-value of 0.22. Which conclusion is appropriate? Explain.

a) There's a 22% chance that the ads worked.

b) There's a 78% chance that the ads worked.

c) There's a 22% chance that the null hypothesis is true.

d) There's a 22% chance that natural sampling variation could produce poll results like these if the use of the one-click feature has increased.

e) There's a 22% chance that natural sampling variation could produce poll results like these if there's really no change in website use.

18. Mutual funds. A mutual fund manager claims that at least 70% of the stocks she selects will increase in price over the next year. We examined a sample of 200 of her selections over the past three years. Our P-value turns out to be 0.03. Which conclusion is appropriate? Explain.

a) There's a 3% chance that the fund manager is correct.

b) There's a 97% chance that the fund manager is correct.

c) There's a 3% chance that a random sample could produce the results we observed, so it's reasonable to conclude that the fund manager is correct.

d) There's a 3% chance that a random sample could produce the results we observed if $p = .7$, so it's reasonable to conclude that the fund manager is not correct.

e) There's a 3% chance that the null hypothesis is correct.

19. Product effectiveness. A pharmaceutical company's old antacid formula provided relief for 70% of the people who used it. The company tests a new formula to see if it is better and gets a P-value of 0.27. Is it reasonable to conclude that the new formula and the old one are equally effective? Explain.

20. Car sales. A German automobile company is counting on selling more cars to the younger market segment—drivers under the age of 20. The company's market researchers survey to investigate whether or not the proportion of today's high school seniors who own their own cars is higher than it was a decade ago. They find a P-value of 0.017. Is it reasonable to conclude that more high school seniors have cars? Explain.

21. False claims? A candy company claims that in a large bag of holiday M&M's® half the candies are red and half the candies are green. You pick candies at random from a bag and discover that of the first 20 you eat, 12 are red.

a) If it were true that half are red and half are green, what is the probability you would have found that at least 12 out of 20 were red?

b) Do you think that half of the M&M's® candies in the bag are really red? Explain.

22. Scratch off. A retail company offers a "scratch off" promotion. Upon entering the store, you are given a card. When you pay, you may scratch off the coating. The company advertises that half the cards are winners and have immediate cash-back savings of $5 (the others offer $1 off any future purchase of coffee in the cafe). You aren't sure the percentage is really 50% winners.

a) The first time you shop there, you get the coffee coupon. You try again and again get the coffee coupon. Do two failures in a row convince you that the true fraction of winners isn't 50%? Explain.

b) You try a third time. You get coffee again! What's the probability of not getting a cash savings three times in a row if half the cards really do offer cash savings?

c) Would three losses in a row convince you that the store is cheating?

We're much more likely to get an average near 3.5 than we are to get one near 1 or 6. Without calculating those probabilities exactly, it's fairly easy to see that the *only* way to get an average of 1 is to get two 1s. To get a total of 7 (for an average of 3.5), though, there are many more possibilities. This distribution even has a name—the *triangular distribution*.

What if we average three dice? We'll simulate 10,000 tosses of three dice and take their average.

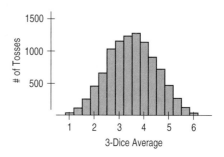

First notice that it's getting harder to have averages near the ends. Getting an average of 1 or 6 with three dice requires all three to come up 1 or 6, respectively. That's less likely than for two dice to come up both 1 or both 6. The distribution is being pushed toward the middle. But what's happening to the shape?

Let's continue this simulation to see what happens with larger samples. Here's a histogram of the averages for 10,000 tosses of five dice.

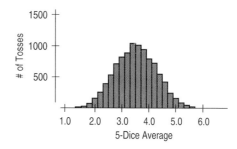

The pattern is becoming clearer. Two things are happening. The first fact we knew already from the Law of Large Numbers, which we saw in Chapter 5. It says that as the sample size (number of dice) gets larger, each sample average tends to become closer to the population mean. So we see the shape continuing to tighten around 3.5. But the shape of the distribution is the surprising part. It's becoming bell-shaped. In fact, it's approaching the Normal model.

Let's skip ahead and try 20 dice. The histogram of averages for throws 10,000 of 20 dice looks like this.

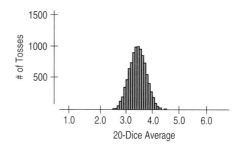

Now we see the Normal shape again (and notice how much smaller the spread is). But can we count on this happening for situations other than dice throws? What kinds of sample means have sampling distributions that we can model with a Normal model? It turns out that Normal models work well amazingly often.

Pierre-Simon Laplace, 1749–1827.

"The theory of probabilities is at bottom nothing but common sense reduced to calculus."

—Laplace, in *Théorie Analytique des Probabilitiés*, 1812

Pierre-Simon Laplace

Laplace was one of the greatest scientists and mathematicians of his time. In addition to his contributions to probability and statistics, he published many new results in mathematics, physics, and astronomy (where his nebular theory was one of the first to describe the formation of the solar system in much the way it is understood today). He also played a leading role in establishing the metric system of measurement.

His brilliance, though, sometimes got him into trouble. A visitor to the Académie des Sciences in Paris reported that Laplace let it be known widely that he considered himself the best mathematician in France. The effect of this on his colleagues was not eased by the fact that Laplace was right.

The Central Limit Theorem

The dice simulation may look like a special situation. But it turns out that what we saw with dice is true for means of repeated samples for almost every situation. When we looked at the sampling distribution of a proportion, we had to check only a few conditions. For means, the result is even more remarkable. There are almost no conditions at all.

Let's say that again: The sampling distribution of *any* mean becomes Normal as the sample size grows. All we need is for the observations to be independent and collected with randomization. We don't even care about the shape of the population distribution![2] This surprising fact was proved in a fairly general form in 1810 by Pierre-Simon Laplace, and caused quite a stir (at least in mathematics circles) because it is so unintuitive. Laplace's result is called the **Central Limit Theorem**[3] (CLT).

Not only does the distribution of means of many random samples get closer and closer to a Normal model as the sample size grows, but *this is true regardless of the shape of the population distribution!* Even if we sample from a skewed or bimodal population, the Central Limit Theorem tells us that means of repeated random samples will tend to follow a Normal model as the sample size grows. Of course, you won't be surprised to learn that it works better and faster the closer the population distribution is to a Normal model. And it works better for larger samples. If the data come from a population that's exactly Normal to start with, then the observations themselves are Normal. If we take samples of size 1, their "means" are just the observations—so, of course, they have a Normal sampling distribution. But now suppose the population distribution is very skewed (like the CEO data from Chapter 3, for example). The CLT works, although it may take a sample size of dozens or even hundreds of observations for the Normal model to work well.

For example, think about a real bimodal population, one that consists of only 0s and 1s. The CLT says that even means of samples from this population will follow a Normal sampling distribution model. But wait. Suppose we have a categorical variable and we assign a 1 to each individual in the category and a 0 to each individual not in the category. Then we find the mean of these 0s and 1s. That's the same as counting the number of individuals who are in the category and dividing by *n*. That mean will be the *sample proportion*, $\hat{p}$, of individuals who are in the category (a "success"). So maybe it wasn't so surprising after all that proportions, like means, have Normal sampling distribution models; proportions are actually just a special case of Laplace's remarkable theorem. Of course, for such an extremely bimodal population, we need a reasonably large sample size—and that's where the Success/Failure condition for proportions comes in.

The Central Limit Theorem (CLT)

The mean of a random sample has a sampling distribution whose shape can be approximated by a Normal model. The larger the sample, the better the approximation will be.

Be careful. We have been slipping smoothly between the real world, in which we draw random samples of data, and a magical mathematical-model world, in which we describe how the sample means and proportions we observe in the real world might behave if we could see the results from every random sample that we might have drawn. Now we have *two* distributions to deal with. The first is the real-world distribution of the sample, which we might display with a histogram (for

---

[2]Technically, the data must come from a population with a finite variance.

[3]The word "central" in the name of the theorem means "fundamental." It doesn't refer to the center of a distribution.

quantitative data) or with a bar chart or table (for categorical data). The second is the math-world *sampling distribution* of the statistic, which we model with a Normal model based on the Central Limit Theorem. Don't confuse the two.

For example, don't mistakenly think the CLT says that the *data* are Normally distributed as long as the sample is large enough. In fact, as samples get larger, we expect the distribution of the data to look more and more like the distribution of the population from which it is drawn—skewed, bimodal, whatever—but not necessarily Normal. You can collect a sample of CEO salaries for the next 1000 years, but the histogram will never look Normal. It will be skewed to the right. The Central Limit Theorem doesn't talk about the distribution of the data from the sample. It talks about the sample *means* and sample *proportions* of many different random samples drawn from the same population. Of course, we never actually draw all those samples, so the CLT is talking about an imaginary distribution—the sampling distribution model.

When the population shape is not unimodal and symmetric it takes longer for the sampling distribution to resemble the Normal. But with a large enough sample, the CLT applies to means and proportions from almost any data set.

JUST CHECKING

The Central Limit Theorem

A supermarket manager examines the amount spent by customers using a self-checkout station. He finds that the distribution of these amounts is unimodal but skewed to the high end because some customers make unusually expensive purchases. He finds the mean spent on each of the 30 days studied and makes a histogram of those values.

1   What shape would you expect for this histogram?

2   If, instead of averaging all customers on each day, he selects the first 10 for each day and just averages those, how would you expect his histogram of the means to differ from the one in (1)?

11.2   The Sampling Distribution of the Mean

The CLT says that the sampling distribution of any mean or proportion is approximately Normal. But which Normal? We know that any Normal model is specified by its mean and standard deviation. For proportions, the sampling distribution is centered at the population proportion. For means, it's centered at the population mean. What else would we expect?

What about the standard deviations? We noticed in our dice simulation that the histograms got narrower as the number of dice we averaged increased. This shouldn't be surprising. Means vary less than the individual observations. Think about it for a minute. Which would be more surprising, having *one* person in your Statistics class who is over 6′9″ tall or having the *mean* of 100 students taking the course be over 6′9″? The first event is fairly rare.[4] You may have seen somebody this tall in one of your classes sometime. But finding a class of 100 whose mean height is over 6′9″ tall just won't happen. Why? *Means have smaller standard deviations than individuals.*

"The n's justify the means."

—APOCRYPHAL STATISTICAL SAYING

---

[4]If students are a random sample of adults, fewer than 1 out of 10,000 should be taller than 6′9″. Why might college students not really be a random sample with respect to height? Even if they're not a perfectly random sample, a college student over 6′9″ tall is still rare.

That is, the Normal model for the sampling distribution of the mean has a standard deviation equal to $SD(\bar{y}) = \dfrac{\sigma}{\sqrt{n}}$ where σ is the standard deviation of the population. To emphasize that this is a standard deviation *parameter* of the sampling distribution model for the sample mean, $\bar{y}$, we write $SD(\bar{y})$ or $\sigma(\bar{y})$.

The Sampling Distribution Model for a Mean

When a random sample is drawn from any population with mean μ and standard deviation σ, its sample mean, $\bar{y}$, has a sampling distribution with the same mean μ but whose standard deviation is $\dfrac{\sigma}{\sqrt{n}}$, and we write $\sigma(\bar{y}) = SD(\bar{y}) = \dfrac{\sigma}{\sqrt{n}}$. No matter what population the random sample comes from, the shape of the sampling distribution is approximately Normal as long as the sample size is large enough. The larger the sample used, the more closely the Normal approximates the sampling distribution model for the mean.

We now have two closely related sampling distribution models. Which one we use depends on which kind of data we have.

- When we have categorical data, we calculate a sample proportion, $\hat{p}$. Its sampling distribution follows a Normal model with a mean at the population proportion, p, and a standard deviation $SD(\hat{p}) = \sqrt{\dfrac{pq}{n}} = \dfrac{\sqrt{pq}}{\sqrt{n}}$.

- When we have quantitative data, we calculate a sample mean, $\bar{y}$. Its sampling distribution has a Normal model with a mean at the population mean, μ, and a standard deviation $SD(\bar{y}) = \dfrac{\sigma}{\sqrt{n}}$.

The means of these models are easy to remember, so all you need to be careful about is the standard deviations. Remember that these are standard deviations of the *statistics* $\hat{p}$ and $\bar{y}$. They both have a square root of n in the denominator. That tells us that the larger the sample, the less either statistic will vary. The only difference is in the numerator. If you just start by writing $SD(\bar{y})$ for quantitative data and $SD(\hat{p})$ for categorical data, you'll be able to remember which formula to use.

FOR EXAMPLE   Working with the sampling distribution of the mean

Suppose that the weights of boxes shipped by a company follow a unimodal, symmetric distribution with a mean of 12 lbs and a standard deviation of 4 lbs. Boxes are shipped in palettes of 10 boxes. The shipper has a limit of 150 lbs for such shipments.

QUESTION   What's the probability that a palette will exceed that limit?

ANSWER   Asking the probability that the total weight of a sample of 10 boxes exceeds 150 lbs is the same as asking the probability that the *mean* weight exceeds 15 lbs. First we'll check the conditions. We will assume that the 10 boxes on the palette are a random sample from the population of boxes and that their weights are mutually independent. We are told that the underlying distribution of weights is unimodal and symmetric, so a sample of 10 boxes should be large enough.

Under these conditions, the CLT says that the sampling distribution of $\bar{y}$ has a Normal model with mean 12 and standard deviation

$$SD(\bar{y}) = \frac{\sigma}{\sqrt{n}} = \frac{4}{\sqrt{10}} = 1.26 \text{ and } z = \frac{\bar{y} - \mu}{SD(\bar{y})} = \frac{15 - 12}{1.26} = 2.38$$

$$P(\bar{y} > 15) = P(z > 2.38) = 0.0087$$

So the chance that the shipper will reject a palette is only .0087—less than 1%.

11.3   How Sampling Distribution Models Work

Both of the sampling distributions we've looked at are Normal. We know for proportions, $SD(\hat{p}) = \sqrt{\dfrac{pq}{n}}$, and for means, $SD(\bar{y}) = \dfrac{\sigma}{\sqrt{n}}$. These are great if we know, or can pretend that we know, p or σ, and sometimes we'll do that.

Often we know only the observed proportion, $\hat{p}$, or the sample standard deviation, s. So of course we just use what we know, and we estimate. That may not seem like a big deal, but it gets a special name. Whenever we estimate the standard deviation of a sampling distribution, we call it a **standard error (SE).**

For a sample proportion, $\hat{p}$, the standard error is:

$$SE(\hat{p}) = \sqrt{\frac{\hat{p}\hat{q}}{n}}.$$

For the sample mean, $\bar{y}$, the standard error is:

$$SE(\bar{y}) = \frac{s}{\sqrt{n}}.$$

You may see a "standard error" reported by a computer program in a summary or offered by a calculator. It's safe to assume that if no statistic is specified, what was meant is $SE(\bar{y})$, the standard error of the mean.

JUST CHECKING

> **3** The entrance exam for business schools, the GMAT, given to 100 students had a mean of 520 and a standard deviation of 120. What was the standard error for the mean of this sample of students?
>
> **4** As the sample size increases, what happens to the standard error, assuming the standard deviation remains constant?
>
> **5** If the sample size is doubled, what is the impact on the standard error?

To keep track of how the concepts we've seen combine, we can draw a diagram relating them. At the heart is the idea that *the statistic itself (the sample proportion or the sample mean) is a random quantity.* We can't know what our statistic will be because it comes from a random sample. A different random sample would have given a different result. This sample-to-sample variability is what generates the sampling distribution, the distribution of all the possible values that the statistic could have had.

We could simulate that distribution by pretending to take lots of samples. Fortunately, for the mean and the proportion, the CLT tells us that we can model their sampling distribution directly with a Normal model.

Figure 11.1   We start with a population model, which can have any shape. It can even be bimodal or skewed (as this one is). We label the mean of this model μ and its standard deviation, σ.

   We draw one real sample (solid line) of size n and show its histogram and summary statistics. We *imagine* (or simulate) drawing many other samples (dotted lines), which have their own histograms and summary statistics.

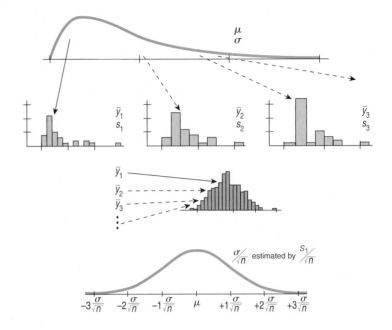

We (imagine) gathering all the means into a histogram.

The CLT tells us we can model the shape of this histogram with a Normal model. The mean of this Normal is μ, and the standard deviation is

$$SD(\bar{y}) = \frac{\sigma}{\sqrt{n}}.$$

The two basic truths about sampling distributions are:

1. Sampling distributions arise because samples vary. Each random sample will contain different cases and, so, a different value of the statistic.
2. Although we can always simulate a sampling distribution, the Central Limit Theorem saves us the trouble for means and proportions.

When we don't know σ, we estimate it with the standard deviation of the one real sample. That gives us the standard error, $SE(\bar{y}) = \dfrac{s}{\sqrt{n}}$.

   Figure 11.1 diagrams the process.

11.4   Gosset and the *t*-Distribution

You've learned how to create confidence intervals for proportions. Now we want to do the same thing for means. For proportions we found the confidence interval as

$$\hat{p} \pm ME.$$

The *ME* was equal to a critical value, z^*, times $SE(\hat{p})$. Our confidence interval for means will look very similar:

$$\bar{y} \pm ME.$$

And our *ME* will be a critical value times $SE(\bar{y})$. So let's put the pieces together.

   The Central Limit Theorem gives us a sampling distribution and a standard deviation for the mean. All we need is a random sample of quantitative data and the true value of the population standard deviation σ.

   But wait. That could be a problem. To compute $\sigma/\sqrt{n}$ we need to know σ. How are we supposed to know σ? Suppose we told you that for 25 young executives the mean value of their stock portfolios is \$125,672. Would that tell you the value of σ? No, the standard deviation depends on how similarly the executives invest, not on how well they invested (the mean tells us that). But we need σ because it's the numerator of the standard deviation of the sample mean: $SD(\bar{y}) = \dfrac{\sigma}{\sqrt{n}}$.

So what can we do? The obvious answer is to use the sample standard deviation, s, from the data instead of σ. The result is the standard error: $SE(\bar{y}) = \dfrac{s}{\sqrt{n}}$.

To find the sampling distribution of $\frac{\bar{y}}{s/\sqrt{n}}$, Gosset simulated it *by hand*. He drew paper slips of small samples from a hat *hundreds of times* and computed the means and standard deviations with a mechanically cranked calculator. Today, you could repeat in seconds on a computer the experiment that took him over a year. Gosset's work was so meticulous that not only did he get the shape of the new histogram approximately right, but he even figured out the exact formula for it from his sample. The formula was not confirmed mathematically until years later by Sir Ronald Aylmer Fisher.

NOTATION ALERT

Ever since Gosset, the letter *t* has been reserved in Statistics for his distribution.

A century ago, people just plugged the standard error into the Normal model, assuming it would work. And for large sample sizes it *did* work pretty well. But they began to notice problems with smaller samples. The extra variation in the standard error was wreaking havoc with the margins of error.

Gosset was the first to investigate this phenomenon. He realized that not only do we need to allow for the extra variation with larger margins of error, but we also need a new sampling distribution model. In fact, we need a whole *family* of models, depending on the sample size, *n*. These models are unimodal, symmetric, and bell-shaped, but the smaller our sample, the more we must stretch out the tails. Gosset's work transformed Statistics, but most people who use his work don't even know his name.

Gosset's *t*

Gosset made decisions about the stout's quality by using statistical inference. He knew that if he used a 95% confidence interval, he would fail to capture the true quality of the batch about 5% of the time. However, the lab told him that he was in fact rejecting about 15% of the good batches. Gosset knew something was wrong, and it bugged him.

Gosset took time off from his job to study the problem and earn a graduate degree in the emerging field of Statistics. He figured out that when he used the standard error $\frac{s}{\sqrt{n}}$, the shape of the sampling model was no longer Normal. He even figured out what the new model was and called it a *t*-distribution.

The Guinness Company didn't give Gosset a lot of support for his work. In fact, it had a policy against publishing results. Gosset had to convince the company that he was not publishing an industrial secret and (as part of getting permission to publish) had to use a pseudonym. The pseudonym he chose was "Student," and ever since, the model he found has been known as **Student's *t***.

> ### Using a Known Standard Deviation
>
> Variation is inherent in manufacturing, even under the most tightly controlled processes. To ensure that parts do not vary too much, however, quality professionals monitor the processes by selecting samples at regular intervals. The mean performance of these samples is measured, and if it lies too far from the desired target mean, the process may be stopped until the underlying cause of the problem can be determined. In silicon wafer manufacturing, the thickness of the film is a crucial measurement. To assess a sample of wafers, quality engineers compare the mean thickness of the sample to the target mean. But, they don't estimate the standard deviation of the mean by using the standard error derived from the same sample. Instead they base the standard deviation of the mean on the historical process standard deviation, estimated from a vast collection of similar parts. In this case, the standard deviation can be treated as "known" and the Normal model can be used for the sampling distribution instead of the *t* distribution.

Gosset's model is always bell-shaped, but the details change with the sample sizes (Figure 11.2). So the Student's *t*-models form a family of related distributions that depend on a parameter known as **degrees of freedom**. We often denote degrees of freedom as df and the model as t_{df}, with the numerical value of the degrees of freedom as a subscript.

Student's *t*-models are unimodal, symmetric, and bell-shaped, just like the Normal model. But *t*-models with only a few degrees of freedom have a narrower peak than the Normal model and have much fatter tails. (See Figure 11.2.) (That's what makes the margin of error bigger.) As the degrees of freedom increase, the *t*-models look more and more like the Normal model. In fact, the

Figure 11.2   The *t*-model (solid curve) with 2 degrees of freedom has fatter tails than the Normal model (dashed curve). So the 68–95–99.7 Rule doesn't work for *t*-models with only a few degrees of freedom.

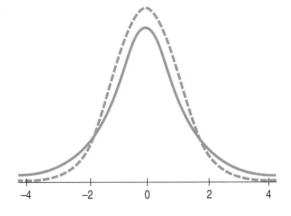

t-model with infinite degrees of freedom is exactly Normal.[5] This is great news if you happen to have an infinite number of data values. Unfortunately, that's not practical. Fortunately, above a few hundred degrees of freedom it's very hard to tell the difference. Of course, in the rare situation that we *know* σ, it would be foolish not to use that information. If we don't have to estimate σ, we can use the Normal model. Typically that value of σ would be based on (lots of) experience, or on a theoretical model. Usually, however, we estimate σ by s from the data and use the *t*-model.

> **z or t?**
>
> If you know σ, use z. (But that almost never happens.) Whenever you use s to estimate σ, use t.

> **Practical Sampling Distribution Model for Means**
>
> When certain conditions are met, the standardized sample mean,
>
> $$t = \frac{\bar{y} - \mu}{SE(\bar{y})}$$
>
> follows a Student's *t*-model with $n - 1$ degrees of freedom. We find the standard error from:
>
> $$SE(\bar{y}) = \frac{s}{\sqrt{n}}.$$

11.5   A Confidence Interval for Means

To make confidence intervals, we need to use Gosset's model. Which one? Well, for means, it turns out the right value for degrees of freedom is df $= n - 1$.

> **One-Sample *t*-Interval**
>
> When the assumptions and conditions are met, we are ready to find the **one-sample *t*-interval for the population mean, μ.** The confidence interval is:
>
> $$\bar{y} \pm t^*_{n-1} \times SE(\bar{y})$$
>
> where the standard error of the mean is:
>
> $$SE(\bar{y}) = \frac{s}{\sqrt{n}}.$$
>
> The critical value t^*_{n-1} depends on the particular confidence level, C, that you specify and on the number of degrees of freedom, $n - 1$, which we get from the sample size.

[5]Formally, in the limit as the number of degrees of freedom goes to infinity.

*Degrees of Freedom—Why $n-1$?

The reason we use $n-1$ degrees of freedom for the t is closely related to why we used $n-1$ when we calculated the standard deviation. We promised back then to say more about that choice later, and this seems like a good time to bring it up.

If only we knew the true population mean, μ, we would find the sample standard deviation using n instead of $n-1$ as:

$$s = \sqrt{\frac{\Sigma (y - \mu)^2}{n}} \text{ and we'd call it } s.$$

We have to use $\bar{y}$ instead of μ, though, and that causes a problem. For any sample, $\bar{y}$ is as close to the data values as possible. Generally the population mean, μ, will be farther away. Think about it. GMAT scores have a population mean of 525. If you took a random sample of 5 students who took the test, their sample mean wouldn't be 525. The five data values will be closer to their own $\bar{y}$ than to 525. So if we use $\Sigma (y - \bar{y})^2$ instead of $\Sigma (y - \mu)^2$ in the equation to calculate s, our standard deviation estimate will be too small. The amazing mathematical fact is that we can compensate for the fact that $\Sigma (y - \bar{y})^2$ is too small just by dividing by $n-1$ instead of by n. So that's all the $n-1$ is doing in the denominator of s. We call $n-1$ the degrees of freedom.

When Gosset corrected the Normal model for the extra uncertainty, the margin of error got bigger, as you might have guessed. When you use Gosset's model instead of the Normal model, your confidence intervals will be just a bit wider. That's just the correction you need. By using the t-model, you've compensated for the extra variability in precisely the right way.

Finding t^*-Values

The Student's t-model is different for each value of degrees of freedom. We might print a table like Table Z (in Appendix B) for each degrees of freedom value, but that's a lot of pages and not likely to be a bestseller. One way to shorten the book is to limit ourselves to 80%, 90%, 95%, and 99% confidence levels. So Statistics books usually have one table of t-model critical values for a selected set of confidence levels. This one does too; see Table T in Appendix B. (You can also find tables on the Internet.)

The t-tables run down the page for as many degrees of freedom as can fit, and, as you can see from Figure 11.3, they are much easier to use than the Normal

Figure 11.3 Part of Table T in Appendix B.

		0.20	0.10	0.05
Two tail probability				
One tail probability		0.10	0.05	0.025
Table T	df			
Values of t_α	1	3.078	6.314	12.706
	2	1.886	2.920	4.303
	3	1.638	2.353	3.182
	4	1.533	2.132	2.776
	5	1.476	2.015	2.571
	6	1.440	1.943	2.447
	7	1.415	1.895	2.365
	8	1.397	1.860	2.306
	9	1.383	1.833	2.262
	10	1.372	1.812	2.228
	11	1.363	1.796	2.201
	12	1.356	1.782	2.179
	13	1.350	1.771	2.160
	14	1.345	1.761	2.145
	15	1.341	1.753	2.131
	16	1.337	1.746	2.120
	17	1.333	1.740	2.110
	18	1.330	1.734	2.101
	19	1.328	1.729	2.093
	⋮	⋮	⋮	⋮
	∞	1.282	1.645	1.960
Confidence levels		80%	90%	95%

tables. But there is only room on the page for a limited number of degrees of freedom. Of course, for *enough* degrees of freedom, the *t*-model gets closer and closer to the Normal, so the tables give a final row with the critical values from the Normal model and label it "∞ df."

FOR EXAMPLE   **Finding a confidence interval for the mean**

According to the Environmental Defense Fund, "Americans are eating more and more salmon, drawn to its rich taste and health benefits. Increasingly they are choosing *farmed* salmon because of its wide availability and low price. But in the last few years, farmed salmon has been surrounded by controversy over its health risks and the ecological impacts of salmon aquaculture operations. Studies have shown that some farmed salmon is relatively higher in contaminants like PCBs than wild salmon, and there is mounting concern over the industry's impact on wild salmon populations."

In a widely cited study of contaminants in farmed salmon, fish from many sources were analyzed for 14 organic contaminants.[6] One of those was the insecticide mirex, which has been shown to be carcinogenic and is suspected of being toxic to the liver, kidneys, and endocrine system. Summaries for 150 mirex concentrations (in parts per million) from a variety of farmed salmon sources were reported as:

$$n = 150; \quad \bar{y} = 0.0913 \text{ ppm}; \quad s = 0.0495 \text{ ppm}$$

QUESTION   The Environmental Protection Agency (EPA) recommends to recreational fishers as a "screening value" that mirex concentrations be no larger than 0.08 ppm. What does the 95% confidence interval say about that value?

ANSWER   Because $n = 150$, there are 149 df. There isn't an entry in Table T for 149 df, so if we're using the table, we'll use the next *smaller* value to be conservative. We find $t^*_{140, 0.025} = 1.977$ (from technology, $t^*_{149, 0.025} = 1.976$), so a 95% confidence interval is

$$\bar{y} \pm t^* \times SE(\bar{y}) = \bar{y} \pm 1.977 \times \frac{s}{\sqrt{n}} = 0.0913 \pm 1.977 \frac{0.0495}{\sqrt{150}} = (0.0833, 0.0993)$$

If this sample is representative (as the authors claim it is), we can be 95% confident that it contains the true value of the mean mirex concentration. Because the interval from 0.0834 to 0.0992 ppm is entirely above the recommended value set by the EPA, we have reason to believe that the true mirex concentration exceeds the EPA guidelines.

11.6   Assumptions and Conditions

Gosset found the *t*-model by simulation. Years later, when Fisher showed mathematically that Gosset was right, he needed to make some assumptions to make the proof work. These are the assumptions we need in order to use the Student's *t*-models.

Independence Assumption

The data values should be independent. There's really no way to check independence of the data by looking at the sample, but we should think about whether the assumption is reasonable.

---

[6]Ronald A. Hites, Jeffery A. Foran, David O. Carpenter, M. Coreen Hamilton, Barbara A. Knuth, and Steven J. Schwager, "Global Assessment of Organic Contaminants in Farmed Salmon," *Science* 9, January 2004: Vol. 303, no. 5655, pp. 226–229.

Randomization Condition: The data arise from a random sample or suitably randomized experiment. Randomly sampled data—and especially data from a Simple Random Sample (SRS)—are ideal.

When a sample is drawn without replacement, technically we ought to confirm that we haven't sampled a large fraction of the population, which would threaten the independence of our selections. In that case, we can check the following condition.

10% Condition: The sample size should be no more than 10% of the population. In practice, though, we often don't mention the 10% Condition when estimating means. Why not? When we made inferences about proportions, this condition was crucial because we usually had large samples. But for means our samples are generally smaller, so this problem arises only if we're sampling from a small population (and then there's a correction formula we could use).

Normal Population Assumption

Student's *t*-models won't work for data that are badly skewed. How skewed is too skewed? Well, formally, we assume that the data are from a population that follows a Normal model. Practically speaking, there's no way to be certain this is true.

And it's almost certainly *not* true. Models are idealized; real data are, well, real. The good news, however, is that even for small samples, it's sufficient to check a condition.

Nearly Normal Condition. The data come from a distribution that is unimodal and symmetric. This is a much more practical condition and one we can check by making a histogram.[7] For small samples, it can be hard to see any distribution shape in the histogram. Unfortunately, the condition matters most when it's hardest to check.

For very small samples ($n < 15$ or so), the data should follow a Normal model pretty closely. Of course, with so little data, it's rather hard to tell. But if you do find outliers or strong skewness, don't use these methods.

For moderate sample sizes (n between 15 and 40 or so), the *t* methods will work well as long as the data are unimodal and reasonably symmetric. Make a histogram to check.

When the sample size is larger than 40 or 50, the *t* methods are safe to use unless the data are extremely skewed. Make a histogram anyway. If you find outliers in the data and they aren't errors that are easy to fix, it's always a good idea to perform the analysis twice, once with and once without the outliers, even for large samples. The outliers may well hold additional information about the data, so they deserve special attention. If you find multiple modes, you may well have different groups that should be analyzed and understood separately.

If the data are extremely skewed, the mean may not be the most appropriate summary. But when our data consist of a collection of instances whose *total* is the business consequence—as when we add up the profits (or losses) from many transactions or the costs of many supplies—then the mean is just that total divided by *n*. And that's the value with a business consequence. Fortunately, in this instance, the Central Limit Theorem comes to our rescue. Even when we must sample from a very skewed distribution, the sampling distribution of our sample mean will be close to Normal, so we can use Student's *t* methods without much worry as long as the sample size is *large enough*.

How large is large enough? Figure 11.4 shows a histogram of CEO compensations ($000) for *Fortune* 500 companies.

---

[7]Or we could check a Normal probability plot.

Figure 11.4   It's hard to imagine a distribution more skewed than these annual compensations from the *Fortune* 500 CEOs.

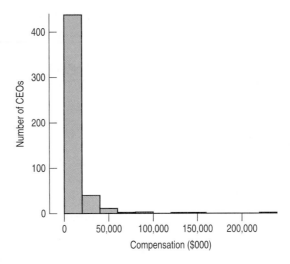

Although this distribution is very skewed, the Central Limit Theorem will make the sampling distribution of the means of samples from this distribution more and more Normal as the sample size grows. Figure 11.5 is a histogram of the means of many samples of 100 CEOs:

Figure 11.5   Even samples as small as 100 from the CEO data set produce means whose sampling distribution is nearly Normal. Larger samples will have sampling distributions even more Normal.

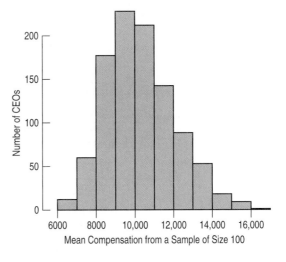

Often, in modern business applications, even if we have a sample of many hundreds, or thousands, we should still be on guard for outliers and multiple modes and we should think about whether the observations are independent. But if the mean is of interest, the Central Limit Theorem works quite well in ensuring that the sampling distribution of the mean will be close to the Normal for samples of this size.

FOR EXAMPLE   **Checking the assumptions and conditions for a confidence interval for means**

Researchers purchased whole farmed salmon from 51 farms in eight regions in six countries. The histogram shows the concentrations of the insecticide mirex in the 150 samples of farmed salmon we examined in the previous example.

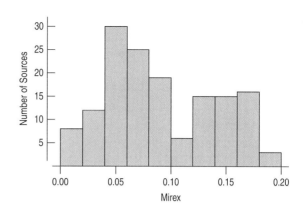

QUESTION   Are the assumptions and conditions for making a confidence interval for the mean mirex concentration satisfied?

ANSWER

✓ **Independence Assumption:** The fish were raised in many different places, and samples were purchased independently from several sources.
✓ **Randomization Condition:** The fish were selected randomly from those available for sale.
✓ **Nearly Normal Condition:** The histogram of the data looks bimodal. While it might be interesting to learn the reason for that and possibly identify the subsets, we can proceed because the sample size is large.

It's okay to use these data about farm-raised salmon to make a confidence interval for the mean.

JUST CHECKING

The alumni organization of your university is trying to get information on the success of their recent graduates, so they have surveyed a sample of graduates. We know that incomes are likely to be skewed to the right (although perhaps not as much as the salaries of CEOs!).

6 If they are successful at obtaining the salaries of only 20 recent graduates, what should they be concerned about when reporting a confidence interval for mean salaries of all recent grads?

7 Why do they need to base these confidence intervals on *t*-models?

8 If they manage to get 60 salaries instead of 20, how will this affect their confidence interval?

GUIDED EXAMPLE   Insurance Profits

Insurance companies take risks. When they insure a property or a life, they must price the policy in such a way that their expected profit enables them to survive. They can base their projections on actuarial tables, but the reality of the insurance business often demands that they discount policies to a variety of customers and situations. Managing this risk is made even more difficult by the fact that until the policy expires, the company won't know if they've made a profit, no matter what premium they charge.

(*continued*)

Profit (in $) from 30 Policies		
222.80	463.35	2089.40
1756.23	−66.20	2692.75
1100.85	57.90	2495.70
3340.66	833.95	2172.70
1006.50	1390.70	3249.65
445.50	2447.50	−397.10
3255.60	1847.50	−397.31
3701.85	865.40	186.25
−803.35	1415.65	590.85
3865.90	2756.94	578.95

A manager wanted to see how well one of her sales representatives was doing, so she selected 30 matured policies that had been sold by the sales rep and computed the (net) profit (premium charged minus paid claims), for each of the 30 policies.

The manager would like you, as a consultant, to construct a 95% confidence interval for the mean profit of the policies sold by this sales rep.

 PLAN

Setup State what we want to know. Identify the variables and their context.

We wish to find a 95% confidence interval for the mean profit of policies sold by this sales rep. We have data for 30 matured policies.

Make a picture. Check the distribution shape and look for skewness, multiple modes, and outliers.

Here's a boxplot and histogram of these values.

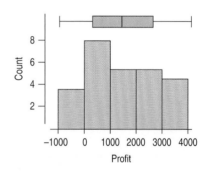

The sample appears to be unimodal and fairly symmetric with profit values between −$1000 and $4000 and no outliers.

Model Think about the assumptions and check the conditions.

✓ **Independence Assumption**

This is a random sample so observations should be independent.

✓ **Randomization Condition**

This sample was selected randomly from the matured policies sold by the sales representative of the company.

✓ **Nearly Normal Condition**

The distribution of profits is unimodal and fairly symmetric without strong skewness.

State the sampling distribution model for the statistic.

We will use a Student's t-model with $n - 1 = 30 - 1 = 29$ degrees of freedom and find a one-sample t-interval for the mean.

DO

Mechanics Compute basic statistics and construct the confidence interval.

Using software, we obtain the following basic statistics:

$$n = 30$$
$$\bar{y} = \$1438.90$$
$$s = \$1329.60$$

Remember that the standard error of the mean is equal to the standard deviation divided by the square root of *n*.

The critical value we need to make a 95% confidence interval comes from a Student's *t*-table, a computer program, or a calculator. We have 30 − 1 = 29 degrees of freedom. So we look up the corresponding *t** value in Table Z.

The standard error of the mean is:

$$SE(\bar{y}) = \frac{s}{\sqrt{n}} = \frac{1329.60}{\sqrt{30}} = \$242.75$$

There are 30 − 1 = 29 degrees of freedom. The manager has specified a 95% level of confidence, so the critical value (from Table T) is 2.045.

The margin of error is:

$$ME = 2.045 \times SE(\bar{y})$$
$$= 2.045 \times 242.75$$
$$= \$496.42$$

The 95% confidence interval for the mean profit is:

$$\$1438.90 \pm \$496.42$$
$$= (\$942.48, \$1935.32)$$

 REPORT

Conclusion Interpret the confidence interval in the proper context.

When we construct confidence intervals in this way, we expect 95% of them to cover the true mean and 5% to miss the true value. That's what "95% confident" means.

MEMO

Re: Profit from policies

From our analysis of the selected policies, we are 95% confident that the true mean profit of policies sold by this sales rep is contained in the interval from \$942.48 to \$1935.32.

Caveat: Insurance losses are notoriously subject to outliers. One very large loss could influence the average profit substantially. However, there were no such cases in this data set.

Cautions about Interpreting Confidence Intervals

Confidence intervals for means offer new, tempting, wrong interpretations. Here are some ways to keep from going astray:

- **Don't say,** "*95% of all the policies* sold by this sales rep have profits between \$942.48 and \$1935.32." The confidence interval is about the *mean*, not about the measurements of individual policies.
- **Don't say,** "We are 95% confident that *a randomly selected policy* will have a net profit between \$942.48 and \$1935.32." This false interpretation is also about individual policies rather than about the *mean* of the policies. We are 95% confident that the *mean* profit of all (similar) policies sold by this sales rep is between \$942.48 and \$1935.32.
- **Don't say,** "The mean profit is \$1438.90 *95% of the time*." That's about means, but still wrong. It implies that the true mean varies, when in fact it is the confidence interval that would have been different had we gotten a different sample.
- **Finally, don't say,** "*95% of all samples* will have mean profits between \$942.48 and \$1935.32." That statement suggests that *this* interval somehow sets a standard for every other interval. In fact, this interval is no more (or less) likely to be correct than any other. You could say that 95% of all possible samples would produce intervals that contain the true mean profit. (The problem is that because we'll never know what the true mean profit is, we can't know if our sample was one of those 95%.)

So, what *should* you say? Since 95% of random samples yield an interval that captures the true mean, you should say:

- "I am 95% confident that the interval from $942.48 to $1935.32 contains the mean profit of all policies sold by this sales representative." It's also okay to make this a little less formal by saying something like:
- "I am 95% confident that the mean profit for all policies sold by this sales rep is between $942.48 and $1935.32."

Remember: Your uncertainty is about the interval, not the true mean. The interval varies randomly. The true mean profit is neither variable nor random—just unknown.

JUST CHECKING

> 9 The alumni organization finds a confidence interval for the mean starting salary of their recent graduates to be ($55,000, $62,000). They release a statement to prospective students saying that 95% of them will earn between $55,000 and $62,000 their first year on the job. Why is this wrong?

11.7   Testing Hypotheses about Means—the One-Sample *t*-Test

The manager we met in the Guided Example above has a more specific concern. Company policy states that if a sales rep's mean profit is below $1500, the sales rep has been discounting too much and will have to adjust his pricing strategy. Is there evidence from this sample that the mean is really less than $1500? This question calls for a hypothesis test called the **one-sample *t*-test for the mean**.

When testing a hypothesis, it's natural to compare the difference between the observed statistic and a hypothesized value to the standard error. For means that looks like: $\dfrac{\bar{y} - \mu_0}{SE(\bar{y})}$. We already know that the appropriate probability model to use is Student's *t* with $n - 1$ degrees of freedom.

> **One-Sample *t*-Test for the Mean**
>
> The conditions for the one-sample *t*-test for the mean are the same as for the one-sample *t*-interval. We test the hypothesis $H_0: \mu = \mu_0$ using the statistic
>
> $$t_{n-1} = \frac{\bar{y} - \mu_0}{SE(\bar{y})},$$
>
> where the standard error of $\bar{y}$ is: $SE(\bar{y}) = \dfrac{s}{\sqrt{n}}$.
>
> When the conditions are met and the null hypothesis is true, this statistic follows a Student's *t*-model with $n - 1$ degrees of freedom. We use that model to obtain a P-value.

GUIDED EXAMPLE   Insurance Profits Revisited

Let's apply the one-sample *t*-test to the 30 mature policies sampled by the manager. From these 30 policies, the management would like to know if there's evidence that the mean profit of policies sold by this sales rep is less than $1500.

PLAN	**Setup** State what we want to know. Make clear what the population and parameter are. Identify the variables and context.	We want to test whether the mean profit of the sales rep's policies is less than $1500. We have a random sample of 30 mature policies from which to judge.

We want to test whether the mean profit of the sales rep's policies is less than $1500. We have a random sample of 30 mature policies from which to judge.

$$H_0: \mu = \$1500$$
$$H_A: \mu < \$1500$$

Setup State what we want to know. Make clear what the population and parameter are.

Identify the variables and context.

Hypotheses We give benefit of the doubt to the sales rep. The null hypothesis is that the true mean profit is equal to $1500. Because we're interested in whether the profit is less, the alternative is one-sided.

Make a graph. Check the distribution for skewness, multiple modes, and outliers.

We checked the histogram of these data in the previous Guided Example and saw that it had a unimodal, symmetric distribution.

Model Check the conditions.

We checked the Randomization and Nearly Normal Conditions in the previous Guided Example.

State the sampling distribution model.

The conditions are satisfied, so we'll use a Student's *t*-model with $n - 1 = 29$ degrees of freedom and a one-sample *t*-test for the mean.

Choose your method.

DO   **Mechanics** Compute the sample statistics. Be sure to include the units when you write down what you know from the data.

Using software, we obtain the following basic statistics:

$$n = 30$$
$$\text{Mean} = \$1438.90$$
$$s = \$1329.60$$
$$t = \frac{1438.90 - 1500}{1329.60/\sqrt{30}} = -0.2517$$

The *t*-statistic calculation is just a standardized value. We subtract the hypothesized mean and divide by the standard error.

We assume the null model is true to find the P-value. Make a picture of the *t*-model, centered at μ_0. Since this is a lower-tail test, shade the region to the left of the observed average profit.

(The observed mean is less than one standard error below the hypothesized value.)

(continued)

The P-value is the probability of observing a sample mean as small as $1438.90 (or smaller) *if* the true mean were $1500, as the null hypothesis states. We can find this P-value from a table, calculator, or computer program.

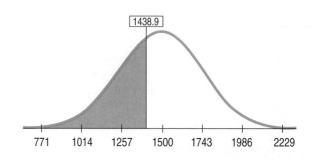

$$\text{P-value} = P(t_{29} < -0.2517) = 0.4015 \ (\text{or from a table } 0.1 < P)$$

REPORT

Conclusion Link the P-value to your decision about H_0, and state your conclusion in context.

MEMO

Re: Sales performance

The mean profit on 30 sampled contracts closed by the sales rep in question has fallen below our standard of $1500, but there is not enough evidence in this sample of policies to indicate that the true mean is below $1500. If the mean were $1500, we would expect a sample of size 30 to have a mean this low about 40.15% of the time.

Notice that the way this hypothesis was set up, the sales rep's mean profit would have to be well below $1500 to reject the null hypothesis. Because the null hypothesis was that the mean was $1500 and the alternative was that it was less, this setup gave some benefit of the doubt to the sales rep. There's nothing intrinsically wrong with that, but keep in mind that it's always a good idea to make sure that the hypotheses are stated in ways that will guide you to make the right business decision.

FOR EXAMPLE   Testing a mean

Summit Projects is a full-service interactive agency based in Hood River, Oregon, that offers companies a variety of website services. Summit recently redesigned a client company's website and wants to show that sales have increased. An analyst selects 58 sales records at random from the client's 2000 access logs and she finds a mean amount spent of $26.05 with a standard deviation of $10.20.

QUESTION   Test the hypothesis that the mean is $24.85 (as it was before the redesign) against the alternative that it has increased.

ANSWER   We can write: $H_0: \mu = \$24.85$ *vs.* $H_A: \mu > \$24.85$. Then

$$t = \frac{(26.05 - 24.85)}{10.2/\sqrt{58}} = 0.896.$$

Because the alternative is *one-sided*, we find $P(t > 0.896)$ with 57 degrees of freedom. From technology, $P(t > 0.896) = 0.1870$, a large P-value. This would not be a surprising value if the hypothesized mean of $24.85 were the true value. Therefore we *fail to reject* the null hypothesis and conclude that there is not sufficient evidence to suggest that the mean has increased from 24.85. Had we used a two-sided alternative, the P-value would have been twice 0.1870 or 0.3740.

Brief Case

Real Estate

A real estate agent is trying to understand the pricing of homes in her area, a region comprised of small to midsize towns and a small city. For each of 1200 homes recently sold in the region, the file **Real Estate sample 1200** holds the following variables:

- *Sale Price* (in $)
- *Lot size* (size of the lot in acres)
- *Waterfront* (Yes, No)
- *Age* (in years)
- *Central Air* (Yes, No)
- *Fuel Type* (Wood, Oil, Gas, Electric, Propane, Solar, Other)
- *Condition* (1 to 5, 1 = Poor, 5 = Excellent)
- *Living Area* (living area in square feet)
- *Pct College* (% in ZIP code who attend a four-year college)
- *Full Baths* (number of full bathrooms)
- *Half Baths* (number of half bathrooms)
- *Bedrooms* (number of bedrooms)
- *Fireplace* (Yes, No)

The agent has a family interested in a four-bedroom house. Using confidence intervals, how should she advise the family on what the average price of a four-bedroom house might be in this area? Compare that to a confidence interval for two-bedroom homes. How much more, on average, does a house that has central air conditioning sell for? Restrict your attention to two-bedroom houses and answer the question again. What about four-bedroom houses? Repeat this investigation for houses with and without fireplaces. What cautions might you give the agent before coming to any overall conclusions?

Explore other questions that might be useful for the real estate agent in knowing how different categorical factors affect the sale price and write up a short report on your findings.

Donor Profiles

A philanthropic organization collects and buys data on their donor base. The full database contains about 4.5 million donors and over 400 variables collected on each, but the data set **Donor Profiles** is a sample of 916 donors and includes the variables:

- *Age* (in years)
- *Homeowner* (H = Yes, U = Unknown)
- *Gender* (F = Female, M = Male, U = Unknown)
- *Wealth* (Ordered categories of total household wealth from 1 = Lowest to 9 = Highest)
- *Children* (Number of children)
- *Donated Last* (0 = Did not donate to last campaign, 1 = Did donate to last campaign)
- *Amt Donated Last* ($ amount of contribution to last campaign)

The analysts at the organization want to know how much people donate on average to campaigns, and what factors might influence that amount. Compare the confidence intervals for the mean *Amt Donated Last* by those known to own

(*continued*)

their homes with those whose homeowner status is unknown. Perform similar comparisons for *Gender* and two of the *Wealth* categories. Write up a short report using graphics and confidence intervals for what you have found. (Be careful not to make inferences directly about the differences between groups. We'll discuss that in Chapter 13. Your inference should be about single groups.)

(The distribution of *Amt Donated Last* is highly skewed to the right, and so the median might be thought to be the appropriate summary. But the median is $0.00 so the analysts must use the mean. From simulations, they have ascertained that the sampling distribution for the mean is unimodal and symmetric for samples larger than 250 or so. Note that small differences in the mean could result in millions of dollars of added revenue nationwide. The average cost of their solicitation is $0.67 per person to produce and mail.)

EXERCISES

SECTION 11.1

1. Games for the iPad have a distribution of prices that is skewed to the high end.

a) Explain why this is what you would expect.
b) Members of the iPad gamers club each own about 50 games. Pat is one such member. What would you expect the shape of the distribution of game prices on her iPad to be?
c) Each club member computes the average price of his or her games. What shape would you expect the distribution of these averages to have?

2. For a sample of 36 houses, what would you expect the distribution of the sale prices to be? A real-estate agent has been assigned 10 houses at random to sell this month. She wants to know whether the mean price of those houses is typical. What, if anything, does she need to assume about the distribution of prices to be able to use the Central Limit Theorem? Are those assumptions reasonable?

3. According to the Gallup Poll, 27% of U.S. adults have high levels of cholesterol. Gallup reports that such elevated levels "could be financially devastating to the U.S. health-care system" and are a major concern to health insurance providers. According to recent studies, cholesterol levels in healthy U.S. adults average about 215 mg/dL with a standard deviation of about 30 mg/dL and are roughly Normally distributed. If the cholesterol levels of a sample of 42 healthy U.S. adults is taken,

a) What shape should the sampling distribution of the mean have?
b) What would the mean of the sampling distribution be?
c) What would its standard deviation be?
d) If the sample size were increased to 100, how would your answers to parts a–c change?

4. As in Exercise 3, cholesterol levels in healthy U.S. adults average about 215 mg/dL with a standard deviation of about 30 mg/dL and are roughly Normally distributed. If the cholesterol levels of a sample of 42 healthy US adults is taken, what is the probability that the mean cholesterol level of the sample

a) Will be no more than 215?
b) Will be between 205 and 225?
c) Will be less than 200?
d) Will be greater than 220?

SECTION 11.3

5. Organizers of a fishing tournament believe that the lake holds a sizable population of largemouth bass. They assume that the weights of these fish have a model that is skewed to the right with a mean of 3.5 pounds and a standard deviation of 2.32 pounds.

a) Explain why a skewed model makes sense here.
b) Explain why you cannot use a Normal model to determine the probability that a largemouth bass randomly selected ("caught") from the lake weighs over 3 pounds.
c) Each contestant catches 5 fish each day. Can you determine the probability that someone's catch averages over 3 pounds? Explain.
d) The 12 contestants competing each caught the limit of 5 fish. What's the standard deviation of the mean weight of the 60 fish caught?
e) Would you be surprised if the mean weight of the 60 fish caught in the competition was more than 4.5 pounds? Use the 68–95–99.7 Rule.

6. In 2008 and 2009, Systemax bought two failing electronics stores, Circuit City and CompUSA. They have kept both the names active and customers can purchase products from either website. If they take a random sample of a mixture of recent purchases from the two websites, the distribution of the amounts purchased will be bimodal.

a) As their sample size increases, what's the expected shape of the distribution of amounts purchased in the sample?
b) As the sample size increases, what's the expected shape of the sampling model for the mean amount purchased of the sample?

SECTION 11.4

7. A survey of 25 randomly selected customers found the following ages (in years):

20	32	34	29	30
30	30	14	29	11
38	22	44	48	26
25	22	32	35	32
35	42	44	44	48

The mean was 31.84 years and the standard deviation was 9.84 years.

a) What is the standard error of the mean?
b) How would the standard error change if the sample size had been 100 instead of 25? (Assume that the sample standard deviation didn't change.)

8. A random sample of 20 purchases showed the following amounts (in $):

39.05	2.73	32.92	47.51
37.91	34.35	64.48	51.96
56.95	81.58	47.80	11.72
21.57	40.83	38.24	32.98
75.16	74.30	47.54	65.62

The mean was $45.26 and the standard deviation was $20.67.

a) What is the standard error of the mean?
b) How would the standard error change if the sample size had been 5 instead of 20? (Assume that the sample standard deviation didn't change.)

9. For the data in Exercise 7:

a) How many degrees of freedom does the *t*-statistic have?
b) How many degrees of freedom would the *t*-statistic have if the sample size had been 100?

10. For the data in Exercise 8:

a) How many degrees of freedom does the *t*-statistic have?
b) How many degrees of freedom would the *t*-statistic have if the sample size had been 5?

SECTION 11.5

11. Find the critical value *t** for:

a) a 95% confidence interval based on 24 df.
b) a 95% confidence interval based on 99 df.

12. Find the critical value *t** for:

a) a 90% confidence interval based on 19 df.
b) a 90% confidence interval based on 4 df.

13. For the ages in Exercise 7:

a) Construct a 95% confidence interval for the mean age of all customers, assuming that the assumptions and conditions for the confidence interval have been met.
b) How large is the margin of error?
c) How would the confidence interval change if you had assumed that the standard deviation was known to be 10.0 years?

14. For the purchase amounts in Exercise 8:

a) Construct a 90% confidence interval for the mean purchases of all customers, assuming that the assumptions and conditions for the confidence interval have been met.
b) How large is the margin of error?
c) How would the confidence interval change if you had assumed that the standard deviation was known to be $20?

SECTION 11.6

15. For the confidence intervals of Exercise 13, a histogram of the data looks like this:

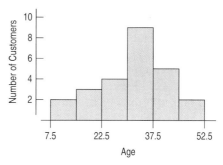

Check the assumptions and conditions for your inference.

16. For the confidence intervals of Exercise 14, a histogram of the data looks like this:

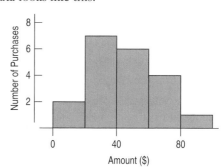

Check the assumptions and conditions for your inference.

SECTION 11.7

17. The owner of the store from Exercise 7 wants to know if the mean age of all customers is 25 years old.

a) What is the null hypothesis?
b) Is the alternative one- or two-sided?
c) What is the value of the test statistic?
d) What is the P-value of the test statistic?
e) What do you conclude at alpha = 0.05?

18. The analyst in Exercise 8 wants to know if the mean purchase amount of all transactions is at least $40.

a) What is the null hypothesis?
b) Is the alternative one- or two-sided?
c) What is the value of the test statistic?
d) What is the P-value of the test statistic?
e) What do you conclude at alpha = 0.05?

19. For the confidence interval in Exercise 13:

a) How large would the sample size have to be to cut the margin of error in half?
b) About how large would the sample size have to be to cut the margin of error by a factor of 10?

20. For the confidence interval in Exercise 14 part a:

a) To reduce the margin of error to about $4, how large would the sample size have to be?
b) How large would the sample size have to be to reduce the margin of error to $0.80?

CHAPTER EXERCISES

21. *t-*models. Using the *t*-tables, software, or a calculator, estimate:

a) the critical value of *t* for a 90% confidence interval with df = 17.
b) the critical value of *t* for a 98% confidence interval with df = 88.

22. *t-*models, part 2. Using the *t* tables, software, or a calculator, estimate:

a) the critical value of *t* for a 95% confidence interval with df = 7.
b) the critical value of *t* for a 99% confidence interval with df = 102.

23. Confidence intervals. Describe how the width of a 95% confidence interval for a mean changes as the standard deviation (*s*) of a sample increases, assuming sample size remains the same.

24. Confidence intervals, part 2. Describe how the width of a 95% confidence interval for a mean changes as the sample size (*n*) increases, assuming the standard deviation remains the same.

25. Confidence intervals and sample size. A confidence interval for the price of gasoline from a random sample of 30 gas stations in a region gives the following statistics:

$$\bar{y} = \$4.49 \quad s = \$0.29$$

a) Find a 95% confidence interval for the mean price of regular gasoline in that region.
b) Find the 90% confidence interval for the mean.
c) If we had the same statistics from a sample of 60 stations, what would the 95% confidence interval be now?

26. Confidence intervals and sample size, part 2. A confidence interval for the price of gasoline from a random sample of 30 gas stations in a region gives the following statistics:

$$\bar{y} = \$4.49 \quad SE(\bar{y}) = \$0.06$$

a) Find a 95% confidence interval for the mean price of regular gasoline in that region.
b) Find the 90% confidence interval for the mean.
c) If we had the same statistics from a sample of 60 stations, what would the 95% confidence interval be now?

27. Marketing livestock feed. A feed supply company has developed a special feed supplement to see if it will promote weight gain in livestock. Their researchers report that the 77 cows studied gained an average of 56 pounds and that a 95% confidence interval for the mean weight gain this supplement produces has a margin of error of ± 11 pounds. Staff in their marketing department wrote the following conclusions. Did anyone interpret the interval correctly? Explain any misinterpretations.

a) 95% of the cows studied gained between 45 and 67 pounds.
b) We're 95% sure that a cow fed this supplement will gain between 45 and 67 pounds.
c) We're 95% sure that the average weight gain among the cows in this study was between 45 and 67 pounds.
d) The average weight gain of cows fed this supplement is between 45 and 67 pounds 95% of the time.
e) If this supplement is tested on another sample of cows, there is a 95% chance that their average weight gain will be between 45 and 67 pounds.

28. Meal costs. A company is interested in estimating the costs of lunch in their cafeteria. After surveying employees, the staff calculated that a 95% confidence interval for the mean amount of money spent for lunch over a period of six months is ($780, $920). Now the organization is trying to write its report and considering the following interpretations. Comment on each.

a) 95% of all employees pay between $780 and $920 for lunch.
b) 95% of the sampled employees paid between $780 and $920 for lunch.
c) We're 95% sure that employees in this sample averaged between $780 and $920 for lunch.

✓ **Randomization Condition:** No randomization was applied, but we are considering these riders involved in accidents to be a representative sample of all riders. We should take care in generalizing our conclusions.

✓ **10% Condition:** These 781 riders are a small sample of a larger population of all young motorcycle riders.

✓ **Success/Failure Condition:** We'd expect $np = 781(0.6) = 468.6$ helmeted riders and $nq = 781(0.4) = 312.4$ non-helmeted. Both are at least 10.

Specify the sampling distribution model and name the test.

The conditions are satisfied, so I can use a Normal model and perform a **one-proportion z-test.**

DO **Mechanics** Find the standard deviation of the sampling model using the hypothesized proportion.

There were 396 helmet wearers among the 781 accident victims.

$$\hat{p} = \frac{396}{781} = 0.507$$

$$SD(\hat{p}) = \sqrt{\frac{p_0 q_0}{n}} = \sqrt{\frac{(0.60)(0.40)}{781}} = 0.0175$$

Find the z-score for the observed proportion.

$$z = \frac{\hat{p} - p_0}{SD(\hat{p})} = \frac{0.507 - 0.60}{0.0175} = -5.31$$

Make a picture. Sketch a Normal model centered at the hypothesized helmet rate of 60%. This is a lower-tail test, so shade the region to the left of the observed rate.

Given this z-score, the P-value is obviously very low.

The observed helmet rate is 5.31 standard deviations below the former rate. The corresponding P-value is less than 0.001.

Find a confidence interval for the proportion.

A 95% confidence interval for the true rate is:

$$\hat{p} \pm z^* \sqrt{\frac{\hat{p}\hat{q}}{n}} = 0.507 \pm 1.96(0.0179) = (0.472, 0.542)$$

REPORT **Conclusion** Link the P-value to your decision about the null hypothesis, and then state your conclusion in context.

MEMO

Re: Helmet compliance rate

The very small P-value says that if the true rate of helmet-wearing among riders under 21 were still 60%, the probability of observing a rate no higher than 50.7% in a sample like this is less than 1 chance in 1000, so I reject the null hypothesis. There is strong evidence that there has been a decline in helmet use among riders under 21. For prediction purposes, a 95% confidence interval for the true compliance rate of under 21 riders is from 47.2% to 54.2%.

There is strong evidence that the rate is no longer 60%, but the small P-value by itself says nothing about how much lower the rate might be. The confidence interval provides that information; the rate seems to be closer to 50% now. Whether a change from 60% to 50% makes an important difference in safety is a judgment that depends on the situation, but not on the P-value. Not coincidentally, on July 1, 2008, Florida required a motorcycle "endorsement" for all motorcycle riders. For riders under 21, that requires a motorcycle safety course. Although only about 70% of motorcycle riders are endorsed, the percentage of unendorsed riders involved in crashes dropped considerably after 2008.[3]

FOR EXAMPLE   Thinking about the P-Value

Many medications have side effects, some of them serious. During a clinical trial, pharmaceutical companies watch for serious side effects and are obligated to report such findings to the U.S. Food and Drug Administration (FDA). The diabetes drug Avandia was approved to treat Type 2 diabetes in 1999. But a 2007 article in the *New England Journal of Medicine* (NEJM) raised concerns that the drug might carry an increased risk of heart attack. The article's author, Dr. Steven E. Nissen, reported that the seven-year risk of heart attack in diabetes patients taking the drug Avandia was increased from the baseline of 20.2% to an estimated risk of 28.9% and said the P-value was 0.03.

QUESTION   Treating 0.202 as p_0, how should the P-value be interpreted in this context?

ANSWER   The P-value $= P(\hat{p} \geq 28.9\% \,|\, p = 20.2\%)$. That is, it's the probability of seeing such a high heart attack rate among the people studied if, in fact, taking Avandia really didn't increase the risk at all.

What to Do with a High P-Value

Insurance companies constantly evaluate medical procedures to make sure their cost is justified. One controversial therapy is therapeutic (or healing) touch (TT), which is taught in many schools of nursing. In therapy, the practitioner moves her hands near, but does not touch, a patient in an attempt to manipulate a "human energy field." Therapeutic touch practitioners believe that by adjusting this field they can promote healing. However, no instrument has ever detected a human energy field, and no experiment has ever shown that TT practitioners can detect such a field.

In 1998, the *Journal of the American Medical Association* published a paper reporting work by a then nine-year-old girl.[4] She had performed a simple experiment in which she challenged 15 TT practitioners to detect whether her unseen hand was hovering over their left or right hand (selected by the flip of a coin).

The practitioners "warmed up" with a period during which they could see the experimenter's hand, and each said that they could detect the girl's human energy field. Then a screen was placed so that the practitioners could not see the girl's hand, and they attempted 10 trials each. Overall, of 150 trials, the TT practitioners were successful only 70 times—a success proportion of 46.7%.

---

[3] www.ridesmartflorida.com
[4] L. Rosa, E. Rosa, L. Sarner, and S. Barrett, "A Close Look at Therapeutic Touch," *JAMA* 279(13) [1 April 1998]: 1005–1010.

The null hypothesis here is that the TT practitioners were just guessing. If that were the case, since the hand was chosen using a coin flip, the practitioners would guess correctly 50% of the time. So the null hypothesis is that $p = 0.5$ and the alternative that they could actually detect a human energy field is (one-sided) $p > 0.5$.

What would constitute evidence that they weren't guessing? Certainly, a very high proportion of correct guesses out of 150 would convince most people. Exactly how high the proportion of correct guesses has to be for you to reject the null hypothesis depends on how small a P-value you need to be convinced (which, in turn, depends on how often you're willing to make mistakes—a topic we'll discuss later in the chapter).

But let's look again at the TT practitioners' proportion. Does it provide any evidence that they weren't guessing? The proportion of correct guesses is 46.7%—that's *less* than the hypothesized value, not greater! When we find $SD(\hat{p}) = 0.041$ (or 4.1%) we can see that 46.7% is almost 1 SD *below* the hypothesized proportion:

$$SD(\hat{p}) = \sqrt{\frac{p_0 q_0}{n}} = \sqrt{\frac{(0.5)(0.5)}{150}} \approx 0.041$$

The observed proportion, $\hat{p}$, is 0.467.

$$z = \frac{\hat{p} - p_0}{SD(\hat{p})} = \frac{0.467 - 0.5}{0.041} = -0.805$$

The observed success rate is 0.805 standard deviations below the hypothesized mean.

$$P = P(z > -0.805) = 0.790$$

If the practitioners had been highly successful, the researchers would have seen a low P-value and would have concluded that they could actually detect a human energy field.

But that's not what happened. What they observed was a $\hat{p} = 0.467$ success rate. The P-value for this proportion is greater than 0.5 because the observed value is on the "wrong" side of the null hypothesis value. Wrong, that is, if you wanted to find evidence against the null hypothesis. To convince anyone that they can detect a human energy field, the practitioners should be doing better than guessing, not worse!

Obviously, the null hypothesis won't be rejected with a large P-value; to reject it, the P-value would have to be quite small. But a P-value of 0.790 seems so big it is almost strange. In fact, for a one-sided test, any time the test statistic is on the "wrong" side of the hypothesis, we know immediately that the P-value is at least 0.50 and we know that we have no evidence to reject the null hypothesis.

Big P-values just mean that what we've observed isn't surprising. That is, the results are in line with our assumption that the null hypothesis models the world, so we have no reason to reject it. A big P-value doesn't prove that the null hypothesis is true, but it certainly offers no evidence that it's *not* true. When we see a large P-value, all we can say is that we "don't reject the null hypothesis."

FOR EXAMPLE More about P-Values

RECAP The question of whether the diabetes drug Avandia increased the risk of heart attack was raised by a study in the *New England Journal of Medicine*. This study estimated the seven-year risk of heart attack to be 28.9% and reported a P-value of 0.03 for a test of whether this risk was higher than the baseline seven-year risk of 20.2%. An earlier study (the ADOPT study) had estimated the seven-year risk to be 26.9% and reported a P-value of 0.27.

QUESTION Why did the researchers in the ADOPT study not express alarm about the increased risk they had seen?

ANSWER A P-value of 0.27 means that a heart attack rate at least as high as the one they observed could be expected in 27% of similar experiments even if, in fact, there were no increased risk from taking Avandia. That's not remarkable enough to reject the null hypothesis. In other words, the ADOPT study wasn't convincing.

12.2   Alpha Levels and Significance

Sometimes we need to make a firm decision about whether or not to reject the null hypothesis. A jury must *decide* whether the evidence reaches the level of "beyond a reasonable doubt." A business must *select* a Web design. You need to decide which section of a Statistics course to enroll in.

When the P-value is small, it tells us that our data are rare *given the null hypothesis*. As humans, we are suspicious of rare events. If the data are "rare enough," we just don't think that could have happened due to chance. Since the data *did* happen, something must be wrong. All we can do now is to reject the null hypothesis.

But how rare is "rare"? How low does the P-value have to be?

We can define "rare event" arbitrarily by setting a threshold for our P-value as we saw in Chapter 10. If our P-value falls below that point, we'll reject the null hypothesis. We call such results *statistically significant*. The threshold is called an **alpha level**. Not surprisingly, it's labeled with the Greek letter α. Common α-levels are 0.10, 0.05, 0.01, and 0.001. You have the option—almost the *obligation*—to consider your alpha level carefully and choose an appropriate one for the situation. If you're assessing the safety of air bags, you'll want a low alpha level; even 0.01 might not be low enough. If you're just wondering whether folks prefer their pizza with or without pepperoni, you might be happy with $\alpha = 0.10$. It can be hard to justify your choice of α, though, so often we arbitrarily choose 0.05.

Sir Ronald Fisher (1890–1962) was one of the founders of modern Statistics.

Where Did the Value 0.05 Come From?

In 1931, in a famous book called *The Design of Experiments*, Sir Ronald Fisher discussed the amount of evidence needed to reject a null hypothesis. He said that it was *situation dependent*, but remarked, somewhat casually, that for many scientific applications, 1 out of 20 *might be* a reasonable value, especially in a *first* experiment—one that will be followed by confirmation. Since then, some people—indeed some entire disciplines—have acted as if the number 0.05 were sacrosanct.

NOTATION ALERT

The first Greek letter, α, is used in Statistics for the threshold value of a hypothesis test. You'll hear it referred to as the alpha level. Common values are 0.10, 0.05, 0.01, and 0.001.

The alpha level is also called the **significance level**. When we reject the null hypothesis, we say that the test is "significant at that level." For example, we might say that we reject the null hypothesis "at the 5% level of significance." You must select the alpha level *before* you look at the data. Otherwise you can be accused of finagling the conclusions by tuning the alpha level to the results after you've seen the data.

What can you say if the P-value does not fall below α? When you have not found sufficient evidence to reject the null according to the standard you have established, you should say: "The data have failed to provide sufficient evidence to reject the null hypothesis." Don't say: "We accept the null hypothesis." You certainly haven't proven or established the null hypothesis; it was assumed to begin with. You *could* say that you have *retained* the null hypothesis, but it's better to say that you've failed to reject it.

> **It Could Happen to You!**
>
> Of course, if the null hypothesis is true, no matter what alpha level you choose, you still have a probability α of rejecting the null hypothesis by mistake. When we do reject the null hypothesis, no one ever thinks that *this* is one of those rare times. As statistician Stu Hunter notes, "The statistician says 'rare events do happen—but not to me!'"

> **Conclusion**
>
> If the P-value $< \alpha$, then reject H_0.
>
> If the P-value $\geq \alpha$, then fail to reject H_0.

Look again at the home field advantage example in Chapter 10. The P-value was <0.001. This is so much smaller than any reasonable alpha level that we can reject H_0. We concluded: "We reject the null hypothesis. There is sufficient evidence to conclude that there is a home field advantage over and above what we expect with random variation." On the other hand, when testing the success rate in the therapeutic touch example, the P-value was 0.790, a very high P-value. In this case we can say only that we have failed to reject the null hypothesis that $p = 0.50$. We certainly can't say that we've proved it, or even that we've accepted it.

The automatic nature of the reject/fail-to-reject decision when we use an alpha level may make you uncomfortable. If your P-value falls just slightly above your alpha level, you're not allowed to reject the null. Yet a P-value just barely below the alpha level leads to rejection. If this bothers you, you're in good company. Many statisticians think it better to report the P-value than to choose an alpha level and carry the decision through to a final reject/fail-to-reject verdict. So when you declare your decision, it's always a good idea to report the P-value as an indication of the strength of the evidence.

> **Practical vs. Statistical Significance**
>
> A large insurance company mined its data and found a statistically significant ($P = 0.04$) difference between the mean value of policies sold in 2001 and those sold in 2002. The difference in the mean values was $0.98. Even though it was statistically significant, management did not see this as an important difference when a typical policy sold for more than $1000. On the other hand, a marketable improvement of 10% in relief rate for a new pain medicine may not be statistically significant unless a large number of people are tested. The effect, which is economically significant, might not be statistically significant. So, always think carefully about the practical consequences of a hypothesis test conclusion.

> **It's in the Stars**
>
> Some disciplines carry the idea further and code P-values by their size. In this scheme, a P-value between 0.05 and 0.01 gets highlighted by a single asterisk (*). A P-value between 0.01 and 0.001 gets two asterisks (**), and a P-value less than 0.001 gets three (***). This can be a convenient summary of the weight of evidence against the null hypothesis, but it isn't wise to take the distinctions too seriously and make black-and-white decisions near the boundaries. The boundaries are a matter of tradition, not science; there is nothing special about 0.05. A P-value of 0.051 should be looked at seriously and not casually thrown away just because it's larger than 0.05, and one that's 0.009 is not very different from one that's 0.011.

Sometimes it's best to report that the conclusion is not yet clear and to suggest that more data be gathered. (In a trial, a jury may "hang" and be unable to return a verdict.) In such cases, it's an especially good idea to report the P-value, since it's the best summary we have of what the data say or fail to say about the null hypothesis.

What do we mean when we say that a test is statistically significant? All we mean is that the test statistic had a P-value lower than our alpha level. Don't be lulled into thinking that "statistical significance" necessarily carries with it any practical importance or impact.

For large samples, even small, unimportant ("insignificant") deviations from the null hypothesis can be statistically significant. On the other hand, if the sample is not large enough, even large, financially or scientifically important differences may not be statistically significant.

When you report your decision about the null hypothesis, it's good practice to report the effect size (the magnitude of the difference between the observed statistic value and the null hypothesis value in the data units) along with the P-value.

FOR EXAMPLE   Setting the α level

Summit Projects is a full-service interactive agency, based in Hood River, Oregon, that offers companies a variety of website services. One of Summit's clients is SmartWool®, which produces and sells wool apparel including the famous SmartWool socks. Summit recently redesigned SmartWool's apparel website and claimed that they increased both the proportion of visits resulting in sales and the average amount spent on the site.

QUESTION   Suppose that an analyst at SmartWool wanted to test if the proportion of visits resulting in a sale from the new website has changed from the 0.20 it was historically. Suppose she also wants to know if the mean sale has increased from the average $24.85 that it was with the old site. To do that she collects a representative sample of 200 visits since the new website went online and finds that the sample proportion is 0.29 with a P-value of 0.00146. From the 58 sales in the sample, she finds that they spent $26.05 on average with a standard deviation of $10.20 for a P-value of 0.1870. What conclusions can she draw if she uses an α level of 0.05?

ANSWER   Using $\alpha = 0.05$, we reject the null hypothesis when the P-value is less than 0.05 and fail to reject when the P-value is greater than or equal to 0.05. For the test of proportion, $P = 0.00146$, which is much less than 0.05 and so we reject the null hypothesis and conclude that the proportion of visits resulting in sales has changed. For the test of means, the P-value is 0.1870, which is greater than 0.05, so we fail to reject the null hypothesis and conclude that there is not enough evidence to say that the mean amount spent has increased.

12.3   Critical Values

When building a confidence interval, we calculated the margin of error as the product of an estimated standard error for the statistic and a critical value. For proportions, we found a **critical value**, z^*, to correspond to our selected confidence level. For means, we found the critical value t^* based on both the confidence level and the degrees of freedom. Critical values can also be used as a shortcut for hypothesis tests. Before computers and calculators were common, P-values were hard to find. It was easier to select a few common alpha levels (0.05, 0.01, 0.001, for example) and learn the corresponding critical values for the Normal model (that is, the critical values corresponding to confidence levels 0.95, 0.99, and 0.999, respectively). Rather than find the probability that corresponded to your observed statistic, you'd just calculate how many standard deviations it was away from the hypothesized value and compare that value directly against these z^* values. (Remember that whenever we measure the distance of a value from the mean in standard deviations, we are finding a z-score.) Any z-score larger in magnitude (that is, more extreme) than a particular critical value has to be less likely, so it will have a P-value smaller than the corresponding alpha.

If we were willing to settle for a flat reject/fail-to-reject decision, comparing an observed z-score with the critical value for a specified alpha level would give a shortcut path to that decision. For the home field advantage example, if we choose $\alpha = 0.05$, then in order to reject H_0, our z-score has to be larger than the one-sided critical value of 1.645. The observed proportion was 4.74 standard deviations above 0.5, so we clearly reject the null hypothesis. This is perfectly correct and does give us a yes/no decision, but it gives us less information about the hypothesis because we don't have the P-value to think about. With technology, P-values are

> **Quick Decisions**
>
> If you need to make a decision on the fly with no technology, remember "2." That's our old friend from the 68–95–99.7 Rule. It's roughly the critical value for testing a hypothesis against a two-sided alternative at $\alpha = 0.05$ using z. In fact, it's just about the t^* critical value with 60 degrees of freedom. The exact critical value for z^* is 1.96, but 2 is close enough for most decisions.

easy to find. And since they give more information about the strength of the evidence, you should report them.

Here are the traditional z^* critical values from the Normal model[5]:

α	1-sided	2-sided
0.05	1.645	1.96
0.01	2.33	2.576
0.001	3.09	3.29

Figure 12.1 When the alternative is one-sided, the critical value puts all of α on one side.

Figure 12.2 When the alternative is two-sided, the critical value splits α equally into two tails.

When testing means, you'll need to know both the α level and the degrees of freedom to find the t^* critical value. With large n, the t^* critical values will be close to the z^* critical values (above) that you use for testing proportions.

FOR EXAMPLE Testing using critical values

QUESTION The analyst at SmartWool (see page 376) finds that the z-value for the sample proportion is 3.182 and the t-value for the sample mean amount sold is 0.896. Using $\alpha = 0.05$, show that the same decisions would have been made using critical values.

ANSWER For the test of proportions, the critical z values at $\alpha = 0.05$ are ± 1.96. Because the z value was 3.182, much larger than 1.96, we reject the null hypothesis.

For the one-sided test of means, with $n = 58$, the critical t value at $\alpha = 0.05$ is 1.676 (using df $= 50$ from a table) or 1.672 (using df $= 57$ from technology). In either case, the t-value of 0.896 is smaller than the critical value, so we fail to reject the null hypothesis, as before.

12.4 Confidence Intervals and Hypothesis Tests

NOTATION ALERT

We've attached symbols to many of the p's. Let's keep them straight.

p is a population parameter—the true proportion in the population.

p_0 is a hypothesized value of p.

$\hat{p}$ is an observed proportion.

p^* is a critical value of a proportion corresponding to a specified α (see page 383).

Confidence intervals and hypothesis tests are built from the same calculations. They have the same assumptions and conditions. You can approximate a hypothesis test by examining the confidence interval. Just ask whether the null hypothesis value is consistent with a confidence interval for the parameter at the corresponding confidence level. Because confidence intervals are naturally two-sided, they correspond to two-sided tests. For example, a 95% confidence interval corresponds

---

[5]In a sense, these are the flip side of the 68–95–99.7 Rule. There we chose simple statistical distances from the mean and recalled the areas of the tails. Here we select convenient tail areas (0.05, 0.01, and 0.001, either on one side or adding both together), and record the corresponding statistical distances.

A Technical Note

For means, you can test a hypothesis by seeing if the null value falls in the appropriate confidence interval. However, for proportions, this isn't *exactly* true. For a confidence interval, we estimate the standard deviation of $\hat{p}$ from $\hat{p}$ itself, making it a *standard error*. For the corresponding hypothesis test, we use the model's *standard deviation* for $\hat{p}$ based on the null hypothesis value p_0. When $\hat{p}$ and p_0 are close, these calculations give similar results. When they differ, you're likely to reject H_0 (because the observed proportion is far from your hypothesized value). In that case, you're better off building your confidence interval with a standard error estimated from the data rather than rely on the model you just rejected.

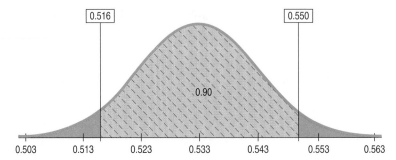

Figure 12.3   The 90% confidence interval is symmetric and leaves 5% on each side. Because the hypothesized value of 0.50 is not a plausible value, we can reject the null hypothesis at $\alpha = 0.05$.

to a two-sided hypothesis test at $\alpha = 5\%$. In general, a confidence interval with a confidence level of $C\%$ corresponds to a two-sided hypothesis test with an α level of $100 - C\%$.

If you are performing a one-sided test at level 0.05, you leave 5% on one side of the null hypothesis. The critical value will then match up with a 90% confidence interval, since that interval leaves 5% on *each* side. Figure 12.3 shows an example. A 90% confidence for the home field advantage is (0.516, 0.550). This contains the plausible values of the true proportion of wins by a home team. Since 0.50 is *not* in the interval, and all values are above 0.05, we can reject the null hypothesis at $\alpha = 0.05$. We use a 90% confidence interval because we wanted a one-sided conclusion.

JUST CHECKING

1 A bank is testing a new method for getting delinquent customers to pay their past-due credit card bills. The standard way was to send a letter (costing about $0.60 each) asking the customer to pay. That worked 30% of the time. The bank wants to test a new method that involves sending a DVD to the customer encouraging them to contact the bank and set up a payment plan. Developing and sending the DVD costs about $10.00 per customer. What is the parameter of interest? What are the null and alternative hypotheses?

2 The bank sets up an experiment to test the effectiveness of the DVD. The DVD is mailed to several randomly selected delinquent customers, and employees keep track of how many customers then contact the bank to arrange payments. The bank just got back the results on their test of the DVD strategy.

A 90% confidence interval for the success rate is (0.29, 0.45). Their old send-a-letter method had worked 30% of the time. Can you reject the null hypothesis and conclude that the method increases the proportion at $\alpha = 0.05$? Explain.

3 Given the confidence interval the bank found in the trial of the DVD mailing, what would you recommend be done? Should the bank scrap the DVD strategy?

4 The mileage rewards program at a major airline company has just completed a test market of a new arrangement with a hotel partner to try to increase engagement of valued customers with the program. The cost to the rewards program of the hotel offer is $35.00 per customer. From the test market, a 95% confidence interval for the revenue generated is ($37.95, $55.05). What does that say about the viability of the new arrangement?

GUIDED EXAMPLE   Credit Card Promotion

The credit card company we met on page 314 wanted to test whether at least 25% of their customers charged $500 or more.

Among the 500 customers, 148 or 29.6% of them charged $500 or more. Instead of a hypothesis test, let's use a confidence interval to test whether the goal of 25% for all customers was met.

PLAN	**Setup** State the problem and discuss the variables and the context.	We want to know whether 25% or more of the customers will spend $500 or more in the next month and qualify for the special program. We will use the data from the same month a year ago to estimate the proportion and see whether the proportion was at least 25%.

Hypotheses The null hypothesis is that the proportion qualifying is 25%. The alternative is that it is higher. It's a one-sided test, so if we use a confidence interval, we'll have to be careful about what level we use.

The statistic is $\hat{p} = 0.296$, the proportion of customers who charged $500 or more.

$$H_0: p = 0.25$$
$$H_A: p > 0.25$$

Model Check the conditions. (Because this is a confidence interval, we use the observed successes and failures to check the Success/Failure condition.)

✓ **Independence Assumption.** Customers are not likely to influence one another when it comes to spending on their credit cards.

✓ **Randomization Condition.** This is a random sample from the company's database.

✓ **10% Condition.** The sample is less than 10% of all customers.

State your method. Here we are using a confidence interval to test a hypothesis.

✓ **Success/Failure Condition.** There were 148 successes and 352 failures, both at least 10. The sample is large enough.

Under these conditions, the sampling model is Normal. We'll create a one-proportion z-interval.

DO	**Mechanics** Write down the given information and determine the sample proportion.	$n = 500$, so

To use a confidence interval, we need a confidence level that corresponds to the alpha level of the test. The level wasn't specifically given, but 0.05 is a typical alpha level to use. If we use $\alpha = 0.05$, we should construct a 90% confidence interval because this is a one-sided test. That will leave 5% on *each* side of the observed proportion. Determine the standard error of the sample proportion and the margin of error. The critical value is $z^* = 1.645$.

$$\hat{p} = \frac{148}{500} = 0.296 \text{ and}$$

$$SE(\hat{p}) = \sqrt{\frac{\hat{p}\hat{q}}{n}} = \sqrt{\frac{(0.296)(0.704)}{500}} = 0.020$$

$$ME = z^* \times SE(\hat{p})$$
$$= 1.645(0.020) = 0.033$$

The confidence interval is estimate ± margin of error.

The 90% confidence interval is 0.296 ± 0.033 or $(0.263, 0.329)$.

REPORT	**Conclusion** Link the confidence interval to your decision about the null hypothesis, then state your conclusion in context.	MEMO **Re: Credit card promotion** Our study of a sample of customer records indicates that between 26.3% and 32.9% of customers charge $500 or more. We are 90%

(continued)

confident that this interval includes the true value. Because the minimum suitable value of 25% is below this interval, we conclude that it is not a plausible value, and so we reject the null hypothesis that only 25% of the customers charge more than $500 a month. The goal appears to have been met assuming that the month we studied is typical.

FOR EXAMPLE   Confidence intervals and hypothesis tests

QUESTION   Construct appropriate confidence intervals for testing the two hypotheses tested by the SmartWool analyst (see page 376) and show how we could have reached the same conclusions from these intervals.

ANSWER   The test of proportion was two-sided, so we construct a 95% confidence interval for the true proportion: $\hat{p} \pm 1.96 \times SE(\hat{p}) = 0.29 \pm 1.96 \times \sqrt{\dfrac{(0.29)(0.71)}{200}} =$ $(0.227, 0.353)$. Since 0.20 is not a plausible value, we reject the null hypothesis.

The test of means is one-sided so we construct a 90% confidence interval, using the t critical value of 1.672:

$$(\bar{y} - t^{*}SE(\bar{y}), \bar{y} + t^{*}SE(\bar{y})) = \left(26.05 - 1.672 \times \frac{10.2}{\sqrt{58}}, 26.05 + 1.672 \times \frac{10.2}{\sqrt{(58)}}\right)$$

$$= (23.81, 28.29)$$

We can see that the hypothesized value of $24.85 is in this interval, so we fail to reject the null hypothesis.

12.5   Two Types of Errors

Nobody's perfect. Even with lots of evidence, we can still make the wrong decision. In fact, when we perform a hypothesis test, we can make mistakes in *two* ways:

I. The null hypothesis is true, but we mistakenly reject it.
II. The null hypothesis is false, but we fail to reject it.

These two types of errors are known as **Type I** and **Type II errors**, respectively. One way to keep the names straight is to remember that we start by assuming the null hypothesis is true, so a Type I error is the first kind of error we could make.

In medical disease testing, the null hypothesis is usually the assumption that a person is healthy. The alternative is that he or she has the disease we're testing for. So a Type I error is a *false positive*—a healthy person is diagnosed with the disease. A Type II error, in which an infected person is diagnosed as disease free, is a *false negative*. These errors have other names, depending on the particular discipline and context.

Which type of error is more serious depends on the situation. In a jury trial, a Type I error occurs if the jury convicts an innocent person. A Type II error occurs if the jury fails to convict a guilty person. Which seems more serious? In medical diagnosis, a false negative could mean that a sick patient goes untreated. A false positive might mean that the person receives unnecessary treatments or even surgery.

In business planning, a false positive result could mean that money will be invested in a project that turns out not to be profitable. A false negative result might mean that money won't be invested in a project that would have been profitable. Which error is worse, the lost investment or the lost opportunity? The answer always depends on the situation, the cost, and your point of view.

Here's an illustration of the situations:

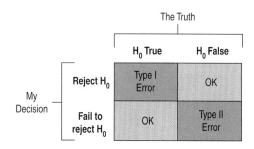

Figure 12.4 The two types of errors occur on the diagonal where the truth and decision don't match. Remember that we *start* by assuming H_0 to be true, so an error made (rejecting it) when H_0 is true is called a Type I error. A Type II error is made when H_0 is false (and we fail to reject it).

How often will a Type I error occur? It happens when the null hypothesis is true but we've had the bad luck to draw an unusual sample. To reject H_0, the P-value must fall below α. When H_0 is true, that happens *exactly* with probability α. So when you choose level α, you're setting the probability of a Type I error to α.

What if H_0 is not true? Then we can't possibly make a Type I error. You can't get a false positive from a sick person. A Type I error can happen only when H_0 is true.

When H_0 is false and we reject it, we have done the right thing. A test's ability to detect a false hypothesis is called the **power** of the test. In a jury trial, power is a measure of the ability of the criminal justice system to convict people who are guilty. We'll have a lot more to say about power soon.

When H_0 is false but we fail to reject it, we have made a Type II error. We assign the letter β to the probability of this mistake. What's the value of β? That's harder to assess than α because we don't know what the value of the parameter really is. When H_0 is true, it specifies a single parameter value. But when H_0 is false, we don't have a specific one; we have many possible values. We can compute the probability β for any parameter value in H_A, but the choice of which one to pick is not always clear.

One way to focus our attention is by thinking about the *effect size*. That is, ask: "How big a difference would matter?" Suppose a charity wants to test whether placing personalized address labels in the envelope along with a request for a donation increases the response rate above the baseline of 5%. If the minimum response that would pay for the address labels is 6%, they would calculate β for the alternative $p = 0.06$.

Of course, we could reduce β for *all* alternative parameter values by increasing α. By making it easier to reject the null, we'd be more likely to reject it whether it's true or not. The only way to reduce *both* types of error is to collect more evidence or, in statistical terms, to collect more data. Otherwise, we just wind up trading off one kind of error against the other. Whenever you design a survey or experiment, it's a good idea to calculate β (for a reasonable α level). Use a parameter value in the alternative that corresponds to an effect size that you want to be able to detect. Too often, studies fail because their sample sizes are too small to detect the change they are looking for.

NOTATION ALERT

In Statistics, α is the probability of a Type I error and β is the probability of a Type II error.

The *Probabilities* of a Type II Error

The null hypothesis specifies a single value for the parameter. So it's easy to calculate the probability of a Type I error. But the alternative gives a whole range of possible values, and we may want to find a β for several of them.

Sample Size and Power

We have seen ways to find a sample size by specifying the margin of error. Choosing the sample size to achieve a specified β (for a particular alternative value) is sometimes more appropriate, but the calculation is more complex and lies beyond the scope of this book.

JUST CHECKING

5 Remember our bank that's sending out DVDs to try to get customers to make payments on delinquent loans? It is looking for evidence that the costlier DVD strategy produces a higher success rate than the letters it has been sending. Explain what a Type I error is in this context and what the consequences would be to the bank.

6 What's a Type II error in the bank experiment context and what would the consequences be?

7 If the DVD strategy *really* works well—actually getting 60% of the people to pay off their balances—would the power of the test be higher or lower compared to a 32% payoff rate? Explain briefly.

8 Recall the mileage program test market of Question 4. Suppose after completing the hotel partnership, the mean revenue per customer is $40.26. Has a Type I or Type II error been made? Explain.

FOR EXAMPLE   Type I and Type II errors

QUESTION   Suppose that a year later, a full accounting of all the transactions at SmartWool (see page 376) finds that 26.5% of visits resulted in sales with an average purchase amount of $26.25. Have any errors been made?

ANSWER   We rejected the null hypothesis that $p = 0.20$ and in fact $p = 0.265$, so we did not make a Type I error (the only error we could have made when rejecting the null hypothesis). For the mean amount, we failed to reject that the mean had increased from $24.85 but actually the mean had increased to $26.25 so we made a Type II error—we failed to reject the null hypothesis when it was false.

12.6   Power

Remember, we can never prove a null hypothesis true. We can only fail to reject it. But when we fail to reject a null hypothesis, it's natural to wonder whether we looked hard enough. Might the null hypothesis actually be false and our test too weak to tell?

When the null hypothesis actually *is* false, we hope our test is strong enough to reject it. We'd like to know how likely we are to succeed. The power of the test gives us a way to think about that. The power of a test is the probability that it correctly rejects a false null hypothesis. When the power is high, we can be confident that we've looked hard enough. We know that β is the probability that a test *fails* to reject a false null hypothesis, so the power of the test is the complement, $1 - \beta$. We might have just written $1 - \beta$, but power is such an important concept that it gets its own name.

Whenever a study fails to reject its null hypothesis, the test's power comes into question. Was the sample size big enough to detect an effect had there been one? Might we have missed an effect large enough to be interesting just because we failed to gather sufficient data or because there was too much variability in the data we could gather? Might the problem be that the experiment simply lacked adequate power to detect their ability?

When we calculate power, we base our calculation on the smallest effect that might influence our business decision. The value of the power depends on how large this effect is. For proportions, that effect size is $p - p_0$; for means it's $\mu - \mu_0$. The power depends directly on the effect size. It's easier to see larger effects, so the further p_0 is from p (or μ is from μ_0), the greater the power.

How can we decide what power we need? Choice of power is more a financial or scientific decision than a statistical one because to calculate the power, we need to specify the alternative parameter value we're interested in. In other words,

Power and Effect Size

When planning a study, it's wise to think about the size of the effect we're looking for. We've called the effect size the difference between the null hypothesis and the observed statistic. In planning, it's the difference between the null hypothesis and a particular alternative we're interested in. It's easier to see a larger effect size, so the power of the study will increase with the effect size.

Once the study has been completed we'll base our business decision on the observed effect size, the difference between the null hypothesis and the observed value.

power is calculated for a particular effect size, and it changes depending on the size of the effect we want to detect.

Graph It!

It makes intuitive sense that the larger the effect size, the easier it should be to see it. Obtaining a larger sample size decreases the probability of a Type II error, and so it increases the power. Finally, it should also makes sense that the more we're willing to accept a Type I error, the less likely we will be to make a Type II error.

Figure 12.5 may help you visualize the relationships among these concepts. Although we'll use proportions to show the ideas, a similar picture and similar statements also hold true for means. Suppose we are testing $H_0: p = p_0$ against the alternative $H_A: p > p_0$. We'll reject the null if the observed proportion, $\hat{p}$, is big enough. By *big enough*, we mean $\hat{p} > p^*$ for some critical value p^* (shown as the red region in the right tail of the upper curve). The upper model shows a picture of the sampling distribution model for the proportion when the null hypothesis is true. If the null were true, then this would be a picture of that truth. We'd make a Type I error whenever the sample gave us $\hat{p} > p^*$ because we would reject the (true) null hypothesis. Unusual samples like that would happen only with probability α.

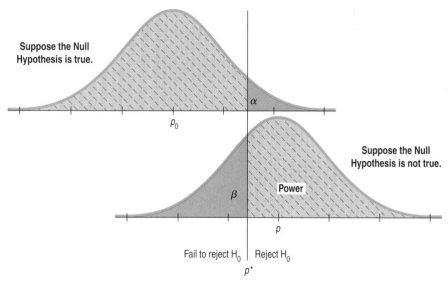

Figure 12.5   The power of a test is the probability that it rejects a false null hypothesis. The upper figure shows the null hypothesis model. We'd reject the null in a one-sided test if we observed a value in the red region to the right of the critical value, p^*. The lower figure shows the model if we assume that the true value is p. If the true value of p is greater than p_0, then we're more likely to observe a value that exceeds the critical value and make the correct decision to reject the null hypothesis. The power of the test is the green region on the right of the lower figure. Of course, even drawing samples whose observed proportions are distributed around p, we'll sometimes get a value in the red region on the left and make a Type II error of failing to reject the null.

In reality, though, the null hypothesis is rarely *exactly* true. The lower probability model supposes that H_0 is not true. In particular, it supposes that the true value is p, not p_0. It shows a distribution of possible observed $\hat{p}$ values around this true value. Because of sampling variability, sometimes $\hat{p} < p^*$ and we fail to reject the (false) null hypothesis. Then we'd make a Type II error. The area under the curve to the left of p^* in the bottom model represents how often this happens. The probability is β. In this picture, β is less than half, so most of the time we *do* make the right decision. The *power* of the test—the probability that we make the right decision—is shown as the region to the right of p^*. It's $1 - \beta$.

We calculate p^* based on the upper model because p^* depends only on the null model and the alpha level. No matter what the true proportion, p^* doesn't change. After all, we don't *know* the truth, so we can't use it to determine the critical value. But we always reject H_0 when $\hat{p} > p^*$.

How often we reject H_0 when it's *false* depends on the effect size. We can see from the picture that if the true proportion were further from the hypothesized value, the bottom curve would shift to the right, making the power greater.

We can see several important relationships from this figure:

- Power $= 1 - \beta$.
- Moving the critical value (p^* in the case of proportions) to the right, reduces α, the probability of a Type I error, but increases β, the probability of a Type II error. It correspondingly reduces the power.
- The larger the true effect size, the real difference between the hypothesized value and the true population value, the smaller the chance of making a Type II error and the greater the power of the test.

If the two proportions (or means) are very far apart, the two models will barely overlap, and we would not be likely to make any Type II errors at all—but then, we are unlikely to really need a formal hypothesis testing procedure to see such an obvious difference.

Reducing Both Type I and Type II Errors

Figure 12.5 seems to show that if we reduce Type I errors, we automatically must increase Type II errors. But there is a way to reduce both. Can you think of it?

If we can make both curves narrower, as shown in Figure 12.6, then the probability of both Type I errors and Type II errors will decrease, and the power of the test will increase.

How can we do that? The only way is to reduce the standard deviations by increasing the sample size. (Remember, these are pictures of sampling distribution models, not of data.) Increasing the sample size works regardless of the true population parameters. But recall the curse of diminishing returns. The standard deviation of the sampling distribution model decreases only as the *square root* of the sample size, so to halve the standard deviations, we must *quadruple* the sample size.

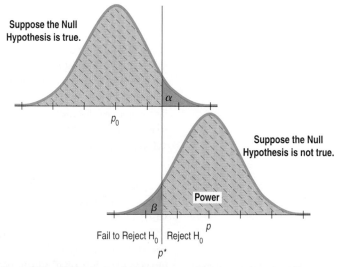

Figure 12.6   Making the standard deviations smaller increases the power without changing the alpha level or the corresponding *z*-critical value. The proportions are just as far apart as in Figure 12.5, but the error rates are reduced. A similar picture could be drawn for testing means.

WHAT CAN GO WRONG? (RECAP)

- **Don't confuse proportions and means.** When you treat your data as categorical, counting successes and summarizing with a sample proportion, make inferences using the Normal model methods. When you treat your data as quantitative, summarizing with a sample mean, make your inferences using Student's *t* methods.

- **Don't base your null hypotheses on what you see in the data.** You are not allowed to look at the data first and then adjust your null hypothesis so that it will be rejected. If the mean spending of 10 customers turns out to be $\bar{y} = \$24.94$ with a standard error of $5, don't form a null hypothesis just big enough so you'll be able to reject it like $H_0: \mu = \$26.97$. The null hypothesis should not be based on the data you collect. It should describe the "nothing interesting" or "nothing has changed" situation.

- **Don't base your alternative hypothesis on the data either.** You should always think about the situation you are investigating and base your alternative hypothesis on that. Are you interested only in knowing whether something has *increased*? Then write a one-tail (upper tail) alternative. Or would you be equally interested in a change in either direction? Then you want a two-tailed alternative. You should decide whether to do a one- or two-tailed test based on what results would be of interest to you, not on what you might see in the data.

- **Don't make your null hypothesis what you want to show to be true.** Remember, the null hypothesis is the status quo, the nothing-is-strange-here position a skeptic would take. You wonder whether the data cast doubt on that. You can reject the null hypothesis, but you can never "accept" or "prove" the null.

- **Don't forget to check the conditions.** The reasoning of inference depends on randomization. No amount of care in calculating a test result can save you from a biased sample. The probabilities you compute depend on the independence assumption. And your sample must be large enough to justify your use of a Normal model.

- **Don't believe too strongly in arbitrary alpha levels.** There's not really much difference between a P-value of 0.051 and a P-value of 0.049, but sometimes it's regarded as the difference between night (having to retain H_0) and day (being able to shout to the world that your results are "statistically significant"). It may just be better to report the P-value and a confidence interval and let the world (perhaps your manager or client) decide along with you.

- **Don't confuse practical and statistical significance.** A large sample size can make it easy to discern even a trivial change from the null hypothesis value. On the other hand, you could miss an important difference if your test lacks sufficient power.

- **Don't forget that in spite of all your care, you might make a wrong decision.** No one can ever reduce the probability of a Type I error (α) or of a Type II error (β) to zero (but increasing the sample size helps).

ETHICS IN ACTION

Many retailers have recognized the importance of staying connected to their in-store customers via the Internet. Retailers not only use the Internet to inform their customers about specials and promotions, but also to send them e-coupons redeemable for discounts.

Shellie Cooper, longtime owner of a small organic food store, specializes in locally produced organic foods and products. Over the years Shellie's customer base has been quite stable, consisting mainly of health-conscious individuals who tend not to be very price sensitive, opting to pay higher prices for better-quality local, organic products.

Faced with increasing competition from grocery chains offering more organic choices, however, Shellie is now thinking of offering coupons. She needs to decide between the newspaper and the Internet. She recently read that the percentage of consumers who use printable Internet coupons is on the rise but, at 15%, is much less than the 40% who clip and redeem newspaper coupons. Nonetheless, she's interested in learning more about the Internet and sets up a meeting with Jack Kasor, a Web

consultant. She discovers that for an initial investment and continuing monthly fee, Jack would design Shellie's website, host it on his server, and broadcast e-coupons to her customers at regular intervals. While she was concerned about the difference in redemption rates for e-coupons vs. newspaper coupons, Jack assured her that e-coupon redemptions are continuing to rise and that she should expect between 15% and 40% of her customers to redeem them. Shellie agreed to give it a try.

After the first six months, Jack informed Shellie that the proportion of her customers who redeemed e-coupons was significantly greater than 15%. He determined this by selecting several broadcasts at random and found the number redeemed (483) out of the total number sent (3000). Shellie thought that this was positive and made up her mind to continue the use of e-coupons.

- Identify the ethical dilemma in this scenario.

- What are the undesirable consequences?

- Propose an ethical solution that considers the welfare of all stakeholders.

WHAT HAVE WE LEARNED?

Learning Objectives

Understand P-values in greater depth.

- A P-value is the conditional probability of observing a statistic value at least as far from the (null) hypothesized value as the one we have actually observed given that the null hypothesis is true.
- A small P-value indicates that the statistic we have observed would be unlikely were the null hypothesis true. That leads us to doubt the null.
- A large P-value just tells us that we have insufficient evidence to doubt the null hypothesis. In particular, it does not prove the null to be true.

Compare P-values to a predetermined α-level to decide whether to reject the null hypothesis.

Be aware of the risks of making errors when testing hypotheses.

- A Type I error can occur when rejecting a null hypothesis if that hypothesis is, in fact, true.
- A Type II error can occur when failing to reject a null hypothesis if that hypothesis is, in fact, false.

Understand the concept of the power of a test.

- We are particularly concerned with power when we fail to reject a null hypothesis.
- The power of a test reports, for a specified effect size, the probability that the test would reject a false null hypothesis.
- Remember that increasing the sample size will generally improve the power of any test.

Terms

Alpha level   The threshold P-value that determines when we reject a null hypothesis. Using an alpha level of α, if we observe a statistic whose P-value based on the null hypothesis is less than α, we reject that null hypothesis.

Critical value	The value in the sampling distribution model of the statistic whose P-value is equal to the alpha level. Any statistic value further from the null hypothesis value than the critical value will have a smaller P-value than α and will lead to rejecting the null hypothesis. The critical value is often denoted with an asterisk, as z^* or t^*, for example.
Power	The probability that a hypothesis test will correctly reject a false null hypothesis. To find the power of a test, we must specify a particular alternative parameter value as the "true" value. For any specific value in the alternative, the power is $1 - \beta$.
Significance level	Another term for the alpha level, used most often in a phrase such as "at the 5% significance level."
Type I error	The error of rejecting a null hypothesis when in fact it is true (also called a "false positive"). The probability of a Type I error is α.
Type II error	The error of failing to reject a null hypothesis when in fact it is false (also called a "false negative"). The probability of a Type II error is commonly denoted β and depends on the effect size.

Brief **Case**

Confidence Intervals and Hypothesis Tests

Using the **Paralyzed Veterans** dataset, construct a 95% confidence interval for the mean age of a potential donor to the Paralyzed Veterans. Test the hypothesis that the mean age is 62 years old. Discuss what the confidence interval says about the hypothesis test. Is the difference meaningful as well? Now take a sample of size 20 from the data set and repeat both the confidence interval and the hypothesis test. Discuss how sample size affects the probability of making errors and the power of a test.

EXERCISES

SECTION 12.1

1. Which of the following are true? If false, explain briefly.

a) A P-value of 0.01 means that the null hypothesis is false.

b) A P-value of 0.01 means that the null hypothesis has a 0.01 chance of being true.

c) A P-value of 0.01 is evidence against the null hypothesis.

d) A P-value of 0.01 means we should definitely reject the null hypothesis.

2. Which of the following are true? If false, explain briefly.

a) If the null hypothesis is true, you'll get a high P-value.

b) If the null hypothesis is true, a P-value of 0.01 will occur about 1% of the time.

c) A P-value of 0.90 means that the null hypothesis has a good chance of being true.

d) A P-value of 0.90 is strong evidence that the null hypothesis is true.

SECTION 12.2

3. Which of the following statements are true? If false, explain briefly.

a) Using an alpha level of 0.05, a P-value of 0.04 results in rejecting the null hypothesis.

b) The alpha level depends on the sample size.

c) With an alpha level of 0.01, a P-value of 0.10 results in rejecting the null hypothesis.

d) Using an alpha level of 0.05, a P-value of 0.06 means the null hypothesis is true.

4. Which of the following statements are true? If false, explain briefly.

a) It is better to use an alpha level of 0.05 than an alpha level of 0.01.

b) If we use an alpha level of 0.01, then a P-value of 0.001 is statistically significant.

c) If we use an alpha level of 0.01, then we reject the null hypothesis if the P-value is 0.001.

d) If the P-value is 0.01, we reject the null hypothesis for any alpha level greater than 0.01.

SECTION 12.3

5. For each of the following situations, find the critical value(s) for z or t.

a) $H_0: p = 0.5$ vs. $H_A: p \neq 0.5$ at $\alpha = 0.05$.
b) $H_0: p = 0.4$ vs. $H_A: p > 0.4$ at $\alpha = 0.05$.
c) $H_0: \mu = 10$ vs. $H_A: \mu \neq 10$ at $\alpha = 0.05$; $n = 36$.
d) $H_0: p = 0.5$ vs. $H_A: p > 0.5$ at $\alpha = 0.01$; $n = 345$.
e) $H_0: \mu = 20$ vs. $H_A: \mu < 20$ at $\alpha = 0.01$; $n = 1000$.

6. For each of the following situations, find the critical value for z or t.

a) $H_0: \mu = 105$ vs. $H_A: \mu \neq 105$ at $\alpha = 0.05$; $n = 61$.
b) $H_0: p = 0.05$ vs. $H_A: p > 0.05$ at $\alpha = 0.05$.
c) $H_0: p = 0.6$ vs. $H_A: p \neq 0.6$ at $\alpha = 0.01$.
d) $H_0: p = 0.5$ vs. $H_A: p < 0.5$ at $\alpha = 0.01$; $n = 500$.
e) $H_0: p = 0.2$ vs. $H_A: p < 0.2$ at $\alpha = 0.01$.

SECTION 12.4

7. Suppose that you are testing the hypotheses $H_0: p = 0.20$ vs. $H_A: p \neq 0.20$. A sample of size 250 results in a sample proportion of 0.25.

a) Construct a 95% confidence interval for p.
b) Based on the confidence interval, at $\alpha = .05$ can you reject H_0? Explain.
c) What is the difference between the standard error and standard deviation of the sample proportion?
d) Which is used in computing the confidence interval?

8. Suppose that you are testing the hypotheses $H_0: p = 0.40$ vs. $H_A: p > 0.40$. A sample of size 200 results in a sample proportion of 0.55.

a) Construct a 90% confidence interval for p.
b) Based on the confidence interval, at $\alpha = .05$ can you reject H_0? Explain.
c) What is the difference between the standard error and standard deviation of the sample proportion?
d) Which is used in computing the confidence interval?

9. Suppose that you are testing the hypotheses $H_0: \mu = 16$ vs. $H_A: \mu < 16$. A sample of size 25 results in a sample mean of 16.5 and a standard deviation of 2.0.

a) What is the standard error of the mean?
b) What is the critical value of t^* for a 90% confidence interval?
c) Construct a 90% confidence interval for μ.
d) Based on the confidence interval, at $\alpha = 0.05$ can you reject H_0? Explain.

10. Suppose that you are testing the hypotheses $H_0: \mu = 80$ vs. $H_A: \mu \neq 80$. A sample of size 61 results in a sample mean of 75 and a standard deviation of 1.5.

a) What is the standard error of the mean?
b) What is the critical value of t^* for a 95% confidence interval?
c) Construct a 95% confidence interval for μ.
d) Based on the confidence interval, at $\alpha = 0.05$ can you reject H_0? Explain.

SECTION 12.5

11. For each of the following situations, state whether a Type I, a Type II, or neither error has been made. Explain briefly.

a) A bank wants to know if the enrollment on their website is above 30% based on a small sample of customers. They test $H_0: p = 0.3$ vs. $H_A: p > 0.3$ and reject the null hypothesis. Later they find out that actually 28% of all customers enrolled.

b) A student tests 100 students to determine whether other students on her campus prefer Coke or Pepsi and finds no evidence that preference for Coke is not 0.5. Later, a marketing company tests all students on campus and finds no difference.

c) A human resource analyst wants to know if the applicants this year score, on average, higher on their placement exam than the 52.5 points the candidates averaged last year. She samples 50 recent tests and finds the average to be 54.1 points. She fails to reject the null hypothesis that the mean is 52.5 points. At the end of the year, they find that the candidates this year had a mean of 55.3 points.

d) A pharmaceutical company tests whether a drug lifts the headache relief rate from the 25% achieved by the placebo. They fail to reject the null hypothesis because the P-value is 0.465. Further testing shows that the drug actually relieves headaches in 38% of people.

12. For each of the following situations, state whether a Type I, a Type II, or neither error has been made.

a) A test of $H_0: \mu = 25$ vs. $H_A: \mu > 25$ rejects the null hypothesis. Later it is discovered that $\mu = 24.9$.

b) A test of $H_0: p = 0.8$ vs. $H_A: p < 0.8$ fails to reject the null hypothesis. Later it is discovered that $p = 0.9$.

c) A test of $H_0: p = 0.5$ vs. $H_A: p \neq 0.5$ rejects the null hypothesis. Later it is discovered that $p = 0.65$.

d) A test of $H_0: p = 0.7$ vs. $H_A: p < 0.7$ fails to reject the null hypothesis. Later is it discovered that $p = 0.6$.

SECTION 12.6

13. Most car engines need at least 87 octane to avoid "knocking" or "pinging," terms used to describe the preignition that can happen when a fuel's octane is too low. An engineer is designing an experiment to raise the octane of an ethanol-based fuel. From previous studies, she thinks that with 8 experimental runs, she will have a power of 0.90 to detect a real increase of 3 points in the mean octane.

a) If the actual increase is only 1 point, will the power be increased or decreased?

b) If she wants the power to be the same, but she is interested in detecting an increase of only 1 point, what will she need to do?

14. A marketing analyst at an Internet book store is testing a new web design which she hopes will increase sales. She wants to randomly send n customers to the new site. She's hoping for an increase of 10% in sales from the new site. She calculates a power of 0.43 for that increase from a sample of 150 customers. Explain to her why she should consider a larger sample size.

CHAPTER EXERCISES

15. Alpha. A researcher developing scanners to search for hidden weapons at airports has concluded that a new device is significantly better than the current scanner. He made this decision based on a test using $\alpha = 0.05$. Would he have made the same decision at $\alpha = 0.10$? How about $\alpha = 0.01$? Explain.

16. Alpha, again. Analysts evaluating a new program to encourage customer retention in a test market find no evidence of an increased rate of retention in a test of 2000 customers. They based this conclusion on a test using $\alpha = 0.01$. Would they have made the same decision at $\alpha = 0.05$? How about $\alpha = 0.001$? Explain.

17. Measles. Health researchers at a large HMO base their cost predictions for measles on the belief that 98% of children have been vaccinated against measles. A random survey of medical records at many schools across the country found that, among more than 13,000 children, only 97.4% had been vaccinated. A statistician would reject the 98% hypothesis with a P-value of P < 0.0001.

a) Explain what the P-value means in this context.

b) The result is statistically significant, but is it important? Comment.

18. Computer skills. A new program may reduce the proportion of employees who fail a computer skills course. The company that developed this program supplied materials and teacher training for a large-scale test involving nearly 8500 employees in several different sites. Statistical analysis of the results showed that the percentage of employees who did not pass the course was reduced from 15.9% to 15.1%. The hypothesis that the program produced no improvement was rejected with a P-value of 0.023.

a) Explain what the P-value means in this context.

b) Even though this program has been shown to be significantly better statistically, why might you not recommend that your company adopt it?

19. Groceries. In January 2011, Yahoo surveyed 2400 U.S. men. Of the men, 1224 identified themselves as the primary grocery shopper in their household.

a) Estimate the percentage of all American males who identify themselves as the primary grocery shopper. Use a 98% confidence interval being sure to check the conditions.

b) A grocery store owner believed that only 45% of men are the primary grocery shopper for their family, and targets his advertising accordingly. He wishes to conduct a hypothesis test to see if the fraction is in fact higher than 45%. What does your confidence interval indicate? Explain.

c) What is the level of significance of this test? Explain.

20. Hard times. In June 2010, a random poll of 800 working men found that 9% had taken on a second job to help pay the bills. (www.careerbuilder.com)

a) Estimate the true percentage of men that are taking on second jobs by constructing a 95% confidence interval.

b) A pundit on a TV news show claimed that only 6% of working men had a second job. Use your confidence interval to test whether his claim is plausible given the poll data.

21. Convenient alpha. An enthusiastic junior executive has run a test of his new marketing program. He reports that it resulted in a "significant" increase in sales. A footnote on his report explains that he used an alpha level of 7.2% for his test. Presumably, he performed a hypothesis test against the null hypothesis of no change in sales.

a) If instead he had used an alpha level of 5%, is it more or less likely that he would have rejected his null hypothesis? Explain.

b) If he chose the alpha level 7.2% so that he could claim statistical significance, explain why this is not an ethical use of statistics.

22. Safety. The manufacturer of a new sleeping pill suspects that it may increase the risk of sleepwalking, which could be dangerous. A test of the drug fails to reject the null hypothesis of no increase in sleepwalking when tested at $\alpha = .01$.

a) If the test had been performed at $\alpha = .05$, would the test have been more or less likely to reject the null hypothesis of no increase in sleepwalking?

b) Which alpha level do you think the company should use? Why?

23. Sales increase. A software engineer at Neverware, a company that replaces computers in schools with terminals connected to a server, is testing a new server to see if mean download times are decreased with the new server. When he compares a random sample of 20 times to the previous standard he gets a t-statistic of -15.

a) Explain what the t-statistic means in this context.
b) Look up the 0.001 lower critical value for a t-statistic with 19 df and state your conclusion about the test.
c) Why did you probably not need to look up the critical value in b) to reach your conclusion?

24. Web finder. Zocdoc.com provides a service to find and make appointments with medical professionals across the United States. Suppose an analyst looking to see if a new web design had improved the percentage of people successfully making appointments found a z-score of 10.23.

a) Explain what the z-statistic means in this context.
b) Look up the 0.001 upper critical value for a z-statistic and state your conclusion about the test.
c) Why did you probably not need to look up the critical value in b) to reach your conclusion?

25. Measles revisited. The analyst in Exercise 17 finds a 98% confidence interval for the true proportion of vaccinated children to be (0.9707, 0.9773).

a) Explain why she can reject the null hypothesis that $p = 0.98$ vs. $p < 0.98$ at $\alpha = 0.01$.
b) Explain why the difference may or may not be important

26. Computer skills again. The health care analyst in Exercise 18 finds a 90% confidence interval for the true proportion of employees who fail the course to be (14.46%, 15.74%).

a) Explain why she can reject the null hypothesis that $p = 0.159$ vs. $p < 0.159$ at $\alpha = 0.05$.
b) Explain why the difference may or may not be important
c) Could you reject the hypothesis that $p = 0.157$? Explain.

27. Loans. Before lending someone money, banks must decide whether they believe the applicant will repay the loan. One strategy used is a point system. Loan officers assess information about the applicant, totaling points they award for the person's income level, credit history, current debt burden, and so on. The higher the point total, the more convinced the bank is that it's safe to make the loan. Any applicant with a lower point total than a certain cutoff score is denied a loan.

We can think of this decision as a hypothesis test. Since the bank makes its profit from the interest collected on repaid loans, their null hypothesis is that the applicant will repay the loan and therefore should get the money. Only if the person's score falls below the minimum cutoff will the bank

reject the null and deny the loan. This system is reasonably reliable, but, of course, sometimes there are mistakes.

a) When a person defaults on a loan, which type of error did the bank make?
b) Which kind of error is it when the bank misses an opportunity to make a loan to someone who would have repaid it?
c) Suppose the bank decides to lower the cutoff score from 250 points to 200. Is that analogous to choosing a higher or lower value of α for a hypothesis test? Explain.
d) What impact does this change in the cutoff value have on the chance of each type of error?

28. Spam. Spam filters try to sort your e-mails, deciding which are real messages and which are unwanted. One method used is a point system. The filter reads each incoming e-mail and assigns points to the sender, the subject, key words in the message, and so on. The higher the point total, the more likely it is that the message is unwanted. The filter has a cutoff value for the point total; any message rated lower than that cutoff passes through to your inbox, and the rest, suspected to be spam, are diverted to the junk mailbox.

We can think of the filter's decision as a hypothesis test. The null hypothesis is that the e-mail is a real message and should go to your inbox. A higher point total provides evidence that the message may be spam; when there's sufficient evidence, the filter rejects the null, classifying the message as junk. This usually works pretty well, but, of course, sometimes the filter makes a mistake.

a) When the filter allows spam to slip through into your inbox, which kind of error is that?
b) Which kind of error is it when a real message gets classified as junk?
c) Some filters allow the user (that's you) to adjust the cutoff. Suppose your filter has a default cutoff of 50 points, but you reset it to 60. Is that analogous to choosing a higher or lower value of α for a hypothesis test? Explain.
d) What impact does this change in the cutoff value have on the chance of each type of error?

29. Second loan. Exercise 27 describes the loan score method a bank uses to decide which applicants it will lend money. Only if the total points awarded for various aspects of an applicant's financial condition fail to add up to a minimum cutoff score set by the bank will the loan be denied.

a) In this context, what is meant by the power of the test?
b) What could the bank do to increase the power?
c) What's the disadvantage of doing that?

30. More spam. Consider again the points-based spam filter described in Exercise 28. When the points assigned to various components of an e-mail exceed the cutoff value you've set, the filter rejects its null hypothesis (that the message is real) and diverts that e-mail to a junk mailbox.

a) In this context, what is meant by the power of the test?
b) What could you do to increase the filter's power?
c) What's the disadvantage of doing that?

31. Homeowners. In 2012, the Gallup Poll reported that only 62% of American families owned their homes, the lowest percentage reported in a decade. Census data reveal that the ownership rate in one small city is even lower. The city council is debating a plan to offer tax breaks to first-time home buyers in order to encourage people to become homeowners. They decide to adopt the plan on a 2-year trial basis and use the data they collect to make a decision about continuing the tax breaks. Since this plan costs the city tax revenues, they will continue to use it only if there is strong evidence that the rate of home ownership is increasing.

a) In words, what will their hypotheses be?
b) What would a Type I error be?
c) What would a Type II error be?
d) For each type of error, tell who would be harmed.
e) What would the power of the test represent in this context?

32. Alzheimer's. Testing for Alzheimer's disease can be a long and expensive process, consisting of lengthy tests and medical diagnosis. A group of researchers (Solomon *et al.*, 1998) devised a 7-minute test to serve as a quick screen for the disease for use in the general population of senior citizens. A patient who tested positive would then go through the more expensive battery of tests and medical diagnosis. The authors reported a false positive rate of 4% and a false negative rate of 8%.

a) Put this in the context of a hypothesis test. What are the null and alternative hypotheses?
b) What would a Type I error mean?
c) What would a Type II error mean?
d) Which is worse here, a Type I or Type II error? Explain.
e) What is the power of this test?

33. Testing cars. A clean air standard requires that vehicle exhaust emissions not exceed specified limits for various pollutants. Many states require that cars be tested annually to be sure they meet these standards. Suppose state regulators double-check a random sample of cars that a suspect repair shop has certified as okay. They will revoke the shop's license if they find significant evidence that the shop is certifying vehicles that do not meet standards.

a) In this context, what is a Type I error?
b) In this context, what is a Type II error?
c) Which type of error would the shop's owner consider more serious?
d) Which type of error might environmentalists consider more serious?

34. Quality control. Production managers on an assembly line must monitor the output to be sure that the level of defective products remains small. They periodically inspect a random sample of the items produced. If they find a significant increase in the proportion of items that must be rejected, they will halt the assembly process until the problem can be identified and repaired.

a) In this context, what is a Type I error?
b) In this context, what is a Type II error?
c) Which type of error would the factory owner consider more serious?
d) Which type of error might customers consider more serious?

35. Cars, again. As in Exercise 33, state regulators are checking up on repair shops to see if they are certifying vehicles that do not meet pollution standards.

a) In this context, what is meant by the power of the test the regulators are conducting?
b) Will the power be greater if they test 20 or 40 cars? Why?
c) Will the power be greater if they use a 5% or a 10% level of significance? Why?
d) Will the power be greater if the repair shop's inspectors are only a little out of compliance or a lot? Why?

36. Production. Consider again the task of the quality control inspectors in Exercise 34.

a) In this context, what is meant by the power of the test the inspectors conduct?
b) They are currently testing 5 items each hour. Someone has proposed that they test 10 instead. What are the advantages and disadvantages of such a change?
c) Their test currently uses a 5% level of significance. What are the advantages and disadvantages of changing to an alpha level of 1%?
d) Suppose that, as a day passes, one of the machines on the assembly line produces more and more items that are defective. How will this affect the power of the test?

37. Equal opportunity? A company is sued for job discrimination because only 19% of the newly hired candidates were minorities when 27% of all applicants were minorities. Is this strong evidence that the company's hiring practices are discriminatory?

a) Is this a one-tailed or a two-tailed test? Why?
b) In this context, what would a Type I error be?
c) In this context, what would a Type II error be?
d) In this context, what is meant by the power of the test?
e) If the hypothesis is tested at the 5% level of significance instead of 1%, how will this affect the power of the test?
f) The lawsuit is based on the hiring of 37 employees. Is the power of the test higher than, lower than, or the same as it would be if it were based on 87 hires?

38. Stop signs. Highway safety engineers test new road signs, hoping that increased reflectivity will make them more visible to drivers. Volunteers drive through a test course with several of the new- and old-style signs and rate which kind shows up the best.

a) Is this a one-tailed or a two-tailed test? Why?
b) In this context, what would a Type I error be?
c) In this context, what would a Type II error be?
d) In this context, what is meant by the power of the test?
e) If the hypothesis is tested at the 1% level of significance instead of 5%, how will this affect the power of the test?
f) The engineers hoped to base their decision on the reactions of 50 drivers, but time and budget constraints may force them to cut back to 20. How would this affect the power of the test? Explain.

39. Software for learning. A Statistics professor has observed that for several years students score an average of 105 points out of 150 on the semester exam. A salesman suggests that he try a statistics software package that gets students more involved with computers, predicting that it will increase students' scores. The software is expensive, and the salesman offers to let the professor use it for a semester to see if the scores on the final exam increase significantly. The professor will have to pay for the software only if he chooses to continue using it.

a) Is this a one-tailed or two-tailed test? Explain.
b) Write the null and alternative hypotheses.
c) In this context, explain what would happen if the professor makes a Type I error.
d) In this context, explain what would happen if the professor makes a Type II error.
e) What is meant by the power of this test?

40. Software, part II. 203 students signed up for the Stats course in Exercise 39. They used the software suggested by the salesman, and scored an average of 108 points on the final with a standard deviation of 8.7 points.

a) Should the professor spend the money for this software? Support your recommendation with an appropriate test.
b) Does this improvement seem to be practically significant?

41. Collections. Credit card companies lose money on cardholders who fail to pay their minimum payments. They use a variety of methods to encourage their delinquent cardholders to pay their credit card balances, such as letters, phone calls and eventually the hiring of a collection agency. To justify the cost of using the collection agency, the agency must collect an average of at least $200 per customer. After a trial period during which the agency attempted to collect from a random sample of 100 delinquent cardholders, the 90% confidence interval on the mean collected amount was reported as ($190.25, $250.75). Given this, what recommendation(s) would you make to the credit card company about using the collection agency?

42. Free gift. A philanthropic organization sends out "free gifts" to people on their mailing list in the hope that the receiver will respond by sending back a donation. Typical gifts are mailing labels, greeting cards, or post cards. They want to test out a new gift that costs $0.50 per item to produce and mail. They mail it to a "small" sample of 2000 customers and find a 90% confidence interval of the mean donation to be ($0.489, $0.879). As a consultant, what recommendation(s) would you make to the organization about using this gift?

43. TV safety. The manufacturer of a metal stand for home TV sets must be sure that its product will not fail under the weight of the TV. Since some larger sets weigh nearly 300 pounds, the company's safety inspectors have set a standard of ensuring that the stands can support an average of over 500 pounds. Their inspectors regularly subject a random sample of the stands to increasing weight until they fail. They test the hypothesis $H_0: \mu = 500$ against $H_A: \mu > 500$, using the level of significance $\alpha = 0.01$. If the sample of stands fails to pass this safety test, the inspectors will not certify the product for sale to the general public.

a) Is this an upper-tail or lower-tail test? In the context of the problem, why do you think this is important?
b) Explain what will happen if the inspectors commit a Type I error.
c) Explain what will happen if the inspectors commit a Type II error.

44. Catheters. During an angiogram, heart problems can be examined via a small tube (a catheter) threaded into the heart from a vein in the patient's leg. It's important that the company that manufactures the catheter maintain a diameter of 2.00 mm. (The standard deviation is quite small.) Each day, quality control personnel make several measurements to test $H_0: \mu = 2.00$ against $H_A: \mu \neq 2.00$ at a significance level of $\alpha = 0.05$. If they discover a problem, they will stop the manufacturing process until it is corrected.

a) Is this a one-sided or two-sided test? In the context of the problem, why do you think this is important?
b) Explain in this context what happens if the quality control people commit a Type I error.
c) Explain in this context what happens if the quality control people commit a Type II error.

45. TV safety, revisited. The manufacturer of the metal TV stands in Exercise 43 is thinking of revising its safety test.

a) If the company's lawyers are worried about being sued for selling an unsafe product, should they increase or decrease the value of α? Explain.
b) In this context, what is meant by the power of the test?
c) If the company wants to increase the power of the test, what options does it have? Explain the advantages and disadvantages of each option.

46. Catheters, again. The catheter company in Exercise 44 is reviewing its testing procedure.

a) Suppose the significance level is changed to $\alpha = 0.01$. Will the probability of a Type II error increase, decrease, or remain the same?
b) What is meant by the power of the test the company conducts?
c) Suppose the manufacturing process is slipping out of proper adjustment. As the actual mean diameter of the catheters produced gets farther and farther above the desired 2.00 mm, will the power of the quality control test increase, decrease, or remain the same?
d) What could they do to improve the power of the test?

47. Two coins. In a drawer are two coins. They look the same, but one coin produces heads 90% of the time when spun while the other one produces heads only 30% of the time. You select one of the coins. You are allowed to spin it *once* and then must decide whether the coin is the 90%- or the 30%-head coin. Your null hypothesis is that your coin produces 90% heads.

a) What is the alternative hypothesis?
b) Given that the outcome of your spin is tails, what would you decide? What if it were heads?
c) How large is α in this case?
d) How large is the power of this test? (*Hint:* How many possibilities are in the alternative hypothesis?)
e) How could you lower the probability of a Type I error and increase the power of the test at the same time?

48. Faulty or not? You are in charge of shipping computers to customers. You learn that a faulty RAM chip was put into some of the machines. There's a simple test you can perform, but it's not perfect. All but 4% of the time, a good chip passes the test, but unfortunately, 35% of the bad chips pass the test, too. You have to decide on the basis of one test whether the chip is good or bad. Make this a hypothesis test.

a) What are the null and alternative hypotheses?
b) Given that a computer fails the test, what would you decide? What if it passes the test?
c) How large is α for this test?
d) What is the power of this test? (*Hint:* How many possibilities are in the alternative hypothesis?)

49. Collections, part 2. The owner of the collection agency in Exercise 41 is quite certain that they can collect more than $200 per customer on average. He urges that the credit card company run a larger trial. Do you think a larger trial might help the company make a better decision? Explain.

50. Free gift, part 2. The philanthropic organization of Exercise 42 decided to go ahead with the new gift. In mailings to 98,000 prospects, the new mailing yielded an average of $0.78. If they had decided based on their initial trial *not* to use this gift, what kind of error would they have made? What aspects of their initial trial might have suggested to you (as their consultant) that a larger trial would be worthwhile?

51. Pricing for competitiveness. SLIX wax is developing a new high performance fluorocarbon wax for cross country ski racing designed to be used under a wide variety of conditions. In order to justify the price marketing wants, the wax needs to be very fast. Specifically, the mean time to finish their standard test course should be less than 55 seconds for the former Olympic champion who is now their consultant. To test it, the consultant will ski the course 8 times.

a) The champion's times are 56.3, 65.9, 50.5, 52.4, 46.5, 57.8, 52.2, and 43.2 seconds to complete the test course. Should they market the wax? Explain.
b) Suppose they decide not to market the wax after the test, but it turns out that the wax really does lower the champion's average time to less than 55 seconds. What kind of error have they made? Explain the impact to the company of such an error.

52. Popcorn. Pop's Popcorn, Inc. needs to determine the optimum power and time settings for their new licorice-flavored microwave popcorn. They want to find a combination of power and time that delivers high-quality popcorn with less than 10% of the kernels left unpopped, on average—a value that their market research says is demanded by their customers. Their research department experiments with several settings and determines that power 9 at 4 minutes is optimum. Their tests confirm that this setting meets the less than 10% requirement. They change the instructions on the box and promote a new money back guarantee of less than 10% unpopped kernels.

a) If, in fact, the setting results in more than 10% kernels unpopped, what kind of error have they made? What will the consequence be for the company?
b) To reduce the risk of making an error, the president (Pop himself) tells them to test 8 more bags of popcorn (selected at random) at the specified setting. They find the following percentage of unpopped kernels: 7, 13.2, 10, 6, 7.8, 2.8, 2.2, 5.2. Does this provide evidence that the setting meets their goal of less than than 10% unpopped? Explain.

JUST CHECKING ANSWERS

1 The parameter of interest is the proportion, p, of all delinquent customers who will pay their bills. $H_0: p = 0.30$ and $H_A: p > 0.30$.

2 At $\alpha = 0.05$, you can't reject the null hypothesis because 0.30 is contained in the 90% confidence interval—it's plausible that sending the DVDs is no more effective than sending letters.

3 The confidence interval is from 29% to 45%. The DVD strategy is more expensive and may not be worth it. We can't distinguish the success rate from 30% given the results of this experiment, but 45% would represent a large improvement. The bank should consider another trial, increasing the sample size to get a narrower confidence interval.

4 The confidence interval suggests that at 95% confidence, even in the worst case, the arrangement will generate a mean profit of at least $\$37.95 - \$35.00 = \$2.95$ per customer. On the other hand, it may generate a profit as high as $\$55.05 - \$35.00 = \$20.05$ per customer.

5 A Type I error would mean deciding that the DVD success rate is higher than 30%, when it isn't. The bank would adopt a more expensive method for collecting payments that's no better than its original, less expensive strategy.

6 A Type II error would mean deciding that there's not enough evidence to say the DVD strategy works when in fact it does. The bank would fail to discover an effective method for increasing revenue from delinquent accounts.

7 Higher; the larger the effect size, the greater the power. It's easier to detect an improvement to a 60% success rate than to a 32% rate.

8 No error has been made. The confidence interval from the test market suggested that the mean revenue was above the $35 cost per customer, and in fact that's what happened.

13

Comparing Two Means

Visa Global Organization

Today, more than one billion people and 24 million merchants use the Visa card in 170 countries worldwide. But back in the early 1950s when the idea of cashless transactions first took hold, only Diners Club and some retailers, notably oil companies, issued charge cards. The vast majority of purchases were made by cash or personal check. Bank of America pioneered its BankAmericard program in Fresno, California, in 1958, and American Express issued the first plastic card in 1959. The idea of a credit "card" really gained momentum a decade later when a group of banks formed a joint venture to create a centralized system of payment. National BankAmericard, Inc. (NBI) took ownership of the credit card system in 1970 and for simplicity and marketability changed its name to Visa in 1976. (The name Visa is pronounced nearly the same way in every language.) That year, Visa processed 679,000 transactions—a volume that is processed on average every four minutes today. As technology changed, so did the credit card industry. By 1986, cardholders were able to use their Visa cards to get cash from ATMs.

Now a global organization, Visa is divided into several regional entities including: Visa Asia Pacific, Visa Canada, Visa Europe, and Visa USA. In the fiscal year ending September 2012, Visa's global network processed 82 billion transactions for a total volume of $6.5 trillion.[1]

---

[1]Source: Visa International Service Association, www.corporate.visa.com.

The credit card business can be extremely profitable. The average American household has eight cards and a total of $7073 in credit card debt. But, since many households have no debt, that average is misleading. Among households that carry credit card debt, the average debt was $15,162 in 2012. Not surprisingly, the credit card business is also intensely competitive. Rival banks and lending agencies are constantly trying to create new products and offers to win new customers, keep current customers, and provide incentives for current customers to charge more on their cards.

Are some credit card promotions more effective than others? For example, do customers spend more using their credit card if they know they will be given "double miles" or "double coupons" toward flights, hotel stays, or store purchases? To answer questions such as this, credit card issuers often perform experiments on a sample of customers, making some of them an *offer* of an incentive, while other customers receive no offer. Promotions cost the company money, so the company needs to estimate the size of any increased revenue to judge whether it is sufficient to cover their expenses. By comparing the performance of the two offers on the sample, they can decide whether the new offer would provide enough potential profit if they were to "roll it out" and offer it to their entire customer base.

Experiments that compare two groups are common throughout both science and industry. Other applications include comparing the effects of a new drug with the traditional therapy, the fuel efficiency of two car engine designs, or the sales of new products on two different customer segments. Usually the experiment is carried out on a subset of the population, often a much smaller subset. Using statistics, we can make statements about whether the means of the two groups differ in the population at large, and how large that difference might be.

13.1   Comparing Two Means

The natural display for comparing the distributions of two groups is side-by-side boxplots (see Figure 13.1). For the credit card promotion, the company judges performance by comparing the *mean* spend lift (the change in spending from before receiving the promotion to after receiving it) for the two samples. If the difference in spend lift between the group that received the promotion and the group that didn't is high enough, this will be viewed as evidence that the promotion worked. Looking at the two boxplots, it's not obvious that there's much of a difference. Can we conclude that the slight increase seen for those who received the promotion is more than just random fluctuation? We'll need statistical inference.

For two groups, the statistic of interest is the difference in the observed means of the offer and no offer groups: $\bar{y}_{Offer} - \bar{y}_{No\ Offer}$. We've offered the promotion to a random sample of cardholders and used another sample of cardholders, who got no special offer, as a control group. We know what happened in our samples, but what we'd really like to know is the difference of the means in the population at large: $\mu_{Offer} - \mu_{No\ Offer}$.

We compare two means in much the same way as we compared a single mean to a hypothesized value. But now both means are statistics, each with its own standard deviation, and the population model parameter of interest is the *difference* between the means. In our example, it's the true difference between the mean spend lift for customers offered the promotion and for customers for

Figure 13.1   Side-by-side boxplots show a small increase in spending for the group that received the promotion.

whom no offer was made. We estimate the difference with $\bar{y}_{Offer} - \bar{y}_{No\ Offer}$. How can we tell if a difference we observe in the sample means indicates a real difference in the underlying population means? We'll need to know the sampling distribution model and standard deviation of the difference. Once we know those, we can build a confidence interval and test a hypothesis just as we did for a single mean.

We have data on 500 randomly selected customers who were offered the promotion and another randomly selected 500 who were not. It's easy to find the mean and standard deviation of the spend lift for each of these groups. From these, we can find the standard deviation of each mean, but that's not what we want. We need the standard deviation of the *difference* in the means. For that, we can use a simple rule: *If the sample means come from independent samples, the variance of their sum or difference is the sum of their variances.*

> ### Variances Add for Sums *and* Differences
>
> At first, it may seem that this can't be true for differences as well as for sums. Here's some intuition about why variation increases even when we subtract two random quantities. Grab a full box of cereal. The label claims that it contains 16 ounces of cereal. We know that's not exact. There's a random quantity of cereal in the box with a mean (presumably) of 16 ounces and some variation from box to box. Now pour a 2-ounce serving of cereal into a bowl. Of course, your serving isn't exactly 2 ounces. There's some variation there, too. How much cereal would you guess was left in the box? Can you guess as accurately as you could for the full box? *After* you pour your bowl, the amount of cereal in the box is still a random quantity (with a smaller mean than before), but you've made it *more variable* because of the uncertainty in the amount you poured. Notice that we don't add the *standard deviations* of these two random quantities. It's the *variance* of the amount of cereal left in the box that's the sum of the two variances.

As long as the two groups are independent, we find the standard deviation of the *difference* between the two sample means by adding their variances and then taking the square root:

$$SD(\bar{y}_1 - \bar{y}_2) = \sqrt{Var(\bar{y}_1) + Var(\bar{y}_2)}$$
$$= \sqrt{\left(\frac{\sigma_1}{\sqrt{n_1}}\right)^2 + \left(\frac{\sigma_2}{\sqrt{n_2}}\right)^2}$$
$$= \sqrt{\frac{\sigma_1^2}{n_1} + \frac{\sigma_2^2}{n_2}}$$

Of course, usually we don't know the true standard deviations of the two groups, σ_1 and σ_2, so we substitute the estimates, s_1 and s_2, and find a *standard error*:

$$SE(\bar{y}_1 - \bar{y}_2) = \sqrt{\frac{s_1^2}{n_1} + \frac{s_2^2}{n_2}}.$$

Just as we did for one mean, we'll use the standard error to judge how big the difference really is. You shouldn't be surprised that, just as for a single mean, the ratio of the difference in the means to the standard error of that difference has a sampling model that follows a Student's *t* distribution.

To do inference, we'll need the degrees of freedom for the Student's *t*-model. Unfortunately, that formula isn't as simple as $n - 1$. The formula is straightforward but doesn't help our understanding much, so we leave it to the computer

An Easier Rule?

The formula for the degrees of freedom of the sampling distribution of the difference between two means is complicated. So some books teach an easier rule: The number of degrees of freedom is always at *least* the smaller of $n_1 - 1$ and $n_2 - 1$ and at most $n_1 + n_2 - 2$. The problem is that if you need to use this rule, you'll have to be conservative and use the lower value. And *that* approximation can be a poor choice because it can give less than *half* the degrees of freedom you're entitled to from the correct formula. So, we don't recommend using it unless you have lots of data.

or calculator. (If you are curious and really want to see the formula, look in the footnote.[2])

A Sampling Distribution for the Difference Between Two Means

We denote the difference in the means of two groups by

$$\mu_1 - \mu_2 = \Delta$$

When the conditions are met (see Section 13.3), the standardized sample difference between the means of two independent groups,

$$t = \frac{(\bar{y}_1 - \bar{y}_2) - \Delta}{SE(\bar{y}_1 - \bar{y}_2)},$$

can be modeled by a Student's t-model with a number of degrees of freedom found with a special formula. We estimate the standard error with

$$SE(\bar{y}_1 - \bar{y}_2) = \sqrt{\frac{s_1^2}{n_1} + \frac{s_2^2}{n_2}}.$$

FOR EXAMPLE   Sampling distribution of the difference of two means

The owner of a large car dealership wants to understand the negotiation process for buying a new car. Cars are given a "sticker price," but that a potential buyer may negotiate a better price is well known. He wonders if there is a difference in how men and women negotiate and who, if either, obtains the larger discount.

The owner takes a random sample of 100 customers from the last six months' sales and finds that 54 were men and 46 were women. On average the 54 men received an average discount of $962.96 with a standard deviation of $458.95; the 46 women received an average discount of $1262.61 with a standard deviation of $399.70.

QUESTION   What is the mean difference of the discounts received by men and women? What is its standard error? If there is no difference between them, does this seem like an unusually large value?

ANSWER   The mean difference is $1262.61 - $962.96 = $299.65. The women received, on average, a discount that was larger by $299.65. The standard error is

$$SE(\bar{y}_{Women} - \bar{y}_{Men}) = \sqrt{\frac{s_{Women}^2}{n_{Women}} + \frac{s_{Men}^2}{n_{Men}}} = \sqrt{\frac{(399.70)^2}{46} + \frac{(458.95)^2}{54}} = \$85.87$$

So, the difference is $299.65/85.87 = 3.49 standard errors away from 0. That sounds like a reasonably large number of standard errors for a Student's t statistic with at least 45 degrees of freedom. (The approximation formula gives 97.94 degrees of freedom.)

---

[2]The result is due to Satterthwaite and Welch.

Satterthwaite, F. E. (1946). "An Approximate Distribution of Estimates of Variance Components," *Biometrics Bulletin* 2: 110–114.

Welch, B. L. (1947). "The Generalization of Student's Problem when Several Different Population Variances are Involved," *Biometrika* 34: 28–35.

$$\mathrm{df} = \frac{\left(\dfrac{s_1^2}{n_1} + \dfrac{s_2^2}{n_2}\right)^2}{\dfrac{1}{n_1 - 1}\left(\dfrac{s_1^2}{n_1}\right)^2 + \dfrac{1}{n_2 - 1}\left(\dfrac{s_2^2}{n_2}\right)^2}$$

This approximation formula usually doesn't even give a whole number. If you are using a table, you'll need a whole number, so round down to be safe. If you are using technology, the approximation formulas that computers and calculators use for the Student's t-distribution can deal with fractional degrees of freedom.

13.2   # The Two-Sample *t*-Test

NOTATION ALERT

Δ_0 (pronounced "delta naught") isn't so standard that you can assume everyone will understand it. We use it because it's the capital Greek letter "D" for "difference."

Now we've got everything we need to construct the hypothesis test, and you already know how to do it. It's the same idea we used when testing one mean against a hypothesized value. Here, we start by hypothesizing a value for the true difference of the means. We'll call that hypothesized difference Δ_0. (It's so common for that hypothesized difference to be zero that we often just assume $\Delta_0 = 0$.) We then take the ratio of the difference in the means from our samples to its standard error and use that ratio to find a P-value from a Student's *t*-model. The test is called the **two-sample *t*-test**.

> **Two-Sample *t*-Test**
>
> When the appropriate assumptions and conditions are met, we test the hypothesis:
> $$H_0: \mu_1 - \mu_2 = \Delta_0$$
> where the hypothesized difference Δ_0 is almost always 0. We use the statistic:
> $$t = \frac{(\bar{y}_1 - \bar{y}_2) - \Delta_0}{SE(\bar{y}_1 - \bar{y}_2)}.$$
> The standard error of $\bar{y}_1 - \bar{y}_2$ is:
> $$SE(\bar{y}_1 - \bar{y}_2) = \sqrt{\frac{s_1^2}{n_1} + \frac{s_2^2}{n_2}}.$$
> When the null hypothesis is true, the statistic can be closely modeled by a Student's *t*-distribution with a number of degrees of freedom given by a special formula. We use that model to compare our *t* ratio with a critical value for *t* or to obtain a P-value.

The Two-Sample *t*-Methods

Two-sample *t*-methods assume that the two groups are independent. This is a crucial assumption. If it's not met, it is not safe to use these methods. One common way for groups to fail independence is when each observation in one group is related to one (and only one) observation in the other group. For example, if we test the *same* subjects before and after an event, or if we measure a variable on both husbands and wives. In that case, the observations are said to be **paired** and you'll need to use the paired *t*-methods discussed in section 13.7.

Sometimes you may see the two-sample *t*-methods referred to as the two-sample **independent** *t*-methods for emphasis. In this book, however, when we say two-sample, we'll always assume that the groups are independent.

> **FOR EXAMPLE** **The *t*-test for the difference of two means**
>
> **QUESTION**   We saw (on page 398) that the difference between the average discount obtained by men and women appeared to be large if we assume that there is no true difference. Test the hypothesis, find the P-value, and state your conclusions.
>
> **ANSWER**   The null hypothesis is: $H_0: \mu_{Women} - \mu_{Men} = 0$ vs.
> $$H_A: \mu_{Women} - \mu_{Men} \neq 0.$$
> The difference in the sample means, $\bar{y}_{Women} - \bar{y}_{Men}$ is \$299.65 with a standard error of 85.87. The *t*-statistic is that difference divided by the standard error:
> $t = \dfrac{\bar{y}_{Women} - \bar{y}_{Men}}{SE(\bar{y}_{Women} - \bar{y}_{Men})} = \dfrac{299.65}{85.87} = 3.49$. The approximation formula gives 97.94
> degrees of freedom (which is close to the maximum possible of $n_1 + n_2 - 2 = 98$). The P-value (from technology) for $t = 3.49$ with 97.94 df is 0.00073. We reject the null hypothesis. There is strong evidence to suggest that the difference in mean discount received by men and women is not 0.

13.3   # Assumptions and Conditions

Before we can perform a two-sample *t*-test, we have to check the assumptions and conditions.

Independence Assumption

We can't *assume* that the data, taken as one big group, come from a homogeneous population because that would mean assuming the means were equal—and we're trying to test that. So, the data in each group must be drawn independently and at random from each group's own homogeneous population separately or generated by a randomized comparative experiment. We should think about whether the independence assumption is reasonable. We can also check two conditions:

> **Randomization Condition:** Data collected with suitable randomization are likely to be independent. For surveys, are the data a representative random sample? For experiments, was the experiment randomized?

> **10% Condition:** We usually check this condition for differences of means only if we have a very small population or an extremely large sample. We needn't worry about it at all for randomized experiments.

Normal Population Assumption

With Student's *t*-models, we need the assumption that the underlying populations are *each* Normally distributed. So we check one condition.

> **Nearly Normal Condition:** We must check normality for *both* groups; a violation by either one violates the condition. As we saw for single sample means, the Normality Assumption matters most when sample sizes are small. When either group is small $(n < 15)$, you should not use these methods if the histogram or Normal probability plot shows skewness. For *n*'s closer to 40, a mildly skewed histogram is OK, but you should remark on any outliers you find and not work with severely skewed data. When both groups are bigger than that, the Central Limit Theorem starts to work, so the Nearly Normal Condition for the data matters less. Even in large samples, however, you should still be on the lookout for outliers, extreme skewness, and multiple modes.

Independent Groups Assumption

To use the two-sample *t*-methods, the two groups we are comparing must be independent of each other. In fact, the test is sometimes called the two *independent samples t*-test. No statistical test can verify that the groups are independent. You have to think about how the data were collected. The assumption would be violated, for example, if one group were comprised of husbands and the other group, their wives. Similarly, if we compared subjects' performances before some treatment with their performances afterward, we'd expect a relationship of each "before" measurement with its corresponding "after" measurement. When the observational units in the two groups are related or matched, *the two-sample methods of this chapter can't be applied.* Instead, we need the methods of section 13.7.

JUST CHECKING

Many office "coffee stations" collect voluntary payments for the food consumed. Researchers at the University of Newcastle upon Tyne performed an experiment to see whether the image of eyes watching would change employee behavior.[3] Each week on the cupboard behind the "honesty box," they alternated pictures of eyes looking at the viewer with pictures of flowers. They measured the consumption of milk to approximate the amount of food consumed and recorded the contributions (in £) each week per liter of milk. The table summarizes their results.

	Eyes	Flowers
n (# weeks)	5	5
$\bar{y}$	0.417 £/liter	0.151 £/liter
s	0.1811	0.067

1 What null hypothesis were the researchers testing?
2 Check the assumptions and conditions needed to test whether there really is a difference in behavior due to the difference in pictures.
3 What alternative hypothesis would you test?
4 The P-value of the test was less than 0.05. State a brief conclusion.

[3]Melissa Bateson, Daniel Nettle, and Gilbert Roberts, "Cues of Being Watched Enhance Cooperation in a Real-World Setting," *Biol. Lett.* Doi:10.1098/rsbl.2006.0509.

FOR EXAMPLE   Checking assumptions and conditions for a two-sample *t*-test

QUESTION   In the example on page 399, we rejected the null hypothesis that the mean discount received by men and women is the same. Here are the histograms of the discounts for both women and men. Check the assumptions and conditions and state any concerns that you might have about the conclusion we reached.

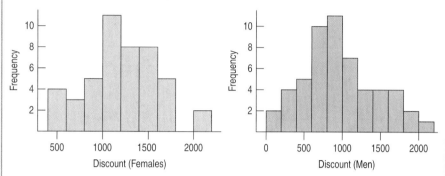

ANSWER   We were told that the sample was random, so the Randomization Condition is satisfied. There is no reason to think that the men's and women's responses are related (as they might be if they were husband and wife pairs) so the Independent Group Assumption is plausible. Because both groups have more than 40 observations, the discounts can be mildly skewed, which is the case. There are no obvious outliers (there is a small gap in the women's distribution, but the observations are not far from the center), so all the assumptions and conditions seem to be satisfied. We have no real concerns about the conclusion we reached that the mean difference is not 0.

GUIDED EXAMPLE   Credit Card Promotions and Spending

Our preliminary market research has suggested that a new incentive may increase customer spending. However, before we invest in this promotion on the entire population of cardholders, let's test a hypothesis on a sample. To judge whether the incentive works, we will examine the change in spending (called the *spend lift*) over a six-month period. We will see whether the *spend lift* for the group that received the offer was greater than the *spend lift* for the group that received no offer. If we observe differences, how can we decide whether these differences are important (or real) enough to justify our costs?

PLAN **Setup** State what we want to know.	We want to know if cardholders who are offered a promotion spend more on their credit card. We have the spend lift (in \$) for a random sample of 500 cardholders who were offered the promotion and for a random sample of 500 customers who were not.
Identify the *parameter* we wish to estimate. Here our parameter is the difference in the means, not the individual group means.	H_0: The mean spend lift for the group who received the offer is the same as for the group who did not:
	$H_0: \mu_{Offer} - \mu_{No\ Offer} = 0$
Identify the *population(s)* about which we wish to make statements.	H_A: The mean spend lift for the group who received the offer is higher:
Identify the variables and context.	$H_A: \mu_{Offer} - \mu_{No\ Offer} > 0$

(continued)

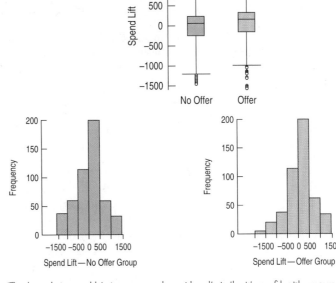

Make a graph to compare the two groups and check the distribution of each group. For completeness, we should report any outliers. If any outliers are extreme enough, we should consider performing the test both with and without the outliers and reporting the difference.

The boxplots and histograms show the distribution of both groups. It looks like the distribution for each group is unimodal and fairly symmetric.

The boxplots indicate several outliers in each group, but we have no reason to delete them, and their impact is minimal.

Model Check the assumptions and conditions.

✓ **Independence Assumption.** We have no reason to believe that the spending behavior of one customer would influence the spending behavior of another customer in the same group. The data report the "spend lift" for each customer for the same time period.

✓ **Randomization Condition.** The customers who were offered the promotion were selected at random.

✓ **Nearly Normal Condition.** The samples are large, so we are not overly concerned with this condition, and the boxplots and histograms show unimodal, symmetric distributions for both groups.

✓ **Independent Groups Assumption.** Customers were assigned to groups at random. There's no reason to think that those in one group can affect the spending behavior of those in the other group.

State the sampling distribution model for the statistic. Here the degrees of freedom will come from the approximation formula in footnote 2.

Under these conditions, it's appropriate to use a Student's t-model.

Specify your method.

We will use a two-sample t-test.

DO

Mechanics List the summary statistics. Be sure to include the units along with the statistics. Use meaningful subscripts to identify the groups.

We know $n_{No\ Offer} = 500$ and $n_{Offer} = 500$.
From technology, we find:

$$\bar{y}_{No\ Offer} = \$7.69 \qquad \bar{y}_{Offer} = \$127.61$$
$$s_{No\ Offer} = \$611.62 \qquad s_{Offer} = \$566.05$$

Use the sample standard deviations to find the standard error of the sampling distribution.

The observed difference in the two means is:

$$\bar{y}_{Offer} - \bar{y}_{No\ Offer} = \$127.61 - \$7.69 = \$119.92$$

The groups are independent, so:

$$SE(\bar{y}_{Offer} - \bar{y}_{No\ Offer}) = \sqrt{\frac{(566.05)^2}{500} + \frac{(611.62)^2}{500}}$$
$$= \$37.27$$

The observed t-value is:

$$t = 119.92/37.27 = 3.218$$

The best alternative is to let the computer use the approximation formula for the degrees of freedom and find the P-value.

with 992.0 df (from technology).

(To use critical values, we could find that the one-sided 0.01 critical value for a t with 992.0 df is $t^* = 2.33$.

Our observed t-value is larger than this, so we could reject the null hypothesis at the 0.01 level.)

Using software to obtain the P-value, we get:

```
Promotional Group     N     Mean    StDev
             No      500     7.69   611.62
             Yes     500   127.61   566.05


Difference = mu(1) − mu(0)
Estimate for difference: 119.9231
t = 3.2178, df = 992.007
One-sided P-value  = 0.0006669
```

REPORT

Conclusion Interpret the test results in the proper context.

MEMO

Re: Credit card promotion

Our analysis of the credit card promotion experiment found that customers offered the promotion spent more than those not offered the promotion. The difference was statistically significant, with a P-*value* < 0.001. So we conclude that this promotion will increase spending. The difference in spend lift averaged $119.92, but our analyses so far have not determined how much income this will generate for the company and thus whether the estimated increase in spending is worth the cost of the offer.

13.4   A Confidence Interval for the Difference Between Two Means

We rejected the null hypothesis that customers' mean spending would not change when offered a promotion. Because the company took a random sample of customers for each group, and our P-value was convincingly small, we concluded this difference is not zero for the population. Does this mean that we should offer the promotion to all customers?

A hypothesis test really says nothing about the size of the difference. All it says is that the observed difference is large enough that we can be confident it isn't zero. That's what the term "statistically significant" means. It doesn't say that the difference is important, financially significant, or interesting. Rejecting a null hypothesis simply says that a value as extreme as the observed statistic is unlikely to have been observed if the null hypothesis were true.

So, what recommendations can we make to the company? Almost every business decision will depend on looking at a range of likely scenarios—precisely the kind of information a confidence interval gives. We construct the confidence interval for the difference in means in the usual way, starting with our observed statistic, in this case $(\bar{y}_1 - \bar{y}_2)$. We then add and subtract a multiple of the standard error $SE(\bar{y}_1 - \bar{y}_2)$ where the multiple is based on the Student's t distribution with the same df formula we saw before.

Confidence Interval for the Difference Between Two Means

When the conditions are met, we are ready to find a **two-sample t-interval** for the difference between means of two independent groups, $\mu_1 - \mu_2$. The confidence interval is:

$$(\bar{y}_1 - \bar{y}_2) \pm t^*_{df} \times SE(\bar{y}_1 - \bar{y}_2),$$

where the standard error of the difference of the means is:

$$SE(\bar{y}_1 - \bar{y}_2) = \sqrt{\frac{s_1^2}{n_1} + \frac{s_2^2}{n_2}},$$

and the degrees of freedom is found by the special formula (see p. 398).

The critical value t^*_{df} depends on the particular confidence level, and on the number of degrees of freedom.

FOR EXAMPLE   A confidence interval for the difference between two means

QUESTION   We've concluded on page 399 that, on average, women receive a larger discount than men at this car dealership. How big is the difference, on average? Find a 95% confidence interval for the difference.

ANSWER   We've seen that the difference from our sample is $299.65 with a standard error of $85.87 and that it has 97.94 degrees of freedom. The 95% critical value for a t with 97.94 degrees of freedom is 1.984.

$$\bar{y}_{Women} - \bar{y}_{Men} \pm t^*_{97.94} SE(\bar{y}_{Women} - \bar{y}_{Men}) = 299.65 \pm 1.984 \times 85.87$$
$$= (\$129.28, \$470.02)$$

We are 95% confident that, on average, women received a discount that is between $129.28 and $470.02 larger than the men at this dealership.

GUIDED EXAMPLE   Confidence Interval for Credit Card Spending

We rejected the null hypothesis that the mean spending in the two groups was equal. But, to find out whether we should consider offering the promotion nationwide, we need to estimate the magnitude of the spend lift.

PLAN	**Setup** State what we want to know.	We want to find a 95% confidence interval for the mean difference in spending between those who are offered a promotion and those who aren't.
	Identify the *parameter* we wish to estimate. Here our parameter is the difference in the means, not the individual group means.	
	Identify the *population(s)* about which we wish to make statements.	We looked at the boxplots and histograms of the groups and checked the conditions before. The same assumptions and conditions are appropriate here, so we can proceed directly to the confidence interval.
	Identify the variables and context.	
	Specify the method.	We will use a two-sample *t*-interval.

DO	**Mechanics** Construct the confidence interval. Be sure to include the units along with the statistics. Use meaningful subscripts to identify the groups.	In our previous analysis, we found:

$$\bar{y}_{No\ Offer} = \$7.69 \qquad \bar{y}_{Offer} = \$127.61$$
$$s_{No\ Offer} = \$611.62 \qquad s_{Offer} = \$566.05$$

The observed difference in the two means is:

$$\bar{y}_{Offer} - \bar{y}_{No\ Offer} = \$127.61 - \$7.69 = \$119.92,$$

and the standard error is:

$$SE(\bar{y}_{Offer} - \bar{y}_{No\ Offer}) = \$37.27$$

From technology, the df is 992.007, and the one-sided 0.025 critical value for *t* with 992.007 df is 1.96. So the 95% confidence interval is:

$$\$119.92 \pm 1.96(\$37.27) = (\$46.87, \$192.97)$$

Using software to obtain these computations, we get:

```
95 percent confidence interval:
 (46.78784, 193.05837)
sample means:
No Offer        Offer
7.690882        127.613987
```

Use the sample standard deviations to find the standard error of the sampling distribution.

The best alternative is to let the computer use the approximation formula for the degrees of freedom and find the confidence interval.

Ordinarily, we rely on technology for the calculations. In our hand calculations, we rounded values at intermediate steps to show the steps more clearly. The computer keeps full precision and is the one you should report. The difference between the hand and computer calculations is about $0.08.

REPORT	**Conclusion** Interpret the confidence interval in the proper context.	MEMO

Re: Credit card promotion experiment

In our experiment, the promotion resulted in an increased spend lift of $119.92 on average. Further analysis gives a 95% confidence interval of ($46.79, $193.06). In other words, we expect with 95% confidence that under similar conditions, the mean spend lift that we achieve when we roll out the offer to all similar customers will be in this interval. We recommend that the company consider whether the values in this interval will justify the cost of the promotion program.

WHO	University students
WHAT	Prices offered to pay for a used camera ($)
WHEN	1990s
WHERE	Cornell University
WHY	To study the effects of friendship on transactions

13.5   The Pooled *t*-Test

If you bought a used camera in good condition from a friend, would you pay the same as you would if you bought the same item from a stranger? A researcher at Cornell University[4] wanted to know how friendship might affect simple sales such as this. She randomly divided subjects into two groups and gave each group descriptions of items they might want to buy. One group was told to imagine buying from a friend whom they expected to see again. The other group was told to imagine buying from a stranger.

Here are the prices they offered to pay for a used camera in good condition.

Price Offered for a Used Camera ($)	
Buying from a Friend	**Buying from a Stranger**
275	260
300	250
260	175
300	130
255	200
275	225
290	240
300	

The researcher who designed the friendship study was interested in testing the impact of friendship on negotiations. Previous theories had doubted that friendship had a measurable effect on pricing, but she hoped to find such an effect. The usual null hypothesis is that there's no difference in means and that's what we'll use for the camera purchase prices.

When we performed *t*-tests earlier in the chapter, we used an approximation formula that adjusts the degrees of freedom downward. Because this is an experiment, we might be willing to make another assumption. The null hypothesis says that whether you buy from a friend or a stranger should have no effect on the mean amount you're willing to pay for a camera. If it has no effect on the means, should it affect the variance of the transactions?

If we're willing to *assume* that the variances of the groups are equal (at least when the null hypothesis is true), then we can use a slightly more powerful method. We **pool** the data to estimate a common variance:

$$s_{pooled}^2 = \frac{(n_1 - 1)\, s_1^2 + (n_2 - 1)\, s_2^2}{(n_1 - 1) + (n_2 - 1)}.$$

Then we substitute this pooled variance in place of each of the variances in the standard error formula, simplifying it:

$$SE_{pooled}(\bar{y}_1 - \bar{y}_2) = \sqrt{\frac{s_{pooled}^2}{n_1} + \frac{s_{pooled}^2}{n_2}} = s_{pooled}\sqrt{\frac{1}{n_1} + \frac{1}{n_2}}.$$

The formula for degrees of freedom for the Student's *t*-model is simpler, too:

$$df = (n_1 - 1) + (n_2 - 1).$$

---

[4]J. J. Halpern (1997). "The Transaction Index: A Method for Standardizing Comparisons of Transaction Characteristics Across Different Contexts," *Group Decision and Negotiation*, 6, no. 6: 557–572.

Substitute the pooled-t estimate of the standard error and its degrees of freedom into the steps of the confidence interval or hypothesis test and you'll be using pooled-t methods.

To use the pooled-t methods, also check the **Equal Variance Assumption** that the variances of the two populations from which the samples have been drawn are equal. An easy way to do that is to compare their boxplots to check whether the boxes are of roughly equal size and that there are no extreme outliers in need of special attention.

Pooled *t*-Test and Confidence Interval for the Difference Between Means

The conditions for the **pooled *t*-test** for the difference between the means of two independent groups are the same as for the two-sample t-test with the additional assumption that the variances of the two groups are the same. We test the hypothesis:

$$H_0: \mu_1 - \mu_2 = \Delta_0,$$

where the hypothesized difference Δ_0 is almost always 0, using the statistic

$$t = \frac{(\bar{y}_1 - \bar{y}_2) - \Delta_0}{SE_{pooled}(\bar{y}_1 - \bar{y}_2)}.$$

The standard error of $\bar{y}_1 - \bar{y}_2$ is:

$$SE_{pooled}(\bar{y}_1 - \bar{y}_2) = s_{pooled}\sqrt{\frac{1}{n_1} + \frac{1}{n_2}},$$

where the pooled variance is:

$$s_{pooled}^2 = \frac{(n_1 - 1)\, s_1^2 + (n_2 - 1)\, s_2^2}{(n_1 - 1) + (n_2 - 1)}.$$

When the conditions are met and the null hypothesis is true, we can model this statistic's sampling distribution with a Student's t-model with $(n_1 - 1) + (n_2 - 1)$ degrees of freedom. We use that model to obtain a P-value for a test or a margin of error for a confidence interval.

The corresponding **pooled-*t* confidence interval** is:

$$(\bar{y}_1 - \bar{y}_2) \pm t_{df}^* \times SE_{pooled}(\bar{y}_1 - \bar{y}_2),$$

where the critical value t^* depends on the confidence level and is found with $(n_1 - 1) + (n_2 - 1)$ degrees of freedom.

GUIDED EXAMPLE   Role of Friendship in Negotiations

The usual null hypothesis in a pooled t-test is that there's no difference in means and that's what we'll use for the camera purchase prices.

(continued)

PLAN

Setup State what we want to know.

Identify the *parameter* we wish to estimate. Here our parameter is the difference in the means, not the individual group means. Identify the variables and context.

We want to know whether people are likely to offer a different amount for a used camera when buying from a friend than when buying from a stranger. We wonder whether the difference between mean amounts is zero. We have bid prices from 8 subjects buying from a friend and 7 subjects buying from a stranger, found in a randomized experiment.

Hypotheses State the null and alternative hypotheses.

The research claim is that friendship changes what people are willing to pay. The natural null hypothesis is that friendship makes no difference.

H_0: The difference in mean price offered to friends and the mean price offered to strangers is zero:

$$\mu_F - \mu_S = 0,$$

H_A: The difference in mean prices is not zero:

$$\mu_F - \mu_S \neq 0.$$

We didn't start with any knowledge of whether friendship might increase or decrease the price, so we choose a two-sided alternative.

Make a graph. Boxplots are the display of choice for comparing groups. We'll also want to check the distribution of each group. Histograms may do a better job.

REALITY CHECK Looks like the prices are higher if you buy from a friend. The two ranges barely overlap, so we'll be pretty surprised if we don't reject the null hypothesis.

Model Think about the assumptions and check the conditions. (Because this is a randomized experiment, we haven't sampled at all, so the 10% Condition doesn't apply.)

✓ **Independence Assumption.** There is no reason to think that the behavior of one subject influenced the behavior of another.

✓ **Randomization Condition.** The experiment was randomized. Subjects were assigned to treatment groups at random.

✓ **Independent Groups Assumption.** Randomizing the experiment gives independent groups.

✓ **Nearly Normal Condition.** Histograms of the two sets of prices show no evidence of skewness or extreme outliers.

Make a picture of the differences. Don't plot separate distributions of the two groups—that would entirely miss the pairing. For paired data, it's the Normality of the differences that we care about. Treat those paired differences as you would a single variable, and check the Nearly Normal condition.

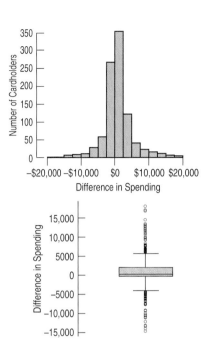

Specify the sampling distribution model.

Choose the method.

The conditions are met, so we'll use a Student's t-model with $(n - 1) = 910$ degrees of freedom, perform a paired t-test, and find a paired t-confidence interval.

DO

Mechanics n is the number of *pairs*, in this case, the number of cardholders.

$\bar{d}$ is the mean difference.

s_d is the standard deviation of the differences.

Make a picture. Sketch a *t*-model centered at the observed mean of 788.18.

Find the standard error and the *t*-score of the observed mean difference. There is nothing new in the mechanics of the paired *t*-methods. These are the mechanics of the *t*-test and *t*-interval for a mean applied to the differences.

The computer output tells us:

$$n = 911 \ pairs$$
$$\bar{d} = \$788.18$$
$$s_d = \$3740.22$$

We estimate the standard error of $\bar{d}$ using:

$$SE(\bar{d}) = \frac{s_d}{\sqrt{n}} = \frac{3740.22}{\sqrt{911}} = \$123.919$$

We find $t = \dfrac{\bar{d} - 0}{SE(\bar{d})} = \dfrac{788.180}{123.919} = 6.36$

A t-statistic with 910 degrees of freedom and a value of 6.36 has a one-sided P-value <0.001.

The critical value for a 95% confidence interval is:

$$t^*_{910} = 1.96$$

The margin of error, $ME = t^*_{910} \times SE(\bar{d})$

$$= 1.96 \times 123.919 = 242.88$$

So a 95% CI is $\bar{d} \pm ME = (\$545.30, \$1031.06)$.

(*continued*)

REPORT

Conclusion Link the results of the confidence interval to the context of the problem.

> MEMO
>
> **Re: Credit card expenditure changes**
>
> In the sample of cardholders studied, the change in expenditures between December and January averaged $788.18, which means that, on average, cardholders spend $788.18 less in January than the month before. There is strong evidence to suggest that the mean difference is not zero and that customers really do spend more in December than January. Although we didn't measure the change for all cardholders in the segment, we can be 95% confident that the true mean decrease in spending from December to January was between $545.30 and $1031.06.

FOR EXAMPLE   The paired *t*-test

Here are some summary statistics from the study undertaken by the car dealership owner (see page 412):

$$\bar{y}_{Frank} = \$414.48 \quad \bar{y}_{Ray} = \$478.88$$
$$SD_{Frank} = \$87.33 \quad SD_{Ray} = \$175.12$$
$$\bar{y}_{Diff} = \$64.40 \quad SD_{Diff} = \$146.74$$

QUESTION   Test the hypothesis that the mean maximum discount that Frank and Ray would give is the same. Give a 95% confidence interval for the mean difference.

ANSWER   We use a paired *t*-test because Frank and Ray were asked to give opinions about the same 30 cars.

$$t_{n-1} = \frac{\bar{d}}{SE(\bar{d})}$$

$$SE(\bar{d}) = \frac{s_d}{\sqrt{n}} = \frac{146.74}{\sqrt{30}} = \$26.79$$

$$t_{29} = \frac{64.40}{26.79} = 2.404$$

which has a (two-sided) P-value of 0.0228. We reject the null hypothesis that the mean difference is 0 and conclude that there is strong evidence to suggest that they are not the same.

A 95% confidence interval:

$$t^*_{29} = 2.045 \text{ at } 95\% \text{ confidence}$$
$$\bar{d} \pm t^*_{29} \times SE(\bar{d}) = 64.40 \pm 2.045 \times 26.79$$
$$= (\$9.61, \$119.19)$$

shows that Ray gives, on average, somewhere between $9.61 and $119.19 more for his maximum discount than Frank does.

WHAT CAN GO WRONG?

- **Watch out for paired data when using the two-sample *t*-test.** The Independent Groups Assumption deserves special attention. Some researcher designs *deliberately* violate the Independent Groups Assumption. For example, suppose you wanted to test a diet program. You select 10 people at random to take part in your diet. You measure their weights at the beginning of the diet and after 10 weeks of the diet. So, you have two columns of weights, one for *before* and one for *after*. But the data are related; each "after" weight goes naturally with the "before" weight for the *same* person. If the samples are *not* independent, you can't use two-sample methods. This is probably the main thing that can go wrong when using two-sample methods.

- **Don't use individual confidence intervals for each group to test the difference between their means.** If you make 95% confidence intervals for the means of each group separately and you find that the intervals don't overlap, you can reject the hypothesis that the means are equal (at the corresponding α level). But, if the intervals do overlap, that doesn't mean that you *can't* reject the null hypothesis. The margin of error for the difference between the means is smaller than the sum of the individual confidence interval margins of error. Comparing the individual confidence intervals is like adding the standard deviations. But we know that it's the variances that we add, and when we do it right, we actually get a more powerful test. So, don't test the difference between group means by looking at separate confidence intervals. Always make a two-sample *t*-interval or perform a two-sample *t*-test.

- **Look at the plots.** The usual (by now) cautions about checking for outliers and non-Normal distributions apply. The simple defense is to make and examine plots (side-by-side boxplots and histograms for two independent samples, histograms of the differences for paired data). You may be surprised how often this simple step saves you from the wrong or even absurd conclusions that can be generated by a single undetected outlier. You don't want to conclude that two methods have very different means just because one observation is atypical.

- **Don't use a paired *t*-method when the samples aren't paired.** When two groups don't have the same number of values, it's easy to see that they can't be paired. But just because two groups have the same number of observations doesn't mean they can be paired, even if they are shown side by side in a table. We might have 25 men and 25 women in our study, but they might be completely independent of one another. If they were siblings or spouses, we might consider them paired. Remember that you cannot *choose* which method to use based on your preferences. Only if the data are from an experiment or study in which observations were paired, can you use a paired method.

- **Don't forget to look for outliers when using paired methods.** For two-sample *t*-methods watch out for outliers in *either* group. For paired *t*-methods, the outliers we care about now are in the differences. A subject who is extraordinary both before and after a treatment may still have a perfectly typical difference. But one outlying difference can completely distort your conclusions. Be sure to plot the differences (even if you also plot the data) when using paired methods.

> **Do What We Say, Not What We Do**
>
> Precision machines used in industry often have a bewildering number of parameters that have to be set, so experiments are performed in an attempt to try to find the best settings. Such was the case for a hole-punching machine used by a well-known computer manufacturer to make printed circuit boards. The data were analyzed by one of the authors, but because he was in a hurry, he didn't look at the boxplots first and just performed t-tests on the experimental factors. When he found extremely small P-values even for factors that made no sense, he plotted the data. Sure enough, there was one observation 1,000,000 times bigger than the others. It turns out that it had been recorded in microns (millionths of an inch), while all the rest were in inches.

ETHICS IN ACTION

Joan Martinez is just beginning her third year as dean of the business school at a small regional university in the midwest. When she joined, the university's president and academic provost expressed concern over dwindling enrollments in the MBA program, and made it clear to her that increasing MBA enrollment was to be her highest priority. She spent her first year evaluating the situation. She discovered that the main reason for the business school's declining enrollments in the MBA program is its location. The region had experienced an economic downturn that forced companies and businesses, many of which had tuition reimbursement programs for their employees, to close or relocate. Given the lack of prospects for increasing MBA enrollments in the traditional regional market, Joan made plans to start an online MBA program.

The university's administration was very enthusiastic about the initiative and approved funding for a new position, Online MBA Director. Joan hired Raj Patel to fill it. Raj not only had considerable experience with online MBA programs, but a proven track record for getting faculty support, something that Joan really needed. Faculty who teach the more quantitative, technical courses had already begun criticizing the initiative. They argued that it would be difficult to achieve desired student learning outcomes in these types of courses using the online mode of delivery. Therefore, Raj's first task as the new Online MBA Director was to change their beliefs.

He remembered that a faculty colleague from his former institution, Rob Lowry, taught finance in a hybrid format: the first half in a traditional classroom and the other half online. Raj contacted him to ask if he would share his test scores (without identifying students) for the mid-term (based on traditional in-class instruction) and the final (based upon online teaching). Rob agreed. Based on test scores for 40 students, Raj calculated the mid-term average as 78.65 and the final exam average as 72.55. Although students' test scores after online instruction were lower, the two-sample t-test revealed that the averages on the two exams were not significantly different ($t = 1.82$, P-value $= 0.073$). Raj felt that these results help make the case that online and in-class instruction are equivalent when it comes to student learning in quantitative business courses, and Joan agreed. She was happy to have these results in time for the next faculty meeting.

- Identify the ethical dilemma in this scenario.

- What are the undesirable consequences?

- Propose an ethical solution that considers the welfare of all stakeholders.

WHAT HAVE WE LEARNED?

Learning Objectives

Know how to test whether the difference in the means of two independent groups is equal to some hypothesized value.

- The two-sample t-test is appropriate for independent groups. It uses a special formula for degrees of freedom.
- The Assumptions and Conditions are the same as for one-sample inferences for means with the addition of assuming that the groups are independent of each other.
- The most common null hypothesis is that the means are equal.

Be able to construct and interpret a confidence interval for the difference between the means of two independent groups.

- The confidence interval inverts the t-test in the natural way.

Know how and when to use pooled t inference methods.

- There is an additional assumption that the variances of the two groups are equal.
- This may be a plausible assumption in a randomized experiment.

Recognize when you have paired or matched samples and use an appropriate inference method.

- Paired t-methods are the same as one-sample t-methods applied to the pairwise differences.
- If data are paired they cannot be independent, so two-sample t and pooled-t methods would not be applicable.

Terms

Paired data
Data are paired when the observations are collected in pairs or the observations in one group are naturally related to observations in the other. The simplest form of pairing is to measure each subject twice—often before and after a treatment is applied. Pairing in experiments is a form of blocking and arises in other contexts. Pairing in observational and survey data is a form of matching.

Paired t-test
A hypothesis test for the mean of the pairwise differences of two groups. It tests the null hypothesis $H_0\colon \mu_d = \Delta_0$, where the hypothesized difference is almost always 0, using the statistic $t = \dfrac{\bar{d} - \Delta_0}{SE(\bar{d})}$ with $n - 1$ degrees of freedom, where $SE(\bar{d}) = \dfrac{s_d}{\sqrt{n}}$ and n is the number of pairs.

Paired t-confidence interval
A confidence interval for the mean of the pairwise differences between paired groups found as $\bar{d} \pm t^*_{n-1} \times SE(\bar{d})$, where $SE(\bar{d}) = \dfrac{s_d}{\sqrt{n}}$ and n is the number of pairs.

Pooled t-interval
A confidence interval for the difference in the means of two independent groups used when we are willing and able to make the additional assumption that the variances of the groups are equal. It is found as:
$$(\bar{y}_1 - \bar{y}_2) \pm t^*_{df} \times SE_{pooled}(\bar{y}_1 - \bar{y}_2),$$
$$\text{where } SE_{pooled}(\bar{y}_1 - \bar{y}_2) = s_{pooled}\sqrt{\frac{1}{n_1} + \frac{1}{n_2}},$$
and the pooled variance is
$$s^2_{pooled} = \frac{(n_1 - 1)\, s^2_1 + (n_2 - 1)\, s^2_2}{(n_1 - 1) + (n_2 - 1)}.$$
The number of degrees of freedom is $(n_1 - 1) + (n_2 - 1)$.

Pooled t-test
A hypothesis test for the difference in the means of two independent groups when we are willing and able to assume that the variances of the groups are equal. It tests the null hypothesis
$$H_0\colon \mu_1 - \mu_2 = \Delta_0,$$
where the hypothesized difference Δ_0 is almost always 0, using the statistic
$$t_{df} = \frac{(\bar{y}_1 - \bar{y}_2) - \Delta_0}{SE_{pooled}(\bar{y}_1 - \bar{y}_2)},$$
where the pooled standard error is defined as for the pooled interval and the degrees of freedom is $(n_1 - 1) + (n_2 - 1)$.

Pooling
Data from two or more populations may sometimes be combined, or *pooled*, to estimate a statistic (typically a pooled variance) when we are willing to assume that the estimated value is the same in both populations. The resulting larger sample size may lead to an estimate with lower sample variance. However, pooled estimates are appropriate only when the required assumptions are true.

Two-sample t-interval
A confidence interval for the difference in the means of two independent groups found as
$$(\bar{y}_1 - \bar{y}_2) \pm t^*_{df} \times SE(\bar{y}_1 - \bar{y}_2), \text{ where}$$
$$SE(\bar{y}_1 - \bar{y}_2) = \sqrt{\frac{s^2_1}{n_1} + \frac{s^2_2}{n_2}}$$
and the number of degrees of freedom is given by the approximation formula in footnote 2 of this chapter, or with technology.

Two-sample t-test
A hypothesis test for the difference in the means of two independent groups. It tests the null hypothesis
$$H_0\colon \mu_1 - \mu_2 = \Delta_0,$$
where the hypothesized difference Δ_0 is almost always 0, using the statistic
$$t_{df} = \frac{(\bar{y}_1 - \bar{y}_2) - \Delta_0}{SE(\bar{y}_1 - \bar{y}_2)},$$
with the number of degrees of freedom given by the approximation formula in footnote 2 of this chapter, or with technology.

TECHNOLOGY HELP: Comparing Two Groups

Two-Sample Methods

Here's some typical computer package output with comments:

May just say "difference of means"

Test Statistic

```
2-Sample t-Test of μ1-μ2 = 0 vs ≠ 0

Difference Between Means = 0.99145299  t-Statistic = 1.540
with 196 df
Fail to reject Ho at Alpha = 0.05
P = 0.1251
```

Some programs will draw a conclusion about the test. Others just give the P-value and let you decide for yourself.

df found from approximation formula and rounded down. The unrounded value may be given, or may be used to find the P-value.

Many programs give far too many digits. Ignore the excess digits.

Some statistics software automatically tries to test whether the variances of the two groups are equal. Some automatically offer both the two-sample-*t* and pooled-*t* results. Ignore the test for the variances; it has little power in any situation in which its results could matter. If the pooled and two-sample methods differ in any important way, you should stick with the two-sample method. Most likely, the Equal Variance Assumption needed for the pooled method has failed.

The degrees of freedom approximation usually gives a fractional value. Most packages seem to round the approximate value down to the next smallest integer (although they may actually compute the P-value with the fractional value, gaining a tiny amount of power).

There are two ways to organize data when we want to compare two independent groups. The first, called **unstacked data**, lists the data in two columns, one for each group. Each list can be thought of as a variable. In this method, the variables in the credit card example would be "Offer" and "No Offer." Graphing calculators usually prefer this form, and some computer programs can use it as well.

The alternative way to organize the data is as **stacked data**. What is the response variable for the credit card experiment? It's the "Spend Lift"—the amount by which customers increased their spending. But the values of this variable in the unstacked lists are in both columns, and actually there's an experiment factor here, too—namely, whether the customer was offered the promotion or not. So we could put the data into two different columns, one with the "Spend Lift"s in it and one with a "Yes" for those who were offered the promotion and a "No" for those who weren't. The stacked data would look like this:

Spend Lift	Offer
969.74	Yes
915.04	Yes
197.57	No
77.31	No
196.27	Yes
…	…

This way of organizing the data makes sense as well. Now the factor and the response variables are clearly visible. You'll have to see which method your program requires. Some packages even allow you to structure the data either way.

The commands to do inference for two independent groups on common statistics technology are not always found in obvious places. The step-by-step instructions contain some starting guidelines.

Paired Methods

Most statistics programs can compute paired-*t* analyses. Some may want you to find the differences yourself and use the one-sample *t*-methods. Those that perform the entire procedure will need to know the two variables to compare. The computer, of course, cannot verify that the variables are naturally paired. Most programs will check whether the two variables have the same number of observations, but some stop there, and that can cause trouble. Most programs will automatically omit any pair that is missing a value for either variable. You must look carefully to see whether that has happened.

As we've seen with other inference results, some packages pack a lot of information into a simple table, but you must locate what you want for yourself. Here's a generic example with comments.

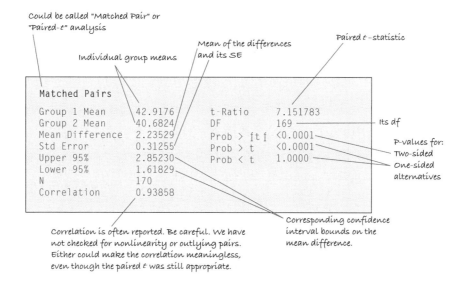

Could be called "Matched Pair" or "Paired-*t*" analysis

Individual group means

Mean of the differences and its SE

Paired *t*-statistic

```
Matched Pairs

Group 1 Mean      42.9176      t-Ratio    7.151783
Group 2 Mean      40.6824      DF         169
Mean Difference    2.23529     Prob > ↑t↑  <0.0001
Std Error          0.31255     Prob > t    <0.0001
Upper 95%          2.85230     Prob < t     1.0000
Lower 95%          1.61829
N                  170
Correlation        0.93858
```

Its df

P-values for:
Two-sided
One-sided
alternatives

Correlation is often reported. Be careful. We have not checked for nonlinearity or outlying pairs. Either could make the correlation meaningless, even though the paired *t* was still appropriate.

Corresponding confidence interval bounds on the mean difference.

Other packages try to be more descriptive. It may be easier to find the results, but you may get less information from the output table.

Groups may have missing values. Only cases with both values present are used in a paired-*t* analysis. You may not learn that from some packages.

Even simple tables can have superfluous numbers such as these.

SD (differences)

SE($\bar{d}$)

```
Paired T for Group 1-Group 2

                   N      Mean    Std Dev   SE(Mean)
Group 1           199     42.62    11.646    0.8255
Group 2           170     40.68    11.414    0.8254
Paired Difference 170      2.235    4.0752   0.31255

95% CI for mean difference: (1.618, 2.852)
T-Test of mean difference = 0(vs ≠ 0): T-Value = 7.1518 P-Value < 0.0001
```

$\bar{d}$

CI corresponds to specified α.

Some packages let you specify the alternative and report only results for that alternative.

t-statistic and its P-value (You may need to calculate $n_d - 1$ for yourself to get the df.)

Computers make it easy to examine the boxplots of the two groups and the histogram of the differences—both important steps. Some programs offer a scatterplot of the two variables. That can be helpful. In terms of the scatterplot, a paired *t*-test is about whether the points tend to be above or below the 45° line $y = x$. (Note that pairing says nothing about whether the scatterplot should be straight. That doesn't matter for our *t*-methods.)

EXCEL

To perform a two-sample *t*-test in Excel using Data Analysis Tool Pack:

- In the **Data** menu, Choose **Data Analysis** (found under Analysis).
- Choose the appropriate *t*-test from the menu.
- Identify the following:
  - The cell range for the data in the two samples (for testing independent groups) or the difference data (for a paired *t*-test).
  - The hypothesized difference.
- Check the box next to Labels if the first row of the data contains labels, and identify where you would like the results to be placed.

To perform a two-sample *t*-test using built-in formulas:

- From Formulas, choose **More functions** > **Statistical** > **T.TEST**, and specify:

  - Array 1 and Array 2 = Location in the spreadsheet of the two groups to compare.

  - Tails of the distribution = 1 for one-tailed test and 2 for two-tailed test.

- Type = 1 for a paired test, 2 for equal variance *t*-test, and 3 for unequal variance *t*-test.

To perform a paired *t*-test in Excel:

- Enter paired data into two columns with one pair in each row.

- In another column, calculate the difference of the values in the two columns.

- Analyze the difference column using a one-sample *t*-test. An example is shown below:

	A	B	C	D	E
1	t-Test of a Mean				
2					**Syntax for Column D**
3	Sample mean	460.38	t Stat	1.89	=(B3-B6)/(B4/B5^0.5)
4	Sample standard deviation	38.83	P(T<=t) one-tail	0.0323	=1-(T.DIST(ABS(D3),(B5-1),1))
5	Sample size	50	t Critical lower one-tail	-1.6766	=T.INV(B7,B5-1)
6	Hypothesized mean	450	t Critical upper one tail	1.6766	=ABS(T.INV(B7,B5-1))
7	Alpha	0.05	P(T<=t) two-tail	0.0646	=2*D4
8			t Critical two-tail	± 2.0096	=T.INV(B7/2,B5-1)

XLSTAT

To conduct a *t* test for the difference between two means:

- Choose **Parametric tests,** and then **Two-sample t-test and z-test.**

- If the two samples are in two separate columns in your workbook, choose the option **One column per sample.**

- If your data are *stacked* (one column lists the data, and the other the group identifier) choose the option **One column per variable.**

- If the data are paired, choose the option **Paired samples.**

- Enter the range of cell data.

- On the **Options** tab, for a test that is not pooled uncheck the box next to **Assume equality.**

The output yields the results of a hypothesis test and a confidence interval for the difference between means.

JMP

To conduct a two-sample *t*-test in JMP:

- From the **Analyze** menu, select **Fit X by Y.**

- Select variables: a **Y, Response** variable that holds the data and an **X, Factor** variable that holds the group names. Click OK, and JMP

will make a dotplot. Be sure that the variable type for the **X, Factor** variable is set to nominal or ordinal.

- Click the Red triangle next to "Oneway Analysis…" and select:

  - *t* **Test** to perform a two-sample *t*-test.

To compute a paired *t*-test using JMP:

- From the **Analyze** menu, select **Matched Pairs.**

- Place two variables containing matched data into **Y, Column.**

Comments:

To perform a pooled *t*-test, select **Means/ANOVA/Pooled *t*** under the red triangle next to "Oneway Analysis…"

MINITAB

To perform a two-sample *t*-test in Minitab:

- From the **Stat** menu, choose the **Basic Statistics** submenu.

- Choose **2t 2-sample t…** and fill in the dialog for:

  - Data in "one column" (unstacked data)

  - Data "two columns" (stacked data) or

  - Summarized data

To conduct a paired *t*-test using Minitab:

- From the **Stat** menu, choose the **Basic Statistics** submenu.
- Choose **t-t Paired t** and fill in the dialog for:
  - Data in "two columns" or
  - Summarized data

Note: For two-sample *t*-tests, the **Graphs** button creates boxplots of your two samples and the **Options** button allows you to conduct either a one-sided or two-sided test or change the confidence level.

To conduct a two-sample *t*-test in SPSS:

- From the **Analyze** menu, choose the **Compare Means** submenu.

- Choose **Independent-Samples t-test.**
- Specify the data variable and grouping variable, click the button under the grouping variable, and identify numerical codes for groups.

Note: SPSS offers both the two-sample and pooled-*t* results in the same table. SPSS expects the data in one variable and group names in the other. If there are more than two group names in the group variable, only the two that are named in the dialog box will be compared.

To perform a paired *t*-test in SPSS:

- From the **Analyze** menu, choose the **Compare Means** submenu.
- Choose **Paired Samples t-test.**
- Highlight the two variables containing the paired data and add to the list.

Brief **Case**

Real Estate

In Chapter 4, we examined the regression of the sales price of a home on its size and saw that larger homes generally fetch a higher price. How much can we learn about a house from the fact that it has a fireplace or more than the average number of bedrooms? Data for a random sample of 1063 homes from the upstate New York area can be found in the file **Saratoga Real Estate**. There are 6 quantitative variables: *Price($)*, *Living Area(sq.ft)*, *Bathrooms(#)*, *Bedrooms(#)*, *Lot Size(Acres)*, and *Age(years)*, and one categorical variable, *Fireplace?* $(1 = Yes; 0 = No)$ denoting whether the house has at least one fireplace. We can use *t*-methods to see, for example, whether homes with fireplaces sell for more, on average, and by how much. For the quantitative variables, create new categorical variables by splitting them at the median or some other splitting point of your choice, and compare home prices above and below this value. For example, the median number of *Bedrooms* of these homes is 2. You might compare the prices of homes with 1 or 2 bedrooms to those with more than 2. Write up a short report summarizing the differences in mean price based on the categorical variables that you created.

Consumer Spending Patterns (Data Analysis)

You are on the financial planning team for monitoring a high spending segment of a credit card. You know that customers tend to spend more during December before the holidays, but you're not sure about the pattern of spending in the months after the holidays. Look at the data set **Consumer spending post holiday**. It contains the monthly credit card spending of 1200 customers during the months December, January, February, March, and April. Report on the spending differences between the months. If you had failed to realize that these are paired data, what difference would that have made in your reported confidence intervals and tests?

EXERCISES

SECTION 13.1

1. A developer wants to know if the houses in two different neighborhoods were built at roughly the same time. She takes a random sample of six houses from each neighborhood and finds their ages from local records. The table shows the data for each sample (in years).

Neighborhood 1	Neighborhood 2
57	50
60	43
46	35
62	53
67	46
56	55

a) Find the sample means for each neighborhood.
b) Find the estimated difference of the mean ages of the two neighborhoods.
c) Find the sample variances for each neighborhood.
d) Find the sample standard deviations for each neighborhood.
e) Find the standard error of the difference of the two sample means.

2. A market analyst wants to know if the new website he designed is showing increased page views per visit. A customer is randomly sent to one of two different websites, offering the same products, but with different designs. Here are the page views from five randomly chosen customers from each website:

Website A	Website B
9	10
4	13
14	2
7	3
2	7

a) Find the sample mean page views for each website.
b) Find the estimated difference of the sample mean page views of the two websites.
c) Find the sample variances for each website.
d) Find the sample standard deviations for each website.
e) Find the standard error of the difference of the sample means.

3. The developer in Exercise 1 hires an assistant to collect a random sample of houses from each neighborhood and finds that the summary statistics for the two neighborhoods look as follows:

Neighborhood 1	Neighborhood 2
$n_1 = 30$	$n_2 = 35$
$\bar{y}_1 = 57.2$ yrs	$\bar{y}_2 = 47.6$ yrs
$s_1 = 7.51$ yrs	$s_2 = 7.85$ yrs

a) Find the estimated mean age difference between the two neighborhoods.
b) Find the standard error of the estimated mean difference.
c) Calculate the t-statistic for the observed difference in mean ages assuming that the true mean difference is 0.

4. Not happy with the previous results, the analyst in Exercise 2 takes a much larger random sample of customers from each website and records their page views. Here are the data:

Website A	Website B
$n_1 = 80$	$n_2 = 95$
$\bar{y}_1 = 7.7$ pages	$\bar{y}_2 = 7.3$ pages
$s_1 = 4.6$ pages	$s_2 = 4.3$ pages

a) Find the estimated mean difference in page visits between the two websites.
b) Find the standard error of the estimated mean difference.
c) Calculate the t-statistic for the observed difference in mean page visits assuming that the true mean difference is 0.

SECTION 13.2

5. For the data in Exercise 1, we want to test the null hypothesis that the mean age of houses in the two neighborhoods is the same. Assume that the data come from a population that is Normally distributed.

a) Using the values you found in Exercise 1, find the value of the t-statistic for the difference in mean ages for the null hypothesis.
b) Calculate the degrees of freedom from the formula in the footnote of page 398.
c) Calculate the degrees of freedom using the rule that df $= \min(n_1 - 1, n_2 - 1)$.
d) Find the P-value using the degrees of freedom from part b. (You can either round the number of df and use a table or use technology or a website).
e) Find the P-value using the degrees of freedom from part d.
f) What do you conclude at $\alpha = 0.05$?

6. For the data in Exercise 2, we want to test the null hypothesis that the mean number of page visits is the same for the two websites. Assume that the data come from a population that is Normally distributed.

a) Using the values you found in Exercise 2, find the value of the *t*-statistic for the difference in mean ages for the null hypothesis.
b) Calculate the degrees of freedom from the formula in the footnote of page 398.
c) Calculate the degrees of freedom using the rule that df $= \min(n_1 - 1, n_2 - 1)$.
d) Find the P-value using the degrees of freedom from part b. (You can either round the number of df and use a table or use technology or a website).
e) Find the P-value using the degrees of freedom from part c.
f) What do you conclude at $\alpha = 0.05$?

7. Using the data in Exercise 3, test the hypothesis that the mean age of houses in the two neighborhoods is the same. You may assume that the ages of houses in each neighborhood follow a Normal distribution.

a) Calculate the P-value of the statistic knowing that the approximation formula gives 62.2 df (you will need to round or use technology).
b) Calculate the P-value of the statistic using the rule that df is at least $min(n_1 - 1, n_2 - 1)$.
c) What do you conclude at $\alpha = 0.05$?

8. Using the data in Exercise 4, test the hypothesis that the mean number of page views from the two websites is the same. You may assume that the number of page views from each website follow a Normal distribution.

a) Calculate the P-value of the statistic knowing that the approximation formula gives 163.6 df.
b) Calculate the P-value of the statistic using the rule that df is at least $\min(n_1 - 1, n_2 - 1)$.
c) What do you conclude at $\alpha = 0.05$?

SECTION 13.4

9. Using the data in Exercise 1, and assuming that the data come from a distribution that is Normally distributed,

a) Find a 95% confidence interval for the mean difference in ages of houses in the two neighborhoods.
b) Is 0 within the confidence interval?
c) What does it say about the null hypothesis that the mean difference is 0?

10. Using the data in Exercise 2, and assuming that the data come from a distribution that is Normally distributed,

a) Find a 95% confidence interval for the mean difference in page views from the two websites.
b) Is 0 within the confidence interval?
c) What does it say about the null hypothesis that the mean difference is 0?

11. Using the summary statistics in Exercise 3, and assuming that the data come from a distribution that is Normally distributed,

a) Find a 95% confidence interval for the mean difference in ages of houses in the two neighborhoods using the df given in Exercise 7.
b) Why is the confidence interval narrower than the one you found in Exercise 9?
c) Is 0 within the confidence interval?
d) What does it say about the null hypothesis that the mean difference is 0?

12. Using the summary statistics in Exercise 4, and assuming that the data come from a distribution that is Normally distributed,

a) Find a 95% confidence interval for the mean difference in page views from the two websites.
b) Why is the confidence interval narrower than the one you found in Exercise 10?
c) Is 0 within the confidence interval?
d) What does it say about the null hypothesis that the mean difference is 0?

SECTION 13.5

13. For the data in Exercise 1,

a) Test the null hypothesis at $\alpha = 0.05$ using the pooled *t*-test. (Show the *t*-statistic, P-value, and conclusion.)
b) Find a 95% confidence interval using the pooled degrees of freedom.
c) Are your answers different from what you previously found in Exercise 9? Explain briefly why or why not.

14. For the data in Exercise 2,

a) Test the null hypothesis at $\alpha = 0.05$ using the pooled *t*-test. (Show the *t*-statistic, P-value, and conclusion.)
b) Find a 95% confidence interval using the pooled degrees of freedom.
c) Are your answers different from what you previously found in Exercise 10? Explain briefly why or why not.

15. For the data in Exercise 3,

a) Test the null hypothesis at $\alpha = 0.05$ using the pooled *t*-test. (Show the *t*-statistic, P-value, and conclusion.)
b) Find a 95% confidence interval using the pooled degrees of freedom.
c) Are your answers different from what you previously found in Exercise 11? Explain briefly why or why not.

16. For the data in Exercise 4,

a) Test the null hypothesis at $\alpha = 0.05$ using the pooled *t*-test. (Show the *t*-statistic, P-value, and conclusion.)
b) Find a 95% confidence interval using the pooled degrees of freedom.

c) Are your answers different from what you previously found in Exercise 12? Explain briefly why or why not.

SECTION 13.6

17. For each of the following scenarios, say whether the data should be treated as independent or paired samples. Explain briefly. If paired, explain what the pairing involves.

a) An efficiency expert claims that a new ergonomic desk chair makes typing at a computer terminal easier and faster. To test it, 15 volunteers are selected. Using both the new chair and their old chair, each volunteer types a randomly selected passage for 2 minutes and the number of correct words typed is recorded.
b) A developer wants to know if the houses in two different neighborhoods have the same mean price. She selects 10 houses from each neighborhood at random and tests the null hypothesis that the means are equal.
c) A manager wants to know if the mean productivity of two workers is the same. For a random selection of 30 hours in the past month, he compares the number of items produced by each worker in that hour.

18. For each of the following scenarios, say whether the data should be treated as independent or paired samples. Explain briefly. If paired, explain what the pairing involves.

a) An efficiency expert claims that a new ergonomic desk chair makes typing at a computer terminal easier and faster. To test it, 30 volunteers are selected. Half of the volunteers will use the new chair and half will use their old chairs. Each volunteer types a randomly selected passage for 2 minutes and the number of correct words typed is recorded.
b) A real estate agent wants to know how much extra a fireplace adds to the price of a house. She selects 25 city blocks. In each block, she randomly chooses a house with a fireplace and one without and records the assessment value.
c) A manager wants to know if the mean productivity of two workers is the same. For each worker, he randomly selects 30 hours in the past month and compares the number of items produced.

SECTION 13.7

19. A supermarket chain wants to know if their "buy one, get one free" campaign increases customer traffic enough to justify the cost of the program. For each of 10 stores they select two days at random to run the test. For one of those days (selected by a coin flip), the program will be in effect. They want to test the hypothesis that there is no mean difference in traffic against the alternative that the program increases the mean traffic. Here are the results in number of customer visits to the 10 stores:

Store #	With Program	Without Program
1	140	136
2	233	235
3	110	108
4	42	35
5	332	328
6	135	135
7	151	144
8	33	39
9	178	170
10	147	141

a) Are the data paired? Explain.
b) Compute the mean difference.
c) Compute the standard deviation of the differences.
d) Compute the standard error of the mean difference.
e) Find the value of the t-statistic.
f) How many degrees of freedom does the t-statistic have?
g) Is the alternative one- or two-sided? Explain.
h) What is the P-value associated with this t-statistic? (Assume that the other assumptions and conditions for inference are met.)
i) At $\alpha = 0.05$, what do you conclude?

20. A city wants to know if a new advertising campaign to make citizens aware of the dangers of driving after drinking has been effective. They count the number of drivers who have been stopped with more alcohol in their systems than the law allows for each day of the week in the week before and the week a month after the campaign starts. Here are the results:

Day of Week	Before	After
M	5	2
T	4	0
W	2	2
Th	4	1
F	6	8
S	14	7
Su	6	7

a) Are the data paired? Explain.
b) Compute the mean difference.
c) Compute the standard deviation of the differences.
d) Compute the standard error of the mean difference.
e) Find the value of the t-statistic.
f) How many degrees of freedom does the t-statistic have?
g) Is the alternative one- or two-sided? Explain.
h) What is the P-value associated with this t-statistic? (Assume that the other assumptions and conditions for inference are met.)
i) At $\alpha = 0.05$, what do you conclude?

21. In order to judge whether the program is successful, the manager of the supermarket chain in Exercise 21 wants to know the plausible range of values for the mean increase in customers using the program. Construct a 90% confidence interval.

22. A new operating system is installed in every workstation at a large company. The claim of the operating system manufacturer is that the time to shut down and turn on the machine will be much faster. To test it an employee selects 36 machines and tests the combined shut down and restart time of each machine before and after the new operating system has been installed. The mean and standard deviation of the differences (before – after) is 23.5 seconds with a standard deviation of 40 seconds.

a) What is the standard error of the mean difference?
b) How many degrees of freedom does the *t*-statistic have?
c) What is the 90% confidence interval for the mean difference?
d) What do you conclude at $\alpha = 0.05$?

CHAPTER EXERCISES

23. Hot dogs and calories. Consumers increasingly make food purchases based on nutrition values. *Consumer Reports* examined the calorie content of two kinds of hot dogs: meat (usually a mixture of pork, turkey, and chicken) and all beef. The researchers purchased samples of several different brands. The meat hot dogs averaged 111.7 calories, compared to 135.4 for the beef hot dogs. A test of the null hypothesis that there's no difference in mean calorie content yields a P-value of 0.124. What would you conclude?

24. Hot dogs and sodium. The *Consumer Reports* article described in Exercise 23 also listed the sodium content (in mg) for the various hot dogs tested. A test of the null hypothesis that beef hot dogs and meat hot dogs don't differ in the mean amounts of sodium yields a P-value of 0.110. What would you conclude?

25. Learning math. The Core Plus Mathematics Project (CPMP) is an innovative approach to teaching mathematics that engages students in group investigations and mathematical modeling. After field tests in 36 high schools over a three-year period, researchers compared the performances of CPMP students with those taught using a traditional curriculum. In one test, students had to solve applied algebra problems using calculators. Scores for 320 CPMP students were compared with those of a control group of 273 students in a traditional math program. Computer software was used to create a confidence interval for the difference in mean scores (*Journal for Research in Mathematics Education*, 31, no. 3, 2000).

```
Conf. level: 95%
Variable: μ(CPMP) − μ(Ctrl)
Interval: (5.573, 11.427)
```

a) What is the margin of error for this confidence interval?
b) If we had created a 98% confidence interval, would the margin of error be larger or smaller?
c) Explain what the calculated interval means in this context.
d) Does this result suggest that students who learn mathematics with CPMP will have (statistically) significantly higher mean scores in applied algebra than those in traditional programs? Explain.

26. Sales performance. A chain that specializes in healthy and organic food would like to compare the sales performance of two of its primary stores in the state of Massachusetts. These stores are both in urban, residential areas with similar demographics. A comparison of the weekly sales randomly sampled over a period of nearly two years for these two stores yields the following information:

Store	N	Mean	StDev	Minimum	Median	Maximum
Store#1	9	242170	23937	211225	232901	292381
Store#2	9	235338	29690	187475	232070	287838

a) Create a 95% confidence interval for the difference in the mean store weekly sales. (df from technology is 15.31)
b) Interpret your interval in context.
c) Does it appear that one store sells more on average than the other store?
d) What is the margin of error for this interval?
e) Would you expect a 99% confidence interval to be wider or narrower? Explain.
f) If you computed a 99% confidence interval, would your conclusion in part c change? Explain.

27. CPMP, again. During the study described in Exercise 25, students in both CPMP and traditional classes took another algebra test that did not allow them to use calculators. The table shows the results. Are the mean scores of the two groups significantly different? Assume that the assumptions for inference are satisfied.

Math Program	n	Mean	SD
CPMP	312	29.0	18.8
Traditional	265	38.4	16.2

a) Write an appropriate hypothesis.
b) Here is computer output for this hypothesis test. Explain what the P-value means in this context.

```
2-Sample t-Test of μ1 − μ2 ≠ 0
t-Statistic = −6.451 w/574.8761 df
P < 0.0001
```

c) State a conclusion about the CPMP program.

28. IT training costs. An accounting firm is trying to decide between IT training conducted in-house and the use of third party consultants. To get some preliminary cost data, each type of training was implemented at two of the firm's offices located in different cities. The table below shows the average annual training cost per employee at each location. Are the mean costs significantly different? Assume that the assumptions for inference are satisfied.

IT Training	n	Mean	SD
In-House	210	$490.00	$32.00
Consultants	180	$500.00	$48.00

a) Write the appropriate hypotheses.
b) Below is computer output for this hypothesis test. Explain what the P-value means in this context.

```
2-Sample t-Test of μ₁ − μ₂ ≠ 0
t-Statistic = −2.38 w/303 df
P = .018
```

c) State a conclusion about IT training costs.

29. Cereal company. CPMP and word problems. The study of the new CPMP mathematics methodology described in Exercise 25 also tested students' abilities to solve word problems. This table shows how the CPMP and traditional groups performed. What do you conclude? (Assume that the assumptions for inference are met.)

Math Program	n	Mean	SD
CPMP	320	57.4	32.1
Traditional	273	53.9	28.5

30. Statistical training. The accounting firm described in Exercise 28 is interested in providing opportunities for its auditors to gain more expertise in statistical sampling methods. They wish to compare traditional classroom instruction with online self-paced tutorials. Auditors were assigned at random to one type of instruction, and the auditors were then given an exam. The table shows how the two groups performed. What do you conclude? (Assume the assumptions for inference are met.)

Program	n	Mean	SD
Traditional	296	74.5	11.2
Online	275	72.9	12.3

31. Trucking company. A trucking company would like to compare two different routes for efficiency. Truckers are randomly assigned to two different routes. Twenty truckers following Route A report an average of 40 minutes, with a standard deviation of 3 minutes. Twenty truckers following Route B report an average of 43 minutes, with a standard deviation of 2 minutes. Histograms of travel times for the routes are roughly symmetric and show no outliers.

a) Find a 95% confidence interval for the difference in average time for the two routes.
b) Will the company save time by always driving one of the routes? Explain.

32. Change in sales. Suppose the specialty food chain from Exercise 26 wants to now compare the change in sales across different regions. An examination of the difference in sales over a 37-week period in a recent year for 8 stores in the state of Massachusetts compared to 12 stores in nearby states reveals the following descriptive statistics for relative increase in sales. (If these means are multiplied by 100, they show % increase in sales.)

```
State      N      Mean      StDev
MA         8      0.0738    0.0666
Other      12     0.0559    0.0503
```

a) Find the 90% confidence interval for the difference in relative increase in sales over this time period.
b) Is there a significant difference in increase in sales between these two groups of stores? Explain.
c) What would you like to see to check the conditions?

33. Cereal company. A food company is concerned about recent criticism of the sugar content of their children's cereals. The data show the sugar content (as a percentage of weight) of several national brands of children's and adults' cereals.

Children's cereals: 40.3, 55, 45.7, 43.3, 50.3, 45.9, 53.5, 43, 44.2, 44, 47.4, 44, 33.6, 55.1, 48.8, 50.4, 37.8, 60.3, 46.6
Adults' cereals: 20, 30.2, 2.2, 7.5, 4.4, 22.2, 16.6, 14.5, 21.4, 3.3, 6.6, 7.8, 10.6, 16.2, 14.5, 4.1, 15.8, 4.1, 2.4, 3.5, 8.5, 10, 1, 4.4, 1.3, 8.1, 4.7, 18.4

a) Write the null and alternative hypotheses.
b) Check the conditions.
c) Find the 95% confidence interval for the difference in means.
d) Is there a significant difference in mean sugar content between these two types of cereals? Explain.

34. Italian wines. Chemical analyses of 1599 red and 4898 white Italian wines revealed the following summary statistics for pH (a measure of acidity):

Type	Count	Mean	St Dev
Red	1599	3.311	0.154
White	4898	3.188	0.151

Is there a difference in pH between red and white wines?

a) Write the null and alternative hypotheses
b) What conditions would you check?
c) Test the hypothesis and find the P-value.
d) Is there a significant difference in pH?

35. Bond funds. Morningstar (www.morningstar.com) selects mutual funds as "Medalist" funds expected to perform well over the long term. You have decided to invest in a bond fund and plan to limit your choice of funds to Morningstar "medalist" funds. But now you must choose between a taxable fund and a municipal bond fund that is at least partially tax-free. Which is better? Here are the % returns for the three-year period leading up to spring of 2013:

Taxable bond funds

10.83, 6.45, 8.52, 10.9, 4.16, 10.48, 6.07, 2.69, 1.24, 1.58, 4.02, 5.64, 6.29, 12.36

Municipal bond funds

8.34, 7.3, 6.07, 6.46, 5.77, 5.89, 5.76, 5.81, 5.12, 5.63 4.71, 5.22, 5.21, 3.12, 4.77, 2.2

a) Write the null and alternative hypotheses.
b) Check the conditions.
c) Test the hypothesis and find the P-value.
d) Is there a significant difference in 3-year returns between these two kinds of funds?

36. Technology adoption. The Pew Internet & American Life Project (www.pewinternet.org/) conducts surveys to gauge how the Internet and technology impact daily life of individuals, families, and communities. In a recent survey Pew asked respondents if they thought that computers and technology give people more or less control over their lives. Companies that are involved in innovative technologies use the survey results to better understand their target market. One might suspect that younger and older respondents might differ in their opinions of whether computers and technology give them more control over their lives. A subset of the data from this survey shows the mean ages of two groups of respondents, those who reported that they believed that computers and technology give them "more" control and those that reported "less" control.

Group	N	Mean	StDev	Min	Q1	Med	Q3	Max
More	74	54.42	19.65	18	41.5	53.5	68.5	99.0
Less	29	54.34	18.57	20	41.0	58.0	70.0	84.0

a) Write the null and alternative hypotheses.
b) Find the 95% confidence interval for the difference in mean age between the two groups of respondents.
c) Is there a significant difference in the mean ages between these two groups? Explain.

37. Product testing. A company is producing and marketing new reading activities for elementary school children that it believes will improve reading comprehension scores. A researcher randomly assigns third graders to an eight-week program in which some will use these activities and others will experience traditional teaching methods. At the end of the experiment, both groups take a reading comprehension exam. Their scores are shown in the back-to-back stem-and-leaf display. Do these results suggest that the new activities are better? Test an appropriate hypothesis and state your conclusion.

New Activities		Control
	1	07
4	2	068
3	3	377
96333	4	12222238
9876432	5	355
721	6	02
1	7	
	8	5

38. Product placement. The owner of a small organic food store was concerned about her sales of a specialty yogurt manufactured in Greece. As a result of increasing fuel costs, she recently had to increase its price. To help boost sales, she decided to place the product on a different shelf (near eye level for most consumers) and in a location near other popular international products. She kept track of sales (number of containers sold per week) for six months after she made the change. These values are shown below, along with the sales numbers for the six months prior to making the change, in stem-and-leaf displays.

	After Change			Before Change
3	2		2	0
3	9		2	899
4	23		3	224
4	589		3	7789
5	0012		4	0000223
5	55558		4	5567
6	00123		5	0
6	67		5	6
7	0			

Do these results suggest that sales are better after the change in product placement? Test an appropriate hypothesis and state your conclusion. Be sure to check assumptions and conditions.

39. Named tropical cyclones 2012. It has been suggested that global climate change may be affecting the frequency of tropical storms. The data here show the number of tropical cyclones (including hurricanes) assigned official names by the National Hurricane Center. Is there evidence of a change?

1995–2001	2002–2012
19, 13, 7, 14, 12, 14, 15	12, 16, 15, 27, 9, 15, 16, 9, 19, 18, 19

a) Write the null and alternative hypotheses.
b) Are the conditions for hypothesis testing satisfied?
c) If so, test the hypothesis.

40. Hurricanes 2012. Exercise 39 considered possible changes in the numbers of tropical cyclones that have grown large enough to be officially named. Regardless of the *number* of storms, has the *fraction* of named storms that grew to hurricane strength changed? Here are those fractions for the same periods as those considered in the previous exercise.

1995–2001	2002–2012
0.579, 0.692, 0.429, 0.714, 0.667, 0.571, 0.600	0.333, 0.438, 0.600, 0.556, 0.556, 0.400, 0.500, 0.333, 0.632, 0.333, 0.526

a) Write the null and alternative hypotheses.
b) Are the conditions for hypothesis testing satisfied?
c) If so, test the hypothesis.

41. Gingko test. A pharmaceutical company is producing and marketing a ginkgo biloba supplement to enhance memory. In an experiment to test the product, subjects were assigned randomly to take ginkgo biloba supplements or a placebo. Their memory was tested to see whether it improved. Here are boxplots comparing the two groups and some computer output from a two-sample t-test computed for the data.

```
2-Sample t-Test of μ_G - μ_p > 0
Difference Between Means = -0.9914
t-Statistic = -1.540 w/196 df
P = 0.9374
```

a) Explain in this context what the P-value means.
b) State your conclusion about the effectiveness of ginkgo biloba.
c) Proponents of ginkgo biloba continue to insist that it works. What type of error do they claim your conclusion makes?

42. Designated hitter 2012. American League baseball teams play their games with the designated hitter rule, meaning that pitchers do not bat. The league believes that replacing the pitcher, traditionally a weak hitter, with another player in the batting order produces more runs and generates more interest among fans. The data provided in the file on the CD include the average numbers of runs scored per game (*Runs per game*) by American League and National League teams for the 2012 season (www.baseball-reference.com).

American League			National League		
Team	R/G	HR	Team	R/G	HR
Los Angeles Angels	4.73	187	Colorado Rockies	4.68	166
Texas Rangers	4.99	200	St. Louis Cardinals	4.72	159
Detroit Tigers	4.48	163	San Francisco Giants	4.43	103
Kansas City Royals	4.17	131	Washington Nationals	4.51	194
New York Yankees	4.96	245	Milwaukee Brewers	4.79	202
Boston Red Sox	4.53	165	Arizona Diamondbacks	4.53	165
Minnesota Twins	4.33	131	Philadelphia Phillies	4.22	158
Chicago White Sox	4.62	211	Los Angeles Dodgers	3.93	116
Cleveland Indians	4.12	136	Cincinnati Reds	4.13	172
Baltimore Orioles	4.40	214	New York Mets	4.01	139
Toronto Blue Jays	4.42	198	Atlanta Braves	4.32	149
Tampa Bay Rays	4.30	175	San Diego Padres	4.02	121
Oakland Athletics	4.40	195	Miami Marlins	3.76	137
Seattle Mariners	3.82	149	Pittsburgh Piarates	4.02	170
			Chicago Cubs	3.78	137
			Houston Astros	3.60	146

a) Create an appropriate display of these data. What do you see?
b) With a 95% confidence interval, estimate the mean number of runs scored by American League teams.
c) With a 95% confidence interval, estimate the mean number of runs scored by National League teams.
d) Explain why you should not use two separate confidence intervals to decide whether the two leagues differ in average number of runs scored.

43. Productivity. A factory hiring people to work on an assembly line gives job applicants a test of manual agility. This test counts how many strangely shaped pegs the applicant can fit into matching holes in a one-minute period. The table summarizes the data by gender of the job applicant. Assume that all conditions necessary for inference are met.

	Male	Female
Number of Subjects	50	50
Pegs Placed:		
Mean	19.39	17.91
SD	2.52	3.39

a) Find 95% confidence intervals for the average number of pegs that males and females can each place.
b) Those intervals overlap. What does this suggest about any gender-based difference in manual agility?
c) Find a 95% confidence interval for the difference in the mean number of pegs that could be placed by men and women.
d) What does this interval suggest about any gender-based difference in manual agility?

e) The two results seem contradictory. Which method is correct: doing two-sample inference, or doing one-sample inference twice?

f) Why don't the results agree?

44. Designated hitter 2012, part 2. Do the data in Exercise 42 suggest that the American League's designated hitter rule may lead to more runs per game scored?

a) Write the null and alternative hypotheses.

b) Find a 95% confidence interval for the difference in mean runs per game, and interpret your interval.

c) Test the hypothesis stated above in part a and find the P-value.

d) Interpret the P-value and state your conclusion. Does the test suggest that the American League scores more runs on average?

45. Water hardness. In an investigation of environmental causes of disease, data were collected on the annual mortality rate (deaths per 100,000) for males in 61 large towns in England and Wales. In addition, the water hardness was recorded as the calcium concentration (parts per million, ppm) in the drinking water. The data set also notes for each town whether it was south or north of Derby. Is there a significant difference in mortality rates in the two regions? Here are the summary statistics.

```
Summary of:        mortality
For categories in: Derby
```

Group	Count	Mean	Median	StdDev
North	34	1631.59	1631	138.470
South	27	1388.85	1369	151.114

a) Test appropriate hypotheses and state your conclusion.

b) The boxplots of the two distributions show a possible outlier among the data north of Derby. What effect might that have had on your test?

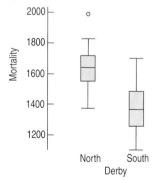

46. Technology investment. The Price-to-Book-value ratio is often used by investors to indicate whether a stock's price is particularly high or low relative to the value of the company. But different market sectors expect different Price/Book values. Here are data on technology companies (biz.yahoo.com/p/8conameu.html accessed in May 2013). We'll compare applications software companies with manufacturers of peripheral equipment. For both, we have taken the logarithm of the Price/Book ratio to make the distributions more nearly symmetric.

Group	Count	Mean	Median	StdDev
Peripherals	19	0.339035	0.264818	0.342258
Software	102	0.566206	0.516535	0.527435

a) State and test appropriate hypotheses and state your conclusion. (So you don't need to compute that strange degrees of freedom formula, the correct df is 36.)

b) Here are boxplots. What more do they tell you about the distributions? Do you think this changes your conclusions in part a?

47. Job satisfaction. A company institutes an exercise break for its workers to see if this will improve job satisfaction, as measured by a questionnaire that was given to a random sample of workers to assess their satisfaction.

Worker Number	Job Satisfaction Index	
	Before	After
1	34	33
2	28	36
3	29	50
4	45	41
5	26	37
6	27	41
7	24	39
8	15	21
9	15	20
10	27	37

a) Identify the procedure you would use to assess the effectiveness of the exercise program and check to see if the conditions allow for the use of that procedure.

b) Test an appropriate hypothesis and state your conclusion.

48. ERP effectiveness. When implementing a packaged Enterprise Resource Planning (ERP) system, many companies report that the module they first install is Financial Accounting. Among the measures used to gauge the effectiveness of their ERP system implementation is acceleration of the financial close process. Below is a sample of 8 companies that report their average time (in weeks) to financial close before and after the implementation of their ERP system.

Company	Before	After
1	6.5	4.2
2	7.0	5.9
3	8.0	8.0
4	4.5	4.0
5	5.2	3.8
6	4.9	4.1
7	5.2	6.0
8	6.5	4.2

a) Identify the procedure you would use to assess the effectiveness of the ERP system and check to see if the conditions allow for the use of that procedure.

b) Test an appropriate hypothesis and state your conclusion.

49. Delivery time. A small appliance company is interested in comparing delivery times of their product during two months. They are concerned that the summer slow-downs in August cause delivery times to lag during this month. Given the following delivery times (in days) of their appliances to the customer for a random sample of 6 orders each month, test if delivery times differ across these two months.

June	54	49	68	66	62	62
August	50	65	74	64	68	72

50. Branding. The *Journal of Applied Psychology* reported on a study that examined whether the content of TV shows influenced the ability of viewers to recall brand names of items featured in the commercials. The researchers randomly assigned volunteers to watch one of three programs, each containing the same nine commercials. One of the programs had violent content, another sexual content, and the third neutral content. After the shows ended, the subjects were asked to recall the brands of products that were advertised. The table shows summaries for how many brands were recalled.

	Program Type		
	Violent	**Sexual**	**Neutral**
n	108	108	108
Mean	2.08	1.71	3.17
SD	1.87	1.76	1.77

a) Do these results indicate that viewer memory for ads may differ depending on program content? Test the hypothesis that there is no difference in ad memory between programs with sexual content and those with violent content. State your conclusion.

b) Is there evidence that viewer memory for ads may differ between programs with sexual content and those with neutral content? Test an appropriate hypothesis and state your conclusion.

51. Ad campaign. You are a consultant to the marketing department of a business preparing to launch an ad campaign for a new product. The company can afford to run ads during one TV show, and has decided not to sponsor a show with sexual content (see Exercise 50). You create a confidence interval for the difference in mean number of brand names remembered between the groups watching violent shows and those watching neutral shows.

```
Two-Sample t
95% CI for μ_viol − μ_neut: (−1.578, −0.602)
```

a) At the meeting of the marketing staff, you have to explain what this output means. What will you say?

b) What advice would you give the company about the upcoming ad campaign?

52. Branding, part 2. In the study described in Exercise 50, the researchers also contacted the subjects again, 24 hours later, and asked them to recall the brands advertised. Results for the number of brands recalled are summarized in the table.

	Program Type		
	Violent	**Sexual**	**Neutral**
No. of Subjects	101	106	103
Mean	3.02	2.72	4.65
SD	1.61	1.85	1.62

a) Is there a significant difference in viewers' abilities to remember brands advertised in shows with violent vs. neutral content?

b) Find a 95% confidence interval for the difference in mean number of brand names remembered between the groups watching shows with sexual content and those watching neutral shows. Interpret your interval in this context.

53. Ad recall. In Exercises 50 and 52, we see the number of advertised brand names people recalled immediately after watching TV shows and 24 hours later. Strangely enough, it appears that they remembered more about the ads the next day. Should we conclude this is true in general about people's memory of TV ads?

a) Suppose one analyst conducts a two-sample hypothesis test to see if memory of brands advertised during violent TV shows is higher 24 hours later. The P-value is 0.00013. What might she conclude?

b) Explain why her procedure was inappropriate. Which of the assumptions for inference was violated?

c) How might the design of this experiment have tainted these results?

d) Suggest a design that could compare immediate brand name recall with recall one day later.

54. Hybrid SUVs. The Chevy Tahoe Hybrid got a lot of attention when it first appeared. It is a relatively high-priced hybrid SUV that makes use of the latest technologies for fuel efficiency. One of the more popular hybrid SUVs on the market is the modestly priced Ford Escape Hybrid. A consumer group was interested in comparing the gas mileage of these two models. In order to do so, each vehicle was driven on the same 10 routes that combined both highway and city streets. The results showed that the mean mileage for the Chevy Tahoe was 29 mpg and for the Ford Escape it was 31 mpg. The standard deviations were 3.2 mpg and 2.5 mpg, respectively.

a) An analyst for the consumer group computed the two-sample t 95% confidence interval for the difference between the two means as $(-0.71, 4.71)$. What conclusion would he reach based on this analysis?

b) Why is this procedure inappropriate? What assumption is violated?

c) In what way do you think this may have impacted the results?

55. The Internet. The National Assessment in Education Program compared science scores for students who had home Internet access with the scores of those who did not, as shown in the graph. They report that the differences are statistically significant.

a) Explain what "statistically significant" means in this context.

b) If their conclusion is incorrect, which type of error did the researchers commit?

c) Does this prove that using the Internet at home can improve a student's performance in science?

d) What companies might be interested in this information?

56. Credit card debt public or private. The average credit card debt carried by college students was compared at public versus private universities. It was reported that a significant difference existed between the two types of institutions and that students at private universities carried higher credit card debt.

a) Explain what "statistically significant" means in this context.

b) If this conclusion is incorrect, which type of error was committed?

c) Does this prove that students who choose to attend public institutions will carry lower credit card debt?

57. Pizza sales. A national food product company believes that it sells more frozen pizza during the winter months than during the summer months. Average weekly sales for a sample of stores in the Baltimore area over a three-year period provided the following data for sales volume (in pounds) during the two seasons.

Season	N	Mean	StDev	Minimum	Maximum
Winter	38	31234	13500	15312	73841
Summer	40	22475	8442	12743	54706

a) How much difference is there between the mean amount of this brand of frozen pizza sold (in pounds) between the two seasons? (Assume that this time frame represents typical sales in the Baltimore area.)

b) Construct and interpret a 95% confidence interval for the difference between weekly sales during the winter and summer months.

c) Suggest factors that might have influenced the sales of the frozen pizza during the winter months.

58. More pizza sales. Here's some additional information about the pizza sales data presented in Exercise 57. It is generally thought that sales spike during the weeks leading up to AFC and NFC football championship games, as well as leading up to the Super Bowl at the end of January each year. If we omit those 6 weeks of sales from this three-year period of weekly sales, the summary statistics look like this.

Season	N	Mean	StDev	Minimum	Maximum
Winter	32	28995	9913	15312	48354
Summer	40	22475	8442	12743	54706

Do sales appear to be higher during the winter months after omitting those weeks most influenced by football championship games?

a) Write the null and alternative hypotheses.

b) Test the null hypotheses and state your conclusion.

c) Suggest additional factors that may influence pizza sales not accounted for in this exercise.

59. Olympic heats 2012. In Olympic running events, preliminary heats are determined by random draw, so we should expect the ability level of runners in the various heats to be about the same, on average. The table gives the times (in seconds) for the 800-m men's run in the 2012 Olympics in London for preliminary heats 1 and 3. Is there any evidence that the mean time to finish is different for randomized heats? Explain. Be sure to include a discussion of assumptions and conditions for your analysis.

Country	Name	Time	Heat
BOT	Nigel Amos	105.9	1
BRA	Fabiano Pecanha	106.3	1
ESP	Luis Alberto Marco	106.9	1
USA	Khadevis Robinson	107.2	1
POL	Marcin Lewandowski	107.6	1
RUS	Ivan Tukhtachev	109.8	1
GUM	Derek Mandell	118.9	1
SUD	Abubaker Kaki	105.5	3
KEN	Timothy Kitum	105.7	3
KSA	Abdulaziz Ladan Mohammed	106.1	3
CUB	Andy González	106.2	3
GBR	Gareth Warburton	107.0	3
HUN	Tamás Kazi	107.1	3
GER	Sören Ludolph	108.6	3
VAN	Arnold Sorina	114.3	3

T 60. Swimming heats 2012. In Exercise 59, we looked at the times in two different heats for the 800-m men's run from the 2012 Olympics. Unlike track events, swimming heats are *not* determined at random. Instead, swimmers are seeded so that better swimmers are placed in later heats. Here are the times (in seconds) for the women's 400-m freestyle from heats 3 and 5.

Country	Name	Time (secs)	Heat
GBR	Rebecca Adlington	245.7	3
USA	Chloe Sutton	247.1	3
ESP	Mireia Belmonte	248.2	3
HUN	Eva Risztov	249.1	3
CHN	Li Xuanxu	250.9	3
ROU	Camelia Potec	251.4	3
GBR	Joanne Jackson	251.5	3
RSA	Wendy Trott	251.6	3
FRA	Camille Muffat	243.3	5
USA	Allison Schmitt	243.3	5
NZL	Lauren Boyle	243.6	5
DEN	Lotte Friis	244.2	5
ESP	Melanie Costa	246.8	5
AUS	Bronte Barratt	248.0	5
HUN	Boglarka Kapas	250.0	5
RUS	Elena Sokolova	252.2	5

Do these results suggest that the mean times of heat 5 are faster than heat 3? Explain. Include a discussion of assumptions and conditions for your analysis.

61. Tee tests. Does it matter what kind of tee a golfer places the ball on? The company that manufactures "Stinger" tees claims that the thinner shaft and smaller head will lessen resistance and drag, reducing spin and allowing the ball to travel farther. Golf Laboratories, Inc. compared the distance traveled by golf balls hit off regular wooden tees to those hit off Stinger tees. All the balls were struck by the same golf club using a robotic device set to swing the

club head at approximately 95 miles per hour. Summary statistics from the test are shown in the table. Assume that 6 balls were hit off each tee and that the data were suitable for inference. Is there evidence that balls hit off the Stinger tees would have a higher initial velocity?

		Total Distance (yards)	Ball Velocity (mph)	Club Velocity (mph)
Regular Tee	**Mean**	227.17	127.00	96.17
	SD	2.14	0.89	0.41
Stinger Tee	**Mean**	241.00	128.83	96.17
	SD	2.76	0.41	0.52

62. Tee tests, part 2. Given the test results on golf tees described in Exercise 61, is there evidence that balls hit off Stinger tees travel farther? Assume that 6 balls were hit off each tee and that the data are suitable for inference.

63. Marketing slogan. A company is considering marketing their classical music as "music to study by." Is this a valid slogan? In a study conducted by some Statistics students, 62 people were randomly assigned to listen to rap music, music by Mozart, or no music while attempting to memorize objects pictured on a page. They were then asked to list all the objects they could remember. Here are summary statistics for each group.

	Rap	Mozart	No Music
Count	29	20	13
Mean	10.72	10.00	12.77
SD	3.99	3.19	4.73

a) Does it appear that it is better to study while listening to Mozart than to rap music? Test an appropriate hypothesis and state your conclusion.
b) Create a 90% confidence interval for the mean difference in memory score between students who study to Mozart and those who listen to no music at all. Interpret your interval.

64. Marketing slogan, part 2. Using the results of the experiment described in Exercise 63, does it matter whether one listens to rap music while studying, or is it better to study without music at all?

a) Test an appropriate hypothesis and state your conclusion.
b) If you concluded there is a difference, estimate the size of that difference with a 90% confidence interval and explain what your interval means.

T 65. Mutual funds returns 2013. You have heard that if you leave your money in mutual funds for a longer period of time, you will see a greater return. So you would like to compare the 3-year and 5-year returns of a random sample of mutual funds to see if indeed, your return is expected to be greater if you leave your money in the funds for 5 years.

a) Using the data provided, check the conditions for this test.
b) Write the null and alternative hypotheses for this test.
c) Test the hypothesis and find the P-value if appropriate.
d) Find a 95% confidence interval for the mean difference.

66. Mutual funds returns 2013, part 2. An investor now tells you that if you leave your money in as long as 10 years, you will see an even greater return, so you would like to compare the 5-year and 10-year returns of a random sample of mutual funds to see if your return is expected to be greater if you leave your money in the funds for 10 years.

a) Using the data provided, check the conditions for this test.
b) Write the null and alternative hypotheses for this test.
c) Test the hypothesis and find the P-value if appropriate.
d) Find a 95% confidence interval for the mean difference.

67. Real estate, two towns. Residents of neighboring towns in a state in the United States have an ongoing disagreement over who lays claim to the higher average price of a single-family home. Since you live in one of these towns, you decide to obtain a random sample of homes listed for sale with a major local realtor to investigate if there is actually any difference in the average home price.

a) Using the data provided on the CD, check the conditions for this test.
b) Write the null and alternative hypotheses for this test.
c) Test the hypothesis and find the P-value.
d) What is your conclusion?

68. Real estate, two towns, bigger sample. Residents of one of the towns discussed in Exercise 67 claim that since their town is much smaller, the sample size should be increased. Instead of random sampling 30 homes, you decide to sample 42 homes from the database to test the difference in the mean price of single-family homes in these two towns.

a) Using the data provided on the CD, check the conditions for this test.
b) Write the null and alternative hypotheses for this test.
c) Test the hypothesis and find the P-value.
d) What is your conclusion? Did the sample size make a difference?
e) Use the pooled t-test to test the hypothesis and compare your answer to parts c and d.

69. Designated hitter 2012, part 3. For the same reasons identified in Exercise 42, a friend of yours claims that the average number of home runs hit per game is higher in the American League than in the National League. Using the same 2012 data as in Exercises 42 and 44, you decide to test your friend's theory.

a) Using the data provided on the CD, check the conditions for this test.

b) Write the null and alternative hypotheses for this test.
c) Test the hypothesis and find the P-value.
d) What is your conclusion?
e) Use the pooled t-test to test the hypothesis and compare your answer to parts c and d.

70. Cloud seeding. It has long been a dream of farmers to summon rain when it is needed for their crops. Crop losses to drought have significant economic impact. One possibility is cloud seeding in which chemicals are dropped into clouds in an attempt to induce rain. Simpson, Alsen, and Eden (*Technometrics*, 1975) report the results of trials in which clouds were seeded and the amount of rainfall recorded. The authors report on 26 seeded (Group 2) and 26 unseeded (Group 1) clouds. Each group has been sorted in order of the amount of rainfall, largest amount first. Here are two possible tests to study the question of whether cloud seeding works.

```
Paired t-Test of μ(1 − 2)
Mean of Paired Differences = −277.4
t-Statistic = −3.641 w/25 dfp = 0.0012
2-Sample t-test of μ1 − μ2
Difference Between Means = −277.4
t-Statistic = −1.998w/33 dfp = 0.0538
```

a) Which of these tests is appropriate for these data? Explain.
b) Using the test you selected, state your conclusion.

71. Online insurance. After seeing countless commercials claiming one can get cheaper car insurance from an online company, a local insurance agent was concerned that he might lose some customers. To investigate, he randomly selected profiles (type of car, coverage, driving record, etc.) for 10 of his clients and checked online price quotes for their policies. The comparisons are shown in the table.

Local	Online	PriceDiff
568	391	177
872	602	270
451	488	−37
1229	903	326
605	677	−72
1021	1270	−249
783	703	80
844	789	55
907	1008	−101
712	702	10

His statistical software produced the following summaries (where *PriceDiff = Local − Online*):

Variable	Count	Mean	StdDev
Local	10	799.200	229.281
Online	10	753.300	256.267
PriceDiff	10	45.900	175.663

At first, the insurance agent wondered whether there was some kind of mistake in this output. He thought the Pythagorean Theorem of Statistics should work for finding the standard deviation of the price differences—in other words, that $SD(Local - Online) = \sqrt{SD^2(Local) + SD^2(Online)}$. But when he checked, he found that

$$\sqrt{(229.281)^2 + (256.267)^2} = 343.864,$$

not 175.663 as given by the software. Tell him where his mistake is.

72. Windy. Alternative sources of energy are of increasing interest throughout the energy industry. Wind energy has great potential. But appropriate sites must be found for the turbines. To select the site for an electricity-generating wind turbine, wind speeds were recorded at several potential sites every 6 hours for a year. Two sites not far from each other looked good. Each had a mean wind speed high enough to qualify, but we should choose the site with a higher average daily wind speed. Because the sites are near each other and the wind speeds were recorded at the same times, we should view the speeds as paired. Here are the summaries of the speeds (in miles per hour):

Variable	Count	Mean	StdDev
site2	1114	7.452	3.586
site4	1114	7.248	3.421
site2 – site4	1114	0.204	2.551

Is there a mistake in this output? Why doesn't the Pythagorean Theorem of Statistics work here? In other words, shouldn't

$$SD(site2 - site4) = \sqrt{SD^2(site2) + SD^2(site4)}?$$

But $\sqrt{(3.586)^2 + (3.421)^2} = 4.956$, not 2.551 as given by the software. Explain why this happened.

73. Online insurance, part 2. In Exercise 71, we saw summary statistics for 10 drivers' car insurance premiums quoted by a local agent and an online company. Here are displays for each company's quotes and for the difference (*Local – Online*):

a) Which of the summaries would help you decide whether the online company offers cheaper insurance? Why?
b) The standard deviation of *PriceDiff* is quite a bit smaller than the standard deviation of prices quoted by either the local or online companies. Discuss why.
c) Using the information you have, discuss the assumptions and conditions for inference with these data.

74. Windy, part 2. In Exercise 72, we saw summary statistics for wind speeds at two sites near each other, both being considered as locations for an electricity-generating wind turbine. The data, recorded every 6 hours for a year, showed each of the sites had a mean wind speed high enough to qualify, but how can we tell which site is best? Here are some displays:

a) The boxplots show outliers for each site, yet the histogram shows none. Discuss why.
b) Which of the summaries would you use to select between these sites? Why?
c) Using the information you have, discuss the assumptions and conditions for paired *t* inference for these data. (*Hint:* Think hard about the independence assumption in particular.)

75. Online insurance, part 3. Exercises 71 and 73 give summaries and displays for car insurance premiums quoted by a local agent and an online company. Test an appropriate hypothesis to see if there is evidence that drivers might save money by switching to the online company.

76. Windy, part 3. Exercises 72 and 74 give summaries and displays for two potential sites for a wind turbine. Test an appropriate hypothesis to see if there is evidence that either of these sites has a higher average wind speed.

77. Employee athletes. An ergonomics consultant is engaged by a large consumer products company to see what they can do to increase productivity. The consultant recommends an "employee athlete" program, encouraging every employee to devote 5 minutes an hour to physical activity. The company worries that the gains in productivity will be offset by the loss in time on the job. They'd like to know if the program increases or decreases productivity. To measure it, they monitor a random sample of 145 employees who word process, measuring their hourly key strokes both before and after the program is instituted. Here are the data:

	Keystrokes per Hour		
	Before	After	Difference (After − Before)
Mean	1534.2	1556.9	22.7
SD	168.5	149.5	113.6
N	145	145	145

a) What are the null and alternative hypotheses?
b) What can you conclude? Explain.
c) Give a 95% confidence interval for the mean change in productivity (as measured by keystrokes per hour).

78. Employee athletes, part 2. A small company, on hearing about the employee athlete program (see Exercise 77) at the large company down the street, decides to try it as well. To measure the difference in productivity, they measure the average number of keystrokes per hour of 23 employees before and after the program is instituted. The data follow:

	Keystrokes per Hour		
	Before	After	Difference (After − Before)
Mean	1497.3	1544.8	47.5
SD	155.4	136.7	122.8
N	23	23	23

a) Is there evidence to suggest that the program increases productivity?
b) Give a 95% confidence interval for the mean change in productivity (as measured by keystrokes per hour).
c) Given this information and the results of Exercise 77, what recommendations would you make to the company about the effectiveness of the program?

79. Exercise equipment. A leading manufacturer of exercise equipment wanted to collect data on the effectiveness of their equipment. An August 2001 article in the journal *Medicine and Science in Sports and Exercise* compared how long it would take men and women to burn 200 calories during light or heavy workouts on various kinds of exercise equipment. The results summarized in the table are the average times for a group of physically active young men and women whose performances were measured on a representative sample of exercise equipment.

		Average Minutes to Burn 200 Calories			
		Hard Exertion		Light Exertion	
		Men	Women	Men	Women
Machine Type	Treadmill	12	17	14	22
	X-C Skier	12	16	16	23
	Stair Climber	13	18	20	37
	Rowing Machine	14	16	21	25
	Exercise Rider	22	24	27	36
	Exercise Bike	16	20	29	44

a) On average, how many minutes longer than a man must a woman exercise at a light exertion rate in order to burn 200 calories? Find a 95% confidence interval.
b) Estimate the average number of minutes longer a woman must work out at light exertion than at heavy exertion to get the same benefit. Find a 95% confidence interval.
c) These data are actually averages rather than individual times. How might this affect the margins of error in these confidence intervals?

80. Market value. Real estate agents want to set correctly the price of a house that's about to go on the real estate market. They must choose a price that strikes a balance between one that is so high that the house takes too long to sell and one that's so low that not enough value will go to the homeowner. One appraisal method is the "Comparative Market Analysis" approach by which the market value of a house is based on recent sales of similar homes in the neighborhood. Because no two houses are exactly the same, appraisers have to adjust comparable homes for such features as extra square footage, bedrooms, fireplaces, upgrading, parking facilities, swimming pool, lot size, location, and so on. The appraised market values and the selling prices of 45 homes from the same region are found on the CD.

a) Test the hypothesis that on average, the market value and the sale price of homes from this region are the same.
b) Find a 95% confidence interval for the mean difference.
c) Explain your findings in a sentence or two in context.

81. Stopping distance. In an experiment on braking performance, a tire manufacturer measured the stopping distance for one of its tire models. On a test track, a car made repeated stops from 60 miles per hour. Twenty tests were run, 10 each on both dry and wet pavement, with results shown in the table. (Note that actual *braking distance*, which takes into account the driver's reaction time, is much longer, typically nearly 300 feet at 60 mph!)

Stopping Distance (ft)	
Dry Pavement	Wet Pavement
145	211
152	191
141	220
143	207
131	198
148	208
126	206
140	177
135	183
133	223

a) Find a 95% confidence interval for the mean dry pavement stopping distance. Be sure to check the appropriate assumptions and conditions, and explain what your interval means.
b) Find a 95% confidence interval for the mean increase in stopping distance on wet pavement. Be sure to check the appropriate assumptions and conditions, and explain what your interval means.

82. Stopping distances, again. For another test of the tires in Exercise 81, the company tried them on 10 different cars, recording the stopping distance for each car on both wet and dry pavement. Results are shown in the following table.

Stopping Distance (ft)		
Car #	Dry Pavement	Wet Pavement
1	150	201
2	147	220
3	136	192
4	134	146
5	130	182
6	134	173
7	134	202
8	128	180
9	136	192
10	158	206

a) Find a 95% confidence interval for the mean dry pavement stopping distance. Be sure to check the appropriate assumptions and conditions, and explain what your interval means.
b) Find a 95% confidence interval for the mean increase in stopping distance on wet pavement. Be sure to check the appropriate assumptions and conditions, and explain what your interval means.

83. Airline "bumping" 2012. Commercial airlines overbook flights, selling more tickets than they have seats, because a sizeable number of reservation holders don't show up in time for their flights. But sometimes, there are more passengers wishing to board than there are seats. Most airlines try to entice travelers to voluntarily give up their seats in return for free travel or other awards, but they do have to "bump" some travelers involuntarily. Of course, they don't like to offend passengers by bumping, so they are constantly trying to improve their systems for predicting how many passengers will show up. Have the rates of "bumping" changed? Here are data on the number of passengers involuntarily denied boarding ("bumping" is not the approved term) per 10,000 passengers during the periods of January to June in 2011 and 2012 by airline.

Involuntary Denied Boarding/10K enplanements		
Airline	2011	2012
JetBlue Airways	0.01	0.01
Virgin America	NA	0.05
Hawaiian Airlines	0.08	0.2
Delta Air Lines	0.29	0.41
Alaska Airlines	1.03	0.62
Frontier Airlines	1.02	0.74
US Airways	1.04	0.74
American Airlines	1.03	0.74
Southwest Airlines	0.78	0.91
Airtran Airways	0.43	0.92
American Eagle Airlines	2.92	1.27
ExpressJet Airlines*	0.76	1.93
United Airlines*	1.08	1.93
Skywest Airlines	0.66	2.07
Mesa Airlines	2.3	2.48

* United Airlines and Continental are combined (following their merger). ExpressJet Airlines and Atlantic Southeast Airlines are combined.

a) Are these paired data? Why or why not?
b) Was there a statistically significant change in the number of passengers involuntarily denied boarding per 10,000 passengers?

84. Grocery prices. WinCo Foods, a large discount grocery retailer in the western United States, promotes itself as the lowest priced grocery retailer. In newspaper ads WinCo Foods published a price comparison for products between WinCo and several competing grocery retailers. One of the retailers compared against WinCo was Walmart, also known as a low price competitor. WinCo selected a variety of products, listed the price of the product charges at each retailer, and showed the sales receipt to prove the prices at WinCo were the lowest in the area. A sample of the products and their price comparison at both WinCo and Walmart are shown in the following table:

Item	WinCo Price	Walmart Price
Bananas (lb)	0.42	0.56
Red Onions (lb)	0.58	0.98
Mini Peeled Carrots (1 lb bag)	0.98	1.48
Roma Tomatoes (lb)	0.98	2.67
Deli Tater Wedges (lb)	1.18	1.78
Beef Cube Steak (lb)	3.83	4.11
Beef Top Round London Broil (lb)	3.48	4.12
Pillsbury Devils Food Cake Mix (18.25 oz)	0.88	0.88
Lipton Rice and Sauce Mix (5.6 oz)	0.88	1.06
Sierra Nevada Pale Ale (12 – 12 oz bottles)	12.68	12.84
GM Cheerios Oat Clusters (11.3 oz)	1.98	2.74
Charmin Bathroom Tissue (12 roll)	5.98	7.48
Bumble Bee Pink Salmon (14.75 oz)	1.58	1.98
Pace Thick & Chunky Salsa, Mild (24 oz)	2.28	2.78
Nalley Chili, Regular w/Beans (15 oz)	0.78	0.78
Challenge Butter (lb quarters)	2.18	2.58
Kraft American Singles (12 oz)	2.27	2.27
Yuban Coffee FAC (36 oz)	5.98	7.56
Totino's Pizza Rolls, Pepperoni (19.8 oz)	2.38	2.42
Rosarita Refried Beans, Original (16 oz)	0.68	0.73
Barilla Spaghetti (16 oz)	0.78	1.23
Sun-Maid Mini Raisins (14 – .5 oz)	1.18	1.36
Jif Peanut Butter, Creamy (28 oz)	2.54	2.72
Dole Fruit Bowl, Mixed Fruit (4 – 4 oz)	1.68	1.98
Progresso Chicken Noodle Soup (19 oz)	1.28	1.38
Precious Mozzarella Ball, Part Skim (16 oz)	3.28	4.23
Mrs. Cubbison Seasoned Croutons (6 oz)	0.88	1.12
Kellogg's Raisin Bran (20 oz)	1.98	2.50
Campbell's Soup at Hand, Cream of Tomato (10.75 oz)	1.18	1.26

a) Do the prices listed indicate that, on average, prices at WinCo are lower than prices at Walmart?

b) At the bottom of the price list, the following statement appears: "Though this list is not intended to represent a typical weekly grocery order or a random list of grocery items, WinCo continues to be the area's low price leader." Why do you think WinCo added this statement?

c) What other comments could be made about the statistical validity of the test on price comparisons given in the ad?

JUST CHECKING ANSWERS

1 $H_0: \mu_{eyes} - \mu_{flowers} = 0$

2 ✓ **Independence Assumption:** The amount paid by one person should be independent of the amount paid by others.

   ✓ **Randomization Condition:** This study was observational. Treatments alternated a week at a time and were applied to the same group of office workers.

   ✓ **Nearly Normal Condition:** We don't have the data to check, but it seems unlikely there would be outliers in either group.

   ✓ **Independent Groups Assumptions:** The same workers were recorded each week, but week-to-week independence is plausible.

3 $H_A: \mu_{eyes} - \mu_{flowers} \neq 0$. An argument could be made for a one-sided test because the research hypothesis was that eyes would improve honest compliance.

4 Office workers' compliance in leaving money to pay for food at an office coffee station was different when a picture of eyes was placed behind the "honesty box" than when the picture was one of flowers.

5 These are independent groups sampled at random, so use a two-sample *t* confidence interval to estimate the size of the difference.

6 If the same random sample of students was sampled both in the first year and again in the fourth year of their university experience, then this would be a paired *t*-test.

7 A male and female are selected from each work group. The question calls for a paired *t*-test.

8 Since we have no reason to believe that public and private companies have equal variances, we should use a two-sample test.

9 Since the same 50 companies are surveyed twice to examine a change in variables over time, this would be a paired *t*-test.

14

Inference for Counts: Chi-Square Tests

SAC Capital

Hedge funds, like mutual funds and pension funds, pool investors' money in an attempt to make profits. Unlike these other funds, however, hedge funds are not required to register with the U.S. Securities and Exchange Commission (SEC) because they issue securities in "private offerings" only to "qualified investors" (investors with either $1 million in assets or annual income of at least $200,000).

Hedge funds don't necessarily "hedge" their investments against market moves. But typically these funds use multiple, often complex, strategies to exploit inefficiencies in the market. For these reasons, hedge fund managers have the reputation for being obsessive traders, and the SEC has recently begun to investigate their practices.

One of the most successful hedge funds is SAC Capital, which was founded by Steven (Stevie) A. Cohen in 1992 with nine employees and $25 million in assets under management (AUM). SAC Capital returned annual gains of 40% or more through much of the 1990s and is now reported to have more than 1000 employees and nearly $14 billion in assets under management. According to *Forbes*, Cohen's $9.3 billion fortune ranks him as the 41st wealthiest American and 117th richest person in the world.

Cohen, a legendary figure on Wall Street, is known for taking advantage of any information he can find and for turning that information into profit. Unlike most hedge funds, which trade by computer and pay fractions of a cent per trade, SAC still trades the "old fashioned way," paying 3 to 5¢. It is generally agreed to be the largest payer of fees on Wall Street, a largesse that may earn it tips from traders.

In March of 2013, SAC agreed to pay (without admitting guilt) a fine of $616 million—the largest fine in the history of the Securities and Exchange Commission—to settle charges of insider trading in just two trades. In October of 2013, SAC pleaded guilty and agreed to pay fines of $1.2B. The government also forced SAC to stop managing money for outside investors. But don't feel too sorry for Mr. Cohen. The firm will continue to manage his fortune of over $9B. He is still the 35th richest man in the United States.

I n a business as competitive as hedge fund management, information is gold. Being the first to have information and knowing how to act on it can mean the difference between success and failure. Hedge fund managers look for small advantages everywhere, hoping to exploit inefficiencies in the market and to turn those inefficiencies into profit.

Wall Street has plenty of "wisdom" about market patterns. For example, investors are advised to watch for "calendar effects," certain times of year or days of the week that are particularly good or bad: "As goes January, so goes the year" and "Sell in May and go away." Some analysts claim that the "bad period" for holding stocks is from the sixth trading day of June to the fifth-to-last trading day of October. Of course, there is also Mark Twain's advice:

> October. This is one of the peculiarly dangerous months to speculate in stocks. The others are July, January, September, April, November, May, March, June, December, August, and February.
> —Mark Twain, Pudd'nhead Wilson, 1894

Day of the Week	Count	% of Day
Monday	4090	19.305
Tuesday	4293	20.263
Wednesday	4317	20.377
Thursday	4253	20.075
Friday	4233	19.980

Table 14.1   The distribution of days of the week among the 21,186 trading days from October 1, 1928 to February 25, 2013. We expect about 20% to fall in each day, with minor variations due to holidays and other events.

One common claim is that stocks show a weekly pattern. For example, some argue that there is a *weekend effect* in which stock returns on Mondays are often lower than those of the immediately preceding Friday. Are patterns such as this real? We have the data, so we can check. Between October 1, 1928 and February 25, 2013, there were 21,186 trading sessions. Let's first see how many trading days fell on each day of the week. It's not exactly 20% for each day because of holidays. The distribution of days is shown in Table 14.1.

Of these 21,186 trading sessions, 11,113, or about 52% of the days, saw a gain in the Dow Jones Industrial Average (DJIA). To test for a pattern, we need a model. The model comes from the supposition that any day is as likely to show a gain as any other. In any sample of positive or "up" days, we should expect to see the same distribution of days as in Table 14.1—in other words, about 19.31% of "up" days would be Mondays, 20.26% would be Tuesdays, and so on. Here is the distribution of days in one such random sample of 1110 "up" days.

Day of the Week	Count	% of Days in the Sample of "Up" days
Monday	195	17.568
Tuesday	223	20.090
Wednesday	239	21.532
Thursday	223	20.090
Friday	230	20.721

Table 14.2   The distribution of days of the week for a sample of 1110 "up" trading days selected at random from October 1, 1928 to February 25, 2013. If there is no pattern, we would expect the proportions here to match fairly closely the proportions observed among all trading days in Table 14.1.

Of course, we expect some variation. We wouldn't expect the proportions of days in the two tables to match exactly. In our sample, the percentage of Mondays in Table 14.2 is slightly lower than in Table 14.1, and the proportion of Fridays is a little higher. Are these deviations enough for us to declare that there is a recognizable pattern?

14.1   Goodness-of-Fit Tests

To address this question, we test the table's **goodness-of-fit**, where *fit* refers to the null model proposed. Here, the null model is that there is no pattern, that the distribution of *up* days should be the same as the distribution of trading days overall. (If there were no holidays or other closings, that would just be 20% for each day of the week.)

Assumptions and Conditions

Data for a goodness-of-fit test are organized in tables, and the assumptions and conditions reflect that. Rather than having an observation for each individual, we typically work with summary counts in categories. Here, the individuals are trading days, but rather than list all 1110 trading days in the sample, we have totals for each weekday.

Counted Data Condition.   The data must be counts for the categories of a categorical variable. This might seem a silly condition to check. But many kinds of values can be assigned to categories, and it is unfortunately common to find the methods of this chapter applied incorrectly (even by business professionals) to proportions or quantities just because they happen to be organized in a two-way table. So check to be sure that you really have counts.

Independence Assumption

Independence Assumption.   The counts in the cells should be independent of each other. You should think about whether that's reasonable. If the data are a random sample you can simply check the randomization condition.

Randomization Condition.   The individuals counted in the table should be a random sample from some population. We need this condition if we want to generalize our conclusions to that population. We took a random sample of 1110 trading days on which the DJIA rose. That lets us assume that the market's performance on any one day is independent of performance on another. If we had selected 1110 consecutive trading days, there would be a risk that market performance on one day could affect performance on the next, or that an external event could affect performance for several consecutive days.

Sample Size Assumption

Sample Size Assumption.   We must have enough data for the methods to work. We usually just check the following condition:

Expected Cell Frequency Condition.   We should expect to see at least 5 individuals in each cell. The expected cell frequency condition should remind you of—and is, in fact, quite similar to—the condition that np and nq be at least 10 when we test proportions.

Chi-Square Model

We have observed a count in each category (weekday). We can compute the number of up days we'd *expect* to see for each weekday if the null model were true. For the trading days example, the expected counts come from the null hypothesis that the up days are distributed among weekdays just as trading days are. Of course, we could imagine almost any kind of model and base a null hypothesis on that model.

> **Expected Cell Frequencies**
>
> Companies often want to assess the relative successes of their products in different regions. However, a company whose sales regions had 100, 200, 300, and 400 representatives might not expect equal sales in all regions. They might expect observed sales to be proportional to the size of the sales force. The null hypothesis in that case would be that the proportions of sales were 1/10, 2/10, 3/10, and 4/10, respectively. With 500 total sales, their expected counts would be 50, 100, 150, and 200.

NOTATION ALERT

We compare the counts *observed* in each cell with the counts we *expect* to find. The usual notation uses *Obs* and *Exp* as we've used here. The expected counts are found from the null model.

To decide whether the null model is plausible, we look at the differences between the expected values from the model and the counts we observe. We wonder: Are these differences so large that they call the model into question, or could they have arisen from natural sampling variability? We denote the *differences* between these observed and expected counts, $(Obs - Exp)$. As we did with variance, we square them. That gives us positive values and focuses attention on any cells with large differences. Because the differences between observed and expected counts generally get larger the more data we have, we also need to get an idea of the *relative* sizes of the differences. To do that, we divide each squared difference by the expected count for that cell.

The test statistic, called the **chi-square (or chi-squared) statistic**, is found by adding up the sum of the squares of the deviations between the observed and expected counts divided by the expected counts:

$$\chi^2 = \sum_{all\ cells} \frac{(Obs - Exp)^2}{Exp}.$$

The chi-square statistic is denoted χ^2, where χ is the Greek letter chi (pronounced kī). The resulting family of sampling distribution models is called the **chi-square models**.

NOTATION ALERT

The only use of the Greek letter χ in Statistics is to represent the chi-square statistic and the associated sampling distribution. This violates the general rule that Greek letters represent population parameters. Here we are using a Greek letter simply to name a family of distribution models and a statistic.

The members of this family of models differ in the number of degrees of freedom. The number of degrees of freedom for a goodness-of-fit test is $k - 1$, where k is the number of cells—in this example, 5 weekdays.

We will use the chi-square statistic only for testing hypotheses, not for constructing confidence intervals. A small chi-square statistic means that our model fits the data well, so a small value gives us no reason to doubt the null hypothesis. If the observed counts don't match the expected counts, the statistic will be large. If the calculated statistic value is large enough, we'll reject the null hypothesis. So the chi-square test is always one-sided. What could be simpler? Let's see how it works.

FOR EXAMPLE Goodness-of-fit test

Atara manages 8 call center operators at a telecommunications company. To develop new business, she gives each operator a list of randomly selected phone numbers of rival phone company customers. She also provides the operators with a script that tries to convince the customers to switch providers. Atara notices that some operators have found more than twice as many new customers as others, so she suspects that some of the operators are performing better than others.

The 120 new customer acquisitions are distributed as follows:

Operator	1	2	3	4	5	6	7	8
New Customers	11	17	9	12	19	18	13	21

QUESTION   Is there evidence to suggest that some of the operators are more successful than others?

ANSWER   Atara has randomized the potential new customers to the operators so the Randomization Condition is satisfied. The data are counts and there are at least 5 expected counts in each cell, so we can apply a chi-square goodness-of-fit test to the null hypothesis that the operator performance is uniform and that each of the operators will convince the same number of customers. Specifically we expect each operator to have converted 1/8 of the 120 customers that switched providers.

Operator	1	2	3	4	5	6	7	8
Observed	11	17	9	12	19	18	13	21
Expected	15	15	15	15	15	15	15	15
Observed-Expected	−4	2	−6	−3	4	3	−2	6
(Obs-Exp)^2	16	4	36	9	16	9	4	36
(Obs-Exp)^2/Exp	16/15 = 1.07	4/15 = 0.27	36/15 = 2.40	9/15 = 0.60	16/15 = 1.07	9/15 = 0.60	4/15 = 0.27	36/15 = 2.40

$$\sum \frac{(Obs - Exp)^2}{Exp} = 1.07 + 0.27 + 2.40 + \cdots + 2.40 = 8.68$$

The number of degrees of freedom is $k - 1 = 7$.

$$P(\chi^2_7 > 8.68) = 0.2765$$

8.68 is not a surprising value for a chi-square statistic with 7 degrees of freedom. So, we fail to reject the null hypothesis that the operators actually find new customers at different rates.

BY HAND The chi-square calculation

Here are the steps to calculate the chi-square statistic:

1. **Find the expected values.** These come from the null hypothesis model. Every null model gives a hypothesized proportion for each cell. The expected value is the product of the total number of observations times this proportion. (The result need not be an integer.)

2. **Compute the residuals.** Once you have expected values for each cell, find the residuals, $Obs - Exp$.

3. **Square the residuals.** $(Obs - Exp)^2$

4. **Compute the components.** Find $\dfrac{(Obs - Exp)^2}{Exp}$ for each cell.

5. **Find the sum of the components.** That's the chi-square statistic,
$$\chi^2 = \sum_{all\ cells} \frac{(Obs - Exp)^2}{Exp}.$$

6. **Find the degrees of freedom.** It's equal to the number of cells minus one.

7. **Test the hypothesis.** Large chi-square values mean lots of deviation from the hypothesized model, so they give small P-values. Look up the critical value from a table of chi-square values such as Table X in Appendix B, or use technology to find the P-value directly.

(continued)

The steps of the chi-square calculations are often laid out in tables. Use one row for each category, and columns for observed counts, expected counts, residuals, squared residuals, and the contributions to the chi-square total:

	A	B	C	D	E	F	G
1	Day	Pop%	Obs	Exp	Resid	Resid^2	Component
2	Monday	0.19305	195	214.28774	-19.28774	372.016806	1.736062
3	Tuesday	0.20263	223	224.92353	-1.92353	3.6999846	0.01645
4	Wednesday	0.20377	239	226.18097	12.81903	164.327567	0.7265312
5	Thursday	0.20075	223	222.82781	-0.17219	0.0296491	0.0001331
6	Friday	0.1998	230	221.77995	8.22005	67.5692381	0.3046679

Table 14.3   Calculations for the chi-square statistic in the trading days example can be performed conveniently in Microsoft Excel 2013. Set up the calculation in the first row and Fill Down, and then find the sum of the rightmost column. The CHIDIST function looks up the chi-square total to find the P-value.

GUIDED EXAMPLE   Stock Market Patterns

We have counts of the "up" days for each day of the week. The economic theory we want to investigate is whether there is a pattern in "up" days. So, our null hypothesis is that across all days in which the DJIA rose, the days of the week are distributed as they are across all trading days. (As we saw, the trading days are not quite *evenly* distributed because of holidays, so we use the *trading days* percentages as the null model.) The alternative hypothesis is that the observed percentages are *not* uniform. The test statistic looks at how closely the observed data match this idealized situation.

PLAN	**Setup** State what you want to know. Identify the variables and context.	We want to know whether the distribution for "up" days differs from the null model (the trading days distribution). We have the number of times each weekday appeared among a random sample of 1110 "up" days.
	Hypotheses State the null and alternative hypotheses. For χ^2 tests, it's usually easier to state the hypotheses in words than in symbols.	H_O: The days of the work week are distributed among the up days as they are among all trading days. H_A: The trading days model does not fit the up days distribution.

Model Think about the assumptions and check the conditions.

✓ **Counted Data Condition** *We have counts of the days of the week for all trading days and for the "up" days.*

✓ **Independence Assumption** *We have no reason to expect that one day's performance will affect another's, but to be safe we've taken a random sample of days. The randomization should make them far enough apart to alleviate any concerns about dependence.*

✓ **Randomization Condition** *We have a random sample of 1110 days from the time period.*

✓ **Expected Cell Frequency Condition** *All the expected cell frequencies are much larger than 5.*

Specify the sampling distribution model.

Name the test you will use.

The conditions are satisfied, so we'll use a χ^2 model with $5 - 1 = 4$ degrees of freedom and do a **chi-square goodness-of-fit test***.*

DO

Mechanics To find the expected number of days, we take the fraction of each weekday from all days and multiply by the number of "up" days.

For example, there were 4090 Mondays out of 21,186 trading days.

So, we'd expect there would be $1110 \times 4090/21186$ or 214.2877 Mondays among the 1110 "up" days.

Each cell contributes a value equal to $\dfrac{(Obs - Exp)^2}{Exp}$ to the chi-square sum.

Add up these components. If you do it by hand, it can be helpful to arrange the calculation in a table or spreadsheet.

The P-value is the probability in the upper tail of the χ^2 model. It can be found using software or a table (see Table X in Appendix B).

Large χ^2 statistic values correspond to small P-values, which would lead us to reject the null hypothesis, but the value here is not particularly large.

The expected values are:

> Monday: 214.28774
> Tuesday: 224.92353
> Wednesday: 226.18097
> Thursday: 222.82781
> Friday: 221.77995

And we observe:

> Monday: 195
> Tuesday: 223
> Wednesday: 239
> Thursday: 223
> Friday: 230

$$\chi^2 = \frac{(195 - 214.28774)^2}{214.28774} + \cdots + \frac{(230 - 221.77995)^2}{221.77995}$$
$$= 2.7838$$

Using Table X in Appendix B, we find that for a significance level of 5% and 4 degrees of freedom, we'd need a value of 9.488 or more to have a P-value less than .05. Our value of 2.7838 is less than that.

Using a computer to generate the P-value, we find:

$$\text{P-value} = P(\chi^2_4 > 2.7838) = 0.5946$$

(continued)

REPORT

Conclusion Link the P-value to your decision. Be sure to say more than a fact about the distribution of counts. State your conclusion in terms of what the data mean.

MEMO

Re: Stock market patterns

Our investigation of whether there are day-of-the-week patterns in the behavior of the DJIA in which one day or another is more likely to be an "up" day found no evidence of such a pattern. Our statistical test indicated that a pattern such as the one found in our sample of trading days would happen by chance about 60% of the time.

We conclude that there is, unfortunately, no evidence of a pattern that could be used to guide investment in the market. We were unable to detect a "weekend" or other day-of-the-week effect in the market.

14.2   Interpreting Chi-Square Values

When we calculated χ^2 for the trading days example, we got 2.7838. That value was not large for 4 degrees of freedom, so we were unable to reject the null hypothesis. In general, what *is* big for a χ^2 statistic?

Think about how χ^2 is calculated. In every cell, any deviation from the expected count contributes to the sum. Large deviations generally contribute more, but if there are a lot of cells, even small deviations can add up, making the χ^2 value larger. So the more cells there are, the higher the value of χ^2 has to be before it becomes significant. For χ^2, the decision about how big is big depends on the number of degrees of freedom.

Unlike the Normal and t families, χ^2 models are skewed. Curves in the χ^2 family change both shape and center as the number of degrees of freedom grows. For example, Figure 14.1 shows the χ^2 curves for 5 and for 9 degrees of freedom.

Figure 14.1   The χ^2 curves for 5 and 9 degrees of freedom.

Notice that the value $\chi^2 = 10$ might seem somewhat extreme when there are 5 degrees of freedom, but appears to be rather ordinary for 9 degrees of freedom. Here are two simple facts to help you think about χ^2 models:

- The mode is at $\chi^2 = $ df $- 2$. (Look at the curves; their peaks are at 3 and 7.)
- The expected value (mean) of a χ^2 model is its number of degrees of freedom. That's a bit to the right of the mode—as we would expect for a skewed distribution.

Goodness-of-fit tests are often performed by people who have a theory of what the proportions *should* be in each category and who believe their theory to be true. In some cases, unlike our market example, there isn't an obvious null hypothesis against which to test the proposed model. So, unfortunately, in those cases, the only null hypothesis available is that the proposed theory is true. And as we know, the hypothesis testing procedure allows us only to reject the null or fail to reject it.

We can never confirm that a theory is in fact true; we can never confirm the null hypothesis.

At best, we can point out that the data are consistent with the proposed theory. But this doesn't prove the theory. The data *could* be consistent with the model even if the theory were wrong. In that case, we fail to reject the null hypothesis but can't conclude anything for sure about whether the theory is true.

> **Why Can't We Prove the Null?**
>
> A student claims that it really makes no difference to your starting salary how well you do in your Statistics class. He surveys recent graduates, categorizes them according to whether they earned an A, B, or C in Statistics, and according to whether their starting salary is above or below the median for their class. He calculates the proportion above the median salary for each grade. His null model is that in each grade category, 50% of students are above the median. With 40 respondents, he gets a P-value of 0.07 and declares that Statistics grades don't matter. But then more questionnaires are returned, and he finds that with a sample size of 70, his P-value is 0.04. Can he ignore the second batch of data? Of course not. If he could do that, he could claim almost any null model was true just by having too little data to refute it.

14.3 Examining the Residuals

Chi-square tests are always one-sided. The chi-square statistic is always positive, and a large value provides evidence against the null hypothesis (because it shows that the fit to the model is *not* good), while small values provide little evidence that the model doesn't fit. In another sense, however, chi-square tests are really many-sided; a large statistic doesn't tell us *how* the null model doesn't fit. In our market theory example, if we had rejected the uniform model, we wouldn't have known *how* it failed. Was it because there were not enough Mondays represented, or was it that all five days showed some deviation from the uniform?

When we reject a null hypothesis in a goodness-of-fit test, we can examine the residuals in each cell to learn more. In fact, whenever we reject a null hypothesis, it's a good idea to examine the residuals. (We don't need to do that when we fail to reject because when the χ^2 value is small, all of its components must have been small.) Because we want to compare residuals for cells that may have very different counts, we standardize the residuals. We know the mean residual is zero,[1] but we need to know each residual's standard deviation. When we tested proportions, we saw a link between the expected proportion and its standard deviation. For counts, there's a similar link. To standardize a cell's residual, we divide by the square root of its expected value:[2]

$$\frac{(Obs - Exp)}{\sqrt{Exp}}.$$

Notice that these **standardized residuals** are the square roots of the components we calculated for each cell, with the plus (+) or the minus (−) sign indicating whether we observed more or fewer cases than we expected.

---

[1] Residual = Observed − Expected. Because the total of the expected values is the same as the observed total, the residuals must sum to zero.

[2] It can be shown mathematically that the square root of the expected value estimates the appropriate standard deviation.

The standardized residuals give us a chance to think about the underlying patterns and to consider how the distribution differs from the model. Now that we've divided each residual by its standard deviation, they are z-scores. If the null hypothesis were true, we could even use the 68–95–99.7 Rule to judge how extraordinary the large ones are.

Ordinarily, you should only look at the residuals if the chi-square value is significantly large. But for illustration, we'll take a peek at the standardized residuals for the trading days data:

	Standardized Residual $= \dfrac{(Obs - Exp)}{\sqrt{Exp}}$
Monday	−1.3176
Tuesday	−0.1283
Wednesday	0.8524
Thursday	0.0115
Friday	0.5520

Table 14.4   Standardized residuals.

As we would expect from the small chi-square value, none of these values is remarkable.

FOR EXAMPLE   **Examining residuals from a chi-square test**

QUESTION   In the call center example (see page 444), examine the residuals to see if any operators stand out as having especially strong or weak performance.

ANSWER   Because we failed to reject the null hypothesis, we don't expect any of the standardized residuals to be large, but we will examine them nonetheless.

The standardized residuals are the square roots of the components (from the bottom row of the table in the Example on page 445).

Standardized Residuals	−1.03	0.52	−1.55	−0.77	1.03	0.77	−0.52	1.55

As we expected, none of the residuals are large. Even though Atara notices that some of the operators enrolled more than twice the number of new customers as others, the variation is typical (within two standard deviations) of what we would expect if all their performances were, in fact, equal.

14.4   The Chi-Square Test of Homogeneity

In Chapter 2 we saw data from a Pew Research survey about social networking in several countries. The question of interest to businesses asked whether respondents had access to and used social networking. Responses were "yes" (use social networking), "no", and "not available". We organized the responses into a contingency table that looked like this:

Country	No	Yes	N/A	Total
Britain	336	529	153	1018
Egypt	70	300	630	1000
Germany	460	340	200	1000
Russia	90	500	420	1010
U.S.	293	506	212	1011
Total	1249	2175	1615	5039

Table 14.5   Responses to a question about use and availability of social networking. ("N/A" = not available)

The natural question to ask is whether there are any differences among the countries (and, if so, what those are). We can start with a stacked bar chart.

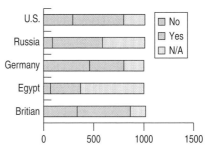

Figure 14.2   The data of Table 14.5 in a stacked bar chart. The bars are easy to compare because they have roughly the same total counts.

In Figure 14.2, Egypt stands out for having less availability of social networking. Germany may have an unusually large number of people saying they don't use social networking despite its availability.

But are the observed differences in the percentages real or just natural sampling variation? Our null hypothesis is that the proportions choosing each alternative are the same for each country. To test that hypothesis, we use a **chi-square test of homogeneity**. This is just another chi-square test. It turns out that the mechanics of the test of this hypothesis are nearly identical to the chi-square goodness-of-fit test we just saw in Section 14.1. The difference is that the goodness-of-fit test compared our observed counts to the expected counts from a *given* model. The test of homogeneity, by contrast, has a null hypothesis that the distributions are the same for all the groups. The test examines the differences between the observed counts and what we'd expect under that assumption of homogeneity.

For example, 529/1018 or 52% of British respondents said that they use social networking. If the distributions were homogeneous across the five countries (as the null hypothesis asserts), then that proportion should be the same for all five countries. So 52% of the 1010 Russian respondents, or 525, would have said that they use social networking. That's the number we'd *expect* under the rule hypothesis.

Working in this way, we (or, more likely, the computer) can fill in expected values for each cell. The following table shows these expected values for each response and each country.

	No	Yes	N/A	Total
Britain	252.328	439.403	326.269	1018
Egypt	247.867	431.633	320.500	1000
Germany	247.867	431.633	320.500	1000
Russia	250.345	435.950	323.705	1010
U.S.	250.593	436.381	324.026	1011
Total	1249	2175	1615	5039

Table 14.6   Expected values for the responses. Because these are theoretical values, they don't have to be integers.

The term *homogeneity* refers to the hypothesis that things are the same. Here, we ask whether the distribution of responses is the same across the five countries. The chi-square test looks for differences large enough to step beyond what we might expect from random sample-to-sample variation. It can reveal a large deviation in a single category or small but persistent differences over all the categories—or anything in between.

Assumptions and Conditions

The assumptions and conditions are the same as for the chi-square test for goodness-of-fit. The **Counted Data Condition** says that these data must be counts. You can never perform a chi-square test on a quantitative variable. For example, if Pew had asked how many hours in a typical day respondents spent on social networking, we wouldn't be able to use a chi-square test to determine whether the mean time expenditures in the five countries were the same.[3]

Independence Assumption.   The counts must be independent of each other. We can check the **Randomization Condition**. Here, we have random samples, so we *can* assume that the observations are independent.

The **Sample Size Assumption** can be checked with the **Expected Cell Frequency Condition**, which says that the expected count in each cell must be at least 5. Here, our samples are certainly large enough.

Following the pattern of the goodness-of-fit test, we compute the component for each cell of the table:

$$\text{Component} = \frac{(Obs - Exp)^2}{Exp}.$$

Summing these components across all cells gives the chi-square value:

$$\chi^2 = \sum_{all\ cells} \frac{(Obs - Exp)^2}{Exp}.$$

The degrees of freedom are different than they were for the goodness-of-fit test. For a test of homogeneity, there are $(R - 1) \times (C - 1)$ degrees of freedom, where R is the number of rows and C is the number of columns.

In our example, we have $4 \times 2 = 8$ degrees of freedom. We'll need the degrees of freedom to find a P-value for the chi-square statistic.

BY HAND   How to find expected values

In a contingency table, to test for homogeneity, we need to find the expected values when the null hypothesis is true. To find the expected value for row i and column j, we take:

$$Exp_{ij} = \frac{Total_{Row\ i} \times Total_{Col\ j}}{Table\ Total}$$

Here's an example:

Suppose we ask 100 people, 40 men and 60 women, to name their magazine preference: *Sports Illustrated*, *Cosmopolitan*, or *The Economist*, with the following result, shown in Microsoft Excel 2013 on the following page.

Large Samples and Chi-Square Tests

Whenever we test any hypothesis, a very large sample size means that small effects have a greater chance of being statistically significant. This is especially true for chi-square tests. So it's important to look at the effect sizes when the null hypothesis is rejected to see if the differences are practically significant. Don't rely only on the P-value when making a business decision. This applies to many of the examples in this chapter which have large sample sizes typical of those seen in today's business environment.

[3]To do that, you'd use a method called Analysis of Variance, which we'll see in Chapter 20.

	A	B	C	D	E
1	Actual	SI	Cosmo	Economist	Total
2	Men	25	5	10	40
3	Women	10	45	5	60
4	Total	35	50	15	100

Then, for example, the expected value under homogeneity for *Men* (row 1) who prefer *The Economist* (column 3) would be:

$$Exp_{13} = \frac{40 \times 15}{100} = 6$$

Performing similar calculations for all cells gives the expected values:

6	Expected	SI	Cosmo	Economist	Total
7	Men	14	20	6	40
8	Women	21	30	9	60
9	Total	35	50	15	100

It is a simple matter to do these calculations in a spreadsheet (as we have done here).

For the social networking data, the chi-square value is 1049, with 8 degrees of freedom. We don't need a table to know that this is large enough to be statistically significant. So we can conclude that these five countries are not homogeneous in the use of social networking.

If you find that simply rejecting the hypothesis of homogeneity is a bit unsatisfying, you're in good company. It's hardly a shock that responses to this question differ from country to country especially with sample sizes this large. What we'd really like to know is where the differences were and how big they were. The test for homogeneity doesn't answer these interesting questions, but it does provide some evidence that can help us. A look at the standardized residuals can help identify cells that don't match the homogeneity pattern.

FOR EXAMPLE   Testing homogeneity

QUESTION   Although annual inflation in the United States has been low for several years, many Americans fear that inflation may return. In May 2010, a Gallup poll asked 680 adults nationwide, "Are you very concerned, somewhat concerned, or not at all concerned that inflation will climb?" Does the distribution of responses appear to be the same for Conservatives as Liberals?

Ideology	Very Concerned	Somewhat Concerned	Not At All Concerned	Total
Conservative	232	83	25	**340**
Liberal	143	126	71	**340**
Total	**375 (55.15%)**	**209 (30.74%)**	**96 (14.12%)**	**680**

(continued)

ANSWER   This is a test of homogeneity, testing whether the distribution of responses is the same for the two ideological groups. The data are counts, the Gallup poll selected adults randomly (stratified by ideology), and all expected cell frequencies are much greater than 5 (see table below).

There are $(3 - 1) \times (2 - 1)$ or 2 degrees of freedom.

If the distributions were the same, we would expect each cell to have expected values that are 55.15%, 30.74%, and 14.12% of the row totals for Very Concerned, Somewhat Concerned, and Not at all Concerned, respectively. These values can be computed explicitly from:

$$Exp_{ij} = \frac{TotalRow_i \times TotalCol_j}{Table\ Total}$$

So, in the first cell (Conservative, Very Concerned):

$$Exp_{11} = \frac{TotalRow_1 \times TotalCol_1}{Table\ Total} = \frac{340 \times 375}{680} = 187.5$$

Expected counts for all cells are:

Expected Numbers	Very Concerned	Somewhat Concerned	Not At All Concerned
Conservative	187.5	104.5	48.0
Liberal	187.5	104.5	48.0

The components $\dfrac{(Obs - Exp)^2}{Exp}$ are:

Components	Very Concerned	Somewhat Concerned	Not At All Concerned
Conservative	10.56	4.42	11.02
Liberal	10.56	4.42	11.02

Summing these gives $\chi^2 = 10.56 + 4.42 + \cdots + 11.02 = 52.00$, which, with 2 df, has a P-value of < 0.0001.

We, therefore, reject the hypothesis that the distribution of responses is the same for Conservatives and Liberals.

14.5   Comparing Two Proportions

In Chapter 2 we saw data from a survey comparing the reasons that men and women watch the Super Bowl. Advertisers spend huge amounts on Super Bowl ads and, consequently, care deeply about who watches them. If we extract the data on the 708 survey respondents who answered and said they would be watching the Super Bowl, we get the data in Table 14.7.

A chi-square test of homogeneity gives 37.26 with 1 degree of freedom. That has a P-value ≤ 0.0001, so we can reject the null hypothesis of no difference.

When we have a 2×2 table like this, we are really just comparing two proportions. In this example, $154/352 = 43.75\%$ of the women and $79/356 = 22.19\%$ of the men say they watch the Super Bowl primarily for the commercials. In this special case of testing the equality of two proportions, there is a z-test, which is equivalent and gives the same P-value.

	Female	Male	Total
Game	198	277	475
Commercials	154	79	233
Total	352	356	708

Table 14.7   Counts of respondents categorized by sex and whether they watch the Super Bowl primarily for the game or for the commercials.

Confidence Interval for the Difference of Two Proportions

The approach of working directly with proportions offers an advantage. As we saw, 43.75% of the women and 22.19% of the men watch the Super Bowl primarily for the commercials. That's a difference of 21.56%.

If we knew the standard error of that quantity, we could use a z-statistic to construct a confidence interval for the true difference in the population. It's not hard to find the standard error. All we need is the formula:[4]

$$SE(\hat{p}_1 - \hat{p}_2) = \sqrt{\frac{\hat{p}_1\hat{q}_1}{n_1} + \frac{\hat{p}_2\hat{q}_2}{n_2}}$$

The confidence interval has the same form as the confidence interval for a single proportion, with this new standard error:

$$(\hat{p}_1 - \hat{p}_2) \pm z^*SE(\hat{p}_1 - \hat{p}_2).$$

Confidence Interval for the Difference of Two Proportions

When the conditions are met, we can find the confidence interval for the difference of two proportions, $p_1 - p_2$. The confidence interval is

$$(\hat{p}_1 - \hat{p}_2) \pm z^*SE(\hat{p}_1 - \hat{p}_2),$$

where we find the standard error of the difference as

$$SE(\hat{p}_1 - \hat{p}_2) = \sqrt{\frac{\hat{p}_1\hat{q}_1}{n_1} + \frac{\hat{p}_2\hat{q}_2}{n_2}}$$

from the observed proportions.

The critical value z^* depends on the particular confidence level that you specify.

For the Super Bowl survey, a 95% confidence interval for the true difference between the proportion of women and the proportion of men preferring the commercials is:

$$(0.4375 - 0.2219) \pm 1.96 \times \sqrt{\frac{0.4375 \times 0.5625}{352} + \frac{0.2219 \times 0.7781}{356}}$$

$$= 0.2156 \pm 0.0674$$

or from 14.82% to 28.30%.

We can be 95% confident that between 14.82% and 28.30% more women than men watch the Super Bowl for the commercials more than for the game.

This confidence interval helps us to address the question of whether the difference matters. That depends on the reason we are asking the question. The confidence interval shows the *effect size*—or at least the interval of plausible values for the effect size. A company planning to advertise on the Super Bowl might consider this difference large enough to consider in designing their ads. Be sure to consider the effect size whenever you make a business decision based on rejecting a null hypothesis.

---

[4]The standard error of the difference is found from the general fact that the variance of a difference of two independent quantities is the *sum* of their variances. See Chapter 6 for details.

FOR EXAMPLE A confidence interval for the difference of proportions

QUESTION In the Gallup poll on inflation (see page 453), 68.2% (232 of 340) of those identifying themselves as Conservative were very concerned about the rise of inflation, but only 42.1% (143 of 340) of Liberals responded the same way. That's a difference of 26.2% in this sample of 680 adults. Find a 95% confidence interval for the true difference.

ANSWER The confidence interval can be found from:

$$(\hat{p}_C - \hat{p}_L) \pm z^* SE(\hat{p}_C - \hat{p}_L) \text{ where } SE(\hat{p}_C - \hat{p}_L) = \sqrt{\frac{\hat{p}_C \hat{q}_C}{n_C} + \frac{\hat{p}_L \hat{q}_L}{n_L}}$$

$$= \sqrt{\frac{(0.682)(0.338)}{340} + \frac{(0.421)(0.579)}{340}} = 0.037.$$

Since we know the 95% confidence critical value for z is 1.96, we have:

$$0.262 \pm 1.96(0.037) = (0.189, 0.335).$$

In other words, we are 95% confident that the proportion of Conservatives who are very concerned by inflation is between 18.9% and 33.5% higher than the same proportion of Liberals.

14.6 Chi-Square Test of Independence

If the importance people place on their personal appearance varies a great deal by age, that might be crucial for the marketing department of a global cosmetics company. Fortunately, we have data. The GfK Roper Reports® Worldwide Survey asked 30,000 consumers in 23 countries about their attitudes on health, beauty, and other personal values. One question participants were asked was how important their personal appearance is to them.

We might think of the different age groups as categories to be compared with a test of homogeneity. But it makes more sense to think of *Age* as a second variable whose value has been measured for each respondent along with his or her response to the appearance question. Asking whether the distribution of responses changes with *Age* now raises the question of whether the variables personal *Appearance* and *Age* are independent.

| | | Age | | | | | | |
		13–19	20–29	30–39	40–49	50–59	60+	Total
Appearance	7—Extremely Important	396	337	300	252	142	93	1520
	6	325	326	307	254	123	86	1421
	5	318	312	317	270	150	106	1473
	4—Average Importance	397	376	403	423	224	210	2033
	3	83	83	88	93	54	45	446
	2	37	43	53	58	37	45	273
	1—Not At All Important	40	37	53	56	36	52	274
	Total	1596	1514	1521	1406	766	637	7440

Table 14.8 Responses to the question about personal appearance by age group.

Whenever we have two variables in a contingency table like this, the natural test is a **chi-square test of independence**. Mechanically, this chi-square test is identical to a test of homogeneity. The difference between the two tests is in how we think of the data and, thus, what conclusion we draw.

Here we ask whether the response to the personal appearance question is independent of age. Remember, that for any two events, **A** and **B**, to be independent, the probability of event **A** given that event **B** occurred must be the same as the probability of event **A**. Here, this means the probability that a randomly selected respondent thinks personal appearance is extremely important doesn't depend on his or her age group. Of course, from a table based on data, the probabilities will never be exactly the same. But to tell whether they are different enough, we use a chi-square test of independence.

Here we have two categorical variables measured on a single population. For the homogeneity test, we had a single categorical variable measured independently on two or more populations. Now we ask a different question: "Are the variables independent?" rather than "Are the groups homogeneous?" These are subtle differences, but they are important when we draw conclusions.

> **Homogeneity or Independence?**
> The only difference between the test for homogeneity and the test for independence is in the decision you need to make.

Assumptions and Conditions

Of course, we still need counts and enough data so that the expected counts are at least five in each cell.

If we're interested in the independence of variables, we usually want to generalize from the data to some population. In that case, we'll need to check that the data are a representative random sample from that population.

GUIDED EXAMPLE   Personal Appearance and Age

We want to help marketers discover whether a person's age influences how they respond to the question: "How important is seeking the utmost attractive appearance to you?" We have the values of *Age* in six age categories. We will view *Age* as a variable, and ask whether the variables *Age* and *Appearance* are independent.

PLAN	**Setup** State what you want to know. Identify the variables and context.	We want to know whether the categorical variables personal *Appearance* and *Age* are statistically independent. We have a contingency table of 7440 respondents from a sample of five countries.

(continued)

Hypotheses State the null and alternative hypotheses.

We perform a test of independence when we suspect the variables may not be independent. We are making the claim that knowing the respondents' age will change the distribution of their response to the question about personal *Appearance*, and testing the null hypothesis that it is *not* true.

H_0: Personal *Appearance* and *Age* are independent.[5]

H_A: Personal *Appearance* and *Age* are not independent.

Model Check the conditions.

✓ **Counted Data Condition** We have counts of individuals categorized on two categorical variables.

✓ **Randomization Condition** These data are from a randomized survey conducted in 30 countries. We have data from five of them. Although they are not an SRS, the samples within each country were selected to avoid biases.

✓ **Expected Cell Frequency Condition** The expected values are all much larger than 5.

The table below shows the expected counts for each cell. The expected counts are calculated exactly as they were for a test of homogeneity; in the first cell, for example, we expect $\frac{1520}{7440} = 20.43\%$ of 1596, which is 326.065.

| | | Expected Values | | | | |
| | | Age | | | | |
	13–19	20–29	30–39	40–49	50–59	60+
7—Extremely Important	326.065	309.312	310.742	287.247	156.495	130.140
6	304.827	289.166	290.503	268.538	146.302	121.664
5	315.982	299.748	301.133	278.365	151.656	126.116
4—Average Importance	436.111	413.705	415.617	384.193	209.312	174.062
3	95.674	90.759	91.178	84.284	45.919	38.186
2	58.563	55.554	55.811	51.591	28.107	23.374
1—Not At All Important	58.777	55.758	56.015	51.780	28.210	23.459

Appearance (row label, vertical)

The stacked bar graph shows that the response seems to be dependent on *Age*. Older people tend to think personal appearance is less important than younger people.

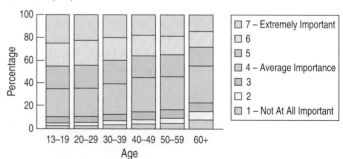

---

[5]As in other chi-square tests, the hypotheses are usually expressed in words, without parameters. The hypothesis of independence itself tells us how to find expected values for each cell of the contingency table. That's all we need.

Specify the model.	(The counts are shown in Table 14.10.)
Name the test you will use.	We'll use a χ^2 model with $(7 - 1) \times (6 - 1) = 30$ df and do a **chi-square test of independence**.

DO	**Mechanics** Calculate χ^2 and find the P-value using software.	$$\chi^2 = \sum_{all\ cells} \frac{(Obs - Exp)^2}{Exp} = 170.7762$$
	The shape of a chi-square model depends on its degrees of freedom. Even with 30 df, this chi-square statistic is extremely large, so the resulting P-value is small.	P-value $= P(\chi^2_{30} > 170.7762) < 0.001$

REPORT | **Conclusion** Link the P-value to your decision. State your conclusion. | MEMO

Re: Investigation of the relationship between age of consumer and attitudes about personal appearance

It appears from our analysis of the Roper survey that attitudes on personal *Appearance* are not independent of *Age*. It seems that older people find personal appearance less important than younger people do (on average in the five countries selected). |

We rejected the null hypothesis of independence between *Age* and attitudes about personal *Appearance*. With a sample size this large, we can detect very small deviations from independence, so it's almost guaranteed that the chi-square test will reject the null hypothesis. Examining the residuals can help you see the cells that deviate farthest from independence. To make a meaningful business decision, you'll have to look at effect sizes as well as the P-value. We should also look at each country's data individually since country to country differences could affect marketing decisions.

Suppose the company was specifically interested in deciding how to split advertising resources between the teen market and the 30–39-year-old market. How much of a difference is there between the proportions of those in each age group that rated personal *Appearance* as very important (responding either 6 or 7)?

For that we'll need to construct a confidence interval on the difference. From Table 14.8, we find that the percentages of those answering 6 and 7 are 45.18% and 39.91% for the teen and 30–39-year-old groups, respectively. The 95% confidence interval is:

$$(\hat{p}_1 - \hat{p}_2) \pm z^* SE(\hat{p}_1 - \hat{p}_2)$$

$$= (0.4518 - 0.3991) \pm 1.96 \times \sqrt{\frac{(0.4518)(0.5482)}{1596} + \frac{(0.3991)(0.6009)}{1521}}$$

$$= (0.018, 0.087), \text{ or } (1.8\% \text{ to } 8.7\%)$$

This is a statistically significant difference, but now we can see that the difference may be as small as 1.8%. When deciding how to allocate advertising expenditures, it is important to keep these estimates of the effect size in mind.

FOR EXAMPLE   A chi-square test of independence

QUESTION   In May 2010, the Gallup poll asked U.S. adults their opinion on whether they are in favor of or opposed to using profiling to identify potential terrorists at airports, a practice used routinely in Israel, but not in the United States. Does opinion depend on age? Or are opinion and age independent? Here are numbers similar to the ones Gallup found (the percentages are the same, but the totals have been changed to make the calculations easier).

			Age		
	18–29	30–49	50–64	65+	Total
Favor	57	66	77	87	287
Oppose	43	34	23	13	113
Total	100	100	100	100	400

ANSWER   The null hypothesis is that *Opinion* and *Age* are independent. We can view this as a test of independence as opposed to a test of homogeneity if we view *Age* and *Opinion* as variables whose relationship we want to understand. This was a random sample and there are at least 5 expected responses in every cell. The expected values are calculated using the formula:

$$Exp_{ij} = \frac{TotalRow_i \times TotalCol_j}{Table\ Total} \Longrightarrow$$

$$Exp_{11} = \frac{TotalRow_1 \times TotalCol_1}{Table\ Total} = \frac{287 \times 100}{400} = 71.75$$

Expected Values			Age		
	18–29	30–49	50–64	65+	Total
Favor	71.75	71.75	71.75	71.75	287
Oppose	28.25	28.25	28.25	28.25	113
Total	100	100	100	100	400

The components are:

Components		Age		
	18–29	30–49	50–64	65+
Favor	3.03	0.46	0.38	3.24
Oppose	7.70	1.17	0.98	8.23

There are $(r - 1) \times (c - 1) = 1 \times 3 = 3$ degrees of freedom. Summing all the components gives:

$$\chi_3^2 = 3.03 + 0.46 + \cdots + 8.23 = 25.19,$$

which has a P-value < 0.0001.

Thus, we reject the null hypothesis and conclude that *Age* and *Opinion* about Profiling are not independent. Looking at the residuals,

Residuals		Age		
	18–29	30–49	50–64	65+
Favor	−1.74	−0.68	0.62	1.80
Oppose	2.78	1.08	−0.99	−2.87

we see a pattern. These two variables fail to be independent because increasing age is associated with more favorable attitudes toward profiling.

Bar charts arranged in *Age* order make the pattern clear:

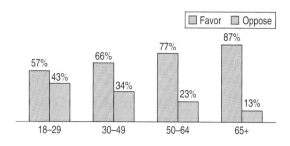

JUST CHECKING

Which of the three chi-square tests would you use in each of the following situations—goodness-of-fit, homogeneity, or independence?

1 A restaurant manager wonders whether customers who dine on Friday nights have the same preferences among the chef's four special entrées as those who dine on Saturday nights. One weekend he has the wait staff record which entrées were ordered each night. Assuming these customers to be typical of all weekend diners, he'll compare the distributions of meals chosen Friday and Saturday.

2 Company policy calls for parking spaces to be assigned to everyone at random, but you suspect that may not be so.

There are three lots of equal size: lot A, next to the building; lot B, a bit farther away; and lot C on the other side of the highway. You gather data about employees at middle management level and above to see how many were assigned parking in each lot.

3 Is a student's social life affected by where the student lives? A campus survey asked a random sample of students whether they lived in a dormitory, in off-campus housing, or at home and whether they had been out on a date 0, 1–2, 3–4, or 5 or more times in the past two weeks.

Chi-Square Tests and Causation

Chi-square tests are common. Tests for independence are especially widespread. Unfortunately, many people interpret a small P-value as proof of causation. We know better. Just as correlation between quantitative variables does not demonstrate causation, a failure of independence between two categorical variables does not show a cause-and-effect relationship between them, nor should we say that one variable *depends* on the other.

The chi-square test for independence treats the two variables symmetrically. There is no way to differentiate the direction of any possible causation from one variable to the other. While we can see that attitudes on personal *Appearance* and *Age* are related, we can't say that getting older *causes* you to change attitudes. And certainly it's not correct to say that changing attitudes on personal appearance makes you older.

Of course, there's never any way to eliminate the possibility that a lurking variable is responsible for the observed lack of independence. In some sense, a failure of independence between two categorical variables is less impressive than a strong, consistent association between quantitative variables. Two categorical variables can fail the test of independence in many ways, including ways that show no consistent pattern of failure. Examination of the chi-square standardized residuals can help you think about the underlying patterns.

WHAT CAN GO WRONG?

- **Don't use chi-square methods unless you have counts.** All three of the chi-square tests apply only to counts. Other kinds of data can be arrayed in two-way tables. Just because numbers are in a two-way table doesn't make them suitable for chi-square analysis. Data reported as proportions or percentages can be suitable for chi-square procedures, *but only after they are converted to counts.* If you try to do the calculations without first finding the counts, your results will be wrong.

- **Beware large samples.** Beware *large* samples? That's not the advice you're used to hearing. The chi-square tests, however, are unusual. You should be wary of chi-square tests performed on very large samples. No hypothesized distribution fits perfectly, no two groups are exactly homogeneous, and two variables are rarely perfectly independent. The degrees of freedom for chi-square tests don't grow with the sample size. With a sufficiently large sample size, a chi-square test can always reject the null hypothesis. But we have no measure of how far the data are from the null model. There are no confidence intervals to help us judge the effect size except in the case of two proportions.

- **Don't say that one variable "depends" on the other just because they're not independent.** "Depend" can suggest a model or a pattern, but variables can fail to be independent in many different ways. When variables fail the test for independence, it may be better to say they are "associated."

ETHICS IN ACTION

Forever Youthful, Inc. specializes in products that contain biologically active ingredients with anti-aging properties often referred to as "cosmeceuticals." Forever Youthful, Inc. has been exclusively focused on skin care. Its line of luxurious creams, masks, and eye treatments, based on various combinations of antioxidants, peptides, and even growth factors, claim to reverse the signs of aging. Michele Kaplan, Vice President for Sales and Marketing, and her team have been very successful in partnering with high-end spas, resorts, and boutiques to deliver Forever Youthful skin care products to its target customer: older wealthy women. Consequently, Michele was the only top level executive to survive the recent restructuring at Forever Youthful after a new president and CEO, J. C. Burnett, was hired.

Under Burnett's leadership the company has begun to move in several different directions. An emerging trend in the anti-aging market is hair care, and Forever Youthful is about to launch a line of expensive shampoos, conditioners, and scalp treatments designed to make hair shiny, full, and younger looking. Michele is excited about the prospects for sales in this new market segment, and she believes the current strategy of targeting high-end distributors, in this case fashionable salons, would work best. However, the new leadership team is proposing that the hair care line of products be sold online direct to customers, arguing that this is more cost-effective because it doesn't require establishing relationships with hair salons.

Michele disagrees. She is concerned about the possible negative consequences of such a move, particularly on the brand's "elite" image, not to mention on her division.

To prove her point, Michele directed her research team to design some questions for gathering data from current and potential customers. Working with some of the businesses that sell Forever Youthful skin care products, clients were interviewed about their online purchasing behaviors and perceptions of brand image as they checked in for appointments. Demographic data were also collected. Based on a sample of 3500 clients, chi-square tests for independence were performed to determine if responses about online shopping and brand image were independent of age category. The results revealed what Michele had expected. Online purchasing behavior is dependent on age. Moreover, level of agreement with the statement "hair products sold online are of inferior quality to those sold in salons" also showed dependence on age. Because Forever Youthful targets older customers, Michele is hopeful that these findings will help convince the team that her strategy is best. She is now looking forward to the next leadership team meeting.

- Identify the ethical dilemma in this scenario.

- What are the undesirable consequences?

- Propose an ethical solution that considers the welfare of all stakeholders.

WHAT HAVE WE LEARNED?

Learning Objectives

Recognize when a chi-square test of goodness-of-fit, homogeneity, or independence is appropriate.

For each test, find the expected cell frequencies.

For each test, check the assumptions and corresponding conditions and know how to complete the test.

- Counted data condition.
- Independence assumption; randomization makes independence more plausible.
- Sample size assumption with the expected cell frequency condition; expect at least 5 observations in each cell.

Interpret a chi-square test.

- Even though we might believe the model, we cannot prove that the data fit the model with a chi-square test because that would mean confirming the null hypothesis.

Examine the standardized residuals to understand what cells were responsible for rejecting a null hypothesis.

Compare two proportions.

State the null hypothesis for a test of independence and understand how that is different from the null hypothesis for a test of homogeneity.

- Both are computed the same way. You may not find both offered by your technology. You can use either one as long as you interpret your result correctly.

Terms

Chi-square models

Chi-square models are skewed to the right. They are parameterized by their degrees of freedom and become less skewed with increasing degrees of freedom.

Chi-square (or chi-squared) statistic

The chi-square statistic is found by summing the chi-square components. Chi-square tests can be used to test goodness-of-fit, homogeneity, or independence.

Chi-square goodness-of-fit test

A test of whether the distribution of counts in one categorical variable matches the distribution predicted by a model. A chi-square test of goodness-of-fit finds

$$\chi^2 = \sum_{all\ cells} \frac{(Obs - Exp)^2}{Exp},$$

where the expected counts come from the predicting model. It finds a P-value from a chi-square model with $n - 1$ degrees of freedom, where n is the number of categories in the categorical variable.

Chi-square test of homogeneity

A test comparing the distribution of counts for two or more groups on the same categorical variable. A chi-square test of homogeneity finds

$$\chi^2 = \sum_{all\ cells} \frac{(Obs - Exp)^2}{Exp},$$

where the expected counts are based on the overall frequencies, adjusted for the totals in each group. We find a P-value from a chi-square distribution with $(R - 1) \times (C - 1)$ degrees of freedom, where R gives the number of categories (rows) and C gives the number of independent groups (columns).

Chi-square test of independence

A test of whether two categorical variables are independent. It examines the distribution of counts for one group of individuals classified according to both variables. A chi-square test of *independence* uses the same calculation as a test of homogeneity. We find a P-value from a chi-square distribution with $(R - 1) \times (C - 1)$ degrees of freedom, where R gives the number of categories in one variable and C gives the number of categories in the other.

Standardized residual

In each cell of a two-way table, a standardized residual is the square root of the chi-square component for that cell with the sign of the *Observed – Expected* difference:

$$\frac{(Obs - Exp)}{\sqrt{Exp}}$$

When we reject a chi-square test, an examination of the standardized residuals can sometimes reveal more about how the data deviate from the null model.

TECHNOLOGY HELP: Chi-Square

Most statistics packages associate chi-square tests with contingency tables. Often chi-square is available as an option only when you make a contingency table. This organization can make it hard to locate the chi-square test and may confuse the three different roles that the chi-square test can take. In particular, chi-square tests for goodness-of-fit may be hard to find or missing entirely. Chi-square tests for homogeneity are computationally the same as chi-square tests for independence, so you may have to perform the mechanics as if they were tests of independence and interpret them afterward as tests of homogeneity.

Most statistics packages work with data on individuals rather than with the summary counts. If the only information you have is the table of counts, you may find it more difficult to get a statistics package to compute chi-square. Some packages offer a way to reconstruct the data from the summary counts so that they can then be passed back through the chi-square calculation, finding the cell counts again. Many packages offer chi-square standardized residuals (although they may be called something else).

EXCEL

To perform a chi-square goodness-of-fit test using Excel:

If you have two parallel columns, one holding observed counts and the other expected counts, follow these steps:

- In columns D through F, you can use spreadsheet calculations and built-in functions to calculate (Obs-Exp), (Obs-Exp)^2, and (Obs-Exp)^2/Exp. Type the following into cells D2, E2, and F2 respectively:
  - =(B2-C2)
  - =D2^2
  - =E2/C2
- Copy the formulas from D2, E2, and F2 and paste into the remainder of the rows in columns D, E, and F.
- Using the =SUM function, add the values contained in the cells in column F to get the χ^2 value.
- The CHISQ.INV.RT and CHISQ.DIST.RT functions can then be used to calculate the critical value and P-value of the chi-square statistic that is calculated. See the image below for commands. Note that the function used to calculate degrees of freedom (=COUNT) should reflect rows containing data.

	A	B	C	D	E	F	G
1	Operator	Observed	Expected	(Obs-Exp)	(Obs-Exp)^2	(Obs-Exp)^2/Exp	**Excel Syntax**
2	1	11	15	-4	16	1.0667	
3	2	17	15	2	4	0.2667	
4	3	9	15	-6	36	2.4000	
5	4	12	15	-3	9	0.6000	
6	5	19	15	4	16	1.0667	
7	6	18	15	3	9	0.6000	
8	7	13	15	-2	4	0.2667	
9	8	21	15	6	36	2.4000	
10					*Chi-Square=*	8.6667	=SUM(F2:F9)
11					*Alpha=*	0.0500	[enter value]
12					*df=*	7	=COUNT(A2:A9)-1
13					χ^2 *critical=*	14.0671	=CHISQ.INV.RT(F11,F12)
14					*p-value=*	0.2775	=CHISQ.DIST.RT(F10,F12)

To perform a chi-square test of independence using Excel:

- Summarize raw data into a row by column pivot table—this will be the observed table. It should have row and column totals and a grand total.
- In the same spreadsheet, create a row by column table that mirrors the observed table without the rows and columns—this will be the expected table.

- In each corresponding cell in the expected table, calculate the expected value. In the example shown on the next page, the formula in cell B11 is =(D5*B7)/D7; repeat this for all cells in the expected table.
- Create a third row by column table that mirrors the observed table without the rows and columns—this will be the table that holds the chi-square calculation for each cell.

- In each corresponding cell in the chi-square table, calculate the chi-square value. In the example shown here, the code for cell B15 =((POWER((B5-B11),2)/B11)); repeat this for all cells in the expected table.

- Below the table, designate cells to hold the values for alpha and degrees of freedom (recall that degrees of freedom for this statistic are [number of rows] −1* [number of columns] −1), and then type in the code to calculate chi-square value, critical chi-square value, and P-value.

	A	B	C	D
1				
2				
3	*Pivot Table*			
4		No AC	AC	Grand Total
5	Old	1055	592	1647
6	New	38	43	81
7	Grand Total	1093	635	1728
8				
9				
10	*Expected Values*	No AC	AC	
11	Old	1041.765625	605.234375	
12	New	51.234375	29.765625	
13				
14	$(O-E)^2/E$ *Values*	No AC	AC	
15	Old	0.168126762	0.28938984	
16	New	3.418577501	5.88426017	
17				
18			Excel Syntax	
19	Chi-Square=	9.7604	=SUM(B15,B16,C15,C16)	
20	Alpha=	0.0500	[enter value]	
21	df=	1	[enter value]	
22	χ^2 critical=	3.8415	=CHISQ.INV.RT(B20,B21)	
23	p-value=	0.0018	=CHISQ.DIST.RT(B19,B21)	

Comments

Excel offers the function CHISQ.TEST (actual_range, expected_range), which computes a chi-square P-value for independence. However, this command will only provide the P-value and no other values. Both ranges are of the form UpperLeftCell: LowerRightCell, specifying two rectangular tables. The two tables must be of the same size and shape. The function is called CHITEST in Excel versions earlier than 2010.

XLSTAT

To perform a chi-square goodness-of-fit test:

- Choose **Parametric Tests**, and then select **Multinomial goodness of fit test**.

- In one column you should have the observed frequencies of the categories of the variable. Enter this under **Frequencies**.

- In another column you should have either the expected frequencies or the proportions. Enter this under either **Expected frequencies** (or expected proportions) and choose the appropriate **data format**.

- Be sure to check the box that says **Chi-square test**.
- Enter in the desired **Significance level**.
- Select **OK**.
- Select **Continue** (if prompted).

To perform a chi-square test for homogeneity:

- Choose **Correlation/Association tests**, and then select **Tests on contingency tables**.
- If your data already are in a contingency table, choose the **Data format** option **Contingency table**.
- If your data are not in a contingency table, choose **Qualitative variables**.
- Enter the cell range of your data.
- On the **Options** tab, check **Chi-square test**.
- On the **Outputs** tab, choose **Proportions/Row** or **Proportions/Column** if you wish to see the conditional distributions.

JMP

To perform a chi-square goodness-of-fit test:

- Select **Analyze > Distribution.**
- Choose a categorical variable for the **Y, Columns** dialog box
- From the red triangle next to the variable, name, select **Test Probabilities** and enter the probabilities you want to test.

To perform other chi-square tests:

- Select **Analyze > Fit Y by X.**
- Choose one variable as the Y, response variable, and the other as the X, factor variable. Both selected variables must be Nominal or Ordinal.
- JMP will make a plot and a contingency table. Below the contingency table, **JMP** offers a **Tests** panel. In that panel, the Chi Square for independence is called **Pearson.** The table also offers the P-value.
- Click on the contingency Table title bar to drop down a menu that offers to include a **Deviation** and Cell **Chi square** in each cell of the table.

Comments

JMP will perform a chi-square analysis for a **Fit Y by X** if both variables are nominal or ordinal (marked with an N or O), but not otherwise. Be sure the variables have the right type. Deviations are the observed—expected differences in counts. Cell chi-squares are the squares of the standardized residuals. Refer to the deviations for the sign of the difference.

MINITAB

From the **Start** menu,

- Choose the **Tables** submenu.
- From that menu, choose **Chi Square Test**....
- In the dialog, identify the columns that make up the table. Minitab will display the table and print the chi-square value and its P-value.

Comments

Alternatively, select the **Cross Tabulation** … command to see more options for the table, including expected counts and standardized residuals.

 SPSS

From the **Analyze** menu,

- Choose the **Descriptive Statistics** submenu.
- From that submenu, choose **Crosstabs**….

- In the Crosstabs dialog, assign the row and column variables from the variable list. Both variables must be categorical.
- Click the **Cells** button to specify that standardized residuals should be displayed.
- Click the **Statistics** button to specify a chi-square test.

Comments

SPSS offers only variables that it knows to be categorical in the variable list for the Crosstabs dialog. If the variables you want are missing, check that they have the right type.

Brief **Case**

Health Insurance

In 2010, the U.S. Congress passed the historic health care reform bill that will provide some type of coverage for the 32 million Americans currently without health care insurance. Just how widespread was the lack of medical coverage? The media claim that the segments of the population most at risk are women, children, the elderly, and the poor. The tables give the number of uninsured (in thousands) by sex, by age, and by household income in 2011.[6] Using the appropriate summary statistics, graphical displays, statistical tests, and confidence intervals, investigate the accuracy of the media's statement using these data. Be sure to discuss your assumptions, methods, results, and conclusions. (Note: some totals between tables may not match exactly due to rounding.)

	Sex		
	Male	**Female**	**Total**
Uninsured	25,571	23,043	**48,614**
Insured	125,604	134,610	**260,214**
Total	**151,175**	**157,653**	**308,828**

		Uninsured	**Insured**	**Total**
Age	**0–17**	6,964	67,143	**74,108**
	18–64	40,959	152,253	**193,212**
	65+	690	40,817	**41,507**
	Total	**48,613**	**260,213**	**308,827**

		Uninsured	**Insured**	**Total**
Household Income	**Less than $25,000**	19,166	51,255	**70,421**
	$25,000 to $49,999	14,714	57,965	**72,679**
	$50,000 to $74,999	7,286	46,445	**53,731**
	$75,000 or more	7,448	104,549	**111,997**
	Total	**48,614**	**260,214**	**308,828**

Loyalty Program

A marketing executive tested two incentives to see what percentage of customers would enroll in a new Web-based loyalty program. The customers were

---

[6]Source: U.S. Census Bureau, Current Population Survey, Annual Social and Economic Supplement, 2011 (www.census.gov/hhes/www/cpstables/032012/health/h01_000.htm).

asked to log on to their accounts on the Web and provide some demographic and spending information. As an incentive, they were offered either Nothing (No Offer), Free flight insurance on their next flight (Free Insurance), or a free companion Airline ticket (Free Flight). The customers were segmented according to their past year's spending patterns as spending primarily in one of five areas: *Travel, Entertainment, Dining, Household,* or *Balanced.* The executive wanted to know whether the incentives resulted in different enrollment rates (*Response*). Specifically, she wanted to know how much higher the enrollment rate for the free flight was compared to the free insurance. She also wanted to see whether *Spending Pattern* was associated with *Response.* Using the data **Loyalty Program**, write up a report for the marketing executive using appropriate graphics, summary statistics, statistical tests, and confidence intervals.

EXERCISES

SECTION 14.1

1. If there is no seasonal effect on human births, we would expect equal numbers of children to be born in each season (winter, spring, summer, and fall). A student takes a census of her statistics class and finds that of the 120 students in the class, 25 were born in winter, 35 in spring, 32 in summer, and 28 in fall. She wonders if the excess in the spring is an indication that births are not uniform throughout the year.

a) What is the expected number of births in each season if there is no "seasonal effect" on births?
b) Compute the χ^2 statistic.
c) How many degrees of freedom does the χ^2 statistic have?

2. At a major credit card bank, the percentages of people who historically apply for the Silver, Gold, and Platinum cards are 60%, 30%, and 10%, respectively. In a recent sample of customers responding to a promotion, of 200 customers, 110 applied for Silver, 55 for Gold, and 35 for Platinum. Is there evidence to suggest that the percentages for this promotion may be different from the historical proportions?

a) What is the expected number of customers applying for each type of card in this sample if the historical proportions are still true?
b) Compute the χ^2 statistic.
c) How many degrees of freedom does the χ^2 statistic have?

SECTION 14.2

3. For the births in Exercise 1,

a) If there is no seasonal effect, about how big, on average, would you expect the χ^2 statistic to be (what is the mean of the χ^2 distribution)?

b) Does the statistic you computed in Exercise 1 seem large in comparison to this mean? Explain briefly.
c) What does that say about the null hypothesis?
d) Find the $\alpha = 0.05$ critical value for the χ^2 distribution with the appropriate number of df.
e) Using the critical value, what do you conclude about the null hypothesis at $\alpha = 0.05$?

4. For the customers in Exercise 2,

a) If the customers apply for the three cards according to the historical proportions, about how big, on average, would you expect the χ^2 statistic to be (what is the mean of the χ^2 distribution)?
b) Does the statistic you computed in Exercise 2 seem large in comparison to this mean? Explain briefly.
c) What does that say about the null hypothesis?
d) Find the $\alpha = 0.05$ critical value for the χ^2 distribution with the appropriate number of df.
e) Using the critical value, what do you conclude about the null hypothesis at $\alpha = 0.05$?

SECTION 14.3

5. For the data in Exercise 1,

a) Compute the standardized residual for each season.
b) Are any of these particularly large? (Compared to what?)
c) Why should you have anticipated the answer to part b?

6. For the data in Exercise 2,

a) Compute the standardized residual for each type of card.
b) Are any of these particularly large? (Compared to what?)
c) What does the answer to part b say about this new group of customers?

SECTION 14.4

7. An analyst at a local bank wonders if the age distribution of customers coming for service at his branch in town is the same as at the branch located near the mall. He selects 100 transactions at random from each branch and researches the age information for the associated customer. Here are the data:

| | **Age** | | | |
	Less than 30	30–55	56 or Older	**Total**
In-Town Branch	20	40	40	**100**
Mall Branch	30	50	20	**100**
Total	**50**	**90**	**60**	**200**

a) What is the null hypothesis?
b) What type of test is this?
c) What are the expected numbers for each cell if the null hypothesis is true?
d) Find the χ^2 statistic.
e) How many degrees of freedom does it have?
f) Find the critical value at $\alpha = 0.05$.
g) What do you conclude?

8. A market researcher working for the bank in Exercise 2 wants to know if the distribution of applications by card is the same for the past three mailings. She takes a random sample of 200 from each mailing and counts the number applying for Silver, Gold, and Platinum. The data follow:

| | **Type of Card** | | | |
	Silver	Gold	Platinum	**Total**
Mailing 1	120	50	30	**200**
Mailing 2	115	50	35	**200**
Mailing 3	105	55	40	**200**
Total	**340**	**155**	**105**	**600**

a) What is the null hypothesis?
b) What type of test is this?
c) What are the expected numbers for each cell if the null hypothesis is true?
d) Find the χ^2 statistic.
e) How many degrees of freedom does it have?
f) Find the critical value at $\alpha = 0.05$.
g) What do you conclude?

SECTION 14.5

9. Markets have become interested in the potential of social networking sites. But they need to understand the demographics of social networking users. Pew Research conducted a survey in late 2012 that addressed these questions. (www.pewinternet.org/Reports/2013/Social-media-users/Social-Networking-Site-Users) That survey found that 525 of 846 surveyed male Internet users use social networking. By contrast 679 of 956 female Internet users use social networking.

a) Find the proportions of male and female Internet users who said they use social networking.
b) What is the difference in proportions?
c) What is the standard error of the difference?
d) Find a 95% confidence interval for the difference between the proportions.

10. From the same survey as in Exercise 9, 294 of the 409 respondents who reported earning less than $30,000 per year said they were social networking users. At the other end of the income scale, 333 of the 504 respondents reporting earnings of $75,000 or more were social networking users.

a) Find the proportions of each income group who are social networking users.
b) What is the difference in proportions?
c) What is the standard error of the difference?
d) Find a 95% confidence interval for the difference between these proportions.

SECTION 14.6

11. The same poll as in Exercise 9 has asked about social networking over several years and for different age groups. Here is a table of responses:

		May-2010	**Aug-2011**	**Aug-2012**	**Total**
Age	18–29	273	277	293	**843**
	30–49	325	362	388	**1075**
	50–64	259	270	314	**843**
	Total	**857**	**909**	**995**	**2761**

a) Under the usual null hypothesis, what are the expected values?
b) Compute the χ^2 statistic.
c) How many degrees of freedom does it have?
d) What do you conclude?

12. To complete the poll reported in Exercise 9, Pew Research surveyed respondents by telephone, drawing a random sample of landlines and another random sample of cell phones. For those numbers that were valid, they report the following:

	Land	**Cell**	**Total**
No Answer/Busy	552	42	**594**
Voicemail	3347	2843	**6190**
Contact	8399	8612	**17,011**
Total	**12,298**	**11,497**	**23,795**

Are the results they find independent of the telephone type?

a) Under the usual null hypothesis, what are the expected values?
b) Compute the χ^2 statistic.
c) How many degrees of freedom does it have?
d) What do you conclude?

CHAPTER EXERCISES

13. Concepts. For each of the following situations, state whether you'd use a chi-square goodness-of-fit test, chi-square test of homogeneity, chi-square test of independence, or some other statistical test.

a) A brokerage firm wants to see whether the type of account a customer has (Silver, Gold, or Platinum) affects the type of trades that customer makes (in person, by phone, or on the Internet). It collects a random sample of trades made for its customers over the past year and performs a test.

b) That brokerage firm also wants to know if the type of account affects the size of the account (in dollars). It performs a test to see if the mean size of the account is the same for the three account types.

c) The academic research office at a large community college wants to see whether the distribution of courses chosen (Humanities, Social Science, or Science) is different for its residential and nonresidential students. It assembles last semester's data and performs a test.

14. Concepts, part 2. For each of the following situations, state whether you'd use a chi-square goodness-of-fit test, a chi-square test of homogeneity, a chi-square test of independence, or some other statistical test.

a) Is the quality of a car affected by what day it was built? A car manufacturer examines a random sample of the warranty claims filed over the past two years to test whether defects are randomly distributed across days of the work week.

b) A researcher for the American Booksellers Association wants to know if retail sales/sq. ft. is related to serving coffee or snacks on the premises. She examines a database of 10,000 independently owned bookstores testing whether retail sales (dollars/sq. ft.) is related to whether or not the store has a coffee bar.

c) A researcher wants to find out whether education level (some high school, high school graduate, college graduate, advanced degree) is related to the type of transaction most likely to be conducted using the Internet (shopping, banking, travel reservations, auctions). He surveys 500 randomly chosen adults and performs a test.

15. Dice. After getting trounced by your little brother in a children's game, you suspect that the die he gave you is unfair. To check, you roll it 60 times, recording the number of times each face appears. Do these results cast doubt on the die's fairness?

Face	Count
1	11
2	7
3	9
4	15
5	12
6	6

a) If the die is fair, how many times would you expect each face to show?

b) To see if these results are unusual, will you test goodness-of-fit, homogeneity, or independence?

c) State your hypotheses.

d) Check the conditions.

e) How many degrees of freedom are there?

f) Find χ^2 and the P-value.

g) State your conclusion.

16. Online Mating. According to recent research (www.nas.org) married couples who met their spouse through an online dating service may have a different divorce rate than those who met "off-line." (Online Mating From Proceedings of the National Academy of Sciences of the United States of America. Copyright (c) 2008 National Academy of Sciences. Reproduced by the permission of National Academy of Sciences.) The survey polled couples who married between 2005 and 2012. The baseline divorce rate (by 2013) for off-line marriages in this cohort is 7.73%. The report gives the following divorce statistics according to the on-line dating service where the couple met:

Service	Couples (*n*)	Divorces/Separations
eHarmony	791	29
Match	775	58
Plenty of Fish	201	20
Yahoo	227	12
Small Sites	777	37

a) If the divorce rate were the same for these couples as for those who met offline, how many divorces would you expect for each group of couples?

b) To test whether these couples are different from offline couples, will you perform a goodness-of-fit test, a test of homogeneity, or a test of independence?

c) State the hypotheses.

d) Check the conditions.

e) Find the standardized residuals and the chi-square components. (Hint: use a spreadsheet to perform the calculations.)

f) State the number of degrees of freedom and find χ^2 and the P-value.

g) State your conclusion.

h) Online dating services are a billion-dollar business in the U.S. Does it change your conclusion to know that the study was funded by eHarmony?

17. Quality control. A company advertises that its premium mixture of nuts contains 10% Brazil nuts, 20% cashews, 20% almonds, 10% hazelnuts, and that the rest are peanuts. You buy a large can and separate the various kinds of nuts. Upon weighing them, you find there are 112 grams of Brazil nuts, 183 grams of cashews, 207 grams of almonds, 71 grams of hazelnuts, and 446 grams of peanuts. You wonder whether your mix is significantly different from what the company advertises.

a) Explain why the chi-square goodness-of-fit test is not an appropriate way to find out.

b) What might you do instead of weighing the nuts in order to use a χ^2 test?

18. Sales rep travel. A sales representative who is on the road visiting clients thinks that, on average, he drives the same distance each day of the week. He keeps track of his mileage for several weeks and discovers that he averages 122 miles on Mondays, 203 miles on Tuesdays, 176 miles on Wednesdays, 181 miles on Thursdays, and 108 miles on Fridays. He wonders if this evidence contradicts his belief in a uniform distribution of miles across the days of the week. Is it appropriate to test his hypothesis using the chi-square goodness-of-fit test? Explain.

19. Maryland lottery. For a lottery to be successful, the public must have confidence in its fairness. One of the lotteries in Maryland is Pick-3 Lottery, where 3 random digits are drawn each day.[7] A fair game depends on every value (0 to 9) being equally likely at each of the three positions. If not, then someone detecting a pattern could take advantage of that and beat the lottery. To investigate the randomness, we'll look at data collected over a recent 32-week period. Although the winning numbers look like three-digit numbers, in fact, each digit is a randomly drawn numeral. We have 654 random digits in all. Are each of the digits from 0 to 9 equally likely? Here is a table of the frequencies. (Maryland State Lottery Agency, www.mdlottery.com)

Group	Count	%
0	62	9.480
1	55	8.410
2	66	10.092
3	64	9.786
4	75	11.468
5	57	8.716
6	71	10.856
7	74	11.315
8	69	10.550
9	61	9.327

a) Select the appropriate procedure.
b) Check the assumptions.
c) State the hypotheses.
d) Test an appropriate hypothesis and state your results.
e) Interpret the meaning of the results and state a conclusion.

20. Employment discrimination? Census data for New York City indicate that 29.2% of the under-18 population is white, 28.2% black, 31.5% Latino, 9.1% Asian, and 2% are of other ethnicities. The New York Civil Liberties Union points out that of 26,181 police officers, 64.8% are white, 14.5% black, 19.1% Hispanic, and 1.4% Asian. Do the police officers reflect the ethnic composition of the city's youth? (Equate Latino with Hispanic.)

a) Select the appropriate procedure.
b) Check the assumptions.
c) State the hypotheses.
d) Test an appropriate hypothesis and state your results.
e) Interpret the meaning of the results and state a conclusion.

21. Titanic. Here is a table showing who survived the sinking of the *Titanic* based on whether they were crew members or passengers booked in first-, second-, or third-class staterooms.

	Crew	First	Second	Third	Total
Alive	212	202	118	178	**710**
Dead	673	123	167	528	**1491**
Total	**885**	**325**	**285**	**706**	**2201**

a) If we draw an individual at random from this table, what's the probability that we will draw a member of the crew?
b) What's the probability of randomly selecting a third-class passenger who survived?
c) What's the probability of a randomly selected passenger surviving, given that the passenger was in a first-class stateroom?
d) If someone's chances of surviving were the same regardless of their status on the ship, how many members of the crew would you expect to have lived?
e) State the null and alternative hypotheses we would test here (and the name of the test).
f) Give the degrees of freedom for the test.
g) The chi-square value for the table is 187.8, and the corresponding P-value is barely greater than 0. State your conclusions about the hypotheses.

22. Promotion discrimination? The table shows the rank attained by male and female officers in the New York City Police Department (NYPD). Do these data indicate that men and women are equitably represented at all levels of the department? (All possible ranks in the NYPD are shown.)

		Male	Female
Rank	**Officer**	21,900	4281
	Detective	4058	806
	Sergeant	3898	415
	Lieutenant	1333	89
	Captain	359	12
	Higher Ranks	218	10

a) What's the probability that a person selected at random from the NYPD is a female?
b) What's the probability that a person selected at random from the NYPD is a detective?
c) Assuming no bias in promotions, how many female detectives would you expect the NYPD to have?

---
[7]Source: Maryland State Lottery Agency, www.mdlottery.com.

Of course, the individual y's are not at these means. In fact, the line will miss most—and usually all—of the plotted points. Some y's lie above the line and some below the line, so like all models, this one makes errors. To account for each individual value of y in our model, we can include these errors, which we denote by ε:

$$y = \beta_0 + \beta_1 x + \varepsilon.$$

This equation has an ε to soak up the deviation at each point, so the model gives a value of y for each value of x. To do hypothesis tests and make confidence intervals, we assume that the errors have a Normal distribution around the line at each x-value, as shown in Figure 15.2.

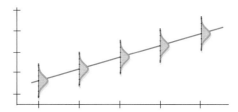

Figure 15.2 There's a distribution of *Prices* for each value of polishing *Time*. The regression model assumes that the means line up perfectly like this, and that the *y*-values are distributed with a Normal model around the line at each *x*-value.

We estimate the β's by finding a regression line, $\hat{y} = b_0 + b_1 x$, as we did in Chapter 4. The residuals, $e = y - \hat{y}$ are the sample-based versions of the errors, ε. We'll use them to help us assess the regression model.

We know that least squares regression will give us reasonable estimates of the parameters of this model from a random sample of data. We also know that our estimates won't be equal to the parameters in the idealized or "true" model. Our challenge is to account for the uncertainty in our estimates by making confidence intervals as we've done for means and proportions. For that, we need to find the standard errors of the slope and intercept.

We expect the estimated slope for any sample, b_1, to be close to—but not actually equal to—the model slope, β_1. If we could see the collection of slopes from many samples (imagined or real) we would see a distribution of values around the true slope. That's the sampling distribution of the slope.

What is the standard deviation of this distribution? That depends on several aspects of our situation: how much the data vary, how solid a basis we have for our estimate, and how much data we have.

- **Spread around the line.** Figure 15.3 shows samples from two populations. Which underlying population would give rise to the more consistent slopes?

Figure 15.3 Which of these scatterplots would give the more consistent regression slope estimate if we were to sample repeatedly from its underlying population?

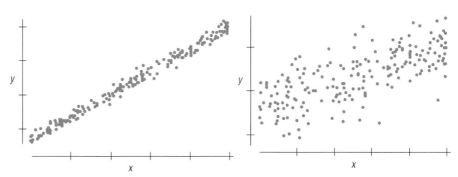

Less scatter around the line means the slope will be more consistent from sample to sample. In Chapter 4, we measured the spread around the line with the **residual standard deviation:**

$$s_e = \sqrt{\frac{\sum (y - \hat{y})^2}{n - 2}}.$$

The less scatter around the line, the smaller the residual standard deviation and the stronger the relationship between x and y.

- **Spread of the x's:** Here are samples from two more populations (Figure 15.4). Which of these would yield more consistent slopes?

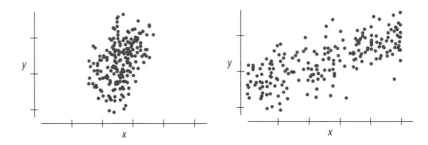

Figure 15.4   Which of these scatterplots would give the more consistent regression slope estimate if we were to sample repeatedly from the underlying population?

A plot like the one on the right has a broader range of x-values, so it gives a more stable base for the slope. We might expect the slopes of samples from situations like that to vary less from sample to sample. A large standard deviation of x, s_x, as in the figure on the right, provides a more stable regression.

- **Sample size.** What about the two scatterplots in Figure 15.5?

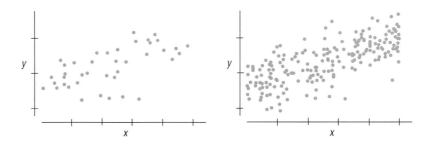

Figure 15.5   Which of these scatterplots would give the more consistent regression slope estimate if we were to sample repeatedly from the underlying population?

It shouldn't shock you that a larger sample size (scatterplot on the right) gives more consistent estimates from sample to sample.

Let's summarize what we've seen in these three figures:

The Standard Error of the Regression Slope

Three aspects of the scatterplot that affect the standard error of the regression slope are:

- Spread around the line: s_e
- Spread of x values: s_x
- Sample size: n

These are in fact the *only* things that affect the standard error of the slope. The formula for the standard error of the slope is:

$$SE(b_1) = \frac{s_e}{s_x\sqrt{n-1}}.$$

The error standard deviation, s_e, is in the *numerator*, since a larger spread around the line *increases* the slope's standard error. On the other hand, the *denominator* has both a sample size term ($\sqrt{n-1}$) and s_x because increasing either of these *decreases* the slope's standard error.

Our goal is a hypothesis test or confidence interval for the slope. The standard deviation of the sampling distribution of the slope is one part, but we need to know the shape of the sampling distribution as well. Here the Central Limit Theorem and Gosset come to the rescue again. We do just what we've done with the mean and proportion. We standardize the estimated slope by subtracting the model value and dividing by the estimated standard error. And just as we did with the mean, we get a Student's t-model, this time with $n - 2$ degrees of freedom:

$$\frac{b_1 - \beta_1}{SE(b_1)} \sim t_{n-2}.$$

> ### The Sampling Distribution for the Regression Slope
> When the conditions are met, the standardized estimated regression slope,
>
> $$t = \frac{b_1 - \beta_1}{SE(b_1)},$$
>
> follows a Student's t-model with $n - 2$ degrees of freedom. We estimate the standard error with $SE(b_1) = \dfrac{s_e}{s_x \sqrt{n - 1}}$, where $s_e = \sqrt{\dfrac{\sum (y - \hat{y})^2}{n - 2}}$, n is the number of data values, and s_x is the standard deviation of the x-values.

What If the Slope Is 0?

If $b_1 = 0$, our prediction is $\hat{y} = b_0 + 0x$, and the equation collapses to just $\hat{y} = b_0$. Now x is nowhere in sight, so y doesn't depend on x at all.

In this case, b_0 would turn out to be $\bar{y}$. Why? Because we know that $b_0 = \bar{y} - b_1 \bar{x}$, and when $b_1 = 0$, that becomes simply $b_0 = \bar{y}$. It turns out, that when the slope is 0, the entire regression equation is just $\hat{y} = \bar{y}$, so for every value of x, we predict the mean value ($\bar{y}$) for y.

Now that we have the standard error of the slope and its sampling distribution, we can test a hypothesis about it and make confidence intervals. The usual null hypothesis about the slope is that it's equal to 0. Why? Well, a slope of zero would say that y doesn't tend to change linearly when x changes—in other words, that there is no linear association between the two variables. If the slope were zero, there wouldn't be much left of our regression equation.

A null hypothesis of a zero slope questions the entire claim of a linear relationship between the two variables, and often that's just what we want to know. In fact, every software package or calculator that does regression simply assumes that you want to test the null hypothesis that the slope is really zero.

> ### The t-Test for the Regression Slope
> When the assumptions and conditions are met, we can test the hypothesis $H_0: \beta_1 = 0$ vs. $H_A: \beta_1 \neq 0$ (or a one-sided alternative hypothesis) using the standardized estimated regression slope,
>
> $$t = \frac{b_1 - \beta_1}{SE(b_1)},$$
>
> which follows a Student's t-model with $n - 2$ degrees of freedom. We can use the t-model to find the P-value of the test.

This is just like every other t-test we've seen: a difference between the statistic and its hypothesized value divided by its standard error. This test is the *t-test* that the regression slope is 0, usually referred to as the ***t*-test for the regression slope**.

Another use of these values might be to make a confidence interval for the slope. We can build a confidence interval in the usual way, as an estimate plus or minus a margin of error. As always, the margin of error is just the product of the standard error and a critical value.

> ### The Confidence Interval for the Regression Slope
> When the assumptions and conditions are met, we can find a confidence interval for β_1 from
>
> $$b_1 \pm t^*_{n-2} \times SE(b_1),$$
>
> where the critical value t^* depends on the confidence level and has $n - 2$ degrees of freedom.

The same reasoning applies for the intercept. We write:

$$\frac{b_0 - \beta_0}{SE(b_0)} \sim t_{n-2}.$$

We could use this statistic to construct confidence intervals and test hypotheses about the intercept, but often the value of the intercept isn't interesting. Most hypothesis tests and confidence intervals for regression are about the slope. But in case you really want to see the formula for the standard error of the intercept, we've parked it in a footnote.[1]

Regression models are almost always found with a computer or calculator. The calculations are too long to do conveniently by hand for data sets of any reasonable size. No matter how the regression is computed, the results are usually presented in a table that has a standard form. Figure 15.6 shows a portion of a typical regression results table, along with annotations showing where the numbers come from.

Figure 15.6 A typical computer regression table presents regression results in a standard format.

15.2 Assumptions and Conditions

Back in Chapter 4 when we fit lines to data, we needed both the **Linearity** and the **Equal Variance Assumptions**. Now, to make inferences about the coefficients of the line, we'll have to assume that the errors are independent and Normally distributed as well.

It is important to check the assumptions and their associated conditions in the right order, so we number the assumptions, and check conditions for each in that order: (1) Linearity Assumption, (2) Independence Assumption, (3) Equal Variance Assumption, and (4) Normal Population Assumption.

1. Linearity Assumption

If the true relationship of two quantitative variables is far from linear and we use a straight line to fit the data, our entire analysis will be useless, so we always check linearity first (and we check the **Quantitative Variable Condition** for both variables as well).

The **Linearity Condition** is satisfied if a scatterplot looks straight. It's generally not a good idea to draw a line through the scatterplot when checking. That can fool your eye into seeing the plot as straighter than it really is. Sometimes it's easier to see violations of this condition by looking at a scatterplot of the residuals

---

[1]$SE(b_0) = s_e \sqrt{\dfrac{1}{n} + \dfrac{\bar{x}^2}{\sum (x - \bar{x})^2}}$

against x or against the predicted values, $\hat{y}$. That plot should have no pattern if the condition is satisfied.

If the scatterplot shows a reasonably straight relationship, we can go on to some assumptions about the errors. If not, we stop here, or consider transforming the variables to make the scatterplot more linear.

2. Independence Assumption

The errors in the true underlying regression model (the ε's) must be independent of each other. As usual, there's no way to be sure that the Independence Assumption is true.

When we care about inference for the regression parameters, it's often because we think our regression model might apply to a larger population. In such cases, we can check the **Randomization Condition** that the individuals are a random sample from that population.

We can also check displays of the regression residuals for evidence of patterns, trends, or clumping, any of which would suggest a failure of independence. In the special case when we have a time series, a common violation of the Independence Assumption is for successive errors to be correlated (autocorrelated). (The error our model makes today may be similar to the one it made yesterday.) We can check this violation by plotting the residuals against time (usually the x-variable for a time series) and looking for patterns.

3. Equal Variance Assumption

The variability of y should be about the same for all values of x. In Chapter 4, we found the standard deviation of the residuals (s_e). Now we need this standard deviation to estimate the standard errors of the coefficients but the residual standard deviation only makes sense if the scatter of the residuals is the same everywhere (else what are we estimating?)

We check the **Equal Spread Condition** by looking at a scatterplot of residuals against either x or $\hat{y}$. Make sure the spread around the line is nearly constant. Be alert for a "fan" shape or other tendency for the variation to grow or shrink in one part of the scatterplot.

If the plot is reasonably straight, the data are independent, and the spread doesn't change, we can move on to the final assumption and its associated condition.

4. Normal Population Assumption

To use a Student's t-model for inference, we must assume the errors around the idealized regression line at each value of x follow a Normal model. As we did before when we used Student's t, we'll settle for the residuals satisfying the **Nearly Normal Condition**.[2] As we have noted before, the Normality Assumption becomes less important as the sample size grows because the model is about means, and the Central Limit Theorem takes over. You can check a histogram of the residuals or look at a **Normal probability plot** (see Section 7.3), which finds deviations from the Normal model more efficiently. Another common failure of Normality is the presence of an outlier. So, we still check the **Outlier Condition**.

Summary of Assumptions and Conditions

We don't expect the assumptions to be exactly true. As George Box said, "all models are wrong." But the linear model is often close enough to be useful as long as the assumptions of the model are reasonably met.

Before we compute the regression, we should check the linearity condition. (You can also look for outliers here.) Then, after we fit the model we should check the rest.

---

[2] *This* is why we check the conditions in order. We check that the residuals are independent and that the variation is the same for all x's before we can lump all the residuals together to check the Normal Condition.

"Truth will emerge more readily from error than from confusion."

—FRANCIS BACON (1561–1626),
English philosopher

So we work in this order:

1. **Make a scatterplot of the data** to check the Linearity Condition and to look for outliers (and always check that the variables are quantitative as well). (This checks the **Linearity Assumption**.)
2. If the data show a reasonably straight relationship, **fit a regression and find the residuals, *e*, and predicted values, *ŷ*.**
3. If you know when the measurements were made, **plot the residuals against time** to check for evidence of patterns that suggest they may not be independent (**Independence Assumption**).
4. **Make a scatterplot of the residuals against *x* or the predicted values.** This plot should have no pattern. Check in particular for any bend (which would suggest that the data weren't that straight after all), for any thickening (or thinning), and, of course, for any unusual observations. (If you discover any errors, correct them or omit those points, and go back to step 1. Otherwise, consider performing two regressions—one with and one without the unusual observations.) (**Equal Variance Assumption**)
5. If the scatterplots look OK, then **make a histogram and Normal probability plot of the residuals** to check the **Nearly Normal** and **Outlier Conditions** (**Normal Population Assumption**).

GUIDED EXAMPLE   Nambé Mills

Now that we have a method to draw inferences from our regression equation, let's try it out on the Nambé Mills data. The slope of the regression gives the impact of *Time* on *Price*. Let's test the hypothesis that the slope is different from zero.

PLAN **Setup** State the objectives. Identify the parameter you wish to estimate. Here our parameter is the slope. Identify the variables and their context.	We want to test the null hypothesis that the price of Nambé Mills items is not related to the time it takes to polish them. We have data for 59 items sold by Nambé Mills. The slope of this relationship will model the relationship between *Time* and *Price*. Our null hypothesis is that the slope of the regression is 0.

Hypotheses Write the null and alternative hypotheses.

H$_0$: The *Price* of an item is not linearly related to the polishing *Time*: $\beta_1 = 0$.
H$_A$: The *Price* is related to the *Time*: $\beta_1 \neq 0$.

Model Check the assumptions and conditions.

Make graphs. Because our scatterplot of *y* versus *x* looks reasonably straight, we can find the least squares regression and plot the residuals.

✓ **Linearity Condition:** There is no obvious curve in the scatterplot of *y* versus *x*.

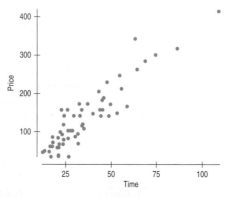

If it is appropriate, we check for suggestions that the Independence Assumption fails by plotting the residuals against time. Patterns or trends in that plot raise our suspicions.

✓ **Independence Assumption:** These data are on 59 different items manufactured by the company. There is no reason to suggest that the error in modeling the price of one item should be influenced by another.

✓ **Randomization Condition:** The data are *not* a random sample, but we assume they are representative of the prices and polishing times of Nambé Mills items.

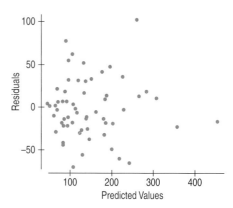

✓ **Equal Spread Condition:** The plot of residuals against the predicted values shows no obvious patterns. The spread is about the same for all predicted values, and the scatter appears random.

✓ **Nearly Normal Condition:** A histogram of the residuals is unimodal and symmetric, and the normal probability plot is reasonably straight.

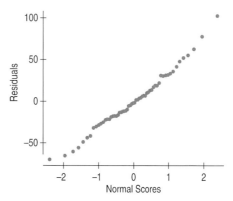

State the sampling distribution model.

Choose the method.

Under these conditions, the sampling distribution of the regression slope can be modeled by a Student's *t*-model with $(n - 2) = 59 - 2 = 57$ degrees of freedom, so we'll proceed with a regression slope *t*-test.

(continued)

Mechanics The regression equation can be found from the formulas in Chapter 4, but regressions are almost always found from a computer program or calculator.

Here's the computer output for this regression.

Variable	Coefficient	SE(coeff)	t-Ratio	P-Value
Intercept	−4.871	9.654	−0.50	0.6159
Time	4.200	0.2385	17.61	<0.0001

$s = 32.54$ R-Sq $= 84.5\%$

The P-values given in the regression output table are from the Student's t-distribution on $(n − 2) = 57$ degrees of freedom. They are appropriate for two-sided alternatives.

The P-value < 0.0001 means that the association we see in the data is unlikely to have occurred by chance. Therefore, we reject the null hypothesis and conclude that there is strong evidence that the Price is linearly related to the polishing Time.

A 95% confidence interval for β_1 is:

Create a confidence interval for the true slope. To obtain the t-value for 57 degrees of freedom, use the t-table at the back of your textbook. The estimated slope and SE for the slope are obtained from the regression output.

$$b_1 \pm t^*_{n-2} \times SE(b_1) = (3.72, 4.68) \$/minute$$

Interpret the interval.

Simply rejecting the standard null hypothesis doesn't guarantee that the size of the effect is large enough to be important.

We can be 95% confident that the price is higher on average, between $3.72 and $4.68 for each additional minute of polishing time. (Technically: we are 95% confident that the interval from $3.72 to $4.68 per minute captures the true rate at which the Price increases with polishing Time.)

 Conclusion State the conclusion in the proper context.

MEMO

Re: Nambé Mills pricing

We investigated the relationship between polishing time and pricing of 59 Nambé Mills items. The regression analysis showed that, on average, the price is higher by $4.20 for every additional minute of polishing time. Assuming that these items are representative, we are 95% confident that the actual price of a metal item manufactured by Nambé Mills is higher by between $3.72 and $4.68 on average for each additional minute of polishing work required.

JUST CHECKING

Companies that market food items conduct research into how and how much people eat. They might, for example, study how big people's mouths tend to be. Researchers measured mouth volume by pouring water into the mouths of subjects who lay on their backs. Unless this is your idea of a good time, it would be helpful to have a model to estimate mouth volume more simply. Fortunately, mouth volume is related to height. (Mouth volume is measured in cubic centimeters and height in meters.)

The data were checked and deemed suitable for regression. Take a look at the computer output below.

```
Summary of Mouth Volume
Mean          60.2704
StdDev        16.8777

Dependent variable is Mouth Volume
R-squared = 15.3%
s = 15.66 with 61 − 2 = 59 degrees of freedom

Variable       Coefficient    SE(coeff)    t-Ratio    P-Value
Intercept       −44.7113        32.16       −1.39      0.1697
Height           61.3787        18.77        3.27      0.0018
```

1 What does the *t*-ratio of 3.27 for the slope tell about this relationship? How does the P-value help your understanding?

2 Would you say that measuring a person's height could reliably be used as a substitute for the wetter method of determining how big a person's mouth is? What numbers in the output helped you reach that conclusion?

3 What does the value of s_e add to this discussion?

*A Hypothesis Test for Correlation

We just tested whether the slope, β_1, was 0. To test it, we estimated the slope from the data and then, using its standard error and the *t*-distribution, measured how far the slope was from 0: $t = \dfrac{b_1 - 0}{SE(b_1)}$. What if we wanted to test whether the *correlation* between x and y is 0? We write ρ for the parameter (true population value) of the correlation, so we're testing H_0: $\rho = 0$. Remember that the regression slope estimate is $b_1 = r\dfrac{s_y}{s_x}$. The same is true for the parameter versions of these statistics: $\beta_1 = \rho\dfrac{\sigma_y}{\sigma_x}$. That means that if the slope is really 0, then the correlation has to be 0, too. So if we test H_0: $\beta_1 = 0$, that's really the same as testing H_0: $\rho = 0$. Sometimes a researcher, however, might want to test correlation without fitting a regression, so you'll see the test of correlation as a separate test (it's also slightly more general), but the results are mathematically the same even though the form looks a little different. Here's the *t*-test for the correlation coefficient.

The *t*-Test for the Correlation Coefficient

When the conditions are met, we can test the hypothesis H_0: $\rho = 0$ vs. H_A: $\rho \neq 0$ using the test statistic:

$$t = r\sqrt{\frac{n-2}{1-r^2}},$$

which follows a Student's *t*-model with $n-2$ degrees of freedom. We can use the *t*-model to find the P-value of the test.

> ## FOR EXAMPLE   Testing correlation
>
> **QUESTION**   The Cornell National Social Survey (CNSS) is a national annual survey of a random sample of 1000 adults in the continental United States. Researchers in various disciplines can submit questions for the survey. According to the Cornell Survey Research Institute's site, sri.cornell.edu/sri/cnss.cfm, the survey is administered by telephone, using a random digit dial (RDD) method. The survey contains a small core of demographic questions, with all remaining questions being generated by Cornell researchers. The interviews average no more than 20 minutes in length and are conducted by the Survey Research Institute. The data are made available to the public and can be used by researchers and business professionals. A chain store that sells electronic equipment is planning a marketing campaign. From the CNSS they find that the correlation between the *Age* of respondents and their *Expenditures on Electronics* is -0.142. Does this indicate a statistically significant association?
>
> **ANSWER**
>
> $$t = -0.142\sqrt{\frac{1000 - 2}{1 - (-0.142)^2}} = -4.53,$$
>
> which is a large enough value to be statistically significant. We can reject the null hypothesis that the true correlation, ρ, is zero.

A test that rejects the null hypothesis for the correlation tells us that there is a real linear relationship between the variables, but it doesn't tell enough. In the For Example, we conclude that the correlation isn't 0, but where do we go from here? For business decisions, we need to know more. We need the information provided by the full regression model. The test that the correlation is zero is equivalent to the test that the slope is zero, but the regression model helps us to understand what's going on and to make real decisions.

15.3   Standard Errors for Predicted Values

Often a business decision will depend not on the value of a slope coefficient, but on a predicted value of the response variable, y, for some given value of x. We saw how to find a predicted value for any value of x back in Chapter 4. This predicted value would be our best estimate, but it's still just an informed guess. Now that we have standard errors, we can use them to construct confidence intervals for the predictions. That makes it possible to report our uncertainty about those predictions honestly—something we'd want to know before relying on them for a decision.

From our model of Nambé Mills items, we can use polishing *Time* to get a reasonable estimate of *Price*. Suppose a manager wanted to estimate the selling *Price* of an item that takes 40 minutes of *Time* to polish. A confidence interval can indicate how precise that prediction is. The precision depends on the question asked, however, and there are two different questions we could ask:

Do we want to know the mean *Price* for *all items* that have a polishing *Time* of 40 minutes?

or,

Do we want to estimate the *Price* for a *particular* item whose polishing *Time* is 40 minutes?

What's the difference between the two questions? The manufacturer might be more interested in the first question which asks about the *mean Price* of all items that take a certain *Time* to polish. But a customer or sales manager might be more interested in the second question—estimating an *individual* item's *Price*.

The predicted *Price* value is the same for both, but one question leads to a much more precise interval than the other. If your intuition says that it's easier to be more precise about the mean than about an individual, you're on the right track. Because, as we have seen, means vary much less than individuals, we can predict the *mean Price* for all items with the same polishing *Time*, more precisely than we can predict the *Price* of a particular item with that polishing *Time*.

Let's start by predicting the mean *Price* for a new *Time*, one that was not necessarily part of the original data set. To emphasize this, we'll call this *x*-value "*x* sub new" and write it x_ν.[3] As an example, we'll take x_ν to be 40 minutes. The regression equation predicts *Price* by $\hat{y}_\nu = b_0 + b_1 x_\nu$. Now that we have the predicted value, we can construct a confidence interval around this number. It has the usual form:

$$\hat{y}_\nu \pm t^*_{n-2} \times SE.$$

The t^* value is the critical value (from Table T or technology) for $n - 2$ degrees of freedom and the specified confidence level.

The Confidence Interval for the Predicted Mean Value

When the conditions are met, we find the confidence interval for the predicted mean value μ_ν at a value x_ν as

$$\hat{y}_\nu \pm t^*_{n-2} \times SE,$$

where the standard error is

$$SE(\hat{\mu}_\nu) = \sqrt{SE^2(b_1) \times (x_\nu - \bar{x}^2) + \frac{s_e^2}{n}}.$$

Figure 15.7 shows the confidence intervals for the mean predictions. In this plot, the intervals for all the mean *Prices* at all values of *Time* are shown together as confidence bands. Notice that the bands get wider as we attempt to predict values that lie farther away from the mean *Time*. (That's due to the $(x_\nu - \bar{x})^2$ term in the SE formula.) As we move away from the mean *x* value, there is more uncertainty associated with our prediction.

Figure 15.7 The confidence intervals for the mean *Price* at a given polishing *Time* are shown as the green dotted lines. Near the mean *Time* (35.8 minutes) our confidence interval for the mean *Price* is narrower than for values far from the mean, like 100 minutes.

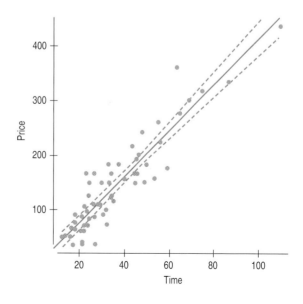

[3]Yes, this is a bilingual pun. The Greek letter ν is called "nu." Don't blame me; my co-author suggested this.

Like all confidence intervals, the width of these confidence intervals varies with the sample size. A larger sample would result in narrower intervals.

The last factor affecting our confidence intervals is the spread of the data around the line. If there were more spread around the line, predictions would be less certain, and the confidence interval bands would be wider.

From Figure 15.7, it's easy to see that most *points* don't fall within the confidence interval bands—and we shouldn't expect them to. These bands show confidence intervals for the *mean*. An even larger sample would have given even narrower bands. Then we'd expect an even smaller percentage of the points to fall within them.

If we want to capture an *individual* price, we need to use a wider interval, called a **prediction interval**. Figure 15.8 shows the prediction intervals for the Nambé Mills data. Prediction intervals are based on the same quantities as the confidence intervals, but the standard error includes an extra term for the spread around the line. As Figure 15.8 shows, these bands also widen as we move from the mean of *x*.

Figure 15.8 Prediction intervals (in red) estimate the interval that contains say, 95% of the distribution of the *y* values that might be observed at a given value of *x*. If the assumptions and conditions hold, then there's about a 95% chance that a particular *y*-value at x_ν will be covered by the interval.

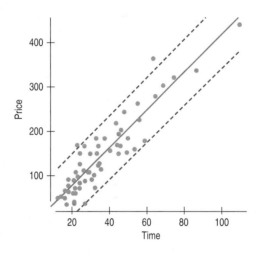

> **The Prediction Interval for an Individual Value**
>
> When the conditions are met, we can find the prediction interval for all values of *y* at a value x_ν as
>
> $$\hat{y}_\nu \pm t^*_{n-2} \times SE,$$
>
> where the standard error is
>
> $$SE(\hat{y}_\nu) = \sqrt{SE^2(b_1) \times (x_\nu - \bar{x})^2 + \frac{s_e^2}{n} + s_e^2}.$$
>
> The critical value t^* depends on the confidence level that you specify.

The good news about confidence intervals for prediction is that they are not hard to find and are provided by most statistics software. The bad news is that intervals for an individual predicted value can be quite wide—often so wide that they are not very useful for a business decision. By contrast, confidence intervals for the mean prediction are often narrow enough to be useful. But you must remember the difference between the two kinds of prediction intervals.

15.4   Using Confidence and Prediction Intervals

How well can our regression model predict the mean price for objects that take 25 minutes to polish? The regression output table provides most of the numbers we need.

```
Variable      Coefficient   SE(coeff)   t-Ratio   P-Value
Intercept       -4.871        9.654      -0.50     0.6159
Time             4.200        0.2385     17.61    <0.0001

s = 32.54   R-Sq = 84.5%
```

The regression model gives a predicted value at $x_\nu = 25$ minutes of:

$$-4.871 + 4.200(25) = \$100.13$$

Many statistics programs can also provide prediction confidence intervals. The 95% confidence interval for the mean price of items with a 25-minute polishing time is ($90.20, $110.06). That may be precise enough to support decisions about where to advertise these products, for example.

But the 95% confidence interval for a particular item with a 25-minute polishing time is ($34.22, $166.04). That's so wide that it serves more as a warning not to believe that the predicted value of $100.13 provides that much information about a single item. Figure 15.9 shows both intervals.

For the details of how the formulas lead to these intervals, see the Math Box.

Figure 15.9 A scatterplot of *Price* versus *Time* with a least squares regression line. The inner lines (green) near the regression line show the extent of the 95% confidence intervals, and the outer lines (red) show the prediction intervals. Most of the points are contained within the prediction intervals (as they should be), but not within the confidence interval for the means.

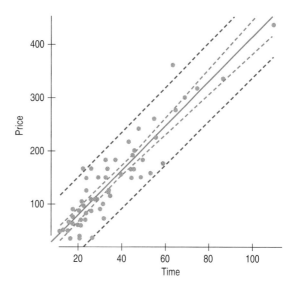

MATH BOX Finding Confidence and Prediction Intervals

We find the standard errors from the formula using the values in the regression output and associated values. (The mean *Polishing Time* in these data is 35.82 minutes.)

$$SE(\hat{\mu}_\nu) = \sqrt{(SE^2(b_1))(x_\nu - \bar{x})^2 + \left(\frac{s_e}{\sqrt{n}}\right)^2}$$

$$= \sqrt{(0.2385)^2(25 - 35.82)^2 + \left(\frac{32.54}{\sqrt{59}}\right)^2} = \$4.96$$

The t^* value that excludes 2.5% in either tail with $59 - 2 = 57$ df is (according to the tables) 2.002.

Putting it all together, the margin of error is:

$$ME = 2.002(4.96) = \$9.93$$

So, the 95% confidence interval is

$$\$100.13 \pm 9.93 = (\$90.20, \$110.06)$$

(continued)

To make a prediction interval for an *individual* item's price with a polishing time of 25 minutes, we use the formula

$$SE(\hat{y}_v) = \sqrt{(SE^2(b_1))(x_v - \bar{x})^2 + \frac{s_e^2}{n} + s_e^2} = \$32.92,$$

and find the ME to be

$$ME = t^* SE(\hat{y}_v) = 2.002 \times 32.92 = \$65.91,$$

and so the prediction interval is

$$\hat{y} \pm ME = 100.13 \pm 65.91 = (\$34.22, \$166.04).$$

WHAT CAN GO WRONG?

With inference, we've put numbers on our estimates and predictions, but these numbers are only as good as the model. Here are the main things to watch out for:

- **Don't fit a linear regression to data that aren't straight.** This is the most fundamental assumption. If the relationship between x and y isn't approximately linear, there's no sense in fitting a straight line to it.

- **Watch out for changing spread.** The common part of confidence and prediction intervals is the estimate of the error standard deviation, the spread around the line. If it changes with x, the estimate won't make sense. Imagine making a prediction interval for these data:

  When x is small, we can predict y precisely, but as x gets larger, it's much harder to pin y down. Unfortunately, if the spread changes, the single value of s_e won't pick that up. The prediction interval will use the average spread around the line, with the result that we'll be too pessimistic about our precision for low x-values and too optimistic for high x-values. A re-expression of y is often a good fix for changing spread.

- **Watch out for non-Normal errors.** When we make a prediction interval for an individual y-value, the Central Limit Theorem can't come to our rescue. For us to believe the prediction interval, the errors must follow the Normal model. Check the histogram and Normal probability plot of the residuals to see if this assumption looks reasonable.

- **Watch out for one-tailed tests.** Because tests of hypotheses about regression coefficients are usually two-tailed, software packages report two-tailed P-values. If you are using that type of software to conduct a one-tailed test about the slope, you'll need to divide the reported P-value by two.

ETHICS IN ACTION

The need for senior care businesses that offer companionship and nonmedical home services is increasing as the U.S. population continues to age. One such franchise, Independent Senior Care, tries to set itself apart from its competitors by offering an additional service to prospective franchisees. In addition to standard information packets that provide tools, training, and mentorship opportunities, Independent Senior Care has an analyst on staff, Allen Ackman, to help prospective franchisees evaluate the feasibility of opening an elder care business in their area.

Allen was contacted recently by Kyle Sennefeld, a recent business school graduate with a minor in gerontology, who is interested in starting a senior care franchise in northeastern Pennsylvania. Allen decides to use a regression model that relates annual profit to the number of residents over the age of 65 that live within a 100-mile radius of a franchise location. Even though the R^2 for this model is small, the slope is statistically significant, and the model is easy to explain to prospective franchisees. Allen sends Kyle a report that estimates the annual profit at Kyle's proposed location. Kyle was excited to see that opening an Independent Senior Care franchise in northeastern Pennsylvania would be a good business decision.

- Identify the ethical dilemma in this scenario.

- What are the undesirable consequences?

- Propose an ethical solution that considers the welfare of all stakeholders.

WHAT HAVE WE LEARNED?

Learning Objectives

Apply your understanding of inference for means using Student's *t* to make inference about regression coefficients.

Know the Assumptions and Conditions for inference about regression coefficients and how to check them, in this order:

- **Linearity Assumption,** checked with the Linearity Condition by examining a scatterplot of *y* vs. *x* or a scatterplot of the residuals plotted against the predicted values.
- **Independence Assumption,** which can't be checked, but is more plausible if the data were collected with appropriate randomization—the Randomization Condition.
- **Equal Variance Assumption,** which requires that the spread around the regression model be the same everywhere. We check it with the Equal Spread Condition, assessed with a scatterplot of the residuals versus the predicted values.
- **Normal Population Assumption,** which is required to use Student's *t*-models unless the sample size is large. Check it with the Nearly Normal Condition by making a histogram or normal probability plot of the residuals.

Know the components of the standard error of the slope coefficient:

- The standard deviation of the residuals, $s_e = \sqrt{\dfrac{\sum (y - \hat{y})^2}{n - 2}}$

- The standard deviation of *x*, $s_x = \sqrt{\dfrac{\sum (x - \bar{x})^2}{n - 1}}$

- The sample size, *n*

Be able to find and interpret the standard error of the slope.

- $SE(b_1) = \dfrac{s_e}{s_x \sqrt{n - 1}}$

- The standard error of the slope is the estimated standard deviation of the sampling distribution of the slope.

State and test the standard null hypothesis on the slope.

- $H_0: \beta_1 = 0$. This would mean that *x* and *y* are not linearly related.

- We test this null hypothesis using the *t*-statistic $t = \dfrac{b_1 - 0}{SE(b_1)}$.

Construct and interpret a confidence interval for the predicted mean value corresponding to a specified value, x_ν.

- $\hat{y}_\nu \pm t^*_{n-2} \times SE(\hat{\mu}_\nu)$, where $SE(\hat{\mu}_\nu) = \sqrt{SE^2(b_1) \times (x_\nu - \bar{x})^2 + \dfrac{s_e^2}{n}}$.

Construct and interpret a confidence interval for an individual predicted value corresponding to a specified value, x_ν.

- $\hat{y}_\nu \pm t^*_{n-2} \times SE(\hat{y}_\nu)$, where $SE(\hat{y}_\nu) = \sqrt{SE^2(b_1) \times (x_\nu - \bar{x})^2 + \dfrac{s_e^2}{n} + s_e^2}$.

Terms

Confidence interval for the predicted mean value

Different samples will give different estimates of the regression model and, so, different predicted values for the same value of x. We find a confidence interval for the mean of these predicted values at a specified x-value, x_ν, as

$$\hat{y}_\nu \pm t^*_{n-2} \times SE(\hat{\mu}_\nu),$$

where

$$SE(\hat{\mu}_\nu) = \sqrt{SE^2(b_1) \times (x_\nu - \bar{x})^2 + \frac{s_e^2}{n}}.$$

The critical value, t^*_{n-2}, depends on the specified confidence level and the Student's t-model with $n - 2$ degrees of freedom.

Confidence interval for the regression slope

When the assumptions are satisfied, we can find a confidence interval for the slope parameter from $b_1 \pm t^*_{n-2} \times SE(b_1)$. The critical value, t^*_{n-2}, depends on the confidence interval specified and on the Student's t-model with $n - 2$ degrees of freedom.

Prediction interval for a future observation

A confidence interval for individual values. Prediction intervals are to observations as confidence intervals are to parameters. They predict the distribution of individual values, while confidence intervals specify likely values for a true parameter. When the assumptions are satisfied, the prediction interval takes the form

$$\hat{y}_\nu \pm t^*_{n-2} \times SE(\hat{y}_\nu),$$

where

$$SE(\hat{y}_\nu) = \sqrt{SE^2(b_1) \times (x_\nu - \bar{x})^2 + \frac{s_e^2}{n} + s_e^2}.$$

The critical value, t^*_{n-2}, depends on the specified confidence level and the Student's t-model with $n - 2$ degrees of freedom. The extra s_e^2 in $SE(\hat{y}_\nu)$ makes the interval wider than the corresponding confidence interval for the mean.

Residual standard deviation

The measure, denoted s_e, of the spread of the data around the regression line:

$$s_e = \sqrt{\frac{\sum (y - \hat{y})^2}{n - 2}} = \sqrt{\frac{\sum e^2}{n - 2}}.$$

t-test for the regression slope

The usual null hypothesis is that the true value of the slope is zero. The alternative is that it is not. A slope of zero indicates a complete lack of linear relationship between y and x.

To test $H_0: \beta_1 = 0$ we find

$$t = \frac{b_1 - 0}{SE(b_1)},$$

where $SE(b_1) = \dfrac{s_e}{s_x \sqrt{n - 1}}$, $s_e = \sqrt{\dfrac{\sum (y - \hat{y})^2}{n - 2}}$, n is the number of cases, and s_x is the standard deviation of the x-values. We find the P-value from the Student's t-model with $n - 2$ degrees of freedom.

TECHNOLOGY HELP: Regression Analysis

All statistics packages make a table of results for a regression. These tables differ slightly from one package to another, but all are essentially the same.

All packages offer analyses of the residuals. With some, you must request plots of the residuals as you request the regression. Others let you find the regression first and then analyze the residuals afterward. Either way, your analysis is not complete if you don't check the residuals with a histogram or Normal probability plot and a scatterplot of the residuals against *x* or the predicted values.

You should, of course, always look at the scatterplot of your two variables before computing a regression.

Regressions are almost always found with a computer or calculator. The calculations are too long to do conveniently by hand for data sets of any reasonable size. No matter how the regression is computed, the results are usually presented in a table that has a standard form. Here's a portion of a typical regression results table, along with annotations showing where the numbers come from.

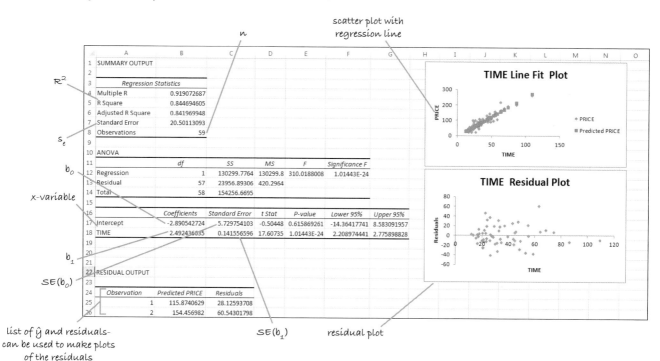

The regression table gives the coefficients (once you find them in the middle of all this other information). This regression (for different items than in the example in the text) predicts Price from Time. The regression equation is

$$\widehat{Price} = -2.891 + 2.492\ Time$$

and the R^2 for the regression is 84.5%.

The column of *t*-ratios gives the test statistics for the respective null hypotheses that the true values of the coefficients are zero. The corresponding P-values are also usually reported.

EXCEL

To perform a regression analysis in Excel:

- From **Data**, select **Data Analysis** and select **Regression.**

- Enter the data range holding the y-variable in the box labeled "Input Y range".

- Enter the range of cells holding the x-variable in the box labeled "Input X range".

- Select the **New Worksheet Ply** option to report results in a new worksheet (or identify output range in current worksheet

or new workbook) and **Labels** if the first row of the data holds the variable labels.

- Select **Residuals**, **Residual Plots**, and **Line Fit Plots** options.

- After the plots are generated, you can delete the predicted values and/or add the least squares line, called a Trendline in Excel, on the Line Fit Plot.
- To obtain a histogram of the residuals, use residuals listed in Excel output to create a histogram using **Data > Data Analysis > Histogram**.

Comments

The *Y* and *X* ranges do not need to be in the same rows of the spreadsheet, although they must cover the same number of cells. But it is a good idea to arrange your data in parallel columns as in a data table to reduce the chance of error. Although the dialog offers a Normal probability plot of the residuals, the data analysis add-in does not make a correct probability plot, so don't use this option.

JMP

To perform a regression analysis in JMP,

- From the **Analyze** menu, select **Fit Y by X**.
- Select variables: a **Y, Response** variable, and an **X, Factor** variable. Both must be continuous (quantitative).
- JMP makes a scatterplot.
- Click on the red triangle beside the heading labeled **Bivariate Fit...** and choose **Fit Line.** JMP draws the least squares regression line on the scatterplot and displays the results of the regression in tables below the plot.
- The portion of the table labeled "Parameter Estimates" gives the coefficients and their standard errors, *t*-ratios, and P-values.

Comments

JMP chooses a regression analysis when both variables are "Continuous." If you get a different analysis, check the variable types.

The Parameter table does not include the residual standard deviation s_e. You can find that as Root Mean Square Error in the Summary of Fit panel of the output.

MINITAB

To compute a regression analysis in Minitab,

- Choose **Regression** from the **Stat** menu.
- Choose **Regression...** from the **Regression** submenu.
- In the Regression dialog, assign the Y-variable to the Response box and assign the X-variable to the Predictors box.
- Click the **Graphs** button.
- In the Regression-Graphs dialog, select **Standardized residuals,** and check **Normal plot of residuals**, **Residuals versus fits**, and **Residuals versus order.**
- Click the **OK** button to return to the Regression dialog.
- Click the **OK** button to compute the regression.

Comments

You can also start by choosing a Fitted Line plot from the **Regression** submenu to see the scatterplot first—usually good practice.

SPSS

To find a regression in SPSS,

- Choose **Regression** from the **Analyze** menu.
- Choose **Linear** from the **Regression** submenu.
- In the Linear Regression dialog that appears, select the Y-variable and move it to the dependent target. Then move the X-variable to the independent target.
- Click the **Plots** button.
- In the Linear Regression Plots dialog, choose to plot the *SRESIDs against the *ZPRED values.
- Click the **Continue** button to return to the Linear Regression dialog.
- Click the **OK** button to compute the regression.

Brief Case

Frozen Pizza

The product manager at a subsidiary of Kraft Foods, Inc. is interested in learning how sensitive sales are to changes in the unit price of a frozen pizza in Dallas, Denver, Baltimore, and Chicago. The product manager has been provided data on both *Price* and *Sales* volume every fourth week over a period of nearly four years for the four cities (**Frozen Pizza**).

Examine the relationship between *Price* and *Sales* for each city. Be sure to discuss the nature and validity of this relationship. Is it linear? Is it negative? Is it significant? Are the conditions of regression met? Some individuals in the product manager's division suspect that frozen pizza sales are more sensitive to price in some cities than in others. Is there any evidence to suggest that? Write up a short report on what you find. Include 95% confidence intervals for the mean *Sales* if the *Price* is $2.50 and discuss how that interval changes if the *Price* is $3.50.

Global Warming?

Every spring, Nenana, Alaska, hosts a contest in which participants try to guess the exact minute that a wooden tripod placed on the frozen Tanana River will fall through the breaking ice. The contest started in 1917 as a diversion for railroad engineers, with a jackpot of $800 for the closest guess. It has grown into an event in which hundreds of thousands of entrants enter their guesses on the Internet and vie for more than $300,000.

Because so much money and interest depends on the time of the ice breakup, it has been recorded to the nearest minute with great accuracy ever since 1917 (**Nenana**). And because a standard measure of breakup has been used throughout this time, the data are consistent. An article in *Science* ("Climate Change in Nontraditional Data Sets," *Science* 294, October 2001) used the data to investigate global warming. Researchers are interested in the following questions. What is the rate of change in the date of breakup over time (if any)? If the ice is breaking up earlier, what is your conclusion? Does this necessarily suggest global warming? What could be other reasons for this trend? What is the predicted breakup date for the year 2020? (Be sure to include an appropriate prediction or confidence interval.) Write up a short report with your answers.

EXERCISES

SECTION 15.1

1. A website that rents movies online recorded the age and the number of movies rented during the past month for some of their customers. Here are their data:

Age	Rentals
35	9
40	8
50	4
65	3
40	10
30	12

Make a scatterplot for these data. What does it tell you about the relationship between these two variables? From computer output, the regression line has $b_0 = 18.9$ and $b_1 = -0.260$.

a) Use the estimated regression equation to predict *Rentals* for all six values of *Age*.
b) Find the residuals e_i.
c) Calculate the residual standard deviation, s_e.

2. A training center, wishing to demonstrate the effectiveness of their methods, tests some of their clients after different numbers of days of training, recording their scores on a sample test. Their data are:

Training Days	Correct Responses
1	4
4	6
8	7
10	9
12	10

The regression model they calculate is

$$\widehat{Correct\ responses} = 3.525 + 0.525\ Training\ days.$$

a) Use the model to predict the correct responses for each number of training days.
b) Find the residuals, e_i.
c) Calculate the residual standard deviation, s_e.

3. For the regression of Exercise 1, find the standard error of the regression slope. Show all three values that go into the calculation.

4. For the regression of Exercise 2, find the standard error of the regression slope. Show all three values that go into the calculation.

5. A data set of 5 observations for *Concession Sales per person* ($) at a theater and *Minutes before the movie begins* results in the following estimated regression model:

$$\widehat{Sales} = 4.3 + 0.265 \, Minutes.$$

The standard error of the regression slope is 0.0454.

a) Compute the value of the *t*-statistic to test if there is a significant relationship between *Sales* and *Minutes*.
b) What are the degrees of freedom associated with the *t*-statistic?
c) What is the P-value associated with the *t*-statistic?
d) At $\alpha = .05$, can you reject the standard null hypothesis for the slope? Explain.

6. A soap manufacturer tested a standard bar of soap to see how long it would last. A test subject showered with the soap each day for 15 days and recorded the *Weight* (in grams) of the soap after the shower. The resulting regression computer output looks, in part, like this:

```
Dependent variable is: Weight
R-squared = 99.5%
s = 2.949

Variable    Coefficient  SE(Coeff)  t-Ratio  P-Value
Intercept   123.141      1.382      89.1     <0.0001
Day         −5.57476     0.1068     −52.2    <0.0001
```

Find the following facts in this output, or determine them from what you know.

a) The standard deviation of the residuals
b) The slope of the regression line
c) The standard error of b_1
d) The P-value appropriate for testing $H_0: \beta_1 = 0$ versus $H_A: \beta_1 \neq 0$
e) Is the null hypothesis rejected at $\alpha = 0.05$?

SECTION 15.2

7. For the data from Exercise 1, which of the following conditions can you check from the scatterplot? Are satisfied?

a) Linearity
b) Independence
c) Equal spread
d) Normal population

8. Here's a scatterplot of the % of income spent on food versus household income for respondents to the Cornell National Social Survey:

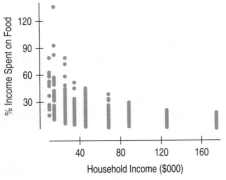

For each of the regression assumptions, state whether it is satisfied, not satisfied, or can't be determined from this plot.

a) Linearity
b) Independence
c) Equal spread
d) Normal population

SECTION 15.3

9. Here are data from a small bookstore.

Number of Salespeople Working	Sales (in $1000's)
2	10
3	11
7	13
9	14
10	18
10	20
12	20
15	22
16	22
20	26
$\bar{x} = 10.4$	$\bar{y} = 17.6$
$SD(x) = 5.64$	$SD(y) = 5.34$

The regression line is:

$$\widehat{Sales} = 8.10 + 0.9134 \, Number \ of \ Salespeople \ Working.$$

The assumptions and conditions for regression are met, and from technology we learn that

$$SE(b_1) = 0.0873 \qquad s_e = 1.477$$

a) Find the predicted *Sales* on a day with 12 employees working.
b) Find a 95% confidence interval for the mean *Sales* on days that have 12 employees working.
c) Find the 95% prediction interval for *Sales* on a day with 12 employees working.

10. The study of external disk drives from Chapter 4, exercise 2 (with the outlier removed) finds the following:

	Capacity (TB)	Price ($)
	0.15	35
	0.25	39.95
	0.32	49.95
	1	75
	2	110
	3	140
	4	325
Mean	1.53	110.7
SD	1.51	102.05

The least squares line was found to be: $\widehat{Price} = 15.112 + 62.417 \, Capacity$ with $s_e = 42.037$ and $SE(b_1) = 11.328$.

a) Find the predicted *Price* of a 2 TB hard drive.

b) Find a 95% confidence interval for the mean *Price* of 2 TB disk drives.
c) Find the 95% prediction interval for the *Price* of a 2 TB hard drive.

SECTION 15.4

11. A survey designed to study how much households spend on eating out finds the following regression model,

$$\widehat{EatOut \ \$/wk} = 17.28 + 0.354 \ HHIncome$$

relating the amount respondents said they spent individually to eat out each week to their household income in $1000's.

a) A 95% prediction interval for a customer with a household income of $80,000 is ($35.60, $55.60). Explain to the restaurant owner how she should interpret this interval.
b) A 95% confidence interval for the mean amount spent weekly to eat out by people with a household income of $80,000 is ($40.60, $50.60). Explain to a restaurant owner how to interpret this interval.
c) Now explain to her why these intervals are different.

12. In Exercise 5, we saw a regression to predict the sales per person at a movie theater in terms of the time (in minutes) before the show. The model was:

$$\widehat{Sales} = 4.3 + 0.265 \ Minutes.$$

a) A 90% prediction interval for sales to a concessions customer 10 minutes before the movie starts is ($4.60, $9.30). Explain how to interpret this interval.
b) A 90% confidence interval for the mean of sales per person 10 minutes before the movie starts is ($6.65, $7.25). Explain how to interpret this interval.
c) Which interval is of particular interest to the concessions manager? Which one is of particular interest to you, the moviegoer?

SECTION 15.5

13. Recall the small bookstore we saw in Exercise 9. The regression line is:

$$\widehat{Sales} = 8.10 + 0.9134 \ Number \ of \ Sales \ People \ Working$$

and the assumptions and conditions for regression are met. Calculations with technology find that

$$s_e = 1.477.$$

a) Find the predicted sales on a day with 500 employees working.
b) Find a 95% prediction interval for the sales on a day with 500 employees working.
c) Are these predictions likely to be useful? Explain.

14. Look back at the prices for the external disk drives we saw in Exercise 10.
The least squares line is $\widehat{Price} = 15.112 + 62.417 \ Capacity$.

The assumptions and conditions for regression are met.

$$SE(b_1) = 11.328$$

a) Disk drives keep growing in capacity. Some tech experts now talk about *Petabyte* (PB = 1000 TB = 1,000,000 GB) drives. What does this model predict that a Petabyte-capacity drive will cost?
b) Find a 95% prediction interval for the price of a 1 PB drive.
c) Are these predictions likely to be useful? Explain.

CHAPTER EXERCISES

15. Online shopping. Several studies have found that the frequency with which shoppers browse Internet retailers is related to the frequency with which they actually purchase products and/or services online. Here are data showing the age of respondents and their answer to the question "How many minutes do you browse online retailers per week?"

Age	Browsing Time (min/wk)
22	492
50	186
44	180
32	384
55	120
60	120
38	276
22	480
21	510
45	252
52	126
33	360
19	570
17	588
21	498

a) Make a scatterplot for these data.
b) Do you think a linear model is appropriate? Explain.
c) Find the equation of the regression line.
d) Check the residuals to see if the conditions for inference are met.

16. Climate change. The Earth has been getting warmer. Most climate scientists agree that one important cause of the warming is the increase in atmospheric levels of carbon dioxide (CO_2), a greenhouse gas. Here is part of a regression analysis of the mean annual CO_2 concentration in the atmosphere, measured in parts per thousand (ppt), at the top of Mauna Loa in Hawaii and the mean annual air temperature over both land and sea across the globe, in degrees Celsius. The scatterplots and residuals plots indicated that the data were appropriate for inference and the response variable is *Temp*.

Variable	Coeff	SE(Coeff)
Intercept	10.707	0.4810
CO2	0.010	0.0013

R-squared = 67.8%
s = 0.0985 with 29 − 2 = 27 degrees of freedom

a) Write the equation of the regression line.
b) Find the value of the correlation. Is there evidence of an association between CO_2 level and global temperature?
c) Find the *t*-value and P-value for the slope. Is there evidence of an association between CO_2 level and global temperature? What do you know from the slope and *t*-test that you might not have known from the correlation?
d) Do you think predictions made by this regression will be very accurate? Explain.

17. Movie budgets. How does the cost of a movie depend on its length? Data on the cost (millions of dollars) and the running time (minutes) for major release films in one recent year are summarized in these plots and computer output:

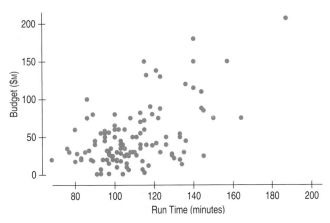

```
Dependent variable is: Budget($M)
R-squared = 15.4%
s = 32.95 with 120 - 2 = 118 degrees of freedom

Variable    Coefficient  SE(Coeff)  t-Ratio  P-Value
Intercept    -31.39        17.12     -1.83    0.0693
Run time       0.71         0.15      4.64   <0.0001
```

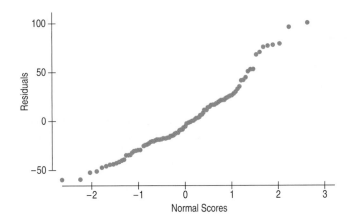

a) Explain in words and numbers what the regression says.
b) The intercept is negative. Discuss its value, taking note of the P-value.
c) The output reports $s = 32.95$. Explain what that means in this context.
d) What's the value of the standard error of the slope of the regression line?
e) Explain what that means in this context.

18. House prices. How does the price of a house depend on its size? Data from Saratoga, New York, on 1064 randomly selected houses that had been sold include data on price ($1000s) and size ($1000 \text{ ft}^2$), producing the following graphs and computer output:

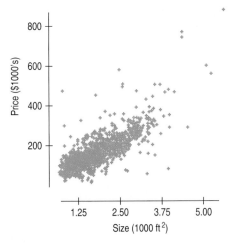

```
Dependent variable is: Price
R-squared = 59.5%
s = 53.79 with 1064 - 2 = 1062 degrees of freedom

Variable    Coefficient  SE(Coeff)  t-Ratio  P-Value
Intercept    -3.1169       4.688     -0.665   0.5063
Size         94.4539       2.393     39.465  <0.0001
```

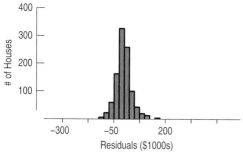

a) Explain in words and numbers what the regression says.

b) The intercept is negative. Discuss its value, taking note of its P-value.

c) The output reports $s = 53.79$. Explain what that means in this context.

d) What's the value of the standard error of the slope of the regression line?

e) Explain what that means in this context.

19. Movie budgets, part 2. Exercise 17 shows computer output examining the association between the length of a movie and its cost.

a) Check the assumptions and conditions for inference.

b) Find a 95% confidence interval for the slope and interpret it.

20. House prices, part 2. Exercise 18 shows computer output examining the association between the sizes of houses and their sale prices.

a) Check the assumptions and conditions for inference.

b) Find a 95% confidence interval for the slope and interpret it.

21. Water hardness. In an investigation of environmental causes of disease, data were collected on the annual mortality rate (deaths per 100,000) for males in 61 large towns in England and Wales. In addition, the water hardness was recorded as the calcium concentration (parts per million, or ppm) in the drinking water. Here are the scatterplot and regression analysis of the relationship between mortality and calcium concentration, where the dependent variable is *Mortality*.

Variable	Coeff	SE(Coeff)
Intercept	1676.36	29.30
Calcium	-3.226	0.485

R-squared = 42.9%
s = 143.0 with 61 − 2 = 59 degrees of freedom

a) Is there an association between the hardness of the water and the mortality rate? Write the appropriate hypothesis.

b) Assuming the assumptions for regression inference are met, what do you conclude?

c) Create a 95% confidence interval for the slope of the true line relating calcium concentration and mortality.

d) Interpret your interval in context.

22. Mutual fund returns 2013. The brief case for Chapter 4 listed the rate of return for 92 mutual funds over the previous 3-year and 5-year periods. It's common for advertisements to carry the disclaimer that "past returns may not be indicative of future performance." Do these data indicate that there was an association between 3-year and 5-year rates of return?

23. Retail trade index. The index of deflated turnover for retail trade shows the activity in volume of the retail trade sector. The United Nations Statistics Division reports Retail trade deflated sales/turnover (seasonally adjusted) with $2005 = 100$. The datafile holds this index for 43 countries for the years 2007–2010.

a) Find a regression model predicting the *2010* index from the index in *2007* for the sample of 43 countries provided by UNSD.

b) Examine the residuals to determine if a linear regression is appropriate.

c) Test an appropriate hypothesis to determine if the association is significant.

d) What percentage of the variability in the *2010 Index* is accounted for by the regression model?

24. Male unemployment 2010. Using unemployment data provided by the United Nations, investigate the association between the male unemployment rate in 2007 and 2010 for a sample of 75 countries.

a) Find a regression model predicting the *2010* rate from the *2007* rate.

b) Examine the residuals to determine if a linear regression is appropriate.

c) Test an appropriate hypothesis to determine if the association is significant.

d) What percentage of the variability in the *2010* rate is accounted for by the *regression model*?

T 25. Used cars. Classified ads in a newspaper offered several used Toyota Corollas for sale. Listed below are the ages of the cars and the advertised prices.

Age (yr)	Prices Advertised ($)
1	13990
1	13495
3	12999
4	9500
4	10495
5	8995
5	9495
6	6999
7	6950
7	7850
8	6999
8	5995
10	4950
10	4495
13	2850

a) Make a scatterplot for these data.
b) Do you think a linear model is appropriate? Explain.
c) Find the equation of the regression line.
d) Check the residuals to see if the conditions for inference are met.

T 26. Property assessments. The following software results provide information about the size (in square feet) of 18 homes in Ithaca, New York, and the city's assessed value of those homes, where the response variable is *Assessment*.

Predictor	Coeff	SE(Coeff)	t-Ratio	P-Value
Intercept	37108.85	8664.33	4.28	0.0006
Size	11.90	4.29	2.77	0.0136

s = 4682.10   R-Sq = 32.5%

Variable	Mean	StdDev
Assessment	60946.7	5527.62
Size	2003.39	264.727

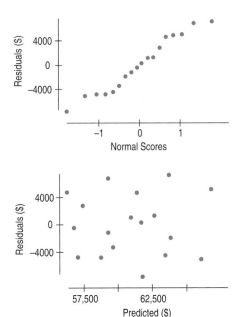

a) Explain why inference for linear regression is appropriate with these data.
b) Is there a significant linear association between the *Size* of a home and its *Assessment*? Test an appropriate hypothesis and state your conclusion.
c) What percentage of the variability in assessed value is accounted for by this regression?
d) Give a 90% confidence interval for the slope of the true regression line, and explain its meaning in the proper context.
e) From this analysis, can we conclude that adding a room to your house will increase its assessed value? Why or why not?
f) The owner of a home measuring 2100 square feet files an appeal, claiming that the $70,200 assessed value is too high. Do you agree? Explain your reasoning.

T 27. Used cars, part 2. Based on the analysis of used car prices you did for Exercise 25, if appropriate, create a 95% confidence interval for the slope of the regression line and explain what your interval means in context.

T 28. Assets and sales. A business analyst is looking at a company's assets and sales to determine the relationship (if any) between the two measures. She has data (in $million) from a random sample of 79 Fortune 500 companies, and obtained the linear regression below:

Predictor	Coeff	SE(Coeff)	t-Ratio	P-Value
Intercept	1867.4	804.5	2.32	0.0230
Sales	0.975	0.099	9.84	<0.0001

s = 6132.59   R-Sq = 55.7%

Use the data provided to find a 95% confidence interval for the slope of the regression line and interpret your interval in context.

T 29. Fuel economy and weight. A consumer organization has reported test data for 50 car models. We will examine the association between the weight of the car (in thousands of pounds) and the fuel efficiency (in miles per gallon). Use the data provided on the disk to answer the following questions, where the response variable is *Fuel Efficiency* (mpg).

a) Create the scatterplot and obtain the regression equation.
b) Are the assumptions for regression satisfied?
c) Write the appropriate hypotheses for the slope.
d) Test the hypotheses and state your conclusion.

T 30. Auto batteries. *Consumer Reports* listed the price (in dollars) and power (in cold cranking amps) of auto batteries. We want to know if more expensive batteries are generally better in terms of starting power. Here are the regression and residual output, where the response variable is *Power*.

```
Dependent variable is: Power
R-squared = 25.2%
s = 116.0 with 33 - 2 = 31 degrees of freedom

Variable    Coefficient   SE(Coeff)   t-Ratio   P-Value
Intercept   384.594       93.55       4.11      0.0003
Price         4.146        1.282      3.23      0.0029
```

a) How many batteries were tested?
b) Are the conditions for inference satisfied? Explain.
c) Is there evidence of a linear association between the price and cranking power of auto batteries? Test an appropriate hypothesis and state your conclusion.
d) Is the association strong? Explain.
e) What is the equation of the regression line?
f) Create a 90% confidence interval for the slope of the true line.
g) Interpret your interval in this context.

T 31. SAT scores. How strong was the association between student scores on the Math and Verbal sections of the old SAT? Scores on this exam ranged from 200 to 800 and were widely used by college admissions offices. Here are summary statistics, regression analysis, and plots of the scores for a graduating class of 162 students at Ithaca High School, where the response variable is *Math Score*.

```
Predictor   Coeff     SE(Coeff)   t-Ratio   P-Value
Intercept   209.55    34.35       6.10      <0.0001
Verbal        0.675    0.057      11.88      <0.0001

s = 71.75      R-Sq = 46.9%
```

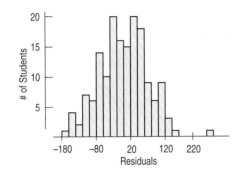

a) Is there evidence of a linear association between *Math* and *Verbal* scores? Write an appropriate hypothesis.
b) Discuss the assumptions for inference.
c) Test your hypothesis and state an appropriate conclusion.

32. Productivity. How strong is the association between labor productivity and labor costs? Data from the Bureau of Labor Statistics for labor productivity, as measured by *Output per Hour*, and *Unit Labor Costs* across 53 industries, are used to examine this relationship (ftp://ftp.bls.gov; accessed June 2013).

a) From a scatterplot, is there evidence of a linear association between *Labor Productivity* and *Unit Labor Costs*? Plot the reciprocal, *Hours per output (000s)*, against *Unit Labor Costs*. Why did the analysts prefer this measure of productivity?
b) Using the reciprocal measure, *Hours per Output (000s)*, test an appropriate null hypothesis and state an appropriate conclusion (assume that assumptions and conditions are now met).

33. Football salaries 2013. Football owners are constantly in competition for good players. The more wins, the more likely that the team will provide good business returns for the owners. The resources that each of the 32 teams has in the National Football League (NFL) vary, but the draft system is designed to counteract the advantages that wealthier teams may have. Is it working or does the size of the payroll matter? Here is the regression output for the 2012/2013 season between the team payroll and the number of wins. (See also Chapter 4, Exercise 33.)

Predictor	Coeff	SE(Coeff)	t-Ratio	P-Value
Intercept	−16.31846	8.49246	−1.922	0.06421
Payroll($M)	0.21875	0.07636	2.865	0.00755

s = 2.779   R-Sq = 21.48%

a) State the hypotheses about the slope.
b) Perform the hypothesis test and state your conclusion in context.
c) Using a statistics program and the data on the DVD, check the assumptions and conditions.

34. Female president. The Gallup organization has, over six decades, periodically asked the following question:

If your party nominated a generally well-qualified person for president who happened to be a woman, would you vote for that person?

We wonder if the proportion of the public who have "no opinion" on this issue has changed over the years. Here is a regression for the proportion of those respondents whose response to this question about voting for a woman president was "no opinion." Assume that the conditions for inference are satisfied and that the response variable is proportion responding *No Opinion*.

Predictor	Coeff	SE(Coeff)	t-Ratio	P-Value
Intercept	7.693	2.445	3.15	0.0071
Year	−0.043	0.035	−1.21	0.2460

s = 2.28   R-Sq = 9.5%

a) State the hypotheses about the slope (both numerically and in words) that describes how voters' thoughts have changed about voting for a woman.
b) Assuming that the conditions for inference are satisfied, perform the hypothesis test and state your conclusion.
c) Examine the scatterplot corresponding to the regression for No Opinion. How does it change your opinion of the trend in "no opinion" responses? Do you think the true slope is negative as shown in the regression output?

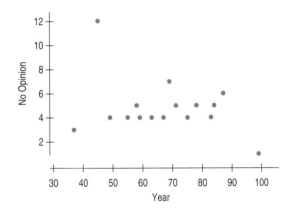

35. Fuel economy and weight, part 2. Consider again the data in Exercise 29 about the gas mileage and weights of cars.

a) Create a 95% confidence interval for the slope of the regression line.
b) Explain in this context what your confidence interval means.

36. SAT scores, part 2. Consider the high school SAT scores data from Exercise 31.

a) Find a 90% confidence interval for the slope of the true line describing the association between Math and Verbal scores.
b) Explain in this context what your confidence interval means.

37. Ozone. The Environmental Protection Agency is examining the relationship between the ozone level (in parts per million) and the population (in millions) of U.S. cities. Part of the regression analysis is shown.

```
Dependent variable is Ozone
R-squared = 84.4%
s = 5.454 with 16 - 2 = 14 df

Variable        Coeff        SE(Coeff)
Intercept       18.892       2.395
Pop             6.650        1.910
```

a) We suspect that the greater the population of a city, the higher its ozone level. Is the relationship statistically significant? Assuming the conditions for inference are satisfied, test an appropriate hypothesis and state your conclusion in context.

b) Do you think that the population of a city is a useful predictor of ozone level? Use the values of both R^2 and s in your explanation.

38. Sales and profits. A business analyst was interested in the relationship between a company's sales and its profits. She collected data (in millions of dollars) from a random sample of Fortune 500 companies and created the regression analysis and summary statistics shown. The assumptions for regression inference appeared to be satisfied.

```
         Profits  Sales    Dependent variable is Profits
Count    79       79       R-squared = 66.2%  s = 466.2
Mean     209.839  4178.29  Variable   Coefficient SE(Coeff)
Variance 635,172  49,163,000 Intercept -176.644   61.16
Std Dev  796.977  7011.63  Sales      0.092498    0.0075
```

a) Is there a statistically significant association between sales and profits? Test an appropriate hypothesis and state your conclusion in context.

b) Do you think that a company's sales serve as a useful predictor of its profits? Use the values of both R^2 and s in your explanation.

39. Ozone, again. Using a statistics program, consider again the relationship between the population and ozone level of U.S. cities that you analyzed in Exercise 37.

a) Give a 90% confidence interval for the approximate increase in ozone level associated with each additional million city inhabitants.

b) For the cities studied, the mean population was 1.7 million people. The population of Boston is approximately 0.6 million people. Predict the mean ozone level for cities of that size with an interval in which you have 90% confidence.

40. More sales and profits. Using a statistics program, consider again the relationship between the sales and profits of Fortune 500 companies that you analyzed in Exercise 38.

a) Find a 95% confidence interval for the slope of the regression line. Interpret your interval in context.

b) Last year, the drug manufacturer Eli Lilly, Inc., reported gross sales of $23 billion (that's $23,000 million). Create a 95% prediction interval for the company's profits, and interpret your interval in context.

41. Tablet computers. In July 2013, cnet.com listed the battery life (in hours) and luminous intensity (i.e., screen brightness, in cd/m²) for a sample of tablet computers. We want to know if screen brightness is associated with battery life. (reviews.cnet.com/8301-19736_7-20080768-251/cnet-updates-tablet-test-results/?tag=contentBody;contentHighlights)

```
Dependent variable is Video battery life (in hours)
R-squared = 4.82%
s = 1.946 with 69 - 2 = 67 degrees of freedom

Variable     Coeff      SE(Coeff)  t-Ratio  P-Value
Intercept    6.21108    0.9609     6.46     6.0001
Brightness   0.00486    0.0026     1.84     0.0699
```

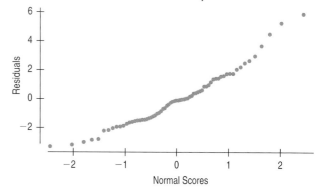

a) How many tablet computers were tested?

b) Are the conditions for inference satisfied? Explain.

c) Is there evidence of an association between maximum brightness of the screen and battery life? Test an appropriate hypothesis and state your conclusion.

d) Is the association strong? Explain.

e) What is the equation of the regression line?

f) Create a 95% confidence interval for the slope of the true line.

g) Interpret your interval in this context.

42. Marketing managers. Are wages for various marketing managerial positions related? One way to determine this is to examine the relationship between the mean hourly wages for two managerial occupations in marketing: sales managers and advertising managers. The average hourly wage for both occupations is reported for all U.S. states and territories by the U.S. Bureau of Labor Statistics (data .bls.gov/oes; Occupational Employment Statistics). Here are the regression analysis results.

```
Predictor         Coeff    SE(Coeff)  t-Ratio  P-Value
Intercept        10.317     4.382      2.35     0.0227
Sales Mgr Avg     0.56349   0.09786    5.76    <0.0001
  Hourly Wage
```

a) State the null and alternative hypothesis under investigation.

b) Assuming that the assumptions for regression inference are reasonable, test the null hypothesis.

c) State your conclusion.

43. Cost index 2011. The *Worldwide Cost of Living Survey* published by *The Economist* provides an index that expresses the cost of living in other cities as a percentage of the New York cost. For example, in 2011, the cost of living index in Tokyo was 161, which means that it was 61% higher than New York. The output shows the regression of the 2011 on the 2010 index for the ten most expensive cities in 2011, where *Index 2011* is the response variable.

```
Predictor    Coeff    SE(Coeff)  t-Ratio  P-Value
Intercept    46.73    15.45      3.02     0.0164
Index 2010    0.744    0.115     6.49     0.0002

s = 3.474   R-Sq = 84.0%
```

a) State the hypotheses about the slope (both numerically and in words).

b) Perform the hypothesis test and state your conclusion in context.

c) Explain what the *R*-squared in this regression means.

d) Do these results indicate that, in general, cities with a higher index in 2010 had a higher index in 2011? Explain.

44. Job growth 2012. *Fortune Magazine* publishes the top 100 companies to work for every year. Among the information listed is the percentage growth in jobs at each company. The period from 2009 to 2011 was a difficult one for job growth in the United States. The output below shows the regression of the 2012 job growth (%) on the 2010 job growth for those companies that appear on both years' lists. (One outlier has been omitted.) *Job Growth 2012* is the response variable (money.cnn.com/magazines/fortune/bestcompanies/; accessed March 2012).

```
Dependent variable is: Job Growth 2012
R-squared = 5.7%
s = 0.0738 with 68 − 2 = 6 degrees of freedom

Variable      Coeff    SE(Coeff)   t-Ratio   P-Value
Intercept    0.0628    0.009       7.00     <0.0001
Job Growth   0.2       0.100       2.00      0.0498
  2010
```

a) State the hypotheses about the slope (both numerically and in words).

b) Assuming that the assumptions for inference are satisfied, perform the hypothesis test and state your conclusion in context.

c) Explain what the *R*-squared in this regression means.

d) Do these results indicate that, in general, companies with a higher job growth in 2010 had a higher job growth in 2012? Explain.

45. Cost index again. In Exercise 43, we examined the *Worldwide Cost of Living Survey* cost of living index for the ten most expensive cities, whose 2011 indices range from Singapore's 137 to Tokyo's 161. Let's add the ten *least* expensive cities to the data. Their 2011 indices range from 46 for Karachi (the least expensive city in 2011) to Dhaka and Manila at 62. Here is the resulting regression:

```
Dependent variable is: Index 2011
R-squared = 99.3%
s = 4.061 with 20 − 2 = 18 degrees of freedom

Predictor    Coeff     SE(Coeff)  t-Ratio  P-Value
Intercept   −2.6787    2.272      −1.18    0.2537
Index 2010   1.1082    0.022      50.1    <0.0001
```

a) Sketch what a scatterplot of *Index2011* vs. *Index2010* is likely to look like. You do not need to see the data.

b) Explain why the R^2 of this regression is higher than the R^2 of the regression in Exercise 43.

46. Job growth again. In Exercise 44, the company Zappos was omitted. Here is a scatterplot of the data with Zappos plotted as an *x*:

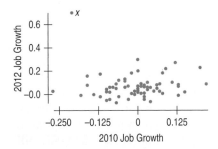

a) In words, what does the outlying point say about Zappos?

b) What effect would this point have on the regression, had it been left with the rest of the data?

c) Using the data on the DVD, find the regression with and without the outlier.

47. Old pitchers. Many factors may affect fans' decision to go to a ball game. Is it possible that fans prefer teams with an older pitching staff?

a) Examine a scatterplot of Attend/Game and PitchAge. Check the conditions for regression.
b) Do you think there is a linear association between Attendance and Pitcher Age?
c) Compute and discuss the regression model.

48. Little League product testing. Ads for a Little League instructional video claimed that the techniques would improve the performances of Little League pitchers. To test this claim, 20 Little Leaguers threw 50 pitches each, and we recorded the number of strikes. After the players participated in the training program, we repeated the test. The following table shows the number of strikes each player threw before and after the training. A test of paired differences failed to show that this training was effective in improving a player's ability to throw strikes. Is there any evidence that the *Effectiveness* (*After − Before*) of the video depends on the player's *Initial Ability* (*Before*) to throw strikes? Test an appropriate hypothesis and state your conclusion. Propose an explanation for what you find.

Number of Strikes (out of 50)			
Before	After	Before	After
28	35	33	33
29	36	33	35
30	32	34	32
32	28	34	30
32	30	34	33
32	31	35	34
32	32	36	37
32	34	36	33
32	35	37	35
33	36	37	32

49. Fuel economy and weight, part 3. Consider again the data in Exercise 29 about the fuel economy and weights of cars.

a) Create a 95% confidence interval for the average fuel efficiency among cars weighing 2500 pounds, and explain what your interval means.
b) Create a 95% prediction interval for the gas mileage you might get driving your new 3450-pound SUV, and explain what that interval means.

50. SAT scores, part 3. Consider the high school SAT scores data from Exercise 31 once more. The mean Verbal score was 596.30 and the standard deviation was 99.52.

a) Find a 90% confidence interval for the mean SAT Math score for all students with an SAT Verbal score of 500.
b) Find a 90% prediction interval for the Math score of the senior class president, if you know she scored 710 on the Verbal section.

51. Little League product testing, part 2. Using the same data provided in Exercise 48, answer the following questions.

a) Find the 95% prediction interval for the effectiveness of the video on a pitcher with an initial ability of 33 strikes.
b) Do you think predictions made by this regression will be very accurate? Explain.

52. Assets and sales, part 2. The analyst in Exercise 28 realized the data were in need of transformation because of the nonlinearity between the variables. Economists commonly take the logarithm of these variables to make the relationship more nearly linear, and she did too. (These are base 10 logs.) The dependent variable is *LogSales*. The conditions for regression inference now appear to be satisfied.

```
Dependent variable is: LogSales
R-squared = 33.9%
s = 0.4278 with 79 − 2 = 77 degrees of freedom

Variable   Coefficient  SE(Coeff)  t-Ratio  P-Value
Intercept     1.303       0.3211     4.06    0.0001
LogAssets     0.578       0.0919     6.28   <0.0001
```

a) Is there a significant linear association between *LogAssets* and *LogSales*? Find the *t*-value and P-value to test an appropriate hypothesis and state your conclusion in context.
b) Do you think that a company's assets serve as a useful predictor of their sales?

53. All the efficiency money can buy 2013. A sample of 61 model-2013 cars from an online information service was examined to see how fuel efficiency (as highway mpg) relates to the cost (Manufacturer's Suggested Retail Price in dollars) of cars. Here are displays and computer output:

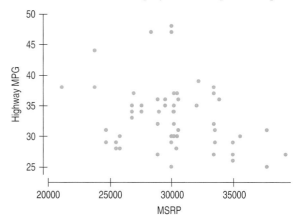

```
Dependent variable is: Highway MPG
R-squared = 10.36%
s = 4,870 with 61 − 2 = 59 degrees of freedom

Variable   Coefficient  SE(Coeff)  t-Ratio  P-Value
Intercept   45.6898      4.849      9.42    <0.0001
MSRP        −0.000416    0.000159  −2.61     0.0114
```

a) State what you want to know, identify the variables, and give the appropriate hypotheses.

b) Check the assumptions and conditions.

c) If the conditions are met, complete the analysis.

54. Energy use and recession. The great recession of 2008 changed spending and energy use habits worldwide. Based on data collected from the United Nations Millennium Indicators Database related to measuring the goal of *ensuring environmental sustainability*, investigate the association between energy use (kg oil equivalent per $1000 GDP) before (2006) and after (2010) the crisis, for a sample of 33 countries (unstats.un.org/unsd/mi/mi_goals.asp; accessed June 2013).

a) Find a regression model showing the relationship between *2010 Energy Use* (reponse variable) and *2006 Energy Use* (predictor variable).

b) Examine the residuals to determine if a linear regression is appropriate.

c) Test an appropriate hypothesis to determine if the association is significant.

d) What percentage of the variability in *2010 Energy Use* is explained by *2006 Energy Use*?

55. Youth employment 2012. Here is a scatterplot showing the regression line, 95% confidence intervals, and 95% prediction intervals, using 2012 youth unemployment data for a sample of 33 nations. The response variable is the *Male Rate*, and the predictor variable is the *Female Rate*.

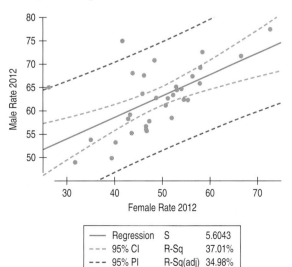

a) Explain the meaning of the 95% prediction intervals in this context.

b) Explain the meaning of the 95% confidence intervals in this context.

c) Using a statistics program, identify any unusual observations, and discuss their potential impact on the regression.

56. Male employment 2012. Here is a scatterplot showing the regression line, 95% confidence intervals, and 95% prediction intervals, using 2011 and 2012 male unemployment data for a sample of 33 nations. The response variable is the *2012-Male Rate*, and the predictor variable is the *2011-Male Rate*.

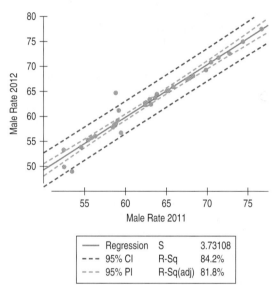

a) Explain the meaning of the 95% prediction intervals in this context.

b) Explain the meaning of the 95% confidence intervals in this context.

c) Using a statistics program, identify any unusual observations, and discuss their potential impact on the regression.

57. Energy use and recession, part 2. Examine the regression and scatterplot showing the regression line, 95% confidence intervals, and 95% prediction intervals using *2006* and *2010 energy use* (kg oil equivalent per $1000 GDP) for a sample of 31 countries first examined in Exercise 54. The response variable is *2010 Energy Use*.

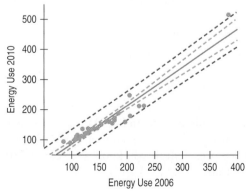

a) Explain the meaning of the 95% prediction intervals in this context.

b) Explain the meaning of the 95% confidence intervals in this context.

You can see the regression model in Exercise 54. The extraordinary point is Iceland. If we set it aside, the model looks like this

```
Response variable is: Energy Use 2010
R squared = 88.6%
s = 13.10 with 32 − 2 = 30 degrees of freedom

Variable     Coefficient  SE(Coeff)  t-Ratio  P-Value
Intercept    5.74436      9.061      0.634    0.5309
Energy 2006  0.921540     0.0605     15.2     <0.0001
```

c) How has setting aside Iceland changed the regression model? How is it likely to affect the intervals discussed in a) and b)?

58. Global reach 2012. The Internet has revolutionized business and offers unprecedented opportunities for globalization. However, the ability to access the Internet varies greatly among different regions of the world. One of the variables the United Nations collects data on each year is *Personal Computers per 100 Population* (unstats.un.org/unsd/cdb/cdb_help/cdb_quick_start.asp) for various countries. Below is a scatterplot showing the regression line, 95% confidence intervals, and 95% prediction intervals using 2000 and 2012 computer adoption (personal computers per 100 population) for a sample of 85 countries. The response variable is *PC/100 2012*.

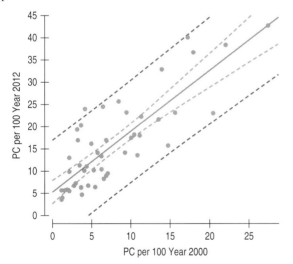

a) Working with the data set on the DVD with the same name as this exercise, find a regression model showing the relationship between personal computer adoption in 2012 *PC/100 2012* (the response variable) and personal computer adoption in 2000 *PC/100 2000* (the predictor variable).

b) Explain the meaning of the 95% prediction intervals in this context.

c) Explain the meaning of the 95% confidence intervals in this context.

59. Seasonal spending. Spending on credit cards decreases after the Christmas spending season (as measured by amount charged on a credit card in December). The data set on the DVD with the same name as this exercise contains the monthly credit card charges of a random sample of 99 cardholders.

a) Build a regression model to predict January spending from December's spending.

b) How much, on average, will cardholders who charged $2000 in December charge in January?

c) Give a 95% confidence interval for the average January charges of cardholders who charged $2000 in December.

d) From part c, give a 95% confidence interval for the average decrease in the charges of cardholders who charged $2000 in December.

e) What reservations, if any, do you have about the confidence intervals you made in parts c and d?

60. Seasonal spending, part 2. Financial analysts know that January credit card charges will generally be much lower than those of the month before. What about the difference between January and the next month? Does the trend continue? The data set on the DVD contains the monthly credit card charges of a random sample of 99 cardholders.

a) Build a regression model to predict February charges from January charges.

b) How much, on average, will cardholders who charged $2000 in January charge in February?

c) Give a 95% confidence interval for the average February charges of cardholders who charged $2000 in January.

d) From part c, give a 95% confidence interval for the average decrease in the charges of cardholders who charged $2000 in January.

e) What reservations, if any, do you have about the confidence intervals you made in parts c and d?

JUST CHECKING ANSWERS

1 A high *t*-ratio of 3.27 indicates that the slope is different from zero—that is, that there is a linear relationship between height and mouth size. The small P-value says that a slope this large would be very unlikely to occur by chance if, in fact, there was no linear relationship between the variables.

2 Not really. The R^2 for this regression is only 15.3%, so height doesn't account for very much of the variability in mouth size.

3 The value of s_e tells the standard deviation of the residuals. Mouth sizes have a mean of 60.3 cubic centimeters. A standard deviation of 15.7 in the residuals indicates that the errors made by this regression model can be quite large relative to what we are estimating. Errors of 15 to 30 cubic centimeters would be common.

16

Understanding Residuals

Kellogg's

John Harvey Kellogg was a physician who ran the Battle Creek Sanitarium. He was an advocate of vegetarian diets and of living without caffeine, alcohol, or sex. He was an early advocate of peanut butter, patenting one of the first devices for making it. But he is best remembered for his work with his brother Will Keith Kellogg. Together, in 1897, they founded the Sanitas Food Company to manufacture whole grain cereals.

At the start of the 20th century, breakfast was typically a large, high-fat meal of eggs and meat for the wealthy and a less nutritious meal of porridge or gruel for the poor. The Kellogg brothers introduced toasted corn flakes as a healthy and affordable alternative. But in 1906, they argued when Will wanted to add sugar to the recipe—an idea that horrified John Harvey. Will founded the Battle Creek Toasted Corn Flake Company, which eventually became the Kellogg Company, using its founder's "W. K. Kellogg" signature as a logo—a marketing concept that survives in the script "Kellogg's" on their boxes to this day.

True to its roots in healthy nutrition, Kellogg's brands include Kashi® health foods, Morningstar Farms® vegetarian foods, and Nutri-Grain® cereal bars. (However, they also make Cocoa Krispies®, Froot Loops®, Cheez-Its®, and Keebler® Cookies.) In 1923, Kellogg hired the first dietitian to work in the food industry, and in the 1930s, Kellogg was the first company to print nutrition information on their boxes. The W. K. Kellogg Institute for Food and Nutrition Research, a world-class research facility, opened in 1997. The company continues to advocate for healthy nutrition, offering advice and education on their website and partnering with organizations such as the American Heart Association.

R egression may be the most widely used Statistics method. It is used every day throughout the world to help make good business decisions. The applications of linear regression are limitless. It can be used to predict customer loyalty, staffing needs at hospitals, sales of automobiles, and almost anything that can be quantified. Because regression is so widely used, it's also widely abused and misinterpreted. This chapter presents examples of regressions in which things are not quite as simple as they may seem at first and shows how you can still use regression to discover what the data have to say.

The residuals from the fitting of a linear regression hold a remarkable amount of information about the model. Remember that a residual is the difference between the actual data and the value we predict for it: $e = y - \hat{y}$. Residuals can help tell you how well the model is performing and provide clues for fixing it if it's not working as well as it could. In this chapter, we'll show a variety of ways in which detecting patterns in the residuals can help you improve the model. Examining residuals can reveal more about the data than was apparent at first, or even second, glance. That's why no regression analysis is ever complete without a display of the residuals and a thorough examination of what they have to say.

16.1 Examining Residuals for Groups

WHO	Breakfast cereals
WHAT	Nutrition information
WHEN	Not stated
WHERE	U.S.

It seems that ever since the Kellogg brothers fought over sugar in breakfast cereals, it has been a concern. Using data from those nutrition labels introduced by Kellogg, we can examine the relationship between the calories in a serving and the amount of sugar (in grams). Figure 16.1 appears to satisfy the conditions for regression; the relationship is linear with no outliers.

The least squares regression model,

$$\widehat{calories} = 89.5 + 2.50 \, sugar$$

has an R^2 of 32%. Figure 16.2 shows the residuals.

Figure 16.1 *Calories* versus *Sugar* content (grams) per serving of breakfast cereal.

Figure 16.2   Residuals for the regression plotted against predicted *Calories*.

At first glance, Figure 16.2 seems to have no particular structure, and as you may remember from Chapter 4, that's exactly what we hope to see. But let's check a histogram of the residuals.

Figure 16.3 The distribution of the regression residuals shows modes above and below the central large mode. These may be worth a second look.

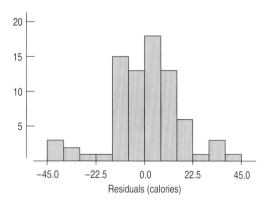

How would you describe the shape of this histogram? It looks like there might be small modes on either side of the central body of the data. A few cereals stand out with larger negative residuals—that is, fewer calories than we might have predicted. And a few stand out with larger positive residuals. Of course, the sample size here is not very large. We can't say for sure that there are three modes, but it's worth a closer look.

Figure 16.4 A scatterplot of the residuals vs. predicted values for the cereal regression. The green x's are cereals whose calorie content is higher than the linear model predicts. The red −'s show cereals with fewer calories than the model predicts. Is there something special about these cereals?

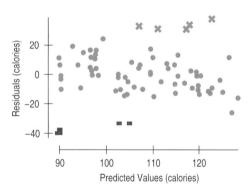

Let's look more carefully at the residuals. Figure 16.4 repeats the scatterplot of Figure 16.2, but with the points in those modes marked. Now we can see that those two groups stand away from the central pattern in the scatterplot. Doing a little more work and examining the data set, we find that the high-residual cereals (green x's) are *Just Right Fruit & Nut; Muesli Raisins, Dates & Almonds; Peaches & Pecans; Mueslix Crispy Blend;* and *Nutri-Grain Almond Raisin*. Do these cereals have something in common? These high-calorie cereals all market themselves as "healthy." This might be surprising, but in fact, "healthy" cereals often contain more fat. They often contain nuts and oil which are "natural" and don't necessarily contain sugar, but are higher in fat than grain and sugar. So, they may have more calories than we might expect from looking at their sugar content alone.

The low-residual (red − 's) cereals are *Puffed Rice*, *Puffed Wheat*, three bran cereals, and *Golden Crisps*. These cereals have fewer calories than we would expect based on their sugar content. We might not have grouped these cereals together before. What they have in common is a low calorie count *relative to their sugar content*—even though their sugar contents are quite different. (They are low calorie because of their shape and structure.)

These observations may not lead us to question the overall linear model, but they do help us understand that other factors may be part of the story. An exploration of residuals often leads us to discover more about individual cases. When we discover groups in our data, we may decide to analyze them separately, using a different model for each group.

Often, more research can help us discover why certain cases tend to behave similarly. Here, certain cereals group together in the residual plot because cereal manufacturers aim cereals at different segments of the market. A common technique used to attract different customers is to place different types of cereals on certain shelves. Cereals for kids tend to be on the "kid's shelf," at their eye level. Toddlers aren't likely to grab a box from this shelf and beg, "Mom, can we please get this *All-Bran with Extra Fiber*?"

How can we take this extra information into account in our analysis? Figure 16.5 shows a scatterplot of *Calories* and *Sugar*, colored according to the shelf on which the cereals were found, with a separate regression line fit for each shelf. Now we can see that the top shelf is unlike the bottom two shelves. We might want to report two regressions, one for the top shelf and one for the bottom two shelves.[1]

Figure 16.5 *Calories* and *Sugars* colored according to the shelf on which the cereal was found in a supermarket, with regression lines fit for each shelf individually. Do these data appear homogeneous? That is, do the cereals seem to all be from the same population of cereals? Or are there kinds of cereals that we might want to consider separately?

FOR EXAMPLE Diamond prices

The price of a jewelry diamond depends on the 4 C's: Carat weight, Cut, Clarity, and Color. Diamond colors are assigned letters from D, for colorless stones, through K, for increasingly more yellow stones. A K-color stone is only faintly yellow and still considered jewelry quality. We've collected a sample of diamond prices from a website. Here is a scatterplot of *Price* vs *Carat Weight* with points colored according to *Color*:

[1]Another alternative is to fit a multiple regression model by adding variables (called dummy or indicator variables) that distinguish the groups. This method will be discussed in Chapter 17.

QUESTION   How does the relationship of *Price* and *Carat Weight* change with *Color*?

ANSWER   For a given *Carat Weight*, diamonds with better (earlier letter) colors are generally worth more. This is not true for every diamond, but it is generally true. There may be greater variability in the middle of the color range with H-color diamonds showing more variability than either D- or K-color stones. There is greater variability for larger (heavier) diamonds.

16.2   Extrapolation and Prediction

Linear models give a predicted value for each case in the data. Put a new *x*-value into the equation, and it gives a predicted value, $\hat{y}$, to go with it. But when the new *x*-value lies far from the data we used to build the regression, how trustworthy is the prediction?

The simple answer is that the farther the new *x*-value is from $\bar{x}$, the center of the *x*-values, the less trust we should place in the predicted value. Once we venture into new *x* territory, such a prediction is called an **extrapolation**. Extrapolations are dangerous because they require the additional—and questionable—assumption that nothing about the relationship between *x* and *y* changes, even at extreme values of *x* and beyond. Extrapolations can get us into deep trouble, especially if we try to predict far into the future.

As a cautionary example, let's examine oil prices from 1972 to 1981.[2] In the mid 1970s, in the midst of an energy crisis, oil prices surged, and long lines at gas stations were common. In 1970, the price of oil was about $3 a barrel. A few years later, it had surged to $15. In 1975, a survey of 15 top econometric forecasting models (built by groups that included Nobel prize-winning economists) found predictions for 1985 oil prices that ranged from $50 to $200 a barrel—which would be $181 to $726(!) dollars a barrel in 2005 dollars. (We shall use constant 2005 dollars from now on, to factor out inflation.) How close were these forecasts? Let's look at Figure 16.6.

> **When the Data Are Years**
>
> We usually don't enter them as four-digit numbers. Here, we used 0 for 1970, 10 for 1980, and so on. It's common to assign 0 to the date of the first observation in our data set if we are working with a time series. Another option is to enter two digits for the year, using 88 for 1988, for instance. Rescaling years like this often makes calculations easier and equations simpler. But be careful; if 1988 is 88, then 2004 is 104 (not 4).

Figure 16.6   The price of oil per barrel in constant (2005) dollars from 1971 to 1982 shows a linear trend increasing at about $7 a year.

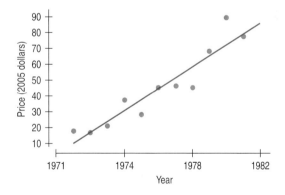

The regression model for the *Price* of oil against *Time* (Years since 1970) for these data is

$$\widehat{Price} = -0.85 + 7.39\ Time,$$

which says that prices increased, on average, $7.39 per year, or nearly $75 in 10 years. If they continued to increase linearly, it would have been easy to predict oil prices. And indeed, many forecasters made that assumption. How well did they do? Well,

---

[2]We will discuss special models for fitting data when *x* is time in Chapter 19, but simple regression models are often used. Even when using more sophisticated methods, the dangers of extrapolation don't disappear.

in the period from 1982 to 1998, oil prices didn't exactly continue that steady increase. In fact, they went down so much that by 1998, prices (adjusted for inflation) were the lowest they'd been since before World War II (Figure 16.7).

Figure 16.7   Time series plot of price of oil in constant (2005) dollars shows a fairly constant decrease over time.

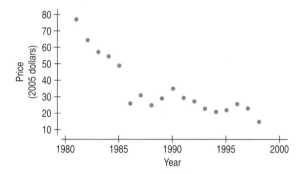

For example, the average price of oil in 1985 turned out to be less than $30 per barrel—not quite the $100 predicted by the model. Extrapolating out beyond the original data by just four years produced some vastly inaccurate forecasts. While the time series plot in Figure 16.7 shows a fairly steady decline, this pattern clearly didn't continue (or oil would be free by now).

In the 1990s, the U.S. government decided to include scenarios in their forecasts. The result was that the Energy Information Administration (EIA) offered *two* 20-year forecasts for oil prices after 1998 in their Annual Energy Outlook (AEO). Both of these scenarios, however, called for relatively modest increases in oil prices (Figure 16.8).

Figure 16.8   This graph, adapted from one by the Energy Information Administration, shows oil prices from 1970 to 1998 with two sets of forecasts for the period 1999 to 2020.

So, how accurate have these forecasts been? Let's compare these predictions to the actual prices in constant (2005) dollars (Figure 16.9).

Figure 16.9   Here are the same EIA forecasts as in Figure 16.8, together with the actual prices from 1981 to 2012. Neither forecast predicted the sharp run-up in the first decade of the 21st century.

The experts seem to have missed the sharp run-up in oil prices in the first decade of the 21st century. Where do you think oil prices will go in the *next* decade? Your guess may be as good as anyone's. Clearly, these forecasts did not take into account many of the unforeseen global and economic events that occurred since 2000. Providing accurate long-term forecasts is extremely difficult.

Extrapolation far from the data is dangerous. Linear models are based on the *x*-values of the data at hand and cannot be trusted beyond that span. Some phenomena do exhibit a kind of structural regularity or inertia that allows us to guess that the currently observed systematic behavior will continue outside this range. When *x* is time, you should be especially wary. Such regularity can't be counted on in phenomena such as stock prices, sales figures, hurricane tracks, or public opinion.

Extrapolating from current trends is a mistake made not only by regression beginners or the naïve. Professional forecasters are prone to the same mistakes, and sometimes the errors are striking. However, because the temptation to predict the future is so strong, our more realistic advice is this:

If you extrapolate far into the future, be prepared for the actual values to be (possibly quite) different from your predictions.

"Prediction is difficult, especially about the future."

—Niels Bohr,
Danish Physicist

Foxtrot © 2002 Bill Amend/Distributed by Universal Uclick. Reprinted with permission. All rights reserved.

FOR EXAMPLE A big diamond

The Cullinan I diamond (the "Star of Africa") owned by the Queen of England is, at 530.20 carats, the largest D-color cut diamond in the world. It is mounted at the head of the scepter with the cross in the British crown jewels.

It has an estimated value of about $400 million. When we restrict our analysis of the diamonds we saw on page 516 to D-color diamonds, the regression model of *Price* on *Carat Weight* is

$$\widehat{Price} = -2129.14 + 8081.12 CaratWt$$

QUESTION What does this model predict for the *Price* of the Cullinan I diamond? Is the estimate of $400 million consistent with this model? Do you think this model should be relied on to establish prices for large diamonds?

ANSWER The predicted price from the model is $4,282,482. That's only about 1/100th the price placed on the diamond itself. The rarity of such large diamonds is likely to make them far more valuable than a model based on much smaller stones could predict. Extrapolation that far from the data on which a model is based is not likely to work well.

16.3   Unusual and Extraordinary Observations

Your credit card company makes money each time you use your card. To encourage you to use your card, the card issuer may offer you an incentive such as airline miles, rebates, or gifts.[3] Of course, this is profitable to the company only if the increased use brings in enough revenue to offset the cost of the incentives. New ideas for offers (referred to as "creatives") are typically tested on a sample of cardholders before they are rolled out to the entire segment or population, a process referred to as a "campaign." Typically, the new offer (the "challenger") is tested against a control group who may be offered nothing or the current best offer ("the champion").

One campaign offered one of the highest-performing market segments an incentive for three months: one redeemable anytime air mile for each dollar spent. After this challenger showed a significant increase in spending compared to the control group during the test period, it was adopted. Analysts hoped that the increase in spending they saw during the test period would continue, but they feared that some cardholders would only change their spending temporarily, with a resulting drop in spending afterward.

However, they were surprised to see that the increase in spending continued well beyond the test period. To investigate, they made a scatterplot like the one shown in Figure 16.10.

Figure 16.10   Spending after the test plotted against spending during the test period reveals a surprising value and a positive regression slope.

The outlying point, at the top of the graph, represents a cardholder who charged nearly $3 million in the month after the test period ended. Remarkably, the point was verified to be a real purchase! Nevertheless, this cardholder is clearly not typical of the rest of credit card users. To determine whether the spending increase persisted, we need to examine the plot without the outlying point (Figure 16.11).

Figure 16.11   A plot of current spending against the spending during the campaign period, with the outlier set aside. Now the slope is negative, and significantly so.

---

[3]There are websites dedicated to finding credit card "deals." Search "credit card rewards."

"Give me a place to stand and I will move the Earth."

—ARCHIMEDES (287–211 BCE)

> **Influence and Leverage**
>
> Influence depends on both the leverage and the residual; a case with high leverage whose y-value sits right on the line fit to the rest of the data is not influential. A case with low leverage but a very large residual can be influential. The only way to be sure is to fit the regression with and without the potential influential point.

"For whoever knows the ways of Nature will more easily notice her deviations; and, on the other hand, whoever knows her deviations will more accurately describe her ways."

—FRANCIS BACON (1561–1626)

Figure 16.12   Bozo the clown's extraordinarily large shoes give his data point high-leverage in the regression of: $\hat{IQ} = 93.3 + 2.08$ *Shoe Size*, even though the R^2 is 25%. Wherever Bozo's IQ happens to be, the regression line will follow.

The plot does show that those with the largest charges during the test period actually spent less in the following month. Just one outlier was capable of changing the slope's direction from strongly negative to strongly positive.

Outliers, Leverage, and Influence

By providing a simple description of how data behave, models help us see when and how data values are unusual. In regression, a point can stand out in two ways. A case can have a large residual, as our $3 million spender certainly did. Points with y-values that are far from the regression model are called **outliers**. Because they are not like the other cases, they deserve special attention.

A data point can also be unusual if its x-value is far from the mean of the x-values. Such a point is said to have high **leverage**. The physical image of a lever is exactly right. The least squares line must pass through $(\bar{x}, \bar{y})$, so you can picture that point as the fulcrum of the lever. Just as sitting farther from the center of a seesaw gives you more leverage, points with values far from $\bar{x}$ pull more strongly on the regression line.

A point with high leverage has the potential to change the regression line but it doesn't always use that potential. If the point is consistent with the trend of the other points, it doesn't change our estimate of the line. By sitting so far from $\bar{x}$ though, it may appear to strengthen the relationship, inflating the correlation and R^2.

How can you tell if a high-leverage point changes the model? Just fit the linear model twice, both with and without the point in question. We say that a point is **influential** if omitting it from the analysis gives a very different model (as the high spender did for the credit card spending in Figure 16.10).[4]

Unusual points in a regression often tell us more about the data and the model than any other cases. Whenever you have—or suspect that you have—influential points, you should fit the linear model to the other cases alone and then compare the two regression models to understand how they differ. A model dominated by a single point is unlikely to be useful for understanding the rest of the cases or for predicting a value for a specified x. The best way to understand unusual points is against the background of the model established by the other data values. Although it is wise to compare a model fit with and without a possibly influential point, that doesn't mean you can just choose the model with the higher R^2. Don't give in to the temptation to delete points simply because they don't fit the line. That can give a false picture of how well the model fits the data. But often the best way to treat interesting cases and subgroups is to note that they are influential and to find out what makes them special.

Not all points with large influence have large residuals. Sometimes, their influence pulls the regression line so close that it makes the residual deceptively small. Influential points like that can have a shocking effect on the regression. Figure 16.12 shows IQ plotted against shoe size from a fanciful study of intelligence and foot size. The outlier is Bozo the clown, known for his large feet and hailed as a comic genius.

Although this is a silly example, it illustrates an important and common potential problem. Almost all of the variance accounted for ($R^2 = 25\%$) is due to *one* point, namely, Bozo. Without Bozo, there is little correlation between shoe size and IQ. If we run the regression after omitting Bozo, we get an R^2 of only 0.7%—a weak linear relationship (as one might expect). One single point exhibits a great influence on the regression analysis.

---

[4]Some textbooks use the term *influential point* for any observation that influences the slope, intercept, or R^2. We'll reserve the term for points that influence the slope.

JUST CHECKING

Each of these scatterplots shows an unusual point. For each, tell whether the point is a high-leverage point, would have a large residual, and/or is influential.

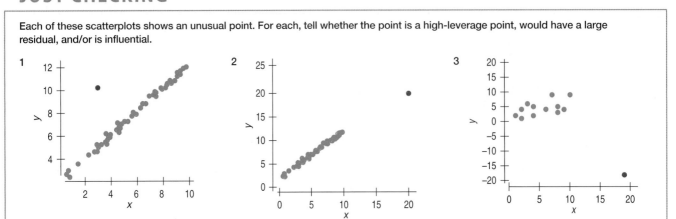

What should you do with a high-leverage point? Sometimes these values are important (they may be customers with extremely high incomes or employees with unusually long service to the company), and they may say more about the relationship between *y* and *x* than any of the other data values. However, at other times, high-leverage points are values that really don't belong with the rest of the data. Such points should probably be omitted, and a linear model found without them for comparison. When in doubt, it's usually best to fit regressions both with and without the points and compare the two models.

- **Warning:** Influential points can hide in plots of residuals. Points with high-leverage pull the line close to them, so they often have small residuals. You'll see influential points more easily in scatterplots of the original data, and you'll see their effects by finding a regression model with and without the points.

FOR EXAMPLE   Colored diamonds

Some true diamonds are colored from inclusions or structural differences. Can the prices of these diamonds be predicted with the models we make for traditional clear diamonds?

One online site lists a black diamond that weighs 2.94 carats for $3050. Black diamonds are true diamonds but may have formed from impacts of comets, asteroids, or meteors rather than from geological pressures deep underground. They are probably best compared to the most-colored K-quality diamonds. Here is a scatterplot of *Price* vs *Carat Weight* for K-color diamonds. The black diamond (shown with a red **X**) has both high leverage and a large residual.

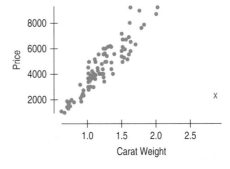

The same site lists a blue diamond that weighs 0.82 carats for $16,500. Blue diamonds are a luxury item, best compared to the best D-color clear diamonds. Here is a scatterplot of *Price* vs *Carat Weight* for D-color diamonds with the blue diamond shown as a red **X**.

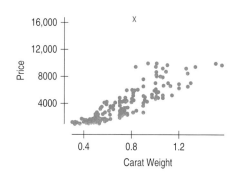

QUESTION   What would be the effect of including these exotic diamonds on regression lines fit to each of these scatterplots?

ANSWER   The black diamond has high leverage because it is heavier than any of the other diamonds considered. It also has a large negative residual because it is much less expensive than a regression for K-color diamonds would predict. As a result, it will pull the regression line down, making the slope smaller.

The blue diamond has a large positive residual because it is much more expensive even than the regression on perfect D-color diamonds would predict. However, because its carat weight is in the middle of the range of weights considered for the regression, it has little leverage. Including this case will increase the intercept slightly, but won't change the slope very much.

16.4   Working with Summary Values

Scatterplots of statistics summarized over groups tend to show less variability than we would see if we measured the same variables on individuals. This is because the summary statistics themselves vary less than the data on the individuals.

Wind power is getting increasing attention as an alternative, carbon-free method of generating electricity. Of course, there must be enough wind to make it cost-effective. In a study to find a site for a wind generator, wind speeds were collected four times a day (at 6:00 A.M., noon, 6:00 P.M., and midnight) for a year at several possible sites. Figure 16.13 plots the wind speeds for two of these sites. The correlation is 0.736.

What would happen to the correlation if we used only one measurement per day? If, instead of plotting four data points for each day, we record an average speed for each day, the resulting scatterplot shows less variation, as Figure 16.14 shows. The correlation for these values increases to 0.844.

Let's average over an even longer time period. Figure 16.15 shows *monthly* averages for the year (plotted on the same scale). Now the correlation is 0.942.

What these scatterplots show is that summary statistics exhibit less scatter than the data on individuals on which they're based and can give us a false impression of how well a line summarizes the data. There's no simple correction for this phenomenon. If we're given summary data, we usually can't get the original values back. You should be a bit suspicious of conclusions based on regressions of summary data. They may look better than they really are.

Another way to reduce the number of points in a data set is to select or sample points rather than average them. This can be especially important with data, such as the wind speeds, that are measured over time. For example, if instead of finding the *mean* for each day, we select just one of the four daily measurements—say the one made at noon on each day. We would have just as many points as in Figure 16.14, but the correlation is 0.730—essentially the same as for the full data. Figure 16.16 shows the relationship.

Figure 16.13   The wind speed at sites 2 and 4 are correlated.

Figure 16.14   Daily average wind speeds show less variation.

Figure 16.15   Monthly averages are even less variable.

Figure 16.16   Selecting only the noon measurements doesn't reduce the variation. Compare this scatterplot to Figures 16.13 and 16.14.

16.5   Autocorrelation

Time series data that are collected at regular time points often have the property that points near each other in time will be related. When values at time t are correlated with values at time t-1 we say the values are **autocorrelated** in the first order. If values are correlated with values two time periods back, we say second-order autocorrelation is present, and so on.

A regression model applied to autocorrelated data will have errors that are not independent, and that violates an assumption for regression. The statistical tests and confidence intervals for the slope depend on independence, and its violation can render these tests and intervals invalid. Fortunately, there is a statistic, called the Durbin-Watson statistic, that can detect first-order autocorrelation from the residuals of a regression analysis.

The Brief Case of Chapter 15 provided data on *Price* and *Sales* volume of frozen pizza for several cities for one week each month. We actually have the data for *every* week in the same three-year period. Here is the regression of *Sales* volume on *Price* for Dallas.

> **Why Is Autocorrelation a Problem?**
>
> When data are highly correlated over time, each data point is similar to those arround it. So each data point provides less additional information than if the points had been independent. All regression inference is based on independent errors so we need to check for autocorrelation.

	Coeff	SE(Coeff)	t-value	P-value
Intercept	139547	11302	12.347	<0.0001
Price	−33527	4308	−7.783	<0.0001

A plot of the residuals against predicted values shows nothing particularly unusual. But because these data points are consecutive weekly data, we should investigate the residuals *vs.* time. In Figure 16.18 (on the next page) we've plotted the *Residuals* against *Week*, consecutively from week 1 to week 156.

It may not be obvious that there's a pattern here. Autocorrelation can be difficult to see in residuals. It does seem, however, that there is a tendency in Figure 16.18 for the residuals to be related to nearby points. Notice the overall positive trend. We shouldn't see such a trend in residuals that are independent of each other.

The **Durbin-Watson statistic e**stimates the autocorrelation by summing squares of consecutive differences and comparing the sum with its expected value under the null hypothesis of no autocorrelation. The Durbin-Watson statistic is computed as follows:

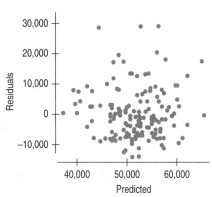

Figure 16.17   A scatterplot of the residuals vs. predicted values for the 156 weeks of pizza sales data reveals no obvious patterns.

$$D = \frac{\sum_{t=2}^{n} (e_t - e_{t-1})^2}{\sum_{t=1}^{n} e_t^2}$$

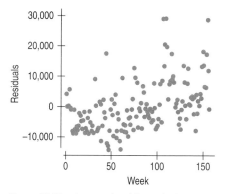

Figure 16.18 A scatterplot of the residuals against weeks for the 156 weeks of pizza sales data seems to show some trend.

Why 0 and 4?

Notice that if the adjacent residuals are equal (perfectly correlated), then the numerator and the value of D equals 0. If, on the other hand, the residuals are equal but have opposite signs (perfectly negatively correlated), then each difference is twice the residual. Then after squaring, the numerator will be 2^2, or four times the denominator.

---

where e_t is the residual at time t. The statistic always falls in the interval from 0 to 4. When the null hypothesis of no autocorrelation is true, the value of D should be 2. Values of D below 2 are evidence of positive autocorrelation, while values of D above 2 indicate possible negative autocorrelation. Positive autocorrelation is more common than negative autocorrelation. How far below or above 2 does D need to be to show "strong" or significant autocorrelation? It may be surprising, but the answer to this question depends only on the sample size, n, and the number of predictors in the regression model, k, which for simple regression is equal to 1.

A standard Durbin-Watson table (see Table D in Appendix B) shows the sample size down the left-hand column, so that each row corresponds to a different sample size n, with the number of predictors k across the top. For each k there are two columns: d_L and d_U. (The significance level of the table is also shown at the top of the page.) The test has several possible outcomes:

If $D < d_L$ (lower critical value), then there is evidence of positive autocorrelation.

If $d_L < D < d_U$, then the test is inconclusive.

If $D > d_U$ (upper critical value), then there is no evidence of positive autocorrelation.

To test negative autocorrelation, we use the same values of d_L and d_U, but we subtract them from 4:

If $D > 4 - d_L$ (lower critical value), then there is evidence of negative autocorrelation.

If $4 - d_L < D < 4 - d_U$, then the test is inconclusive.

If $D < 4 - d_U$ (upper critical value), then there is no evidence of negative autocorrelation.

We usually rely on technology to compute the statistic. For the pizza example, we have $n = 156$ weeks and one predictor (*Price*), so $k = 1$. The value of D is $D = 0.8812$. Using the table in Appendix B, we find the largest value of n listed is $n = 100$, and at $\alpha = 0.05$, $d_L = 1.65$. Because our value is less than that, we conclude that there is evidence of positive autocorrelation. (A software package would find the P-value to be <0.0001.) We conclude that the residuals are *not* independent but that residuals from one week have a positive correlation with the residuals from the preceding week. The standard errors and test for the slope are not valid since we don't have independence.

FOR EXAMPLE Gemstone imports

The U.S. Geological Survey reports facts about a range of mineral and material commodities (minerals.usgs.gov/ds/2005/140/) including gemstones. From their report, we find that imports of gemstones increased between 1990 and 2011:

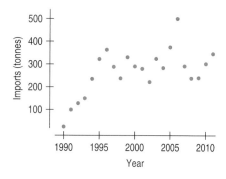

(continued)

A regression gives the following:

```
Dependent variable is:  Imports
R squared = 36.0%  R squared (adjusted)  =  32.8%
s = 83.78 with 22 − 2 = 20 degrees of freedom
```

Variable	Coefficient	SE(Coeff)	t-ratio	P-value
Intercept	−18615.6	5632	−3.31	0.0035
Year	9.43924	2.815	3.35	0.0032

The Durbin-Watson statistic is $D = 0.92$.

QUESTION   Why should we check the Durbin-Watson statistic for this analysis? What does the statistic say about these data?

ANSWER   The data are a time series. For time series there is always a possibility of autocorrelation, which we test for with the Durbin-Watson statistic. A value of 0.92 for a regression with $n = 22$ and one predictor is below the lower limit (d_L) for significance, which we can find from Table D in Appendix B to be 1.24. So we conclude that there is evidence of a positive autocorrelation in these data. We should not rely on the standard errors calculated for this regression.

Time series methods (see Chapter 19) attempt to deal with the problem of autocorrelation by modeling the errors. Another solution is to find a predictor variable that accounts for some of the autocorrelation and removes the dependence in the residuals (see Chapter 18). A simple solution that often works is to sample from the time series so that the values are more distant in time and thus less likely to be correlated. If we take every fourth week of data (as we did in Chapter 15), starting at week 4, from the Dallas pizza data, our regression becomes:

	Coeff	SE(Coeff)	t-ratio	P-value
Intercept	148350	22266	6.663	<0.0001
Price	−36762	8583	−4.283	0.000126

Now, $D = 1.617$. With $n = 39$, the upper critical value d_U is 1.54. Since our new value of D is larger than that, we see no evidence of autocorrelation. Output from technology shows the P-value:

```
Durbin-Watson test
D = 1.6165, P = 0.098740
```

We should feel more comfortable basing our confidence and prediction intervals on this model.

16.6   Transforming (Re-expressing) Data

Linearity

Increasing gas prices and concern for the environment have led to increased attention to automobile fuel efficiency. The most important factor in fuel efficiency is the weight of the car.

The relationship is strong ($R^2 = 81.6\%$), clearly negative, and apparently linear. The regression equation

$$\widehat{Fuel\ Efficiency} = 48.7 - 8.4\ Weight$$

says that fuel efficiency drops by 8.4 mpg per 1000 pounds, starting from a value of 48.7 mpg. We check the **Linearity Condition** by plotting the residuals versus either the x variable or the predicted values.

The scatterplot of the residuals against *Weight* (Figure 16.20) holds a surprise. Residual plots should have no pattern, but this one has a bend. Look at Figure 16.19. The scatter of points isn't really straight. There's a slight bend to the plot, but the bend is much easier to see in the residuals.

Figure 16.19 *Fuel Efficiency* (mpg) *vs. Weight* (thousands of pounds) shows a strong, apparently linear, negative trend.

Figure 16.20 Plotting residuals against weight reveals a bend. The bend can be seen if you look carefully at the original scatterplot, but here it's easier to see.

When the relationship isn't straight, we shouldn't fit a regression or summarize the strength of the association with correlation. But often we can make the relationship straighter. All we have to do is **re-express (or transform)** one or both of the variables with a simple function. In this case, there's a natural function. In the U.S., automobile fuel efficiency is measured in miles per gallon. But throughout the rest of the world, things are different. Not only do other countries use metric measures, and thus kilometers and liters, but they measure fuel efficiency in liters per 100 kilometers. That's the *reciprocal* of miles per gallon (times a scale constant). That is, the gas amount (gallons or liters) is in the numerator, and the distance (miles or kilometers) is now in the denominator.

There's no reason to prefer one form or the other, so let's try the (negative) reciprocal form. The residuals look better as well. (See Figures 16.21 and 16.22.)

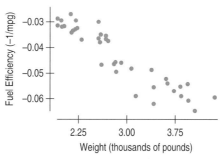

Figure 16.21 The reciprocal of *Fuel Efficiency vs. Weight* is straighter.

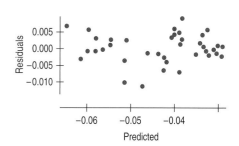

Figure 16.22 Residuals from the regression of *Fuel Efficiency (-1/mpg)* on *Weight* show less bend.

There's a clear improvement using the reciprocal, so we should use the reciprocal as the response in our regression model.

Are we allowed to re-express fuel efficiency as its reciprocal? For these data, it seems like a good idea. After all, we chose a form of the variable used by most people in the world. The general idea of transforming data to improve and simplify its structure extends beyond straightening scatterplots. In fact, you use

WHO	77 large companies
WHAT	*Assets, Sales,* and *Market Sector*
UNITS	$1,000,000
WHEN	1986
WHY	To examine distribution of *Assets* for the top *Forbes* 500 companies

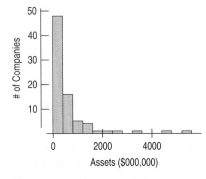

Figure 16.23   The distribution of the *Assets* of large companies is skewed to the right. Data on wealth often look like this.

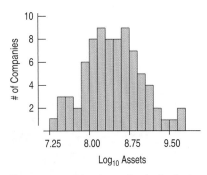

Figure 16.24   Taking logs makes the distribution more symmetric.

Figure 16.25   Assets of large companies by *Market Sector*. It's hard to compare centers or spreads, and there seem to be a number of high outliers.

re-expressions in everyday life. How fast can you go on a bicycle? If you measure your speed, you probably do it in distance per time (miles per hour or kilometers per hour). In 2005, during a 12-mile-long time trial in the Tour de France, Dave Zabriskie averaged nearly 35 mph (54.7 kph), beating Lance Armstrong by 2 seconds. You probably realize that's a tough act to follow. It's fast. You can tell that at a glance because you have no trouble thinking in terms of distance covered per time.

If you averaged 12.5 mph (20.1 kph) for a mile run, would that be fast? Would it be fast for a 100-meter dash? Even if you run the mile often, you probably have to stop and calculate. Although we measure speed of bicycles in distance per time, we don't usually measure running speed that way. Instead, we re-express it as the *reciprocal*—time per distance (minutes per mile, seconds per 100 meters, etc.). Running a mile in under 5 minutes (12 mph) is fast. A mile at 16 mph would be close to the world record (that's a 3-minute 45-second mile).

The point is that there is no single natural way to measure speed. In some cases, we use distance traveled per time, and in other cases, we use the reciprocal. It's just because we're used to thinking that way in each case, not because one way is correct. It's important to realize that the way these quantities are measured is not sacred. It's usually just convenience or custom. When we re-express a quantity to make it satisfy certain conditions, we may either leave it in those new units when we explain the analysis to others or convert it back to the original units.

Goals of Re-expression

We re-express data for several reasons. Each of these goals helps make the data more suitable for analysis by our methods. We'll illustrate each goal by looking at data about large companies.

Goal 1   *Make the distribution of a variable (as seen in its histogram, for example) more symmetric.* It's easier to summarize the center of a symmetric distribution, and for nearly symmetric distributions, we can use the mean and standard deviation. If the distribution is unimodal, then the resulting distribution may be closer to the Normal model, allowing us to use the 68–95–99.7 Rule.

Figure 16.23 shows the *Assets* of 77 large companies as reported by *Forbes*.

The skewed distribution is made much more symmetric by taking logs (see Figure 16.24).

Goal 2   *Make the spread of several groups (as seen in side-by-side boxplots) more alike,* even if their centers differ. Groups that share a common spread are easier to compare. We'll see methods later in the book that can be applied only to groups with a common standard deviation. We saw an example of re-expression for comparing groups with boxplots in Chapter 3.

Here are the *Assets* of these companies by *Market Sector*.

Taking logs makes the individual boxplots more symmetric and gives them spreads that are more nearly equal.

Figure 16.26 After re-expressing using logs, it's much easier to compare across *Market Sectors*. The boxplots are more symmetric, most have similar spreads, and the companies that seemed to be outliers before are no longer extraordinary. Two new outliers have appeared in the finance sector. They are the only companies in that sector that are not banks.

This makes it easier to compare *Assets* across *Market Sectors*. It can also reveal problems in the data. Some companies that looked like outliers on the high end turned out to be more typical. But two companies in the Finance sector now stick out. They are not banks. Unlike the rest of the companies in that sector, they may have been placed in the wrong sector, but we couldn't see that in the original data.

Goal 3 *Make the form of a scatterplot more nearly linear:* Linear scatterplots are easier to describe. The value of re-expressing data to straighten a relationship is that we can fit a linear model once the relationship is straight.

Here are *Assets* plotted against the logarithm of *Sales*.

Figure 16.27 *Assets* vs. log *Sales* shows a positive association (bigger sales goes with bigger *Assets*) with a bent shape.

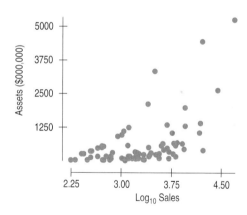

Note that the plot of *Assets* versus log *Sales* shows that the points go from tightly bunched at the left to widely scattered at the right—a "fan" shape. The plot's shape is bent. Taking logs makes the relationship much more linear (see Figure 16.28). If we re-express the company *Assets* using logarithms, we get a graph that shows a more linear association. Also note that the "fan" shape has disappeared and the variability at each value of *x* is about the same.

Figure 16.28 Log *Assets* vs. log *Sales* shows a positive linear association.

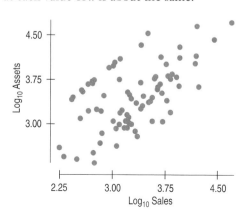

Goal 4 *Make the scatter in a scatterplot or residual plot spread out evenly rather than following a fan shape.* Having an even scatter is a condition of many methods of Statistics, as we'll see in later chapters. This goal is closely related to Goal 2, but it often comes along with Goal 3. Indeed, a glance back at the scatterplot (Figure 16.27) shows that the plot for *Assets* is much more spread out on the right than on the left, while the plot for log *Assets* (Figure 16.28) has roughly the same variation in log *Assets* for any *x*-value.

FOR EXAMPLE   Re-expressing diamond prices

When we first looked at diamond prices (on page 516), we noted that we needed to model prices for different color diamonds separately. In other examples, we restricted attention to either the D- or K-color diamonds at either end of the color spectrum. Here is a scatterplot of *Price* vs *Carat Weight* for the E- and F-color stones:

QUESTION   Which assumptions for regression are violated in this plot?

ANSWER   The relationship is not straight. It also spreads out more on the right than on the left.

16.7   The Ladder of Powers

We've seen that taking logs or reciprocals can improve an analysis of relationships. Other transformations can be helpful too, but how do we know which re-expression to use? We could use trial and error to choose a re-expression, but there's an easier way. We can choose our re-expressions from a family of simple mathematical expressions that move data toward our goals in a consistent way. This family includes the most common ways to re-express data. More important, the members of the family line up in order, so that the farther you move away from the original data (the "1" position), the greater the effect on the data. This fact lets you search systematically for a transformation that works—stepping a bit farther from "1" or taking a step back toward "1" as you see the results.

Where to start? It turns out that certain kinds of data are more likely to be helped by particular re-expressions. Knowing that gives you a good place to start your search for a mathematical expression. We call this collection of re-expressions the **Ladder of Powers.** The following table shows some of the most useful powers with each one specified as a single value.

Power	Name	Comment
2	*The square of the data values,* y^2	Try this for unimodal distributions that are skewed to the left.
1	The raw data—no change at all. This is "home base." The farther you step from here up or down the ladder, the greater the effect.	Data that can take on both positive and negative values with no bounds are less likely to benefit from re-expression.
1/2	The square root of the data values $\sqrt{y}$	Counts often benefit from a square root re-expression. For counted data, start here.
"0"	Although mathematicians define the "0-th" power differently, for us the place is held by the logarithm.	Measurements that cannot be negative, and especially values that grow by percentage increases such as salaries or populations, often benefit from a log re-expression. When in doubt, start here. If your data have zeros, try adding a small constant to all values before finding the logs.
−1/2	The (negative) reciprocal square root $-1/\sqrt{y}$	An uncommon re-expression, but sometimes useful. Changing the sign to take the *negative* of the reciprocal square root preserves the direction of relationships, which can be a bit simpler.
−1	The (negative) reciprocal, $-1/y$	Ratios of two quantities (miles per hour, for example) often benefit from a reciprocal. (you have about a 50-50 chance that the original ratio was taken in the "wrong" order for simple statistical analysis and would benefit from re-expression.) Often, the reciprocal will have simple units (hours per mile). Change the sign if you want to preserve the direction of relationships. If your data have zeros, try adding a small constant to all values before finding the reciprocal.

The Ladder of Powers orders the *effects* that the re-expressions have on data. If you try, say, taking the square roots of all the values in a variable and it helps, but not enough, then moving farther down the ladder to the logarithm or reciprocal root will have a similar effect on your data, but even stronger. If you go too far, you can always back up. But don't forget—when you take a negative power, the *direction* of the relationship will change. You can always change the sign of the response if you want to keep the same direction.

FOR EXAMPLE   Finding a re-expression for diamond prices

We have seen (on page 530) that the relationship between *Price* and *Carat Weight* is not linear and spreads out toward the right side of the plot. We can re-express *Price*, hoping to improve these problems. Here are three possible re-expressions of *Price*: square root, $\log_{10}$, and (negative) reciprocal.

(*continued*)

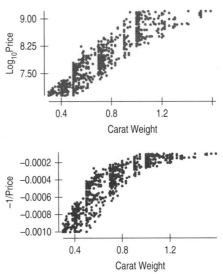

QUESTION   Which of these does the best job of making the relationship linear? Does the plot indicate that we have satisfied the regression assumptions?

ANSWER   The relationship of $\log_{10}$ *Price* to *Carat Weight* is much more linear and the spread has evened out across the plot. A regression of $\log_{10}$ *Price* on *Carat Weight* would be appropriate.

GUIDED EXAMPLE   Commercial Real Estate

What determines the value of commercial real estate? In Chapter 4 we used a simple linear relationship with an R^2 of 62.4% to see that living area was a good predictor of the value of a family home. Does the same relationship hold for commercial property? Are other factors important?

We have available data on 286 commercial properties in and around a major U.S. city.

PLAN

Plan State your objective. Identify the quantitative variables you wish to examine. Define each variable. (State the W's.)

Our objective is to investigate the association between the *Price* of a commercial property ($M) and its *Size* (square ft).

We have data for 286 commercial properties in and around a major U.S. city. We will build and diagnose a regression model.

Plot the data.

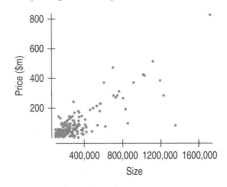

Check the conditions for regression.

✓ **Quantitative Variable Condition:** Both variables are quantitative.

✓ **Linearity Condition:** The scatterplot is straight enough.

✓ **Outlier Condition:** There are no obvious outliers.

✓ **Equal Spread Condition:** The plot fans out to the right. That makes us suspect skewness, so we'll look at a histogram:

REALITY CHECK It isn't surprising to find that *Price* is skewed to the high end. Variables like this that cannot get too small but have no real limit on the upper end are often skewed like this.

The skewness of *Price* suggests a re-expression to make the distribution more nearly symmetric and to even out the spread in the scatterplot.

DO

We will investigate re-expressions of the variables.

A histogram of $\text{Log}_{10}(\text{Price})$ is much more symmetric:

Log_{10} is easier to interpret than the natural log. The $\log_{10}$ of 1,000,000 is 6; the $\log_{10}$ of 10,000,000 is 7. So these prices are mostly between \$1M and \$100M, with some near \$1B ($\log_{10} = 9$).

(Rather than find the log of *Price* in \$M, we used the original *Price* in \$ to aid interpretation.)

The scatterplot of $\text{Log}_{10}(\text{Price})$ vs. *Size* is not straight:

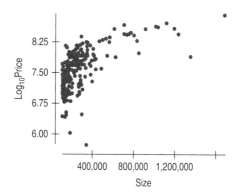

(continued)

It seems natural to try a square root re-expression for a variable like *Size* that is measured in squared units (ft^2):

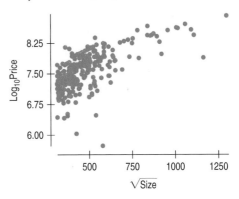

This is an improvement, but still not straight. We'll try the next two steps on the Ladder of Powers: log and $-1/\sqrt{y}$:

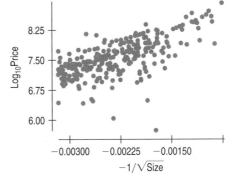

We change the sign when we take the reciprocal to preserve the direction—here a positive relationship.

The log and (negative) reciprocal root look good. We'll pick the reciprocal root but could just as well have used the log.

A regression fit to this relationship looks like this:

```
Dependent variable is: Log₁₀(Price)
R² = 45.7%    R²(adjusted) = 45.5%
s = 0.3484 with 286 − 2 = 284 df
```

Variable	Coeff	SE(Coeff)	t-ratio	P-value
Intercept	8.842	0.0857	103	<0.0001
$-1/\sqrt{\text{Size}}$	561.375	36.34	15.4	<0.0001

a) The Durbin-Watson statistic for this analysis is 0.73. Consult Table D in Appendix B and complete the test at $\alpha = 0.05$.

b) What do you conclude from this test?

SECTION 16.6

15. A scatterplot of *Salary* against *Years Experience* for some employees, and the scatterplot of residuals against predicted *Salary* from the regression line are shown in the figures. On the basis of these plots, would you recommend a re-expression of either *Salary* or *Years Experience*? Explain.

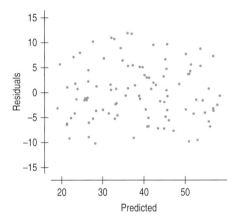

16. A study of homes looking at the relationship between *Age* of a home and *Price* produced the following scatterplot. A regression was fit to the data as shown below.

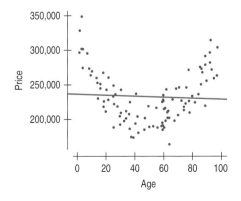

On the basis of this plot, would you advise using this regression? Explain.

17. A small company has developed an improved process for making solar panels. The company needs to set its prices and wants those prices to reflect the efficiencies of producing larger batches. The data show the following:

#Units	Cost per Unit
10	7.389
20	6.049
30	4.953
40	4.055
50	3.320
60	2.718
70	2.459
80	2.225
90	2.013
100	1.822
120	1.648
140	1.491
160	1.349
180	1.221
200	1.105

A scatterplot of *Cost per Unit* vs. *#Units* looks like this:

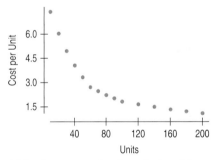

What should be done to make the relationship more nearly linear?

18. One possible model for the manufacturing process of Exercise 17 is the following:

```
Dependent variable is: Log(Cost per unit)
R squared = 90.1%  R squared (adjusted) = 89.3%
s = 0.0841 with 15 − 2 = 13 degrees of freedom

Variable    Coefficient  SE(Coeff)  t-ratio P-value
Intercept     0.7618      0.0405     18.8   <0.0001
#Units       -0.0041      0.0004    -10.9   <0.0001
```

Using this model, predict the cost per unit in a batch of 300.

SECTION 16.7

19. A quickly growing company shows the following scatterplot of customers vs. time (in months).

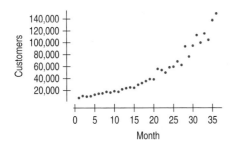

a) What re-expression might you suggest for the number of customers?

b) What power in the ladder of powers does that correspond to?

20. For the regression in Exercise 19:

A student tries taking the reciprocal of customers and produces the plot shown below:

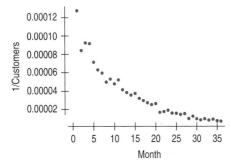

a) Would you recommend this transformation? Why or why not?

b) What would you suggest?

CHAPTER EXERCISES

T 21. Age at first marriage 2011. Weddings are one of the fastest growing businesses; about $40 billion is spent on weddings in the United States each year. But demographics may be changing, and this could affect wedding retailers' marketing plans. Is there evidence that the age at which women get married has changed over the past 100 years? The scatterplot shows the trend in age at first marriage for American women. (U.S. Census Bureau; www.census.gov)

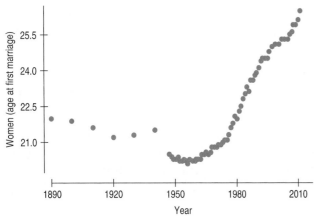

a) Do you think there is a clear pattern? Describe the trend.

b) Is the association strong?

c) Is the correlation high? Explain.

d) Do you think a linear model is appropriate for these data? Explain.

T 22. Smoking. Even with campaigns to reduce smoking, Americans still consume more than four packs of cigarettes per month per adult (libraries.ucsd.edu/ssds/pub/CTS/tobacco/sales). The Centers for Disease Control and Prevention track cigarette smoking in the United States. How has the percentage of people who smoke changed since the danger became clear during the last half of the 20th century? The scatterplot shows percentages of smokers among men 18–24 years of age, as estimated by surveys. (Centers for Disease Control and Prevention; www.cdc.gov/nchs/)

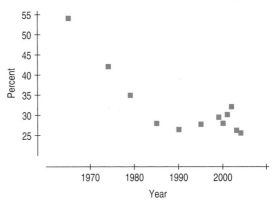

a) Do you think there is a clear pattern? Describe the trend.

b) Is the association strong?

c) Is a linear model appropriate for these data? Explain.

T 23. Human Development Index (HDI) 2012. The United Nations Development Programme (UNDP) collects data in the developing world to help countries solve global and national development challenges. In the UNDP annual Human Development Report, you can find data on over 100 variables for each of 197 countries worldwide. One summary measure used by the agency is the Human Development Index (HDI), which attempts to summarize in a single number the progress in health, education, and economics of a country. In 2012, the HDI was as high as 0.955 for Norway and as low as 0.304 for the Congo and Niger. The gross domestic product per capita (GDPPC), by contrast, is often used to summarize the *overall* economic strength of a country. Is the HDI related to the GDPPC? Here is a scatterplot of *HDI* against *GDPPC*.

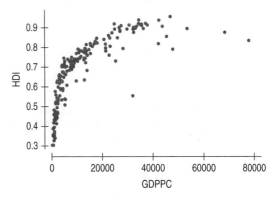

a) Explain why fitting a linear model to these data would be misleading.
b) If you fit a linear model to the data, what do you think a scatterplot of residuals versus predicted *HDI* will look like?
c) There are two outliers, Qatar and Luxembourg with very high *GDPPC*'s and Equitorial Guinea with a very low *HDI* for its GDPPC. Will setting these points aside improve the model substantially? Explain.

24. Human Development Index 2012, part 2. The United Nations Development Programme (UNDP) uses the Human Development Index (HDI) in an attempt to summarize in one number the progress in health, education, and economics of a country. The number of Internet accounts per 1000 people is positively associated with economic progress in a country. Can that be used to predict the HDI? Here is a scatterplot of *HDI* against Internet subscribers:

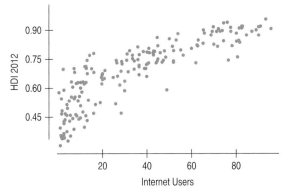

a) Explain why fitting a linear model to these data might be misleading.
b) If you fit a linear model to the data, what do you think a scatterplot of residuals versus predicted *HDI* will look like?

25. Good model? In justifying his choice of a model, a consultant says "I know this is the correct model because $R^2 = 99.4\%$."

a) Is this reasoning correct? Explain.
b) Does this model allow the consultant to make accurate predictions? Explain.

26. Bad model? An intern who has created a linear model is disappointed to find that her R^2 value is a very low 13%.

a) Does this mean that a linear model is not appropriate? Explain.
b) Does this model allow the intern to make accurate predictions? Explain.

27. Movie budgets. Here's a scatterplot of the production budgets (in millions of dollars) vs. the running time (in minutes) for a collection of major movies. Dramas are plotted in red and all other genres are plotted in blue. A separate least squares regression line has been fitted to each group. For the following questions, just examine the plot:

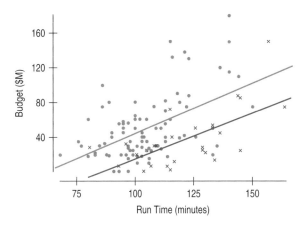

a) What are the units for the slopes of these lines?
b) In what way are dramas and other movies similar with respect to this relationship?
c) In what way are dramas different from other genres of movies with respect to this relationship?

28. Movie revenues. How does what a movie earns relate to its run time? Will audiences pay more for a longer film? Does the relationship depend on the type of film?

The scatterplot shows the relationship for the films in Exercise 27 between *U.S. Gross* earnings and *Run Time*. Dramas are plotted with purple dots, comedies with green squares, horror/thriller/action films with blue diamonds, and adventure movies with orange crosses. Regression lines have been drawn for each type of movie.

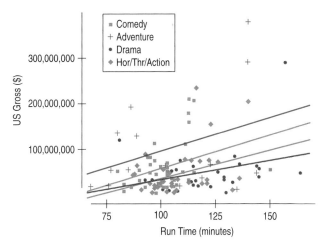

a) In what ways is the relationship between run times and U.S. Gross similar for the four kinds of films?
b) How do the gross receipts of adventure films (the red line on top) differ from those of comedies (the green line below the red)? Discuss both the slopes and the intercepts.
c) The film *Harry Potter and the Goblet of Fire* is the purple point in the upper right. If it were omitted from this analysis, how might that change your conclusions about dramas?

29. Oakland passengers. Much attention has been paid to the challenges faced by the airline industry. Patterns in customer demand are an important variable to watch. The scatterplot below, created in Excel, shows the number of passengers departing from Oakland (CA) airport month by month since the start of 1997. Time is shown as years since 1990, with fractional years used to represent each month. (Thus, June of 1997 is 7.5—halfway through the 7th year after 1990.) www.oaklandairport.com

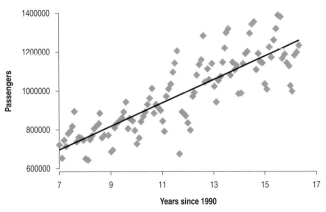

Here's a regression and the residuals, created in Excel 2013, plotted against *Years since 1990*:

SUMMARY OUTPUT
Dependent Variable is: Passengers

Regression Statistics	
R Square	0.711
Standard Error	104330
Coefficients	
Intercept	282584
Years since 1990	59704.4

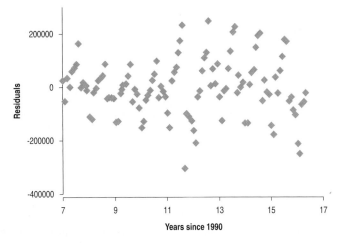

a) Interpret the slope and intercept of the regression model.
b) What does the value of R^2 say about how successful the model is?
c) Interpret s_e in this context.
d) Compute the Durbin-Watson statistic and comment.
e) Would you use this model to predict the numbers of passengers in 2010 (*YearsSince1990 = 20*)? Explain.

f) There's a point near the middle of this time span with a large negative residual. Can you explain this outlier?

30. Tracking hurricanes 2012. Like many businesses, The National Hurricane Center also participates in a program to improve the quality of data and predictions by government agencies. They report their errors in predicting the path of hurricanes. The following scatterplot shows the trend in 48-hour tracking errors since 1970. (www.nhc.noaa.gov/verification/pdfs/1970-present_OFCL_ATL_annual_trk_errors_noTDs.pdf)

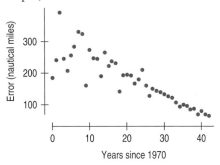

```
Dependent variable is: Error
R-squared = 75.4%  s = 39.10

Variable       Coeff
Intercept      294.138
Years-1970      -5.392
```

a) Interpret the slope and intercept of the regression model.
b) Interpret s_e in this context.
c) If the Center had a goal of achieving an average tracking error of 50 nautical miles by 2015, will they make it? Explain.
d) Use technology to compute the Durbin-Watson statistic and comment.
e) What cautions would you state about your conclusion?

31. Unusual points. Each of the four scatterplots a–d that follow shows a cluster of points and one "stray" point. For each, answer questions 1–4:
1) In what way is the point unusual? Does it have high leverage, a large residual, or both?
2) Do you think that point is an influential point?
3) If that point were removed from the data, would the correlation become stronger or weaker? Explain.
4) If that point were removed from the data, would the slope of the regression line increase, decrease, or remain the same? Explain.

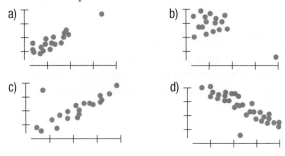

32. More unusual points. Each of the following scatterplots a–d shows a cluster of points and one "stray" point. For each, answer questions 1–4:

1) In what way is the point unusual? Does it have high leverage, a large residual, or both?
2) Do you think that point is an influential point?
3) If that point were removed from the data, would the correlation become stronger or weaker? Explain.
4) If that point were removed from the data, would the slope of the regression line increase, decrease, or remain the same? Explain.

33. The extra point. The scatterplot shows five blue data points at the left. Not surprisingly, the correlation for these points is $r = 0$. Suppose *one* additional data point is added at one of the five positions suggested below in green. Match each point (a–e) with the correct new correlation from the list given.

1) −0.90
2) −0.40
3) 0.00
4) 0.05
5) 0.75

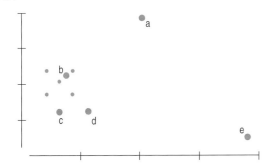

34. The extra point, part 2. The original five points in Exercise 33 produce a regression line with slope 0. Match each of the green points (a–e) with the slope of the line after that one point is added:

1) −0.45
2) −0.30
3) 0.00
4) 0.05
5) 0.85

35. What's the cause? A researcher gathering data for a pharmaceutical firm measures blood pressure and the percentage of body fat for several adult males and finds a strong positive association. Describe three different possible cause-and-effect relationships that might be present.

36. What's the effect? Published reports about violence in computer games have become a concern to developers and distributors of these games. One firm commissioned a study of violent behavior in elementary-school children. The researcher asked the children's parents how much time each child spent playing computer games and had their teachers rate each child's level of aggressiveness when playing with other children. The researcher found a moderately strong positive correlation between computer game time and aggressiveness score. But does this mean that playing computer games increases aggression in children? Describe three different possible cause-and-effect explanations for this relationship.

37. Heating cost. Small businesses must track every expense. A flower shop owner tracked her costs for heating and related it to the average daily Fahrenheit temperature, finding the model $\widehat{Cost} = 133 - 2.13\, Temp$. The residuals plot for her data is shown.

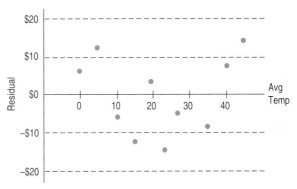

a) Interpret the slope of the line in this context.
b) Interpret the *y*-intercept of the line in this context.
c) During months when the temperature stays around freezing, would you expect cost predictions based on this model to be accurate, too low, or too high? Explain.
d) What heating cost does the model predict for a month that averages 10°?
e) During one of the months on which the model was based, the temperature did average 10°. What were the actual heating costs for that month?
f) Do you think the home owner should use this model? Explain.
g) Would this model be more successful if the temperature were expressed in degrees Celsius? Explain.

38. Fuel economy. How does the speed at which a car drives affect fuel economy? Owners of a taxi fleet, watching their bottom line sink beneath fuel costs, hired a research firm to tell them the optimal speed for their taxis to drive. Researchers drove a compact car for 200 miles at speeds ranging from 35 to 75 miles per hour. From their data, they created the model $\widehat{Fuel\ Efficiency} = 32 - 0.1\, Speed$ and created this residual plot:

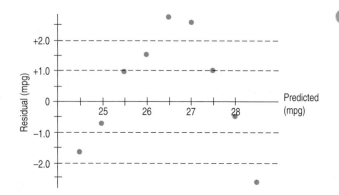

a) Interpret the slope of this line in context.
b) Explain why it's silly to attach any meaning to the *y*-intercept.
c) When this model predicts high *Fuel Efficiency*, what can you say about those predictions?
d) What *Fuel Efficiency* does the model predict when the car is driven at 50 mph?
e) What was the actual *Fuel Efficiency* when the car was driven at 45 mph?
f) Do you think there appears to be a strong association between *Speed* and *Fuel Efficiency*? Explain.
g) Do you think this is the appropriate model for that association? Explain.

T 39. Historical interest rates. Here's a plot showing the federal rate on 3-month Treasury bills from 1950 to 1980, and a regression model fit to the relationship between the *Rate* (in %) and *Years since 1950*. (www.gpoaccess.gov/eop/)

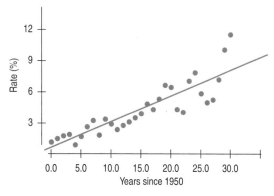

```
Dependent variable is: Rate
R-squared = 77.4%   s = 1.239

Variable          Coeff
Intercept         0.640282
Year-1950         0.247637
```

a) What is the correlation between *Rate* and *Year*?
b) Interpret the slope and intercept.
c) What does this model predict for the interest rate in the year 2000?
d) Compute the Durbin-Watson statistic and comment.
e) Would you expect this prediction to have been accurate? Explain.

T 40. Age at first marriage 2011, part 2. In Exercise 21 we looked at the age at which women married as one of the variables considered by those selling wedding services. Another variable of concern is the *difference* in age of the two partners. The graph shows the ages of both men and women at first marriage. (www.census.gov)

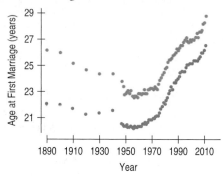

Clearly, the pattern for men is similar to the pattern for women. But are the two lines getting closer together?

Here is a timeplot showing the *difference* in average age (men's age – women's age) at first marriage, the regression analysis, and the associated residuals plot.

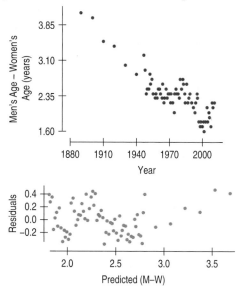

```
Dependent variable is: Age Difference
R-squared = 74.9%   s = 0.2346

Variable          Coeff
Constant          32.9679
Year              −0.01549
```

a) What is the correlation between *Age Difference* and *Year*?
b) Interpret the slope of this line.
c) Predict the average age difference in 2020.
d) Compute the Durbin-Watson statistic and comment.
e) Describe reasons why you might not place much faith in that prediction.

T 41. Modern interest rates. In Exercise 39 you investigated the federal rate on 3-month Treasury bills between 1950 and

1980. The scatterplot below shows that the trend changed dramatically after 1980, so we've built a new regression model that includes only the data since 1980 (from $x = 30$ and on in the plot below).

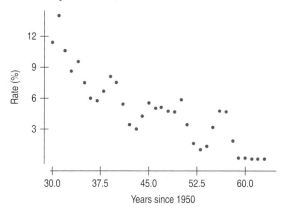

Years since 1950

```
Dependent variable is: Rate
R-squared = 78.3%  s = 1.644

Variable      Coeff
Intercept     19.2024
Year-50       -0.30871
```

a) How does this model compare to the one in Exercise 39?
b) What does this model estimate the interest rate to have been in 2000? How does this compare to the rate you predicted in Exercise 39?
c) Do you trust this newer predicted value? Explain.
d) Given these two models, what would you predict the interest rate on 3-month Treasury bills will be in 2020?

42. Age at first marriage 2011, part 3. Has the trend of decreasing difference in age at first marriage seen in Exercise 40 gotten stronger recently? Here are the scatterplot and residual plot for the data from 1975 through 2011, along with a regression for just those years.

```
Dependent variable is: Men - Women
R-squared = 51.9%  s = 0.2143
```

```
Variable      Coeff
Intercept     42.5662
Year          -0.0203
```

a) Why is R^2 higher for the first model (in Exercise 40)?
b) Is this linear model appropriate for the post-1975 data? Explain.
c) What does the slope say about marriage ages since 1975?
d) Explain why it's not safe to interpret the *y*-intercept.

43. Colorblind. Although some women are colorblind, this condition is found primarily in men. An advertisement for socks marked so they were easy for someone who was colorblind to match started out "There's a strong correlation between sex and colorblindness." Explain in statistics terms why this isn't a correct statement (whether or not it might be a good ad).

44. New homes. A real estate agent collects data to develop a model that will use the *Size* of a new home (in square feet) to predict its *Sale Price* (in thousands of dollars). Which of these is most likely to be the slope of the regression line: 0.008, 0.08, 0.8, or 8? Explain.

45. Residuals. Suppose you have fit a linear model to some data and now take a look at the residuals. For each of the following possible residuals plots, tell whether you would try a re-expression and, if so, why.

46. Residuals, part 2. Suppose you have fit a linear model to some data and now take a look at the residuals. For each of the following possible residuals plots, tell whether you would try a re-expression and, if so, why.

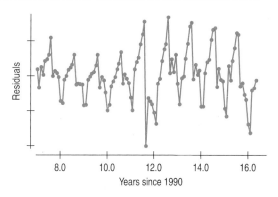

47. Oakland passengers, part 2. In Exercise 29, we created a linear model describing the trend in the number of passengers departing from Oakland (CA) airport each month since the start of 1997. Here's the residual plot, but with lines added to show the order of the values in time:

a) Can you account for the pattern shown here?
b) Would a re-expression help us deal with this pattern? Explain.

48. Home Depot sales. The home retail industry experienced relatively consistent annual growth until the economic crisis of 2006. Here is a scatterplot of the *Net Sales* ($B) of *The Home Depot* from 1995 through 2004, along with a regression and a time series plot of the residuals.

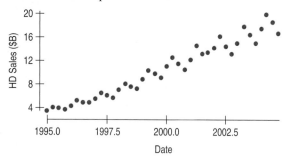

```
Dependent variable is: HDSales
R-squared = 95.5%
s = 1.044 with 40 - 2 = 38 degrees of freedom

Variable      Coeff      SE(Coeff)   t-ratio   P-value
Constant    -3234.87      114.4       -28.3    <0.0001
Date           1.62283     0.0572      28.4    <0.0001
```

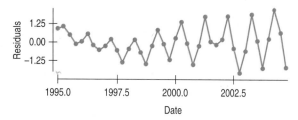

a) What does the R^2 value in the regression mean?
b) What features of the residuals should be noted with regards to this regression?
c) What features of the residuals might be dealt with by a re-expression? Which ones would not be helped by a re-expression?
d) Can you use the regression model to help in your understanding of the growth of this market?

49. Models. For each of the models listed below, predict y when $x = 2$.

a) $\hat{y} = 1.2 + 0.8x$
b) $\widehat{\ln y} = 1.2 + 0.8x$
c) $\widehat{\sqrt{y}} = 1.2 + 0.8x$
d) $\widehat{1/y} = 1.2 + 0.8x$
e) $\hat{y} = 1.2x^{0.8}$

50. More models. For each of the models listed below, predict y when $x = 2$.

a) $\hat{y} = 1.2 + 0.8 \log x$
b) $\log \hat{y} = 1.2 + 0.8x$

c) $\hat{y} = 1.2 + 0.8\sqrt{x}$
d) $\hat{y} = 1.2(0.8^x)$
e) $\hat{y} = 0.8x^2 + 1.2x + 1$

51. Models, again. Find the predicted value of y, using each model for $x = 10$.

a) $\hat{y} = 2 + 0.8 \ln x$
b) $\widehat{\log y} = 5 - 0.23x$
c) $\dfrac{1}{\sqrt{\hat{y}}} = 17.1 - 1.66x$

52. Models, last time. Find the predicted value of y, using each model when $x = 4$.

a) $\hat{y} = 10 + \sqrt{x}$
b) $\dfrac{1}{\hat{y}} = 14.5 - 3.45x$
c) $\sqrt{\hat{y}} = 3.0 + 0.5x$

53. Lobsters 2012. According to the Maine Department of Marine Resources, in 2012 more than 126,000,000 pounds of lobster were landed in Maine—a catch worth more than $338.9M. The lobster fishing industry is carefully controlled and licensed, and facts about it have been recorded for more than a century, so it is an important industry that we can examine in detail. We'll look at annual data (available at www.maine.gov/dmr) from 1950 through 2012.

The value of the annual lobster catch has grown. Here's a scatterplot of the value in millions of dollars over time:

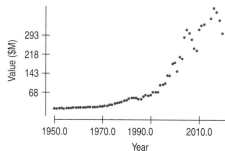

a) Which regression assumptions and conditions appear to be violated according to this plot?

Here's a scatterplot of the *log* of the value:

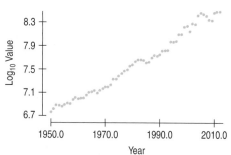

b) Discuss the same assumptions as in part a. Does taking logs make these data suitable for regression?

After performing a regression on the log values, we obtain the following plot of residuals:

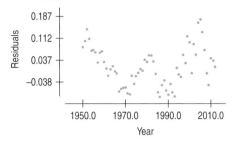

c) Discuss what this plot shows. Would a different transformation be likely to do better than the *log*? Explain.

54. Lobsters 2012, part 2. Lobster are caught in traps, which are baited and left in the open ocean. Licenses to fish for lobster are limited, there is a small additional fee for each trap in use, and there are limits on the numbers of traps that can be placed in each of seven fishing zones. But those limits have changed over time. Here's a scatterplot of the number of traps per licensed lobster fisher over time:

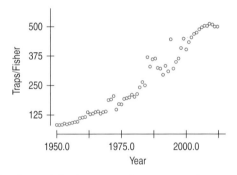

a) Does this plot satisfy the regression assumptions and conditions? Explain.

A regression of *Traps/Fisher* vs. *Year* yields the following plot of residuals:

b) What can you see in the plots of residuals that may not have been clear in the original scatterplot of the data?

55. Lobsters 2012, part 3. Here's a regression model relating the *logValue* of the annual Maine lobster catch to the number of licensed lobster *Fishers* since 1985:

```
Dependent variable is:  LogValue
R squared = 17.6%
s = 0.2752 with 28 − 2 = 26 degrees of freedom
```

Variable	Coefficient	SE(Coeff)	t-ratio	P-value
Intercept	0.94028	0.5120	13.6	<0.0001
Fishers	1.88720e-4	0.0001	2.35	0.0265

a) The number of licensed lobster fishers has fluctuated over the years between roughly 5000 and 10,000. Recently the number has been just over 7000. But licenses are in demand (and tightly restricted). What does this model predict the value of the catch would be in a year if there were 10,000 licensed fishers? (Take care to interpret the coefficient correctly and to compute the inverse of the log transformation.)
b) Interpret the slope coefficient. Do more fishers cause a higher valued harvest? Suggest alternative explanations.

56. Lobsters 2012, part 4. Of course, what matters most to the individual entrepreneur—the licensed commercial lobster fisher—is the price of lobster. Here's an analysis relating that price ($/lb) to the number of traps (millions) since 1950:

```
Dependent variable is:  Price/lb
R squared = 93.4%
s = 0.3147 with 63 − 2 = 61 degrees of freedom
```

Variable	Coefficient	SE(Coeff)	t-ratio	P-value
Intercept	−0.251127	0.0844	−2.98	0.0042
Traps(M)	1.22756	0.0417	29.4	<0.0001

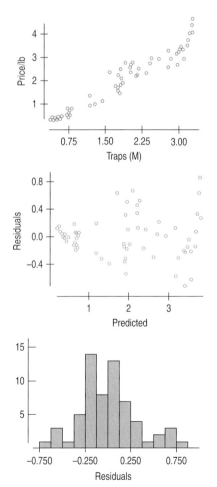

a) Are the assumptions and conditions for regression inference satisfied?
b) What does the coefficient of *Traps* mean in this model? Does it predict that licensing more traps would cause an increase in the price of lobster? Suggest some alternative explanations.

57. GDP 2013. The scatterplot shows the gross domestic product (GDP) of the United States in trillions of dollars plotted against years since 1950.

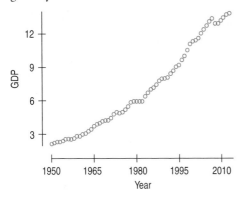

A linear model fit to the relationship looks like this:

```
Dependent variable is:  GDP($T)
R squared = 96.7%  R squared (adjusted) = 96.7%
s = 0.6874 with 64 - 2 = 62 degrees of freedom

Variable   Coefficient   SE(Coeff)   t-ratio   P-value
Intercept  -387.843       9.217       -42.1    <0.0001
Year         0.199268     0.0047       42.8    <0.0001
```

a) Does the value 96.7% suggest that this is a good model? Explain.
b) Here's a scatterplot of the residuals. Now do you think this is a good model for these data? Explain?

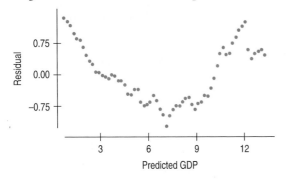

58. GDP 2013, part 2. Consider again the post-1950 trend in U.S. GDP we examined in Exercise 57. Here are a regression and residual plot when we use the log of GDP in the model. Is this a better model for GDP? Explain.

```
Dependent variable is:  Log GDP
R squared = 99.1%  R squared (adjusted) = 99.1%
s = 0.0241 with 64 - 2 = 62 degrees of freedom

Variable   Coefficient  SE(Coeff)  t-ratio   P-value
Intercept  -26.2401      0.3225     -81.4    <0.0001
Year         0.013634    0.0002      83.8    <0.0001
```

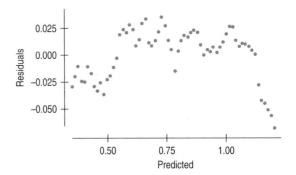

59. Logs (not logarithms). Many professions use tables to determine key quantities. The value of a log is based on the number of board feet of lumber the log may contain. (A board foot is the equivalent of a piece of wood 1 inch thick, 12 inches wide, and 1 foot long. For example, a 2″ × 4″ piece that is 12 feet long contains 8 board feet.) To estimate the amount of lumber in a log, buyers measure the diameter inside the bark at the smaller end. Then they look in a table based on the Doyle Log Scale. The table below shows the estimates for logs 16 feet long.

Diameter of Log	8″	12″	16″	20″	24″	28″
Board Feet	16	64	144	256	400	576

a) What transformation of *Board Feet* makes this relationship linear?
b) Based on a linear regression using this transformation, How much lumber would you estimate that a log 10 inches in diameter contains?
c) What does this model suggest about logs 36 inches in diameter?

T 60. Life expectancy. Life insurance rates are based on life expectancy values compiled for large demographic groups. But with improvements in medical care and nutrition, life expectancies have been changing. Here is a table from the National Vital Statistics Report that gives the Life Expectancy for white males in the United States every decade during the last century (1 = 1900 to 1910, 2 = 1911 to 1920, etc.). Consider a linear model to predict future increases in life expectancy. Would re-expressing either variable make a better model?

Decade	1	2	3	4	5	6	7	8	9	10
Life exp.	48.6	54.4	59.7	62.1	66.5	67.4	68.0	70.7	72.7	74.9

T 61. OECD GDP. The Organization for Economic Cooperation and Development (OECD) is an organization comprised of thirty countries. To belong, a country must support the principles of representative democracy and a free market economy. How have these countries grown in the decade from 1988 to 1998–2000? Here are the GDP per capita for 24 of the OECD members (in year 2000 dollars). (www.sba.gov/advo/research/rs264tot.pdf)

Country	1988 GDP/ Capita	1998–2000 GDP/ Capita
Australia	18,558	23,713
Austria	25,626	31,192
Belgium	24,204	30,506
Canada	19,349	22,605
Denmark	31,517	38,136
Finland	25,682	31,246
France	24,663	29,744
Germany	27,196	32,256
Greece	10,606	13,181
Ireland	13,050	27,282
Italy	17,339	20,710
Japan	36,301	44,154
Korea	7038	12,844
Mexico	3024	3685
Netherlands	23,159	30,720
New Zealand	15,480	17,979
Norway	28,241	37,934
Portugal	8935	12,756
Spain	12,879	17,197
Sweden	26,634	30,873
Switzerland	43,375	46,330
Turkey	2457	2947
United Kingdom	17,676	22,153
United States	25,324	31,296

Make a model of 1998–2000 GDP/Capita in terms of 1988 GDP/Capita. Plot the residuals and discuss any concerns you may have.

62. Orange production. Orange growers know that the larger an orange the higher the price it will bring. But as the number of oranges on a tree increases, the fruit tends to be smaller. Here's a table of that relationship. Create a model for this relationship, and express any concerns you may have.

Number of Oranges/Tree	Average Weight/ Fruit (lb)
50	0.60
100	0.58
150	0.56
200	0.55
250	0.53
300	0.52
350	0.50
400	0.49
450	0.48
500	0.46
600	0.44
700	0.42
800	0.40
900	0.38

63. Human Development Index 2012, part 3. In Exercise 23 we saw that the United Nations Development Programme (UNDP) uses the Human Development Index (HDI) in an attempt to summarize the progress in health, education, and economics of a country with one number. The gross domestic product per capita (GDPPC) attempts to summarize the wealth produced by a country in one number. Here is a plot of *GDPPC* against *HDI*:

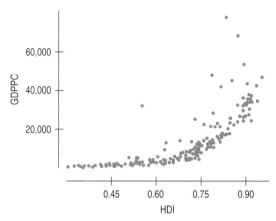

GDPPC is measured in dollars. Incomes and other economic measures tend to be highly right skewed. Taking logs often makes the distribution more unimodal and symmetric. Compare the histogram of *GDPPC* to the histogram of *log(GDPPC)*.

64. Human Development Index 2012, part 4. In Exercise 63 we examined the relationship between *log(GDPPC)* and *HDI*. The number of Internet users (per 1000 people) is also positively associated with economic progress in a country. Here's a scatterplot of *Internet users* (subscribers per 1000 people) against *HDI*:

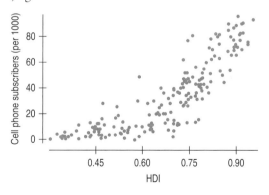

a) *Internet Users* is a count of subscribers (per 1000). What re-expression is often useful for counts? Examine the histogram of *Internet Users* and the histogram of *Internet Users* using the re-expression you suggested. Comment.
b) Use the re-expression in a) for the scatterplot against *HDI*. Comment.
c) Would you feel confident using this relationship to predict the number of *Internet Users* based on the *HDI*?

65. Lobsters 2012, part 5. How has the number of licensed lobster fishers changed? Here's a plot of the number of *Fishers vs. Year*:

This plot isn't straight. Would a transformation help? If so, which one? If not, why not?

66. Lobsters 2012, part 6. How has the price of a lobster changed? Here's a plot tracking the price of lobster per pound in constant year 2000 dollars.

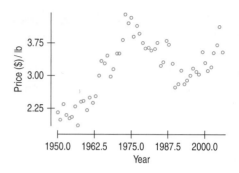

This plot is not straight. Would a transformation help? If so, which one? If not, why not?

JUST CHECKING ANSWERS

1 Not high-leverage, not influential, large residual
2 High-leverage, not influential, small residual
3 High-leverage, influential, not large residual
4 None
5 Logarithm

17

Multiple Regression

Zillow.com

Zillow.com is a real estate research site, founded in 2005 by Rich Barton and Lloyd Frink. Both are former Microsoft executives and founders of Expedia.com, the Internet-based travel agency. Zillow collects publicly available data and provides an estimate (called a Zestimate®) of a home's worth. The estimate is based on a model of the data that Zillow has been able to collect on a variety of predictor variables, including the past history of the home's sales, the location of the home, and characteristics of the house such as its size and number of bedrooms and bathrooms.

The site is enormously popular among both potential buyers and sellers of homes. According to Rismedia.com, Zillow is one of the most-visited U.S. real estate sites on the Web, with approximately 5 million unique users each month. These users include more than one-third of all mortgage professionals in the U.S.—or approximately 125,000—in any given month. Additionally, 90% of Zillow users are homeowners, and two-thirds are either buying and selling now, or plan to in the near future.

How exactly does Zillow figure the worth of a house? According to the Zillow.com site, "We compute this figure by taking zillions of data points—much of this data is public—and entering them into a formula. This formula is built using what our statisticians call 'a proprietary algorithm'—big words for 'secret formula.' When our statisticians developed the model to determine home values, they explored how homes in certain areas were similar (i.e., number of bedrooms and baths, and a myriad of other details) and then looked at the relationships between actual sale prices and those home details." These relationships form a pattern, and they use that pattern to develop a model to estimate a market value for a home. In other words, the Zillow statisticians use a model, most likely a regression model, to predict home value from the characteristics of the house. We've seen how to predict a response variable based on a single predictor. That's been useful, but the types of business decisions we'll want to make are often too complex for simple regression.[1] In this chapter, we'll expand the power of the regression model to take into account many predictor variables into what's called a multiple regression model. With our understanding of simple regression as a base, getting to multiple regression isn't a big step, but it's an important and worthwhile one. Multiple regression is probably the most powerful and widely used statistical tool today.

As anyone who's ever looked at house prices knows, house prices depend on the local market. To control for that, we will restrict our attention to a single market. We have a random sample of 1057 home sales from the public records of sales in upstate New York, in the region around the city of Saratoga Springs. The first thing often mentioned in describing a house for sale is the number of bedrooms. Let's start with just one predictor variable. Can we use *Bedrooms* to predict home *Price*?

WHO	Houses
WHAT	Sale price (dollars) and other facts about the houses
WHERE	Upstate New York near Saratoga Springs
WHY	To understand what influences housing prices and how to predict them

Figure 17.1   Side-by-side boxplots of *Price* against *Bedrooms* show that price increases, on average, with more bedrooms.

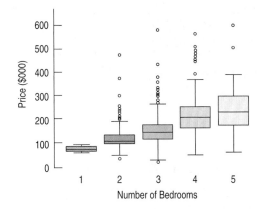

The number of *Bedrooms* is a quantitative variable, but it holds only a few values (from 1 to 5 in this data set). So a scatterplot may not be the best way to examine the relationship between *Bedrooms* and *Price*. In fact, at each value for *Bedrooms* there is a whole distribution of prices. Side-by-side boxplots of *Price* against *Bedrooms* (Figure 17.1) show a general increase in price with more bedrooms, and an approximately linear growth.

Figure 17.1 also shows a clearly increasing spread from left to right, violating the Equal Spread Condition, and that's a possible sign of trouble. For now, we'll proceed cautiously. We'll fit the regression model, but we will be cautious about using inference methods for the model. Later we'll add more variables to increase the power and usefulness of the model.

---

[1]When we need to note the difference, a regression with a single predictor is called a **simple regression**.

A linear regression model of *Price* on *Bedrooms* gives the model

$$\widehat{Price} = 14349.48 + 48218.91 \times Bedrooms.$$

The model tells us that, on average, we'd expect the price to be higher by almost $50,000 for each bedroom in the house, as we can see from the slope value of $48,218.91. But the R^2 for this regression is only 21.4%. So the regression model accounts for about 21.4% of the variation in house prices. Perhaps some of the other facts about these houses can account for portions of the remaining variation.

The standard deviation of the residuals is $s = 68,432$, which tells us that the model only does a modestly good job of accounting for the price of a home. Approximating with the 68–95–99.7 Rule, we'd guess that only about 68% of home prices predicted by this model would be within $68,432 of the actual price. That's not likely to be close enough to be useful for a home buyer.

17.1   The Multiple Regression Model

For simple regression, we wrote the predicted values in terms of one predictor variable:

$$\hat{y} = b_0 + b_1 x.$$

To include more predictors in the model, we simply write the same regression model with more predictor variables. The resulting **multiple regression** looks like this:

$$\hat{y} = b_0 + b_1 x_1 + b_2 x_2 + \cdots + b_k x_k$$

where b_0 is still the intercept and each b_k is the estimated coefficient of its corresponding predictor x_k. Although the model doesn't look much more complicated than a simple regression, it isn't practical to determine a multiple regression by hand. This is a job for a statistics program on a computer. Remember that for simple regression, we found the coefficients for the model using the least squares solution, the one whose coefficients made the sum of the squared residuals as small as possible. For multiple regression, a statistics package does the same thing and can find the coefficients of the least squares model easily.

If you know how to find the regression of *Price* on *Bedrooms* using a statistics package, you can probably just add another variable to the list of predictors in your program to compute a multiple regression. A multiple regression of *Price* on the two variables *Bedrooms* and *Living Area* generates a multiple regression table like this one.

```
Response variable: Price
R² = 57.8%
s = 50142.4 with 1057 − 3 = 1054 degrees of freedom
Variable       Coeff       SE(Coeff)   t-ratio   P-value
Intercept      20986.09    6816.3       3.08      0.0021
Bedrooms       −7483.10    2783.5      −2.69      0.0073
Living Area       93.84       3.11     30.18     <0.0001
```

Table 17.1 Multiple regression output for the linear model predicting *Price* from *Bedrooms* and *Living Area*.

You should recognize most of the numbers in this table, and most of them mean what you expect them to. The value of R^2 for a regression on two variables gives the fraction of the variability of *Price* accounted for by both predictor variables together. With *Bedrooms* alone predicting *Price*, the R^2 value was 21.4%, but this model accounts for 57.8% of the variability in *Price* and the standard deviation of the residuals is now $50,142.40. We shouldn't be surprised that the variability explained by the model has gone up. It was for this reason—the hope of accounting for some of that leftover variability—that we introduced a second predictor. We also shouldn't be surprised that the size of the house, as measured by *Living Area*, also contributes to a good prediction of house prices. Collecting the coefficients of the multiple regression of *Price* on *Bedrooms* and *Living Area* from Table 17.1, we can write the estimated regression as:

$$\widehat{Price} = 20,986.09 - 7,483.10 Bedrooms + 93.84 Living\ Area.$$

As before, we define the residuals as:

$$e = y - \hat{y}.$$

The standard deviation of the residuals is still denoted s (or also sometimes s_e to distinguish it from the standard deviation of y). The degrees of freedom is the number of observations ($n = 1057$) minus one for each coefficient estimated:

$$df = n - k - 1,$$

where k is the number of predictor variables and n is the number of cases. For this model, subtract 3 (the two coefficients and the intercept). To find the standard deviation of the residuals, use that number of degrees of freedom in the denominator:

$$s_e = \sqrt{\frac{\sum (y - \hat{y})^2}{n - k - 1}}.$$

For each predictor, the regression output shows a coefficient, its standard error, a *t*-ratio, and the corresponding P-value. As with simple regression, the **t-ratio** measures how many standard errors the coefficient is away from 0. Using a Student's t-model, we can find its P-value and use that to test the null hypothesis that the true value of the coefficient is 0.

What's different? With so much of the multiple regression looking just like simple regression, why devote an entire chapter to the subject?

There are several answers to this question. First, and most important, is that the meaning of the coefficients in the regression model has changed in a subtle, but important, way. Because that change is not obvious, multiple regression coefficients are often misinterpreted. And that can lead to dangerously wrong decisions.

Second, multiple regression is an extraordinarily versatile model, underlying many widely used statistics methods. A sound understanding of the multiple regression model will help you to understand these other applications as well.

Third, multiple regression offers you a first glimpse into statistical models that use more than two quantitative variables. The real world is complex. Simple models are a great start, but they're not detailed enough to be useful for understanding, predicting, and making business decisions in many real-world situations. Models that use several variables can be a big step toward realistic and useful modeling of complex phenomena and relationships.

FOR EXAMPLE   The multiple regression model

A large clothing store has recently sent out a special catalog of Fall clothes, and Leiram, its marketing analyst, wants to find out which customers responded to it and which ones bought the most. She plans to conduct an RFM (Recency, Frequency, Monetary) analysis. The RFM method is based on the principle that

80% of your business comes from the best 20% of your customers, and states that the following attributes will be useful predictors of who the best customers will be:

- How *recently* the customer has purchased (Recency)
- How *frequently* the customer shops (Frequency)
- How *much* the customer spends (Monetary)

For each customer, Leiram has information for the past 5 years on: *Date of Last Purchase*, *Number of Purchases*, and *Total Amount Spent.* In addition, she has demographic information including *Age*, *Marital Status*, *Sex*, *Income*, and *Number of Children.* She chooses a random sample of 149 customers who bought something from the catalog and who have purchased at least 3 times in the past 5 years (*Number of Purchases*). She wants to model how much they bought from the new catalog (*Respond Amount*).

Leiram fits the following multiple regression model to the response variable *Respond Amount*:

```
Response Variable: Respond Amount
R² = 91.48%  Adjusted R² = 91.31%
s = 18.183 with 149 − 4 = 145 degrees of freedom
```

Variable	Coeff	SE(Coeff)	t-ratio	P-value
Intercept	111.01	6.459	17.187	<0.0001
Income	0.00091	0.00012	7.643	<0.0001
Total Amount Spent	0.154	0.00852	18.042	<0.0001
Number of Purchases	−14.81	0.716	−20.695	<0.0001

QUESTIONS How much of the variation in *Respond Amount* is explained by this model? What does the term $s = 18.183$ mean? Which variables seem important in the model?

ANSWERS This model has an R^2 of 91.48% which means that the model has explained 91.48% of the variation in *Respond Amount* using the three predictors: *Income*, *Total Amount Spent*, and *Number of Purchases*. The term $s = 18.183$ means that the standard deviation of the residuals is about $18.18. Using the 68–95–99.7 Rule we know that most prediction errors will be no larger than about $36.36. All terms seem important in this model since all three have very large *t*-ratios and correspondingly small P-values.

17.2 Interpreting Multiple Regression Coefficients

It makes sense that both the number of bedrooms and the size of the living area would influence the price of a house. We'd expect both variables to have a positive effect on price—houses with more bedrooms typically sell for more money, as do larger houses. But look at the coefficient for *Bedrooms* in the multiple regression equation. It's negative: −7483.10. How can it be that the coefficient of *Bedrooms* in the multiple regression is negative? And not just slightly negative, its *t*-ratio is large enough for us to be quite confident that the true value is really negative. Yet we saw the coefficient was clearly positive when *Bedrooms* was the sole predictor in the model (Figure 17.2).

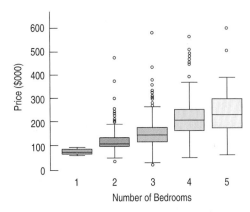

Figure 17.2 The slope of *Bedrooms* is positive. Each is worth about $48,000 in the price of a house as the simple regression model estimated.

Figure 17.3 For the 96 houses with *Living Area* between 2500 and 3000 square feet, the slope of *Price* on *Bedrooms* is negative. For each additional bedroom, restricting data to homes of this size, we would predict that the house's *Price* was about $17,800 lower.

The explanation of this apparent paradox is that in a multiple regression, coefficients have a more subtle meaning. Each coefficient takes into account the other predictor(s) in the model.

To see how variables can interact, let's look at a group of similarly sized homes and examine the relationship between *Bedrooms* and *Price* just for houses with 2500 to 3000 square feet of living area (Figure 17.3). For houses of this size, those with *fewer* bedrooms have a higher price, on average, than those with more bedrooms. This makes sense when we think about houses in terms of *both*. A 2500-square-foot house with five bedrooms would have either relatively small, cramped bedrooms or not much common living space. The same size house with only three bedrooms could have larger, more attractive bedrooms and still have adequate common living space. What the coefficient of *Bedrooms* says in the multiple regression is that, after accounting for living area, houses with more bedrooms tend to sell for a *lower* price—that the pattern for moderate-size homes is generally true across all sizes.

JUST CHECKING

Body fat percentage is an important health indicator, but it is difficult to measure accurately. One way to do so is via dual energy X-ray absorpitometry (DEXA) at a cost of several hundred dollars per image. Insurance companies want to know if body fat percentage can be estimated from easier-to-measure characteristics such as *Height* and *Weight*. A scatterplot of *Percent Body Fat* against *Height* for 250 adult men shows no pattern, and the correlation is -0.03 which is not statistically significant. A multiple regression using *Height (inches)*, *Age (years)*, and *Weight (pounds)* finds the following model:

```
              Coeff      SE(Coeff)    t-ratio    P-value
Intercept     57.27217   10.39897      5.507     <0.0001
Height        -1.27416    0.15801     -8.064     <0.0001
Weight         0.25366    0.01483     17.110     <0.0001
Age            0.13732    0.02806      4.895     <0.0001
```

s = 5.382 on 246 degrees of freedom
Multiple R-squared: 0.584,
F-statistic: 115.1 on 3 and 246 DF, P-value: <0.0001

1 Interpret the R^2 of this regression model.

2 Interpret the coefficient of *Age*.

3 How can the coefficient of *Height* have such a small P-value in the multiple regression when the correlation between *Height* and *Percent Body Fat* was not statistically distinguishable from zero?

Of course, without taking *Living Area* into account, *Price* tends to go *up* with more bedrooms. But that's because *Living Area* and *Bedrooms* are related. Multiple regression coefficients must always be interpreted in terms of the other predictors in the model. That can make their interpretation more subtle, more complex, and more challenging, but it is also what makes multiple regression so versatile and effective. The more sophisticated interpretations are more appropriate.

People often make another error when interpreting coefficients. Regression coefficients should not be interpreted causally. A regression model describes the world as measured by the data, but it can't say very much about what would happen if things were changed. For example, this analysis cannot tell a homeowner how much the price of his home will change if he combines two of his four bedrooms into a new master bedroom. And it can't be used to predict whether adding a 100-square-foot child's bedroom onto the house would increase or decrease its value. The model simply reports the relationship between the number of *Bedrooms* and *Living Area* and *Price* for existing houses. As always with regression, you should be careful not to assume causation between the predictor variables and the response.

FOR EXAMPLE Interpreting multiple regression coefficients

QUESTION In the regression model of *Respond Amount*, interpret the intercept and the regression coefficients of the three predictors.

ANSWER The model says that from a base of $111.01 of spending, customers (who have purchased at least 3 times in the last 12 months), on average, spent $0.91 for every $1000 of *Income* (after accounting for *Number of Purchases* and *Total Amount Spent*), $0.154 for every dollar they have spent in the past 5 years (after accounting for *Income* and *Number of Purchases*), but $14.81 less for every additional purchase that they've made in the last 5 years (after accounting for *Income* and *Total Amount Spent*). It is important to note especially that the coefficient in *Number of Purchases* is negative, but only after accounting for both *Income* and *Total Amount Spent*.

17.3 Assumptions and Conditions for the Multiple Regression Model

We can write the multiple regression model, numbering the predictors arbitrarily (the order doesn't matter), writing betas for the model coefficients (which we will estimate from the data), and including the errors in the model:

$$y = \beta_0 + \beta_1 x_1 + \beta_2 x_2 + \cdots + \beta_k x_k + \varepsilon.$$

The assumptions and conditions for the multiple regression model are nearly the same as for simple regression, but with more variables in the model, we'll have to make a few changes, as described in the following sections.

Linearity Assumption

We are fitting a linear model.[2] For that to be the right kind of model for this analysis, we need to verify an underlying linear relationship. But now we're thinking about

---

[2] By *linear* we mean that each *x* appears simply multiplied by its coefficient and added to the model, and that no *x* appears in an exponent or some other more complicated function. That ensures that as we move along any *x*-variable, our prediction for *y* will change at a constant rate (given by the coefficient) if nothing else changes.

several predictors. To confirm that the assumption is reasonable, we'll check the Linearity Condition for *each* of the predictors.

Linearity Condition.   Scatterplots of *y* against each of the predictors are reasonably straight. The scatterplots need not show a strong (or any) slope; just check to make sure that there isn't a bend or other nonlinearity. For the real estate data, the scatterplot is linear in both *Bedrooms* and *Living Area*.

As in simple regression, it's a good idea to check the residual plot for any violations of the linearity condition. Fit the regression and plot the residuals against the predicted values (Figure 17.4), checking to make sure there are no patterns—especially bends or other nonlinearities.

Figure 17.4   A scatterplot of residuals against the predicted values shows no obvious pattern.

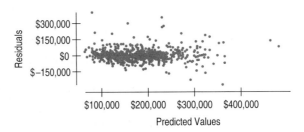

Independence Assumption

As with simple regression, the errors in the true underlying regression model must be independent of each other. As usual, there's no way to be sure that the Independence Assumption is true, but you should think about how the data were collected to see if that assumption is reasonable. You should check the randomization condition as well.

Randomization Condition.   Ideally, the data should arise from a random sample or randomized experiment. Randomization assures us that the data are representative of some identifiable population. If you can't identify the population, you can interpret the regression model as a description of the data you have, but you can't interpret the hypothesis tests at all because such tests are about a regression model for a specific population. Regression methods are often applied to data that were not collected with randomization. Regression models fit to such data may still do a good job of modeling the data at hand, but without some reason to believe that the data are representative of a particular population, you should be reluctant to believe that the model generalizes to other situations.

We also check the regression residuals for evidence of patterns, trends, or clumping, any of which would suggest a failure of independence. In the special case when one of the *x*-variables is related to time (or is itself *Time*), be sure that the residuals do not have a pattern when plotted against that variable. In addition to checking the plot of residuals against the predicted values, we recommend that you check the individual plots of the residuals against each of the explanatory, or *x*, variables in the model. These individual plots can yield important information on necessary transformations, or re-expressions, for the predictor variables.

The real estate data were sampled from a larger set of public records for sales during a limited period of time. The error the model makes in predicting one is not likely to be related to the error it makes in predicting another.

Equal Variance Assumption

The variability of the errors should be about the same for all values of *each* predictor. To see whether this assumption is valid, look at scatterplots and check the Equal Spread Condition.

Equal Spread Condition. The same scatterplot of residuals against the predicted values (Figure 17.4) is a good check of the consistency of the spread. We saw what appeared to be a violation of the equal spread condition when *Price* was plotted against *Bedrooms* (Figure 17.2). But here in the multiple regression, the problem has dissipated when we look at the residuals. Apparently, much of the tendency of houses with more bedrooms to have greater variability in prices was accounted for in the model when we included *Living Area* as a predictor.

If residual plots show no pattern, if the errors are plausibly independent, and if the plots of residuals against each *x*-variable don't show changes in variation, you can feel good about interpreting the regression model. Before testing hypotheses, however, you must check one final assumption: the normality assumption.

Normality Assumption

We assume that the errors around the idealized regression model at any specified values of the *x*-variables follow a Normal model. We need this assumption so that we can use a Student's *t*-model for inference. As with other times when we've used Student's *t*, we'll settle for the residuals satisfying the Nearly Normal Condition. As with means, the assumption is less important as the sample size grows. For large data sets, you have to be careful only of extreme skewness or large outliers. These inference methods will work well even when the residuals are moderately skewed, if the sample size is large. If the distribution of residuals is unimodal and symmetric, there is little to worry about.[3]

Nearly Normal Condition. Because there is only one set of residuals, this is the same set of conditions we had for simple regression. Look at a histogram or Normal probability plot of the residuals.

Figure 17.5 A histogram of the residuals shows a unimodal, symmetric distribution, but the tails seem a bit longer than one would expect from a Normal model. The Normal probability plot confirms that.

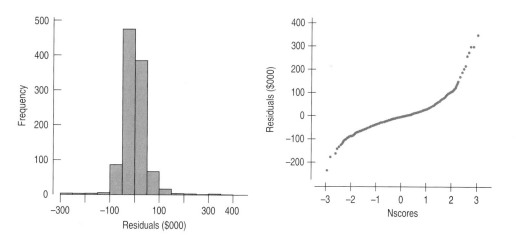

The histogram of residuals in the real estate example certainly looks unimodal and symmetric. The Normal probability plot has some bend on both sides, which indicates that the residuals in the tails straggle away from the center more than Normally distributed data would. However, as we have said before, the Normality Assumption becomes less important as the sample size grows, and here we have no skewness and more than 1000 cases. (The Central Limit Theorem helps our confidence intervals and tests based on the *t*-statistic to be valid when we have large samples.)

Let's summarize all the checks of conditions that we've made and the order in which we've made them.

---

[3]The only time we need strict adherence to the Normality Assumption of the errors is when finding prediction intervals for individuals in multiple regression. Because they are based on individual Normal probabilities and not the Central Limit Theorem, the errors must closely follow a Normal model.

1. Check the Linearity Condition with scatterplots of the *y*-variable against each *x*-variable.
2. If the scatterplots are straight enough, fit a multiple regression model to the data. (Otherwise, either stop or consider re-expressing an *x*-variable or the *y*-variable.)
3. Find the residuals and predicted values.
4. Make a scatterplot of the residuals against the predicted values (and ideally against each predictor variable separately). These plots should look patternless. Check, in particular, for any bend (which would suggest that the data weren't all that straight after all) and for any changes in variation. If there's a bend, consider re-expressing the *y* and/or the *x* variables. If the variation in the plot grows from one side to the other, consider re-expressing the *y*-variable. If you re-express a variable, start the model fitting over.
5. Think about how the data were collected. Was suitable randomization used? Are the data representative of some identifiable population? If the data are measured over time, check for evidence of patterns that might suggest they're not independent by plotting the residuals against time to look for patterns.
6. If the conditions check out this far, feel free to interpret the regression model and use it for prediction.
7. Make a histogram and Normal probability plot of the residuals to check the Nearly Normal Condition. If the sample size is large, the Normality is less important for inference, but always be on the lookout for skewness or outliers.

JUST CHECKING

> **4** Give two ways that we use histograms to support the construction, inference, and understanding of multiple regression models.
>
> **5** Give two ways that we use scatterplots to support the construction, inference, and understanding of multiple regression models.
>
> **6** What role does the Normal model play in the construction, inference, and understanding of multiple regression models?

FOR EXAMPLE Assumptions and conditions for multiple regression

Here are plots of *Respond Amount* against the three predictors, a plot of the residuals against the predicted values from the multiple regression, a histogram of the residuals, and a Normal probability plot of the residuals. Recall that the data come from a random sample of customers who both responded to the catalog and who had purchased at least 3 times in the past 5 years.

QUESTION   Do the assumptions and conditions for multiple regression appear to have been met?

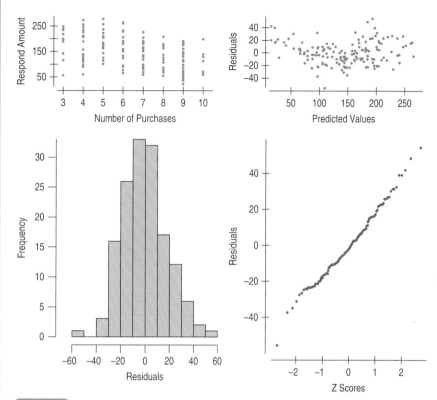

ANSWER   Because the sample is random, the randomization condition is satisfied and we assume the responses are independent. The plots of *Respond Amount* against each predictor are reasonably linear with the possible exception of *Number of Purchases*. There may also be some curvature and increasing spread in the residual plot. The histogram of residuals is unimodal and symmetric with no extreme outliers. The Normal probability plot shows that the distribution is fairly Normally distributed. The conditions are not completely satisfied and we should proceed somewhat cautiously especially with regard to *Number of Purchases*.

GUIDED EXAMPLE   Housing Prices

Zillow.com attracts millions of users each month who are interested in finding out how much their house is worth. Let's see how well a multiple regression model can do. The variables available include:

Price	The price of the house as sold in 2002
Living Area	The size of the living area of the house in square feet
Bedrooms	The number of bedrooms
Bathrooms	The number of bathrooms (a half bath is a toilet and sink only)
Age	Age of the house in years
Fireplaces	Number of fireplaces in the house

PLAN	**Setup** State the objective of the study. Identify the variables.	We want to build a model to predict house prices for a region in upstate New York. We have data on *Price* ($), *Living Area* (sq ft), *Bedrooms* (#), *Bathrooms* (#), *Fireplaces* (#), and *Age* (in years).

(continued)

Model Think about the assumptions and check the conditions.

Linearity Condition

To fit a regression model, we first require linearity. Scatterplots (or side-by-side boxplots) of *Price* against all potential predictor variables are shown.

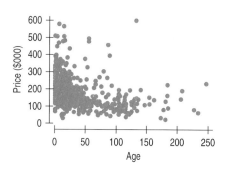

Remarks

There are a few anomalies in the plots that deserve discussion. The plot of *Price* against *Bathrooms* shows a positive relationship, but it is not quite linear. There seem to be two slopes, one from 1–2 bathrooms and then a steeper one from 2–4. For now, we'll proceed cautiously, realizing that any slope we find will average these two. The plot of *Price* against *Fireplaces* shows an outlier—an expensive home with four fireplaces. We tried setting this home aside and running the regression without it, but its influence on the coefficients was not large, so we decided to include it in the model. The plot of *Price* against *Age* shows that there may be some curvature. We may want to consider re-expressing *Age* to improve the linearity of the relationship.

✓ **Independence Assumption.** We can regard the house prices as being independent of one another. The error the regression model makes in predicting one isn't likely to be related to the error it will make in predicting another.

✓ **Randomization Condition.** These 1057 houses are a random sample of a much larger set.

✓ **Equal Spread Condition.** A scatterplot of residuals vs. predicted values shows no evidence of changing spread. There is a group of homes whose residuals are larger (both negative and positive) than the vast majority. This is also seen in the long tails of the histogram of residuals.

We need the Nearly Normal Condition only if we want to do inference and the sample size is not large. If the sample size is large, as it is here, we need the distribution to be Normal only if we plan to produce prediction intervals.

✓ **Nearly Normal Condition, Outlier Condition.** The histogram of residuals is unimodal and symmetric, but long tailed. The Normal probability plot supports that.

(continued)

Under these conditions, we can proceed with caution to a multiple regression analysis. We will return to some of our concerns about curvature in some plots in the discussion.

DO

Mechanics We always fit multiple regression models with computer software. An output table like this one isn't exactly what any of the major packages produce, but it is enough like all of them to look familiar.

Here is some computer output for the multiple regression, using all five predictors.

	Coeff	SE(Coeff)	t-ratio	P-value
Intercept	15712.702	7311.427	2.149	0.03186
Living Area	73.446	4.009	18.321	<0.0001
Bedrooms	−6361.311	2749.503	−2.314	0.02088
Bathrooms	19236.678	3669.080	5.243	<0.0001
Fireplaces	9162.791	3194.233	2.869	0.00421
Age	−142.740	48.276	−2.957	0.00318

Residual standard error: 48615.95 on 1051 degrees of freedom
Multiple R-squared: 0.6049.
F-statistic: 321.8 on 5 and 1051 DF, P-value: <0.0001

The estimated equation is:

$$\widehat{Price} = 15{,}712.70 + 73.45\,Living\ Area - 6361.31\,Bedrooms +$$
$$19{,}236.68\,Bathrooms + 9162.79\,Fireplaces - 142.74\,Age$$

All of the P-values are small which indicates that even with five predictors in the model, all are contributing. The R^2 value of 60.49% indicates that more than 60% of the overall variation in house prices has been accounted for by this model. The residual standard error of $48,620 gives us a rough indication that we can predict the price of a typical home to within about $2 \times \$48{,}620 = \$97{,}240$. That seems too large to be useful, but the model does give some idea of the price of a home.

REPORT

Summary and Conclusions Summarize your results and state any limitations of your model in the context of your original objectives.

MEMO

Re: Regression analysis of home price predictions

A regression model of *Price* on *Living Area, Bedrooms, Bathrooms, Fireplaces,* and *Age* accounts for 60.5% of the variation in the price of homes in upstate New York. The residual standard deviation is $48,620. A statistical test of each coefficient shows that each one is almost certainly not zero, so each of these variables appears to be a contributor to the price of a house.

This model reflects the common wisdom in real estate about the importance of various aspects of a home. An important variable not included is the location, which every real estate agent knows is crucial to pricing a house. This is ameliorated by the fact that all these houses are in the same general area. However, knowing more specific information about where they are located would almost certainly help the model. The price found from this model is to be used as a starting point for comparing a home with comparable homes in the area.

The model may be improved by re-expressing one or more of the predictors, especially *Age* and *Bathrooms*. We recommend caution in interpreting the coefficients across the entire range of these predictors.

17.4   Testing the Multiple Regression Model

There are several hypothesis tests in the multiple regression output, but all of them talk about the same thing. Each is concerned with whether the underlying model parameters (the slopes and intercept) are actually zero. The first of these hypotheses is one we skipped over for simple regression (for reasons that will be clear in a minute).

Now that we have more than one predictor, there's an overall test we should perform before we consider inference for the coefficients. We ask the global question: Is this multiple regression model any good at all? If home prices were set randomly or based on other factors than those we have as predictors, then the best estimate would just be the mean price.

To address the overall question, we'll test the null hypothesis that all the slope coefficients are zero:

$$H_0: \beta_1 = \cdots = \beta_k = 0 \text{ vs. } H_A: \text{at least one } \beta \neq 0.$$

We can test this hypothesis with an **F-test**. (It's the generalization of the *t*-test to more than one predictor.) The sampling distribution of the statistic is labeled with the letter F (in honor of Sir Ronald Fisher). The F-distribution has two degrees of freedom, k, the number of predictors, and $n - k - 1$. In the Guided Example, there were $k = 5$ predictors and $n = 1057$ homes, which means that the F-value of 321.8 has 5 and $1057 - 5 - 1 = 1051$ degrees of freedom. The regression output (page 568) shows that it has a P-value < 0.0001. The null hypothesis is that all the coefficients are 0, in which case the regression model predicts no better than the mean. The alternative is that at least one coefficient is non-zero. The test is one-sided—bigger F-values mean smaller P-values. If the null hypothesis were true, the F-statistic would have a value near 1. The F-statistic here is quite large, so we can easily reject the null hypothesis and conclude that the multiple regression model for predicting house prices with these five variables is better than just using the mean.[4]

Once we check the F-test and reject its null hypothesis—and, if we are being careful, *only* if we reject that hypothesis—we can move on to checking the test statistics for the individual coefficients. Those tests look like what we did for the slope of a simple regression in Chapter 15. For each coefficient, we test the null hypothesis that the slope is zero against the (two-sided) alternative that it isn't zero. The regression table gives a standard error for each coefficient and the ratio of

F-test for Simple Regression?

Why didn't we check the F-test for simple regression? In fact, we did. When you do a simple regression with statistics software, you'll see the F-statistic in the output. But for simple regression, it gives the same information as the *t*-test for the slope. It tests the null hypothesis that the slope coefficient is zero, and we already test that with the *t*-statistic for the slope. In fact, the square of that *t*-statistic is equal to the F-statistic for the simple regression, so it really is the identical test.

---

[4]To know how big the F-value has to be, we need a table of F-values. There are F tables in the back of the book, and most regression tables include a P-value for the F-statistic.

the estimated coefficient to its standard error. If the assumptions and conditions are met (and now we need the Nearly Normal Condition or a large sample), these ratios follow a Student's t-distribution:

$$t_{n-k-1} = \frac{b_j - 0}{SE(b_j)}.$$

Where did the degrees of freedom $n - k - 1$ come from? We have a rule of thumb that works here. The degrees of freedom value is the number of data values minus the number of estimated coefficients, minus 1 for the intercept. For the house price regression on five predictors, that's $n - 5 - 1$. Almost every regression report includes both the t-statistics and their corresponding P-values.

We can build a confidence interval in the usual way, with an estimate plus or minus a margin of error. As always, the margin of error is the product of the standard error and a critical value. Here the critical value comes from the t-distribution on $n - k - 1$ degrees of freedom, and the standard errors are in the regression table. So a confidence interval for each slope β_j is:

$$b_j \pm t_{n-k-1}^* \times SE(b_j).$$

The tricky parts of these tests are that the standard errors of the coefficients now require harder calculations (so we leave it to technology), and the meaning of a coefficient, as we have seen, depends on all the other predictors in the multiple regression model.

That last point is important. If we fail to reject the null hypothesis for a multiple regression coefficient, it does *not* mean that the corresponding predictor variable has no linear relationship to y. It means that the corresponding predictor contributes nothing to modeling y *after allowing for all the other predictors.*

The multiple regression model looks so simple and straightforward. It *looks* like each β_j tells us the effect of its associated predictor, x_j, on the response variable, y. But that is not true. This is, without a doubt, the most common error that people make with multiple regression. In fact:

- The coefficient β_j in a multiple regression can be quite different from zero even when it is possible there is no simple linear relationship between y and x_j.
- It is even possible that the multiple regression slope changes sign when a new variable enters the regression. We saw this for the *Price* on *Bedrooms* real estate example when *Living Area* was added to the regression.

So we'll say it once more: The coefficient of x_j in a multiple regression depends as much on the *other* predictors as it does on x_j. Failing to interpret coefficients properly is the most common error in working with regression models.

FOR EXAMPLE Testing a multiple regression model

Leiram tries another model, adding the variable *Age* to see if that improves the model:

```
Response Variable: Respond Amount
R² = 91.50%; Adjusted R² = 91.23%
s = 18.179 with 149 − 5 = 144 degrees of freedom
```

Variable	Coeff	SE(Coeff)	t-ratio	P-value
Intercept	114.91	9.244	12.439	<0.0001
Income	0.00091	0.00012	7.619	<0.0001
Total Amount Spent	0.154	0.00855	18.007	<0.0001
Number of Purchases	−14.79	0.719	−20.570	<0.0001
Age	−0.1264	0.2144	−0.5898	0.5563

QUESTION Has the variable *Age* improved the model? Would you leave the term in? Comment.

ANSWER Of course, we would like to see the residual plots, but given this output it appears that although the R^2 value has increased from 0.9148 to 0.9150, the *t*-ratio for *Age* is only −0.5898 with a P-value of 0.5563. This indicates that there is no evidence to suggest that the slope for *Age* is different from 0. We cannot reject that null hypothesis. There is no reason to leave *Age* in this model.

17.5 Adjusted R^2 and the F-statistic

In Chapter 15, for simple linear regression, we interpreted R^2 as the variation in *y* accounted for by the model. The same interpretation holds for multiple regression, where now the model contains more than one predictor variable. The R^2 value tells us how much (as a fraction or percentage) of the variation in *y* is accounted for by the model with all the predictor variables included.

There are some relationships among the standard error of the residuals, s_e, the F-ratio, and R^2 that are useful for understanding how to assess the value of the multiple regression model. To start, we can write the standard error of the residuals as:

$$s_e = \sqrt{\frac{SSE}{n - k - 1}},$$

where $SSE = \sum e^2$ is called the **Sum of Squared Residuals** (or errors—the E is for error). A larger SSE (and thus s_e) means that the residuals are more variable and that our predictions will be correspondingly less precise.

We can look at the total variation of the response variable, *y*, which is called the **Total Sum of Squares** and is denoted SST: $SST = \sum (y - \bar{y})^2$. For any regression model, we have no control over SST, but we'd like SSE to be as small as we can make it by finding predictor variables that account for as much of that variation as possible. In fact, we can write an equation that relates the total variation SST to SSE:

$$SST = SSR + SSE,$$

where $SSR = \sum (\hat{y} - \bar{y})^2$ is called the **Regression Sum of Squares** because it comes from the predictor variables and tells how much of the total variation in the response is due to the regression model. For a model to account for a large portion of the variability in *y*, SSR should be large and SSE should be small. In fact, R^2 is just the ratio of SSR to SST:

$$R^2 = \frac{SSR}{SST} = 1 - \frac{SSE}{SST}.$$

When the SSE is nearly 0, the R^2 value will be close to 1.

In Chapter 15, we saw that for the relationship between two quantitative variables, testing the standard null hypothesis about the correlation coefficient,

Mean Squares

Whenever a sum of squares is divided by its degrees of freedom, the result is called a mean square. For example, the Mean Square for Error, which you may see written as MSE, is found as $SSE/(n - k - 1)$. It estimates the variance of the errors.

Similarly $SST/(n - 1)$ divides the total sum of square by *its* degrees of freedom. That is sometimes called the Mean Square for Total and denoted MST. We've seen this one before; the MST is just the variance of y.

And SSR/k is the Mean Square for Regression.

$H_0: \rho = 0$, was equivalent to testing the standard null hypothesis about the slope, $H_0: \beta_1 = 0$. A similar result holds here for multiple regression. Testing the overall hypothesis tested by the F-statistic, $H_0: \beta_1 = \beta_2 = \cdots = \beta_k = 0$, is equivalent to testing whether the true multiple regression R^2 is zero. In fact, the F-statistic for testing that all the slopes are zero can be found as:

$$F = \frac{R^2/k}{(1 - R^2)/(n - k - 1)} = \frac{\dfrac{SSR}{SST}\dfrac{1}{k}}{\dfrac{SSE}{SST}\dfrac{1}{n - k - 1}} = \frac{SSR/k}{SSE/(n - k - 1)} = \frac{MSR}{MSE}.$$

In other words, using an F-test to see whether any of the true coefficients is different from 0 is equivalent to testing whether the R^2 value is different from zero. A rejection of either hypothesis says that at least one of the predictors accounts for enough variation in y to distinguish it from noise. Unfortunately, the test doesn't say which slope is responsible. You must look at individual t-tests on the slopes to determine that. Because removing one predictor variable from the regression equation can change any number of slope coefficients, it is not straightforward to determine the right subset of predictors to use. We'll return to that problem when we discuss model selection in Chapter 18.

R^2 and Adjusted R^2

Adding a predictor variable to a multiple regression equation does not always increase the amount of variation accounted for by the model, but it can never reduce it. Adding new predictor variables will always keep the R^2 value the same or increase it. It can never decrease it. But, even if the R^2 value grows, that doesn't mean that the resulting model is a better model or that it has greater predictive ability. If you have a model with k predictors (all of which have statistically significant coefficients at some α level) and want to see if including a new variable, x_{k+1}, is warranted, you could fit the model with all $k + 1$ variables and simply test the slope of the added variable with a t-test of the slope.

This method can test whether the most recently added variable adds significantly to the model, but choosing the "best" subset of predictors is not necessarily straightforward. We'll discuss strategies for model selection in Chapter 18. The trade-off between a small (parsimonious) model and one that fits the data well is one of the great challenges of any serious model-building effort. Various statistics have been proposed to provide guidance for this search, and one of the most common is called adjusted R^2. **Adjusted** R^2 imposes a "penalty" for each new term that's added to the model in an attempt to make models of different sizes (numbers of predictors) comparable. It differs from R^2 because it can shrink when a predictor is added to the regression model or grow when a predictor is removed if the predictor in question doesn't contribute usefully to the model. It can even be negative.

For a multiple regression with k predictor variables and n cases, it is defined as

$$R^2_{adj} = 1 - (1 - R^2)\frac{n - 1}{n - k - 1} = 1 - \frac{SSE/(n - k - 1)}{SST/(n - 1)}.$$

In the Guided Example, the regression of *Price* on *Bedrooms, Bathrooms, Living Area, Fireplaces,* and *Age* resulted in an R^2 of 0.6049. All the coefficients had P-values well below 0.05. The adjusted R^2 value for this model is 0.6030. Adding the variable *Lot Size* to the model gives the following regression model:

	Coeff	SE(Coeff)	t-ratio	P-value
Intercept	15360.011	7334.804	2.094	0.03649
Living Area	73.388	4.043	18.154	<0.00001
Bedrooms	−6096.387	2757.736	−2.211	0.02728
Bathrooms	18824.069	3676.582	5.120	<0.00001
Fireplaces	9226.356	3191.788	2.891	0.00392
Age	−152.615	48.224	−3.165	0.00160
Lot Size	847.764	1989.112	0.426	0.67005

Residual standard error: 48440 on 1041 degrees of freedom
Multiple R-squared: 0.6081, Adjusted R-squared: 0.6059
F-statistic: 269.3 on 6 and 1041 DF, P-value: <0.0001

The most striking feature of this regression table as compared to the one in the Guided Example on page 568, is that although most of the coefficients have changed very little, the coefficient of *Lot Size* is far from significant, with a P-value of 0.670. Yet, the adjusted R^2 value is actually higher than for the previous model. This is why we warn against putting too much faith in this statistic. Especially for large samples, the adjusted R^2 does not always adjust downward enough to make sensible model choices. The other problem with comparing these two models is that 9 homes had missing values for *Lot Size*, which means that we're not comparing the models on exactly the same data set. When we matched the two models on the smaller data set, the adjusted R^2 value actually did "make the right decision" but just barely—0.6059 versus 0.6060 for the model without *Lot Size*. One might expect a larger difference considering we added a variable whose *t*-ratio is much less than 1.

The lesson to be learned here is that there is no "correct" set of predictors to use for any real business decision problem, and finding a reasonable model is a process that takes a combination of science, art, business knowledge, and common sense. Look at the adjusted R^2 value for any multiple regression model you fit, but be sure to think about all the other reasons for including or not including any given predictor variable. We will have much more to say about this important subject in Chapter 18.

FOR EXAMPLE R^2 and adjusted R^2

QUESTION   The model for *Respond Amount* that included *Age* as a predictor (see For Example on page 570) had an adjusted R^2 value of 0.9123 (or 91.23%) The original model (see For Example on page 558) had an adjusted R^2 value of 0.9131. Explain how that is consistent with the decision we made to drop *Age* from the model.

ANSWER   The *t*-ratio indicated that the slope for *Age* was not significantly different from 0, and thus that we should drop *Age* from the model. Although the R^2 value for the model that included *Age* was slightly higher, the adjusted R^2 value was slightly lower. Adjusted R^2 adds a penalty for each added term that allows us to compare models of different sizes. Because the adjusted R^2 value for the smaller model (without *Age*) is higher than the larger model (with *Age*), it indicates that the inclusion of *Age* is not justified, which is consistent with the recommendation from the *t*-ratio.

*17.6   The Logistic Regression Model

Business decisions often depend on whether something will happen or not. Will my customers leave my wireless service at the end of their subscription? How likely is it that my customers will respond to the offer I just mailed? The response variable is either Yes or No—a dichotomous response. By definition, that's a categorical response, so we can't use linear regression methods to predict it.

If we coded this categorical response variable by giving the Yes values the value 1 and the No values the value 0, we could "pretend" that it's quantitative and try to fit a linear model. Let's imagine that we're trying to model whether someone will respond to an offer based on how much they spent in the last year at our company. The regression of *Purchase (1 = Yes: 0 = No)* on *Spending* might look like Figure 17.6.

The model shows that as past spending increases, something having to do with responding to the offer increases. Look at *Spending* near $500. Nearly all the customers who spend that much responded to the offer, while for those customers who spent less than $100 last year, almost none responded. The line seems to show the proportion of those responding for different values of *Spending*. Looking at the plot, what would you predict the proportion of responders to be for those that spent about $225? You might say that the proportion was about 0.50.

Figure 17.6 A linear model of *Respond to Offer* shows that as *Spending* increases, the proportion of customers responding to the offer increases as well. Unfortunately, the line predicts values outside the interval (0,1), but those are the only sensible values for proportions or probabilities.

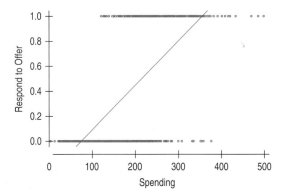

What's wrong with this interpretation? We know proportions (or probabilities) must lie between 0 and 1. But the linear model has no such restrictions. The line crosses 1.0 at about $350 in *Spending* and goes below 0 at about $75 in *Spending*. However, by transforming the probability, we can make the model behave better and get more sensible predictions for all values of *Spending*. We could just cut off all values greater than 1 at 1 and all values less than 0 at 0. That would work fine in the middle, but we know that things like customer behavior don't change that abruptly. So we'd prefer a model that curves at the ends to approach 0 and 1 gently. That's likely to be a better model for what really happens. A simple function is all we need. There are several that can do the job, but one common model is the logistic regression model. Here is a plot of the logistic regression model predictions for the same data.

Figure 17.7 A logistic regression model of *Respond to Offer* on *Spending* predicts values between 0 and 1 for the proportion of customers who *Respond* for all values of *Spending*.

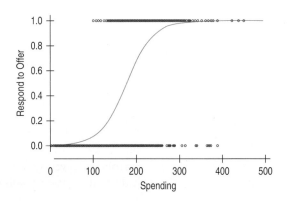

For many values of *Spending*, especially those near the mean value of *Spending*, the predictions of the probability of responding are similar for the linear and logistic models, but the logistic transformation approaches the limits at 0 and 1 smoothly. A logistic regression is an example of a nonlinear regression model. The computer finds the coefficients by solving a system of equations that in some ways mimic the least squares calculations we did for linear regression. The **logistic regression** model looks like this:

$$\ln\left(\frac{p}{1-p}\right) = \beta_0 + \beta_1 x_1 + \cdots + \beta_k x_k.$$

where ln( ) denotes the natural logarithm and p is the probability of a "success."

In other words, it's not the probabilities themselves that are modeled by a (multiple) regression model, but a transformation (the logistic function) of the probabilities. When the probabilities are transformed back and plotted, we get an S-shaped curve (when plotted against each predictor), as seen in Figure 17.7.

As with multiple regression, computer output for a logistic regression model provides estimates for each coefficient, standard errors, and a test for whether the coefficient is zero. Unlike multiple regression, the coefficients for each variable are tested with a Chi-square statistic[5] rather than a *t*-statistic, and the overall R^2 is no longer available. (Some computer programs use a *z*-statistic to test individual coefficients. The tests are equivalent.) Because the probabilities are not a linear function of the predictors, it is more difficult to interpret the coefficients. The fitted logistic regression equation can be written:

$$\ln\left(\frac{\hat{p}}{1-\hat{p}}\right) = b_0 + b_1 x_1 + \cdots + b_k x_k.$$

Some researchers try to interpret the logistic regression equation directly by realizing that the expression on the left of the logistic regression equation, $\ln\left(\frac{\hat{p}}{1-\hat{p}}\right)$, can be thought of as the predicted log (base e) odds of the outcome. This is sometimes denoted $\text{logit}(\hat{p})$. The higher the log odds, the higher the probability. Negative log odds indicate that the probability is less than 0.5 because then $\frac{p}{1-p}$ will be less than 1 and thus have a negative logarithm. Positive log odds indicate a probability greater than 0.5. If the coefficient of a particular predictor is positive, it means that higher values of it are associated with higher log odds and thus a higher probability of the response. So, the *direction* is interpretable in the same way as a multiple regression coefficient. But an increase of one unit of the predictor *increases* the predicted *log odds* by an amount equal to the coefficient of that predictor, after allowing for the effects of all the other predictors. It does not increase the predicted *probability* by that amount.

The transformation back to probabilities is straightforward, but nonlinear. Once you have fit the logistic regression equation

$$\ln\left(\frac{\hat{p}}{1-\hat{p}}\right) = \text{logit}(\hat{p}) = b_0 + b_1 x_1 + \cdots + b_k x_k,$$

you can find the individual probability estimates from the equation:

$$\hat{p} = \frac{1}{1 + e^{-(b_0 + b_1 x_1 + \cdots + b_k x_k)}} = \frac{e^{(b_0 + b_1 x_1 + \cdots + b_k x_k)}}{1 + e^{(b_0 + b_1 x_1 + \cdots + b_k x_k)}}.$$

Log Odds

Racetrack enthusiasts know that when p is a probability, $\frac{p}{1-p}$ is the *odds* in favour of a success. For example, when the probability of success, $p = 1/3$, we'd get the ratio $\frac{1/3}{2/3} = \frac{1}{2}$. We'd say that the odds in favour of success are 1:2 (or we'd probably say the odds *against* it are 2:1). Logistic regression models the *logarithm* of the odds as a linear function of *x*. In fact, nobody really thinks in terms of the log of the odds ratio. But it's the combination of that ratio and the logarithm that gets us the nice S-curved shape. What is important is that we can work backward from a log odds ratio to get the probability—which is often easier to think about.

---

[5]Yes, the same sampling distribution model as we used in Chapter 14.

The assumptions and conditions for fitting a logistic regression are similar to multiple regression. We still need the independence assumption and randomization condition. We no longer need the linearity or equal spread condition. However, it's a good idea to plot the response variable against each predictor variable to make sure that there are no outliers that could unduly influence the model. A customer who both spent $10,000 and responded to the offer could possibly change the shape of the curve shown in Figure 17.7. However, residual analysis for logistic regression models is beyond the scope of this book.

FOR EXAMPLE   Logistic regression

Leiram wants to build a model to predict *whether* a customer will respond to the new catalog offer. The variable *Respond* indicates 1 for responders and 0 for nonresponders. After trying several models, she settles on the following logistic regression model:

```
Response Variable: Respond

Variable                      Coeff     SE(Coeff)   z-value    P-value
Intercept                    -3.298     0.4054      -8.136     <0.0001
Age                           0.08365   0.012226     6.836     <0.0001
Days Since Last Purchase      0.00364   0.000831     4.378     <0.0001
```

QUESTIONS   Interpret the model. Would you keep both predictor variables in the model? Why? Who would be more likely to respond, a 20-year-old customer who has recently purchased another item, or a 50-year-old customer who has not purchased in a year?

ANSWERS   The model says:

$$\text{logit}(\hat{p}) = -3.298 + 0.08365\ Age + 0.00364\ Days\ Since\ Last\ Purchase,$$

which means that the probability of responding goes up with both *Age* and *Days Since Last Purchase*. Both terms have large z-values and correspondingly low P-values, which indicate that they contribute substantially to the model. We should keep both terms. Because both terms are positively associated with increasing (log) odds of purchasing, both an older person and one who has *not* purchased recently are more likely to respond. A 50-year-old who has not purchased recently would be more likely to respond than the 20-year-old who has.

GUIDED EXAMPLE   Time on Market

A real estate agent used information on 1115 houses, such as we used in our multiple regression Guided Example. She wants to predict whether a house sold in the first 3 months it was on the market based on other variables. The variables available include:

Sold	1 = Yes—the house sold within the first 3 months it was listed; 0 = No, it did not sell within 3 months.
Price	The price of the house as sold in 2002.
Living Area	The size of the living area of the house in square feet
Bedrooms	The number of bedrooms
Bathrooms	The number of bathrooms (a half bath is a toilet and sink only)
Age	Age of the house in years
Fireplaces	Number of fireplaces in the house

PLAN

Setup State the objective of the study. Identify the variables.

Model Think about the assumptions and check the conditions.

We want to build a model to predict whether a house will sell within the first 3 months it's on the market based on *Price* ($), *Living Area* (sq ft), *Bedrooms* (#), *Bathrooms* (#), *Fireplaces* (#), and *Age* (years). Notice that now *Price* is a predictor variable in the regression.

Outlier Condition

To fit a logistic regression model, we check that there are no outliers in the predictors that may unduly influence the model.

Here are scatterplots of *Sold* (1 = Yes; 0 = No) against each predictor. (Plots of *Sold* against the variables *Bathrooms*, *Bedrooms*, and *Fireplaces* are uninformative because these predictors are discrete.)

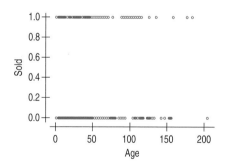

✓ **Outlier Condition.** There do not seem to be any outliers in the predictors. Of course, there can't be any in the response variable; it is only 0 or 1.

✓ **Independence Assumption.** We can regard the house prices as being independent of one another since they come from a fairly large geographic area.

✓ **Randomization Condition.** These 1115 houses are a random sample from a larger collection of houses.

We can fit a logistic regression predicting *Sold* from the six predictor variables.

(continued)

DO

Mechanics We always fit logistic regression models with computer software. An output table like this one isn't exactly what any of the major packages produce, but it is enough like all of them to look familiar.

Here is the computer output for the logistic regression using all six predictors.

	Coeff	SE(Coeff)	z-value	P-value
Intercept	−3.222e+00	3.826e−01	−8.422	<0.0001
Living Area	−1.444e−03	2.518e−04	−5.734	<0.0001
Age	4.900e−03	2.823e−03	1.736	0.082609
Price	1.693e−05	1.444e−06	11.719	<0.0001
Bedrooms	4.805e−01	1.366e−01	3.517	0.000436
Bathrooms	−1.813e−01	1.829e−01	−0.991	0.321493
Fireplaces	−1.253e−01	1.633e−01	−0.767	0.442885

The estimated equation is:

$$\text{logit}(\hat{p}) = -3.22 - 0.00144\,Living\ Area$$
$$+\ 0.0049\,Age + 0.0000169\,Price$$
$$+\ 0.481\,Bedrooms - 0.181\,Bathrooms$$
$$-\ 0.125\,Fireplaces$$

Three of the P-values are quite small, two are large (*Bathrooms* and *Fireplaces*), and one is marginal (*Age*). After examining several alternatives, we chose the following model.

	Coeff	SE(Coeff)	z-value	P-value
Intercept	−3.351e+00	3.601e−01	−9.305	<0.0001
Living Area	−1.574e−03	2.342e−04	−6.719	<0.0001
Age	6.106e−03	2.668e−03	2.289	0.022102
Price	1.672e−05	1.428e−06	11.704	<0.0001
Bedrooms	4.631e−01	1.354e−01	3.421	0.000623

The estimated logit equation is:

$$\text{logit}(\hat{p}) = -3.351 - 0.00157\,Living\ Area$$
$$+\ 0.00611\,Age + 0.0000167\,Price$$
$$+\ 0.463\,Bedrooms$$

Strategies for model selection will be discussed in Chapter 18.

While interpretation is difficult, it appears that for a house of a given size (and age and bedrooms), higher-priced homes may have a higher chance of selling within 3 months. For a house of given size and price and age, having more bedrooms may be associated with a greater chance of selling within 3 months.

REPORT

Summary and Conclusions Summarize your results and state any limitations of your model in the context of your original objectives.

MEMO

Re: Logistic regression analysis of selling

A logistic regression model of *Sold* on various predictors was fit, and a model based on *Living Area*, *Bedrooms*, *Price*, and *Age* found that these four predictors were statistically significant in predicting the probability that a house will sell within 3 months. More thorough analysis to understand the meaning of the coefficients is needed, but each of these variables appears to be an important predictor of whether the house will sell quickly.

However, knowing more specific information about other characteristics of a house and where it is located would almost certainly help the model.

WHAT CAN GO WRONG?

Interpreting Coefficients

- **Don't claim to "hold everything else constant" for a single individual.** It's often meaningless to say that a regression coefficient says what we expect to happen if all variables but one were held constant for an individual and the predictor in question changed. While it's mathematically correct, it often just doesn't make any sense. For example, in a regression of salary on years of experience, years of education, and age, subjects can't gain a year of experience or get another year of education without getting a year older. Instead, we *can* think about all those who satisfy given criteria on some predictors and ask about the conditional relationship between y and one x for those individuals.

- **Don't interpret regression causally.** Regressions are usually applied to observational data. Without deliberately assigned treatments, randomization, and control, we can't draw conclusions about causes and effects. We can never be certain that there are no variables lurking in the background, causing everything we've seen. Don't interpret b_1, the coefficient of x_1 in the multiple regression, by saying: "If we were to change an individual's x_1 by 1 unit (holding the other x's constant), it would change his y by b_1 units." We have no way of knowing what applying a change to an individual would do.

- **Be cautious about interpreting a regression model as predictive.** Yes, we do call the x's predictors, and you can certainly plug in values for each of the x's and find a corresponding *predicted value*, $\hat{y}$. But the term "prediction" suggests extrapolation into the future or beyond the data, and we know that we can get into trouble when we use models to estimate $\hat{y}$ values for x's not in the range of the data. Be careful not to extrapolate very far from the span of your data. In simple regression, it was easy to tell when you extrapolated. With many predictor variables, it's often harder to know when you are outside the bounds of your original data.[6] We usually think of fitting models to the data more as modeling than as prediction, so that's often a more appropriate term.

- **Be careful when interpreting the signs of coefficients in a multiple regression.** Sometimes our primary interest in a predictor is whether it has a positive or negative association with y. As we have seen, though, the sign of the coefficient also depends on the other predictors in the model. Don't look at the sign in isolation and conclude that "the direction of the relationship is positive (or negative)." Just like the value of the coefficient, the sign is about the relationship after allowing for the linear effects of the other predictors. The sign of a variable can change depending on which other predictors are in or out of the model. For example, in the regression model for house prices, we saw the coefficient of *Bedrooms* change sign when *Living Area* was added to the model as a predictor. It isn't correct to say either that houses with more bedrooms sell for more on average or that they sell for less. The truth is more subtle and requires that we understand the multiple regression model.

- **If a coefficient's *t*-statistic is not significant, don't interpret it at all.** You can't be sure that the value of the corresponding parameter in the underlying regression model isn't really zero.

---

[6]With several predictors we can wander beyond the data because of the *combination* of values even when individual values are not extraordinary. For example, houses with 1 bathroom and houses with 5 bedrooms can both be found in the real estate records, but a single house with 5 bedrooms and only 1 bathroom would be quite unusual. The model we found is not appropriate for predicting the price of such an extraordinary house.

WHAT ELSE CAN GO WRONG?

- **Don't fit a linear regression to data that aren't straight.** This is the most fundamental regression assumption. If the relationship between the x's and y isn't approximately linear, there's no sense in fitting a linear model to it. What we mean by "linear" is a model of the form we have been writing for the regression. When we have two predictors, this is the equation of a plane, which is linear in the sense of being flat in all directions. With more predictors, the geometry is harder to visualize, but the simple structure of the model is consistent; the predicted values change consistently with equal size changes in any predictor.

  Usually we're satisfied when plots of y against each of the x's are straight enough. We'll also check a scatterplot of the residuals against the predicted values for signs of nonlinearity.

- **Watch out for changing variance in the residuals.** The estimate of the error standard deviation shows up in all the inference formulas. But that estimate assumes that the error standard deviation is the same throughout the extent of the x's so that we can combine all the residuals when we estimate it. If s_e changes with any x, these estimates won't make sense. The most common check is a plot of the residuals against the predicted values. You can also check plots of residuals against several of the predictors. If they show a thickening and especially if they also show a bend, then consider re-expressing y.

- **Make sure the errors are nearly Normal.** All of our inferences require that, unless the sample size is large, the true errors be modeled well by a Normal model. Check the histogram and Normal probability plot of the residuals to see whether this assumption looks reasonable.

- **Watch out for high-influence points and outliers.** We always have to be on the lookout for a few points that have undue influence on our model, and regression is certainly no exception. Chapter 19 discusses this issue in greater depth.

ETHICS IN ACTION

Alpine Medical Systems, Inc. is a large provider of medical equipment and supplies to hospitals, doctors, clinics, and other health care professionals. Alpine's VP of Marketing and Sales, Kenneth Jadik, asked one of the company's analysts, Nicole Haly, to develop a model that could be used to predict the performance of the company's sales force.

Based on data collected over the past year, as well as records kept by Human Resources, she considered five potential independent variables: (1) gender, (2) starting base salary, (3) years of sales experience, (4) personality test score, and (5) high school grade point average. The dependent variable (sales performance) is measured as the sales dollars generated per quarter.

In discussing the results with Nicole, Kenneth asks to see the full regression model with all five independent variables included. Kenneth notes that a t-test for the coefficient of gender shows no significant effect on sales performance and recommends that it be eliminated from the model. Nicole reminds him of the company's history of offering lower starting base salaries to women, recently corrected under court order. If instead, starting base salary is removed from the model, gender is statistically significant, and its coefficient indicates that women on the sales force outperform men (taking into account the other variables). Kenneth argues that because gender is not significant when all predictors are included, it is the variable that should be omitted.

- Identify the ethical dilemma in this scenario.

- What are the undesirable consequences?

- Propose an ethical solution that considers the welfare of all stakeholders

WHAT HAVE WE LEARNED?

Learning Objectives

Know how to perform a multiple regression, using the technology of your choice.

- Technologies differ, but most produce similar-looking tables to hold the regression results. Know how to find the values you need in the output generated by the technology you are using.

Understand how to interpret a multiple regression model.

- The meaning of a multiple regression coefficient depends on the other variables in the model. In particular, it is the relationship of y to the associated x after removing the linear effects of the other x's.

Be sure to check the Assumptions and Conditions before interpreting a multiple regression model.

- The **Linearity Assumption** asserts that the form of the multiple regression model is appropriate. We check it by examining scatterplots. If the plots appear to be linear, we can fit a multiple regression model.
- The **Independence Assumption** requires that the errors made by the model in fitting the data be mutually independent. Data that arise from random samples or randomized experiments usually satisfy this assumption.
- The **Equal Variance Assumption** states that the variability around the multiple regression model should be the same everywhere. We usually check the **Equal Spread Condition** by plotting the residuals against the predicted values. This assumption is needed so that we can pool the residuals to estimate their standard deviation, which we will need for inferences about the regression coefficients.
- The **Normality Assumption** says that the model's errors should follow a Normal model. We check the **Nearly Normal Condition** with a histogram or normal probability plot of the residuals. We need this assumption to use Student's t models for inference, but for larger sample sizes, it is less important.

Know how to state and test hypotheses about the multiple regression coefficients.

- The standard hypothesis test for each coefficient is

$$H_0: \beta_j = 0 \text{ vs.}$$
$$H_A: \beta_j \neq 0$$

- We test these hypotheses by referring the test statistic

$$\frac{b_j - 0}{SE(b_j)}$$

to the Student's t distribution on $n - k - 1$ degrees of freedom, where k is the number of coefficients estimated in the multiple regression.

Interpret other associated statistics generated by a multiple regression.

- R^2 is the fraction of the variation in y accounted for by the multiple regression model.
- Adjusted R^2 attempts to adjust for the number of coefficients estimated.
- The F-statistic tests the overall hypothesis that the regression model is of no more value than simply modeling y with its mean.
- The standard deviation of the residuals,

$$s_e = \sqrt{\frac{\sum e^2}{n - k - 1}}$$

provides an idea of how precisely the regression model fits the data.

Terms	
Adjusted R^2	An adjustment to the R^2 statistic that attempts to allow for the number of predictors in the model. It is sometimes used when comparing regression models with different numbers of predictors: $$R_{adj}^2 = 1 - (1 - R^2)\,\frac{n-1}{n-k-1} = 1 - \frac{SSE/(n-k-1)}{SST/(n-1)}.$$
F-test	The F-test is used to test the null hypothesis that the overall regression is no improvement over just modeling y with its mean: $$H_0: \beta_1 = \cdots = \beta_k = 0. \text{ vs } H_A: \text{at least one } \beta \neq 0$$ If this null hypothesis is not rejected, then you should not proceed to test the individual coefficients.
*Logistic regression	A regression model that models a binary (0/1) response variable based on quantitative predictor variables.
Multiple regression	A linear regression with two or more predictors whose coefficients are found by least squares. When the distinction is needed, a least squares linear regression with a single predictor is called a *simple regression*. The multiple regression model is: $y = \beta_0 + \beta_1 x_1 + \cdots + \beta_k x_k + \varepsilon$.
Regression Sum of Squares, SSR	A measure of the total variation in the response variable due to the model. $SSR = \sum (\hat{y} - \bar{y})^2$.
Sum of Squared Errors or Residuals, SSE	A measure of the variation in the residuals. $SSE = \sum (y - \hat{y})^2$.
Total Sum of Squares, SST	A measure of the variation in the response variable. $SST = \sum (y - \bar{y})^2$. Note that $\dfrac{SST}{n-1} = Var(y)$.
t-ratios for the coefficients	The t-ratios for the coefficients can be used to test the null hypotheses that the true value of each coefficient is zero against the alternative that it is not. The t distribution is also used in the construction of confidence intervals for each slope coefficient.

TECHNOLOGY HELP: Regression Analysis

All statistics packages make a table of results for a regression. The table for multiple regression looks very similar to the table for simple regression.

Most packages offer to plot residuals against predicted values. Some will also plot residuals against the x's. With some packages, you must request plots of the residuals when you request the regression. Others let you find the regression first and then analyze the residuals afterward. Either way, your analysis is not complete if you don't check the residuals with a histogram or Normal probability plot and a scatterplot of the residuals against the x's or the predicted values. In most packages, the commands to obtain residuals and residual plots are the same for single and multiple regression.

Multiple regressions are always found with a computer or programmable calculator. Before computers were available, a full multiple regression analysis could take months or even years of work.

EXCEL

- Select **Data Analysis** from the **Analysis Group** on the Data Tab.
- Select **Regression** from the **Analysis Tools** list.
- Click the **OK** button.
- Enter the data range holding the y-variable in the box labeled **Y-range**.
- Enter the range of cells holding the x-variables in the box labeled **X-range**.
- Select the **New Worksheet Ply** option.
- Select **Residuals** options. Click the **OK** button.

Comments

Although the Excel Data Analysis dialog offers a Normal probability plot of the residuals, the data analysis add-in does not make a correct probability plot, so don't use this option.

XLSTAT

- In **Modeling Data** menu, choose **Linear Regression**.
- Enter *y*-variable and *x*-variable cell ranges.
- Specify desired statistics in Outputs and Charts tabs, respectively.

Comments

For both Excel and XLStat, the Y and X cell ranges do not need to be in the same rows of the spreadsheet, although they must cover the same number of cells. It is a good idea to arrange your data in parallel columns as in a data table. The X-variables must be in adjacent columns. No cells in the data range may hold nonnumeric values or be left blank.

JMP

- From the **Analyze** menu, select **Fit Model**.
- Put the response variable in the **Y** dialog box and the predictor variables in the **Add** dialog box under **Construct Model Effects**.
- Click on **Run Model**.

Comments

JMP chooses a regression analysis when the response variable is "Continuous." The predictors can be any combination of quantitative or categorical. If you get a different analysis, check the variable types.

MINITAB

- Choose **Regression** from the **Stat** menu.
- Choose **Regression …** from the **Regression** submenu.
- In the Regression dialog, assign the Y-variable to the Response box and assign the X-variables to the Predictors box.
- Click the **Graphs** button.
- In the Regression-Graphs dialog, select **Standardized residuals**, and check **Normal plot of residuals** and **Residuals versus fits**.
- Click the **OK** button to return to the Regression dialog.
- Click the **OK** button to compute the regression.

SPSS

- Choose **Regression** from the **Analyze** menu.
- Choose **Linear** from the **Regression** submenu.
- When the Linear Regression dialog appears, select the Y-variable and move it to the dependent target. Then move the X-variables to the independent target.
- Click the **Plots** button.
- In the Linear Regression Plots dialog, choose to plot the *SRESIDs against the *ZPRED values.
- Click the **Continue** button to return to the Linear Regression dialog.
- Click the **OK** button to compute the regression.

Brief **Case**

Golf Success

Professional sports, like many other professions, require a variety of skills for success. That makes it difficult to evaluate and predict success. Fortunately, sports provide examples we can use to learn about modeling success because of the vast amount of data which are available. Here's an example.

What makes a golfer successful? The game of golf requires many skills. Putting well or hitting long drives will not, by themselves, lead to success. Success in golf requires a combination of skills. That makes multiple regression a good candidate for modeling golf achievement.

A number of Internet sites post statistics for the current PGA players. We have data for 181 top players of 2013 in the file **Golfers 2013**.

All of these players earned money on the tour, but they didn't all play the same number of events. And the distribution of earnings is quite skewed. So it's a good idea to take logs of Earnings/Event as the response variable.

The variables in the data file include:

Log$/E	The logarithm of earnings per event
Greens in Regulation	Greens in Regulation. Percentage of holes played in which the ball is on the green with two or more strokes left for par.
Putt Average	Average number of putts per hole in which the green was reached in regulation.
Save pct	Each time a golfer hits a bunker by the side of a green but needs only one or two additional shots to reach the hole, he is credited with a save. This is the percentage of opportunities for saves that are realized.
Yds/Drive	Average Drive Distance (yards). Measured as averages over pairs of drives in opposite directions (to account for wind).
Driving Acc	Drive Accuracy. Percent of drives landing on the fairway.

Investigate these data. Find a regression model to predict golfers' success (measured in log earnings per event). Write a report presenting your model including an assessment of its limitations. Note: Although you may consider several intermediate models, a good report is about the model you think best, not necessarily about all the models you tried along the way while searching for it.

EXERCISES

SECTION 17.1

1. A house in the upstate New York area from which the chapter data was drawn has 2 bedrooms and 1000 square feet of living area. Using the multiple regression model found in the chapter,

$$\widehat{Price} = 20{,}986.09 - 7483.10 Bedrooms + 93.84 Living\ Area.$$

a) Find the price that this model estimates.
b) The house just sold for $135,000. Find the residual corresponding to this house.
c) What does that residual say about this transaction?

2. A candy maker surveyed chocolate bars available in a local supermarket and found the following least squares regression model:

$$\widehat{Calories} = 28.4 + 11.37 Fat(g) + 2.91 Sugar(g).$$

a) The hand-crafted chocolate she makes has 15g of fat and 20g of sugar. How many calories does the model predict for a serving?
b) In fact, a laboratory test shows that her candy has 227 calories per serving. Find the residual corresponding to this candy. (Be sure to include the units.)
c) What does that residual say about her candy?

SECTION 17.2

3. What can predict how much a motion picture will make? We have data on a number of recent releases that includes the *USGross* (in $M), the *Budget* ($M), the *Run Time* (minutes), and the average number of *Stars* awarded by reviewers. The first several entries in the data table look like this:

Movie	USGross ($M)	Budget ($M)	Run Time (minutes)	Stars
White Noise	56.094360	30	101	2
Coach Carter	67.264877	45	136	3
Elektra	24.409722	65	100	2
Racing Stripes	49.772522	30	110	3
Assault on Precinct 13	20.040895	30	109	3
Are We There Yet?	82.674398	20	94	2
Alone in the Dark	5.178569	20	96	1.5
Indigo	51.100486	25	105	3.5

We want a regression model to predict *USGross*. Parts of the regression output computed in Excel look like this:

```
Dependent variable is: USGross($)
R squared = 47.4%  R squared (adjusted) = 46.0%
s = 46.41 with 120 − 4 = 116 degrees of freedom

Variable    Coefficient  SE(Coeff)  t-ratio  P-value
Intercept   −22.9898     25.70      −0.895   0.3729
Budget($)   1.13442      0.1297     8.75     <0.0001
Stars       24.9724      5.884      4.24     <0.0001
Run Time    −0.403296    0.2513     −1.60    0.1113
```

a) Write the multiple regression equation.
b) What is the interpretation of the coefficient of *Budget* in this regression model?

4. A middle manager at an entertainment company, upon seeing the analysis of Exercise 3, concludes that the longer you make a movie, the less money it will make. He argues that his company's films should all be cut by 30 minutes to improve their gross. Explain the flaw in his interpretation of this model.

SECTION 17.3

5. For the movies examined in Exercise 4, here is a scatterplot of *USGross* vs. *Budget*:

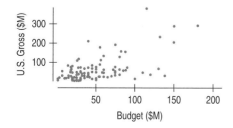

What (if anything) does this scatterplot tell us about the following Assumptions and Conditions for the regression?

a) Linearity condition
b) Equal Spread condition
c) Normality assumption

6. For the movies regression, here is a histogram of the residuals. What does it tell us about these Assumptions and Conditions?

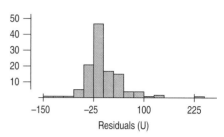

a) Linearity condition
b) Nearly Normal condition
c) Equal Spread condition

SECTION 17.4

7. In the regression output for the movies of Exercise 3,

a) What is the null hypothesis tested for the coefficient of *Stars* in this table?
b) What is the *t*-statistic corresponding to this test?
c) What is the P-value corresponding to this *t*-statistic?
d) Complete the hypothesis test. Do you reject the null hypothesis?

8. a) What is the null hypothesis tested for the coefficient of *Run Time* in the regression of Exercise 3?
b) What is the *t*-statistic corresponding to this test?
c) Why is this *t*-statistic negative?
d) What is the P-value corresponding to this *t*-statistic?
e) Complete the hypothesis test. Do you reject the null hypothesis?

SECTION 17.5

9. In the regression model of Exercise 3,

a) What is the R^2 for this regression? What does it mean?
b) Why is the "Adjusted R Square" in the table different from the "R Square"?

10. Here is another part of the regression output for the movies in Exercise 3:

```
Source      Sum of Squares  df   Mean Square  F-ratio
Regression  224995          3    74998.4      34.8
Residual    249799          116  2153.44
```

a) Using the values from the table, show how the value of R^2 could be computed. Don't try to do the calculation, just show what is computed.
b) What is the F-statistic value for this regression?
c) What null hypothesis can you test with it?
d) Would you reject that null hypothesis?

CHAPTER EXERCISES

The next 12 exercises consist of two sets of 6 (one even-numbered, one odd-numbered). Each set guides you through a multiple regression analysis. We suggest that you do all 6 exercises in a set. Remember that the answers to the odd-numbered exercises can be found in the back of the book.

11. Police salaries 2013. Is the amount of violent crime related to what police officers are paid? The U.S. Bureau of Labor Statistics publishes data on occupational employment and wage estimates (www.bls.gov/oes/) for each of the 50 states. Here are data released from 2011 to 2013. The variables are:

Violent Crime (crimes per 100,000 population)
Police Officer Wage (mean $/hr)
Graduation Rate (%)

One natural question to ask of these data is how police officer wages are related to violent crime across these states.

First, here are plots and background information.

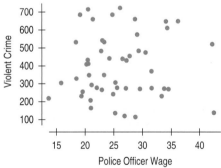

Correlations			
	Violent Crime	**Graduation Rate**	**Police Officer Wage**
Violent Crime	1.000		
Graduation Rate	−0.473	1.000	
Police Officer Wage	0.051	−0.473	1.000

a) Name and check (to the extent possible) the regression assumptions and their corresponding conditions.
b) If we found a regression to predict *Violent Crime* just from *Police Officer Wage*, what would the R^2 of that regression be?

12. Ticket prices. On a typical night in New York, about 25,000 people attend a Broadway show, paying an average price of more than $75 per ticket. *Variety* (www.variety.com), a news weekly that reports on the entertainment industry, publishes statistics about the Broadway show business. The data file on the disk holds data about shows on Broadway for most weeks of a recent three-year period. (A few weeks are missing data.) The following variables are available for each week:

Receipts ($ million)
Paid Attendance (thousands)
 # Shows
Average Ticket Price ($)

Viewing this as a business, we'd like to model *Receipts* in terms of the other variables.

First, here are plots and background information.

Correlations				
	Receipts	**Paid Attendance**	**# Shows**	**Average Ticket Price**
Receipts ($M)	1.000			
Paid Attendance	0.961	1.000		
# Shows	0.745	0.640	1.000	
Average Ticket Price	0.258	0.331	−0.160	1.000

a) Name and check (to the extent possible) the regression assumptions and their corresponding conditions.

b) If we found a regression to predict *Receipts* only from *Paid Attendance*, what would the R^2 of that regression be?

13. Police salaries, part 2. Here's a multiple regression model for the variables considered in Exercise 11.

```
Dependent variable is: Violent Crime
R squared = 22.41%  R squared (adjusted) = 19.10%
s = 156.9 with 47 degrees of freedom
```

Source	Sum of Squares	df	Mean Square	F-ratio
Regression	334246	2	167123	6.786
Residual	1157508	47	24628	

Variable	Coeff	SE(Coeff)	t-ratio	P-value
Intercept	1370.22	292.180	4.690	<0.0001
Police Officer Wage	0.7947	3.598	0.221	0.8262
Graduation Rate	−12.641	3.451	−3.663	0.00063

a) Write the regression model.
b) What does the coefficient of *Police Officer Wage* mean in the context of this regression model?
c) In a state in which the average police officer wage is $20/hour and the high school graduation rate is 70%, what does this model estimate the violent crime rate would be?
d) Is this likely to be a good prediction? Why do you think that?

14. Ticket prices, part 2. Here's a multiple regression model for the variables considered in Exercise 12:[7]

```
Dependent variable is: Receipts($M)
R squared = 99.9%  R squared (adjusted) = 99.9%
s = 0.0931 with 74 degrees of freedom
```

Source	Sum of Squares	df	Mean Square	F-ratio
Regression	484.789	3	161.596	18634
Residual	0.641736	74	0.008672	

Variable	Coeff	SE(Coeff)	t-ratio	P-value
Intercept	−18.320	0.3127	−58.6	<0.0001
Paid Attendance	0.076	0.0006	126.7	<0.0001
# Shows	0.0070	0.0044	1.59	0.116
Average Ticket Price	0.24	0.0039	61.5	<0.0001

a) Write the regression model.
b) What does the coefficient of *Paid Attendance* mean in this regression? Does that make sense?
c) In a week in which the paid attendance was 200,000 customers attending 30 shows at an average ticket price of $70, what would you estimate the receipts would be?
d) Is this likely to be a good prediction? Why do you think that?

_____

[7]Some values are rounded to simplify the exercises. If you recompute the analysis with your statistics software you may see slightly different numbers.

15. Police salaries, part 3. Using the regression table in Exercise 13, answer the following questions.

a) How was the *t*-ratio of 0.221 found for *Police Officer Wage*? (Show what is computed using numbers from the table.)
b) How many states are used in this model. How do you know?
c) The *t*-ratio for *Graduation Rate* is negative. What does that mean?

16. Ticket prices, part 3. Using the regression table in Exercise 14, answer the following questions.

a) How was the *t*-ratio of 126.7 found for *Paid Attendance*? (Show what is computed using numbers found in the table.)
b) How many weeks are included in this regression? How can you tell?
c) The *t*-ratio for the intercept is negative. What does that mean?

17. Police salaries, part 4. Consider the coefficient of *Police Officer Wage* in the regression table of Exercise 13.

a) State the standard null and alternative hypotheses for the true coefficient of *Police Officer Wage*.
b) Test the null hypothesis (at $\alpha = 0.05$) and state your conclusion.

18. Ticket prices, part 4. Consider the coefficient of *# Shows* in the regression table of Exercise 14.

a) State the standard null and alternative hypotheses for the true coefficient of *# Shows*.
b) Test the null hypothesis (at $\alpha = 0.05$) and state your conclusion.
c) A Broadway investor challenges your analysis. He points out that the scatterplot of *Receipts* vs. *# Shows* in Exercise 12 shows a strong linear relationship and claims that your result in part a can't be correct. Explain to him why this is not a contradiction.

19. Police salaries, part 5. A Senate aide accepts your analysis in Exercise 17 but claims that it demonstrates that if the state pays police more, it will actually *increase* the rate of violent crime. Explain why this interpretation is not a valid use of this regression model. Offer some alternative explanations.

20. Ticket prices, part 5. The investor in Exercise 18 now accepts your analysis but claims that it demonstrates that it doesn't matter how many shows are playing on Broadway; receipts will be essentially the same. Explain why this interpretation is not a valid use of this regression model. Be specific.

21. Police salaries, part 6. Here are some plots of residuals for the regression of Exercise 13.

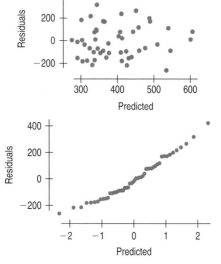

Which of the regression conditions can you check with these plots?

Do you find that those conditions are met?

T 22. Ticket prices, part 6. Here are some plots of residuals for the regression of Exercise 14.

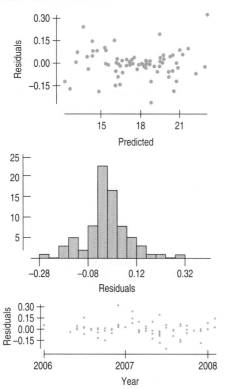

Which of the regression conditions can you check with these plots?

Do you find that those conditions are met?

23. Real estate prices. A regression was performed to predict selling *Price* of houses in dollars from their *Area* in

square feet, *Lotsize* in square feet, and *Age* in years. The R^2 is 92%. The equation from this regression is given here.

$$Price = 169,328 + 35.3\,Area + 0.718\,Lotsize - 6543\,Age$$

One of the following interpretations is correct. Which is it? Explain what's wrong with the others.

a) Each year a house ages, it is worth $6543 less.
b) Every extra square foot of area is associated with an additional $35.50 in average price, for houses with a given lot size and age.
c) Every additional dollar in price means lot size increases 0.718 square feet.
d) This model fits 92% of the data points exactly.

24. Wine prices. Many factors affect the price of wine, including such qualitative characteristics as the variety of grape, location of winery, and label. Researchers developed a regression model considering two quantitative variables: the tasting score of the wine and the age of the wine (in years) when released to market. They found the following regression equation, with an R^2 of 65%, to predict the price (in dollars) of a bottle of wine.

$$Price = 6.25 + 1.22\,Tasting\ Score + 0.55\,Age$$

One of the following interpretations is correct. Which is it? Explain what's wrong with the others.

a) Each year a bottle of wine ages, its price increases about $.55.
b) This model fits 65% of the points exactly.
c) For a unit increase in tasting score, the price of a bottle of wine increases about $1.22.
d) After allowing for the age of a bottle of wine, a wine with a one unit higher tasting score can be expected to cost about $1.22 more.

25. Appliance sales. A household appliance manufacturer wants to analyze the relationship between total sales and the company's three primary means of advertising (television, magazines, and radio). All values were in millions of dollars. They found the following regression equation.

$$Sales = 250 + 6.75\,TV + 3.5\,Radio + 2.3\,Magazine$$

One of the following interpretations is correct. Which is it? Explain what's wrong with the others.

a) If they did no advertising, their income would be $250 million.
b) Every million dollars spent on radio makes sales increase $3.5 million, all other things being equal.
c) Every million dollars spent on magazines increases TV spending $2.3 million.
d) Sales increase on average about $6.75 million for each million spent on TV, after allowing for the effects of the other kinds of advertising.

26. Wine prices, part 2. Here are some more interpretations of the regression model to predict the price of wine developed in Exercise 24. One of these interpretations is correct. Which is it? Explain what is wrong with the others.

a) The minimum price for a bottle of wine that has not aged is $6.25.
b) The price for a bottle of wine increases on average about $.55 for each year it ages, after allowing for the effects of tasting score.
c) Each year a bottle of wine ages, its tasting score increases by 1.22.
d) Each dollar increase in the price of wine increases its tasting score by 1.22.

27. Cost of pollution. What is the financial impact of pollution abatement on small firms? The U.S. government's Small Business Administration studied this and reported the following model.

$$Pollution\ abatement/employee = -2.494 - 0.431$$
$$\ln(Number\ of\ Employees) + 0.698 \ln(Sales)$$

Pollution abatement is in dollars per employee.

a) The coefficient of ln(*Number of Employees*) is negative. What does that mean in the context of this model? What does it mean that the coefficient of ln(*Sales*) is positive?
b) The model uses the (natural) logarithms of the two predictors. What does the use of this transformation say about their effects on pollution abatement costs?

T **28.** OECD economic regulations. A study by the U.S. Small Business Administration used historical data to model the GDP per capita of 24 of the countries in the Organization for Economic Cooperation and Development (OECD) (Crain, M. W., *The Impact of Regulatory Costs on Small Firms*, available at www.sba.gov/advocacy/7540/49291). One analysis estimated the effect on GDP of economic regulations, using an index of the degree of OECD economic regulation and other variables. They found the following regression model.

$$\widehat{GDP/Capita(1998-2002)} = 10487 - 1343\ OECD$$

$$Economic\ Regulation\ Index + 1.078\ GDP/Capita(1988)$$
$$- 69.99\ Ethno\text{-}linguistic\ Diversity\ Index$$
$$+ 44.71\ Trade\ as\ share\ of\ GDP\ (1998-2002)$$
$$- 58.4\ Primary\ Education\ (\%Eligible\ Population)$$

All *t*-statistics on the individual coefficients have P-values < 0.05, except the coefficient of *Primary Education*.

a) The researchers hoped to show that more regulation leads to lower GDP/Capita. Does the coefficient of the OECD Economic Regulation Index demonstrate that? Explain.
b) The F-statistic for this model is 129.61 (5, 17 df). What do you conclude about the model?
c) If *GDP/Capita(1988)* is removed as a predictor, then the F-statistic drops to 0.694 and none of the *t*-statistics

is significant (all P-values > 0.22). Reconsider your interpretation in part a.

29. Home prices. Many variables have an impact on determining the price of a house. A few of these are size of the house (square feet), lot size, and number of bathrooms. Information for a random sample of homes for sale in the Statesboro, Georgia, area was obtained from the Internet. Regression output modeling the asking price with square footage and number of bathrooms gave the following result.

```
Dependent Variable is: Asking Price
s = 67013   R-Sq = 71.1%   R-Sq(adj) = 64.6%
```

Predictor	Coeff	SE(Coeff)	t-ratio	P-value
Intercept	−152037	85619	−1.78	0.110
Baths	9530	40826	0.23	0.821
Area	139.87	46.67	3.00	0.015

Analysis of Variance

Source	DF	SS	MS	F	P-value
Regression	2	99303550067	49651775033	11.06	0.004
Residual	9	40416679100	4490742122		
Total	11	1.39720E+11			

a) Write the regression equation.
b) How much of the variation in home asking prices is accounted for by the model?
c) Explain in context what the coefficient of Area means.
d) The owner of a construction firm, upon seeing this model, objects because the model says that the number of bathrooms has no effect on the price of the home. He says that when *he* adds another bathroom, it increases the value. Is it true that the number of bathrooms is unrelated to house price? (*Hint:* Do you think bigger houses have more bathrooms?)

30. Home prices, part 2. Here are some diagnostic plots for the home prices data from Exercise 29. These were generated by a computer package and may look different from the plots generated by the packages you use. (In particular, note that the axes of the Normal probability plot are swapped relative to the plots we've made in the text. We only care about the pattern of this plot, so it shouldn't affect your interpretation.) Examine these plots and discuss whether the assumptions and conditions for the multiple regression seem reasonable.

Normal Probability Plot

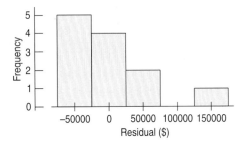

31. Secretary performance. The AFL-CIO has undertaken a study of 30 secretaries' yearly salaries (in thousands of dollars). The organization wants to predict salaries from several other variables. The variables to be considered potential predictors of salary are:

$X1$ = months of service

$X2$ = years of education

$X3$ = score on standardized test

$X4$ = words per minute (wpm) typing speed

$X5$ = ability to take dictation in words per minute

A multiple regression model with all five variables was run on a computer package, resulting in the following output.

Variable	Coeff	Std. Error	t-value
Intercept	9.788	0.377	25.960
X1	0.110	0.019	5.178
X2	0.053	0.038	1.369
X3	0.071	0.064	1.119
X4	0.004	0.0307	0.013
X5	0.065	0.038	1.734

$s = 0.430$ R-sq $= 0.863$

Assume that the residual plots show no violations of the conditions for using a linear regression model.

a) What is the regression equation?

b) From this model, what is the predicted salary (in thousands of dollars) of a secretary with 10 years (120 months) of experience, 9th grade education (9 years of education), 50 on the standardized test, 60 wpm typing speed, and the ability to take 30 wpm dictation?

c) Test whether the coefficient for words per minute of typing speed (X4) is significantly different from zero at $\alpha = 0.05$.

d) How might this model be improved?

e) A correlation of age with salary finds $r = 0.682$, and the scatterplot shows a moderately strong positive linear association. However, if X6 = Age is added to the multiple regression, the estimated coefficient of age turns out to be $b_6 = -0.154$. Explain some possible causes for this apparent change of direction in the relationship between age and salary.

32. Wal-Mart revenue. Here's a regression of monthly revenue of Wal-Mart Corp, relating that revenue to the Total U.S. Retail Sales, the Personal Consumption Index, and the Consumer Price Index.

Dependent variable is: Wal-Mart_Revenue
R squared = 66.7% R squared (adjusted) = 63.8%
s = 2.327 with 39 − 4 = 35 degrees of freedom

Source	Sum of Squares	df	Mean Square	F-ratio
Regression	378.749	3	126.250	23.3
Residual	189.474	35	5.41354	

Variable	Coeff	SE(Coeff)	t-ratio	P-value
Intercept	87.0089	33.60	2.59	0.0139
Retail Sales	0.000103	0.000015	6.67	<0.0001
Persnl Consmp	0.00001108	0.000004	2.52	0.0165
CPI	−0.344795	0.1203	−2.87	0.0070

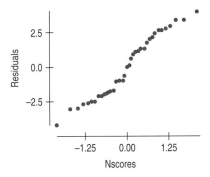

a) Write the regression model.

b) Interpret the coefficient of the Consumer Price Index (CPI). Does it surprise you that the sign of this coefficient is negative? Explain.

c) Test the standard null hypothesis for the coefficient of CPI and state your conclusions.

T 33. Gross domestic product. The gross domestic product (GDP) is an important measure of the overall economic strength of a country. GDP per capita makes comparisons between different size countries more meaningful. A researcher looking at GDP, fit the following model based on an educational variable, *Primary School Completion Rate (%)*, and finds:

Dependent variable is: *GDP per Capita*
R squared = 3.44%
s = 15945.46 with 96 − 1 = 95 df

Term	Estimate	Std Error	t-Ratio	P-value
Intercept	1935.5693	5987.938	0.320	0.7472
Primary Completion Rate	122.3288	66.8131	1.830	0.0703

a) Explain to the researcher why, on the basis of the regression summary, she might want to consider other predictor variables in the model.

b) Explain why you are not surprised that the sign of the slope is positive.

The researcher adds two variables to the regression and finds:

Dependent variable is: *GDP per Capita*
R squared = 80.00%
s = 7327.65 with 96 − 4 = 92 df

Term	Estimate	SE(Coeff)	t-Ratio	P-value
Intercept	2775.98251	2803.32606	0.99	0.3247
Cell phones/ 100 people	92.84968	37.38697	2.48	0.0148
Internet users per 100 people (2004)	480.49061	54.04020	8.89	<0.0001
Primary completion rate	−63.28454	32.25614	−1.96	0.0528

c) Explain how the slope of *Primary completion rate* can now be negative.

34. Lobster industry 2012, revisited. In Chapter 16, Exercise 53 predicted the annual value of the Maine lobster industry catch from the number of licensed lobser fishers. The lobster industry is an important one in Maine, with annual landings worth about $300,000,000 and employment consequences that extend throughout the state's economy. We saw in Chapter 16 that it was best to transform Value by logarithms. Here's a more sophisticated multiple regression to predict the logValue from other variables published by the Maine Department of Marine Resources (maine.gov/dmr). The predictors are number of *Traps* (millions), number of licensed *Fishers*, and *Pounds/Trap* during the years 1957 to 2012.

Dependent variable is: LogValue
R squared = 97.5% R squared (adjusted) = 97.4%
s = 0.0801 with 56 − 4 = 52 degrees of freedom

Source	Sum of Squares	df	Mean Square	F-ratio
Regression	13.2861	3	4.4287	690.108
Residual	0.33370	52	0.00642	

Variable	Coeff	SE(Coeff)	t-ratio	P-value
Intercept	0.85601	0.08766	9.77	<0.0001
Traps(M)	0.56347	0.01245	45.26	<0.0001
Fishers	−0.0000444	0.00000953	−4.67	<0.0001
Pounds/ Trap	0.00381	0.00145	2.62	0.0114

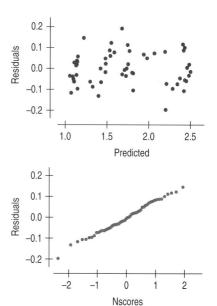

a) Write the regression model.

b) Are the assumptions and conditions met?

c) Interpret the coefficient of *Fishers*. Would you expect that restricting the number of lobstering licenses to even fewer fishers would increase the value of the harvest?

d) State and test the standard null hypothesis for the coefficient of *Pounds/Trap*. Scientists claim that this is an important predictor of the harvest. Do you agree?

35. Lobster industry 2012, revisited, part 2. In Chapter 16, Exercise 54 predicted the price ($/lb) of lobster harvested in the Maine lobster fishing industry. Here's a multiple regression to predict the *Price* from the number of *Traps* (millions), the number of *Fishers*, and *Pounds/Trap* during the years 1957 to 2012.

Dependent variable is: Price/lb
R squared = 94.2% R squared (adjusted) = 93.8%
s = 0.2850 with 56 − 4 = 52 degrees of freedom

Source	Sum of Squares	df	Mean Square	F-ratio
Regression	68.3949	3	22.7983	280.70
Residual	4.2234	52	0.0812	

Variable	Coefficient	SE(Coeff)	t-ratio	P-value
Intercept	1.0942	0.3118	3.51	0.0009
Traps(M)	1.2357	0.0443	27.90	<0.0001
Fishers	−0.000149	0.0000339	−4.40	<0.0001
Pounds/ Trap	−0.0180	0.00517	−3.47	0.0011

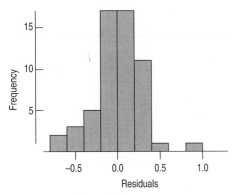

a) Write the regression model.

b) Are the assumptions and conditions met?

c) State and test the standard null hypothesis for the coefficient of *Pounds/Trap.* Use the standard α-level of .05 and state your conclusion.

d) Does the coefficient of *Pounds/Trap* mean that when the pounds per trap declines the price will increase?

e) This model has an adjusted R^2 of 93.8%. The previous model of Chapter 16, Exercise 56, had an adjusted R^2 of 91.6%. What does adjusted R^2 say about the two models?

T 36. HDI. In 1990, the United Nations created a single statistic, the Human Development Index or HDI, to summarize the health, education, and economic status of countries. Using data from 96 countries, here is a multiple regression model trying to predict *HDI.*

```
Dependent variable is: HDI
R squared = 98.23%
s = 0.024 with 96 - 8 = 88 df
```

Term	Estimate	Std Error	t-Ratio	P-value
Intercept	0.09010	0.04208	2.14	0.0351
Expected years of schooling (yrs)	0.01376	0.00176	7.79	<0.0001
Life expectancy at birth (years)	0.00333	0.00063	5.32	<0.0001
Maternal mortality ratio (deaths per 100000 live births)	-0.000120	0.0000254	-4.74	<0.0001
Mean years of schooling of adults (years)	0.01686	0.00166	10.19	<0.0001
Population urban (%)	0.000745	0.000181	4.13	<0.0001
GDP Per Capita	0.000000802	0.000000263	3.05	0.003
Cell phones/ 100 people	0.000460	0.000141	3.26	0.0016

a) Write the regression model.

b) Are the assumptions and conditions met?

c) State and test the standard null hypothesis for the coefficient of *Expected Years of Schooling.* Use the standard-level of $\alpha = 0.05$ and state your conclusion.

d) What effects do your observation in response to part b have on your test in part c?

T 37. Wal-Mart revenue, part 2. Wal-Mart is the second largest retailer in the world. The data file on the disk holds monthly data on Wal-Mart's revenue, along with several possibly related economic variables.

a) Using computer software, find the regression equation predicting Wal-Mart revenues from the *Retail Index,* the Consumer Price index (*CPI*), and *Personal Consumption.*

b) Does it seem that Wal-Mart's revenue is closely related to the general state of the economy?

T 38. Wal-Mart revenue, part 3. Consider the model you fit in Exercise 37 to predict Wal-Mart's revenue from the Retail Index, CPI, and Personal Consumption index.

a) Plot the residuals against the predicted values and comment on what you see.

18

Building Multiple Regression Models

Bolliger and Mabillard

The story is told that when John Wardley, the award-winning concept designer of theme parks and roller coasters, including *Nitro* and *Oblivion*, was about to test the roller coaster *Nemesis* for the first time, he asked Walter Bolliger, the president of the coaster's manufacturer, B&M, "What if the coaster stalls? How will we get the trains back to the station?" Bolliger replied, "Our coasters never stall. They always work perfectly the first time." And, of course, it did work perfectly.

Roller coaster connoisseurs know that Bolliger & Mabillard Consulting Engineers, Inc. (B&M) is responsible for some of the most innovative roller coasters in the business. The company was founded in the late 1980s when Walter Bolliger and Claude Mabillard left Intamin AG, where they had designed the company's first stand-up coaster. B&M has built its reputation on innovation. They developed the first "inverted" roller coaster in which the train runs under the track with the seats attached to the wheel carriage and pioneered "diving machines," which feature a vertical drop, introduced first with *Oblivion*.

B&M coasters are famous among enthusiasts for particularly smooth rides and for their reliability, easy maintainability, and excellent safety record. Unlike some other manufacturers, B&M does not use powered launches, preferring, as do many coaster connoisseurs, gravity-powered coasters. B&M is an international leader in the roller coaster design field, having designed 24 of the top 50 steel roller coasters on the 2009 Golden Ticket Awards list and 3 of the top 10 in the 2013 Awards.

WHO	Roller coasters
WHAT	See Table 18.1 for the variables and their units.
WHERE	Worldwide
WHEN	All were in operation in 2013.
WHY	To understand characteristics that affect speed and duration

Theme parks are big business. In the United States alone, there are nearly 500 theme and amusement parks that generate over $10 billion a year in revenue. The U.S. industry is fairly mature, but parks in the rest of the world are still growing. Europe now generates more than $1 billion a year from their theme parks, and Asia's industry is growing fast. Although theme parks have started to diversify to include water parks and zoos, rides are still the main attraction at most parks, and at the center of the rides is the roller coaster. Engineers and designers compete to make them bigger and faster. For a two-minute ride on the fastest and best roller coasters, fans will wait for hours.

Can we learn what makes a roller coaster fast? What are the most important design considerations in getting the fastest coaster? Here are data on some of the fastest roller coasters in the world today:

Name	Park	Country	Type	Duration (sec)	Speed (mph)	Height (ft)	Drop (ft)	Length (ft)	Inversion?
New Mexico Rattler	Cliff's Amusement Park	USA	Wooden	75	47	80	75	2750	No
Fujiyama	Fuji-Q Highlands	Japan	Steel	216	80.8	259.2	229.7	6708.67	No
Goliath	Six Flags Magic Mountain	USA	Steel	180	85	235	255	4500	No
Great American Scream Machine	Six Flags Great Adventure	USA	Steel	140	68	173	155	3800	Yes
Hangman	Wild Adventures	USA	Steel	125	55	115	95	2170	Yes
Hayabusa	Tokyo SummerLand	Japan	Steel	108	60.3	137.8	124.67	2559.1	No
Hercules	Dorney Park	USA	Wooden	135	65	95	151	4000	No
Hurricane	Myrtle Beach Pavilion	USA	Wooden	120	55	101.5	100	3800	No

A small selection of coasters from the larger data set available on the CD.

Table 18.1 Facts about some roller coasters. (Source: The Roller Coaster Database at www.rcdb.com.)

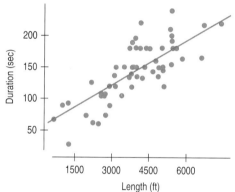

Figure 18.1 The relationship between *Duration* and *Length* looks strong and positive. On average, *Duration* increases linearly with *Length*.

- *Type* indicates what kind of track the roller coaster has. The possible values are "wooden" and "steel." (The frame usually is of the same construction as the track, but doesn't have to be.)
- *Duration* is the duration of the ride in seconds.
- *Speed* is top speed in miles per hour.
- *Height* is maximum height above ground level in feet.
- *Drop* is greatest drop in feet.
- *Length* is total length of the track in feet.
- *Inversions* reports whether riders are turned upside down during the ride. It has the values "yes" or "no."

Customers not only want the ride to be fast; they also want it to last. It makes sense that the longer the track is, the longer the ride will last. Let's have a look at *Duration* and *Length* to see what the relationship is.

```
Dependent variable is: Duration
R-squared = 62.0%  R-squared (adjusted) = 61.4%
s = 27.23 with 63 − 2 = 61 degrees of freedom

Source      Sum of Squares   DF   Mean Square   F-ratio
Regression  73901.7           1   73901.7       99.6
Residual    45243.7          61    741.700

Variable    Coefficient   SE(Coeff)   t-ratio   P-value
Intercept   53.9348       9.488       5.68      <0.0001
Length       0.0231       0.0023      9.98      <0.0001
```

Table 18.2 The regression of *Duration* on *Length* looks strong, and the conditions seem to be met.

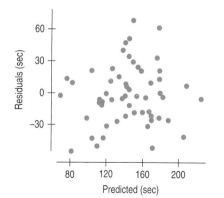

Figure 18.2 Residuals from the regression in Table 18.2.

As the scatterplots of the variables (Figure 18.1) and residuals (Figure 18.2) show, the regression conditions seem to be met, and the regression makes sense; we'd expect longer tracks to give longer rides. Starting from the intercept at about 53.9 seconds, the duration of the ride increases, on average, by 0.0231 seconds per foot of track—or 23.1 seconds more for each 1000 additional feet of track.

18.1   Indicator (or Dummy) Variables

Of course, there's more to these data. One interesting variable might not be one you'd naturally think of. Many modern coasters have "inversions" where riders get turned upside down, with loops, corkscrews, or other devices. These inversions add excitement, but they must be carefully engineered, and that enforces some speed limits on that portion of the ride. Riders like speed, but they also like inversions which affect both the speed and the duration of the ride. We'd like to add the information of whether the roller coaster has an inversion to our model. Until now, all our predictor variables have been quantitative. Whether or not a roller coaster has an inversion is a categorical variable ("yes" or "no"). Let's see how to introduce the categorical variable *Inversions* as a predictor in our regression model. Figure 18.3 shows the same scatterplot of *Duration* against *Length*, but now with the roller coasters that have inversions shown as red x's and those without shown as blue dots. There's a separate regression line for each type of roller coaster.

Figure 18.3   The two lines fit to coasters with (red x's) and without (blue dots) inversions are roughly parallel.

It's easy to see that, for a given length, the roller coasters with inversions take a bit longer and that for each type of roller coaster, the slopes of the relationship between duration and length are not quite equal but are similar. If we split the data into two groups—coasters without inversions and those with inversions—and compute the regression for each group, the output looks like this:

```
Dependent variable is: Duration
Cases selected according to: No inversions
R-squared = 69.4%  R-squared (adjusted) = 68.5%
s = 25.12 with 38 − 2 = 36 degrees of freedom
```

Variable	Coefficient	SE(Coeff)	t-ratio	P-value
Intercept	25.9961	14.10	1.84	0.0734
Length	0.0274	0.003	9.03	<0.0001

```
Dependent variable is: Duration
Cases selected according to: Inversions
R-squared = 70.5%  R-squared (adjusted) = 69.2%
s = 23.20 with 25 − 2 = 23 degrees of freedom
```

Variable	Coefficient	SE(Coeff)	t-ratio	P-value
Intercept	47.6454	12.50	3.81	0.0009
Length	0.0299	0.004	7.41	<0.0001

Table 18.3   The regressions computed separately for the two types of roller coasters show similar slopes but different intercepts.

As the scatterplot showed, the slopes are very similar, but the intercepts are different. When we have a situation like this with roughly parallel regressions for each group,[1] there's an easy way to add the group information to a single regression model. We create a new variable that *indicates* what type of roller coaster we have, giving it the value 1 for roller coasters that have inversions and the value 0 for those that don't. (We could have reversed the coding; it's an arbitrary choice.[2]) Such variables are called **indicator variables** or *indicators* because they indicate which category each case is in. They are also often called **dummy variables**. When we add our new indicator, *Inversions*, to the regression model as a second variable, the multiple regression model looks like this.

> *Inversions* = 1 if a coaster has inversions.
> *Inversions* = 0 if not.

```
Dependent variable is: Duration
R-squared = 70.4%  R-squared (adjusted) = 69.4%
s = 24.24 with 63 − 3 = 60 degrees of freedom

Variable     Coefficient   SE(Coeff)   t-ratio   P-value
Intercept    22.3909       11.39       1.97       0.0539
Length        0.0282        0.0024     11.7      <0.0001
Inversions   30.0824        7.290       4.13     <0.0001
```

Table 18.4   The regression model with a dummy, or indicator, variable for Inversions.

This looks like a better model than the simple regression for all the data. The R^2 is larger, the *t*-ratios of both coefficients are large, and now we can understand the effect of inversions with a single model without having to compare two regressions. (The residuals look reasonable as well.) But what does the coefficient for *Inversions* mean? Let's see how an indicator variable works when we calculate predicted values for two of the roller coasters listed in Table 18.1.

Name	Park	Country	Type	Duration	Speed	Height	Drop	Length	Inversion?
Hangman	Wild Adventures	USA	Steel	125	55	115	95	2170	Yes
Hayabusa	Tokyo SummerLand	Japan	Steel	108	60.3	137.8	124.67	2559.1	No

Ignoring the variable *Inversions* for the moment, the model (in Table 18.4) says that for all coasters, the predicted *Duration* is:

$$22.39 + 0.0282 \, Length + 30.08 \, Inversions.$$

Now remember that for this indicator variable, the value 1 means that a coaster has an inversion, while a 0 means it doesn't. For *Hayabusa*, with no inversion, the value of *Inversions* is 0, so the coefficient of *Inversions* doesn't affect the prediction at all. With a length of 2259.1 feet, we predict its duration as:[3]

$$22.39 + 0.0282 \, (2559.1) + 30.08 \times 0 = 94.56 \text{ seconds},$$

which is close to its actual duration of 108 seconds. The *Hangman* (with a length of 2170 feet) has an inversion, and so the model predicts an "additional" 30.0824 seconds for its duration:

$$22.39 + 0.0282 \, (2170.0) + 30.08 \times 1 = 113.66 \text{ seconds}.$$

That compares well with the actual duration of 125 seconds.

---

[1] The fact that the individual regression lines are nearly parallel is a part of the Linearity Condition. You should check that the lines are nearly parallel before using this method or read on to see what to do if they are not parallel enough.

[2] Some implementations of indicator variables use 1 and −1 for the levels of the categories.

[3] We round coefficient values when we write the model and sometimes, as here, when we show calculations in the text. But, in general, we recommend calculating with full precision, rounding only at the end of the calculation.

Notice how the indicator works in the model. When there is an inversion (as in *Hangman*), the value 1 for the indicator causes the amount of the indicator's coefficient, 30.08, to be *added* to the prediction. When there is no inversion (as in *Hayabusa*), the indicator is 0, so nothing is added. Looking back at the scatterplot, we can see that this is exactly what we need. The difference between the two lines is a vertical shift of about 30 seconds. This may seem a bit confusing at first because we usually think of the coefficients in a multiple regression as slopes. For indicator variables, however, they act differently. They're vertical shifts that keep the slopes for the other variables apart.

An indicator variable that is 0 or 1 can only shift the line up and down. It can't change the slope, so it works only when we have lines with the same slope and different intercepts.

Indicators for Three or More Categories

Business and economic variables such as *Month* or *Socioeconomic Class* may have several levels, not just two. You can construct indicators for a categorical variable with several levels by constructing a separate indicator for each of these levels. There's just one thing to keep in mind. If a variable has k levels, you can create only $k - 1$ indicators. You have to choose one of the k categories as a "baseline" and *leave out* its indicator. Then the coefficients of the other indicators can be interpreted as the amount by which their categories differ from the baseline, after allowing for the linear effects of the other variables in the model. (There are ways to code the variables so that each is compared to the overall mean. See the comment in Footnote 2.)

For the two-category variable *Inversions*, we used "no inversion" as the baseline, and coasters with an inversion got a 1. We needed only one variable for two levels. If we wished to represent *Month* with indicators, we would need 11 of them. We might, for example, define *January* as the baseline and make indicators for *February*, *March*, . . . , *November*, and *December*. Each of these indicators would be 0 for all cases except for the ones that had that value for the variable *Month*.

Why couldn't we use a single variable with "1" for *January*, "2" for *February*, and so on? That would require the pretty strict assumption that the responses to the months are linear and equally spaced—that is, that the change in our response variable from January to February is the same in both direction and amount as the change from July to August. That's a pretty severe restriction and usually isn't true. Using 11 indicators releases the model from that restriction even though it adds complexity to the model.

Once you've created multiple indicator variables (up to $k - 1$) for a categorical variable with k levels, it often helps to combine levels with similar characteristics and with similar relationships with the response. This can help keep the number of variables in a multiple regression from exploding.

FOR EXAMPLE   Indicator variables

In Chapter 16 we looked at data on the prices of diamonds (see page 516). Although, in general, higher carat weight means higher cost, *Carat Weight* is not the only factor that determines a diamond's price. A typical diamond is pale yellow. The less color a diamond has, the higher its color grade and—generally—its price. We want to build a model that incorporates both *Carat Weight* and *Color* to predict a diamond's price. The data here are a collection of 749 diamonds: *Weight* is between 0.3 and 1.4 carats; color grades are D (highest possible), G (medium), and K (fairly low). As before, we'll use $Log_{10}Price$ as the response to make the relationship more linear. Here are scatterplots of *Price* and $Log_{10}Price$ versus *Carat Weight* for these diamonds:

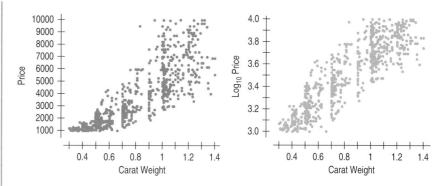

A linear model for $Log_{10}Price$ on *Carat Weight* alone finds:

```
Response Variable: Log₁₀Price
R² = 77.39%  Adjusted R² = 77.36%
s = 0.1364 with 749 - 2 = 747 degrees of freedom
```

```
Variable      Coeff      SE(Coeff)   t-ratio   P-value
Intercept     2.76325    0.01532     180.42    <0.0001
Carat.Weight  0.90020    0.01780      50.56    <0.0001
```

Here is a scatterplot of $Log_{10}Price$ vs. *Carat Weight* showing the three different color grades (D, G, and K):

To account for the differences, two indicator variables were created:

$$Color\ D = 1 \text{ if } Color = \text{D and 0 otherwise}$$
$$Color\ G = 1 \text{ if } Color = \text{G and 0 otherwise}$$

A multiple regression of $Log_{10}Price$ was run with three predictors: *Carat Weight, Color D,* and *Color G*

Here is the output:

```
Response Variable: Log₁₀Price
R² = 85.66%  Adjusted R² = 85.61%
s = 0.1088 with 749 - 4 = 745 degrees of freedom
```

```
Variable      Coeff      SE(Coeff)   t-ratio   P-value
Intercept     2.43978    0.01981     123.14    <0.0001
Carat.Weight  1.02865    0.01589      64.75    <0.0001
ColorD        0.29405    0.01424      20.65    <0.0001
ColorG        0.21883    0.01278      17.12    <0.0001
```

QUESTIONS   For the three colors of diamonds, what are the models that predict $Log_{10}Price$? Does the addition of the indicator variables for the colors seem like a good idea? Why are there only two indicator variables?

ANSWERS   The indicator variable adds amounts to the intercept value for the two color levels, D and G. Since diamonds of color K have both dummy variables set to 0, the equation for diamonds with *Color K* is simply:

$$\widehat{Log_{10}Price} = 2.440 + 1.029\ Carat\ Weight$$

(continued)

For diamonds with *Color G*, we add 0.219 to the intercept, so:

$$\widehat{Log_{10}Price} = (2.440 + 0.219) + 1.029\ Carat\ Weight = 2.659 + 1.029\ Carat\ Weight$$

Similarly for diamonds with *Color D*, we add 0.294 to the intercept, so:

$$\widehat{Log_{10}Price} = (2.440 + 0.294) + 1.029\ Carat\ Weight = 2.734 + 1.029\ Carat\ Weight$$

Both indicator variables are highly significant, which means that the differences in intercept are large enough to justify the addition of the variables.

With 3 levels of color, we need only 2 indicator variables. (In general *k* levels require *k* − 1 indicators.)

18.2 Adjusting for Different Slopes— Interaction Terms

WHO	Burger King menu items
WHAT	Calories, Carbohydrates, Protein, Type of item
WHEN	Current
WHERE	Posted in stores and online
WHY	Informing customers

Even consumers of fast food are increasingly concerned with nutrition. So, like many restaurant chains, Burger King publishes the nutrition details of its menu items on its website (www.bk.com). Many customers count calories or carbohydrates. Of course, these are likely to be related to each other. We can examine that relationship in Burger King foods by looking at a scatterplot.

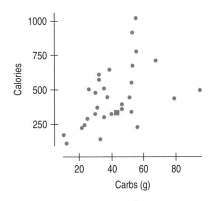

Figure 18.4 *Calories* of Burger King foods plotted against *Carbs* seems to fan out.

It's not surprising to see that an increase in *Carbs* is associated with more *Calories*, but the plot seems to thicken as we move from left to right. Could there be something else going on?

We can divide Burger King foods into two groups, coloring those with meat (including chicken and fish) with red x's and those without meat with blue dots. Looking at the regressions for each group, we see a different picture:

Figure 18.5 Plotting the meat-based and nonmeat items separately, we see two distinct linear patterns.

Burger King

James McLamore and David Edgerton, graduates of the Cornell University School of Hotel Administration, opened their first Burger King (BK) restaurant in 1954. McLamore had been impressed with the assembly-line–based production innovated by Dick and Mac MacDonald. BK grew in the Miami area and then expanded nationally through franchising. Pillsbury acquired BK in 1967 and expanded it internationally. After a number of owners, BK was purchased by private investors and taken public. The initial public offering (IPO) in 2006 generated $425 million in revenue—the largest IPO of a U.S.-based restaurant chain on record.

Clearly, meat-based items contribute more calories from their carbohydrate content than do other Burger King foods. But unlike Figure 18.3, when the lines were parallel, we can't account for the kind of difference we see here by just including a dummy variable in a regression. It isn't just the intercepts of the lines that are different; they have entirely different slopes.

We'll start, as before, by constructing the indicator for the two groups, *Meat*, which is 1 for foods that contain meat and 0 for the others. The variable *Meat* can adjust the intercepts of the two lines. To adjust the slopes, we have to construct another variable—the *product* of *Meat* and the predictor variable *Carbs*. The coefficient of this **interaction term** in a multiple regression gives an adjustment to the slope for the cases in the indicated group. The resulting variable *Carbs*Meat* has the value of *Carbs* for foods containing meat (those coded 1 in the *Meat* indicator) and the value 0 for the others. By including this interaction variable in the model, we can adjust the slope of the line fit to the meat-containing foods. Here's the resulting analysis:

```
Dependent variable is: Calories
R-squared = 78.1%  R-squared (adjusted) = 75.7%
s = 106.0 with 32 − 4 = 28 degrees of freedom
```

Source	Sum of Squares	DF	Mean Square	F-ratio
Regression	1119979	3	373326	33.2
Residual	314843	28	11244.4	

Variable	Coefficient	SE(Coeff)	t-ratio	P-value
Intercept	137.395	58.72	2.34	0.0267
Carbs(g)	3.93317	1.113	3.53	0.0014
Meat	−26.1567	98.48	−0.266	0.7925
Carbs*Meat	7.87530	2.179	3.61	0.0012

Table 18.5 The regression model with both an indicator variable and an interaction term.

What does the coefficient for the indicator *Meat* do? It provides a different intercept to separate the meat and nonmeat items at the origin (where *Carbs* = 0). Each group has its own slope, but the two lines nearly meet at the origin, so there seems to be no need for an additional intercept adjustment. The difference of 26.16 calories is small. That's why the coefficient for the indicator variable *Meat* has a small *t*-ratio (−0.266).

By contrast, the coefficient of the interaction term, *Carbs*Meat*, says that the slope relating calories to carbohydrates is steeper by 7.88 calories per carbohydrate gram for meat-containing foods than for meat-free foods. Its small P-value suggests that this difference is real. Overall, the regression model predicts calories to be:

$$137.40 + 3.93 \, Carbs − 26.16 \, Meat + 7.88 \, Carbs{*}Meat.$$

Let's see how these adjustments work. A BK Whopper has 53 grams of carbohydrates and is a meat dish. The model predicts its *Calories* as:

$$137.40 + 3.93 \times 53 − 26.16 \times 1 + 7.88 \times 53 \times 1 = 737.2 \text{ calories,}$$

not far from the measured calorie count of 680. By contrast, the Veggie Burger, with 43 grams of carbohydrates, has value 0 for *Meat* and so has a value of 0 for *Carbs*Meat* as well. Those indicators contribute nothing to its predicted calories:

$$137.40 + 3.93 \times 43 − 26.16 \times 0 + 7.88 \times 0 \times 43 = 306.4 \text{ calories,}$$

close to the 330 measured officially.

FOR EXAMPLE Adding interaction terms

After adding the indicator variables for *Color*, which showed different intercepts for the three different color levels, an analyst wonders if the slopes for the three color levels might be different as well, so she adds two more predictors, *ColorD*Carat Weight* and *ColorG*Carat Weight* to the model (see page 602). The regression output shows:

```
Response Variable: Log10Price
R-squared = 85.77%  Adjusted R-squared = 85.67%
s = 0.1085 with 749 − 6 = 743 degrees of freedom

Variable             Coeff      SE(Coeff)   t-ratio   P-value
Intercept            2.54151    0.06000     42.361    <0.0001
Carat.Weight         0.92968    0.05734     16.212    <0.0001
ColorD               0.16466    0.06302      2.613     0.00916
ColorG               0.12656    0.06287      2.013     0.04448
Carat.Weight*ColorD  0.14076    0.06356      2.215     0.02709
Carat.Weight*ColorG  0.08809    0.06095      1.445     0.14877
```

QUESTION   Based on this, what model might you use to predict $Log_{10}Price$?

ANSWERS   The only significant interaction term is the one for *ColorD* by *Carat Weight*, so we probably don't need different slopes for levels *G* and *K*. We should refit the regression without the interaction term *ColorG*Carat Weight*. When we do, we find that the term for *Carat Weight*ColorD* is marginally significant. The decision whether to include it is a judgment call. To make a final decision, we should also consider residual analysis and diagnostics. For the sake of simplicity we will proceed with the simpler model with only the indicator variables and not the interaction (the model fit in the previous example).

JUST CHECKING

A researcher in the Human Resource department wants to study the relationships among *Salary, Years Experience, Education,* and *Gender*. For *Education,* there are 3 levels: high school or some college (*HS*), college grad (*BA*), and post graduate (*PG*).

1 If she wants to account for differences in the relationship between *Salary* and *Years Experience* for men and women, what terms should she enter in the regression?

2 If she wants to study the differences in the relationship between *Salary* and *Years Experience* for different *Education* levels, how many indicator variables will she need for *Education*?

18.3   Multiple Regression Diagnostics

We often use regression analyses to make important business decisions. By working with the data and creating models, we can learn a great deal about the relationships among variables. As we saw with simple regression, sometimes we can learn as much from the cases that *don't* fit the model as from the bulk of cases that do. Extraordinary cases often tell us more just by the ways in which they fail to conform and the reasons we can discover for those deviations. If a case doesn't conform to the others, we should identify it and, if possible, understand why it is different. In simple regression, a case can be extraordinary by standing away from the model in the *y* direction or by having unusual values in an *x*-variable. In multiple regression, it can also be extraordinary by having an unusual *combination* of values in the *x*-variables. Just as in simple regression, large deviations in the *y* direction show up in the residuals as outliers. Deviations in the *x*'s show up as *leverage*.

Leverage

In a regression of a single predictor and a response, it's easy to see if a value has high leverage, because it's far from the mean of the *x* values in a scatterplot. In a multiple regression with *k* predictor variables, things are more complicated. A point might actually not be far from any of the *x* means and yet still exert large leverage because it has an unusual *combination* of predictor values. Even a graphics program designed to display points in high dimensional spaces may not make it obvious. Fortunately, we can calculate leverage values for each case. These are standard for most multiple regression programs.

The **leverage** of a case is easy to understand. For any case, add 1 to its *y*-value. Recompute the regression, and see how much the *predicted* value of the case changes. The amount of the change is the leverage. It can never be greater than 1 or less than 0. A point with zero leverage has no effect at all on the regression slope, although it does participate in the calculations of the intercept, R^2, *s*, and the *F*- and *t*-statistics. The leverage of the ith point in a data set is often denoted by h_i.

A point with high leverage may not actually influence the regression coefficients if it follows the pattern of the model set by the other points, but it's worth examining simply because of its *potential* to do so. Looking at leverage values can be an effective way to discover cases that are extraordinary on a combination of *x*-variables. In business, such cases often deserve special attention.

There are no tests for whether the leverage of a case is too large. The average leverage value among all cases in a regression is $1/n$, but that doesn't give us much of a guide. Some packages use rules of thumb to indicate high leverage values.[4] Another common approach is to just make a histogram of the leverages. Any case whose leverage stands out in a histogram of leverages probably deserves special attention. You may decide to leave the case in the regression or to see how the regression model changes when you delete the case, but you should be aware of its potential to influence the regression.

We've already seen that the *Duration* of a roller coaster ride depends linearly on its *Length*. But even more than a long ride, roller coaster customers like speed. So, rather than predict the duration of a roller coaster ride, let's build a model for how fast it travels. A multiple regression with two predictors shows that both the total *Height* and the *Drop* (the maximum distance from the top to the bottom of the largest drop in the ride) are important factors:

```
Dependent variable is: Speed
R-squared = 85.5%  R-squared (adjusted) = 85.1%
s = 4.608 with 76 − 3 = 73 degrees of freedom

Source        Sum of Squares   DF   Mean Square   F-ratio
Regression    9140.89           2   4570.44       215.24
Residual      1550.10          73     21.23

Variable    Coefficient    SE(Coeff)    t-ratio    P-value
Intercept   37.01333       1.47723      25.06      <0.0001
Height       0.0658136     0.01911       3.44       0.0010
Drop         0.1254037     0.018878      6.64      <0.0001

The estimated regression equation is
```
$$\widehat{Speed} = 37.01 + 0.066\,Height + 0.125\,Drop.$$

Table 18.6　A multiple regression of *Speed* on *Height* and *Drop*. Both coefficients are significant.

The regression certainly seems reasonable.

---

[4]One common rule for determining when a leverage is large is to indicate any leverage value greater than $3(k + 1)/n$, where *k* is the number of predictors.

Standard Error

In some software regression tables, the standard deviation of the residuals, which we denote s_e, is called a "standard error." In this book, "standard error" refers to the estimated standard deviation of a statistic, and we denote it SE(*statistic*). The standard deviation of the residuals is not a standard error. Although it is a data-based estimate of a standard deviation, it is not the standard deviation of an estimated statistics. Other statistics programs call this value the residual standard error or root mean square error. Remember that it's the estimated standard deviation of the residuals, not a summary.

A histogram of the leverage values, however, shows something interesting:

Figure 18.6 The distribution of leverage values shows a few high values and one extraordinarily high-leverage point.

The case with very high leverage is a coaster called *Oblivion*, a steel roller coaster in England that opened as the world's first "vertical drop coaster" in 1998. What's unusual about *Oblivion* is that its *Height* is only about 65 feet above ground (placing it below the median), and yet it drops 180 feet to achieve a top speed of 68 mph. The unique feature of *Oblivion* is that it plunges *underground* nearly 120 feet. So when considered together, its height and drop are a very unusual combination.

Figure 18.7 A plot of the two predictors shows why *Oblivion* has high leverage.

Leverage points can affect not only the coefficients of the model, but also our choice of whether to include a predictor in a regression model as well. The more complex the regression model, the more important it is to look at high-leverage values and their effects.

Residuals and Standardized Residuals

Residuals are not all alike. Consider a point with leverage 1.0. That's the highest a leverage can be, and it means that the line follows the point perfectly. So, a point like that must have a zero residual. And since we know the residual exactly, that residual has zero standard deviation. This tendency is true in general: The larger the leverage, the smaller the standard deviation of its residual. When we want to compare values that have differing standard deviations, it's a good idea to standardize them. We can do that with the regression residuals, dividing each one by an estimate of its own standard deviation. Such standardized residuals are called **studentized residuals**.[5] In a simple regression, it makes little difference, but for a multiple regression, it's a good idea to examine studentized residuals rather than the simple residuals to check the Nearly Normal Condition and the Equal Spread Condition. Any studentized residual that stands out from the others deserves your attention.

It may occur to you that we've always plotted the *unstandardized* residuals when we made regression models. We treated them as if they all had the same

_____

[5]There's more than one way to studentize residuals according to how you estimate the standard deviation of the residuals. You may find statistics packages referring to *externally studentized residuals* and *internally studentized residuals*. The *externally studentized* version follows a *t*-distribution, so those are the ones we recommend.

standard deviation when we checked the Nearly Normal Condition. It turns out that this was a simplification. It didn't matter much for simple regression, but for multiple regression models, it's a better idea to use the studentized residuals when checking the Nearly Normal Condition and when making scatterplots of residuals against predicted values.

Influence Measures

A case that has *both* high leverage and a large studentized residual may have changed the regression model substantially all by itself. Such a case is said to be **influential**. An influential case cries out for special attention because removing it is likely to give a different regression model. The surest way to tell whether a case is influential is to try leaving it out[6] and see how much the regression model changes. You should call a case "influential" if omitting it changes the regression model by enough to matter for *your* purposes.

To identify possibly influential cases, check the leverage and studentized residuals. Two statistics that combine leverage and studentized residuals into a single measure of influence, **Cook's Distance** (Cook's D) and **DFFITS**, are offered by many statistics programs. You should examine a histogram of these measures and pay special attention to any case with an extraordinarily large value because it may be exerting a lot of influence on your regression model.

A histogram of the Cook's Distances from the model in Table 18.6 shows a few influential values:

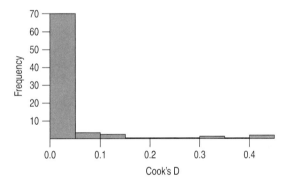

Here are coasters with the four highest values of Cook's D.

Name	Type	Duration	Speed	Height	Drop	Length	Inversions	Cook's D
HyperSonic XLC	Steel	NA	80	165	133	1560	0	0.1037782
Oblivion	Steel	NA	68	65	180	1222	0	0.1124114
Volcano, The Blast Coaster	Steel	NA	70	155	80	2757	1	0.3080218
Xcelerator	Steel	62	82	205	130	2202	0	0.4319336

Table 18.7   Coasters with high Cook's D.

In addition to the *Oblivion*, Cook's Distance singles out three other coasters: *HyperSonic XLC*; *Volcano, The Blast Coaster*; and *Xcelerator*. A little research finds that these three coasters *are* different as well. Our model found that *Height* and *Drop* significantly influence a coaster's *Speed*. But these three coasters have something extra—a hydraulic catapult that accelerates the coasters more than gravity

---

[6]Or, equivalently, include an indicator variable that selects only for that case. See the discussion in the next section.

alone. In fact, the *Xcelerator* reaches 82 mph in 2.3 seconds, using only 157 feet of track to launch it. Removing the three accelerator coasters from the model has a striking effect:

```
Variable    Coeff       SE(Coeff)   t-ratio   P-value
Intercept   36.47453    1.06456     34.262    <0.0001
Drop         0.17519    0.01493     11.731    <0.0001
Height       0.01600    0.01507      1.062     0.292

s = 3.307 on 70 degrees of freedom
R-squared = 92.5%  Adjusted R-squared = 92.3%
F = 429.5 on 2 and 70 DF, P-value: <0.0001
```

Table 18.8   Removing the three blast coasters has made *Height* no longer important to the model. A simple regression model, such as in Table 18.9, may be a more effective summary than the model with two predictor variables.

The *Height* of the coaster is no longer a statistically significant predictor, so we might choose to omit that variable.

```
Variable    Coeff       SE(Coeff)   t-ratio   P-value
Intercept   36.743925   1.034798    35.51     <0.0001
Drop         0.189474   0.006475    29.26     <0.0001

s = 3.31 on 71 degrees of freedom
R-squared = 92.3%  Adjusted R-squared = 92.2%
F = 856.3 on 1 and 71 DF, P-value: <0.0001
```

Table 18.9   A simple linear regression model without the three blast coasters and with *Height* deleted.

Indicators for Influence

One good way to examine the effect of an extraordinary case on a regression is to construct a special indicator variable that is zero for all cases *except* the one we want to isolate. Including such an indicator in the regression model has the same effect as removing the case from the data, but it has two special advantages. First, it makes it clear to anyone looking at the regression model that we have treated that case specially. Second, the *t*-statistic for the indicator variable's coefficient can be used as a test of whether the case is influential. If the P-value is small, then that case really didn't fit well with the rest of the data. Typically, we name such an indicator with the identifier of the case we want to remove. Here's the last roller coaster model in which we have removed the influence of the three blast coasters by constructing indicators for them instead of by removing them from the data. Notice that the coefficient for drop is just the same as the ones we found by omitting the cases.

```
Dependent variable is: Speed
R-squared = 92.7%  R-squared (adjusted) = 92.3%
s = 3.310 with 76 − 5 = 71 degrees of freedom

Variable    Coeff      SE(Coeff)   t-ratio   P-value
Intercept   36.7439    1.035       35.5      <0.0001
Drop         0.189474  0.0065      29.3      <0.0001
Xcelerator  20.6244    3.334        6.19     <0.0001
HyperSonic  18.0560    3.334        5.42     <0.0001
Volcano     18.0981    3.361        5.38     <0.0001
```

Table 18.10   The P-values for the three indicator variables confirm that each of these roller coasters doesn't fit with the others.

Diagnosis Wrapup

What have we learned from diagnosing the regression? We've discovered four roller coasters that may be strongly influencing the model. And for each of them, we've been able to understand why and how it differed from the others. The oddness of *Oblivion* plunging into a hole in the ground may have caused us to value *Drop* as a predictor of *Speed* more than *Height*. The three influential cases with high Cook's D values turned out to be different from the other roller coasters because they are "blast coasters" that don't rely only on gravity for their acceleration. Although we can't count on always discovering why influential cases are special, diagnosing influential cases raises the question of what about them might be different and can help us understand our model better.

When a regression analysis has cases that have both high leverage and large studentized residuals, it would be irresponsible to report only the regression on all the data. You should also compute and discuss the regression found with such cases removed, and discuss the extraordinary cases individually if they offer additional insight. If your interest is to understand the world, the extraordinary cases may tell you more than the rest of the model. If your only interest is in the model (for example, because you hope to use it for prediction), then you'll want to be certain that the model wasn't determined by only a few influential cases, but instead was built on the broader base of the body of your data.

FOR EXAMPLE   Regression diagnostics

Two other measures of quality of a diamond (see page 602) are its *Table* size and *Depth*; both are expressed as percentages. *Table* size is the ratio of the flat top part (the table) diameter to the diameter of the stone. *Depth* is the ratio of the distance from table to bottom (culet) to the diameter. The output of the regression of $Log_{10}Price$ on *Carat Weight, Color D, Color G, Table,* and *Depth* shows:

```
Response Variable: Log10Price
R-squared = 85.92%  Adjusted R-squared = 85.82%
s = 0.1080 with 749 − 6 = 743 degrees of freedom
```

Variable	Coeff	SE(Coeff)	t-ratio	P-value
Intercept	3.464326	0.322336	10.748	<0.0001
Carat.Size	1.031627	0.015799	65.295	<0.0001
ColorD	0.291119	0.014214	20.481	<0.0001
ColorG	0.213842	0.012760	16.759	<0.0001
Table	−0.008497	0.002345	−3.623	0.000311
Depth	−0.008638	0.003765	−2.294	0.022043

Influence measures can be adversely affected by indicator variables, so studentized residuals, Cook's Distance, and leverage were all calculated on this model without the indicator variables for *Color*.

Here are the histograms and boxplots for these three measures. Several points have unusually high values on one or more measures.

(continued)

The analyst identified 5 diamonds that had high leverage (1) or Cook's Distance (4). Two of these also had large studentized residuals. Indicator variables were created for these 5 points and a regression was run with these new variables:

```
Variable      Coeff    SE(Coeff)   t-ratio   P-value
Intercept     4.5658   0.3972      11.49     <0.0001
Carat Size    0.9125   0.0177      51.54     <0.0001
Depth        -0.0190   0.0047      -4.04     <0.0001
Table        -0.0111   0.0029      -3.84      0.0001
Diamond 1     0.0478   0.1343       0.36      0.7221
Diamond 2     0.0837   0.1344       0.62      0.5336
Diamond 3    -0.1332   0.1361      -0.98      0.3283
Diamond 4    -0.3205   0.1346      -2.38      0.0176
Diamond 5    -0.4284   0.1346      -3.18      0.0015
```

QUESTION   What would you do next?

ANSWER   The indicator variables indicated that of the 5 suspected high influence points, only Diamonds 4 and 5 actually influence the regression. Run the regression again without these two points to see what coefficients change. If there is anything identifiably different about these two diamonds, set them aside or create a new variable for the newly identified characteristic (if possible) that distinguishes these diamonds.

18.4   Building Regression Models

When many possible predictors are available, we will naturally want to select only a few of them for a regression model. But which ones? The first and most important thing to realize is that often there is no such thing as the "best" regression model. In fact, no regression model is "right." Often, several alternative models may be useful or insightful. The "best" for one purpose may not be best for another, and the one with the highest R^2 may not be best for many purposes.

Multiple regressions are subtle. The coefficients often don't mean what they may appear to mean at first. The choice of which predictors to use determines almost everything about the regression. Predictors interact with each other, which complicates interpretation and understanding. So it is usually best to build a parsimonious model, using as few predictors as you can. On the other hand, we don't want to leave out predictors that are theoretically or practically important. Making this trade-off is the heart of the challenge of selecting a good model.[7] The best

---

[7]This trade-off is sometimes referred to as Occam's Razor after the medieval philosopher William of Occam.

regression models, in addition to satisfying the assumptions and conditions of multiple regression, have:

- Relatively few predictors, to keep the model simple.
- A relatively high R^2, indicating that much of the variability in y is accounted for by the regression model.
- A relatively small value of s_e, the standard deviation of the residuals, indicating that the magnitude of the errors is small.
- Relatively small P-values for the F- and t-statistics, showing that the overall model is better than a simple summary with the mean and that the individual coefficients are reliably different from zero.
- No cases with extraordinarily high leverage that might dominate and alter the model.
- No cases with extraordinarily large residuals, and studentized residuals that appear to be nearly Normal. Outliers can alter the model and certainly weaken the power of any test statistics, and the Nearly Normal Condition is required for inference.
- Predictors that are reliably measured and relatively unrelated to each other.

The term "relatively" in this list is meant to suggest that you should favor models with these attributes over others that satisfy them less, but of course, there are many trade-offs and no absolute rules. In addition to favoring predictors that can be measured reliably, you may want to favor those that are less expensive to measure, especially if your model is intended for prediction with values not yet measured.

It should be clear from this discussion that the selection of a regression model calls for judgment. This is yet another of those decisions in Statistics that just can't be made automatically. Indeed, it is one that we shouldn't want to make automatically; there are so many aspects of what makes a model useful that human judgment is necessary to make a final choice. Nevertheless, there are tools that can help by identifying potentially interesting models.

Best Subsets and Stepwise Regression

How can we find the best multiple regression model? The list of desirable features we just looked at should make it clear that there is no simple definition of the "best" model. The choice of a multiple regression model always requires judgment to choose among potential models. Sometimes it can help to look at models that are "good" in some arbitrary sense to understand some possibilities, but such models should never be accepted blindly.

If we choose a single criterion such as finding a model with the highest adjusted R^2, then, for modest size data sets and a modest number of potential predictors, it is actually possible for computers to search through *all* possible models. The method is called a **best subsets regression**. Often the computer reports a collection of "best" models: the best with three predictors, the best with four, and so on.[8] Of course, as you add predictors, the R^2 can never decrease, but the improvement may not justify the added complexity of the additional predictors. One criterion that might help is to use adjusted R^2. Best subsets regression programs usually offer a choice of criteria, and of course, different criteria usually lead to different "best" models.

---

[8] Best subsets regressions don't actually compute every regression. Instead, they cleverly exclude models they know to be worse than some they've already examined. Even so, there are limits to the size of the data and number of variables they can deal with comfortably.

Although best subsets programs are quite clever about computing far fewer than all the possible alternative models, they can become overwhelmed by more than a few dozen possible predictors or very many cases. So, unfortunately, they aren't useful in many data mining applications. (We'll discuss those more in Chapter 24.)

Another alternative is to have the computer build a regression "stepwise." In a **stepwise regression**, at each step, a predictor is either added to or removed from the model. The predictor chosen to add is the one whose addition increases the adjusted R^2 the most (or similarly improves some other measure such as an F-statistic). The predictor chosen to remove is the one whose removal reduces the adjusted R^2 least (or similarly loses the least on some other measure). The hope is that by following this path, the computer can settle on a good model. The model will gain or lose a predictor only if that change in the model makes a big enough change in the performance measure. The changes stop when no more changes pass the criterion.

Best subsets and stepwise methods offer both a final model and information about the paths they followed. The intermediate stage models can raise interesting questions about the data and suggest relationships that you might not have thought about. Some programs offer the chance for you to make choices as the process progresses. By interacting with the process at each decision stage, you can exclude a variable that you judge inappropriate for the model (even if including it would help the statistic being optimized) or include a variable that wasn't the top choice at the next step, if you think it is important for your purposes. Don't let a variable that doesn't make sense enter the model just because it has a high correlation, but at the same time, don't exclude a predictor just because you didn't initially think it was important. (That would be a good way to make sure that you never learn anything new.) Finding the balance between these two choices underlies the art of successful model building and makes it challenging.

Unlike best subset methods, stepwise methods can work even when the number of potential predictors is so large that you can't examine them individually. In such cases, using a stepwise method can help you identify potentially interesting predictors, especially when you use it sequentially.

Both methods are powerful. But as with many powerful tools, they require care when you use them. You should be aware of what the automated methods *fail* to do: They don't check the Assumptions and Conditions. Some, such as the independence of the cases, you can check before performing the analyses. Others, such as the Linearity Condition and concerns over outliers and influential cases, must be checked for each model. There's a risk that automated methods will be influenced by nonlinearities, by outliers, by high leverage points, by clusters, and by the need for constructed dummy variables to account for subgroups.[9] And these influences affect not just the coefficients in the final model, but the *selection* of the predictors themselves. If there is a case that is influential for even one possible multiple regression model, a best subsets search is guaranteed to consider that model (because it considers *all* possible models) and have its decision influenced by that one case.

- **Choosing the Wrong "Best" Model.** Here's a simple example of how stepwise and best subsets regressions can go astray. We might want to find a regression to model *Horsepower* in a sample of cars from the car's engine size (*Displacement*) and its *Weight*. The simple correlations are in the table at left.

	HP	Disp	Wt
Horsepower	1.000		
Displacement	0.872	1.000	
Weight	0.917	0.951	1.000

---

[9]This risk grows dramatically with larger and more complex data sets—just the kind of data for which these methods can be most helpful.

Because *Weight* has a slightly higher correlation with *Horsepower*, stepwise regression will choose it first. Then, because *Weight* and engine size (*Displacement*) are so highly correlated, once *Weight* is in the model, *Displacement* won't be added to the model. And a best subsets regression will prefer the regression on *Weight* because it has a higher R^2 and adjusted R^2. But *Weight* is, at best, a lurking variable leading to both the need for more horsepower and a larger engine. Don't try to tell an engineer that the best way to increase horsepower is to add weight to the car and that the engine size isn't important! From an engineering standpoint, *Displacement* is a far more appropriate predictor of *Horsepower*, but stepwise regression can't find that model.

Challenges in Building Regression Models

The data set used to construct the regression in the Guided Example of Chapter 17 originally contained more than 100 variables on more than 10,000 houses in the upstate New York area. Part of the challenge in constructing models is simply preparing the data for analysis. A simple scatterplot can often reveal a data value mistakenly coded, but with hundreds of potential variables, the task of checking the data for accuracy, missing values, consistency, and reasonableness can become the major part of the effort. We will return to this issue when we discuss data mining in Chapter 24.

Another challenge in building large models is Type I error. Although we've warned against using 0.05 as an unquestioned guide to statistical significance, we have to start somewhere, and this critical value is often used to test whether a variable can enter (or leave) a regression model. Of course, using 0.05 means that about 1 in 20 times, a variable whose contribution to the model may be negligible will appear as significant. Using something more stringent than 0.05 means that potentially valuable variables may be overlooked. Whenever we use automatic methods (stepwise, best subsets, or others), the actual number of different models considered becomes huge, and the probability of a Type I error grows with it. There is no easy remedy for this problem. Building a model that includes predictors that actually contribute to reducing the variation of the response and avoiding predictors that simply add noise to the predictions is the challenge of modern model building. Much current research is devoted to criteria and automatic methods to make this search easier and more reliable, but for the foreseeable future, you will need to use your own judgment and wisdom in addition to your statistical knowledge to build sensible useful regressions.

FOR EXAMPLE Stepwise regression

In addition to the predictor variables from the last example (page 611) we also have information on the quality of the *Cut* (4 grades: *Good, Very Good, Excellent,* and *Ideal*) and the quality of the *Clarity* (7 grades: *VVS2, VVS1,VS2, VS1, SI2, SI1,* and *IF*). A model was fit to predict $Log_{10}Price$ from all the predictors we have available: *Carat Weight, Color, Cut, Clarity, Depth,* and *Table* on all 749 diamonds. A backward elimination of terms was performed, and the following model was selected:

```
Response Variable: Log10Price
R-squared = 94.46%  Adjusted R-squared = 94.37%
s = 0.06806 with 749 − 13 = 736 degrees of freedom
```

(continued)

Variable	Coeff	SE(Coeff)	t-ratio	P-value
Intercept	2.437903	0.014834	164.349	<0.0001
Carat.Weight	1.200301	0.011365	105.611	<0.0001
ColorD	0.342888	0.009107	37.649	<0.0001
ColorG	0.254024	0.008159	31.135	<0.0001
CutGood	−0.028884	0.011133	−2.594	0.00966
CutVeryGood	−0.015374	0.005503	−2.793	0.00535
CutIdeal	0.012127	0.010022	1.210	0.22662
ClaritySI1	−0.237850	0.011736	−20.267	<0.0001
ClaritySI2	−0.312076	0.012454	−25.058	<0.0001
ClarityVS1	−0.130431	0.012118	−10.764	<0.0001
ClarityVS2	−0.178439	0.011684	−15.273	<0.0001
ClarityVVS1	−0.064518	0.012445	−5.184	<0.0001
ClarityVVS2	−0.076747	0.011878	−6.461	<0.0001

QUESTION   Compare this model with the model based only on *Carat Weight* and *Color* from the first example with indicator variables for *Color*.

ANSWER   This new model has several advantages over the simpler model. First, the residual standard error is now 0.068 $\log_{10}$ dollars, a decrease from 0.109 $\log_{10}$ dollars. (We can transform that back to dollars as $10^{0.068} = \$1.17$—quite a small standard deviation.)

Correspondingly, the R^2 is now 94.46% compared to 85.66%. Nearly all the terms are highly statistically significant. The one exception is the indicator for the *Ideal* level of *Cut*. We could consider omitting this indicator (which would then combine the levels *Excellent* and *Ideal*), but for simplicity we will leave it as is. Before deploying this model, however, we should look at all the assumptions and conditions, which we will do in the final example of this chapter.

GUIDED EXAMPLE   Housing Prices

Let's return to the upstate New York data set to predict house prices, this time using a sample of 1734 houses and 16 variables.

The variables available include:

Price The price of the house as sold in 2002

Lot Size The size of the land in *acres*

Waterfront An indicator variable coded as 1 if the property contains waterfront, 0 otherwise

Age The age of the house in *years*

Land Value The assessed value of the property without the structures

New Construct An indicator variable coded as 1 if the house is new construction, 0 otherwise

Central Air An indicator variable coded as 1 if the house has central air conditioning, 0 otherwise

Fuel Type A categorical variable describing the main type of fuel used to heat the house:

   1 = None; 2 = Gas; 3 = Electric; 4 = Oil; 5 = Wood; 6 = Solar; 7 = Unknown/Other

Heat Type A categorical variable describing the heating system of the house:

   1 = None; 2 = Forced Hot Air; 3 = Hot Water; 4 = Electric

Sewer Type	A categorical variable describing the sewer system of the house:
	1 = None/Unknown; 2 = Private (Septic System); 3 = Commercial/Public
Living Area	The size of the living area of the house in *square feet*
Pct College	The percent of the residents of the zip code that attended four-year college (from the U.S. Census Bureau)
Bathrooms	The *number* of bathrooms
Bedrooms	The *number* of bedrooms
Fireplaces	The *number* of fireplaces

PLAN

Setup State the objective of the study.

Identify the variables.

Model Think about the assumptions and check the conditions. A scatterplot matrix is a good way to examine the relationships for the quantitative variables.

We want to build a model to predict house prices for a region in upstate New York. We have data on *Price* (\$), and 15 potential predictor variables selected from a much larger list.

✓ **Linearity Condition.** To fit a regression model, we first require linearity. (Scatterplots of *Price* against *Living Area, Age, Bedrooms, Bathrooms,* and *Fireplaces* are similar to the plots shown in the regression of Chapter 17 and are not shown here.)

✓ **Independence Assumption.** We can regard the errors as being independent of one another since the houses themselves were a random sample.

✓ **Randomization Condition.** These 1734 houses are a random sample of a much larger set. That supports the idea that the errors are independent.

To check equal variance and Normality, we usually find a regression and examine the residuals. Linearity is all we need for that.

Remarks

Examination of *Fuel Type* showed that there were only 6 houses that did not have categories 2, 3, or 4.

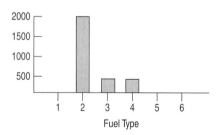

All six of those also had *Heat Type* 1. We decided to set these 6 houses aside, leaving three categories of each variable. So we can use two dummy variables for each. We now have 17 potential predictor variables.

We started by fitting a model to all of them.

Because there are 7 levels of Fuel Type, we expect to need 6 indicator variables. We can use *None* as the baseline. *Fuel2* has the value 1 for Gas and 0 for all other types, *Fuel3* has value 1 for Electric and 0 for all other types. As the bar chart shows, only 6 houses have values other than 2, 3, and 4. So we can omit those cases and use just 2 indicators, *Fuel2* and *Fuel3* indicating Gas and Electric respectively, leaving Oil as the baseline. The 6 houses (out of over 1700) set aside have a very small impact on the model.

(continued)

```
Dependent variable is: Price
R-squared = 65.1%  R-squared (adjusted) = 64.8%
s = 58408 with 1728 − 18 = 1710 degrees of freedom
```

Variable	Coeff	SE(Coeff)	t-ratio	P-value
Intercept	18794.0	23333	0.805	0.4207
Lot.Size	7774.34	2246	3.46	0.0006
Waterfront	119046	15577	7.64	<0.0001
Age	−131.642	58.54	−2.25	0.0246
Land.Value	0.9258	0.048	19.4	<0.0001
New.Construct	−45234.8	7326	−6.17	<0.0001
Central.Air	9864.30	3487	2.83	0.0047
Fuel Type[2]	4225.35	5027	0.840	0.4008
Fuel Type[3]	−8148.11	12906	−0.631	0.5279
Heat Type[2]	−1185.54	12345	−0.096	0.9235
Heat Type[3]	−11974.4	12866	−0.931	0.3521
Sewer Type[2]	4051.84	17110	0.237	0.8128
Sewer Type[3]	5571.89	17165	0.325	0.7455
Living.Area	75.769	4.24	17.9	<0.0001
Pct.College	−112.405	151.9	0.740	0.4593
Bedrooms	−4963.36	2405	2.06	0.0392
Fireplaces	768.058	2992	0.257	0.7975
Bathrooms	23077.4	3378	6.83	<0.0001

✓ **Equal Spread Condition.** A scatterplot of the studentized residuals against predicted values shows no thickening or other patterns. There is a group of homes whose residuals are larger (both negative and positive) than the vast majority, whose studentized residual values are larger than 3 or 4 in absolute value. We'll revisit them after we've selected our model.

We need the Nearly Normal Condition only if we want to do inference and the sample size is not large. If the sample size is large, we need the distribution to be Normal only if we plan to produce prediction intervals.

✓ **Nearly Normal Condition, Outlier Condition.** The histogram of residuals is unimodal and symmetric, but slightly long tailed.

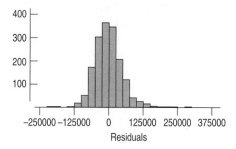

Under these conditions, we can proceed to search for a suitable multiple regression model using a subset of the predictors. We will return to some of our concerns in the discussion.

DO **Mechanics** We first let the stepwise program proceed backward from the full model on all 17 predictors.

Here is the computer output for the multiple regression, starting with all 17 predictor variables and proceeding backward until no more candidates were nominated for exclusion.

```
Dependent variable is: Price
R-squared = 65.1%  R-squared (adjusted) = 64.9%
s = 58345 with 1728 − 12 = 1716 degrees of freedom

Variable         Coeff        SE(Coeff)   t-ratio   P-value
Intercept        9643.14      6546        1.47      0.1409
Lot.Size         7580.42      2049        3.70      0.0002
Waterfront       119372       15365       7.77      <0.0001
Age              −139.704     57.18       −2.44     0.0147
Land.Value       0.921838     0.0463      19.9      <0.0001
New.Construct    −44172.8     7159        −6.17     <0.0001
Central.Air      9501.81      3402        2.79      0.0053
Heat Type[2]     10099.9      4048        2.50      0.0127
Heat Type[3]     −791.243     5215        −0.152    0.8794
Living.Area      75.9000      4.124       18.4      <0.0001
Bedrooms         −4843.89     2387        −2.03     0.0426
Bathrooms        23041.0      3333        6.91      <0.0001
```

The estimated equation is:

$$Price = 9643.14 + 7580.42\,LotSize$$
$$+ 119{,}372\,Waterfront - 139.70\,Age$$
$$+ 0.922\,LandValue$$
$$- 44{,}172.8\,NewConstuction$$
$$+ 9501.81\,CentralAir$$
$$+ 10099.9\,Heat\ Type2$$
$$- 791.24\,Heat\ Type3$$
$$+ 75.90\,Living\ Area$$
$$- 4843.89\,Bedrooms$$
$$+ 23041\,Bathrooms$$

Nearly all of the P-values are small which indicates that even with 11 predictors in the model, most are contributing. The exception is the indicator for Heat Type 3 which is *Hot Water*. We could consider dropping this indicator and combining those houses with those that have levels 1 (None) and 4 (Electricity). However, for simplicity we have left the model as the stepwise search found it. The R^2 value of 65.1% indicates that more than 65% of the overall variation in house prices has been accounted for by this model and the fact that the adjusted R^2 has actually increased, suggest that we haven't removed any important predictors from the model. The residual standard error of $58,345 gives us a rough indication that we can predict the price of a home to within about $2 \times \$58{,}345 = \$116{,}690$. If that's close enough to be useful, then our model is potentially useful as a price guide.

Remarks

We also tried running the stepwise regression program forward and obtained the same model. There are some houses that have large studentized residual values and some that have somewhat large leverage, but omitting them from the model did not significantly change the coefficients. We can use this model as a starting basis for pricing homes in the area.

(continued)

REPORT

Summary and Conclusions
Summarize your results and state any limitations of your model in the context of your original objectives.

MEMO

Re: Regression analysis of home price predictions

A regression model of *Price* on 11 predictors accounts for about 65% of the variation in the price of homes in these data from upstate New York. Tests of each coefficient show that each of these variables appears to be an aspect of the price of a house.

This model reflects the common wisdom in real estate about the importance of various aspects of a home. An important variable not included is the location, which every real estate agent knows is crucial to pricing a house. This is ameliorated by the fact that all these houses are in the same general area. However, knowing more specific information about where they are located would probably improve the model. The price found from this model can be used as a starting point for comparing a home with comparable homes in the area.

As with all multiple regression coefficients, when we interpret the effect of a predictor, we must take account of all the other predictors and be careful not to suggest a causal relationship between the predictor and the response variable. Here are some interesting features of the model. It appears that among houses with the same values of the other variables, those with waterfront access are worth on average about $119,000 more. Among houses with the same values of the other variables, those with more bedrooms have lower sales prices by, on average, $4800 for each bedroom, while among those with the same values of the other variables, those with more bathrooms have higher prices by, on average, $23,000 per bathroom. Not surprisingly, the value of the land is positively associated with the sale price, accounting for, on average, about $0.92 of the sale price for each $1 of assessed land value among houses that are otherwise alike on the other variables.

This model reflects the prices of 1728 homes in a random sample of homes taken in this area.

18.5 Collinearity

Anyone who has shopped for a home knows that houses with more rooms generally cost more than houses with fewer rooms. A simple regression of *Price* on *Rooms* for the New York houses shows:

```
Variable    Coeff      SE(Coeff)   t-ratio   P-value
Intercept   53015.6    6424.3       8.252    <0.0001
Rooms       22572.9     866.7      26.046    <0.0001
```

An additional room seems to be "worth" about $22,600 on average to these homes. We can also see that the *Living Area* of a house is an important predictor. Each square foot is worth about $113.12:

```
Variable      Coeff       SE(Coeff)   t-ratio   P-value
Intercept     13439.394   4992.353     2.692    0.00717
Living Area     113.123      2.682    42.173    <0.0001
```

Finally, the *Price* increases with the number of *Bedrooms*, with each *Bedroom* worth, on average, $48,218:

Variable	Coeff	SE(Coeff)	t-ratio	P-value
Intercept	59863	8657	6.915	<0.0001
Bedrooms	48218	2656	18.151	<0.0001

But, when we put more than one of these variables into a regression equation simultaneously, things can change. Here's a regression with both *Living Area* and *Bedrooms*:

Variable	Coeff	SE(Coeff)	t-ratio	P-value
Intercept	36667.895	6610.293	5.547	<0.0001
Living Area	125.405	3.527	35.555	<0.0001
Bedrooms	−14196.769	2675.159	−5.307	<0.0001

Now, it appears that each bedroom is associated with a *lower* sale *Price*.

This type of coefficient change often happens in multiple regression and can seem counterintuitive. When two predictor variables are correlated, their coefficients in a multiple regression (with both of them present) can be quite different from their simple regression slopes. In fact, the coefficient can change from being significantly positive to significantly negative with the inclusion of one correlated predictor, as is the case here with *Bedrooms* and *Living Area*. The problem arises when one of the predictor variables can be predicted well from the others. This phenomenon is called **collinearity**.[10]

Collinearity in the predictors can have other consequences in a multiple regression. If instead of adding *Bedrooms* to the model, we add *Rooms*, we see a different outcome:

Variable	Coeff	SE(Coeff)	t-ratio	P-value
Intercept	11691.586	5521.253	2.118	0.0344
Living Area	110.974	3.948	28.109	<0.0001
Rooms	783.579	1056.568	0.742	0.4584

The coefficient for *Living Area* has hardly changed at all. It still shows that a house costs about $111 per square foot, but now the P-value of the coefficient for *Rooms* says that it is indistinguishable from 0. With the addition of *Living Area* to the model the coefficient for *Rooms* changed from having a *t*-statistic over 25, with a very small P-value (in the simple regression) to having a P-value of 0.458. Notice also that the standard errors of the coefficients have increased. The standard error of *Living Area* increased from 2.68 to 3.95. That may not seem like much, but it's an increase of nearly 50%.

This variance inflation of the coefficients is another consequence of collinearity. The stronger the correlation between predictors, the more the variance of their coefficients increases when both are included in the model. Sometimes this effect can change a coefficient from statistically significant to indistinguishable from zero.

Data sets in business often have related predictor variables. General economic variables, such as interest rates, unemployment rates, GDP, and other productivity measures are highly correlated. The choice of which predictors to include in the model can significantly change the coefficients, their standard errors, and their P-values, making both selecting regression models and interpreting them difficult.

> **What the Coefficients Tell Us When Predictors Are Correlated**
>
> Sometimes we can understand what the coefficients are telling us even in such paradoxical situations. Here, it seems that a house that allocates more of its living area to bedrooms (and correspondingly less to other areas) will be worth less.
>
> In the second example, we see that more rooms don't make a house worth more if they just carve up the existing living area. The value of more rooms we saw before was probably because houses with more rooms tend to have more living area as well.

---

[10]You may see also this problem called "multicollinearity."

How can we detect and deal with collinearity? Let's look at a regression among just the predictor variables. If we regress *Rooms* on *Bedrooms* and *Living Area* we find:

```
Variable        Coeff    SE(Coeff)    t-ratio    P-value
Intercept       0.680    0.141          4.821    <0.0001
Bedrooms        0.948    0.057         16.614    <0.0001
Living Area     0.009    0.000         25.543    <0.0001

s = 1.462 on 1725 degrees of freedom
R-squared = 60.2%  Adjusted R-squared = 60.15%
F = 1304 on 2 and 1725 DF, P-value: <0.0001
```

Look at the R^2 for that regression. What does it tell us? Since R^2 is the fraction of variability accounted for by the regression, in this case, that's the fraction of the variability in *Rooms* accounted for by the other two predictors.

Now we can be precise about collinearity. If that R^2 were 100%, we'd have perfect collinearity. *Rooms* would then be perfectly predictable from the other two predictors and so could tell us nothing new about *Price* because it didn't vary in any way not already accounted for by the predictors already in the model. In fact, we couldn't even perform the calculation. Its coefficient would be indeterminate, and its standard error would be infinite. (Statistics packages usually print warnings when this happens.[11]) Conversely, if the R^2 were 0%, then *Rooms* would bring entirely new information to the model, and we'd have no collinearity at all.

Clearly, there's a range of possible collinearities for each predictor. The statistic that measures the degree of collinearity of the jth predictor with the others is called the **Variance Inflation Factor (VIF)** and is found as:

$$VIF_j = \frac{1}{1 - R_j^2}.$$

The R_j^2 here shows how well the jth predictor can be predicted by the other predictors. The $1 - R_j^2$ term measures what that predictor has left to bring to the regression model. If R_j^2 is high, then not only is that predictor superfluous, but it can damage the regression model. The VIF tells how much the variance of the coefficient has been inflated due to collinearity. The higher the VIF, the higher the standard error of its coefficient and the less it can contribute to the regression model. Since R_j^2 can't be less than zero, the minimum value of the VIF is 1.0. The VIF takes into account the influence of all the other predictors—and that's important. You can't judge whether you have a collinearity problem simply by looking at the correlations among the predictors because those only consider each "pair" of predictors.

As a final blow, when a predictor is collinear with the other predictors, it's often difficult to figure out what its coefficient means in the multiple regression. We've blithely talked about "removing the effects of the other predictors," but now when we do that, there may not be much left. What is left is not likely to be about the original predictor, but more about the fractional part of that predictor not associated with the others. In a regression of *Horsepower* on *Weight* and *Engine Size*, once we've removed the effect of *Weight* on *Horsepower*, *Engine Size* doesn't tell us anything *more* about *Horsepower*. That's certainly not the same as saying that *Engine Size* doesn't tell us anything at all about *Horsepower*. It's just that most cars with big engines also weigh a lot. So *Engine Size* may be telling us mostly about sporty cars that have larger engines than expected for their weight.

---

[11]Excel does not. It gives 0 as the estimate of most values and a NUM! warning for the standard error of the coefficient.

To summarize, when a predictor is collinear with the other predictors in the model, two things can happen:

1. Its coefficient can be surprising, taking on an unanticipated sign or being unexpectedly large or small.
2. The standard error of its coefficient can be large, leading to a smaller *t*-statistic and correspondingly large P-value.

One telltale sign of collinearity is the paradoxical situation in which the over-all F-test for the multiple regression model is significant, showing that at least one of the coefficients is significantly different from zero, and yet all of the individual coefficients have small *t*-values, each in effect, denying that *it* is the significant one.

What should you do about a collinear regression model? The simplest cure is to remove some of the predictors. That both simplifies the model and generally improves the *t*-statistics. If several predictors give pretty much the same information, removing some of them won't hurt the model's ability to describe the response variable. Which should you remove? Keep the predictors that are most reliably measured, least expensive to find, or even those that are politically important. Another alternative that may make sense is to construct a new predictor by combining variables. For example, several different measures of a product's durability (perhaps for different parts of it) could be added together to create a single durability measure.

Facts about Collinearity

- The collinearity of any predictor with the others in the model can be measured with its Variance Inflation Factor.
- High collinearity leads to the coefficient being poorly estimated and having a large standard error (and correspondingly low *t*-statistic). The coefficient may seem to be the wrong size or even the wrong sign.
- Consequently, if a multiple regression model has a high R^2 and large *F*, but the individual *t*-statistics are not significant, you should suspect collinearity.
- Collinearity is measured in terms of the R_j^2 between a predictor and *all* of the other predictors in the model. It is not measured in terms of the correlation between any two predictors. Of course, if two predictors are highly correlated, then the R_j^2 with even more predictors must be at least that large and will usually be even higher.

JUST CHECKING

> **3** In a study of *Salary*, a regression on several variables shows high collinearity of *Age* and *Years Experience*. Explain why this might be and what you would do about it.

18.6 Quadratic Terms

WHO Downhill racers in the 2002 Winter Olympics

WHAT Time, Starting Position

WHEN 2002

WHERE Salt Lake City

After the women's downhill ski racing event at the 2002 Winter Olympic Games in Salt Lake City, Picabo Street of the U.S. team was disappointed with her 16th place finish after she'd posted the fastest practice time. Changing snow conditions can affect finish times, and in fact, the top seeds can choose their starting positions and try to guess when the conditions will be best. But how much impact was there? On the day of the women's downhill race, it was unusually sunny. Skiers expect conditions to improve and then, as the day wears on, to deteriorate, so they try to pick the optimum time. But their calculations were upset by a two-hour delay. Picabo Street chose to race in 26th position. By then conditions had turned around, and the slopes had begun to deteriorate. Was that the reason for her disappointing finish?

The regression in Table 18.11 seems to support her point. Times did get slower as the day wore on.

```
Dependent variable is: Time
R-squared = 37.9%  R-squared (adjusted) = 36.0%
s = 1.577 with 35 − 2 = 33 degrees of freedom

Variable    Coeff       SE(Coeff)   t-ratio   P-value
Intercept   100.069     0.5597      179       <0.0001
StartOrder    0.108563  0.0242        4.49    <0.0001
```

Table 18.11   Time to ski the women's downhill event at the 2002 Winter Olympics depended on starting position.

But a plot of the residuals warns us that the linearity assumption isn't met.

Figure 18.8   The residuals reveal a bend.

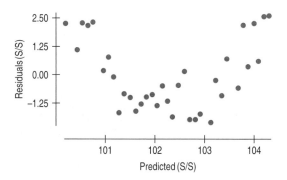

If we plot the data, we can see that re-expression can't help us because as the skiers expected, the times first trended down and then turned around and increased.

Figure 18.9   The original data trend down and then up. That kind of bend can't be improved with re-expression.

How can we use regression here? We can introduce a squared term to the model:

$$\widehat{Time} = b_0 + b_1 startorder + b_2 startorder^2.$$

The fitted function is a *quadratic*, which can follow bends like the one in these data. Table 18.12 has the regression table.

```
Dependent variable is: Time
R-squared = 83.3%  R-squared (adjusted) = 82.3%
s = 0.8300 with 35 − 3 = 32 degrees of freedom
```

Source	Sum of Squares	df	Mean Square	F-ratio
Regression	110.139	2	55.0694	79.9
Residual	22.0439	32	0.688871	

Variable	Coeff	SE(Coeff)	t-ratio	P-value
Intercept	103.547	0.4749	218	<0.0001
StartOrder	−0.367408	0.0525	−6.99	<0.0001
StartOrder^2	0.011592	0.0012	9.34	<0.0001

Table 18.12 A regression model with a quadratic term fits these data better.

This model fits the data better. Adjusted R^2 is 82.3%, up from 36.0% for the linear version. And the residuals look generally unstructured, as Figure 18.10 shows.

Figure 18.10 The residuals from the quadratic model show no structure.

However, one problem remains. In the new model, the coefficient of *Start Order* has changed from significant and positive to significant and negative. As we've just seen, that's a signal of possible collinearity. Quadratic models often have collinearity problems because for many variables, x and x^2 are highly correlated. In these data, *Start Order* and *Start Order^2* have a correlation of 0.97.

There's a simple fix for this problem. Instead of using *Start Order^2*, we can use $(\text{Start Order} - \overline{\text{Start Order}})^2$. The form with the mean subtracted has a *zero* correlation with the linear term. Table 18.13 shows the resulting regression. (Writing *Start Order* as *SO* for brevity.)

```
Dependent variable is: Time
R-squared = 83.3%  R-squared (adjusted) = 82.3%
s = 0.8300 with 35 − 3 = 32 degrees of freedom
```

Source	Sum of Squares	df	Mean Square	F-ratio
Regression	110.139	2	55.0694	79.9
Residual	22.0439	32	0.688871	

Variable	Coeff	SE(Coeff)	t-ratio	P-value
Intercept	98.7493	0.3267	302	<0.0001
StartOrder	0.104239	0.0127	8.18	<0.0001
(SO-mean)^2	0.011592	0.0012	9.34	<0.0001

Table 18.13 Using a centered quadratic term alleviates the collinearity.

The predicted values and residuals are the same for these two models,[12] but the coefficients of the second one are easier to interpret.

[12]This can be shown algebraically for any quadratic model with a centered squared term.

So, did Picabo Street have a valid complaint? Well, times did increase with start order, but (from the quadratic term), they decreased before they turned around and increased. Picabo's start order of 26 has a predicted time of 101.83 seconds. Her performance at 101.17 was better than predicted, but her residual of −0.66 is not large in magnitude compared to that for some of the other skiers. Skiers who had much later starting positions *were* disadvantaged, but Picabo's start position was only slightly later than the best possible one (about 16th according to this model), and her performance was not extraordinary by Olympic standards.

One final note: Quadratic models can do an excellent job of fitting curved patterns such as this one. But they are particularly dangerous to use for extrapolating beyond the range of the *x*-values. So you should use them with care.

FOR EXAMPLE Quadratic terms

We have fit a model of $Log_{10}Price$ to *Carat Weight*, *Color*, *Cut*, and *Clarity*. (See page 615.) The R^2 is an impressive 94.46%. The 749 diamonds are a random sample of diamonds of three *Color* levels and of *Weight* between 0.3 and 1.5 carats. We transformed *Price* using the log (base 10) to linearize the relationship with *Carat Weight*. However, a plot of residuals vs. predicted values reveals:

There appears to be a curved relationship between residuals and predicted values. What happens if we add $(Carat\ Weight)^2$ as a predictor?

Here's the regression output:

```
Response Variable: Log10Price
R-squared = 97.31%  Adjusted R-squared = 97.27%
s = 0.04741 with 749 − 14 = 735 degrees of freedom
```

Variable	Coeff	SE(Coeff)	t-ratio	P-value
Intercept	2.040547	0.017570	116.138	<0.0001
Carat.Weight	2.365036	0.042400	55.780	<0.0001
Carat.Weight²	−0.699846	0.025028	−27.962	<0.0001
ColorD	0.347479	0.006346	54.755	<0.0001
ColorG	0.252336	0.005683	44.398	<0.0001
CutGood	−0.038896	0.007763	−5.010	<0.0001
CutIdeal	0.016165	0.006982	2.315	0.020877
CutVery Good	−0.014988	0.003834	−3.910	0.000101
ClaritySI1	−0.286641	0.008359	−34.292	<0.0001
ClaritySI2	−0.353371	0.008800	−40.155	<0.0001
ClarityVS1	−0.161288	0.008513	−18.947	<0.0001
ClarityVS2	−0.215559	0.008246	−26.141	<0.0001
ClarityVVS1	−0.077703	0.008682	−8.950	<0.0001
ClarityVVS2	−0.103078	0.008327	−12.378	<0.0001

The plot of residuals against predicted values shows:

A histogram, boxplot, and Normal probability plot of the residuals show:

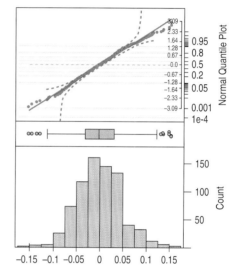

QUESTION Summarize this regression and comment on its appropriateness for predicting the price of diamonds (of this *Carat Weight*).

ANSWER The model for $Log_{10}Price$ is based on *Carat Weight*, *Carat Weight²*, *Color (3 levels)*, *Cut (4 levels)*, and *Clarity (7 levels)*. The R^2 for this model is 97.31% (97.27% adjusted), and the residual standard deviation is only 0.047 (in $Log_{10}Price$). Every term included in the model is statistically significant. The assumptions and conditions of multiple regression are all met. The residuals appear to be symmetric and roughly Normal. The inclusion of the squared term for *Carat Weight* has eliminated the pattern in the plot of residuals vs. predicted values. This model seems appropriate to use for other diamonds of this *Carat Weight*.

Regression Roles

We build regression models for a number of reasons. One reason is to model how variables are related to each other in the hope of understanding the relationships. Another is to build a model that might be used to predict values for a response variable when given values for the predictor variables. When we hope to understand, we are particularly interested in simple, straightforward models in which predictors are as unrelated to each other as possible. We are especially happy when the *t*-statistics are large, indicating that the predictors each contribute to the model.

By contrast, when prediction is our goal, we are more likely to care about the overall R^2. Good prediction occurs when much of the variability in y is accounted for by the model. We might be willing to keep variables in our model that have relatively small t-statistics simply for the stability that having several predictors can provide. We care less whether the predictors are related to each other because we don't intend to interpret the coefficients anyway, so collinearity is less of a concern.

In both roles, we may include some predictors to "get them out of the way." Regression offers a way to approximately control for factors when we have observational data because each coefficient estimates a relationship *after removing the effects* of the other predictors. Of course, it would be better to control for factors in a randomized experiment, but in the real world of business that's often just not possible.

WHAT CAN GO WRONG?

- **Be alert for collinearity when you set aside an influential point.** Removing a high-influence point may have surprising consequences. Sometimes variables are collinear *except* when the point is there, so removing it actually introduces collinearity. In this case, you should consider removing one of the variables from the model. On the other hand, sometimes variables are collinear only because of one outlying point, so removing it removes the collinearity—and probably results in a more useful regression model.

- **Beware missing data.** Values may be missing or unavailable for any case in any variable. In simple regression, when the cases are missing for reasons that are unrelated to the variable we're trying to predict, that's not a problem. We just analyze the cases for which we have data. But when several variables participate in a multiple regression, any case with data missing on any of the variables will be omitted from the analysis. You can unexpectedly find yourself with a much smaller set of data than you started with. Be especially careful, when comparing regression models with different predictors, that the cases participating in the models are the same.

- **Don't forget linearity.** The **Linearity Assumption** requires linear relationships among the variables in a regression model. As you build and compare regression models, be sure to plot the data to check that it is straight. Violations of this assumption make everything else about a regression model invalid.

- **Check for parallel regression lines.** When you introduce an indicator variable for a category, check the underlying assumption that the other coefficients in the model are essentially the same for both groups. If not, consider adding an interaction term.

ETHICS IN ACTION

F red Barolo heads a travel company that offers, among other services, customized travel packages. These packages provide a relatively high profit margin for his company, but Fred worries that a weakened economic outlook will adversely affect this segment of his business.

He read in a recent Travel Industry Association report that there is increasing interest among U.S. leisure travelers in trips focused on a unique culinary and wine-related experience. To gain an understanding of travel trends in this niche market, he seeks advice from a market analyst, Smith Nebbiolo, whose firm also handles promotional campaigns. Smith has access to several databases, some through membership with the Travel Industry Association and others through the U.S. Census Bureau and Bureau of Economic Analysis.

Smith suggests developing a model to predict demand for culinary wine-related travel, and Fred agrees. As the dependent variable, Smith uses the monthly dollar amount spent on travel packages advertised as culinary wine experiences. He considers a number of monthly economic indicators such as gross domestic product (GDP) and personal consumption expenditures (PCE); variables related to the travel industry (e.g., the American Consumer Satisfaction Index (ACSI) for airlines and hotels, etc.); and factors specific to culinary and wine travel experiences such as advertising expenditure and price. With so many variables, Smith uses an automatic stepwise procedure to select among them.

The final model Smith presents to Fred does not include any monthly economic indicators; ACSI for airlines and hotels are included as was advertising expenditure for these types of trips. Fred and Smith discuss how it appears that the economy has little effect on this niche travel market and how Fred should start thinking of how he will promote his new culinary wine-related travel packages.

- Identify the ethical dilemma in this scenario.

- What are the undesirable consequences?

- Propose an ethical solution that considers the welfare of all stakeholders.

WHAT HAVE WE LEARNED?

Learning Objectives

Use indicator (dummy) variables intelligently.

- An indicator variable that is 1 for a group and 0 for others is appropriate when the slope for that group is the same as for the others, but the intercept may be different.
- If the slope for the indicated group is different, then it may be appropriate to include an interaction term in the regression model.
- When there are three or more categories, use a separate indicator variable for each, but leave one out to avoid collinearity.

Diagnose multiple regressions to expose any undue influence of individual cases.

- Leverage measures how far a case is from the mean of all cases when measured on the x-variables.
- The leverage of a case tells how much the predicted value of that case would change if the y-value of that case were changed by adding 1 and nothing else in the regression changed.
- Studentized residuals are residuals divided by their individual standard errors. Externally studentized residuals follow a t-distribution when the regression assumptions are satisfied.
- A case is influential if it has both sufficient leverage and a large enough residual. Removing an influential case from the data will change the model in ways that matter to your interpretation or intended use. Measures such as *Cook's D* and *DFFITS* combine leverage and studentized residuals into a single measure of influence.
- By assigning an indicator variable to a single influential case, we can remove its influence from the model and test (using the P-value of its coefficient) whether it is in fact influential.

Build multiple regression models when many predictors are available.

- Seek models with few predictors, a relatively high R^2, a relatively small residual standard deviation, relatively small P-values for the coefficients, no cases that are unduly influential, and predictors that are reliably measured and relatively unrelated to each other.

- Automated methods for seeking regression models include Best Subsets and Stepwise regression. Neither one should be used without carefully diagnosing the resulting model.

Recognize collinearity and deal with it to improve your regression model. Collinearity occurs when one predictor can be well predicted from the others.

- The R^2 of the regression of one predictor on the others is a suitable measure. Alternatively, the *Variance Inflation Factor*, which is based on this R^2, is often reported by statistics programs.
- Collinearity can have the effect of making the P-values for the coefficients large (not significant) even though the overall regression fits the data well.
- Removing some predictors from the model or making combinations of those that are collinear can reduce this problem.

Consider fitting quadratic terms in your regression model when the residuals show a bend. Re-expressing y is another option, unless the bent relationship between y and the x's is not monotonic.

Recognize why a particular regression model is fit.

- We may want to understand some of the individual coefficients.
- We may simply be interested in prediction and not be concerned about the coefficients themselves.

Terms

Best subsets regression	A regression method that checks all possible combinations of the available predictors to identify the combination that optimizes an arbitrary measure of regression success.
Collinearity	When one (or more) of the predictors can be fit closely by a regression on the other predictors, we have collinearity. When collinear predictors are in a regression model, they may have unexpected coefficients and often have inflated standard errors (and correspondingly small t-statistics).
Cook's Distance	A measure of the influence of a single case on the coefficients in a multiple regression.
DFFITS	A measure of the influence of a single case on a multiple regression model.
Indicator variable (dummy variable)	A variable constructed to indicate for each case whether it is in a designated group or not. Usually the values are 0 and 1, where 1 indicates group membership.
Influential case	A case is *influential* on a multiple regression model if, when it is omitted, the model changes by enough to matter for your purposes. (There is no specific amount of change defined to declare a case influential.) Cases with high leverage and large studentized residual are likely to be influential.
Interaction term	A variable constructed by multiplying a predictor variable by an indicator variable. An interaction term adjusts the slope of that predictor for the cases identified by the indicator.
Leverage	A measure of the amount of influence an individual case has on the regression. Moving a case in the y direction by 1 unit (while changing nothing else) will move its predicted value by the leverage. The leverage of the ith case is denoted h_i.
Stepwise regression	An automated method of building regression models in which predictors are added to or removed from the model one at a time in an attempt to optimize a measure of the success of the regression. Stepwise methods rarely find the best model and are easily affected by influential cases, but they can be valuable in winnowing down a large collection of candidate predictors.
Studentized residual	When a residual is divided by an estimate of its standard deviation, the result is a studentized residual. The type of studentized residual that has a t-distribution is an *externally studentized residual*.
Variance inflation factor (VIF)	A measure of the degree to which a predictor in a multiple regression model is collinear with other predictors. It is based on the R^2 of the regression of that predictor on all the other predictors in the model:

$$VIF_j = \frac{1}{1 - R_j^2}$$

TECHNOLOGY HELP: Building Multiple Regression Models

Statistics packages differ in how much information they provide to diagnose a multiple regression. Most packages provide leverage values. Many provide far more, including statistics that we have not discussed. But for all, the principle is the same. We hope to discover any cases that don't behave like the others in the context of the regression model and then to understand why they are special.

Many of the ideas in this chapter rely on the concept of examining a regression model and then finding a new one based on your growing understanding of the model and the data. Regression diagnosis is meant to provide steps along that road. A thorough regression analysis may involve finding and diagnosing several models.

Statistics software will omit from a regression analysis any case that is missing a value on any variable in the model. As a result, when variables are added to or removed from a model, the cases in that model may change in subtle ways.

EXCEL

Excel and XLStat do not offer diagnostic statistics with its regression function.

Comments
Although the dialog offers a Normal probability plot of the residuals, the data analysis add-in does not make a correct probability plot, so don't use this option. The "standardized residuals" are just the residuals divided by their standard deviation (with the wrong df), so they too should be ignored.

XLSTAT

XLStat can handle both qualitative (indicator) and quantitative explanatory variables. To use stepwise regression:

- Choose **Modeling data**.
- Select all desired explanatory variables in the dialog box for **Linear regression**.
- On the **Options** tab, XLStat gives you options for building a **Best model** using various criteria, or building a model based on significance in a **stepwise** or **forward** or **backward** direction.

JMP

- From the **Analyze** menu select **Fit Model**.
- Specify the response, Y. Assign the predictors, X, in the **Construct Model Effects** dialog box.
- Click on **Run Model**.
- Click on the red triangle in the title of the Model output to find a variety of plots and diagnostics available.

Comments
JMP chooses a regression analysis when the response variable is "Continuous."

In JMP, stepwise regression is a *Personality* of the **Model Fitting** platform; it is found in the upper right of the **Model Specification**

dialog. Stepwise provides several options including forward, backward, and mixed selection and can find best subsets with an **All Possible Models** command, accessible from the red triangle drop-down menu on the stepwise control panel after you've selected a stepwise regression analysis.

MINITAB

- Choose **Regression** from the **Stat** menu.
- Choose **Regression...** from the **Regression** submenu.
- In the Regression dialog, assign the Y variable to the Response box and assign the X-variables to the Predictors box.
- Click on the **Options** button to obtain the VIF in the regression output.
- In the Regression **Storage** dialog, you can select a variety of diagnostic statistics. They will be stored in the columns of your worksheet.
- Click the **OK** button to return to the Regression dialog.
- To specify displays, click **Graphs**, and check the displays you want.
- Click the **OK** button to return to the Regression dialog.
- Click the **OK** button to compute the regression.

Comments
You will probably want to make displays of the stored diagnostic statistics. Use the usual Minitab methods for creating displays.

Minitab also offers both stepwise and best subsets regression from the **Regression** dialog. Indicate the response variable, the predictors eligible for inclusion, and any predictors that you wish to force into the model.

SPSS

- Choose **Regression** from the **Analyze** menu.
- Choose **Linear** from the **Regression** submenu.
- When the Linear Regression dialog appears, select the Y-variable and move it to the dependent target. Then move the X-variables to the independent target.
- Click the **Save** button.
- In the Linear Regression Save dialog, choose diagnostic statistics. These will be saved in your worksheet along with your data.
- Click the **Continue** button to return to the Linear Regression dialog.
- Click the **OK** button to compute the regression.

Comments
SPSS offers stepwise methods (use the **Method** drop-down menu), but not best subsets (in the student version). Click on the **Statistics** button to find collinearity diagnostics and on the **Save** button for influential point diagnostics. (The residuals SPSS calls "Studentized deleted" are the externally studentized residuals that we've recommended in this chapter.) You may want to plot the saved diagnostics using SPSS's standard graphics methods.

Brief Case

Building Models

The Paralyzed Veterans of America (PVA) is a philanthropic organization sanctioned by the U.S. government to represent the interests of those veterans who are disabled. (For more information on the PVA see the opening of Chapter 24.) To generate donations, the PVA sends out greeting cards and mailing address labels periodically with their requests for donations. To increase their efficiency, they would like to be able to model the amount of donations based on past giving and demographic variables on their donors. The data set **PVA** contains data on 3648 donors who gave to a recent solicitation. There are 26 predictor variables and 1 response variable. The response variable (GIFTAMNT) is the amount of money donated by the donor to the last solicitation. Find a model from the 26 predictor variables using any model selection procedure you like to predict this amount. The variables include:

Variables based on the donor's zipcode

> MALEVET (% Male veterans)
>
> VIETVETS (% Vietnam Veterans)
>
> WWIIVETS (% WWII veterans)
>
> LOCALGOV (% Employed by local government)
>
> STATEGOV (% Employed by state government)
>
> FEDGOV (% Employed by federal government)

Variables specific to the individual donor

> HOMEOWNER (N = No; Y = Yes)
>
> HIT (Number of times donor has responded to mail order offers other than PVA's)
>
> CARDPROM (Number of card promotions received lifetime)
>
> MAXADATE (Date of most recent promotion received in YYMM Year Month format)
>
> NUMPROM (Number of promotions received lifetime)
>
> CARDPRM12 (Number of card promotions received in last 12 months)
>
> NUMPRM12 (Number of promotions received in last 12 months)
>
> NGIFTALL (Number of gifts given lifetime to date)
>
> CARDGIFT (Number of gifts to card promotions given lifetime to date)
>
> MINRAMNT (Amount of smallest gift to date in $)
>
> MINRDATE (Date associated with the smallest gift to date—YYMM format)
>
> MAXRAMNT (Amount of largest gift to date in $)
>
> MAXRDATE (Date associated with the largest gift to date—YYMM format)
>
> LASTGIFT (Amount of most recent gift in $)
>
> AVGGIFT (Average amount of gifts to date in $)
>
> CONTROLN (Control number—unique record identifier)
>
> HPHONE_D (Indicator variable for presence of a published home phone number: 1 = Yes; 0 = No)
>
> CLUSTER2 (Marketing Cluster Code—nominal field)
>
> CHILDREN (Number of children living at home)

Response variable

> GIFTAMNT (Response variable—amount of last gift in $)

Be sure to include exploratory data analysis and evaluate the relationship among these variables using graphical and correlation analysis to guide you in building your regression models. Write a report summarizing your analysis.

EXERCISES

SECTION 18.1

1. For each of the following, show how you would code dummy (or indicator) variables to include in a regression model.

a) Company unionization status (Unionized, No Union)
b) Gender (Female, Male)
c) Account Status (Paid on time, Past Due)
d) Political party affiliation (Democrat, Republican, Other)

2. A marketing manager has developed a regression model to predict quarterly sales of his company's down jackets based on price and amount spent on advertising. An intern suggests that he include an indicator (dummy) variable for the Fall quarter.

a) How would you code such a variable? (What values would it have for each quarter?)
b) Why does the intern's suggestion make sense?
c) Do you think a regression with the indicator variable for Fall would model down jacket sales better than one without that predictor?

3. Do movies of different types have different rates of return on their budgets? Here's a scatterplot of Gross Revenue in US ($M) vs. Budget ($M) for recent movies whose MPAA Rating is either PG (blue) or R (red):

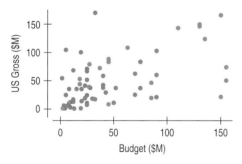

a) Why might a researcher want to use an indicator variable for the MPAA Rating?
b) What would the data values in such an indicator variable be?

4. Here is the regression for Exercise 3 with an indicator variable:

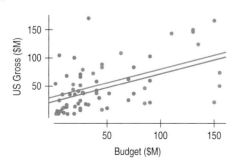

Dependent variable is: USGross($M)
R-squared = 0.193, Adjusted R-squared: 0.166
s = 37.01 with 62 − 3 = 59 degrees of freedom

Variable	Coefficient	SE(Coeff)	t-ratio	P-value
Intercept	49.2642	12.5736	3.918	0.000235
Budget	0.3292	0.1264	2.605	0.011612
R Rating	−12.4871	11.2145	−1.113	0.270018

a) Write out the regression model.
b) In this regression, the variable *R Rating* is an indicator variable that is 1 for movies that have an R rating. How would you interpret the coefficient of *R Rating*?
c) What null hypothesis can we test with the *t*-ratio for *R Rating*?
d) Can you reject the null hypothesis of part c? Explain.

5. For each of the following, show how you would code dummy (indicator) variables to include in a regression model.

a) Type of residence (Apartment, Condominium, Townhouse, Single family home)
b) Employment status (Full-time, Part-time, Unemployed)

6. A marketing manager has developed a regression model to predict quarterly sales of his company's mid-weight microfiber jackets based on price and amount spent on advertising. An intern suggests that he include indicator (dummy) variables for each quarter.

a) How would you code the variables? (How many dummy variables do you need? What values would they have?)
b) Why does the intern's suggestion make sense?
c) Do you think a regression with the indicator variables would model jacket sales better than one without those predictors?

SECTION 18.2

7. Are R rated movies as profitable as those rated PG-13? Here's scatterplot of USGross ($M) vs. Budget ($M) for PG-13 (green) and R (purple) rated movies

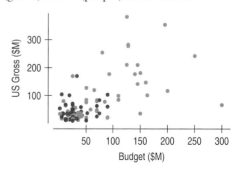

a) How would you code the indicator variable? (Use PG-13 as the base level.)
b) How would you construct the interaction term variable?

8. Here is the scatterplot of the variables in Exercise 7 with regression lines added for each kind of movie:

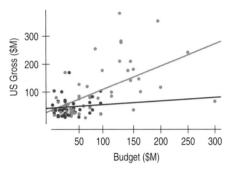

The regression model is:

```
Dependent variable is: USGross($M)
R-squared = 0.3674, Adjusted R-squared: 0.3491
s = 58.24 with 107 − 3 = 104 degrees of freedom
```

Variable	Coefficient	SE(Coeff)	t-ratio	P-value
Intercept	34.0262	10.6595	3.192	0.00187
Budget	0.7902	0.1143	6.912	<0.0001
R Rating	9.9217	18.8666	0.526	0.60009
Budget*R Rating	−0.6679	0.3798	−1.758	0.08163

a) Write out the regression model.
b) In this regression, the variable *Budget*R Rating* is an interaction term. How would you interpret its coefficient?
c) What null hypothesis can we test with the *t*-ratio for *Budget*R Rating*?
d) Would you reject that hypothesis at 0.05? What do you conclude?

SECTION 18.3

9. For the regression model in Exercise 8, the leverage values look like this:

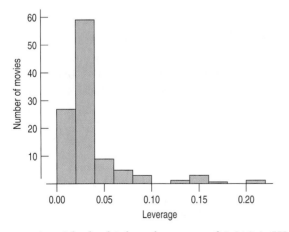

The movie with the highest leverage of 0.219 is Walt Disney's *John Carter*, which grossed $66M but had a budget of $300M.

If the budget for *John Carter* had been $1M higher than it was (and everything else remained the same), how much would the model's prediction of *John Carter*'s U.S. gross revenue change?

10. For the same regression as in Exercise 9, the Cook's Distances look like this:

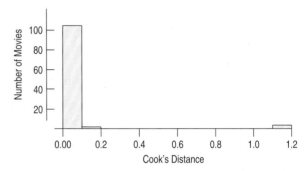

The outlier, once again, is *John Carter*, whose budget was more than $200M more than its gross revenue in the U.S. Setting this movie aside and rerunning the regression from Exercise 8, we find:

```
Dependent variable is: USGross($M)
R-squared = 0.4635, Adjusted R-squared: 0.4478
s = 53.89 with 106 − 3 = 103 degrees of freedom
```

Variable	Coefficient	SE(Coeff)	t-ratio	P-value
Intercept	21.6562	10.2755	2.108	0.0375
Budget	1.0224	0.1188	8.607	<0.0001
R Rating	22.2916	17.6941	1.260	0.2106
Budget*R Rating	−0.9001	0.3556	−2.531	0.0129

a) What are the main differences between this model with *John Carter* removed and the model from Exercise 7 with it included?
b) Which model do you prefer? Explain briefly.

SECTION 18.4

11. An analyst wants to build a regression model to predict spending from the following four predictor variables: *Past Spending, Income, Net Worth* and *Age*. A correlation matrix of the four predictors shows:

	Income	Net Worth	Age
Past Spending	0.442	0.433	0.446
Income		0.968	0.992
Net Worth			0.976

Why might a stepwise regression search not find the same model as an "all subsets" regression?

12. The analyst in Exercise 11 fits the model with the four predictor variables. The regression output shows:

```
Response Variable: Spending
R² = 84.92%  Adjusted R² = 84.85%
s = 48.45 with 908 - 5 = 903 degrees of freedom
```

Variable	Coeff	SE(Coeff)	t-ratio	P-value
Intercept	−3.738e + 00	1.564e + 01	−0.239	0.811
Past Spending	1.063e − 01	4.203e − 03	25.292	<0.0001
Income	1.902e − 03	3.392e − 04	5.606	<0.0001
Networth	2.900e − 05	3.815e − 05	0.760	0.447
Age	6.065e − 01	7.631e − 01	0.795	0.427

a) How many observations were used in the regression?

b) What might you do next?

c) Is it clear that *Income* is more important to predicting *Spending* than *Networth*? Explain.

SECTION 18.5

13. The analyst from Exercise 11, worried about collinearity, regresses *Age* against *Past Spending*, *Income*, and *Networth*. The output shows:

```
Response Variable: Age
R² = 98.75%  Adjusted R² = 98.74%
s = 2.112 with 908 - 4 = 904 degrees of freedom
```

Variable	Coeff	SE(Coeff)	t-ratio	P-value
(Intercept)	2.000e + 01	1.490e − 01	134.234	<0.0001
Past Spending	3.339e − 04	1.828e − 04	1.826	0.0681
Income	3.811e − 04	7.610e − 06	50.079	<0.0001
Networth	2.420e − 05	1.455e − 06	16.628	<0.0001

What is the VIF for *Age*?

14. If the VIF for *Networth* in the regression of Exercise 11 was 20.83, what would the R^2 be from the regression of *Networth* on *Age*, *Income*, and *Past Spending*?

SECTION 18.6

15. A collection of houses in a neighborhood of Boston shows the following relationship between *Price* and *Age* of the house:

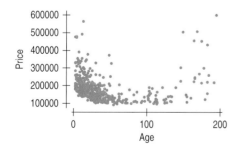

a) Describe the relationship between *Price* and *Age*. Explain what this says in terms of house prices.

b) A linear regression of *Price* on *Age* shows that the slope for *Age* is not statistically significant. Is *Price* unrelated to *Age*? Explain.

c) What might you do instead?

16. A regression model from the collection of houses in Exercise 15 shows the following:

Variable	Coeff	SE(Coeff)	t-ratio	P-value
Intercept	217854.85	4197.417	51.90	<0.0001
Age	−1754.254	127.3356	−13.78	<0.0001
(Age-38.5122)²	20.401223	1.327713	15.37	<0.0001

a) The slope of *Age* is negative. Does this indicate that older houses cost less, on average? Explain.

b) Why did the model subtract 38.5122 from *Age* in the quadratic term?

CHAPTER EXERCISES

17. *Pizza ratings.* Manufacturers of frozen foods often reformulate their products to maintain and increase customer satisfaction and sales. So they pay particular attention to evaluations of their products in comparison to their competitors' products. Frozen pizzas are a major sector of the frozen food market, accounting for an average of $3.1 billion in sales in the five-year period from 2008 to 2012 (www.companiesandmarkets.com). The prestigious Consumer's Union rated frozen pizzas for flavor and quality, assigning an overall score to each brand tested. A regression model to predict the Consumer's Union score from Calories, Type (1 = cheese, 0 = pepperoni), and fat content gives the following result:

```
Dependent variable is: Score
R-squared = 28.7%  R-squared (adjusted) = 20.2%
s = 19.79 with 29 - 4 = 25 degrees of freedom
```

Source	Sum of Squares	df	Mean Square	F-ratio
Regression	3947.34	3	1315.78	3.36
Residual	9791.35	25	391.654	

Variable	Coeff	SE(Coeff)	t-ratio	P-value
Intercept	−148.817	77.99	−1.91	0.0679
Calories	0.743023	0.3066	2.42	0.0229
Type	15.6344	8.103	1.93	0.0651
Fat	−3.89135	2.138	−1.82	0.0807

a) What is the interpretation of the coefficient of *Type* in this regression? According to these results, what type would you expect to sell better—cheese or pepperoni?

b) What displays would you like to see to check assumptions and conditions for this model?

18. *Traffic delays.* The Texas Transportation Institute (tti.tamu.edu) studies traffic delays. They estimate that in the year 2011, 498 urban areas experienced 5.5 billion vehicle hours of delay, resulting in 2.9 billion gallons of wasted fuel and $121 billion in lost productivity and fuel costs. That's about 0.7% of the nation's GDP that year. Data the institute published for the year 2001 include information on the *Total Delay per Person* (hours per year spent delayed by traffic), the *Average Arterial Road Speed* (mph), the *Average Highway Road Speed* (mph), and the *Size* of the city (small, medium, large, very large). The regression model based on these variables looks like this. The variables *Small*,

Large, and *Very Large* are indicators constructed to be 1 for cities of the named size and 0 otherwise.

```
Dependent variable is: Delay/person
R-squared = 79.1%  R-squared (adjusted) = 77.4%
s = 6.474 with 68 − 6 = 62 degrees of freedom

Source       Sum of Squares  df  Mean Square  F-ratio
Regression   9808.23          5  1961.65       46.8
Residual     2598.64         62  41.9135

Variable     Coeff     SE(Coeff)  t-ratio  P-value
Intercept    139.104   16.69       8.33    <0.0001
HiWay MPH     −1.07347  0.2474     −4.34    <0.0001
Arterial MPH  −2.04836  0.6672     −3.07     0.0032
Small         −3.58970  2.953      −1.22     0.2287
Large          5.00967  2.104       2.38     0.0203
Very Large     3.41058  3.230       1.06     0.2951
```

a) Why is there no coefficient for *Medium*?

b) Explain how the coefficients of *Small*, *Large*, and *Very Large* account for the size of the city in this model.

19. Pizza ratings, part 2. Here's a scatterplot of the residuals against predicted values for the regression model found in Exercise 17.

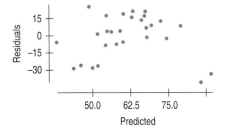

a) The two extraordinary points in the lower right are *Reggio's* and *Michelina's*, two gourmet brands. Interpret these points.

b) Do you think these two pizzas are likely to be influential in the regression. Would setting them aside be likely to change the coefficients? What other statistics might help you decide?

20. Traffic delays, part 2. Here's a scatterplot of the residuals from the regression in Exercise 18 plotted against mean *Highway mph.*

a) The point plotted with an x is Los Angeles. Read the graph and explain what it says about traffic delays in Los Angeles and about the regression model.

b) Is Los Angeles likely to be an influential point in this regression?

21. Walmart revenue. Each week about 100 million customers—nearly one-third of the U.S. population—visit one of Walmart's U.S. stores. How does Walmart's revenue relate to the state of the economy in general? Before 2009, Walmart reported sales each month, but since then it has switched to quarters. Here's a regression table predicting Walmart's monthly revenue ($Billion) from the end of 2003 through the start of 2007 from the consumer price index (*CPI*), and a scatterplot of the relationship.

```
Dependent variable is: WM_Revenue
R-squared = 11.4%  R-squared (adjusted) = 9.0%
s = 3.689 with 39 − 2 = 37 degrees of freedom

Variable   Coeff      SE(Coeff)  t-ratio  P-value
Intercept  −24.4085   19.25      −1.27     0.2127
CPI          0.071792  0.0330     2.18     0.0358
```

A scatterplot can give us some clues as to why they turned away from monthly reporting.

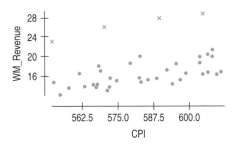

a) The points plotted with x are the December values. We can construct a variable that is "1" for those four values and "0" otherwise. What is such a variable called?

Here's the resulting regression.

```
Dependent variable is: WM_Revenue
R-squared = 80.3%  R-squared (adjusted) = 79.2%
s = 1.762 with 39 − 3 = 36 degrees of freedom

Variable   Coeff      SE(Coeff)  t-ratio  P-value
Intercept  −34.7755   9.238      −3.76     0.0006
CPI          0.087707  0.0158     5.55    <0.0001
December    10.4905    0.9337     11.2    <0.0001
```

b) What is the interpretation of the coefficient of the constructed variable *December*?

c) What additional assumption is required to include the variable *December* in this model? Is there reason to believe that it is satisfied?

22. Baseball attendance. Pedro Martinez, who retired from Major League Baseball in 2012, had a stellar career, helping the Boston Red Sox to their first World Series title in 86 years in 2004. The next year he became a free agent and the New York Mets picked him up for $53 million for 4 years. Even after the move to New York, Martinez had his own fans. Possibly, he attracted more fans to the ballpark when he pitched at home, helping to justify his multimillion dollar contract. Was there really a "Pedro effect" in attendance? We have data for the Mets home games of the 2005 season. The regression has the following predictors:

Weekend	1 if game is on a weekend day or night, 0 otherwise
Yankees	1 if game is against the Yankees (a hometown rivalry), 0 otherwise
Rain Delay	1 if the game was delayed by rain (which might have depressed attendance), 0 otherwise
Opening Day	1 for opening day, 0 for the others
Pedro Start	1 if Pedro was the starting pitcher, 0 otherwise

Here's the regression.

```
Dependent variable is: Attendance
R-squared = 53.9%  R-squared (adjusted) = 50.8%
s = 6998 with 80 - 6 = 74 degrees of freedom
```

Variable	Coeff	SE(Coeff)	t-ratio	P-value
Intercept	28896.9	1161	24.9	<0.0001
Weekend	9960.50	1620	6.15	<0.0001
Yankees	15164.3	4218	3.59	0.0006
Rain Delay	−17427.9	7277	−2.39	0.0192
Opening Day	24766.1	7093	3.49	0.0008
Pedro Start	5428.02	2017	2.69	0.0088

a) All of these predictors are of a special kind. What are they called?

b) What is the interpretation of the coefficient for *Pedro Start*?

c) If we're primarily interested in Pedro's effect on attendance, why is it important to have the other variables in the model?

d) Could Pedro's agent claim, based on this regression, that his man attracts more fans to the ballpark? What statistics should he cite?

T 23. Pizza ratings, part 3. In Exercise 19, we raised questions about two gourmet pizzas. After removing them, the resulting regression looks like this.

```
Dependent variable is: Score
R-squared = 64.4%  R-squared (adjusted) = 59.8%
s = 14.41 with 27 - 4 = 23 degrees of freedom
```

Source	Sum of Squares	df	Mean Square	F-ratio
Regression	8649.29	3	2883.10	13.9
Residual	4774.56	23	207.590	

Variable	Coeff	SE(Coeff)	t-ratio	P-value
Intercept	−363.109	72.15	−5.03	<0.0001
Calories	1.56772	0.2824	5.55	<0.0001
Type	25.1540	6.214	4.05	0.0005
Fat	−8.82748	1.887	−4.68	0.0001

A plot of the residuals against the predicted values for this regression looks like this. It has been colored according to the *Type* of pizza.

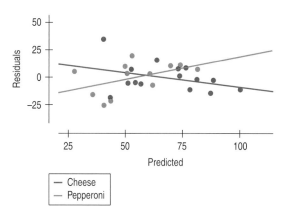

a) What does this plot say about how the regression model deals with these two types of pizza?

We constructed another variable consisting of the indicator variable *Type* multiplied by *Calories*. Here's the resulting regression.

```
Dependent variable is: Score
R-squared = 73.1%  R-squared (adjusted) = 68.2%
s = 12.82 with 27 - 5 = 22 degrees of freedom
```

Source	Sum of Squares	df	Mean Square	F-ratio
Regression	9806.53	4	2451.63	14.9
Residual	3617.32	22	164.424	

Variable	Coeff	SE(Coeff)	t-ratio	P-value
Intercept	−464.498	74.73	−6.22	<0.0001
Calories	1.92005	0.2842	6.76	<0.0001
Type	183.634	59.99	3.06	0.0057
Fat	−10.3847	1.779	−5.84	<0.0001
Type*Cals	−0.461496	0.1740	−2.65	0.0145

b) Interpret the coefficient of *Type*Cals* in this regression model.

c) Is this a better regression model than the one in Exercises 17 and 19?

T 24. Traffic delays, part 3. Here's a plot of the Studentized residuals from the regression model of Exercise 18 plotted against *ArterialMPH*. The plot is colored according to *City Size* (Small, Medium, Large, and Very Large), and regression lines are fit for each city size.

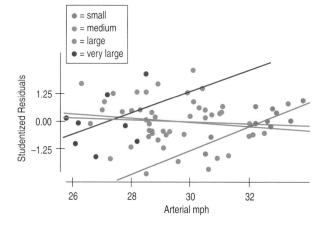

a) The model in Exercise 18 includes indicators for city size. Considering this display, have these indicator variables accomplished what is needed for the regression model? Explain.

Here is another model that adds two new constructed variables to the model in Exercise 18. They are the product of *ArterialMPH* and *Small* and the product of *ArterialMPH* and *VeryLarge*.

```
Dependent variable is: Delay/person
R-squared = 80.7%  R-squared (adjusted) = 78.5%
s = 6.316 with 68 − 8 = 60 degrees of freedom
```

Source	Sum of Squares	df	Mean Square	F-ratio
Regression	10013.0	7	1430.44	35.9
Residual	2393.82	60	39.8970	

Variable	Coeff	SE(Coeff)	t-ratio	P-value
Intercept	153.110	17.42	8.79	<0.0001
HiWayMPH	−1.02104	0.2426	−4.21	<0.0001
ArterialMPH	−2.60848	0.6967	−3.74	0.0004
Small	−125.979	66.92	−1.88	0.0646
Large	4.89837	2.053	2.39	0.0202
VeryLarge	−89.4993	63.25	−1.41	0.1623
AM*Sml	3.81461	2.077	1.84	0.0712
AM*VLg	3.38139	2.314	1.46	0.1491

b) What does the predictor *AM*Sml* (*ArterialMPH* by *Small*) do in this model? Interpret the coefficient.

c) Does this model improve on the model in Exercise 18? Explain.

25. Insurance (life expectancy). Insurance companies base their premiums on many factors, but basically all the factors are variables that predict life expectancy. Life expectancy varies from place to place. Here's a regression that models *Life Expectancy* in terms of other demographic variables. The variables are *Murder* rate per 100,000, *HighSchool Graduation* rate in %, *Income* per capita in dollars, *Illiteracy* rate per 1000, and *Life Expectancy* in years.

```
Dependent variable is: Life exp
R-squared = 67.0%  R-squared (adjusted) = 64.0%
s = 0.8049 with 50 − 5 = 45 degrees of freedom
```

Source	Sum of Squares	df	Mean Square	F-ratio
Regression	59.1430	4	14.7858	22.8
Residual	29.1560	45	0.647910	

Variable	Coeff	SE(Coeff)	t-ratio	P-value
Intercept	69.4833	1.325	52.4	<0.0001
Murder	−0.261940	0.0445	−5.89	<0.0001
HSGrad	0.046144	0.0218	2.11	0.0403
Income	$1.24948e−4$	0.0002	0.516	0.6084
Illiteracy	0.276077	0.3105	0.889	0.3787

a) The state with the highest leverage and largest Cook's Distance is Alaska. It is plotted with an x in the residuals plot. Here are a scatterplot of the residuals, a normal probability plot of the leverage values, and a histogram of Cook's distance values. What evidence do you have from these diagnostic plots that Alaska might be an influential point?

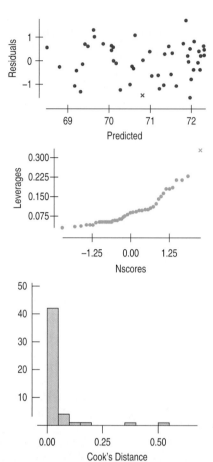

Here's another regression with a dummy variable for Alaska added to the regression model.

```
Dependent variable is: Life exp
R-squared = 70.8%  R-squared (adjusted) = 67.4%
s = 0.7660 with 50 − 6 = 44 degrees of freedom
```

Source	Sum of Squares	df	Mean Square	F-ratio
Regression	62.4797	5	12.4959	21.3
Residual	25.8193	44	0.586802	

Variable	Coeff	SE(Coeff)	t-ratio	P-value
Intercept	67.6377	1.480	45.7	<0.0001
Murder	−0.250395	0.0426	−5.88	<0.0001
HSGrad	0.055792	0.0212	2.63	0.0116
Illiteracy	0.458607	0.3053	1.50	0.1401
Income	$3.68218e−4$	0.0003	1.46	0.1511
Alaska	−2.23284	0.9364	−2.38	0.0215

b) What does the coefficient for the dummy variable for Alaska mean? Is there evidence that Alaska is an outlier in this model?

c) Which model would you prefer for understanding or predicting *Life Expectancy*? Explain.

19

Time Series Analysis

Whole Foods Market®

In 1978, twenty-five-year-old John Mackey and twenty-one-year-old Rene Lawson Hardy borrowed $45,000 from family and friends to open the doors of a small natural foods store they named SaferWay in Austin, Texas. Two years later, they joined forces with Clarksville Natural Grocery to open the first Whole Foods Market. With 10,500 square feet of floor space and a staff of 19, their store was large in comparison to other health food stores of the time.

During the next 15 years, Whole Foods Market grew rapidly, in part due to several mergers and acquisitions. Among the stores they acquired were Wellspring Grocery, Bread & Circus, Mrs. Gooch's Natural Foods, and Fresh Fields Markets. Since 2000, Whole Foods has expanded outside of North America with the purchase of seven Fresh & Wild stores in the United Kingdom. In 2007, they merged with Wild Oats of Boulder, Colorado. The firm has continued to grow both by opening new stores and by acquiring related firms, and by 2013 had nearly 60,000 employees in 352 locations.

In spite of its wholesome image, the company has not been without controversy. It has been threatened from time to time with national boycotts for issues as varied as opinions by its CEO on health care, business practices, labor issues, treatment of animals, and most recently, suspension of employees, allegedly for speaking Spanish.

Criticized for selling genetically modified (GMO) foods, Whole Foods announced in March 2013, "that by 2018, all products in our U.S. and Canadian stores must be labeled to indicate whether they contain genetically modified organisms (GMOs)."[1]

[1]Source: Official Whole Foods Market website: www.wholefoodsmarket.com.

T he decade of the 1990s was a period of growth for most companies, but unlike firms in many other industries, Whole Foods Market continued to grow into the next decade. Here is a time series plot showing the quarterly Sales ($M) plotted by quarter since 1995. If you were asked to summarize the trend in *Sales* over this decade what would you say?

Figure 19.1   Quarterly Sales (in $M) for Whole Foods from 1995 to 2013.

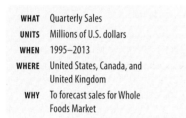

WHAT	Quarterly Sales
UNITS	Millions of U.S. dollars
WHEN	1995–2013
WHERE	United States, Canada, and United Kingdom
WHY	To forecast sales for Whole Foods Market

Clearly, sales at Whole Foods Market, Inc. grew between 1995 and 2013, starting at below $250 million and reaching more than $3 billion per quarter. But we'd like to be able to say something more than that, and ultimately, we'd like to *model* the growth. Time series models are primarily built for predicting into the near future. Some also offer interpretable coefficients.

Corporations often look at time series plots to examine prior patterns in the data and to forecast future values. The executives at Whole Foods Market, Inc. might be interested in understanding patterns in *Sales* to:

- Plan inventory and distribution of goods
- Schedule hiring and staffing
- Understand the impact of seasons, or time of the year, on sales
- Develop advertising campaigns
- Forecast profits and plan corporate strategy

Suppose that you are an analyst at Whole Foods Market, Inc. and you have been asked to forecast *Sales* for the next four quarters. How can you analyze the time series to produce accurate forecasts of *Sales*? How can you measure accuracy and compare your different forecasting models?

19.1   What Is a Time Series?

The Whole Foods sales are recorded each financial quarter, and we're interested in the growth of sales over time. Whenever we have data recorded sequentially over time, and we consider *Time* to be an important aspect of the data, we have a **time series**.[2] Most time series are equally spaced at roughly regular intervals, such as monthly, quarterly, or annually.[3] The Whole Foods sales data in Figure 19.1 are a time series measured quarterly. The fiscal year at Whole Foods Market, Inc. starts on or near September 30, so, unlike many companies, the first fiscal quarter reports sales for the end of the calendar year.

Because a time series is likely to be revealed to us sequentially and only up to the present, most time series methods use prior values of a series to predict

---

[2]Actually, the methods of this chapter can be applied to any values that are ordered.
[3]Some series, such as those recording values for trading days or on the first day of each month, are not exactly equally spaced. If there are actual gaps in a time series, researchers use a variety of methods to fill in the missing observations before analyzing the data.

future values. Some methods describe the overall pattern in the series and predict that it will continue, at least for a short while. Other methods estimate *time series models* that identify structured components like trends and seasonal fluctuation in the series and model those. Some introduce external variables to help predict the response, as in regression, while others simply look at the prior values in the series to try to discern patterns.[4] The objective of most time series analyses is to provide **forecasts** of future values of the time series. Of course, predicting the future is valuable to business decision makers, so time series methods are widely used.

Time series analysis is a rich and sophisticated topic. This chapter can do little more than survey the field and give you a taste of how time series are special. If you want to understand time series in depth, we recommend taking a course devoted to the topic.

19.2 Components of a Time Series

When we examined the distribution of a single variable, we looked at its shape, center, and spread. When we looked at scatterplots of two variables, we asked about the direction, form, and strength. For a time series, we look for the trend, seasonal patterns, and long-term cycles. Some time series exhibit some of these components, some show all of them, and others have no particular large-scale structure at all.

The Trend Component

Look at the time series plot of the Whole Foods *Sales* data in Figure 19.1. What overall pattern are the *Sales* following? Not only have sales at Whole Foods Market been increasing, but they seem to be accelerating. Of course, there are fluctuations around this pattern, but viewed over more than a decade, the overall trend is clear. We'd describe the direction as positive, and the shape as curving upwards. This overall pattern is the **trend component** of the time series. This is often the most interesting aspect of a time series. For example, it is what an investor would want to know about.

Most series have an increasing or decreasing trend with other fluctuations around the trend. Some, however, just fluctuate randomly, much like residual plots from a successful regression. If a series shows no particular trend over time and has a relatively consistent mean, it is said to be **stationary in the mean**.

If the trend grows roughly linearly, we can use the linear regression methods of Chapter 15 to estimate the linear component. We'll do that later in this chapter. (You may wonder if we can use regression for data in which successive errors are not likely to be independent. But if we don't plan to test the coefficients against the standard regression null hypothesis, we don't need any regression assumptions other than linearity.)

The Seasonal Component

Many time series fluctuate regularly. Sales of skis, for example, are always higher in the fall and lower in the spring. Sales of swimsuits peak in the summer. The **seasonal component** of a time series is the part of the variation in a time series that fluctuates in a way that is roughly stable over time with respect to timing, direction, and magnitude. In Figure 19.1, you can easily find that kind of consistent pattern around the general trend. In particular, the first quarter of every fiscal year records more sales than the adjacent quarters, but these fluctuations are relatively

Quarterly data often show a seasonal component that repeats every 4 points. The red trace exhibits such a seasonal fluctuation overlaying a linear trend.

---

[4]Advanced models, such as dynamic regression models or distributed lag models, are outside the scope of this text.

small compared to the overall trend. Because seasonal components are usually related to external patterns they are generally stable and predictable. For example, a retail outlet can forecast sales for the next holiday season from information about the previous holiday season and the overall trend. Even though the retail environment may change, they know that this year's holiday season will look more like last year's holiday season than like last April's sales. Typically seasonal components repeat annually, but patterns that repeat more frequently (for example, hourly energy use by a company during a 24-hour period) are still called seasonal components and are modeled with the same methods. A **deseasonalized**, or seasonally adjusted, series is one from which the seasonal component has been removed.

The time between peaks of a seasonal component is referred to as the **period**. The period is independent of the actual timing of peaks and valleys. For example, many retail companies' sales spike during the holiday season in December, and sales of water skis peak in early summer, but both have a seasonal period of one year.

Cyclical Component

Regular cycles in the data with periods longer than one year are referred to as **cyclical components**. Economic and business cycles can sometimes be modeled, but often we do little more than describe them. If a cyclical component can be related to a predictable phenomenon, then it can be modeled based on some regular behavior or by introducing a variable that represents that predictable phenomenon, and adding it to whatever model we are building for the time series.

Irregular Component

We will see a number of ways to model time series. Just as we did with linear models and regression in Chapter 4, in this chapter we'll find that the residuals—the part of the data *not* fit by the model—can be informative. In time series modeling, these residuals are called the **irregular component**. As with regression residuals, it's a good idea to plot the irregular component to look for extraordinary cases or other unexpected patterns. Often our interest in the irregular component is in how variable it is, whether that variability changes over time, and whether there are any outliers or spikes that may deserve special attention. A time series that has a relatively constant variance is said to be **stationary in the variance**.

To summarize, we identify four *components* of a time series:

1. Trend component (T)
2. Seasonal component (S)
3. Cyclical component (C)
4. Irregular component (I)

Table 19.1 provides a summary of the components as applied to the Whole Foods *Sales* data.

Even though some time series exhibit only two or one of these components, or even none, an understanding of them can help us structure our understanding of a time series. Just as we look at the direction, form, and strength of a scatterplot, remembering to think about the trend, seasonal, and cyclical parts of a time series can clarify our view of a time series.

Modeling Time Series

I have seen the future and it is just like the present, only longer.

—KEHLOG ALBRAN,
" THE PROFIT"

Methods for forecasting a time series fall into two general classes. Smoothing methods work from the bottom up. They try to "smooth out" the irregular component so any underlying patterns will be easier to see. They have the advantage that they don't assume that there is a trend or seasonal component—and indeed, they'll

Component	Description	Rationale	Period Length
Trend	Positive and nonlinear	Overall increase in sales, with a change in the rate of increase of sales in the last 7 years	
Seasonal	Peaks every first quarter in 1995 through 2013	Larger sales in first quarter; reason unknown at present	4 quarters—yearly
Cyclical	No evidence of cycle, although some impact of the economic downturn in 2008 and divestment of Wild Oats	Could be due to economic cycles and factors, such as inflation, interest rates, and employment that might impact consumer spending	No expected period length
Irregular	Random fluctuations in data	Due to irregular or unpredictable events, such as mergers and acquisitions of other companies, or natural disasters, such as floods	No regular repeating pattern; no period

Table 19.1 Time series components terms applied to the series *Sales* for Whole Foods Market, Inc. from 1995 to 2013.

work even when no seasonal component is present and the trend is complex. For example, we can use smoothing methods on a time series that has only a general cyclical component but no clear trend or seasonal fluctuations to model. The disadvantage of smoothing methods is that they can forecast only the immediate future. Lacking a model of behaviors that can be trusted to continue (such as a seasonal component based on calendar shopping patterns or temperature variation over the year), smoothing models don't have a basis for long-term forecasting. Instead, they rely on the assumption that most time series show patterns that vary more slowly than each successive observation, so the next value in the future will resemble the most recent ones.

When we can discern a trend or both a trend and seasonal component, we'll often prefer regression-based modeling methods. These use the methods of multiple regression we've learned in Chapters 17 and 18 to estimate each component's contribution to the time series and to build a model for the time series. As with any regression-based model, models of this kind can be used to forecast for any value of *Time* and thus can generate forecasts further into the future than one time period. However, as always, we'll need to be cautious with such extrapolations.

The next sections discuss several kinds of smoothing methods, followed by a discussion of regression-based models. Although the smoothing methods don't explicitly use the time series components, it is a good idea to keep them in mind. The regression models explicitly estimate the components as a basis for building the models.

FOR EXAMPLE   Truck border crossings in Alaska

The U.S. Department of Transportation Statistics records border crossings into each state on the U.S. border. Commercial traffic, in particular, can be of great interest to businesses that ship to and from Alaska and to economists and investors concerned with those businesses. Here are the border crossings by trucks for Alaska, recorded each month from 1999 through 2009.

(continued)

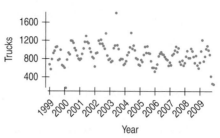

QUESTION   Describe the components of this time series.

ANSWER   Trend: Generally constant; there may be some slight downward trend from 2002 onward.

Seasonal: Strong seasonal component each 12 months, possibly reflecting the difficulty of driving in Alaska in the winter.

Cyclic: Not enough data to see any long-term cycles; trucking should reflect business cycles to some extent.

Irregular: There is clearly some random fluctuation around the seasonal and trend patterns. There are also a few outlying points that may be worth investigating.

19.3   Smoothing Methods

Most time series contain some random fluctuations that vary up and down rapidly—often for consecutive observations. But, precisely because they are random, these fluctuations provide no help in forecasting. Even if we believe that a time series will continue to fluctuate randomly, we can't predict *how* it will do so. The only aspects of a time series that we have any hope of predicting are those that vary either regularly or slowly. One way to identify these aspects is to smooth away the rapid random fluctuations.[5] To forecast the value of a time series in the future, we want to identify the underlying, consistent behavior of the series. In many time series, these slower changes have a kind of inertia. They change and fluctuate, but recent behavior is often a good indication of behavior in the near future. Smoothing methods damp down random fluctuations and try to reveal the underlying behavior so we can use it to forecast values in the immediate future.

The time series for the daily value of the Dow Jones Industrial Average in 2012 (Figure 19.2) shows no regular repeating patterns and no evidence of a regular seasonal effect. But it does show rapid fluctuations and some evidence of longer-term movements.

Figure 19.2   Daily closing value of the DJIA in 2012 shows no seasonal pattern.

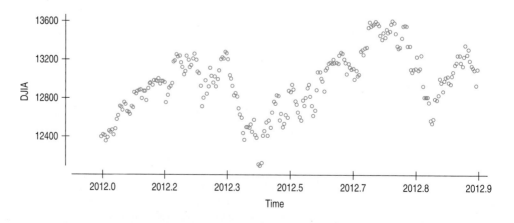

[5]To an engineer, this would be separating the signal from the rapidly varying noise.

Methods for smoothing out the apparently random fluctuations generally work by averaging adjacent values in the series. We know from Chapter 11 that means vary less than the underlying data. We can use that principle to find values that are typical of the local value of the series while varying less than the original data.

Simple Moving Average Methods

The most commonly used smoothing method is the method of **moving averages**. A moving average replaces each value in a time series by an average of the adjacent values. The number of values we use to construct the averages is called the *length* of the moving average (*L*). Almost every stock tracking service on the Internet offers a variety of moving averages (often with 50-, 100-, and 200-day lengths) to help track stock movements.

A moving average simply uses the mean of the previous *L* values as the fitted value at each time. Because it focuses on only the recent values, a moving average with a short length can respond to rapid changes in a time series. A moving average with a longer length will respond more slowly. The general form of a moving average is:

$$\widetilde{y}_t = \frac{\sum\limits_{i=t-L+1}^{t} y_i}{L}$$

The length, *L*, of a moving average is a subjective choice, but it must be specified when discussing a moving average. We write MA(*L*) for a moving average of length *L*, indicate the range of values involved in the sum with subscripts below and above the summation sign, and use the tilde to denote a moving average calculated from a sequence of data values.

Let's begin by using a moving average of length of 5 on the DJIA series to illustrate the calculation. The data are in Table 19.2 and the formulas to calculate the smoothed stock price for the fifth and sixth day in the series are:

$$\widetilde{\text{Price}}_5 = \frac{\sum\limits_{1}^{5} \text{Price}_t}{5} = \frac{12397.38 + 12418.42 + \cdots + 12392.69}{5} = 12396.82$$

and

$$\widetilde{\text{Price}}_6 = \frac{\sum\limits_{2}^{6} \text{Price}_t}{5} = \frac{12418.42 + 12415.70 + \cdots + 12462.47}{5} = 12409.84$$

The MA(5) smoothed stock price for each day in the series in 2012 is computed from that day's closing price and the preceding four daily closing prices using similar formulas. If we instead select $L = 15$ for our moving averages, then the calculations will average the 15 previous closing prices (including today's price). Table 19.2 shows the computed values for the two moving averages using $L = 5$ and $L = 15$ and the actual closing price of the DJIA for the first 30 days when the market was open in 2012.

There are no moving averages for the first $(L - 1)$ days in the series for each moving average model. What happens to the moving average as the length, *L*, increases? Of the two smoothed series produced by computing moving averages for the daily DJIA value using $L = 5$ and $L = 15$, Figure 19.3 shows that the moving average series with the greater length is smoother. That should be what you expected. Of course, a smoother series is not necessarily a better model for the data

Summarizing and Predicting

If we just want to summarize the patterns in a time series, a centered moving average will usually be a better choice. A centered moving average summarizes each value in a time series with the mean of the L/2 values on either side. A centered MA will track a time series with a strong trend better than one that uses only previous values, but it can't provide a forecast because it would need the L/2 values in the future to provide a smooth value for the most recent observation.

Differing Answers

The smoother-based analyses in this chapter were calculated in Excel 2013. Similar analyses calculated in other packages may differ due to different assumptions about starting and ending values.

Dow	MA5	MA15
12397.38		
12418.42		
12415.70		
12359.92		
12392.69	12396.82	
12462.47	12409.84	
12449.45	12416.05	
12471.02	12427.11	
12422.06	12439.54	
12482.07	12457.41	
12578.95	12480.71	
12623.98	12515.62	
12720.48	12565.51	
12708.82	12622.86	
12675.75	12661.60	12505.28
12756.96	12697.20	12529.25
12734.63	12719.33	12550.33
12660.46	12707.32	12566.65
12653.72	12696.30	12586.23
12632.91	12687.74	12602.25
12716.46	12679.64	12619.18
12705.41	12673.79	12636.25
12862.23	12714.15	12662.33
12845.13	12752.43	12690.53
12878.20	12801.49	12716.94
12883.95	12834.98	12737.27
12890.46	12871.99	12755.04
12801.23	12859.79	12760.42
12874.04	12865.58	12771.44
12878.28	12865.59	12784.94

Table 19.2   Moving Averages for $L = 5$, or MA(5), and $L = 15$, or MA(15), for the closing DJIA values for the first 30 trading days of 2012.

because it has a hard time following the series when it changes rapidly. Look, for example, at the two times during the year the DJIA fell rapidly, but the MA(15) smooth changed too slowly, running above the data for several weeks before it "caught up."

Figure 19.3   A time series plot of the daily Dow Jones Industrial Average closing values in 2012 (in red) with MA(5) (in yellow) and MA(15) (in blue) forecasts superimposed. The moving average with the smaller length, $L = 5$, follows the data more closely while the moving average with the longer length is smoother.

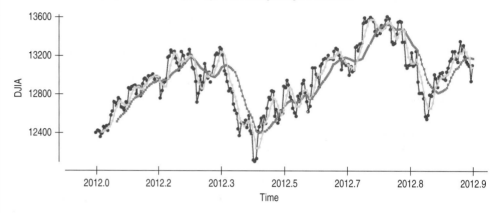

> **Smoothed Values and Forecast Values**
>
> To model the smooth pattern that we think might underlie a time series, it makes sense to include the observed value at time t in calculating the smooth value we'll plot at that time point. There's little sense in ignoring information that we have.
>
> When we forecast the next value, that most recent smoothed value is a good choice since it is recent and incorporates information from several recent time periods, damping out the short-term fluctuations.
>
> We use a tilde to denote the smoothed values. We follow the convention from regression of using a hat to denote a predicted value.

To obtain a forecast for a new time point, analysts use the last average in the series:

$$\hat{y}_{t+1} = \tilde{y}_t$$

This is the **simple moving average forecast**. Of course, this method can forecast only one time period into the future, for $Time = t + 1$. (You can repeat that value as a forecast beyond period $t + 1$, but unless the time series is essentially unstructured and horizontal, it won't be a very good forecast.) If the length of the moving average is 1 ($L = 1$), then the forecast is simply that the next value will be the same as the previous one, $\hat{y}_{t+1} = y_t$. As the simplest forecast, this is called the **naïve forecast**.

Often, moving averages are used primarily as summaries of how a time series is changing. The length selected depends on the purpose of the analysis. If the focus is on long-term behavior, a longer moving average is appropriate. But an analyst interested in shorter-term changes would choose a shorter length. Sometimes (as you can see in the sidebar on page 651) analysts compare a shorter-length moving average and one with a longer length, hoping to learn something from how they compare.

One potential problem with a moving average is that, as we know from Chapter 3, means can be affected by outliers. An outlier in a time series would be a spike in the series far from the adjacent values. Such a spike will contaminate all of the averages in which it participates, spreading its influence over a number of values.

Weighted Moving Averages

In a simple moving average, we just average the most recent L values. But we can benefit from a more sophisticated averaging scheme. We can assign a *weight* to each

Moving averages are widely used in so-called technical analyses of the stock market. Many investors believe that the movement of a short-term (such as a 15- or 50-day) moving average compared to a long-term (typically the 100- or 200-day) moving average measures the "momentum" of the price and provides guidance as to whether to buy or sell the stock or mutual fund. Because averages with more observations vary less than those with fewer observations, many analysts believe that the longer term average should carry more weight in the analysis. So, when a short-term moving average falls below, or "crosses over," the long-term moving average, it's a bearish (sell) signal called a "death cross." On the other hand, when the short-term moving average breaks above the long-term, it's a bullish (buy) signal called a "golden cross." Note, however, that neither of these signals has ever been proven to provide reliable information about the future performance of a stock or mutual fund.

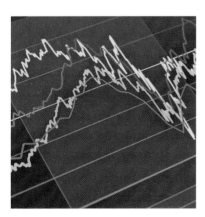

value according to how far it is before the current value. The result is a *weighted* average. In a weighted average, each value is multiplied by a *weight* before they are added up, and the total is divided by the sum of the weights:

$$\widetilde{y}_t = \frac{\sum w_i y_{t-i}}{\sum w_i}$$

The weights might be specified, or they might be found as part of the smoothing process.

Weighted moving averages form a very general class of smoothers.[6] We will consider two types of weighted moving average smoothers that are commonly used on time series data, exponential smoothers and autoregressive moving averages.

FOR EXAMPLE   The value of the euro

The euro is the second-most traded currency (after the dollar), so its value relative to other currencies is of great interest. One euro was equal to one U.S. dollar when the new European currency was launched on January 1, 1999. Since that time the value has fluctuated. On October 26, 2000, one euro cost $0.8252. But on July 15, 2008, it was as high as $1.5990. As the time series plot of 50 weekly euro/dollar values between July 1, 2012 and June 9, 2013, shows, recent fluctuations show little pattern, so smoothing methods may be the best approach to short-term prediction of euro values.

Here are some of those euro values in dollars for the weeks of July and August 2012.

Date	Value ($)
Jul 2, 2012–Jul 8, 2012	1.2508
Jul 9, 2012–Jul 15, 2012	1.2257
Jul 16, 2012–Jul 22, 2012	1.2243
Jul 23, 2012–Jul 29, 2012	1.2186
Jul 30, 2012–Aug 5, 2012	1.2291
Aug 6, 2012–Aug 12, 2012	1.2353
Aug 13, 2012–Aug 19, 2012	1.232
Aug 20, 2012–Aug 26, 2012	1.245
Aug 27, 2012–Sep 2, 2012	1.2536

QUESTION   Find a 3-term moving average for these data and predict the value for the next week.

(continued)

[6]In this general form, these smoothers are known as *linear smoothers*. They are important in engineering and finance.

Date	Value ($)	MA(3)
Jul 2, 2012–Jul 8, 2012	1.2508	
Jul 9, 2012–Jul 15, 2012	1.2257	
Jul 16, 2012–Jul 22, 2012	1.2243	1.2336
Jul 23, 2012–Jul 29, 2012	1.2186	1.2229
Jul 30, 2012–Aug 5, 2012	1.2291	1.2240
Aug 6, 2012–Aug 12, 2012	1.2353	1.2277
Aug 13, 2012–Aug 19, 2012	1.232	1.2321
Aug 20, 2012–Aug 26, 2012	1.245	1.2374
Aug 27, 2012–Sep 2, 2012	1.2536	1.2435

The prediction is $1.2435.

Exponential Smoothing Methods

Smoothing methods summarize each value of a time series with an average of recent values. In many time series, recent values of the series are more relevant for modeling than older ones. So a weighted moving average that weights the more recent values more heavily than the older ones makes sense. Exponential smoothing does just that. **Exponential smoothing** is a weighted moving average with weights that decline exponentially into the past. The most recent data are weighted the most and the most distant data are weighted the least. This model is the **single-exponential smoothing (SES) model**:

$$\tilde{y}_t = \alpha y_t + (1 - \alpha)\tilde{y}_{t-1}$$

The choice of the weight α is up to the data analyst, although it is usually restricted to $0 < \alpha < 1$. When $\alpha = 0.50$, the current data point and the entire set of historical data (all points before the current one) are weighted equally. If $\alpha = 0.75$, then historical data are weighted only 25% and the current value has more weight at 75%. If the objective is to produce forecasts that are stable and smoother, then choose a smoothing coefficient closer to zero. If, however, the objective is to react to volatile events rapidly, then choose a smoothing coefficient close to one.[7]

Unlike a simple moving average, exponential smoothing uses *all* previous values, although distant ones typically get very small weight. If we expand the calculation, we can see that the smoothed value at time t is a *weighted* average of the current value and all the previous values, with the weights depending on a smoothing coefficient, α:

$$\tilde{y}_t = \alpha y_t + \alpha(1 - \alpha)y_{t-1} + \alpha(1 - \alpha)^2 y_{t-2} + \alpha(1 - \alpha)^3 y_{t-3} + \cdots.$$

As with the moving average model, we use $\tilde{y}_t$ as our prediction for time $t + 1$.

Figure 19.4 shows the DJIA values again, this time with exponentially smoothed values using $\alpha = 0.75$ and $\alpha = 0.10$. You can see that the curve computed using the larger α follows the original series closely. By contrast, the curve computed using the smaller α is smoother, but doesn't follow rapid changes in the series such as the sharp price drop in June.

---

[7]The initial smoothed value to get the algorithm started is either the initial observed value ($\tilde{y}_1 = y_1$) or the average of some of the initial values. In Minitab, for example, the initial smoothed value is equal to the average of the first six observations. We have used the initial value for the examples here.

Figure 19.4 The DJIA with exponential smoothing models ($\alpha = 0.75$ in purple, $\alpha = 0.10$ in yellow). The model with the larger alpha follows the data more closely, and the model with the smaller alpha is smoother.

19.4 Summarizing Forecast Error

Whenever we model a time series, it is natural to ask how closely the model fits the series. A closely related question is how well the model *forecasts* the series. For smoothing models, we use the most recent model value as the forecast for the next time period. When we make a plot of the data and the smoothed series, we usually plot the smoothed value $\tilde{y}_t$ at time t. But if we are interested in the error the model makes when trying to forecast each value, we must compare the data value y_t not to $\tilde{y}_t$, but rather to $\hat{y}_t$, which is actually equal to $\tilde{y}_{t-1}$. We can find a **forecast error** for each time in the series for which we have such a forecast:

$$e_t = (y_t - \hat{y}_t)$$

When there is a particular forecast of interest, it makes sense to look at the forecast error, e_t. More often, we ask about the overall success of a model at forecasting for a time series. That calls for a summary of the forecast errors and, as often happens in statistics, we have several summaries to choose among

In Chapter 17, we found the **mean squared error (MSE)** to summarize the magnitude of the errors. We can use a similar calculation for the forecast errors:

$$MSE = \frac{1}{n}\Sigma(y_t - \hat{y}_t)^2$$

The MSE penalizes large forecast errors because the errors are squared. It also has the problem that it is not in the same units as the data, but rather in the square of those units. We can address both of these problems by summing the *absolute values* of the errors. That gives the **mean absolute deviation (MAD)**:

$$MAD = \frac{1}{n}\Sigma|y_t - \hat{y}_t|$$

The most common approach to measuring forecast error compares the absolute errors to the magnitude of the estimated quantities and sums up the *proportions* of the values that are in error. Multiplying the proportions by 100 gives the **absolute percentage error (APE)**. If we average the APE for all the forecasts, we have the **mean absolute percentage error (MAPE)**:

$$MAPE = 100 \times \frac{1}{n}\Sigma\frac{|y_t - \hat{y}_t|}{|y_t|}$$

The MAPE is expressed in percent, so it doesn't depend on the units of the y variable. If you choose to rescale y, both the MSE and MAD will change, but the MAPE will remain the same.

In summary, MSE resembles the error measures we've used for regression models, but it isn't in the same units as the data. MAD is in the same units as the data, but that means that it will be rescaled if the measurements are rescaled. MAPE is a percentage relating the size of the errors to the magnitudes of the data values.

Date	DJIA	SES(.10)	Forecast(.10)	Error(.10)	SES(.75)	Forecast(.75)	Error(.75)	AbsErr(.10)	AbsErr(.75)
Monday, February 11, 2013	13971.24	13823.3785	13806.9495	164.290517	13974.18	13982.99	−11.75	164.290517	11.7476554
Tuesday, February 12, 2013	14018.70	13842.9107	13823.3785	195.321465	14007.57	13974.18	44.52	195.321465	44.5230861
Wednesday, February 13, 2013	13982.91	13856.9106	13842.9107	139.999318	13989.07	14007.57	−24.66	139.999318	24.6592285
Thursday, February 14, 2013	13973.39	13868.5586	13856.9106	116.479387	13977.31	13989.07	−15.68	116.479387	15.6848071
Friday, February 15, 2013	13981.76	13879.8787	13868.5586	113.201448	13980.65	13977.31	4.45	113.201448	4.44879822
Tuesday, February 19, 2013	14035.67	13895.4578	13879.8787	155.791303	14021.91	13980.65	55.02	155.791303	55.0221996
Wednesday, February 20, 2013	13927.54	13898.666	13895.4578	32.0821728	13951.13	14021.91	−94.37	32.0821728	94.3744501
Thursday, February 21, 2013	13880.62	13896.8614	13898.666	−18.046044	13898.25	13951.13	−70.51	18.0460444	70.5136125
Friday, February 22, 2013	14000.57	13907.2323	13896.8614	103.70856	13974.99	13898.25	102.32	103.70856	102.321597
Monday, February 25, 2013	13784.17	13894.9261	13907.2323	−123.0623	13831.87	13974.99	−190.82	123.062296	190.819601

	$\alpha = .1$	$\alpha = .75$
MAD	206.806	89.8830937
MSE	64973.88	15049.0208
MAPE	1.955	0.84277661

Table 19.3 The initial DJIA values in the series along with smoothed values reported as forecasts one period ahead for two models. For this series, the single-exponential smoothing (SES) model with the larger coefficient ($\alpha = 0.75$) has a larger forecast error.

Table 19.3 shows forecast error for two different single-exponential smoothing (SES) models over the final 10 days of the DJIA values along with the MAD, MSE, and MAPE computed for the entire time series from 2002 to 2013.

FOR EXAMPLE   Forecast errors

QUESTION   For the euro values in the example on page 651, find the forecasts, the errors, and the measures of forecast error.

ANSWER

Date	Value ($)	MA(3)	Forecast	Error
Jul 16, 2012–Jul 22, 2012	1.2243	1.2336		
Jul 23, 2012–Jul 29, 2012	1.2186	1.2229	1.2336	−0.0150
Jul 30, 2012–Aug 5, 2012	1.2291	1.2240	1.2229	0.0062
Aug 6, 2012–Aug 12, 2012	1.2353	1.2277	1.2240	0.0113
Aug 13, 2012–Aug 19, 2012	1.232	1.2321	1.2277	0.0043
Aug 20, 2012–Aug 26, 2012	1.245	1.2374	1.2321	0.0129
Aug 27, 2012–Sep 2, 2012	1.2536	1.2435	1.2374	0.0162
Sep 3, 2012–Sep 9, 2012	1.2634	1.2540	1.2435	0.0199

MSE	0.0002
MAD	0.01225238
MAPE	0.98573126

19.5   Autoregressive Models

Simple moving averages and exponential smoothing methods are good choices for time series with no regular long-term patterns. But if some patterns are present—even if they don't rise to the level of a well-structured seasonal fluctuation—we may want to choose weights that facilitate modeling that structure—something that exponential smoothing can find difficult to do. Such weights might even be negative. (Imagine a series with values that alternated up and down for successive times. A good weighted average would give a negative weight to the most recent value and a positive weight to the one before that.)

But how can we find appropriate weights and how can we choose among the huge number of possible weights? It turns out that we can use the methods of multiple regression we saw in Chapters 17 and 18, along with the fact that the data come to us in time sequence order, to discover weights for a weighted moving average smoother. We shift the data by a time period or a few time periods. This shift is known as *lagging*, and the resulting variables are called *lagged variables*. For example, Table 19.4 shows the first 15 values of the daily DJIA values in 2012 along with the lagged values for lags of one, two, three, and four days.

DJIA	DJIA$_{lag1}$	DJIA$_{lag2}$	DJIA$_{lag3}$	DJIA$_{lag4}$
12397.38	*	*	*	*
12418.42	12397.38	*	*	*
12415.70	12418.42	12397.38	*	*
12359.92	12415.70	12418.42	12397.38	*
12392.69	12359.92	12415.70	12418.42	12397.38
12462.47	12392.69	12359.92	12415.70	12418.42
12449.45	12462.47	12392.69	12359.92	12415.70
12471.02	12449.45	12462.47	12392.69	12359.92
12422.06	12471.02	12449.45	12462.47	12392.69
12482.07	12422.06	12471.02	12449.45	12462.47
12578.95	12482.07	12422.06	12471.02	12449.45
12623.98	12578.95	12482.07	12422.06	12471.02
12720.48	12623.98	12578.95	12482.07	12422.06
12708.82	12720.48	12623.98	12578.95	12482.07

Table 19.4   The lagged values for the first 15 days in the DJIA 2012 time series for one, two, three, and four days.

If we fit a regression to predict a time series from its lag1 and lag2 versions,

$$\hat{y} = b_0 + b_1 y_{lag1} + b_2 y_{lag2},$$

each predicted value, $\hat{y}_t$, is just a sum of the two previous values, y_{lag1} and y_{lag2} (plus a constant) weighted by the fitted coefficients b_1 and b_2. That's just a weighted moving average with weights found by the regression.

But wait. Regression methods assume that the errors are mutually independent. And this method works only if recent values can help predict current ones, which makes it likely that recent errors will be like the current one. Isn't this a violation of the regression model? Well, yes and no. The independence assumption is certainly required for inference on the coefficients, for example, to test the standard null hypothesis that the true coefficient is zero. But we're not doing inference here; we're just building a model. And for that purpose, the failure of independence is really more an opportunity than a problem.

In fact, we can specifically account for the association of cases with previous ones. The correlation between a series and a **lagged** version of the same series that is offset by a fixed number of time periods is called **autocorrelation**.[8] Table 19.5 shows some autocorrelations for the DJIA series.

	DJIA	Lag1	Lag2	Lag3	Lag4
DJIA	1.000				
Lag1	0.956	1.000			
Lag2	0.910	0.956	1.000		
Lag3	0.862	0.910	0.957	1.000	
Lag4	0.815	0.862	0.911	0.957	1.000

Table 19.5 Autocorrelations of the DJIA daily values for all of 2012 for lags 1, 2, 3, and 4.

A regression model that is based on an average of prior values in the series weighted according to a regression on lagged versions of the series, is called an **autoregressive model.** A model based on only the first lagged variable is called a first-order autoregressive model, often abbreviated as AR(1).

A pth-order autoregressive model has the form:

$$\hat{y} = b_0 + b_1 y_{lag1} + \cdots + b_p y_{lag\,p}.$$

For the DJIA series, we find the coefficients for a fourth-order autoregressive model from a multiple regression of the series on its first four lagged values, as shown in Table 19.6.

```
Dependent variable is: DJIA
249 total cases of which 4 are missing
R squared = 91.0%  R squared (adjusted) = 90.9%
s = 94.96 with 245 - 5 = 240 degrees of freedom

Variable      Coefficient    SE(Coeff)    t-ratio    P-value
Intercept     733.345        256.1         2.86       0.0046
Lag1            0.978554       0.0649      15.1       <0.0001
Lag2            0.008051       0.0916       0.088      0.9300
Lag3           -0.042241       0.0918      -0.460      0.6457
Lag4           -0.000682       0.0648      -0.011      0.9916
```

Table 19.6 A fourth-order autoregressive model for the DJIA series. Note that there are 249 values in the series but, because lagged variables have missing values at the beginning of the series, there are only 245 complete cases.

The resulting fourth-order autoregressive model is

$$\hat{y}_t = 733.345 + 0.978554 y_{lag1} + 0.008051 y_{lag2} - 0.042241 y_{lag3} - 0.000682 y_{lag4}$$

Looking at the coefficients, we can see that the model puts most of its weight on the data value just preceding the one we're estimating (the lag 1 value).

Figure 19.5 The DJIA series with an AR(4) model.

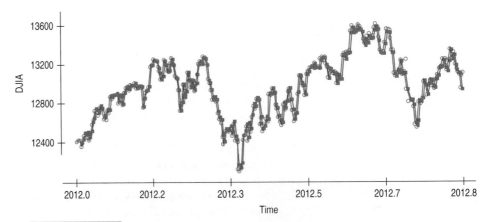

We can use an autoregressive model to predict the next value in a time series, but, to predict further into the future, we must substitute predicted values in the lag variables, which of course is likely to make our errors larger.

FOR EXAMPLE   An autoregressive model for the euro

QUESTION   Find and interpret an autoregressive model for the euro prices.

ANSWER

```
Dependent variable is: Value($)
50 total cases of which 2 are missing
R squared = 90.3%  R squared (adjusted) = 89.9%
s = 0.0104 with 48 − 3 = 45 degrees of freedom
```

Variable	Coefficient	SE(Coeff)	t-ratio	P-value
Intercept	0.106611	0.0595	1.79	0.0799
Lag1	1.25427	0.1429	8.78	< 0.0001
Lag2	−0.336069	0.1411	−2.38	0.0215

Both the lag1 and lag2 terms are significant, suggesting that changes in the value of the euro show short-term serial correlation; today's value is much like yesterday's.

Unlike simple moving average models and single exponential smoothing models, AR models can follow time series that have seasonal fluctuations. The AR method will assign a larger weight to lags that correspond to the period of the fluctuation. For example, AR models will tend to predict quarterly sales that show a seasonal cycle by assigning a large weight to the lag4 version of the series, so sales in the same quarter of the previous year are counted heavily.

Of course, because AR models are regression models, you should plot the residuals. For time series, residuals are usually plotted against time rather than against predicted values.

JUST CHECKING

J. Crew is a clothing company known for its preppy fashions, including jeans, khakis, and other basic items sold to young professionals through its catalogs, websites, and some 260 retail and outlet stores in the United States. (Michelle Obama shops there.) We have their reported quarterly revenue from Q1 2003 through 2007. Here's a time series plot:

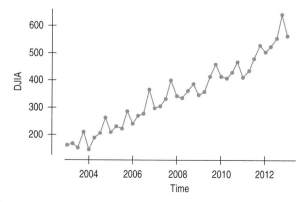

1. Which time series components do you see in this plot?
2. The final four values for 2012 are

Q1 2012	503.5
Q2 2012	525.5
Q3 2012	555.8
Q4 2012	642.9

   Given these four values, where on the graph would the final value of a 4-point simple moving average be? Do you think it would be a good prediction for Q1 of 2013?

3. If the exponential smooth value for Q3 of 2012 is 550, what is the exponential smooth value of Q4 when an α of 0.5 is used?

4. If you wished to fit an autoregressive model, how many terms should you include? Why?

Random Walks

All moving average models include the special naïve model that predicts that the next value will be the same as the current one. For an autoregressive model, when the coefficient of y_{lag1} is close to one and the estimated intercept is close to zero, the first-order autoregressive model is approximately

$$\hat{y}_{t+1} = y_t$$

The naïve forecast model is the best we can do when the underlying time series has no other structure. A series with no other structure can be described as just adding a random kick to the previous value:

$$y_{t+1} = y_t + e_t$$

where the "e" are independent random values with some distribution. The "e" are sometimes referred to as "white noise." This kind of time series is called a **random walk** because each new value can be thought of as a random step away from the previous value.

Time series that are modeled by a random walk can have rapid and sudden changes in direction, but they also may have long periods of runs up or down that can be mistaken for cycles.[9] Random walks include series such as the assets of a gambler over time, the location of a molecule in a gas, and the path taken by a foraging animal. The random walk hypothesis in finance predicts that in an efficient market, stock prices should follow a random walk.[10,11] There is a large literature dealing with random walks. They show up in mathematics, economics, finance, and physics, as well as other fields.

GUIDED EXAMPLE   Comparing Time Series Methods

The Home Depot chain of home improvement stores grew in the 1980s and 1990s faster than any other retailer in history. By 2005, it was the second largest retailer in the United States. But its extraordinary record of growth was slowed by the financial crisis of 2008. How do different methods of modeling time series compare for understanding these data?

PLAN

Setup State your objective. Identify the quantitative variables you wish to examine. Report the time frame over which the data have been collected and define each variable.

We want to build time series models for quarterly sales at The Home Depot from 1995 through 2012. We have quarterly sales ($ Billion).

---

[9]This is one reason we recommended that the identification of cycles be based on theory, on established patterns, or on other variables.

[10]The fact that only the first term in the AR(4) model on page 656 was significant supports the random walk theory for stock prices.

[11]Princeton economist Burton Malkiel made the random walk theory of the stock market famous in his book *A Random Walk Down Wall Street: The Time-Tested Strategy for Successful Investing*, first published in 1973. The theory originated in the 1950s with Maurice Kendall, a British statistician.

Plot Plot the time series and clearly label the axes to identify the scale and units.

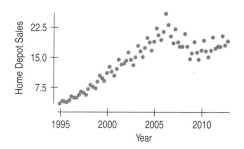

Model Think about the assumptions and check the conditions.

These are quantitative data measured over time at consistent intervals. So it is appropriate to use time series methods.

There was a consistent increasing trend until the end of 2006. After that, sales fell sharply. They appear to have been recovering. Throughout this period, however, there are fluctuations around the trend that appear to be seasonal because they repeat every four quarters. Some smoothing methods may have difficulty with the seasonal fluctuations, but they are likely to be successful at following the sudden change in fortunes following 2006.

DO

Mechanics, Part 1 Try a moving average. For data with a strong seasonal component, such as these, a moving average length that is a multiple of the period is a good idea. But series with a strong trend, such as this one, won't be fit well by an uncentered moving average.

Here is a simple moving average of length 4:

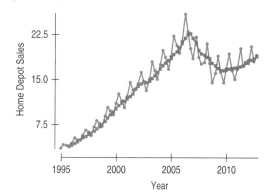

Evaluate how well this method fits the series.

We can also calculate

MAD = 1.134
MSE = 2.209
MAPE = 7.756

Make a forecast for Q1 2013.

The program offers a forecast of 18.908 $B for the first quarter of 2013.

Mechanics, Part 2 Exponential smoothing can be a good compromise between a simple moving average smoother and a fit with a seasonal component.

In series with a strong trend such as this one, exponential smooths will inevitably lag behind the data.

Let's try an exponential smooth. Now we have to choose a smoothing weight. We'll use $\alpha = 0.5$, which weights the current data value equally with all the rest in the past. Here's the result from a computer-generated smooth:

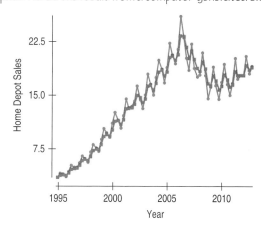

(continued)

Evaluate how well this model fits.

MAD = 0.7277
MSE = 0.8677
MAPE = 5.043

Forecast sales for Q1 2013.

The smoother generates a prediction of 18.8928 $B for the first quarter of 2013.

Mechanics, Part 3 An autoregressive model is a multiple regression on the series itself lagged, or offset, by 1, 2, or more time periods. When we know that there is a seasonal component, it is important to include the corresponding lag—here lag4. This model has terms for each lag.

Now let's fit an autoregressive model. Because we know that the seasonal pattern is 4 quarters long, we'll fit four terms, using multiple regression to find the smoothing weights:

```
Dependent variable is:  HDSales
72 total cases of which 4 are missing
R squared = 94.2%  R squared (adjusted) = 93.8%
s = 1.319 with 68 − 5 = 63 degrees of freedom
```

Variable	Coefficient	SE(Coeff)	t-ratio	P-value
Intercept	1.69432	0.4721	3.59	0.006
Lag1	0.469540	0.1124	4.18	<0.0001
Lag2	−0.255134	0.1245	−2.05	0.0446
Lag3	0.223335	0.1284	1.74	0.0869
Lag4	0.487104	0.1123	4.34	<0.0001

The AR(4) model is

$$\hat{y}_t = 1.694 + 0.4695 y_{t-1} - 0.255 y_{t-2} + 0.223 y_{t-3} + 0.487 y_{t-4}$$

Plot the fit.

Plot the residuals.

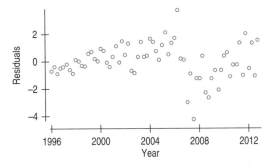

The forecast errors show some disturbance around the time of the financial crisis. Because sales at that time stopped resembling previous behavior with respect to growth, lagged versions of the series were less successful predictors.

Calculate fit measures and a prediction.

MAD = 0.952
MSE = 1.1612
MAPE = 6.517

A predicted value for the first quarter of 2013 is:

$$1.694 + 0.4695 \times 17.61$$
$$- 0.225 \times 19.226 + 0.2233$$
$$\times 19.237 + 0.487 \times 18.348 = 19.317$$

REPORT

Conclusion Compare the advantages and disadvantages of the time series methods. Be sure to state your interpretations in the proper context.

MEMO

Re: Time series analyses of The Home Depot quarterly sales

We compared several time series methods to fit quarterly data on sales at The Home Depot for the period from 1995 through 2012. The actual sales in Q1 of 2013 were $19.124B.

The different methods had differing strengths and weaknesses. The moving average method smooths out most of the seasonal effects and because it lags behind the series, has trouble modeling the sudden change in 2007, but it provides a good description of the trend.

The exponential smoothing method follows the seasonal pattern more closely, and has the best average error.

The autoregressive method seems to have the greatest difficulty following the sudden adjustment in 2007. It appears to be getting back on track as growth resumed in the most recent years.

Each of these methods is within about 1% in its prediction for the first quarter of 2013.

19.6 Multiple Regression–based Models

We noted earlier that some time series have identifiable components; a trend, a seasonal component, and possibly a cyclical component. Simple moving average models work best on time series that lack any consistent structures like these. Exponential smoothing models don't usually follow a seasonal component well either. Autoregressive moving averages can follow all of these components provided the length of the smoother is at least as long as the period of the seasonal or cyclical component.

When some or all of these components are present, we can gain two distinct advantages by modeling them directly. First, we may be able to forecast beyond the immediate next time period—something the smoothing models can't do easily. Second, we may be able to understand the components themselves and reach a deeper understanding of the time series itself.

Modeling the Trend Component When a time series has a **linear trend**, the natural thing to do is to model it with a regression. If the trend is linear, a linear regression of y_t on *Time* can model the trend. The residuals would then be a *detrended* version of the time series.

During its period of record growth until about 2006, the Home Depot sales seem to have a roughly linear trend. We can't fit a linear model to the entire series, but we can model that period of initial growth. The regression to estimate the trend for 1995 to the end of 2005 is in Table 19.7.

```
Dependent variable is: HDSales
R squared = 95.5%  R squared (adjusted) = 95.4%
s = 1.044 with 40 - 2 = 38 degrees of freedom

Variable    Coeff     SE(Coeff)  t-ratio  P-value
Intercept   2.67102   0.3241      8.24    <0.0001
Time        0.405707  0.0143     28.4     <0.0001
```

Table 19.7 Estimating the trend component in the Home Depot sales data by regression for the period of record growth up to 2006.

One attractive feature of a regression-based model is that the coefficient of *Time* can be interpreted directly as the change in *y* (here, Home Depot Sales) *per* time unit (here, quarters). The trend in Home Depot sales was that they increased by 0.405 billion dollars per quarter.

By contrast, we saw in Figure 19.1 that the Whole Foods sales data *don't* have a linear trend. As we learned in Chapter 16, we can often improve the linearity of a relationship with a re-expression. The re-expression that most often works for time series is the logarithm. That's because many time series grow or shrink exponentially. Typically, the bigger you are, the larger the absolute increment in your profits. Growth by a consistent percentage is *exponential growth*. For example, if sales each year are 5% higher than the previous year, then the overall growth will be exponential. And the logarithm makes exponential growth linear. Figure 19.6 shows the result of taking logs in the Whole Foods data.

Figure 19.6   The logarithm of Whole Foods quarterly Sales is linear over time.

The corresponding model for the trend is

```
Dependent variable is: LogSales
R squared = 96.9%  R squared (adjusted) = 96.9%
s = 0.0687 with 74 − 2 = 72 degrees of freedom

Variable      Coefficient    SE(Coeff)    t-ratio    P-value
Intercept      −139.924       2.999        −46.7      <0.0001
Year              0.071282    0.0015         47.6      <0.0001
```

Table 19.8   A regression model for the trend in LogSales of Whole Foods. Taking logs has made the relationship more nearly linear.

Now the interpretation of the trend coefficient is different. Adding 0.071282 to the logarithm of sales each year is the same as multiplying sales by $10^{0.071282} \approx 1.18$. And that's an increase of 18 percent. So we can say that Whole Foods Market's sales were increasing by 18 percent per year.[12]

Re-expressing the Whole Foods quarterly sales data by logarithms reveals a second advantage of the re-expression. The seasonal fluctuations evident in Figure 19.1 grew in magnitude as the sales themselves grew. But in Figure 19.6, those fluctuations are nearly constant in size. That will make them much easier to model. And, although it is visible in Figure 19.1, the "adjustment" in sales growth due to the financial crisis of 2008 is much easier to see in Figure 19.6. It appears that after the crisis, sales growth has been slower than it had been before 2008.

Which Log?

Financial models that talk about exponential growth usually describe them using the constant $e = 2.71828$, and its corresponding inverse function is the *natural* logarithm, written *ln*. When we re-express data to improve linearity, we usually prefer the base-10 logarithm, written *log* or log_{10}, because it is a bit easier to interpret. Which should you use? In fact, it doesn't matter at all. For all values, $ln(y) = log(y) \times ln(10)$, so the two functions differ only by a scale factor—a constant that doesn't affect our analyses. For consistency with our earlier analyses, we'll use base-10 logarithm here.

---

[12]Of course, if you use natural logarithms rather than base-10 logarithms, the function that returns to the original units is e^b where *b* is the Trend coefficient. But the interpretation of the result (and, allowing for rounding error, the value itself) will be the same.

> **Recording *Time***
>
> The Whole Foods Market sales are reported quarterly, but the time variable here is *Year*. The time variable in a time series often is just a count of the number of time periods (weeks, months, quarters, etc.) since the series began. So, the periods are often recorded as 1, 2, 3, . . . as we did for The Home Depot sales data. If we want to use the actual date as the predictor variable and we have quarterly data, we need to express each time period as a fractional year, such as 1995.0, 1995.25, 1995.5, ... The only difference this will make is in interpreting the coefficients. Moving average methods take no note of how time is recorded, but when you use a regression-based model, you must be aware of that so you can interpret the *Time* coefficient correctly.
>
> For example, if we had used a time variable that counted 1, 2, 3, . . . in the regression instead of fractional year, the slope coefficient would have been 1/4 of the one we found and it would have estimated the *quarterly* growth in log sales rather than the annual growth.

Modeling the Seasonal Component   Figure 19.6 shows that the Whole Foods data have a strong seasonal component. Every fourth quarter there's a spike. That's not unusual in time series related to retail sales. The simplest version of a seasonal component is one that adds a different value to the series (in addition to the trend) for each season. We can see that this is a good description of the Whole Foods data; the first fiscal quarter is above the overall trend by roughly the same amount each year. Figure 19.7 shows the pattern.

Figure 19.7 The logarithm of Whole Foods quarterly sales. Each quarter is displayed in its own color and has a regression line fit to it. The lines differ almost exclusively by a shift up or down. The change in growth due to the financial crisis is evident. We'll want to take note of that in our analyses.

As we learned in Chapter 18, a pattern such as the one shown in Figure 19.7 can be modeled by introducing an indicator or dummy variable for each season. For example, we can define our indicator variables to be:

$Q_1 = 1$ in quarter 1 and 0, otherwise

$Q_2 = 1$ in quarter 2 and 0, otherwise, and

$Q_3 = 1$ in quarter 3 and 0, otherwise.

Recall from Chapter 18 that for a categorical variable with k levels to enter a regression model we use $k - 1$ indicator variables. We can't use all k because that would create a collinearity. So we leave out one of them. It doesn't really matter which one we choose to leave out, but because the omitted one becomes the standard of comparison, we often choose the one that is the most typical. The intercept coefficient will estimate a level for the period "left out," and the coefficient of each indicator variable estimates the shift up or down in the series relative to that base level. With four quarters, we use three indicator variables. For this example, we'll arbitrarily choose to leave out the indicator for Q4. Then cases in Q4 will have the value zero for all three of our indicator variables (Q_1, Q_2, and Q_3) and the mean adjustment relative to the trend will be estimated by the intercept (b_0). In any other quarter, the adjustment relative to Q4 will be the coefficient for that quarter's indicator variable.

FOR EXAMPLE   A regression model for truck border crossings

QUESTION   Find and interpret a multiple regression model for the Alaska truck border crossing data from the example on page 647. (The data are in the file **Trucks**.)

ANSWER   The model is:

```
Dependent variable is: Trucks
R squared = 54.2%  R squared (adjusted) = 49.6%
s = 156.7 with 132 − 13 = 119 degrees of freedom
```

Variable	Coefficient	SE(Coeff)	t-ratio	P-value
Intercept	27539.6	8719	3.16	0.0020
Decimal Year	−13.3027	4.350	−3.06	0.0028
Jan	−187.342	46.93	−3.99	0.0001
Feb	−160.325	46.93	−3.42	0.0009
Mar	−2.03334	46.93	−0.043	0.9655
May	129.728	46.94	2.76	0.0066
Jun	311.474	46.95	6.63	<0.0001
Jul	195.491	46.97	4.16	<0.0001
Aug	125.531	50.71	2.48	0.0147
Sep	23.3453	47.00	0.497	0.6203
Oct	−4.27389	47.03	−0.091	0.9277
Nov	−139.893	47.05	−2.97	0.0036
Dec	−209.693	47.08	−4.45	<0.0001

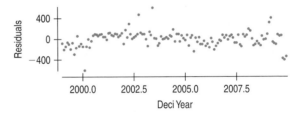

The model finds that the trend is declining over time, but only by about 13 trucks per month per year. (The units of the series are "Trucks per month.") The coefficient of the trend indicates that 13 fewer trucks cross the border each month than in the previous year, after allowing for the (very substantial) seasonal pattern. The model estimates a strong seasonal pattern with crossings low in winter months (November to February) and high in the summer (May to August)—not a surprising pattern for Alaska.

Additive and Multiplicative Models

Adding indicator variables to the regression of a time series on *Time* turns what was a simple one-predictor regression, such as we dealt with in Chapter 4, into a multiple regression, such as those we learned about in Chapter 17. If we model the original values, we have added the seasonal component (in the form of dummy variables) to the trend component (in the form of an intercept coefficient and a regression with the *Time* variable as a predictor). We can write $\hat{y}_t = T + S$.

This is an **additive model** because the components are added up in the model. For example, we've seen that Sales from The Home Depot seem to grow linearly during its period of record growth between 1995 and the end of 2005. And we've noted a seasonal pattern. Table 19.9 shows the regression that models those sales in terms of a trend component and three quarterly dummy variables.

```
Dependent variable is: HDSales
R squared = 98.7%  R squared(adjusted) = 98.5%
s = 0.5915 with 40 − 5 = 35 degrees of freedom

Variable   Coeff     SE(Coeff)  t-ratio  P-value
Intercept  1.38314   0.2534      5.46    <0.0001
Time       0.410336  0.0081     50.4     <0.0001
Q1         1.22191   0.2657      4.60    <0.0001
Q2         2.41907   0.2650      9.13    <0.0001
Q3         1.14944   0.2647      4.34    <0.0001
```

Table 19.9   A regression to model Home Depot sales with a trend component and three dummy variables representing a seasonal component in an additive model.

The model contains a trend component that predicts growth at about \$0.41B per quarter with adjustments for each quarter that are consistent over the entire time period. For example, because Q4 is the quarter without a dummy variable, sales in Q4 are predicted to be on average $1.38 + 0.41\,Time$ billion dollars. The seasonal dummy variable coefficients adjust the predictions for each quarter by adding the value of their coefficients to the intercept. For example, sales in Q1 are predicted to be $1.38 + 0.41\,Time + 1.22 = \$2.60B + 0.41\,Time$ (see Figure 19.8). But you can see from Figure 19.8 that the seasonal fluctuations are small early in the series and grow larger later in the series—a pattern this model doesn't fit.

Figure 19.8   Sales at The Home Depot with predictions from the additive model. The model predicts a consistent seasonal component although the seasonal component of the data varies.

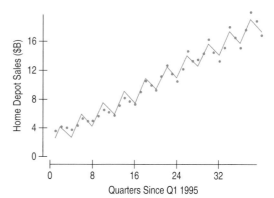

Quarters Since Q1 1995

When we examined the Whole Foods sales data, we saw that we could straighten the trend and make the seasonal fluctuations more nearly the same size by finding the *logarithm*. We can still find a multiple regression, using the re-expressed response variable. The model is in Table 19.10.

```
Dependent variable is: LSI
R squared = 98.8%  R squared (adjusted) = 98.8%
s = 0.0434 with 74 − 5 = 69 degrees of freedom

Variable   Coefficient  SE(Coeff)  t-ratio  P-value
Intercept  −147.856     2.239      −66.0    <0.0001
Year         0.075217   0.0011      67.4    <0.0001
Q1           0.156682   0.0153      10.3    <0.0001
Q2           0.040523   0.0152       2.67   0.0094
Q3           0.035156   0.0156       2.25   0.0276
```

Table 19.10   A regression model for the logarithm of the Whole Foods quarterly Sales data with trend and seasonal components

However, the residuals from this regression sound a warning.

Figure 19.9   The residuals from the regression model of Table 19.10.

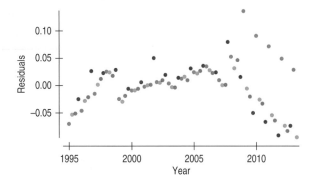

After 2007, sales dropped off sharply. The regression model's assumption of linearity has been violated. If we wish to use regression models, we'd do better to fit one to the pre-2008 data and another to the more recent data.

Here's the fit to the data from 1995 through 2007:

```
Dependent variable is: Log WFSales
R squared = 99.6%  R squared (adjusted) = 99.6%
s = 0.0188 with 52 − 5 = 47 degrees of freedom

Variable   Coeff       SE(Coeff)   t-ratio   P-value
Constant   −156.488    1.396       −112      <0.0001
Year          0.079541   0.0007      114      <0.0001
Q1            0.132511   0.0074       17.9     <0.0001
Q2            0.016969   0.0074        2.30     0.0261
Q3            0.012885   0.0074        1.75     0.0874
```

Table 19.11   A regression model for the logarithm of the initial years of the Whole Foods quarterly Sales data with trend and seasonal components.

> **Logarithms Reminder**
>
> Logarithms have the special property that they turn multiplication into addition. Before technology, that made them a workhorse tool. To understand why a model for the logarithm of a series is a *multiplicative* model, recall that
>
> If
> $$y = T \times S$$
> then
> $$\log(y) = \log(T) + \log(S)$$

> The terms *exponential model* and *multiplicative model* are equivalent for these models and can be used interchangeably.

Now, however, there's a difference in the model. Because we are modeling the logarithm of sales, when we think in terms of the sales themselves, the model components are multiplied rather than added, so we have a **multiplicative model**,

$$\hat{y} = T \times S.$$

Although we acknowledge that the terms in a multiplicative model are multiplied, we always fit the multiplicative model by taking logs, changing the form to an additive model that can be fit by multiple regression.

As we observed earlier, seasonal fluctuations are often proportional to the overall level of the values in the series. The largest coefficient is for Q1. The Q1 lift in sales in a multiplicative model is a *proportion* of overall sales, not a fixed additive increment. Specifically, it is $10^{0.1325} \approx 1.36$—about 36% higher than the sales at that time. Because the sales themselves were growing (at 20% per year), this 36% lift grew as well, in dollar terms. But after taking logs, it is a constant lift, and easier to model.

Look back at the Whole Foods sales in Figure 19.1 on page 644. You can see this growth in the size of the seasonal component in the plot as well as in the trend. Taking logs not only turns exponential growth into linear growth, but it also tends to stabilize the size of the seasonal fluctuations.

Cyclical and Irregular Components

Many time series are more complex than the trend and seasonal components can model. The Dow Jones series of Figure 19.2 on page 648 is one example. Models of time series components are usually said to include two additional components, a cyclical component and an irregular component. Consistent with their form for the trend and seasonal components, we write for additive models:

$$\hat{y}_t = T + S + C + I,$$

and for multiplicative models:

$$\hat{y}_t = T \times S \times C \times I.$$

The Cyclical Component   Long-term business cycles may influence economic and financial time series. Other time series may be influenced by other long-term fluctuations. Whenever there is a business, economic, or physical cycle whose cause is understood and can be relied on, we should look for an external or **exogenous** variable to model the cycle. The regression models we've been considering can accommodate such additional predictors naturally.

Just calling a long-term fluctuation in the data that isn't fit by the trend or seasonal component a "cyclical component" doesn't add much to our understanding. Cyclical patterns may not be immediately evident in the data, so it is wise to compute and plot the residuals, known for time series models as the irregular component.

Irregular Components   The irregular components are the residuals—what's left over after we fit all the other components. We should examine them to check any assumptions and also to see if there might be other patterns apparent in the residuals that we might model. For multiple regression, most statistics programs plot the residuals against the predicted values, but for time series models, it is essential to plot them against *Time*. Figure 19.10 shows the residuals of the initial years of the Whole Foods data plotted against year. Two quarters stand out. Both extraordinary quarters are fourth quarters of their years, which suggests that our seasonal model may need to be improved.[13] We also see a possible cyclical pattern with a period of about 4 years. This might be something worth investigating to see if we can add a component to our model.

Figure 19.10   The irregular component, or residuals, of the multiplicative model for the Whole Foods sales. In the beginning years, growth was apparently faster than after 1999 or so. There are also a couple of quarters that deserve attention: Q4 of 2001 and Q4 of 2007 which were underestimated.

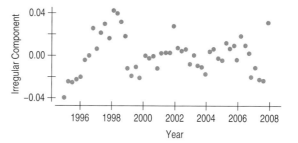

FOR EXAMPLE   **Additive and multiplicative models**

> QUESTION   Is the model for Alaska truck border crossings in the previous example (see page 664) an additive or a multiplicative model? Describe the components. Which month was left out? Why?
>
> ANSWER   This is an additive model. There is an overall negative trend of -13.3 truck crossings per month per year. There is a strong seasonal pattern, fit by the indicator
>
> *(continued)*

---

[13] It's possible to include an indicator (dummy) variable to model a specific event in time. Doing so is known as intervention analysis.

variables for month. April was left out. One month had to be left out to avoid collinearity among the indicator variables.[14] There are generally fewer border crossings between October and March and more between April and September—probably due to the difficulty of driving in the winter in Alaska.

The residuals show no cyclic pattern. The irregular component shown in the residuals has a few outlying months that may deserve looking into. (For example, January of 2000 was a month with particularly heavy snows in Alaska.)

JUST CHECKING

Continuing our analysis of the J. Crew revenue data from the previous Just Checking (page 657), here is a regression fitting a linear model to predict *Revenue* ($M):

```
Dependent variable is: Revenue
R squared = 97.2%  R squared (adjusted) = 96.9%
s = 21.75 with 40 − 5 = 35 degrees of freedom
```

Variable	Coefficient	SE(Coeff)	t-ratio	P-value
Intercept	191.904	9.316	20.6	<0.0001
Q#since 2003	10.0017	0.2993	33.4	<0.0001
Q1	−65.1649	9.766	−6.67	<0.0001
Q2	−59.5866	9.744	−6.12	<0.0001
Q3	−48.8483	9.730	−5.02	<0.0001

5 Locate and interpret the trend coefficient.

6 Why is there no term for Q4?

7 Is the average value for Q4 higher or lower than the other three quarters? Why?

Forecasting with Regression-based Models

Regression models are easy to use for forecasting because they give us a formula. It is easy to substitute future values for *Time*, for the appropriate dummy variables, and for any exogenous variables and calculate a predicted value. Unlike smoothing models, regression-based models can forecast beyond the next time period. But any kind of forecast is uncertain, and the uncertainty grows the further we extrapolate, so it's wise to limit forecasts to the near term. The forecast error measures we discussed in Section 19.4 apply equally well to regression models and are computed from the residuals (or Irregular component.)

> **Were Car Makers' Boom Years Just a Bubble?**
>
> Sales of automobiles reached a high of 17.4 million in 2000 and remained near 17 million for another five years. The *Wall Street Journal* (May 20, 2008, page 1) reported, "Heads of General Motors Corp. and Toyota said the U.S. was entering a golden age of the automobile. In 2003, Toyota's head of North American sales predicted the industry would soon be selling 20 million vehicles a year. They were wrong. Sales started falling in 2006 and this year are expected to be right back where they were in the 1990s, at just over 15 million."

---

[14]April was selected by technology because it was alphabetically first. That's not a particularly good reason. You should be alert for arbitrary decisions by technology like this.

The most reliable part of a regression time series model may be the seasonal component—especially when it is driven by fairly regular economic or environmental phenomena. We can reasonably expect those patterns to continue into the future, so we can feel comfortable basing longer-term forecasts on them. A company that sees large fourth-quarter holiday season sales can probably count on higher fourth-quarter sales even several years in the future.

The trend component is less reliable. As much as we might like to think that a growing company will continue to grow, it should be clear that no company can grow forever and that the economy may experience sudden shocks that change the business climate. Exponential growth is even harder to maintain. Changes in the trend can be quite sudden. The business news is filled with stories of companies whose growth "suddenly" stopped or slowed, of products whose sales unexpectedly shot up and then, just as unexpectedly fell back, and of economic predictions by experts that, in retrospect, look ill-informed. While long-term government forecasts can be found for such reliable indicators as the Gross Domestic Product (GDP) and Disposable Income (DI), long-term forecasts should be made with great care. Changes in the economy or the market cannot be anticipated by the trend component, and can change a company's business quite suddenly.

The reliability of cyclical components for forecasting is something you must simply judge for yourself based on your knowledge and understanding of the underlying economic cycles. An empirical cycle that is not understood makes a risky basis for prediction. A cycle that is understood and is due to underlying phenomena that are stable over time would be a more reliable component of a forecast.

GUIDED EXAMPLE   Comparing Time Series Methods, Part 2

In 2010, the People's Republic of China became the world's second largest economy. China is the largest foreign holder of U.S. public debt. Trade between the two largest economies of the world is an important factor in the global economy. Forecasting U.S. imports from China is important because it is a key factor in the health of the U.S. economy. We have quarterly data starting in 1995. Let's try the regression models to see how well they do.

PLAN	**Setup** State your objective. Identify the quantitative variables you wish to examine. Report the time frame over which the data have been collected and define each variable.	*We want to build regression-based time series models for the logarithm of U.S. imports from China. Because we have already concluded that the exponential growth in imports calls for taking logarithms, we will fit a multiplicative model.*

(continued)

Plot Plot the time series and clearly label the axes to identify the scale and units.

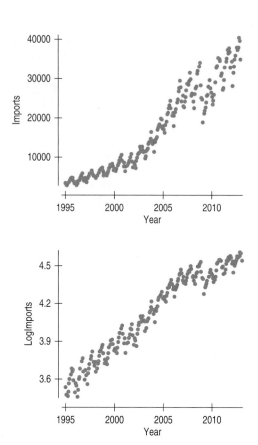

Model Think about the assumptions and check the conditions.

This is a time series recording quantitative values.

There is a consistent, increasing trend and fluctuations around it that may be seasonal. However, it is clearly growing exponentially. The logarithm is much more nearly linear. So we should take logs and fit a multiplicative model.

DO **Mechanics** Fit a multiplicative model with trend and seasonal terms.

```
Dependent variable is: LogImports
R squared = 96.6%  R squared (adjusted) = 96.4%
s = 0.0625 with 216 − 13 = 203 degrees of freedom
```

Variable	Coefficient	SE(Coeff)	t-ratio	P-value
Intercept	−118.340	1.641	−72.1	<0.0001
Year	0.061102	0.0008	74.6	<0.0001
Feb	−0.061534	0.0208	−2.96	0.0035
March	−0.062441	0.0208	−3.00	0.0030
April	−0.025918	0.0208	−1.24	0.2146
May	6.30778e-4	0.0208	0.030	0.9759
June	0.026409	0.0208	1.27	0.2061
July	0.049512	0.0208	2.38	0.0183
Aug	0.069299	0.0208	3.33	0.0010
Sep	0.072621	0.0208	3.49	0.0006
Oct	0.085385	0.0208	4.10	<0.0001
Nov	0.037045	0.0208	1.78	0.0768
Dec	−0.022210	0.0208	−1.07	0.2877

Plot the fit vs. the data (here on the log scale) and the residuals.

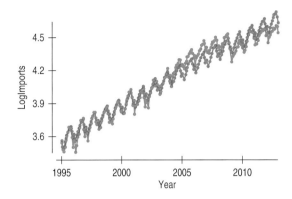

The data are the blue series and the model is the more regular red pattern.

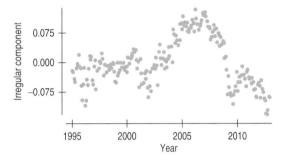

The Irregular component shows that the growth in imports slowed during the financial crisis of 2008.

MAD = 0.049
MSE = 0.0391
MAPE = 1.1614

To make a prediction with a multiplicative model, we use the inverse function of the logarithm.

Forecast for January 2013 is easy to find because January is the indicator that was left out. We calculate
2013 × 0.061102 − 118.340 = 4.6583 corresponding to $10^{4.6583}$ = $45,533M.

REPORT

Conclusion Compare the advantages and disadvantages of the time series models. Be sure to state your interpretations in the proper context.

MEMO

Re: Time series analyses of U.S. imports from China

A multiplicative regression model fit to the monthly data on U.S. imports from China for the period from 1995 through 2012 provides a reasonable fit. However, its greatest value is to highlight the fact that the nature of the series changed with the financial crisis of 2008. Models that expect a consistent pattern, such as the regression models, can't follow sudden changes as well as smoothers.

The actual imports in January 2013 were $37,172M.

To obtain a better prediction, it might be better to model only the years since 2011; however, such a short series might not have sufficient data for reliable model-fitting.

19.7   Choosing a Time Series Forecasting Method

We've considered several methods for modeling and forecasting time series. How can you choose from among them the ones that fit your needs? Your choice depends both on the nature of your data and on what you hope to learn from the data.

Simple moving averages demand the least of the data. You can apply them to almost any time series. However:

- They can forecast well only for the next time period. Longer forecasts just repeat the single forecast value.
- They are sensitive to spikes or outliers in the series, and can smear the shock of a spike across several adjacent time periods.
- They don't do well on series that have a strong trend, tending to lag behind the trend.

Exponential smoothing methods also make few assumptions about the data. They have the advantage of controlling the importance of recent values relative to older ones, and do a good job of following the movement of a time series. However:

- They can forecast well only for the next time period. Longer forecasts just repeat the single forecast value.
- They are sensitive to spikes or outliers in the series.
- They don't do well on series that have a strong trend, tending to lag behind the trend.

Autoregressive models use automatically determined weights to allow them to follow time series that may have regular fluctuations, such as a seasonal component, or series with a consistent trend. However:

- They can forecast for a limited span before they must "recycle" forecast values to use them to make more distant forecasts.
- They are sensitive to spikes or outliers in two different ways. Those outliers will influence the regression that determines the smoothing weights. And then again, when the smoothing is done, the effect of spikes in the series can be spread out, contaminating several points.

Regression-based models estimate the trend and seasonal components by regression against *Time* and using dummy variables to represent the seasonal period. They can incorporate exogenous variables to help model business cycles and other phenomena. And, unlike moving average models, they can forecast into the future. However:

- You must decide whether to fit an additive model to the time series (if the trend is linear and the seasonal fluctuations have a consistent size) or to re-express the series by logarithms and fit the resulting multiplicative model.
- Because they are based on regression, these models are sensitive to outliers and failures of linearity. Because they use dummy variables to estimate the seasonal effects, those effects must be consistent in magnitude during the time covered by the data.
- Forecasts depend on the continuation of the trend and seasonal patterns. Although seasonal patterns may be reliable, trends are difficult to forecast and hazardous to assume beyond the near future. Cycles are best forecast when they are based on some identifiable (and predictable) phenomenon.

19.8 Interpreting Time Series Models: The Whole Foods Data Revisited

When you use a time series model based on moving averages, you can (and should) summarize the patterns seen in the series and any patterns noticed in the residuals around the smooth trend. But time series models based on regression encourage us to interpret the coefficients.

Many time series of retail sales have a strong seasonal component. We've seen some in this chapter. But one of those, the quarterly sales at Whole Foods, is problematic. No, there's no problem with the models we've fit. But there is a problem if we interpret them without thinking.

Why should there be a seasonal spike in Whole Foods' sales? Food isn't a seasonal item. To be honest, it took the authors a while before we asked this question. That sent us back to the original source—the quarterly reports posted online by Whole Foods Market. Now that we were looking for it, we realized that Whole Foods Market divides its financial year into three quarters of 12 weeks and one of 16 weeks. The spike is entirely due to this bookkeeping anomaly. You can check for yourself; the seasonal peaks are $16/12 = 1.33$ times as big as the other quarters—almost exactly what the multiplicative model estimated them to be.

That doesn't invalidate any of our models. We'd still have to allow for the seasonal peak to model Whole Foods sales. But it is a cautionary tale that warns us not to jump to conclusions when interpreting our models.

WHAT CAN GO WRONG?

- **Don't use a linear trend model to describe a nonlinear trend.** Be sure to examine the scatter of the observations around the linear trend line to determine if there is a pattern. A curved pattern may indicate a need to transform the series. Plot the residuals. Variation in the residuals that increases when the central value is higher is a sign of a need to take logarithms. Series that grow or shrink by a constant percentage each time period are exponential and should be transformed before fitting a model.

- **Don't use a trend model for short-term forecasting.** Trend models are most effective for long-term forecasting and are rarely the best models to forecast one or two time periods ahead. Be aware that forecast errors are greater for long-term forecasting.

- **Don't use a moving average or an exponential model for long-term forecasting.** Smoothing models are most effective for short-term forecasting because they require continuous updating as new values in the time series are observed. However, it is less important to transform an exponentially trending series for these models because they base their predictions on recent values.

- **Don't ignore autocorrelation if it is present.** Look at correlations among the lagged versions of the time series. Compute the Durbin-Watson statistic, and make residual plots to identify autocorrelation but don't limit your attention to lag1 autocorrelation (as Durbin-Watson does). If present, then try using lagged variables to model the time series.

ETHICS IN ACTION

GoLearn is a new social networking site designed mainly for college students who have an interest in study abroad. Students from both within and outside the United States are beginning to join, although the majority of users are from the United States. U.S. students are typically interested in short-term semester or summer programs, while those who come to the United States from other countries tend to stay long-term and pursue degrees. GoLearn provides its users a place to "gather" around this common interest and share experiences, information, photos, and advice. It also hopes to attract others to the site, including organizations that sponsor international study (e.g., host universities, consortiums), families who serve as hosts for exchange students, and agencies that provide financial support (e.g., aid and grants).

GoLearn was the brainchild of Charlie Gavigan, president and CEO, who credits his own study abroad experience for changing his life. He founded GoLearn nearly three years ago starting with investments from the "3 Fs" (Family, Friends, and Fools). With a small staff of programmers, graphic designers, and marketing people, the start-up launched the site, initiated a pilot program with students from 20 regional colleges, and created some buzz through local interviews and blogs. The site is periodically updated with new features, and the number of users has been climbing steadily.

Having just concluded a round with angel investors, Charlie knows that it is time to pursue venture capitalists to get the investments needed to take GoLearn to the next level. One area in which progress has been lackluster is attracting advertisers to the site. If GoLearn wants to increase its chances for securing venture capitalist funds, Charlie and his team will need to have more advertisers on board. So Charlie and Pat Conrad, the head of marketing and sales, sit down to discuss some strategies for increasing advertisers on the site. A common concern expressed by many of the potential advertisers Pat had visited was simply the number of users on the site. They believe that GoLearn is too narrow in scope and will not grow at a rate comparable to other popular social networks.

Since the number of GoLearn users had been increasing over time, Charlie asked Pat to fit a trend line to these data. Charlie thought it would be a good idea to have such a model available to show advertisers the projected growth in users. Pat did just that, using the monthly number of users since GoLearn went live. He then checked the residuals and noticed a curvature. So he transformed the data by logs and got a better fitting model. However, when he used each model to project the future growth in GoLearn users, the linear trend provided higher numbers. He thought it best not to apply the log transformation. After all, this would be more difficult to explain to prospective advertisers.

- Identify the ethical dilemma in this scenario.

- What are the undesirable consequences?

- Propose an ethical solution that considers the welfare of all stakeholders.

WHAT HAVE WE LEARNED?

Learning Objectives

Be able to recognize when data are in a time series.

- A *time series* consists of data recorded sequentially over time, usually at equally spaced intervals.
- Time series analyses often attempt to provide forecasts of future values of the series.

Recognize the four components of a time series.

- The Trend component measures the overall tendency of the series to increase or decrease. It is ordinarily estimated as the slope of a regression against *Time*.
- The Seasonal component measures regular, repeating fluctuations. Often these are due to seasons of the year, but the term applies to any such regular fluctuation. Seasonal components are often estimated by introducing indicator (dummy) variables in a regression model.
- The Cyclic component accounts for such things as long-term business cycles.
- The Irregular component is the random fluctuation around the time series model. It corresponds to the residuals from a time series model.

Use smoothing methods to see past random fluctuations (noise) in a time series to detect an underlying smoother pattern (signal).

- Simple Moving Average methods average a relatively small number of adjacent values to obtain a smooth value for each time period.
- Weighted Moving Average methods introduce weights. Because the weights can determine the behavior of the smoother, these are a very general class of time series methods.
- Exponential smoothing methods are weighted moving averages with weights that decline exponentially into the past.
- Autoregressive models use regression methods, predicting the time series from versions of the same series offset, or *lagged*, in time. The result is a weighted moving average method in which the weights are estimated from the data.

Estimate and report forecast error with statistics such as MSE, MAD, and MAPE.

Use multiple regression methods to model a structured time series, using *Time*, indicator variables for the Seasonal component, and exogenous variables that might account for the Cyclic component.

- Multiple regression models have the advantage that they can provide forecasts farther into the future.
- *Additive Model*s estimate the components using multiple regression methods to find a model in which the estimates are added to yield the predicted values.
- Multiplicative models for a time series model the series as a product of its components.
- Multiplicative models are ordinarily estimated by taking the logarithm of the time series values and then using multiple regression as for additive models.

Terms

Absolute percentage error (APE)	A measure of the error of a forecast: $$APE = \frac{|y_t - \hat{y}_t|}{|y_t|}$$
Additive model	A model for a time series that models the series with a sum of all or some of the following terms: a trend, a seasonal pattern, and a cyclical pattern.
Autocorrelation	The correlation between a data sequence, such as a time series, and that same sequence offset (or lagged) by one or more positions. Autocorrelation is one measure of association over time among the individual cases.
Autoregressive model	A pth-order autoregressive model has the form: $$\hat{y} = b_0 + b_1 y_{lag1} + \cdots + b_p y_{lag\,p}.$$
Cyclical component	The part of a model for a time series that describes regular repeating fluctuations with a period longer than a year (or whatever the base period for the seasonal component is).
Deseasonalized	A time series that has had a seasonal component estimated and subtracted.
Exogenous	Variables that are not part of a time series but nevertheless might be helpful in modeling it.
Exponential model	A model for a time series that grows exponentially. It is estimated by transforming the response variable by the logarithm: $$\widehat{log(y)} = b_0 + b_1 Time + other\ terms.$$
Exponential smoothing, Single exponential smoothing (SES model)	An exponential smoother has the form $$\tilde{y}_t = \alpha y_t + (1 - \alpha)\tilde{y}_{t-1}$$ or equivalently, $$\tilde{y}_t = \alpha y_t + \alpha(1 - \alpha)y_{t-1} + \alpha(1 - \alpha)^2 y_{t-2} + \alpha(1 - \alpha)^3 y_{t-3} \ldots$$ The parameter α determines how the smoother behaves. Larger values of α give more weight to recent values of the series. Smaller values give more weight to more distant values.
Forecast	Many analyses of time series attempt to forecast future values. We denote a forecast value $\hat{y}_t$.
Forecast error	The difference between the observed value and the forecasted value for a particular time in a time series: $$e_t = y_t - \hat{y}_t.$$

Irregular component	The part of a time series model that describes random, or unpredictable, behavior; the residuals.
Lagged series	A time series shifted in time by one or more time units.
Linear trend model	A time series model that assumes a constant rate of increase (or decrease) over time: $$\hat{y} = b_0 + b_1 t.$$
Mean absolute deviation (MAD)	A measure of forecast error of the form: $$MAD = \frac{1}{n}\Sigma\,|y_t - \hat{y}_t|.$$
Mean absolute percentage error (MAPE)	A measure of forecast error of the form: $$MAPE = 100 \times \frac{1}{n}\Sigma\frac{|y_t - \hat{y}_t|}{|y_t|}.$$
Mean squared error (MSE)	A measure of forecast error of the form: $$MSE = \frac{1}{n}\Sigma\,(y_t - \hat{y}_t)^2.$$
Moving average	An estimate that uses the arithmetic average of the prior L values in a time series to forecast the next value $$\tilde{y}_t = \frac{\sum\limits_{i=t-L+1}^{t} y_i}{L}.$$
Multiplicative model	A classical time series model consisting of four components, $$\hat{y} = T \times S \times C \times I,$$ where T is the trend component, S is the seasonal component, C is the cyclic component, and I is the irregular component.
Naïve forecast	Forecasting that the next value in a time series will be equal to the current one: $$\hat{y}_{t+1} = y_t.$$
Period	The time between peaks of a regular oscillation in a time series.
Random walk	A time series that exhibits random periods of upturns and downturns and is best modeled using a naïve forecast.
Seasonal component	The part of a model for a time series that fits a regular pattern that has a period of less than or equal to 12 months.
Simple moving average forecast	A simple moving average averages L consecutive values of a time series, where L is the length of the moving average. When the final L values have been averaged, the resulting smooth value for time t can be used to forecast the series for time $t + 1$. (See Moving average.)
Single exponential smoothing (SES) model	(See Exponential smoothing.)
Stationary in the mean	A time series that has a relatively constant mean value over the time frame of the series is said to be stationary in the mean.
Stationary in the variance	A time series that has a relatively constant variance is said to be stationary in the variance. This is equivalent to the Equal Spread condition. (If a time series is simply said to be stationary, most often what is meant is that it has stationary variance.)
Time series	A time series is data recorded sequentially over time at roughly equally spaced intervals.
Trend component	The part of a model for a time series that fits long-term changes in the mean of the series.

```
Dependent variable is: International
R squared = 59.9%  R squared (adjusted) = 49.7%
s = 13540 with 60 - 13 = 47 degrees of freedom
```

Variable	Coeff	SE(Coeff)	t-ratio	P-value
Intercept	175289	6580	26.639	<0.0001
Time	104	103	1.009	0.318049
Feb	−12411	8564	−1.449	0.153943
Mar	−4284	8566	−0.500	0.619369
Apr	−39269	8569	−4.583	<0.0001
May	−32214	8574	−3.757	0.000474
Jun	−23988	8579	−2.796	0.007468
Jul	−11384	8586	−1.326	0.191275
Aug	4737	8594	0.551	0.584075
Sep	−12792	8603	−1.487	0.143706
Oct	−10780	8614	−1.252	0.216944
Nov	−17519	8625	−2.031	0.047919
Dec	14338	8638	1.660	0.103617

a) Interpret the P-value for the *Time* coefficient.

b) The R^2 for this model is lower than for the model fit to domestic visitors in Exercise 39. Does that mean that an exponential trend model would do better?

c) International tourists often visit Hawaii in January. How can you tell that from this model?

d) Even though the R^2 for this model is lower than the corresponding R^2 for the model fit in Exercise 39 to domestic tourist visits, you might feel more comfortable predicting the number of international visitors for April 2007 with this model than you did predicting the number of domestic visitors with the previous model. Explain why.

41. Oakland passengers. The Port of Oakland airport reports the number of passengers passing through each month. At first glance, this is just simple growth, but by recognizing the series as a time series, we may learn more. The following plot was created in **Excel 2013**.

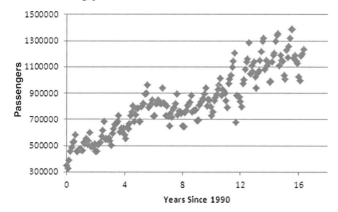

The increasing spread of the data suggests that a multiplicative model may fit better.

Here's an exponential trend model with seasonal (monthly) dummy variables.

```
Dependent variable is: LogPassengers
R squared = 92.4%  R squared (adjusted) = 91.9%
s = 0.0358 with 194 - 13 = 181 degrees of freedom
```

Variable	Coeff	SE(Coeff)	t-ratio	P-value
Intercept	5.64949	0.0101	558	<0.0001
Years since '90	0.024929	0.0006	45.2	<0.0001
Feb	−0.013884	0.0127	−1.10	0.2747
Mar	0.048429	0.0127	3.82	0.0002
Apr	0.049028	0.0125	3.93	0.0001
May	0.066227	0.0125	5.30	<0.0001
Jun	0.082862	0.0127	6.54	<0.0001
Jul	0.095295	0.0127	7.52	<0.0001
Aug	0.121779	0.0127	9.61	<0.0001
Sep	0.029382	0.0127	2.32	0.0216
Oct	0.049596	0.0127	3.91	0.0001
Nov	0.039649	0.0127	3.13	0.0020
Dec	0.043545	0.0127	3.44	0.0007

a) Interpret the slope.

b) Interpret the intercept.

c) Which months have the lowest traffic at Oakland airport? (Hint: Consider all 12 months.)

Here's a plot of the residuals from the model fit to the Oakland airport passengers, created in **Excel**:

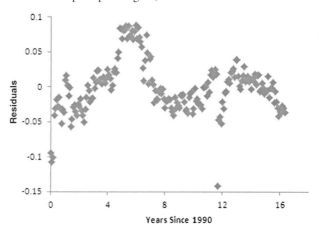

d) What components would you now say are in this series?

42. Monthly gas prices. We have seen that gas prices can fluctuate. But during some periods they have moved consistently. Here are the data extracted for one week of each month from January 2002 to May 2007.

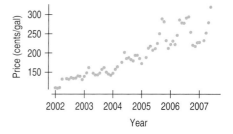

The bend in the plot and the increasing variation suggest a multiplicative model. Here is a multiplicative model with seasonal dummy variables for months.

```
Dependent variable is: Log price
R squared = 92.0%  R squared (adjusted) = 90.2%
s = 0.0377 with 66 - 13 = 53 degrees of freedom
```

Variable	Coeff	SE(Coeff)	t-ratio	P-value
Intercept	2.04566	0.0164	125	<0.0001
Year since 2002	0.071754	0.0030	24.2	<0.0001
Feb	0.002682	0.0210	0.128	0.8988
Mar	0.030088	0.0210	1.43	0.1574
Apr	0.053455	0.0210	2.55	0.0138
May	0.058316	0.0210	2.78	0.0075
Jun	0.044912	0.0221	2.03	0.0471
Jul	0.055008	0.0221	2.49	0.0159
Aug	0.061186	0.0221	2.77	0.0077
Sep	0.057329	0.0221	2.60	0.0122
Oct	0.039903	0.0221	1.81	0.0764
Nov	0.012609	0.0221	0.571	0.5704
Dec	−0.085243	0.0221	−0.386	0.7011

a) Interpret the slope.
b) Interpret the intercept.
c) In what month of the year are gas prices highest?

43. Oakland outlier. The plot of residuals in Exercise 41 shows an outlier that wasn't as evident in the data. The outlier is September 2001. Clearly, this wasn't a typical month for air travel. Here are three models fit to this series, a single exponential smooth, a 12-point moving average, and the fitted values from the seasonal regression model of Exercise 41. Discuss how each deals with the outlier.

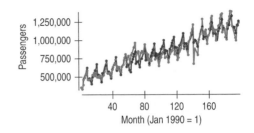

The remaining exercises require the use of statistics software. Statistics packages vary in their capabilities and in the default decisions that some make. As a result, depending upon which package you choose, your answers may differ from those in the back of the book.

T 44. E-commerce. Quarterly e-commerce retail sales (in millions of dollars) in the United States are provided. (Source: U.S. Census Bureau; www.census.gov.) Use this time series to answer the following questions.

a) Fit a linear trend model to this series but do not use the last two quarters (Q4 2007 and Q1 2008).
b) Fit an exponential trend model to this series but do not use the last two quarters.
c) Use both models to forecast the quarterly values for Q4 2007 and Q1 2008. Which model produces better forecasts?
d) What other time series components (besides trend) are likely present in this series?

T 45. E-commerce, part 2.

a) Fit a linear trend model with dummy variables for the seasonal effect to the e-commerce data in Exercise 44.
b) Fit an exponential trend (multiplicative) model with dummy variables to these data.
c) Which model fits better?

T 46. Monthly gas prices, part 3. Using the data from Exercise 42, develop and compare the following models.

a) Fit an appropriate autoregressive model by testing for the significance of each autoregressive term.
b) Obtain a forecast for the week of May 28, 2007.
c) Compare your forecast to the actual value (by computing APE).
d) Do you think this is an appropriate model for forecasting this time series?

T 47. Oil prices. A time series plot of monthly crude oil price ($/barrel) from January 2001 to March 2007 is shown here.

Using these data,

a) Fit a first-order autoregressive model.
b) Obtain a forecast for March 2007.

48. Oil prices, again. Return to the oil price data of Exercise 47.

a) Find a linear model for this series.
b) Find an exponential (multiplicative) model for this series.
c) For the model of Exercise 47 and the models of parts a and b, compute the MAPE. Which model did best? Given the plot in Exercise 47, explain why.
d) Use these methods to forecast the crude oil price for April 2007. The April price was $60.48. Which forecast was closest? Does that mean it's the best model?

49. U.S. unemployment 2013. Following is the time series plot for the monthly U.S. *Unemployment rate* (%) from January 2003 to June 2013. These data have been seasonally adjusted (meaning that the seasonal component has already been removed).

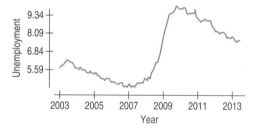

a) What time series components do you observe in this series?
b) Develop a 6-month and 12-month moving average model for this series.
c) Fit a single exponential smoothing model ($\alpha = .7$) to this series.
d) Comment on how these models do with these data.

50. U.S. unemployment rate 2013, part 2. Using the data from Exercise 49 develop and compare the following models:

a) Fit a regression model with just Year as the predictor.
b) Add a lag1 component to the model of (a). How does it change the coefficient of Year?
c) Add lag2 and lag3 components to the model. How do the coefficients change?
d) Can you account for these changes? (Hint: Find the correlations among the Rate and lagged versions of the Rate.)

51. Hawaii tourism 2013. In Exercise 39, we fit a linear regression for the number of monthly domestic visitors to Hawaii (for the years 2002 through 2006) using *Time* and dummy variables for the months as predictors. The R^2 value was 96.6% and a residual plot against *Time* would show no discernible pattern. The data set for this exercise contains the same data for the period January 2000 through May 2013.

a) Fit the linear model from Exercise 39 to this entire time period.
b) Would you use this model? Explain.
c) The impact of what two major events can you see in the plot of residuals against *Time*?

52. Hawaii tourism 2013, part 2. In Exercise 40, we fit a linear regression for the number of monthly international visitors to Hawaii (for the years 2002 through 2006) using *Time* and dummy variables for the months as predictors. The R^2 value was 59.9% and a residual plot against *Time* would show a few low outliers, but no discernible pattern. The data set for this exercise contains the same data for the period January 2000 through May 2013.

a) Fit the linear model from Exercise 40 to this entire time period.
b) Is the trend term statistically significant?
c) Would you use this model? Explain.
d) Why does the no trend model from Exercise 40 no longer work?

JUST CHECKING ANSWERS

1 Trend and seasonal.

2 The value is the mean of the final 4 values, about 557. It might be a bit low as a prediction.

3 $(550 + 642.9)/2 = 596.45$.

4 Four terms because there is a strong seasonal component with period 4.

5 10.0017. Revenue grew at about 10 million dollars per quarter.

6 Dummy variables require that we leave one out.

7 Higher. The four quarterly effects have to sum to zero and the other are all negative.

Case **Study**

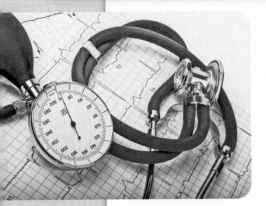

Health Care Costs

Heart disease is the leading cause of death for both men and women. According to the Centers for Disease Control and Prevention, as of 2013, about 715,000 heart attacks occur in the United States each year.[1] The cost of cardiovascular diseases in the United States, including health care expenditures and lost productivity from deaths and disability, is estimated to be more than $444 billion each year.

Many businesses have seen their cost for health insurance grow beyond bounds. Negotiations with insurance companies can depend, in part, on the demographics of a company's workforce. To understand the relationship between costs and other variables, companies must understand how factors such as age and sex can help predict health costs. Because diseases and therapies vary greatly, it is best to build a separate model for each disease group. And, of course, heart disease is near the top of the list as an important condition to predict.

Models for health care costs can help in predicting and controlling costs. The data file **Heart Attack Costs** holds records for 12,844 patients admitted to hospitals in the Northeast United States with a diagnosis of acute myocardial infarction (heart attack; AMI). The data are available from Medicare records for public use. These data provide a good example of the kinds of models we can build to understand and predict health care expenses.

The variables available in this dataset are:

Charges: the total hospital charges in dollars.

Age: in years

Sex: coded M for males, F for females

Diagnosis: the International Classification of Diseases, 10th revision, Clinical Modification code. These codes tell which part of the heart was affected.

DRG: the Diagnosis Related Group, which groups together patients with similar management. In this data set there are three different DRGs.

> 121: patients with AMIs and cardiovascular complications who did not die.
>
> 122: patients with AMIs without cardiovascular complications who did not die.
>
> 123: patients with AMIs who died.

LOS: hospital length of stay in days.

Died: 1 for patients who died in hospital and a 0 otherwise.

Build a model to predict *Charges*. Here are some things to consider in building the model:

1. Should *Charges* be re-expressed? Examine displays and find a suitable re-expression.

2. Should *LOS* be re-expressed? Are there unusual features of the distribution that may deserve special attention?

3. Some of these records may hold errors or otherwise be extraordinary. Make appropriate displays and set aside records that may not be reliable.

---

[1]www.cdc.gov/chronicdisease/resources/publications/AAG/dhdsp.htm

4. How do men and women differ? Consider, for example, the distribution of *Age* for male and female patients. Should you introduce *Sex* as a variable in your model? How will you do that?

5. Can you use *DRG* in your regression model as it is presented here, or should it be recoded in some way? *Diagnosis* raises similar questions. If our purpose is to predict costs based on demographic information, should these variables be predictors in our model?

6. Ultimately, how well can you predict *Charges*? Consider not just the R^2, but also the s_e. (Be sure to transform the s_e back to dollars if you are working with a transformed version of *Cost*.) Discuss how well your model predicts health care costs due to heart attack.

20

Design and Analysis of Experiments and Observational Studies

Capital One

Not everyone graduates first in their class at a prestigious business school. But even doing that won't guarantee that the first company you start will become a Fortune 500 company within a decade. Richard Fairbank managed to do both. When he graduated from Stanford Business School in 1981, he wanted to start his own company, but, as he said in an interview with the *Stanford Business Magazine*, he had no experience, no money, and no business ideas. So he went to work for a consulting firm. Wanting to be on his own, he left in 1987 and landed a contract to study the operations of a large credit card bank in New York. It was then that he realized that the secret lay in data. He and his partner, Nigel Morris, asked themselves, "Why not use the mountains of data that credit cards produce to design cards with prices and terms to satisfy different customers?" But they had a hard time selling this idea to the large credit card issuers. At the time all cards carried the same interest rate—19.8% with a $20 annual fee, and almost half of the population didn't qualify for a card. And credit issuers were naturally resistant to new ideas.

Finally, Fairbank and Morris signed on with Signet, a regional bank that hoped to expand its modest credit card operation. Using demographic and financial data about Signet's customers, they designed and tested combinations of card features that allowed them to offer credit to customers who previously didn't qualify. Signet's credit card business grew and, by 1994, was spun off as Capital One with a market capitalization of $1.1B. By contrast, twenty years later, Capital One's revenues were $24.1B and its market capitalization was $33.7B.

Fairbank also introduced "scientific testing." Capital One designs experiments to gather data about customers. For example, customers who hear about a better deal than the one their current card offers may phone, threatening to switch to another bank unless they get a better deal. To help identify which potential card-hoppers were serious, Fairbank designed an experiment. When a card-hopper called, the customer service agent's computer randomly ordered one of three actions: match the claimed offer, split the difference in rates or fees, or just say no. In that way the company could gather data on who switched, who stayed, and how they behaved. Now when a potential card-hopper phones, the computer can give the operator a script specifying the terms to offer—or instruct the operator to bid the card-hopper a pleasant good-bye.

Fairbank attributes the phenomenal success of Capital One to their use of such experiments. According to Fairbank, "Anyone in the company can propose a test and, if the results are promising, Capital One will rush the new product or approach into use immediately." Why does this work for Capital One? Because, as Fairbank says, "We don't hesitate because our testing has already told us what will work."

Capital One weathered the financial crisis of 2008 better than most banks, selling their mortgage business and repaying the federal bailout by July 2009. In February 2012, it acquired ING Bank and in November announced that ING Direct would become Capital One 360. The firm was named by *Fortune* as one of the top 100 companies to work for in 2013. However, the previous July, Capital One was fined by the Consumer Financial Protection Bureau for "misleading millions of customers" about paying for extra services like payment protection and credit monitoring when receiving a new card. The company agreed to refund $150M to customers and pay $55M in fines.[1]

20.1   Observational Studies

Fairbank started by analyzing the data that had already been collected by the credit card company. These data weren't from designed studies of customers. He simply *observed* the behavior of customers from the data that were already there. Such studies are called **observational studies**. Many companies collect data from customers with "frequent shopper" cards, which allow the companies to record each purchase. A company might study that data to identify associations between customer behavior and demographic information. For example, customers with pets might tend to spend more. The company can't conclude that owning a pet *causes* these customers to spend. People who have pets may also have higher incomes on average or be more likely to own their own homes. Nevertheless, the company may decide to make special offers targeted at pet owners.

Observational studies are used widely in public health and marketing because they can reveal trends and relationships. Observational studies that study an outcome in the present by delving into historical records are called **retrospective studies**.

---

[1]BBC Business News, 18 July 2012, www.bbc.co.uk/news/business

When Fairbank looked at the accumulated experiences of Signet bank's credit card customers, he started with information about which customers earned the bank the most money and sought facts about these customers that could identify others like them, so he was performing a retrospective study. Retrospective studies can often generate testable hypotheses because they identify interesting relationships although they can't demonstrate a causal link.

When it is practical, a somewhat better approach is to observe individuals over time, recording the variables of interest and seeing how things turn out. For example, if we thought pet ownership might be a way to identify profitable customers, we might start by selecting a random sample of new customers and ask whether they have a pet. We could then track their performance and compare those who own pets to those who don't. Identifying subjects in advance and collecting data as events unfold would make this a **prospective study**. Prospective studies are often used in public health, where by following smokers or runners over a period of time we may find that one group or the other develops emphysema or arthritic knees (as you might expect), or dental cavities (which you might not anticipate).

Although an observational study may identify important variables related to the outcome we are interested in, there is no guarantee that it will find the right or the most important related variables. People who own pets may differ from the other customers in ways that we failed to observe. It may be this difference—whether we know what it is or not—rather than owning a pet in itself that leads pet owners to be more profitable customers. It's just not possible for observational studies, whether prospective or retrospective, to demonstrate a causal relationship. That's why we need experiments.

FOR EXAMPLE   Observational studies

Amtrak launched its high-speed train, the Acela, in December 2000. Not only is it the only high-speed line in the United States, but it currently is the only Amtrak line to operate at a profit. The Acela line generates about one quarter of Amtrak's entire revenue.[2] The Acela is typically used by business professionals because of its fast travel times, high fares, business class seats, and free Wi-Fi. As a new member of the marketing department for the Acela, you want to boost young ridership of the Acela. You examine a sample of last year's customers for whom you have demographic information and find that only 5% of last year's riders were 21 years old or younger, but of those, 90% used the Internet while on board as opposed to 37% of riders older than 21 years.

QUESTION   What kind of study is this? Can you conclude that Internet use is a factor in deciding to take the Acela?

ANSWER   This is a retrospective observational study. Although we can compare rates of Internet use between those older and younger than 21 years, we cannot come to any conclusions about why they chose to ride the Acela.

JUST CHECKING

In early 2007, a larger-than-usual number of cats and dogs developed kidney failure; many died. Initially, researchers didn't know why, so they used an observational study to investigate.

1   Suppose that, as a researcher for a pet food manufacturer, you are called on to plan a study seeking the cause of this problem. Specify how you might proceed. Would your study be prospective or retrospective?

---

[2] Amtrak News Release ATK–09–074, October 2009.

20.2   Randomized, Comparative Experiments

Experiments are the only way to show cause-and-effect relationships convincingly, so they are a critical tool for understanding what products and ideas will work in the marketplace. An **experiment** is a study in which the experimenter *manipulates* attributes of what is being studied and observes the consequences. Usually, the attributes, called **factors**, are manipulated by being set to particular **levels** and then allocated or assigned to individuals. An experimenter identifies at least one factor to manipulate and at least one response variable to measure. Often the observed **response** is a quantitative measurement such as the amount of a product sold. However, responses can be categorical ("customer purchased"/ "customer didn't purchase"). The combination of factor levels assigned to a subject is called that subject's **treatment**.

The individuals on whom or which we experiment are known by a variety of terms. Humans who are experimented on are commonly called **subjects** or **participants**. Other individuals (rats, products, fiscal quarters, company divisions) are commonly referred to by the more generic term **experimental units**.

You've been the subject of marketing experiments. Every credit card offer you receive is actually a combination of various factors that specify your "treatment," the specific offer you get. For example, the factors might be *Annual Fee, Interest Rate*, and *Communication Channel* (e-mail, direct mail, phone, etc.). The particular treatment you receive might be a combination of *no Annual Fee* and a *moderate Interest Rate* with the offer being sent by *e-mail*. Other customers receive different treatments. The response might be categorical (do you accept the offer of that card?) or quantitative (how much do you spend with that card during the first three months you have it?).

Two key features distinguish an experiment from other types of investigations. First, the experimenter actively and deliberately manipulates the factors to specify the treatment. Second, the experiment assigns the subjects to those treatments at *random*. The importance of **random assignment** may not be immediately obvious. Experts, such as business executives and physicians, may think that they know how different subjects will respond to various treatments. In particular, marketing executives may want to send what they consider the best offer to their best customers, but this makes fair comparisons of treatments impossible and invalidates the inference from the test. Without random assignment, we can't perform the hypothesis tests that allow us to conclude that differences among the treatments were responsible for any differences we observed in the responses. By using random assignment to ensure that the groups receiving different treatments are comparable, the experimenter can be sure that these differences are *due* to the differences in treatments. There are many stories of experts who were certain they knew the effect of a treatment and were proven wrong by a properly designed study. In business, it is important to get the facts rather than to just rely on what you may think you know from experience.

FOR EXAMPLE   A marketing experiment

After finding out that most young riders of the Acela use the Internet while on board (see page 695), you decide to perform an experiment to see how to encourage more young people to take the Acela. After purchasing a mailing list of 16,000 college students, you decide to randomly send 1/4 a coupon worth 10% off their next Acela ride (*Coupon*), 1/4 a 5000-mile Amtrak mile bonus card (*Card*), and 1/4 a free Netflix download during their next Acela trip (*Movie*). The remaining 4000 students will receive no offer (*No Offer*). You plan to monitor the four groups to see which group travels most during the 12 months after sending the offer.

QUESTIONS   What kind of study is this? What are the factors and levels? What are the subjects? What is the response variable?

ANSWERS   This is an experiment because the factor (type of offer) has been manipulated. The four levels are *Coupon*, *Card*, *Movie*, and *No Offer*. The subjects are 16,000 college students. Each of four different offers will be distributed randomly to 1/4 of the college students. The response variable is *Miles Traveled* during the next 12 months on the Acela.

20.3   The Four Principles of Experimental Design

There are four **principles of experimental design**.

1. **Control.** We control sources of variation other than the factors we are testing by making conditions as similar as possible for all treatment groups. In a test of a new credit card, all alternative offers are sent to customers at the same time and in the same manner. Otherwise, if gas prices soar, the stock market drops, or interest rates spike dramatically during the study, those events could influence customers' responses, making it difficult to assess the effects of the treatments. So an experimenter tries to make any other variables that are not manipulated as alike as possible. Controlling extraneous sources of variation reduces the variability of the responses, making it easier to discern differences among the treatment groups.

    There is a second meaning of control in experiments. A bank testing the new creative idea of offering a card with special discounts on chocolate to attract more customers will want to compare its performance against one of their standard cards. Such a baseline measurement is called a control treatment, and the group that receives it is called the **control group**.

2. **Randomize.** In any true experiment, subjects are assigned treatments at random. Randomization allows us to equalize the effects of unknown or uncontrollable sources of variation. Although randomization can't eliminate the effects of these sources, it spreads them out across the treatment levels so that we can see past them. Randomization also makes it possible to use the powerful methods of inference to draw conclusions from your study. Randomization protects us even from effects we didn't know about. Perhaps women are more likely to respond to the chocolate benefit card. We don't need to test equal numbers of men and women—our mailing list may not have that information. But if we randomize, that tendency won't contaminate our results. There's an adage that says "Control what you can, and randomize the rest."

3. **Replicate.** Replication shows up in different ways in experiments. Because we need to estimate the variability of our measurements, we must make more than one observation at each level of each factor. Sometimes that just means making repeated observations. But, as we'll see later, some experiments combine two or more factors in ways that may permit a single observation for each *treatment*—that is, each combination of factor levels. When such an experiment is repeated in its entirety, it is said to be *replicated*. Repeated observations at each treatment are called **replicates**. If the number of replicates is the same for each treatment combination, we say that the experiment is **balanced**.

    A second kind of replication is to repeat the entire experiment for a different group of subjects, under different circumstances, or at a different time. Experiments do not require, and often can't obtain, representative random samples from an identified population. Experiments study the consequences of different levels of their factors. They rely on the random assignment of treatments to the subjects to generate the sampling distributions and to control for other possibly contaminating variables. When we detect a significant difference in response among treatment groups, we can conclude that it is due to the difference in treatments. However, we should take care in generalizing that result too broadly if we've only studied a specialized population. A special offer of accelerated checkout lanes for regular customers may attract more business in December, but it may not be effective in July. Replication in a variety of circumstances can increase our confidence that our results apply to other situations and populations.

4. **Block.** Sometimes we can identify a factor not under our control whose effect we don't care about, but which we suspect might have an effect either on our response variable or on the ways in which the factors we are studying affect that response. Perhaps men and women will respond differently to our chocolate offer. Or maybe customers with young children at home behave differently than those without. Platinum card members may be tempted by a premium offer much more than standard card members. Factors like these can account for some of the variation in our observed responses because subjects at different levels respond differently. But we can't *assign* them at random to subjects. So we deal with them by grouping, or **blocking**, our subjects together and, in effect, analyzing the experiment separately for each block. Such factors are called **blocking factors**, and their levels are called **blocks**. Blocking in an experiment is like stratifying in a survey design. Blocking reduces variation by comparing subjects within these more homogenous groups. That makes it easier to discern any differences in response due to the factors of interest. In addition, we may want to study the effect of the blocking factor itself. Blocking is an important compromise between randomization and control. However, unlike the first three principles, blocking is not required in all experiments.

JUST CHECKING

Following concerns over the contamination of its pet foods by melamine, which had been linked to kidney failure, a manufacturer now claims its products are safe. You are called on to design the study to demonstrate the safety of the new formulation.

2 Identify the treatment and response.

3 How would you implement control, randomization, and replication?

FOR EXAMPLE Experimental design principles

QUESTION Explain how the four principles of experimental design are used in the Acela experiment described in the previous section (see page 696).

ANSWER Control: It is impossible to control other factors that may influence a person's decision to use the Acela. However, a control group—one that receives no offer—will be used to compare to the other three treatment levels.

Randomization: Although we can't control the other factors (besides *Offer*) that may influence a person's decision to use the Acela, by randomizing which students receive which offer, we hope that the influences of all those other factors will average out, enabling us to see the effect of the four treatments.

Replication: We will send each type of offer to 4000 students. We hope that the response is high enough that we will be able to see differences in *Miles Traveled* among the groups. This experiment is balanced since the number of subjects is the same for all four treatments.

Blocking: We have not blocked the experiment. Possible blocking factors might include demographic variables such as the region of the student's home or college, their sex, or their parent's income.

20.4   Experimental Designs

Completely Randomized Designs

When each of the possible treatments is assigned to at least one subject at random, the design is called a **completely randomized design**. This design is the simplest and easiest to analyze of all experimental designs. A diagram of the procedure can help in thinking about experiments. In this experiment, the subjects are assigned at random to the two treatments.

Figure 20.1   The simplest randomized design has two groups randomly assigned two different treatments.

Randomized Block Designs

When one of the factors is a blocking factor, complete randomization isn't possible. We can't randomly assign factors based on people's behavior, age, sex, and other attributes. But we may want to block by these factors to reduce variability and to understand their effect on the response. When we have a blocking factor, we randomize the subject to the treatments *within each block*. This is called a **randomized block design**. In the following experiment, a marketer wanted to know the effect of two types of offers in each of two segments: a high spending group and a low spending group. The marketer selected 12,000 customers *from each group* at random and then randomly assigned the three treatments to the 12,000 customers *in each group* so that 4000 customers in each segment received each of the three treatments. A display makes the process clearer.

Figure 20.2   This example of a randomized block design shows that customers are randomized to treatments within each segment, or block.

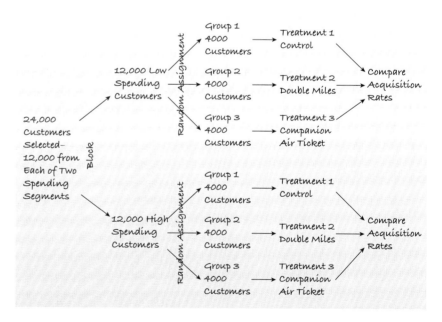

Factorial Designs

An experiment with more than one manipulated factor is called a **factorial design**. A full factorial design contains treatments that represent all possible combinations of all levels of all factors. That can be a lot of treatments. With only three factors, one at 3 levels, one at 4, and one at 5, there would be $3 \times 4 \times 5 = 60$ different treatment combinations. So researchers typically limit the number of levels to just a few.

It may seem that the added complexity of multiple factors is not worth the trouble. In fact, just the opposite is true. First, if each factor accounts for some of the variation in responses, having the important factors in the experiment makes it *easier* to discern the effects of each. Testing multiple factors in a single experiment makes more efficient use of the available subjects. And testing factors together is the only way to see what happens at *combinations* of the levels.

An experiment to test the effectiveness of offering a $50 coupon for free gas may find that the coupon increases customer spending by 1%. Another experiment finds that lowering the interest rate increases spending by 2%. But unless some customers were offered *both* the $50 free gas coupon *and* the lower interest rate, the analyst can't learn whether offering both together would lead to still greater spending or less.

When the combination of two factors has a different effect than you would expect by adding the effects of the two factors together, that phenomenon is called an **interaction**. If the experiment does not contain both factors, it is impossible to see interactions. That can be a major omission because such effects can have the most important and surprising consequences in business.

FOR EXAMPLE   Designing an experiment

Continuing the example from page 698, you are considering splitting up the students into two groups before mailing the offers: those who live or go to school in the Northeast corridor, where the Acela operates, and those who don't. Using home and school zip codes, you split the original 12,000 students into those groups and find that they split 4000 in the Northeast corridor and 8000 outside. You plan to randomize the treatments within those two groups and you'll monitor them to see if this factor, *NE corridor*, affects their *Miles Traveled* as well as the type of offer they receive.

QUESTION   What kind of design would this be? Diagram the experiment.

ANSWER   It is a randomized block experiment with *NE corridor* as the blocking factor.

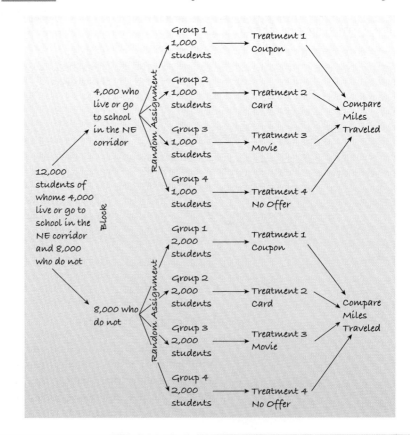

GUIDED EXAMPLE   Designing a Direct Mail Experiment

At a major credit card bank, management has been pleased with the success of a recent campaign to cross-sell Silver card customers with the new SkyWest Gold card. But you, as a marketing analyst, think that the revenue of the card can be increased by adding three months of double miles on SkyWest to the offer, and you think the additional gain in charges will offset the cost of the double miles. You want to design a marketing experiment to find out what the difference will be in revenue if you offer the double miles. You've also been thinking about offering a new version of the miles called "use anywhere miles," which can be transferred to other airlines, so you want to test that version as well.

You also know that customers receive so many offers that they tend to disregard most of their direct mail. So, you'd like to see what happens if you send the offer in a shiny gold envelope with the SkyWest logo prominently displayed on the front. How can we design an experiment to see whether either of these factors has an effect on charges?

 PLAN   State the problem.

We want to study two factors to see their effect on the revenue generated for a new credit card offer.

Response Specify the response variable.

Revenue is a percentage of the amount charged to the card by the cardholder. To measure the success, we will use the monthly charges of customers who receive the various offers. We will use the three months after the offer is sent out as the collection period and use the total amount charged per customer during this period as the response.

Factors Identify the factors you plan to test.

Levels Specify the levels of the factors you will use.

We will offer customers three levels of the factor *Miles* for the SkyWest Gold card: *Regular* (no additional) *Miles*, *Double Miles*, and *Double Use Anywhere Miles*. Customers will receive the offer in the *Standard Envelope* or the new SkyWest *Logo Envelope* (factor *Envelope*).

Experimental Design Observe the principles of design:

Control any sources of variability you know of and can control.

Randomly assign experimental units to treatments to equalize the effects of unknown or uncontrollable sources of variation.

Replicate results by placing more than one customer (usually many) in each treatment group.

We will send out all the offers to customers at the same time (in mid September) and evaluate the response as total charges in the period October through December.

A total of 30,000 current Silver card customers will be randomly selected from our customer records to receive one of the six offers.

✓ *Regular Miles* with *Standard Envelope*

✓ *Double Miles* with *Standard Envelope*

✓ *Double Use Anywhere Miles* with *Standard Envelope*

✓ *Regular Miles* with *Logo Envelope*

✓ *Double Miles* with *Logo Envelope*

✓ *Double Use Anywhere Miles* with *Logo Envelope*

(*continued*)

Make a Picture A diagram of your design can help you think about it.

Specify any other details about the experiment. You must give enough details so that another experimenter could exactly replicate your experiment.

It's generally better to include details that might seem irrelevant because they may turn out to make a difference.

Specify how to measure the response.

On January 15, we will examine the total card charges for each customer for the period October 1 through December 31.

DO

Once you collect the data, you'll need to display them (if appropriate) and compare the results for the treatment groups. (Methods of analysis for factorial designs will be covered later in the chapter.)

REPORT

To answer the initial question, we ask whether the differences we observe in the means (or proportions) of the groups are meaningful.

Because this is a randomized experiment, we can attribute significant differences to the treatments. To do this properly, we'll need methods from the analysis of factorial designs covered later in the chapter.

MEMO

Re: Test mailing for creative offer and envelope

The mailing for testing the Double Miles and Logo Envelope ideas went out on September 17. On January 15, once we have total charges for everyone in the treatment groups, I would like to call the team back together to analyze the results to see:

✓ *Whether offering Double Miles is worth the cost of the miles*

✓ *Whether the Double Use Anywhere Miles are worth the cost*

✓ *Whether the Logo Envelope increased spending enough to justify the added expense*

20.5 Issues in Experimental Design

Blinding and Placebos

Blinding by Misleading

Social science experiments can sometimes blind subjects by disguising the purpose of a study. One of the authors participated as an undergraduate volunteer in one such (now infamous) psychology experiment. The subjects were told that the experiment was about 3-D spatial perception and were assigned to draw a model of a horse and were randomly assigned to a room alone or in a group. While they were busy drawing, a loud noise and then groaning were heard coming from the room next door. The *real* purpose of the experiment was to see whether being in a group affects how people reacted to the apparent disaster. The horse was only a pretext. The subjects were blind to the treatment because they were misled.

Humans are notoriously susceptible to errors in judgment—all of us. When we know what treatment is assigned, it's difficult not to let that knowledge influence our response or our assessment of the response, even when we try to be careful.

Suppose you were trying to sell your new brand of cola to be stocked in a school's vending machines. You might hope to convince the committee designated to make the choice that students prefer your less expensive cola, or at least that they can't taste the difference. You could set up an experiment to see which of the three competing brands students prefer (or whether they can tell the difference at all). But people have brand loyalties. If they know which brand they are tasting, it might influence their rating. To avoid this bias, it would be better to disguise the brands as much as possible. This strategy is called **blinding** the participants to the treatment. Even professional taste testers in food industry experiments are blinded to the treatment to reduce any prior feelings that might influence their judgment.

But it isn't just the subjects who should be blind. Experimenters themselves often subconsciously behave in ways that favor what they believe. It wouldn't be appropriate for you to run the study yourself if you have an interest in the outcome. People are so good at picking up subtle cues about treatments that the best (in fact, the only) defense against such biases in experiments on human subjects is to keep anyone who could affect the outcome or the measurement of the response from knowing which subjects have been assigned to which treatments. So, not only should your cola-tasting subjects be blinded, but also you, as the experimenter, shouldn't know which drink is which—at least until you're ready to analyze the results.

There are two main classes of individuals who can affect the outcome of the experiment:

- Those who could influence the results (the subjects, treatment administrators, or technicians)
- Those who evaluate the results (judges, experimenters, etc.)

When all the individuals in either one of these classes are blinded, an experiment is said to be **single-blind**. When everyone in both classes is blinded, we call the experiment **double-blind**. Double-blinding is the gold standard for any experiment involving both human subjects and human judgment about the response.

Placebos and Authority

The placebo effect is stronger when placebo treatments are administered with authority or by a figure who appears to be an authority. "Doctors" in white coats generate a stronger effect than salespeople in polyester suits. But the placebo effect is not reduced much, even when subjects know that the effect exists. People often suspect that they've gotten the placebo if nothing at all happens. So, recently, drug manufacturers have gone so far in making placebos realistic that they cause the same side effects as the drug being tested! Such "active placebos" usually induce a stronger placebo effect. When those side effects include loss of appetite or hair, the practice may raise ethical questions.

Often simply applying *any* treatment can induce an improvement. Every parent knows the medicinal value of a kiss to make a toddler's scrape or bump stop hurting. Some of the improvement seen with a treatment—even an effective treatment—can be due simply to the act of treating. To separate these two effects, we can sometimes use a control treatment that mimics the treatment itself. A "fake" treatment that looks just like the treatments being tested is called a **placebo**. Placebos are the best way to blind subjects so they don't know whether they have received the treatment or not. One common version of a placebo in drug testing is a "sugar pill." Especially when psychological attitude can affect the results, control group subjects treated with a placebo may show an improvement.

The fact is that subjects treated with a placebo sometimes improve. It's not unusual for 20% or more of subjects given a placebo to report reduction in pain, improved movement, or greater alertness or even to demonstrate improved health or performance. This **placebo effect** highlights both the importance of effective blinding and the importance of comparing treatments with a control. Placebo controls are so effective that you should use them as an essential tool for blinding whenever possible.

JUST CHECKING

The pet food manufacturer we've been following hires you to perform the experiment to test whether their new formulation is safe and nutritious for cats and dogs.

4 How would you establish a control group?

5 Would you use blinding? How? (Can or should you use double-blinding?)

6 Both cats and dogs are to be tested. Should you block? Explain.

The best experiments are usually:

- Randomized
- Double-blind
- Comparative
- Placebo-controlled

Confounding and Lurking Variables

A credit card bank wanted to test the sensitivity of the market to two factors: the annual fee charged for a card and the annual percentage rate charged. The bank selected 100,000 people at random from a mailing list and sent out 50,000 offers with a low rate and no fee and 50,000 offers with a higher rate and a $50 annual fee. They discovered that people preferred the low-rate, no-fee card. No surprise. In fact, customers signed up for that card at over twice the rate as the other offer. But the question the bank really wanted to answer was: "How much of the change was due to the rate, and how much was due to the fee?" Unfortunately, there's simply no way to separate out the two effects with that experimental design.

If the bank had followed a factorial design in the two factors and sent out all four possible different treatments—low rate with no fee; low rate with $50 fee; high rate with no fee, and high rate with $50 fee—each to 25,000 people, it could have learned about both factors and could have also learned about the interaction between rate and fee. But we can't tease apart these two effects because the people who were offered the low rate were also offered the no-fee card. When the levels of one factor are associated with the levels of another factor, we say that the two factors are **confounded**.

Confounding can also arise in well-designed experiments. If some other variable not under the experimenter's control but associated with a factor has an effect on the response variable, it can be difficult to know which variable is really responsible for the effect. A shock to the economic or political situation that occurs during a marketing experiment can overwhelm the effects of the factors being tested. Randomization will usually take care of confounding by distributing uncontrolled factors over the treatments at random. But be sure to watch out for potential confounding effects even in a well-designed experiment.

Confounding may remind you of the problem of lurking variables that we discussed in Chapter 4. Confounding variables and lurking variables are alike in that they interfere with our ability to interpret our analyses simply. Each can mislead us, but they are not the same. A lurking variable is associated with two variables in such a way that it creates an apparent, possibly causal relationship between them. By contrast, confounding arises when a variable associated with a factor has an effect on the response variable, making it impossible to separate the effect of the factor from the effect of the confounder. Both confounding and lurking variables are outside influences that make it harder to understand the relationship we are modeling.

20.6   Analyzing a Design in One Factor— The One-Way Analysis of Variance

The most common experimental design used in business is the single factor experiment with two levels. Often these are known as champion/challenger designs because typically they're used to test a new idea (the challenger) against the current version (the champion). In this case, the customers offered the champion are the control group, and the customers offered the challenger (a special deal, a new offer, a new service, etc.) are the test group. As long as the customers are randomly assigned to the two groups, we already know how to analyze data from experiments like these. When the response is quantitative, we can test whether the means are equal with a two-sample *t*-test, and if the response is 0-1 (yes/no), we would test whether the two proportions are equal using a two proportion *z*-test.

But those methods can compare only two groups. What happens when we introduce a third level into our single factor experiment? Suppose an associate in a percussion music supply company, *Tom's Tom-Toms*, wants to test ways to increase the amount purchased from the catalog the company sends out every three months. He decides on three treatments: a coupon for free drum sticks with any purchase, a free practice pad, and a $50 discount on any purchase. The response will be the dollar amount of sales per customer. He decides to keep some customers as a control group by sending them the catalog without any special offer. The experiment is a single factor design with four levels: no coupon, coupon for free drum sticks, coupon for the practice pad, and $50 coupon. He assigns the same number of customers to each treatment randomly.

Now the hypothesis to test isn't quite the same as when we tested the difference in means between two independent groups. To test whether all *k* means are equal, the hypothesis becomes:

$$H_0: \mu_1 = \mu_2 = \cdots = \mu_k$$
$$H_A: \textit{at least one mean is different}$$

The test statistic compares the variance of the means to what we'd expect that variance to be based on the variance of the individual responses. Figure 20.3 illustrates the concept. The differences among the means are the same for the two sets of boxplots, but it's easier to see that they are different when the underlying variability is smaller.

Figure 20.3 The means of the four groups in the left display are the same as the means of the four groups in the right display, but the differences are much easier to see in the display on the right because the variation within each group is less.

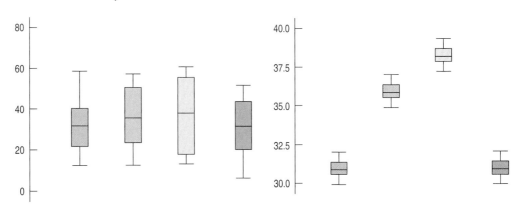

Why is it easier to see that the means[3] of the groups in the display on the right are different and much harder to see it in the one on the left? It is easier because we

---

[3]Of course the boxplots show medians at their centers, and we're trying to find differences among means. But for roughly symmetric distributions like these, the means and medians are very close.

naturally compare the differences *between* the group means to the variation *within* each group. In the picture on the right, there is much less variation within each group so the differences among the group means are evident.

This is exactly what the test statistic does. It's the ratio of the variation among the group means to the variation within the groups. When the numerator is large enough, we can be confident that the differences among the group means are greater than we'd expect by chance, and reject the null hypothesis that they are equal. The test statistic is called the *F*-statistic in honor of Sir Ronald Fisher, who derived the sampling distribution for this statistic. The *F*-statistic showed up in multiple regression (Chapter 17) to test the null hypothesis that all slopes were zero. Here, it tests the null hypothesis that the means of all the groups are equal.

The **F-statistic** compares two quantities that measure variation, called *mean squares*. The numerator measures the variation *between* the groups (treatments) and is called the **Mean Square due to Treatments (MSTr)**. The denominator measures the variation *within* the groups, and is called the **Mean Square due to Error (MSE)**. The *F*-statistic is their ratio:

$$F_{k-1,\,N-k} = \frac{MSTr}{MSE}$$

We reject the null hypothesis that the means are equal if the *F*-statistic is too big. The critical value for deciding whether *F* is too big depends both on its degrees of freedom and the α-level you choose. Every **F-distribution** has two degrees of freedom, corresponding to the degrees of freedom for the mean square in the numerator and for the mean square (usually the MSE) in the denominator. Here, the MSTr has $k - 1$ degrees of freedom because there are k groups. The MSE has $N - k$ degrees of freedom where N is the total number of observations. Rather than compare the *F*-statistic to a specified critical value, we could find the P-value of this statistic and reject the null hypothesis when that value is small.

This analysis is called an **Analysis of Variance (ANOVA)**, but the hypothesis is actually about *means*. The null hypothesis is that the means are all equal. The collection of statistics—the sums of squares, mean squares, *F*-statistic, and P-value—are usually presented in a table, called the **ANOVA table**, like this one:

Source	DF	Sum of Squares	Mean Square	F-Ratio	Prob > F
Treatment (Between)	$k - 1$	SSTr	MSTr	MSTr/MSE	P-value
Error (Within)	$N - k$	SSE	MSE		
Total	$N - 1$	SST			

Table 20.1   An ANOVA table displays the treatment and error sums of squares, mean squares, *F*-ratio, and P-value.

- **How does the Analysis of Variance work?** When looking at side-by-side boxplots to see whether we think there are real differences between treatment means, we naturally compare the variation *between* the groups to the variation *within* the groups. The variation between the groups indicates how large an effect the treatments have. The variation within the groups shows the underlying variability. To model those variations, the one-way ANOVA decomposes the data into several parts: the grand average, the treatment effects, and the residuals.

$$y_{ij} = \bar{\bar{y}} + (\bar{y}_i - \bar{\bar{y}}) + (y_{ij} - \bar{y}_i).$$

We can write this as we did for regression as

$$data = predicted + residual.$$

To estimate the variation *between* the groups we look at how much their means vary. The SSTr (sometimes called the *between* sum of squares) captures it like this:

$$SSTr = \sum_{i=1}^{k} n_i(\bar{y}_i - \bar{\bar{y}})^2$$

where $\bar{y}_i$ is the mean of group i, n_i is the number of observations in group i, $\bar{\bar{y}}$ is the overall mean of all observations and there are k groups.

We compare the *SSTr* to how much variation there is *within* each group. The SSE captures that like this:

$$SSE = \sum_{i=1}^{k} (n_i - 1)s_i^2$$

where s_i^2 is the sample variance of group i.

To turn these estimates of variation into variances, we divide each sum of squares by its associated degrees of freedom:

$$MSTr = \frac{SSTr}{k - 1}$$

$$MSE = \frac{SSE}{N - k}$$

Remarkably (and this is Fisher's real contribution), these two variances estimate the *same* variance when the null hypothesis is true. When it is false (and the group means differ), the MSTr gets larger.

The *F*-statistic tests the null hypothesis by taking the ratio of these two mean squares:

$$F_{k-1,\,N-k} = \frac{MSTr}{MSE},$$ and rejecting the hypothesis if the ratio is too large.

The critical value and P-value depend on the two degrees of freedom $k - 1$ and $N - k$.

Let's look at an example. For the summer catalog of the percussion supply company *Tom's Tom-Toms*, 4000 customers were selected at random to receive one of four offers:[4] *No Coupon*, *Free Sticks* with purchase, *Free Pad* with purchase, or *Fifty Dollars* off next purchase. All the catalogs were sent out on March 15 and sales data for the month following the mailing were recorded.

The first step is to plot the data. Here are boxplots of the spending of the four groups for the month after the mailing:

Figure 20.4 Boxplots of the spending of the four groups show that the coupons seem to have stimulated spending.

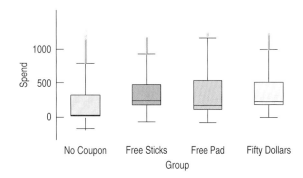

---

[4] Realistically, companies often select equal (and relatively small) sizes for the treatment groups and consider all other customers as the control. To make the analysis easier, we'll assume that this experiment considered only 1000 "control" customers. Adding more controls wouldn't increase the power very much anyway.

Here are summary statistics for the four groups:

Summary			
Groups	Median	Mean	SD
No Coupon	$0.00	$216.68	$390.58
Free Sticks	$233.00	$385.87	$331.10
Free Pad	$157.50	$339.54	$364.17
Fifty Dollars	$232.00	$399.95	$337.07

The ANOVA table shows the components of the calculation of the F-test.

ANOVA					
Source of Variation	SS	df	MS	F	P-value
Between Groups	20825966	3	6941988.66	54.6169	<0.0001
Within Groups	507905263	3996	127103.42		
Total	528731229	3999			

Table 20.2 The ANOVA table shows that the F-statistic has a very small P-value, so we can reject the null hypothesis that the means of the four treatments are equal.

The very small P-value is an indication that the differences we saw in the box-plots are not due to chance, so we reject the null hypothesis of equal means and conclude that the four means are not equal.

FOR EXAMPLE   Analyzing a one-way design

You decide to implement the simple one factor completely randomized design sending out four offers (*Coupon, Card, Movie,* or *No Offer*) to 4000 students each (see page 696). A year later you collect the results and find the following table of means and standard deviations:

Level	Number	Mean	Std Dev	Std Err Mean	Lower 95%	Upper 95%
Coupon	4000	15.17	72.30	1.14	12.93	17.41
Card	4000	11.53	62.62	0.99	9.59	13.47
Movie	4000	13.29	66.51	1.05	11.22	15.35
No Offer	4000	9.03	50.99	0.81	7.45	10.61

An ANOVA table shows:

Source	DF	Sum of Squares	Mean Square	F Ratio	Prob > F
Offer	3	81,922.26	27,307.42	6.75	0.0002
Error	15,996	64,669,900.04	4,042.88		
Total	15,999	64,751,822.29			

QUESTION   What conclusions can you draw from these data?

ANSWER   From the ANOVA table, it looks like the null hypothesis that all the means are equal is strongly rejected. The average number of miles traveled seems to have increased (from those receiving *No Offer*) about 2.5 miles for students receiving the *Card*, about 4.26 miles for students receiving the free *Movie*, and a little more than 6 miles for those students receiving the *Coupon*.

20.7   Assumptions and Conditions for ANOVA

Whenever we compute P-values and make inferences about a hypothesis, we need to make assumptions and check conditions to see if the assumptions are reasonable. The ANOVA is no exception. Because it's an extension of the two-sample *t*-test, many of the same assumptions apply.

Independence Assumption

The groups must be independent of each other. No test can verify this assumption. You have to think about how the data were collected. The individual observations must be independent as well.

We check the **Randomization Condition**. Did the experimental design incorporate suitable randomization? We were told that the customers were assigned to each treatment group at random.

Equal Variance Assumption

ANOVA assumes that the true variances of the treatment groups are equal. We can check the corresponding **Similar Variance Condition** in various ways:

- Look at side-by-side boxplots of the groups to see whether they have roughly the same spread. It can be easier to compare spreads across groups when they have the same center, so consider making side-by-side boxplots of the residuals. If the groups have differing spreads, it can make the pooled variance—the MSE—larger, reducing the *F*-statistic value and making it less likely that we can reject the null hypothesis. So the ANOVA will usually fail on the "safe side," rejecting H_0 less often than it should. Because of this, we usually require the spreads to be quite different from each other before we become concerned about the condition failing. If you've rejected the null hypothesis, this is especially true.

- Look at the original boxplots of the response values again. In general, do the spreads seem to change systematically with the centers? One common pattern is for the boxes with bigger centers to have bigger spreads. This kind of systematic trend in the variances is more of a problem than random differences in spread among the groups and should not be ignored. Fortunately, such systematic violations are often helped by re-expressing the data. If, in addition to spreads that grow with the centers, the boxplots are skewed with the longer tail stretching off to the high end, then the data are pleading for a re-expression. Try taking logs of the dependent variable for a start. You'll likely end up with a much cleaner analysis.

- Look at the residuals plotted against the predicted values. Often, larger predicted values lead to larger magnitude residuals. This is another sign that the condition is violated. If the residual plot shows more spread on one side or the other, it's usually a good idea to consider re-expressing the response variable. Such a systematic change in the spread is a more serious violation of the equal variance assumption than slight variations of the spreads across groups.

Figure 20.5   A plot of the residuals against the predicted values from the ANOVA shows no sign of unequal spread.

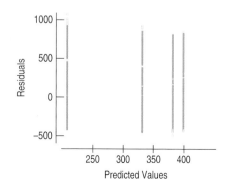

Normal Population Assumption

As we saw for *t*-tests, the *F*-test requires that the underlying errors follow a Normal model. As before when we faced this assumption, we'll check a corresponding **Nearly Normal Condition**.

Technically, we need to assume that the Normal model is reasonable for the populations underlying each treatment group. We can (and should) look at the side-by-side boxplots for indications of skewness. Certainly, if they are all (or mostly) skewed in the same direction, the Nearly Normal Condition fails (and re-expression is likely to help). However, in many business applications, sample sizes are quite large, and when that is true, the Central Limit Theorem implies that the sampling distribution of the means may be nearly Normal in spite of skewness. Fortunately, the *F*-test is conservative. That means that if you see a small P-value it's probably safe to reject the null hypothesis for large samples even when the data are nonnormal.

Check Normality with a histogram or a Normal probability plot of all the residuals together. Because we really care about the Normal model within each group, the Normal Population Assumption is violated if there are outliers in any of the groups. Check for outliers in the boxplots of the values for each treatment.

The Normal Probability plot for the *Tom's Tom-Toms* residuals holds a surprise.

Figure 20.6   A normal probability plot shows that the residuals from the ANOVA of the *Tom's Tom-Toms* data are clearly not normal.

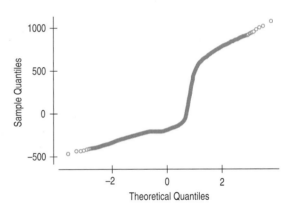

Investigating further with a histogram, we see the problem.

Figure 20.7   A histogram of the residuals reveals bimodality.

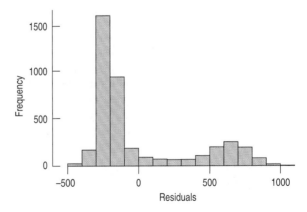

The histogram shows clear bimodality of the residuals. If we look back to histograms of the spending of each group, we can see that the boxplots failed to reveal the bimodal nature of the spending.

The manager of the company wasn't surprised to hear that the spending is bimodal. In fact, he said, "We typically have customers who either order a complete new drum set, or who buy accessories. And, of course, we have a large group of customers who choose not to purchase anything during a given quarter."

These data (and the residuals) clearly violate the Nearly Normal Condition. Does that mean that we can't say anything about the null hypothesis? No. Fortunately, the sample sizes are large, and there are no individual outliers that have undue influence on the means. With sample sizes this large, we can appeal to the Central Limit Theorem and still make inferences about the means. In particular, we are safe in rejecting the null hypothesis. When the Nearly Normal Condition is not satisfied, the *F*-test will tend to fail on the safe side and be less likely to reject the null. Since we have a very small P-value, we can be fairly sure that the differences we saw were real. On the other hand, we should be very cautious when trying to make predictions about individuals rather than means.

Figure 20.8 The spending appears to be bimodal for all the treatment groups. There is one mode near $1000 and another larger mode between $0 and $200 for each group.

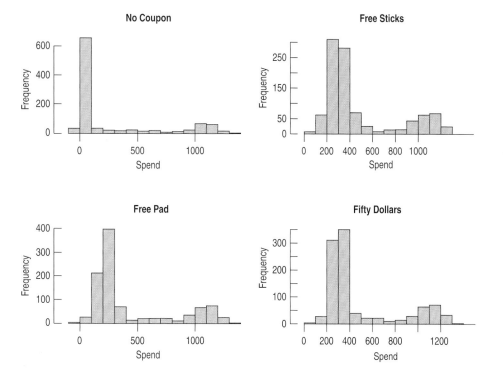

FOR EXAMPLE Assumptions and conditions for ANOVA

Closer examination of the miles data from the Acela project (see page 696) shows that only about 5% of the students overall actually took the Acela, so the *Miles Traveled* are about 95% 0's and the other values are highly skewed to the right.

QUESTION Are the assumptions and conditions for ANOVA satisfied?

(continued)

> ANSWER The responses are independent since the offer was randomized to the students on the mailing list. The distributions of *Miles Traveled* by *Offer* are highly right skewed. Most of the entries are zeros. This could present a problem, but because the sample size is so large (4000 per group), the inference is valid (a simulation shows that the averages of 4000 are Normally distributed). Although the distributions are right skewed, there are no extreme outliers that are influencing the group means. The variances in the four groups also appear to be similar. Thus, the assumptions and conditions appear to be met. (An alternative analysis might be to focus on the *Miles Traveled* only of those who actually took the Acela. The conclusion of the ANOVA would remain the same).

JUST CHECKING

Your experiment to test the new pet food formulation has been completed. One hypothesis you have tested is whether the new formulation is different in nutritional value (measured by having veterinarians evaluate the test animals) from a standard food known to be safe and nutritious. The ANOVA has an *F*-statistic of 1.2, which (for the degrees of freedom in your experiment) has a P-value of 0.87. Now you need to make a report to the company.

7 Write a brief report. Can you conclude that the new formulation is safe and nutritious?

*20.8   Multiple Comparisons

Simply rejecting the null hypothesis is almost never the end of an Analysis of Variance. Knowing that the means are different leads to the question of which ones are different and by how much. Tom, the owner of *Tom's Tom-Toms*, would hardly be satisfied with a consultant's report that told him that the offers generated different amounts of spending, but failed to indicate which offers did better and by how much.

We'd like to know more, but the *F*-statistic doesn't offer that information. What can we do? If we can't reject the null hypothesis, there's no point in further testing. But if we can reject the null hypothesis, we can do more. In particular, we can test whether any pairs or combinations of group means differ. For example, we might want to compare treatments against a control or against the current standard treatment.

We could do *t*-tests for any pair of treatment means that we wish to compare. But each test would have some risk of a Type I error. As we do more and more tests, the risk that we'll make a Type I error grows. If we do enough tests, we're almost sure to reject one of the null hypotheses by mistake—and we'll never know which one.

There is a solution to this problem. In fact, there are several solutions. As a class, they are called methods for **multiple comparisons**. All multiple comparisons methods require that we first reject the overall null hypothesis with the ANOVA's *F*-test. Once we've rejected the overall null, we can think about comparing several— or even all—pairs of group means.

One such method is called the **Bonferroni method**. This method adjusts the tests and confidence intervals to allow for making many comparisons. The result is a wider margin of error (called the **minimum significant difference, or MSD**) found by replacing the critical *t*-value *t** with a slightly larger number. That makes the confidence intervals wider for each pairwise difference and the corresponding

Carlo Bonferroni (1892–1960) was a mathematician who taught in Florence. He wrote two papers in 1935 and 1936 setting forth the mathematics behind the method that bears his name.

Type I error rates lower for each test, and it keeps the overall Type I error rate at or below α.

The Bonferroni method distributes the error rate equally among the confidence intervals. It divides the error rate among J confidence intervals, finding each interval at confidence level $1 - \dfrac{\alpha}{J}$ instead of the original $1 - \alpha$. To signal this adjustment, we label the critical value t^{**} rather than t^*. For example, to make the six confidence intervals comparing all possible pairs of offers at our overall α risk of 5%, we'd use

$$1 - \frac{0.05}{6} = 1 - 0.0083 = 0.9917$$

for α instead of 0.95. So we look up the critical t value with $\alpha = 0.0083/2$ and 3996 df and find $t^{**} = 2.640$. The ME would then become:

$$ME = 2.64 \times 356.52 \sqrt{\frac{1}{1000} + \frac{1}{1000}} = 42.09$$

This change doesn't affect our *decision* that each offer increases the mean sales compared to the *No Coupon* group, but it does adjust the confidence intervals for the differences between all groups pairs.

For example, if we compare the *Free Sticks* offer to the *Free Pad* offer, the difference between their average sales is now

$$(385.87 - 339.54) \pm 42.09 = (\$4.24, \$88.42).$$

The confidence interval says that the *Free Sticks* offer generated between $4.24 and $88.42 more sales per customer on average than the *Free Pad* offer. To make a valid business decision, the company should now calculate their expected *profit* based on the confidence interval. Suppose they make 8% profit on sales. Then, multiplying the confidence interval

$$0.08 \times (\$4.24, \$88.42) = (\$0.34, \$7.07)$$

we find that the *Free Sticks* generate between $0.34 and $7.07 profit per customer on average. So, if the *Free Sticks* cost $1.00 more than the pads, the confidence interval for profit would be:

$$(\$0.34 - \$1.00, \$7.07 - \$1.00) = (-\$0.66, \$6.07)$$

There is a possibility that the *Free Sticks* may actually be a less profitable offer. The company may decide to take the risk or to try another test with a larger sample size to get a more precise confidence interval.

Many statistics packages assume that you'd like to compare all pairs of means. Some will display the result of these comparisons in a table such as the one to the left. This table indicates that the top two are indistinguishable, that all are distinguishable from *No Coupon*, and that *Free Pad* is also distinguishable from the other three.

The subject of multiple comparisons is a rich one because of the many ways in which groups might be compared. Most statistics packages offer a choice of several methods. When your analysis calls for comparing all possible pairs, consider a multiple comparisons adjustment such as the Bonferroni method. If one of the groups is a control group, and you wish to compare all the other groups to it, there are specific methods (such as Dunnett's methods) available. Whenever you look at differences after rejecting the null hypothesis of equal means, you should consider using a multiple comparisons method that attempts to preserve the *overall* α risk.

Fifty Dollars	$399.95	A		
Free Sticks	$385.87	A		
Free Pad	$339.54		B	
No Coupon	$216.68			C

Table 20.3 The output shows that the two top-performing offers are indistinguishable in terms of mean spending, but that the Free Pad is distinguishable from both those two and from *No Coupon*.

FOR EXAMPLE   Multiple comparisons

You perform a multiple comparison analysis using the Bonferroni correction on the Acela data (see page 708) and the output looks like:

Offer			Mean
Coupon	A		15.17
Movie	A		13.29
Card	A	B	11.53
No Offer		B	9.03

QUESTION   What can you conclude?

ANSWER   From the original ANOVA we concluded that the means were not all equal. Now it appears that we can say that the mean *Miles Traveled is* greater for those receiving the *Coupon* or the *Movie* than those receiving *No Offer*, but we cannot distinguish the mean *Miles Traveled* between those receiving the *Card* or *No Offer*.

A further analysis only of those who actually took the Acela during the 12 months shows a slightly different story:

Coupon	A			300.37
Card	A	B		279.50
Movie		B		256.74
No Offer			C	206.40

Here we see that all offers can be distinguished from the *No Offer* group and that the *Coupon* group performed better than the group receiving the free *Movie*. Of those using the Acela, the *Coupon* resulted in nearly 100 more miles traveled on average during the year of those taking the Acela at least once.

20.9   ANOVA on Observational Data

So far we've applied ANOVA only to data from designed experiments. That application is appropriate for several reasons. The primary one is that randomized comparative experiments are specifically designed to compare the results for different treatments. The overall null hypothesis, and the subsequent tests on pairs of treatments in ANOVA, address such comparisons directly. In addition, the **Equal Variance Assumption** (which we need for all of the ANOVA analyses) is often plausible in a randomized experiment because when we randomly assign subjects to treatments, all the treatment groups start out with the same underlying variance of the experimental units.

Sometimes, though, we just can't perform an experiment. When ANOVA is used to test equality of group means from observational data, there's no *a priori* reason to think the group variances might be equal at all. Even if the null hypothesis of equal means were true, the groups might easily have different variances. But you can use ANOVA on observational data if the side-by-side boxplots of responses for each group show roughly equal spreads and symmetric, outlier-free distributions.

Observational data tend to be messier than experimental data. They are much more likely to be unbalanced. If you aren't assigning subjects to treatment groups, it's harder to guarantee the same number of subjects in each group. And because

> **Balance**
> Recall that a design is called *balanced* if it has an equal number of observations for each treatment level.

you are not controlling conditions as you would in an experiment, things tend to be, well, less controlled. The only way we know to avoid the effects of possible lurking variables is with control and randomized assignment to treatment groups, and for observational data, we have neither.

ANOVA is often applied to observational data when an experiment would be impossible or unethical. (We can't randomly break some subjects' legs, but we *can* compare pain perception among those with broken legs, those with sprained ankles, and those with stubbed toes by collecting data on subjects who have already suffered those injuries.) In such data, subjects are already in groups, but not by random assignment.

Be careful; if you have not assigned subjects to treatments randomly, you can't draw *causal* conclusions even when the *F*-test is significant. You have no way to control for lurking variables or confounding, so you can't be sure whether any differences you see among groups are due to the grouping variable or to some other unobserved variable that may be related to the grouping variable.

Because observational studies often are intended to estimate parameters, there is a temptation to use pooled confidence intervals for the group means for this purpose. Although these confidence intervals are statistically correct, be sure to think carefully about the population that the inference is about. The relatively few subjects that you happen to have in a group may not be a simple random sample of any interesting population, so their "true" mean may have only limited meaning.

20.10 Analysis of Multifactor Designs

In our direct mail example, we looked at two factors: *Miles* and *Envelope*. *Miles* had three levels: *Regular Miles*, *Double Miles*, and *Double Use Anywhere Miles*. The factor *Envelope* had two levels: *Standard* and new *Logo*. The three levels of *Miles* and the two levels of *Envelope* resulted in six treatment groups. Because this was a completely randomized design, the 30,000 customers were selected at random, and 5000 were assigned at random to each treatment.

Three months after the offer was mailed out, the total charges on the card were recorded for each of the 30,000 cardholders in the experiment. Here are boxplots of the six treatment groups' responses, plotted against each factor.

If you look closely, you may be able to discern a very slight increase in the *Total Charges* for some levels of the factors, but it's very difficult to see. There are two reasons for this. First, the variation due to each factor gets in the way of seeing the

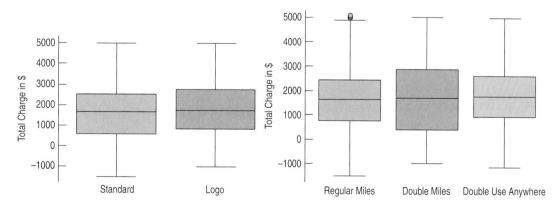

Figure 20.9 Boxplots of *Total Charge* by each factor. It is difficult to see the effects of the factors for two reasons. First, the other factor hasn't been accounted for, and second, the effects are small compared to the overall variation in charges.

effect of the other factor. For example, each customer in the boxplot for the *Logo Envelope* got one of three different offers. If those offers had an effect on spending, then that increased the variation within the *Logo* treatment group. Second, as is typical in a marketing experiment of this kind, the effects are very small compared to the variability in people's spending. That's why companies use such a large sample size.

The Analysis of Variance for two factors removes the effects of each factor from consideration of the other. It can also model whether the factors interact, increasing or decreasing the effect. In our example, it will separate out the effect of changing the levels of *Miles* and the effect of changing the levels of *Envelope*. It will also test whether the effect of the *Envelope* is the same for the three different *Miles* levels. If the effect is different, that's called an interaction effect between the two factors.

The details of the calculations for the two-way ANOVA with interaction are less important than understanding the summary, the model, and the assumptions and conditions under which it's appropriate to use the model. For a one-way ANOVA, we calculated three sums of squares (SS): the Total SS, the Treatment SS, and the Error SS. For this model, we'll calculate five: the Total SS, the SS due to Factor A, the SS due to Factor B, the SS due to the interaction, and the Error SS.

Let's suppose we have a levels of factor A, b levels of factor B, and r replicates at each treatment combination. In our case, $a = 2, b = 3, r = 5000$, and $a \times b \times r = N$ is 30,000. Then the ANOVA table will look like this.

Source	DF	Sum of Squares	Mean Square	F-Ratio	Prob $>$ F
Factor A	$a - 1$	SSA	MSA	MSA/MSE	P-value
Factor B	$b - 1$	SSB	MSB	MSB/MSE	P-value
Interaction	$(a - 1) \times (b - 1)$	SSAB	MSAB	MSAB/MSE	P-value
Error	$ab(r - 1)$	SSE	MSE		
Total (Corrected)	$N - 1$	SST			

Table 20.4   An ANOVA table for a replicated two-factor design with a row for each factor's sum of squares, interaction sum of square, error, and total.

There are now three null hypotheses—one that asserts that the means of the levels of factor A are equal, one that asserts that the means of the levels of factor B are all equal, and one that asserts that the effects of factor A are *constant* across the levels of factor B (or vice versa). Each P-value is used to test the corresponding hypothesis.

Here is the ANOVA table for the marketing experiment.

Source	DF	Sum of Squares	Mean Square	F-Ratio	Prob $>$ F
Envelope	1	203,090,000	203,090,000	133.68	$<$.0001
Miles	2	201,150,000	100,575,000	66.20	$<$.0001
Miles $\times$ Envelope	2	1,505,200	752,600	0.50	0.61
Error	29,994	45,568,000,000	1,519,237		

Table 20.5   The ANOVA table for the marketing experiment. Both the effect of *Miles* and *Envelope* are highly significant, but the interaction term is not.

From the ANOVA table, we can see that both the *Miles* and the *Envelope* effects are highly significant, but that the interaction term is not. An **interaction plot,** a plot of means for each treatment group, is essential for sorting out what these P-values mean.

Figure 20.10 An interaction plot of the *Miles* and *Envelope* effects. The parallel lines show that the effects of the three *Miles* offers are roughly the same over the two different *Envelopes* and therefore that the interaction effect is small.

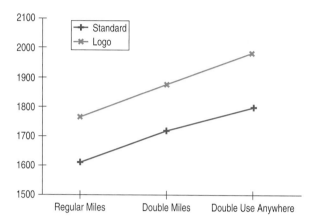

The interaction plot shows the mean *Charges* at all six treatment groups. The levels of one of the factors, in this case *Miles*, are shown on the *x*-axis, and the mean *Charges* of the groups for each *Envelope* level are shown at each *Miles* level. The means of each level of *Envelope* are connected for ease of understanding. Notice that the effect of *Double Miles* over *Regular Miles* is about the same for both the *Standard* and *Logo Envelopes.* And the same is true for the *Double Use Anywhere* miles. This indicates that the effect of *Miles* is constant for the two different *Envelopes.* The lines are parallel, which indicates that there is no interaction effect.

We reject the null hypothesis that the mean *Charges* at the three different levels of *Miles* are equal (with P-values < 0.0001), and also we reject that the mean *Charges* for *Standard* and *Logo* are the same (with P-value < 0.0001). We have no evidence, however, to suggest that there is an interaction between the factors.

After rejecting the null hypotheses, we can create a confidence interval for any particular treatment mean or perform a hypothesis test for the difference between any two means. If we want to do several tests or confidence intervals, we will need to use a multiple comparisons method that adjusts the size of the confidence interval or the level of the test to keep the *overall* Type I error rate at the level we desire.

When the interaction term is not significant, we can talk about the overall effect of either factor. Because the effect of *Envelope* is roughly the same for all three *Miles* offers (as we know by virtue of not rejecting the hypothesis that the interaction effect is zero), we can calculate and interpret an overall *Envelope* effect. The means of the two *Envelope* levels are:

Logo $1871.75   *Standard* $1707.19

and so the *Logo* envelope generated a difference in average charge of $1871.75 − $1707.19 = $164.56. A confidence interval for this difference is ($136.66, $192.45), which the analysts can use to decide whether the added cost of the *Logo* envelope is worth the expense.

But when an interaction term *is* significant, we must be very careful not to talk about the effect of a factor, *on average,* because the effect of one factor *depends* on the level of the other factor. In that case, we always have to talk about the factor effect at a specific level of the other factor, as we'll see in the next example.

FOR EXAMPLE Multifactor designs

QUESTION   Suppose that you had run the randomized block design from Section 20.4 (see page 700). You would have had two levels of the (blocking) factor *NE Corridor* (*NE* or *not*) and the same four levels of *Offer* (*Coupon, Card, Movie,* and *No Offer*). The ANOVA shows a significant interaction effect between *NE Corridor* and *Offer*. Explain what that means. An analysis of the two groups (*NE* and *not*) separately shows that for the *NE* group, the P-value for testing the four offers is <0.0001 but for the *not* NE group, the P-value is 0.2354. Is this consistent with a significant interaction effect? What would you tell the marketing group?

ANSWER   A significant interaction effect implies that the effect of one factor is not the same for the levels of another. Thus, it is saying that the effect of the four offers is not the same for those living in the NE corridor as it is for those who do not. The separate analysis explains this further. For those who do not live in the NE, the offers do not significantly change the average number of miles they travel on the Acela. However, for those who live or go to school in the NE, the offers have an effect. This could impact where Amtrak decides to advertise the offers, or to whom they decide to send them.

MATH BOX

- **How does two-way Analysis of Variance work?** In two-way ANOVA, we have two factors. Each treatment consists of a level of each of the factors, so we write the individual responses as y_{ij}, to indicate the ith level of the first factor and the jth level of the second factor. The more general formulas are no more informative; just more complex. We will start with an unreplicated design with one observation in each treatment group (although in practice, we'd always recommend replication if possible). We'll call the factors A and B, each with a and b levels, respectively. Then the total number of observations is $n = a \times b$.

  For the first factor (factor A), the *Treatment Sum of Squares*, SSA, is the same as we calculated for one-way ANOVA:

  $$SSA = \sum_{i=1}^{a} b(\bar{y}_i - \bar{\bar{y}})^2 = \sum_{j=1}^{b} \sum_{i=1}^{a} (\bar{y}_i - \bar{\bar{y}})^2$$

  where b is the number of levels of factor B, $\bar{y}_i$ is the mean of all subjects assigned level i of factor A (regardless of which level of factor B they were assigned), and $\bar{\bar{y}}$ is the *overall* mean of all observations. The mean square for treatment A (MSA) is

  $$MSA = \frac{SSA}{a-1}.$$

  The treatment sum of squares for the second factor (B) is computed in the same way, but of course the treatment means are now the means for each level of this second factor:

  $$SSB = \sum_{j=1}^{b} a(\bar{y}_j - \bar{\bar{y}})^2 = \sum_{i=1}^{a} \sum_{j=1}^{b} (\bar{y}_j - \bar{\bar{y}})^2, \text{ and}$$

  $$MSB = \frac{SSB}{b-1}$$

where a is the number of levels of factor A, and $\bar{\bar{y}}$, as before, is the overall mean of all observations. $\bar{y}_j$ is the mean of all subjects assigned the jth level of factor B.

The SSE can be found by subtraction:

$$SSE = SST - (SSA + SSB)$$

where

$$SST = \sum_{i=1}^{a}\sum_{j=1}^{b} (y_{ij} - \bar{\bar{y}})^2.$$

The mean square for error is $MSE = \dfrac{SSE}{N - (a + b - 1)}$, where $N = a \times b$.

There are now two F-statistics, the ratio of each of the treatment mean squares to the MSE, which are associated with each null hypothesis.

To test whether the means of all the levels of factor A are equal, we would find a P-value for $F_{a-1,\, N-(a+b-1)} = \dfrac{MSA}{MSE}$. For factor B, we would find a P-value for $F_{b-1,\, N-(a+b-1)} = \dfrac{MSB}{MSE}$.

If the experiment is replicated (say r times), we can also estimate the interaction between the two factors, and test whether it is zero. The sums of squares for each factor have to be multiplied by r. Alternatively they can be written as a (triple) sum where the sum is now over factor A, factor B, and the replications:

$$SSA = \sum_{k=1}^{r}\sum_{j=1}^{b}\sum_{i=1}^{a} (\bar{y}_i - \bar{\bar{y}})^2 \text{ and } SSB = \sum_{k=1}^{r}\sum_{i=1}^{a}\sum_{j=1}^{b} (\bar{y}_j - \bar{\bar{y}})^2.$$

We find the sum of squares for the interaction effect AB as:

$$SSAB = \sum_{k=1}^{r}\sum_{j=1}^{b}\sum_{i=1}^{a} (\bar{y}_{ij} - \bar{y}_i - \bar{y}_j + \bar{\bar{y}})^2, \text{ and}$$

$$MSAB = \frac{SSAB}{(a-1)(b-1)}.$$

The SSE is the sum of the squared residuals:

$$SSE = \sum_{k=1}^{r}\sum_{j=1}^{b}\sum_{i=1}^{a} (y_{ijk} - \bar{y}_{ij})^2 \text{ and } MSE = \frac{SSE}{ab(r-1)}.$$

There are now three F-statistics associated with the three hypotheses (factor A, factor B, and the interaction). They are the ratios of each of these mean squares with the MSE:

$$F_{a-1,\, ab(r-1)} = \frac{MSA}{MSE}, F_{b-1,\, ab(r-1)} = \frac{MSB}{MSE}, \text{ and } F_{(a-1)(b-1),\, ab(r-1)} = \frac{MSAB}{MSE}.$$

Note that $N = r \times a \times b$ is the total number of observations in the experiment.

GUIDED EXAMPLE   A Follow-up Experiment

After analyzing the data, the bank decided to go with the *Logo* envelope, but a marketing specialist thought that more *Miles* might increase spending even more. A new test was designed to test both the type of *Miles* and the amount. Again, total *Charge* in three months is the response.

PLAN State the problem.	We want to study the two factors *Miles* and *Amount* to see their effect on the revenue generated for a new credit card offer.
Response Specify the response variable.	To measure the success, we will use the monthly charges of customers who receive the various offers. We will use the three months after the offer is sent out as the collection period and the total amount charged per customer during this period as the response.
Factors Identify the factors you plan to test.	We will offer each customer one of the two levels of the factor *Miles* for the SkyWest Gold card: *SkyWest Miles* or *Use Anywhere Miles*. Customers are offered three levels of *Miles*: *Regular Miles, Double Miles,* and *Triple Miles.*
Levels Specify the levels of the factors you will use.	We will send out all the offers to customers at the same time (in mid March) and evaluate the response as total charges in the period April through June.
Experimental Design Specify the design.	A total of 60,000 current Gold card customers will be randomly selected from our customer records to receive one of the six offers.

✓ *Regular SkyWest Miles*
✓ *Double SkyWest Miles*
✓ *Triple SkyWest Miles*
✓ *Regular Use Anywhere Miles*
✓ *Double Use Anywhere Miles*
✓ *Triple Use Anywhere Miles*

Make a Picture A diagram of your design can help you think about it. We could also draw this diagram like the one on page 702 with 6 treatment groups, but now we are thinking of the design as having two distinct factors that we wish to evaluate individually, so this form gives the right impression.

On June 15, we will examine the total card charges for each customer for the period April 1 through June 30.

Specify any other experimental details. You must give enough details so that another experimenter could exactly replicate your experiment.

It's generally better to include details that might seem irrelevant than to leave out matters that could turn out to make a difference.

Specify how to measure the response and your hypotheses.

We want to measure the effect of the two types of Miles and the three award amounts.

The three null hypotheses are:

H_O: *The mean charges for Sky West Miles and Use Anywhere Miles are the same (the means for Miles are equal).*

H_O: *The mean charges for Regular Miles, Double Miles, and Triple Miles are the same (the means for Amount are equal).*

H_O: *The effect of Miles is the same for all levels of Amount (and vice-versa) (no interaction effect).*

The alternative for the first hypothesis is that the mean Charges for the two levels of Miles are different.

The alternative for the second hypothesis is that at least one of the mean charges for the three levels of Amount is different.

The alternative for the third hypothesis is that there is an interaction effect.

Plot Examine the boxplots and interaction plots.

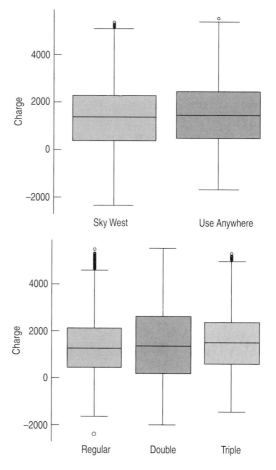

Boxplots by each factor show that there may be a slight increase in charges due to the Use Anywhere Miles and the Amount of Miles offered, but the differences are hard to see because of the intrinsic variation in Charges.

(continued)

There are some outliers apparent in the boxplots, but none exerts a large influence on its group mean, so we will leave them in.

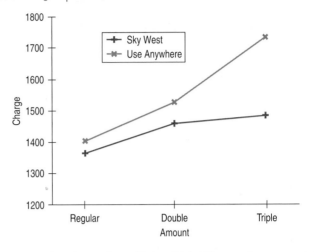

The interaction plot shows that offering *Triple Miles* may have a much larger effect for *Use Anywhere Miles* than for *Sky West Miles*.

Assumptions and Conditions
Think about the assumptions and check the conditions.

✓ **Independence Assumption, Randomization Condition.** The experiment was randomized to current cardholders.
✓ **Similar Variance Condition.** The boxplots show that the variances across all groups are similar. (We can recheck with a residual plot after fitting the ANOVA model.)
✓ **Outlier Condition.** There are some outliers, but none appear to be exerting undue influence on the group means.

DO   Show the ANOVA table.

Source	Df	SS	MS	*F*-Ratio	P-Value
Miles	1	103,576,768	103,576,768	61.6216	<0.0001
Amount	2	253,958,660.1	126,979,330	75.5447	<0.0001
Miles × Amount	2	64,760,963.01	32,380,481.51	19.2643	<0.0001
Error	29,994	50,415,417,459	1,680,850		
Total	29,999	50,837,713,850			

Check the remaining conditions on the residuals.

✓ **Nearly Normal Condition.** A histogram of the residuals shows that they are reasonably unimodal and symmetric.

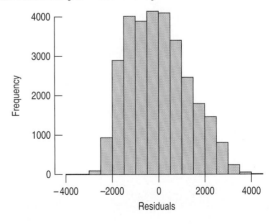

Under these conditions, it is appropriate to interpret the *F*-ratios and their *P*-values.

Discuss the results of the ANOVA table.

The *F*-ratios are all large, and the *P*-values are all very small, so we reject all three null hypotheses. Because the interaction effect is significant, we cannot talk about the overall effect of the amount of miles but must make the discussion specific to the type of *Miles* offered.

Show a table of means, possibly with confidence intervals or tests from an appropriate Multiple Comparisons method.

Level				Mean
Use Anywhere, Triple	A			1732.21
Use Anywhere, Double		B		1526.93
Sky West, Triple		B		1484.34
Sky West, Double		B	C	1460.20
Use Anywhere, Regular			C	D	1401.89
Sky West, Regular				D	1363.94

REPORT

To answer the initial question, we ask whether the differences we observe in the means of the groups are meaningful.

Because this is a randomized experiment, we can attribute significant differences to the treatments.

MEMO

Re: Test mailing for creative offer and envelope

The mailing for testing the Triple Miles initiative went out in March, and results on charges from April through June were available in early July. We found that *Use Anywhere Miles* performed better than the standard *Sky West Miles*, but that the amount they increased charges depended on the amount offered.

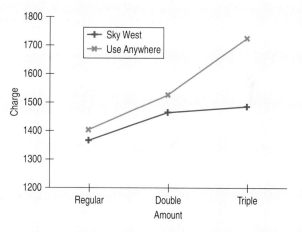

As we can see, *Triple Miles* for the *Sky West Miles* didn't increase *Charge* significantly and is probably not worth the added expense. However, *Triple Miles* for the *Use Anywhere Miles* generated an average $205 more in average *Charge* (with a confidence interval from $131 to $279). Even at the low end of this interval, we feel that the added revenue of the *Triple Miles* justifies their cost.

Be sure to make recommendations based on the context of your business decision.

In summary, we recommend offering *Triple Miles* for the *Use Anywhere Miles* offers but would keep the *Double Miles* offer for the *Sky West Miles*.

WHAT CAN GO WRONG?

- **Don't give up just because you can't run an experiment.** Sometimes we can't run an experiment because we can't identify or control the factors. Sometimes it would simply be unethical to run the experiment. (Consider randomly assigning employees to two environments—one where workers were exposed to massive amounts of cigarette smoke and one a smoke-free environment—to see differences in health and productivity.) If we can't perform an experiment, often an observational study is a good choice.

- **Beware of confounding.** Use randomization whenever possible to ensure that the factors not in your experiment are not confounded with your treatment levels. Be alert to confounding that cannot be avoided, and report it along with your results.

- **Bad things can happen even to good experiments.** Protect yourself by recording additional information. An experiment in which the air-conditioning failed for two weeks, affecting the results, was saved by recording the temperature (although that was not originally one of the factors) and estimating the effect the higher temperature had on the response.[5] It's generally good practice to collect as much information as possible about your experimental units and the circumstances of the experiment. For example, in the direct mail experiment, it would be wise to record details of the general economy and any global events (such as a sharp downturn in the stock market) that might affect customer behavior.

- **Don't spend your entire budget on the first run.** Just as it's a good idea to pretest a survey, it's always wise to try a small pilot experiment before running the full-scale experiment. You may learn, for example, how to choose factor levels more effectively, about effects you forgot to control, and about unanticipated confounding.

- **Watch out for outliers.** One outlier in a group can change both the mean and the spread of that group. It will also inflate the Error Mean Square, which can influence the F-test. The good news is that ANOVA fails on the safe side by losing power when there are outliers. That is, you are less likely to reject the overall null hypothesis if you have (and leave) outliers in your data, so they are not likely to cause you to make a Type I error.

- **Watch out for changing variances.** The conclusions of the ANOVA depend crucially on the assumptions of independence and constant variance and (somewhat less seriously as the number of observations in each group increases) on Normality. If the conditions on the residuals are violated, it may be necessary to re-express the response variable to approximate these conditions more closely. ANOVA benefits so greatly from a judiciously chosen re-expression that the choice of a re-expression might be considered a standard part of the analysis.

- **Be wary of drawing conclusions about causality from observational studies.** ANOVA is often applied to data from randomized experiments for which causal conclusions are appropriate. If the data are not from a

---

[5]R. D. DeVeaux and M. Szelewski, "Optimizing Automatic Splitless Injection Parameters for Gas Chromatographic Environmental Analysis," *Journal of Chromatographic Science* 27, no. 9 (1989): 513–518.

b) Form the *F*-statistic by dividing the two mean squares.

c) The P-value of this *F*-statistic turns out to be 0.00000949. What does this say about the null hypothesis of equal means?

d) What assumptions have you made to answer part c?

e) What would you like to see to justify the conclusions of the *F*-test?

f) What is the average size of the error standard deviation in particulate emissions?

45. Cereal shelf placement. Supermarkets often place similar types of cereal on the same supermarket shelf. The shelf placement for 77 cereals was recorded as well their sugar content. Does sugar content vary by shelf? Here's a boxplot and an ANOVA table.

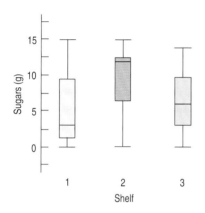

Source	DF	Sum of Squares	Mean Square	F-ratio	P-value
Shelf	2	248.4079	124.204	7.3345	0.0012
Error	74	1253.1246	16.934		
Total	76	1501.5325			

Level	n	Mean	StdDev
1	20	4.80000	4.57223
2	21	9.61905	4.12888
3	36	6.52778	3.83582

a) What kind of design or study is this?

b) What are the null and alternative hypotheses?

c) What does the ANOVA table say about the null hypothesis? (Be sure to report this in terms of sugar content and shelf placement.)

d) Can we conclude that cereals on shelf 2 have a different mean sugar content than cereals on shelf 3? Can we conclude that cereals on shelf 2 have a different mean sugar content than cereals on shelf 1? What can we conclude?

e) To check for significant differences between the shelf means, we can use a Bonferroni test, whose results are shown at the top of the next column. For each pair of shelves, the difference is shown along with its standard error and significance level. What does it say about the questions in part d?

Dependent Variable: SUGARS
Bonferroni

(I) SHELF	(J) SHELF	Mean Difference (I-J)	Std. Error	P-value	95% Confidence Interval Lower Bound	95% Confidence Interval Upper Bound
1	2	-4.819	1.2857	0.001	-7.969	-1.670
	3	-1.728	1.1476	0.409	-4.539	1.084
2	1	4.819	1.2857	0.001	1.670	7.969
	3	3.091	1.1299	0.023	0.323	5.859
3	1	1.728	1.1476	0.409	-1.084	4.539
	2	-3.091	1.1299	0.023	-5.859	-0.323

46. Cereal shelf placement, part 2. We also have data on the protein content on the 77 cereals in Exercise 45. Does protein content vary by shelf? Here's a boxplot and an ANOVA table.

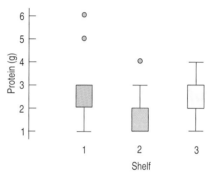

Source	DF	Sum of Squares	Mean Square	F-ratio	P-value
Shelf	2	12.4258	6.2129	5.8445	0.0044
Error	74	78.6650	1.0630		
Total	76	91.0909			

Level	n	Mean	StdDev
1	20	2.65000	1.46089
2	21	1.90476	0.99523
3	36	2.86111	0.72320

a) What kind of design or study is this?

b) What are the null and alternative hypotheses?

c) What does the ANOVA table say about the null hypothesis? (Be sure to report this in terms of protein content and shelf placement.)

d) Can we conclude that cereals on shelf 2 have a lower mean protein content than cereals on shelf 3? Can we conclude that cereals on shelf 2 have a lower mean protein content than cereals on shelf 1? What can we conclude?

e) To check for significant differences between the shelf means, we can use a Bonferroni test, whose results are shown here. For each pair of shelves, the difference is shown along with its standard error and significance level. What does it say about the questions in part d?

Dependent Variable: PROTEIN
Bonferroni

(I) SHELF	(J) SHELF	Mean Differ- ence (I-J)	Std. Error	P- value	95% Confidence Interval	
					Lower Bound	Upper Bound
1	2	0.75	0.322	0.070	−0.04	1.53
	3	−0.21	0.288	1.000	−0.92	0.49
2	1	−0.75	0.322	0.070	−1.53	0.04
	3	−0.96	0.283	0.004	−1.65	−0.26
3	1	0.21	0.288	1.000	−0.49	0.92
	2	0.96	0.283	0.004	0.26	1.65

47. Automotive safety. The National Highway Transportation Safety Administration runs crash tests in which stock automobiles are crashed into a wall at 35 mph with dummies in both the passenger and the driver's seats. The THOR Alpha crash dummy is capable of recording 134 channels of data on the impact of the crash at various sites on the dummy. In this test, 335 cars are crashed. The response variable is a measure of head injury. Researchers want to know whether the seat the dummy is sitting in affects head injury severity, as well as whether the type of car affects severity. Here are boxplots for the 2 different *Seats* (*driver, passenger*) and the 6 different *Size* classifications (*compact, light, medium, mini, pickup, van*).

An interaction plot shows:

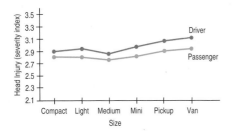

A scatterplot of residuals vs. predicted values shows:

The ANOVA table follows:

Source	DF	Sum of Squares	Mean Square	F-ratio	P-value
Seat	1	0.88713	0.88713	25.501	<0.0001
Size	5	1.49253	0.29851	8.581	<0.0001
Seat × Size	5	0.07224	0.01445	0.415	0.838
Error	282	9.8101	0.03479		
Total	293	12.3853			

a) State the null hypotheses about the main effects (in words, not symbols).
b) Are the conditions for two-way ANOVA met?
c) If so, perform the hypothesis tests and state your conclusion. Be sure to state it in terms of head injury severity, seats, and vehicle types.

48. Gas additives. An experiment to test a new gasoline additive, *Gasplus*, was performed on three different cars: a sports car, a minivan, and a hybrid. Each car was tested with both *Gasplus* and regular gas on 10 different occasions, and their gas mileage was recorded. Here are the boxplots.

A two-way ANOVA with interaction model was run, and the following ANOVA table resulted.

Source	DF	Sum of Squares	Mean Square	F-ratio	P-value
Type	2	23175.4	11587.7	2712.2	<0.0001
Additive	1	92.1568	92.1568	21.57	<0.0001
Interaction	2	51.8976	25.9488	6.0736	0.0042
Error	54	230.711	4.27242		
Total	59	23550.2			

A plot of the residuals vs. predicted values showed:

What conclusions about the additive and car types do you draw? Do you see any potential problems with the analysis?

JUST CHECKING ANSWERS

1 Gather reports from veterinarians and pet hospitals. Look into the histories of sick animals. This would be a retrospective observational study.

2 Treatment: Feed the new food and a previously tested, known to be safe, food to pets.

Response: Judge the health of the animals, possibly by having a veterinarian examine them before and after the feeding trials.

3 Control by choosing similar animals. Perhaps choose just one breed and test animals of the same age and health. Treat them otherwise the same in terms of exercise, attention, and so on.

Randomize by assigning animals to treatments at random.

Replicate by having more than one animal fed each formulation.

4 A control group could be fed a standard laboratory food, if we have one known to be safe. Otherwise we could prepare a special food in our test kitchens to be certain of its safety.

5 The veterinarian evaluating the animals should be blind to the treatments. For double-blinding, all technicians handling the animals should also be blinded. That would require making the control food look as much like the test food as possible.

6 Yes. Test dogs and cats separately.

7 No. We have failed to reject the hypothesis of a difference, but that's all we can conclude. There is insufficient evidence to discern any difference. But that should be sufficient for the company's purposes.

21

Quality Control

Sony

In 1945, at the end of World War II, Masaru Ibuka started a radio repair shop in a bombed-out building in Tokyo. The next year, Akio Morita joined him and together they founded a company called Tokyo Tsushin Kogyo K.K. (or Tokyo Communication Engineering Company), which built Japan's first tape recorder. In the early 1950s, Ibuka traveled to the United States and convinced Bell Labs to license its transistor technology to his Japanese company, which then released Japan's first commercially produced transistor radio. The next May, the company released a new radio with a slim design and improved sound quality. In 1957, it came out with the TR-63—the smallest transistor radio in commercial production. By all accounts, it was a worldwide commercial success.

With increasing international sales, Ibuka and Morita knew they needed a simpler name for their company. Unfortunately, the name Totsuko didn't work well in English, and their initials, TKK, were already in use by a railroad company, so Ibuka and Morita worked to find a word that didn't exist in any language but would be easy to remember. Finally, they combined the Latin word for sound, *sonus*, with the American word *sonny*, which was a popular word meaning boy or young man in the 1950s. From this Sony was born in 1958.

Sony is now one of the world's most recognized brands with sales of more than $57 billion for the fiscal year ending March 31, 2013. It employs more than 146,000 people worldwide.

Unfortunately for the young Sony Corporation, in the 1950s, the phrase "Made in Japan" was synonymous with cheap and shoddily made. Japan's manufacturing capabilities had been destroyed in the latter part of World War II. To rebuild its economy as quickly as possible, Japan started producing and exporting large quantities of inexpensive goods, including electronic products. A rumor often heard in the United States after the war was that Japan had renamed one of its towns Usa so that it could stamp "Made in Usa" on its products. Although this urban legend was false (in fact the town of Usa on the island of Kyushu existed long before WWII) the shoddy quality of the Japanese goods gave credence to the story and kept it alive for years.

The United States sent General Douglas MacArthur to oversee the rebuilding of Japan after the war ended. Realizing the importance of reversing Japan's poor quality image, he recruited two key players, W. Edwards Deming and Joseph Juran, who had both been active in the field of quality control in the United States. In addition, he enlisted the help of Homer Sarasohn to help rebuild the communication infrastructure of Japan.

Just after World War II, Japanese manufacturing plants were designed to produce radios using vacuum tube technology. In early trial runs, Sarasohn was shocked to find that yields were commonly less than 10%. In other words, 90% of the vacuum tubes produced were defective. Even more shocking was that the Japanese were not surprised and had little understanding of quality; other than the Zero fighter (known as the best carrier-based fighter jet in the world at that time), their engineering designs were often flawed with low production yields. Sarasohn decided to work more closely with the plant managers on improving quality at their plants.

One day, Sarasohn made a visit to the Tokyo Communication Engineering Company, a new start-up factory that was building radio equipment because equipment owed to Sarasohn was overdue. When he arrived at the factory, he found chaos. When the owners (Ibuka and Morita) heard of the surprise inspection, they raced to see Sarasohn in Tokyo who gave them one more chance to prove that they could learn something about quality and apply it to their factory. Luckily Ibuka and Morita learned their lesson, and this young company was the company that eventually changed its name to the Sony Corporation.

These quality control efforts in Japan proved enormously fruitful. In the 30 years after WWII, Japan became a world leader in manufacturing, and today Japanese products consistently rank among the world's highest quality. The United States, the world leader in quality in the 1950s, saw its market share in electronics and automobiles shrink at the expense of Japan in this same time period.

Today, manufacturing has shifted from Japan, Germany, and the United States to China. In 2006, China replaced the United States as the world's largest exporter. Unfortunately, quality control issues often plague Chinese manufacturing. News stories about baby formula and pet food tainted with melamine, toys painted with lead paint, and tires that fail at high speed alarm consumers worldwide. The head of China's top quality-control agency quit in the midst of the scandal about tainted milk in 2008. Quality control continues to be of vital importance to worldwide manufacturing.

21.1   A Short History of Quality Control

The desire to make quality products is part of human nature. Several millennia ago, the builders of the Great Pyramid of Giza had to produce blocks of incredible uniformity to build a pyramid whose four sides were perpendicular to within 3.5 arc seconds. During the Middle Ages in Europe, guilds were formed, in part to enforce quality control on craftsmen but also to punish those who tried to pass off inferior goods. The manufacture of money has long relied on quality control to guarantee

Walter A. Shewhart (1891–1967) was an early pioneer of quality methods. Before his arrival at the Western Electric Company, quality control consisted of inspecting products and removing defective items. Shewhart introduced statistical methods including the quality control chart which bears his name.

Because he helped Japanese industrial leaders rebuild after World War II and to shed the image of Japanese products as cheap and shoddy, W. Edwards Deming (1900–1993) is known as the father of the Japanese postwar industrial revival. He was also regarded by many as the leading quality guru in the United States until his death in 1993.

that the same amount of precious metal is used in each coin. In seventeenth century England, Samuel Pepys wrote in his famous diary of his inspection of quality at The Royal Mint.

Statistical methods for quality control were pioneered in the 1920s at the Bell Telephone Laboratories in the United States (where they were used in producing telephone equipment at the company's Western Electric subsidary) and at roughly the same time at the General Electric Company in the United Kingdom. Quality control today is a tool in the larger effort of continual process improvement in both the manufacturing and service industries. In this view, work is a process on which data can be gathered and studied. This study can then lead to improvement in the process, which ideally will have an impact on both customer satisfaction and the company's bottom line. The process improvement strategy includes understanding the process, collecting the data, assessing the process, eliminating causes of variation, studying the cause and effect of relationships within the process, and implementing changes. In this chapter we will study some tools used in the assessment of the process data to investigate whether the process has changed, either in its mean or in its variation.

Walter A. Shewhart was a statistician and engineer working at Bell Laboratories in the early part of the twentieth century, responsible for improving the quality of the manufactured telephones. As early as 1924, he introduced a chart in an internal Bell Labs memo to graphically display variation in a process over time. The kind of chart he used, a time plot of a measure of quality, became known as a **control chart**, or sometimes a **Shewhart chart,** in his honor. In the same memo, he defined the fundamental rule of **statistical process control (SPC)**: "Variation from common-cause systems should be left to chance, but special causes of variation should be identified and eliminated."

Shewhart's insight was that the variation we see in manufacturing arises from two distinct sources. Some of the random fluctuations are *intrinsic* to the process or **common-cause variation**. Others, which are not, are called **special-cause variation.** When special-cause variation is present, the process is said to be **out of control**. The short-term focus of quality control is to detect and correct the special causes of variation. The long-term focus of continual quality improvement is to reduce the amount of variation from the common causes. Shewhart suggested a system of analysis based on the scientific method specifically to address the special-cause issue, but which has also been used as the basis for continual quality improvement.

The term *control chart* is somewhat of a misnomer. Certainly one can't control a process simply by graphing measurements of it over time. The term *quality control* became popular in the latter part of the twentieth century and control charts were an important tool in the quality control effort. More recent views of process improvement view the process as evolving toward higher and higher quality (and less variation) and so the term quality "control" is almost passé. The American Society for Quality Control (ASQC) changed its name in the 1980s to the American Society for Quality (ASQ) when its members realized that their methods could be part of a more general movement toward excellence in the organization.

In 1950, when W. Edwards Deming replaced Sarasohn in Japan, he taught the Shewhart principles and process to Japanese managers. The process became codified into four distinct stages: Plan, Do, Check, and Act—known as the PDCA cycle. In the *Plan* stage, the manager identifies and describes the process to be improved and suggests improvements. In the *Do* stage, the manager implements on a pilot level the improvement strategies. In the *Check* stage, the manager examines variation to see if the improvement strategies have been successful. Finally, in the *Act* stage, depending on the results of the Check stage, the manager implements the improvement strategies on a large scale. These stages are completed continuously and repeatedly, so that they form a cycle, or some say a spiral, of quality improvement.[1]

---

[1]Some organizations use a modification of this known as the Define-Measure-Analyze-Improve-Control (DMAIC) cycle.

Figure 21.1   The Shewhart PDCA Cycle.

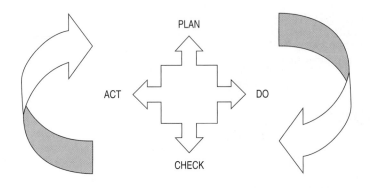

Control and Specification Limits

Shewhart's idea for monitoring the variability in a process was based on probability theory. He knew that if the common-cause variation in a process was Normally distributed, there would be only a small probability that an individual value could be farther than certain limits from the mean. To monitor the process, Shewhart advocated plotting measurements of the process over time, looking for evidence that the process might change and slip "out of control." He called such a plot a control chart, although they are often referred to as Shewhart charts. Typical examples of measurements for manufactured parts are characteristics such as thickness or size, weight, color, or electrical properties, just to name a few possibilities. Before starting to monitor the process, however, the process must first be stable, or "in control"—that is, both the mean and the standard deviation must be constant. Then, if an observation deviates far enough from the mean, it could be taken as a signal that either the process mean or standard deviation has changed.

Here is a control chart for 15 observations from an automobile manufacturing plant. The measurements are the diameters of a bolt used to fasten the car door to the chassis. The desired mean of the bolts' diameters is 23 mm:

Figure 21.2   A control chart for 15 diameters of bolts with a desired mean of 23 mm.

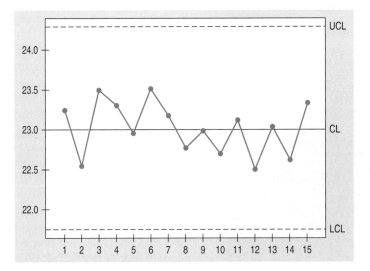

The main idea of using a control chart to monitor a process is that if the process stays in control, observations will stay within a certain distance of the mean (at least with very high probability). However, if the process mean or standard deviation changes, then the observations will start to drift, and, by monitoring the process, we will be able to discover that change. The question then becomes how far the observations must drift before we decide that the process has changed. So, for every process, **control limits** need to be established to decide when to take action.

When points fall outside of the control limits, this provides a signal that the process may have changed and some action is needed. We will discuss how to define the control limits and the various rules for deciding when action is needed in the rest of this chapter.

Using a control chart to monitor a process can be viewed as a graphical hypothesis test. The null hypothesis is that the process has not changed (both the mean and variance are constant). Various rules are used to decide when a signal has occurred (for example, an observation that falls more than 3σ from the mean is a common rule). When such a signal occurs, we reject the null hypothesis and conclude that a change has taken place. Of course, like all hypothesis tests, both Type I and Type II errors are always possible. In this context, a Type I error is a **false alarm**, requiring an unnecessary adjustment to the process. A Type II error is a failure to see a change in the process. The trade-off between the two types of errors and their relative costs in particular settings give rise to the many different rules for deciding when to reject the null hypothesis and declare a change in the process. Of course, rules that make it easier to reject the hypothesis will result in more false alarms and rules that make it harder will allow processes to drift farther (on average) before a signal is produced. Rules are often judged by how long they run, on average, without a false alarm when the process is in control. This is called the in-control **average run length** or **ARL**.

Control limits are based on the data themselves, and for that reason it is imperative that the process be in control before starting the monitoring process. Sometimes, however, quality concerns impose *external* limits on the process as well. For example, the diameters of the bolts must fall between certain limits or they just won't work. Limits such as these are **specification limits** because they are based on external specifications and not on how well the parts are actually produced. These upper and lower specification limits are abbreviated as USL and LSL respectively. To understand how well the process is behaving compared to the specification limits, studies known as **process capability studies** are undertaken. Quality control practitioners use these studies to understand the relationships between the specification limits and the actual process parameters (mean and variance). Several different **process capability indices** measuring different aspects of the relationship are commonly used.

Process capability studies can be performed only when the process is in control. In other words, these studies involve only the common-cause variation and not special-cause variation. As long as the observations stay between the LSL and USL, the parts will meet specification. Ideally we would want the upper and lower specification limits to be as far from the process mean as is economically feasible. That width can be measured by USL − LSL. If the process can be centered at the desired mean, then by the 68–95–99.7 Rule, we know that observations farther than 3σ from the mean will be rare. The ratio $C_p = \dfrac{USL - LSL}{6\sigma}$ measures the ratio of the entire specification range (both sides of the mean) to 6 times the standard deviation of the actual process variation. A process with a C_p value of 1.0 would therefore just satisfy the 3σ on each side of the mean criteria and translates to about one observation in about 370 falling outside the specification limits, which is considered too often for most modern manufacturing and service industries. Usually it is recommended that C_p be at least 1.25, and sometimes as high as 2.0, but the actual choice depends on the economics of the situation and the type of industry. The larger this C_p value, the smaller the chance of an observation falling outside the specification limits. A large value of C_p indicates a process with a large potential to produce parts within the specification limits.

In any real process, no matter how stable, the mean will drift slightly even when the process is in control. Because C_p does not explicitly use the location of the mean it tends to overestimate the potential of the process when the mean is not centered and can be misleading. A measure known as C_{pk} is often used instead. When the process mean and standard deviation are known, C_{pk} is defined as:

$$C_{pk} = \min\left[\frac{USL - \mu}{3\sigma}, \frac{\mu - LSL}{3\sigma}\right]$$

Using a period during which the process is in control to estimate the process parameters gives rise to the estimated value of C_{pk}.

$$\hat{C}_{pk} = \min\left[\frac{USL - \hat{\mu}}{3\hat{\sigma}}, \frac{\hat{\mu} - LSL}{3\hat{\sigma}}\right]$$ where the hats indicate that the parameters

are estimated from the process data. Most studies recommend that the estimates of process capability be based on at least 50 observations. As with C_p the choice of how large a value of C_{pk} is acceptable or desired depends on the situation and the associated costs but values below 1.0 are rarely acceptable. Some industries (such as the automotive manufacturing industry) have specific guidelines that they publish. It is also important to remember that these indices rely heavily on the assumption that all observations are Normally distributed.

FOR EXAMPLE   **Capability indices**

Fudge requires fairly strict adherence to a sequence of boiling sugar in milk until it reaches a certain consistency and then beating the mixture while it cools so that it acquires a smooth, creamy texture. A small candy company about 100 miles north of New York City ships fudge worldwide. If its fudge mix has a stable consistency, workers can control the weight of the fudge by simply timing how long they pour the warm fudge into the box prior to shipping. They would like the labeled 18 oz. box of fudge to contain no more than 18.5 oz. of fudge and no less than 17.9 oz. From the last 100 batches, they estimate the standard deviation of the weights to be 0.1 oz. with a mean of 18.1 oz.

QUESTION   Perform a process capability analysis on the fudge shop and comment on your findings.

ANSWER

Our estimate of C_p is $\hat{C}_p = \dfrac{USL - LSL}{6\hat{\sigma}} = \dfrac{18.5 - 17.9}{6(0.1)} = \dfrac{0.6}{0.6} = 1.0$. Our estimate

of C_{pk} is $\hat{C}_{pk} = \min\left[\dfrac{USL - \hat{\mu}}{3\hat{\sigma}}, \dfrac{\hat{\mu} - LSL}{3\hat{\sigma}}\right] = \min\left[\dfrac{18.5 - 18.1}{3(0.1)}, \dfrac{18.1 - 17.9}{3(0.1)}\right]$

$= \min\left[\dfrac{0.4}{0.3}, \dfrac{0.2}{0.3}\right] = 0.67$. The C_p value shows that if the weights are Normally

distributed and the mean is centered, about 1 in 370 boxes will exceed the limits. This is a low C_p value, but it may be acceptable in this industry. However, the mean is not centered between the two limits and the C_{pk} value of 0.67 is too low. The candy company should work to center the mean and/or lower the standard deviation of the weights.

21.2   Control Charts for Individual Observations (Run Charts)

The Sony Corporation of the 1950s used transistors and tubes for their electronic equipment, but nearly all their products today rely on computer chips. And almost all computer chips in use today are built on silicon wafers. Silicon is a natural semiconductor—it can be used both as a conductor of electricity and an insulator to prevent conduction. It is also relatively inexpensive and plentiful.

The basic source of silicon is sand, which can be purified to produce chips that are 99.9999% pure silicon. Although there are many different kinds of chips (RAM, processors, etc.), they are all built from the basic silicon wafer. Making a wafer involves a number of steps, all of which must be carried out as consistently as possible to ensure the chip will be able to perform reliably, regardless of its final function. During the manufacturing process a variety of performance characteristics must be checked. These include physical measurements such as thickness, chemical properties involving purity, and electrical properties such as conductance. All of these have specifications depending on the type of chip being produced. Because billions of chips are manufactured worldwide every year, maintaining quality control on chip manufacturing is big business.

Silicon wafers are produced in varying thicknesses, depending on their diameter. For photovoltaic use, a typical wafer is about 100–200 mm square with a thickness of $200 - 300 \mu$m. The mean target thickness of the particular wafer whose production is studied here is 300 μm. One way to ensure quality is to keep the thickness as consistent as possible. We will use 250 past measurements of the process which has been judged to be in control to establish control limits. Here are the summary statistics and a histogram:

```
maximum    392.423
quartile   325.067
median     298.521
quartile   277.030
minimum    221.838
Mean       301.111
Std Dev     32.990
```

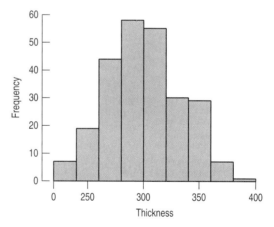

Figure 21.3 A histogram of the thickness shows a nearly Normal distribution centered at 300 μm.

Because the process has been judged to be in control, we can use the statistics from these data to develop control limits. We will base the mean at 300 μm, the desired thickness. The standard deviation of these measurements is 32.99. Using 33 μm as the standard deviation, (σ), the 68–95–99.7 Rule states that, as long as the process remains stable, only about 0.3% or 3 of 1000 observations will fall outside of 3σ from the mean. Using 3σ the lower and upper control limits would be

$$\mu - 3\sigma = 300 - 99 = 201 \text{ and } \mu + 3\sigma = 300 + 99 = 399 \ \mu\text{m}.$$

Using these control limits, a control chart can be monitored to see whether the process stays in control. Here are the subsequent 50 thicknesses of the wafer manufacturing process:

Figure 21.4 A control chart of individual observations shows no evidence that the process has slipped out of control. The 3σ lower (LCL) and upper (UCL) control limits are shown as dotted lines. The center line is denoted CL.

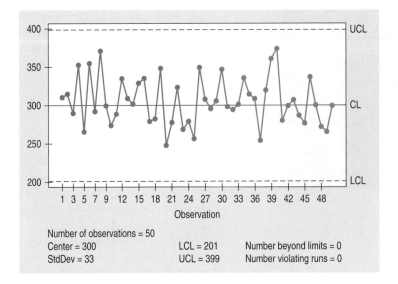

Number of observations = 50
Center = 300   LCL = 201   Number beyond limits = 0
StdDev = 33   UCL = 399   Number violating runs = 0

Figure 21.4 shows a control chart for individual observations (sometimes called a **run chart**), where a measurement is made on every product being produced. As we check each observation we are really performing a graphical hypothesis test, with the null hypothesis that the mean is 300 μm, and the (two-sided) alternative that it has changed to something else. The change may be abrupt, caused perhaps by a breakdown of a machine or the introduction of an impurity, in which case it is called a **level shift**. Or, the change might be gradual, in which case it is called a **trend**. We'll reject the null hypothesis if any point lies outside the 3σ control limits. The use of 3σ control limits as a standard is fairly widespread in the United States, while the United Kingdom and Europe tend to use other multiples of σ that depend on the specified probability of a Type I error, or false alarm signal. Using 3σ control limits will give rise to a false alarm rate of about 0.003 (using $1 - 0.997$ from the 68–95–99.7 Rule), or more precisely, 0.0027. That's the probability of any *single* observation giving rise to a false alarm. Even a process that is perfectly in control will have observations farther than 3σ from the mean, eventually (in fact, about 3 times in every 1000 observations). The average time between alarms for a process is called the **average run length** or **ARL**. The average time between *false* alarms for a process in control is called the **in-control ARL**. We want as large an in-control ARL as possible, but at the same time, we'd like the ARL for a process that is out-of-control to be short. The in-control ARL can be calculated by taking the reciprocal of the false alarm probability. For the 3σ rule, the in-control ARL is:

$$ARL_0 = \frac{1}{p} = \frac{1}{0.0027} = 370.37.$$

On average, we would expect to see a false alarm about every 370 observations for a process that is in control.

If the process mean shifts we'd like the control chart to show an alarm. If the chart shows the process staying in control, that's a Type II error. As in any hypothesis testing situation, the probability of the Type II error depends on how many observations have occurred since the process went out of control and how large the shift is (the effect size). Balancing Type I and Type II errors is an economic decision and depends on the control limits and the rule for deciding when a process has changed. The ability of any chart to detect shifts can be described by its **operating-characteristic (OC) curve** or equivalently by comparing the in-control and out-of-control ARLs. We describe shifts in mean in terms of standard deviations. If the process shifts only one standard deviation, the probability of noticing the shift on the next observation will be very small. If the shift were quite large, say, 5σ, we should be surprised if we didn't see it immediately. Here is an OC curve for the run chart just described:

Figure 21.5 The operating-characteristic curve for a run chart. For a shift of 3σ the probability of not detecting it on the next observation is about 0.50.

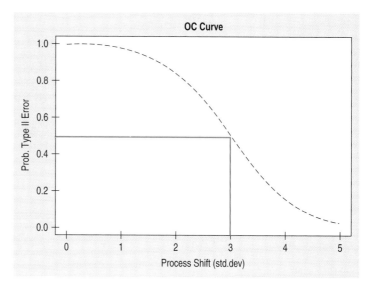

Even though the probability of detecting a shift of 3σ is only about 0.5 on the *next* observation, the probability of a Type II error after two observations is about $0.5 \times 0.5 = 0.25$, and the probability of failing to detect the shift after 5 observations is $(0.5)^5 = 0.031$. More observations, of course, help guard against making errors.

In addition to the simple 3σ rule, there are many other rules commonly used in industry with different OC curves, and different ARLs. The Western Electric *Statistical Quality Control Handbook* (WECO, 1956) became a standard reference for quality control methods. It suggests several rules for deciding whether a process is out-of-control:

1. One point outside of the 3σ control limits on either side
2. Two out of three consecutive points beyond the 2σ "warning limits"
3. Four out of five consecutive points beyond 1σ from the mean
4. Eight (or seven) points in a row on the same side of the mean
5. Six points in a row increasing (or decreasing)
6. Fourteen points in a row alternatively increasing and decreasing

These rules are commonly used in practice. Some are available in commonly used software (notably Excel and Minitab), which implement several other rules as well. You may see eight or even ten rules used by software to detect a possible shift in the process. Deciding which combination of rules to use involves a trade-off between false alarms and failure to detect process changes. If the simple 3σ rule is the only one used, the in-control ARL before a false alarm, as we have seen, is about 370. If all 6 WECO rules are implemented, the ARL drops to about 92 observations between false alarms, but decreases the out-of-control ARL as well. Using more rules only decreases both ARLs even more. Each user has to decide whether the ability to detect shifts faster is worth the price of more frequent false alarms. It is also important to note that these tests rely crucially on the assumption that the observations themselves are well-modeled by a Normal distribution. In the next section, we will plot *averages* of several observations and the Central Limit Theorem will help somewhat with this restrictive assumption.

FOR EXAMPLE   Runs charts

QUESTION   After the report in the example on page 748, the candy company makes some changes to the pouring process and thinks that the mean is now 18.15 oz. and the standard deviation is 0.08 oz. Using these parameter values, construct a runs chart for the following weights of recent batches and comment on whether the process is in control.

18.03	18.00	18.12	17.81	18.23
18.11	18.23	18.19	18.00	18.05
18.12	18.05	18.14	18.16	18.11
18.19	18.26	18.11	18.15	18.07
18.04	18.14	18.00	18.21	18.12

ANSWER

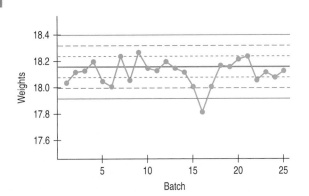

It appears that the process is not yet in control. The weight of batch 16 is too low and, in fact, it is outside both the 3σ and the lower specification limit of 17.90.

21.3   Control Charts for Measurements: $\overline{X}$ and R Charts

Although the run chart of the last section is the easiest to implement and to understand, it is not usually practical to measure *every* item coming down a production line, or every phone call coming into a call center, especially if the testing is destructive. Nor are all observations Normally distributed. As an alternative, a sample is taken at periodic intervals and, typically, the *mean* of that sample is plotted. A chart of these sample means is called an $\overline{X}$ **chart** (pronounced "X bar chart" and often written as x-bar or xbar chart).

For detecting a shift in the mean, the $\overline{X}$ chart has several advantages over the run chart. A practical advantage is that it tests less frequently. Even more important, the averages from a sample of size n are more nearly Normal than individual observations, so that the basic assumption of the control chart that gives us the probabilities of a false alarm and other characterisitcs is more likely to be met. Because the sample sizes used in an $\overline{X}$ chart are usually small, however, it still relies somewhat on the underlying measurements being approximately Normal. Very skewed distributions will make the $\overline{X}$ chart inaccurate for detecting out-of-control signals.

When the standard deviation is assumed to be known (perhaps based on a large amount of past data), the implementation of the $\overline{X}$ chart is essentially the same as the individual control chart. Because a sample mean has a standard deviation of $\frac{\sigma}{\sqrt{n}}$ rather than σ, the 3σ control limits for the $\overline{X}$ chart become:

$$LCL = \mu - 3\frac{\sigma}{\sqrt{n}}$$

$$UCL = \mu + 3\frac{\sigma}{\sqrt{n}}$$

For the wafer data, if we continue to use $\mu = 300$, and $\sigma = 33$, and take a 5-item sample at regular intervals, the control limits become:

$$LLC = \mu - 3\frac{\sigma}{\sqrt{n}} = 300 - 3\left(\frac{33}{\sqrt{5}}\right) = 255.7\ \mu\text{m}$$

$$ULC = \mu + 3\frac{\sigma}{\sqrt{n}} = 300 + 3\left(\frac{33}{\sqrt{5}}\right) = 344.3\ \mu\text{m}$$

Here is an $\overline{X}$ chart for 25 samples of size 5 from the wafer production process:

Figure 21.6   An $\overline{X}$ chart for 25 samples of size 5. The process appears to be in control because all sample means are within the control limits. This particular chart use two of the Western Electric rules and reports *Number beyond limits* (rule #1) and *Number violating runs* (variant of rule #4—7 on same side of mean).

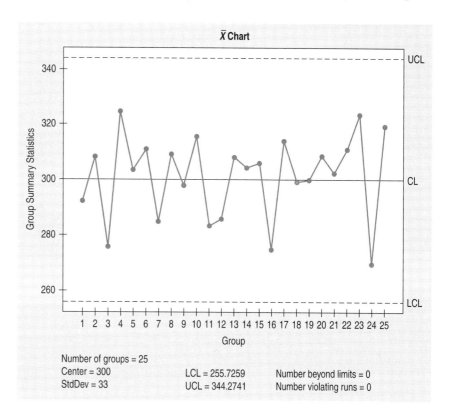

Up to now, we have assumed that the past data are numerous, so the mean and standard deviation of the process are known. In practice, we may not have this information, and we will have to estimate both μ and σ. These estimates should be based on as much data as possible—20 to 25 samples at a minimum—and, of course, the process must be in control. If we have k samples of size n, then we can use the average of the averages, called $\overline{\overline{X}}$ (X double bar), to get our estimate of μ:

$$\overline{\overline{X}} = \frac{\overline{X}_1 + \cdots + \overline{X}_k}{k}.$$

If no external center were desired, $\overline{\overline{X}}$ would be the center of our control chart.

To find the control limits, we still need an estimate of the standard deviation, σ. This is typically done by technology, or from the standard deviation of a large in-control sample, but can also be found by using the ranges of the samples rather than their standard deviations. Recall that the range of a sample is defined as the maximum minus the minimum:

$$R = max - min.$$

For Normally distributed data when no other reliable estimate of the standard deviation is available, we can use a well-known relationship between the range of a sample and its standard deviation. The mean of the ratio $\dfrac{R}{\sigma}$ is a constant denoted d_2, which depends on the sample size (and is given for various sample sizes in Table R in Appendix B). Using this constant, an estimate of σ is found from $\hat{\sigma} = \dfrac{\overline{R}}{d_2}$ where

$$\overline{R} = \frac{R_1 + \cdots + R_k}{k}.$$

The limits of the control chart then become:

$$LCL = \overline{\overline{X}} - 3\frac{\hat{\sigma}}{\sqrt{n}} = \overline{\overline{X}} - 3\frac{\overline{R}}{d_2\sqrt{n}}$$

$$UCL = \overline{\overline{X}} + 3\frac{\hat{\sigma}}{\sqrt{n}} = \overline{\overline{X}} + 3\frac{\overline{R}}{d_2\sqrt{n}}$$

Suppose that instead of the 250 individual measurements we used previously to establish μ and σ, we had used the first half of these as a calibration set and then monitored the rest of the samples. In total we have 50 samples of size 5. From the first 25 samples of size 5 we compute their means and ranges and find:

$$\overline{\overline{X}} = 295.27; \overline{R} = 81.32.$$

To compute the control limits, we have $n = 5$, and $d_2 = 2.326$, and so:

$$LCL = 295.27 - 3\left(\frac{81.32}{2.326\sqrt{5}}\right) = 248.36$$

$$UCL = 295.27 + 3\left(\frac{81.32}{2.326\sqrt{5}}\right) = 342.18$$

These are not very far from the control limits we found by assuming that the mean and standard deviation were known. But often control limits have to be adjusted as new information about the process performance becomes available. Quality control charting involves learning about a process as well as monitoring it. A more modern approach to process monitoring uses control charts to monitor the *inputs* to the process instead of just the measurements (outputs). In this way of thinking, if the critical inputs to the process are in control, the resulting outputs will be as well.

As we saw with run charts, the power for detecting a shift depends on the size of the process shift. For $\overline{X}$ charts it also depends on the sample size. To choose an appropriate sample size, quality control monitors examine the operating characteristic curves such as the one shown in Figure 21.7 based on the wafer data. Both the process shift and sample size can be used to find the probability of a Type II error for the next sample.

In general, we care about both the level of the process and consistency in variation. Although an $\overline{X}$ chart will detect increases in the standard deviation, for more information, the ranges themselves are plotted in what is known as an **R chart**. The procedure for setting up the R chart is very similar to the $\overline{X}$ chart. The only new element is finding the standard deviation of the range. Fortunately, for Normally

Figure 21.7   Operating characteristic curves for the wafer data $\bar{X}$ chart. For any proposed value of the process shift (in standard deviations), operators can examine different sample sizes to determine a good sample size with a reasonable probability of a Type II error. For example, for a 1.5σ shift, a sample size of more than 10 would be necessary to produce a probability of a Type II error below 0.10.

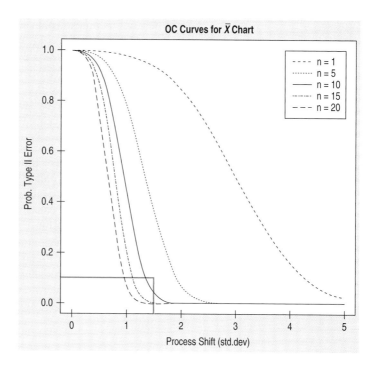

distributed data, the relationship between σ and R is well known. There is a new parameter d_3, that depends on the sample size as did d_2. If we assume σ is known, we can find the standard deviation of the range directly by: $\sigma_R = d_3\sigma$. If we need to estimate σ, we can use $\hat{\sigma} = \dfrac{\bar{R}}{d_2}$ as before:

$$\hat{\sigma}_R = d_3 \frac{\bar{R}}{d_2}$$

We center the range chart at $\bar{R}$, so the control limits:

$$LCL = \bar{R} - 3\sigma_R$$
$$UCL = \bar{R} + 3\sigma_R$$

become:

$$LCL = \bar{R} - 3d_3\frac{\bar{R}}{d_2}$$
$$UCL = \bar{R} + 3d_3\frac{\bar{R}}{d_2}$$

(If we are given both the mean and standard deviation from the process history and wish to establish limits for R, we can alternatively use $R = d_2\sigma$ as the center line.)

Using our 25 samples of size 5 with $\bar{R} = 81.32$, and finding d_3 for $n = 5$ to be 0.864, we have: $\hat{\sigma}_R = d_3 \dfrac{\bar{R}}{d_2} = 0.864 \dfrac{81.32}{2.326} = 30.21$. (Had we assumed $\sigma = 33$ we would have $\sigma_R = 0.864(33) = 28.51$, not far from the value we obtained.) This gives us lower and upper control limits for the range of:

$$LCL = \bar{R} - 3d_3\frac{\bar{R}}{d_2} = 81.32 - 3(30.21) = -9.31$$

$$UCL = \bar{R} + 3d_3\frac{\bar{R}}{d_2} = 81.32 + 3(30.21) = 171.95$$

Because a range can never be negative, we set the lower limit at 0.

Target Values

When using target or known values for the process mean and standard deviation the center lines and 3σ control limits are particularly easy to find.

For $\bar{X}$ charts:
center line: μ

UCL: $\mu + 3\sigma/\sqrt{n}$
LCL: $\mu - 3\sigma/\sqrt{n}$

For R charts:
center line: $d_2\sigma$

UCL: $d_2\sigma + 3\,d_3\sigma$
LCL: $d_2\sigma - 3\,d_3\sigma$

where d_2 and d_3 are found in Table R for sample size n.

When not using external values for the process mean and standard deviation, these formulas can (and in industry usually are) simplified by noticing that we can collect the constants and rewrite the limits more simply as:

$$LCL = \overline{R} - 3d_3\frac{\overline{R}}{d_2} = \overline{R}\left(1 - 3\frac{d_3}{d_2}\right) = D_3\overline{R}$$

$$UCL = \overline{R} + 3d_3\frac{\overline{R}}{d_2} = \overline{R}\left(1 + 3\frac{d_3}{d_2}\right) = D_4\overline{R}$$

So now the upper and lower limits for the $\overline{R}$ chart are just multiples of $\overline{R}$ (and are found in Table R). For small sample sizes, $D_3 = 0$ which automatically sets the lower range limit 0. (These simplications should not be used if you want to base the limits on an *external* value of the process standard deviation or mean.)

For $n = 5$, $D_3 = 0$ and $D_4 = 2.114$ so $LCL = 0$ and $UCL = 2.114\,(81.32) = 171.91$, nearly the same (accounting for rounding) as we found before.

For R charts, the first four WECO rules are often used, although some adaptations for the fact that the chart is generally asymmetric exist as well. The chart below uses rules 1 and 4 (with seven) as it did for the $\overline{X}$ chart. Monitoring the next 25 samples, we see that the range stayed in control:

Figure 21.8 An R chart for 25 samples of size 5. The process appears to be in control in terms of variation because all sample ranges are within the control limits.

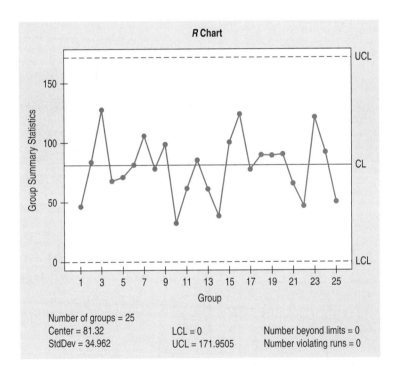

An alternative to the R chart is the **S chart**, which uses the standard deviations of samples rather than their ranges. The most common use of $\overline{X}$ and S charts occurs when the sample sizes are moderately large (where the range loses statistical efficiency—around $n = 10$ or 12) or when the sample size varies and the ranges of different samples are not comparable. The formulas for finding the control limits for both $\overline{X}$ and S are complicated and are usually left to technology to calculate. We refer the interested reader to any number of excellent books on quality control.

In this section we have seen how to establish the most common control limits for $\overline{X}$ and R charts. $\overline{X}$ and R charts are the most commonly used charts for measuring quantitative values and are used together to monitor both changes in the mean and the spread of a process. However, it should be pointed out that the more rules one uses for detecting signals, the smaller the in-control ARL will be. So, using more of the Western Electric rules or using $\overline{X}$ and R charts together will decrease the time to detect a true signal, but will increase the number of false alarms as well. Important alternatives to the $\overline{X}$ charts have been developed, among which the two most widely used are the cumulative sum (CUSUM) and exponentially weighted moving average (EWMA) charts.

The CUSUM chart plots the cumulative sums of all the deviations of the values from the target mean. If the process stays in control, that sum should stay near 0 (although its variance will increase). If the process drifts, the sum will start to accumulate the differences (on one side of the target mean or the other). Because the variance of a sum increases even when the process is in control, the control limits are not lines equally spaced from the mean, but a V-shaped mask that moves as the number of observations increases. The EWMA chart, like the exponential smoothing method of Chapter 19, weights recent observations more heavily so that past observations have decreasing importance as time rolls on. Both of these charts have been shown to provide advantages over $\overline{X}$ charts for many real-world situations.

Finally, it is important to point out that not all process changes are undesirable. In fact, in modern quality control, much emphasis is placed on reducing process variation. A shift indicating that the range (or standard deviation) has decreased would almost certainly be viewed as beneficial.

FOR EXAMPLE $\overline{X}$ and *R* charts

The fudge makers (see page 748) make more changes to the process and wonder if they have been successful in getting the process under control. They still desire a mean of 18.1 oz. and a process standard deviation of 0.08 oz. Here are the average weights and ranges of 25 batches of size 5:

Batch	Mean	Range	Batch	Mean	Range
1	18.104	0.13	14	18.076	0.20
2	18.014	0.09	15	18.152	0.15
3	18.138	0.14	16	18.114	0.31
4	18.108	0.31	17	18.180	0.36
5	18.118	0.12	18	18.086	0.26
6	18.112	0.18	19	18.104	0.40
7	18.216	0.15	20	18.074	0.20
8	18.332	0.62	21	18.122	0.24
9	18.434	0.19	22	18.146	0.12
10	18.146	0.29	23	18.104	0.36
11	18.032	0.22	24	18.136	0.16
12	18.102	0.39	25	18.104	0.08
13	18.112	0.21			

QUESTIONS   Using $\overline{X}$ and R charts with the desired mean of 18.15 oz. and the desired standard deviation of 0.08 oz., does the process seem to be in control now? If not, when did the process seem to slip out of control?

ANSWERS   For the $\overline{X}$ chart, we use 18.15 as the center line and the desired process standard deviation of 0.08. The control limits are found at

$$\mu \pm 3\frac{\sigma}{\sqrt{5}} = 18.15 \pm 3\frac{0.08}{\sqrt{5}} = 18.15 \pm 0.107 = 18.043 \;and\; 18.257.$$

(continued)

Here is the $\overline{X}$ chart of the 25 batches:

For the ranges, we use the desired process mean and standard deviation as well. So the center is

$$center = d_2\sigma = 2.326(0.08) = 0.186$$
$$LCL = center - 3(d_3\sigma) = 0.186 - 3(0.864 \times 0.08) = -0.021 \Rightarrow 0$$
$$UCL = center + 3(d_3\sigma) = 0.186 + 3(0.864 \times 0.08) = 0.393$$

Here is the R chart:

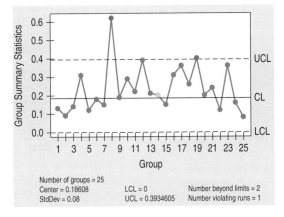

The process is out of control both in mean and variation. Batches 2 and 11 were too low, and 8 and 9 were too high. Batches 8 and 19 had ranges too high and by Batch 14, there were seven ranges on the same side of the center line. The candy company clearly needs to study the process to bring it into control.

21.4   Actions for Out-of-Control Processes

Once a process has been determined to be "out of control," it does not necessarily mean that something is "wrong" with the process. It simply means that a signal has occurred indicating a possible change in the system. An action should be taken to understand the source of the special-cause variation. If the change is determined not to be beneficial, however, those in charge of the process must act quickly to resolve the problem. In the case of a detrimental change, an out-of-control signal may necessitate stopping production of the process until the cause has been determined and a correction put into place. This is the "Act" part of the Shewhart Cycle and a crucial step for process management.

For an established manufacturing process there may be an **out-of-control action plan (OCAP)** in place based on past experience. An operator seeing an out-of-control signal would consult the OCAP and take the steps outlined in it and then continue monitoring the process to see if the process regained an in-control state.

If no such plan exists, as would be the case for a new process, an investigation of possible causes is undertaken. The full details of such an investigation are beyond the scope of this text, but the basic steps involve:

- Forming a team of all those involved in the process to discuss and enumerate the possible causes of the shift. A powerful tool in this effort is the **cause-and-effect diagram** (sometimes called an Ishikawa or fishbone diagram) that helps organize the possible causes and helps prioritize them for further analysis. (See Figure 21.9.)
- If no simple cause can be determined it may be necessary to commence a series of experiments using the most probable causes as the factors. There are efficient designs that can accommodate as many as a dozen or more possible factors in the initial investigation of possible causes.
- Once the most likely cause has been identified, and the optimal value for that factor has been determined, the process inputs are changed in an attempt to drive the process back into control.
- The monitoring process is restarted in the hope that the problem has been resolved, and the Shewhart cycle starts again.

Understanding and controlling processes is a large area of activity in both the manufacturing and service industries involving the efforts of many people in the organization. The American Society for Quality (www.asq.org) provides a wealth of information on the subject.

Figure 21.9 Cause-and-effect diagram for a production problem involving faulty welding between a detector and its base in a gas chromatograph. After a control chart showed the process was out of control, a team was assembled and together they listed 5 potential areas to investigate for process improvement: Materials, Personnel, Welding, Welding Methods, and the Machines involved. For each area, three to four potential factors were listed. From here, the team designed a series of experiments in the factors deemed most likely to affect weld breakage. The factors were manipulated and the resulting weld breakage was measured. Eventually it was determined that the alloy used by one of the suppliers had changed. When the company insisted that the supplier use the alloy that historically had been used for the weld, the problem disappeared.

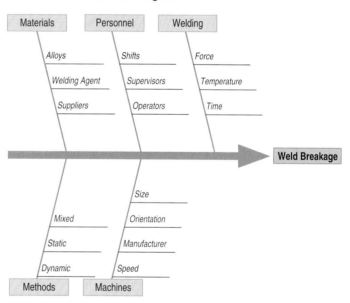

Cause-and-Effect Diagram

FOR EXAMPLE   Actions for out-of-control processes

The fudge company (see page 748) wants to bring its process under control and assembles a team of bakers, process engineers, and marketing staff. The team discusses possible factors influencing the weight and groups them into four main categories:

Raw materials (sugar, butter, milk, flavorings)
Oven (oven temperature, pan temperature, time)
Process (timing of stir, amount of stir, pouring of fudge)
Container (pan material, pan size)

QUESTION   Organize these possible factors into a fishbone (Ishikawa) diagram to help them design experiments using these factors.

(continued)

ANSWER

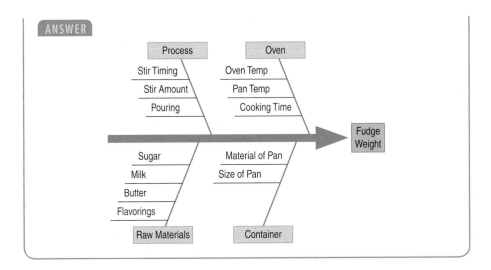

GUIDED EXAMPLE   KomTek Technologies

KomTek Technologies produces hip prosthetics in the United States with more than 60% of the U.S. market share. Founded in 1984, KomTek Technologies specializes in the production of nickel- and cobalt-based super alloys—specifically in the production of prosthetic devices. This manufacturing firm sells hip joints to five biomedical companies and these account for 30% to 40% of the firm's annual revenue. This firm uses a cobalt chromium alloy to forge the joints, which are heated in a furnace and then beaten or hammered into shape. Because prosthetic hips are costly to manufacture, the firm produces them only when a customer places an order. The average size of an order is typically between 200 and 600 pieces.[2]

Each part of the manufacturing process is monitored and controlled and the corporation has implemented a rigorous program to assist with quality control. Toward the end of the manufacturing process, dimples need to be hammered into each hip joint to enhance the fit. Occasionally, this hammering process causes the center line to be off-center. The tip length of this dimple is a crucial measurement to monitor.

A major customer that accounts for nearly 40% to 50% of the total hip joint sales at the firm recently placed an order for 1200 prosthetic hips—a larger than usual order. Following the manufacturing and shipment of these hips for this customer, the team at the firm responsible for quality control noticed that their overall cost for filling this order was high. The team members realized that the order was larger than usual, but they need to figure how and why the cost was so high. There was some concern by management that quality control monitoring may not have been in place for the latter part of this order. In particular, there was some suspicion that the last 230 or so hip joints had not been subjected to rigorous quality control.

We want to establish control limits for $\overline{X}$ and R charts for the *Tip Length* and investigate the recent production run to understand why the cost of recent orders has been high.

PLAN   **Setup** State the objectives.

Identify the type of data you are examining.

We want to examine the variation in the Tip Length of the distal hip for the latter part of a recent large customer order to look for possible quality control issues. The tip length spec is 0.25 cm so we will use this as the center line. To start the monitoring process, we have data from 50 samples of size 5 from previous orders, when the process was judged to be in control (the calibration period), to use to establish our control limits.

---

[2]This example is based on 1998 case study written by J. Hunt, E. Landry, and J. Rao as part of the Babson College case series. The data and setting used in this example are based on the actual case study, but the data have been modified and the conclusions are fictitious.

DO **Mechanics** We can compute the limits using the specs provided by the company.

For the calibration period the overall mean is $\bar{\bar{X}} = 0.2507$ inch. We will use 0.25, the specified length, as the center line. A histogram of these 250 observations shows a unimodal and symmetric distribution:

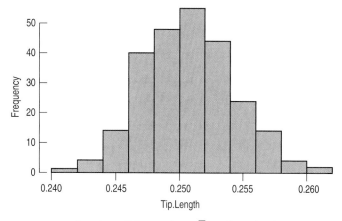

The average range for these 50 samples is $\bar{R} = 0.00847$ cm. Using the range to estimate sigma, we have:

$$\hat{\sigma} = \frac{\bar{R}}{d_2} = \frac{0.00847}{2.326} = 0.0036 \text{ cm}$$

Our initial control limits for $\bar{X}$ are therefore:

$$LCL = \mu - 3\frac{\hat{\sigma}}{\sqrt{n}} = 0.25 - 3\left(\frac{0.0036}{\sqrt{5}}\right)$$
$$= 0.2452 \text{ cm}$$
$$UCL = \mu + 3\frac{\hat{\sigma}}{\sqrt{n}} = 0.25 + 3\left(\frac{0.0036}{\sqrt{5}}\right)$$
$$= 0.2548 \text{ cm}$$

We use software to create the $\bar{X}$ control chart.

The $\bar{X}$ chart for the calibration data is shown here for completeness (although, of course, we would not expect to see problems here because these are the data on which the limits are based):

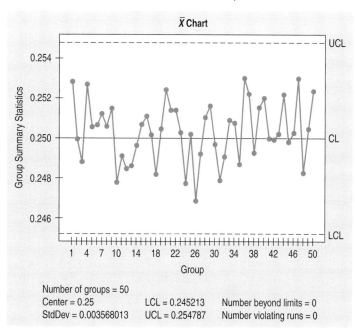

Number of groups = 50
Center = 0.25   LCL = 0.245213   Number beyond limits = 0
StdDev = 0.003568013   UCL = 0.254787   Number violating runs = 0

(continued)

We use technology to create the R chart on the calibration data.

Similarly, we show the R chart for the calibration period. For this period $\bar{R} = 0.00847$. To establish control limits for the R chart we use

$$LCL = D_3\bar{R} = 0(0.00847) = 0$$
$$UCL = D_4\bar{R} = 2.114(0.00847) = 0.0179$$

as the control limits.

Examine the $\bar{X}$ and R charts for the recent order.

Using these limits, we now create $\bar{X}$ and R charts for 100 hip joints in the latter part of the recent order, starting with unit 970 (20 samples of size 5). The $\bar{X}$ chart shows several problems:

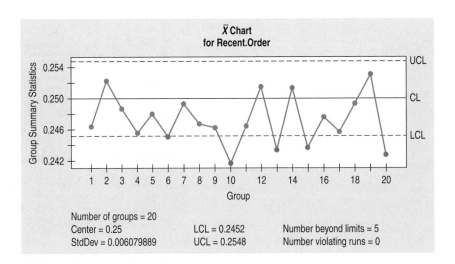

There are 5 samples whose average tip length falls below the LCL. In addition, there were 9 samples in a row below the center line starting with sample 3. This should have been a signal that the process mean had shifted and some intervention should have taken place.

The *R* chart shows similar problems:

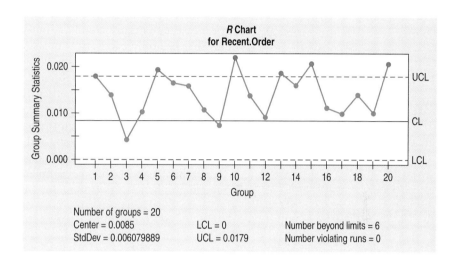

There are 6 samples whose range is too large (outside of the UCL). Starting with the first sample, this should have been a sign that something had changed with the process.

REPORT

Conclusion State the conclusion in the context of the problem.

MEMO

Re: Patterns of tip length

We investigated the variation in the length of the distal tip for this unusually large customer order. It is clear that quality control for the latter part of this order was lax. Several samples from units 970 to 1070 had average tip lengths that were too short. In addition, the volatility in the process also seems to have increased. The quality team notes that the length of the distal tip must be monitored using sampling during the process and the equipment should be checked, recalibrated, and/or changed after every violation of the limits in either the $\overline{X}$ or *R* charts.

Follow up

Following this incident, the team was assembled to try to diagnose the problem. None of the inputs to the machine that produces the part seemed to have changed. However, using a fishbone diagram, many possible causes of the problem were identified. After intensive discussion, four factors deemed most likely to affect tip length were selected for further study. An experiment testing these was designed and run. The analysis of the data showed that the tensile strength needed to be increased. A subsequent run of 50 tips showed that the problem had been resolved by this adjustment.

21.5   Control Charts for Attributes: p Charts and c Charts

We've seen several examples of quantitative measurements that are used to assess quality. For manufacturing processes these might include physical characteristics such as the thickness or diameter of a silicon wafer. In service industries, we might want to measure the length of time a customer has to wait to talk to a representative at a call center or how long it has been since they used one of our branches. Quantitative measurements are common, but we may want to monitor the quality of a process that has only categorical measurements such as color, or product type. The most common type of categorical measurements used in quality control are **dichotomous**—or yes/no—**variables**. Examples of these include whether a part is defective or nondefective or whether the customer has rated a phone call as satisfactory or not. In such cases, we can monitor the *proportion* of defective items in the sample. If it is determined that the proportion of defectives has increased, the special-cause variation will be investigated and the process will be adjusted to reduce variation. The control chart of proportions is called a **p chart**.

Recall that, if we assume the samples are independent, the standard deviation of a sample proportion $\hat{p}$ (writing q for $(1 - p)$) is:

$$SD(\hat{p}) = \sqrt{\frac{pq}{n}}.$$

If we know the desired proportion p, we can use this to establish 3σ control limits for the sample proportion:

$$LCL = p - 3\sqrt{\frac{pq}{n}}$$

$$UCL = p + 3\sqrt{\frac{pq}{n}}$$

In practice, however, we usually use the data from a period believed to be in control to estimate p and then use this value to monitor future data. As we did for $\overline{X}$ charts, we start by taking k samples of size n as our calibration data and base our control limits on the results. We'll call the average proportion of defective items from our k samples $\bar{p} = \dfrac{\hat{p}_1 + \cdots + \hat{p}_k}{k}$. Recall that when we didn't know p, we used the sample proportion to find the standard error:

$$SE(\hat{p}) = \sqrt{\frac{\hat{p}\hat{p}}{n}}.$$

We can use the same formula to estimate the standard deviation and find the control limits by using $\bar{p}$ in place of $\hat{p}$:

$$LCL = \bar{p} - 3\sqrt{\frac{\bar{p}\,\bar{q}}{n}}$$

$$UCL = \bar{p} + 3\sqrt{\frac{\bar{p}\,\bar{q}}{n}}$$

As with R charts, if the lower limit is negative, we set it to 0.

The usual point outside of the 3σ rule indicates a process that may be out of control. As with $\overline{X}$ charts there are a variety of alternative rules (WECO). Minitab, for example, uses the following four:

1. One point outside of the 3σ lines
2. Nine points in a row outside of 1σ on the same side

3. Six increasing or decreasing points in a row
4. Fourteen points in a row that alternate up and down

For example, suppose that a wafer is defective if its film thickness is either too thin ($<250\,\mu$m) or too thick ($>350\,\mu$m). If we use 25 samples of size 50 as our calibration set we find $\bar{p} = 0.1544$ and so

$$LCL = \bar{p} - 3\sqrt{\frac{\bar{p}\,\bar{q}}{n}} = 0.1544 - 3\sqrt{\frac{0.1544 \times 0.8456}{50}} = 0.001$$

$$UCL = \bar{p} + 3\sqrt{\frac{\bar{p}\,\bar{q}}{n}} = 0.1544 + 3\sqrt{\frac{0.1544 \times 0.8456}{50}} = 0.308$$

The p chart for the next 25 samples shows no evidence of a change in the proportion:

Figure 21.10 A p chart based on 25 samples of size 50 with an average proportion defective of 0.1544. The process appears to be in control in terms of variation because all sample proportions for the 25 samples after the initial calibration are within the control limits.

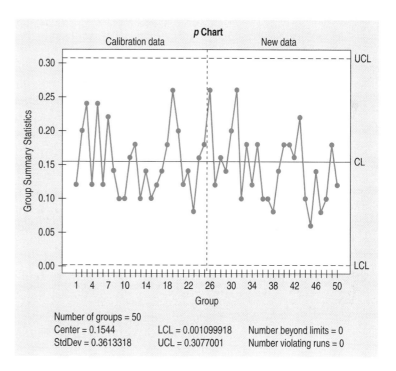

(Some computer programs have the ability to accommodate variable sample sizes for p charts, even though the control limits will vary with the sample size. If the sample sizes don't vary widely, it is also possible to use the average sample size and keep the control limits constant.)

Another variation on this type of monitoring focuses on the number of defective items in each sample rather than the proportion. This process is tracked in a **c chart**. The c chart should be used when the occurrence of a defective is *rare*. Then, the probabilities can be based on the Poisson model rather than the Binomial, which can lead to better ability to detect shifts. Because the standard deviation of a Poisson variable with mean μ is $\sqrt{\mu}$, we find the control limits easily. If the standard number of defects c is known we could simply use the 3σ control limits:

$$LCL = c - 3\sqrt{c}$$
$$UCL = c + 3\sqrt{c}$$

When no standard is given, we find the average number of defectives, $\bar{c}$, from k samples of size n and use that in the control limits centered at $\bar{c}$:

$$LCL = \bar{c} - 3\sqrt{\bar{c}}$$
$$UCL = \bar{c} + 3\sqrt{\bar{c}}$$

A more serious type of defect in wafer manufacturing is the failure of a die, the integrated circuit that eventually becomes a chip. If the number of failed dies per wafer is too great, the wafer is scrapped. If the number of scrapped wafers becomes too large, the process may need to be recalibrated or examined for other problems.

Suppose that for a period in which the process was in control, the average number of scrapped wafers was 1.44 in 1000. Then, in subsequent samples of size 500 we would expect 0.72 defects per sample. The control limits then become:

$$LCL = \bar{c} - 3\sqrt{\bar{c}} = 0.72 + 3\sqrt{0.72} = -1.826$$
$$UCL = \bar{c} + 3\sqrt{\bar{c}} = 0.72 + 3\sqrt{0.72} = 3.266$$

Figure 21.11   A c chart based on the same 25 samples of size 50 with an average number of defectives of 0.72. The process appears to be in control in terms of variation because all sample counts of defectives for the 25 samples after the initial calibration are within the control limits. Notice that the bottom control limit has been set to 0 because 3 standard deviations below 0.72 was negative.

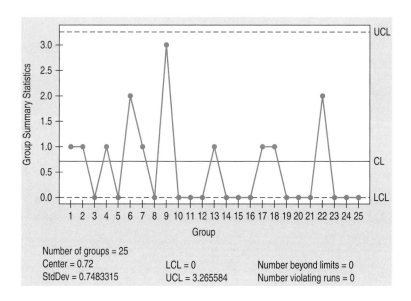

Number of groups = 25
Center = 0.72
StdDev = 0.7483315
LCL = 0
UCL = 3.265584
Number beyond limits = 0
Number violating runs = 0

FOR EXAMPLE   Control charts for attributes

The fudge company (see page 748) solicits customer feedback by surveys and phone interviews. One of the questions asks how satisfied customers were with the fudge on a scale from 1 to 5 with 1 = Very Dissatisfied; 2 = Dissatisfied; 3 = Neither Satisfied nor Dissatisfied; 4 = Satisfied; 5 = Very Satisfied. They want 80% or more of their customers to be "Very Satisfied." Here are the percentages saying "Very Satisfied" from the last 15 surveys of 100 people.

Number responding "5" out of 100: 78 78 88 77 76 79 85 75 81 88 86 74 76 81 75

QUESTION   Is the process "in control"?

ANSWER   Using a p chart with center line $p = 0.8$ the control lines are:

$$LCL = p - 3\sqrt{\frac{pq}{n}} = 0.8 - 3\sqrt{\frac{(.8)(.2)}{100}} = 0.68$$

$$UCL = p + 3\sqrt{\frac{pq}{n}} = 0.8 + 3\sqrt{\frac{(.8)(.2)}{100}} = 0.92$$

From the p chart, it appears that the process is in control.

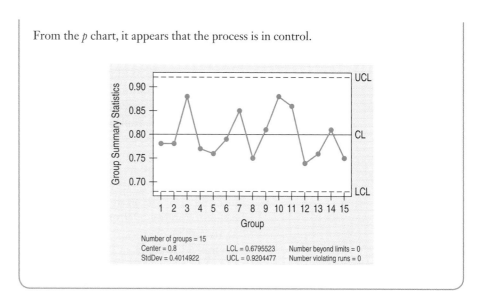

21.6   Philosophies of Quality Control

As U.S. industry saw its global market share slip in the 1970s and 1980s, and worldwide customers began to rely on Japanese and German products for high quality, a renaissance of interest in quality improvement sprang up all over the United States. During this time, many similar quality philosophies, acronyms, and gurus competed for the attention of top management. Most of them share three common ideas from statistical thinking as outlined by the Statistics Division of the American Society for Quality (ASQ):

- All work occurs in a system of interconnected processes,
- Variation exists in all processes, and
- Understanding and reducing variation are keys to success.[3]

Although the United States and Britain were the birthplace of modern quality control, the efforts of the quality movement in Japan caught the attention of U.S. industry in the decades after WWII. Deming is often credited for much of the success of Japan's manufacturing in the latter part of the twentieth century.

Deming ambitiously shared his ideas of concentrating on the customer and cutting costs by concentrating on quality in all aspects of the company in an effort to reduce waste and raise efficiency. Deming also suggested that the Japanese use market research—a new field in the United States and virtually unknown at the time in Japan—to help satisfy the needs of the customers. At the core of market research was the concept of random sampling to understand customers' desires and needs. Deming also conveyed the idea that managers need to take responsibility for quality control. He taught the Shewhart cycle and explained the importance of managers "acting" on the analytical information provided by the quality control tools. Deming also explained the importance of viewing the supplier as a partner and of building cooperative relationships, so that the supplier, producer, and customer all form a network. The teachings of Deming's philosophy can be summarized as **total quality management (TQM)**, although the term was not used until 1974 by one of the Deming Prize recipients.[4] TQM extends the theory of quality control in that it encompasses the total organization, uses quality control methods, and

W. Edwards Deming

W. Edwards Deming was decorated by the Emperor of Japan with the Second Order Medal of the Sacred Treasure in 1960 for his decade of contributions to Japanese production, and the Japanese created the annual Deming Prize in his honor for recognition of achievements in producing a quality product. Dr. Deming was a member of the International Statistical Institute and was elected to the National Academy of Engineering.

---

[3]Glossary of Statistical Terms, Quality Press 1996.
[4]The American Society for Quality (ASQ) maintains that the term *TQM* was initially used by the U.S. Naval Air Systems Command in 1984 to describe the management approach to quality used in Japan because they did not like the term Total Quality Control.

focuses on the leadership provided by management to ensure long-term success, by focusing on customer satisfaction. It is a broad approach that seeks to improve all areas of the business to better satisfy the customer. The philosophy of TQM plays a central role in the Criteria for Performance Excellence, published in 1988, and the Baldrige National Quality Program (BNQP) that provides benchmarks for quality for organizations today.

Six Sigma® is another business improvement approach that focuses more on the identification and elimination of defects or special-cause variation in business processes. Six Sigma was developed at Motorola during the 1980s but was picked up, expanded, and spread to other industries by General Electric and Allied Signal. Like other quality philosophies, the basis for the Six Sigma approach and philosophy was the early work of Shewhart, Deming, and others who furthered their efforts in the 1970s and 1980s.

All control charts are based on the idea that the process should be monitored to catch individual items or batches that are out of control. The core idea of Six Sigma is to reduce variation in the process to the point that inspection is no longer necessary. If the standard deviation can be made small enough so that the specification limits defining what it means for a part to be out of control are 4½ standard deviations from the mean, then the probability of an out-of-control observation is only about 6 in 1,000,000. In real-life processes, the mean of the process can shift somewhat as well. To account for that the developers of Six Sigma added an allowance of a 1½ standard deviation (sigma) shift. In this case, to achieve the 6 in 1,000,000 probability, the standard deviation has to be so small that 6 standard deviations are still within the control limit. This corresponds to a C_{pk} value of 2.0. At this point, it is no longer necessary (in theory) to monitor the process with control charts for inspection because the probability of being out of control is so small. Although this was the original idea of Six Sigma, it has become a much broader philosophy and approach to quality as practiced by large firms such as the General Electric Company. There is a hierarchy of experts (known as Black Belts) who, after being trained in the Six Sigma philosophy, act as internal quality consultants on a wide variety of quality issues.

ETHICS IN ACTION

Trax, one of the leading manufacturers of bicycles in the United States, is interested in expanding its line to include high-end road bikes. One of the features of high-end bikes, and one that avid cyclists pay top dollar for, is the use of super-light carbon fiber frames. Trax is currently in the process of selecting a supplier for these frames. Potential suppliers were asked to provide reports that included statistical process control (SPC) and capability data on their carbon fiber frame production processes.

Trax had specified the weight for these frames to be between 2 and 3 pounds with a target mean of 2.5 pounds. John Dickinson, Vice President of Operations, was in charge of summarizing the information contained in these reports to present at an upcoming senior management meeting at which a final decision on a supplier would be made.

As he reviewed the reports, he noticed that one supplier, DBS, could provide the frames at a much lower cost than its competitors. Eager to save the company money, he carefully considered this supplier's SPC and process capability data. John was pleased with their $\overline{X}$ and R charts for weight that indicated the process was stable (in statistical control). He was also pleased to be able to verify from these charts that their reported process standard deviation is only 0.1 pounds and that the C_p index of 1.67 indicates that they would be able to easily meet Trax's weight requirement. While he did notice that the process mean was a bit off target (at 2.8 rather than 2.5 pounds), he decided that the significant cost savings that Trax would realize by choosing this supplier outweighed any potential negative consequences of a shifted process mean. John decided that he would present only cost data and the C_p index for the suppliers under consideration, and conclude his presentation at the senior management meeting with a recommendation that Trax choose DBS as its supplier of carbon frames. He believed that the team would be quite impressed with his cost-saving recommendation.

- Identify the ethical dilemma in this scenario.

- What are the undesirable consequences?

- Propose an ethical solution that considers the welfare of all stakeholders.

WHAT HAVE WE LEARNED?

Learning Objectives

Understand the principles of quality control.

- A process is in control if the aspects being followed stay within the control limits established for them.
- When a process drifts out of control, it is important to recognize the fact so that adjustments can be made promptly. But we hope to avoid making too many false alarms, so a balance must be found.

Use run charts to track individual observations.

- A level shift flags a sudden change. A trend is a more gradual change.
- The ability of a chart to detect shifts is described by its operating characteristics (OC) curve.
- The Western Electric Handbook specified several rules for deciding when a process is out of control.

Use $\overline{X}$, R, and S charts to track a process by plotting the means, and ranges or standard deviations of small samples drawn from the process.

- The control limits are often based on estimated standard deviations and means.
- The S chart, which uses the standard deviations of the samples rather than their ranges is more appropriate than the R chart used when the samples are moderately large.

Understand the basic steps in creating an out-of-control action plan (OCAP).

- A cause-and-effect diagram helps organize possible causes and prioritize them for further analysis.
- It may be necessary to perform experiments to determine the cause of the problem.
- Once a cause is identified, process inputs can be adjusted to drive the process back into control.
- The monitoring process can then be restarted.

Use p charts and c charts to track processes that have categorical measurements.

- A p chart tracks proportions using control limits based on the standard deviation of a proportion.
- A c chart tracks the number of defective items in a process.

Understand the basic philosophies of quality control, such as Total Quality Management (TQM) and Six Sigma®, and how they are applied to improve business performance and quality.

Terms

Average run length (ARL)	The in-control ARL is the average time between false alarms, calculated by taking the reciprocal of the false alarm probability. The out-of-control ARL is the average number of runs until a signal is detected. It depends on the state of the process while out of control.
c chart	A control chart that displays the counts, or number, of occurrences of defectives (or nondefectives if rare) in samples taken from a process over time.
C_p	A process capability index that measures the ratio of the specification limit range to 6 times the standard deviation of the process without taking into consideration possible drift of the process: $$C_p = \frac{USL - LSL}{6\sigma}$$
C_{pk}	A process capability index that measures what the process is capable of producing, estimated by: $$\hat{C}_{pk} = \min\left[\frac{USL - \hat{\mu}}{3\hat{\sigma}}, \frac{\hat{\mu} - LSL}{3\hat{\sigma}}\right]$$
Common-cause variation	Variation characterized by apparent random fluctuations around an average level within specified limits called control limits.
Control chart or Shewhart chart	A graph that displays variation by plotting individual measurements or sample statistics taken from a process over time, sometimes referred to as a Shewhart chart.
Control limits	Horizontal lines drawn on a control chart. Various rules are used to determine when a process is out of control depending on the specific control chart.
Dichotomous variable	A categorical variable that has only two possible outcomes such as success or failure. Also called a yes/no variable.

False alarm	A Type I error indicating that the process is out of control, when in actuality, it was due only to common-cause variation.
Level shift	A sudden and sustained shift in the mean of the measurements being monitored.
Operating-characteristic (OC) curve	A chart that shows the probability of failing to see a process shift (a Type II error) plotted against the size of the shift (in standard deviation units).
Out of control	The presence of special-cause variation in a process.
Out-of-control Action Plan (OCAP)	A set of instructions to follow for well-established processes indicating what action to take following an out-of-control signal.
p chart	A control chart that displays the proportion of defectives (or nondefectives) in samples taken from a process over time.
Process Capability Study	A study that compares the variability of the process to the specification limits imposed on the process by external concerns. Two of the most common process capability indices are C_p and C_{pk}.
R chart	A control chart that plots the ranges of samples taken from a process over time.
Run chart	A control chart that displays individual measurements from a process taken over time.
S chart	A control chart that plots the standard deviations of samples drawn from a process. It may be preferred to the R chart when the samples are relatively large (10 or more).
Six Sigma®	A quality control philosophy based on reducing variation to the point where inspection sampling is no longer necessary. The philosophy's name comes from the fact that if specification limits (plus possible drift) are 6 standard deviations from the control center line, the chances of an out-of-control part are negligible.
Special-cause variation	Causes of variation that are not intrinsic to the process and thus whose presence is important to detect.
Specification limits	Limits above (and/or below) which a measurement should not lie, imposed by external considerations.
Statistical process control (SPC)	The examination of variation in a process over time to identify sources of variation.
Total quality management	Extends the theory of quality control to include the total organization and the leadership of management.
Trend	The gradual shift of a process mean.
$\overline{X}$ or x-bar chart	Control chart that displays the averages of samples taken from a process over time.

TECHNOLOGY HELP: Quality Control Charts

EXCEL

Excel does not offer quality control charts. A number of third-party add-ins and templates are available.

XLSTAT

To implement control charts for desired bounds:

- From the XLStat tab, choose the **XLStat-SPC** toolbar.
- Select either **Subgroup charts** (for x-bar and r charts) or **Attribute charts** (for p and c charts).
- Select the desired chart from the **Mode** tab in the dialog box.
- Under the General tab, type the data range into the **Data** field.

If your data have sampled values in rows for each sample, choose the **Data Format Columns**.

- In the **Options** tab, you can type in your UCL and LCL directly, but if you leave these fields blank, XLStat will compute these for you.

- If you have a specific value for the mean, type it in. Under the **Estimation** tab, choose **R bar** as the **method for sigma**.

JMP

From the **Analyze** menu select the **Quality and Process** submenu. There you will find a variety of control charts and quality control analysis methods.

MINITAB

From the **Stat** menu, select the **Control Charts** submenu. There you will find an additional level of submenus offering Variables Charts for Subgroups, Variables Charts for Individuals, Attributes charts, and Time Weighted charts. Standard control chart types are found within these submenus.

SPSS

From the **Analyze** menu, select the **Quality Control** submenu. Selecting **Control Charts** from that submenu brings up a dialog box from which you can select the chart type and specify other details.

Brief **Case**

Laptop Touchpad Quality

Consumers always seem to want thinner and lighter electronic products, and computer laptops are no exception. One of the challenges of producing extremely thin and light laptops is the manufacturing of the touch pads. In particular, touch pads are difficult to align. A common complaint is that one corner is higher or lower than another, resulting in what is known as "tilting." Tilting makes navigation difficult, so touch pad manufacturers have strict limits on the amount of tilting that they will allow in a pad.

A company producing touch pads will want to ensure that the pads are flat to within a certain acceptable tolerance. One possible measure is the total deviation from flatness as measured by the maximum difference in height between any two corners (in mm). In the data file **QC Control** you will find this flatness measure for 250 touch screens produced during a period that was judged to be in control.

Using the mean and standard deviation from this control period, examine the next 150 samples of 5 pads (in the data file **QC Production**). Using various quality control rules and appropriate graphs, do you think the process is still in control? Explain.

Instead of samples of size 5 suppose they had used a run chart on the individual pads. Would your answer change? Explain.

Suppose the engineers establish 14 mm as the maximum flatness deviation they will tolerate and want to use that as an upper specification limit. Does your answer change now? Explain.

A qualitative measure is clarity of the pad. Batches of 100 pads are produced and defects are counted where defect is defined as a pad that does not pass the clarity test. From a period that was deemed to be in control, the mean number of defects per 100 was 0.5. Using this mean, determine whether the process stayed in control for the next 50 batches (**QC Clarity**).

EXERCISES

SECTION 21.1

1. A producer of beverage containers wants to ensure that a liquid at 90°C will lose no more than 4°C after 30 minutes. Containers are selected at random and subjected to testing. Historical data shows the standard deviation to be 0.2°C. The quality control team has set 3.5 and 4.5°C as the specification limits. Here are the data from the last 12 containers tested:

Container #	Temperature Loss (°C)	Container #	Temperature Loss (°C)
1	3.89	7	4.22
2	3.71	8	4.02
3	4.14	9	4.48
4	4.12	10	3.93
5	3.74	11	3.87
6	3.99	12	3.94

a) Make a control chart of these data using the specification limits given.
b) Does the process seem to be in control?
c) What is the value of C_p for the process?
d) Given this value of C_p, what recommendations might you make to the quality control team?

2. A computer screen manufacturing process must produce screens of uniform size. In particular, for a new tablet, the screen should be 10.1 inches long. The engineers have set 10.16 and 10.04 as the upper and lower specifications on screen length. If the actual process standard deviation is 0.01 inches,

a) What is the value of C_p for the process?
b) What might you recommend to the engineers given this value of C_p?

SECTION 21.2

3. For the data in Exercise 1, instead of the specification limits,

a) Use the historical standard deviation to set up 1, 2, and 3σ limits and draw the control chart.
b) Are any points outside the 3σ limits on either side?
c) Are two of three consecutive points outside of 2σ on either side?
d) Are four out of five consecutive points outside of 1σ on either side?
e) Are there eight points in a row on the same side of the mean?
f) Are any six points in a row increasing (or decreasing)?
g) Are any fourteen points in a row alternatively increasing and decreasing?
h) Based on your answers to parts b–g, what do you conclude?

4. For the data in Exercise 1, suppose the historical standard deviation had been 0.1°C instead of 0.2°C. How would that change your answers to the questions in Exercise 3?

SECTION 21.3

5. A process to make dental floss produces spools with a desired mean length of 91.4 m (100 yds). The historical standard deviation is 1 cm (0.01 m). If samples of size 5 are taken and measured,

a) What is the standard deviation of the sample mean?
b) How long (or short) would a sample mean have to be to fall outside the 3σ limit?
c) How would the answers to parts a and b change if the sample were of size 10?

6. As in Exercise 5, a process to make dental floss produces spools with a desired mean length of 91.4 m (100 yds). The historical standard deviation is 1 cm (0.01 m). If samples of size 5 are taken and measured,

a) What is the center line for the R chart?
b) What is the standard deviation of the sample range?
c) How large (or small) would the sample range have to be to fall outside the 3σ limit?

SECTION 21.5

7. One of the ways in which the dental floss discussed in Exercise 5 can fail is if it snaps when pulled with a certain tension. Historically, only 2% of the tested floss snaps. Suppose boxes of size 50 are selected at random to be tested.

a) What is the standard deviation for the sample proportion from a box of 50?
b) What are the upper and lower 3σ control limits?
c) How many packages in a box of 50 would have to fail for a process to be declared out of control using the 3σ control limits?

8. Rather than use the proportion of packages that contain defective floss, another quality control inspector simply counts the number of packages. If historically, only 1 package out of 50 is defective,

a) What is the standard deviation of the number of defective packages?
b) What are the upper and lower 3σ control limits on the number of defectives?
c) How does the upper limit compare to the upper limit in Exercise 7, part c?

CHAPTER EXERCISES

9. Super Glue®. Cyanoacrylates, the generic name for several compounds with strong adhesive properties, were invented during WWII during experiments to make a special extra-clear plastic suitable for gun sights. They didn't work for gun sights, however, because they stuck to everything. They were first commercialized by the Eastman Kodak company in the 1950s and are now sold under the names Super Glue and Krazy® Glue. They are often sold in small quantities, typically 2-oz. tubes. The manufacturers want to ensure that the same quantity of glue goes into each tube so they monitored the process from the past three weeks (when there were no production problems) and calculate the mean and standard deviation weight from 50 tubes. If they use those quantities to calculate future limits for quality control monitoring, are they constructing control or specification limits? Explain.

10. MLB®. Major League Baseball (MLB) requires that a ball used in a major league game weigh between 5 and 5.25 oz. (www.MLB.com). Rawlings® is the official supplier of baseballs for MLB. In their production process, do they treat 5 and 5.25 oz. as control or specification limits? Explain.

11. Pole vault. Pole vault technology has evolved considerably since the times of the ancient Greeks and even more recently as new materials have found their way into pole manufacturing. There are currently no regulations on the composition of poles although for safety reasons, there are restrictions on the amount of bend depending on the vaulter's weight. On the other hand, safety considerations have led to the U.S. National High School Federation (NHSF) to require that high school vault landing pads must be no less than 6.0 m wide and 6.15 m long. Should the manufacturers of landing pads treat these as specification or control limits? Explain.

12. Milk production. Whether pasteurized or raw, both the European Economic Council (EEC) and the U.S. Food and Drug Administration (USFDA) require that milk sold to consumers contain no more than 10 coliform bacteria per mL of milk (www.cdfa.ca.gov). Should dairies take this as a control or specification limit when applying quality control to milk production? Explain.

13. Observatories. The two Gemini observatories (www .gemini.edu) were built and are operated by a partnership of seven countries including the United States, United Kingdom, Canada, Chile, Australia, Brazil, and Argentina. Astronomers in each of these countries are able to apply for time on the telescopes for scientific research. Gemini sets strict technical requirements on many aspects of the filters used on the telescope including a strict requirement that they be extremely flat—their total deviation from absolute flatness must be no more than 30 nm as measured by the root mean square deviation. How should filter manufacturers view this requirement, as a control or specification limit? Explain.

14. DVD production. Plastic covers for DVDs must be manufactured with enough precision so that a DVD can properly fit into the cover. Specifically, the diameter of the central plastic piece over which the DVD is placed must not vary more than a certain amount. A manufacturer has been producing DVD covers for several months and has had no complaints from its customers. It decides to use the past 2 months of data to estimate the mean and standard deviation of the process. Are the limits for quality monitoring based on these quantities control or specification limits? Explain.

15. Roulette. An observer at the roulette wheel in Monte Carlo notices that there seems to be no pattern to the numbers that come up during an entire evening. Is this an example of special- or common-cause variation? Explain.

16. Pennsylvania lottery. In 1980, millions of viewers watched as the number 666 was drawn for the Pick 3 Pennsylvania lottery. Although as likely as any other number, lottery authorities and local bookmakers became suspicious when they noticed that a large number of tickets were purchased for the eight numbers 444, 446, 464, 466, 644, 646, 664, and 666. Soon, a handful of players came forward to claim approximately $1.8 million of the then-record $3.5 million payout. Officials eventually discovered that 8 of the 10 balls were weighted, giving them almost no chance to be selected in the drawing. Is this an example of special- or common-cause variation? Explain.

17. Out-of-control rules. Most control charts use three sigmas (standard deviations) to set the upper and lower control limits. For a run chart, what is the probability that an observation would fall beyond 3σ from the mean based on random chance variation alone? What assumptions do you have to make to answer this?

18. Out-of-control rules, part 2. Instead of one observation outside of 3σ from the mean as in Exercise 17, suppose a quality control engineer decides to use only the run chart rule that the system is out of control if 8 observations in a row lie on the same side of the mean. What is the probability that this would happen based on random chance variation alone? What assumptions do you have to make to answer this?

19. Basketballs. A company that makes basketballs has the motto: "Our basketballs are ready to play." Therefore, it is important to the company that the basketballs are inflated with the proper amount of air when shipped. Most basketballs are inflated to 7 to 9 pounds per square inch. From a set of calibration data, the following statistics were measured:

$$\overline{\overline{X}} = 8.05$$
$$\overline{R} = 0.65$$

Recently the company selected a random basketball from its production line at four different time periods over its normal production day. The results were recorded and listed in the following table.

	Shift			
	8:00–10:00 AM	**10:00 AM**	**Noon–2:00 PM**	**2:00–4:00**
Day 1	8.05	8.49	7.59	7.90
Day 2	8.16	7.62	7.71	7.90
Day 3	8.30	8.07	8.14	8.12
Day 4	7.55	8.82	8.12	8.18
Day 5	8.18	7.76	7.70	7.65
Day 6	7.88	7.90	7.99	7.62
Day 7	8.01	8.02	7.32	8.10
Day 8	8.32	7.89	8.62	7.89
Day 9	7.94	7.75	7.58	7.74
Day 10	7.38	7.47	7.93	7.73
Day 11	7.44	7.84	7.87	8.33
Day 12	8.30	8.04	7.94	8.09
Day 13	8.46	8.20	7.93	7.89
Day 14	8.10	8.38	8.08	7.80
Day 15	7.70	7.68	8.25	8.40
Day 16	8.32	7.98	7.65	8.32
Day 17	8.13	7.96	8.21	8.51
Day 18	7.69	8.07	7.55	8.26
Day 19	7.86	8.55	8.05	7.63
Day 20	7.97	8.08	7.89	7.97
Day 21	8.73	7.84	7.94	8.07
Day 22	8.14	7.56	7.97	7.86
Day 23	7.64	7.89	7.47	7.66
Day 24	8.33	7.87	7.89	7.62
Day 25	8.00	7.61	7.65	7.39
Day 26	7.31	8.66	7.71	7.29
Day 27	7.58	7.95	8.13	8.52
Day 28	7.91	8.53	7.86	7.96
Day 29	8.34	8.10	8.45	8.16
Day 30	8.04	8.25	7.13	8.12

a) Create an $\overline{X}$ chart based on the calibration data statistics for these 30 samples.
b) Create an R chart based on the calibration data statistics for these 30 samples.
c) Assuming that the process was in control during the calibration period, is the company's process for filling its basketball with the proper amount of air in control?

20. Rulers. A company that traditionally made rulers and yardsticks is setting up a manufacturing process to make metersticks. Obviously, accuracy is important for their new product. The company runs a 24-hour production process. Using a calibration set of data they found:

$$\overline{\overline{X}} = 1.000$$
$$\overline{R} = 0.0016$$

They took a sample of 3 metersticks each hour and recorded the results in the following table.

	Sample 1	Sample 2	Sample 3
Hour 1	0.9983	1.0007	1.0010
Hour 2	1.0005	1.0011	1.0014
Hour 3	1.0002	0.9995	0.9997
Hour 4	1.0004	1.0016	1.0007
Hour 5	1.0014	0.9994	1.0008
Hour 6	0.9990	0.9996	0.9984
Hour 7	1.0014	1.0010	1.0017
Hour 8	1.0017	1.0002	1.0002
Hour 9	1.0003	1.0008	0.9993
Hour 10	0.9998	1.0002	0.9992
Hour 11	0.9985	1.0002	1.0006
Hour 12	1.0003	1.0012	0.9994
Hour 13	0.9998	1.0013	0.9995
Hour 14	1.0000	0.9994	0.9992
Hour 15	1.0005	0.9999	1.0016
Hour 16	1.0019	1.0018	1.0010
Hour 17	0.9993	0.9994	0.9993
Hour 18	1.0020	1.0000	0.9978
Hour 19	1.0007	1.0005	0.9991
Hour 20	1.0009	1.0005	0.9999
Hour 21	1.0002	0.9998	1.0021
Hour 22	1.0019	0.9986	0.9996
Hour 23	1.0011	1.0003	0.9993
Hour 24	0.9993	1.0010	1.0001

a) Create an $\overline{X}$ chart based on the calibration data statistics for these 24 hourly samples.
b) Create an R chart based on the calibration data statistics for these 24 hourly samples.

c) Assuming that the process was in control during the calibration period, is the company's process for making accurate meter sticks out of control?

21. Graphite production. A graphite manufacturer makes long rolls of flexible graphite to be used to seal components in combustion engines. The specifications state that the mean strength should be 21.2 ounces per square yard with a standard deviation of 0.29. Further specifications state that no roll should have strength less than 20.2 or more than 22.2 ounces per square yard. If there is a defect in terms of the strength of the graphite rolls, the seal will not hold. After the roll is created, a beta scanner takes readings of the basis weight in ounces per square yard. The data is separated into 3 lanes with 20 scans in each lane. A sample consists of one roll from each lane. The results from 20 samples follow:

Sample	Lane 1	Lane 2	Lane 3
1	20.65	21.01	20.76
2	21.27	21.53	21.53
3	21.69	21.53	21.14
4	21.06	20.38	20.62
5	21.18	21.29	20.95
6	21.14	21.01	21.37
7	20.89	20.63	21.24
8	21.73	21.39	20.87
9	21.55	21.34	21.17
10	21.72	21.97	21.84
11	21.26	20.77	21.24
12	21.05	20.70	20.87
13	22.23	22.09	21.62
14	21.27	21.71	21.89
15	21.60	21.03	20.68
16	21.37	21.29	21.13
17	21.19	21.80	21.36
18	21.56	21.64	21.67
19	21.12	20.56	20.57
20	20.88	20.57	20.37

a) Using the given mean and standard deviation, create an $\overline{X}$ chart for these samples.
b) Using the given mean and standard deviation, create an R chart for these samples.
c) Is the company's process for making flexible graphite sheets out of control?
d) Do all the rolls meet the specification limits?

Sample	Lane 1	Lane 2	Lane 3	Lane 4	Lane 5	Lane 6	Lane 7	Lane 8	Lane 9	Lane 10
1	21.56	21.59	21.26	21.16	21.01	21.10	21.22	20.95	20.78	20.66
2	21.42	21.54	21.43	21.44	20.99	21.10	20.78	21.17	21.21	21.10
3	21.48	21.23	21.19	21.34	21.63	21.47	21.18	21.05	21.21	21.22
4	21.14	21.26	21.57	21.34	21.36	21.37	21.42	21.48	21.14	21.02
5	21.53	21.26	21.43	21.26	20.95	20.86	20.99	20.90	20.69	20.80
6	21.40	21.26	21.19	21.38	21.57	21.30	20.97	20.72	20.78	20.70
7	21.84	21.51	21.71	21.34	21.38	21.32	21.32	21.05	20.57	20.27
8	21.83	21.83	21.56	21.17	20.74	20.83	21.00	21.35	21.54	21.41
9	21.60	21.57	21.44	20.99	20.60	20.83	20.85	20.90	21.14	21.36
10	21.84	21.93	21.99	21.97	21.57	21.56	21.17	20.89	21.20	21.28
11	21.96	21.50	21.48	21.37	21.57	21.68	21.82	21.65	21.20	21.19
12	21.27	21.53	21.31	21.22	21.33	21.31	21.46	21.68	21.69	21.52
13	22.03	21.90	22.02	21.46	21.34	21.35	21.44	21.84	21.55	21.63
14	21.30	21.36	21.28	21.29	21.00	20.82	20.55	20.48	20.46	20.68
15	21.65	21.18	20.77	20.98	20.92	20.99	21.27	21.56	21.72	21.67
16	21.46	21.52	21.47	21.45	21.31	21.76	21.92	21.34	21.11	21.19
17	21.72	21.69	21.77	21.44	21.13	21.12	20.91	20.60	20.69	21.07
18	21.67	22.02	21.78	21.34	21.00	20.80	20.30	20.54	20.59	21.16
19	21.44	21.28	21.15	20.97	20.85	21.17	21.87	21.67	21.59	21.20
20	21.38	21.32	20.91	21.10	21.17	21.58	21.53	21.54	21.12	20.69
21	21.23	21.30	21.57	21.42	21.52	21.42	20.90	20.85	20.60	20.71
22	21.65	21.33	21.44	21.27	21.06	20.80	20.82	20.84	20.98	21.22
23	21.59	21.58	21.13	21.34	21.57	21.47	21.55	21.83	21.56	21.02
24	20.92	20.74	20.30	20.07	20.48	20.39	20.81	20.90	21.18	21.18
25	21.02	21.03	21.00	21.04	21.15	21.10	21.24	21.09	21.25	20.86

T 22. Graphite production, 10 lanes. The same graphite manufacturer from Exercise 21 uses an alternative process to make rolls. For this process the data are separated into 10 lanes—a sample consists of one roll from each lane. The results of 25 samples are shown in the table at the top of the page.

a) Using the same mean and standard deviation as given in Exercise 21, create an $\overline{X}$ chart for these samples.
b) Using the mean and standard deviation as in Exercise 21, create an R chart for these samples.
c) Is the company's process for making flexible graphite sheets in control?
d) Are all of these rolls within the specification limits?

T 23. Defect monitoring. The following data are from a production process that makes 250 units each hour. The data were collected over a normal 12-hour shift one day. The data are shown in the table at the right.

Using the first 10 hours as the calibration period,

a) Calculate the center line of the p chart.
b) Calculate the upper control limit of the p chart.
c) Calculate the lower control limit of the p chart.

d) Create a p chart for the samples from the second set of 10 hours.
e) Is this process out of control?

Hour	No. of Defects	Sample Size
1	17	250
2	15	250
3	12	250
4	20	250
5	13	250
6	12	250
7	19	250
8	14	250
9	14	250
10	18	250
11	17	250
12	16	250
13	19	250
14	22	250
15	18	250
16	13	250
17	23	250
18	17	250
19	22	250
20	19	250

T 24. Defect monitoring, second product. The following data are from a production process that makes approximately 250 units each hour. The data were collected over a normal 12-hour shift one day. Historical data shows the proportion of defects to be 6.21%. Either use technology to accommodate the different sample sizes, or use 250 as an approximation for all of them.

Hour	No. of Defects	Sample Size
1	13	241
2	18	265
3	17	256
4	14	249
5	20	221
6	19	276
7	12	244
8	15	261
9	12	259
10	17	243
11	14	237
12	16	257
13	18	252
14	19	260
15	17	245
16	20	255
17	19	262
18	14	244
19	22	270
20	18	254

Assuming the process was previously in control,

a) Calculate the center line.
b) Create a *p* chart for these samples.
c) Is this process out of control?

T 25. Computer chip manufacturing. MediaChip manufactures computer chips specifically for MP3 players. The process uses sophisticated lasers to imprint several hundred chips on a single silicon "wafer." While the process is completely automated and set in a clean room environment, a batch of chips can contain imperfections that render the chips useless. This results in significant cost overruns. MediaChip would like to use a control chart to monitor their manufacturing process. Presently, the production level is set to 250 wafers per day. The average number of defects that can be tolerated is 1.7 per day. The number of defective wafers was tracked and recorded in the following table.

Day	Defects	Day	Defects
1	1	11	3
2	1	12	3
3	2	13	2
4	0	14	2
5	2	15	1
6	2	16	2
7	2	17	1
8	3	18	2
9	2	19	2
10	2	20	1

a) Create a *c* chart.
b) Is MediaChip's manufacturing process in control?

T 26. Faulty pixels. In LCD screens, every attempt is made to make sure that all pixels illuminate when they receive a signal, but it is impossible to ensure that every pixel in a large screen will actually work. A screen is determined to be defective if more than 2 pixels fail to light. Every week 500 screens are randomly selected and a quality control team member counts the number of defective screens. Out of 500 screens, management would like an average of no more than 5 defective screens. The results for the last 50 weeks are shown in the following table.

Week	Defective Screens	Week	Defective Screens	Week	Defective Screens
1	5	18	4	35	6
2	6	19	4	36	6
3	4	20	4	37	7
4	5	21	3	38	3
5	1	22	3	39	8
6	7	23	5	40	5
7	1	24	3	41	7
8	4	25	7	42	5
9	3	26	10	43	5
10	4	27	5	44	5
11	4	28	11	45	5
12	6	29	2	46	8
13	4	30	3	47	3
14	3	31	2	48	6
15	4	32	5	49	4
16	1	33	11	50	4
17	4	34	9		

a) Create a *c* chart.
b) Is the number of defective screens out of control? Comment.

27. Patient complaints. The following data were collected from the number of patient complaints from a small medical service facility over a two-week period. The past year the average number of complaints was 4.57. The management team would like to use that as a baseline for monitoring.

Day	1	2	3	4	5	6	7	8	9	10	11	12	13	14
Complaints	3	6	1	2	12	5	7	0	4	6	3	5	2	8

Based on last year, using a *c* chart:

a) What is the center line?
b) Calculate the upper control limit.
c) Calculate the lower control limit.
d) Create the *c* chart for this two-week period.
e) Is this process out of control?

28. Patient forms. The medical facility in Exercise 27 also keeps track of the number of errors found when transcribing information from patient forms. Last year the average number of errors was 1.26 per day which the facility found acceptable. Here are the past two weeks' data:

Day	1	2	3	4	5	6	7	8	9	10	11	12	13	14
Errors	1	2	1	2	1	2	5	3	3	2	0	3	5	5

Based on last year, using a *c* chart:

a) What is the center line?
b) Calculate the upper control limit.
c) Calculate the lower control limit.
d) Create the *c* chart for this two-week period.
e) Is this process out of control?

29. Baseball circumferences. Baseballs used in the major leagues in the United States must adhere to strict standards. One such standard is that the circumference must be between 9 and 9.25 inches. One could look at this standard as a target circumference of 9.125 inches with a tolerance of $+/-0.125$ inches. These data (shown at the bottom of the page) were taken from a random sample of 50 baseballs from a large production batch. The actual circumference and deviation from the target circumference are listed.

Using the specification limits as the control limits,

a) Create a run chart for the baseballs' circumferences.
b) Is the process for making baseballs in terms of their circumference in control?
c) How many baseballs produced were out of spec?
d) When should the quality team have investigated the production process?

Sample	Circumference	Deviation	Sample	Circumference	Deviation
1	8.998	−0.127	26	9.121	−0.004
2	9.181	0.056	27	9.111	−0.014
3	9.147	0.022	28	9.130	0.005
4	9.182	0.057	29	9.116	−0.009
5	9.087	−0.038	30	9.035	−0.090
6	9.154	0.029	31	9.188	0.063
7	9.108	−0.017	32	9.092	−0.033
8	9.109	−0.016	33	9.078	−0.047
9	9.141	0.016	34	9.101	−0.024
10	9.093	−0.032	35	9.113	−0.012
11	9.142	0.017	36	9.087	−0.038
12	9.140	0.015	37	9.054	−0.071
13	9.125	0.000	38	9.177	0.052
14	9.175	0.050	39	9.058	−0.067
15	8.985	−0.140	40	9.179	0.054
16	9.119	−0.006	41	9.147	0.022
17	9.140	0.015	42	9.123	−0.002
18	9.109	−0.016	43	9.097	−0.028
19	9.190	0.065	44	9.108	−0.017
20	9.087	−0.038	45	9.214	0.089
21	9.046	−0.079	46	9.140	0.015
22	9.108	−0.017	47	9.151	0.026
23	9.188	0.063	48	9.041	−0.084
24	9.125	0.000	49	9.061	−0.064
25	9.114	−0.011	50	9.162	0.037

30. Baseball weights. Baseballs used in the major leagues in the United States must adhere to strict standards. One such standard is that the weight must be between 5 and 5.25 ounces. One could look at this standard as a target weight of 5.125 ounces with a tolerance of $+/-0.125$ ounces. The following data were taken from a random sample of 50 baseballs from a large production batch. The actual weight and deviation from the target weight are listed.

Using the specification limits as the control limits,

a) Create a run chart for the baseballs' weights.
b) Is the process for making baseballs in control?
c) How many baseballs produced were out of spec?
d) When should the quality team have investigated the production process?

Sample	Weight (oz.)	Deviation	Sample	Weight (oz.)	Deviation
1	5.060	−0.065	26	5.073	−0.052
2	5.014	−0.111	27	5.133	0.008
3	5.118	−0.007	28	5.075	−0.050
4	5.098	−0.027	29	4.971	−0.154
5	5.069	−0.056	30	5.121	−0.004
6	5.159	0.034	31	5.013	−0.112
7	5.099	−0.026	32	5.181	0.056
8	5.031	−0.094	33	5.151	0.026
9	5.067	−0.058	34	5.124	−0.001
10	5.122	−0.003	35	5.044	−0.081
11	5.243	0.118	36	5.054	−0.071
12	5.149	0.024	37	5.020	−0.105
13	5.124	−0.001	38	5.063	−0.062
14	5.077	−0.048	39	5.163	0.038
15	5.178	0.053	40	5.122	−0.003
16	5.165	0.040	41	5.127	0.002
17	5.156	0.031	42	5.016	−0.109
18	5.121	−0.004	43	5.132	0.007
19	5.056	−0.069	44	5.091	−0.034
20	5.127	0.002	45	5.165	0.040
21	5.100	−0.025	46	5.097	−0.028
22	5.057	−0.068	47	5.121	−0.004
23	5.173	0.048	48	5.165	0.040
24	5.160	0.035	49	5.185	0.060
25	5.126	0.001	50	5.173	0.048

22

Nonparametric Methods

i4cp

When Rensis Likert ("Lick-urt") (1903–1981) was studying for his PhD in Psychology, he developed a scale for recording opinions with 5 or 7 ordered categories, now known as a *Likert scale*, and demonstrated its value. Likert scales are now widely used, especially for measurements that are ordered information with no quantitative values or units.

Likert was a founder of the Institute for Social Research (ISR) at the University of Michigan, and directed the Institute from its founding in 1946 until 1970. The Institute specializes in research on organizations. While he was at ISR, Likert helped found the Human Resource Institute (HRI) to work with companies such as GE, GM, and IBM to develop human resource planning. The Institute developed metrics for measuring the value of human capital and return on investment in human capital—work called Human Resource Accounting.

In 2006, HRI was acquired by the Institute for Corporate Productivity (i4cp), currently the world's largest vendor-free network of corporations focused on improving workforce productivity. i4cp maintains a staff of more than 20 full-time analysts and researchers and runs an Executives-in-Residence program. i4cp performs and publishes surveys of organizations focused on Human Resource information.

Questions that survey opinion often present respondents with a choice of five or seven ordered alternatives. They'll ask something like "Thinking about your recent car rental experience, would you say that you were

Very satisfied
Satisfied
Neither satisfied nor dissatisfied
Dissatisfied
or
Very dissatisfied"

Data recorded on a *Likert scale* such as this can be quite useful, but it has one major disadvantage. It isn't quantitative. Specifically, although we can be reasonably sure that a response of "Satisfied" is more favorable than a response of "Neither," we can't tell whether the difference between "Very satisfied" and "Satisfied" is the same, in any sense, as the difference between "Dissatisfied" and "Very dissatisfied."

If, for example, we hope to anticipate which customers are likely to return or identify which of our locations lead to less customer satisfaction, we should be very cautious if we want to find a difference in means or compare boxplots.

In fact, we can be reasonably certain that there will be an occasional customer whose dissatisfaction with his experience will be quite extreme and (we hope) some whose joy with their rental experience exceeds all bounds. Our questionnaire can't record such extreme responses.

Another method, which can give a bit more discrimination, would be to ask customers to assign grades—A, A−, B+, and so on—to their rental experience, specifying that the grades can run from A+ (for extreme satisfaction) to F (for extreme dissatisfaction).

22.1   Ranks

Suppose we have such grades for 6 customers from one location and 5 from another location rating their car rental experience. They might look like this:

Airport	Main Street
C+	B
B−	C
A−	D−
D+	B+
A+	C+
B+	

Table 22.1 Customer grades for two car rental sites.

We can get a clearer understanding of our customers' opinions if we *rank* these values. To rank values, all we need to do is put them in order. It doesn't really matter whether we assign rank "1" to the lowest value and count up or assign rank "1" to the highest value and count down—but we should make clear which we choose. Of course, we can always rank any quantitative values, but ranks have the additional advantage that we can assign them even if we have no more than a clear ordering, as we do here.

Airport	Rank	Main Street	Rank
C+	4.5	B	7
B−	6	C	3
A−	10	D−	1
D+	2	B+	8.5
A+	11	C+	4.5
B+	8.5		

Table 22.2 Customer grades with their ranks.

We can assign rank 1 to the lowest grade—here a D−. If there are any ties, we simply give all the values that are tied the *average* rank they are at. In this example, there are two C+ grades and two B+ grades, so those get ranks of 4.5 (averaging 4 and 5) and 8.5, respectively.

To assign these ranks, all we did was to put all the grades in order:

D−	D+	C	C+	C+	B−	B	B+	B+	A−	A+
1	2	3	4.5	4.5	6	7	8.5	8.5	10	11

Table 22.3 All the grades in order. Red indicates the Main Street location.

Because they are "grades," they have no numeric value, but they do have a clear order. The ranks in Table 22.3 order all the grades from the worst (a D− assigned rank 1) to the best (an A+ assigned rank 11). Of course, we could have just as easily assigned the ranks in the opposite order; for our purposes it makes no difference.

Such a ranking can be used whenever we have data that can be placed in order. Of course, that includes data that have numeric values as well as data that tell us no more than the order.

22.2 The Wilcoxon Rank-Sum/ Mann-Whitney Statistic

The manager of the company wants to know whether satisfaction levels differ between these two locations. In formal terms, she wants to test a hypothesis:

H_0: The locations have the same typical satisfaction.

vs.

H_A: The locations differ in typical satisfaction.

How can we perform such a test? The key is that we'll give up an aspect of hypothesis testing that we've maintained for all the inference methods we've seen so far. In all other methods, a null hypothesis specified a parameter and a null value for that parameter. The parameter was a number that specified something about the distribution of values in a population. Thus, for example, we might hypothesize a value for a mean or for a difference between two means. The parameters would be the underlying population mean or the means of the two populations from which two samples had been drawn.

But with only grades, no parameters are available. Indeed, it might be hard to say just exactly what it would mean for customers to be more satisfied at one location compared to the other. If *all* the grades for one location were better than

Wilcoxon or Mann-Whitney?
Frank Wilcoxon first proposed this test to compare equal-size groups. H. B. Mann and D. R. Whitney extended it to work with groups of unequal size. Because it is more general, the Mann-Whitney name for the test is the one you are most likely to find in statistics software.

the grades for the other, we'd be pretty sure which was the better one. That would show up clearly when we ranked the grades together. And if the grades alternated from one location to the other when we put them all in order, we'd probably conclude that there wasn't much difference.

So we need a statistic that measures where the data stand between the extremes of clearly favoring one site and showing no difference between them.

We'll start by computing the sum of the ranks (called the *rank sums*) in each group. In general, we can call them T_1 and T_2, but it helps to name them. In the example, $T_{Airport} = 42$ and $T_{Main Street} = 24$.

The sum of all of the ranks for 11 customers, 1 to 11, is $1 + 2 + 3 + \cdots + 11 = 66$. There is a formula for this: The sum of the first n integers 1, 2, up to n is equal to $n(n + 1)/2$. So, $T_{Airport} + T_{Main Street} = 66$ and, in general, if you know one rank sum, the other is completely determined.

We don't need to compare rank sums with each other. The rank sum for one of the groups tells the whole story. So we can pick one rank sum and ask whether this is unusually big or small. The conventional choice is to pick the rank sum that has the smaller sample. That's the Main Street location in this example.

What do we know about this rank sum? It could be as small as $1 + 2 + 3 + 4 + 5 = 15$ or as big as $11 + 10 + 9 + 8 + 7 = 45$. You might guess that its expectation (under H_0) would be right in the middle of these two values—that is, equal to 30—and you'd be right. Under the null hypothesis that the two groups are drawn from the same population, the rankings in either sample are a random selection from all of the rankings, so each sample should, on average, receive its fair share of the ranks. The Main Street sample has 5 of the 11 grades, so its expected rank sum is 5/11 of 66, the sum of all the ranks. That's 30.

So we know that the rank sum of 24, which we have for the Main Street location, is a bit low. But to test the hypothesis we must determine whether it is unusually low. That is, if H_0 were true, how likely would it be to find a rank sum of 24 or less for a comparison like this? That probability would be a P-value because it gives the probability of observing the statistic value we have observed—or something more extreme—if the null hypothesis were true.

When we needed a P-value before, we relied on the Central Limit Theorem or a similar result to find the sampling distribution of our statistic when the underlying parameter took on the value in the null hypothesis. But now we have no parameter and no distribution. Methods that work without estimating a parameter are called **nonparametric**. Those that don't rely on a sampling distribution are called **distribution-free**.

But the lack of a sampling distribution is no problem. When dealing with ranks rather than with quantitative values, there are only so many possibilities. In particular, we can consider *all possible* rankings. Under the null hypothesis, each of them is equally likely. So we can calculate what fraction of them would give rank sums less than 24. Fortunately, the "we" here is the computer, which does the work for us. The results are in Table W1 in Appendix B. The "W" is because this test is called the **Wilcoxon rank-sum** test or the **Mann-Whitney** test. The table gives critical values for the rank sum of the sample with fewer observations. The rank sum for the smaller sample here is 24. From the table, for samples of size 5 and 6, the closest value to 24 is 20 and the probability beyond that is 0.05. The manager has chosen a two-sided alternative hypothesis, so we'll double that value and conclude that the probability of a difference this great is more than 0.10. We wouldn't reject the null hypothesis, so we can't conclude that there's a significant difference in customer satisfaction between these two sites.

Using the Central Limit Theorem for Larger Groups

Table W1 only goes as far as groups of 10. What can we do for larger groups? The Central Limit Theorem comes to the rescue. We know from the CLT that means tend to be normally distributed as the sample size grows, and that this happens more quickly for well-behaved, unimodal population distributions with no skewness or outliers. If a mean has a Normal sampling distribution, then so does the sum of the values before dividing by n. (After all, n is a constant and can't change the distribution.) So when we add up the ranks, that rank sum will tend toward a Normal sampling distribution as the number of ranks in the sum grows. And we know that the ranks can't be badly distributed. After all, under the null hypothesis, they are Uniformly distributed, so there are no outliers or long tails. A sum of even 10 ranks has a sampling distribution that is close enough to Normal for our purposes. All we need to know is the mean and standard deviation, and we can find those easily:

For groups 1 and 2, with corresponding rank sums, T_1 and T_2,

$$E(T_i) = n_i(n_1 + n_2 + 1)/2 \text{ and } Var(T_i) = n_1 n_2(n_1 + n_2 + 1)/12 \; [i = 1 \text{ or } 2]$$

So we can find a P-value directly from the Normal tables (or with the 68–95–99.7 Rule).

When to Use the Wilcoxon/Mann-Whitney Test

The Wilcoxon test applies to situations, such as the customer-provided grades in our example, in which we can't use means. (The Mann-Whitney version is the version that is appropriate when the groups differ in size.) Data consisting only of grades or ordered categories is one example. We might also choose to replace numeric values with their ranks, for example, because we feared that there may be extreme outliers in the data.

These tests make no assumptions about the distribution of the data or the errors. That frees us from checking the corresponding assumptions. But what do we pay for these advantages? Statisticians evaluate statistical methods in terms of their *power*; the ability of the test to reject a false null hypothesis. When it is possible to perform both a parametric and a nonparametric test (because we have quantitative measurements) reducing the data to ranks and using the Wilcoxon/Mann-Whitney test will have about 95% of the power of a corresponding two-sample t-test. And, as we have seen, often outliers are interesting in their own right. An analysis that simply ignores them may miss an important fact or instance.

Assumptions and Conditions

Nonparametric methods require no assumptions about distributions. However, we still have some assumptions about the structure of the data:

Independence Assumption. The data values are mutually independent. Appropriate randomization in data collection (checked with the **Randomization Condition**) is one way to accomplish this.

Independent Groups Assumption. The two groups must be independent of each other.

The hypotheses may seem kind of vague. But it's a feature of the method that it doesn't test properties of any population parameter. That's what makes it a *nonparametric* method.

Wilcoxon Rank-Sum/Mann-Whitney Test

When the Assumptions are satisfied, we can test:

H_0: the two samples are from the same distribution

vs.

H_A: one distribution is shifted in location higher or lower than the other.

Calculate T = the rank sum for the smaller sample. Then, estimate the P-value using tables of critical values or the normal approximation, if either sample size is off the table.

FOR EXAMPLE   Comparing two groups

QUESTION   In Section 16.7 we saw data on commercial properties in a large U.S. city. One variable available for those properties is a "quality" ranking into one of 6 categories, with 1 as the "best" and 6 as the "worst." A realtor wanted to know how that quality index related to the "extras" available such as food service on site, an atrium, or a fitness center. He grouped the properties into two categories: those that had no more than one of these extras and those that had more than one. How can he use a nonparametric method to compare the quality rankings of the two groups?

ANSWER   To compare the quality rankings for these two groups he used the Mann-Whitney extension of the Wilcoxon rank-sum test. (Most statistics software packages offer Mann-Whitney rather than Wilcoxon because it doesn't require equal-size groups and is therefore more general.) The Minitab results are typical of those from a statistics package:

```
W = 21642.5
Test of Extras = NoExtras vs Extras not = NoExtras is
significant at 0.0008
The test is significant at 0.0003 (adjusted for ties)
```

The realtor concluded that these extras might be an effective quick method of judging the quality of commercial properties in this city.

GUIDED EXAMPLE   Buying from a Friend

In Chapter 13 we first looked at data from a study that examined how friendship might affect bargaining and negotiation. The researcher set up an experiment to test whether there is an effect. Subjects were randomly assigned to imagine purchasing a camera from a friend, and others were assigned to imagine purchasing the same camera from a stranger. They were asked to make a single bid. The table shows their bids. The two groups were separated and were blind to the purpose of the study. The question of interest is whether there is a difference between what people tend to offer to a friend and what they would offer to a stranger.

Price Offered for a Used Camera ($)	
Buying from a Friend	**Buying from a Stranger**
275	260
300	250
260	175
300	130
255	200
275	225
290	240
300	

| | PLAN | Setup State the objectives.

Check the assumptions and conditions. | We want to test whether people tend to offer a different amount to a friend than they would offer to a stranger when making a purchase offer.

The subjects in this experiment were randomly assigned individually to either imagine dealing with a friend or with a stranger. That randomization allows us to assume both independence among the subjects and between the two groups. That's the only assumption we'll need to perform a non-parametric test.

The null hypothesis is that the two groups are the same—that there's no difference in offering price between those negotiating with a friend and those negotiating with a stranger. |

| DO | Mechanics Rank the data from the two groups together. | We start by ranking all the bids as a single group. We give average ranks to ties: |

Data	130	175	200	225	240	250	255	260	260	275	275	290	300	300	300
Rank	1	2	3	4	5	6	7	8.5	8.5	10.5	10.5	12	14	14	14
Group	S	S	S	S	S	S	F	S	F	F	F	F	F	F	F

Now we add up the ranks of the smaller (Strangers) group:
$$1 + 2 + 3 + 4 + 5 + 6 + 8.5 = 29.5$$

From Table W1, the critical value for a two-sided test at $\alpha = 0.05$ and groups of 7 and 8 is 39. Our observed rank sum is less than this so we can reject the null hypothesis and conclude that there is, in fact, a difference in the two groups.

| REPORT | Conclusion State the conclusion in the context of the problem. | MEMO

Re: Friendship in negotiations

We investigated whether friendship has an influence on what negotiators are willing to bid for a mid-priced object—in our experiment, a camera. We analyzed data from a randomized single-blind experiment using a nonparametric Wilcoxon rank-sum test and found that there is a statistically significant difference. Negotiators appear to bid more when buying from a friend than when buying from a stranger. |

22.3 Kruskal-Wallace Test

Suppose now that we have more than two independent groups to compare. We need a generalization of the Wilcoxon test. For example, we may have customer grades for *three* car rental locations. Now the null hypothesis is that all three sites are rated equally. The alternative hypothesis is that they aren't—but without specifying exactly how they might differ. These hypotheses are similar to those in the one-way Analysis of Variance (see Chapter 20). The manager wants to know of any differences among these locations. The **Kruskal-Wallace** test provides a nonparametric method. First, we rank all of the data values together, assigning average ranks to tied values. We then sum up these ranks for each group and calculate

Site 1	Site 2	Site 3
D	C	C
D	D	A
C	B	C
D	B	B
C	C	A
C	D	C
C	C	D
C	C	B
B	B	D
C	C	A

$$H = \frac{12}{N(N+1)} \sum \frac{T_i^2}{n_i} - 3(N+1)$$

where the T_i are the rank sums for each group and N is the *total* number of values.

The test says that we can reject the null hypothesis H_0: all populations are identical

$$\text{if } H > \chi^2_{k-1,\,\alpha}$$

where χ^2 denotes the chi-square distribution, and k is the number of groups we are comparing. The chi-square distribution is a large-sample approximation (like the use of Normal for the Wilcoxon rank-sum test). For very small samples, you may want to consult a table of critical values.[1]

FOR EXAMPLE   Comparing several groups

The realtor of the example on page 784 catalogued four features of interest to his health-oriented clientele (green construction, atrium, food service on site, and fitness center) in the commercial properties. Properties had between none and four of the features.

QUESTION   Did the overall quality measure provided for these properties reflect these differences?

ANSWER   The quality measures are just ordered categories with no units, so a Kruskal-Wallace test is appropriate. The Minitab results are:

```
Features  N     Median  Ave Rank     Z
0         69    4.000   176.9       3.86
1         70    3.000   145.0       0.17
2         91    3.000   136.7      -0.95
3         50    3.000   117.2      -2.48
4          6    2.000    64.2      -2.37
Overall  286            143.5

H = 22.50  DF = 4  P < 0.0001
H = 22.94  DF = 4  P < 0.0001  (adjusted for ties)
```

The realtor notes from the detailed output that having none of these features corresponds to much lower quality (recall that quality = 1 is top so a high number rank is poor quality), but that the difference between 3 and 4 features is slight.

GUIDED EXAMPLE   Customer Satisfaction

A car rental company wants to compare customer satisfaction at three of its rental sites. They have a simple survey that asks customers to grade them on an A to F scale when they return their cars. Are there differences among the three sites?

---

[1]You can find these on the Internet. For example, at faculty.virginia.edu/kruskal-wallis/

PLAN	**Setup** State the objectives of the study.	The objective is to compare customer satisfaction for all three sites. We'll test the following hypothesis: H_O : The centers of all groups are the same. H_A : At least one of the centers is different from the others. We have three groups. It is reasonable to assume that the customers at the three sites are mutually independent. That's all we need to perform a Kruskal-Wallace test.

DO Rank all the values together, assigning average ranks to values that are tied, just as we did before.

Order	Data	Rank	Order	Data	Rank
1	A	2.0	16	C	16.5
2	A	2.0	17	C	16.5
3	A	2.0	18	C	16.5
4	B	6.5	19	C	16.5
5	B	6.5	20	C	16.5
6	B	6.5	21	C	16.5
7	B	6.5	22	C	16.5
8	B	6.5	23	C	16.5
9	B	6.5	24	D	27.0
10	C	16.5	25	D	27.0
11	C	16.5	26	D	27.0
12	C	16.5	27	D	27.0
13	C	16.5	28	D	27.0
14	C	16.5	29	D	27.0
15	C	16.5	30	D	27.0

Sum the ranks within each group

Site 1	Rank	Site 2	Rank	Site 3	Rank
D	27.0	C	16.5	C	16.5
D	27.0	D	27.0	A	2.0
C	16.5	B	6.5	C	16.5
D	27.0	B	6.5	B	6.5
C	16.5	C	16.5	A	2.0
C	16.5	D	27.0	C	16.5
C	16.5	C	16.5	D	27.0
C	16.5	C	16.5	B	6.5
B	6.5	B	6.5	D	27.0
C	16.5	C	16.5	A	2.0
	186.5		156.0		122.5

(continued)

Calculate the corresponding test statistic H:

$$H = \frac{12}{N(N+1)} \sum \frac{T_i^2}{n_i} - 3(N+1)$$

Where N is the total number of observations from all samples, n_i are the individual sample sizes, and T_i is the sum of the ranks in the ith group.

The Kruskal-Wallis test rejects the null hypothesis when the value of H is large, yielding a small P-value.

$$H = \frac{12}{N(N+1)} \left(\frac{T_1^2}{n_1} + \frac{T_2^2}{n_2} + \frac{T_3^2}{n_3} \right) - 3(N+1)$$
$$= \frac{12}{30(30+1)} \left(\frac{186.5^2}{10} + \frac{156^2}{10} + \frac{122.5^2}{10} \right)$$
$$-3(30+1)$$
$$= 2.64$$

The critical value is approximately 5.99, so we can't reject the null hypothesis.

REPORT

MEMO

Re: Customer ratings

An examination of customer ratings from three rental sites did not reveal any significant difference in customer satisfaction.

22.4 Paired Data: The Wilcoxon Signed-Rank Test

Companies that devise tests for students (e.g., for college applications) and for professional certification have been looking to online testing as a way to increase efficiency, save money, and provide results to test takers more rapidly. But there is a natural concern about whether someone taking a test at a computer screen will achieve the same result as he or she would taking the test with pencil and paper.

A testing company devised an experiment to investigate the problem. Researchers randomly assigned subjects to take one of two tests (form A or form B) either electronically or with pencil and paper. Subjects then took the *other* test using the other method. The two forms had been designed to be equivalent in difficulty, but nevertheless, that equivalence was checked as part of the experiment. Our concern is whether subjects did equally well with each testing method. Table 22.4 on the next page gives the results.

We have two test scores for each subject. Clearly these are paired because they are two scores from the same subject. How can we tell whether there is a difference in methods? (Technically the test concerns the median of the differences).

The tests we've examined so far require that the groups being compared be mutually independent. What can we do when they are naturally paired? We saw paired data in Chapter 13, where we used methods based on Student's t. A nonparametric method suitable for paired data is the **Wilcoxon signed-rank test**.

First we find the pairwise difference for each subject. Then set aside any ties (zero differences) and, using the new count of cases, rank the absolute values of the differences. Under the null hypothesis that the two testing methods are the same, we'd expect these ranks to appear about equally between the groups. Sum up the ranks for the positive differences (T^+) and for all the negative differences (T^-). We can concentrate on the smaller of these two totals, and call it T. This is our test statistic. A table of critical values for the statistic will tell us if it is sufficiently small to reject the null hypothesis. With large numbers of pairs, a normal approximation for T is also possible.

For our example, $T^+ = 3 + 3 + 7.5 + 7.5 + 7.5 + 7.5 + 11 + 11 + 14 + 16 = 88$ and $T^- = 3 + 3 + 3 + 11 + 13 + 15 + 17 = 65$ so our test statistic is

Subject	Online	Paper	Difference
1	13	14	−1
2	13	10	3
3	8	16	−8
4	14	15	−1
5	16	17	−1
6	11	14	−3
7	12	9	3
8	12	12	0
9	16	16	0
10	14	7	7
11	13	8	5
12	13	11	2
13	17	15	2
14	13	11	2
15	14	13	1
16	9	9	0
17	9	15	−6
18	15	14	1
19	12	16	−4
20	10	8	2

Table 22.4 Test scores with two testing methods

$T = 65$. Consulting Table W2 in Appendix B, we see that critical values for $n = 17$ are all substantially less than 65, so we can't reject the null hypothesis.

Assumptions and Conditions: As with our previous consideration of paired data, the primary assumption is that the data are appropriately paired. You can't just match up values arbitrarily. On the other hand, if the data are paired, you should not use methods that assume independent groups. There's no condition to check here; you just have to think it through.

Because this is a nonparametric test, the only other assumption is that the differences are mutually independent.

FOR EXAMPLE   Paired data

The Lake County, Illinois, Health Department experimented with a flexible four-day work week. For a year, the department recorded the mileage driven by 11 field workers on an ordinary five-day work week. Then it changed to a flexible four-day work week and recorded mileage for another year.[2] Here are the data:

Name	5-Day Mileage	4-Day Mileage
Jeff	2798	2914
Betty	7724	6112
Roger	7505	6177
Tom	838	1102
Aimee	4592	3281
Greg	8107	4997
Larry G.	1228	1695
Tad	8718	6606
Larry M.	1097	1063
Leslie	8089	6392
Lee	3807	3362

QUESTION Do flexible schedules change the demand for resources?

ANSWER These data are clearly paired. And we have no particular reason to assume Normal distributions. We can use a Wilcoxon signed-rank test to compare the mileages. The results are:

H_0: Median(5-day mileage − 4-day mileage) = 0 vs
H_A: Median(5-day mileage − 4-day mileage) ≠ 0

$T^+ = 56$ and $T^- = 10$, so $T = 10$.

From Table W2, the critical value for $n = 11$, and $\alpha = 0.05$ is 11 and for $\alpha = 0.01$ is 7, so $P < 0.05$ but not < 0.01 (In fact, from technology we find $P = 0.0420$).

So based on this test we can conclude that there is a difference in mileage.

[2]Charles S. Catlin, "Four-day Work Week Improves Environment," *Journal of Environmental Health*, Denver, 59:7.

GUIDED EXAMPLE   Do Hormones Boost Profits?

"Hormones may boost profits" read the headline of science reporter Anne McIlroy's article in the Toronto *Globe & Mail* on April 15, 2008. Is this true? To examine the question, Canadian researcher John Coates took saliva samples in the morning, twice a day for eight days, from 17 men working on a London mid-size trading floor (trading a wide range of assets, with largest exposure to German interest rate futures), in June 2005, and classified each trader according to whether his testosterone level was high or low on that day (compared with the trader's median over the period). High testosterone days differed from trader to trader, and high days differed from low days on average by 25% in testosterone level. He also recorded the profits or losses (P&L) in pounds sterling of each trader during 11 A.M.–4 P.M. daily. (Coates JM, Herbert J. *PNAS* 2008;105:6167–6172. Copyright © National Academy of Sciences. Reproduced by the permission of National Academy of Sciences.)

PLAN	**Setup** State the objectives.	We want to perform a test to determine if there is evidence of a testosterone effect on traders' daily profits. For each trader, we have recorded a profit (or loss) average for his high-testosterone days (testosterone level above his own median) during this 8-day period in June 2005, and another profit average for his low-testosterone days during this 8-day period.

Check the assumptions and conditions.

Hypotheses State the null and alternative hypotheses.

H_O: There is no difference in the distribution of profits between high testosterone days and low testosterone days.

H_A: Profits tend to be either generally higher or generally lower on a trader's high testosterone days than on his low testosterone days.

Model Think about the assumptions and check any conditions.

The data are paired. The researcher took an average on both high and low testosterone days for the same trader, so each trader gives us paired responses.

It is reasonable to assume that the traders are independent of each other, although this is not a random sample of traders.

Coates provided the following data from his study. We've added the pairwise differences.

Trader	P&L Low 11 A.M. testosterone	P&L High 11 A.M. testosterone	Difference
1	127	−63	−190
2	113	725	612
3	−2	−5	−3
4	−292	1780	2072
5	−98	262	360
6	−1308	1401	2709
7	88	2092	2004
8	361	887	526
9	−700	2500	3200
10	143	82	−61
11	1448	1547	99

(continued)

Trader	P&L Low 11 A.M. testosterone	P&L High 11 A.M. testosterone	Difference
12	1625	7000	5375
13	−127	38	165
14	−2066	1941	4007
15	183	268	85
16	483	513	30
17	−115	−4	111

Select a method

The differences include some extraordinarily large values. A nonparametric method would be more appropriate for these data. We'll use a Wilcoxon signed-rank test.

DO

Mechanics Compute the difference for each trader (in the previous table). Throw out any zero differences.

n is the number of pairs = # of traders

List the differences in order of magnitude. Sum the ranks for the positive and negative differences. Clearly here the latter will be smaller, so we compute only that rank sum.

Here are the differences, in order by magnitude, with ranks shown underneath.

−3	30	−61	85	99	111	165	−190	360
1	2	3	4	5	6	7	8	9

526	612	2004	2072	2709	3200	4007	5375
10	11	12	13	14	15	16	17

Determine if T is smaller than its expectation under the null, by either using the table of exact critical values or technology.

The sum of the ranks for negative differences is $1 + 3 + 8 = 12$. The sum of the first four positive differences is already > 12, so $T = 12$. According to table W2, the critical value with $n = 17$ and $\alpha = 0.01$ is 23. Since $T < 23$, we know $P < 0.01$ (from technology $P = 0.0011$). We can therefore reject the null hypothesis and conclude that the median testosterone levels are different.

REPORT

Conclusion State the conclusion in the context of the problem.

MEMO

Re: Hormones and trading

We investigated whether testosterone levels have a measurable effect on the success of traders. We found that there was a statistically significant difference: when traders' testosterone levels were higher, they were more successful.

*22.5 Friedman Test for a Randomized Block Design

Chapter 20 discussed experimental design and the Analysis of Variance. There is a nonparametric alternative for ANOVA as well. Suppose that we have a randomized block design, with more than two treatments to compare. (If we had only two, we'd use methods for paired data.) We need a generalization of the Wilcoxon Signed Rank.

Micky Parker, the owner of *Mick's Comicks*, a store that deals in collector's comic books and memorabilia, wondered what method to use to attract customers into his store. He decided to compare three methods:

- Coupons distributed on the street by a model dressed as a super hero
- A sale announced by a large sign in the window
- Music from movies based on comics played loud enough to be heard in the street

Micky reasons that customer traffic is different in the morning, in the afternoon, and in the evening, so he decides to block on time of day. On three weekdays, he randomly decides which method to use for each time of day. After three days, his customer counts look like the table at left (top).

The method we'll use for these data is the Friedman test. Again, we need to convert to ranks, but now we *rank separately within each block*, yielding the ranks (in parentheses) shown in the the table at left (bottom).

We wish to test for significant variation among the treatment rank sums. The Friedman statistic is:

$$F = \frac{12}{bk(k+1)}\sum T_i^2 - 3b(k+1)$$

where T_i are the rank sums for the various treatments (6,9,3 in our example), b is the number of blocks, and k is the number of treatments.

We reject H_0: all treatments are identical, at approximate significance level α if:

$$F > \chi^2_{k-1,\,\alpha}$$

This is an approximate result. There are tables of exact critical values available for small sample sizes, but this approximation works well for most cases.

	Treatment		
Block	**Coupons**	**Sale**	**Music**
Morning	9	12	2
Afternoon	5	10	4
Evening	7	11	1

	Treatment		
Block	**Coupons**	**Sale**	**Music**
Morning	9(2)	12(3)	2(1)
Afternoon	5(2)	10(3)	4(1)
Evening	7(2)	11(3)	1(1)
Rank Sums	6	9	3

22.6   Kendall's Tau: Measuring Monotonicity

In the chapters on correlation and regression, we used a linear model to describe the relationship between two quantitative variables. Sometimes, however, we are primarily concerned with the *direction* of the association, but not particularly worried about whether the form of the relationship is linear. In other situations, we may have data measured on a Likert scale or other data that gives only information about order and not about quantitative value.

A restaurant owner might wonder whether adding more salt really does make fried potatoes taste better. It may be impossible to measure "how much better," but it is certainly possible to ask customers which of several plates of fries they like best and least.

A consistent trend is called *monotone*. Of course, real data are rarely so simple as to line up in a perfect monotone trend. But we can measure how close our data are to overall monotonicity. The statistic we use is **Kendall's τ** (that's a Greek tau).

Kendall's tau measures monotonicity directly. For each pair of points in a scatterplot, it records only whether the slope of a line between those two points is positive, negative, or zero. (If the points have the same *x*-value, the slope between them is ignored.) In a monotone plot, these pairwise slopes would all be positive or all be negative. In a nonmonotone plot, the counts of positive and negative slopes will tend to balance out. Tau (often written with the Greek letter τ) is the difference between the number of positive slopes and the number of negative slopes divided by the total number of slopes between pairs.

Obviously, tau can take values between -1.0 and $+1.0$. If every pairwise slope is negative, then tau will equal -1.0, and the plot will show a single stream of

Maurice Kendall

Sir Maurice Kendall (1907–1983) was a prominent statistician, writer, and teacher. He made significant contributions to the study of randomness (developing tests for randomness that are still used), the theory of statistics, and rank-based statistics. He also served as director of the World Fertility Study, for which the United Nations awarded him their peace medal.

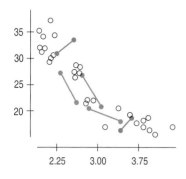

Figure 22.1   For each pair of points, Kendall's tau records whether the slope between them is positive (red), negative (blue), or zero.

A Monotonous Relationship?
You probably think of monotonous as *boring*. A monotone relationship shares the same root, but it's only the *sameness* that's important. A monotone relationship is one that increases or decreases consistently (but it doesn't have to be boring).

points trending consistently downward. If every pairwise slope is positive, then tau will equal +1.0, and the plot will show a single stream of points trending consistently upward. In a generally horizontal plot or one that goes up and then down, the counts of positive and negative slopes will balance out and tau will be near zero. For the example in Figure 22.1 the value of tau is −0.787.

Kendall's tau is easy to understand, but is not the kind of statistic that we calculate by hand. Usually, we let the computer do that work. You can get an idea of why by considering how to find Kendall's tau by hand. First, for every *pair* of points record whether it is *concordant*—that is, with a positive slope between the two points, or *discordant*—having a negative slope. If n_c is the number of concordant points, and n_d the number of discordant points, then

$$\tau = \frac{n_c - n_d}{\frac{1}{2}n(n-1)}$$

This is a simple formula, so why don't we typically find tau by hand? The denominator, $\frac{1}{2}n(n-1)$, is the number of pairs to check. That number can get very large for even modest size data sets.

FOR EXAMPLE **Estimating association for ordered categories**

In Chapters 16 (page 522 and later) and 18 (page 602 and later) we looked at data on diamond prices and quality. The methods of those chapters could only deal with color as a category. But diamond colors are ordered with D as the best and later letters labeling lower-quality colors, so it makes sense to ask whether prices change consistently with color quality. We can rank the colors, assigning rank 1 to color D, 2 to color E, and so on. Of course, these ranks have no measurement units, so a least squares regression would make no sense. But it is appropriate to use Kendall's tau to assess the association between *Price* and *Color rank*.

QUESTION   What is Kendall's tau for these data, and what does it mean?

ANSWER   Kendall's tau for these data is 0.175. It seems that lower-quality (later letters; higher rank) colors are associated with *higher* prices!

QUESTION   That doesn't make sense. How can we explain this apparent anomaly?

ANSWER   These diamonds are not all the same *Carat weight*. Perhaps larger diamonds of the best color are harder to find. If we restrict our analysis to diamonds that are 1.0 carat in weight, we find that Kendall's tau for the selected diamonds is −0.463. That indicates a strong association with "better" colors associated with higher prices.

22.7   Spearman's Rho

One of the problems we have seen with the correlation coefficient is that it is very sensitive to violations of the Linearity Condition. Both outliers and bends in the data make it impossible to interpret correlation. **Spearman's rho** (often denoted by the Greek letter ρ) can deal with both of these problems. Rho replaces the original data values with their ranks within each variable. That is, it replaces the lowest value in x by the number 1, the next lowest value by 2, and so on, until the highest value is assigned the value n. The same ranking method is applied to the y-variable. A scatterplot of the y-ranks against the x-ranks shows the same general trend as the original data, going up whenever the data went up and down whenever the data went down. If the original scatterplot shows a consistent but bent trend, however, the scatterplot of the ranks is likely to be more nearly linear. And if either variable has an extreme

Figure 22.2 Spearman's rho finds the correlation of the *ranks* of the two variables.

Charles Edward Spearman, FRS (1863–1945) was an English psychologist known for work in statistics, as a pioneer of factor analysis, and for Spearman's rank correlation coefficient. He also did fundamental work on measure of human intelligence.

outlying value, the ranking process keeps it from being extreme by just counting it as the highest or lowest value, ignoring how extreme it really is.

Spearman's rho is the correlation of the two rank variables. Because this is a correlation coefficient, it must be between −1.0 and 1.0.

Both Kendall's tau and Spearman's rho have advantages over the correlation coefficient *r*. For one, they can be used even when we know only the ranks. Also, they measure the consistency of the trend between the variables without insisting that the trend be linear.

They have the added advantage that they are not much affected by outliers. Spearman's rho limits the outlier to the value of its rank, and Kendall's tau cares only about the sign of each slope between points, not how steep it might be. Neither tau nor rho is changed at all by re-expressing variables by functions that don't alter the order of values (that is, by just the sort of functions we might use to straighten a scatterplot). But, unlike the correlation coefficient, neither statistic can be used as a base for more advanced or complex methods, so they tend to be specialized methods used when we care primarily about consistent trend between two variables.

FOR EXAMPLE   Estimating association when there are outliers

How are the prices of commercial properties related to the number of stories high they are? A scatterplot for the commercial properties in one city that are built with masonry construction looks like this:

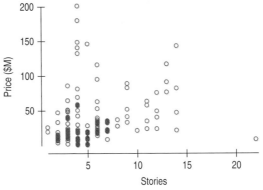

QUESTION   The linearity assumption is clearly not satisfied by these data, and there is one building of more than 20 stories with a low price that is likely to be influential. What is an appropriate way to summarize the relationship between *Price* and *Stories*?

ANSWER   The standard (Pearson) correlation for these data is 0.280, but it wouldn't be right to interpret it. The high leverage case on the right and the two particularly expensive buildings at the top of the plot are both likely to influence the value of the correlation. Both violate the linearity assumption. Spearman's rho is more appropriate because it is based on the ranks so it doesn't require an assumption of linearity and can deal with outliers in either direction. Spearman's rho for these properties is 0.467. That's probably a better assessment of association.

22.8   When Should You Use Nonparametric Methods?

Nonparametric methods such as those discussed in this chapter (there are others) are particularly valuable when your data contain only information about order. But they can also be valuable for quantitative data—especially when the quantitative variables violate one or more of our assumptions and conditions.

Translating quantitative values to ranks protects us from the influence of outliers (which simply become the "biggest one" without being extreme), from the effects of two or more modes in the data (because the ranks ignore modes), and from skewed distributions and nonlinear relationships. They "charge" for this service by being a bit less powerful than corresponding parametric methods when the assumptions and conditions of those methods *are* met. But when those assumptions are violated, nonparametric methods can be not only more powerful, but also more appropriate. It is unwise to use methods when their underlying assumptions are not met.

On the other hand, the choice of nonparametric methods should not be made to ignore or hide features of the data. For example, although nonparametric methods can protect us from the influence of an outlier, we know already that outliers often hold valuable information themselves. You should certainly examine any outliers even if you elect to then use a nonparametric method. Similarly, nonparametric methods can protect us from the effects of a bimodal variable (where parametric methods assumed a nearly Normal distribution). But if the data are bimodal, they may be trying to tell us that we have two fundamentally different sub-groups in the data. It would be wise not to ignore that information.

Although nonparametric methods are appropriate for skewed data and nonlinear relationships, it may be more effective to re-express one or more variables to improve symmetry and straighten relationships. (See Sections 3.11 and 4.11.) The resulting models using the re-expressed variables may be simpler, more useful, and have wider applicability.

Of course, statistics software makes it easy to try two or more approaches and compare the results. That is never a bad approach.

WHAT CAN GO WRONG?

- **Don't forget to check independence.** Nonparametric methods are free of many of the assumptions and conditions we check for other methods, but they are not entirely free of assumptions. The assumption that the cases are independent is especially important when P-values and critical values are determined by probability calculations based on the assumption that all orderings are equally likely.

- **Don't degrade your data unnecessarily.** If you have quantitative data that satisfy the assumptions and conditions of statistics methods such as *t*-tests, correlation, regression, and ANOVA, you are generally better off using those methods rather than the corresponding nonparametric methods. Working with the ranks rather than measurements inevitably throws away some information in return for protection from outliers and violations of other assumptions.

ETHICS IN ACTION

Admiral Oil & Gas Corporation, headquartered in Houston, is the most recognizable of the companies that moved into Pennsylvania to drill for gas from the Marcellus shale formation. While geologists suspected that this formation contained large reserves of natural gas, with some estimates indicating it is enough to satisfy U.S. consumption for 14 years, it was not cost effective to extract until the techniques of horizontal drilling and hydraulic fracturing were improved. The economic impact of gas drilling on the region is undeniable, with a substantial transfer of wealth to landowners (mostly dairy farmers), an increase in jobs related to the industry, and an influx of workers stimulating the housing and local retail markets.

Yet, there is strong opposition to developing this resource. Those against it are concerned about the harmful effects on the environment and public health from the release of naturally

(continued)

occurring radioactive material during the drilling process and the waste water from toxic fracturing. Consequently, Admiral has found it necessary to work at upholding a good public image. It has made substantial financial contributions to various local charities and organizations, the latest being a leadership gift to kick off the fund raising campaign for a new hospital project. It has produced a number of ads that stress Admiral's safety record, its partnerships with local businesses, and its open, honest, and transparent way of doing business.

But Admiral is always searching for new ways to enhance its reputation. At a recent brainstorming session of the PR department, Lisa Cummings, a relatively new hire, suggested the possibility of developing a game. She had just read an article published in *PennEnergy* (June 3, 2013; www.pennenergy.com) about "Power Matrix," an online game developed by Siemens that makes the public aware of sustainable energy alternatives and portrays the company as socially responsible. While the specifics of the game would need to be worked out, the group seemed to like the idea, at least in theory. Jeff Greenwood, V.P. of Communications, had his reservations; he thought that the costs of developing an online game would outweigh the in-

tended benefits. Nonetheless, he decided to go along with the group's recommendation to at least consider it as an option.

Jeff then arranged for a small group of local residents to participate in an information-gathering session. During this session, he asked their opinions about various strategies to improve the public's perception about gas drilling. Eight residents participated, and one task involved rating the effectiveness of several approaches, which included online gaming. Because the sample was so small, Jeff knew that he needed to analyze the data using a nonparametric method. He chose the Wilcoxon rank-sum test to compare the effectiveness ratings for online gaming to the other methods considered (e.g., public service announcements). The results revealed no significant differences. Jeff is not surprised. It now appears that the PR department won't be able to justify this option as a means for improving Admiral's image.

- Identify the ethical dilemma in this scenario.

- What are the undesirable consequences?

- Propose an ethical solution that considers the welfare of all stakeholders.

WHAT HAVE WE LEARNED?

Learning Objectives

Recognize when nonparametric methods may be appropriate.
- Data recorded as ranks without units can usually be best analyzed with nonparametric methods.
- Data with unusual distributions or for which we can't reasonably make the assumptions about the distribution as required by parametric methods call for distribution-free (nonparametric) methods.
- Situations in which the question being asked is best answered by a nonparametric method.

The Wilcoxon rank-sum statistic, also called the Mann-Whitney statistic, tests whether two independent groups have the same or different typical ranks for some variable.
- The test requires only that the individuals and the two groups be independent.

The Kruskal-Wallace test compares three or more groups.

The Wilcoxon signed-rank test is appropriate for paired data.

Kendall's tau measures the degree on monotonicity in the relationship between two variables.
- It can be applied to two quantitative variables if the question of interest is about monotonicity—and especially if we suspect or know that the linearity assumption required by regression and Pearson correlation is not satisfied.
- It can be applied to rank data, where it is not appropriate to apply least squares methods at all.

Spearman's rho measures the correlation between the ranks of two variables.

- It can be used even when the relationship is not linear or when outliers are present in either variable.
- It can be used when one or both variables consist of ranks.

Terms	
Distribution-free methods	Statistical tests that are not based on the sampling distribution of parameters. See Nonparametric methods.
Kendall's tau	A statistic that measures how close the relationship between two variables is to being monotone
Kruskal-Wallis test	A statistical test that uses the sums of the ranks for the groups that are being compared
Mann-Whitney test	See Wilcoxon rank-sum test.
Nonparametric methods	Statistical tests that investigate characteristics of populations without using specific parameters; these tests use the sign or the rank of the data rather than the specific numerical value of the variable, and they can also be used with ordinal data (categorical data with a logical order such as survey results based on a scale)
Spearman's rho	A correlation computed on the ranks of data values rather than their numeric values
Wilcoxon rank-sum test	(also referred to as **Mann-Whitney**) A statistical method used to test for the differences between population centers: whether the median of the difference between two variables is less than, equal to, or greater than zero
Wilcoxon signed-rank test	A statistical test used to test the difference between two related measurements or samples

TECHNOLOGY HELP: Nonparametric Methods

EXCEL

Ranking can be performed with the Excel built-in functions RANK.AVG and RANK.EQ. Each of these functions will provide a rank for one observation within a list of numbers. In the case of ties, RANK.AVG will assign the average rank and RANK.EQ will assign the top rank of the set of values.

Excel does not offer nonparametric analysis methods. A number of third-party add-ins and templates are available.

XLSTAT

To conduct the Wilcoxon Rank Sum/Mann-Whitney test or the Wilcoxon signed-rank test for two samples:

- Choose **Nonparametric tests**, and then select **Comparison of two samples**.
- Choose the **Mann-Whitney test** option on the **General** tab for the Wilcoxon Rank Sum test. See the dialog box below.

To conduct a Kruskal-Wallace test,

- Choose **Nonparametric tests, and** then select **Comparison of k samples** for the Kruskal-Wallace test.

- If the data are unstacked and the samples are of unequal sizes, choose the option **Remove the observations** from the **Missing data** tab.

To find Kendall and Spearman coefficients:

- Choose **Similarity/Dissimilarity matrices** from the **Describing data** tab. See the dialog box below.

- Be sure **Quantitative** is selected under Data (for Kendall and Spearman coefficients)

- From the drop-down menu, choose the appropriate procedure.

 JMP

To conduct a Wilcoxon test in JMP:

- Open Data.

- Select **Fit Y by X** and enter X and Y variables for analysis.

- Expand the Red triangle menu in the **Fit Y by X** output.

Wilcoxon and other nonparametric methods are found under the Nonparametric submenu.

Comment:

Other nonparametric methods are available in JMP but will be found in different menus, depending on the desired analysis and the type of parametric test that is most similar.

MINITAB

Nonparametric tests can be found in Minitab under the **Stat Menu > Nonparametrics**.

SPSS

Nonparametric tests can be found in SPSS in the **Analysis Menu > Nonparametric Tests**. Other nonparametric tests can be found as checkbox options in related analysis dialogs. For example, in the **Analyze > Correlate** option, Spearman's Rho appears as a checkbox; in the **Crosstab** options, a Kendal's τ can be found.

Brief **Case**

Real Estate Reconsidered

In Chapters 4 and 13 we considered what factors might contribute to the price of a home. In Chapter 4 we looked at living area and in Chapter 13 we considered such features as whether the home had a fireplace or more than 2 bedrooms. In those initial analyses, we used correlation and regression and Student's t-based methods. However, a careful look at the data reveals that the assumptions required by those methods are dubious. The data file is **Real Estate**. Return to those questions, this time using appropriate nonparametric methods. Specifically, consider:

Does the price for homes with a fireplace differ significantly from the price for homes without fireplaces? Make an appropriate display and discuss whether a nonparametric method is preferable to a *t*-test. Select an appropriate nonparametric test and compare the results.

Does the price for homes depend on the number of bedrooms? Code the bedrooms as 1, 2, 3, or 4 or more. Make an appropriate display and discuss whether nonparametric methods are preferable to an ANOVA for comparing central values of these groups. Perform an appropriate nonparametric test and report on your findings.

Does the price of a home depend on its living area? Make a scatterplot and discuss whether a nonparametric method would be more appropriate than Pearson correlation for discussing this question. Select an appropriate method, and discuss your conclusions.

EXERCISES

SECTION 22.1

1. Which of the following variables are ranks? For those that are not ranks, give the units.

a) Student ratings of a course on a 5-point Likert scale.
b) Students' letter grades in that course.
c) Students' point scores on the final exam.

2. Which of the following variables are ranks? For those that are not ranks, give the units.

a) U.S. change by size: dime, penny, nickel, quarter, half dollar, dollar.
b) U.S. change by value: penny, nickel, dime, quarter, half dollar, dollar.
c) The change in your pocket by year minted.

SECTION 22.2

3. For which one of the following situations would a Wilcoxon rank-sum (or Mann-Whitney) test be appropriate?

a) Comparing the ratings of a new product on a 5-point Likert scale by a panel of consumers to their ratings of a competitor's product on the same scale.
b) Comparing the sweetness of a diet drink (rated from 1 to 10) as judged by a panel of teenage tasters and a panel of adult tasters.
c) Judging whether the height of the water at high tide at a marina increases more or less consistently as the phase of the moon changes from new to full.
d) Testing whether the distributions of the ratings of a new distance learning course were the same as rated (on the usual 5-point Likert scale) by Freshmen, Sophomores, Juniors, and Seniors who had taken the course.
e) Estimating the association between the value of homes and their age in a community known to have a number of very expensive mansions.

4. For which one of the following situations would a Wilcoxon rank-sum (or Mann-Whitney) test be appropriate?

a) The Mohs scale rates the hardness of minerals. If one mineral can scratch another, it is judged to be harder. (Diamond, the hardest mineral, is a 10.) Is hardness related to the weight of a $1 \times 1 \times 1$ cm cube of the mineral?
b) Each member of a group of professional chefs rates the quality of a basket of organic vegetables on a 5-point scale. The same chefs then rate the quality of a basket of non-organic vegetables on the same scale. Are the organic veggies rated higher?
c) During its initial release, is there an association between the number of downloads of a new smartphone game and the number of hours since it has been released?
d) The Richter scale measures the damage potential of earthquakes. Some scientists think it is best used for judging the relative size of earthquakes and not their absolute size. Are earthquakes around the Pacific "ring of fire" rim stronger in general than those around the Atlantic? Compare earthquakes over a recent 5-year period.
e) A dog's intelligence can be judged roughly by how many times a new command must be repeated until it is learned. A researcher trained several dogs of each of 4 different breeds, teaching them 3 new commands. Are the breeds equally "intelligent"?

SECTION 22.3

5. For which one of the following situations would a Kruskal-Wallace test be appropriate?

a) Comparing the ratings of a new product on a 5-point Likert scale by a panel of consumers to their ratings of a competitor's product on the same scale.

b) Comparing the sweetness of a diet drink (rated from 1 to 10) as judged by a panel of teenage tasters and a panel of adult tasters.

c) Judging whether the height of the water at high tide at a marina increases more or less consistently as the phase of the moon changes from new to full.

d) Testing whether the distributions of the ratings of a new distance learning course were the same as rated (on the usual 5-point Likert scale) by Freshmen, Sophomores, Juniors, and Seniors who had taken the course.

e) Estimating the association between the value of homes and their age in a community known to have a number of very expensive mansions.

6. For which one of the following situations would a Kruskal-Wallace test be appropriate?

a) The Mohs scale rates the hardness of minerals. If one mineral can scratch another, it is judged to be harder. (Diamond, the hardest mineral, is a 10.) Is hardness related to the weight of a $1 \times 1 \times 1$ cm cube of the mineral?

b) Each member of a group of professional chefs rates the quality of a basket of organic vegetables on a 5-point scale. The same chefs then rate the quality of a basket of non-organic vegetables on the same scale. Are the organic veggies rated higher?

c) During its initial release, is there an association between the number of downloads of a new smartphone game and the number of hours since it has been released?

d) The Richter scale measures the damage potential of earthquakes. Some scientists think it is best used for judging the relative size of earthquakes and not their absolute size. Are earthquakes around the Pacific "ring of fire" rim stronger in general than those around the Atlantic? Compare earthquakes over a recent 5-year period.

e) A dog's intelligence can be judged roughly by how many times a new command must be repeated until it is learned. A researcher trained several dogs of each of 4 different breeds, teaching them 3 new commands. Are the breeds equally "intelligent?"

SECTION 22.4

7. For which one of the following situations would a Wilcoxon signed-rank test be appropriate?

a) Comparing the ratings of a new product on a 5-point Likert scale by a panel of consumers to their ratings of a competitor's product on the same scale.

b) Comparing the sweetness of a diet drink (rated from 1 to 10) as judged by a panel of teenage tasters and a panel of adult tasters.

c) Judging whether the height of the water at high tide at a marina increases more or less consistently as the phase of the moon changes from new to full.

d) Testing whether the distributions of the ratings of a new distance learning course were the same as rated (on the usual 5-point Likert scale) by Freshmen, Sophomores, Juniors, and Seniors who had taken the course.

e) Estimating the association between the value of homes and their age in a community known to have a number of very expensive mansions.

8. For which one of the following situations would a Wilcoxon signed-rank test be appropriate?

a) The Mohs scale rates the hardness of minerals. If one mineral can scratch another, it is judged to be harder. (Diamond, the hardest mineral, is a 10.) Is hardness related to the weight of a $1 \times 1 \times 1$ cm cube of the mineral?

b) Each member of a group of professional chefs rates the quality of a basket of organic vegetables on a 5-point scale. The same chefs then rate the quality of a basket of non-organic vegetables on the same scale. Are the organic veggies rated higher?

c) During its initial release, is there an association between the number of downloads of a new smartphone game and the number of hours since it has been released?

d) The Richter scale measures the damage potential of earthquakes. Some scientists think it is best used for judging the relative size of earthquakes and not their absolute size. Are earthquakes around the Pacific "ring of fire" rim stronger in general than those around the Atlantic? Compare earthquakes over a recent 5-year period.

e) A dog's intelligence can be judged roughly by how many times a new command must be repeated until it is learned. A researcher trained several dogs of each of 4 different breeds, teaching them 3 new commands. Are the breeds equally "intelligent?"

SECTION 22.6

9. For which one of the following situations would Kendall's tau be appropriate?

a) Comparing the ratings of a new product on a 5-point Likert scale by a panel of consumers to their ratings of a competitor's product on the same scale.

b) Comparing the sweetness of a diet drink (rated from 1 to 10) as judged by a panel of teenage tasters and a panel of adult tasters.

c) Judging whether the height of the water at high tide at a marina increases more or less consistently as the phase of the moon changes from new to full.

d) Testing whether the distributions of the ratings of a new distance learning course were the same as rated (on the usual 5-point Likert scale) by Freshmen, Sophomores, Juniors, and Seniors who had taken the course.

e) Estimating the association between the value of homes and their age in a community known to have a number of very expensive mansions.

10. For which one of the following situations would Kendall's tau be appropriate?

a) The Mohs scale rates the hardness of minerals. If one mineral can scratch another, it is judged to be harder. (Diamond, the hardest mineral, is a 10.) Is hardness related to the weight of a $1 \times 1 \times 1$ cm cube of the mineral?

b) Each member of a group of professional chefs rates the quality of a basket of organic vegetables on a 5-point scale. The same chefs then rate the quality of a basket of non-organic vegetables on the same scale. Are the organic veggies rated higher?

c) During its initial release, is there an association between the number of downloads of a new smartphone game and the number of hours since it has been released?

d) The Richter scale measures the damage potential of earthquakes. Some scientists think it is best used for judging the relative size of earthquakes and not their absolute size. Are earthquakes around the Pacific "ring of fire" rim stronger in general than those around the Atlantic? Compare earthquakes over a recent 5 year period.

e) A dog's intelligence can be judged roughly by how many times a new command must be repeated until it is learned. A researcher trained several dogs of each of 4 different breeds, teaching them 3 new commands. Are the breeds equally "intelligent?"

SECTION 22.7

11. For which one of the following situations would Spearman's rho be appropriate?

a) Comparing the ratings of a new product on a 5-point Likert scale by a panel of consumers to their ratings of a competitor's product on the same scale.

b) Comparing the sweetness of a diet drink (rated from 1 to 10) as judged by a panel of teenage tasters and a panel of adult tasters.

c) Judging whether the height of the water at high tide at a marina increases more or less consistently as the phase of the moon changes from new to full.

d) Testing whether the distributions of the ratings of a new distance learning course were the same as rated (on the usual 5-point Likert scale) by Freshmen, Sophomores, Juniors, and Seniors who had taken the course.

e) Estimating the association between the value of homes and their age in a community known to have a number of very expensive mansions.

12. For which one of the following situations would Spearman's rho be appropriate?

a) The Mohs scale rates the hardness of minerals. If one mineral can scratch another, it is judged to be harder.

(Diamond, the hardest mineral, is a 10.) Is hardness related to the weight of a $1 \times 1 \times 1$ cm cube of the mineral?

b) Each member of a group of professional chefs rates the quality of a basket of organic vegetables on a 5-point scale. The same chefs then rate the quality of a basket of non-organic vegetables on the same scale. Are the organic veggies rated higher?

c) During its initial release, is there an association between the number of downloads of a new smartphone game and the number of hours since it has been released?

d) The Richter scale measures the damage potential of earthquakes. Some scientists think it is best used for judging the relative size of earthquakes and not their absolute size. Are earthquakes around the Pacific "ring of fire" rim stronger in general than those around the Atlantic? Compare earthquakes over a recent 5 year period.

e) A dog's intelligence can be judged roughly by how many times a new command must be repeated until it is learned. A researcher trained several dogs of each of 4 different breeds, teaching them 3 new commands. Are the breeds equally "intelligent?"

CHAPTER EXERCISES

13. Product testing. A company is producing and marketing new reading activities for elementary school children that it believes will improve reading comprehension scores. A researcher randomly assigns third graders to an eight-week program in which some will use these activities and others will experience traditional teaching methods. At the end of the experiment, both groups take a reading comprehension exam. Their scores are shown in the back-to-back stem-and-leaf display.

a) Do these results suggest that the new activities are better? Test an appropriate hypothesis with a Wilcoxon (or Mann-Whitney) rank-sum test and state your conclusion.
b) How would you re-design this study? What nonparametric method would be appropriate then?

New Activities		Control
	1	07
4	2	068
3	3	377
96333	4	12222238
9876432	5	355
721	6	02
1	7	
	8	5

14. Product placement. The owner of a small organic food store was concerned about her sales of a specialty yogurt manufactured in Greece. As a result of increasing fuel costs, she recently had to increase its price. To help boost sales, she decided to place the product on a different shelf (near eye level for most consumers) and in a location near other popular international products. She kept track of sales (number of containers sold per week) for six months after she made the change. The values are shown below, along with the sales numbers for the six months prior to making the change, in stem-and-leaf displays.

After Change		Before Change	
3	2	2	0
3	9	2	899
4	23	3	224
4	589	3	7789
5	0012	4	0000223
5	55558	4	5567
6	00123	5	0
6	67	5	6
7	0		

Do these results suggest that sales are better after the change in product placement? Test an appropriate hypothesis and state your conclusion. Be sure to check assumptions and conditions.

15. Cereal sugar. A food company is concerned about recent criticism of the sugar content of their children's cereals. The data show the sugar content (as a percentage of weight) of several national brands of children's and adults' cereals. Are children's cereals really different from adults' cereals in sugar content?

Children's cereals: 40.3, 55, 45.7, 43.3, 50.3, 45.9, 53.5, 43, 44.2, 44, 47.4, 44, 33.6, 55.1, 48.8, 50.4, 37.8, 60.3, 46.6

Adults' cereals: 20, 30.2, 2.2, 7.5, 4.4, 22.2, 16.6, 14.5, 21.4, 3.3, 6.6, 7.8, 10.6, 16.2, 14.5, 4.1, 15.8, 4.1, 2.4, 3.5, 8.5, 10, 1, 4.4, 1.3, 8.1, 4.7, 18.4

a) Write the null and alternative hypotheses.
b) Check the conditions for a Wilcoxon rank-sum (or Mann-Whitney) test.
c) Complete the test and report your conclusion.
d) Make histograms of each group. Discuss whether you would choose a nonparametric test for these data or a two-sample t-test.

16. Foreclosure rates. Home foreclosures were up 47% in March 2008 compared to the previous year (realestate.msn .com; MSN Real Estate, April 2008). The data show home foreclosure rates (as % change from the previous year) for a sample of cities in two regions of the United States, the Northeast and the Southwest.

Northeast: 2.99, −2.36, 3.03, 1.01, 5.77, 9.95, −3.52, 7.16, −3.34, 4.75, 5.25, 6.21, 1.67, −2.45, −0.55, 3.45, 4.50, 1.87, −2.15, −0.75

Southwest: 10.15, 23.05, 18.95, 21.16, 17.45, 12.67, 13.75, 29.42, 11.45, 16.77, 12.67, 13.69, 25.81, 21.16, 19.67, 11.88, 13.67, 18.00, 12.88

a) Write the null and alternative hypotheses.

b) Check the conditions for a Wilcoxon rank-sum (or Mann-Whitney) test.
c) Complete the test and report your conclusion.
d) Make histograms of each group. Discuss whether you would choose a nonparametric test for these data or a two-sample t-test (as in Chapter 13).

17. Trophy sizes. The table gives the names, dates first awarded, and heights (inches) of major trophies and awards in sports and entertainment. The America's Cup, awarded for sailing, claims to be the oldest such award. The first five were created in the 19th century (which ended in 1900, not in 1899). The others were created after a gap of 26 years. When the creation of new awards was begun again, were the trophies the same size? Compare the two groups with an appropriate nonparametric measure. Complete the test at $\alpha = 0.10$.

Award	Year	Size
America's Cup	1851	27
Kentucky Derby	1875	22
Wimbledon Men's Singles	1887	18.5
Stanley Cup	1892	35.2
Davis Cup	1900	42
Ryder Cup	1927	17
Oscar	1929	13.5
Jules Rimet Trophy (Word Cup Soccer)	1929	14
Heisman Trophy	1935	15
Primetime Emmy	1949	15.5
Vince Lombardi Trophy	1967	22
Commissioner's Trophy (World Series)	1967	24
Larry O'Brien NBA Trophy	1977	24
Webb Ellis Cup (Rugby)	1987	15

18. Designated hitter 2012. American League baseball teams play their games with the designated hitter rule, meaning that pitchers do not bat. The league believes that replacing the pitcher, traditionally a weak hitter, with another player in the batting order produces more runs and generates more interest among fans. Below are the average numbers of runs scored per game by American League and National League teams for the 2012 season.

National League	Runs	American League	Runs
Colorado Rockies	4.68	Los Angles Angels	4.73
St. Louis Cardinals	4.72	Texas Rangers	4.99
San Francisco Giants	4.43	Detroit Tigers	4.48
Washington Nationals	4.51	Kanas City Royals	4.17
Milwaukee Brewers	4.79	New York Yankees	4.96
Arizona Diamondbacks	4.53	Boston Red Sox	4.53
Philadelphia Phillies	4.22	Minnesota Twins	4.33
Los Angeles Dodgers	3.93	Chicago White Sox	4.62
Cincinnati Reds	4.13	Cleveland Indians	4.12
New York Mets	4.01	Baltimore Orioles	4.40
Atlanta Braves	4.32	Toronto Blue Jays	4.42
San Diego Padres	4.02	Tampa Bay Rays	4.30

(continued)

National League	Runs	American League	Runs
Miami Marlins	3.76	Oakland Athletics	4.40
Pittsburgh Pirates	4.02	Seattle Mariners	3.82
Chicago Cubs	3.78		
Houston Astros	3.6		

Use a Mann-Whitney method to test whether there is really a difference in number of runs scored.

19. Freshman 15. Cornell Professor of Nutrition David Levitsky recruited students from two large sections of an introductory health course to test the validity of the "Freshman 15" theory that students gain 15 pounds their first year. Although they were volunteers, they appeared to match the rest of the freshman class in terms of demographic variables such as sex and ethnicity. The students were weighed during the first week of the semester, then again 12 weeks later.

Subject Number	Initial Weight	Terminal Weight	Subject Number	Initial Weight	Terminal Weight
1	171	168	35	148	150
2	110	111	36	164	165
3	134	136	37	137	138
4	115	119	38	198	201
5	150	155	39	122	124
6	104	106	40	146	146
7	142	148	41	150	151
8	120	124	42	187	192
9	144	148	43	94	96
10	156	154	44	105	105
11	114	114	45	127	130
12	121	123	46	142	144
13	122	126	47	140	143
14	120	115	48	107	107
15	115	118	49	104	105
16	110	113	50	111	112
17	142	146	51	160	162
18	127	127	52	134	134
19	102	105	53	151	151
20	125	125	54	127	130
21	157	158	55	106	108
22	119	126	56	185	188
23	113	114	57	125	128
24	120	128	58	125	126
25	135	139	59	155	158
26	148	150	60	118	120
27	110	112	61	149	150
28	160	163	62	149	149
29	220	224	63	122	121
30	132	133	64	155	158
31	145	147	65	160	161
32	141	141	66	115	119
33	158	160	67	167	170
34	135	134	68	131	131

a) Use a Wilcoxon signed-rank test to test whether these students' weights changed. State your hypotheses, check conditions, and complete the test (with technology).

b) Would you prefer the nonparametric test, or the paired *t*-test asked for in Chapter 13? Explain.

20. Job satisfaction. A company institutes an exercise break for its workers to see whether this will have any effect on job satisfaction, as measured by a questionnaire that assesses workers' satisfaction. Scores for 10 randomly selected workers before and after the implementation of the exercise program are shown in the following table.

Worker Number	Job Satisfaction Index Before	After
1	34	33
2	28	36
3	29	50
4	45	41
5	26	37
6	27	41
7	24	39
8	15	21
9	15	20
10	27	37

a) Identify a nonparametric procedure you could use to assess the effectiveness of the exercise program and check to see whether the conditions allow for the use of that procedure.

b) Test an appropriate hypothesis and state your conclusion.

21. ERP effectiveness. When implementing a packaged Enterprise Resource Planning (ERP) system, many companies report that the module they first install is Financial Accounting. Among the measures used to gauge the effectiveness of their ERP system implementation is acceleration of the financial close process. Below is a sample of 8 companies that report their average time (in weeks) to financial close before and after the implementation of their ERP system. In Chapter 13, we saw these data:

Company	Before	After
1	6.5	4.2
2	7.0	5.9
3	8.0	8.0
4	4.5	4.0
5	5.2	3.8
6	4.9	4.1
7	5.2	6.0
8	6.5	4.2

Use a Wilcoxon signed-rank test to see whether the ERP system seems to be effective.

22. Online insurance. A local insurance agent was concerned that he might lose customers to online discount insurance sites. To investigate, he randomly selected profiles (type of car, coverage, driving record, etc.) for 10 of his clients and checked online price quotes for their policies. The comparisons are shown in the table.

Local	Online	PriceDiff
568	391	177
872	602	270
451	488	−37
1229	903	326
605	677	−72
1021	1270	−249
783	703	80
844	789	55
907	1008	−101
712	702	10

Identify an appropriate nonparametric method to compare the two sets of prices and complete the test.

T **23.** Friday the 13th, traffic. In 1993 the *British Medical Journal* published an article titled, "Is Friday the 13th Bad for Your Health?" Researchers in Britain examined how Friday the 13th affects human behavior. One question was whether people tend to stay at home more on Friday the 13th—an issue of great concern, for example, to restaurants and theaters. The data in the table are the number of cars passing Junctions 9 and 10 on the M25 motorway for consecutive Fridays (the 6th and 13th) for five different periods.

Year	Month	6th	13th
1990	July	134,012	132,908
1991	September	133,732	131,843
1991	December	121,139	118,723
1992	March	124,631	120,249
1992	November	117,584	117,263

Identify and use an appropriate nonparametric test to judge whether there is a significant difference in traffic between consecutive Fridays when one is the 13th.

T **24.** Friday the 13th, accidents. The researchers in Exercise 23 also examined the number of people admitted to emergency rooms for vehicular accidents on 12 Friday evenings (6 each on the 6th and 13th).

Year	Month	6th	13th
1989	October	9	13
1990	July	6	12
1991	September	11	14
1991	December	11	10
1992	March	3	4
1992	November	5	12

Is Friday the 13th "unlucky"? Hospital emergency rooms need to plan for any increased "business" if they can. Use an appropriate nonparametric test to decide whether there is really a difference between consecutive Fridays when one of them is a 13th.

T **25.** Cuckoos and quality control. Cuckoos lay their eggs in the nests of other (host) birds. The eggs are then adopted and hatched by the host birds. But the potential host birds lay eggs of different sizes. Does the cuckoo change the size of her eggs for different foster species? The numbers in the table are lengths (in mm) of cuckoo eggs found in nests of three different species of other birds. The data are drawn from the work of O. M. Latter in 1902 and were used in a fundamental textbook on statistical quality control by L. H. C. Tippett (1902–1985), one of the pioneers in that field.

Cuckoo Egg Length (MM)		
Foster Parent Species		
Sparrow	Robin	Wagtail
20.85	21.05	21.05
21.65	21.85	21.85
22.05	22.05	21.85
22.85	22.05	21.85
23.05	22.05	22.05
23.05	22.25	22.45
23.05	22.45	22.65
23.05	22.45	23.05
23.45	22.65	23.05
23.85	23.05	23.25
23.85	23.05	23.45
23.85	23.05	24.05
24.05	23.05	24.05
25.05	23.05	24.05
	23.25	24.85
	23.85	

Use a Kruskal-Wallace test to decide whether cuckoos really do adjust the size of their eggs.

26. Analgesics. A pharmaceutical company tested three formulations of a pain relief medicine for migraine headache sufferers. For the experiment, 27 volunteers were selected and 9 were randomly assigned to one of three drug formulations. The subjects were instructed to take the drug during their next migraine headache episode and to report their pain on a scale of $1 = $ no pain to $10 = $ extreme pain, 30 minutes after taking the drug.

Drug	Pain	Drug	Pain	Drug	Pain
A	4	B	6	C	6
A	5	B	8	C	7
A	4	B	4	C	6
A	3	B	5	C	6
A	2	B	4	C	7
A	4	B	6	C	5
A	3	B	5	C	6
A	4	B	8	C	5
A	4	B	6	C	5

a) Use the Kruskal-Wallace test to judge whether there is a difference among the analgesics.

b) What aspect of these data may make the Kruskal-Wallace test more appropriate for these data than the ANOVA methods of Chapter 20?

27. Crowdedness. In a *Chance* magazine article (Summer 2005), Danielle Vasilescu and Howard Wainer used data from the United Nations Center for Human Settlements to investigate aspects of living conditions for several countries. Among the variables they looked at were the country's per capita gross domestic product (*GDP*, in $) and *Crowdedness*, defined as the average number of persons per room living in homes there. This scatterplot displays these data for 56 countries:

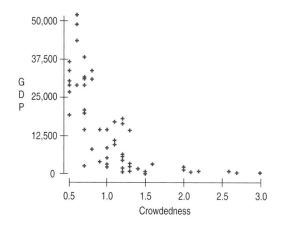

a) The value of Kendall's tau is -0.626. What does this tell us about the association?

b) The value of Spearman's rho is -0.804. What does this tell us about the association?

c) What about these data would make the nonparametric measures appropriate choices?

28. Basebal salaries 2009. Baseball is big business, and the top salaries have become quite large. The highest salaries (in millions of dollars per season) for some notable players since 1980 are given in the following table:

Player	Year	Salary ($M)
Nolan Ryan	1980	1.0
George Foster	1982	2.0
Kirby Puckett	1990	3.0
Jose Canseco	1990	4.7
Roger Clemens	1991	5.3
Ken Griffey, Jr.	1986	8.5
Albert Belle	1997	11.0
Pedro Martinez	1998	12.5
Mike Piazza	1999	12.5
Mo Vaughn	1999	13.3
Kevin Brown	1999	15.0
Carlos Delgado	2001	17.0
Alex Rodriguez	2001	22.0
Manny Ramirez	2004	22.5
Alex Rodriguez	2005	26.0
Derek Jeter	2006	20.6
Jason Giambi	2007	23.4
Alex Rodriguez	2009	33.0

a) Kendall's tau for these data is 0.887. What does that say about these data?

b) Based on that result, would you predict that salaries will continue to rise? Explain.

29. The Home Depot. Here are data that relate *Sales* at The Home Depot and *Housing Starts*, for quarters during its period of rapid growth between 1995 and 2004.

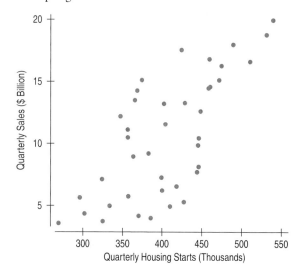

a) Would Kendall's τ or Pearson correlation be the more appropriate summary? Explain.

b) What could we learn from Kendall's tau that we wouldn't learn from the Pearson correlation?

T 30. Carbon footprint. Here are data relating the carbon footprint (tons of CO_2 per year) to the new Environmental Protection Agency (EPA) highway mileage for 82 family sedans as reported by the U.S. government (www.fueleconomy.gov/feg/byclass.htm). The car with the highest highway mpg and lowest carbon footprint is the Toyota Prius.

a) Would Spearman's rho be an appropriate summary of the strength of the association shown here?
b) Find rho for the full data and for the relationship with the Prius removed. Comment.

T 31. Income and housing. The Office of Federal Housing Enterprise Oversight (www.ofheo.gov) collects data on various aspects of housing costs around the United States. Here is a scatterplot of the *Housing Cost Index* versus the *Median Family Income* for each of the 50 states. The correlation is 0.65.

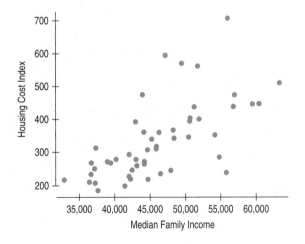

For these data Kendall's tau is 0.51. Does that provide proof that by raising the median income in a state, the Housing Cost Index will rise as a result? Explain what Kendall's tau says and does not say.

T 32. Interest rates and mortgages. Since 1980, average mortgage interest rates have fluctuated from a low of under 4% to a high of over 14%. Is there a relationship between the amount of money people borrow and the interest rate that's offered? Here is a scatterplot of *Total Mortgages* in the United States (in millions of 2005 dollars) versus *Interest Rate* at various times over 26 years. The correlation is −0.84.

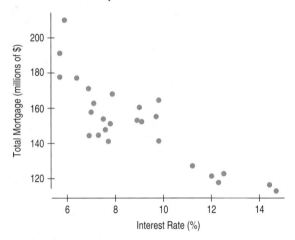

For these data Kendall's tau is −0.61. Does that provide proof that if mortgage rates are lowered, people will take out more mortgages? Explain what Kendall's tau says and does not say.

23

Decision Making and Risk

Data Description, inc.

Small businesses are 99.7 percent of all U.S. firms. They generate more than half of the private non-farm gross domestic product and create 60 to 80 percent of net new jobs (www.sba.gov). Here's the story of one such firm.

Data Description was founded in 1985 to develop, market, and support the Data Desk® statistics program.[1] Personal computers were becoming more widely available, and graphical desktop interfaces offered new and exciting opportunities for data analysis and graphics. Data Desk was introduced in 1986 for the newly released Macintosh computer and released for the PC in 1997, with expanded capabilities for analysis, and the ability to work efficiently with large (several million case) data sets. Data Description then launched *ActivStats*, a multimedia education product on DVD, which pioneered multimedia teaching in statistics and led to the development of MediaDX, a development platform that deploys a full array of media, narration, animation, video, sound, and interactive tools for teaching.

Data Description employs both a local staff and programmers who work remotely from other parts of the country and "telecommute." In these ways, it is typical of many technologically centered small businesses relying on the Internet for development, marketing, and customer support and competing with larger firms by staying fast and flexible.

---

[1]Because Data Description was founded by Paul Velleman, one of our co-authors, we have been able to gain access to business decisions that would ordinarily not be publicly available.

Company president John Sammis notes that the Internet has enabled small businesses such as Data Description to compete with larger international firms and that decisions about how best to use the Internet are key to competing successfully. By its twentieth anniversary, Data Description (www.datadesk.com), based in Ithaca, New York, was providing software and services to education and business clients throughout the world.

W e make decisions every day, often without knowing how they will turn out. Most of our daily decisions have no serious consequences. But the decisions a business makes determine the success or failure of the venture. The consequences of business decisions can often be quantified in monetary terms, but the costs and benefits themselves often depend on events beyond the control or foresight of decisionmakers. Decisions must be made nevertheless. How can people make intelligent decisions when they don't know for certain what the future holds?

One decision facing Data Description (as with many high-tech companies) is how best to provide technical support for its customers. In the past, Data Description has relied on its thorough documentation, a built-in help system, and free telephone support. But as its user base has grown, telephone-based customer support has become a significant expense. Data Description's president, John Sammis, must decide whether to invest in developing an online FAQ (Frequently Asked Questions) help system as the first line of defense for customer support, to continue free telephone support through the help desk, or to hire and train additional telephone support staff and charge customers for it. For a small business, decisions such as these carry significant costs, but making the right decision can be the difference between keeping customers happy and losing them to larger competitors.

23.1   Actions, States of Nature, and Outcomes

We refer to the alternative choices we can make for a decision as **actions.** Actions are mutually exclusive; if you choose one course of action, you haven't chosen the others. We'll call Data Descriptions' choices:

- Online FAQ
- Free Help Desk
- Pay Help Desk

The facts about the world that affect the consequences of each action are called **states of nature**, or sometimes just **states.** We often simplify the states to make it easier to understand the decision alternatives. We know, for example, that the economy isn't just "good" or "bad," and the number of customers can be any value in some reasonable range. But we'll simplify by grouping the states of nature into a few categories and treating them as discrete possibilities.

For Data Description, the *states of nature* concern the type of question coming into the Help Desk. Management classifies them into two basic types:

- Simple
  or
- Complex

A simple question is one that can be answered with an online FAQ system alone. A complex question requires either human technical support by telephone or backup e-mail support for FAQ users.

Each *action* has consequences that depend on the *state of nature* that actually occurs. These consequences are called the **outcomes** or **payoffs** (because usually in business the consequence can be measured in money).

To make informed decisions, Data Description president John Sammis must estimate the costs and benefits of each action under each state of nature. According to his estimates:

- The FAQ system can answer a simple question for about $3.50. A complex question can't be answered by the FAQ system and needs additional resources. Unfortunately the back-up system is slow and the marketing manager estimates that this would cost about $15 in goodwill and future business. Adding that to the FAQ system cost gives a total cost of $18.50 for a complex question.
- A live telephone support person costs about $10 per question whether it is simple or complex.
- Charging the customer $3 for the telephone support could defray some of the cost, but it might upset a customer with only a simple question. That resulting ill will will cost the company an estimated $15 for each simple question. On the other hand, customers with a complex question might be happy to pay for the telephone support, so the net cost for them would be $7.

FOR EXAMPLE Actions, states of nature, and outcomes

Pat needs to purchase airplane tickets to fly home at the end of the term. The last exam schedule slot is Friday at 3 p.m. Exams are scheduled centrally at Pat's school, and there is no alternative time to take exams. Pat simply must be there. A ticket to fly out on Thursday costs $750. An advanced-purchase ticket for Saturday morning costs $900, but, the end of term being a busy time, Pat doubts this option will be available for many more days. If the exam is scheduled on Thursday or Friday, Pat would have to sacrifice the ticket and purchase a new one for $1200.

QUESTIONS

What are the actions in this decision process?

What are the states of nature?

What are the outcomes?

ANSWERS

The actions are purchasing a ticket for Thursday or Saturday.

The states of nature are the exam being scheduled before Thursday or afterwards.

The outcomes are $750 for a Thursday ticket and early exam, $900 for a Saturday ticket, and $1950 for a Thursday ticket but late exam.

23.2 Payoff Tables and Decision Trees

We can summarize the actions, states of nature, and corresponding payoffs in a **payoff table**. Table 23.1 shows the payoff table for Data Description's decision about customer support. Customer support is an expense, so all the entries in the payoff table are costs, which Data Description hopes to keep to a minimum. The table shows the costs for a single tech support request.

		State of Nature	
		Simple Question	Complex Question
Action	FAQ	$3.50	$18.50
	Free Help Desk	$10.00	$10.00
	Pay Help Desk	$15.00	$7.00

Table 23.1   A payoff table showing costs of actions for two states of nature. Note that these are costs and not profits. As "payoffs," they might be written as negative values, but it is simpler to just remember that we want to *minimize* costs. Payoff tables of profits look to *maximize* values.

The payoff table is easy to read, but it doesn't display the sequential nature of the decision process. Another way to display this information that shows the dynamics of the decision-making process is with a **decision tree**. The decision tree mimics the actual decision-making process by showing actions first followed by the possible states of nature and finally the outcomes that would result from each combination (Figure 23.1).

Figure 23.1   A decision tree for the customer support decision.

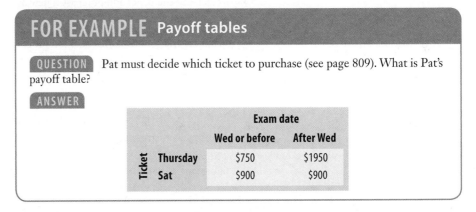

Action	State	Outcome
FAQ	Simple	$3.50
	Complex	$18.50
Free Help	Simple	$10.00
	Complex	$10.00
Pay Help	Simple	$15.00
	Complex	$7.00

The decision process moves from left to right through the decision tree. The decisionmaker chooses an action (indicated by a square node), determining which branch of the tree to follow. The circle nodes indicate branches due to the state of nature, which lie outside the control of the decisionmaker. The tree can expand to show decisions with any (reasonable) number of actions and states of nature.

> **Node Shapes**
>
> The square node, or decision node, indicates that a decision must be made. The circular node, or chance node, indicates a choice made by nature.

FOR EXAMPLE   Payoff tables

QUESTION   Pat must decide which ticket to purchase (see page 809). What is Pat's payoff table?

ANSWER

		Exam date	
		Wed or before	**After Wed**
Ticket	**Thursday**	$750	$1950
	Sat	$900	$900

23.3   Minimizing Loss and Maximizing Gain

A conservative approach to decision making would look at the worst possible loss and try to minimize it. Here are the outcomes for each decision and the greatest cost for each.

		State of Nature		
		Simple Question	**Complex Question**	**Greatest Cost**
Action	**FAQ**	$3.50	$18.50	$18.50
	Free Help Desk	$10.00	$10.00	$10.00
	Pay Help Desk	$15.00	$7.00	$15.00

Table 23.2   The greatest cost for each decision.

The decision to go with a FAQ could cost the company as much as $18.50 when complex calls come in, and the decision for a pay help desk could cost up to $15.00.

The safe choice—the one that minimizes the maximum cost—is the free help desk. This is known as the **minimax choice**. (If we are maximizing the minimum return, this can be called a maximin strategy.)

Of course, one could take the other extreme position and try for the maximum gain (or, equivalently here, the minimum cost). In this table, that would call for committing to a FAQ system (and hoping that the calls were simple). Such a choice is known as the **maximax** (when maximizing return) or the **minimin** (when minimizing cost) choice.

Choosing actions based on worst and best case scenarios rarely leads to the best business decision. Instead, successful small business executives rely on knowing their market so they can make less absolute decisions. A more realistic modeling approach takes into account how frequently the decisionmaker expects to experience each of the states of nature, and finds the optimum under that model.

> ### FOR EXAMPLE   Minimizing loss and maximizing gain
>
> **QUESTIONS**   Recall Pat's payoff table for purchasing an airplane ticket from the example on page 810. What is Pat's minimax choice?
>
> What is Pat's minimin choice?
>
> **ANSWERS**   Pat's minimax choice, minimizing the worst cost, is to purchase a Saturday ticket.
>
> Pat's minimin choice, minimizing the minimum cost, is to purchase a Thursday ticket.

23.4   The Expected Value of an Action

How can Data Description choose an action to maximize profit (or minimize loss)? They can be pretty sure that they'll get a mix of both simple and complex questions. Decisionmakers often estimate the *probability* of a state of nature based on their understanding of their business. Such probabilities can be *subjective* probabilities or can be grounded in data, and viewed as the *frequentist* probabilities we've used earlier in this book. In either case they express the expert's opinion of and belief in the relative likelihood of the states. We'll write $P(s_j)$ for the probability of the jth state of nature.

As with all probabilities, we need to check that the probabilities are *legitimate*. If there are N states of nature, then we require that:

$$P(s_j) \geq 0 \text{ for all } j,$$

$$\sum_{j=1}^{N} P(s_j) = 1.$$

If the probabilities are legitimate, then we can find the **expected value (EV)** of action a_i in essentially the same way as we found the expected value of a discrete random variable in Chapter 6:[2]

$$EV(a_i) = \sum_{j=1}^{N} o_{ij} P(s_j),$$

where there are N possible states of nature and o_{ij} is the outcome or payoff of action i when the state of nature is s_j.

---

[2]In Chapter 6 we computed the EV for one action, such as investing in a CD. This chapter extends this concept by computing and comparing EVs for different actions.

At Data Description, about 40% of the questions are simple, so managers assigned a probability of 0.4 that a support question will be simple and a probability of 0.6 that it will be complex. To compute the expected value, we start by placing the probabilities on the decision tree in the appropriate place. With these values in place, we can find the expected value of each of the actions. The probabilities are associated with each state of nature and are the same regardless of the action. We place these values on the branches associated with each state of nature, repeated for each one of the possible actions (the circle nodes).

For each combination of outcome and probability, we calculate its contribution to the expected value $P(s_j) \times o_{ij}$. Because only one state of nature can occur for each call, the states of nature are disjoint. We can therefore find the expected value for each action by summing the contributions over all the states of nature, in this case Simple and Complex (see Figure 23.2).

Figure 23.2 Calculating the expected value of each action using a decision tree.

From the expected values in Figure 23.2, it appears that expanding free telephone support may be the best action because it costs Data Description the *least*. The expected value of that action is a cost of $10.00.

FOR EXAMPLE **Expected value of purchasing a ticket**

Pat guesses that the course in question has an exam scheduled on the last 2 days of exam period only about 20% of the time (see page 809).

QUESTION   What is the expected value of purchasing a Thursday ticket?

ANSWER $0.8 \times 750 + 0.2 \times 1950 = \$990$

23.5   Expected Value with Perfect Information

Unfortunately, we can't predict the state of nature with certainty. But it can be informative to consider what it costs us to live with the uncertainty. If we knew the true state of nature—rather than just the probable state of nature—how much might that be worth to us? To help quantify that, let's consider a single customer support question. Knowing whether it was simple or complex would enable us to take the optimal action in each case. For a simple question we'd offer online FAQ support and the "payoff" would be $3.50. For a complex question we'd provide paid telephone support costing the company $7.00.

Using the probabilities of the two states of nature, we can calculate the expected value of this optimal strategy as:

$$0.6 \times \$7.00 + 0.4 \times \$3.50 = \$5.60$$

This is called the **expected value with perfect information** and is sometimes denoted *EVwPI*.

By contrast, the expected value of the optimal strategy that we calculated without knowing the state of nature was $10.00. The absolute value of the difference between these two quantities is called the **expected value of perfect information.**

$$EVPI = |EVwPI - EV|$$

In our example, this difference is $|\$5.60 - \$10.00| = \$4.40$. (Notice the absolute value in that calculation. Information should increase profit or, as in our example, reduce costs. Either way, the *value* of information is positive.) Our lack of perfect knowledge about the state of nature costs us $4.40 per call. The expected value of information, EVPI, gives the maximum amount the company might be willing to pay for perfect information about the outcome.

FOR EXAMPLE EVwPI and EVPI

QUESTIONS Recall from the example on page 809 that Pat is purchasing an airplane ticket; the payoff table is in the example on page 810. What is Pat's EVwPI? What is the EVPI?

ANSWERS With perfect information, Pat would purchase the early ticket for $750 80% of the time and the late ticket for $900 20% of the time for an EVwPI of $0.8 \times 750 + 0.2 \times 900 = \$780$.
The EVPI is then $|\$780 - \$990| = \$210$.

23.6 Decisions Made with Sample Information

Usually the costs and profits—the payoffs—of alternative actions under various states of nature can be estimated fairly well, because they depend on business-related events and actions that are well understood. By contrast, the probabilities assigned to the states of nature may be based only on expert judgment. These probabilities are sometimes called **prior probabilities** because they are determined before obtaining any additional information on the states of nature. A survey of customers, however, or a planned experiment might provide information that could bring the probabilities closer to reality and make for a more informed decision. Revised probabilities are also called **posterior probabilities**. Should the decisionmaker first gather data to help estimate the probabilities of the states of nature? That's a decision in itself. Surveys and experiments cost money, and the resulting information may not be worth the expense. We can incorporate the decision to gather data into the overall decision process. First, it is worthwhile to ask whether useful information is even possible. If the states of nature in the decision process are about the future health of the economy or the future value of the Dow Jones Industrial Average, it is not likely that we can learn very much new. But market research surveys of customers and trial marketing incentives can often provide useful data.

To improve their estimates of the probabilities making up the mix of simple and complex questions, Data Description could collect data about their customers. Would the added expense of that work be worthwhile? It depends on whether the information about customers helps to predict the likelihood of each type of question. Suppose they could classify their users into those who are *technically sophisticated* users and those who are *beginners*. That information might be useful because for *technically sophisticated* users, Data Description thinks that 75% of the questions will be complex but for *beginners*, that percentage is only 40%. Knowing how to classify their customers will help them make the right decision.

These probabilities are *conditional* probabilities of the kind we first saw in Chapter 5. We write:

$$P(\text{Complex}\,|\,\text{Sophisticated}) = 0.75; P(\text{Simple}\,|\,\text{Sophisticated}) = 0.25$$
$$P(\text{Complex}\,|\,\text{Beginner}) = 0.40; P(\text{Simple}\,|\,\text{Beginner}) = 0.60$$

In each case, we know the missing probability from the requirement that the probabilities sum to one.

Now our decision tree must include both the decision of whether or not to conduct the study and the possible outcomes of the study (if it is conducted), each with its appropriate conditional probability. Figure 23.3 shows the results. The costs in Figure 23.3 are the same ones we've used all along from Table 23.1. The expected values when there is no study are those worked out previously in Figure 23.2.

This decision process has two sets of decision nodes. The first decision is whether to conduct the study. The second is what action to take given the information from the study (if available). The outcome of the study is a chance node because we don't know *a priori* what the study will tell us.

To determine a decision strategy we compute the expected payoff at the end of each branch of the tree following the same methods we used before and now using the estimated probabilities that might come from the study. In this example, if we perform the study and it shows that sophisticated users are more common, we'll choose a pay help desk at a cost of $9.00. If we perform the study but it shows that beginners are the norm, we'll choose the FAQ system, at a cost of $9.50. If

Figure 23.3   A decision tree including a customer history study. For each decision node under each circumstance, the optimal (in this example, lowest cost) alternative is indicated in color, and the corresponding consequence is assigned as the expected value for that alternative EV's for the No Study branch are from Figure 23.2.

we don't perform the study at all, our optimal choice was the free phone help at a cost of $10.00. In this example, both alternatives following the study are less costly than the nonstudy choice, so it appears that any information the study may provide will save the company money. To be more precise, however, the company can go further and estimate the likelihood of the study's outcome. This will give the company an estimate of the **expected value with sample information** and help them estimate the potential worth of the study.

For example, if they think there's a probability of 0.8 that the study will show that most users are now technically sophisticated (and, correspondingly, a probability of 0.2 that it would find that beginners are the norm), then the expected value of the decision with that sample information would be:

$$EVwSI = 0.8 \times \$9.00 + 0.2 \times \$9.50 = \$9.10$$

The absolute value of the difference between this payoff and the payoff without the study is the **expected value of sample information**.

$$EVSI = |EVwSI - EV| = |\$9.10 - \$10.00| = \$0.90$$

An analysis like this can help us understand the value of sample information. It tells us that a study of this sort is likely to be worth about $0.90 per technical support question in its ability to help the company choose the optimal action.

23.7   Estimating Variation

In Chapter 3, we said that means should always be reported with an associated standard deviation, but thus far we've found expected values (which are, after all, means) without finding the corresponding standard deviations. The expected values tell the decisionmaker which action is likely to be worth the most. But to assess the *risk* of the decision, a decisionmaker must understand whether the likely outcome of the decision will always be close to that expected value or whether it might be quite different. We assess that risk by finding the standard deviation of the outcome.

Recall that the calculation of the expected value of an action is:

$$EV(a_i) = \sum_{j=1}^{N} o_{ij} P(s_j),$$

where there are N possible states of nature, o_{ij} is the outcome or payoff of action i when the state of nature is s_j, and $P(s_j)$ is the probability of the jth state of nature. We saw the equivalent formula for expected value in Chapter 6. The corresponding formulas for variance and **standard deviation** (also seen in Chapter 6) are:

$$Var(a_i) = \sum_{j=1}^{N} (o_{ij} - EV(a_i))^2 P(s_j),$$
$$\text{and } SD(a_i) = \sqrt{Var(a_i)}.$$

To calculate some values, we'll need the outcomes and probabilities we saw earlier and the expected values we calculated for the actions. Recall that Data Description thinks the probability of a simple question is 0.40 and of a complex question is 0.60. The payoffs for each state of nature and action were first given in Table 23.1. Now we also have expected values found from those payoffs and probabilities. Table 23.3 summarizes them.

	State of Nature		
	Simple Question **$P = 0.40$**	**Complex Question** **$P = 0.60$**	**$EV(a_i)$**
FAQ	$3.50	$18.50	$12.50
Free Help Desk	$10.00	$10.00	$10.00
Pay Help Desk	$15.00	$7.00	$10.20

*(left label: Action)*

Table 23.3   The payoff table for the customer support decision along with the expected values computed earlier. Recall that these are costs and thus could be written as negative values. Of course, for finding a standard deviation, writing these as negative numbers would give the same result.

Now, for example, the standard deviation of the outcome for the FAQ action is

$$SD(FAQ) = \sqrt{(3.50 - 12.50)^2 \times 0.40 + (18.50 - 12.50)^2 \times 0.60} = \$7.35$$

and the standard deviation of the Pay Help Desk option is

$$SD(Pay\ Help) = \sqrt{(15.00 - 10.20)^2 \times 0.4 + (7.00 - 10.20)^2 \times 0.6} = \$3.92$$

The standard deviation of the Free Help Desk option is zero. (Can you see why?)

In the customer support example, the choice to rely on an online FAQ system has higher variability. That may make it a less desirable alternative even in situations where its expected value seems to be optimal.

One way to combine the expected value and standard deviation is to find their ratio, the **coefficient of variation**.

$$CV(a_i) = \frac{SD(a_i)}{EV(a_i)}.$$

For the customer support example, the CVs are 0.588 for online FAQ, 0 for Free Help, and 0.384 for Pay Help. Actions with smaller CVs are generally seen as less risky, and may be preferred for that reason by some people. You can see why Data Description may prefer Free Help even though it may be more expensive; the company can predict its cost regardless of the state of nature.

One action may dominate another if its worst outcome is still better than the best outcome for the other. In such cases, the better action should be chosen regardless of how much variation it may have. **Dominance** is defined as the situation in which one decision alternative is never an optimal action regardless of the state of nature. A dominated action can be eliminated as a variable option or strategy.

Some discussions of risk prefer to concentrate on the expected value rather than the standard deviation, so they look at the reciprocal of the CV and give it the name **return to risk ratio**

$$RRR(a_i) = \frac{1}{CV(a_i)} = \frac{EV(a_i)}{SD(a_i)}.$$

The RRR can't be computed for actions with zero standard deviation, because they have no risk. Generally, actions with higher RRR are favored because they are less risky for their expected return. The units of RRR are dollars returned per dollar at risk.

FOR EXAMPLE   Estimating variation

Pat must decide about purchasing a ticket (see the example on page 809 for background).

QUESTION   Find the standard deviation of Pat's outcome. What is the RRR of purchasing a Thursday ticket?

ANSWER   For Thursday ticket:

$$\sqrt{(750 - 990)^2 \times 0.8 + (1950 - 990)^2 \times 0.2} = 480$$

For Saturday ticket, SD = 0

$$\text{RRR(Thursday)} = \frac{EV(Thursday)}{SD(Thursday)} = \frac{990}{480} = 2.06$$

23.8 Sensitivity

One weakness of the methods we've discussed here is that they require that you estimate—subjectively or by research—probabilities of states of nature. You may wish to assess the *sensitivity* of your conclusions about the expected value and standard deviation of alternative actions to the probabilities in your model. One way to do this is to re-compute those values with slightly (or even substantially) different probabilities. If the decision advised by the model doesn't change, you can be more confident in it. But if small changes in the probabilities result in large differences in the estimated value of the action alternatives, you should take great care and not rely too heavily on your decision analysis.[3]

For example, if the probability of a complex question were 0.8 rather than 0.6, would that change the decision? Table 23.4 shows the calculations.

		State of Nature		
		Simple Question $P = 0.20$	Complex Question $P = 0.80$	$EV(a_i)$
Action	**FAQ**	$3.50	$18.50	$15.50
	Free Help Desk	$10.00	$10.00	$10.00
	Pay Help Desk	$15.00	$7.00	$8.60

Table 23.4   Alternative calculations (compare with Table 23.3) with different probabilities for the states of nature.

It seems that the best decision would change if the probability of a complex question were as large as 0.8. The decisionmakers at Data Description should consider how sensitive these expected values are to their probabilities by finding the SD and EV for a plausible range of probabilities and then think about how certain they are about those estimated probabilities.

FOR EXAMPLE   Assessing sensitivity

Pat is making a decision about whether to purchase a cheaper ticket with a risk of having to purchase another if there's a conflict with the final exam (see the example on page 809).

QUESTIONS
How sensitive is Pat's decision? Suppose, for example, that the probability of a late exam were only 0.1. How would that change the expected values?

ANSWER   The EV of the Thursday ticket would now be $870, less than the EV of the Saturday ticket (which would still be $900).

---

[3]If you completed the Brief Case at the end of Chapter 6, you have already conducted a small sensitivity analysis.

23.9   Simulation

Another alternative to assessing the sensitivity of a decision model to the choice of probabilities is to simulate the model for a variety of plausible probability values. Rather than specify single probabilities, you can specify a distribution of plausible values. You can then run a *simulation* in which the computer draws states of nature at random according to your distribution of probabilities and evaluates the consequences. This approach can deal with much more complex decision models than those we've discussed here. The result of the simulation is not a single decision but a distribution of outcomes. Such a distribution may be a more appropriate description for a decisionmaker than any single expected value.

Programs such as *@Risk* (www.palisade.com/) and Crystal Ball (www.oracle.com/us/products/applications/crystalball/overview/index.html) provide ways for you to specify actions, states of nature, and the associated probabilities and outcomes and then use simulation methods to generate distributions of outcomes.

GUIDED EXAMPLE   **Insurance Services**

InterCon Travel Health is a Toronto-based company that provides services to health insurers of foreign tourists who travel to the United States and Canada.[4] The primary focus of InterCon is to act as an interface between local health providers and the overseas insurance company who insured the tourist should the traveler find himself or herself in need of medical attention. The customer base of sick or injured tourists is potentially profitable because most tourists who fall ill require only minor treatment and rarely come back for expensive follow-up visits. So InterCon can pass savings along to the foreign insurer by facilitating claim management and payment and can collect processing fees from these insurance companies in return.

Currently, InterCon charges a processing fee of 9.5%, collected partly from the medical providers and partly from the foreign insurers. It has experienced an average annual growth of 3%. However, to help with rising costs, they may consider increasing the processing fee from 9.5% to 10.5%. Although this would generate additional revenue, they would also incur the risk of losing contracts with insurers and health care providers. Table 23.5 gives the company's estimates of the impact of a change in rates on the annual growth in claims depending on the strength of foreign tourism.

		State of Nature	
		Weak Tourism $P = 0.40$	Strong Tourism $P = 0.60$
Action	9.5% Fee	$54.07M	$56.23M
	10.5% Fee	$52.97M	$54.56M

Table 23.5   InterCon's estimates of the impact on the annual growth in claims for two different actions (changes in rate) under two possible states of nature (strong or weak tourism).

What would be the best choice for the company?

---

[4]This example is based on the case by G. Truman, D. Pachamanova, and M. Goldstein entitled "InterCon Travel Health Case Study" in *Journal of the Academy of Business Education*, Vol. 8, Summer 2007, pp. 17–32.

	PLAN	**Setup** State the objective of the study.	We want to evaluate the two alternative actions the company is considering.
		Identify the variables.	We have estimates of the outcomes and the probabilities of two states of nature: weak or strong tourism.
		Model Think about the assumptions and check the conditions.	The only condition to check is that the probabilities are legitimate; $0.40 + 0.60 = 1.0$, and 0.4 and 0.6 are both between 0 and 1.

DO

Mechanics The calculations of expected value and standard deviation are straightforward.

Action	P	State	Outcome	$o_{ij}P(s)$	$EV(a_i)$
9.5% fee	0.4	Weak	$54.07M	$21.63M	
					$55.37M
	0.6	Strong	$56.23M	$33.74M	
10.5% fee	0.4	Weak	$52.97M	$21.19M	
					$53.93M
	0.6	Strong	$54.56M	$32.74M	

It can help to diagram the decision process with a tree diagram.

For example:

$$0.4 \times \$54.07M = \$21.63M$$
$$\$21.63M + \$33.74M = \$55.37M$$

Standard deviations:

For 9.5% fee:

$$(o_{ij} - EV(a_i)) \qquad\qquad (o_{ij} - EV(a_i))^2 P(s_j)$$
$$(54.07 - 55.37) = -1.30 \quad (-1.30)^2 \times 0.4 = 0.676$$
$$(56.23 - 55.37) = 0.86 \quad (0.86^2) \times 0.6 = 0.444$$
$$SD = \sqrt{0.676 + 0.444}$$
$$= \$1.06M$$

For 10.5% fee:

$$SD = \$0.774M$$
$$RRR\,(9.5\%\ fee) = 55.37/1.06 = 52.24$$
$$RRR\,(10.5\%\ fee) = 53.93/0.774 = 69.23$$

REPORT

Summary and Conclusions Summarize your results and state any limitations of your model in the context of your original objectives.

MEMO

Re: Recommendations for processing fee rate

The expected value of the alternative with the lower processing fee rate is slightly higher ($55.37 million compared to $53.92 million). However, because it has a smaller standard deviation, the return to risk ratio (RRR) at the higher processing fee rate of 10.5% is 69.22; while at the lower rate, it is only 52.24.

Because one action has the better expected value but the other seems less risky, the company should determine the impact of the downside of their decision and evaluate the probability estimates for the strength of the foreign tourism industry.

23.10   More Complex Decisions

The methods of this chapter can be extended to decisions that are more complex and that may have second or third stages conditional on the outcomes of the first decisions. For example, customer support questions might be handled best by an initial online FAQ system that then offers customers with complex questions a choice of free e-mail support or paid telephone support. To work out the expected values for these choices, we'd need to estimate the probabilities of a customer with a complex question choosing free e-mail or paid telephone support—something with which the company has no prior experience.

Or the probabilities may be changed by a change in circumstances. When the company releases an upgraded version, technical support calls increase, but there's a higher probability of simple calls. As the customer base learns the new version, their questions generally become more sophisticated.

WHAT CAN GO WRONG?

- **Decision trees do not tell the decisionmaker the correct decision.** Models can be useful, but they are based on assumptions. Decision trees model the expected outcome and risk for each decision. The best decision depends on the level of risk the decisionmaker is willing to accept, as well as the state of nature that occurs.

- **The computation of the expected values and standard deviations are sensitive to the probabilities.** The probabilities required by the calculations of expected value and standard deviation may be reliably based on past experience or data, or they may just represent the subjective judgment of the decisionmaker. Don't trust them blindly. Using a decision model and ignoring the sensitivity of the model to different probabilities can lead to poor decisions and misleading conclusions. One way to address the problem is to solve the model with a range of plausible probabilities to assess how sensitive the conclusions are to the choice of probabilities. Another way is to use software that simulates the results for randomly generated probabilities from an appropriate distribution.

- **Be sure that the probabilities are legitimate and that the action choices are disjoint.** The calculations in this chapter depend upon both of these being true.

ETHICS IN ACTION

Nelson Greene develops real estate in the southwestern United States. His next planned project is to build a housing development on a parcel of land in New Mexico, not far from Santa Fe. However, with the recent decline in housing prices, particularly in areas of the southwest like Las Vegas, Nelson is reconsidering his decision.

He set up a meeting with some key individuals, including Tom Barnick, a representative from the township supervisors. Tom and the township council were positive about the proposed development since it would provide increased tax revenue. So Tom wanted to influence Nelson to go forward with the development.

Tom had some analysis prepared, which he presented at the meeting. Based on several assumptions, including the probabilities associated with different housing market conditions in New Mexico (improving, worsening, or staying the same), the analysis showed a positive expected payoff for going forward with the project. Tom mentioned that the probabilities were obtained from a small group of housing market experts, although they had difficulty reaching consensus. Nelson noticed that not all the payoffs associated with going forward with the project were positive for each possible market condition, but the positive expected payoff made him view the project more favorably.

- Identify the ethical dilemma in this scenario.
- What are the undesirable consequences?
- Propose an ethical solution that considers the welfare of all stakeholders.

WHAT HAVE WE LEARNED?

Learning Objectives	**Assess costs and benefits of various actions given possible states of nature.**
	• Use judgment or data.

Estimate the likelihood of the possible states of nature.
- Use data, if they are available.
- Confirm that probabilities are legitimate.

Evaluate likely outcomes (costs and benefits) of decisions when faced with uncertainty about the state of nature.
- Make a decision tree and find the expected value of actions.
- Evaluate the relative risk of alternative decisions.

Terms	
Action	Alternative choices that one can make for a decision.
Coefficient of variation	The coefficient of variation (CV) of each decision shows the "$ at risk" for each "$ returned": $$CV(a_i) = SD(a_i)/EV(a_i).$$
Decision tree	A decision tree organizes the actions, states of nature, and outcomes to display the sequence of the elements in a decision.
Dominance	An alternative dominates when it pays off at least as much as (or costs less than) the alternative it dominates in all states of nature.
Expected value (EV)	The expected value of an action under uncertain states of nature is: $$EV(a_i) = \sum_{j=1}^{N} o_{ij} P(s_j)$$ where there are N possible states of nature and o_{ij} is the outcome or payoff of action i when the state of nature is s_j.
Expected value of perfect information (EVPI)	The difference between the expected value with perfect information (EVwPI) and the expected value (without perfect information) of the strategy (EV): $$EVPI = |EVwPI - EV|$$
Expected value with perfect information (EVwPI)	The expected value of a hypothetical strategy assuming that the states of nature are known.
Expected value of sample information (EVSI)	The difference between the expected value with sample information (EVwSI) and the expected value (without sample information) of the strategy (EV): $$EVSI = |EVwSI - EV|$$
Expected value with sample information (EVwSI)	The expected value of a hypothetical strategy given probabilities of the states of nature estimated from sample data.

Maximax choice (or strategy)	The action that maximizes the maximum possible return across all states of nature in a payoff table.
Minimax choice (or strategy)	The action that minimizes the maximum possible cost across all states of nature in a payoff table.
Minimin choice (or strategy)	The action that minimizes the minimum possible cost across all states of nature in a payoff table.
Outcome (or payoff)	The consequence of an action combined with a state of nature, usually expressed in monetary units (positive or negative).
Payoff table	A table containing the actions, states of nature, and the corresponding payoffs for each combination of the two.
Return to risk ratio	The return to risk ratio (RRR) measures the expected return of an action relative to the risk, represented by its standard deviation: $$RRR(a_i) = 1/CV = EV(a_i)/SD(a_i).$$
Standard deviation of an action, Variance of an action	The standard deviation of an action measures the variability of possible outcomes, calculated in terms of their estimated probabilities of occurring. The standard deviation is the square root of the variance: $$Var(a_i) = \sum_{j=1}^{N} (o_{ij} - EV(a_i))^2 P(s_j)$$ $$SD(a_i) = \sqrt{Var(a_i)}$$
States of nature	The facts about the world that affect the consequences of an action, usually summarized into a few possible values.

Brief Case

Texaco-Pennzoil

"Oil is big business." A classic example of this is the Texaco-Pennzoil court case, which appeared in the book *Making Hard Decisions*[5] and in a subsequent case study by T. Reilly and N. Sharpe (2001). In 1984, a merger was hammered out between two oil giants, Pennzoil and Getty Oil. Before the specifics had been agreed to in a written and binding form, another oil giant—Texaco—offered Getty Oil more money. Ultimately, Getty sold out to Texaco.

Pennzoil immediately sued Texaco for illegal interference, and in late 1985 was awarded $11.1 billion—an enormous award at the time. (A subsequent appeal reduced the award to $10.3 billion.) The CEO of Texaco threatened to fight the judgment all the way to the U.S. Supreme Court, citing improper negotiations held between Pennzoil and Getty. Concerned about bankruptcy if forced to pay the required sum of money, Texaco offered Pennzoil $2 billion to settle the case. Pennzoil considered the offer, analyzed the alternatives, and decided that a settlement price closer to $5 billion would be more reasonable.

The CEO of Pennzoil had a decision to make. He could make the low-risk decision of accepting the $2 billion offer, or he could decide to make the counteroffer of $5 billion. If Pennzoil countered with $5 billion, what are the possible outcomes? First, Texaco could accept the offer. Second, Texaco could refuse to negotiate and demand settlement in the courts. Assume that the courts could order one of the following:

[5]Clemen, R. T. and Reilly, T. (2001), *Making Hard Decisions*, New York: Brooks/Cole

- Texaco must pay Pennzoil $10.3 billion.
- Texaco must pay Pennzoil's figure of $5 billion.
- Texaco wins and pays Pennzoil nothing.

The award associated with each outcome—whether ordered by the court or agreed upon by the two parties—is what we will consider to be the "payoff" for Pennzoil. To simplify Pennzoil's decision process, we make a few assumptions. First, we assume that Pennzoil's objective is to maximize the amount of the settlement. Second, the likelihood of each of the outcomes in this high-profile case is based on similar cases. We will assume that there is an even chance (50%) that Texaco will refuse the counteroffer and go to court. According to a *Fortune* article,[6] the CEO of Pennzoil believed that should the offer be refused, Texaco had a chance to win the case with appeals, which would leave Pennzoil with high legal fees and no payoff. Based on prior similar court cases and expert opinion, assume that there is also a 50% probability that the court will order a compromise and require Texaco to pay Pennzoil the suggested price of $5 billion. What are the remaining options for the court? Assume that the probabilities of the other two alternatives—Pennzoil receiving the original total award ($10.3 billion) or Pennzoil getting nothing—are almost equal, with the likelihood of the original verdict being upheld slightly greater (30%) than the likelihood of reversing the decision (20%).

Evaluate the expected payoff and risk of each decision for Pennzoil.

Insurance Services, Revisited

InterCon Travel Health is a Toronto-based company that provides services to health insurers of foreign tourists who travel to the United States and Canada.[7] As described in the Guided Example in this chapter, the primary focus of InterCon is to act as an interface between local health providers and the overseas insurance company who insured the tourist should the traveler find himself or herself in need of medical attention. The customer base of sick or injured tourists is potentially profitable because most tourists who fall ill require only minor treatment and rarely come back for expensive follow-up visits. Therefore, InterCon can pass savings along to the foreign insurer by facilitating claim management and payment and can collect processing fees from these insurance companies in return.

Currently, this Canadian company charges a processing fee of 9.5% (collected partly from the medical providers and partly from the foreign insurers) and has experienced an average annual growth rate of 3%. However, a backlog of claims and a cyclical pattern to the claims (due to high tourist seasons) has caused a delay in filing claims with the foreign insurers, resulting in a number of noncollectible claims. In addition, while the growing company has been trying to keep costs to a minimum, they are considering adding a new information technology system to help them streamline the process. Most of the company's revenue comes from claims for inpatient hospital stays, which average approximately $10,000. These claims represent 20% of InterCon's claims, but over 80% of its claim revenue. The remaining claims arise from clinic and emergency room visits. Currently, the company has about 20,000 annual claims, so the associated revenue is estimated to be as follows.

---

[6]*Fortune*, May 11, 1987, pp. 50–58.

[7]This case is based on the case by G. Truman, D. Pachamanova, and M. Goldstein entitled "InterCon Travel Health Case Study" in *Journal of the Academy of Business Education*, Vol. 8, Summer 2007, pp. 17–32.

(*continued*)

Claim Class	# Claims by Class	% of Total	Average Claim Amount	Claim Revenue ($M)	% of Total	Fee Rate	Fees ($M)
Class A	4000	20%	$10000	$40.0	85%	9.5%	$3.8
Class B	6000	30%	$1000	$6.0	13%	9.5%	$0.57
Class C	10000	50%	$100	$1.0	2%	9.5%	$0.095
Total (Annual)	20000			$47.0			$4.465

To help with rising costs, this firm may consider raising the processing fee as high as 11.0%. While this would generate additional revenue, the firm would also incur the risk of losing contracts with insurers and health care providers. Here are estimates of the impact of a change in rates on the annual growth in claims depending on the strength of foreign tourism (reverse of the strength of the U.S. economy) for the 9.5% processing fee rate. Find the payoffs (total revenue) for the 11.0% fee rate based on the preceding table and the growth rates provided.

Foreign Tourism	Probability	Processing Fee Rate at 9.5%		Processing Fee Rate at 11.0%	
		Growth Rate	Payoff ($)	Growth Rate	Payoff ($)
Weak	0.40	3%	54069129	1%	??
Strong	0.60	4%	56231894	3%	??

What is the expected revenue for the respective fee alternatives based on the growth rate and total income from claims and fees? Suppose the manager gets new information and revises the probabilities for the strength of tourism to be even at 50-50. What are the new values for expected revenue, CV, and return to risk ratio?

EXERCISES

SECTION 23.1

1. Which of the following are Actions and which are States of Nature?

a) Whether Unemployment is above or below 10%.
b) Whether a new product should be brought to market before or after the beginning of the fiscal year.
c) Whether to tell employees to stay home because of a blizzard.

2. Which of the following are Actions and which are States of Nature?

a) Whether to invest in solar energy companies.
b) Whether your chief competitor decides to launch a new advertising campaign.
c) Whether the decision you made to out-source manufacturing last year turned out to be the cost-saver you thought it would be.

SECTION 23.2

3. You are called on to decide how your company should produce its new cell phone screen defroster (for use by skiers and others spending time out of doors in the cold.) You develop the following cost matrix ($000's):

	State of Nature (State of the Economy)		
Production	Recession	Stable	Expansion
Out-source	220	350	300
In-house	150	240	390

Draw the corresponding decision tree.

4. Here is a decision tree for the profits (in $000's) you project for your sales of the cell phone screen defroster, depending on the weather this coming winter and your choice of advertising method:

Action	State	Outcome
Point of Sale	Warm	550
	Moderate	600
	Cold	710
Magazine	Warm	410
	Moderate	590
	Cold	800
Internet	Warm	750
	Moderate	710
	Cold	590

Write out the corresponding profit matrix.

SECTION 23.3

5. For the cost matrix of Exercise 3,

a) What is the minimax choice?
b) What is the minimin choice?

6. For the decision tree of Exercise 4,

a) What is the maximin choice?
b) What is the maximax choice?

SECTION 23.4

7. For the cost matrix of Exercise 3,

a) Suppose $P(Recession) = 0.2$, $P(Stable) = 0.2$, and $P(Expansion) = 0.6$. What is the expected value of each action?
b) What is the best choice using the expected-value approach?

8. For the decision tree of Exercise 4,

a) Suppose $P(Warm) = 0.5$, $P(Moderate) = 0.3$, and $P(Cold) = 0.2$. What is the expected value of each action?
b) What is the best choice using the expected-value approach?

SECTION 23.7

9. For the probabilities of Exercise 7 and the cost matrix of Exercise 3, using the expected values you found in Exercise 7, compute the standard deviation of values associated with each action and the corresponding coefficient of variation.

10. For the probabilities of Exercise 8 and the decision tree of Exercise 4, using the expected values found in Exercise 8, compute the standard deviations of the values associated with each action and the corresponding coefficient of variation.

CHAPTER EXERCISES

11. Flight decision. You are planning a trip home at the end of the semester and need to make plane reservations soon. However, you've just had a preliminary interview with a consulting firm that seemed to go very well. There's a chance that they will want you to stay for a few days at the end of the semester for a round of interviews at their offices, which will mean you'll have to change the date of the flight if you make the reservation now. Suppose that you can purchase a changeable fare for $750 or a nonrefundable fare for $650 for which a change costs $150. Construct a payoff table for this set of actions using total cost as the "payoff."

12. Product introduction. A small company has the technology to develop a new personal data assistant (PDA), but it worries about sales in the crowded market. They estimate that it will cost $600,000 to develop, launch, and market the product. Analysts have produced revenue estimates for three scenarios: If sales are high, they will sell $1.2M worth of the phones; if sales are moderate, they will sell $800,000 worth; and if sales are low, they will sell only $300,000 worth. Construct a payoff table for this set of actions using net profit as the "payoff." Don't forget the possible action of doing nothing.

13. Advertising strategies. After a series of extensive meetings, several of the key decisionmakers for a small marketing firm have produced the following payoff table (expected profit per customer) for various advertising strategies and two possible states of the economy.

		Consumer Confidence	
		Rising	Falling
Action	Prime Time Ad	$20.00	$2.00
	Targeted Web Marketing	$12.00	$10.00
	Direct Mail Piece	$10.00	$15.00

Construct a decision tree for this payoff table.

14. Energy investment. An investment bank is thinking of investing in a start-up alternative energy company. They can become a major investor for $6M, a moderate investor for $3M, or a small investor for $1.5M. The worth of their investment in 12 months will depend on how the price of oil behaves between then and now. A financial analyst produces the following payoff table with the net worth of their investment (predicted worth − initial investment) as the payoff.

		Price of Oil		
		Substantially Higher	**About the Same**	**Substantially Lower**
Action	**Major investment**	$5,000,000	$3,000,000	−$2,000,000
	Moderate investment	$2,500,000	$1,500,000	−$1,000,000
	Small investment	$1,000,000	$500,000	−$100,000

Construct a decision tree for this payoff table.

15. Flight decision tree. Construct a decision tree for the payoff table in Exercise 11.

16. Product introduction tree. Construct a decision tree for the payoff table in Exercise 12.

17. Flight decision expected value. If you think the probability of being called for an interview is 0.30, calculate the expected value of each action in Exercise 15. Which is the better action in this case?

18. Product introduction expected value. An analyst for the company in Exercise 12 thinks the probabilities of high, moderate, and low sales are 0.2, 0.5, and 0.3, respectively. In this case calculate the expected value of each action. Which is the best action in this case?

19. Flight decision, part 4. For the decision of Exercise 11, you've just learned that you are on the short list and now estimate the chance that you'll be called for an interview is 0.70. Does that change your choice of actions?

20. Product introduction, part 4. For the product launch decision of Exercise 12, the economy isn't looking that good. Your very cautious boss says that he thinks there's a 60% chance of low sales, and a 30% chance of moderate sales. Which course should the company follow?

21. Advertising strategies decisions. For the payoff table in Exercise 13, find the action with the highest expected value.

a) If forecasters think the probability of rising consumer confidence is 0.70, what is its expected value?
b) What action would have the highest expected value if they think the probability of rising consumer confidence is only 0.40?

22. Energy investment decisions.

a) For the payoff table in Exercise 14, find the investment strategy under the assumption that the probability that the price of oil goes substantially higher is 0.4 and that the probability that it goes substantially lower is 0.2.
b) What if those two probabilities are reversed?

23. Advertising strategies EVPI.

a) For the advertising strategies of Exercise 21 and using the probability of 0.70 for rising consumer confidence, what is the Expected Value of Perfect Information (EVPI)?
b) What is the EVPI if the probability of rising consumer confidence is only 0.40?

24. Energy investment EVPI. For the energy investment of Exercise 22 and using both of the probabilities considered in that exercise, find the Expected Value of Perfect Information.

25. Advertising strategies with information. The company from Exercises 13, 21, and 23 has the option of hiring an economics consulting firm to predict consumer confidence. The company has already considered that the probability of rising consumer confidence could be as high as 0.70 or as low as 0.40. They could ask the consultants for their choice between those two probabilities, or they could just pick a probability in the middle, such as .50, and choose a strategy based on that.

a) Draw the decision tree including the decision to hire the consultants.
b) Would the consultants' information be useful? Explain.
c) The company thinks there's an equal chance of either of the consulting alternatives being what the consultants report. What's the value to the company (per customer) of the extra information?

26. Energy investment with information. The company in Exercises 14, 22, and 24 could send a team to Saudi Arabia to obtain additional information about the probabilities that oil will increase or decrease in price. They hope that the fact-finding trip would choose between the two alternatives considered in Exercise 22, or they could just estimate that the probabilities are equal.

a) Make a decision tree for these decisions.
b) Should the company send the fact-finding trip? Explain.
c) The company's experts estimate that if they send the fact-finding mission, there's a 70% chance that they'll conclude there's a 0.4 probability of higher oil prices. What would the value of the additional information be to the company?

27. Investing in equipment. *KickGrass Lawncare* is a service that cares for lawns in a large, affluent community. Shawn Overgrowth, the owner, is considering the purchase of new zero-turn riding lawn tractors, which would allow him to expand his business. The tractors cost $6300 each, and he would purchase two of them. Another alternative is to purchase three additional mowers of the current type to add to his current equipment. Those would cost $475 apiece. Or he could face the coming gardening season with his existing equipment. Shawn estimates that in a good growing season, the tractors would allow him to expand his business by $40,000. But if the summer is hot and dry (so lawns don't grow) or cold and wet (ditto), he'd only be able to add about $15,000 in contracts. If he purchases the mowers, he could expand his business by $10,000 in a good year or by just $5000 in a bad one. And if he spends nothing, he won't expand his business. In a bad year, his income would contract by about $1000.

Construct a payoff table and tree diagram for Shawn's decision. Don't forget to include his expenses in the calculations.

28. Market segmentation. Demand and price are related; raising prices typically lowers demand. Many companies understand that if they can *segment* their market and offer different prices to different segments, they can often capture more revenue. *Aaron'sAir* is a small commuter airline. They typically charge $150 for a one-way flight between a resort island they serve and the mainland. In times of low, medium, and high demand, Aaron (the owner and pilot) estimates that he'll sell 100, 200, or 500 seats per week, respectively. He is considering offering two different fares based on whether his customers stay over a Saturday night on the island. He thinks that business travelers coming to the island for conferences and retreats would typically not stay, but vacationers would. He expects that the low fare will attract additional customers. However, he anticipates that some of his regular customers will also pay less. The two fares would be $90 and $210. Aaron estimates that in times of low demand he'd sell 30 high-fare and 80 low-fare tickets—revenue of $30 \times \$210 + 80 \times \$90 = \$13,500$. In times of medium demand, he estimates 110 high-fare and 250 low-fare tickets, for an estimated revenue of $45,600. And in times of high demand, he expects 500 low-fare customers and 250 high-fare customers, yielding $97,500.

Make a payoff table and decision tree for this decision.

29. Investing in equipment, maxes and mins. Shawn Overgrowth, whom we met in Exercise 27, is an entrepreneur who is optimistic about the growing season. What choice should he make to maximize his return? His assistant, Lance Broadleaf, is very conservative, and argues that *Kick-Grass* should minimize their potential downside results. Which alternative decision does he argue for?

30. Market segmentation minimax. Aaron, who we met in Exercise 28, tends to be optimistic about business conditions. What is his maximax strategy that would maximize his results?

31. "Weather" or not to invest in equipment. Shawn Overgrowth, from Exercise 27, estimates that the probability of a good growing season is 0.70. Based on that:

a) Find the EV for his actions.
b) Find the standard deviations.
c) Compute the RRRs. Which action is preferred based on the RRRs?

32. Market segmentation and chance. *Aaron'sAir* (see Exercises 28 and 30) estimates that high-demand periods (which depend on the weather and on bookings for conferences) occur with probability .3 and medium demand periods occur with probability .5. The rest are low-demand periods.

a) What's the expected value of each of Aaron's alternative actions?
b) What are the standard deviations for each action?
c) What are the RRRs? Based on the RRRs, what action is best?

33. Equipment and data. Shawn, of Exercises 27, 29, and 31, could obtain long-range predictions of the growing conditions for next summer. He thinks that those might show a probability of good growing conditions as low as 50% or as high as 80%. If he doesn't obtain those predictions, he'll make a decision based on his previous estimates (see Exercise 31).

a) Draw the decision tree.
b) If Shawn thinks there's a 60% chance the long-range predictions will predict a 50% chance of good conditions, find the corresponding EVwSI.
c) Should Shawn purchase the long-range predictions?

34. Segments and surveys. *Aaron'sAir* (see Exercises 28, 30, and 32) could purchase a market survey from a firm that has advised the island tourist and conference bureau. He thinks their projections would help him determine whether the probability of high demand might be as high as .5 or as low as .2, with the corresponding probabilities for medium demand being .3 and .4. If he doesn't purchase the market survey, he'll make a decision based on his previous best estimates (see Exercise 32).

a) Draw the decision tree.
b) Aaron thinks the market survey is likely to be optimistic. He'd estimate a 65% probability that it would predict the higher (.5) probability of high demand. What would be the EVwSI?
c) If the consultant's report costs $2000, should Aaron pay for it?

35. Investment strategy. An investor is considering adding a stock to her portfolio. Assuming she buys 100 shares, here is an estimated payoff table for the alternative stocks if she holds onto them for six months. The value of the stock depends on whether or not an acquisition is approved for one of the companies, since the companies are actually competitors. She estimates the probability of an acquisition to be 0.3.

	Acquisition?	
	Yes (0.3)	No (0.7)
Stock A	$5000	−$1000
Stock B	−$500	$3500

a) Compute the EV for each alternative decision.
b) Compute the SD for each decision.
c) Compute the CV and RRR for each decision.
d) Which stock would you choose and why?

36. Mutual fund investing. An investor is considering how to invest her money. She has two options—either a domestic mutual fund that only invests in blue chip stocks or an international aggressive mutual fund that invests in young technical firms. The payoff (profit) after one year for these investments depends on the state of the economy.

	Economy	
	Improves (0.5)	**Declines (0.5)**
Domestic Mutual Fund	$1500	$1000
International Mutual Fund	$3500	−$1000

a) Compute the EV for each alternative decision.
b) Compute the SD for each decision.
c) Compute the CV and RRR for each decision.
d) Which mutual fund would you invest in and why?

37. Bicycle sales. A bicycle shop owner is deciding which products to stock. His distributor will give him a deal if he buys more of the same kind of bike. The payoff table shows monthly sales for a high-end bike (selling at $950) or a moderately priced bike (selling at $500). Based on past experience, the shop owner makes the following assumption about the demand for the high-end bike. Demand will be low, moderate, or high with probabilities 0.3, 0.5, and 0.2, respectively. He also assumes that if demand is low for the high-end bike, it will be higher for the moderately priced bike.

	Demand for High-End Bike		
	Low Demand (0.3)	**Moderate Demand (0.5)**	**High Demand (0.2)**
High-End Bike	$1900	$4750	$7600
Moderately Priced Bike	$4000	$2500	$1000

a) Compute the EV for each alternative product (decision).
b) Compute the SD for each decision.
c) Compute the CV and RRR for each decision.
d) Which bike would you stock and why?

38. Bicycle sales, part 2. The bike shop owner has now done a bit more research and believes that the demand for high-end bikes has shifted, so that now the low demand is 50% likely and the high demand is only 10% likely. How does this change your responses to Exercise 37? Find the new RRR. Does your recommendation to the shop owner change?

24

Introduction to Data Mining

Paralyzed Veterans of America

The Paralyzed Veterans of America (PVA) is a philanthropic and service organization chartered by the U.S. government to serve the needs of U.S. veterans who suffer from spinal cord injury or disease. Since 1946, PVA has raised money to support a variety of activities, including advocacy for veterans' health care, research and education in spinal cord injury and disease, and support for veterans' benefits and rights.

PVA raises money in a variety of ways, but the majority of their fund-raising comes from direct mail campaigns, in which they send free address labels or greeting cards to potential donors on their mailing list and request a donation for receiving these gifts.

PVA sends out regular solicitations to a list of more than four million donors. In 2012, PVA received about $150 million in donations, but the effort cost them over $33 million in postage, administrative, and gift expenses. Most of that money was spent on mailings to people who never responded. In fact, in any one solicitation, groups like PVA are lucky to get responses from more than a few percent of the people they contact. Response rates for commercial companies such as large credit card banks are so low that they often measure responses not in percentage points, but in basis points—hundredths of a percent. If the PVA could avoid mailing to just half of the people who won't respond, they could save $17 million a year and produce only half as much wasted paper. Can statistical methods help them decide who should get what mail?

24.1   The Big Data Revolution

You learned about Big Data in Chapter 1, and you hear about it on the news almost every day. The technological advances of the past few decades have enabled us to capture information virtually everywhere and automatically. When you visit a social networking site, data about you, your likes, your photos, your friends, and your habits are uploaded to servers, waiting for analysis. Your smartphone sends information about the calls you make, the texts you send, and even your location to central servers. Whether this information is being used in a prudent way by the government is the subject of recent news and citizen concerns,[1] but the collection of data by business, science, and government is exploding and will continue to explode into the foreseeable future. And these data will be used to solve problems using techniques that are based on the methods you've learned to master in this course.

Terms like *data mining*, *data science*, and *analytics* are really just describing the application of techniques that are built on the methods that you've learned in this course to large data sets. In Chapter 1, we defined **data mining** as the process that uses a variety of data analysis tools to discover patterns and relationships in data to help build useful models and make predictions. The more general term **business analytics** (or sometimes simply *analytics*) describes any use of statistical analysis to drive business decisions from data, whether the purpose is predictive or simply descriptive. **Big data** is a term for data sets so large and complex that it becomes difficult to use traditional methods to capture, store, visualize, and analyze them. But the definition of how "big" the database should be to qualify keeps changing with advancing computer speeds and storage capabilities.

What can companies hope to learn from all these data, and how do they analyze them? With information about the transactions you make, the websites you visit, and the social media you interact with, retailers can customize offers to you and predict when and how to deliver those offers to maximize the chance that you will purchase. Advertisers can place their message in specific channels to maximize the impact for the group of consumers they are targeting.

The Obama presidential campaign used analytics rather than conventional wisdom to determine when and where to place ads during the fall of 2012. As part of their sophisticated targeting operations, they bought "detailed data on TV viewing by millions of cable subscribers, showing which channels they were watching, sometimes on a second-by-second basis."[2] The campaign then "used a third-party company to match viewing data to its own internal list of voters and poll responses," helping to make the most out of their advertising budget during the final weeks of the 2012 campaign. The *New York Times* reported that the system "allowed Mr. Obama's team to direct advertising with a previously unheard-of level of efficiency,"[3] with some analysts crediting this data mining with Obama's victory.

Most of the models used in analytics and data mining are based on the regression ideas that you've studied. But because data mining has benefited from work in other fields as well, it has a much richer set of tools than those in this book. Some of the techniques enable more automatic re-expressions and more flexible fitting than the multiple regression and time series methods you saw in Chapters 17, 18, and 19, but they are based on the same ideas. The skills you've acquired by learning to fit models, diagnose them, and assess their limitations already prepare you to start entering the world of big data.

---

[1] "Momentum Builds Against N.S.A. Surveillance," *New York Times*, July 28, 2013.
[2] "Obama Campaign Took Unorthodox Approach to Ad Buying," *Washington Post*, November 14, 2012.
[3] "Secret of the Obama Victory? Rerun Watchers, for One Thing," *New York Times*, November 12, 2012.

24.2 Direct Marketing

Direct mail, often called "junk mail," generates about four million tons of paper waste per year. Direct e-mail, often called "spam," accounts for 95% of all e-mails according to The European Network and Information Security Agency (ENISA). Companies use direct mail and e-mail because, compared to other options, it is inexpensive and effective. To make it more effective, companies want to identify people who are most likely to respond. In other words, the companies would like to *target* their promotions and offers.

To help them decide how likely a customer might be to respond to a particular offer, a company might build a model to estimate the probability. The data used to build the model is usually a combination of data on customers that the company has collected and other data that it has bought. Data mining techniques can help companies direct their mailings to people more likely to respond to the solicitations. For example, analysts might use past customer behavior and other demographic information and build a model (or models) to predict who is most likely to respond. Techniques like multiple linear and logistic regression play an important role in these analyses, but if the number of variables is too large, researchers might use more sophisticated methods to reduce the number of predictor variables to a manageable size first.

Companies and philanthropic organizations collect an incredible amount of information about their customers. You've contributed to this data gathering yourself, perhaps without even knowing it. Every time you purchase something with a credit card, use a loyalty card at a supermarket, order by phone or on the Internet, or call an 800 number, your transaction is recorded. For a credit card company, this **transactional data** might contain hundreds of entries a year for each customer. For a philanthropic organization, the data might also include a history of when solicitations were sent, whether the donor responded to each solicitation, and how much they contributed. For a credit card bank, the transactional data would include every purchase the customer made. Every time a transaction is attempted, information is sent back to the transactional database to check that the card is valid, has not been reported stolen, and that the credit limit of the customer has not been exceeded—that's why there's a small delay before your transaction is approved every time you charge something. Although companies collect transactional data to facilitate the transactions themselves, they recognize that these data hold a wealth of information about their business. The challenge is to find ways to extract—to mine—that information.

In addition to transactional data, companies often have separate databases containing information about customers and about products (inventory, price, and shipping costs, for example). The databases can be linked to each other in a relational database. The properties of relational databases and some simple examples were discussed in Chapter 1.

The variables in the customer database are of two types: individual and regional. The individual variables are typically first gathered when the customer opens an account, registers on a website, or fills out a warranty card and are specific to that customer. They might include **demographic variables** such as a customer's age, income, and number of children. The company can add to these variables others that arise from the customer's interactions with the company, including some that may summarize variables in the transactional database. For example, the total amount spent each month might be a variable in the customer database that is updated from the customer's individual purchases, stored in the transactional database. The company might also purchase additional demographic data. Some demographic data are based on zip codes and can be obtained from agencies like the U.S. Census Bureau. These data can provide information on the average income, education, home value, and ethnic composition of the neighborhood in which a customer lives, but are not customer-specific.

Customer-specific data can also be purchased from a variety of commercial organizations. For example, a credit card company may want to send out an offer of free flight insurance to customers who travel frequently. To help know which customers those are, the company may buy information about customers' magazine subscriptions to identify customers who subscribe to travel or leisure magazines. The sharing and selling of individual information is controversial and raises privacy concerns, especially when the purchased data involve health records and personal information. In fact, concerns over the sharing of health data in the United States led to a set of strict guidelines known as HIPAA (Health Insurance Portability and Accountability Act) regulations. Restrictions on the collection and sharing of information about customers vary widely from country to country.

The PVA customer database[4] is a typical mix of variables. It contains 481 variables on each donor. There are 479 potential predictor variables and two responses: *TARGET_B*, a 0/1 variable which indicates whether the donor contributed to the most recent campaign and *TARGET_D* which gives the dollar amount of the contribution. Table 24.1 shows the first 18 records for a subset of the 481 variables found in the PVA data. We can guess what some of the variables mean from their names, but others are more mysterious.

ODATEDW	OSOURCE	TCODE	STATE	ZIP	DOB	RFA_2A	AGE	OWN	INC	SEX	WEALTH	AVGGIFT	TARGET_B	TARGET_D
9401	L16	2	GA	30738	6501	F	33	U	5	F	2	11.66667	0	0
9001	L01	1	MI	49028	2201	F	76	H	1	M	2	8.777778	0	0
8601	DNA	1	TN	37079	0	E		U	1	M		8.619048	1	10
8601	AMB	1	WI	53719	3902	G	59			M		16.27273	0	0
8601	EPL	2	TX	79925	1705	E	81	H	2	F	6	10.15789	0	0
8701	LIS	1	IN	46771	0	F				M		8.871333	0	0
9201	GRI	1	IL	60016	1807	F	79	H	4	M	6	13.8	0	0
9401	HOS	0	KS	67218	5001	G	48	U	7	F	7	18.33333	0	0
8901	DUR	0	MI	48304	1402	F	84	H	7	M	9	12.90909	0	0
8601	AMB	0	FL	34746	1412	F	83	H	2	F	3	9.090909	0	0
9501	CWR	2	LA	70582	0	D		U	5	F		5.8	0	0
9501	ARG	0	MI	48312-	4401	E	54			F		8	0	0
8601	ASC	0	TX	75644	2401	G	74	U	7	F		13.20833	0	0
9501	DNA	28	CA	90059	2001	E	78	H	1	F		10	0	0
9201	SYN	0	FL	33167	1906	F	79	U	2	M	3	10.09091	0	0
9401	MBC	2	MO	63084	3201	F	66	H	5	F		10	0	0
9401	HHH	28	WI	54235	0	F		H	7	F		20	0	0
9101	L02	28	AL	36108	4006	F	58	H	5	F		10.66667	0	0

Table 24.1   Part of the customer records from the PVA data set. Shown here are 15 of the 481 variables and 18 of the nearly 100,000 customer records used in the 1998 KDD (Knowledge Discovery and Data Mining) data mining competition.[5] The actual PVA customer database contains several million customer records.

[4]The PVA made some of their data available for the 1998 Knowledge Discovery and Data Mining (KDD) contest. The object of the contest was to build a model to predict which donors should receive the next solicitation based on demographic and past giving information. The results were presented at the KDD conference (www.kdnuggets.com). The variables discussed in this chapter are some of the ones that PVA made available. We have used various subsets of the PVA dataset in previous chapters, sometimes changing the variable names for clarity. The entire dataset can be found at the University of California at Irvine Data Repository: kdd.ics.uci.edu/databases/kddcup98/kddcup98.html
[5]The KDD Cup is the leading Data Mining competition in the world and is organized by the SIGKDD interest group of the ACM (Association for Computing Machinery).

Information about the variables, including their definitions, how they are collected, the date of collection, etc. is collectively called **metadata**. The variables in the PVA data set shown on the previous page are typical of the types of data found in the customer records of many companies. We shouldn't be surprised to find out that *AGE* is the donor's age measured in years and that *ZIP* is the donor's postal zip code. But without the metadata, it would be hard to know that *TCODE* is the code used before the title on the address label (0 = blank; 1 = Mr.; 2 = Mrs.; 28 = Ms., and so on) or that *RFA_2A* is a summary of past giving.

About 10% of the PVA variables describe past giving behavior collected by the PVA itself. More than half of the variables are regional data based on zip codes, most likely purchased from the Census Bureau. The rest of the variables are donor-specific, either gathered by the PVA or purchased from other organizations.

Sometimes disparate databases are gathered or merged in a central repository called a **data warehouse**. Maintaining the data warehouse is a huge job, and companies spend millions of dollars each year for the software, hardware, and technical personnel to do just that. Once a company has invested in creating and maintaining a data warehouse, it's only natural that they would want to get as much value as they can from it. For example, at PVA, analysts might use the data to build models to predict who will respond to a direct mail campaign; a credit card company, similarly, might want to predict who is most likely to accept an offer for a new credit card or services.

24.3 The Goals of Data Mining

The purpose of data mining is to extract useful information hidden in these large databases. With a database as large as a typical data warehouse, that search can be like looking for a needle in a haystack. How can analysts hope to find what they're looking for? They may start their search by using a sequence of queries to deduce facts about customer behavior, asking specific questions based on the data. Guided by their knowledge of the specific business, they may try a query-driven approach, asking a series of specific questions to deduce patterns. Such an approach is **online analytical processing** or **OLAP**. Analysts in sales, marketing, budgeting, inventory, and finance often use OLAP to answer specific questions involving many variables. An OLAP question for the PVA might be: "How many customers under the age of 65 with incomes between $40,000 and $60,000 in the Western region who have not donated in the previous two years gave more than $25 to the most recent solicitation?" Although OLAP is efficient in answering such multivariable queries, it is question-specific. OLAP produces answers for specific queries, typically as tables, but does not build a predictive model, and so it is not appropriate to generalize using OLAP.

In contrast to an OLAP query, the outcome of a data mining analysis is a **predictive model**—a model that uses predictor variables to predict a response. For a quantitative response variable (as in linear regression), the model will predict the *value* of the response, whereas for a categorical response, the model estimates the probability that the response variable takes on a certain value (as in logistic regression). Both linear and logistic multiple regressions are common tools of a data miner. Like all statistical models and unlike query-based methods such as OLAP, data mining generalizes to other similar situations through its predictive model. For example, an analyst using an OLAP query might find that customers in a certain age group responded to a recent product promotion. But without building a model, the analyst can't understand the relationship between the customer's age and the success of the promotion, and thus may be unable to predict how the product will do with a larger set of customers. The goal of a data mining project is to increase business understanding and knowledge by building a model to answer a specific set of questions raised at the beginning of the project.

Data mining is similar to traditional statistical analysis in that it involves exploratory data analysis and modeling. However, there are several aspects of data mining that distinguish it from more traditional statistical analysis. Although there is no consensus on exactly what data mining is and how it differs from statistics, some of the most important differences include:

- **The size of the databases.** Although no particular size is required for an analysis to be considered data mining, an analysis involving only a few hundred cases or only a handful of variables would not usually be considered data mining.
- **The exploratory nature of data mining.** Unlike a statistical analysis that might test a hypothesis or produce a confidence interval, the outcome of a data mining effort is typically a model used for prediction. Usually, the data miner is not interested in the values of the parameters of a specific model or in testing hypotheses.
- **The data are "happenstance."** In contrast to data arising from a designed experiment or survey, the typical data on which data mining is performed have not been collected in a systematic way. Thus, warnings not to confuse association with causation are especially pertinent for data mining. Moreover, the sheer number of variables involved makes any search for relationships among variables prone to Type I errors.
- **The results of a data mining effort are "actionable."** For business applications, there should be a consensus of what the problem of interest is and how the model will help solve the problem. There should be an action plan in place for a variety of possible outcomes of the model. Exploring large databases out of curiosity or just to see what they contain is not likely to be productive.
- **The modeling choices are automatic.** Typically the data miner will try several different types of models to see what each has to say, but doesn't want to spend a lot of time choosing which variables to include in the model or making the kinds of choices one might make in a more traditional statistical analysis. Unlike the analyst who wants to understand the terms in a stepwise regression, the data miner is more concerned with the predictive ability of the model. As long as the resulting model can help make decisions about who should receive the next offer, who is best suited for an online coupon, or who is most likely to switch cable providers next month, the data miner is likely to be satisfied.

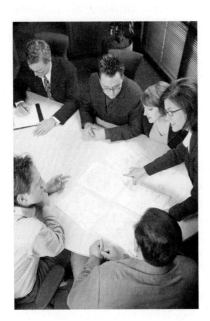

24.4   Data Mining Myths

Data mining software usually contains a variety of exploratory and model-building tools and a graphical user interface designed to guide the user through the data mining process. Some people buy data mining software hoping that the tools will find information in their databases and write reports that spew knowledge with little or no effort or input from the user. Software vendors often capitalize on this hope by exaggerating the capabilities and the automatic nature of data mining to increase sales of their software. Data mining can often *assist* the analyst to find meaningful patterns and help predict future customer behavior, but the more the analyst knows about his or her business, the more likely he or she will be successful using data mining. Data mining is not a magic wand that can overcome poor data quality or collection. A product may have tools for detecting outliers and may be able to impute (assign a value for) missing data values, but all the issues you learned about good statistical analysis are still relevant for data mining.

Here are some of the more common myths about what data mining can do.

- **Myth 1:** Find answers to unasked questions

    Even though data mining can build a model to help answer a specific question, it does not have the ability to answer questions that haven't been asked. In fact, formulating a precise question is a key first step in any data mining project.

$40,000?" If the answer is yes, move down to the right. For these cases, *Debt* is the next variable split, this time at $10,000. If this customer's *Debt* exceeded $10,000 move down and to the right again. The tree estimates that customers like this (both *Household Income* > $40,000 and *Debt* > $10,000) defaulted at a rate of 5% (0.05). Just to the left are customers whose *Household Income* was > $40,000 but whose *Debt* was ≤ $10,000. They defaulted at a rate of 1%. For customers with incomes less than $40,000 (the left branch of the first split), the next variable split was not *Debt*, but *Job*. For those who have been at their job more than 5 years, the default rate was 6%, but was 11% for those with less time at their present job. The modeler may, at this point, label the outcomes as *risk* categories, for example by calling 1% *Very low*, 5 and 6% *Moderate*, and 11% *High*.

Figure 24.2   Part of a tree model on a hypothetical examination of mortgage default. The tree selects *Household Income* as the most important variable to split on and selects $40,000 as the cut point. For those customers whose income is more than $40,000, *Debt* is the next most important variable, while for those whose income is less than $40,000, how long they've held their current job is more important.

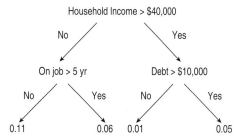

Tree models are very easy to implement and, in principle, are easy to interpret. They have the advantage of showing their logic clearly and are easy to explain to people who don't have a deep background in statistics. Even when they aren't used as a final model in a data mining project, they can be very useful for selecting a smaller subset of variables on which to do further analysis.

Unlike many other data mining algorithms, a tree can handle a great number of potential predictor variables, both categorical and quantitative. This makes it a great model for starting a data mining project. The modeler can then choose whether to use this model as a final model for predicting the response, or to use the variables suggested by the tree as inputs to other models that are more computationally intensive and less able to handle very large numbers of predictors.

FOR EXAMPLE Decision tree

Decision trees are calculated by data mining software. Several different algorithms may be used, but the important thing to know is how to understand what the resulting decision tree says about the data. Figure 24.3 shows a tree model found for the PVA data using *TARGET_B* as a response variable. *TARGET_B* is "YES" if the donor contributed to the most recent solicitation and "NO" if not.

QUESTION   What can we learn about the PVA data from this decision tree?

ANSWER   The goal of the decision tree is to characterize those potential donors who responded to the most recent solicitation with a donation. The PVA tree model starts at the root node with all 94,649 customers (listed under Count in the top box of the figure).

The first branching of the tree is according to the variable *RFA_4*, a variable that summarizes past giving. The algorithm identifies this as the best single predictor of *TARGET_B*. So, the first split occurs by splitting the levels of that variable into two groups, with 29,032 customers split to the left and the remaining 65,617 customers to the right. You can tell that because *RFA_4* is listed first in both boxes of the first split. The variable *RFA_4* comprises codes that contain information on how recently the

(continued)

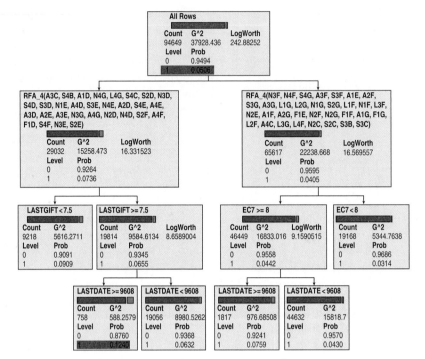

Figure 24.3   Part of a tree model run on the PVA data using JMP® software.

last gift solicitation was received, how frequently the donor has given, and how large the last gift was. (Examples of these codes are A3C, S4B, etc., seen in parentheses after the variable name in the output display). The percentages next to the levels 0 and 1 indicate the proportion of those who donated or not (*TARGET_B 1 or 0*, respectively) in each node. So although only 7.36% of those in the left node contributed, that was almost twice the 4.05% in the right node who contributed.

The tree continues to split each subpopulation. Notice that the variable chosen to split the left branch of the tree (*LASTGIFT*) is not the same as the variable chosen to split the right branch (*EC7*). The terminal nodes are found in the bottom row. The terminal node at the bottom left of the figure shows that 12.4% of the 758 potential donors in this small subgroup donated, a substantial improvement over the average of all potential donors (5.06%) shown in the root node at the top. Even at this stage of the analysis, if the PVA directed their solicitations to names on their list that satisfied the conditions found in the path through the tree to this node, they might reduce their costs and increase their yield substantially.

It's interesting to see that of the 479 potential predictor variables, 3 of the top 4 variables selected by the decision tree algorithm involve past giving history rather than demographics. *RFA_4* is a summary of past giving, *LASTGIFT* measures the amount of the last gift, and *LASTDATE* reports how recently the donor made the last gift. Only *EC7* is a demographic variable, measuring the percentage of residents in the donor's zip code that have at least a bachelor's degree. By letting the tree grow further, we could grow the list of potential predictors to 20 or 30, a much larger number than shown here, but still a manageable subset of the original 479 variables.

Neural Networks

Another popular data mining tool is the multilayer perceptron or (artificial) **neural network**. This algorithm sounds more impressive than it really is. Although it was inspired by models that tried to mimic the function of the brain, it's really just an automatic, flexible, nonlinear regression tool. That is, it models a single response variable with a function of some number of predictor variables but, unlike multiple regression,

RFA_2A	2.31%
RFA_2	1.64%
RFA_2F	1.27%
LASTDATE	1.18%
INCOME	1.03%
PEPSTRFL	1.00%
ADATE_4	0.83%
ADATE_3	0.74%
RDATE_7	0.73%
LIFESRC	0.73%
HVP1	0.69%
RDATE_6	0.61%
DMA	0.55%
GENDER	0.54%
RDATE_3	0.51%

Table 24.2 The top fifteen variables ranked in importance by the neural network node in Clementine®. The importance percentages indicate relative importance only and are not meant to be interpreted in an absolute sense.

it constructs a more complex function for the relationship. This can have the advantage of fitting the data better but has the disadvantage that complex functions are harder to interpret and understand. Indeed, modelers often don't even look at the models themselves. There are certainly things to be learned by studying how neural networks build models, but, for our purposes, we'll view them as "black box" models—models that don't produce an equation or graphical display that we can examine, but simply predict the response without much information about *how* it's doing it.

Even though they are black boxes, neural network algorithms do leave some clues. A listing of the most important variables is a common output feature, and some neural network software even provide plots of the predicted relationships between the response and the most important variables as measured by how much the predictions change when the variable is deleted. Table 24.2 shows a list of the top fifteen variables in the PVA problem ranked by "importance" from a neural network output in a data mining software package called Clementine®.

Many other algorithms are used by data miners, and new ones are being developed all the time. Typically, a data miner will build several different models and then test them before selecting one to use, or the data miner might decide to form a "committee" of models, combining the output from several models, much in the way a CEO might take input from a group of advisors in order to make a decision. For a classification problem, the final prediction for a case might be the class that's predicted most often by the models in the committee. For a regression problem, the prediction might simply be the average prediction of all the models in the committee. Averaging models provides protection against choosing the "wrong" model, but usually at a cost of not being able to interpret the resulting predictions. Finding the best ways to combine many different models is an active and exciting area of current research in data mining.

24.8 The Data Mining Process

Data mining projects require a number of different skills. For that reason, a data mining project should be a team effort. No one person is likely to have the business knowledge, computer and database management skills, software expertise, and statistical training needed for all the steps in the process. Because data mining projects tend to be complex, it's useful to map out the steps for a successful project. A group of data mining experts have shared their combined expertise in a project called the Cross Industry Standard Process for Data Mining (CRISP-DM). A CRISP-DM schematic of the data mining cycle appears in Figure 24.4.

Figure 24.4 A picture of the CRISP-DM data mining process.

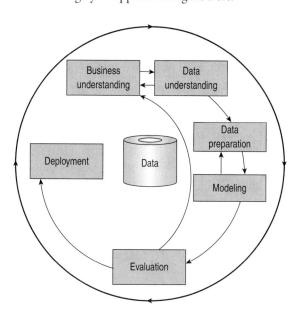

In this schematic, the process starts with the *Business understanding* phase. This is where the problem to be addressed is carefully articulated. It is best to have a specific problem before starting. A goal of understanding how to best manage customers sounds good but is not precise enough for a data mining project. A better, more specific question might be to understand which customers are most likely to switch cell phone providers in the next three months. It's important to have all the members of the data mining team involved at this stage, and the team should be representative of all parts of the business that may be affected by the resulting business decisions. If key constituents aren't represented, the model might not answer the right question. It can't be overemphasized how important it is to have consensus on a precise, correctly formulated problem to be addressed before continuing with the data mining effort.

The phase of *Data understanding* is central to the entire data mining project. If you want to know which customers are likely to switch providers, you have to understand your data and have data that can support such an exploration. For example, you'll need a sample that contains both customers who have recently switched and those who have been loyal customers for some time. There should also be variables in the database that could reasonably explain or predict the behavior. The choice of those variables has to rely on the business knowledge of the team. At the beginning of the project, it's best to include all the variables that might be useful, but keep in mind that having *too* many variables can make the model selection phase more difficult. It is crucial to understand the data warehouse, what it contains, and what its limitations are at this stage.

Once the variables have been selected and the response variable(s) agreed upon, it's time to begin the *Data preparation* phase for modeling. As mentioned earlier, this can be a time-consuming part of the process and is likely to be a team effort. Investigating missing values, correcting wrong and inconsistent entries, reconciling data definitions, and merging data sources are all challenging issues. Some of these can be handled automatically, while others require painstaking detailed analysis. The team will have to decide how much effort is reasonable to make the data set as complete and reliable as possible, given the time and resource constraints of the project.

Once the data have been prepared, the analysts begin the *Modeling* phase by exploring and developing models. If the number of variables is very large, a preliminary model (such as a tree) might be considered in order to narrow the candidate predictor variables down to a reasonable number. If the number of predictors is small enough, modelers can use traditional graphical analysis (histograms, bar charts) for each variable to start and then investigate the relationship between each predictor and the response with bivariate graphs (scatterplots, boxplots, or segmented bar charts, depending on the variable types). The more knowledge of the data and variables that goes into the model, the higher the chance of success for the project.

The analysts should now have several models that fit the response variable with differing levels of accuracy in the training set. Once the analyst has several models that seem reasonable (based on domain knowledge and performance on the training set), the *Evaluation* phase can begin. Looking at the structure of the models and deciding what predictors are important for each model should give the analysts information about how the predictors can predict the response variable of interest. In the *Evaluation* phase, the candidate models are tested against the test set, and various criteria are used to judge the models. For example, for a regression problem with a quantitative response, the sum of squares of the residuals from predicting the response on the test set might be compared. For a (two-level) classification problem, the two types of errors that arise (predicting YES when the true response is NO and vice versa) are weighed. Different costs on the two types of errors might be warranted, and the total cost of misclassification should reflect that. At this point, the business question that motivated the project should be revisited.

Does the model help to answer the question? If not, it may be necessary to go back to one of the previous steps to investigate why that happened.

If the model (or average of several models) seems to give insight into the business problem, then it's time for the *Deployment* phase. Usually, that means using the model to predict an outcome on a larger data set than the original, or on more recent data than were used to build the model. The reason that so many phases of the CRISP-DM diagram have arrows both to and from them is that this process is not a straightforward movement through the phases—it is an iterative and interconnected process. Knowledge gained at any phase may trigger a reexamination of an earlier phase. Even the "final" phase, deployment, is not really final. In many business situations, the environment changes rapidly, so models can become stale quickly. Although a data mining project is complex and involves the efforts of many people, mapping out the different phases can help assure that the project is as successful as possible.

24.9 Summary

There are many similarities between the modeling process of data mining and the basic approach to modeling that you've been learning throughout this book. What makes data mining different really has to do with the large number of algorithms and types of models available to the data miner and with the size and complexity of the data sets. But most of what makes a data mining project successful would make any statistical analysis successful. The same principles of understanding and exploring variables and their relationships are key to both processes. A famous statistician, Jerry Friedman, was once asked if there was a difference between statistics and data mining. Before answering, he asked if the questioner wanted the long answer or the short answer. Because the response was "the short answer," Jerry said simply, "No." We never got to hear the long answer, but we suspect it may have contained some of the differences discussed in this chapter.

Having a good set of statistical and data analysis tools is a great beginning to becoming a successful data miner. Being willing to learn new techniques, whether they come from statistics, computer science, machine learning, or other disciplines, is essential. Learning to work with other people whose skills complement yours will not only make the task more pleasant, but also is key to a successful data mining project. The need to understand the information contained in large databases will increase in the years ahead, so it will continue to be important to know about this rapidly growing field.

WHAT CAN GO WRONG?

- **Be sure that the question to be answered is specific.** Make sure that the business question to be addressed is specific enough so that a model can help to answer it. A goal as vague as "improving the business" is not likely to lead to a successful data mining project.

- **Be sure that the data have the potential to answer the question.** Check the variables to see whether a model can reasonably be built to predict the response. For example, if you want to know which type of customers are going to a particular Web page, make sure that data are being collected that link the Web page to the customer visiting the site.

- **Beware of overfitting to the data.** Because data mining tools are powerful and because the data sets used to train them are usually large, it is easy to think you're fitting the data well. Make sure you validate the model on a test set—a data set not used to fit the model.

- **Make sure that the data are ready to use in the data mining model.** Typically, data warehouses contain data from several different sources. It's important to confirm that variables with the same name actually measure the same thing in two different databases. Missing values, incorrect entries, and different time scales are all challenges to be overcome before the data can be used in the model building phase.

- **Don't try it alone.** Data mining projects require a variety of skills and a lot of work. Assembling the right team of people to carry out the effort is crucial.

ETHICS IN ACTION

With U.S. consumers becoming more environmentally conscious, there has been an explosion of eco-friendly products on the market. One notable entry has been the gas-electric hybrid car.

A large nonprofit environmental group would like to target customers likely to purchase hybrid cars in the future with a message expressing the urgency to do so sooner rather than later. They understand that direct mailings are very effective in this regard, but staying true to their environmental concerns, they want to avoid doing a nontargeted mass mailing.

The executive team met to discuss the possibility of using data mining to help identify their target audience. The initial discussion revolved around data sources. Although they have several databases on demographics and transactional informa-

tion for consumers who have purchased green products and donated to organizations that promote sustainability, someone suggested that they get data on contributions to political parties. After all, there was a Green party, and Democrats tend to be more concerned about environmental issues than Republicans. Another member of the team was genuinely surprised that this was even possible. She wondered how ethical it is to use information about individuals that they may assume is being kept confidential.

- Identify the ethical dilemma in this scenario.

- What are the undesirable consequences?

- Propose an ethical solution that considers the welfare of all stakeholders.

WHAT HAVE WE LEARNED?

Learning Objectives

Understand the uses and value of data mining in business.

Recognize data mining approaches.

- OLAP approaches answer specific questions about data in a database that may involve many variables.
- Predictive model approaches build complex models that attempt to predict a response.

Be aware that data preparation is essential to sound data mining.

- Data must be cleaned of errors and impossible or implausible values.
- Missing values may be a serious issue.
- Data preparation may take the majority of time and effort devoted to a data mining project.

Be able to articulate the goal of a data mining project and understand that data mining efforts differ according to the kind of dependent variable.

- When the goal is to predict a quantitative response, the problem is called a regression problem.
- When the goal is to classify individuals according to a categorical variable, the problem is called a classification problem.

Be aware of the variety of models and algorithms that are used to build predictive models.

- Tree models build interpretable models that select predictor variables and split points to best predict the response in either a regression or classification problem.

- Neural networks build black box models that use all the predictor variables for both regression and classification problems.
- Many other data mining algorithms are used as well, and new competitors are continually being developed.

Understand that successful data mining is a team effort that requires a variety of skills.

- Defining the problem and objective of interest is crucial for success.
- The CRISP data mining process provides a good outline for a data mining project.

Terms

Algorithm	A set of instructions used for calculation and data processing. The algorithm specifies how the model is built from the data.
Big Data	The collection and analysis of data sets so large and complex that traditional methods typically brought to bear on the problem would be overwhelmed.
Business analytics (or analytics or predictive analytics)	The process of using statistical analysis and modeling to make predictions and drive business decisions.
Classification problem	A prediction problem that involves a categorical response variable. (See also regression problem.)
Data mining	A process that uses a variety of data analysis tools to discover patterns and relationships in data that are useful for making predictions.
Data preparation	The process of cleaning data and checking its accuracy prior to modeling. Data preparation includes investigating missing values, correcting wrong and inconsistent entries, and reconciling data definitions.
Data warehouse	A digital repository for several large databases.
Decision tree (data mining version)	A model that predicts either a categorical or quantitative response in which the branches represent variable splits and the terminal nodes provide the predicted value.
Demographic variable	A variable containing information about a customer's personal characteristics or the characteristics of the region in which the customer lives. Commonly used demographics include age, income, race, and education.
Metadata	Information about the data including when and where the data were collected.
Neural network	A model based on analogies with human brain processing that uses combinations of predictor variables and nonlinear regression to predict either a categorical or quantitative response variable.
Online analytical processing (OLAP)	An approach for providing answers to queries that typically involve many variables simultaneously.
Predictive model	A model that provides predictions for the response variable.
Regression problem	A prediction problem that has a quantitative response variable. (See classification problem.)
Supervised problem	A classification or regression problem in which the analyst is given a set of data for which the response is known to use to build a model.
Terminal node	The final leaves of a decision tree where the predictions for the response variable are found.
Test set	The data set used in a supervised classification or regression problem *not used* to build the predictive model. The test set is withheld from the model building stage of the process, and the model's predictions on the test set are used to evaluate the model performance.
Training set	The data set used in a supervised classification or regression problem to build the predictive model.
Transactional data	Data describing an event involving a transaction, usually an exchange of money for goods or services.
Unsupervised problem	A problem, unlike classification or regression problems, where there is no response variable. The goal of an unsupervised problem is typically to put similar cases together into homogeneous groups or clusters.

Marketing Experiment

Many credit cards offer "free" miles to entice customers to increase the use of their cards. These miles can be exchanged for flights or hotel rooms, depending on the type of card, and the miles are very popular among card-holders. The miles are not free to the credit card company, however, which must pay the airline or hotel chain for the services provided to the customer in exchange for the miles.

To help evaluate how much revenue a new campaign that offers double miles might generate on a standard miles card, a marketing analyst ran an experiment on 4800 cardholders, half of whom were randomly chosen to receive the new card with the double-miles offer (*Miles* = Double Miles) and half of whom were using the standard card (*Miles* = Standard Miles).

The analyst had also read some research that claimed that making cardholders enroll on the Internet increases their awareness of the card and will "engage" the customer more, leading to increased use of the card. So, she gave half of each group the requirement to enroll the card on the Internet before the miles would be earned (*Enroll* = Yes or No).

Finally, cardholders are segmented into three types of users: those who use the card mainly for retail purchases (*Cardholder Segment* = Retail), those who use the card mainly for travel and leisure purchases (*Cardholder Segment* = Travel & Leisure), and those who the company is unable to segment (*Cardholder Segment* = Unspecified).

To measure effectiveness of the factors, the marketing analyst measures the increase in spending after three months of the program (*Spend Lift*).

The data set **Market Experiment** contains the data for the 4800 cardholders in the experiment. The variables are:

> *Miles:* coded Double Miles or Standard Miles
> *Enroll:* coded Yes if enrollment is required; No otherwise
> *Cardholder Segment:* coded Retail, Travel & Leisure, or Unspecified
> *Spend Lift ($):* the amount of increased or decreased use of the card after three months of the program

The analyst wants to know if any of the factors are important for understanding card use. Build a model to predict *Spend Lift* using the three predictor variables. Here are some things to consider:

1. Examine displays to see if the conditions of your model are satisfied.

2. Are any of the interactions of the variables significant?

3. If the three-way interaction is important, consider running separate models for the three levels of *Cardholder Segment*. Use interaction plots for each segment to understand whether the two-way interaction between *Miles* and *Enroll* changes for the three segments.

4. Keep in mind that the credit card company gains about $0.02 profit on every dollar of in-creased spending. Assume that adding double miles costs $0.005 for each mile awarded, but Internet enrollment is essentially free.

5. Write a report giving recommendations on whether the double-miles program is successful. Be sure to include confidence intervals for the effects and the profit to the company for both the *Miles* and *Enroll* factor effect. What effect does the cardholder segment have on your recommendations?

Answers

CHAPTER 1

SECTION EXERCISE ANSWERS

1. a) Each row represents a different house. It is a case.
   b) There are 7 variables including the house identifier.

3. a) House_ID is an identifier (categorical, not ordinal). Neighborhood is categorical (nominal). Mail_ZIP is categorical (nominal – ordinal in a sense, but only on a national level). Acres is quantitative (units – acres). Yr_Built is quantitative (units – year). Full_Market_Value is quantitative (units – dollars). Size is quantitative (units – square feet).
   b) These data are cross-sectional. All variables were measured at about the same time.

5. It is not clear if the data were obtained from a survey. They are certainly not from an experiment. Most likely they are just a collection of recent sales. We don't know if those sales are representative of all sales, so we should be cautious in drawing conclusions from these data about the housing market in general.

CHAPTER EXERCISE ANSWERS

7. Answers will vary.

9. *Who*—college students; *What*—2025 opinion and whether they'd purchase an electric vehicle; *When*—current; *Where*—your location; *Why*—Automobile manufacturer wants college student opinions; *How*—survey; *Variables*—There are 2 categorical variables. "Whether they'd purchase" is ordinal. The data are cross-sectional.

11. Answers will vary.

13. *Who*—MBA applicants at school in northeast US; *What*—sex, age, whether or not they accepted, whether or not they attended, and the reasons; *When*—not specified; *Where*—School in the Northeastern United States; *Why*—The researchers wanted to investigate any patterns in female acceptance and attendance; *How*—Data obtained internally from admissions office; *Variables*—There are 5 variables. Sex, whether or not they accepted, whether or not they attended, and the reasons are all categorical variables; only age (years) of applicant is quantitative. The data are a cross section.

15. *Who*—experiment volunteers; *What*—herbal cold remedy or sugar solution, and cold severity; *When*—not specified; *Where*—major pharmaceutical firm; *Why*—Scientists were testing the efficacy of a herbal compound on the severity of the common cold; *How*—The scientists set up an experiment; *Variables*—There are 2 variables. Type of treatment (herbal or sugar solution) is categorical, and severity rating is quantitative; *Concerns*—The severity of a cold seems subjective and difficult to quantify. Also, the scientists may feel pressure to report negative findings about the herbal product. The data are cross-sectional and from a designed experiment.

17. *Who*—vineyards; *What*—size of vineyard (possibly in acres), number of years in existence, state, varieties of grapes grown, average case price (probably in dollars), gross sales (probably in dollars), and percent profit; *When*—not specified; *Where*—not specified; *Why*—Business analysts hoped to provide information that would be helpful to producers of U.S. wines; *How*—not specified; *Variables*—There are 5 quantitative variables and 2 categorical variables. Size of vineyard, number of years in existence, average case price, gross sales, and percent profit are quantitative variables. State and variety of grapes grown are categorical variables. The data are a cross section collected in a designed survey.

19. *Who*—every model of automobile in the United States; *What*—vehicle manufacturer, vehicle type, weight (probably in pounds), horsepower (in horsepower), and gas mileage (in miles per gallon) for city and highway driving; *When*—This information is collected currently; *Where*—United States; *Why*—The Environmental Protection Agency uses the information to track fuel economy of vehicles; *How*—The data is collected from the manufacturer of each model; *Variables*—There are 6 variables. City mileage, highway mileage, weight, and horsepower are quantitative variables. Manufacturer and type of car are categorical variables. The data are a cross section.

21. *Who*—restaurants; *What*—% of customers liking restaurant, average meal cost ($), food rating (0–30), decor rating (0–30), service rating (0–30). *When*—current; *Where*—United States; *Why*—service to provide information for consumers; *How*—not specified; *Variables*—There are 5 variables. % liking and average cost are quantitative. Ratings (food, decor, and service) are ordered categories. The data are a cross section.

23. *Who*—students in an MBA statistics class; *What*—total personal investment in stock market ($), number of different stocks held, total invested in mutual funds ($), and name of each mutual fund; *When*—not specified; *Where*—School in the Northeastern United States; *Why*—The information was collected for use in classroom illustrations; *How*—An online survey was conducted. Presumably, participation was required for all members of the class; *Variables*—There are 4 variables. Name of mutual fund is a categorical variable. Number of stocks held, total amount invested in market ($), and in mutual funds ($) are quantitative variables. The data are a cross section.

25. *Who*—Indy 500 races; *What*—year, winner, car, time (hours), speed (mph), and car #. *When*—1911–2012; *Where*—Indianapolis, Indiana; *Why*—It is interesting to examine the trends in Indy 500 races; *How*—Official statistics are kept for the race every year; *Variables*—There are 6 variables. Winner, car, and car # are categorical variables. Year, time, and speed are quantitative variables. The quantitative variables can be viewed as time series.

27. Each row should be a single mortgage loan. Columns hold the borrower's name (which identifies the rows) and amount.

29. Each row is a week. Columns hold week number (to identify the row), sales prediction, sales, and difference.

31. Cross-sectional.

33. Time series.

CHAPTER 2

SECTION EXERCISE ANSWERS

1. a) Frequency table:

None	AA	BA	MA	PhD
164	42	225	52	29

   b) Relative frequency table (divide each number by 512 and multiply by 100):

None	AA	BA	MA	PhD
32.03%	8.20%	43.95%	10.16%	5.66%

3. a)

b)

c)

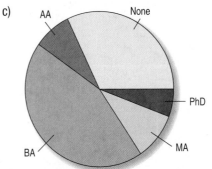

5. a) The vast majority of employees have either no college degree or a bachelor's degree (32% and 44%, respectively). About 10% have master's degrees, 8% have associate's degrees, and nearly 6% have PhDs.

   b) I would not be comfortable generalizing this to any other division or company. These data were collected only from my division. Other companies might have vastly different educational distributions.

7. a)

	Totals
<1 Year	95
1–5 Years	205
More Than 5 Years	212

   b) Yes

None	AA	BA	MA	PhD
164	42	225	52	29

9. a)

Percent	None	AA	BA	MA	PhD
<1 Year	6.1	7.1	22.2	38.5	41.4
1–5 Years	25.6	21.4	49.8	51.9	51.7
More Than 5 Years	68.3	71.4	28.0	9.6	6.9

b) No. The distributions look quite different. More than $^2/_3$ of those with no college degree have been with the company longer than 5 years, but almost none of the PhDs (less than 7%) have been there that long.

c)

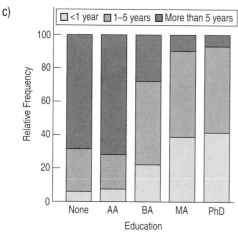

d) It's possible to see it in the table, but the stacked bar chart makes the differences much clearer.
e) A mosaic plot would display the different counts for each degree type. Areas of the plot representing each cell would then reflect the cell counts accurately.

CHAPTER EXERCISE ANSWERS

11. Answers will vary.

13. Answers will vary.

15. a) Yes, the categories divide a whole.
   b) Coca-Cola.

17. a) The pie chart does a better job of showing portions of a whole.
   b) There is no bar for "Other."

19. a) Yes, it is reasonable to assume that heart and respiratory disease caused approximately 38% of U.S. deaths in this year, since there is no possibility for overlap. Each person could only have one cause of death.
   b) Since the percentages listed add up to 73.7%, other causes must account for 26.3% of U.S. deaths.
   c) A bar graph or pie chart would be appropriate if a category for Other with 26.3% were added.

21. Cisco systems continues to dominate the market for desktop conferencing. Citrix and Microsoft are battling for second place. A pie chart or bar chart would be appropriate.

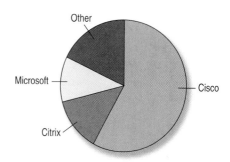

23. a) They don't total 100%. Others must have refused to answer or didn't know.
   b)

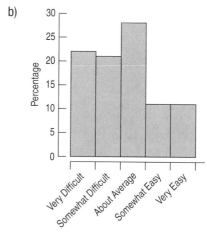

   c) Only if the "other" category were added.
   d) Answers will vary. Nearly half (43%) of business owners said that it would be somewhat or very difficult to obtain credit. Only 22% said it would be somewhat or very easy. Of the remaining, 28% said it would be about average and 7% didn't answer.

25. The bar chart shows that grounding is the most frequent cause of oil spillage for these 455 spills, and allows the reader to rank the other types as well. If being able to differentiate between close counts is required, use the bar chart. The pie chart is also acceptable as a display, but it's difficult to tell whether, for example, a greater percentage of spills is caused by grounding or collisions. To showcase the causes of oil spills as a fraction of all 455 spills, use the pie chart.

27. a) 31%
   b) Because the bars do not start at zero, it looks like India's percentage is about 6 times as big, but in fact, it's not even twice as big.
   c) Start the percentages at 0% on the vertical axis, not 40%.

d)

e) The percentage of people who say that wealth is important to them is highest in China and India (around 70%), followed by France (around 60%) and then the United States and United Kingdom where the percentage was only about 45%.

29. a) They must be column percentages because the sums are greater than 100% across the rows and all the columns add to 100%.

b)

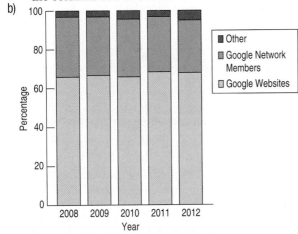

c) The main source of revenue for Google is from their own websites, which in 2008 was 66%, and increased to 69% by 2011. The second largest source is from other network websites which decreased from 31% in 2008 to 27% in 2012. Licensing and other revenue was 3% in 2008, but since 2008 has been 3 to 5%.

31. a) 45.1%
b) 34.9%
c) 5.3%
d) 59.8%
e) 41.3%
f) 65.8%
g) Companies that reported a positive change on October 24 were more likely to report a negative change for the year than companies who reported a negative change on October 24.

33. a) 11.5%
b) 45.5%

c) 18.2%
d) 2009 was 11.2%; 2010 was 8.2%; change = 3.0% fewer in 2010.

35. a) 4.8% G; 30.2% PG; 36.5% PG-13; 28.6% R or NC-17
b) 0% G; 2.3% PG; 45.5% PG-13; 52.3% R or NC-17

c)

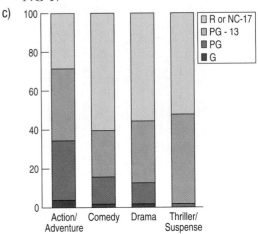

d) *Genre* and *Rating* are not independent. Thriller/Horror movies are nearly all PG-13 or R/NC-17, but 35% of Action/Adventure movies were either G or PG in 2011. Comedy is over 60% R or NC-17 in this year, while Action/Adventure was only 28.6%.

37. a) 62.7%
b) 62.8%
c) 62.5%
d) 23.9% from Asia, 1.9% Europe, 7.8% Latin America, 3.7% Middle East, and 62.7% North America.
e) The column percentages are given in the table.

		MBA Program		
		Two-Yr	Evening	Total
	Asia	18.90	31.73	**23.88**
	Europe	3.05	0.00	**1.87**
Origin	**Latin America**	12.20	0.96	**7.84**
	Middle East	3.05	4.81	**3.73**
	North America	62.80	62.50	**62.69**
	Total	**100.00**	**100.00**	**100.00**

f) No. The distributions appear to be different. For example, the percentage from Latin America among those in Two-Year programs is nearly 12.2% while for those in Evening programs it is less than 1%.

39. a) 5.5%
b) 5%
c) 4.5%
d) 53%
e) 71%
f) Here are row percentages:

	G	PG	PG-13	R/NC17	Total
2008–2012	4%	30%	54%	12%	100.0%
2003–2007	5%	22%	58%	15%	100.0%

The distributions are quite similar, although there were more PG and slightly fewer PG-13 and R/NC17 films in the more recent 5 years than the previous.

41. The study by the University of Texas Southwestern Medical Center provides evidence of an association between having a tattoo and contracting hepatitis C. Around 33% of the subjects who were tattooed in a commercial parlor had hepatitis C, compared with 13% of those tattooed elsewhere, and only 3.5% of those with no tattoo. If having a tattoo and having hepatitis C were independent, we would have expected these percentages to be roughly the same.

43. a) 66%
  b) It is higher.
  c) No, because we're not given counts or totals.
  d) Young (18–34 year-old) women appear to consider being professionally successful more important in their lives than do young men. But older respondents showed no difference by sex.

45. a)

	Caucasian	Hispanic	African-American	Other
Population	66.0%	16.0%	12.0%	6.0%
Moviegoers	63.0%	19.0%	12.0%	6.0%
Tickets	56.0%	26.0%	11.0%	7.0%

  b) The distributions of moviegoers are quite similar to the population as a whole, but Hispanics seem to buy proportionally more tickets and Caucasians fewer. Hispanics appear to go to the movies more often, on average, than Caucasians.

47. a) 14.25%
  b) 58.7%
  c) Younger women are more likely than older women to say that professional success is important to them.

49. a) The marginal totals have been added to the table:

		Hospital Size		
		Large	Small	Total
Procedure	Major Surgery	120 of 800	10 of 50	130 of 850
	Minor Surgery	10 of 200	20 of 250	30 of 450
	Total	130 of 1000	30 of 300	160 of 1300

160 of 1300, or about 12.3% of the patients had a delayed discharge.
  b) Major surgery patients were delayed 15.3% of the time.
     Minor surgery patients were delayed 6.7% of the time.
  c) Large hospital had a delay rate of 13%.
     Small hospital had a delay rate of 10%.
     The small hospital has the lower overall rate of delayed discharge.
  d) Large hospital: Major surgery 15% and Minor surgery 5%.
     Small hospital: Major surgery 20% and minor surgery 8%.
     Even though the small hospital had the lower overall rate of delayed discharge, the large hospital had a lower rate of delayed discharge for each type of surgery.
  e) Yes. While the overall rate of delayed discharge is lower for the small hospital, the large hospital did better with *both* major surgery and minor surgery.
  f) The small hospital performs a higher percentage of minor surgeries than major surgeries. 250 of 300 surgeries at the small hospital were minor (83%). Only 200 of the large hospital's 1000 surgeries were minor (20%). Minor surgery had a lower delay rate than major surgery (6.7 to 15.3%), so the small hospital's overall rate was artificially inflated. The larger hospital is the better hospital when comparing discharge delay rates.

51. a) 1284 applicants were admitted out of a total of 3014 applicants. 1284/3014 = 42.6%
  b) 1022 of 2165 (47.2%) of males were admitted. 262 of 849 (30.9%) of females were admitted.

		Males Accepted (of Applicants)	Females Accepted (of Applicants)	Total
Program	1	511 of 825	89 of 108	600 of 933
	2	352 of 560	17 of 25	369 of 585
	3	137 of 407	132 of 375	269 of 782
	4	22 of 373	24 of 341	46 of 714
	Total	1022 of 2165	262 of 849	1284 of 3014

  c) Since there are four comparisons to make, the table shown on the next page organizes the percentages of males and females accepted in each program. Females are accepted at a higher rate in every program.

Program	Males	Females
1	61.9%	82.4%
2	62.9%	68.0%
3	33.7%	35.2%
4	5.9%	7.0%

d) The comparison of acceptance rate within each program is most valid. The overall percentage is an unfair average. It fails to take the different numbers of applicants and different acceptance rates of each program. Women tended to apply to the programs in which gaining acceptance was difficult for everyone. This is an example of Simpson's Paradox.

CHAPTER 3
SECTION EXERCISE ANSWERS

1. a)

b)

c)

d) 1|14
    2|0225699
    3|0002224558
    4|244488

3. a) Unimodal
   b) Around 35 years old
   c) Fairly symmetric
   d) No outliers.

5. a) About the same. The distribution is fairly symmetric.
   b) 31.84 years
   c) 32 years

7. a) Q1 = 26; Q3 = 38 (Answers may vary slightly.)
   b) Q1 = 25.5; Q3 = 40
   c) IQR = 12 years
   d) SD = 9.84 years

9. a) The distribution is skewed to the right. There are a few negative values. The range is about $6000. Center around $2000; IQR around $2000.
   b) The mean will be larger because the distribution is right skewed.
   c) Because of the skewness, the median is a better summary.

11. a) 11 has a z-score of −2.12; 48 has a z-score of +1.64.
    b) The min, 11, is more extreme.
    c) 61.36 years old

13. a)

    b) No.
    c) 38 + 1.5*12 = 56 years old

15. a) Skewed to the right, since the mean is much greater than the median.
    b) Yes, at least one high outlier, since 250 is far greater than Q3 + 1.5 IQRs.
    c) We don't know how far the high whisker should go because we don't know the largest value inside the fence, or where other possible outliers might be.

17. The ages of the women are generally higher than those of the men by about 10 years. As the boxplot shows, more than 3/4 of the women are older than all the men.

19. Sales in Location #1 were higher than sales in Location #2 in nearly every week. The company might want to compare other stores in locations like these to see if this phenomenon holds true for other locations.

21. The upper outlier limit is
$123 + 1.5*(123 - 44.9) = 240.15$.
The lower outlier limit is
$44.9 - 1.5*(123 - 44.9) < 0$. Yes, the maximum value is an outlier. We should look at a boxplot to know how to proceed.

23. a) Yes.
   b) No—data are from a single time point.
   c) No—response is "time" but measured at only one time point.
   d) Yes.

25. A logarithmic transformation might make the distribution of revenues more symmetric.

CHAPTER EXERCISE ANSWERS

27. Answers will vary.

29. a) It is symmetric, with a center between 14.5 and 15 inches. *Size* varies from 12.5 inches to 17.5 inches and has no outliers.
   b) The bin from 14.5 to 15 and the bin from 15 to 15.5
   c) Men in the bin from 14.5 to 15 would need a 15.5 inch shirt. Those in the 15 to 15.5 bin would need a 16 inch shirt. So, 15.5 and 16 inches.

31. a) The distribution is unimodal (possibly bimodal) and skewed to the left. The median return is around 5% (6.8%). More than 6.8%. Half of the funds returned between 0% and 10%.
   b) About 75% of the funds returned less than the 10% returned by the S&P index.

33. a)

Min.	1st Qu.	Median	3rd Qu.	Max.
−4.14	1.75	6.68	10.08	14.58

   b) Median is 6.68%; IQR is 8.33%.

   d) The histogram (not shown here) shows the asymmetry of the distribution better than the boxplot.

35. Answers may vary slightly, depending on the stem used. The skewness of the distribution, the gap and the high outlier are all evident.

```
O | 111111122223333333444444
O | 55666678
1 | 03
1 | 5
2 |
2 | 5
```
Key: $0|8 = 80$ acres

37. a) Wayne Gretzky—Games played per season

```
8 | 000000122
7 | 8899
7 | 0344
6 |
6 | 4
5 |
5 |
4 | 58
4 |
```
Key: $7|8 = 78$ games
(Stem and leaf could also be displayed with smaller numbers on top.)

   b)

   c) The distribution of the number of games played per season by Wayne Gretzky is skewed to the low end and has low outliers. The median is 79, and the range is 37 games.

d) There are two outlier seasons with 45 and 48 games. He may have been injured. The season with 64 games is also separated by a gap.

39. a) The median because the distribution is skewed.
b) Lower, because the distribution is skewed toward the low end.
c) That display is not a histogram. It's a time series plot using bars to represent each point. The histogram should split up the number of games played into bins, not display the number of games played over time.

41. a) Descriptive Statistics: Price ($)

Minimum	Q1	Median	Q3	Maximum
2.21	2.51	2.61	2.72	3.05

b) Range = max − min = 3.05 − 2.21 = $0.84;
IQR = Q3 − Q1 = 2.72 − 2.51 = $0.21

c)

d) Symmetric with one high outlier. The mean is $2.62, with a standard deviation of $0.156.
e) There is one unusually high price that is greater than $3.00 per frozen pizza.

43. As we can see from the histogram and boxplot,

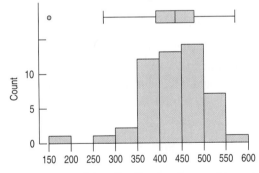

the main part of the distribution is roughly unimodal and symmetric, but there is a low outlier (District of Columbia). Without the District of Columbia (which is not a state), the median consumption is 438 gal/capita. Fifty percent of the states have consumption between 394 and 479 gal/capita.

45. a) 1611 yards
b) Between Quartile 1 = 5585.75 yards, and Quartile 3 = 6131 yards.
c) The distribution of golf course lengths appears roughly symmetric, so the mean and the standard deviation are appropriate.

d) The distribution of the lengths of all the golf courses in Vermont is roughly unimodal and symmetric. The mean length of the golf courses is approximately 5900 yards and the standard deviation is 386.6 yards.

47. a) A boxplot is shown. A histogram would also be appropriate.

b) Descriptive Statistics: Sales ($) (Different statistics software may yield slightly different results.)

Variable	N	Mean	SE Mean	StDev	Minimum
Sales ($)	18	107845	11069	46962	62006

Q1	Median	Q3	Maximum
73422.5	95975	112330.0	224504

The mean sale is $107,845, and the median is $95,975. The mean is higher because the outliers pull it up.
c) The median because the distribution has outliers.
d) The standard deviation of the distribution is $46,962 and the IQR is $38,907.50. (Answers may vary slightly due to different quartile algorithms.)
e) The IQR because the outliers inflate the standard deviation.
f) The mean would decrease. The standard deviation would decrease. The median and IQR would be less affected.

49. A histogram shows that the distribution is unimodal and skewed to the left. There do not appear to be any outliers. The median failure rate for these 17 models is 16.2%. The middle 50% of the models have failure rates between 10.87% and 21.2%. The best rate is 3.17% for the 60GB Video model, and the worst is the 40GB Click Wheel at 29.85%.

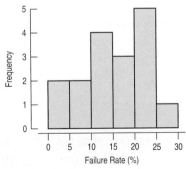

51. a) Gas prices generally increased over the nine-year period except for the dip in 2009. The distribution of prices in 2003 appears symmetric with a relatively small spread. Median prices rose in 2006, fell slightly by 2009 and then increased to new highs in 2012. There are low outliers in 2009 and 2012, but they appear to be quite near the lower fences.

b) The distribution of gas prices in 2003 were most stable because it has the smallest IQR. Prices in 2006 and 2009 were least stable.

53. a) There is one wine in Seneca more expensive than any other.

b) Both Cayuga and Seneca produce cheaper wines than Keuka, but Seneca has several high outliers.

c) Keuka Lake.

d) Cayuga Lake vineyards and Seneca Lake vineyards have approximately the same average price of about $15 a bottle, while a typical Keuka Lake vineyard has a price near $22. Keuka Lake vineyards have consistently high prices between about $18 and $26 a bottle. Cayuga Lake vineyards have prices from $13 to $19, and Seneca Lake vineyards have highly variable prices from about $12 to over $30.

55. a) The median speed is the speed at which 50% of the winning horses ran slower. Find 50% on the left, move straight over to the graph and down to a speed of about 36 mph.

b) Q1 = 34.5 mph; Q3 = 36.5 mph

c) Range = 7 mph
   IQR = 2 mph

d)

Derby Speeds

e) The distribution of winning speeds in the Kentucky Derby is skewed to the left. The lowest winning speed is just under 31 mph, and the fastest speed is about 37.5 mph. The median speed is approximately 36 mph, and 75% of winning speeds are above 34.5 mph. Only a few percent of winners have had speeds below 33 mph.

57. a) Class 3.

b) Class 3.

c) Class 3 because it is the most highly skewed. Median is higher.

d) Class 1.

e) Probably Class 1. But without the actual scores, it is impossible to calculate the exact IQRs.

59. There is an extreme outlier for the slow-speed drilling. One hole was drilled almost an inch away from the center of the target! If that distance is correct, the engineers at the computer production plant should investigate the slow-speed drilling process closely. It may be plagued by extreme, intermittent inaccuracy. The outlier in the slow-speed drilling process is so extreme that no graphical display can display the distribution in a meaningful way while including that outlier. That distance should be removed before looking at a plot of the drilling distances.

   With the outlier removed, we can see that the slow drilling process is more accurate. The greatest distance from the target for the slow drilling process, 0.000098 inches, is still more accurate than the smallest distance for the fast drilling process, 0.000100 inches.

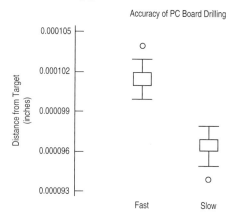

61. a) The mean of 54.41 is meaningless. These are categorical values.

b) Typically, the mean and standard deviation are influenced by outliers and skewness.

c) No. Summary statistics are only appropriate for quantitative data.

63. Although the numbers are not large, it appears that Bond funds performed worse, and more consistently than the other funds. The Domestic Equity funds appear to have performed best except for one low outlier. The lower quartile of the Domestic Equity funds are higher than the medians of the other types of funds.

65. a) Even though MLS ID numbers are categorical identifiers, they are assigned sequentially, so this graph has some information. Most of the houses listed long ago have sold and are no longer listed.

b) A histogram is generally not an appropriate display for categorical data.

67. a)

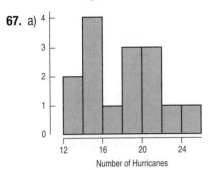

Number of Hurricanes

b) The distribution is fairly uniform considering the small numbers in each bin. There do not appear to be any decades that would be considered to be outliers.

c)

Decade

d) This graph does not support the claim that the number of hurricanes has increased in recent decades.

69. What is the *x*-axis? If it is time, what are the units? Months? Years? Decades? How is "productivity" measured?

71. The house that sells for $400,000 has a *z*-score of $(400,000 - 167,900)/77,158 = 3.01$, but the house with 4000 sq. ft. of living space has a *z*-score of $(4000 - 1819)/663 = 3.29$. So it's even more unusual.

73. U.S. *z*-scores are -0.04 and 1.63, total $= 1.59$. Ireland *z*-scores are 0.25 and 2.77, total 3.02. So Ireland "wins" the consumption battle.

75. a) The histogram shows the distribution is strongly skewed to the right and possibly bimodal with one mode just over $1 and another near $2.75.

Price ($)

b) Prices were relatively stable until the late 1990s when they started increasing. They increased steadily from 2002 until 2008 (the financial crisis) when they dropped precipitously before increasing steadily again until mid 2011. Since then, they have been moderately decreasing.

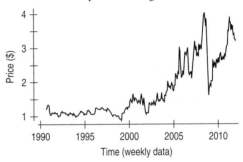

Time (weekly data)

c) The time series plot is more informative because the prices have changed so much over time.

77. a) The bimodality of the distribution.

b) The trend over time.

c) The time series plot because it reveals much more of the structure of the data. The rates are not stationary.

d) Unemployment decreased from 2004 to 2007 from just over 6% to just under 5%. It then increased steadily until 2010 when it reached nearly 10%. Since then it has decreased to about 8%.

79. a) The distribution is skewed. That makes it difficult to estimate anything meaningful from the graph.

b) Transform these data using either square roots or logs.

CHAPTER 4
SECTION EXERCISE ANSWERS

1. a)

Number of Sales People Working

b) Positive.
c) Linear.
d) Strong.
e) No.

3. a) Years of experience.
b) Salary.
c) Salary.

5. a) True.
   b) False. It will not change the correlation.
   c) False. Correlation has no units.

7. Correlation does not demonstrate causation. The analyst's argument is that sales staff cause sales. However, the data may reflect the store hiring more people as sales increase, so any causation would run the other way.

9. a) False. The line usually touches none of the points. We minimize the sum of the squared errors.
   b) True.
   c) False. It is the sum of the squares of all the residuals that is minimized.

11. a) $2 \times 0.965 = 1.93$ SDs
   b) $17.6 + 1.93 \times 5.34 = 27.906$ or \$27,906
   c) 0.965 SDs below the mean
   d) \$12,447

13. a) $b_1 = 0.914$ if found by hand. $b_1 = 0.913$ if found by technology. (Difference is due to rounding error.)
   b) It means that an additional 0.914 (\$1000) or \$914 of sales is associated with each additional sales person working.
   c) $b_0 = 8.10$
   d) It would mean that, on average, we expect sales of 8.10 (\$1000) or \$8100 with 0 sales people working. Doesn't really make sense in this context.
   e) $\widehat{Sales} = 8.10 + 0.914 \, Number \, of \, Sales \, People \, Working$
   f) \$24.55 (\$1000) or \$24,550. (24,540 if using the technology solution.)
   g) 0.45 (\$1000) or \$450. (\$460 with technology.)
   h) Underestimated.

15. The winners may be suffering from regression to the mean. Perhaps they weren't really better than other rookie executives, but just happened to have a lucky year.

17. a) Thousands of dollars.
   b) 2.77 (the largest residual in magnitude).
   c) 0.07 (the smallest residual in magnitude).

19. $R^2 = 93.12\%$. About 93% of the variance in *Sales* can be accounted for by the regression of *Sales* on *Number of Sales Workers*.

21. 16, 16, 36, 49, 49, 64, 100. They are skewed to the high end.

CHAPTER EXERCISE ANSWERS

23. a) Number of text messages: explanatory; cost: response. To predict cost from number of text messages. Positive direction. Linear shape. Possibly an outlier for contracts with fixed cost for texting.
   b) Fuel efficiency: explanatory; sales volume: response. To predict sales from fuel efficiency. There may be no association between mpg and sales

volume. Environmentalists hope that a higher mpg will encourage higher sales, which would be a positive association. We have no information about the shape of the relationship.
   c) Neither variable is explanatory. Both are responses to the lurking variable of temperature.
   d) Price: explanatory variable; demand: response variable. To predict demand from price. Negative direction. Linear shape in a narrow range, but curved over a larger range of prices.

25. a) None.
   b) 3 and 4
   c) 2, 3, and 4
   d) 2 and 4
   e) 3 and 1

27. a)

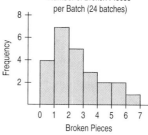

   b) Unimodal, skewed to the right. The skewness.
   c) The positive, somewhat linear relation between batch number and broken pieces.

29. a) 0.006
   b) 0.777
   c) -0.923
   d) -0.487

31. a) *Price*.
   b) *Sales*.
   c) Sales decrease by 24,369.49 pounds for every additional dollar charged.
   d) It is just a base value. It means nothing because stores won't set their price to \$0.
   e) 56,572.32 pounds
   f) 3427.69 pounds

33. a) *Salary*.
   b) *Wins*.
   c) On average, teams who spend \$1M more in salary win, 0.219 games more.
   d) Number of wins predicted for a team that spends \$0 on salaries. This is not meaningful here.
   e) 2.19 games more
   f) Slightly worse. They are expected to win 9.96 games.
   g) -1.96 games
   h) Not very useful. The residual standard deviation says that we can not predict better than about $+/-5$ games. For a prediction of 8 games won,

that's 3 to 13 games. All but 2 teams that year were already in that range.

35. About 47,084 pounds

37. "Packaging" isn't a variable. At best, it is a category. There's no basis for computing a correlation.

39. The model is meaningless because the variable *Region* is not quantitative. The slope makes no sense because *Region* has no units. The boxplot comparisons are useful but the regression is meaningless.

41. a) There is a strong negative linear association between Carbon Footprint and Highway mpg.
   b) Quantitative variables, straight enough. The hybrid cars are far from the rest of the data. But they are mostly in line with the linear pattern. It is correct to regard them as outliers or not; that's a matter of judgment.
   c) $r = -0.941$; Removing the hybrids reduces the correlation. Data values far from the main body of the data and in line with the linear trend tend to increase correlation and may make it misleading.

43. a) Positive association.
   b) Plot is not linear, violating the linearity condition. There may be an outlier at 17 rooms.

45. a) The variables are both quantitative (with units % of GDP), the plot is reasonably straight, but there are a couple of outliers that influence the fit (especially 2009). The spread is roughly constant (although the spread is large). We should be cautious in interpreting the model too strictly.
   b) About 31.6% of the variation in the growth rates of developing countries is accounted for by the growth rates of developed countries.
   c) Years 1970–2011

47. a) $\overline{Growth\ (Developing\ Countries)} = 3.38 + 0.468$ *Growth (Developed Countries)*
   b) The predicted growth of developing countries in years of 0 growth in developed countries. Yes, this makes sense.
   c) On average, GDP in developed countries increased 0.468% for a 1% increase in growth in developed countries.
   d) 5.25%
   e) More; we would predict 4.62%.
   f) 1.47%

49. a) Yes, the scatterplot is straight enough, variables are quantitative and there are no outliers.
   b) Teams that score more runs generally have higher attendance but the relationship is only moderately strong, with a correlation of 0.477.
   c) There is a positive association, but correlation doesn't imply causation.

51. a) The predicted value of the money *Flow* if the *Return* was 0%.
   b) An increase of 1% in mutual fund return was associated with an increase of $771 million in money flowing into mutual funds.
   c) $9747 million
   d) −$4747 million; overestimated.

53. a) Model seems appropriate. Residual plot looks fine.
   b) Model not appropriate. Relationship is nonlinear.
   c) Model not appropriate. Spread is increasing.

55. There are two outliers that inflate the R^2 value and affect the slope and intercept. Without those two points, the R^2 drops from 79% to about 31%. The analyst should set aside those two customers and refit the model.

57. 0.03. For every $1000 increase in ad expenditure, sales are most likely to increase by $30,000.

59. a) R^2 is an indication of the strength of the model, not the appropriateness of the model.
   b) The agent should have said, "The model predicts that annual sales will be $10 million when $1.5 million is spent on advertising."

61. a) Quantitative variable condition: Both variables are quantatitive (*GPA* and *Starting Salary*).
   b) Linearity condition: Examine a scatterplot of *Starting Salary* by *GPA*.
   c) Outlier condition: Examine the scatterplot.
   d) Equal spread condition: Plot the regression residuals versus predicted values.

63. a)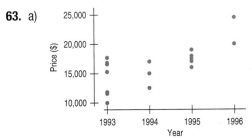
   b) There is a strong, positive, association between *Price* and *Year* of used BMW 850CSi's with some upward curvature.
   c) Yes, but with caution because of the curvature.
   d) 0.757
   e) 57.3% of the variability in *Price* of a used BMW 850 can be accounted for by the *Year* the car was made.
   f) The relationship is not perfect. Other factors, such as options, condition, and mileage, may account for some of the variability in price.

65. a) The association between cost of living in 2013 and 2007 is very weak. There are no outliers. The scatterplot indicates that the linear model is appropriate but not likely to reveal much.

b) 7.0% of the variability in cost of living in 2013 can be explained by variability in cost of living in 2007.

c) -0.26

d) $\overline{Index\ 2013} = 191.6 - 0.683\ \overline{Index\ 2007}$

e) Moscow was predicted to have an index of $191.6 - .683(134.4) = 99.80$, but the 2013 index was only 81.58, so the residual is $81.58 - 99.80 = -18.22\%$.

67. a) 0.578

b) CO_2 levels account for 33.4% of the variation in mean temperature.

c) $\overline{Mean\ Temperature} = 15.3066 + 0.004\ CO_2$

d) The predicted mean temperature has been increasing at an average rate of 0.004 degrees (C)/ppm of CO_2.

e) One *could* say that with no CO_2 in the atmosphere, there would be a temperature of 15.3066 degrees Celsius, but this is extrapolation to a nonsensical point.

f) No.

g) Predicted 16.7626 degrees C.

CHAPTER 5

SECTION EXERCISE ANSWERS

1. a) Independent (unless a large group of one gender comes to the ATM machine together).

b) Independent. The last digit of one student's SS number provides no information about another.

c) Not independent. How you perform on one test provides information about other tests.

3. a) Won't work, but won't hurt. Each number drawn is equally likely and independent of the others, so this set of numbers is just as likely as any other in the next drawing.

b) Won't work, but won't hurt. Each number drawn is equally likely and independent of the others and of previous drawings, so the previous winners are just as likely as any other in the next drawing.

5. a) 0.40

b) 0.60

c) $0.60^2 = 0.36$

d) $0.60 + 0.60 - (0.36) = 0.84$ or $1 - (0.4^2) = 0.84$

7. a) $755/1200 = 0.629$

b) Marginal.

c) $210/1200 = 0.175$

d) Joint.

9. a) $210/500 = 0.42$

b) $210/755 = 0.278$

c) $415/500 = 0.83$

11. a) $100\% - 30\% = 70\%$

b) Joint.

c)

		Online Banking		
		Yes	**No**	
Age	**Under 50**	0.25	0.15	**0.40**
	50 or Older	0.05	0.55	**0.60**
		0.30	**0.70**	**1.00**

d) $0.25/0.40 = 0.625$

e) No, because the conditional probability of banking online for those under 50 is 0.625. The probability of banking online is 0.30 which is not the same.

13. a)

b) 3.7%

c) 0.405

15. a) White: 0.68, Black: 0.11, Hispanic/Latino/Other: 0.21; White Male: 0.54, White Female: 0.46; Black Male: 0.52, Black Female: 0.48; Hispanic/Latino/Other Male: 0.58, Hispanic/Latino/Other Female: 0.42.

b) 0.0528

c) 0.46

d) 0.6893

CHAPTER EXERCISE ANSWERS

17. a) Individual outcomes can't be predicted, although in the long run the relative frequencies may be known (and for a roulette wheel should be equal.)

b) This is likely a personal probability expressing his degree of belief that there will be a new high.

19. a) There is no such thing as the "law of averages." The overall probability of an airplane crash does not change due to recent crashes.

b) There is no such thing as the "law of averages." The overall probability of an airplane crash does not change due to a period in which there were no crashes.

21. a) It would be foolish to insure your neighbor's house for $300. Although you would probably simply collect $300, there is a chance you could end up paying much more than $300. That risk is not worth the $300.

b) The insurance company insures many people. The overwhelming majority of customers pay and never have a claim. The few customers who do have a claim are offset by the many who simply send their premiums without a claim. The relative risk to the insurance company is low.

23. a) Yes.

b) Yes.

c) No, probabilities sum to more than 1.

d) Yes.

e) No, sum isn't 1 and one value is negative.

25. 0.078

27. The events are disjoint. Use the addition rule.

a) 0.72

b) 0.89

c) 0.28

29. a) 0.5184

b) 0.0784

c) 0.4816

31. a) The repair needs for the two cars must be independent of one another.

b) This may not be reasonable. An owner may treat the two cars similarly, taking good (or poor) care of both. This may decrease (or increase) the likelihood that each needs to be repaired.

33. a) 0.68

b) 0.32

c) 0.04

35. a) The events are disjoint (an M&M can't be two colors at once), so use the addition rule where applicable.

i) 0.30

ii) 0.30

iii) 0.90

iv) 0

b) The events are independent (picking out one M&M doesn't affect the outcome of the next pick), so use the multiplication rule.

i) 0.027

ii) 0.128

iii) 0.512

iv) 0.271

37. a) Disjoint.

b) Independent.

c) No. Once you know that one of a pair of disjoint events has occurred, the other one cannot occur, so its probability has become zero.

39. a) 0.125

b) 0.125

c) 0.875

d) Independence.

41. a) 0.0225

b) 0.092

c) 0.00008

d) 0.556

43. a) Your thinking is correct. There are 47 cards left in the deck, 26 black and only 21 red.

b) This is not an example of the Law of Large Numbers. The card draws are not independent.

45. a) 0.39

b) 0.82

47. a) 0.642

b) 0.035

c) $1 - (410 + 815)/1270$

49. a)

b) 0.16

c) 0.667

51. a) $P(\text{Tweet and} <30) = P(\text{Tweet}) \times P(<30 \mid \text{Tweet}) = 0.15 * 0.5 = 0.075$

b) Using Bayes's theorem, $P(\text{tweet} \mid <30) = P(\text{tweet and} <30)/P(\text{tweet}) = 0.075/0.15 = 0.5$

53. a) 0.10

b) 0.17

c) 0.026

d) 0.24

55. a) 0.1062

b) 0.4469

c) 0.0785

57. a) 0.11

b) 0.27

c) 0.407

d) 0.344

59. No. 28.8% of men with OK blood pressure have high cholesterol, but 40.7% of men with high blood pressure have high cholesterol.

61. a) 0.026
b) 0.84
c) 0.20
d) 0.053
e) 0.554
f) $P(\text{more time} \mid <25 \text{ years}) = 0.158$. $P(\text{more time}) = 0.10$. Since not equal, they are not independent.

63. a) 0.47
b) 0.266
c) $P(\text{pool}) = 0.21$, $P(\text{pool} \mid \text{garage}) = 0.266$. Having a garage and a pool are not independent events.
d) $P(\text{pool and garage}) = 0.17$. Having a garage and a pool are not disjoint eventxs.

65. a) 0.71
b) $P(<500\text{K} \mid 2 \text{ Br}) = 0$. $P(<500\text{K}) = 0.71$. Since not equal, they are not independent.

67. a) 15.4%
b) 11.4%
c) 73.9%
d) 18.5%

*69. a)

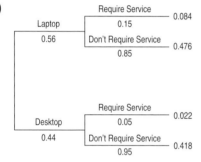

b) 10.6%
c) 0.792

CHAPTER 6
SECTION EXERCISE ANSWERS

1. a) Discrete.
b) Yes/no.

3. 0.7

5. 0.781

7. a) $19
b) $7

9. a) $\mu = 30; \sigma = 6$
b) $\mu = 26; \sigma = 5$
c) $\mu = 30; \sigma = 5.39$
d) $\mu = -10; \sigma = 5.39$

11. a) 110 and 12.
b) 450 and 40.
c) 190 and 14.422.
d) X and Y are independent for the SD calculation, but not necessarily for the sum.

13. a) Yes. Outcomes are independent with probability $p = 1/6$. The outcomes are {getting a 6} and {not getting a 6}.
b) No. More than two outcomes are possible.
c) No. The chance of a woman (or man) changes depending on who has already been picked.
d) Yes, assuming responses (and cheating) are independent among the students.

15. Yes.

17. Geometric; $p = 0.287$

19. a) 0.5488
b) 0.4512

CHAPTER EXERCISE ANSWERS

21. a) $1, 2, \ldots, n$
b) Discrete.

23. a) 1.7
b) 0.9

25. a) 2.25 lights
b) 1.26 lights

27. a) No, the probability he wins the second changes depending on whether he won the first.
b) 0.42
c) 0.08
d)

X	0	1	2
$P(X = x)$	0.42	0.50	0.08

e) $E(X) = 0.66$ tournaments; $\sigma = 0.62$ tournaments.

29. a) No, the probability of one battery being dead will depend on the state of the other one since there are only 10 batteries.

b)

Number Good	0	1	2
P(number good)	$\left(\dfrac{3}{10}\right)\left(\dfrac{2}{9}\right) = \dfrac{6}{90}$	$\left(\dfrac{3}{10}\right)\left(\dfrac{7}{9}\right) + \left(\dfrac{7}{10}\right)\left(\dfrac{3}{9}\right) = \dfrac{42}{90}$	$\left(\dfrac{7}{10}\right)\left(\dfrac{6}{9}\right) = \dfrac{42}{90}$

c) $\mu = 1.4$ batteries
d) $\sigma = 0.61$ batteries

31. $\mu = E$ (total wait time) $= 74.0$ seconds
$\sigma = SD$ (total wait time) ≈ 20.57 seconds
(Answers to standard deviation may vary slightly due to rounding of the standard deviation of the number of red lights each day.) The standard deviation may be calculated only if the stoplights are independent of each other. This seems reasonable.

33. a) $\mu = 13.6, \sigma = 2.55$
  b) Assuming the hours are independent of each other.
  c) A typical 8-hour day will have about 11 to 16 repair calls.
  d) 19 or more repair calls would be a lot! That's more than two standard deviations above average.

35. a) B = number basic; D = number deluxe; Net Profit= 120B + 150D − 200
  b) $928.00
  c) $187.45
  d) Mean—no; SD—yes (sales are independent).

37. a) $50
  b) $100

39. a) Let X_i = price of ith Hulk figure sold; Y_i = price of ith Iron Man figure sold; Insertion Fee = \$0.55; $T =$ Closing Fee $= 0.0875(X_1 + X_2 + \cdots + X_{19} + Y_1 + \cdots + Y_{13})$; Net Income $= (X_1 + X_2 + \cdots + X_{19} + Y_1 + \cdots + Y_{13}) - 32(0.55) - 0.0875(X_1 + X_2 + \cdots + X_{19} + Y_1 + \cdots + Y_{13})$
  b) $\mu = E$ (net income) = \$313.24
  c) $\sigma = SD$ (net income) = \$6.625
  d) Yes, to compute the standard deviation.

41. a) No, these are not Bernoulli trials. The possible outcomes are 1, 2, 3, 4, 5, and 6. There are more than two possible outcomes.
  b) Yes, these may be considered Bernoulli trials. There are only two possible outcomes: Type A and not Type A. Assuming the 120 donors are representative of the population, the probability of having Type A blood is 43%. The trials are not independent because the population is finite, but the 120 donors represent less than 10% of all possible donors.
  c) No, these are not Bernoulli trials. The probability of choosing a man changes after each promotion and the 10% condition is violated.
  d) No, these are not Bernoulli trials. We are sampling without replacement, so the trials are not independent. Samples without replacement may be considered Bernoulli trials if the sample size is less than 10% of the population, but 500 is more than 10% of 3000.
  e) Yes, these may be considered Bernoulli trials. There are only two possible outcomes: sealed properly and not sealed properly. The probability that a package is unsealed is constant at about 10%, as long as the packages checked are a representative sample of all.

43. a) 0.0819
  b) 0.0064
  c) 0.16
  d) 0.992

45. $E(X) = 14.29$, so 15 patients

47. a) 0.078 pixels
  b) 0.280 pixels
  c) 0.374
  d) 0.012

49. a) 0.293
  b) 0.3597
  c) 0.347

51. a) 0.0745
  b) 0.502
  c) 0.211
  d) 0.0166
  e) 0.0179
  f) 0.9987

53. a) A uniform; all numbers should be equally likely to be selected.
  b) 0.5
  c) 0.001

55. a) The Poisson model.
  b) 0.9502
  c) 0.0025

57. a) 0.65
  b) 0.75
  c) 7.69 picks

59. a) $\mu = 10.44, \sigma = 1.16$
  b) 0.812
  c) 0.475
  d) 0.00193
  e) 0.998

CHAPTER 7

SECTION EXERCISE ANSWERS

1. In economics she scored 1.25 standard deviations above the mean. On the math exam she scored 1.50 standard deviations above the mean, so she did "better" on the math exam.

3. You scored 2.2 standard deviations above the mean.

5. a) According to the 68–95–99.7 Rule, only 5% of the distribution is beyond 2 standard deviations from the mean, so only 2.5% is more than 2 standard deviations above the mean. So less than 3% of the distribution is above a z-score of 2.20. You qualify.

b) You need to assume that the distribution is unimodal and symmetric for the 68–95–99.7 Rule to apply.

7. a)

b) 18.6 to 31.0 mpg
c) 16%
d) 13.5%
e) less than 12.4 mpg

9. a) 6.68%
b) 98.78%
c) 71.63%
d) 61.71%

11. a) 0.842
b) −0.675
c) −1.881
d) −1.645 to 1.645

13. Yes. The histogram is unimodal and symmetric and the Normal probability plot is straight.

15. a) $\mu = E(\text{miles remaining}) = 164$ miles
$\sigma = SD(\text{miles remaining}) \approx 19.80$ miles
b) 0.580

17. a) 0.141 (0.175 with continuity correction)
b) Answers may vary. That's a fairly high proportion, but the decision depends on the relative costs of not selling seats and bumping passengers.

19. a) A uniform; all numbers should be equally likely to be selected.
b) 0.02
c) 0.10

21. a) $\lambda = 1/3$.
b) 0.811

CHAPTER EXERCISE ANSWERS

23. a) 16%
b) 50%
c) 95%
d) 0.15%

25. a) 6.2%
b) 8.0%
c) 2.6%
d) $4.4\% < x < 8.0\%$

27. a) 50%
b) 16%
c) 2.5%
d) More than 1.298 is more unusual.

29. a) $x > 1.233$
b) $x < 1.190$
c) $(1.104 < x < 1.276)$
d) $x < 1.104$

31. a) 36.9% (using technology).
b) 78.1%
c) 99.8%
d) 0.003%

33. a) $x > 8.51\%$
b) $x < 4.69\%$
c) $5.26\% < x < 7.14\%$
d) $x > 4.69\%$

35. a) 5.74%
b) 10.39%
c) 2.43%

37. a) 79.58
b) 18.50
c) 95.79
d) −2.79

39. $z_{\text{SAT}} = 1.30$; $z_{\text{ACT}} = 2$. The ACT score is the better score because it is farther above the mean in standard deviation units than the SAT score.

41. Any Job Satisfaction score more than 2 standard deviations below the mean or less than $100 - 2(12) = 76$ might be considered unusually low. We would expect to find someone with a Job Satisfaction score less than $100 - 3(12) = 64$ very rarely.

43. a) About 16%
b) One standard deviation below the mean is −1.27 hours, which is impossible.
c) Because the standard deviation is larger than the mean, the distribution is strongly skewed to the right, not symmetric.

45. a)

b) 30.85%
c) 17.00%
d) IQR = Q3 − Q1 = 32.38
e) Above 212.87 points.

47. a) To know about their consistency and how long they might last. Standard deviation measures variability, which translates to consistency in everyday use. A type of battery with a small standard deviation would be more likely to have life spans close to their mean life span than a type of battery with a larger standard deviation.

b) The second company's batteries have a higher mean life span, but a larger standard deviation, so they have more variability. The decision is not clear-cut. The first company's batteries are not likely to fail in less than 21 months, but that wouldn't be surprising for the second company. But the second company's batteries could easily last longer than 39 months—a span very unlikely for the first company.

49. CEOs can have between 0 and maybe 40 (or possibly 50) year's experience. A standard deviation of 1/2 year is impossible because many CEOs would be 10 or 20 SDs away from the mean, whatever it is. An SD of 16 years would mean that 2 SDs on either side of the mean is plus or minus 32, for a range of 64 years. That's too high. So, the SD must be 6 years.

51. a) 1 oz
b) 0.5 oz
c) 0.023
d) $\mu = 4$ oz, $\sigma = 0.5$ oz
e) 0.159
f) $\mu = 12.3$ oz, $\sigma = 0.54$ oz

53. a) 12.2 oz
b) 0.51 oz
c) 0.058

55. a) $\mu = 37.6$ min, $\sigma = 3.7$ min
b) No, 30 min is more than 2 SDs below the mean.

57. a) $\mu = 1920$, $\sigma = 48.99$; $P(T > 2000) = 0.051$
b) $\mu = \$220$, $\sigma = 11.09$; No—$300 is more than 7 SDs above the mean.
c) $P(D - \frac{1}{2}C > 0) \approx 0.26$

59. 0.053 or 0.066 using continuity correction

61. 0.025 or 0.0296 using continuity correction

63. a) 0.5
b) 0.25

65. a) The Poisson model
b) The exponential model
c) 1/3 minutes
d) 0.0473

CHAPTER 8
SECTION EXERCISE ANSWERS

1. a) False. Sampling error cannot be avoided, even with unbiased samples.
b) True.
c) True.
d) False. Randomization will match the characteristics in a way that is unbiased. We can't possibly think of all the characteristics that might be important or match our sample to the population on all of them.

3. a) Organic farmers in the northeast United States.
b) NOFA membership listing.
c) Proportion who think global climate change is affecting crop yield.
d) Simple random sample.

5. a) No. It would be nearly impossible to get exactly 500 males and 500 females by random chance.
b) Stratified sample, stratified by whether the respondent is male or female.

7. Systematic sample.

9. a) Population—Human resources directors of *Fortune* 500 companies.
b) Parameter—Proportion who don't feel surveys intruded on their work day.
c) Sampling Frame—List of HR directors at *Fortune* 500 companies.
d) Sample—23% who responded.
e) Method—Attempted census (nonrandom).
f) Bias—Hard to generalize because who responds is related to the question itself (nonresponse bias).

11. a) Organic farmers in the Northeast.
b) The members who attended the recent symposium.
c) The sampling frame is not necessarily representative of the entire group of farmers. Those who attended the symposium may have different opinions from those who didn't. His sample isn't random and may be biased toward those most interested in the topic. Finally, the script is biased and may lead to an estimate of a higher proportion who think government should be doing more to fight global warming than is true within the population.

13. a) Answers will vary. Question 1 seems appropriate. Question 2 predisposes the participant to agree that $50 is a reasonable price, and does not seem appropriate.
b) Question 1 is the more neutrally worded. Question 2 is biased in its wording.

15. a) True.
b) False. Often parts of the population are not sampled.

c) False. Measurement error refers to inaccurate responses. Sampling error refers to sample-to-sample variability.

d) True.

17. a) This is a multistage design, with a cluster sample at the first stage and a simple random sample for each cluster.

b) If any of the three churches you pick at random is not representative of all churches then you'll introduce sampling error by the choice of that church.

CHAPTER EXERCISE ANSWERS

19. a) Voluntary response.

b) We have no confidence at all in estimates from such studies.

21. a) The population of interest is all adults in the United States.

b) The sampling frame is U.S. adults with telephones. Because they use computers to generate random numbers from all possible numbers this seems representative.

23. a) Population—U.S. teens.

b) Parameter—Proportion who have access to computers and proportion who generally access the Internet by cell phone.

c) Sampling Frame—not specified.

d) Sample—802 teens and parents.

e) Method—Not specified. Probably a random digit dialed survey.

f) Bias—If teens were interviewed in front of their parents, it might have biased their responses.

25. a) Population—Adults.

b) Parameter—Proportion who think drinking and driving is a serious problem.

c) Sampling Frame—Bar patrons.

d) Sample—Every 10th person leaving the bar.

e) Method—Systematic sampling.

f) Bias—Those interviewed had just left a bar. They probably think drinking and driving is less of a problem than do adults in general.

27. a) Population—Soil around a former waste dump.

b) Parameter—Concentrations of toxic chemicals.

c) Sampling Frame—Accessible soil around the dump.

d) Sample—16 soil samples.

e) Method—Not clear.

f) Bias—Don't know if soil samples were randomly chosen. If not, may be biased toward more or less polluted soil.

29. a) Population—Snack food bags.

b) Parameter—Weight of bags, proportion passing inspection.

c) Sampling Frame—All bags produced each day.

d) Sample—10 randomly selected cases, 1 bag from each case for inspection.

e) Method—Multistage sampling.

f) Bias—Should be unbiased.

31. Bias. Only people watching the news will respond, and their preference may differ from that of other voters. The sampling method may systematically produce samples that don't represent the population of interest.

33. a) Voluntary response. Only those who both see the ad *and* feel strongly enough will respond.

b) Cluster sampling. One town may not be typical of all.

c) Attempted census. Will have nonresponse bias.

d) Stratified sampling with follow-up. Should be unbiased.

35. a) This is a systematic sample.

b) It is likely to be representative of those waiting for the roller coaster. Indeed, it may do quite well if those at the front of the line respond differently (after their long wait) than those at the back of the line.

c) The sampling frame is patrons willing to wait for the roller coaster on that day at that time. It should be representative of the people in line, but not of all people at the amusement park.

37. Only those who think it worth the wait are likely to be in line. Those who don't like roller coasters are unlikely to be in the sampling frame, so the poll won't get a fair picture of whether park patrons overall would favor still more roller coasters.

39. a) Biased toward yes because of "pollute." "Should companies be responsible for any costs of environmental cleanup?"

b) Biased toward no because of "enforce" and "strict." "Should companies have dress codes?"

41. a) Not everyone has an equal chance. People with unlisted numbers, people without phones, and those at work cannot be reached. There may be a slight bias against people from large households.

b) Generate random numbers and call at random times.

c) Under the original plan, those families in which one person stays home are more likely to be included. Under the second plan, many more are included. People without phones are still excluded.

d) It improves the chance of selected households being included.

e) This takes care of phone numbers. Time of day may be an issue. People without phones are still excluded.

43. a) Answers will vary.

b) The amount of change you typically carry. Parameter is the true mean amount of change. Population is the amount on each day around noon.

c) Population is now the amount of change carried by your friends. The average estimates the mean of these amounts.

d) Possibly for your class. Probably not for larger groups. Your friends are likely to have similar needs for change during the day.

45. a) Assign numbers 001 to 120 to each order. Use random numbers to select 10 transactions to examine.

b) Sample proportionately within each type. (Do a stratified random sample.)

47. a) Select three cases at random; then select one jar randomly from each case.

b) Use random numbers to choose three cases from numbers 61 through 80; then use random numbers between 1 and 12 to select the jar from each case.

c) No. Multistage sampling.

49. a) Depends on the Yellow Pages listings used. If from regular (line) listings, this is fair if all doctors are listed. If from ads, probably not, as those doctors may not be typical.

b) Not appropriate. This cluster sample will probably contain listings for only one or two business types.

CHAPTER 9
SECTION EXERCISE ANSWERS

1. a) Normal.

b) 0.36

c) They wouldn't change. The shape is still approximately Normal and the mean is still the true proportion.

3. a) 0.0339

b) 0.5

c) 0.842 (0.843 using a rounded answer from part a)

d) 0.01

e) 0.039

5. Yes. Assuming the survey is random, they should be independent. We don't know the true proportion, so we can't check np and nq, but we have observed 10 successes, and 30 failures which is sufficient.

7. a) 0.0357

b) 400

9. a) p is the proportion of all backpacks entering the stadium which contain alcoholic beverages; $\hat{p}$ is the proportion in the sample $\hat{p} = 17/130 = 13.08\%$. Yes. This seems to be a random sample.

b) p is the proportion of all visitors to the website who approve of recent bossnapping. $\hat{p}$ is the proportion in the sample $\hat{p} = 49.2\%$. No. This is a volunteer sample and may be biased.

c) This question is about the mean weight, not a proportion. The methods of this chapter are not appropriate.

11. a) 0.35

b) 0.034

c) (0.283, 0.417)

13. a) False. Doesn't make sense. Workers are not proportions.

b) True.

c) False. Our best guess is 0.48 not 0.95.

d) False. Our best guess is 0.48, but we're not sure that's correct.

e) False. The statement should be about the true proportion, not future samples.

15. a) Narrower. (0.295, 0.405) (using 1.645 standard errors on each side)

b) Narrower. (0.296, 0.404)

c) Wider. (0.263, 0.437) (using 2.576 standard errors on each side).

d) 4 times as large: 800 students.

17. a) About 2401 (using 1.96 standard errors)

b) About 4148 (using 2.576 standard errors)

c) About 385 (using 1.96 standard errors)

19. a) 141

b) 318

c) 564

CHAPTER EXERCISE ANSWERS

21. All the histograms are centered near 0.05. As n gets larger, the histograms approach the Normal shape, and the variability in the sample proportions decreases.

23. a)

n	Observed mean	Theoretical mean	Observed st. dev.	Theoretical st. dev.
20	0.0497	0.05	0.0479	0.0487
50	0.0516	0.05	0.0309	0.0308
100	0.0497	0.05	0.0215	0.0218
200	0.0501	0.05	0.0152	0.0154

b) They are all quite close to what we expect from the theory.

c) The histogram is unimodal and symmetric for $n = 200$.

d) The success/failure condition says that np and nq should both be at least 10, which is not satisfied until $n = 200$ for $p = 0.05$. The theory predicted my choice.

25. a) Symmetric, because probabilities of success and failure are equal.

b) 0.5

c) Standard deviation would be 0.125

d) $np = 8 < 10$

27. a) About 68% should have proportions between 0.4 and 0.6, about 95% between 0.3 and 0.7, and about 99.7% between 0.2 and 0.8.

b) $np = 12.5, nq = 12.5$; both are ≥ 10.

c)

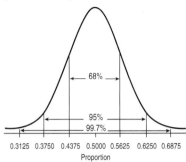

$np = nq = 32$; both are ≥ 10. Samples are random, but stock movements might not be independent.

d) Becomes narrower (less spread around 0.5).

29. a) This is a fairly unusual result: about 2.28 SDs above the mean.

b) The probability of that is about 0.012. So, in a class of 100 it is certainly reasonable that one person would do this well.

31. a)

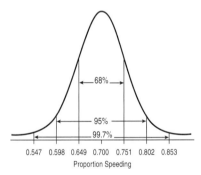

b) Both $np = 56$ and $nq = 24 \geq 10$. Drivers *may* be independent of each other, but if flow of traffic is very fast, they may not be. Or weather conditions may affect all drivers. In these cases they may get more or fewer speeders than they expect.

33. a) Assume that these children are typical of the population. They can be considered a random sample that represents fewer than 10% of all children. We expect 20.4 nearsighted and 149.6 not; both are at least 10.

b)

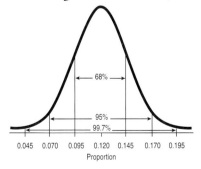

c) Probably between 12 and 29.

35. a) $\mu = 7\%, \sigma = 1.8\%$

b) Assume that clients pay independently of each other, that we have a random sample of all possible clients, and that these represent less than 10% of all possible clients. $np = 14$ and $nq = 186$ are both at least 10.

c) 0.048

37.

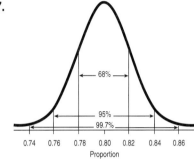

These are not random samples, and not all colleges may be typical (representative). $np = 320, nq = 80$ are large enough.

39. Yes; if their students were typical, a retention rate of $551/603 = 91.4\%$ would be 7 standard deviations above the expected rate of 80%.

41. 0.212. Reasonable that those polled are independent of each other and represent less than 10% of all potential voters. We assume the sample was selected at random. Success/Failure Condition met: $np = 208, nq = 192$. Both ≥ 10.

43. 0.088 using $N(0.08, 0.022)$ model.

45. a) Not correct. This implies certainty.

b) Not correct. Different samples will give different results. Most likely, none of the samples will have *exactly* 88% on-time orders.

c) Not correct. A confidence interval says something about the unknown population proportion, not the sample proportion in different samples.

d) Not correct. In this sample, we *know* that 88% arrived on time.

e) Not correct. The interval is about the parameter, not about the days.

47. a) False.

b) True.

c) True.

d) False.

49. We are 90% confident that between 29.9% and 47.0% of U.S. cars are made in Japan.

51. a) 0.025 or 2.5%

b) The pollsters are 90% confident that the true proportion of adults who do not use e-mail is within 2.5% of the estimated 38%.

c) A 99% confidence interval requires a larger margin of error. In order to increase confidence, the interval must be wider.

d) 0.039 or 3.9%.

e) Smaller margins of error will give us less confidence in the interval.

53. a) (12.7%, 18.6%)

b) We are 95% confident that between 12.7% and 18.6% of all accidents involve teenage drivers.

c) About 95% of all random samples of size 582 will produce intervals that contain the true proportion of accidents involving teenage drivers.

d) Contradicts—the interval is completely below 20%.

55. Probably nothing. Those who bothered to fill out the survey are a voluntary response sample, which may be biased.

57. This was a random sample of less than 10% of all Internet users; there were $703 \times 0.18 = 127$ successes and 576 failures, both at least 10. We are 95% confident that between 15.2% and 20.8% of Internet users have downloaded music from a site that was not authorized. (Answer could be 15.2% to 20.9% if $n = 127$ is used instead of 0.18).

59. a) $385/550 = 0.70$; 70% of U.S. chemical companies in the sample are certified.

b) This was a random sample, but we don't know if it is less than 10% of all U.S. chemical companies; there were $550(0.70) = 385$ successes and 165 failures, both at least 10. We are 95% confident that between 66.2% and 73.8% of the chemical companies in the United States are certified. It appears that the proportion of companies certified in the United States is less than in Canada.

61. a) There may be response bias based on the wording of the question.

b) (45.5%, 51.5%)

c) The margin of error based on the pooled sample is smaller, since the sample size is larger.

63. a) This was a random sample of less than 10% of all English children; there were $2700(0.20) = 540$ successes and 2160 failures, both at least 10; (18.2%, 21.8%).

b) We are 98% confident that between 18.2% and 21.8% of English children are deficient in vitamin D.

c) About 98% of random samples of size 2700 will produce confidence intervals that contain the true proportion of English children that are deficient in vitamin D.

d) No. The interval says nothing about causation.

65. a) This was a random sample of less than 10% of all companies in Vermont; there were 12 successes and 0 failures, which is not greater than 10, so the sample is not large enough.

b) Sample is not large enough to compute CI.

67. a) This was a random sample of less than 10% of all self-employed taxpayers; there were 20 successes and 206 failures, both at least 10.

b) (5.1%, 12.6%)

c) We are 95% confident that between 5.1% and 12.6% of all self-employed individuals had their tax returns audited in the past year.

d) If we were to select repeated samples of 226 individuals, we'd expect about 95% of the confidence intervals we created to contain the true proportion of all self-employed individuals who were audited.

69. a) The 95% confidence interval for the true proportion of all 18- to 29-year-olds who believe the U.S. is ready for a woman president will be about twice as wide as the confidence interval for the true proportion of all U.S. adults, since it is based on a sample about one-fourth as large. (Assuming approximately equal proportions.)

b) This was a random sample of less than 10% of all U.S. 15- to 29-year-old-adults; there were $250 \times 0.62 = 155$ successes and 95 failures, both at least 10. We are 95% confident that between 56.0% and 68.0% of 18- to 29-year-olds believe the U.S. is ready for a woman president.

71. a) This was a random sample of less than 10% of all Internet users; there were $703(0.64) = 450$ successes and 253 failures, both at least 10. We are 90% confident that between 61.0% and 67.0% of Internet users would still buy a CD.

b) In order to cut the margin of error in half, they must sample 4 times as many users; $4 \times 703 = 2812$ users.

73. 1801

75. 384 total, using $p = 0.15$

77. Since $z^* \approx 1.634$, which is close to 1.645, the pollsters were probably using 90% confidence.

79. This was a random sample of less than 10% of all customers; there were 67 successes and 433 failures, both at least 10. From the data set, $\hat{p} = 67/500 = 0.134$. We are 95% confident that the true proportion of customers who spend $1000 per month or more is between 10.4% and 16.4%.

CHAPTER 10
SECTION EXERCISE ANSWERS

1. a) Let p = probability of winning on the slot machine. H_0: $p = 0.01$ vs. H_A: $p \neq 0.01$.

b) Let p = proportion of patients cured by the new drug. H_0: $p = 0.3$ vs. H_A: $p \neq 0.3$.

c) Let p = proportion of clients now using the website. H_0: $p = 0.4$ vs. H_A: $p \neq 0.4$.

3. a) False. A high P-value shows that the data are consistent with the null hypothesis, but provides no evidence for rejecting the null hypothesis.

b) False. It results in rejecting the null hypothesis, but does not prove that it is false.

c) False. A high P-value shows that the data are consistent with the null hypothesis but does not prove that the null hypothesis is true.

d) False. Whether a P-value provides enough evidence to reject the null hypothesis depends on the risk one is willing to accept.

5. a) $SE(\hat{p}) = \sqrt{\dfrac{p_0 q_0}{n}} = \sqrt{\dfrac{(0.35)(0.65)}{300}} = 0.028$

b) $z = \dfrac{\hat{p} - p_0}{SD(\hat{p})} = \dfrac{0.46 - 0.35}{0.028} = 3.93$

c) Yes, that's an unusually large z-value.

7. a) H_0: $p = 0.40$ vs. H_A: $p \neq 0.40$. Two-sided.

b) H_0: $p = 0.42$ vs. H_A: $p > 0.42$. One-sided.

c) H_0: $p = 0.50$ vs. H_A: $p > 0.50$. One-sided.

9. a) The drug may not be approved for use, and people would miss out on a beneficial product.

b) The drug will go into production and people will suffer the side effect.

CHAPTER EXERCISE ANSWERS

11. a) Let p be the percentage of products delivered on time. H_0: $p = 0.90$ vs. H_A: $p > 0.90$.

b) Let p be the proportion of houses taking more than 3 months to sell. H_0: $p = 0.50$ vs. H_A: $p > 0.50$.

c) Let p be the error rate. H_0: $p = 0.02$ vs. H_A: $p < 0.02$.

13. Statement d is correct.

15. If the rate of seat-belt usage after the campaign is the same as the rate of seat-belt usage before the campaign, there is a 17% chance of observing a rate of seat-belt usage after the campaign this large or larger in a sample of the same size by natural sampling variation alone.

17. Statement e is correct.

19. No, we can say only that there is a 27% chance of seeing the observed effectiveness just from natural sampling if $p = 0.7$. There is no *evidence* that the new formula is more effective, but we can't conclude that they are equally effective.

21. a) 0.186 using the normal model.

b) It seems reasonable to think there really may have been half of each. We would expect to get 12 or more reds out of 20 more than 15% of the time, so there's no real evidence that the company's claim is not true. The two sided P-value is greater than 0.30.

23. a) Conditions are satisfied: random sample; less than 10% of population; more than 10 successes and failures; $z = -5.93$. Yes, strong evidence that the proportion has changed. $P < 0.001$.

b) (0.4994, 0.5606); we are 95% confident that the true proportion of U.S. investors who believe the price of energy is hurting the U.S. investment climate is between 49.9% and 56.1%.

25. 1. Use p, not $\hat{p}$, in hypotheses.

2. The question is about *failing* to meet the goal. H_A should be $p < 0.96$.

3. Did not check $nq = (200)(0.04) = 8$. Since $nq < 10$, the Success/Failure condition is violated. Didn't check the 10% condition.

4. $\hat{p} = \dfrac{188}{200} = 0.94$; $SD(\hat{p}) = \sqrt{\dfrac{p_0 q_0}{n}}$

$= \sqrt{\dfrac{(0.96)(0.04)}{200}} \approx 0.014$

The student used $\hat{p}$ and $\hat{q}$ instead of p_0 and q_0.

5. z is incorrect; should be $z = \dfrac{0.94 - 0.96}{0.014} \approx -1.43$.

6. $P = P(z < -1.43) = 0.076$

7. There is only weak evidence that the new system has failed to meet the goal.

27. a) Let p = the proportion of children with genetic abnormalities. H_0: $p = 0.05$ vs. H_A: $p > 0.05$.

b) SRS (not clear from information provided); $384 < 10\%$ of all children; $np = (384)(0.05) = 19.2 > 10$ and $nq = (384)(0.95) = 364.8 > 10$.

c) $z = 6.28, P < 0.0001$

d) If 5% of children have genetic abnormalities, the chance of observing 46 children with genetic abnormalities in a random sample of 384 children is essentially 0.

e) Reject H_0. There is strong evidence that more than 5% of children have genetic abnormalities.

f) We don't know that environmental chemicals cause genetic abnormalities, only that the rate is higher now than in the past.

29. a) Let p = the proportion of Americans concerned about global warming in 2012 (0.55). $H_0: p = 0.55$ vs. $H_A: p > 0.55$.

b) It is reasonable to assume that Gallup uses random sampling. $1022 < 10\%$ of the population of U.S. adults; $np = (1022)(0.55) = 562.1 > 10$ and $nq = (1022)(0.45) = 459.9 > 10$.

c) $z = 1.928, P = 0.027$

d) Reject H_0. There is evidence to suggest that the proportion of Americans concerned about global warming has increased from 2012 to 2013.

e) This result is statistically significant, but it's not clear that this is a trend that will continue.

31. a) SRS (not clear from information provided); $1000 < 10\%$ of all workers; $n\hat{p} = 520 > 10$ and $n\hat{q} = 480 > 10$; $(0.489, 0.551)$; we are 95% confident that between 48.9% and 55.1% of workers have invested in individual retirement accounts.

b) Let p = the proportion of workers who have invested. $H_0: p = 0.44$ vs. $H_A: p \neq 0.44$; $np_0 = 440 > 10$ and $nq_0 = 560 > 10$. $z = (0.52 - 0.44)/$ sqrt$(0.44*0.56/1000) = 5.096$; $P < 0.001$. There is strong evidence that the proportion of workers who have invested in individual retirement accounts was not 44%. In fact, our sample indicates an increase in the percentage of adults who invest in individual retirement accounts.

33. Let p = the proportion of cars with faulty emissions. $H_0: p = 0.20$ vs. $H_A: p > 0.20$; two conditions are not satisfied: $22 > 10\%$ of the population of 150 cars and $np = (22)(0.20) = 4.4 < 10$. It's not a good idea to proceed with a hypothesis test.

35. Let p = the proportion of readers interested in an online edition. $H_0: p = 0.25$ vs. $H_A: p > 0.25$; SRS; $500 < 10\%$ of all potential subscribers; $np = (500)(0.25) = 125 > 10$ and $nq = (500)(0.75) = 375 > 10$; $z = 1.24, P = 0.1076$. Since the P-value is high, we fail to reject H_0. There is insufficient evidence to suggest that the proportion of interested readers is greater than 25%. The magazine should not publish the online edition.

37. Let p = the proportion of female executives. $H_0: p = 0.40$ vs. $H_A: p < 0.40$; data are for all executives in this company and may not be able to be generalized to all companies; $np = (43)(0.40) = 17.2 > 10$ and $nq = (43)(0.60) = 25.8 > 10$; $z = -1.31, P = 0.0955$. Since the P-value is high, we fail to reject H_0. There is insufficient evidence to suggest proportion of female executives is any different from the overall proportion of 40% female employees at the company.

39. Let p = the proportion of first-time home buyers with income $<\$40,000$. $H_0: p = 0.15$ vs.

$H_A: p > 0.15$; assume that the home buyers are independent of each other (i.e., not related); $100 < 10\%$ of all home buyers; $np = (100)(0.15) = 15 > 10$ and $nq = (100)(0.85) = 85 > 10$; $z = 2.80, P = 0.0026$. Since the P-value is low, we reject H_0. There is strong evidence that the proportion of home buyers with income $<\$40,000$ is greater than 15%.

41. H_0: These MBA students are exposed to unethical practices at a similar rate to others in the program $(p = 0.30)$.

H_A: These students are exposed to unethical practices at a different rate than other students $(p \neq 0.30)$.

There is no reason to believe that students' rates would influence others; the professor considers this class typical of other classes; $120 < 10\%$ of all students in the MBA program; $np = (120)(0.30) = 36 > 10$ and $nq = (120)(0.7) = 84 > 10; z = -0.717, P = 0.4732$. Since the P-value is very large, we fail to reject the null hypothesis. There is little evidence that the rate at which these students are exposed to unethical business practices is different from that reported in the study.

43. a) $z = -0.729$

b) P-value = 0.2330. Do not reject the null hypothesis.

c) We conclude that the percent of U.S. investors concerned about a politically divided government has not changed significantly between the two surveys.

45. a) One-tailed; we are testing to see if a decrease in the dropout rate is associated with the software.

b) H_0: The dropout rate does not change following the use of the software $(p = 0.13)$.

H_A: The dropout rate decreases following the use of the software $(p < 0.13)$.

One student's decision about dropping out should not influence another's decision in general; this year's class of 203 students is probably representative of all statistics students; $203 < 10\%$ of all students; $np = (203)(0.13) = 26.39 > 10$ and $nq = (203)(0.87) = 176.61 > 10; z = -3.21, P = 0.0007$. Since the P-value is very low, we reject H_0. There is strong evidence that the dropout rate has dropped since use of the software program was implemented. As long as the professor feels confident that this class of statistics students is representative of all potential students, then he should buy the program.

d) The chance of observing 11 or fewer dropouts in a class of 203 is only 0.07% if the dropout rate is really 13%.

CHAPTER 11

SECTION EXERCISE ANSWERS

1. a) Prices cannot be less than 0, but there is nothing to prevent some from being expensive, so they are likely to be skewed to the high end.

   b) It should resemble the population distribution and be skewed to the right.

   c) Nearly Normal. The Central Limit Theorem tells us this.

3. a) Normal.

   b) 215 mg/dL

   c) 4.63 mg/dL

   d) Only c would change, to 3.0 mg/dL.

5. a) One would expect many small fish and a few large ones.

   b) We don't know the exact distribution, but we know it is skewed, so it can't be Normal.

   c) Probably not. With a skewed distribution, a sample of size 5 is not large enough to use the Central Limit Theorem.

   d) The standard deviation is 0.30.

   e) 4.5 pounds is more than 3 standard deviations above the mean, so by the 68–95–99.7 rule, it would happen less than 0.15% of the time.

7. a) 1.968 years

   b) 0.984 years (half as large)

9. a) 24

   b) 99

11. a) 2.064

   b) 1.984

13. a) (27.78, 35.90) years

   b) 4.06 years

   c) (27.92, 35.76) years. Slightly narrower.

15. Independence: The data were from a random survey and should be independent.
Randomization: the data were selected randomly.
10% Condition: These customers are fewer than 10% of the customer population.
Nearly Normal: The histogram is unimodal and symmetric, which is sufficient.

17. a) $H_0: \mu = 25$

   b) Two-sided; $H_A: \mu \neq 25$

   c) $t_{24} = 3.476$

   d) P-value < 0.002 or P-value $= 0.00195$

   e) Reject the null. There is strong evidence the mean age is not 25.

19. a) Four times as big, or $n = 100$.

   b) 100 times as big, or $n = 2500$.

CHAPTER EXERCISE ANSWERS

21. a) 1.74

   b) 2.37

23. As the variability of a sample increases, the width of a 95% confidence interval increases, assuming that the sample size remains the same.

25. a) ($4.382, $4.598)

   b) ($4.400, $4.580)

   c) ($4.415, $4.565)

27. a) Not correct. A confidence interval is for the mean weight gain of the population of all cows. It says nothing about individual cows.

   b) Not correct. A confidence interval is for the mean weight gain of the population of all cows, not individual cows.

   c) Not correct. We don't need a confidence interval about the average weight gain for cows in this study. We are certain that the mean weight gain of the cows in this study is 56 pounds.

   d) Not correct. This statement implies that the average weight gain varies. It doesn't.

   e) Not correct. This statement implies that there is something special about our interval, when this interval is actually one of many that could have been generated, depending on the cows that were chosen for the sample.

29. The assumptions and conditions for a *t*-interval are not met. With a sample size of only 20, the distribution is too skewed. There is also a large outlier that is pulling the mean higher.

31. a) The data are a random sample of all days; the distribution is unimodal and symmetric with no outliers.

   b) ($122.20, $129.80)

   c) We are 90% confident that the interval $122.20 to $129.80 contains the true mean daily income of the parking garage.

   d) 90% of all random samples of size 44 will produce intervals that contain the true mean daily income of the parking garage.

   e) $128 is a plausible value.

33. a) We can be more confident that our interval contains the mean parking revenue.

   b) Wider (and less precise) interval.

   c) By collecting a larger sample, they could create a more precise interval without sacrificing confidence.

35. a) (2230.4, 2469.6)

   b) The assumptions and conditions that must be satisfied are:

      1 Independence: probably OK.

      2 Nearly Normal condition: can't tell.

      3 Sample size of 51 is large enough.

c) We are 95% confident the interval $2230.4 to $2469.6 contains the true mean increase in sales tax revenue.

Examples of what the interval *does not* mean: The mean increase in sales tax revenue is $2350 95% of the time. 95% of all increases in sales tax revenue increases will be between $2230.4 and $2469.6. There's 95% confidence the next small retailer will have an increase in sales tax revenue between $2230.4 and $2469.6.

37. a) Given no time trend, the monthly on-time departure rates should be independent. Though not a random sample, these months should be representative, and they're fewer than 10% of all months. The histogram looks unimodal, but slightly left-skewed; not a concern with this large sample.
b) (80.22, 81.29)
c) We can be 90% confident that the interval from 80.22 to 81.29 holds the true mean monthly percentage of on-time flight departures.

39. a) The histogram of the lab fees shows 2 extreme outliers, so with the outliers included, the conditions for inference are violated.
b) With the outliers left in, the 95% confidence interval is (44.9, 81.6) minutes. If we remove the two extreme outliers, it is (54.6, 68.4).

In either case, we would be reluctant to conclude that the mean is above 55 minutes. The sample size is small and the presence of two large outliers advises us to be cautious about conclusions from this sample.

41. a) The assumptions and conditions that must be satisfied are:
The data come from a nearly normal distribution. The air samples were selected randomly, and there is no bias present in the sample.
b) The histogram of air samples is not nearly normal, but the sample size is large, so inference is OK.

43. a) $14.90 - 11.6$ or ± 3.3 miles per hour
b) We can find the needed sample size from: $1.96 \times 8/2 = \sqrt{n}$. $(7.84)^2 = n = 61.46$ use 62.

45. a) Interval: $653 to $707
b) The confidence interval suggests the mean audit cost is now greater than $650.

47. a) The timeplot shows no pattern, so it seems that the measurements are independent. Although this is not a random sample, an entire year is measured, so it is likely that we have representative values. We certainly have fewer than 10% of all possible wind readings. The histogram appears nearly normal.

b) A 95% confidence interval for the true mean speed is (7.795, 8.243) mph. Because there are many plausible values below 8 mph, we can not be confident that the true mean is at least 8 mph. We would not recommend that the turbine be placed here.

49. The 1% P-value means that, if the mean monthly sales due to online purchases has not changed, there is a 1% chance (or 1 out of every 100 samples) that the resulting mean sales would occur assuming the historical mean for sales. This is rare and considered to be a significant value.

51. a) $H_0: \mu = 23.3$ years; $H_A: \mu > 23.3$ years
b) The randomization condition: The 40 online shoppers were selected randomly. Nearly normal condition: the distribution of the sample should be examined to check for serious skewness or outliers but the sample of 40 shoppers is large enough that it should be safe to proceed.
c) P-value = 0.145
d) If the mean age of shoppers remains at 23.3 years, there is a 14.5% chance of getting a sample mean of 24.2 years or older simply from natural sampling variation.
e) There is not enough evidence to suggest that the mean age of online shoppers has increased from the mean of 23.3 years.

53. a) Random sample. Nearly Normal Condition is reasonable by examining a Normal probability plot. The histogram is roughly unimodal (although somewhat uniform) and symmetric with no outliers. (Show your plot.)
b) (114.9, 148.8) calories
c) The mean number of calories in a serving of vanilla yogurt is between 115 and 149, with 95% confidence. We conclude that the diet guide's claim of 120 calories is toward the lower end, but is reasonable.

CHAPTER 12
SECTION EXERCISE ANSWERS

1. a) False. It provides evidence against it but does not show it is false.
b) False. The P-value is not the probability that the null hypothesis is true.
c) True
d) False. Whether a P-value provides enough evidence to reject the null hypothesis depends on the risk of a type I error that one is willing to assume (the α level).

3. a) True.
b) False. The alpha level is set independently and does not depend on the sample size.

c) False. The P-value would have to be less than 0.01 to reject the null hypothesis.

d) False. It simply means we do not have enough evidence at that alpha level to reject the null hypothesis.

5. a) $z = \pm 1.96$
   b) $z = 1.645$
   c) $t = \pm 2.03$
   d) $z = 2.33$; n is not relevant for critical values for z.
   e) $z = -2.33$

7. a) $(0.196, 0.304)$
   b) No, because 0.20 is a plausible value.
   c) The SE is based on $\hat{p}$, so:
   $$SE(\hat{p}) = \sqrt{\frac{\hat{p}\hat{q}}{n}} = \sqrt{\frac{(0.25)(0.75)}{250}} = 0.0274.$$
   The SD is based on the hypothesized value 0.20, so
   $$SD(\hat{p}) = \sqrt{\frac{p_0 q_0}{n}} = \sqrt{\frac{(0.20)(0.80)}{250}} = 0.0253.$$
   d) The SE since it is sample based.

9. a) $SE = \dfrac{s}{\sqrt{n}} = \dfrac{2.0}{\sqrt{25}} = 0.4$
   b) t^* with 24 df for a 90% confidence interval is 1.711.
   c) $(15.82, 17.18)$
   d) No, we fail to reject H_0 (one-sided) at $\alpha = 0.05$ because 16.0 is in the corresponding two-sided 90% confidence interval.

11. a) Type I error. The actual value is not greater than 0.3 but they rejected the null hypothesis.
    b) No error. The actual value is 0.50, which was not rejected.
    c) Type II error. The actual value was 55.3 points, which is greater than 52.5.
    d) Type II error. The null hypothesis was not rejected, but it was false. The true relief rate was greater than 0.25.

13. a) All other things being equal, the power is reduced when trying to detect a smaller effect size.
    b) She should use a larger sample size to keep the power the same.

15. At $\alpha = 0.10$ he would have made the same decision because the P-value was < 0.05 (and so < 0.10). But if $\alpha = 0.01$ he will reach the same decision only if the P-value is also < 0.01.

17. a) There is basically zero chance of seeing a sample proportion as low as 97.4% vaccinated by natural sampling variation if 98% have really been vaccinated.
    b) We conclude that p is below 0.98, but a 95% confidence interval would suggest that the true proportion is between $(0.971, 0.977)$. Most likely, a decrease from 98% to 97.6% would not be

considered important. On the other hand, with 1,000,000 children a year vaccinated, even 0.1% represents about 1000 kids—so this may very well be important.

19. a) No mention of an SRS or randomization, so proceed with caution; successes and failures both > 10; $(0.486, 0.534)$.
    b) Because 45% is not in the interval we have strong evidence that more than 45% of men identify themselves as the primary grocery shopper.
    c) $\alpha = 0.01$; it's an upper tail test based on a 98% confidence interval.

21. a) Less likely
    b) Alpha levels must be chosen *before* examining the data. Otherwise the alpha level could always be selected to reject the null hypothesis.

23. a) The mean download time is 15 standard errors below the hypothesized mean.
    b) $t_{19,.001} = -3.5794$. Since $-15 < -3.5794$, we can reject H_0 at $\alpha < 0.001$.
    c) We know that 15 standard errors is very unlikely no matter how many degrees of freedom there are.

25. a) The value 0.98 lies above the interval which leaves 1% of the plausible values on that side. So she can reject the null hypothesis that $p = 0.98$.
    b) The true value may be as high as 97.73%. She would need to do a cost analysis to see what the cost of an extra 0.27% measles cases would mean to her company.

27. a) Type II error.
    b) Type I error.
    c) By making it easier to get the loan, the bank has reduced the alpha level.
    d) The risk of a Type I error is decreased and the risk of a Type II error is increased.

29. a) Power is the probability that the bank denies a loan that would not have been repaid.
    b) Raise the cutoff score.
    c) A larger number of trustworthy people would be denied credit, and the bank would miss the opportunity to collect interest on those loans.

31. a) The null is that the level of home ownership remains the same. The alternative is that it rises.
    b) The city concludes that home ownership is on the rise, but in fact the tax breaks don't help.
    c) The city abandons the tax breaks, but home ownership is actually increasing.
    d) A Type I error causes the city to forego tax revenue, while a Type II error withdraws help from those who might have otherwise been able to buy a home.

e) The power of the test is the city's ability to detect an actual increase in home ownership.

33. a) It is decided that the shop is not meeting standards when it is.
b) The shop is certified as meeting standards when it is not.
c) Type I.
d) Type II.

35. a) The probability of detecting a shop that is not meeting standards.
b) 40 cars. Larger n.
c) 10%. More chance to reject H_0.
d) A lot. Larger differences are easier to detect.

37. a) One-tailed. The company wouldn't be sued if "too many" minorities were hired.
b) Deciding the company is discriminating when it is not.
c) Deciding the company is not discriminating when it is.
d) The probability of correctly detecting actual discrimination.
e) Increases power.
f) Lower, since n is smaller.

39. a) One-tailed. The software is supposed to increase the final exam scores.
b) $H_0: \mu = 105$; $H_A: \mu > 105$
c) He buys the software when it doesn't help students.
d) He doesn't buy the software when it does help students.
e) The probability of correctly deciding the software is helpful.

41. Given this confidence interval, we cannot reject the null hypothesis of a mean $200 collection using $\alpha = 0.05$. However, the confidence interval suggests that there may be a large upside potential. The collection agency may be collecting as much as $250 per customer on average, or as little as $190 on average. If the possibility of collecting $250 on average is of interest to them, they may want to collect more data.

43. a) Upper-tail. We want to show it will hold 500 pounds (or more) easily.
b) They will decide the stands are safe when they're not.
c) They will decide the stands are unsafe when they are in fact safe.

45. a) Decrease α. This means a smaller chance of declaring the stands safe if they are not.
b) The probability of correctly detecting that the stands are capable of holding more than 500 pounds.
c) Decrease the standard deviation—probably costly. Increase the sample size—takes more time for

testing and is costly. Increase α—more Type I errors. Increase the "design load" to be well above 500 pounds—again, costly.

47. a) H_A: The coin is the 30% heads coin.
b) Reject the null hypothesis if the coin comes up tails—otherwise fail to reject.
c) $P(\text{tails given the null hypothesis}) = 0.1 = \alpha$
d) $P(\text{tails given the alternative hypothesis}) = \text{power} = 0.70$
e) Spin the coin more than once and base the decision on the sample proportion of heads.

49. Yes, there is a large ($50) upside potential. The larger trial will likely narrow the confidence interval and make the decision clearer.

51. a) $H_0: \mu = 55$; $H_A: \mu < 55$; Independence assumption: Since the times are not randomly selected, we will assume that the times are independent and representative of all the champion's times. Nearly Normal condition: The histogram of the times is unimodal and roughly symmetric; P-value = 0.235; fail to reject H_0. There is insufficient evidence to conclude the mean time is less than 55 seconds. They should not market the new ski wax.
b) Type II error. They won't market a competitive wax and thus lose the potential profit from having done so.

CHAPTER 13
SECTION EXERCISE ANSWERS

1. a) $\bar{y}_1 = 58.0$ years; $\bar{y}_2 = 47.0$ years
b) 11 years
c) $s_1^2 = 50$; $s_2^2 = 54$
d) $s_1 = 7.07$ years; $s_2 = 7.35$ years
e) 4.16 years

3. a) 9.6 years
b) 1.91 years
c) 5.03

5. a) 2.64
b) 9.985
c) 5
d) 0.0247
e) 0.0459
f) For either method of calculating df, there is reasonably strong evidence to suggest that we reject the null hypothesis and conclude that the mean age of houses is not the same in the two neighborhoods.

7. a) <0.001
b) <0.001
c) In both cases, reject H_0. There is very strong evidence to suggest that there is a difference in the mean ages of houses in the two neighborhoods.

9. a) (1.72, 20.28) years
   b) No.
   c) It suggests that we should reject H_0 since 0 is not a plausible value for the true mean difference.

11. a) (5.77, 13.43) years
   b) The sample sizes are larger.
   c) No.
   d) It suggests that we should reject H_0 since 0 is not a plausible value for the true mean difference.

13. a) $t = 2.642$; P-value $= 0.0246$. Reject H_0 and conclude that there is sufficient evidence to suggest that the true means are different.
   b) (1.72, 20.28) years
   c) Not really. Because the standard deviations are fairly close, the two methods will result in essentially the same confidence intervals and hypothesis tests.

15. a) $t = 5.01$; P-value < 0.001. Reject H_0. There is strong evidence to reject the hypothesis that the means are equal.
   b) (5.77, 13.43) years
   c) Very close to previous results because the standard deviations are fairly close. In such a case, the two methods will result in essentially the same confidence intervals and hypothesis tests.

17. a) Paired. Each pair consists of a volunteer using each chair.
   b) Not paired. The samples are random within each neighborhood.
   c) Paired. Each pair consists of an hour in which the productivity of the two workers is compared.

19. a) Yes, each pair is a store in which the customers with and without the program are compared.
   b) 3 customers
   c) 4.52 customers
   d) 1.43 customers
   e) 2.098
   f) 9
   g) One-sided. They want to know if traffic increased.
   h) 0.0327
   i) We can reject the null hypothesis. There is evidence of an increase in traffic.

21. (0.379, 5.621) customers

CHAPTER EXERCISE ANSWERS

23. The P-value is too high to reject H_0 at any reasonable α-level.

25. a) 2.927 points
   b) Larger.
   c) We are 95% confident that the mean score for the CPMP math students will be between 5.573 and 11.427 points higher on this assessment than the mean score of the traditional students.

   d) Since the entire interval is above 0, there is strong evidence that students who learn with CPMP will have higher mean scores in applied algebra than those in traditional programs.

27. a) $H_0: \mu_C - \mu_T = 0$; $H_A: \mu_C - \mu_T \neq 0$
   b) If the mean scores for the CPMP and traditional students are really equal, there is less than a 1 in 10,000 chance of seeing a difference as large or larger than the observed difference of 9.4 points just from natural sampling variation.
   c) There is strong evidence that the CPMP students have a different mean score than the traditional students. The evidence suggests that the CPMP students have a lower mean score.

29. $H_0: \mu_C - \mu_T = 0$; $H_A: \mu_C - \mu_T \neq 0$
   P $= 0.1602$; fail to reject H_0. There is no evidence that the CPMP students have a different mean score on the word problems test than the traditional students.

31. a) (1.36, 4.64); df $= 33.1$
   b) Since the CI does not contain 0, there is evidence that Route A is faster on average.

33. a) $H_0: \mu_C - \mu_A = 0$; $H_A: \mu_C - \mu_A \neq 0$
   b) Independent groups assumption: The percentage of sugar in the children's cereals is unrelated to the percentage of sugar in adult cereals. Randomization condition: It is reasonable to assume that the cereals are representative of all children's cereals and adult cereals, in regard to sugar content. Nearly Normal condition: The histogram of adult cereal sugar content is skewed to the right, but the sample sizes are reasonably large. The Central Limit Theorem allows us to proceed.
   c) (32.49, 40.80)%
   d) Since the 95% confidence interval does not contain 0, we can conclude that the mean sugar content for the two cereals is significantly different at the 5% level of significance.

35. a) $H_0: \mu_{\text{Taxable}} - \mu_{\text{Municipal}} = 0$
      $H_A: \mu_{\text{Taxable}} - \mu_{\text{Municipal}} \neq 0$
   b) Distributions are symmetric. Funds are independent. Outliers in boxplot not severe enough to cause concern.

c) Difference Between Means $= 1.055$
t-Statistic $= 1.020$ w/16.54 df
$P = 0.3225$

d) There does not appear to be a significant difference between these types of funds.

37. $H_0: \mu_N - \mu_C = 0$; $H_A: \mu_N - \mu_C > 0$. Independent groups assumption: Student scores in one group should not have an impact on the scores of students in the other group. Randomization condition: Students were randomly assigned to classes. Nearly Normal condition: The histograms of the scores are unimodal and symmetric. $P = 0.017$; reject H_0. There is evidence that the students taught using the new activities have a higher mean score on the reading comprehension test than the students taught using traditional methods.

39. a) $H_0: \mu_{1995–2001} - \mu_{2002–2012} = 0$
$H_A: \mu_{1995–2001} - \mu_{2002–2012} \neq 0$

b) Both time periods have values that show as possible outliers in boxplots, but neither one seems particularly extreme. The two time periods are plausibly independent.

c) Performing a two-sample t-test, $t = -1.210$ with 15 df, $P = 0.245$. Fail to reject H_0.

41. a) If the mean memory scores for people taking ginkgo biloba and people not taking it are the same, there is a 93.74% chance of seeing a difference in mean memory score this large or larger simply from natural sampling variability.

b) Since the P-value is so high, there is no evidence that the mean memory test score for ginkgo biloba users is higher than the mean memory test score for non-users.

c) Type II.

43. a) Males: (18.67, 20.11) pegs; females: (16.95, 18.87) pegs

b) It may appear to suggest that there is no difference in the mean number of pegs placed by males and females, but a two-sample t-interval should be constructed to assess the difference in mean number of pegs placed.

c) (0.29, 2.67) pegs

d) We are 95% confident that the mean number of pegs placed by males is between 0.29 and 2.67 pegs higher than the mean number of pegs placed by females.

e) Two-sample t-interval.

f) If you attempt to use two confidence intervals to assess a difference in means, you are actually adding standard deviations. But it's the variances that add, not the standard deviations. The two-sample difference of means procedure takes this into account.

45. a) $H_0: \mu_N - \mu_S = 0$; $H_A: \mu_N - \mu_S \neq 0$
$t = 6.47$, df $= 53.49$, $P < 0.001$

Since the P-value is low, we reject H_0. There is strong evidence that the mean mortality rate is different for towns north and south of Derby. There is evidence that the mortality rate north of Derby is higher.

b) The possible outlier slightly raised the mean and inflated the variance for North Derby. The t-statistic is large and the outlier not particularly extreme, so omitting that point would likely make little difference in our conclusion.

47. a) Paired data assumption: The data are before and after job satisfaction rating for the same workers. Randomization condition: The workers were randomly selected to participate. Nearly Normal condition: A histogram of differences between before and after job satisfaction ratings is roughly unimodal and symmetric.

b) $H_0: \mu_d = 0$; $H_A: \mu_d > 0$; $t = 3.60$; df $= 9$; P-value $= 0.0029$; reject H_0. There is evidence that the mean job satisfaction rating has increased since the implementation of the exercise program.

49. Independent groups assumption: Assume that orders in June are independent of orders in August. Independence assumption: Orders were a random sample. Nearly normal condition: Hard to check with small sample, but no outliers. H_0: $\mu_J - \mu_A = 0$; $H_A: \mu_J - \mu_A > 0$; $t = -1.17$; $P = 0.136$; fail to reject H_0. Thus, although the mean delivery time during August is higher, the difference in delivery time from June is not significant. A larger sample may produce a different statistical result, but the size of the difference may not be important from a business standpoint.

51. a) We are 95% confident that the mean number of brand names remembered by viewers of shows with violent content will be between 1.6 and 0.6 lower than the mean number of brand names remembered by viewers of shows with neutral content.

b) If they want viewers to remember their brand names, they should consider advertising on shows with neutral content, as opposed to shows with violent content.

53. a) She might attempt to conclude that the mean number of brand names recalled is greater after 24 hours.

b) The groups are not independent. They are the same people, asked at two different time periods.

c) A person with high recall right after the show might tend to have high recall 24 hours later as well. Also, the first interview may have helped the people to remember the brand names for a longer period of time than they would have otherwise.

d) Randomly assign half of the group watching that type of content to be interviewed immediately after watching, and assign the other half to be interviewed 24 hours later.

55. a) The differences that were observed between the group of students with Internet access and those without were too great to be attributed to natural sampling variation.
b) Type I.
c) No. There may be many other factors.
d) It might be used to market computer services to parents.

57. a) 8759 pounds
b) Independent groups assumption: Sales in different seasons should be independent. Randomization condition: Not a random sample of weeks, but it is of stores. Nearly Normal condition: Can't verify, but we will proceed cautiously. We are 95% confident that the interval 3630.54 to 13,887.39 pounds contains the true difference in mean sales between winter and summer.
c) Weather and sporting events may impact pizza sales.

59. Because runners are assigned to heats at random, we expect there to be no statistically significant difference between the heats.

Boxplots show only a small difference in medians. But both heats had a high outlier time, making a formal test problematic.

61. $H_0: \mu_S - \mu_R = 0$; $H_A: \mu_S - \mu_R > 0$. Assuming the conditions are satisfied, it is appropriate to model the sampling distribution of the difference in means with a Student's t-model, with 7.03 degrees of freedom (from the approximation formula). $t = 4.57$; $P = 0.0013$; reject H_0. There is strong evidence that the mean ball velocity for Stinger tees is higher than the mean velocity for regular tees.

63. a) $H_0: \mu_M - \mu_R = 0$; $H_A: \mu_M - \mu_R > 0$. Independent groups assumption: The groups are not related in regards to memory score. Randomization condition: Subjects were randomly assigned to groups. Nearly Normal condition: We don't have the actual data. We will assume that the distributions of the populations of memory test scores are Normal. $t = -0.70$; df = 45.88; $P = 0.7563$; fail to reject H_0. There is no evidence that the mean number of objects remembered by those who listen to Mozart is higher than the mean number of objects remembered by those who listen to rap music.
b) We are 90% confident that the mean number of objects remembered by those who listen to Mozart is between 0.19 and 5.35 objects lower than the mean of those who listened to no music.

65. a) Paired data assumption: These data are paired as they are the 3- and 5-year returns of the same mutual funds. Randomization condition: random sample of funds. Nearly Normal condition: Histogram of differences is slightly skewed left, but we will proceed with caution.
b) $H_0: \mu_{5yr} - \mu_{3yr} = 0$; $H_A: \mu_{5yr} - \mu_{3yr} > 0$
c) In fact the mean paired difference is -9.58, so the P-value will be higher than 0.50. (The actual one-sided P-value is nearly 1.0.)
d) A confidence interval between 9.17% and 9.99% has a 95% chance of capturing the true mean difference.

67. a) Independent groups assumption: The prices in the two towns are not related. Randomization condition: Each sample was a random sample of prices. Nearly Normal condition: Both histograms are reasonably unimodal and symmetric with no outliers, so will use the two-sample t-test.
b) $H_0: \mu_1 = \mu_2$; $H_A: \mu_1 \neq \mu_2$
c) $t = -0.58$; $P = 0.567$; fail to reject H_0.
d) We conclude that the mean price of homes in these two towns is not significantly different.

69. a) Independent groups assumption: The home runs hit in different leagues are independent. Randomization condition: Not a random sample, but we will assume it's representative. Nearly Normal condition: Both histograms are reasonably unimodal and symmetric with no outliers.
b) $H_0: \mu_{AL} - \mu_{NL} = 0$; $H_A: \mu_{AL} - \mu_{NL} > 0$
c) $t = 2.32$; $P = 0.0146$
d) We can conclude that the mean number of home runs is higher, on average, in the American League. We reject the null hypothesis.
e) $t = 2.36$; df = 28; $P = 0.0128$. Same conclusion as in part d.

71. Adding variances requires that the variables be independent. These price quotes are for the same cars, so they are paired. Drivers quoted high insurance premiums by the local company will be likely to get a high rate from the online company, too.

73. a) The histogram—we care about differences in price.
   b) Insurance cost is based on risk, so drivers are likely to see similar quotes from each company, making the differences relatively smaller.
   c) The price quotes are paired; they were for a random sample of fewer than 10% of the agent's customers; the histogram of differences looks approximately Normal.

75. $H_0: \mu_{\text{Local}-\text{Online}} = 0$; $H_A: \mu_{\text{Local}-\text{Online}} > 0$; $t = 0.826$ with 9 df. With a P-value of 0.215, we cannot reject the null hypothesis. These data don't provide evidence that online premiums are lower, on average.

77. a) $H_0: \mu_d = 0$; $H_A: \mu_d \neq 0$
   b) $t_{144} = 2.406$; 2-sided $P = 0.017$
      We are able to reject the null hypothesis (with a P-value of 0.017) and conclude that mean number of keystrokes per hour has changed.
   c) 95% CI for mean keystrokes per hour $22.7 \pm t_{0.025,\,144} s / \sqrt{n} = (4.05, 41.35)$

79. a) Paired data assumption: The data are paired by type of exercise machine. Randomization condition: Assume that the men and women participating are representative of all men and women in terms of number of minutes of exercise required to burn 200 calories. Nearly Normal condition: The histogram of differences between women's and men's times is roughly unimodal and symmetric. We are 95% confident that women take an average of 4.8 to 15.2 minutes longer to burn 200 calories than men when exercising at a light exertion rate.
   b) Nearly Normal condition: There is no reason to think that this histogram does not represent differences drawn from a Normal population. We are 95% confident that women exercising with light exertion take an average of 4.9 to 20.4 minutes longer to burn 200 calories than women exercising with hard exertion.
   c) Since these data are averages, we expect the individual times to be more variable. Our standard error would be larger, resulting in a larger margin of error.

81. a) Randomization condition: These stops are probably representative of all such stops for this type of car, but not for all cars. Nearly Normal condition: A histogram of the stopping distances is roughly unimodal and symmetric. We are 95% confident that the mean dry pavement stopping distance for this type of car is between 133.6 and 145.2 feet.
   b) Independent groups assumption: The wet pavement stops and dry pavement stops were made under different conditions and not paired in any way. Randomization condition: These stops are probably representative of all such stops for this type of car, but not for all cars. Nearly Normal condition: The histogram of wet pavement stopping distances is more uniform than unimodal, but no outliers. We are 95% confident that the mean stopping distance on wet pavement is between 50.4 and 75.6 feet longer than the mean stopping distance on dry pavement.

83. a) The data are paired. They are for the same airlines in two different years and our concern is about whether the involuntary DB rate has changed. We would measure improvement for each airline.
   b) Boxplots are *not* the appropriate display because the data are paired. Here is a histogram of the pairwise differences.

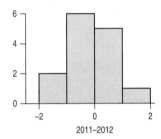

2011–2012

A paired *t*-test finds a mean of paired differences (2011–2012) of −0.11. The corresponding *t* statistic is −0.5466 with 13df. That gives a P-value of 0.5939, which is not small enough to conclude that there is a real difference.

CHAPTER 14
SECTION EXERCISE ANSWERS

1. a) (30, 30, 30, 30), 30 for each season
   b) 1.933
   c) 3

3. a) 3
   b) No, it's smaller than the mean.
   c) It would say that there is no evidence to reject the null hypothesis that births are distributed uniformly across the seasons.
   d) 7.815
   e) Do not reject the null hypothesis. As in part c, there is no evidence to suggest that births are not distributed uniformly across the seasons.

5. a) $(-0.913, 0.913, 0.365, -0.365)$

b) No, they are quite small for z-values.

c) Because we did not reject the null hypothesis, we shouldn't expect any of the standardized residuals to be large.

7. a) The age distributions of customers at the two branches are the same.

b) Chi-square test of homogeneity.

c)

	Age			
	Less Than 30	**30–55**	**56 or Older**	**Total**
In-Town Branch	25	45	30	100
Mall Branch	25	45	30	100
Total	50	90	60	200

d) 9.778

e) 2

f) 5.991

g) Reject H_0 and conclude that the age distributions at the two branches are not the same.

9. a) Men 62%, women 71%

b) Difference = 9%

c) SE = 0.022

d) (0.046, 0.133) or 4.6% to 13.3%

11. a)

	May-2010	**Aug-2011**	**Aug-2012**	**Total**
18–29	261.663	277.540	303.798	843
30–49	333.674	353.921	387.405	1075
50–64	261.663	277.540	303.798	843
Total	857	909	995	2761

b) 1.861

c) 4

d) We cannot reject the null hypothesis, the growth in use of social networking over these three years appears to be independent of age groups.

CHAPTER EXERCISE ANSWERS

13. a) Chi-square test of independence; One sample, two variables. We want to see if the variable *Account type* is independent of the variable *Trade type*.

b) Some other statistical test; the variable *Account size* is quantitative, not counts.

c) Chi-square test of homogeneity; we have two samples and one variable, *Courses*. We want to see if the distribution of *Courses* is the same for the two groups.

15. a) 10

b) Goodness-of-fit.

c) H_0: The die is fair. (All faces have $p = 1/6$.)
H_A: The die is not fair. (Some faces are more or less likely to come up than others.)

d) Count data; rolls are random and independent of each other; expected frequencies are all greater than 5.

e) 5

f) $\chi^2 = 5.600; P = 0.3471$

g) Since $P = 0.3471$ is high, fail to reject H_0. There is not enough evidence to conclude that the die is unfair.

17. a) Weights are quantitative, not counts.

b) Count the number of each type of nut, assuming the company's percentages are based on counts rather than weights (which is not clear).

19. a) Goodness-of-fit.

b) Count data; assume the lottery mechanism uses randomization and guarantees independence; expected frequencies are all greater than 5.

c) H_0: Likelihood of drawing each numeral is equal.
H_A: Likelihood of drawing each numeral is *not* equal.

d) $\chi^2 = 6.46$; df = 9; $P = 0.693$; fail to reject H_0.

e) The P-value says that if the drawings were in fact fair, an observed chi-square value of 6.46 or higher would occur about 69% of the time. This is not unusual at all, so we won't reject the null hypothesis that the values are uniformly distributed. The variation that we observed seems typical of that expected if the digits were drawn equally likely.

21. a) 40.2%

b) 8.1%

c) 62.2%

d) 285.48

e) Chi-square test of independence. H_0: Survival was independent of status on the ship. H_A: Survival was not independent of the status.

f) 3

g) We reject the null hypothesis. Survival depended on status. We can see that first-class passengers were more likely to survive than passengers of any other class.

23. a) Independence.

b) H_0: College choice is independent of birth order.
H_A: There is an association between college choice and birth order.

c) Count data; not a random sample of students, but assume that it is representative; expected counts are low for both the Social Science and Professional Colleges for both third and fourth or higher birth order. We'll keep an eye on these when we calculate the standardized residuals.

d) 9

e) With a P-value this low, we reject the null hypothesis. There is some evidence of an association between birth order and college enrollment.

f) None are particularly large, but 4 cells have expected counts less than 5, so we should be cautious in making conclusions. Perhaps we should group 3 with 4 or more and redo the analysis. Unfortunately, 3 of the 4 largest standardized residuals are in cells with expected counts less than 5. We should be very wary of drawing conclusions from this test.

25. a) Chi-square test for homogeneity.
   b) Count data; assume random assignment to treatments (although not stated); expected counts are all greater than 5.
   c) H_0: The proportion of infection is the same for each group.
      H_A: The proportion of infection is different among the groups.
   d) $\chi^2 = 7.776$; df $= 2$; $P = 0.02$; reject H_0
   e) Since the P-value is low, we reject the null hypothesis. There is strong evidence of difference in the proportion of urinary tract infections for cranberry juice drinkers, lactobacillus drinkers, and women that drink neither of the two beverages.
   f) The standardized residuals are:

	Cranberry	Lactobacillus	Control
Infection	−1.87276	1.191759	0.681005
No infection	1.245505	−0.79259	−0.45291

   The significant difference appears to be primarily due to the success of cranberry juice.

27. a) Homogeneity.
   b) H_0: The numbers of families spending each amount on eating out did not change between 2008 and 2010.
   c) Yes.
   d) We can reject the null hypothesis at the 0.05 level. There appears to be a difference in the distribution of expenses for eating out.
   e) In 2010, more families opted for spending less than \$50/week eating out and fewer chose to spend more than that. There was a noticeable drop in large (more than \$150/week) expenditures.

29. a) $P = 0.3766$. With a P-value this high, we fail to reject. There is not enough evidence to conclude that either men or women are more likely to make online purchases of books.
   b) Type II.
   c) $(-4.09\%, 10.86\%)$

31. a) $P < 0.001$. There is strong evidence that the proportions of the two groups are not equal.
   b) $(0.096, 0.210)$ (proportion of old − proportion of young)

33. a) The standard error of the difference in proportions is 0.0094, but the difference in proportions is 0.009, which is about one standard error. That is not a statistically significant difference.
   b) A 90% CI is 0.009 ± 0.0155.

35. This is a test of homogeneity. The null hypothesis in either case is that there was no change over the three years. Chi-square $= 24.33$ with 8 df $P = 0.0020$, so the null hypothesis is rejected.

37. a) Chi-square test for homogeneity.
   b) Count data; adult respondents were surveyed randomly; expected counts are all greater than 5.
   c) H_0: The distribution of attitudes about the importance of financial success was the same for men and women 18 to 34 years old.
      H_A: The distribution of attitudes was not the same.
   d) $\chi^2 = 17.43$; df $= 3$; $P = 0.0006$
   e) The P-value is small so we reject the null hypothesis and conclude that men and women in this age group have different attitudes about the importance of this type of success.

39. a) A test of independence would be appropriate.
   b) The data are counts; no cells are too small.
   c) $\chi^2 = 14.43$ with 2 df $P = 0.0007$
   d)

	No	Yes
Yes	−1.22856	1.53931
No	2.01107	−2.51975
Retired	0.250431	−0.313775

   e) Those who are employed are more likely to own stock than either those who are not employed or those who are retired.

41. a)

	Men	Women
Excellent	6.667	5.333
Good	12.778	10.222
Average	12.222	9.778
Below Average	8.333	6.667

   Count data; assume that these executives are representative of all executives that have ever completed the program; expected counts are all greater than 5.
   b) Decreased from 4 to 3.
   c) $\chi^2 = 9.306$; $P = 0.0255$. Since the P-value is low, we reject the null hypothesis. There is evidence that the distributions of responses about the value of the program for men and women executives are different.

43. H_0: There is no association between race and the section of the apartment complex in which people live.
   H_A: There is an association between race and the section of the apartment complex in which people live.

Count data; assume that the recently rented apartments are representative of all apartments in the complex; expected counts are all greater than 5.

$\chi^2 = 14.058$; df $= 1$; $P < 0.001$.

Since the P-value is low, we reject the null hypothesis. There is strong evidence of an association between race and the section of the apartment complex in which people live. An examination of the components shows us that blacks are less likely to rent in Section A (component $= 6.2215$) and that blacks are more likely to rent in Section B (component $= 5.0517$).

45. $\hat{p}_B - \hat{p}_A = 0.206$
95% CI $= (0.107, 0.306)$

47. a) Chi-square test for independence.
b) Count data; assume that the sample was taken randomly; expected counts are all greater than 5.
c) H_0: Outsourcing is independent of industry sector.
H_A: There is an association between outsourcing and industry sector.
d) $\chi^2 = 2815.968$; df $= 9$; P-value is essentially 0.
e) Since the P-value is so low, we reject the null hypothesis. There is strong evidence of an association between outsourcing and industry sector.

49. a) Chi-square test for homogeneity. (Could be independence if the categories are considered exhaustive.)
b) Count data; assume that the sample was taken randomly; expected counts are all greater than 5.
c) H_0: The distribution of employee job satisfaction level attained is the same for different management styles.
H_A: The distribution of employee job satisfaction level attained is different for different management styles.
d) $\chi^2 = 178.453$; df $= 12$; P-value is essentially 0.
e) Since the P-value is so low, we reject the null hypothesis. There is strong evidence that the distribution of employee job satisfaction level attained is different across management styles. Generally, exploitative authoritarian management is more likely to have lower levels of employee job satisfaction than consultative or participative styles.

51. Assumptions and conditions for test of independence satisfied. H_0: Reading online journals or blogs is independent of generation. H_A: There is an association between reading online journals or blogs and generation. $\chi^2 = 48.408$; df $= 8$; $P < 0.001$. We reject the null hypothesis and conclude that reading online journals or blogs is not independent of generational age.

53. Chi-square test of homogeneity (unless these two types of firms are considered the only two types in which case it's a test of independence).
Count data; assume that the sample was random; expected counts are all greater than 5.

H_0: Systems used have same distribution for both types of industry.
H_A: Distributions of type of system differs in the two industries.
$\chi^2 = 157.256$; df $= 3$; P-value is essentially 0.
Since the P-value is low, we can reject the null hypothesis and conclude that the type of ERP system used differs across industry type. Those in manufacturing appear to use more of the inventory management and ROI systems.

55. Chi-square test of independence.
Count data; we assume that this time period is representative; expected counts are less than 5 in three cells, but very close.
H_0: GDP % change is independent of Region of the United States.
H_A: GDP % change is not independent of Region of the United States.
$\chi^2 = 19.0724$; df $= 3$; $P < 0.001$.
The P-value is low so we reject the null hypothesis and conclude that GDP % change and Region are not independent. The result seems clear enough even though the expected counts of 3 cells were slightly below 5.

CHAPTER 15
SECTION EXERCISE ANSWERS

1. a) 9.8, 8.5, 5.9, 2.0, 8.5, 11.1
b) $-0.8, -0.5, -1.9, 1.0, 1.5, 0.9$
c) 1.46

3. $s_x = 12.5167, s_e = 1.46, n = 6, SE(b_1) = 0.052$

5. a) 5.837
b) 3
c) 0.01
d) Yes, the P-value is smaller than 0.05.

7. a) Linearity: the plot appears linear.

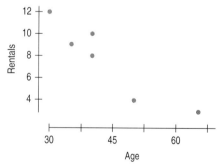

b) Independence: It is likely that the customers are independent. It is likely that errors made by the regression will be independent.
c) Equal spread: the plot appears to have a consistent spread.
d) Normality: We can't tell from what we know.

9. **a)** 19.06 ($1000)
   b) $19.06 \pm 1.12 = (17.94, 20.19)$ in $1000's
   c) $19.06 \pm 3.59 = (15.47, 22.65)$ in $1000's

11. **a)** 95% of potential customers in the community from households that have annual incomes of $80,000 can be expected to spend between $35.60 and $55.60 eating out each week. Pricing an individual meal in this range might attract that demographic.
   b) We can be 95% confident that the mean amount spent weekly by individuals whose household incomes are $80,000 is between $40.60 and $50.60. The mean is a summary for this demographic.
   c) We can estimate means more accurately than we can estimate values for individuals. That's why the confidence interval for the mean is narrower than the corresponding interval for an individual.

13. **a)** 464.8 ($000)
   b) $464.8 \pm 97.52 = (366.2, 563.4)$ in $1000
   c) No. Extrapolating what their sales might be with 500 employees based on data with between 2 and 20 employees working is likely to be very wrong.

CHAPTER EXERCISE ANSWERS

15. **a)**

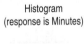

Scatterplot of Minutes vs. Age

   b) This scatterplot appears to have curvature at both ends of the age distribution so a linear regression may not be completely appropriate.
   c) The regression equation is
$$\widehat{Minutes} = 750 - 11.5 \, Age.$$
   d) The residual plots are:

Histogram
(response is Minutes)

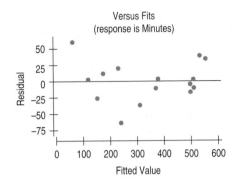

Versus Fits
(response is Minutes)

The nearly normal condition is satisfied. There may be some curvature to the residual plot.

17. **a)** $\widehat{Budget} = -31.39 + 0.71 \, Run \, Time$. The model suggests that movies cost about $710,000 per minute to make.
   b) A negative starting value makes no sense, but the P-value of 0.07 indicates that we can't discern a difference between our estimated value and zero. The statement that a movie of zero length should cost $0 makes sense.
   c) Amounts by which movie costs differ from predictions made by this model vary, with a standard deviation of about $33 million.
   d) 0.15$M/min
   e) If we constructed other models based on different samples of movies, we'd expect the slopes of the regression lines to vary, with a standard deviation of about $150,000 per minute.

19. **a)** The scatterplot looks straight enough, the residuals look random and roughly normal, and the residuals don't display any clear change in variability although there may be some increasing spread.
   b) I'm 95% confident that the cost of making longer movies increases at a rate of between 0.41 and 1.01 million dollars per minute. (CI is 0.41 to 1.02 using raw data.)

21. **a)** H_0: There is no linear relationship between calcium concentration in water and mortality rates for males. ($\beta_1 = 0$) H_A: There is a linear relationship between calcium concentration in water and mortality rates for males. ($\beta_1 \neq 0$)
   b) $t = -6.65, P < 0.0001$; reject the null hypothesis. There is strong evidence of a linear relationship between calcium concentration and mortality. Towns with higher calcium concentrations tend to have lower mortality rates.
   c) For 95% confidence, use $t^*_{59} \approx 2.001$, or estimate from the table $t^*_{50} \approx 2.009$; $(-4.20, -2.26)$.
   d) We are 95% confident that the average mortality rate decreases by between 2.26 and 4.20 deaths per 100,000 for each additional part per million of calcium in drinking water.

23. a) $\widehat{2010Index} = 33.187 + 0.6869 \times 2007Index$

b) The plot tends to thicken, but the regression is otherwise OK.

c) The P-value for the slope is 0.0025. That is small enough to be confident that the true slope is not zero.

d) $R^2 = 21.2\%$

25. a)

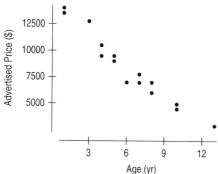

b) Yes, the plot seems linear.

c) $\widehat{Advertised\ Price} = 14286 - 959 \times Age$

d)

The residual plot shows some possible curvature. Inference may not be valid here, but we will proceed (with caution).

27. Based on these data, we are 95% confident that a used car's *Price* decreases between \$819.50 and \$1098.50 per year.

29. a)

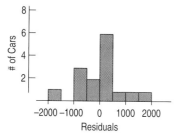

$\widehat{mpg} = 48.7393 - 8.21362\,(weight)$

b) Yes, the conditions seem satisfied. Histogram of residuals is unimodal and symmetric; residual plot looks okay, but some "thickening" of the plot with increasing values. There may be one possible outlier.

c) H_0: There is no linear relationship between the weight of a car and its fuel efficiency. ($\beta_1 = 0$)
H_A: There is a linear relationship between the weight of a car and its mileage. ($\beta_1 \neq 0$)

d) $t = -12.2$, df $= 48$, $P < 0.0001$; reject the null hypothesis. There is strong evidence of a linear relationship between weight of a car and its mileage. Cars that weigh more tend to have lower gas mileage.

31. a) H_0: There is no linear relationship between SAT Verbal and Math scores. ($\beta_1 = 0$)
H_A: There is a linear relationship between SAT Verbal and Math scores. ($\beta_1 \neq 0$)

b) Assumptions seem reasonable, since conditions are satisfied. Residual plot shows no patterns (one outlier); histogram is unimodal and roughly symmetric.

c) $t = 11.9$, df $= 160$, $P < 0.0001$; reject the null hypothesis. There is strong evidence of a linear relationship between SAT Verbal and Math scores. Students with higher SAT Verbal scores tend to have higher SAT Math scores.

33. a) $H_0: \beta_1 = 0$ vs. $H_A: \beta_1 \neq 0$

b) The P-value of 0.0076 shows strong evidence to reject the null hypothesis. It seems that higher salaries are associated with more wins.

c) However, there are two teams with low salaries and only 2 wins. Without those teams, the P-value is 0.396, and would lead us not to reject the null hypothesis. It seems that there is little relationship between salary and wins excluding those two teams.

35. a) $(-9.57, -6.86)$ mpg per 1000 pounds

b) We are 95% confident that the mean mileage of cars decreases by between 6.86 and 9.57 miles per gallon for each additional 1000 pounds of weight.

37. a) H_0: No linear relationship between *Population* and *Ozone*, $\beta_1 = 0$.
H_A: *Ozone* increases with *Population*, $\beta_1 > 0$.
$t = 3.48$; P-value $= 0.0018$. With a P-value so low, we reject H_0. These data show evidence that *Ozone* increases with *Population*.

b) Yes. *Population* accounts for 84% of the variability in *Ozone* level, and *s* is just over 5 parts per million.

39. a) Based on this regression, each additional million residents corresponds to an increase in average ozone level of between 3.29 and 10.01 ppm, with 90% confidence.

b) The mean *Ozone* level for cities with 600,000 people is between 18.47 and 27.29 ppm, with 90% confidence.

41. a) 69 tablets.
  b) Yes. The scatterplot is roughly linear with lots of scatter; plot of residuals vs. predicted values shows no overt patterns; Normal probability plot of residuals is reasonably straight.
  c) H_0: No linear relationship between *Battery Life* and *Screen Brightness*, $\beta_1 = 0$. H_A: *Battery Life* is associated with *Screen Brightness*, $\beta \neq 0$. $t = 1.842$; P-value $= 0.070$. There is a slight *positive* association between *Screen Brightness* and *Battery Life*, but the P-value is too large to conclude that it did not occur by chance.
  d) Not particularly. $R^2 = 4.82\%$ and $s = 1.946$ hours. Since the range of battery life is only about 9 hours, an s of 1.946 is quite large.
  e) *Hours* $= 6.21 + 0.0049$ *Screen Brightness*
  f) $(-0.00041, 0.0101)$ hours per cd/m^2 units
  g) *Battery life* increases, on average, between -0.00041 and 0.0101 *hours* per one cd/m^2 units, with 95% confidence.

43. a) $H_0: \beta_1 = 0$ (There is no linear relationship between the 2011 index and the 2010 index.) vs. $H_A: \beta_1 \neq 0$ (There is a linear relationship.)
  b) The P-value is very small, so we can reject the null hypothesis and conclude that expensive cities continue to be expensive.
  c) 84% of the variation in the cost of living index in 2011 can be accounted for by the index in 2010.
  d) Yes, the slope is positive and statistically significant.

45. a) The plot has a cluster of expensive cities in the upper right and a cluster of inexpensive cities in the lower left with a large gap between them.
  b) The R^2 is inflated by the large separation of the two groups.

47. a)

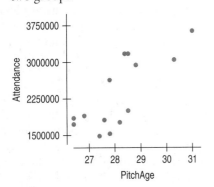

b) Yes, there appears to be a linear association
c) Dependent variable is: Attend/G
   R-squared = 59.3% R-squared (adjusted) = 55.9%
   s = 6025 with 14 − 2 = 12 degrees of freedom

Variable	Coeff	SE(Coeff)	t-Ratio	P-Value
Intercept	−120463	35750	−3.37	0.0056
PitchAge	5305.56	1269	4.18	0.0013

Teams with pitchers who are a year older tend to have about 5305 more fans on average at each game.

49. a) We are 95% confident that the mean fuel efficiency of cars that weigh 2500 pounds is between 27.34 and 29.07 miles per gallon.
  b) We are 95% confident that a car weighing 3450 pounds will have fuel efficiency between 15.44 and 25.36 miles per gallon.

51. a) $(-4.99, 5.29)$
  b) Yes, it will probably be accurate, but not very useful since most of the pitchers fall in to this range.

53. a) We'd like to know if there is a linear association between *Price* and *Highway MPG* in cars. We have data on 2012 model-year cars giving their highway mpg and retail price. $H_0: \beta_1 = 0$ (no linear relationship between *Price* and *Highway MPG*); $H_A: \beta_1 \neq 0$.
  b) The scatterplot shows that the Straight Enough Condition is reasonably satisfied. The residual plots show no particular pattern, so we can continue.
  c) We find a moderately strong, negative linear relationship between efficiency and price. An increase in price of $1000 is associated, on average, with a decrease of 0.42 highway mpg.

55. a) The 95% prediction interval shows the interval of uncertainty for a single country's predicted male unemployment rate, given its female unemployment rate.
  b) The 95% confidence interval shows the interval of uncertainty for the mean male unemployment rate given a sample of female unemployment rates. Because this is an interval for an average, the variation or uncertainty is less, so the interval is narrower.
  c) The two outliers are Mexico and Turkey, whose female rate is much lower than the male rate. There is no obvious justification for removing them, but the model would be stronger without them.

57. a) The 95% prediction interval shows the interval of uncertainty for the predicted energy use in 2010 based on energy use in 2006 for a single country.
  b) The 95% confidence interval shows the interval of uncertainty for the mean energy use in 2010 based on the same energy use in 2006 for a sample of countries.

Because this is an interval for an average, the variation or uncertainty is less, so the interval is narrower.

c) The outlier is Iceland. It does impact the regression. After removing it, the slope is lowered to 0.922 (SE 0.06) and the intercept becomes 5.744 (SE 9.06). The R^2 is lowered to 88.6% from 91.3%. The standard deviation of the residuals is now 13.10, which is much smaller than the original 22.53. This will make the intervals narrower and our predictions more precise.

59. a) $\widehat{Jan} = 120.73 + 0.6995\,Dec$. We are told this is an SRS. One cardholder's spending should not affect another's. These are quantitative data with no apparent bend in the scatterplot. The residual plot shows some increased spread for larger values of January charges. A histogram of residuals is unimodal and slightly skewed to the right with several high outliers. We will proceed cautiously.

b) $1519.73

c) ($1330.24, $1709.24)

d) ($290.76, $669.76)

e) The residuals show increasing spread, so the confidence intervals may not be valid. I would be skeptical of interpreting them too literally.

CHAPTER 16

SECTION EXERCISE ANSWERS

1. The different cardholder segments are not scattered at random throughout the scatter plot. Each segment may have a different relationship.

3. Yes, it is clear that the relationship between January and December spending is not the same for all five segments. Using one overall model to predict January spending would be very misleading.

5. a) 464.6 ($000)

b) No. Extrapolating what their sales might be with 500 employees based on data with between 2 and 20 employees working is likely to be very wrong.

7. a) $354,472

b) An extrapolation this far from the data is unreliable.

9. a) $\widehat{Sales} = 14.32 + 0.297\,Number\,of\,Sales\,People\,Working$

b) The intercept is higher and the slope is much lower.

c) High leverage and influential.

d) Not really. The line is so influenced by the new point that it passes close to it.

11. a)

Quarter	Sales ($M)	Predicted	Residual
1	12	19.02	−7.02
2	41	23.89	17.11
3	15	28.76	−13.76
4	48	33.63	14.37
5	25	38.5	−13.5
6	55	43.37	11.63
7	23	48.24	−25.24
8	69	53.11	15.89
9	51	57.98	−6.98
10	80	62.85	17.15
11	54	67.72	−13.72
12	87	72.59	14.41
13	64	77.46	−13.46
14	94	82.33	11.67
15	62	87.2	−25.2
16	108	92.07	15.93

b)

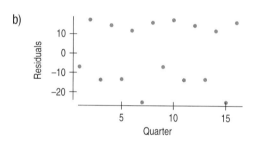

c) $D = 3.62$

d) 1.10, 1.37

e) No. $D > 1.37$

f) Yes. $D > 4 - 1.10$

13. a) $d_L = 1.48, d_U = 1.57$. The observed value is less than d_L so we can reject the null hypothesis of no autocorrelation.

b) The statistic tests for time-related correlation. We can conclude that there is evidence of positive autocorrelation.

15. No. The scatterplot shows a linear relationship and the residual plot has no obvious pattern. No transformation is suggested.

17. A re-expression is called for. Taking the log or reciprocal of *Cost per Unit* would probably improve the linearity.

19. a) Log

b) 0

21. a) The trend appears to be somewhat linear up to about 1940, but from 1940 to about 1970 the trend appears to be nonlinear. From 1975 or so to about 1995, the trend appears to be linear.
b) Relatively strong for certain periods.
c) No, as a whole the graph is clearly nonlinear. Within certain periods (1975 to about 1995) the correlation is high.
d) Overall, no. You could fit a linear model to the period from 1975 to about 1995, but why? You don't need to interpolate, since every year is reported, and extrapolation seems dangerous.

23. a) The relationship is not straight.
b) It will be curved downward.
c) No. The relationship will still be curved.

25. a) No. We need to see the scatterplot first to see if the conditions are satisfied.
b) No. in spite of the high R^2, the linear model might still be inappropriate.

27. a) Millions of dollars per minute of run time.
b) Budgets for dramas increase, on average, at the same rate per minute as other movies.
c) Regardless of run time, dramas cost less by about $30 million.

29. a) The use of Oakland airport has been growing at about 59,700 passengers/year, starting from about 283,000 in 1990.
b) 71% of the variation in passengers is accounted for by this model.
c) Errors in predictions based on this model have a standard deviation of 104,330 passengers.
d) DW = 0.912; Strong evidence of autocorrelation.
e) No, that would extrapolate too far from the years we've observed, and the series is autocorrelated.
f) The negative residual is September 2001. Air traffic was artificially low following the attacks on 9/11.

31. a) 1) High leverage, small residual.
2) No, not influential for the slope.
3) Correlation would decrease because outlier has large z_x and z_y, increasing correlation.
4) Slope wouldn't change much because the outlier is in line with other points.
b) 1) High leverage, probably small residual.
2) Yes, influential.
3) Correlation would weaken and become less negative because scatter would increase.
4) Slope would increase toward 0, since outlier makes it negative.
c) 1) Some leverage, large residual.
2) Yes, somewhat influential.
3) Correlation would strengthen, since scatter would decrease.
4) Slope would increase slightly.

d) 1) Little leverage, large residual.
2) No, not influential.
3) Correlation would become stronger and become more negative because scatter would decrease.
4) Slope would change very little.

33. 1) e   2) d   3) c   4) b   5) a

35. Perhaps high blood pressure causes high body fat, high body fat causes high blood pressure, or both could be caused by a lurking variable such as a genetic or lifestyle issue.

37. a) *Cost* decreases by $2.13 per degree of average daily *Temp*. So warmer temperatures indicate lower costs.
b) For an avg. monthly temperature of 0°F, the cost is predicted to be $133.
c) Too high; the residuals (observed − predicted) around 32°F are negative, showing that the model overestimates the costs.
d) $111.7
e) About $105.7
f) No, the residuals show a definite curved pattern. The data are probably not linear.
g) No, there would be no difference. The relationship does not depend on the units.

39. a) 0.88
b) Interest rates during this period grew at about 0.25% per year, starting from an interest rate of about 0.64%.
c) Substituting 50 in the model yields a predicted value of about 13%.
d) DW = 0.9527; P-value = 0.002; Strong evidence of autocorrelation.
e) Not really. Extrapolating 20 years beyond the end of these data would be dangerous and unlikely to be accurate. Errors are autocorrelated as well.

41. a) The two models both fit well, but they have very different slopes and intercepts.
b) This model predicts the interest rate in 2000 to be 3.76%, lower than the other model predicts.
c) We can trust the new predicted value because it is in the middle of the data used for the regression.
d) The best answer is "I can't predict that."

43. *Sex* and *Colorblindness* are both categorical variables, not quantitative. Correlation is meaningless for them, but we can say that the variables are associated.

45. a) No re-expression needed.
b) Re-express to straighten the relationship.
c) Re-express to equalize spread.

47. a) There's an annual pattern, so the residuals cycle up and down.

b) No, this kind of pattern can't be helped by re-expression.

49. a) 2.8 **b)** 16.44 **c)** 7.84 **d)** 0.36 **e)** 2.09

51. a) 3.842 **b)** 501.187 **c)** 4.0

53. a) Linearity condition violated. Possibly increased variation at higher values. Independence may be in doubt since this is a time series.

b) This plot looks both straighter and more consistent in variation.

c) The residuals show a pattern, but it tracks up and down and could not be improved by an alternative transformation.

55. a) About $672,000,000

b) *logValue* grows at 0.0001915 per licensed *Fisher*. Possibly more fishers cause a more valuable harvest, but greater value would likely attract more fishers, so the causation might run the other way. Or improving technology could both lead to more value and attract more fishers.

57. a) Although nearly 97% of the variation in GDP can be accounted for by this model, we should examine a scatterplot of the residuals to see if it's appropriate.

b) No. The residuals show clear curvature.

59. a)

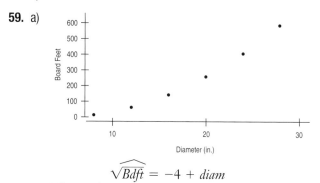

$$\widehat{\sqrt{Bdft}} = -4 + diam$$

The model is exact.

b) 36 board feet.

c) 1024 board feet.

61. Dependent variable is: 1998 GDP/Cap
R-squared = 94.2% R-squared (adjusted) = 93.9%
s = 2803 with 24 − 2 = 22 degrees of freedom

Source	Sum of Squares	df	Mean Square	F-ratio
Regression	2800375675	1	2800375675	356
Residual	172861656	22	7857348	

Variable	Coeff	SE(Coeff)	t-ratio	P-value
Intercept	3295.80	1307	2.52	0.0194
88 GDP CAP	1.090	0.058	18.9	<0.0001

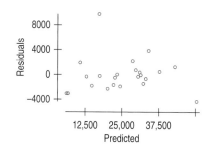

The regression has a high R^2 but the residuals show two influential points, Ireland with the largest positive residual and Switzerland with the largest negative residual. Assuming the data for these countries are correct, they should be set aside from the analysis and further work done to understand why each is unusual. Reports both with and without the outliers should be compared.

63. The histogram is much more unimodal and symmetric after we take logs.

65. The plot cannot be straightened by a transformation because it is not a simple monotonically increasing or decreasing shape, but rather it oscillates up and down.

CHAPTER 17
SECTION EXERCISE ANSWERS

1. a) $99,859.89
    b) $35,140.11
    c) The house sold for about $35,100 more than our estimate.

3. a) $\widehat{USGross} = -22.9898 + 1.13442 Budget + 24.9724 Stars - 0.403296 RunTime$
    b) After allowing for the effects of *RunTime* and *Stars*, each million dollars spent making a film yields about 1.13 million dollars in gross revenue.

5. a) Linearity: The plot is reasonably linear with no bends.
    b) Equal spread: The plot fails the Equal Spread condition. It is much more spread out to the right than on the left.
    c) Normality: A scatterplot of two of the variables doesn't tell us anything about the distribution of the residuals.

7. a) $H_0: \beta_{Stars} = 0$
    b) $t = 4.24$
    c) $P \leq 0.0001$
    d) Reject the null hypothesis and conclude that the coefficient of *Stars* is not zero.

9. a) $R^2 = 0.474$ or 47.4%
       About 47.4% of the variation in *USGross* is accounted for by the least squares regression on *Budget*, *RunTime*, and *Stars*.
    b) Adjusted R^2 accounts for the number of predictors, so it differs from R^2, which does not.

CHAPTER EXERCISE ANSWERS

11. a) Linearity: The scatterplots show little pattern, but are not nonlinear.
       Independence: States are not a random sample, but they may be independent of each other.
       Equal variance: The scatterplots do not appear to have a changing spread.
       Normality: To check the Nearly Normal condition, we'll need to look at the residuals; we can't check it with these plots.
    b) 0.26%

13. a) $\widehat{Violent\ Crime} = 1370.22 + 0.795\ Police\ Officer\ Wage - 12.641\ Graduation\ Rate$
    b) After allowing for the effects of graduation rate (or, alternatively, among states with similar graduation rates), states with higher police officer wages have more crime at the rate of 0.7953 crimes per 100,000 for each dollar per hour of average wage.
    c) 501.244 crimes per 100,000
    d) Not very good; R^2 is only 22.4% and $s = 156.9$.

15. a) $0.221 = \dfrac{0.7947}{3.598}$
    b) 50 states. There are 47 degrees of freedom and that's equal to $n - k - 1$. With two predictors, $50 - 2 - 1 = 47$.
    c) The *t*-ratio is negative because the coefficient is negative.

17. a) $H_0: \beta_{Officer\ Wage} = 0$ $H_A: \beta_{Officer\ Wage} \neq 0$
    b) $P = 0.8262$; that's not small enough to reject the null hypothesis at $\alpha = .05$ and conclude that the coefficient is discernibly different from zero.

19. This is a causal interpretation, which is not supported by regression. For example, among states with high graduation rates, it may be that those with higher violent crime rates choose (or are obliged) to spend more to hire police officers, or that states with higher costs of living must pay more to attract qualified police officers but also have higher crime rates. Moreover, the coefficient of *Police Wage* can not be distinguished from 0.

21. Constant variance condition: may be met by the residuals vs. predicted plot (but some may judge otherwise). Nearly Normal condition: met by the Normal probability plot

23. a) Doesn't mention other predictors; suggests direct relationship
    b) Correct
    c) Can't predict *x* from *y*
    d) Incorrect interpretation of R^2

25. a) Extrapolates far from the data
    b) Suggests a perfect relationship
    c) Can't predict one explanatory variable from another
    d) Correct

27. a) The sign of the coefficient for ln(*number of employees*) is negative. This means that for businesses that have the same amount of sales, those with more employees spend less per employee on pollution abatement on average. The sign of the coefficient for ln(*sales*) is positive. This means that for businesses with the same number of employees, those with larger sales spend more on pollution abatement on average.
    b) The logarithms mean that the effects become less severe (in dollar terms) as companies get larger either in sales or in number of employees.

29. a) $\widehat{Price} = -152,037 + 9530\ Baths + 139.87\ Area$
    b) $R^2 = 71.1\%$
    c) For houses with the same number of bathrooms, each square foot of area is associated with an increase of $139.87 in the price of the house, on average.
    d) The regression model says that for houses of the same size, those with more bathrooms are not

priced higher. It says nothing about what would happen if a bathroom were added to a house. That would be a predictive interpretation, which is not supported by regression.

31. a) The regression equation is: $\widehat{Salary} = 9.788 + 0.110\ Service + 0.053\ Education + 0.071\ Test\ Score + 0.004\ Typing\ wpm + 0.065\ Dictation\ wpm$

b) $Salary = 29.205$ or $29,205$

c) The *t*-value is 0.013 with 24 df. P-value $= 0.9897$ which is not significant at $\alpha = 0.05$.

d) Take out the explanatory variable for typing speed since it is not significant.

e) *Age* is likely to be collinear with several of the other predictors already in the model. For example, secretaries with longer terms of *Service* will probably also be older.

33. a) This model explains less than 4% of the variation in *GDP per Capita*. The P-value is not particularly low.

b) Because more education is generally associated with a higher standard of living, it is not surprising that the simple association between *Primary Completion Rate* and GDP is positive

c) The coefficient now is measuring the association between *GDP/Capita* and *Primary Completion Rate* after accounting for the two other predictors.

35. a) $\widehat{Price} = 1.094 + 1.236\ Traps\ (M) - 0.000149\ Fishers - 0.0180\ Pounds/Trap$

b) The residuals show greater spread on the right and their distribution shows a possible outlier on the high end. We might wonder whether values from year to year are mutually independent. We should interpret the model with caution.

c) $H_0: \beta_{Pounds/Trap} = 0, H_A: \beta_{Pounds/Trap} \neq 0$; the P-value is 0.0011. It appears that *Pounds/Trap* does contribute to the model.

d) No. We can't draw causal conclusions from a regression. A change in *Pounds/Trap* would likely affect other variables in the model.

e) Adjusted R^2 says to prefer the more complex model.

37. a)
```
R squared = 66.7% R squared (adjusted) = 63.8%
    s = 2.327 with 39 - 4 = 35 degrees of freedom
```

Variable	Coeff	SE(Coeff)	t-ratio	P-value
Intercept	87.0089	33.60	2.59	0.0139
CPI	−0.344795	0.1203	−2.87	0.0070
Personal Consumption	1.10842e−5	4.403e−6	2.52	0.0165
Retail Sales	1.03152e−4	1.545e−5	6.67	<0.0001

$\widehat{Revenue} = 87.0 - 0.344\ CPI + 0.000011$ *Percsonal Consumption* $+ 0.0001\ Retail\ Sales$

b) R^2 is 66.7%, and all *t*-ratios are significant. It looks like these variables can account for much of the variation in Wal-Mart revenue.

39. a) $\widehat{Logit(Drop)} = 0.4419 + 0.0379\ Age - 0.0468$ *HDRS*

b) 0.1749

c) 0.544

d) 2.342

e) 0.912

41. *Displacement* and *Bore* would be good predictors. Relationship with *Wheelbase* isn't linear.

43. a) Yes, R^2 of 90.9% says that most of the variability of *MSRP* is accounted for by this model.

b) No, a regression model may not be inverted in this way.

45. a) Yes, R^2 is very large.

b) The value of *s*, 3.140 calories, is very small compared with the initial standard deviation of *Calories*. This indicates that the model fits the data quite well, leaving very little variation unaccounted for.

c) A true value of 100% would indicate zero residuals, but with real data such as these, it is likely that the computed value of 100% is rounded up from a slightly lower value.

CHAPTER 18
SECTION EXERCISE ANSWERS

1. a) Unionized $= 1$, No Union $= 0$ (or the reverse)

b) Female $= 1$, Male $= 0$ (or the reverse)

c) Paid on time $= 1$, Past Due $= 0$ (or the reverse)

d) Two variables. One variable could have Democrat $= 1$, 0 otherwise and another Republican $= 1$ and 0 otherwise.

3. a) To make two different intercepts for the two types of movie.

b) If R then 1; If PG then 0

5. (One possible answer for each: other equivalent codings are possible.)

a) Three variables: One variable that is 1 for Apartment, 0 for others. One that is 1 for Condo, 0 for others. One that is 1 for Townhouse, 0 for others.

b) Two variables: One that is 1 for Full-time, 0 for others. One that is 1 for Part-time, 0 for others.

7. a) If *PG-13 then* 0; If *R then* 1

b) The interaction term is the product of the indicator variable and the Budget variable.

9. A bit more than $0.2M (actually, $0.219M). This is a fundamental property of leverage.

11. Because of the high correlation between several of the predictor variables, a stepwise search might find a very different model from the best of the all subsets model.

13. 80.00

15. a) It is curved upward at both extremes of *Age*. It says that the most expensive homes are either quite new or very old.
   b) No. Although the relationship is not linear in *Age*, it is probably quadratic.
   c) Add a quadratic term in (Age^2).

17. a) Cheese pizzas (*Type* 1) scored about 15.6 points higher, after allowing for the effects of calories and fat. Cheese pizzas can be expected to sell better than pepperoni pizzas based on these results.
   b) Scatterplots of the data and of residuals to check linearity and constant variance; a histogram or probability plot of residuals to check normality.

19. a) Both pizzas are predicted to have high scores. But both have scores more than 30 points lower than predicted.
   b) Yes, their unusually large predicted values indicate that they must be different from the other pizzas in some ways, and their large (negative) residuals indicate that they would pull on the regression. It might be helpful to see leverage values or Cook's Distance values for these points.

21. a) An indicator or "dummy" variable
   b) Sales are about 10.5 billion dollars higher in December, after accounting for the *CPI*.
   c) Must assume that the slope is the same for the December points as for the others. That appears to be true in the scatterplot.

23. a) There are different slopes for the two types.
   b) This is an interaction term. It says that cheese pizzas (*Type* 1) have scores that grow less rapidly with *Calories* (a slope 0.46 smaller) than do pepperoni pizzas.
   c) The adjusted R^2 for this model is higher than the adjusted R^2 for the previous model. Also, the *t*-ratios are larger. Overall, this looks like a more successful regression model.

25. a) Large Cook's Distance suggests that Alaska is influential. Its leverage is high, and its residual is one of the largest in magnitude (very negative.)
   b) After allowing for the other predictors, Alaska's life expectancy is 2.23 years lower than the model predicts from the other states. The P-value of 0.02 says that Alaska is an outlier because the coefficient of the dummy variable is significantly not zero.

c) The model is better (higher adjusted R^2, smaller standard deviation of residuals) when Alaska is removed from the model with a dummy variable.

27. a) Because the P-value for *Rent Index* is so high, we should consider dropping it from the model.
   b) The adjusted R^2 value is the same and it has fewer predictors. All predictors have P-values below 0.05.
   c) Because the P-value for *Rent Index* was high.
   d) The 3 variable model has the same adjusted R^2 with one less predictor variable. However, there is, in fact, very little difference between the models. They make roughly the same predictions and have very similar coefficients.

29. a) Lesotho has an unusually high level of public health expenditures. Djibouti has a very low number of Internet users and low expected years of schooling. Singapore has a low expenditure for health given the predictor values. Cuba has an extraordinarily high public health expenditure for its predictor variables and Eritrea is low on all three variables.
   b) Answers may vary. The coefficients don't change a great deal, but the R^2 increases from 55.17% to 69.80%. It's a more accurate model without these points, but there may be no justification for just deleting them. It's best to report both models.

31. a) The equal spread condition shows that the equal variance assumption is violated.
   b) Try a re-expression of *US Gross*, perhaps log.
   c) The new model shows that by using the log(*US Gross*) as the response, neither the interaction nor the dummy variable are necessary. The simpler model just uses *Budget* as the predictor. The residual plot looks much better.

33. a) Bahrain has a relatively high number of *Cell phones/100* people, but a very low *Primary Completion Rate*. Burkina Faso has the lowest (negative?) *Primary Completion Rate* and low *Internet Users/100* people. Israel has the highest number of *Cell phones/100 people* and Luxembourg has the highest *GDP per Capita* and high *Cell phones/100 people*.
   b) Consider verifying the data (especially the negative *Primary Completion Rate*) and running a new model without these points to see the impact they make on the model selection and the coefficients.

35. The two countries with the largest leverage values are Chad (0.3624) and Luxembourg (0.2708). Chad also has an extremely high Cook's distance value. Chad, with a very low HDI score, has very low life expectancy, high maternal mortality, low schooling, and very few cell phone users. Luxembourg is nearly the opposite, with the highest *GDP per capita* of any country in the data set.

CHAPTER 19
SECTION EXERCISE ANSWERS

1. a) Yes
b) No, not vs. time
c) No, for each worker, not over time
d) Yes

3. a)

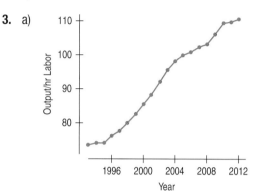

b) Trend: positive, slightly curved, strong.
c) No evidence of a seasonal component.

5. a)
```
*
0.9700
0.9560
0.9465
0.9895
1.0370
1.0995
1.1905
1.2455
1.1970
1.1135
1.0580
```

b) 1.058

7. 2.32% (If your value was negative, you forgot the absolute value.)

9.
```
*
0.963
0.977
0.935
0.958
1.021
1.053
1.146
1.235
1.256
1.138
1.089
```

11. 1.0012

13. a) Dummy or indicator variable.
b) A set of indicator variables must omit one to avoid collinearity.

15. a) The 200-day moving average will be smoother.
b) The SES model using $\alpha = 0.10$ is smoother.
c) When the α is raised from 0.10 to 0.80, the most recent data point is weighted more heavily, so the model responds more quickly and is not as smooth.

17. a) Random walk, so use AR(1) or naïve forecast.
b) Exponential model
c) Seasonal dummy variable model, or AR model that uses sales from the same quarter in prior years (lag4).

19. a) 22,988 $M
b) 21,270 $M

21. a) 475.88 $/tonne
b) 481.20 $/tonne
c) 17.53%, 16.60%

23. a) Irregular
b) Second graph

25. The 2-quarter moving average is shown in A and fits better. This series has a strong, consistent trend component, so a longer-span moving average is dragged down below the series.

27. a) $2.676B
b) APE = 7.7% (underforecast)
c) Forecast is $3.515B; APE = 3.34% (overforecast).

29. a) 136.206
b) 1.94%
c) 135.97; the AR model prediction is closer.

31. a) 112
b) The forecast will be over 100%, which is not possible.

33. a) Irregular components and possible cycles.
b) No. This could be a local artifact. We would want some independent reason to believe in a 14-week cycle.
c) It wouldn't be wise to use this model for prediction unless we had some reason to believe in the 14-week cycle.

35. a) $1.1 million
b) Q3
c) Q4
d) Sales on average are $0.5 million greater in Q4 than in Q1.

37. a) A positive trend component and a seasonal component
b) Walmart revenues have been increasing at about $0.145 billion per month.
c) Revenues in December tend to be about $11.56 billion more than in January (the base month).

d) $19.3028 billion

e) October is the only month in which Walmart revenues are typically lower than they are in January, after allowing for the overall growth trend in revenue.

39. a) The P-value indicates that the slope of the time trend is significantly different from zero.

b) The coefficient for November is not significantly different from zero, so it should not be interpreted.

c) Yes. Many of the month indicators are highly signficant.

d) 470,773

41. a) The log of the number of passengers grew at 0.0249 per month.

b) In January 1990 there were about $10^{5.64949} = 446,159$ passengers.

c) January and February; we can tell that January is low because it is the base for the dummy variables and the other coefficients are positive.

d) Trend, seasonal, and possibly an 8-year cyclic component.

43. The single exponential smooth is pulled down by the outlier. The moving average spreads out the effect of the outlier across several months. The seasonal regression is not noticeably affected. (The September dummy coefficient absorbs the effect and spreads it out over other Septembers, but that isn't evident in the plot.)

45. a)
```
Dependent variable is: E-Commerce Sales (Millions $)
R squared = 96.9%  R squared (adjusted) = 96.4%
s = 1740 with 34 − 5 = 29 degrees of freedom
```

Variable	Coeff	SE(Coeff)	t-ratio	P-value
Intercept	2022.8	777.4	2.60	0.014
Time	900.138	30.45	29.6	<0.0001
Q2	−486.223	845.9	−0.575	0.5699
Q3	−709.611	845.4	0.839	0.4081
Q4	3288.03	820.7	4.01	0.0004

Note: Choosing a different quarter as the base quarter will yield a different model, but one with the same R^2.

b)
```
Dependent variable is: logE-commerce Sales
R squared = 98.7%  R squared (adjusted) = 98.5%
s = 0.0297 with 34 − 5 = 29 degrees of freedom
```

Variable	Coeff	SE(Coeff)	t-ratio	P-value
Intercept	3.73222	0.0136	274	<0.0001
Time	0.024502	0.0005	47.1	<0.0001
Q2	−2.63785e-3	0.0145	−0.182	0.8566
Q3	−5.43049e-3	0.0145	−0.376	0.7099
Q4	0.072158	0.0140	5.14	<0.0001

c) The multiplicative model fits better judging from R^2 or adjusted R^2.

47. a) The regression equation is $\overparen{\text{Crude Price}}$ ($/Bar) = 0.809 + 0.991 lag1.

b) Forecast is 53.26.

49. a) Irregular and cyclical; note that since these are de-seasonalized data, we are unable to observe the seasonal component.

b) Check on graph below

c) Key:

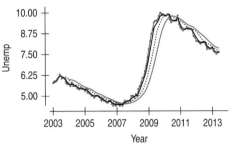

d) The exponential smooth fits the data most closely. The moving average smoothers lag behind the large movements in the unemployment rate.

51. a)
```
R squared = 69.5%  R squared (adjusted) = 67.0%
s = 34260 with 161 − 13 = 148 degrees of freedom
```

Variable	Coefficient	SE(Coeff)	t-ratio	P-value
Intercept	331767.84	10243.52	32.388	<0.0001
Time	531.37	58.14	9.140	<0.0001
Feb	10513.49	12948.92	0.812	0.418142
Mar	64524.62	12949.31	4.983	<0.0001
Apr	29200.97	12949.97	2.255	0.025606
May	26785.10	12950.88	2.068	0.040361
Jun	88457.52	13195.59	6.704	<0.0001
Jul	120284.30	13195.46	9.116	<0.0001
Aug	92049.70	13195.59	6.976	<0.0001
Sep	−29294.74	13195.97	−2.220	0.027941
Oct	3442.89	13196.61	0.261	0.794538
Nov	−5470.94	13197.51	−0.415	0.679076
Dec	46271.85	13198.66	3.506	0.000603

b) No. The time plot shows that the trend is not a simple linear one. The residual plot shows major changes in the behavior of the time series. A simple linear model is no longer adequate.

c) You can see both 9/11 (Sept 2001) and the impact of the 2008 financial crisis on the number of visitors.

CHAPTER 20
SECTION EXERCISE ANSWERS

1. a) Retrospective

b) Prospective

3. Experimental units: Cookies

Treatments: Chocolate chip choice (milk, dark, semi-sweet)

Response: Rating by trained testers

Randomization: Random presentation to the tasters

5. Control: All other aspects of the recipes were kept the same

Randomization: Cookies presented to tasters in random order

Replication: 10 tasters did the rating

7.

9. Single-blind. Customers were blind to treatments, but the kitchen staff knew.

11. a) 3, 36, and 39
b) 321.90
c) 285.36
d) 8.94

13. a) Chips (milk, dark, semi), and Oil (butter, margarine)
b) 6 treatments: milk/butter, dark/butter, semi/butter, milk/margarine, dark/margarine, semi/margarine
c) It would mean that the effect of the oil (butter vs. margarine) on ratings was not the same for the different chocolate types, (or vice versa).

CHAPTER EXERCISE ANSWERS

15. a) Temperature, Washing time, Detergent
b) Temperature (Hot, Cold), Washing time (Short, Long), Detergent (Standard, New).
c) Whiteness as measured by an optical scanner

17. a) Both detergents should be tested under the same conditions to ensure that the results are comparable.
b) It will be impossible to generalize to cold water washing.
c) Treatments should be run in random order to ensure that no other unforeseen influences could affect the response in a systematic way.

19. a) The differences among the Mozart and quiet groups were more than would have been expected from ordinary sampling variation.

b)

c) The Mozart group seems to have the smallest median difference and thus the *least* improvement, but there does not appear to be a significant difference.
d) No, the difference does not seem significant compared with the usual variation.

21. a) Observational; randomly select a group of children, ages 10 to 13, have them taste the cereal, and ask if they like the cereal.
b) Answers may vary. Get volunteers ages 10 to 13. Each volunteer will taste one cereal, randomizing the assignment. Compare the percentage of favorable ratings for each cereal.

c) Answers may vary. From the volunteers, identify the children who watch Frump and identify the children who do not watch Frump. Use a blocked design to reduce variation in cereal preference that may be associated with watching the Frump cartoon.

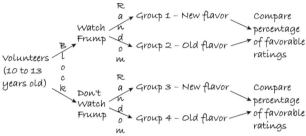

23. a) The students were not randomly assigned. Those who signed up for the prep course may be a special group whose scores would have improved anyway.
b) Answers may vary. Find a group of volunteers who are willing to participate. Give all volunteers the SAT exam. Randomly assign the subjects to the review or no review group. Give the tutoring to one group. After a reasonable time, retest both groups. Check to see that the tutored group had a significant improvement in scores when compared with the no review group.
c) After the volunteers have taken the first SAT exam, separate the volunteers into blocks of low, average, and high SAT exam score performance. Now assign half of each block to the review and half to the no review groups. Give the tutoring. Now retest all groups. Compare the differences between treatments for each block.

25. a) The null hypothesis is that the mean *Mileage* for all cylinder levels is the same. The alternative is that not all means are equal.
b) Randomization not specified, so inference is not clear. The spreads of the four groups look very different. The response variable probably should be re-expressed before proceeding with an Analysis of Variance. Consider omitting the single 5-cylinder car from the study since it is the only one in its group. Boxplots appear symmetric, but other plots should be used to check the Nearly Normal Condition.

27. a) H_0: Mean cell phone adoption rates are equal in the three regions.
H_A: Mean cell phone adoption rates are not all equal in the three regions.
b) Countries were selected randomly from the three regions, so the randomization condition is met. However, boxplots suggest the spreads may differ, and show several outliers, which may require attention. Other plots should be used to check the Nearly Normal Condition.

29. a) $H_0: \mu_1 = \mu_2 = \mu_3 = \mu_4 = \mu_5 = \mu_6$ (That is, each of the tellers takes, on average, the same amount of time to serve a customer.) vs. the alternative that not all means are equal. Here μ_k refers to the mean *Time* it takes *Teller k* to serve a customer.

b) With a P-value of 0.19, we can't reject the null hypothesis.

c) No, because we do not reject the null hypothesis, we cannot perform multiple comparisons.

31. a) Observational; the factor was not deliberately manipulated.

b) Retrospective; using previously collected data.

c) H_0: Mean responses to the e-security questions are all equal for the three types of community.
H_A: Mean responses to the e-security questions are not all equal for the three types of community.

d) $F = 6.24$

e) With such a small P-value, we can reject the null hypothesis and conclude that mean responses to the e-security question are not all equal for the three types of community. A causal link cannot be established because this is an observational study.

33. a) Experimental

b) Drug

c) Reported pain level (1 to 10)

d)

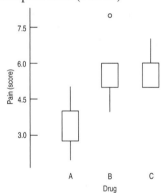

Analysis of Variance

Source	DF	Sum of Squares	Mean Square	F-ratio	P-value
Drug	2	28.2222	14.1111	11.9062	0.0003
Error	24	28.4444	1.1852		
Total	26	56.6666			

35. a) Experiment; the factors are deliberately manipulated to specify treatments, and the subjects are assigned to the treatments randomly.

b) Website trustworthiness measured on a 10-point scale.

c) There are two factors: (1) website configuration with respect to assurance and (2) type of product purchased.

d) There are nine treatments.

e) H_0: The mean *trustworthiness ratings* of websites are the same for those *with a third-party assurance seal, a self-proclaimed assurance displayed*, and *no assurance seal*.

H_0: The mean *trustworthiness* of websites is the same for online purchases of *books, cameras,* and *insurance*.

H_0: There is no interaction effect. (The effect of each factor is the same at all levels of the other factor.)

37. a) Observational study.

b) The mean DJIA closing is roughly the same each day of the week. The mean DJIA closing is roughly the same each month. Differences in days are no different from month to month.

c) There is no apparent difference in DJIA according to day of the week.

d) There does appear to be a difference from month to month.

e) There is no interaction between day of the week and month.

39. a) Observational study; the factors are not deliberately manipulated to specify treatments.

b) Boxplots of the hourly wages by both manager type and region indicate that the equal variance assumption is reasonable. Also, the boxplots indicate fairly symmetric distributions. However, other plots should be used to check the Nearly Normal Condition once the model has been fit. The states were randomly selected from the three regions, so the randomization condition is satisfied.

c) Based on the P-values, we can conclude that there is no significant interaction effect. There is no evidence that the mean hourly wages are different across the three regions but are different for sales and advertising managers.

d) Yes, because the interaction effect is not significant.

41. a) Experiment; the machine setting factor was deliberately manipulated. Shift is a blocking factor.

b) Size error of the part is the response variable.

c) There are nine treatments.

d) There is no significant interaction effect so we can conclude that both the Shift and the Machine Setting appear to have a significant effect. However, from this table alone, we cannot determine which of these effects is more important.

43. a) $MST = 8.65; MSE = 0.0767$

b) $F = 112.78$

c) The data provide very strong evidence that the means are not equal.

d) We have assumed that the experimental runs were performed in random order, that the variances of the treatment groups are similar, and that the residuals are nearly Normal.

e) A boxplot of the *Scores* by *Method*, a plot of residuals vs. predicted values, a Normal probability plot, and a histogram of the residuals.

f) $s_p = \sqrt{0.0767} = 0.277$ points

45. a) An observational study

b) The null hypothesis is that the mean *Sugar Content* is the same for the cereals on each *Shelf*. The alternative is that not all the means are equal.

c) The P-value of 0.0012 provides strong evidence that the mean *Sugar Content* is not the same for each *Shelf*.

d) We cannot conclude that cereals on *Shelf* 2 have a different mean *Sugar Content* than cereals on *Shelf* 3 or that cereals on *Shelf* 2 have a different mean *Sugar Content* than cereals on *Shelf* 1. We can conclude only that the means are not all equal.

e) The Bonferroni test shows that at $\alpha = .05$ the shelves are different, except for Shelf 1 and Shelf 3, which are not discernibly different. Now we can conclude that the mean *Sugar Content* of cereals on *Shelf* 2 is *not* equal to the mean *Sugar Content* on *Shelf* 1 and *Shelf* 3. In other words, we can conclude from this test what we wanted to conclude in part d.

47. a) H_0: Head injuries are, on average, about the same regardless of the size of the car
H_0: Which seat you sit in doesn't affect the degree of head injury.

b) The conditions appear to be met. We assume the data were collected independently, the boxplots show that the variance is roughly constant, and there are no patterns in the scatterplot of residuals vs. predicted values.

c) There is no significant interaction. The P-values for both *Seat* and *Size* are <0.0001. Thus, we reject both the null hypotheses and conclude that both the *Seat* and the *Size* of car affect the severity of head injury.

CHAPTER 21

SECTION EXERCISE ANSWERS

1. a)

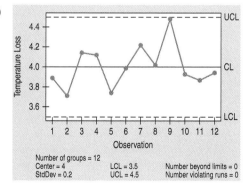

b) Yes, but one container was quite close to the upper limit.

c) 0.833

d) They need to decrease the process standard deviation. There is too great a chance that a container will fall outside the specification limits.

3. a)

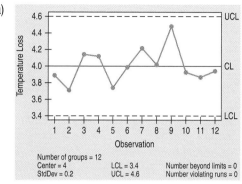

b) No.
c) No.
d) No.
e) No.
f) No.
g) No.
h) The process seems to be in control.

5. a) 0.00447 m (or 0.447 cm)
b) Outside (91.387, 91.413) m
c) $SD(\overline{X}) = 0.00316$m; Outside (91.391, 91.409) m

7. a) 0.0198
b) (0, 0.0794)
c) 4 (round up 3.97)

9. These would be control limits because they are based on the process itself and not on external criteria.

11. These are lower specification limits set by the NHSF below which no pad should fall.

13. This is an upper specification limit set by Gemini.

15. This is common-cause variation based on random fluctuations.

17. 0.0027 based on the observations being Normal.

19. a) and b)

$$\overline{\overline{X}} = 8.05; \quad \overline{R} = 0.65 \Rightarrow \hat{\sigma} = \frac{\overline{R}}{d_2} = \frac{0.65}{2.059} = 0.316$$

$\overline{X}$ *chart*: $LCL: 8.05 - 3\left(\frac{0.316}{\sqrt{4}}\right) = 7.576$

$UCL: 8.05 + 3\left(\frac{0.316}{\sqrt{4}}\right) = 8.524$

R *chart*: $LCL = 0(0.65) = 0$
$UCL = 2.282(0.65) = 1.483$

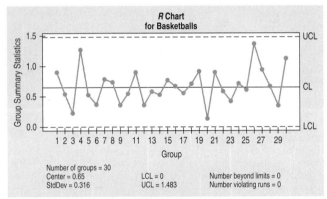

c) Both charts indicate that the process is in control as defined by the calibration period.

21. a) and b)

$$\mu = 21.2; \ \sigma = 0.29 \Rightarrow \sigma_R = d_3\sigma = 0.888 \times 0.29 = 0.258$$

$$\overline{X} \text{ chart:} \quad LCL = \mu - 3\frac{\sigma}{\sqrt{n}} = 21.2 - 3\frac{0.29}{\sqrt{3}} = 20.70$$

$$UCL = \mu + 3\frac{\sigma}{\sqrt{n}} = 21.2 + 3\frac{0.29}{\sqrt{3}} = 21.70$$

Center line: $\overline{R} = d_2\sigma = 1.693 \times 0.29 = 0.491$

R chart: $LCL = D_3\overline{R} = 0$

$$UCL = D_4\overline{R} = 2.574(0.491) = 1.264$$

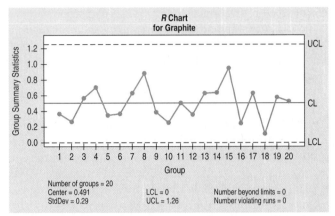

c) The process is out of control. Although the R chart appears to be in control, the $\overline{X}$ chart shows numerous samples outside the 3σ limits.

d)

All but one of the samples meets the specification limits.

23. a) 0.0616
b) 0.1072
c) 0.0160
d) See the following chart.
e) The process seems to be in control.

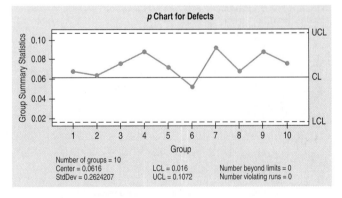

25. a) See the following chart.

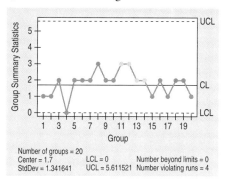

Number of groups = 20
Center = 1.7   LCL = 0   Number beyond limits = 0
StdDev = 1.341641   UCL = 5.611521   Number violating runs = 4

  b) Although no day exceeds the upper control limit, there are more than 9 days on the same side of the desired center line. The process appears to be out of control.

27. a) 4.57
  b) 10.99
  c) 0
  d) See the following chart.
  e) The process is not in control on day 5.

29. a)

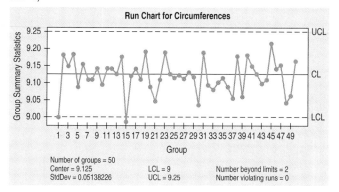

Number of groups = 50
Center = 9.125   LCL = 9   Number beyond limits = 2
StdDev = 0.05138226 UCL = 9.25   Number violating runs = 0

  b) No, there are two balls that are too small.
  c) Two.
  d) Right away. The first ball produced was too small.

CHAPTER 22
SECTION EXERCISE ANSWERS

 1. a) Ranks
  b) Ranks
  c) Not ranks—units are points earned on the exam.

 3. b

 5. d

 7. a

 9. c (possibly e)

11. e (possibly c)

13. a) The assumptions and conditions are met. The experiment was randomized, so the groups are independent and the individual participants are in-dependent. From technology we find that P = 0.01, which is small enough to reject the null hypothesis.
  b) It would be better to design this as a before/after study, testing the children at the start of the teaching period, then randomly assigning them to treatment groups, and finally testing them again and com-paring their results. An appropriate nonparametric method would be the Wilcoxon signed-rank test.

15. a) H_0: Distributions of sugar content have the same center.
      H_A: They have different centers.
  b) We don't know whether these cereals are a random sample from any particular population, but they are likely to be mutually independent.
  c) $P < 0.001$ (according to technology). We can re-ject the null hypothesis and conclude that there is a difference in sugar content.
  d) The distribution for Adults' cereals is skewed but the distribution for Children's cereals is symmetric. The skewness is a mild violation of the nearly Nor-mal condition for the *t*-test, but we can't re-express one without re-expressing the other the same way, and that would make the currently symmetric dis-tribution skewed. The nonparametric method is a better choice.

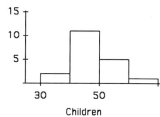

17. Use a Mann-Whitney test

```
Variable     n      median
size19th     5      27.00
size20th     9      15.50
W = 54.5
```

```
Test of medians equal vs medians not equal is
significant at 0.0278
Reject the null at α = 0.10
```

19. a) The subjects are not randomly selected, but are probably representative of the larger population of Freshmen. They are almost surely independent of each other.

H_0: No change over time; the median change is 0.
H_A: Change over time.
$P < 0.001$.

b) The *paired t*-test is probably more appropriate here because all assumptions and conditions it requires are met and it can provide a confidence interval for weight change, which would be a more complete response.

21. $N = 8$, N for test $= 7$.
$T = 2.5$. From Table, one sided 0.05 critical value is 4, so $P < 0.05$ (from technology $P = 0.031$). Reject the null hypothesis. ERP appears to be effective.

23. Wilcoxon signed-rank test
$N = 5$; $T^+ = 15$; $T^- = 0$: $T = 0$
For $\alpha = 0.05$ no critical value exists (sample is too small). From technology, $P = 0.0625$. So, do not reject the null hypothesis.

25.
```
species    N    Median   Ave Rank      Z
Robin      16   22.55      19.2      −1.46
Sparrow    14   23.05      26.7       1.26
Wagtail    15   23.05      23.7       0.24
Overall    44              23.0

H = 2.51  DF = 2  P = 0.285
H = 2.55  DF = 2  P = 0.279 (adjusted for ties)
```

Do not reject the null hypothesis.

27. a) The relationship is strongly monotonic.
b) There is a strong association between GDP and Crowdedness.
c) The association is not linear, so Pearson correlation is not appropriate.

29. a) Because the plot shows some bending, Kendall's tau may be more appropriate.
b) Tau tells us how consistently sales at The Home Depot grow as housing starts grow, but not the amount by which they grow.

31. Kendall's tau tells us that there is a fairly consistent positive association between the housing cost index and median family income. But it does not allow any conclusions about causation.

CHAPTER 23
SECTION EXERCISE ANSWERS

1. a) State of Nature
b) Action
c) Action

3.

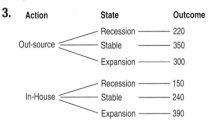

Action	State	Outcome
Out-source	Recession	220
	Stable	350
	Expansion	300
In-House	Recession	150
	Stable	240
	Expansion	390

5. a) Out-source
b) In-house

7. a) $EV(\text{Out-source}) = 294$, $EV(\text{In-house}) = 312$
b) Out-source

9. $SD(\text{Out-source}) = 41.76$, $CV(\text{Out-source}) = 0.14$,
$SD(\text{In-house}) = 99.68$, $CV(\text{In-house}) = 0.32$

11.

		Stay for Interview	
		No	**Yes**
Action	**Fully Changeable Fare**	$750	$750
	Nonrefundable Fare	$650	$800

13.

15.

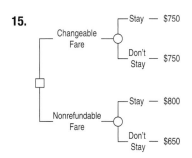

17. EV(Fully Changeable Fare) = \$750
EV(Nonrefundable Fare) = \$695
Choose the nonrefundable fare because we want to minimize the expected cost.

19. EV(Fully Changeable Fare) = \$750, EV(not changeable) is now \$755, so the changeable fare is a better choice.

21. a) If P(rising confidence) = 0.70, EV(Prime Time) = \$14.60. EV(Targeted Web Marketing) = \$11.40; EV(Direct Mail) = \$11.50
Choose Prime Time since expected payoff is highest.
b) If P(rising confidence) = 0.40, EV(Prime Time) = \$9.20; EV(Targeted Web Marketing) = \$10.80; EV(Direct Mail) = \$13.
Choose Direct Mail in this case since expected payoff is highest.

23. a) \$3.90
b) \$4.00

25. a)

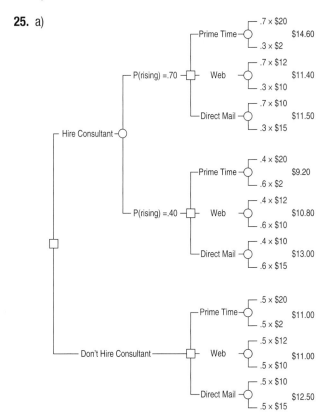

b) Yes, both alternatives with information have a better return.
c) \$1.30

27.

		Growing Season	
		Good	**Bad**
Purchase Decision	**2 Tractors**	\$27,400	\$2400
	3 Mowers	\$8575	\$3575
	No Purchase	\$0	−\$1000

29. Shawn favors Tractors, with an upside gain of \$27,400. Lance prefers the Mowers, whose worst result is \$3575.

31. a) and b)

		EV	**SD**	**RRR**
Purchase Decision	**2 Tractors**	\$19,900.00	11,456.44	1.737
	3 Mowers	\$7075.00	2291.28	3.088
	No Purchase	−\$300.00	458.26	−0.655

c) Purchasing Mowers has the highest RRR, which is preferred.

33. a)

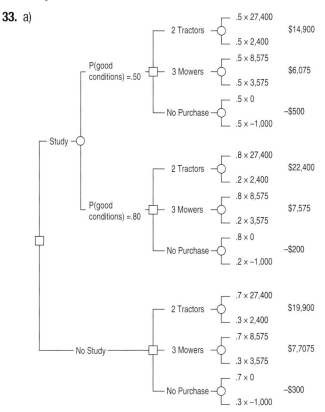

b) \$17,900
c) No. In all scenarios, the Tractors investment seems the best course to take.

35. a)   EV(Stock A) = \$800; EV(Stock B) = \$2300
  b)   SD(Stock A) = \$2749.55;
       SD(Stock B) = \$1833.03
  c)   CV(Stock A) = 3.437; CV(Stock B) = 0.797;
       RRR(Stock A) = 0.291; RRR(Stock B) = 1.255
  d)   Stock B; it has a higher expected value and a lower
       SD. Its RRR is much higher, which shows it has a
       better reward to risk ratio.

37. a)   EV(High-End Bike) = \$4465; EV(Moderately-
       Priced Bike) = \$2650
  b)   SD(High-End Bike) = \$1995.00;
       SD(Moderately-Priced Bike) = \$1050.00
  c)   CV(High-End Bike) = 0.447; CV(Moderately-
       Priced Bike) = 0.396; RRR(High-End Bike) =
       2.238; RRR(Moderately-Priced Bike) = 2.524
  d)   Answers may vary. The high-end bike has a much
       higher EV, but also a higher SD. Its RRR is lower
       but is very close to the moderately-priced bike.
       The decision will depend on the store owner's ap-
       petite for risk.

Tables and Selected Formulas

Table D

Critical Values d_L and d_U of the Durbin–Watson Statistic (Critical Values are One-Sided) [a]

α = 0.05

n	k = 1 d_L	k = 1 d_U	k = 2 d_L	k = 2 d_U	k = 3 d_L	k = 3 d_U	k = 4 d_L	k = 4 d_U	k = 5 d_L	k = 5 d_U
15	1.08	1.36	.95	1.54	.82	1.75	.69	1.97	.56	2.21
16	1.10	1.37	.98	1.54	.86	1.73	.74	1.93	.62	2.15
17	1.13	1.38	1.02	1.54	.90	1.71	.78	1.90	.67	2.10
18	1.16	1.39	1.05	1.53	.93	1.69	.82	1.87	.71	2.06
19	1.18	1.40	1.08	1.53	.97	1.68	.86	1.85	.75	2.02
20	1.20	1.41	1.10	1.54	1.00	1.68	.90	1.83	.79	1.99
21	1.22	1.42	1.13	1.54	1.03	1.67	.93	1.81	.83	1.96
22	1.24	1.43	1.15	1.54	1.05	1.66	.96	1.80	.86	1.94
23	1.26	1.44	1.17	1.54	1.08	1.66	.99	1.79	.90	1.92
24	1.27	1.45	1.19	1.55	1.10	1.66	1.01	1.78	.93	1.90
25	1.29	1.45	1.21	1.55	1.12	1.66	1.04	1.77	.95	1.89
26	1.30	1.46	1.22	1.55	1.14	1.65	1.06	1.76	.98	1.88
27	1.32	1.47	1.24	1.56	1.16	1.65	1.08	1.76	1.01	1.86
28	1.33	1.48	1.26	1.56	1.18	1.65	1.10	1.75	1.03	1.85
29	1.34	1.48	1.27	1.56	1.20	1.65	1.12	1.74	1.05	1.84
30	1.35	1.49	1.28	1.57	1.21	1.65	1.14	1.74	1.07	1.83
31	1.36	1.50	1.30	1.57	1.23	1.65	1.16	1.74	1.09	1.83
32	1.37	1.50	1.31	1.57	1.24	1.65	1.18	1.73	1.11	1.82
33	1.38	1.51	1.32	1.58	1.26	1.65	1.19	1.73	1.13	1.81
34	1.39	1.51	1.33	1.58	1.27	1.65	1.21	1.73	1.15	1.81
35	1.40	1.52	1.34	1.58	1.28	1.65	1.22	1.73	1.16	1.80
36	1.41	1.52	1.35	1.59	1.29	1.65	1.24	1.73	1.18	1.80
37	1.42	1.53	1.36	1.59	1.31	1.66	1.25	1.72	1.19	1.80
38	1.43	1.54	1.37	1.59	1.32	1.66	1.26	1.72	1.21	1.79
39	1.43	1.54	1.38	1.60	1.33	1.66	1.27	1.72	1.22	1.79
40	1.44	1.54	1.39	1.60	1.34	1.66	1.29	1.72	1.23	1.79
45	1.48	1.57	1.43	1.62	1.38	1.67	1.34	1.72	1.29	1.78
50	1.50	1.59	1.46	1.63	1.42	1.67	1.38	1.72	1.34	1.77
55	1.53	1.60	1.49	1.64	1.45	1.68	1.41	1.72	1.38	1.77
60	1.55	1.62	1.51	1.65	1.48	1.69	1.44	1.73	1.41	1.77
65	1.57	1.63	1.54	1.66	1.50	1.70	1.47	1.73	1.44	1.77
70	1.58	1.64	1.55	1.67	1.52	1.70	1.49	1.74	1.46	1.77
75	1.60	1.65	1.57	1.68	1.54	1.71	1.51	1.74	1.49	1.77
80	1.61	1.66	1.59	1.69	1.56	1.72	1.53	1.74	1.51	1.77
85	1.62	1.67	1.60	1.70	1.57	1.72	1.55	1.75	1.52	1.77
90	1.63	1.68	1.61	1.70	1.59	1.73	1.57	1.75	1.54	1.78
95	1.64	1.69	1.62	1.71	1.60	1.73	1.58	1.75	1.56	1.78
100	1.65	1.69	1.63	1.72	1.61	1.74	1.59	1.76	1.57	1.78

α = 0.01

n	k = 1 d_L	k = 1 d_U	k = 2 d_L	k = 2 d_U	k = 3 d_L	k = 3 d_U	k = 4 d_L	k = 4 d_U	k = 5 d_L	k = 5 d_U
15	.81	1.07	.70	1.25	.59	1.46	.49	1.70	.39	1.96
16	.84	1.09	.74	1.25	.63	1.44	.53	1.66	.44	1.90
17	.87	1.10	.77	1.25	.67	1.43	.57	1.63	.48	1.85
18	.90	1.12	.80	1.26	.71	1.42	.61	1.60	.52	1.80
19	.93	1.13	.83	1.26	.74	1.41	.65	1.58	.56	1.77
20	.95	1.15	.86	1.27	.77	1.41	.68	1.57	.60	1.74
21	.97	1.16	.89	1.27	.80	1.41	.72	1.55	.63	1.71
22	1.00	1.17	.91	1.28	.83	1.40	.75	1.54	.66	1.69
23	1.02	1.19	.94	1.29	.86	1.40	.77	1.53	.70	1.67
24	1.04	1.20	.96	1.30	.88	1.41	.80	1.53	.72	1.66
25	1.05	1.21	.98	1.30	.90	1.41	.83	1.52	.75	1.65
26	1.07	1.22	1.00	1.31	.93	1.41	.85	1.52	.78	1.64
27	1.09	1.23	1.02	1.32	.95	1.41	.88	1.51	.81	1.63
28	1.10	1.24	1.04	1.32	.97	1.41	.90	1.51	.83	1.62
29	1.12	1.25	1.05	1.33	.99	1.42	.92	1.51	.85	1.61
30	1.13	1.26	1.07	1.34	1.01	1.42	.94	1.51	.88	1.61
31	1.15	1.27	1.08	1.34	1.02	1.42	.96	1.51	.90	1.60
32	1.16	1.28	1.10	1.35	1.04	1.43	.98	1.51	.92	1.60
33	1.17	1.29	1.11	1.36	1.05	1.43	1.00	1.51	.94	1.59
34	1.18	1.30	1.13	1.36	1.07	1.43	1.01	1.51	.95	1.59
35	1.19	1.31	1.14	1.37	1.08	1.44	1.03	1.51	.97	1.59
36	1.21	1.32	1.15	1.38	1.10	1.44	1.04	1.51	.99	1.59
37	1.22	1.32	1.16	1.38	1.11	1.45	1.06	1.51	1.00	1.59
38	1.23	1.33	1.18	1.39	1.12	1.45	1.07	1.52	1.02	1.58
39	1.24	1.34	1.19	1.39	1.14	1.45	1.09	1.52	1.03	1.58
40	1.25	1.34	1.20	1.40	1.15	1.46	1.10	1.52	1.05	1.58
45	1.29	1.38	1.24	1.42	1.20	1.48	1.16	1.53	1.11	1.58
50	1.32	1.40	1.28	1.45	1.24	1.49	1.20	1.54	1.16	1.59
55	1.36	1.43	1.32	1.47	1.28	1.51	1.25	1.55	1.21	1.59
60	1.38	1.45	1.35	1.48	1.32	1.52	1.28	1.56	1.25	1.60
65	1.41	1.47	1.38	1.50	1.35	1.53	1.31	1.57	1.28	1.61
70	1.43	1.49	1.40	1.52	1.37	1.55	1.34	1.58	1.31	1.61
75	1.45	1.50	1.42	1.53	1.39	1.56	1.37	1.59	1.34	1.62
80	1.47	1.52	1.44	1.54	1.42	1.57	1.39	1.60	1.36	1.62
85	1.48	1.53	1.46	1.55	1.43	1.58	1.41	1.60	1.39	1.63
90	1.50	1.54	1.47	1.56	1.45	1.59	1.43	1.61	1.41	1.64
95	1.51	1.55	1.49	1.57	1.47	1.60	1.45	1.62	1.42	1.64
100	1.52	1.56	1.50	1.58	1.48	1.60	1.46	1.63	1.44	1.65

[a] n = number of observations; k = number of independent variables.

Source: This table is reproduced from Biometrika, 41 (1951): 173 and 175, with the permission of the Biometrika Trustees.

Table F

Numerator df

$\alpha = .01$	1	2	3	4	5	6	7	8	9	10	11	12	13	14	15	16	17	18	19	20	21	22
1	4052.2	4999.3	5403.5	5624.3	5764.0	5859.0	5928.3	5981.0	6022.4	6055.9	6083.4	6106.7	6125.8	6143.0	6157.0	6170.0	6181.2	6191.4	6200.7	6208.7	6216.1	6223.1
2	98.50	99.00	99.16	99.25	99.30	99.33	99.36	99.38	99.39	99.40	99.41	99.42	99.42	99.43	99.43	99.44	99.44	99.44	99.45	99.45	99.45	99.46
3	34.12	30.82	29.46	28.71	28.24	27.91	27.67	27.49	27.34	27.23	27.13	27.05	26.98	26.92	26.87	26.83	26.79	26.75	26.72	26.69	26.66	26.64
4	21.20	18.00	16.69	15.98	15.52	15.21	14.98	14.80	14.66	14.55	14.45	14.37	14.31	14.25	14.20	14.15	14.11	14.08	14.05	14.02	13.99	13.97
5	16.26	13.27	12.06	11.39	10.97	10.67	10.46	10.29	10.16	10.05	9.96	9.89	9.82	9.77	9.72	9.68	9.64	9.61	9.58	9.55	9.53	9.51
6	13.75	10.92	9.78	9.15	8.75	8.47	8.26	8.10	7.98	7.87	7.79	7.72	7.66	7.60	7.56	7.52	7.48	7.45	7.42	7.40	7.37	7.35
7	12.25	9.55	8.45	7.85	7.46	7.19	6.99	6.84	6.72	6.62	6.54	6.47	6.41	6.36	6.31	6.28	6.24	6.21	6.18	6.16	6.13	6.11
8	11.26	8.65	7.59	7.01	6.63	6.37	6.18	6.03	5.91	5.81	5.73	5.67	5.61	5.56	5.52	5.48	5.44	5.41	5.38	5.36	5.34	5.32
9	10.56	8.02	6.99	6.42	6.06	5.80	5.61	5.47	5.35	5.26	5.18	5.11	5.05	5.01	4.96	4.92	4.89	4.86	4.83	4.81	4.79	4.77
10	10.04	7.56	6.55	5.99	5.64	5.39	5.20	5.06	4.94	4.85	4.77	4.71	4.65	4.60	4.56	4.52	4.49	4.46	4.43	4.41	4.38	4.36
11	9.65	7.21	6.22	5.67	5.32	5.07	4.89	4.74	4.63	4.54	4.46	4.40	4.34	4.29	4.25	4.21	4.18	4.15	4.12	4.10	4.08	4.06
12	9.33	6.93	5.95	5.41	5.06	4.82	4.64	4.50	4.39	4.30	4.22	4.16	4.10	4.05	4.01	3.97	3.94	3.91	3.88	3.86	3.84	3.82
13	9.07	6.70	5.74	5.21	4.86	4.62	4.44	4.30	4.19	4.10	4.02	3.96	3.91	3.86	3.82	3.78	3.75	3.72	3.69	3.66	3.64	3.62
14	8.86	6.51	5.56	5.04	4.69	4.46	4.28	4.14	4.03	3.94	3.86	3.80	3.75	3.70	3.66	3.62	3.59	3.56	3.53	3.51	3.48	3.46
15	8.68	6.36	5.42	4.89	4.56	4.32	4.14	4.00	3.89	3.80	3.73	3.67	3.61	3.56	3.52	3.49	3.45	3.42	3.40	3.37	3.35	3.33
16	8.53	6.23	5.29	4.77	4.44	4.20	4.03	3.89	3.78	3.69	3.62	3.55	3.50	3.45	3.41	3.37	3.34	3.31	3.28	3.26	3.24	3.22
17	8.40	6.11	5.19	4.67	4.34	4.10	3.93	3.79	3.68	3.59	3.52	3.46	3.40	3.35	3.31	3.27	3.24	3.21	3.19	3.16	3.14	3.12
18	8.29	6.01	5.09	4.58	4.25	4.01	3.84	3.71	3.60	3.51	3.43	3.37	3.32	3.27	3.23	3.19	3.16	3.13	3.10	3.08	3.05	3.03
19	8.18	5.93	5.01	4.50	4.17	3.94	3.77	3.63	3.52	3.43	3.36	3.30	3.24	3.19	3.15	3.12	3.08	3.05	3.03	3.00	2.98	2.96
20	8.10	5.85	4.94	4.43	4.10	3.87	3.70	3.56	3.46	3.37	3.29	3.23	3.18	3.13	3.09	3.05	3.02	2.99	2.96	2.94	2.92	2.90
21	8.02	5.78	4.87	4.37	4.04	3.81	3.64	3.51	3.40	3.31	3.24	3.17	3.12	3.07	3.03	2.99	2.96	2.93	2.90	2.88	2.86	2.84
22	7.95	5.72	4.82	4.31	3.99	3.76	3.59	3.45	3.35	3.26	3.18	3.12	3.07	3.02	2.98	2.94	2.91	2.88	2.85	2.83	2.81	2.78
23	7.88	5.66	4.76	4.26	3.94	3.71	3.54	3.41	3.30	3.21	3.14	3.07	3.02	2.97	2.93	2.89	2.86	2.83	2.80	2.78	2.76	2.74
24	7.82	5.61	4.72	4.22	3.90	3.67	3.50	3.36	3.26	3.17	3.09	3.03	2.98	2.93	2.89	2.85	2.82	2.79	2.76	2.74	2.72	2.70
25	7.77	5.57	4.68	4.18	3.85	3.63	3.46	3.32	3.22	3.13	3.06	2.99	2.94	2.89	2.85	2.81	2.78	2.75	2.72	2.70	2.68	2.66
26	7.72	5.53	4.64	4.14	3.82	3.59	3.42	3.29	3.18	3.09	3.02	2.96	2.90	2.86	2.81	2.78	2.75	2.72	2.69	2.66	2.64	2.62
27	7.68	5.49	4.60	4.11	3.78	3.56	3.39	3.26	3.15	3.06	2.99	2.93	2.87	2.82	2.78	2.75	2.71	2.68	2.66	2.63	2.61	2.59
28	7.64	5.45	4.57	4.07	3.75	3.53	3.36	3.23	3.12	3.03	2.96	2.90	2.84	2.79	2.75	2.72	2.68	2.65	2.63	2.60	2.58	2.56
29	7.60	5.42	4.54	4.04	3.73	3.50	3.33	3.20	3.09	3.00	2.93	2.87	2.81	2.77	2.73	2.69	2.66	2.63	2.60	2.57	2.55	2.53
30	7.56	5.39	4.51	4.02	3.70	3.47	3.30	3.17	3.07	2.98	2.91	2.84	2.79	2.74	2.70	2.66	2.63	2.60	2.57	2.55	2.53	2.51
32	7.50	5.34	4.46	3.97	3.65	3.43	3.26	3.13	3.02	2.93	2.86	2.80	2.74	2.70	2.65	2.62	2.58	2.55	2.53	2.50	2.48	2.46
35	7.42	5.27	4.40	3.91	3.59	3.37	3.20	3.07	2.96	2.88	2.80	2.74	2.69	2.64	2.60	2.56	2.53	2.50	2.47	2.44	2.42	2.40
40	7.31	5.18	4.31	3.83	3.51	3.29	3.12	2.99	2.89	2.80	2.73	2.66	2.61	2.56	2.52	2.48	2.45	2.42	2.39	2.37	2.35	2.33
45	7.23	5.11	4.25	3.77	3.45	3.23	3.07	2.94	2.83	2.74	2.67	2.61	2.55	2.51	2.46	2.43	2.39	2.36	2.34	2.31	2.29	2.27
50	7.17	5.06	4.20	3.72	3.41	3.19	3.02	2.89	2.78	2.70	2.63	2.56	2.51	2.46	2.42	2.38	2.35	2.32	2.29	2.27	2.24	2.22
60	7.08	4.98	4.13	3.65	3.34	3.12	2.95	2.82	2.72	2.63	2.56	2.50	2.44	2.39	2.35	2.31	2.28	2.25	2.22	2.20	2.17	2.15
75	6.99	4.90	4.05	3.58	3.27	3.05	2.89	2.76	2.65	2.57	2.49	2.43	2.38	2.33	2.29	2.25	2.22	2.18	2.16	2.13	2.11	2.09
100	6.90	4.82	3.98	3.51	3.21	2.99	2.82	2.69	2.59	2.50	2.43	2.37	2.31	2.27	2.22	2.19	2.15	2.12	2.09	2.07	2.04	2.02
120	6.85	4.79	3.95	3.48	3.17	2.96	2.79	2.66	2.56	2.47	2.40	2.34	2.28	2.23	2.19	2.15	2.12	2.09	2.06	2.03	2.01	1.99
140	6.82	4.76	3.92	3.46	3.15	2.93	2.77	2.64	2.54	2.45	2.38	2.31	2.26	2.21	2.17	2.13	2.10	2.07	2.04	2.01	1.99	1.97
180	6.78	4.73	3.89	3.43	3.12	2.90	2.74	2.61	2.51	2.42	2.35	2.28	2.23	2.18	2.14	2.10	2.07	2.04	2.01	1.98	1.96	1.94
250	6.74	4.69	3.86	3.40	3.09	2.87	2.71	2.58	2.48	2.39	2.32	2.26	2.20	2.15	2.11	2.07	2.04	2.01	1.98	1.95	1.93	1.91
400	6.70	4.66	3.83	3.37	3.06	2.85	2.68	2.56	2.45	2.37	2.29	2.23	2.17	2.13	2.08	2.05	2.01	1.98	1.95	1.92	1.90	1.88
1000	6.66	4.63	3.80	3.34	3.04	2.82	2.66	2.53	2.43	2.34	2.27	2.20	2.15	2.10	2.06	2.02	1.98	1.95	1.92	1.90	1.87	1.85

Denominator df

Table F (cont.)

													Numerator df									
$\alpha = .01$	23	24	25	26	27	28	29	30	32	35	40	45	50	60	75	100	120	140	180	250	400	1000
1	6228.7	6234.3	6239.9	6244.5	6249.2	6252.9	6257.1	6260.4	6266.9	6275.3	6286.4	6295.7	6302.3	6313.0	6323.7	6333.9	6339.5	6343.2	6347.9	6353.5	6358.1	6362.8
2	99.46	99.46	99.46	99.46	99.46	99.46	99.46	99.47	99.47	99.47	99.48	99.48	99.48	99.48	99.48	99.49	99.49	99.49	99.49	99.50	99.50	99.50
3	26.62	26.60	26.58	26.56	26.55	26.53	26.52	26.50	26.48	26.45	26.41	26.38	26.35	26.32	26.28	26.24	26.22	26.21	26.19	26.17	26.15	26.14
4	13.95	13.93	13.91	13.89	13.88	13.86	13.85	13.84	13.81	13.79	13.75	13.71	13.69	13.65	13.61	13.58	13.56	13.54	13.53	13.51	13.49	13.47
5	9.49	9.47	9.45	9.43	9.42	9.40	9.39	9.38	9.36	9.33	9.29	9.26	9.24	9.20	9.17	9.13	9.11	9.10	9.08	9.06	9.05	9.03
6	7.33	7.31	7.30	7.28	7.27	7.25	7.24	7.23	7.21	7.18	7.14	7.11	7.09	7.06	7.02	6.99	6.97	6.96	6.94	6.92	6.91	6.89
7	6.09	6.07	6.06	6.04	6.03	6.02	6.00	5.99	5.97	5.94	5.91	5.88	5.86	5.82	5.79	5.75	5.74	5.72	5.71	5.69	5.68	5.66
8	5.30	5.28	5.26	5.25	5.23	5.22	5.21	5.20	5.18	5.15	5.12	5.09	5.07	5.03	5.00	4.96	4.95	4.93	4.92	4.90	4.89	4.87
9	4.75	4.73	4.71	4.70	4.68	4.67	4.66	4.65	4.63	4.60	4.57	4.54	4.52	4.48	4.45	4.41	4.40	4.39	4.37	4.35	4.34	4.32
10	4.34	4.33	4.31	4.30	4.28	4.27	4.26	4.25	4.23	4.20	4.17	4.14	4.12	4.08	4.05	4.01	4.00	3.98	3.97	3.95	3.94	3.92
11	4.04	4.02	4.01	3.99	3.98	3.96	3.95	3.94	3.92	3.89	3.86	3.83	3.81	3.78	3.74	3.71	3.69	3.68	3.66	3.64	3.63	3.61
12	3.80	3.78	3.76	3.75	3.74	3.72	3.71	3.70	3.68	3.65	3.62	3.59	3.57	3.54	3.50	3.47	3.45	3.44	3.42	3.40	3.39	3.37
13	3.60	3.59	3.57	3.56	3.54	3.53	3.52	3.51	3.49	3.46	3.43	3.40	3.38	3.34	3.31	3.27	3.25	3.24	3.23	3.21	3.19	3.18
14	3.44	3.43	3.41	3.40	3.38	3.37	3.36	3.35	3.33	3.30	3.27	3.24	3.22	3.18	3.15	3.11	3.09	3.08	3.06	3.05	3.03	3.02
15	3.31	3.29	3.28	3.26	3.25	3.24	3.23	3.21	3.19	3.17	3.13	3.10	3.08	3.05	3.01	2.98	2.96	2.95	2.93	2.91	2.90	2.88
16	3.20	3.18	3.16	3.15	3.14	3.12	3.11	3.10	3.08	3.05	3.02	2.99	2.97	2.93	2.90	2.86	2.84	2.83	2.81	2.80	2.78	2.76
17	3.10	3.08	3.07	3.05	3.04	3.03	3.01	3.00	2.98	2.96	2.92	2.89	2.87	2.83	2.80	2.76	2.75	2.73	2.72	2.70	2.68	2.66
18	3.02	3.00	2.98	2.97	2.95	2.94	2.93	2.92	2.90	2.87	2.84	2.81	2.78	2.75	2.71	2.68	2.66	2.65	2.63	2.61	2.59	2.58
19	2.94	2.92	2.91	2.89	2.88	2.87	2.86	2.84	2.82	2.80	2.76	2.73	2.71	2.67	2.64	2.60	2.58	2.57	2.55	2.54	2.52	2.50
20	2.88	2.86	2.84	2.83	2.81	2.80	2.79	2.78	2.76	2.73	2.69	2.67	2.64	2.61	2.57	2.54	2.52	2.50	2.49	2.47	2.45	2.43
21	2.82	2.80	2.79	2.77	2.76	2.74	2.73	2.72	2.70	2.67	2.64	2.61	2.58	2.55	2.51	2.48	2.46	2.44	2.43	2.41	2.39	2.37
22	2.77	2.75	2.73	2.72	2.70	2.69	2.68	2.67	2.65	2.62	2.58	2.55	2.53	2.50	2.46	2.42	2.40	2.39	2.37	2.35	2.34	2.32
23	2.72	2.70	2.69	2.67	2.66	2.64	2.63	2.62	2.60	2.57	2.54	2.51	2.48	2.45	2.41	2.37	2.35	2.34	2.32	2.30	2.29	2.27
24	2.68	2.66	2.64	2.63	2.61	2.60	2.59	2.58	2.56	2.53	2.49	2.46	2.44	2.40	2.37	2.33	2.31	2.30	2.28	2.26	2.24	2.22
25	2.64	2.62	2.60	2.59	2.58	2.56	2.55	2.54	2.52	2.49	2.45	2.42	2.40	2.36	2.33	2.29	2.27	2.26	2.24	2.22	2.20	2.18
26	2.60	2.58	2.57	2.55	2.54	2.53	2.51	2.50	2.48	2.45	2.42	2.39	2.36	2.33	2.29	2.25	2.23	2.22	2.20	2.18	2.16	2.14
27	2.57	2.55	2.54	2.52	2.51	2.49	2.48	2.47	2.45	2.42	2.38	2.35	2.33	2.29	2.26	2.22	2.20	2.18	2.17	2.15	2.13	2.11
28	2.54	2.52	2.51	2.49	2.48	2.46	2.45	2.44	2.42	2.39	2.35	2.32	2.30	2.26	2.23	2.19	2.17	2.15	2.13	2.11	2.10	2.08
29	2.51	2.49	2.48	2.46	2.45	2.44	2.42	2.41	2.39	2.36	2.33	2.30	2.27	2.23	2.20	2.16	2.14	2.12	2.10	2.08	2.07	2.05
30	2.49	2.47	2.45	2.44	2.42	2.41	2.40	2.39	2.36	2.34	2.30	2.27	2.25	2.21	2.17	2.13	2.11	2.10	2.08	2.06	2.04	2.02
32	2.44	2.42	2.41	2.39	2.38	2.36	2.35	2.34	2.32	2.29	2.25	2.22	2.20	2.16	2.12	2.08	2.06	2.05	2.03	2.01	1.99	1.97
35	2.38	2.36	2.35	2.33	2.32	2.30	2.29	2.28	2.26	2.23	2.19	2.16	2.14	2.10	2.06	2.02	2.00	1.98	1.96	1.94	1.92	1.90
40	2.31	2.29	2.27	2.26	2.24	2.23	2.22	2.20	2.18	2.15	2.11	2.08	2.06	2.02	1.98	1.94	1.92	1.90	1.88	1.86	1.84	1.82
45	2.25	2.23	2.21	2.20	2.18	2.17	2.16	2.14	2.12	2.09	2.05	2.02	2.00	1.96	1.92	1.88	1.85	1.84	1.82	1.79	1.77	1.75
50	2.20	2.18	2.17	2.15	2.14	2.12	2.11	2.10	2.08	2.05	2.01	1.97	1.95	1.91	1.87	1.82	1.80	1.79	1.76	1.74	1.72	1.70
60	2.13	2.12	2.10	2.08	2.07	2.05	2.04	2.03	2.01	1.98	1.94	1.90	1.88	1.84	1.79	1.75	1.73	1.71	1.69	1.66	1.64	1.62
75	2.07	2.05	2.03	2.02	2.00	1.99	1.97	1.96	1.94	1.91	1.87	1.83	1.81	1.76	1.72	1.67	1.65	1.63	1.61	1.58	1.56	1.53
100	2.00	1.98	1.97	1.95	1.93	1.92	1.91	1.89	1.87	1.84	1.80	1.76	1.74	1.69	1.65	1.60	1.57	1.55	1.53	1.50	1.47	1.45
120	1.97	1.95	1.93	1.92	1.90	1.89	1.87	1.86	1.84	1.81	1.76	1.73	1.70	1.66	1.61	1.56	1.53	1.51	1.49	1.46	1.43	1.40
140	1.95	1.93	1.91	1.89	1.88	1.86	1.85	1.84	1.81	1.78	1.74	1.70	1.67	1.63	1.58	1.53	1.50	1.48	1.46	1.43	1.40	1.37
180	1.92	1.90	1.88	1.86	1.85	1.83	1.82	1.81	1.78	1.75	1.71	1.67	1.64	1.60	1.55	1.49	1.47	1.45	1.42	1.39	1.35	1.32
250	1.89	1.87	1.85	1.83	1.82	1.80	1.79	1.77	1.75	1.72	1.67	1.64	1.61	1.56	1.51	1.46	1.43	1.41	1.38	1.34	1.31	1.27
400	1.86	1.84	1.82	1.80	1.79	1.77	1.76	1.75	1.72	1.69	1.64	1.61	1.58	1.53	1.48	1.42	1.39	1.37	1.33	1.30	1.26	1.22
1000	1.83	1.81	1.79	1.77	1.76	1.74	1.73	1.72	1.69	1.66	1.61	1.58	1.54	1.50	1.44	1.38	1.35	1.33	1.29	1.25	1.21	1.16

Denominator df

Table F (cont.)

Numerator df

α = .05	1	2	3	4	5	6	7	8	9	10	11	12	13	14	15	16	17	18	19	20	21	22
1	161.4	199.5	215.7	224.6	230.2	234.0	236.8	238.9	240.5	241.9	243.0	243.9	244.7	245.4	245.9	246.5	246.9	247.3	247.7	248.0	248.3	248.6
2	18.51	19.00	19.16	19.25	19.30	19.33	19.35	19.37	19.38	19.40	19.40	19.41	19.42	19.42	19.43	19.43	19.44	19.44	19.44	19.45	19.45	19.45
3	10.13	9.55	9.28	9.12	9.01	8.94	8.89	8.85	8.81	8.79	8.76	8.74	8.73	8.71	8.70	8.69	8.68	8.67	8.67	8.66	8.65	8.65
4	7.71	6.94	6.59	6.39	6.26	6.16	6.09	6.04	6.00	5.96	5.94	5.91	5.89	5.87	5.86	5.84	5.83	5.82	5.81	5.80	5.79	5.79
5	6.61	5.79	5.41	5.19	5.05	4.95	4.88	4.82	4.77	4.74	4.70	4.68	4.66	4.64	4.62	4.60	4.59	4.58	4.57	4.56	4.55	4.54
6	5.99	5.14	4.76	4.53	4.39	4.28	4.21	4.15	4.10	4.06	4.03	4.00	3.98	3.96	3.94	3.92	3.91	3.90	3.88	3.87	3.86	3.86
7	5.59	4.74	4.35	4.12	3.97	3.87	3.79	3.73	3.68	3.64	3.60	3.57	3.55	3.53	3.51	3.49	3.48	3.47	3.46	3.44	3.43	3.43
8	5.32	4.46	4.07	3.84	3.69	3.58	3.50	3.44	3.39	3.35	3.31	3.28	3.26	3.24	3.22	3.20	3.19	3.17	3.16	3.15	3.14	3.13
9	5.12	4.26	3.86	3.63	3.48	3.37	3.29	3.23	3.18	3.14	3.10	3.07	3.05	3.03	3.01	2.99	2.97	2.96	2.95	2.94	2.93	2.92
10	4.96	4.10	3.71	3.48	3.33	3.22	3.14	3.07	3.02	2.98	2.94	2.91	2.89	2.86	2.85	2.83	2.81	2.80	2.79	2.77	2.76	2.75
11	4.84	3.98	3.59	3.36	3.20	3.09	3.01	2.95	2.90	2.85	2.82	2.79	2.76	2.74	2.72	2.70	2.69	2.67	2.66	2.65	2.64	2.63
12	4.75	3.89	3.49	3.26	3.11	3.00	2.91	2.85	2.80	2.75	2.72	2.69	2.66	2.64	2.62	2.60	2.58	2.57	2.56	2.54	2.53	2.52
13	4.67	3.81	3.41	3.18	3.03	2.92	2.83	2.77	2.71	2.67	2.63	2.60	2.58	2.55	2.53	2.51	2.50	2.48	2.47	2.46	2.45	2.44
14	4.60	3.74	3.34	3.11	2.96	2.85	2.76	2.70	2.65	2.60	2.57	2.53	2.51	2.48	2.46	2.44	2.43	2.41	2.40	2.39	2.38	2.37
15	4.54	3.68	3.29	3.06	2.90	2.79	2.71	2.64	2.59	2.54	2.51	2.48	2.45	2.42	2.40	2.38	2.37	2.35	2.34	2.33	2.32	2.31
16	4.49	3.63	3.24	3.01	2.85	2.74	2.66	2.59	2.54	2.49	2.46	2.42	2.40	2.37	2.35	2.33	2.32	2.30	2.29	2.28	2.26	2.25
17	4.45	3.59	3.20	2.96	2.81	2.70	2.61	2.55	2.49	2.45	2.41	2.38	2.35	2.33	2.31	2.29	2.27	2.26	2.24	2.23	2.22	2.21
18	4.41	3.55	3.16	2.93	2.77	2.66	2.58	2.51	2.46	2.41	2.37	2.34	2.31	2.29	2.27	2.25	2.23	2.22	2.20	2.19	2.18	2.17
19	4.38	3.52	3.13	2.90	2.74	2.63	2.54	2.48	2.42	2.38	2.34	2.31	2.28	2.26	2.23	2.21	2.20	2.18	2.17	2.16	2.14	2.13
20	4.35	3.49	3.10	2.87	2.71	2.60	2.51	2.45	2.39	2.35	2.31	2.28	2.25	2.22	2.20	2.18	2.17	2.15	2.14	2.12	2.11	2.10
21	4.32	3.47	3.07	2.84	2.68	2.57	2.49	2.42	2.37	2.32	2.28	2.25	2.22	2.20	2.18	2.16	2.14	2.12	2.11	2.10	2.08	2.07
22	4.30	3.44	3.05	2.82	2.66	2.55	2.46	2.40	2.34	2.30	2.26	2.23	2.20	2.17	2.15	2.13	2.11	2.10	2.08	2.07	2.06	2.05
23	4.28	3.42	3.03	2.80	2.64	2.53	2.44	2.37	2.32	2.27	2.24	2.20	2.18	2.15	2.13	2.11	2.09	2.08	2.06	2.05	2.04	2.02
24	4.26	3.40	3.01	2.78	2.62	2.51	2.42	2.36	2.30	2.25	2.22	2.18	2.15	2.13	2.11	2.09	2.07	2.05	2.04	2.03	2.01	2.00
25	4.24	3.39	2.99	2.76	2.60	2.49	2.40	2.34	2.28	2.24	2.20	2.16	2.14	2.11	2.09	2.07	2.05	2.04	2.02	2.01	2.00	1.98
26	4.23	3.37	2.98	2.74	2.59	2.47	2.39	2.32	2.27	2.22	2.18	2.15	2.12	2.09	2.07	2.05	2.03	2.02	2.00	1.99	1.98	1.97
27	4.21	3.35	2.96	2.73	2.57	2.46	2.37	2.31	2.25	2.20	2.17	2.13	2.10	2.08	2.06	2.04	2.02	2.00	1.99	1.97	1.96	1.95
28	4.20	3.34	2.95	2.71	2.56	2.45	2.36	2.29	2.24	2.19	2.15	2.12	2.09	2.06	2.04	2.02	2.00	1.99	1.97	1.96	1.95	1.93
29	4.18	3.33	2.93	2.70	2.55	2.43	2.35	2.28	2.22	2.18	2.14	2.10	2.08	2.05	2.03	2.01	1.99	1.97	1.96	1.94	1.93	1.92
30	4.17	3.32	2.92	2.69	2.53	2.42	2.33	2.27	2.21	2.16	2.13	2.09	2.06	2.04	2.01	1.99	1.98	1.96	1.95	1.93	1.92	1.91
32	4.15	3.29	2.90	2.67	2.51	2.40	2.31	2.24	2.19	2.14	2.10	2.07	2.04	2.01	1.99	1.97	1.95	1.94	1.92	1.91	1.90	1.88
35	4.12	3.27	2.87	2.64	2.49	2.37	2.29	2.22	2.16	2.11	2.07	2.04	2.01	1.99	1.96	1.94	1.92	1.91	1.89	1.88	1.87	1.85
40	4.08	3.23	2.84	2.61	2.45	2.34	2.25	2.18	2.12	2.08	2.04	2.00	1.97	1.95	1.92	1.90	1.89	1.87	1.85	1.84	1.83	1.81
45	4.06	3.20	2.81	2.58	2.42	2.31	2.22	2.15	2.10	2.05	2.01	1.97	1.94	1.92	1.89	1.87	1.86	1.84	1.82	1.81	1.80	1.78
50	4.03	3.18	2.79	2.56	2.40	2.29	2.20	2.13	2.07	2.03	1.99	1.95	1.92	1.89	1.87	1.85	1.83	1.81	1.80	1.78	1.77	1.76
60	4.00	3.15	2.76	2.53	2.37	2.25	2.17	2.10	2.04	1.99	1.95	1.92	1.89	1.86	1.84	1.82	1.80	1.78	1.76	1.75	1.73	1.72
75	3.97	3.12	2.73	2.49	2.34	2.22	2.13	2.06	2.01	1.96	1.92	1.88	1.85	1.83	1.80	1.78	1.76	1.74	1.73	1.71	1.70	1.69
100	3.94	3.09	2.70	2.46	2.31	2.19	2.10	2.03	1.97	1.93	1.89	1.85	1.82	1.79	1.77	1.75	1.73	1.71	1.69	1.68	1.66	1.65
120	3.92	3.07	2.68	2.45	2.29	2.18	2.09	2.02	1.96	1.91	1.87	1.83	1.80	1.78	1.75	1.73	1.71	1.69	1.67	1.66	1.64	1.63
140	3.91	3.06	2.67	2.44	2.28	2.16	2.08	2.01	1.95	1.90	1.86	1.82	1.79	1.76	1.74	1.72	1.70	1.68	1.66	1.65	1.63	1.62
180	3.89	3.05	2.65	2.42	2.26	2.15	2.06	1.99	1.93	1.88	1.84	1.81	1.77	1.75	1.72	1.70	1.68	1.66	1.64	1.63	1.61	1.60
250	3.88	3.03	2.64	2.41	2.25	2.13	2.05	1.98	1.92	1.87	1.83	1.79	1.76	1.73	1.71	1.68	1.66	1.65	1.63	1.61	1.60	1.58
400	3.86	3.02	2.63	2.39	2.24	2.12	2.03	1.96	1.90	1.85	1.81	1.78	1.74	1.72	1.69	1.67	1.65	1.63	1.61	1.60	1.58	1.57
1000	3.85	3.00	2.61	2.38	2.22	2.11	2.02	1.95	1.89	1.84	1.80	1.76	1.73	1.70	1.68	1.65	1.63	1.61	1.60	1.58	1.57	1.55

Denominator df

Table F (cont.)

Numerator df

$\alpha = .05$

Denominator df	23	24	25	26	27	28	29	30	32	35	40	45	50	60	75	100	120	140	180	250	400	1000
1	248.8	249.1	249.3	249.5	249.6	249.8	250.0	250.1	250.4	250.7	251.1	251.5	251.8	252.2	252.6	253.0	253.3	253.4	253.6	253.8	254.0	254.2
2	19.45	19.45	19.46	19.46	19.46	19.46	19.46	19.46	19.46	19.47	19.47	19.47	19.48	19.48	19.48	19.49	19.49	19.49	19.49	19.49	19.49	19.49
3	8.64	8.64	8.63	8.63	8.63	8.62	8.62	8.62	8.61	8.60	8.59	8.59	8.58	8.57	8.56	8.55	8.55	8.55	8.54	8.54	8.53	8.53
4	5.78	5.77	5.77	5.76	5.76	5.75	5.75	5.75	5.74	5.73	5.72	5.71	5.70	5.69	5.68	5.66	5.66	5.65	5.65	5.64	5.64	5.63
5	4.53	4.53	4.52	4.52	4.51	4.50	4.50	4.50	4.49	4.48	4.46	4.45	4.44	4.43	4.42	4.41	4.40	4.39	4.39	4.38	4.38	4.37
6	3.85	3.84	3.83	3.83	3.82	3.82	3.81	3.81	3.80	3.79	3.77	3.76	3.75	3.74	3.73	3.71	3.70	3.70	3.69	3.69	3.68	3.67
7	3.42	3.41	3.40	3.40	3.39	3.39	3.38	3.38	3.37	3.36	3.34	3.33	3.32	3.30	3.29	3.27	3.27	3.26	3.25	3.25	3.24	3.23
8	3.12	3.12	3.11	3.10	3.10	3.09	3.08	3.08	3.07	3.06	3.04	3.03	3.02	3.01	2.99	2.97	2.97	2.96	2.95	2.95	2.94	2.93
9	2.91	2.90	2.89	2.89	2.88	2.87	2.87	2.86	2.85	2.84	2.83	2.81	2.80	2.79	2.77	2.76	2.75	2.74	2.73	2.73	2.72	2.71
10	2.75	2.74	2.73	2.72	2.72	2.71	2.70	2.70	2.69	2.68	2.66	2.65	2.64	2.62	2.60	2.59	2.58	2.57	2.57	2.56	2.55	2.54
11	2.62	2.61	2.60	2.59	2.59	2.58	2.58	2.57	2.56	2.55	2.53	2.52	2.51	2.49	2.47	2.46	2.45	2.44	2.43	2.43	2.42	2.41
12	2.51	2.51	2.50	2.49	2.48	2.48	2.47	2.47	2.46	2.44	2.43	2.41	2.40	2.38	2.37	2.35	2.34	2.33	2.33	2.32	2.31	2.30
13	2.43	2.42	2.41	2.41	2.40	2.39	2.39	2.38	2.37	2.36	2.34	2.33	2.31	2.30	2.28	2.26	2.25	2.25	2.24	2.23	2.22	2.21
14	2.36	2.35	2.34	2.33	2.33	2.32	2.31	2.31	2.30	2.28	2.27	2.25	2.24	2.22	2.21	2.19	2.18	2.17	2.16	2.15	2.15	2.14
15	2.30	2.29	2.28	2.27	2.27	2.26	2.25	2.25	2.24	2.22	2.20	2.19	2.18	2.16	2.14	2.12	2.11	2.11	2.10	2.09	2.08	2.07
16	2.24	2.24	2.23	2.22	2.21	2.21	2.20	2.19	2.18	2.17	2.15	2.14	2.12	2.11	2.09	2.07	2.06	2.05	2.04	2.03	2.02	2.02
17	2.20	2.19	2.18	2.17	2.17	2.16	2.15	2.15	2.14	2.12	2.10	2.09	2.08	2.06	2.04	2.02	2.01	2.00	1.99	1.98	1.98	1.97
18	2.16	2.15	2.14	2.13	2.13	2.12	2.11	2.11	2.10	2.08	2.06	2.05	2.04	2.02	2.00	1.98	1.97	1.96	1.95	1.94	1.93	1.92
19	2.12	2.11	2.11	2.10	2.09	2.08	2.08	2.07	2.06	2.05	2.03	2.01	2.00	1.98	1.96	1.94	1.93	1.92	1.91	1.90	1.89	1.88
20	2.09	2.08	2.07	2.07	2.06	2.05	2.05	2.04	2.03	2.01	1.99	1.98	1.97	1.95	1.93	1.91	1.90	1.89	1.88	1.87	1.86	1.85
21	2.06	2.05	2.05	2.04	2.03	2.02	2.02	2.01	2.00	1.98	1.96	1.95	1.94	1.92	1.90	1.88	1.87	1.86	1.85	1.84	1.83	1.82
22	2.04	2.03	2.02	2.01	2.00	2.00	1.99	1.98	1.97	1.96	1.94	1.92	1.91	1.89	1.87	1.85	1.84	1.83	1.82	1.81	1.80	1.79
23	2.01	2.01	2.00	1.99	1.98	1.97	1.97	1.96	1.95	1.93	1.91	1.90	1.88	1.86	1.84	1.82	1.81	1.81	1.79	1.78	1.77	1.76
24	1.99	1.98	1.97	1.97	1.96	1.95	1.95	1.94	1.93	1.91	1.89	1.88	1.86	1.84	1.82	1.80	1.79	1.78	1.77	1.76	1.75	1.74
25	1.97	1.96	1.96	1.95	1.94	1.93	1.93	1.92	1.91	1.89	1.87	1.86	1.84	1.82	1.80	1.78	1.77	1.76	1.75	1.74	1.73	1.72
26	1.96	1.95	1.94	1.93	1.92	1.91	1.91	1.90	1.89	1.87	1.85	1.84	1.82	1.80	1.78	1.76	1.75	1.74	1.73	1.72	1.71	1.70
27	1.94	1.93	1.92	1.91	1.90	1.90	1.89	1.88	1.87	1.86	1.84	1.82	1.81	1.79	1.76	1.74	1.73	1.72	1.71	1.70	1.69	1.68
28	1.92	1.91	1.91	1.90	1.89	1.88	1.88	1.87	1.86	1.84	1.82	1.80	1.79	1.77	1.75	1.73	1.71	1.71	1.70	1.68	1.67	1.66
29	1.91	1.90	1.89	1.88	1.88	1.87	1.86	1.85	1.84	1.83	1.81	1.79	1.77	1.75	1.73	1.71	1.70	1.69	1.68	1.67	1.66	1.65
30	1.90	1.89	1.88	1.87	1.86	1.85	1.85	1.84	1.83	1.81	1.79	1.77	1.76	1.74	1.72	1.70	1.68	1.68	1.66	1.65	1.64	1.63
32	1.87	1.86	1.85	1.84	1.84	1.83	1.82	1.82	1.80	1.79	1.77	1.75	1.74	1.71	1.69	1.67	1.66	1.65	1.64	1.63	1.61	1.60
35	1.84	1.83	1.82	1.82	1.81	1.80	1.79	1.79	1.77	1.76	1.74	1.72	1.70	1.68	1.66	1.63	1.62	1.61	1.60	1.59	1.58	1.57
40	1.80	1.79	1.78	1.77	1.77	1.76	1.75	1.74	1.73	1.72	1.69	1.67	1.66	1.64	1.61	1.59	1.58	1.57	1.55	1.54	1.53	1.52
45	1.77	1.76	1.75	1.74	1.73	1.73	1.72	1.71	1.70	1.68	1.66	1.64	1.63	1.60	1.58	1.55	1.54	1.53	1.52	1.51	1.49	1.48
50	1.75	1.74	1.73	1.72	1.71	1.70	1.69	1.69	1.67	1.66	1.63	1.61	1.60	1.58	1.55	1.52	1.51	1.50	1.49	1.47	1.46	1.45
60	1.71	1.70	1.69	1.68	1.67	1.66	1.66	1.65	1.64	1.62	1.59	1.57	1.56	1.53	1.51	1.48	1.47	1.46	1.44	1.43	1.41	1.40
75	1.67	1.66	1.65	1.64	1.63	1.63	1.62	1.61	1.60	1.58	1.55	1.53	1.52	1.49	1.47	1.44	1.42	1.41	1.40	1.38	1.37	1.35
100	1.64	1.63	1.62	1.61	1.60	1.59	1.58	1.57	1.56	1.54	1.52	1.49	1.48	1.45	1.42	1.39	1.38	1.36	1.35	1.33	1.31	1.30
120	1.62	1.61	1.60	1.59	1.58	1.57	1.56	1.55	1.54	1.52	1.50	1.47	1.46	1.43	1.40	1.37	1.35	1.34	1.32	1.30	1.29	1.27
140	1.61	1.60	1.58	1.57	1.56	1.56	1.55	1.54	1.53	1.51	1.48	1.46	1.44	1.41	1.38	1.35	1.33	1.32	1.30	1.29	1.27	1.25
180	1.59	1.58	1.57	1.56	1.55	1.54	1.53	1.52	1.51	1.49	1.46	1.44	1.42	1.39	1.36	1.33	1.31	1.30	1.28	1.26	1.24	1.22
250	1.57	1.56	1.55	1.54	1.53	1.52	1.51	1.50	1.49	1.47	1.44	1.42	1.40	1.37	1.34	1.31	1.29	1.27	1.26	1.23	1.21	1.18
400	1.56	1.54	1.53	1.52	1.51	1.50	1.50	1.49	1.47	1.45	1.42	1.40	1.38	1.35	1.32	1.28	1.26	1.25	1.23	1.20	1.18	1.15
1000	1.54	1.53	1.52	1.51	1.50	1.49	1.48	1.47	1.46	1.43	1.41	1.38	1.36	1.33	1.30	1.26	1.24	1.22	1.20	1.17	1.14	1.11

Table F (cont.)

Numerator df

$\alpha = .1$	1	2	3	4	5	6	7	8	9	10	11	12	13	14	15	16	17	18	19	20	21	22
1	39.9	49.5	53.6	55.8	57.2	58.2	58.9	59.4	59.9	60.2	60.5	60.7	60.9	61.1	61.2	61.3	61.5	61.6	61.7	61.7	61.8	61.9
2	8.53	9.00	9.16	9.24	9.29	9.33	9.35	9.37	9.38	9.39	9.40	9.41	9.41	9.42	9.42	9.43	9.43	9.44	9.44	9.44	9.44	9.45
3	5.54	5.46	5.39	5.34	5.31	5.28	5.27	5.25	5.24	5.23	5.22	5.22	5.21	5.20	5.20	5.20	5.19	5.19	5.19	5.18	5.18	5.18
4	4.54	4.32	4.19	4.11	4.05	4.01	3.98	3.95	3.94	3.92	3.91	3.90	3.89	3.88	3.87	3.86	3.86	3.85	3.85	3.84	3.84	3.84
5	4.06	3.78	3.62	3.52	3.45	3.40	3.37	3.34	3.32	3.30	3.28	3.27	3.26	3.25	3.24	3.23	3.22	3.22	3.21	3.21	3.20	3.20
6	3.78	3.46	3.29	3.18	3.11	3.05	3.01	2.98	2.96	2.94	2.92	2.90	2.89	2.88	2.87	2.86	2.85	2.85	2.84	2.84	2.83	2.83
7	3.59	3.26	3.07	2.96	2.88	2.83	2.78	2.75	2.72	2.70	2.68	2.67	2.65	2.64	2.63	2.62	2.61	2.61	2.60	2.59	2.59	2.58
8	3.46	3.11	2.92	2.81	2.73	2.67	2.62	2.59	2.56	2.54	2.52	2.50	2.49	2.48	2.46	2.45	2.45	2.44	2.43	2.42	2.42	2.41
9	3.36	3.01	2.81	2.69	2.61	2.55	2.51	2.47	2.44	2.42	2.40	2.38	2.36	2.35	2.34	2.33	2.32	2.31	2.30	2.30	2.29	2.29
10	3.29	2.92	2.73	2.61	2.52	2.46	2.41	2.38	2.35	2.32	2.30	2.28	2.27	2.26	2.24	2.23	2.22	2.22	2.21	2.20	2.19	2.19
11	3.23	2.86	2.66	2.54	2.45	2.39	2.34	2.30	2.27	2.25	2.23	2.21	2.19	2.18	2.17	2.16	2.15	2.14	2.13	2.12	2.12	2.11
12	3.18	2.81	2.61	2.48	2.39	2.33	2.28	2.24	2.21	2.19	2.17	2.15	2.13	2.12	2.10	2.09	2.08	2.08	2.07	2.06	2.05	2.05
13	3.14	2.76	2.56	2.43	2.35	2.28	2.23	2.20	2.16	2.14	2.12	2.10	2.08	2.07	2.05	2.04	2.03	2.02	2.01	2.01	2.00	1.99
14	3.10	2.73	2.52	2.39	2.31	2.24	2.19	2.15	2.12	2.10	2.07	2.05	2.04	2.02	2.01	2.00	1.99	1.98	1.97	1.96	1.96	1.95
15	3.07	2.70	2.49	2.36	2.27	2.21	2.16	2.12	2.09	2.06	2.04	2.02	2.00	1.99	1.97	1.96	1.95	1.94	1.93	1.92	1.92	1.91
16	3.05	2.67	2.46	2.33	2.24	2.18	2.13	2.09	2.06	2.03	2.01	1.99	1.97	1.95	1.94	1.93	1.92	1.91	1.90	1.89	1.88	1.88
17	3.03	2.64	2.44	2.31	2.22	2.15	2.10	2.06	2.03	2.00	1.98	1.96	1.94	1.93	1.91	1.90	1.89	1.88	1.87	1.86	1.86	1.85
18	3.01	2.62	2.42	2.29	2.20	2.13	2.08	2.04	2.00	1.98	1.95	1.93	1.92	1.90	1.89	1.87	1.86	1.85	1.84	1.84	1.83	1.82
19	2.99	2.61	2.40	2.27	2.18	2.11	2.06	2.02	1.98	1.96	1.93	1.91	1.89	1.88	1.86	1.85	1.84	1.83	1.82	1.81	1.81	1.80
20	2.97	2.59	2.38	2.25	2.16	2.09	2.04	2.00	1.96	1.94	1.91	1.89	1.87	1.86	1.84	1.83	1.82	1.81	1.80	1.79	1.79	1.78
21	2.96	2.57	2.36	2.23	2.14	2.08	2.02	1.98	1.95	1.92	1.90	1.87	1.86	1.84	1.83	1.81	1.80	1.79	1.78	1.78	1.77	1.76
22	2.95	2.56	2.35	2.22	2.13	2.06	2.01	1.97	1.93	1.90	1.88	1.86	1.84	1.83	1.81	1.80	1.79	1.78	1.77	1.76	1.75	1.74
23	2.94	2.55	2.34	2.21	2.11	2.05	1.99	1.95	1.92	1.89	1.87	1.84	1.83	1.81	1.80	1.78	1.77	1.76	1.75	1.74	1.74	1.73
24	2.93	2.54	2.33	2.19	2.10	2.04	1.98	1.94	1.91	1.88	1.85	1.83	1.81	1.80	1.78	1.77	1.76	1.75	1.74	1.73	1.72	1.71
25	2.92	2.53	2.32	2.18	2.09	2.02	1.97	1.93	1.89	1.87	1.84	1.82	1.80	1.79	1.77	1.76	1.75	1.74	1.73	1.72	1.71	1.70
26	2.91	2.52	2.31	2.17	2.08	2.01	1.96	1.92	1.88	1.86	1.83	1.81	1.79	1.77	1.76	1.75	1.73	1.72	1.71	1.71	1.70	1.69
27	2.90	2.51	2.30	2.17	2.07	2.00	1.95	1.91	1.87	1.85	1.82	1.80	1.78	1.76	1.75	1.74	1.72	1.71	1.70	1.70	1.69	1.68
28	2.89	2.50	2.29	2.16	2.06	2.00	1.94	1.90	1.87	1.84	1.81	1.79	1.77	1.75	1.74	1.73	1.71	1.70	1.69	1.69	1.68	1.67
29	2.89	2.50	2.28	2.15	2.06	1.99	1.93	1.89	1.86	1.83	1.80	1.78	1.76	1.75	1.73	1.72	1.71	1.69	1.68	1.68	1.67	1.66
30	2.88	2.49	2.28	2.14	2.05	1.98	1.93	1.88	1.85	1.82	1.79	1.77	1.75	1.74	1.72	1.71	1.70	1.69	1.68	1.67	1.66	1.65
32	2.87	2.48	2.26	2.13	2.04	1.97	1.91	1.87	1.83	1.81	1.78	1.76	1.74	1.72	1.71	1.69	1.68	1.67	1.66	1.65	1.64	1.64
35	2.85	2.46	2.25	2.11	2.02	1.95	1.90	1.85	1.82	1.79	1.76	1.74	1.72	1.70	1.69	1.67	1.66	1.65	1.64	1.63	1.62	1.62
40	2.84	2.44	2.23	2.09	2.00	1.93	1.87	1.83	1.79	1.76	1.74	1.71	1.70	1.68	1.66	1.65	1.64	1.62	1.61	1.61	1.60	1.59
45	2.82	2.42	2.21	2.07	1.98	1.91	1.85	1.81	1.77	1.74	1.72	1.70	1.68	1.66	1.64	1.63	1.62	1.60	1.59	1.58	1.58	1.57
50	2.81	2.41	2.20	2.06	1.97	1.90	1.84	1.80	1.76	1.73	1.70	1.68	1.66	1.64	1.63	1.61	1.60	1.59	1.58	1.57	1.56	1.55
60	2.79	2.39	2.18	2.04	1.95	1.87	1.82	1.77	1.74	1.71	1.68	1.66	1.64	1.62	1.60	1.59	1.58	1.56	1.55	1.54	1.53	1.53
75	2.77	2.37	2.16	2.02	1.93	1.85	1.80	1.75	1.72	1.69	1.66	1.63	1.61	1.60	1.58	1.57	1.55	1.54	1.53	1.52	1.51	1.50
100	2.76	2.36	2.14	2.00	1.91	1.83	1.78	1.73	1.69	1.66	1.64	1.61	1.59	1.57	1.56	1.54	1.53	1.52	1.50	1.49	1.48	1.48
120	2.75	2.35	2.13	1.99	1.90	1.82	1.77	1.72	1.68	1.65	1.63	1.60	1.58	1.56	1.55	1.53	1.52	1.50	1.49	1.48	1.47	1.46
140	2.74	2.34	2.12	1.99	1.89	1.82	1.76	1.71	1.68	1.64	1.62	1.59	1.57	1.55	1.54	1.52	1.51	1.50	1.48	1.47	1.46	1.45
180	2.73	2.33	2.11	1.98	1.88	1.81	1.75	1.70	1.67	1.63	1.61	1.58	1.56	1.54	1.53	1.51	1.50	1.48	1.47	1.46	1.45	1.44
250	2.73	2.32	2.11	1.97	1.87	1.80	1.74	1.69	1.66	1.62	1.60	1.57	1.55	1.53	1.51	1.50	1.49	1.47	1.46	1.45	1.44	1.43
400	2.72	2.32	2.10	1.96	1.86	1.79	1.73	1.69	1.65	1.61	1.59	1.56	1.54	1.52	1.50	1.49	1.47	1.46	1.45	1.44	1.43	1.42
1000	2.71	2.31	2.09	1.95	1.85	1.78	1.72	1.68	1.64	1.61	1.58	1.55	1.53	1.51	1.49	1.48	1.46	1.45	1.44	1.43	1.42	1.41

Denominator df

Table F (cont.)

Numerator df

$\alpha = .1$	23	24	25	26	27	28	29	30	32	35	40	45	50	60	75	100	120	140	180	250	400	1000
1	61.9	62.0	62.1	62.1	62.1	62.2	62.2	62.3	62.3	62.4	62.5	62.6	62.7	62.8	62.9	63.0	63.1	63.1	63.1	63.2	63.2	63.3
2	9.45	9.45	9.45	9.45	9.45	9.46	9.46	9.46	9.46	9.46	9.47	9.47	9.47	9.47	9.48	9.48	9.48	9.48	9.49	9.49	9.49	9.49
3	5.18	5.18	5.17	5.17	5.17	5.17	5.17	5.17	5.17	5.16	5.16	5.16	5.15	5.15	5.15	5.14	5.14	5.14	5.14	5.14	5.14	5.1
4	3.83	3.83	3.83	3.82	3.82	3.82	3.82	3.82	3.81	3.81	3.80	3.80	3.80	3.79	3.78	3.78	3.78	3.77	3.77	3.77	3.77	3.76
5	3.19	3.19	3.19	3.18	3.18	3.18	3.18	3.17	3.17	3.16	3.16	3.15	3.15	3.14	3.13	3.13	3.12	3.12	3.12	3.11	3.11	3.11
6	2.82	2.82	2.81	2.81	2.81	2.81	2.80	2.80	2.80	2.79	2.78	2.77	2.77	2.76	2.75	2.75	2.74	2.74	2.74	2.73	2.73	2.72
7	2.58	2.58	2.57	2.57	2.56	2.56	2.56	2.56	2.55	2.54	2.54	2.53	2.52	2.51	2.51	2.50	2.49	2.49	2.49	2.48	2.48	2.47
8	2.41	2.40	2.40	2.40	2.39	2.39	2.39	2.38	2.38	2.37	2.36	2.35	2.35	2.34	2.33	2.32	2.32	2.31	2.31	2.30	2.30	2.30
9	2.28	2.28	2.27	2.27	2.26	2.26	2.26	2.25	2.25	2.24	2.23	2.22	2.22	2.21	2.20	2.19	2.18	2.18	2.18	2.17	2.17	2.16
10	2.18	2.18	2.17	2.17	2.17	2.16	2.16	2.16	2.15	2.14	2.13	2.12	2.12	2.11	2.10	2.09	2.08	2.08	2.07	2.07	2.06	2.06
11	2.11	2.10	2.10	2.09	2.09	2.08	2.08	2.08	2.07	2.06	2.05	2.04	2.04	2.03	2.02	2.01	2.00	2.00	1.99	1.99	1.98	1.98
12	2.04	2.04	2.03	2.03	2.02	2.02	2.01	2.01	2.01	2.00	1.99	1.98	1.97	1.96	1.95	1.94	1.93	1.93	1.92	1.92	1.91	1.91
13	1.99	1.98	1.98	1.97	1.97	1.96	1.96	1.96	1.95	1.94	1.93	1.92	1.92	1.90	1.89	1.88	1.88	1.87	1.87	1.86	1.86	1.85
14	1.94	1.94	1.93	1.93	1.92	1.92	1.92	1.91	1.91	1.90	1.89	1.88	1.87	1.86	1.85	1.83	1.83	1.82	1.82	1.81	1.81	1.80
15	1.90	1.90	1.89	1.89	1.88	1.88	1.88	1.87	1.87	1.86	1.85	1.84	1.83	1.82	1.80	1.79	1.79	1.78	1.78	1.77	1.76	1.76
16	1.87	1.87	1.86	1.86	1.85	1.85	1.84	1.84	1.83	1.82	1.81	1.80	1.79	1.78	1.77	1.76	1.75	1.75	1.74	1.73	1.73	1.72
17	1.84	1.84	1.83	1.83	1.82	1.82	1.81	1.81	1.80	1.79	1.78	1.77	1.76	1.75	1.74	1.73	1.72	1.71	1.71	1.70	1.70	1.69
18	1.82	1.81	1.80	1.80	1.79	1.79	1.79	1.78	1.78	1.77	1.75	1.74	1.74	1.72	1.71	1.70	1.69	1.69	1.68	1.67	1.67	1.66
19	1.79	1.79	1.78	1.78	1.77	1.77	1.76	1.76	1.75	1.74	1.73	1.72	1.71	1.70	1.69	1.67	1.67	1.66	1.65	1.65	1.64	1.64
20	1.77	1.77	1.76	1.76	1.75	1.75	1.74	1.74	1.73	1.72	1.71	1.70	1.69	1.68	1.66	1.65	1.64	1.64	1.63	1.62	1.62	1.61
21	1.75	1.75	1.74	1.74	1.73	1.73	1.72	1.72	1.71	1.70	1.69	1.68	1.67	1.66	1.64	1.63	1.62	1.62	1.61	1.60	1.60	1.59
22	1.74	1.73	1.73	1.72	1.72	1.71	1.71	1.70	1.69	1.68	1.67	1.66	1.65	1.64	1.63	1.61	1.60	1.60	1.59	1.58	1.58	1.57
23	1.72	1.72	1.71	1.70	1.70	1.69	1.69	1.69	1.68	1.67	1.66	1.64	1.64	1.62	1.61	1.59	1.59	1.58	1.57	1.57	1.56	1.55
24	1.71	1.70	1.70	1.69	1.69	1.68	1.68	1.67	1.66	1.65	1.64	1.63	1.62	1.61	1.59	1.58	1.57	1.57	1.56	1.55	1.54	1.54
25	1.70	1.69	1.68	1.69	1.67	1.67	1.66	1.66	1.65	1.64	1.63	1.62	1.61	1.59	1.58	1.56	1.56	1.55	1.54	1.54	1.53	1.52
26	1.68	1.68	1.67	1.67	1.66	1.66	1.65	1.65	1.64	1.63	1.61	1.60	1.59	1.58	1.57	1.55	1.54	1.54	1.53	1.52	1.52	1.51
27	1.67	1.67	1.66	1.65	1.65	1.64	1.64	1.64	1.63	1.62	1.60	1.59	1.58	1.57	1.55	1.54	1.53	1.53	1.52	1.51	1.50	1.50
28	1.66	1.66	1.65	1.64	1.64	1.63	1.63	1.63	1.62	1.61	1.59	1.58	1.57	1.56	1.54	1.53	1.52	1.51	1.51	1.50	1.49	1.48
29	1.65	1.65	1.64	1.63	1.63	1.62	1.62	1.62	1.61	1.60	1.58	1.57	1.56	1.55	1.53	1.52	1.51	1.50	1.50	1.49	1.48	1.47
30	1.64	1.64	1.63	1.63	1.62	1.62	1.61	1.61	1.60	1.59	1.57	1.56	1.55	1.54	1.52	1.51	1.50	1.49	1.49	1.48	1.47	1.46
32	1.63	1.62	1.62	1.61	1.60	1.60	1.59	1.59	1.58	1.57	1.56	1.54	1.53	1.52	1.50	1.49	1.48	1.47	1.47	1.46	1.45	1.44
35	1.61	1.60	1.60	1.59	1.58	1.58	1.57	1.57	1.56	1.55	1.53	1.52	1.51	1.50	1.48	1.47	1.46	1.45	1.44	1.43	1.42	1.42
40	1.58	1.57	1.57	1.56	1.56	1.55	1.55	1.54	1.53	1.52	1.51	1.49	1.48	1.47	1.45	1.43	1.42	1.42	1.41	1.40	1.39	1.38
45	1.56	1.55	1.55	1.54	1.53	1.53	1.52	1.52	1.51	1.50	1.48	1.47	1.46	1.44	1.43	1.41	1.40	1.39	1.38	1.37	1.37	1.36
50	1.54	1.54	1.53	1.52	1.52	1.51	1.51	1.50	1.49	1.48	1.46	1.45	1.44	1.42	1.41	1.39	1.38	1.37	1.36	1.35	1.34	1.33
60	1.52	1.51	1.50	1.49	1.49	1.49	1.48	1.48	1.47	1.45	1.44	1.42	1.41	1.40	1.38	1.36	1.35	1.34	1.33	1.32	1.31	1.30
75	1.49	1.49	1.48	1.47	1.47	1.46	1.45	1.45	1.44	1.43	1.41	1.40	1.38	1.37	1.35	1.33	1.32	1.31	1.30	1.29	1.27	1.26
100	1.47	1.46	1.45	1.44	1.44	1.43	1.43	1.42	1.41	1.40	1.38	1.37	1.35	1.34	1.32	1.29	1.28	1.27	1.26	1.25	1.24	1.22
120	1.46	1.45	1.43	1.43	1.43	1.42	1.41	1.41	1.40	1.39	1.37	1.35	1.34	1.32	1.30	1.28	1.26	1.26	1.24	1.23	1.22	1.20
140	1.45	1.44	1.42	1.42	1.42	1.41	1.41	1.40	1.39	1.38	1.36	1.34	1.33	1.31	1.29	1.26	1.25	1.24	1.23	1.22	1.20	1.19
180	1.43	1.43	1.41	1.40	1.40	1.40	1.39	1.39	1.38	1.36	1.34	1.33	1.32	1.29	1.27	1.25	1.23	1.22	1.21	1.20	1.18	1.16
250	1.42	1.41	1.40	1.39	1.39	1.39	1.38	1.37	1.36	1.35	1.33	1.31	1.30	1.28	1.26	1.23	1.22	1.21	1.19	1.18	1.16	1.14
400	1.41	1.40	1.39	1.38	1.38	1.37	1.37	1.36	1.35	1.34	1.32	1.30	1.29	1.26	1.24	1.21	1.20	1.19	1.17	1.16	1.14	1.12
1000	1.40	1.39	1.38	1.37	1.37	1.36	1.36	1.35	1.34	1.32	1.30	1.29	1.27	1.25	1.23	1.20	1.18	1.17	1.15	1.13	1.11	1.08

Denominator df

Table R

n	d_2	d_3	D_3	D_4
2	1.128	0.852	0	3.267
3	1.693	0.888	0	2.574
4	2.059	0.880	0	2.282
5	2.326	0.864	0	2.114
6	2.534	0.848	0	2.004
7	2.704	0.833	0.076	1.924
8	2.847	0.820	0.136	1.864
9	2.970	0.808	0.184	1.816
10	3.078	0.797	0.223	1.777
11	3.173	0.787	0.256	1.744
12	3.258	0.779	0.283	1.717
13	3.336	0.771	0.307	1.693
14	3.407	0.763	0.328	1.672
15	3.472	0.756	0.347	1.653
16	3.532	0.750	0.363	1.637
17	3.588	0.744	0.378	1.622
18	3.640	0.738	0.391	1.608
19	3.689	0.734	0.403	1.597
20	3.735	0.728	0.415	1.585
21	3.778	0.724	0.425	1.575
22	3.819	0.721	0.434	1.566
23	3.858	0.716	0.443	1.557
24	3.895	0.711	0.451	1.548
25	3.931	0.709	0.459	1.541

Two-tail probability		0.20	0.10	0.05	0.02	0.01	
One-tail probability		0.10	0.05	0.025	0.01	0.005	
Table T	df						df
Values of t_α	1	3.078	6.314	12.706	31.821	63.657	1
	2	1.886	2.920	4.303	6.965	9.925	2
	3	1.638	2.353	3.182	4.541	5.841	3
	4	1.533	2.132	2.776	3.747	4.604	4
	5	1.476	2.015	2.571	3.365	4.032	5
	6	1.440	1.943	2.447	3.143	3.707	6
	7	1.415	1.895	2.365	2.998	3.499	7
	8	1.397	1.860	2.306	2.896	3.355	8
	9	1.383	1.833	2.262	2.821	3.250	9
	10	1.372	1.812	2.228	2.764	3.169	10
	11	1.363	1.796	2.201	2.718	3.106	11
	12	1.356	1.782	2.179	2.681	3.055	12
	13	1.350	1.771	2.160	2.650	3.012	13
	14	1.345	1.761	2.145	2.624	2.977	14
	15	1.341	1.753	2.131	2.602	2.947	15
	16	1.337	1.746	2.120	2.583	2.921	16
	17	1.333	1.740	2.110	2.567	2.898	17
	18	1.330	1.734	2.101	2.552	2.878	18
	19	1.328	1.729	2.093	2.539	2.861	19
	20	1.325	1.725	2.086	2.528	2.845	20
	21	1.323	1.721	2.080	2.518	2.831	21
	22	1.321	1.717	2.074	2.508	2.819	22
	23	1.319	1.714	2.069	2.500	2.807	23
	24	1.318	1.711	2.064	2.492	2.797	24
	25	1.316	1.708	2.060	2.485	2.787	25
	26	1.315	1.706	2.056	2.479	2.779	26
	27	1.314	1.703	2.052	2.473	2.771	27
	28	1.313	1.701	2.048	2.467	2.763	28
	29	1.311	1.699	2.045	2.462	2.756	29
	30	1.310	1.697	2.042	2.457	2.750	30
	32	1.309	1.694	2.037	2.449	2.738	32
	35	1.306	1.690	2.030	2.438	2.725	35
	40	1.303	1.684	2.021	2.423	2.704	40
	45	1.301	1.679	2.014	2.412	2.690	45
	50	1.299	1.676	2.009	2.403	2.678	50
	60	1.296	1.671	2.000	2.390	2.660	60
	75	1.293	1.665	1.992	2.377	2.643	75
	100	1.290	1.660	1.984	2.364	2.626	100
	120	1.289	1.658	1.980	2.358	2.617	120
	140	1.288	1.656	1.977	2.353	2.611	140
	180	1.286	1.653	1.973	2.347	2.603	180
	250	1.285	1.651	1.969	2.341	2.596	250
	400	1.284	1.649	1.966	2.336	2.588	400
	1000	1.282	1.646	1.962	2.330	2.581	1000
	∞	1.282	1.645	1.960	2.326	2.576	∞
Confidence levels		80%	90%	95%	98%	99%	

Two tails

One tail

Table W1

Critical Values of T_L and T_U for the Wilcoxon Rank Sum Test: Independent Samples

Test statistic is the rank sum associated with the smaller sample (if equal sample sizes, either rank sum can be used). Reject the null hypothesis at the indicated α level if the test statistic falls below the lower bound, T_L, or above the upper bound, T_U. For groups larger than 10, use the Normal approximation given in the text.

a. $\alpha = .025$ one-tailed; $\alpha = .05$ two-tailed

n_1 n_2	3		4		5		6		7		8		9		10	
	T_L	T_U	T_L	T_U	T_L	T_U	T_L	T_U	T_L	T_U	T_L	T_U	T_L	T_U	T_L	T_U
3	5	16	6	18	6	21	7	23	7	26	8	28	8	31	9	33
4	6	18	11	25	12	28	12	32	13	35	14	38	15	41	16	44
5	6	21	12	28	18	37	19	41	20	45	21	49	22	53	24	56
6	7	23	12	32	19	41	26	52	28	56	29	61	31	65	32	70
7	7	26	13	35	20	45	28	56	37	68	39	73	41	78	43	83
8	8	28	14	38	21	49	29	61	39	73	49	87	51	93	54	98
9	8	31	15	41	22	53	31	65	41	78	51	93	63	108	66	114
10	9	33	16	44	24	56	32	70	43	83	54	98	66	114	79	131

a. $\alpha = .05$ one-tailed; $\alpha = .10$ two-tailed

n_1 n_2	3		4		5		6		7		8		9		10	
	T_L	T_U	T_L	T_U	T_L	T_U	T_L	T_U	T_L	T_U	T_L	T_U	T_L	T_U	T_L	T_U
3	6	15	7	17	7	20	8	22	9	24	9	27	10	29	11	31
4	7	17	12	24	13	27	14	30	15	33	16	36	17	39	18	42
5	7	20	13	27	19	36	20	40	22	43	24	46	25	50	26	54
6	8	22	14	30	20	40	28	50	30	54	32	58	33	63	35	67
7	9	24	15	33	22	43	30	54	39	66	41	71	43	76	46	80
8	9	27	16	36	24	46	32	58	41	71	52	84	54	90	57	95
9	10	29	17	39	25	50	33	63	43	76	54	90	66	105	69	111
10	11	31	18	42	26	54	35	67	46	80	57	95	69	111	83	127

Source: From F. Wilcoxon and R. A. Wilcox, "Some Rapid Approximate Statistical Procedures," 1964. Copyright © 1964 by BASF Corporation.

Table W2

Critical Values of T in the Wilcoxon Paired Difference Signed-Rank Test. Reject the null hypothesis at the indicated α levels if the test statistic is smaller than the corresponding critical value.

One-Tailed	Two-Tailed	$n = 5$	$n = 6$	$n = 7$	$n = 8$	$n = 9$	$n = 10$
$\alpha = .05$	$\alpha = .10$	1	2	4	6	8	11
$\alpha = .025$	$\alpha = .05$		1	2	4	6	8
$\alpha = .01$	$\alpha = .02$			0	2	3	5
$\alpha = .005$	$\alpha = .01$				0	2	3
		$n = 11$	$n = 12$	$n = 13$	$n = 14$	$n = 15$	$n = 16$
$\alpha = .05$	$\alpha = .10$	14	17	21	26	30	36
$\alpha = .025$	$\alpha = .05$	11	14	17	21	25	30
$\alpha = .01$	$\alpha = .02$	7	10	13	16	20	24
$\alpha = .005$	$\alpha = .01$	5	7	10	13	16	19
		$n = 17$	$n = 18$	$n = 19$	$n = 20$	$n = 21$	$n = 22$
$\alpha = .05$	$\alpha = .10$	41	47	54	60	68	75
$\alpha = .025$	$\alpha = .05$	35	40	46	52	59	66
$\alpha = .01$	$\alpha = .02$	28	33	38	43	49	56
$\alpha = .005$	$\alpha = .01$	23	28	32	37	43	49
		$n = 23$	$n = 24$	$n = 25$	$n = 26$	$n = 27$	$n = 28$
$\alpha = .05$	$\alpha = .10$	83	92	101	110	120	130
$\alpha = .025$	$\alpha = .05$	73	81	90	98	107	117
$\alpha = .01$	$\alpha = .02$	62	69	77	85	93	102
$\alpha = .005$	$\alpha = .01$	55	61	68	76	84	92
		$n = 29$	$n = 30$	$n = 31$	$n = 32$	$n = 33$	$n = 34$
$\alpha = .05$	$\alpha = .10$	141	152	163	175	188	201
$\alpha = .025$	$\alpha = .05$	127	137	148	159	171	183
$\alpha = .01$	$\alpha = .02$	111	120	130	141	151	162
$\alpha = .005$	$\alpha = .01$	100	109	118	128	138	149
		$n = 35$	$n = 36$	$n = 37$	$n = 38$	$n = 39$	
$\alpha = .05$	$\alpha = .10$	214	228	242	256	271	
$\alpha = .025$	$\alpha = .05$	195	208	222	235	250	
$\alpha = .01$	$\alpha = .02$	174	186	198	211	224	
$\alpha = .005$	$\alpha = .01$	160	171	183	195	208	
		$n = 40$	$n = 41$	$n = 42$	$n = 43$	$n = 44$	$n = 45$
$\alpha = .05$	$\alpha = .10$	287	303	319	336	353	371
$\alpha = .025$	$\alpha = .05$	264	279	295	311	327	344
$\alpha = .01$	$\alpha = .02$	238	252	267	281	297	313
$\alpha = .005$	$\alpha = .01$	221	234	248	262	277	292
		$n = 46$	$n = 47$	$n = 48$	$n = 49$	$n = 50$	
$\alpha = .05$	$\alpha = .10$	389	408	427	446	466	
$\alpha = .025$	$\alpha = .05$	361	379	397	415	434	
$\alpha = .01$	$\alpha = .02$	329	345	362	380	398	
$\alpha = .005$	$\alpha = .01$	307	323	339	356	373	

Source: From F. Wilcoxon and R. A. Wilcox, "Some Rapid Approximate Statistical Procedures," 1964. Copyright © 1964 by BASF Corporation.

Right-tail probability

		0.10	0.05	0.025	0.01	0.005
Table X	df					
Values of χ_α^2	1	2.706	3.841	5.024	6.635	7.879
	2	4.605	5.991	7.378	9.210	10.597
	3	6.251	7.815	9.348	11.345	12.838
	4	7.779	9.488	11.143	13.277	14.860
	5	9.236	11.070	12.833	15.086	16.750
	6	10.645	12.592	14.449	16.812	18.548
	7	12.017	14.067	16.013	18.475	20.278
	8	13.362	15.507	17.535	20.090	21.955
	9	14.684	16.919	19.023	21.666	23.589
	10	15.987	18.307	20.483	23.209	25.188
	11	17.275	19.675	21.920	24.725	26.757
	12	18.549	21.026	23.337	26.217	28.300
	13	19.812	22.362	24.736	27.688	29.819
	14	21.064	23.685	26.119	29.141	31.319
	15	22.307	24.996	27.488	30.578	32.801
	16	23.542	26.296	28.845	32.000	34.267
	17	24.769	27.587	30.191	33.409	35.718
	18	25.989	28.869	31.526	34.805	37.156
	19	27.204	30.143	32.852	36.191	38.582
	20	28.412	31.410	34.170	37.566	39.997
	21	29.615	32.671	35.479	38.932	41.401
	22	30.813	33.924	36.781	40.290	42.796
	23	32.007	35.172	38.076	41.638	44.181
	24	33.196	36.415	39.364	42.980	45.559
	25	34.382	37.653	40.647	44.314	46.928
	26	35.563	38.885	41.923	45.642	48.290
	27	36.741	40.113	43.195	46.963	49.645
	28	37.916	41.337	44.461	48.278	50.994
	29	39.087	42.557	45.722	59.588	52.336
	30	40.256	43.773	46.979	50.892	53.672
	40	51.805	55.759	59.342	63.691	66.767
	50	63.167	67.505	71.420	76.154	79.490
	60	74.397	79.082	83.298	88.381	91.955
	70	85.527	90.531	95.023	100.424	104.213
	80	96.578	101.879	106.628	112.328	116.320
	90	107.565	113.145	118.135	124.115	128.296
	100	118.499	124.343	129.563	135.811	140.177

Table Z	SECOND DECIMAL PLACE IN Z										
Areas under the standard Normal curve	0.09	0.08	0.07	0.06	0.05	0.04	0.03	0.02	0.01	0.00	z
										0.0000†	−3.9
	0.0001	0.0001	0.0001	0.0001	0.0001	0.0001	0.0001	0.0001	0.0001	0.0001	−3.8
	0.0001	0.0001	0.0001	0.0001	0.0001	0.0001	0.0001	0.0001	0.0001	0.0001	−3.7
	0.0001	0.0001	0.0001	0.0001	0.0001	0.0001	0.0001	0.0001	0.0002	0.0002	−3.6
	0.0002	0.0002	0.0002	0.0002	0.0002	0.0002	0.0002	0.0002	0.0002	0.0002	−3.5
	0.0002	0.0003	0.0003	0.0003	0.0003	0.0003	0.0003	0.0003	0.0003	0.0003	−3.4
	0.0003	0.0004	0.0004	0.0004	0.0004	0.0004	0.0004	0.0005	0.0005	0.0005	−3.3
	0.0005	0.0005	0.0005	0.0006	0.0006	0.0006	0.0006	0.0006	0.0007	0.0007	−3.2
	0.0007	0.0007	0.0008	0.0008	0.0008	0.0008	0.0009	0.0009	0.0009	0.0010	−3.1
	0.0010	0.0010	0.0011	0.0011	0.0011	0.0012	0.0012	0.0013	0.0013	0.0013	−3.0
	0.0014	0.0014	0.0015	0.0015	0.0016	0.0016	0.0017	0.0018	0.0018	0.0019	−2.9
	0.0019	0.0020	0.0021	0.0021	0.0022	0.0023	0.0023	0.0024	0.0025	0.0026	−2.8
	0.0026	0.0027	0.0028	0.0029	0.0030	0.0031	0.0032	0.0033	0.0034	0.0035	−2.7
	0.0036	0.0037	0.0038	0.0039	0.0040	0.0041	0.0043	0.0044	0.0045	0.0047	−2.6
	0.0048	0.0049	0.0051	0.0052	0.0054	0.0055	0.0057	0.0059	0.0060	0.0062	−2.5
	0.0064	0.0066	0.0068	0.0069	0.0071	0.0073	0.0075	0.0078	0.0080	0.0082	−2.4
	0.0084	0.0087	0.0089	0.0091	0.0094	0.0096	0.0099	0.0102	0.0104	0.0107	−2.3
	0.0110	0.0113	0.0116	0.0119	0.0122	0.0125	0.0129	0.0132	0.0136	0.0139	−2.2
	0.0143	0.0146	0.0150	0.0154	0.0158	0.0162	0.0166	0.0170	0.0174	0.0179	−2.1
	0.0183	0.0188	0.0192	0.0197	0.0202	0.0207	0.0212	0.0217	0.0222	0.0228	−2.0
	0.0233	0.0239	0.0244	0.0250	0.0256	0.0262	0.0268	0.0274	0.0281	0.0287	−1.9
	0.0294	0.0301	0.0307	0.0314	0.0322	0.0329	0.0336	0.0344	0.0351	0.0359	−1.8
	0.0367	0.0375	0.0384	0.0392	0.0401	0.0409	0.0418	0.0427	0.0436	0.0446	−1.7
	0.0455	0.0465	0.0475	0.0485	0.0495	0.0505	0.0516	0.0526	0.0537	0.0548	−1.6
	0.0559	0.0571	0.0582	0.0594	0.0606	0.0618	0.0630	0.0643	0.0655	0.0668	−1.5
	0.0681	0.0694	0.0708	0.0721	0.0735	0.0749	0.0764	0.0778	0.0793	0.0808	−1.4
	0.0823	0.0838	0.0853	0.0869	0.0885	0.0901	0.0918	0.0934	0.0951	0.0968	−1.3
	0.0985	0.1003	0.1020	0.1038	0.1056	0.1075	0.1093	0.1112	0.1131	0.1151	−1.2
	0.1170	0.1190	0.1210	0.1230	0.1251	0.1271	0.1292	0.1314	0.1335	0.1357	−1.1
	0.1379	0.1401	0.1423	0.1446	0.1469	0.1492	0.1515	0.1539	0.1562	0.1587	−1.0
	0.1611	0.1635	0.1660	0.1685	0.1711	0.1736	0.1762	0.1788	0.1814	0.1841	−0.9
	0.1867	0.1894	0.1922	0.1949	0.1977	0.2005	0.2033	0.2061	0.2090	0.2119	−0.8
	0.2148	0.2177	0.2206	0.2236	0.2266	0.2296	0.2327	0.2358	0.2389	0.2420	−0.7
	0.2451	0.2483	0.2514	0.2546	0.2578	0.2611	0.2643	0.2676	0.2709	0.2743	−0.6
	0.2776	0.2810	0.2843	0.2877	0.2912	0.2946	0.2981	0.3015	0.3050	0.3085	−0.5
	0.3121	0.3156	0.3192	0.3228	0.3264	0.3300	0.3336	0.3372	0.3409	0.3446	−0.4
	0.3483	0.3520	0.3557	0.3594	0.3632	0.3669	0.3707	0.3745	0.3783	0.3821	−0.3
	0.3859	0.3897	0.3936	0.3974	0.4013	0.4052	0.4090	0.4129	0.4168	0.4207	−0.2
	0.4247	0.4286	0.4325	0.4364	0.4404	0.4443	0.4483	0.4522	0.4562	0.4602	−0.1
	0.4641	0.4681	0.4721	0.4761	0.4801	0.4840	0.4880	0.4920	0.4960	0.5000	−0.0

† For $z \le -3.90$ the areas are 0.0000 to four decimal places.

Table Z (cont.)

Areas under the standard Normal curve

	SECOND DECIMAL PLACE IN Z									
z	0.00	0.01	0.02	0.03	0.04	0.05	0.06	0.07	0.08	0.09
0.0	0.5000	0.5040	0.5080	0.5120	0.5160	0.5199	0.5239	0.5279	0.5319	0.5359
0.1	0.5398	0.5438	0.5478	0.5517	0.5557	0.5596	0.5636	0.5675	0.5714	0.5753
0.2	0.5793	0.5832	0.5871	0.5910	0.5948	0.5987	0.6026	0.6064	0.6103	0.6141
0.3	0.6179	0.6217	0.6255	0.6293	0.6331	0.6368	0.6406	0.6443	0.6480	0.6517
0.4	0.6554	0.6591	0.6628	0.6664	0.6700	0.6736	0.6772	0.6808	0.6844	0.6879
0.5	0.6915	0.6950	0.6985	0.7019	0.7054	0.7088	0.7123	0.7157	0.7190	0.7224
0.6	0.7257	0.7291	0.7324	0.7357	0.7389	0.7422	0.7454	0.7486	0.7517	0.7549
0.7	0.7580	0.7611	0.7642	0.7673	0.7704	0.7734	0.7764	0.7794	0.7823	0.7852
0.8	0.7881	0.7910	0.7939	0.7967	0.7995	0.8023	0.8051	0.8078	0.8106	0.8133
0.9	0.8159	0.8186	0.8212	0.8238	0.8264	0.8289	0.8315	0.8340	0.8365	0.8389
1.0	0.8413	0.8438	0.8461	0.8485	0.8508	0.8531	0.8554	0.8577	0.8599	0.8621
1.1	0.8643	0.8665	0.8686	0.8708	0.8729	0.8749	0.8770	0.8790	0.8810	0.8830
1.2	0.8849	0.8869	0.8888	0.8907	0.8925	0.8944	0.8962	0.8980	0.8997	0.9015
1.3	0.9032	0.9049	0.9066	0.9082	0.9099	0.9115	0.9131	0.9147	0.9162	0.9177
1.4	0.9192	0.9207	0.9222	0.9236	0.9251	0.9265	0.9279	0.9292	0.9306	0.9319
1.5	0.9332	0.9345	0.9357	0.9370	0.9382	0.9394	0.9406	0.9418	0.9429	0.9441
1.6	0.9452	0.9463	0.9474	0.9484	0.9495	0.9505	0.9515	0.9525	0.9535	0.9545
1.7	0.9554	0.9564	0.9573	0.9582	0.9591	0.9599	0.9608	0.9616	0.9625	0.9633
1.8	0.9641	0.9649	0.9656	0.9664	0.9671	0.9678	0.9686	0.9693	0.9699	0.9706
1.9	0.9713	0.9719	0.9726	0.9732	0.9738	0.9744	0.9750	0.9756	0.9761	0.9767
2.0	0.9772	0.9778	0.9783	0.9788	0.9793	0.9798	0.9803	0.9808	0.9812	0.9817
2.1	0.9821	0.9826	0.9830	0.9834	0.9838	0.9842	0.9846	0.9850	0.9854	0.9857
2.2	0.9861	0.9864	0.9868	0.9871	0.9875	0.9878	0.9881	0.9884	0.9887	0.9890
2.3	0.9893	0.9896	0.9898	0.9901	0.9904	0.9906	0.9909	0.9911	0.9913	0.9916
2.4	0.9918	0.9920	0.9922	0.9925	0.9927	0.9929	0.9931	0.9932	0.9934	0.9936
2.5	0.9938	0.9940	0.9941	0.9943	0.9945	0.9946	0.9948	0.9949	0.9951	0.9952
2.6	0.9953	0.9955	0.9956	0.9957	0.9959	0.9960	0.9961	0.9962	0.9963	0.9964
2.7	0.9965	0.9966	0.9967	0.9968	0.9969	0.9970	0.9971	0.9972	0.9973	0.9974
2.8	0.9974	0.9975	0.9976	0.9977	0.9977	0.9978	0.9979	0.9979	0.9980	0.9981
2.9	0.9981	0.9982	0.9982	0.9983	0.9984	0.9984	0.9985	0.9985	0.9986	0.9986
3.0	0.9987	0.9987	0.9987	0.9988	0.9988	0.9989	0.9989	0.9989	0.9990	0.9990
3.1	0.9990	0.9991	0.9991	0.9991	0.9992	0.9992	0.9992	0.9992	0.9993	0.9993
3.2	0.9993	0.9993	0.9994	0.9994	0.9994	0.9994	0.9994	0.9995	0.9995	0.9995
3.3	0.9995	0.9995	0.9995	0.9996	0.9996	0.9996	0.9996	0.9996	0.9996	0.9997
3.4	0.9997	0.9997	0.9997	0.9997	0.9997	0.9997	0.9997	0.9997	0.9997	0.9998
3.5	0.9998	0.9998	0.9998	0.9998	0.9998	0.9998	0.9998	0.9998	0.9998	0.9998
3.6	0.9998	0.9998	0.9999	0.9999	0.9999	0.9999	0.9999	0.9999	0.9999	0.9999
3.7	0.9999	0.9999	0.9999	0.9999	0.9999	0.9999	0.9999	0.9999	0.9999	0.9999
3.8	0.9999	0.9999	0.9999	0.9999	0.9999	0.9999	0.9999	0.9999	0.9999	0.9999
3.9	1.0000[†]									

[†] For $z \geq 3.90$, the areas are 1.0000 to four decimal places.

ROW					TABLE OF RANDOM DIGITS					
1	96299	07196	98642	20639	23185	56282	69929	14125	38872	94168
2	71622	35940	81807	59225	18192	08710	80777	84395	69563	86280
3	03272	41230	81739	74797	70406	18564	69273	72532	78340	36699
4	46376	58596	14365	63685	56555	42974	72944	96463	63533	24152
5	47352	42853	42903	97504	56655	70355	88606	61406	38757	70657
6	20064	04266	74017	79319	70170	96572	08523	56025	89077	57678
7	73184	95907	05179	51002	83374	52297	07769	99792	78365	93487
8	72753	36216	07230	35793	71907	65571	66784	25548	91861	15725
9	03939	30763	06138	80062	02537	23561	93136	61260	77935	93159
10	75998	37203	07959	38264	78120	77525	86481	54986	33042	70648
11	94435	97441	90998	25104	49761	14967	70724	67030	53887	81293
12	04362	40989	69167	38894	00172	02999	97377	33305	60782	29810
13	89059	43528	10547	40115	82234	86902	04121	83889	76208	31076
14	87736	04666	75145	49175	76754	07884	92564	80793	22573	67902
15	76488	88899	15860	07370	13431	84041	69202	18912	83173	11983
16	36460	53772	66634	25045	79007	78518	73580	14191	50353	32064
17	13205	69237	21820	20952	16635	58867	97650	82983	64865	93298
18	51242	12215	90739	36812	00436	31609	80333	96606	30430	31803
19	67819	00354	91439	91073	49258	15992	41277	75111	67496	68430
20	09875	08990	27656	15871	23637	00952	97818	64234	50199	05715
21	18192	95308	72975	01191	29958	09275	89141	19558	50524	32041
22	02763	33701	66188	50226	35813	72951	11638	01876	93664	37001
23	13349	46328	01856	29935	80563	03742	49470	67749	08578	21956
24	69238	92878	80067	80807	45096	22936	64325	19265	37755	69794
25	92207	63527	59398	29818	24789	94309	88380	57000	50171	17891
26	66679	99100	37072	30593	29665	84286	44458	60180	81451	58273
27	31087	42430	60322	34765	15757	53300	97392	98035	05228	68970
28	84432	04916	52949	78533	31666	62350	20584	56367	19701	60584
29	72042	12287	21081	48426	44321	58765	41760	43304	13399	02043
30	94534	73559	82135	70260	87936	85162	11937	18263	54138	69564
31	63971	97198	40974	45301	60177	35604	21580	68107	25184	42810
32	11227	58474	17272	37619	69517	62964	67962	34510	12607	52255
33	28541	02029	08068	96656	17795	21484	57722	76511	27849	61738
34	11282	43632	49531	78981	81980	08530	08629	32279	29478	50228
35	42907	15137	21918	13248	39129	49559	94540	24070	88151	36782
36	47119	76651	21732	32364	58545	50277	57558	30390	18771	72703
37	11232	99884	05087	76839	65142	19994	91397	29350	83852	04905
38	64725	06719	86262	53356	57999	50193	79936	97230	52073	94467
39	77007	26962	55466	12521	48125	12280	54985	26239	76044	54398
40	18375	19310	59796	89832	59417	18553	17238	05474	33259	50595

Selected Formulas

$Range = Max - Min$
$IQR = Q3 - Q1$
Outlier Rule-of-Thumb: $y < Q1 - 1.5 \times IQR$ or $y > Q3 + 1.5 \times IQR$

$$\bar{y} = \frac{\sum y}{n}$$

$$s = \sqrt{\frac{\sum (y - \bar{y})^2}{n - 1}}$$

$$z = \frac{y - \mu}{\sigma} \text{ (model based)} \qquad z = \frac{y - \bar{y}}{s} \text{ (data based)}$$

$$r = \frac{\sum z_x z_y}{n - 1}$$

$$\hat{y} = b_0 + b_1 x \qquad \text{where } b_1 = r\frac{s_y}{s_x} \text{ and } b_0 = \bar{y} - b_1\bar{x}$$

$P(\mathbf{A}) = 1 - P(\mathbf{A}^C)$
$P(\mathbf{A} \text{ or } \mathbf{B}) = P(\mathbf{A}) + P(\mathbf{B}) - P(\mathbf{A} \text{ and } \mathbf{B})$
$P(\mathbf{A} \text{ and } \mathbf{B}) = P(\mathbf{A}) \times P(\mathbf{B}|\mathbf{A})$

$$P(\mathbf{B}|\mathbf{A}) = \frac{P(\mathbf{A} \text{ and } \mathbf{B})}{P(\mathbf{A})}$$

If $\mathbf{A}$ and $\mathbf{B}$ are independent, $P(\mathbf{B}|\mathbf{A}) = P(\mathbf{B})$

$E(X) = \mu = \sum x \cdot P(x) \qquad Var(X) = \sigma^2 = \sum (x - \mu)^2 P(x)$
$E(X \pm c) = E(X) \pm c \qquad Var(X \pm c) = Var(X)$
$E(aX) = aE(X) \qquad Var(aX) = a^2 Var(X)$
$E(X \pm Y) = E(X) \pm E(Y) \qquad Var(X \pm Y) = Var(X) + Var(Y)$
$\qquad\qquad\qquad\qquad\qquad\qquad$ if X and Y are independent

Geometric: $\quad P(x) = q^{x-1}p \qquad \mu = \frac{1}{p} \qquad \sigma = \sqrt{\frac{q}{p^2}}$

Binomial: $\quad P(x) = {}_nC_x p^x q^{n-x} \quad \mu = np \quad \sigma = \sqrt{npq}$

$\hat{p} = \frac{x}{n} \qquad \mu(\hat{p}) = p \qquad SD(\hat{p}) = \sqrt{\frac{pq}{n}}$

Poisson probability model for successes: Poisson (λ)
$\lambda = $ mean number of successes.
$X = $ number of successes.

$$P(X = x) = \frac{e^{-\lambda}\lambda^x}{x!}$$

Expected value: $\qquad E(X) = \lambda$
Standard deviation: $\qquad SD(X) = \sqrt{\lambda}$

Sampling distribution of $\bar{y}$:
(CLT) As n grows, the sampling distribution approaches the Normal model with

$$\mu(\bar{y}) = \mu_y \qquad SD(\bar{y}) = \frac{\sigma}{\sqrt{n}}$$

Inference:

Confidence interval for parameter $=$ ***statistic*** $\pm$ ***critical value*** $\times$ ***SE***(***statistic***)

$$\text{Test statistic} = \frac{statistic - parameter}{SD(statistic)}$$

Parameter	Statistic	SD (statistic)	SE (statistic)
p	$\hat{p}$	$\sqrt{\dfrac{pq}{n}}$	$\sqrt{\dfrac{\hat{p}\hat{q}}{n}}$
μ	$\bar{y}$	$\dfrac{\sigma}{\sqrt{n}}$	$\dfrac{s}{\sqrt{n}}$
$\mu_1 - \mu_2$	$\bar{y}_1 - \bar{y}_2$	$\sqrt{\dfrac{\sigma_1^2}{n_1} + \dfrac{\sigma_2^2}{n_2}}$	$\sqrt{\dfrac{s_1^2}{n_1} + \dfrac{s_2^2}{n_2}}$
μ_d	$\bar{d}$	$\dfrac{\sigma_d}{\sqrt{n}}$	$\dfrac{s_d}{\sqrt{n}}$
σ_ε	$s_e = \sqrt{\dfrac{\sum(y - \hat{y})^2}{n-2}}$	(divide by $n - k - 1$ in multiple regression)	
β_1	b_1	(in simple regression)	$\dfrac{s_e}{s_x \sqrt{n-1}}$
μ_ν	$\hat{y}_\nu$	(in simple regression)	$\sqrt{SE^2(b_1) \cdot (x_\nu - \bar{x})^2 + \dfrac{s_e^2}{n}}$
y_ν	$\hat{y}_\nu$	(in simple regression)	$\sqrt{SE^2(b_1) \cdot (x_\nu - \bar{x})^2 + \dfrac{s_e^2}{n} + s_e^2}$

Pooling: For testing difference between proportions: $\hat{p}_{pooled} = \dfrac{y_1 + y_2}{n_1 + n_2}$

For testing difference between means: $s_p = \sqrt{\dfrac{(n_1 - 1)s_1^2 + (n_2 - 1)s_2^2}{n_1 + n_2 - 2}}$

Substitute these pooled estimates in the respective SE formulas for both groups when assumptions and conditions are met.

Chi-square: $\chi^2 = \sum \dfrac{(Obs - Exp)^2}{Exp}$

Assumptions for Inference	And the Conditions That Support or Override Them

Proportions (z)

- **One sample**
  1. Individuals are independent.
  2. Sample is sufficiently large.

  1. SRS and $n < 10\%$ of the population.
  2. Successes and failures each ≥ 10.

Means (t)

- **One Sample** (df $= n - 1$)
  1. Individuals are independent.
  2. Population has a Normal model.

  1. SRS and $n < 10\%$ of the population.
  2. Histogram is unimodal and symmetric.*

- **Matched pairs** (df $= n - 1$)
  1. Data are matched.
  2. Individuals are independent.
  3. Population of differences is Normal.

  1. (Think about the design.)
  2. SRS and $n < 10\%$ OR random allocation.
  3. Histogram of differences is unimodal and symmetric.*

- **Two independent samples** (df from technology)
  1. Groups are independent.
  2. Data in each group are independent.
  3. Both populations are Normal.

  1. (Think about the design.)
  2. SRSs and $n < 10\%$ OR random allocation.
  3. Both histograms are unimodal and symmetric.*

Distributions/Association (χ^2)

- **Goodness of fit** (df $=$ # of cells $- 1$; one variable, one sample compared with population model)
  1. Data are counts.
  2. Data in sample are independent.
  3. Sample is sufficiently large.

  1. (Are they?)
  2. SRS and $n < 10\%$ of the population.
  3. All expected counts ≥ 5.

- **Homogeneity** [df $= (r - 1)(c - 1)$; many groups compared on one variable]
  1. Data are counts.
  2. Data in groups are independent.
  3. Groups are sufficiently large.

  1. (Are they?)
  2. SRSs and $n < 10\%$ OR random allocation.
  3. All expected counts ≥ 5.

- **Independence** [df $= (r - 1)(c - 1)$; sample from one population classified on two variables]
  1. Data are counts.
  2. Data are independent.
  3. Sample is sufficiently large.

  1. (Are they?)
  2. SRSs and $n < 10\%$ of the population.
  3. All expected counts ≥ 5.

Regression with k predictors (t, df $= n - k - 1$)

- **Association** of each quantitative predictor with the response variable
  1. Form of relationship is linear.

  2. Errors are independent.
  3. Variability of errors is constant.

  4. Errors follow a Normal model.

  1. Scatterplots of y against each x are straight enough. Scatterplot of residuals against predicted values shows no special structure.
  2. No apparent pattern in plot of residuals against predicted values.
  3. Plot of residuals against predicted values has constant spread, doesn't "thicken."
  4. Histogram of residuals is approximately unimodal and symmetric, or Normal probability plot is reasonably straight.*

Analysis of Variance (F, df dependent on number of factors and number of levels in each)

- **Equality** of the mean response across levels of categorical predictors
  1. Additive Model (if there are 2 factors with no interaction term).

  2. Independent errors.
  3. Equal variance across treatment levels.

  4. Errors follow a Normal model.

  1. Interaction plot shows parallel lines (otherwise include an interaction term if possible).
  2. Randomized experiment or other suitable randomization.
  3. Plot of residuals against predicted values has constant spread. Boxplots (partial boxplots for 2 factors) show similar spreads.
  4. Histogram of residuals is unimodal and symmetric, or Normal probability plot is reasonably straight.

* Less critical as n increases

Quick Guide to Inference

Plan			Do				Report
Inference about?	**One group or two?**	**Procedure**	**Model**	**Parameter**	**Estimate**	**SE**	**Chapter**
Proportions	One sample	1-Proportion z-Interval	z	p	$\hat{p}$	$\sqrt{\dfrac{\hat{p}\hat{q}}{n}}$	9
		1-Proportion z-Test				$\sqrt{\dfrac{p_0 q_0}{n}}$	10
Means	One sample	t-Interval t-Test	t df = $n-1$	μ	$\bar{y}$	$\dfrac{s}{\sqrt{n}}$	11
	Two independent groups	2-Sample t-Test 2-Sample t-Interval	t df from technology	$\mu_1 - \mu_2$	$\bar{y}_1 - \bar{y}_2$	$\sqrt{\dfrac{s_1^2}{n_1} + \dfrac{s_2^2}{n_2}}$	13
	Matched pairs	Paired t-Test Paired t-Interval	t df = $n-1$	μ_d	$\bar{d}$	$\dfrac{s_d}{\sqrt{n}}$	13
Distributions (one categorical variable)	One Sample	Goodness-of-Fit	χ^2 df = *cells* − 1			$\sum \dfrac{(Obs - Exp)^2}{Exp}$	14
	Many independent groups	Homogeneity χ^2 Test	χ^2 df = $(r-1)(c-1)$				
Independence (two categorical variables)	One sample	Independence χ^2 Test					
Association (two quantitative variables)	One sample	Linear Regression t-Test or Confidence Interval for β		β_1	b_1	$\dfrac{s_e}{s_x \sqrt{n-1}}$ (compute with technology)	15, 16
		*Confidence Interval for μ_ν	t df = $n-2$	μ_ν	$\hat{y}_\nu$	$\sqrt{SE^2(b_1) \cdot (x_\nu - \bar{x})^2 + \dfrac{s_e^2}{n}}$	
		*Prediction Interval for y_ν		y_ν	$\hat{y}_\nu$	$\sqrt{SE^2(b_1) \cdot (x_\nu - \bar{x})^2 + \dfrac{s_e^2}{n} + s_e^2}$	
Association (one quantitative and two or more categorical variables)	One sample	Multiple Regression t-test or Confidence interval for each β_j	t df = $n - (k+1)$	β_j	b_j	(from technology)	17, 18
		F test for regression model	F df = k and $n - (k+1)$			MST/MSE	18
Association (one quantitative and two or more categorical variables)	Two or more	ANOVA	F df = $k-1$ and $N-k$			MST/MSE	20

Photo Acknowledgments

Meet the Authors
Page vi, (Norean Sharpe) courtesy of Norean Radke Sharpe; (Richard D. De Veaux), Courtesy of Richard De Veaux; (Paul Velleman) courtesy of Paul F. Velleman.

Chapter 1
Page 1, Anton Balazh/Shutterstock; Page 6, Margo Harrison/Shutterstock; Page 7, Pearson Education, Inc. Page 14, Lightpoet/Fotolia.

Chapter 2
Page 19, Tim Draper/DK Images; Page 22, (bottom), Courtesy of Keen Shoes/Photo © Ben Moon; Page 31, Adisa/Shutterstock; Page 39, Feng Yu/Shutterstock.

Chapter 3
Page 49, Richard Drew/AP Images; Page 62, Lindasj22/Shutterstock; Page 64, Pressmaster/Shutterstock; Page 66, Africa Studio/Fotolia; Page 76, *Ithaca Times*; Page 82, Artazum and Iriana Shiyan/Shutterstock.

Chapter 4
Page 97, David Parker/Alamy; Page 101, Library of Congress Prints and Photographs Division [LC-USZ62-61365]; Page 104, Vectorlib/Shutterstock; Page 106, Crystal Kirk/Shutterstock; Page 112 (top), Alamy (bottom), Pearson Education, Inc. Page 119, Andy Dean Photography/Shutterstock; Page 126, Harald Hoiland Tjostheim/Shutterstock; Page 131, Michael Shake/Fotolia.

Chapter 5
Page 147, Laitr Keiows/Fotolia; Page 150, Interfoto/Alamy; Page 151, Matthew Mawson/Alamy; Page 156, Adam Rountree/AP Images; Page 162, Artazum/Shutterstock; Page 163, Kim Steele/Getty Images; Page 170, Yuri Arcurs/Shutterstock.

Chapter 6
Page 181, Kroomjai/Shutterstock; Page 185, Steve Design/Shutterstock; Page 191, *Calvin & Hobbes* © 1993 Watterson. Distributed by Universal Uclick. Reprinted with permission. All rights reserved. Page 192, Photos 12/Alamy; Page 195, Keith Brofsky/Photodisc/Getty Images; Page 202, Elena Elisseeva/Shutterstock.

Chapter 7
Page 209, Gary/Fotolia; Page 217, David Buffington/Blend Images/Getty Images; Page 222, Walter Hodges/Digital Vision/Getty Images; Page 233, iStock/Thinkstock.

Chapter 8
Page 243, Bettmann/Corbis; Page 245, Michael Lamotte/Cole Group/Getty Images; Page 250, Digital Vision/Getty Images; Page 252, Tatiana Popova/Shutterstock; Page 254, *Calvin & Hobbes* © 1993 Watterson. Distributed by Universal Uclick. Reprinted with permission. All rights reserved. Page 258, *The Wizard of Id* © 2001 John L. Hart/Distributed by Creators Syndicate. Reprinted with permission. All rights reserved. Page 262, Goodluz/Shutterstock.

Chapter 9
Page 271, Bertys30/Fotolia; Page 276, Galina Barskaya/Shutterstock; Page 283, *Garfield* © 1999 Jim Davis/Distributed by Universal Uclick. Reprinted with permission. All rights reserved. Page 284, Ittel/Sipa/Newscom; Page 288, Michael Blann/Photodisc/Getty Images; Page 304 (Case Study), Jim Pruitt/Shutterstock.

Chapter 10
Page 305, Mark III Photonics/Shutterstock; Page 309, IE235/Image Source Plus/Alamy; Page 314, Tischenko Irina/Shutterstock; Page 317, Richard Paul Kane/Shutterstock; Page 323, Luoman/Getty Images.

Chapter 11
Page 331, Tom Norring/Danita Delimont/Alamy; Page 334, Elk-Opid/Photos12/Alamy; Page 339, Courtesy of the International Statistical Institute; Page 345, Sapsiwai/Shutterstock; Page 349, Jim Lopes/Shutterstock; Page 357, Scott Leigh/E+/Getty Images.

Chapter 12
Page 367, Niday Picture Library/Alamy; Page 370, AlcelVision/Fotolia; Page 372, Paul Velleman; Page 374, A. Barrington Brown/Photo Researchers, Inc. Page 378, Tischenko Irina/Shutterstock; Page 387, Tristan Hawke/PhotoStockFile/Alamy.

Chapter 13
Page 395, Goodshoot/Getty Images; Page 397, Peter Cade/Goodshoot/Getty Images; Page 400, (top) Yt/iStockphoto, (second from top) Bestweb/Shutterstock, (third from top) Shell/iStockphoto, (fourth from top) Inga Dudkina/Dreamstime, (fifth from top) Paha L/iStockphoto, (sixth from top) Plamen Petrov/Dreamstime, (seventh from top) Alexeys/iStockphoto, (eighth from top) Jorg Hackemann/Shutterstock, (ninth from top) Jason Stitt/Shutterstock, (bottom) Ronyzmbow/Dreamstime; Page 401, JupiterImages/Getty Images; Page 404, Turtix/

Shutterstock; **Page 406**, Leegudim/Shutterstock; **Page 407**, Monkey Business Images/Getty Images; **Page 413**, Ariel Skelley/Blend Images/Getty Images; **Page 423**, M. Eric Honeycutt/E+/Getty Images.

Chapter 14

Page 441, Ken Graff/Getty Images; **Page 446**, Tischenko Irina/Shutterstock; **Page 457**, Minerva Studio/Fotolia; **Page 466**, Jakub Jirsák/Fotolia; **Page 478** (Case Study), WavebreakmediaMicro/Fotolia.

Chapter 15

Page 479 and 486, Courtesy of Nambé; **Page 495**, Peter Teller/Getty Images; **Page 498**, Larry Crowe/AP Images; **Page 499**, Pearson Education, Inc.

Chapter 16

Page 513, Dmitry Pichugin/Fotolia; **Page 519**, (top) Heather A. Craig/Shutterstock, (middle), *Foxtrot* © 2002 Bill Amend/Distributed by Universal Uclick. Reprinted with permission. All rights reserved. (bottom), Bridgeman Art Library; **Page 521**, World History Archive/Image Asset Management Ltd./Alamy **Page 523**, Michael Betts/Getty Images; **Page 528**, Bryn Lennon/Getty Images; **Page 532**, Pete Spiro/Shutterstock; **Page 539**, Tentacle/Fotolia.

Chapter 17

Page 555, David Hughes/Shutterstock; **Page 559**, Monkey Business/Fotolia; **Page 565**, Rob Marmion/Shutterstock; **Page 574**, Yamini Chao/Digital Vision/Getty Images; **Page 576**, iStockphoto; **Page 584**, Djtaylor/Fotolia.

Chapter 18

Page 597, Rachael Grazias/Shutterstock; **Page 598**, Shutterstock; **Page 600**, Shutterstock; **Page 604**, Joao Virissimo/Shutterstock; **Page 607**, Andrew Fox/Alamy; **Page 616**, Maisna/Fotolia; **Page 624**, Scott Markewitz/Getty Images; **Page 632**, Anke van Wyk/Shutterstock.

Chapter 19

Page 643, Monticellllo/Fotolia; **Page 651**, Dambuster/Fotolia; **Page 658**, Shutterstock; **Page 669**, Alan Novelli/Alamy; **Page 673**, Shutterstock; **Page 677**, Petrovish9/Getty Images; **Page 690**, (Case Study), Stephan Morrosch/Fotolia.

Chapter 20

Page 693, Bertys30/Fotolia; **Page 701**, Victor Burnside/Thinkstock; **Page 707**, I. Pilon/Shutterstock; **Page 712**, Pearson Education, Inc. **Page 720**, Dmitriy K/Fotolia; **Page 730**, Aleksey Stemmer/Fotolia.

Chapter 21

Page 743, Mark Eite/Aflo Co., Ltd./Alamy; **Page 745**, (top) Pearson Education, Inc. (bottom) Catherine Karnow/Corbis; **Page 749**, Joanchang/Shutterstock; **Page 760**, Skyhawk/Shutterstock; **Page 771**, Stefan Kiefer/Imagebroker/Alamy.

Chapter 22

Page 779, Dragon Images/Shutterstock; **Page 784**, Floresco Productions/Corbis; **Page 786**, Luke Macgregor/Reuters/Corbis; **Page 790**, Olivier/Shutterstock; **Page 794**, Pearson Education, Inc. **Page 798**, Diane39/iStockphoto.

Chapter 23

Page 807, (top) Courtesy of Data Description, (middle) Chris Schmidt/E+/Getty Images; **Page 818**, Paul Matthew Photography/Shutterstock; **Page 822**, DNY59/E+/Getty Images.

Chapter 24

Page 829, Phattman/Fotolia; **Page 834**, Plush Studios/Vetta/Getty Images; **Page 846**, Michaeljung/Fotolia.

Subject Index

Note: Page numbers in **boldface** indicate chapter-level topics; FE indicates For Example; and n indicates a footnote

10% Condition
  for comparing means, 400
  for confidence intervals, 282
  independence and, 191
  for paired data, 412
  sampling distribution models, 275
  for Student's *t*-models, 343
68–95–99.7 Rule
  applying, 212FE
  critical values and, 377n
  defined, 211–212

A

Abscissa (*x*-axis), 101
Absolute percentage error (APE), 653
Actions
  in decision-making, 808–809,
    809FE
  defined, 808
  estimating variation of, 815–816,
    816FE–817FE
  expected values of, 811–812,
    812FE
  for out-of-control process, 758–759,
    759FE–763FE
  outcomes of, 808–809, 809FE
  standard deviation of, 815–816,
    816FE–817FE
ActivStats Multimedia Assistant, 807
Addition Rule
  defined, 154, 154FE
  for expected values of random
    variables, 187
  General Addition Rule, 155,
    155FE
  for variances of random variables,
    188
Additive model, 664–666, 667FE
Adjusted *R*2, 571–573, 573FE
AIG (American International Group),
  49–59, 66FE–67FE
Albran, Kehlog, 646
Algorithms, data mining, 837–841
Alpha levels
  defined, 374
  in hypothesis testing, 374–377,
    376FE
  of test, 316

Alternative hypothesis
  defined, 307
  one-sided, 314
  P-value and, 313–314
  two-sided, 313
Amazon.com, 2, 4, 97–98
American Express, 395
American International Group (AIG),
  49–59, 66FE–67FE
American Society for Quality (ASQ),
  745, 767
ANOVA (Analysis of Variance),
  693–741
  analysis of multifactor designs,
    715–717, 718FE
  assumptions and conditions,
    709–711, 711FE–712FE
  on the computer, 729–730
  Equal Variance Assumption, 709,
    714
  F-statistic, 573, 706–707
  functionality, 705–708, 708FE
  Independence Assumption, 709
  Mean Square due to Error,
    706–707
  Mean Square due to Treatment,
    706–707
  multiple comparisons, 712–713,
    714FE
  Nearly Normal Condition,
    710–711
  nonparametric methods and,
    791–792
  Normal Population Assumption,
    710–711
  on observational data, 714–715
  Randomization Condition, 709
  Similar Variance Condition, 709
  two-way, 718–719
ANOVA tables, 706
Archimedes, 521
Area codes, 6–7
Area principle, 22–23
Armstrong, Lance, 528
Association(s)
  linear, 99, 103, 105
  Brief Case, 131–132
  negative direction, 99
  positive direction, 99

Assumptions
  for ANOVA, 709–711, 711FE–712FE
  for chi-square tests, 443, 457–459
  for confidence intervals, 281–282,
    282FE, 342–344, 344FE–345FE
  defined, 114
  Equal Variance Assumption, 407,
    484–486, 562–563, 709, 714
  goodness-of-fit tests, 443–444
  for homogeneity tests, 452–453
  Independence Assumption, 114–115,
    275, 281, 342–343, 399–400,
    411–412, 443, 452, 485–486, 562,
    709, 783
  for independence tests, 457–459
  Independent Groups Assumption,
    400, 783
  for linear regression, 114–115
  Linearity Assumption, 115, 484–486,
    561–562
  for means, 399–400
  for multiple regression, 561–564,
    564FE–565FE
  for nonparametric methods, 783
  Normal Population Assumption, 343–
    344, 400, 412, 485–486, 710–711
  Normality Assumption, 563–564
  for paired data, 411–412
  Paired Data Assumption, 411
  for regression, 485–486
  Sample Size Assumption, 275, 282,
    443, 452
  sampling distribution models, 275,
    276FE
  Student's *t*-models, 342–347
  for two-sample *t*-test, 401FE
  Wilcoxon signed-rank test, 788
Attributes, control charts for, 764–766,
  766FE–767FE
Autocorrelation, 524–526,
  525FE–526FE, 656
Autoregressive model, 655–658,
  657FE, 672
Average run length (ARL), 747, 750
Axis
  coordinates of, 101
  origin, 101
  x-axis, 101
  y-axis, 101

Note: Page numbers in **boldface** indicate chapter-level topics; FE indicates For Example; and n indicates a footnote

Note: Page numbers in **boldface** indicate chapter-level topics; FE indicates For Example; and n indicates a footnote

Note: Page numbers in **boldface** indicate chapter-level topics; FE indicates For Example; and n indicates a footnote

Note: Page numbers in **boldface** indicate chapter-level topics; FE indicates For Example; and n indicates a footnote

Note: Page numbers in **boldface** indicate chapter-level topics; FE indicates For Example; and n indicates a footnote

Note: Page numbers in **boldface** indicate chapter-level topics; FE indicates For Example; and n indicates a footnote

Note: Page numbers in **boldface** indicate chapter-level topics; FE indicates For Example; and n indicates a footnote

Note: Page numbers in **boldface** indicate chapter-level topics; FE indicates For Example; and n indicates a footnote

Note: Page numbers in **boldface** indicate chapter-level topics; FE indicates For Example; and n indicates a footnote

Note: Page numbers in **boldface** indicate chapter-level topics; FE indicates For Example; and n indicates a footnote

Note: Page numbers in **boldface** indicate chapter-level topics; FE indicates For Example; and n indicates a footnote

Note: Page numbers in **boldface** indicate chapter-level topics; FE indicates For Example; and n indicates a footnote

Note: Page numbers in **boldface** indicate chapter-level topics; FE indicates For Example; and n indicates a footnote

Note: Page numbers in **boldface** indicate chapter-level topics; FE indicates For Example; and n indicates a footnote

Note: Page numbers in **boldface** indicate chapter-level topics; FE indicates For Example; and n indicates a footnote